THE
MIDDLE
EAST

THE MIDDLE EAST

Seventh Edition

Revised to Include a Persian Gulf Crisis Supplement

Washington, D.C.

Congressional Quarterly Inc.

Congressional Quarterly Inc., an editorial research service and publishing company, serves clients in the fields of news, education, business, and government. It combines Congressional Quarterly's specific coverage of Congress, government, and politics with the more general subject range of an affiliated service, Editorial Research Reports.

Congressional Quarterly publishes the *Congressional Quarterly Weekly Report* and a variety of books, including college political science textbooks under the CQ Press imprint and public affairs paperbacks on developing issues and events. CQ also publishes information directories and reference books on the federal government, national elections, and politics, including the *Guide to the Presidency*, the *Guide to Congress*, the *Guide to the U.S. Supreme Court*, the *Guide to U.S. Elections*, *Politics in America*, and *Congress A to Z: CQ's Ready Reference Encyclopedia*. The *CQ Almanac*, a compendium of legislation for one session of Congress, is published each year. *Congress and the Nation*, a record of government for a presidential term, is published every four years.

CQ publishes the *Congressional Monitor*, a daily report on current and future activities of congressional committees, and several newsletters including *Congressional Insight*, a weekly analysis of congressional action, and *Campaign Practices Reports*, a semimonthly update on campaign laws.

An electronic online information system, Washington Alert, provides immediate access to CQ's databases of legislative action, votes, schedules, profiles, and analyses.

Copyright © 1991 Congressional Quarterly Inc.
1414 22nd Street, N.W., Washington, D.C. 20037

Printed in the United States of America

Library of Congress Cataloging-in-Publication Data

The Middle East. -- 7th ed.
    p.   cm.
    "Revised to include a Persian Gulf Crisis supplement."
    Includes bibliographical references.
    ISBN 0-87187-630-2
    1. Middle East--Politics and government--1979- I. Congressional Quarterly, inc.
DS63.1.M484   1991
956.05'3--dc20   91-13516
                              CIP

Editor: Daniel C. Diller
Associate Editors: John L. Moore, Kerry Kern
Major Contributors: Beth B. Grill, Max Gross, Ian L.
    Todreas
Contributors: Geoffrey Aronson, Sally Ann Baynard,
    Joseph A. Davis, John Felton, Hoyt Gimlin,
    Edward Hossain Kajani, Amy S. Meyers,
    John R. Undeland
Proofreader: Kristen Carpenter Stoever
Index: Jane F. Maddocks
Cover: Design, Jack Auldridge; Photo, Richard
    Quataert/Folio Inc.
Graphics: Paula Anderson, William Clipson, Dmitri
    Lipczenko, George Rebh, Dan Sherbo

Editors' Note to the Persian Gulf Supplement Edition

Most of the material in this printing of *The Middle East, Seventh Edition*, was prepared in 1989 before Iraq's 1990 invasion of Kuwait, which precipitated the Persian Gulf crisis and the ensuing war. The contents of Chapters 1 through 7, the country profiles, and the appendix remain unchanged from the original seventh edition and must be read with that in mind. To the original text we have added, at the end of the volume, new material that examines the Gulf crisis in detail. The supplementary material, which begins on page 315, is new to this printing of the book. The index at the end of the volume has been updated to cover the original and the supplementary material.

Congressional Quarterly Editors
March 1991

Table of Contents

1 The Middle East in the 1990s   1
2 Arab-Israeli Conflict   7
3 U.S. and Soviet Mideast Policies   39
4 Arms Sales: A Thriving Bazaar   69
5 Persian Gulf: A Fragile Balance   87
6 Mideast Oil: An Uncertain Future   101
7 Fourteen Centuries of Islam   123
Country Profiles
    Egypt   139
    Iran   149
    Iraq   159
    Israel   167
    Jordan   177
    Lebanon   183
    Libya   197
    Persian Gulf States   205
    Saudi Arabia   215
    Syria   223
    Yemens   231
Appendix
    Sketches of Middle East Leaders   239
    Major Events, 1900-1944   247
    Chronology of Events, 1945-1989   249
    Documents   301
Supplement: The Persian Gulf Crisis
    The Persian Gulf Crisis   315
    Chronology of the Gulf Crisis   355
    Documents on the Gulf Crisis   369
Bibliography   391
Index   397

Tables and Charts

U.S. Arms Sales, 1950-1987   73
United States Assistance to the Middle East, 1946-1988   77
Arms Sales to Middle East, North Africa   85
Petroleum Supply and Disposition, 1986   103
World Oil Consumption   104
Estimated Crude Oil and Natural Gas Proved Reserves   105
Share of U.S. Oil Consumption Supplied by Imports   107
Crude Oil Prices, 1973-1988   108
U.S. Petroleum Imports from OPEC Nations, 1964-1984   111
Major Petroleum Producing Countries of the World   113
OPEC Oil Revenues, 1974-1988   117
OPEC Crude Oil Production, 1979-1987   121
American Hostages in Lebanon   297
Iraq's Major Weapons Suppliers   337

Maps

West Bank and Gaza Strip   2
UN Partition of 1947   41
Israel After 1948-1949 War   41
Middle East After 1967 War   47
U.S., Soviet Military in the Middle East   71
Strait of Hormuz   89
Oil Pipelines in the Middle East   95
Shatt al-Arab   97
Persian Gulf Region   97
Gulf Cooperation Council Member States   99
Egypt   139, 141
Iran   149, 151
Iraq   159, 161
Israel   167, 169
Jordan   177, 179
Lebanon   183, 185
Libya   197, 199
Persian Gulf States   205
Saudi Arabia   215, 217
Syria   223, 225
North and South Yemen   231, 233, 235
The Middle East   316
Kuwait Under Iraqi Occupation   338
Troop Buildup   340
Ground War to Liberate Kuwait   345

The Middle East in the 1990s

Throughout history the Middle East has been a rich and diverse region of enormous cultural significance. It has spawned three of the world's great religions—Christianity, Islam, and Judaism—and has provided many other contributions to civilization. In the twentieth century the discovery of the largest petroleum deposits in the world made the Middle East vital to the international economy.

The region is also strategically important because of its oil assets, its location on the southern flank of the Soviet Union at the crossroads of three continents, and the client relationships between the United States and Israel and between the Soviet Union and several Arab states. What happens there affects not only local peoples and nations but also the entire world.

More than any other area, the Middle East is afflicted with major conflicts that seem to defy solution. Disputes between Arabs and Israelis, Iranians and Iraqis, and other antagonists go beyond disagreements over territory or fears concerning a rival's geopolitical and economic goals. The combatants in these squabbles often hate each other because of decades of mutual hostilities and ethnic, religious, and cultural prejudices. Constructing long-term settlements requires not only carefully drawn compromises backed by international guarantees, but also fundamental changes in the attitudes of people toward their enemies. Thus burdened, progress toward resolving the region's conflicts comes only in small steps.

Since the end of World War II the Arab-Israeli conflict has been the central political issue in the Middle East. Through the 1970s the Arabs and Israelis fought four major wars and numerous smaller battles that demonstrated the intractability of the conflict and threatened to involve outside powers. In addition, the Arab-Israeli conflict caused or exacerbated other upheavals in the region, such as the Jordanian civil war in 1970 and the Lebanese civil war in 1975.

In 1979 the Iranian Revolution, the U.S. embassy hostage crisis in Tehran, a second round of oil price increases, and the Soviet invasion of Afghanistan converged to focus the world's attention on the Persian Gulf. Since then the problems of the Gulf region have seemed as critical as the Arab-Israeli conflict. In particular, the Iran-Iraq war underscored the volatility as well as the strategic and economic importance of the Persian Gulf. Touched off in September 1980 by Iraq's invasion of Iran, the eight-year war threatened the flow of oil through the Gulf and ulti-

mately involved the United States and other countries outside the region. The continuing hostility between Iran and Iraq, the regional arms race, the importance of oil to the world economy, and superpower competition in the area all ensure that the Gulf will remain strategically important.

In the four years since the sixth edition of the *The Middle East* was published, the area that this seventh edition examines has seen continued strife. Although no major Arab-Israeli war was fought, terrorism remained a constant threat, key states engaged in an accelerated arms race, and Palestinians in the West Bank and Gaza Strip began a sustained uprising against Israel's occupation that seemed to deepen hostilities between the two groups. Further conflict, terrorism, and internal unrest appeared to be unavoidable in the 1990s.

Nevertheless, local and international developments created some optimism that progress toward peace could be achieved. Iran and Iraq concluded a cease-fire, the Soviets withdrew from Afghanistan and appeared willing to become constructively involved in the Middle East peace process, and the public moderation of the Palestine Liberation Organization (PLO) led to its formal renunciation of terrorism and consequently to the opening of a dialogue with the United States. Whether the next decade will produce a more stable and peaceful Middle East depends on the efforts of both the international community and the nations and groups directly involved.

The Intifada

In November 1987 Arab leaders met in Amman, Jordan, to discuss a common approach to ending the Iran-Iraq war. The summit was notable for its minimal attention to the Arab-Israeli conflict. Iran's determination to continue its war with Iraq, its deadly attacks on shipping in the Persian Gulf, and its efforts to export its version of Moslem fundamentalism had caused moderate Arab leaders to regard Iran as the most immediate threat to their nations' security. The final communiqué of the summit chastised Tehran for its pursuit of the war in the face of international condemnation, denounced Iran's "aggression," declared the league's solidarity with Iraq, and called on the international community to "adopt the necessary measures to make the Iranian regime respond to the peace calls." The Arab-Israeli conflict was discussed, but it was clearly a secondary concern.

In this atmosphere, the Palestinians in the West Bank and Gaza Strip began in December 1987 a popular uprising against Israel's occupation of those territories. The uprising came to be known as the *intifada*. Palestinian youths went into the streets and hurled rocks and molotov cocktails at Israeli soldiers. Israel's army tried to put down the rebellion, but it could not succeed without using a level of force that would ensure world condemnation. Even so, Israeli forces frequently beat and arrested young rock throwers and enforced strict curfews. By the end of the first year of the intifada about three hundred fifty Palestinians had been killed. The uprising had dramatically changed the nature of the Arab-Israeli conflict by shifting Israel's greatest threat from the surrounding Arab states to Palestinians living inside Israeli-occupied territory.

For more than two decades hundreds of thousands of Palestinians had made their homes in areas Israel occupied during the 1967 Six-Day War. Although Israel had not annexed these territories, it maintained tight military control over them and established Jewish settlements, which indicated to many Arabs that Israel never intended to relinquish them. In 1977 the conservative Likud party gained control of the government. Its leaders accelerated the pace of Jewish settlement on the West Bank and declared that they would not give up the occupied territories. Palestinian nationalists, however, demanded that Israel withdraw from the territories and allow the establishment of a Palestinian state in the West Bank and Gaza Strip. The intifada was seen as being motivated primarily by the frustrations of local Palestinians with Israel's hard-line position toward the territories and their dismal economic conditions.

Palestinians quickly came to see that for several reasons the intifada was their strongest lever against Israel. First, it kept the Palestinian problem in the international spotlight, forcing world leaders to become involved in the Middle East peace process. Second, the protesters' resilience and televised pictures of Israeli troops using lethal force against Palestinian youths increased world sympathy for the Palestinian cause. Third, the uprising forced Israel to expend resources to contain the rebellion. Fourth, it caused minor disruptions in the flow of Palestinian labor into Israel and diminished the value of the West Bank and Gaza Strip markets for Israeli industry. Finally, the uprising caused many Israelis to doubt the morality of their nation's occupation of the territories. In short, the intifada threatened to turn a strategic asset into an economic, political, and public relations liability. Palestinians hoped that the prospect of the intifada's continuing for years would eventually make Israelis more accommodating on the issues of relinquishing the occupied territories and accepting the establishment of a Palestinian state.

The intifada also affected the Arab-Israeli peace process by inducing Jordan's King Hussein to renounce his government's claims to the West Bank. He announced on July 31, 1988, that the PLO was "the sole legitimate representative of the Palestine people." He severed Jordan's administrative and legal links to the West Bank and declared later that Jordan would no longer pay the salaries of about twenty-one thousand West Bank civil servants. Hussein's renunciation appeared to be motivated primarily by his desire to insulate Jordan's Palestinian population from the destabilizing effects of the intifada and his recognition that Palestinians in the West Bank did not favor a federation with Jordan.

Hussein's bombshell stunned Israeli and U.S. leaders. Israel had long considered negotiations with King Hussein regarding the fate of the occupied territories as the best way to achieve some type of peace settlement while avoiding contact with the PLO. Hussein's withdrawal seemed to preclude, or at least complicate, this option. Similarly, the United States regarded Hussein as an essential player in any Middle East peace settlement. If he remained aloof from the peace process, the United States would have to consider other avenues of negotiation.

Reassessment by the PLO

The intifada forced Israel and Jordan to reconsider their strategies, and it compelled the PLO, which is based outside the territories and claims to represent Palestinians everywhere, to reassess its approach to Israel. Because the intifada was a spontaneous movement that the PLO had not engineered, the uprising threatened to undermine PLO influence in the West Bank and Gaza. Unless the PLO leadership could produce diplomatic progress toward realization of Palestinian statehood, it would lose credibility in the territories with the Palestinians who were dying for the cause. The PLO especially feared being replaced as the patron of Palestinians by Islamic fundamentalist groups that showed increasing popularity in the occupied territories.

After some initial confusion the PLO leadership under Chairman Yasir Arafat endorsed the intifada and claimed credit for it. Even though the PLO had not launched the intifada, which in some respects demonstrated a frustra-

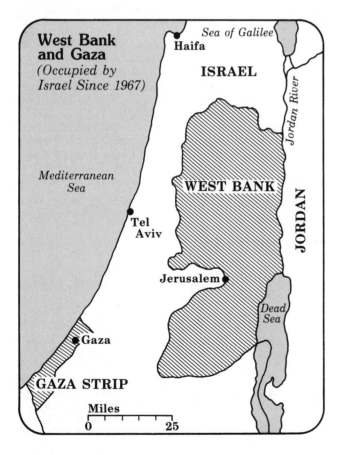

West Bank and Gaza
(Occupied by Israel Since 1967)

Sea of Galilee
Haifa
ISRAEL
Jordan River
Mediterranean Sea
WEST BANK
Tel Aviv
JORDAN
Jerusalem
Dead Sea
Gaza
GAZA STRIP
Miles
0   25

tion with PLO policy, most Palestinians in the occupied territories regarded the PLO as their sole legitimate representative. The PLO used threats and intimidation to discourage unauthorized contacts between local Arab leaders and Israeli officials. If Israel was going to negotiate an end to the intifada, there was little chance that it could avoid talking to the PLO. The PLO also increased its international diplomatic activity in an effort to take advantage of world sympathy for the Palestinian cause generated by the uprising.

Nevertheless, the intifada put pressure on the PLO to make progress toward establishing a Palestinian homeland. On November 15, 1988, in Algiers the Palestine National Council (PNC), the PLO's parliament-in-exile, declared the existence of an independent Palestinian state in the West Bank and Gaza Strip. Although Israel's continued occupation of the territories obviously prevented the establishment of such a state, many nations recognized the new Palestinian nation, thereby increasing the international stature of the PLO.

U.S.-PLO Dialogue

The refusal of the United States to negotiate with the PLO had been a longstanding element of American Middle East policy. Successive U.S. administrations guaranteed Israel that the United States would not talk to the PLO until it recognized Israel's right to exist, accepted UN Security Council resolutions 242 and 338, and renounced the use of terrorism. At the PNC's Algiers meeting the council expressed its acceptance of all of these conditions. The Reagan administration, however, called the PNC's acceptance ambiguous. It declined to take any action toward opening a dialogue with the PLO until the statement was more explicit. During the next twenty-nine days PLO Chairman Arafat inched toward using the precise wording demanded by U.S. officials, while moderate Arab leaders urged Washington to begin a dialogue. In a December 14 press conference Arafat finally made a statement that satisfied the Reagan administration. Secretary of State George P. Shultz announced later that day that the United States would open talks with PLO representatives in Tunis.

The U.S. decision delighted Palestinians and shocked Israelis, who remained skeptical of the PLO's sincerity. Although the U.S.-PLO dialogue produced no significant breakthroughs during its first ten months, the fact that the two sides were talking put pressure on Israel to advance its own peace proposals. The talks also encouraged PLO moderation by giving the organization something to lose if it reneged on its pledge not to resort to terrorism.

War and Peace

Although these developments had changed the rules and the setting of Middle East politics, a general peace between Israel and the Arabs still seemed a distant dream. The Arabs appeared unwilling to settle for anything less than the establishment of a Palestinian state in the West Bank and Gaza Strip, while Israel's current leadership vowed that it would never give up the occupied territories. Moreover, Prime Minister Yitzhak Shamir and his Likud party remained publicly opposed to any negotiations with the PLO. They rejected the idea of an international peace

Defining the Middle East

The Middle East is not a precisely defined area of the world. It is sometimes referred to as the "Near East" or "Southwest Asia," but not everyone agrees on what countries should be included within these geographic designations. If the Middle East is defined solely as the Arab states and Israel, Iran would be excluded. If it is thought to comprise Israel and the predominantly Moslem states, then all the North African states—Algeria, Tunisia, Morocco, and Libya—plus the Sudan, Afghanistan, Pakistan, and Turkey—would have to be included.

This book focuses on those countries that American readers most often associate with the Middle East and that have had a continuing and central role in two issues of critical importance to U.S. foreign policy: the Arab-Israeli conflict and the security of the Persian Gulf and its oil resources. These nations are Egypt, Iran, Iraq, Israel, Jordan, Lebanon, Libya, Saudi Arabia, Syria, North and South Yemen, Bahrain, Kuwait, Oman, Qatar, and the United Arab Emirates.

conference attended by either the PLO or the Soviet Union. Although most Israeli citizens did not favor such a hard line toward negotiations, they still were skeptical that Israel could give up the territories soon without jeopardizing its security.

While the Arab-Israeli conflict continued its slow burn during the late 1980s, some areas of the Middle East made progress toward ending armed conflict. Fighting in Beirut, however, intensified and spread throughout Lebanon because warring factions were unable to construct a political compromise.

Iran-Iraq War

Perhaps the most encouraging event in the Middle East during this period was the cease-fire in the Iran-Iraq war. The war, which had killed more than a million people by most estimates, showed few signs of abating as late as 1987. In July 1988, however, an economically and militarily exhausted Iran grudgingly accepted a UN-sponsored cease-fire after Iraq began having success on the battlefield.

The end of the war brought relief to neighboring Gulf nations, whose oil industries and domestic stability had been threatened by the conflict. After the war Iraq began trying to reassert itself as a leader of the Arab world, while Iran debated its own domestic course. Talks on a final settlement of the conflict, however, made little progress.

Libya

Libya's military adventures in Chad also came to an end in 1988. The outmanned and outgunned Chadian army supported by French and U.S. aid frustrated Libyan attempts to consolidate and expand military gains in Chad. In 1987 the Chadian army even staged raids inside Libya. Under increasing international pressure, Libyan leader Muammar Qaddafi decided to cut his losses. In May 1988 he announced that he would end the armed conflict with the Chadian government of President Hissene Habre. The two governments established diplomatic relations with each other on October 3 of that year.

Lebanon

The 1985 Israeli withdrawal from Lebanon engendered hope that the Lebanese people could construct a political compromise that would halt the fighting that had continued intermittently since the 1975 civil war. The chaotic factional warfare in Lebanon persisted, however, and in 1989 it reached a new level of intensity. For months Syrian forces traded devastating artillery fire with Lebanese Christians under Gen. Michel Aoun, who had vowed to expel the Syrians from his country. The artillery duels killed hundreds of Lebanese, destroyed most of the structures in Beirut that had survived the previous years of war, and made living a normal life impossible.

Lebanon's troubles were complicated by the activities of foreign powers, which competed for influence in the tiny country. Israel maintained its security zone in southern Lebanon and regularly launched retaliatory raids into the area. Syria continued to seek military dominance over its neighbor, while rival Iraq provided aid to Lebanese Christian forces fighting the Syrians. In addition, the Iranian government promoted its brand of Islamic fundamentalism in Lebanon and supported Lebanese Shi'ite groups holding Western hostages.

Economic Difficulties

The economies of the Middle East suffered during the late 1980s, primarily because of the collapse of oil prices in 1986. Oil-rich nations such as Saudi Arabia and Kuwait, which seemingly could generate unlimited wealth during the early part of the decade, suddenly were forced to make cuts in development projects and government services. The pinch was felt throughout the Middle East as these nations had less money to buy goods, services, and labor from their neighbors. Oil producers also cut back on aid sent to other Arab states.

Beyond the oil glut, conflicts in the region consumed the resources of several nations. Iran and Iraq poured money into their war efforts, Syria maintained an expensive presence in Lebanon, and Israel was forced to spend hundreds of millions of dollars on operations in southern Lebanon and on efforts to control the intifada. In general, expenditures on advanced weaponry constituted a drain on the budgets of most Middle East nations. Other problems that threatened Middle Eastern economies included a population boom in many countries, massive foreign debt, and the scarcity of water resources.

Oil Industry

Between 1973 and the early 1980s petroleum-producing nations enjoyed a seller's market, in which oil prices rose dramatically. During the mid-1980s, however, the market turned to the advantage of buyers as supply met and exceeded demand. With that change came downward pressure on oil prices and a weakening of the political and economic leverage enjoyed by oil-rich Middle East nations.

By 1986 members of the Organization of Petroleum Exporting Countries (OPEC) had virtually abandoned their cartel efforts to prop up oil prices and were competing to hold on to customers. Oil prices dropped from nearly $40 a barrel in 1981 to only $12 in the summer of 1986. Although oil prices recovered somewhat during the late 1980s, the export incomes of Middle East oil producers remained far below what they were before the 1986 crash. The collapse of the oil market forced the oil-exporting nations of the Middle East to scale back expensive development projects and seek new sources of income. Economic diversification became a priority of many oil-rich states.

Regional Cooperation

Besides trying to diversify, the nations of the Middle East have attempted to enhance their economic prospects through regional cooperation. In 1981 Saudi Arabia, Kuwait, Oman, Bahrain, Qatar, and the United Arab Emirates formed the Gulf Cooperation Council, which promotes economic cooperation among its members and enhances their mutual security.

During 1989 steps were taken by Arab nations to create two other economic blocs. The first was the Arab Cooperation Council, made up of Egypt, Iraq, Jordan, and North Yemen. The second was the Maghreb Union, formed by Morocco, Algeria, Tunisia, Libya, and Mauritania. Members' representatives said the new groups would aid economic integration and would construct common markets to reduce trade barriers.

Dangers and Opportunities

As always in the Middle East, the greatest danger is an outbreak of war. Notwithstanding the turmoil of the intifada, the chances of a general war between Israel and its neighbors appear to have been reduced during the late 1980s. Israel's peaceful relationship with Egypt has continued despite many disagreements between the two nations. The PLO's gains on the diplomatic front have decreased the possibility that the organization soon will abandon the international peace process in favor of a military solution to its quest for a homeland. Although fighting continues in Lebanon among domestic factions backed by various foreign powers, Israel's experiences in that country have made it less disposed to be drawn into a large-scale war there.

These developments, however, do not preclude the possibility of war. Every decade since Israel was established has seen a major Arab-Israeli war. The mutual hatreds, prejudices, and historical grievances that exist between Israel and the Arabs, the seemingly intractable issue of Palestinian statehood, and a regional arms race that shows no signs of slowing combine to make another war an almost constant threat. In such an environment, progress toward a peace settlement is vital. The riskiest strategy for both sides may be avoiding compromise in favor of pressing status quo demands and conditions.

A renewal of hostilities between Iran and Iraq is also a real possibility, although both nations have been exhausted by the war and would like to be able to concentrate on other domestic and foreign objectives. The possibility of further fighting exists because the war did not settle the main issues that led to the conflict—control of the Shatt al-Arab waterway, the willingness of each country to support rebel movements in the other, and the struggle for economic and political leadership of the Gulf region. The death of Ayatollah Ruhollah Khomeini has diminished the Iranian desire to overthrow the regime of Saddam Hussein, but the two governments remain enemies and rivals, and neither side will soon forgive the other for acts of brutality and aggression committed during the war.

Arab Reacceptance of Egypt

One of the most overlooked events of the late 1980s was Egypt's return to the Arab fold. Following its 1979 treaty with Israel, Egypt had been expelled from the Arab League. Of the twenty-one Arab League nations, only Oman, Somalia, and the Sudan continued to maintain full diplomatic relations with the ostracized state; Jordan and Djibouti reestablished ties in 1985. The growing threat from Iran, however, prompted other Arab leaders to reconsider Egypt's role in Middle East politics. Egypt, with more than one quarter of the people in the Arab world, was easily the most populous Arab nation. Egypt's half-million troops also constituted the largest peacetime army of any Arab state. Most Arab leaders came to believe that Egypt's military and economic strength was needed as a counterweight to Iran.

At the November 1987 Amman summit, Arab leaders agreed that "diplomatic relations between any Arab League member state and the Arab Republic of Egypt is a sovereign act decided by each state in accordance with its constitution and laws." Within a year most Arab states had restored ties with Egypt.

Egypt's reintegration not only gave Arab states more confidence that they could withstand Iranian aggression, but it also implied a more flexible attitude toward Israel on the part of the moderate Arab leaders who had pressed for Egypt's rehabilitation. Although Arab leaders were not ready to endorse the Camp David accords, they no longer felt it necessary to condemn Egypt for making peace with Israel. The renewed participation of Egypt in the general Arab-Israeli peace process gave greater weight to the moderate Arab positions of Saudi Arabia and Jordan and it increased pressure on Israel to seek a negotiated settlement.

The Death of Khomeini

By far the most significant leadership change during the second half of the 1980s occurred with the death of Ayatollah Khomeini, the top spiritual and political leader of Iran, on June 3, 1989. He had been the guiding force behind the Iranian Revolution and had led the revolutionary government through ten turbulent years that included the U.S. embassy hostage crisis, many instances of Iranian-supported terrorism, and the war with Iraq. His passing presented Iran and its neighbors with both dangers and opportunities.

So long as Khomeini was alive, Iran was unlikely to turn away from its support of terrorism and its efforts to export its Islamic revolution to neighboring nations. These activities had made Iran a pariah to much of the world, including most of the Gulf states. Yet Khomeini's unifying presence as the undisputed political and religious leader of Iran prevented underlying disputes among Iran's leadership from surfacing. Many Western analysts speculated that after Khomeini died Iran would experience domestic terrorism, leadership struggles, factional fighting, and perhaps even civil war. In the immediate aftermath of Khomeini's death, however, his political heirs avoided the overt factional strife that had been predicted.

Moreover, reputed moderates led by newly elected president Ali Akbar Hashemi Rafsanjani and supported by Khomeini's successor as Iran's top spiritual leader, Ayatollah Ali Khamenei, appeared to have prevailed in the initial maneuvering for power. Rafsanjani indicated that he would focus on economic reconstruction, rather than on promoting revolutionary activity abroad. He also concluded a multibillion-dollar economic reconstruction agreement with the Soviet Union and hinted at increasing economic and political contacts with the West. It was unclear, however, whether Rafsanjani's intention to focus on internal reconstruction would lead to a decrease in Iran's support for terrorist activities.

Internal Dissent

Few Middle Eastern nations are immune to serious internal dissent. During a four-month period in late 1988 and early 1989, two of the longest-lasting regimes in the region survived grave internal threats. Reports indicated that in December 1988 President Saddam Hussein of Iraq weathered a military coup attempt that caused the government to execute a number of military personnel. King Hussein of Jordan withstood a different kind of unrest. In April 1989, while the king was on a diplomatic mission to the United States, Jordanians rioted for ten days to protest price increases on certain staples. The riots resulted in dozens of deaths and forced Jordan's prime minister, Zeid Rifai, to resign.

Throughout the Middle East, ethnic and religious minorities seeking greater autonomy or enhanced political rights—such as the Kurds in Iran and Iraq, the Shi'ites in Saudi Arabia and Kuwait, and the Copts in Egypt—have created domestic tensions that challenge, and in some cases threaten, Middle Eastern leaders. And Islamic fundamentalism remains a strong force of opposition to modernization and Westernization in many nations of the region.

Middle East Arms Race

Even if the potential for war in the short term has been reduced, the consequences of a future war have been multiplied by the Middle East's regional arms race, which escalated during the late 1980s. There are no controls on sales of conventional weapons to Middle East nations, and weapons producers have been willing to sell increasingly sophisticated weapons systems, including surface-to-surface missiles, to countries in the region. Moreover, when one weapons supplier has refused to sell weapons to a nation for political or security reasons, the buyer can turn to numerous other suppliers for comparable weapons. The result has been an unrestrained arms race that not only could increase the devastation of a Middle East war but also could trigger a war by upsetting power balances and inducing nations to launch preemptive strikes.

By far the most dangerous potential development in the Middle East arms race would be the acquisition of nuclear weapons by several states. As of 1989 Israel was the only country known to have a nuclear arsenal, although the

Israeli government does not acknowledge the existence of its nuclear weapons. Other states—such as Iraq, Syria, and Libya—have nuclear weapons programs or have tried to buy a nuclear weapon. While the nuclear arsenals of the superpowers have helped to provide deterrence and stability during the post-World War II period (especially since the 1960s when the Soviets achieved nuclear parity), it would be difficult to establish a similar atmosphere of stability in a nuclearized Middle East because nuclear weapons arsenals would be small and vulnerable, the relatively short distances between countries would make adequate warning of attack difficult, and the intense hostilities between nations would cause leaders to constantly fear a nuclear attack.

Although international constraints on the transfer of nuclear technology have been somewhat successful in slowing the development of nuclear weapons, many Middle East nations have developed the capacity to produce chemical weapons. Arab nations have ignored calls from the West asking them to resist building and deploying chemical arms. Arab leaders have responded that such efforts are necessary to provide a deterrent against Israel's substantial nuclear and chemical arsenal.

Iraq's use of poison gas against its Kurdish minority and Iranian troops demonstrated that chemical weapons are a current threat, not just a long-range problem. Several times during the Gulf war, Iraq resorted to chemical weapons to help repel Iranian "human wave" assaults. Iran reportedly also used chemical weapons, though less frequently than Iraq. Then in August and September 1988, after Iran had agreed to a cease-fire, Iraq used chemical weapons as part of a military campaign to cripple the Kurdish resistance movement within its borders. The Iraqi attacks killed or wounded thousands of Kurds and drove tens of thousands of Kurdish civilians to seek refuge in Turkey.

Libya also became the subject of a chemical weapons controversy. In December 1988 the United States accused that country of building a huge factory near Rabta to produce chemical weapons. Libyan leader Qaddafi maintained that the facility would make only pharmaceuticals, but the United States rejected the explanation and sought international sanctions against Libya. The subsequent disclosure that a West German company had helped Libya to build the facility demonstrated the difficulty of controlling the spread of weapons technology.

2

Arab-Israeli Conflict

For more than forty years, the world has nervously monitored the seemingly unresolvable conflict between Israel and its Arab neighbors. On at least seven occasions the conflict has erupted into outright war, leaving thousands dead, maimed, or homeless. One such war, in 1973, appeared to bring the superpowers close to a nuclear confrontation, when President Richard Nixon, worried about possible Soviet intervention, put American forces on worldwide alert.

In between the hot wars, lower-level hostilities have continued. Acts of terrorism, preemptive and retaliatory raids, other forms of special operations, civil strife, hostile propaganda, and mutual recriminations have become part of daily life in the region. World leaders have sought to mediate the conflict, usually with minimal success. Days and even weeks are given to debates at the United Nations and other international forums on issues associated with the conflict.

The Arab-Israeli conflict also has spawned other regional conflicts, such as the Jordanian civil war in September 1970 and the unresolved Lebanese civil war of the mid-1970s. These apparently local, domestic conflicts too have attracted intensive international attention and involvement, largely because of their association with the Arab-Israeli conflict.

The growth during the late 1960s of an increasingly autonomous and organized national movement among Arab refugees who were driven from or fled Palestine during the 1948 Arab-Israeli war gravely complicated what previously had been perceived as a conflict between Israel and neighboring Arab states. Although the armed cadres of the Palestinian nationalist movement posed no conventional threat to Israel, they were a destabilizing force in the countries where the movement was able to take root. Moreover, their use of commercial aircraft hijackings, bombings of international airports, hostage incidents, and continual acts of sabotage and terrorism in Israel itself drew international attention to their cause, even while tending to discredit it in the eyes of most Westerners whose support for Israel has been greatest. Although most of the world recoiled at the terrorist acts of Palestinian groups, it became increasingly clear in the 1970s and 1980s that the "Palestinian problem" was an integral part of the Arab-Israeli conflict and needed resolution as a part of the overall settlement. So wide-ranging have the ramifications of the Arab-Israeli conflict sometimes been that the problem often is perceived as an international, rather than simply a regional, issue. As such, its ultimate resolution, if one is possible, may require a vigorous international effort. There is doubt, however, that an international settlement that is not completely acceptable to the principal parties could be imposed. The historic proclivity of radical parties from both sides to resort to terrorist tactics to express their grievances implies that any effort to impose a settlement could be met by continued resistance.

Some of the conflict's issues, such as the ultimate status of Jerusalem, are so profound and divisive that a reasonable settlement may not be possible. If so, then the conflict will fester into the indefinite future, aggravating regional as well as international relations and producing crises that could involve the superpowers. Yet because of the risks and consequences of the conflict, efforts to understand its origins, history, and basic issues, and to seek ways to ameliorate it, if not resolve it, will continue.

Origins of the Conflict

The Middle East is the inheritor of five-thousand years of history. The ancient connection of the people of Israel with the land of Palestine is an integral part of the region's history. The Roman destruction of the Second Temple in Jerusalem in A.D. 70 and the forced dispersal of the Jews from Palestine left the Jewish people scattered around the world. Although many Jews assimilated into the many countries of their diaspora, for nearly two-thousand years a significant number retained their Jewish identity and each year concluded Passover ceremonies with the determined prayer, "Next year in Jerusalem." The prophetic concept of an eventual ingathering of the Jewish exiles into the land of their origin influenced the beliefs and expectations of many Jews and Christians in the West.

Zionism, the political movement among European Jewry that led, beginning in the late nineteenth century, to increased Jewish migration to Palestine and ultimately to the successful establishment of an independent Israeli state in 1948, had its roots in specific conditions in nineteenth-century Europe. The growth across Europe and ultimately throughout the world of the idea of nationalism as an ideological basis for political organization caused many to ponder the ultimate meaning of Jewish identity in an age of emerging nation-states. Continuing anti-Semitism throughout most of Europe, culminating in the Nazi holocaust of European Jewry during World War II, finally led most Jews and a great many others in the West to view with favor the idea of an independent Jewish state in Palestine, where more than half a million Jews had established themselves by the end of the war.

Establishing a Jewish state in Palestine, however, was not a simple matter. Much had happened there during the nearly two-thousand years of Jewish diaspora. Since the rise of Islam in the seventh century, the Middle East had become largely an Islamic region, and the inhabitants of Palestine, Syria, Iraq, Egypt, and the Arabian Peninsula were now nearly all Arabs. Islam, a religion closely akin to both Judaism and Christianity, also had laid claim to Jerusalem as one of its holy cities. Most Arabs believed that, as "People of the Book," Jews, like Christians, were free to live peaceably in Arab areas so long as they recognized Arab-Islamic sovereignty. The Arabs, however, did not believe that Jews had a right to an independent state of their own on land that was now part of the Arab-Islamic world. From its inception, therefore, the Zionist movement faced general opposition in the Middle East, not only from the Arab inhabitants of Palestine but also from the larger Arab world of which Palestine was considered a part.

The Arabs of Palestine were ill-equipped to meet the challenge posed by the determined Zionist movement. For four centuries, since 1516, the Ottoman Empire had ruled Palestine. Ottoman rule, although Islamic in character, was fundamentally oppressive and aimed at extracting as much wealth as possible from an increasingly impoverished Arab peasantry. As the twentieth century began, Palestine, like most Arab societies, was seriously underdeveloped. Moreover, long centuries of relatively oppressive foreign rule had fragmented the Palestinian Arabs politically and trained them effectively in the virtues of political accommodation. As a result, the Palestinian Arabs had no tradition of independent political organization, and although they were disturbed by the Zionist movement, they lacked effective political institutions to secure their own rights and interests.

The European powers, meanwhile, were competing for influence and domination in local regions throughout the rapidly declining Ottoman Empire. The European Zionists recognized that they could advance their cause by backing the imperial aims of the European power most likely to prevail in the contest for influence in Palestine. This ambition was achieved in the last days of World War I, when Great Britain concluded that support for the Zionist movement would significantly serve its imperial interests in the Middle East. On November 2, 1917, the British government issued what has come to be known as the Balfour Declaration, named after Lord Arthur James Balfour, the British foreign minister who enunciated it:

> His Majesty's Government views with favor the establishment in Palestine of a national home for the Jewish people, and will use their best endeavors to facilitate the achievement of this object, it being clearly understood that nothing shall be done which may prejudice the civil and religious rights of existing non-Jewish communities in Palestine, or the rights and political status enjoyed by Jews in any other country.

Many observers regard this declaration as the beginning of what has come to be known as the Arab-Israeli conflict, which still eludes resolution nearly three-quarters of a century later.

The British Mandate

The Balfour Declaration committed Great Britain to support the establishment of an independent Jewish state, a goal the fledgling Zionist movement had been seeking since its first meeting in Basel, Switzerland, in 1897. Other powers, including France and the United States, soon issued resolutions of support for the principles enunciated in the Balfour Declaration. In July 1922 the League of Nations adopted the British mandate for Palestine, which incorporated the principles of the Balfour Declaration within its text. Article Two of the mandate document states:

> The Mandatory shall be responsible for placing the country under such political, administrative and economic conditions as will secure the establishment of the Jewish national home, as laid down in the preamble, and the development of self-governing institutions, and also for safeguarding the civil and religious rights of all the inhabitants of Palestine, irrespective of race and religion.

With the official implementation of the British mandate in September 1923, the road was opened for unrestricted Jewish migration to Palestine and the establishment of legally sanctioned institutions that were to culminate in the state of Israel twenty-five years later.

Barriers to a Jewish State

Even with such international support, however, the large-scale Jewish settlement of Palestine and eventual establishment of an independent Jewish state was not inevitable. Although the Zionist movement at this time received considerable support, this backing was more idealistic than practical. In addition, Jews in general during the 1920s simply did not leap at the chance to emigrate to Palestine. Indeed, after an initial surge of migration in 1924 and 1925, the yearly number of Jewish settlers arriving in Palestine fell to an average of between 2,500 and 5,000—hardly a sufficient number to repopulate a land and transform its basic national character. Only after the 1933 German elections that brought Hitler and the Nazi party to power was there a significant increase in Jewish migration, brought on by a growing belief among Jews that a Jewish national home was needed.

The considerable ideological conflict and political factionalism within the early Yishuv (the Jewish settlement in Palestine) also threatened the Zionist movement. Socialist-labor Zionists, mainly from Eastern Europe and Russia, sought to collectivize all economic activity of the Yishuv while totally Judaizing it to the detriment of Arab labor. The labor Zionists often clashed with private Jewish capitalists and investors who hired Arab labor and criticized the labor Zionists for placing socialism above the effort to create a Jewish state. Both these Jewish groups were opposed by an even larger body of Orthodox Jews who opposed the whole Zionist vision of a Jewish state as being inconsistent with their spiritualist view of religion. In addition, conflicts between the leadership of the Yishuv and the Zionist leadership abroad also threatened the unity of the Zionist enterprise.

Another factor inhibiting the progress of the Zionist movement in Palestine was the coincidental growth of nationalist sentiment among the Arabs. The emergence of such sentiment predated World War I and gave rise first to movements opposed to continued Ottoman Turkish rule, and after the war to the imposition of European rule through the League of Nations mandate system. During the war the British had capitalized on the existence of Arab nationalist sentiment by striking an agreement with Hussein ibn Ali (Sherif Hussein) of Mecca, who had led an Arab revolt against the Turks in support of British military operations in Palestine and Syria. In return for this support Henry McMahon, the British high commissioner in Egypt, had promised Hussein British support for an Arab kingdom under his rule after the war. Such a kingdom with its capital at Damascus did come into being briefly in 1919, but it was suppressed in July 1920 by French forces acting to assert France's control over Lebanon and Syria in accordance with its own League of Nations mandate over these areas.

This division of the Arab Middle East into French and British spheres of influence resulted from wartime negotiations. While the British were negotiating with Hussein in 1915 and 1916 and making promises of support for an Arab kingdom after the war, the British and French in 1916 signed the Sykes-Picot agreement that set aside Lebanon and Syria as areas of French interest, while giving Britain a free hand in the Arab region to the south.

The final sorting out of the conflicting promises made in the Hussein-McMahon correspondence, the Sykes-Picot agreement, and the Balfour Declaration came in the Paris peace talks after the war. During these talks Hussein's son, Faisal, who had been proclaimed king of the new Arab state in Damascus, expressed his willingness to collaborate with the Zionists and to accept the principle of a Jewish national home in Palestine. This brief possibility of Arab-Zionist cooperation quickly faded, however, with the overthrow of Faisal's kingdom by France in 1920.

With the demise of the Arab kingdom, Arab nationalist hopes that had been nurtured during the war turned to bitterness. Although some Arabs collaborated with the French and British during the 1920s and 1930s, an increasingly strong nationalist movement promoted strikes, demonstrations, occasional acts of terrorism, and other forms of resistance against European rule. To the nationalists, the European division of the Middle East into several countries was perceived as part of a larger Western strategy to divide and rule the Arab world and to prevent nationalist aspirations from being realized. Many Arabs also perceived Western support for Zionist aspirations in Palestine as an aspect of this strategy, aimed at creating a Western-sponsored base in the Arab world that would legitimize a permanent Western presence in the region to sustain and defend the Jewish national home. The between-wars struggle against European colonial domination, therefore, included opposition to Jewish migration to Palestine as well as to the perpetuation of the mandate system. Arab opposition to Zionist aspirations, consequently, had a pan-Arab character and influenced Arab opinion far beyond the boundaries of Palestine, which, then as now, constituted the central theater of the Arab-Israeli conflict.

A final factor that threatened the Zionist movement was British policy itself. Although Britain remained committed to the promises of the Balfour Declaration, successive British governments amended it in response to Arab nationalist challenges, both within Palestine and beyond. The first major compromise came at the Cairo Conference in March 1921, which was convened by Winston Churchill, then British colonial secretary, to seek ways to consolidate British authority in both Palestine and Iraq in the face of growing Arab nationalist opposition and the

Who Is a Palestinian?

The word "Palestine" is of Roman origin, referring to the biblical land of the Philistines. The term fell into disuse for centuries, but the British revived it as an official designation for the area that the League of Nations mandated to their supervision in 1920, following the World War I breakup of the Turkish-Ottoman Empire. The League of Nations approved the terms of the mandate—including the pledges made by Britain in the 1917 Balfour Declaration—on July 24, 1922.

The British mandate also applied to Transjordan (now Jordan). Transjordan lay entirely to the east of the Jordan River; Palestine lay entirely to the west of the river.

Because the league's mandate applied to both regions, however, the argument was made that "Palestinian" applied to persons east as well as west of the Jordan River and that the designation applied not just to the Arab inhabitants—as is the common practice today—but also to Jews and Christians living in the former mandated area.

Palestine as a legal entity ceased to exist in 1948 when Britain, unable to control Arab-Jewish hostility and the influx of Jewish immigrants to Palestine, relinquished its mandate and Israel declared its independence on May 14. The United Nations had voted in 1947 to partition Palestine into Arab and Jewish sectors.

During 1948-1949 Israel enlarged its territory in a war of independence with neighboring Arab nations. But it did not take control of all Palestine. One region, the West Bank, came under the control of Jordan, which later annexed the territory, and another, the Gaza Strip, came under Egyptian control. These territories, however, were subsequently occupied by Israel during the Six-Day War of 1967.

need to cut costs of colonial administration. The conference decided to install Faisal, the recently deposed Arab king in Damascus, as king of Iraq. In addition, to further appease the embittered supporters of Faisal, the original Palestine mandate was divided at the Jordan River and Faisal's brother, Abdullah, was installed as king in eastern Palestine, which now took the name Transjordan. After this decision Transjordan was no longer open to Jewish migration and settlement, a circumstance that some Zionists saw as a betrayal of the British promise in the Balfour Declaration and a contravention of its responsibilities under the terms of its League of Nations mandate.

British Reassessment

A major outbreak of Arab-Jewish violence around the Wailing Wall in Jerusalem in August 1929 spread to other parts of Palestine and led the British government to take still another look at its policy in Palestine. Two consecutive investigative reports (the Shaw Report of March 1930 and the Hope-Simpson Report of May 1930) concluded that insufficient attention was being paid to the second half of the British obligations under its mandate charter, namely "ensuring the rights and positions" of the non-Jewish inhabitants of Palestine. Both reports recommended restrictions on Jewish migration and limitations on future land transfers to "non-Arabs." The British government accepted these recommendations in the subsequent Passfield White Paper of October 1930. This new policy position provoked a political furor in England, however, and appeared to threaten the survival of the government of Prime Minister Ramsay MacDonald. The prime minister subsequently issued a letter repudiating the white paper, and the perceived threat to Zionist aspirations in Palestine passed. The events, however, indicated to both Arabs and Jews that the British commitment to a Jewish national home in Palestine was not without limits.

Finally, following the upsurge in Jewish migration that accompanied the rise to power of the Nazi party in Germany in the mid-1930s, new violence erupted in 1936 that again led the British government to review its position in Palestine. The "Arab Revolt" of 1936-1939, which in some respects was analogous to the Palestinian *intifada* of the late 1980s, was the first major outbreak of Arab-Israeli hostilities, although British authorities were present as a dominant third party to deal with it. The apparent irreconcilability of Zionist aspirations with Arab nationalist claims finally led the Peel Commission in July 1937 to recommend the partition of Palestine into Jewish and Arab states. This was the first time partition had been officially advocated as a potential solution to the emerging conflict in Palestine. The Peel Commission's recommendation of partition, however, was rejected by the Arabs, and Zionist leaders, although accepting the principle of partition, objected to the limited territory that had been allotted to the Jewish state. The British government again reviewed its position and in May 1939 issued a final white paper, which effectively ended Britain's open-ended commitment to the establishment of the Jewish national home in Palestine.

Historians generally agree that, with the clouds of World War II looming over Europe, Britain's perceptions of its strategic interests in the Middle East now favored positions that would not alienate Arab nationalist sentiment. The British wanted to prevent the Arabs from looking to the Nazis as potential liberators from British control. Consequently, the 1939 white paper, which remained the basis of British policy in Palestine until the end of the British mandate in 1948, emphasized meeting Arab demands more than satisfying Zionist aspirations. It rejected the concept of partition and foresaw the establishment of an independent Palestine state within ten years. During this period the British government in Palestine proposed to develop self-governing institutions that would include Arabs and Jews, even if both sides refused to collaborate. More importantly, however, the white paper enunciated the principle that the Jewish national home could be established only with Arab consent, and it proposed that the Jewish national home be established within the independent Palestine state. Regarding Jewish immigration, 25,000 immigrants would be admitted immediately; over the next five years it would be restricted to 15,000 a year; and after the five-year period future Jewish immigration would occur only with Arab consent. Jewish land purchases and settle-

ments also were restricted to the coastal and lowland areas of Palestine and were not permitted in the hilly and mountainous areas of the country. Finally, if after the ten-year period Palestine still seemed unready for independence, Britain would undertake another review to determine what course of action it would take.

Despite its clear effort to satisfy Arab demands without totally abandoning its prior commitments to the Zionist movement, the 1939 white paper was rejected both by the Arabs and the Zionists. The Arabs opposed it because it did not totally halt Jewish migration and failed to grant immediate political independence to Palestine. The new British policy, however, did prevent further major outbreaks of Arab rebellion, although British military action had effectively suppressed the three-year Arab revolt by early 1939. The Zionists too rejected the white paper on the grounds that it constituted a violation of international law, namely the League of Nations mandate, which they believed obligated Britain to use its authority on behalf of Zionist goals. The Zionists believed that the British government had abandoned its commitment to the Jewish national home, and they vowed to resist the new British policy in Palestine, even while lending support to the British war effort in Europe and North Africa.

Jewish Self-Reliance

The challenges faced by the Zionist movement led its Yishuv component toward increasing self-reliance, even though the Jewish settlement in Palestine remained dependent on diaspora Jewry for financial assistance, migration, and political activism on behalf of the Zionist cause outside of Palestine. During the early 1920s, institutions for organizing the Jewish presence in Palestine had been established. The most significant of these were the Jewish National Fund, which purchased land for Zionist settlement; the Keren Hayesod, a second fund that financed development projects on behalf of the Yishuv; the Histadrut, a countrywide labor organization that gradually became the dominant force in Yishuv and later Israeli affairs; and finally the Haganah, the forerunner of the Israel Defense Force. Overseeing all these activities after 1929 was the Jewish Agency, whose headquarters were in Jerusalem rather than in London, where the World Zionist Organization previously had exerted primary executive authority over affairs of the Yishuv. Increasingly through the 1930s and 1940s, Yishuv figures, notably David Ben-Gurion, Israel's first prime minister, strengthened their influence over the Jewish Agency and the Zionist movement.

Against this developing organization of the Jewish community in Palestine, the Arabs had no counterpart. Divided among various factions that reflected the rivalries among Palestine's traditional notable families, the Arabs generally reacted negatively to British rule and Jewish enterprise instead of constructing a positive political program of their own. Although some Arabs favored collaboration with the British as a means of co-opting British favor, they were usually intimidated into silence by more radical leaders who favored boycotts and general strikes to demand immediate political independence for Palestine. Many militant Arab nationalists were arrested by the British, or they fled abroad before World War II, just as British policy was becoming more supportive of Arab concerns.

Because Arab attacks during the revolt were directed against British authority as well as the Jewish presence, the British began to rely on Jews to perform police duties on their behalf. A Jewish settlement police was raised, trained, armed, and paid by the British to guard isolated Jewish settlements. Most of the Jews organized for this purpose turned out to be members of the Haganah, the secret and illegal paramilitary force being raised by the Yishuv. Police duties gave the Haganah a legal cover for conducting military training and carrying weapons.

The Haganah had since its origins in the early 1920s amounted to little more than a paper organization formally grouping local village defense committees. In 1936 as a consequence of the Arab revolt, however, one thousand men were selected for a standing force available for service anywhere in Palestine. Infiltrated into the British police, they gained useful training, acquired arms, and undertook special operations of their own against Arab groups involved in the revolt. At the same time, a rival Jewish militia, the Irgun Zvai Leumi, was formed under the leadership of Ze'ev Jabotinsky, a political opponent of the socialist-labor Zionists who dominated the politics of the Yishuv and controlled the Haganah. Less restrained than the Haganah, the Irgun favored more forceful tactics, including terrorism, against the Arabs.

The issuance of the British 1939 white paper put Palestinian Jewry on a collision course with the British and strengthened the resolve of the Yishuv to maintain and strengthen the still-secret and illegal Haganah. The restrictions on Jewish immigration into Palestine at a time of extreme anti-Semitism in Nazi-dominated Europe led the Haganah to facilitate illegal immigration in opposition to British policy. At the same time, however, the Haganah collaborated with the British by providing about 27,000 Jews to serve with British forces against Nazi Germany during World War II. This service provided further training and experience to the armed forces of the Yishuv.

A second result of the 1939 white paper was a decision of the World Zionist Organization to broaden its base of international support. No longer confident of British guarantees, the Zionist movement increasingly looked to the United States as a source of funds and political support. At the Biltmore Conference in New York City in May 1942, organized to mobilize the support of the large American Jewish community, resolutions were adopted that called for the United States to support the opening of Palestine to Jewish migration, to recognize the Jewish Agency in Jerusalem as the sole authority in control of immigration and the economic development of Palestine, and to recognize all of Palestine after the war as "a Jewish Commonwealth integrated in the structure of the new democratic world." This appeal had great success, and Great Britain soon found itself increasingly on the defensive in matters pertaining to Palestine, especially after knowledge of the Nazi holocaust of European Jewry began surfacing during the second half of 1942.

End of the British Mandate

The quest for a Jewish homeland in Palestine reached a climax during the three years following the end of World War II. With thousands of displaced Jews from the war living in refugee camps, Britain came under great international pressure, encouraged by the Zionists, to admit them to Palestine. At the same time, the Haganah, the Irgun, and a third breakaway Jewish militia known as the Stern Gang inaugurated a guerrilla campaign against the British in Palestine that included the use of terrorism. Britain was unable to maintain central authority in Palestine and unwilling to

Who Is an Arab?

It is not easy to define accurately the term "Arab." The British geographer W. B. Fisher, in his book *The Middle East: A Physical, Social and Regional Geography*, states: "From the point of view of the anthropologist, it is impossible to speak with accuracy either of an Arab or of a Semitic people. Both terms connote a mixed population varying widely in physical character and in racial origin, and are best used purely as cultural and linguistic terms, respectively." Thus the so-called Arab countries are those that share a common culture and speak Arabic as the primary language.

As Islam spread from the Arabian Peninsula there took place Arabization and Islamization—processes that are closely linked but not identical. Peter Mansfield writes in *The Arabs: A Comprehensive History* that "Arabization began some two centuries before the Prophet Muhammad, with the overflow of Arabian tribes into Syria and Iraq, and reached its greatest impulse during the first decades of the Arab Empire. Islamization lasted much longer and still continues today, especially in Africa."

The Arab countries are Egypt, Syria, Jordan, Lebanon, Iraq, Saudi Arabia, North and South Yemen, Kuwait, Bahrain, Oman, Qatar, a loose group of tiny sheikdoms on the Persian Gulf that form the United Arab Emirates, and the North African countries collectively known as the Maghreb—Morocco, Algeria, Tunisia, and Libya.

Islam is the predominant religion today in all of these countries. That in itself, however, does not define an Arab nation. Turkey, Iran, Afghanistan, Pakistan, Indonesia, the Sudan, and Somalia are Islamic, but not Arab. Similarly, not all Arabs are Moslems. Lebanon's population includes close to a million Arab Christians. In several other Middle Eastern countries there are significant Arab Christian minorities—some with ancestral roots antedating the Moslem conquests and others converted by missionaries. There are also several non-Arab Moslem minorities in the Middle East, including the Kurds in parts of Iraq, Iran, and Turkey.

reverse the policy enunciated in its 1939 white paper because of perceived British interests among the newly independent Arab states of the region. The British government saw no resolution to its predicament and decided to get out of Palestine. In February 1947 it announced that it would end its responsibilities under the mandate and refer the problem to the newly formed United Nations, from which its legitimacy as mandatory power derived.

Thus ended the British mandate for Palestine, a colonial enterprise that had been undertaken to serve British interests in the Middle East by fostering the establishment of a Jewish national home in Palestine. As Arab nationalists, including those of Palestine, strove with increasing success to achieve political independence and an end of European colonial rule in the Middle East, Britain perceived its interests to be associated with the maintenance of satisfactory relations with the newly independent Arab states. These, like the Palestinian Arabs, opposed Jewish migration and resisted any thought that Palestine might be partitioned into two states. Unable to satisfy either Zionist aspirations as promised in the Balfour Declaration three decades earlier or the demands of the Palestinian Arabs, who had the support of their Arab neighbors, Britain turned the matter over to the international community. The United Nations would have to devise a resolution of the problem if violence in Palestine were to be avoided.

Partition of Palestine, 1948 War

At the United Nations a special commission was appointed in May 1947 to investigate the situation in Palestine and to recommend action to the General Assembly. Known as the United Nations Special Committee on Palestine (UNSCOP), the commission was composed of representatives of eleven countries: Australia, Canada, Czechoslovakia, Guatemala, India, Iran, Mexico, the Netherlands, Peru, Sweden, and Yugoslavia. Feted and warmly received by the Zionists and boycotted completely by the Arab leadership in Palestine, the committee concluded that the British mandate should be terminated and that Palestine should be granted independence.

The implacable attitudes expressed by Arabs and Jews, however, led the committee to recommend partition as the basis for granting Palestinian independence. Members of the commission differed on how partition should be implemented. The minority report (India, Iran, Yugoslavia) recommended "an independent federal state" with its capital at Jerusalem, composed of two autonomous political entities (Arab and Jewish), but united by a central government that would include both Arab and Jewish representatives. The majority report recommended the establishment of two sovereign states, joined in an economic federation, but with Jerusalem having a separate status as an international city under UN administration.

The commission presented its report in August 1947, and after nearly three months the General Assembly voted on it. The newly independent Arab states that were now members of the assembly, while favoring Palestinian independence, opposed partition in any form. In the end, however, they supported the UNSCOP minority report in an effort to head off the majority recommendation. Zionist forces and their supporters favored the full partition plan and exerted extreme diplomatic pressure to obtain the votes even of countries whose delegates had gone on record against partition.

Following numerous postponements and delays until the requisite two-thirds vote could be obtained, UN General Assembly Resolution 181, adopting the majority recommendation of the UNSCOP report, was passed on November 29, 1947, by a vote of 33-13, with 10 abstentions.

The United Nations decision on the partition of Palestine was greeted with joy and celebration among Jews around the world, since it provided international sanction for the establishment of a Jewish state. The UN vote, however, caused Arab-Jewish hostilities to erupt throughout Palestine, as Arabs struggled to prevent implementation of the partition plan, and the forces of the Yishuv fought to ensure its implementation. On December 3, 1947, Great Britain, which had abstained from voting on the UN resolution, announced it was unwilling to implement a policy that it had not supported and that lacked support from both sides of the conflict. Britain declared that it would evacuate Palestine on May 15, 1948. On the same day, the two-year-old League of Arab States (Arab League) declared its united opposition to the partition of Palestine and encouraged league members to intervene in support of the Arab cause in Palestine.

With Arabs far outnumbering Jews in Palestine, especially with the support of the armies of neighboring Arab states behind them, it seemed unlikely that the Yishuv could prevail on its determination to establish a Jewish state. In early 1948 the Jewish population of Palestine, which lived mainly in that portion of the country assigned to the Jewish state by the UN resolution, numbered slightly over 600,000, whereas the Arabs numbered about 1,300,000. At least 500,000 Arabs lived alongside Jews in the sector allotted to the Jewish state.

The Arabs, however, lacked institutions of self-government that the Yishuv had been creating since the early 1920s. The Jewish Haganah in late 1947 numbered about 43,000. Consisting mainly of "home guards" who, although not well trained, were well organized to defend established Jewish settlements, the Haganah also possessed a rudimentary mobile field force of about 11,000, many of whose members had served with the British army during World War II. In addition the Irgun, now led by future Israeli prime minister Menachem Begin, fielded a militia numbering about 5,000, while the terrorist organization LEHI (the Stern Gang) included several hundred fighters.

Against these elements of the Yishuv, the Arabs also had forces that could be construed as "village militias," but these lacked central direction. Closely monitored by the British since the Arab revolt in the 1930s, the Arabs found it impossible to develop coordinated military activity until after the November 1947 partition resolution. At that time, two different Arab forces gradually were established. The first, sponsored by Hajj Amin al-Husseini, the leader of the 1936 Arab revolt, who remained in Cairo and was prohibited by the British from returning to Palestine, was the Holy War Army. Never larger than 5,000 loosely coordinated fighters in various parts of the country, Husseini's forces lacked the support of the Arab League, which sponsored a second force, the Arab Liberation Army (ALA). Composed of about 3,800 volunteers from the various Arab countries, including about 1,000 from Palestine, its units entered northern Palestine during January-May 1948. Still a third force in Palestine were elements of Jordan's Arab Legion that remained under British authority, and therefore officially neutral. After Britain's departure on May 15, 1948, the Arab Legion came under Jordanian control.

Fighting during December 1947 and early 1948 consisted mainly of low-level guerrilla operations—sniping, ambushes, and acts of terrorism—as Jewish forces sought to hold the main roads linking Jewish settlements in Palestine. In February 1948 the leadership of the Yishuv announced a general mobilization, and in April the Haganah, which heretofore had conducted mainly defensive operations, went on the offensive. Operating in accordance with what was known as "Plan D," Haganah strategy was to secure control of all territory allotted to the Jewish state by the UN resolution prior to the departure of the British. This involved seizing all Arab towns and villages in the Jewish sector and expelling as many of the Arab inhabitants as possible. The Haganah also attempted to secure the road connecting the Jewish sector with West Jerusalem, where nearly one-fifth of the Jewish inhabitants of Palestine lived.

Jewish forces quickly proved victorious, seizing control of Tiberias on April 18, Haifa on April 22, Safed on May 10, and Jaffa on May 13. In the process, whether voluntarily or not (the issue has always been controversial), some 300,000 of the 500,000 Arabs living in the Jewish sector became refugees by May 15, fleeing to other parts of Palestine or neighboring Arab countries. Historians generally agree that a systematic massacre on April 9 of some 250 Arab inhabitants of Dayr Yassin, a village overlooking the road to Jerusalem, conducted by the Irgun and Stern Gang, helped to create the psychological climate that encouraged the refugees to flee.

Israel Proclaimed

As the British mandate came to a formal end and the last British forces evacuated Jerusalem on May 15, the armed forces of the Yishuv had laid effective claim to virtually all the territory allocated to it under the terms of the partition resolution. On May 14 David Ben-Gurion, head of the Jewish Agency, formally proclaimed the establishment of Israel as an independent state. Both the United States and the Soviet Union quickly recognized the new state of Israel, as did most other members of the United Nations. Of the Western states, only Great Britain delayed recognizing Israel, waiting until January 30, 1949, to recognize the Jewish state.

At this point, if the recently independent Arab states surrounding Israel had acquiesced to the Jewish state's existence, the Arab-Jewish conflict in Palestine might have been effectively ended. The Arabs of Palestine were not in a position to continue the conflict, and an independent Palestinian Arab state prescribed by the UN partition could have emerged. Although Israel had gained control of territory assigned to it in the UN resolution, it had failed to secure control of the road to Jerusalem, and it was possible that Jerusalem could have emerged as the neutral, UN-administered city envisioned by the partition resolution. Earlier hostilities between Jews and Arabs and the Arab states' commitment to their Palestinian brethren, however, made compromise impossible. As they had vowed and had been preparing to do since December 1947, the contiguous Arab states—Egypt, Saudi Arabia, Syria, Transjordan, and Lebanon, as well as Iraq—sent contingents of their armies into Palestine on May 15, as the last British forces were departing.

The 1948 War

The entrance of the Arab armies transformed what had been fundamentally a religious-ethnic conflict in Palestine into a wider war among all the newly established states of the region. Conflicting Arab objectives resulted in uncoordinated military strategies that the new Israeli state was able to exploit to its advantage. In the process, the cause of the Palestine Arabs was submerged in the wider conflict. When the fighting subsided, the Palestine Arabs found themselves living under Israeli, Jordanian, or Egyptian rule, or as displaced refugees in hastily constructed camps around the margins of Israel's newly established, somewhat expanded frontiers. The Arab Palestinians not only failed to keep Israel from being established as a state, they also lost what had been assigned to them in the UN partition resolution.

Despite the attack on Israel by six Arab armies, the armed forces of Israel, now formally reincorporated as the Israel Defense Force on May 26, 1948, continued to hold a distinct manpower advantage. By this time Israel now fielded a mobile army of nine brigades with 25,000 front-line troops that would grow to nearly 80,000 by the end of the year. Historians generally agree that initially the Arabs held the edge in terms of aircraft, armored vehicles, and artillery, but Israel quickly overcame these deficiencies following the British withdrawal from Palestine. With the British departure, restrictions on Jewish immigration also were lifted, and Israel significantly increased its pool of available manpower.

The Arab-Israeli war of 1948 developed in three phases. During the first phase (May 15-June 11), Israel conducted primarily defensive operations that succeeded in halting Arab offensive thrusts into Israeli territory. Unable to break through Jordanian defenses defending the road to Jerusalem, Israel also managed to construct a secondary road, the so-called Burma Road, that enabled Jerusalem to be resupplied, thus securing West Jerusalem for Israel. A UN-brokered cease-fire gave time to all sides, especially Israel, to rearm, reorganize, train, and plan for the second phase of the war. When the truce ended on July 6, primarily because of Syrian and Egyptian unwillingness to extend it, Israel had greatly improved its military position in terms of weapons, manpower, and organization.

During this second phase (July 6-19), Israel took the offensive and delivered several crushing defeats to the various Arab armies. It took Lod and Ramle in central Palestine and Nazareth in the north, all areas designated for the Arab state in the UN partition plan. A determined Israeli effort to capture East (Arab) Jerusalem had failed by the time a second United Nations cease-fire was imposed on July 19.

This second cease-fire was meant to be permanent until final armistices were signed, but it left Egyptian and Jordanian forces in control of the Negev, which the UN partition resolution had assigned to Israel. Determined not to lose the Negev, Israel on October 15 seized the pretext of Egyptian sniping at an Israeli convoy to resume offensive operations that eventually isolated Egyptian forces. The withdrawal of Egyptian forces from the Negev following a new cease-fire on January 7, 1949, opened the way for complete Israeli occupation of the Negev, which it accomplished on March 6-10, 1949. Meanwhile, on October 29-31, 1948, Israel also resumed offensive operations in the north and quickly defeated Syrian, Lebanese, and ALA forces located there, bringing all of Galilee under Israeli control. This further usurpation of territory assigned to the proposed Arab state by the UN partition resolution was soon complemented by the de facto annexation in December of the remaining portion of Arab Palestine (the West Bank) by King Abdullah of Jordan. As the war ended, Egyptian forces remained in occupation of the Gaza Strip, but unlike Jordan they never annexed it.

Effectively defeated by Israel and unable to continue the war, the Arab states finally signed United Nations-sponsored armistice agreements: Egypt on February 25,

Jewish Heritage Unites an Israel . . .

Like the United States, Israel is a country founded and developed by immigrants from many different ethnic and cultural backgrounds. Israel's Jewish population in 1986 was almost as hybrid as America's. Since its founding in 1948, Israel has attracted more than 1.5 million settlers from one-hundred countries.

Israel has encouraged this "ingathering" of Jews from all parts of the world, counting on their common Jewish heritage to help cement their union with other Israelis—a task that has presented many difficulties. This drawing-together is the essence of Zionism, which might be called "the founding religion" of Israel. But even Zionism came under scrutiny in the 1980s.

Zionism is rooted in the nationalist zeal that swept Eastern Europe in the late nineteenth century. It emerged from a ferment of nationalist, socialist, populist, and utopian ideas that were inflaming the youth of that time. As nationalists, the Jews were not unlike other minority groups chafing under foreign rule within the Russian and Austro-Hungarian empires. The Jews had a special impetus, however, because of anti-Semitic persecutions.

Earliest Settlements

The first Jewish settlements in Palestine arose through the efforts of Jews who in 1882 formed an organization called "Lovers of Zion." (Zion is the hill in Jerusalem on which King David's palace is said to have stood.) These young Jews conceived the idea of sending groups of colonists to Palestine, then a neglected backwater of the Ottoman Empire, to establish Jewish communities in the land of their forebears. The movement got its start when Theodor Herzl, a Viennese journalist, wrote *Der Judenstaat,* the rationale for creation of a Jewish state. He later founded the Zionist movement as it exists today. *(Israel profile, p. 167)*

"I imagine that the Jews will always have sufficient enemies, just as every other nation," Herzl wrote. "But once settled in their own land, they can never again be scattered all over the world."

Palestine at that time had a Jewish population of about 25,000, mostly descendants of refugees from the Spanish Inquisition and pious pilgrims who had come to the Holy Land to pray and die. They were poor, religious, and lived separatist lives among the largely Arab Moslem population. The resident Jews looked with hostility on the new arrivals, whom they considered dangerous radicals and religious renegades. The newcomers were equally repelled by a life style that seemed to contain the worst aspects of the ghetto life from which they had fled.

The new arrivals moved beyond the squalid towns to the sparsely populated coastal plains, "a silent, mournful expanse, ravaged by centuries of warfare, fever, piracy and neglect," as Amos Elon describes it in his 1972 book, *The Israelis: Founders and Sons.* This was the ancient land of the Philistines. Ruins of antiquity lay under shifting sand dunes. Much of the area was malarial swampland.

Despite the unpromising scene and the difficult climate, a succession of immigrants succeeded over the next few decades in founding several dozen communities. Land was purchased from absentee owners with funds that came largely from philanthropy. Many could not stand the rigors and emigrated, but those who remained managed to establish agricultural communities, although they came to depend increasingly on Arab laborers.

The Jewish settlement of Palestine was marked by numerous waves of immigration, known by the Hebrew word *aliyah,* meaning ascension (to Zion). The first aliyah, 1882-1903, brought in some 20,000 to 30,000 Jews. The second aliyah, 1905-1914, which brought 35,000 to 40,000 settlers, was the formative one that set the tone for the future nation. Immigrants of this period produced the first leaders of independent Israel, among them David Ben-Gurion and Isaac Ben-Zvi, later prime minister and president, respectively.

The first twentieth-century immigrants were young Jews in their late teens or early twenties, burning with zeal to create a utopia. They believed that only through socialism could a society be created free of the evils of selfishness, materialism, exploitation, and the aberrations that produced anti-Semitism. "What had so dismally failed in Russia (in the abortive revolution of 1905) some now hoped would succeed in one of the most destitute corners of the Ottoman Empire—a safe haven for Jews, and a new paradise," wrote Elon.

Although not religious in the traditional sense, the immigrants were driven by an intense, near-mystical devotion to their cause. Working the soil for them was not merely a pioneering necessity, but a sacred mission. They scorned all luxury, wearing the plainest clothes and eating the simplest food.

Founding of Kibbutzim

"The immigrants of the second aliyah brought with them to Palestine not only their powerful ties to Jewish history and traditions as well as to contemporary political and social movements . . . in their countries of origin, but also ideologies and principles concerning the nature and institutions of the Jewish

... of Many Nationalities and Languages

community and society they intended to create," wrote Judah Matras in a 1970 study in *Integration and Development in Israel*. This wave of immigrants, he claimed, "did in fact later become the political, social, economic, and ideological backbone of the Jewish community in Palestine, and large sectors of life in Israel today are organized around institutions created by immigrants arriving in the second aliyah."

These were the founders of the *kibbutzim*, collective farms that Elon described as "the single most powerful cultural force of the entire Zionist enterprise." The first kibbutz, Degania, was founded in 1910 on swampland near Lake Tiberias; it was the cheapest land available.

The kibbutz idea appealed to the most ardent idealists among the pioneers, and soon many agricultural collectives were established. Although the kibbutzim never held more than 10 to 12 percent of the Jewish population of Palestine, they created the national ideal of the tough, vital, selflessly dedicated, sun-bronzed farmer-soldier and patriot. The kibbutz provided the nation with some of its governing elite and many of its best soldiers. Tales of their heroism are legendary. Although only 4 percent of today's Israeli population has ever lived on a kibbutz, kibbutz members accounted for one-fourth of the Israeli fatalities in the 1967 Arab-Israeli war.

World War I Immigration

World War I brought Jewish immigration to a halt. Furthermore, the Turkish regime, which was on the side of the Central Powers, expelled many Jews who had come from the Allied nations. Other Jews left voluntarily because of deteriorating economic conditions. During World War I the Jewish population of Palestine dropped from 85,000 to 56,000. After the war ended, however, a third aliyah got under way, encouraged by the Balfour Declaration of November 2, 1917, in which the British government expressed sympathy for the Jewish dream of a homeland. Britain in 1917 was the occupying power in Palestine and from 1920 ruled the region under a League of Nations mandate.

Between 1919 and 1923, this third aliyah brought 35,000 Jews to Palestine. This group was composed mainly of Russians, whose motives were similar to those of the prewar pioneers.

The fourth aliyah, 1924-1931, brought some 82,000 immigrants, mainly middle-class Jews from Poland. "An economic depression, combined evidently with anti-Semitism, touched off widespread economic, social and political sanctions and discrimination against the Jews in Poland," according to Matras. Another factor was new U.S. legislation restricting immigration from Eastern Europe. Jewish

immigrants from Asia and Africa rose from less than 5 percent of the total coming to Palestine during the third aliyah to 12 percent during the fourth.

Impact of Nazi Persecution

The fifth aliyah, 1932-1938, was massive. In all, 217,000 Jews came to Palestine in those years. The rise of nazism in Germany and its expansionist moves in Central Europe occasioned the first sizable influx of immigrants from Germany and Austria, as well as from Czechoslovakia, Hungary, and Greece. The Nazi threat also accounted in large part for a renewed flow, totaling 91,000, from Poland. Unlike the pioneers, who were young, unattached, and eager to work the soil, the aliyah of the 1930s included large numbers of settled middle-class families, headed by men who had made their mark in business and in the professions. This group established a number of businesses and cultural institutions that are still important in Israeli society.

Throughout the entire period of Jewish settlement, large numbers of immigrants decided not to stay in Palestine. Nevertheless, by the end of 1938 the Jewish population had risen to 413,000.

Arabs protested the influx of Jews, and the British government responded by reducing immigration quotas and restricting Jewish land purchases. This policy, set forth in a British government white paper on May 17, 1939, remained in force throughout World War II. Nevertheless, 75,000 Jews entered Palestine during the war years, 29,000 of them illegally. By the end of the war in 1945, the Jewish population of Palestine stood at 564,000.

Post-World War II Immigrants

The next wave of immigration drew mainly from the 200,000 homeless Jews—Russian, Polish, and German—who were living in so-called displaced persons camps after World War II. In the years 1946-1948 about 61,000 came to Palestine, nearly half of them slipping through a blockade the British had imposed to halt further immigration. The ban drew protests from a world haunted by the revelations of Hitler's death camps, and it provided an additional ingredient fueling a three-sided civil war that developed among the Jews, the British, and the Arabs.

A hard-pressed Britain notified the United Nations in 1947 that it could no longer continue its role in Palestine and planned to withdraw its forces. With the ending of the British mandate, Jews in Palestine declared the existence of the state of Israel. Within three years Israel's population doubled to 1.4 million, 75 percent of it foreign-born.

1949; Lebanon on March 23; Jordan on April 3; and Syria on July 20. Israel had emerged as an independent state in the region, successfully defended its borders, expanded its assigned territory, and gained general international recognition. With Israel's acquisition of areas allotted to the proposed Arab state and Jordan's annexation of most of the rest of it, the Arab state envisioned in the resolution was left without territory. Moreover, out of Palestine's prewar Arab population of 1,300,000, approximately half had become refugees, either in the West Bank or Gaza or neighboring Arab countries. Jerusalem, moreover, emerged as a divided city, partitioned into Israeli and Jordanian sectors, rather than the united city under international administration proposed by the UN resolution.

Israel refused to negotiate away any of the gains it had made during the war to achieve a durable peace. The Arab states were similarly unwilling to conclude durable peace agreements with Israel. Despite the decisiveness of Israel's victory, therefore, the Arab-Israeli conflict continued.

Early Arab-Israeli Relations

The nearly two decades between the establishment of Israel and the Arab-Israeli war of June 1967 was a time of momentous change in the Middle East. The newly established Jewish state, inhabited by many European emigrés who were highly motivated to build the new state and defend it, was better equipped and more effectively organized to take advantage of post-World War II developments in technology and communications than the more traditional societies of its Arab neighbors. Liberated from the constraints of British rule, Israel embarked on a period of nation building that gradually transformed it into the most technologically advanced state in the region. Unrestricted immigration also led to rapid population growth during the early years of Israeli independence—from a Jewish population of 717,000 in November 1948 to nearly two million by 1961. Many of these immigrants were Jews from the Arab countries. From 1950 onward, the Israeli government insisted that the influx of Jews from Arab countries amounted to a population exchange that freed Israel from responsibility toward the Palestine Arabs who became refugees during the 1948 Israeli war of independence.

For the Arab states surrounding Israel, however, the defeat of their armies by the new Jewish state was perceived as a disaster. So overwhelming did the defeat appear that the legitimacy of every Arab regime was seriously undermined, an era of general Arab political instability was inaugurated, and a popular desire to obtain revenge for the insult of 1948 fueled Arab political rhetoric for the next two decades. Under such circumstances the transformation of the various Arab-Israeli armistice agreements into a permanent peace settlement proved impossible, despite growing Israeli power and the absence of a credible Arab threat.

Unable to force compliance with the UN partition resolution of November 1947, the UN General Assembly in December 1948 established the Conciliation Commission for Palestine to mediate the Arab-Israeli conflict. Consisting of France, Turkey, and the United States and headed by UN acting mediator Ralph Bunche, the commission presided over negotiations on the island of Rhodes. Its efforts led to the various Arab-Israeli armistice agreements. The commission was unable, however, to transform these agreements into a broader peace settlement. The Arab states insisted on negotiating as a unified bloc, while Israel would only negotiate with each individual Arab state. In addition, Israel rebuffed Arab demands for repatriation of Palestinian refugees. Finally, while some Arab leaders privately indicated their willingness to resolve the conflict in return for some territorial concession by Israel, the beleaguered Israeli government adamantly refused to give up any territory, especially after its formal admission into the United Nations on May 11, 1949.

Israel's refusal to permit even a partial repatriation of Arab refugees and the Arab states' refusal to grant them citizenship created an enormous refugee problem. In response, the United Nations in 1950 established the UN Relief and Works Agency (UNRWA) to fund and administer refugee camps in Lebanon, Syria, Jordan, the West Bank, and Gaza. The camps, which soon became permanent, demonstrated the impotence of the international community in leading the conflicting parties toward an overall settlement.

Regional Arms Race

Aware of the unstable political situation that had emerged after the unresolved 1948 Arab-Israeli war, Great Britain, France, and the United States in May 1950 announced a Tripartite Declaration in which they agreed to limit arms supplies to the various parties of the Arab-Israeli conflict and to insist on a political rather than a military solution to the problem. This early effort to contain a potential arms race soon broke down, however, when Israel in 1954 concluded a major arms agreement with France. On February 28, 1955, Israel made use of its newly strengthened armed forces to launch a successful raid against an Egyptian position in the Gaza Strip. Ostensibly undertaken in retaliation for continuing border incidents by unknown Arab refugees, the raid was carried out primarily to demonstrate Israeli military strength and the futility of continued Arab nonrecognition of Israel.

Instead of intimidating Egypt into recognizing the permanence of Israel, however, the Gaza raid, along with other similar Israeli retaliatory raids into Arab territory, provoked the new military leadership in Egypt, headed by Col. Gamal Abdel Nasser, to seek a reliable source of arms for itself. Nasser preferred to obtain arms from the West, especially from the United States, which was seeking to draw Egypt into a Western-sponsored Middle East alliance system. When President Dwight D. Eisenhower refused to provide arms on terms that Egypt would accept, however, Nasser turned to the Soviets. The subsequent Soviet-Egyptian arms agreement, announced on September 27, 1955, marked the final collapse of the Tripartite Declaration arms limitation policy, gave impetus to the developing French-Israeli arms relationship, undercut U.S. efforts to contain Soviet influence in the Middle East, and provoked tensions that led to renewed war between Israel and Egypt in November 1956.

Barriers to Peace

Despite continuing diplomatic efforts by the United Nations, United States, and Great Britain to diminish tensions and suggest plans for an overall Arab-Israeli settlement, a variety of factors combined to thwart peace efforts. Foremost among them was the pattern of border clashes and incidents that developed almost from the moment the

1949 armistice agreements were signed. In the beginning these clashes were often begun by Arab villagers on one side of the armistice line whose lands and crops had ended up on the Israeli side of the unofficially established Israeli border. The border incidents, however, gradually evolved into more organized attempts at sabotage and violence by refugee elements, who even in the early 1950s, began to coalesce into various resistance groups. Arab governments sometimes supported these groups, but more often governments sought to control them.

Israel tended to hold the appropriate Arab government responsible for patrolling the Arab side of the border, but Arab governments generally were unable or unwilling to perform this task. Israel's adoption in 1952 of a more aggressive reprisal policy led the Arab states to enhance their defensive preparations.

Israel's sense of isolation and vulnerability during the early 1950s was fueled by Arab rhetoric calling for its destruction, an Arab League—sponsored boycott on trade with Israel and ultimately on any international company doing business with Israel, and frequent Egyptian blockades of sea traffic to or from Israel through the Strait of Tiran or the Suez Canal. The Soviet-Egyptian arms agreement of September 1955 dramatically increased Israeli fears of the Arabs' potential military capabilities. Pressure in Israel grew for a large preemptive strike against Egypt, mainly to secure Sharm al-Sheikh, the western flank of the Strait of Tiran, before Egypt could integrate its new weapons into its armed forces. Israel also signed a major new arms agreement with France.

Western Hostility toward Egypt

Israel's growing desire to attack Egypt was made increasingly feasible because of developing Western hostility toward Egypt's new military government, increasingly dominated from 1954 by Nasser. France viewed Nasser as an enemy because of the moral and material support he offered to the Algerian resistance fighters who opposed French rule in North Africa. Great Britain also was alarmed by the nationalist policies of Nasser, who sought to end the British presence in Egypt and the Suez Canal Zone. Nasser also resisted British efforts to organize the Baghdad Pact, a Western-supported alliance (Turkey, Iraq, Iran, Pakistan) intended to check the expansion of Soviet influence in the Middle East.

Finally, the United States, whose policy was to encourage Egypt's inclusion in any Western alliance formed in the region, gradually became disenchanted with Nasser's policies as well. His official acceptance of Soviet arms assistance in September 1955, his refusal to lift a blockade against Israeli shipping through the Strait of Tiran and the Suez Canal, and his recognition of Communist China in May 1956 were all considered blows to U.S. interests. Nasser's recognition of China, however, was the act that led the U.S. secretary of state, John Foster Dulles, on July 20, 1955, to withdraw promised financing for the proposed Aswan High Dam, the principal symbol of Nasser's ambitious plans for Egypt's agricultural and economic development. Although Dulles's move was probably a bargaining maneuver aimed at forcing Nasser to take more seriously U.S. interests in the region, Nasser unexpectedly reacted on July 26 by nationalizing the French- and British-owned Suez Canal Company. This action led Great Britain and France to begin preparations for a joint military operation to take back the canal.

Unable to secure support for an Anglo-French military intervention from the United States, which preferred a negotiated settlement of the Suez crisis, the two Western allies and Israel adopted a strategy of deception. Israel would launch an attack on Egyptian forces in the Sinai and appear to threaten the canal. At this point Great Britain and France would intervene to separate the warring parties, reoccupying the Suez Canal in the process. The operation was timed for late October 1956, when the Soviet Union was preoccupied with the uprising in Hungary and the United States was faced with presidential elections. The British and French believed the elections would prevent the Eisenhower administration from taking any action against Israel.

1956 Suez Crisis

In accordance with the prearranged secret plan, Israel launched its offensive against Egyptian positions in the Sinai on October 29. The attack included an Israeli paratroop drop near the Mitla Pass to give the appearance of a threat to the Suez Canal. The transparency of the allied strategy was evident on the following day, however, when France and Great Britain jointly issued an ultimatum demanding an immediate cease-fire, a withdrawal of Egyptian and Israeli forces from opposite sides of the Suez Canal, and Egyptian acceptance of a temporary occupation by French and British forces of the Suez Canal Zone to separate the belligerents and to ensure freedom of shipping through the canal. At this point, Israeli-Egyptian hostilities had barely begun near the Israeli frontier, far from the Suez Canal, and Egypt would have had to evacuate its 30,000-man force from the Sinai to observe the terms of the cease-fire.

Israel quickly indicated its acceptance of the ultimatum, while Nasser rejected it but issued orders that in the event of an Anglo-French attack on Egypt, all forces in the Sinai were to be withdrawn to defend the canal. These orders were implemented on the nights of October 31 and November 1, following French and British air attacks against Egyptian airfields on October 31. The withdrawal of Egyptian forces from the Sinai, coupled with the decimation of the Egyptian air force by the allied air attacks, opened the way for Israel's complete occupation of the Sinai Peninsula, almost without a fight, which it achieved by the morning of November 5.

Meanwhile, on November 1 the United Nations General Assembly adopted a United States—sponsored resolution calling for an immediate cease-fire, a withdrawal of Israeli forces behind the 1949 armistice lines, the reopening of the Suez Canal (which Egypt had closed), and all other United Nations members (that is, Great Britain and France) "to refrain from introducing military goods into the area." Egypt immediately accepted this call for a cease-fire, but Israel, Britain, and France would not, the latter two because they had not yet introduced ground forces in the Suez Canal area, which they were able to do only by November 5. Finally caving in to both international and domestic pressure, Great Britain accepted the United Nations cease-fire effective at midnight on November 6-7, long before it had been able to achieve its military objectives in the Suez Canal Zone, but well after Israeli objectives had been achieved. Israel and France also accepted the cease-fire.

Of the three attackers, Israel alone had achieved its military objectives in the 1956 Suez crisis. Nevertheless, as in 1949, it was unable to translate military victory into a lasting political settlement. Under strong pressure from the United Nations, and especially from the United States and the Soviet Union, to withdraw unconditionally from all territories it had occupied during the conflict, Israel ultimately did so. The last Israeli troops left Gaza on March 9, 1957. The last French and British troops had left Egypt on December 22, 1956.

In return for Israel's evacuation of the Sinai, Israel and Egypt accepted the presence on the Egyptian side of the Israeli-Egyptian armistice line of a United Nations Emergency Force (UNEF), which began arriving in mid-November 1956. The force's mission was to help protect Israel's southern frontier from further Arab attacks as well as to ensure freedom of Israeli navigation through the Strait of Tiran. These being two primary goals of its 1956 war against Egypt, Israel in fact profited from its military campaign. It failed, however, to secure a general peace treaty as a result of the war or explicit Arab recognition of its legitimacy as an existing state. Therefore, it remained technically at war with Egypt, as with the rest of the Arab world.

Arab Rivalries

Despite the lack of an overall settlement of the Arab-Israeli conflict, the years immediately following the Suez crisis witnessed a significant downturn in Arab-Israeli tensions. This was primarily due to Arab preoccupation with inter-Arab politics and rivalries. Although anti-Israeli sentiment remained the staple of Arab political rhetoric, Israel took a back seat to instability and other problems that afflicted Arab regimes.

Despite the military defeat Egypt had suffered during the Suez crisis, Nasser emerged from its aftermath as a popular hero for many Arabs. Whatever the military outcome of the war, the political result was that Britain and France, the traditional colonial powers in the Arab world, had been humiliated. Moreover, the Egyptian nationalization of the Suez Canal received permanent international recognition, Israel had been denied any territorial expansion, and Nasser was seen as the leader capable of restoring Arab unity and pride. Pro-Nasser parties and groups, perhaps encouraged by Egyptian funds, sprang up throughout the Arab world. Nasser enjoyed an era of leadership in the Arab world that lasted until Egypt's humiliating defeat in the Arab-Israeli war of 1967.

The popularity of Nasser and what came to be known as "Nasserism" provoked crises in several Arab countries during the late 1950s and early 1960s. Pro-Nasser groups and other opponents raised challenges to King Hussein's rule in Jordan that led to British intervention in support of the king in both 1957 and 1958. In February 1958 Syrian politicians, inspired by Nasser, came to Cairo offering their country as part of a Nasser-led United Arab Republic (UAR). This political union of Egypt and Syria lasted three years until disgruntled Syrian officers reclaimed Syrian sovereignty through a successful military coup in September 1961.

Inspired by the union of Egypt and Syria, large numbers of Lebanese in 1958 demonstrated in favor of union with the UAR. The subsequent destabilization of the existing Lebanese government led to United States intervention during the summer in support of continued Lebanese sovereignty. Almost simultaneously, military officers in Iraq, again influenced by the example set by Nasser's Egypt, overthrew their pro-Western monarchy and withdrew Iraq from the Baghdad Pact. Rather than join the new United

Arab Republic, however, the new military regime emphasized Iraqi independence and began to vie with Nasser for moral leadership in the Arab world.

Finally, in September 1962 pro-Nasser elements in the North Yemen military overthrew their traditional monarchy, leading ultimately to Egyptian military intervention against the Saudi-financed royalist opposition, which the new Yemeni military regime could not subdue. The heavy Egyptian commitment in soldiers, money, and materiel in North Yemen seriously drained Egyptian resources and decreased Nasser's capability to conduct a successful war against Israel in 1967.

Despite continuing popular support in the Arab world, by the mid-1960s Nasser experienced strained relations with other Arab regimes. Relations with Saudi Arabia were the most hostile because of the conflict in Yemen, but Jordan and Iraq also had disputes with Egypt. Successive Syrian regimes also sought to establish their legitimacy among the Arab masses by advancing their own revolutionary credentials, leaning either toward Egypt or Iraq.

In the midst of these Arab disputes, any Arab threat to Israel seemed remote. It was true that with Soviet support and assistance, Egypt and Syria were arming themselves for a potential third round of hostilities against Israel. The Jewish state, however, continued its reliable arms relationship with France and was developing its own arms manufacturing industry. In addition it was gradually building its highly trained citizen army to meet future Arab military challenges. Israeli victories in 1948 and 1956 also provided a measure of deterrence against an Arab attack. Even as late as the spring of 1967, the possibility of an Arab-Israeli war did not appear likely. Yet out of the conflicts spawned by developing inter-Arab rivalries lay the seeds of the war that broke out on June 5, 1967.

The Six-Day War of 1967

Two developments in 1964 led to the gradual revival of Arab-Israeli border tensions that culminated in the Six-Day War of 1967. An Israeli project to divert water from the Sea of Galilee along an aqueduct to the Negev Desert led Syria to call for joint Arab action against the Israeli effort. Seeking to reassert his credentials as leader of the Arab world, Nasser called for a meeting of Arab heads of state under the auspices of the Arab League in Cairo. This first Arab summit convened in January 1964 and announced two significant decisions. The first was general Arab support for Syria to divert sections of the Jordan River lying in its territories, a step that would diminish the amount of water flowing into Israel. As Syrian construction crews began to undertake this project in late 1964, however, Israeli air strikes forced them to halt work.

The second decision taken at the Arab summit was the formal establishment of the Palestine Liberation Organization (PLO). Since the 1956 Suez crisis, many stateless Palestinian refugees from the 1948 war had been organizing political groups and attempting to mobilize public sentiment for their return to what was now Israel. In general, they still looked to the Arab regimes to help them achieve this mission, but many became increasingly skeptical about the capability and the will of the Arab governments to keep the issue alive.

Some Palestinians, such as George Habash, a leader of the Arab National Movement (ANM), which he had helped establish in Beirut in the early 1950s, believed that general revolutionary upheaval and the achievement of Arab unity was a precondition for overcoming Israeli intransigence. Soon after the formation of the PLO in 1964, Habash established a Palestinian wing of the ANM known as the National Front for the Liberation of Palestine (NFLP—later to be called the Popular Front for the Liberation of Palestine, or PFLP). Still others, such as Yasir Arafat's Fatah (Conquest) organization, established about 1959, took the view that the Arabs of Palestinian origin had to develop their own independent political capacity, distinct from the Arab states, to foster an eventual return of the lands lost in 1948.

The proliferation and appeal of such groups led Nasser to favor the establishment of a formal Palestinian organization within the Arab League structure. In this way he sought to channel Palestinian irredentist energies into another base of support for himself and his leadership in the Arab world. At the same time he sought to exert control over the Palestinian movement. The language of the summit communiqué establishing the PLO was significant. Where previous gatherings of Arab officials since 1949 had called for the "application of the United Nations resolutions" on the issue, that is, that Israel should accept border rectifications and the return of Arab refugees, the new formulation called for "the liberation of Palestine," thus implying a resolution of the Arab-Israeli conflict through military force.

Mounting Tensions

Nasser wanted to avoid direct confrontation with Israel in 1964 and refrained from mobilizing general Arab support against Israel's effort to stop Syria's water diversion project. Unable to count on Nasser's backing, Syria responded by providing arms and training to Yasir Arafat's Fatah organization, which began undertaking sabotage operations against Israel. The Fatah operations, which caused little damage but resulted in some Israeli casualties, continued through 1965 and escalated in 1966 and 1967. Complicating the problem for Israel was the fact that although the attacks originated in Syria, the missions were conducted over Jordan's West Bank armistice line with Israel. In accordance with its traditional policy, therefore, Israel held Jordan responsible for failing to control its border. In November 1966, after a particularly serious incident in which several Israelis were killed, Israel retaliated against the village of Samu near Hebron in the West Bank.

During this period tensions also had risen along the Syrian-Israeli frontier because of Syrian shelling of Israeli settlements from elevated positions in the Golan Heights. Although UN observers often held Israeli settlers responsible for these incidents because of their efforts to farm disputed territories whose status had not been resolved in the 1949 armistice agreement, the Syrian shells nevertheless often hit areas outside of the disputed zones, including established Israeli settlements. Finally, a particularly intensive Syrian shelling on April 7, 1967, escalated into an air battle in which Israeli pilots shot down six Syrian aircraft.

Syrian and Jordanian reaction to these mounting tensions focused on criticism of Nasser. They accused him of hiding behind the UNEF troops along his armistice line with Israel and of being more interested in his empire in Yemen than in helping confront the common Israeli enemy. The regimes in Jordan and Syria, despite their own rivalry,

in effect dared Nasser to assert his self-proclaimed leadership of the Arab world.

The terrorist attacks against Israel were not deterred by Israeli counterstrikes, and in early May 1967 the Israeli government announced that it was considering more decisive action, especially against Syria. Rumors of Israeli preparations for war along the Syrian border, apparently spread by Moscow, raised a challenge that Nasser could not avoid. On May 16 he demanded the withdrawal of the UNEF from the Sinai and began reinforcing Egyptian troops near the frontier with Israel. On May 22 Nasser announced his intention to reestablish the blockade of the Strait of Tiran at the entrance to the Gulf of Aqaba. This last action, which violated the terms of the 1956 agreement that ended the Suez crisis, was considered an act of war by the Israeli government.

War fever began to grip the Arab world, fueled by Jordan's decision on May 30 to join a mutual defense pact with Syria and Egypt. The latter two had entered into such an agreement the previous November. Meanwhile, paralyzed by indecision, the Israeli government fell, and on June 1 a new national unity government was formed that included Moshe Dayan, the architect of Israel's 1956 military campaign, as minister of defense.

With historical hindsight, it now seems possible that if Israel had not launched hostilities on June 5, no war would have occurred in 1967. Nevertheless, any diplomatic settlement of the crisis, which U.S. officials were trying to arrange, would likely have been reached at Israel's expense. Although Nasser insisted that any outbreak of war would be initiated by Israel, other Arab leaders spoke of destroying Israel. Egyptian movements in the Sinai also appeared to indicate a plan to break through the Negev to create a land corridor linking Egypt and Jordan, a goal of Egyptian diplomacy since 1949. Terrorist operations against Israel also would not likely have ended with a diplomatic settlement. Finally, Israeli military strategy, grounded in a perception of the country's geographic vulnerability, placed an emphasis on capturing the initiative by launching a preemptive first strike. These factors combined to lead the new Israeli government to decide to go to war.

Israel Attacks

During the Six-Day War Israel executed a brilliant military strategy that resulted in its reconquest of the Sinai peninsula, and the conquest of Jordan's West Bank and Syria's Golan Heights. Achieving total surprise, Israel launched its military campaign on June 5 at 8:45 a.m. (Egyptian time), after dawn alerts had ended at Egyptian airfields and the Cairo rush hour was in full swing. In three hours of precise wave attacks. Israeli aircraft struck Egyptian airfields, destroying about 300 of the 430 aircraft in the Egyptian inventory. Then during the noon hour and early afternoon, similar attacks destroyed the air forces of Jordan and Syria and Iraqi aircraft deployed at a major airfield in western Iraq. The achievement of immediate Israeli air superiority enabled the outmanned Israeli ground forces to have the decisive advantage in the land battles that followed.

Meanwhile Israeli ground forces launched a multipronged attack into the Sinai. Unlike the campaign of 1956, which was designed to confront static Egyptian defensive positions, the 1967 attack aimed at breaking through Egyptian lines, severing lines of communication, and finally destroying the Egyptian army as it tried to retreat. With

The Rise of Arab Nationalism ...

The faint beginnings of Arab nationalism can be traced back to the nineteenth century, when it was strongest among Christian Arabs, who did not identify fully with the larger Islamic community and who were more susceptible to Western ideas. The British occupation of Egypt in 1882 sparked development of nationalism there, but until World War I it was the Moslem faith that supplied the predominant bulwark against the encroaching West.

As a popular movement, Arab nationalism first developed from 1908 to 1914 with the Young Turks' rise to power in the Ottoman Empire. The Young Turks advocated a constitution providing for the fusion of the different races of the empire into a single, Ottoman democracy. Once in control, however, the Young Turks used their power to promote Turkish interests and to rule the empire on the tenet of Turkish racial supremacy. In response, Arab leaders formed secret societies in Beirut, Cairo, and Paris and called for Arab political autonomy within the empire. Arab efforts culminated in the convening of the 1913 Paris Congress, at which the Young Turks agreed to the Arabs' request on the basis of further negotiation. The defeat of the Ottomans in World War I and the occupation of the Arab Middle East by the victorious European powers, however, provided the Arabs with an even stronger desire to pursue political autonomy.

At the beginning of the war, most Moslem Arabs favored the Turks against the Allied powers. But in 1916 the British organized an Arab revolt, immortalized by the adventures and writings of T. E. Lawrence. Bedouin troops supported the British forces advancing through Palestine and Syria. Their leaders had been promised Arab independence, but once the war ended the Allied powers were reluctant to give up their control. Instead, the Arabs of the former Ottoman Empire found themselves divided into a series of states governed under British or French mandates. The mandates, as formalized by the League of Nations between 1922 and 1924, provided that the British and French would administer and develop the territories until they were ready for independence.

The British were given control of Palestine, Jordan, and Iraq. Both Transjordan (the area to the east of the Jordan River) and Iraq were ruled by Arab kings—under the supervision of British advisers and troops. Palestine was run by a British commissioner who, under the League of Nations mandate, was allowed to begin developing a national home for the Jews. Syria, which then included what later became Lebanon, was administered by the French. In 1923 the British agreed to independence for Egypt, but it retained advisers and the right to station troops to oversee the Suez Canal. Iraq's independence came with the end of the British mandate in 1932.

The situation in the Arabian Peninsula was different. The strength of the Ottoman Turks had never penetrated deeply there. There was a major rivalry for power between King Hussein, ruler of the Hijaz, and Ibn Saud, ruler of Najd. The French and British were content to let them fight it out, and in 1927 Ibn Saud became sovereign over both Najd and the Hijaz.

Between the world wars Saudi Arabia, while independent, was too inward-looking to lead the move for Arab unity that had begun during World War I. The other states, under their tutelary rulers, were concerned with achieving a greater degree of independence from occupying powers rather than with working for pan-Arab nationalism.

The pan-Arab movement was reawakened by World War II. The Arabs in 1939 had progressed beyond the complete servitude of 1914 to a semi-autonomous existence based on treaties with Britain and France. The war removed the French from Syria and Lebanon and the Italians from Libya, leaving Britain the only colonial power in the Middle East. Arab nationalism intensified, and the eventual end of the British role appeared inescapable.

Near the end of the war the Hashemite Arab leaders of Iraq and Syria proposed to unite several Arab countries under their leadership. Non-Hashemite Arabs and the British opposed the plans. They supported instead the formation of a loose federation of the Arab states that would safeguard national sovereignties but enable them to work for the common interest. The federation concept grew out of two conferences among Egypt, Saudi Arabia, Yemen, Transjordan, Syria, Lebanon, and Iraq and became known as the Arab League.

The Arab League

The birth of the first pan-Arab organization in 1944 stirred high hopes among many Arabs, but its capacity for action turned out to be considerably less than many had hoped. The seven original states were unequal in wealth and prestige and had differing political goals. None wanted to sacrifice its own sovereignty to a federal ideal, and there were destructive personal rivalries among the rulers of Egypt, Saudi Arabia, Jordan, and Iraq.

The one area in which members of the league were in complete agreement in the early years was opposition to growing Jewish claims to Palestine. After the United Nations voted to partition Palestine in 1947, the Arab League declared war against the new state of Israel. But instead of acting in a truly coordinated fashion, each Arab state tried to help a particular client group in an effort to emerge as the champion of the Palestinian Arab cause. This uncoordinated and conflicting effort led to the Arabs'

... and Efforts toward Unification

defeat in the first Arab-Israeli war, bitter feuds among the Arab governments, and the influx of unwanted Arab refugees into other Arab countries.

The 1948 war and subsequent emergence of Egypt as the leader in the Arab League wiped out British designs of a British-Hashemite plan for Arab unity and, consequently, British influence in the league. The formation in Gaza of the All-Palestinian government under Egyptian aegis, Jordan's annexation of eastern Palestine (which the league condemned and only two countries recognized), and a breakdown in the Syrian government in 1949 threatened to bring down the Arab League completely. It was resuscitated, however, by the signing of a mutual security pact aimed at protecting Syria from the ambitions of the Hashemite kings.

Neither the mutual security pact nor any other collective action by the league was of great practical value. Nevertheless, the league did perform some useful functions. In his book *From War to War,* Middle East authority Nadav Safran speculates that the league "gave the idea of pan-Arabism an institutionalized expression that made it part of Arab daily life." During the 1950s it also was responsible for useful administrative and cultural initiatives.

The Arab League has remained an important Arab forum, though one where rival Arab countries often displayed more disunity than unity. Currently the league has twenty-two members, including the Palestine Liberation Organization (PLO). Egypt was expelled in 1979 after President Anwar Sadat signed the Egyptian-Israeli peace treaty, but it was welcomed back into the organization in May 1989. Notably, when Syrian forces were used beginning in mid-1976 to quell the destructive Lebanese civil war, they did so under the colors of the Arab League.

The Arab League members as of late 1989:

Algeria	Palestine Liberation
Bahrain	Organization
Djibouti	Qatar
Egypt	Saudi Arabia
Iraq	Somalia
Jordan	Sudan
Kuwait	Syria
Lebanon	Tunisia
Libya	United Arab Emirates
Mauritania	Yemen Arab Republic
Morocco	Yemen, People's Democratic
Oman	Republic of

The league set up more than twenty specialized agencies and institutions and sponsored other projects such as the Arab Common Market and various funds and financial organizations. Its two most notable successes have been the Economic Unity Council and the Boycott of Israel Office.

The factionalism of the Arab League and its failure to meet primary goals have been reflected in the larger history of the Arab world since World War II. As the British systematically gave up their remaining control, the newly independent nations endured dictatorships, coups, assassinations, and abdications. Moreover, the Arab countries were continually interfering in each others' affairs. Egypt, for example, attempted to instigate or support revolutions in Syria, Lebanon, Iraq, Jordan, Saudi Arabia, and Yemen. Egypt became involved in a full-scale war in Yemen during the 1960s and at one point had as many as seventy thousand troops there. Almost all of the Arab countries at some time were involved in machinations intended to bolster one state against another. Until 1973 attempts to achieve fruitful pan-Arab cooperation ended in failure.

For much of the postwar period, Egypt, the most populous state, sought to lead the Arab world. In 1952 the monarchy was overthrown and supplanted by a military dictatorship headed by Gamal Abdel Nasser, a vigorous and charismatic figure. Nasser emerged as the champion of Arab nationalism, but his feuds with other leaders often made him a divisive force in the region. President Anwar Sadat, his successor, however, broke with the pan-Arab ideologues and advocated an Egyptian nationalist philosophy. This approach was dramatically exemplified by his trip to Jerusalem and the signing of the Egyptian-Israeli peace treaty in 1979.

Other Unification Attempts

Since World War II there have been several unsuccessful attempts to form federations of Arab states. Syria and Egypt in 1958 united in a common government to form the United Arab Republic. The federation was ended by a Syrian coup in 1961. Nasser threatened the Syrians but was powerless to act; Syria's nearest point was 130 miles from Egypt. Subsequent efforts to unite Syria and Iraq, since they were both controlled by the Ba'ath party, also fell apart owing to disagreement over the implementation of Ba'athist principles. Syria, Egypt, and Libya in 1971 formed a loose Federation of Arab Republics. Plans for an actual merger of Libya and Egypt collapsed in 1973.

On September 10, 1980, the leaders of Libya and Syria agreed to merge their countries. But the merger still has not been realized, because of disagreements over how it should be implemented.

Libya and Morocco agreed August 14, 1985, to form a union of their two states, but in 1986 Libya renounced the agreement after Morocco's King Hassan held talks with Israel's Prime Minister Shimon Perez.

complete air superiority, the Israeli strategy proved highly effective. Egypt unconditionally accepted a UN Security Council request for a cease-fire on June 9. By this time, however, Israel had achieved full control of the Sinai Peninsula and the Jordanian West Bank.

The circumstances and motivations of Israel's attack on Jordan are less clear. Forty-five minutes after launching its air strikes against Egypt, Israel sent a message through UN mediators to the Jordanian king informing him that Israel would not attack the West Bank unless Jordan attacked first. Nevertheless, deceived by Nasser that Egypt was destroying the Israeli air force rather than being destroyed by it, Hussein ordered his artillery to open fire on various targets in Israel, apparently before receiving the Israeli message. Although this firing did not constitute a prelude to Jordanian offensive operations, it did supply a pretext for Israel to attack the West Bank.

Israeli military action against the West Bank began at 11:15 a.m. on June 5, shortly before its destruction of the Jordanian air force. The capture of East Jerusalem was the first Israeli priority. Fierce fighting around the city occurred June 5 and 6. Realizing the weakness of his position, the Jordanian commander in Jerusalem withdrew his forces during the night of June 6, and unopposed Israeli forces took control of the city the next morning. Meanwhile, Israeli columns moved in from the north, west, and south against Jordanian forces concentrated at Nablus. Aided by air superiority, they gradually overcame Jordanian resistance and converged on Nablus on June 7. Virtually surrounded by approaching Israeli forces, and with their morale broken, the defenders of Nablus fled in a disorganized fashion across the Jordan River, leaving Israel in effective control of the West Bank. At 8:00 that evening, both Jordan and Israel accepted the UN appeal for a cease-fire, fully a day and a half before the cease-fire concluded in the Sinai. Israel now took up the problem of Syria.

Syria, whose actions and policies had done so much to provoke the war, did little once hostilities had started. After the destruction of its air force on June 5, Syrian military movements were vulnerable to Israeli interdiction. As the magnitude of Israel's victories in the Sinai and West Bank became apparent, the Syrian government planned at the appropriate moment to accept the UN call for a cease-fire, which it did at 5:20 p.m. on June 8. Since the outbreak of the war four days earlier, however, Syrian artillery from the Golan Heights had kept Israeli forces and settlements under constant bombardment. The Israeli government faced strong public pressure from its population in the north and from army units in its northern territorial command to do something to silence the Syrian guns. Accordingly, without informing the rest of his government, Israeli defense minister Moshe Dayan ordered the army to attack Syria as soon as its units were ready on June 9. Syria may have accepted the cease-fire on June 8, but as Dayan later remarked wryly in his memoirs, it "went into effect a day and a half later."

Despite the formidable obstacle posed by the Golan Heights, Israeli columns advanced up the Heights without faltering, although they faced withering fire from dug-in Syrian positions along their routes. The Syrian government in Damascus sent an immediate protest concerning Israel's violation of the cease-fire to the United Nations and issued orders for its front-line units to withdraw from the Golan Heights to defensive positions near the capital. This withdrawal began even before the Israelis reached the crest of the Heights on the afternoon of June 9. Consequently,

when Israel resumed operations the following morning, its units swept to their designated military objectives without opposition. Having achieved its military objectives, Israel accepted the UN cease-fire at 6:30 p.m. on June 10, the sixth day of the war.

Aftermath of the War

The results of the Six-Day War greatly complicated the Arab-Israeli conflict. Before the war the key issues were quite simple: the final settlement of Israel's borders and the ultimate disposition of the Arab refugees. After the war several new issues emerged. Among these were the terms by which the Sinai Peninsula would be returned to Egypt and the Golan Heights to Syria; the status of the West Bank and Gaza Strip; the status of Jerusalem, which Israel now proclaimed to be the reunited capital of Israel and not subject to negotiation. Two other results of the war also would affect profoundly the Arab-Israeli conflict in the coming years. The war increased international involvement in the Middle East, especially that of the United States and the Soviet Union, and stimulated a sense of national identity among the Palestinian refugees of 1948 as well as among the Arabs living under Israeli occupation. This national identity eventually led to calls for Palestinian national self-determination.

Except for East Jerusalem, which it immediately annexed, Israel initially expressed its official willingness to return the territories it had occupied during the war. The Israeli government, however, stated that it would permit no return to the prewar status quo that had provided the conditions for the war to erupt in the first place. Israel insisted on negotiated peace agreements with its Arab neighbors in exchange for the occupied territories. In this view, Israel received the support of the United States, which in 1956 had insisted on Israel's unconditional withdrawal from the Sinai.

The Arab states convened an Arab summit in Khartoum in August 1967 and, by contrast, adopted the position that Israel should withdraw from the occupied territories without further conditions. Because the principle of the "inadmissibility of the acquisition of territory by war" was enshrined in the United Nations Charter, they expected the international community to support the Arab position. Unlike the United States, the Soviet Union, which had broken diplomatic relations with Israel during the war, did so. Moscow also agreed to rearm Egypt and Syria, a gesture that strengthened their resolve to hold fast to the principles enunciated at the Khartoum summit: "no peace with Israel, no recognition of Israel, no negotiations with it, and insistence on the rights of the Palestinian people in their own country."

UN Resolution 242

In an effort to reconcile these positions, the United States and the Soviet Union, now deeply immersed in the Arab-Israeli imbroglio, sought to reach agreement on a framework for encouraging a settlement of the conflict. The result of their effort was United Nations Security Council Resolution 242 adopted on November 22, 1967. *(Text, Appendix, p. 301)*

Emphasizing the "inadmissibility of the acquisition of territory by war and the need to work for a just and lasting peace in which every state in the area can live in security," the resolution also stressed that a "just and lasting peace" should include the application of both the following principles: "(i) Withdrawal of Israeli armed forces from territories occupied in the recent conflict; (ii) Termination of all claims or states of belligerency and respect for and acknowledgment of the sovereignty, territorial integrity and political independence of every State in the area and their right to live in peace within secure and recognized boundaries free from threats or acts of force." Other principles enunciated in the resolution included freedom of navigation through international waterways in the area; a just settlement of the refugee problem; establishment of demilitarized zones, if necessary, to guarantee the territorial inviolability and the political independence of every state in the area.

Although the resolution clearly linked the establishment of peace with Israeli withdrawal, any insistence on direct negotiations among the hostile parties was notably missing from the text. The resolution concluded, however, by requesting the appointment of a special UN representative to conduct negotiations with the various parties in accordance with its provisions.

Gunnar Jarring, Sweden's ambassador to the Soviet Union, was appointed to mediate between the Arabs and Israel, but his efforts to secure movement in the peace process soon failed. Egypt, although it grudgingly accepted the UN resolution, mainly at Soviet insistence, held fast to the view that Jarring should focus solely on Israeli withdrawal. Syria, on the other hand, refused to accept the resolution at this time and continued to support Palestinian resistance groups willing to make raids into Israel. These hard-line attitudes, meanwhile, strengthened the hands of a rapidly growing body of Israelis who called for retention of the territories, or most of them. They claimed that the territories were needed for Israeli security because the Arabs would never agree to peace. Some Israelis also claimed that because the territories were part of historic Israel, they should not be returned in any case.

In the face of continued Israeli occupation of the territories, King Hussein tolerated the growth of Palestinian resistance organizations in Jordan. He had accepted Resolution 242, but he saw the organizations as a means of deterring any Israeli effort to annex the West Bank, which technically remained part of his kingdom.

The emergence of an increasingly significant Palestinian-based guerrilla movement against Israel proved to be one of the most salient new features of the Arab-Israeli conflict in the years after the 1967 war. The rapidly growing community of Palestinian Arab refugees was increasingly drawn to the idea, most effectively articulated by Yasir Arafat's Fatah organization, that the Palestinians needed to forge their own independent political identity in order to secure their liberation. The growth of such attitudes, however, was to bring them into conflict not only with Israel but also with their host states, especially those where their movement was able to take root.

War of Attrition

As it became clear that the Jarring mission was not going to be successful and that Israel was consolidating its hold on the occupied territories, Nasser decided to renew military confrontation with Israel as a means of retaining superpower interest in the conflict. His determination to secure Israel's withdrawal from the Sinai on his own terms rather than Israel's was strengthened by continuing Soviet military assistance. By the summer of 1968 the Egyptian inventory of military hardware was superior in quality and quantity to what it had been on the eve of the 1967 war. Accordingly, in September 1968, Egypt began intensive artillery barrages of Israeli positions along the entire length of the Suez Canal. The tactic failed to raise an international response, however, and Israeli retaliation by air attacks against civilian targets and helicopter raids deep in Egyptian territory indicated the need for better defensive preparations. In addition, the Israelis built stronger fortified positions, the so-called Bar-Lev Line, along the east bank of the canal.

To meet these challenges, Nasser evacuated civilians from the Egyptian cities along the canal and began building, with Soviet assistance, an elaborate air defense network to counter Israeli air superiority. When these preparations were in place, he formally announced and launched on March 8, 1969, a "War of Attrition" against Israeli forces on the canal. Nasser now hoped to weaken Israeli resolve by resorting to an extended conflict that would inflict unacceptable Israeli casualties and destroy the Bar-Lev Line, making it possible for Egyptian forces to cross the canal and establish a beachhead in the Sinai.

Heavy Egyptian bombardment and Israeli counterfire continued for about eighty days. When in July an Egyptian commando unit succeeded in crossing the canal and inflicting heavy Israeli casualties, Israel decided to commit its air force. The Israeli air force sent a commando unit to destroy a key radar installation that controlled parts of Egypt's extensive air defense system. Then Israeli jets followed up with ten days of intensive air attacks causing great damage to Egyptian artillery and surface-to-air missile systems. This action made it possible for Israeli warplanes to strike virtually at will against Egyptian positions.

The War of Attrition continued, however, with no end in sight. Israel in early 1970 decided to expand the war with deep-penetration bombing of targets in the Egyptian interior. These actions led Nasser to seek increased Soviet support, which in due course was provided. Moscow sent Soviet personnel to help Egypt operate certain portions of its air defense system and to fly newly supplied Soviet aircraft. The influx of Soviet personnel soon improved Egyptian air defenses but provoked at least one instance of aerial combat between Israeli and Soviet pilots in which the Israelis were victorious. Most importantly for Nasser, however, the Soviet role prompted a new U.S. initiative aimed at implementing a cease-fire in the conflict.

This was the Rogers Plan, named after U.S. Secretary of State William Rogers, who enunciated it. Firmly grounded in UN Resolution 242, it called for a cease-fire that included a memorandum of understanding that both Egypt and Israel agreed with the resolution as a basis for further negotiations.

Both Egypt and Jordan accepted the Rogers Plan, but Israel refused to make any commitment to withdrawal before negotiations and rejected it. Only after the United States applied strong pressure, promised continuing military assistance, and guaranteed that it would not insist on a full withdrawal to the 1967 borders did Israel finally agree to accept the Rogers proposal. Even then the Israeli decision provoked a minor government crisis when several cabinet members, including Menachem Begin, resigned from the government rather than be associated with it. Nevertheless, a cease-fire was implemented on August 8, 1970, but not before Nasser had been able to obtain from Israel a commitment in principle, guaranteed by the United States, to withdraw its forces from the Sinai.

1973 War

A few weeks after the cease-fire agreement with Israel, Nasser died in September 1970, and Anwar Sadat was chosen to replace him as president of Egypt. Although Sadat had been among the Free Officer cadre that had overthrown King Farouk in 1952 and had been part of Nasser's leadership council from the beginning, he was different from Nasser in many ways. He was less ideological and had a more relaxed style of leadership. He also proved to be less wedded to the concept of pan-Arabism and more oriented toward purely Egyptian interests. Many observers at the time thought of him as a transitional leader. Few thought he would last as president, partly because he seemed to lack Nasser's dynamic personality.

Following the achievement of an Egyptian-Israeli cease-fire, the United States focused on reviving UN Ambassador Gunnar Jarring's efforts to secure a full implementation of UN Resolution 242. In February 1971 Jarring asked Sadat to enter into a peace agreement with Israel on the basis of the UN Resolution. Sadat readily agreed, accepting even the principle of settling the refugee question on the basis of existing UN resolutions, a stance that was at variance with the policy of the PLO.

Israel, however, rejected Sadat's terms, indicating that it did not accept full withdrawal to prewar lines. It also refused to accept a negotiation process mediated by a third party, insisting on direct negotiations without preconditions. In rejecting Sadat's offer at this time, however, the Israelis gravely underestimated the new Egyptian president. He would in time achieve precisely what he now offered, but at a considerable cost to Israel. Soon after the breakdown of this mediation effort, Jarring abandoned his effort to achieve a settlement on the basis of UN Resolution 242.

Preparations for War

As time passed, Sadat concluded that the new geopolitical situation produced by the 1967 war would not be reversed by diplomacy. As early as 1971 he began to prepare for war. Even as he did so he continued to privately communicate to the United States his desire to achieve a negotiated settlement. Sadat also made contacts with Hafez al-Assad, the new president of Syria, who eagerly supported the concept of a two-front war needed by both countries if a war against Israel were to achieve success. They and their staffs held many planning meetings concerning the war under the cover of talks concerning a Libyan-proposed Federation of Arab Republics embracing Egypt, Syria, Libya, and the Sudan.

Receiving sufficient arms from the Soviet Union was the key condition needed by both leaders for a decision on war. Although the youthful Libyan leader Col. Muammar Qaddafi was excluded from the plans of Assad and Sadat, his generous infusions of Libyan oil wealth contributed significantly to the rearming of both countries. Sadat became frustrated by the slowness of Soviet arms deliveries, due, he believed, to U.S.-Soviet efforts to achieve détente, even while U.S. arms continued to flow to Israel. In July 1972 he took the surprising step of expelling all 21,000 Soviet military advisers and operations personnel serving in Egypt. Ironically this step caused the Soviets to speed up weapons deliveries to both Egypt and Syria—to Egypt in an attempt to win back Sadat's favor, and to Syria in order not to lose Assad's favor. The expulsion also made a

favorable impression in Washington and seemed to diminish chances that Egypt could soon launch a war against Israel. By November 30, 1972, however, according to his memoirs, Sadat felt confident enough in his military preparedness to make his "firm decision" to go to war.

Arabs Attack

At precisely 2:05 p.m. on Saturday, October 6, 1973, the high Jewish Holy Day of Yom Kippur, Egypt and Syria jointly launched their war on Israel. The Israeli high command, despite sufficient intelligence, was caught by surprise, having misinterpreted the evidence of an impending attack until just hours before it occurred. In accordance with a meticulously planned and methodically executed operation, nearly 90,000 Egyptian troops, supported by intense artillery barrages and aerial bombardments, crossed the Suez Canal, overran existing Israeli defenses, and established defensive beachheads along the length of the canal's east bank. By the time Israeli mobilization could produce sufficient forces to counterattack on October 8, the Egyptian defensive positions had been made virtually impregnable. An elaborate air defense system behind the canal effectively neutralized Israeli air strike capability over the Egyptian positions. Meanwhile, effective deployment of antitank weapons neutralized the second principal element of Israel's military superiority, its capability in mobile armored warfare.

Golan Heights Fighting

As it became clear that Sadat's intention was to consolidate his newly won defensive position and not strike off across the Sinai, Israel turned its attention to the Syrian front. Simultaneously with the Egyptian offensive, Syria had thrown 35,000 troops and 800 tanks against Israeli defenses on the Golan Heights. Unlike the Egyptian strategy—which was to establish a strong position on the east bank of the Suez Canal, defend it, and use the crisis to consolidate its gains in subsequent negotiations—the Syrian objective was to drive the Israelis off the Golan Heights and to recapture the territory that had been lost in 1967. From October 6 to October 13, the Golan front remained the principal theater of the war as Israel devoted the bulk of its resources to holding its position there. In close and bitter fighting, the Syrians almost achieved their objective before breaking off offensive operations on October 9, after Israeli reinforcements had reestablished a firm defensive line at the crest of the Heights.

Israeli ground forces played the key role in defending Israeli positions in the Golan Heights. During the first days of the war, the Israeli air force faced a network of surface-to-air missiles and antiaircraft artillery similar to the one that had successfully challenged its control of the air over the Sinai front. By October 8, however, as the Sinai front began to stabilize, the Israelis, at great cost to their aircraft and pilots, undertook a systematic effort to destroy the Syrian air defense system. By October 11, Israel once again had achieved general control of the air. That day Israeli ground forces went on the offensive to recapture territories lost so far in the war and to carry the battle beyond the cease-fire line of 1967 toward the Syrian capital.

Despite a brave defense, Syria was unable to contain the advance of an Israeli salient along the eastern base of Mount Hermon toward Damascus. Syrian forces withdrew under fire to an established defensive line at Sasa and prepared to defend the approaches to Damascus with the support of newly arrived Iraqi and Jordanian units. Having reestablished its control of the battlefield and created a pressure point within Syria to absorb future Arab counterattacks, Israel after October 13 broke off offensive operations and turned its attention to the Sinai front.

Israeli Counterattack in the Sinai

Even before turning back the Syrian offensive on the Golan, the Israelis had been planning their counteroffensive at the Suez Canal. It called for a breakthrough and crossing of the canal at Deversoir, just north of the Great Bitter Lake. The Israeli high command had hoped that their own attack would be preceded by an Egyptian thrust from the bridgehead into the Sinai. Israel hoped to blunt the Egyptian offensive and take advantage of the confusion to drive through Egyptian lines to the designated crossing point at the canal. When Egyptian forces failed to cooperate and remained secure in their well-defended position, Israel prepared for its breakthrough anyway for the night of October 14.

Meanwhile, as Syrian forces had begun to come under extreme Israeli pressure on October 11, President Assad had appealed to Sadat to attack in the Sinai. In their prewar planning, Assad had understood that Sadat contemplated a deeper drive into the Sinai. When this did not come, he began to feel betrayed. Egypt had indeed planned such an expanded offensive across the Suez, but not until its elaborate air defense system had been transported across the canal. Sadat resisted launching the offensive until his relations with Syria had reached the breaking point. Finally, against the advice of his generals, and after it was too late to relieve the Syrian front, Sadat ordered an October 14 Egyptian offensive to capture the Giddi and Mitla passes, thus providing Israel with precisely the opportunity that so far had been denied them.

The Egyptian forces advanced beyond their air defense cover and under an ill-conceived plan toward an increasingly strong and well-prepared Israeli army whose own plans hoped for just such an Egyptian strategic miscalculation. In the Sinai nearly 1,000 Egyptian tanks and 800 Israeli tanks, the latter now supported by air cover, fought the largest armored battle since World War II. Israeli tactics and superior mobility succeeded in blunting the Egyptian advance, inflicting heavy casualties and causing confusion in the Egyptian ranks that allowed the Israelis to implement their own plan to cross to the west bank of the canal.

On the night of October 15 a small Israeli force commanded by Gen. Ariel Sharon broke through a gap in the Egyptian defenses, bridged the canal, and reached the west side by the morning of October 16. For two more days, however, intense fighting continued as Egyptian forces attempted to close the gap. Finally, by the afternoon of October 17, after nearly forty-eight hours of continuous battle, a much larger Israeli force succeeded in clearing the gap, opening the way for a major crossing of the canal and the establishment of an effective Israeli beachhead on its western side. For two more days the Israelis struggled to consolidate the beachhead and bring in more forces to strengthen the position while Egyptian forces encircling the beachhead attempted desperately to destroy it.

On October 19, Israeli forces on the western bank of the canal drove south along the canal toward Suez. Their goal was to trap the Egyptian Third Army on the east bank of the canal. When the UN-sponsored cease-fire came into effect in the evening of October 22, however, Israeli forces had been able to push only half way toward their goal against determined Egyptian resistance. Despite Israeli acceptance of the cease-fire, fighting continued in this sector until October 25 when Israeli units had effectively cut all supply lines serving the Third Army. Continued shelling and several other last-ditch efforts to secure final positions also occurred on the Golan front after the October 22 cease-fire.

Cease-Fire

As the war ended, none of the participants had achieved the kind of military victory it would have preferred. Yet all had fought tenaciously and had achieved partial successes. There was no clear winner as had been the case in previous Arab-Israeli wars.

Syrian President Assad was furious with Sadat for agreeing to the cease-fire. In his view, the Syrian army was about to recapture the initiative from the Israelis. Beginning on October 8, a massive Soviet airlift of resupplies to both Egypt and Syria had begun, and Syrian units on the Golan front had been reequipped and had a tight ring around the Israeli salient pointing toward Damascus. Units from Morocco, Iraq, Jordan, and Saudi Arabia also had taken places along the front, and Israeli forces had been substantially weakened because of redeployment in the Sinai. Unable to fight alone without continued pressure on the Egyptian front, however, Assad also finally agreed to the cease-fire.

Israel also was not satisfied with its gains on the Egyptian front, and it continued to fight on for three days after its official acceptance of the cease-fire.

It was primarily Egypt that took the lead in responding to international appeals for a cease-fire, but only after it had become clear that the tide was turning against the Arabs. On October 16, after the disastrous Egyptian defeat in the Sinai, but before he had information about the Israeli breakthrough across the canal, Sadat in a major television and radio broadcast expressed his willingness to accept a cease-fire if Israel withdrew from all the territories occupied in 1967. In addition, however, he expressed willingness to attend a postwar peace conference with Israel and to endeavor to convince the other Arab states to participate also.

As the war had continued, it increasingly became the focus of great power concern, facilitating communication between Washington and Moscow, even as U.S.-Soviet tensions mounted. On October 21, in response to a U.S. congressional decision to appropriate $2.2 billion for a major military arms package for Israel, the states comprising the Organization of Arab Petroleum Exporting Countries (OAPEC), led by Saudi Arabia, announced a general boycott of oil sales to the United States.

After Sadat issued a strong appeal on October 19 to the Soviet Union to help him in arranging a cease-fire, the Soviets urgently requested that U.S. Secretary of State Henry Kissinger visit Moscow. There, after two days of negotiations, procedures were agreed upon for a cease-fire and future negotiations. Presented to the United Nations Security Council, it was passed by unanimous vote on October 22 as Resolution 338. *(Text, Appendix, p. 301)*

Nevertheless, when Israel continued its effort, despite the cease-fire, to consolidate its position on the west bank of the canal, Moscow protested to Washington, suggesting the urgent dispatch of Soviet and U.S. troops to police the cease-fire and to implement the provisions of Resolution 338. If the U.S. disagreed, the Kremlin continued, the Soviet Union was prepared to act alone. U.S. President Nixon, at the advice of Kissinger, interpreted the Soviet communication as an ultimatum and placed U.S. forces on worldwide alert to face down the Soviet challenge. Although the Arab-Israeli war was effectively over, the conflict still seemed to have the potential to threaten global nuclear war. The nuclear crisis probably was more artificial than real, and it passed quickly, as tensions diminished after the halting of Israeli offensive operations on October 25.

Disengagement Agreements

Despite the joint U.S.-Soviet role in bringing an end to the 1973 war, U.S. Secretary of State Kissinger emerged as the central mediator in postwar negotiations. This was due in part to Kissinger's determination to keep the Soviet Union out of the negotiations, but it was also due to a growing perception among the Arabs, especially Sadat, that only the United States was in a position to extract compromises from Israel that the Arabs, even with Soviet support, could not obtain by themselves. As long as support for UN Security Council Resolution 242, which called for Israeli withdrawal from occupied territories, remained an element of U.S. policy, a basis for achieving this objective through diplomatic means continued.

In addition to demanding an immediate cease-fire in the 1973 war, UN Security Council Resolution 338 did reiterate the objective of the consenting parties to implement Resolution 242 in all its parts. Moreover, unlike Resolution 242, 338 also called for negotiations "between the parties concerned under appropriate auspices aimed at establishing a just and durable peace in the Middle East." Sadat was prepared to participate in such negotiations, and under the rubric of "appropriate auspices" a role was provided for Henry Kissinger.

Repeatedly traveling between the Arab capitals and Israel, Kissinger engaged in what came to be called "shuttle diplomacy." Kissinger's efforts gradually produced a series of "disengagement agreements." A first agreement on October 28, 1973, secured Israel's assent to relief for Egypt's encircled Third Army. A subsequent agreement on November 11 committed both Egypt and Israel to implement Security Council resolutions 242 and 338 and to stabilize the cease-fire.

Finally on January 18, 1974, Kissinger's diplomacy resulted in the "Disengagement of Forces Agreement," which significantly reduced the chances of a surprise attack by either side. In it, Israel consented to withdraw its forces from the west bank of the Suez Canal. In return, Egypt accepted a stringent limitation on the number of its forces permitted on the east bank of the canal and a withdrawal of its surface-to-air missiles (a key component of its success in the war) and long-range artillery to a line thirty kilometers behind the demilitarized zone now established between the Egyptian and Israeli forces. A similar limitation was also placed on Israeli forces near the canal. United Nations Disengagement Observer Forces (UNDOF) were to be stationed in the demilitarized zone to monitor compliance with the agreement.

Following the Egyptian-Israeli agreements, Kissinger focused on negotiations between Syria and Israel. Sadat's decision to agree to provisions that reduced the chances for a renewed two-front war weakened Assad's negotiating position. So also did Sadat's promise to Kissinger to encourage the Arab oil-producing states to lift their boycott on sales of petroleum to the United States, which they did on March 18, 1974. As with Sadat, Kissinger's assurances that the United States would work for implementation of resolutions 242 and 338 enabled him to secure Assad's acceptance of a Syrian-Israeli "Separation of Forces" agreement on May 31.

In accordance with this agreement, Israel withdrew from the salient it had occupied during the war and gave up a narrow band of land it had captured in 1967, including the town of Qunaitra. This zone, however, became a demilitarized buffer zone controlled by UNDOF units established to monitor the agreement. On each side of the buffer zone Syrian and Israeli zones with restricted numbers of personnel and weapons also were established. Finally, in a separate agreement with Kissinger, Assad promised not to permit Palestinian guerrilla attacks on Israel along the Golan front, something he had never permitted in any case, despite general support for the guerrillas in neighboring Lebanon and Jordan.

Continuing efforts by Kissinger during the summer of 1974 to further the Arab-Israeli peace process were overshadowed by U.S.-Soviet summit talks, a Turkish invasion of Cyprus, and President Nixon's resignation because of the Watergate scandal. Issues were further complicated by the Arab League's decision made in October 1974 at a summit in Rabat, Morocco, endorsing the PLO as the sole legitimate representative of the Palestinian people. *(Text, Appendix, p. 301)*

The implication of this position from the Arab perspective was that, although Egypt and Syria were free to pursue recovery of territories lost to Israel in 1967, collective Arab policy toward a general resolution of the Arab-Israeli conflict was to focus on arrangements reached between the PLO and Israel. The Arabs' support of the PLO's claims to be the legitimate representative of all those Palestine Arabs living either as refugees outside of Israel or under Israeli occupation directly contradicted Israel's policy, buttressed by Resolution 338, of seeking peace through direct negotiations with its neighboring Arab states. In addition, Israel positively opposed negotiations with the PLO because of the latter's denial of Israel's right to exist and its opposition to resolutions 242 and 338.

Sinai II

Kissinger's shuttle diplomacy resulted in a second Israeli-Egyptian disengagement agreement (Sinai II) on September 4, 1975. In this agreement Israel agreed to a further withdrawal of its forces from the Mitla and Giddi passes and the Abu Rudais oil fields to a new cease-fire line. Egyptian forces were permitted to move up to the line Israel had previously occupied. In between, a new UNDOF-monitored buffer zone was established, and early warning electronic monitoring systems operated by American technicians were put in place to warn both governments of any violations of the agreement.

The agreement also imposed limitations on forces in zones adjoining the neutral buffer zone, and both Israel and Egypt promised to observe their continuing cease-fire and to abjure the use of force or military blockade against one another. Egypt also agreed to allow Israel to use the Suez Canal for the passage of nonmilitary cargoes, and both countries pledged to continue negotiations toward a final peace settlement. Despite the guarantees embodied in the Sinai II accord, however, Israel's acceptance of them was conditional on two side memorandums signed by Kissinger. The first provided guarantees of continued U.S. economic and military assistance to Israel. In the second, the United States promised not to "recognize or negotiate with the PLO so long as the PLO does not recognize Israel's right to exist and does not accept Security Council Resolutions 242 and 338."

With the signing of the Sinai II accord, Kissinger's ability to advance the Arab-Israeli peace process came to an end. The position of the United States and Israel not to negotiate with the PLO was at odds with what now had become a collective Arab stand. In addition, President Assad was especially disturbed by the implications of Sinai II for Syria. He feared that Egypt's agreement with Israel undermined his own effort to secure a return of the Golan Heights. As a result, he refused to cooperate with U.S. peacemaking and joined with Iraq, Algeria, Libya, South Yemen, and the PLO in a new alliance called the Rejectionist Front, which condemned Sadat's increasing accommodation with Israel and sought to undermine it.

Role of the PLO

The growing importance of the PLO as a factor in the Arab-Israeli conflict in the years after 1967 was a function of the emerging sense of Palestinian identity. The PLO formed by the Arab summit of 1964 had been intended to be merely a bureaucratic arm of the Arab League, then effectively controlled by President Nasser of Egypt. Despite this effort to establish control of the Palestinian movement, however, the various independent resistance groups springing up in the 1950s and 1960s had avoided being dominated by the Arab League. When Arafat's Fatah began operations in Israel in the mid-1960s, contributing to the 1967 war, it had done so for itself, as well as on behalf of Syria, and not as an element of the PLO.

Only after the war, in February 1969, did the various commando groups seek and receive admission into the organization. By this time, however, they had become strong enough to take over the organization. Yasir Arafat, head of the largest Palestinian organization, became PLO chairman, a position he has never been forced to relinquish, despite many challenges to his leadership. Under his chairmanship the PLO, in accordance with Fatah policy, strove to be an independent political actor in inter-Arab relations. At the same time, Arafat's independence was constrained by the perceived need to maintain unity within the Palestinian movement and consensus among the different commando organizations belonging to the PLO.

The various commando groups were able to assert their control over the PLO because of the moral support, funds, and recruits that began to flow toward them, especially Fatah, in the period following the 1967 war. As the Arab regimes slowly recovered from their military debacle and sought to regain their losses, the commando groups kept the Arab-Israeli conflict alive by launching raids and acts of terrorism in Israel or the occupied territories.

PLO in Jordan and Lebanon

Jordan and Lebanon, where the largest numbers of refugees were located, were the two countries where the Palestinian movement and the resistance groups thrived. An incident in Jordan soon after the 1967 war greatly contributed to the fortunes of Arafat's Fatah. A major Israeli reprisal against the Jordanian town of Karameh in March 1968 encountered stiff resistance from Fatah fighters supported by Jordanian artillery. Although the Israeli unit accomplished its mission, it sustained many casualties. Arafat was able to claim that his fighters had fought more bravely than any of the Arab armies a few months earlier. The Karameh incident brought great attention to Fatah and drew many new recruits into the organization. Further Israeli reprisals in Jordan and Lebanon now began to have the same effect, strengthening the resistance groups that gradually began to take control of the Palestinian refugee camps in those countries.

A major rival of Arafat at this time was George Habash, the leader of the PFLP. His organization was imbued with a far more revolutionary philosophy than Arafat's. It called for the overthrow of discredited Arab regimes and the unification of the Arab world under revolutionary leadership as a means to achieve the liberation of Palestine. In July 1968 the PFLP embarked on a new strategy to bring international attention to the Palestinian problem. It began hijacking Israeli El Al passenger aircraft and then aircraft of other Western airlines that serviced Israel. The purpose was to highlight the seriousness of the Arab-Israeli conflict and the intensity of its Palestinian dimension. Although these and subsequent acts of international terrorism did draw international attention to the Palestinian problem and the hapless condition of the Arab refugees the commando leaders claimed to represent, they also provoked international outrage and tended to discredit the Palestinian movement.

A government crisis in Lebanon in 1969 led to a new status for the PLO in that country. A developing pattern of PLO-Israeli violence over Lebanon's southern boundary with Israel provoked the crisis. Many Lebanese wanted their government to deal forcibly with the Palestinian fighters and disarm them. Still others lent support to the Palestinian cause and demanded that the government demonstrate solidarity with the PLO by mobilizing a stronger army to resist Israeli incursions. The result was political paralysis and a government crisis that was resolved only by the intervention of President Nasser of Egypt. Through his mediation, the "Cairo Agreement" was reached in October 1969. It spelled out specified areas of operation for the PLO in southern Lebanon and placed the Palestinian refugee camps under PLO control. Even though the Cairo Agreement resolved the immediate crisis, it amounted to a significant infringement on Lebanese sovereignty by giving the PLO virtual state-within-a-state status in Lebanon. It also strengthened Arafat's effort to be treated as an independent actor in inter-Arab politics.

A similar crisis developed in Jordan in 1970. Tensions between the army and the PLO that had increased throughout the year finally erupted into civil war in September, following the PFLP hijacking of four international airliners. The Palestinian hijackers had forced the planes to land at a remote airfield outside the Jordanian capital. When the crisis had passed and all hostages on the airliners had been released, King Hussein unleashed his army against the Palestinian guerrillas in his country. They were defeated after ten days of fighting. This setback for the PLO, which was remembered as "Black September," made Lebanon the sole remaining center of PLO organizational activity in its struggle against Israel.

Palestine Liberation Organization Factions ...

The Palestine Liberation Organization (PLO) was established in 1964 at the first Palestine National Congress with the sponsorship of the Arab League. By 1968, when the PLO adopted the Palestine National Covenant as its charter, the PLO had become the center of Arab efforts to regain a Palestinian homeland from Israel through political and military means. The PLO also has acted as a "government" representing Palestinians who live under Israeli occupation and those who are settled throughout the world.

Yasir Arafat

The PLO has developed political institutions that attempt to achieve consensus among its member organizations. The most important of these institutions are the Palestine National Council (PNC), a Palestinian parliament in exile, which meets periodically to debate PLO policy and strategy, and the PLO Executive Committee (EC), a twelve- to fifteen-member group chosen by the PNC to direct the PLO's day-to-day activities. Between these two governing bodies is the PLO Central Committee (CC), also selected by the PNC, with which the EC consults on matters of policy between meetings of the PNC. Finally, under the EC is a series of executive departments (comparable to government ministries such as foreign affairs, information, or finance) that implement the decisions of the EC, CC, and PNC.

The PLO's internal politics are complicated by the diverse objectives, interests, and philosophies of its member organizations. Since 1968 Yasir Arafat, head of the Fatah organization, the largest and most prominent of the PLO's eight member groups, has dominated the institutions of the PLO from his position as chairman. His capacity for independent leadership has been constrained, however, by his policy of seeking consensus among the constituent groups in order to maintain PLO unity. For example, since 1975 Arafat has declared his opposition to terrorism

as an instrument of armed struggle against Israel, but as PLO chairman he has been unable to impose this view because of the opposition of several groups. Even now, some groups have stated their acceptance of (but not agreement with) the PNC's November 1988 renunciation of terrorism.

Fatah. Fatah (Arabic for "conquest"), founded in 1959, is the largest and oldest PLO member organization. Arafat has dominated Fatah, which has always advocated a strongly Palestinian nationalist ideology, in contrast to the pan-Arabism or Marxism advocated by many of its rivals. Fiercely independent, it has sought support from every Arab country but has resisted affiliation with any. Having no ambitions beyond Palestine, it has received the bulk of Arab support over the years, an important factor in Arafat's ability to appeal to the majority of Palestinians. Most of the PLO's top leaders are members of Fatah.

Fatah Uprising. Led by Abu Musa (Col. Sa'id Musa al-Muragha), this group consists mainly of Palestinian soldiers who served in the Jordanian army until the Jordanian-PLO civil war in 1970. Incorporated into Fatah as the Yarmuk Brigade after that conflict, they opposed Arafat's decision to leave Beirut in 1982 and chose to go to Syria rather than be scattered elsewhere in the Arab world. Fiercely anti-Jordanian, they opposed Arafat's attempts to develop a negotiating strategy with King Hussein and rose in mutiny against Arafat's leadership of the PLO in the spring of 1983. The Fatah Uprising was supported by Syrian president Hafez Assad, who hoped to weaken Arafat's control of the PLO. Abu Musa and his anti-Arafat allies expelled Arafat's forces from northern Lebanon in December 1983. More ideologically committed than Arafat to the total liberation of Palestine, this group opposes his diplomatic strategies but finds itself unable to act independently because of its reliance on Syria.

Popular Front for the Liberation of Palestine (PFLP). Founded in 1967 and led by George Habash, the PFLP has long been Fatah's principal rival for leadership of the PLO. Like Fatah, it seeks to remain independent of ties to any Arab regime,

Between 1949 and 1967 Lebanon had remained aloof from the Arab-Israeli conflict. Its emergence as the principal arena of the Israeli-PLO conflict placed strains on the Lebanese political system, which eventually led to civil war in 1975. Meanwhile, Lebanon increasingly became the center of PLO operations against Israel, both across Israel's borders and abroad, and the various PLO groups operating in Lebanon became targets of Israeli reprisals.

Growing International Stature

During the early 1970s the PLO's support among Palestinian Arabs both outside and within Israel continued to grow. Arab and other governments increasingly accepted the PLO as the legitimate political representative of the unabsorbed refugees of the 1948 war with Israel. The strength and appeal of the PLO among the refugees and in

... Vary in Loyalty or Opposition to Arafat

most of which it considers corrupt and reactionary. Unlike Fatah, however, it has a strongly neo-Marxist orientation, but in a pan-Arab context. Considered the Palestinian branch of the old Arab Nationalist movement (ANM) of the 1950s and 1960s, it has its closest relationship with the Yemeni Socialist party (YSP), the ruling party of South Yemen, which was the Yemeni branch of the ANM. The PFLP, now headquartered in Syria, has a long history of antagonism toward Arab regimes, and it maintains precarious relations with both Fatah and Syria.

Democratic Front for the Liberation of Palestine (DFLP). Formed in 1968 and led by Nayef Hawatmeh, the DFLP was an offshoot of the PFLP. The split was led by the left wing of the PFLP, which considered the PFLP too bourgeois and its ideology too colored by Arab nationalism. The DFLP still commands respect as one of the three largest PLO factions.

Popular Front for the Liberation of Palestine-General Command (PFLP-GC). Also formed in 1968 as a splinter group of the PFLP, the General Command is led by Ahmed Jabril, a former Palestinian officer in the Syrian army. Tired of the dialectical arguments of the PFLP and DFLP ideologues, Jabril formed his own group to concentrate on military strategy in the struggle against Israel. It has been responsible for many of the most violent attacks on Israelis conducted by the PLO groups. Supported by both Syria and Libya, for which it may have committed terrorist operations, it rejects the idea of a diplomatic settlement with Israel. Some analysts have suggested that the PFLP-GC was responsible for the sabotage of Pan Am Flight 103 over Lockerbie, Scotland, in December 1988, although evidence remains circumstantial and Jabril has denied PFLP-GC involvement.

Palestine Liberation Front (PLF). A very small group formed as an offshoot of the PFLP-GC in 1977, the PLF seemed to specialize in unique forms of commando operations against Israel, such as attacks by glider or hot air balloons. Following the 1982 PLO evacuation from Lebanon, it split into three components—one in Syria, one in Libya, and one, led by PLF leader Muhammad Abu'l Abbas, in Tunis at PLO headquarters. Because of his loyalty to the greater PLO, Abu'l Abbas was elected to the PLO EC at the Seventeenth PNC meeting in Jordan in November 1984. In October 1985, PLF members hijacked the *Achille Lauro* cruise liner, and the United States accused Abu'l Abbas of being the mastermind behind the operation. Although the terrorist operation compromised Arafat's negotiating strategy with King Hussein of Jordan at the time, Arafat remained loyal to Abu'l Abbas, who stayed on the PLO EC until the Nineteenth PNC in Algiers in November 1988. American protests concerning his presence—at a time when the PLO was trying to demonstrate its renunciation of terrorism—led Arafat finally to drop him from the Executive Committee.

Saiqa. Saiqa (Arabic for "thunderbolt") was founded by the Syrian Ba'ath party in 1968 and is considered the Palestinian wing of the Ba'ath party under the overall authority of President Assad of Syria. Its current leader, Isam al-Qadi, lacks the independence of most other leaders of the Palestinian resistance groups and represents Syrian interests in the PLO.

Arab Liberation Front (ALF). Founded in 1969 to counter Saiqa and Syrian influence in Palestinian political councils, the ALF for the most part has worked within the PLO to protect Iraqi interests. The ALF is a tiny organization, in part because of the relatively small number of Palestinians living in Iraq. Following the PLO's expulsion from Lebanon in 1982, all ALF fighters went to Iraq. Continued strong Iraqi support for Arafat in his struggle against Syria and Syrian-controlled PLO groups has ensured a seat for ALF leader Abd al-Rahim Ahmed on the PLO Executive Council.

Popular Palestinian Struggle Front (PPSF). A minuscule faction created in 1968 by its leader, Bahjat Abu Gharbiyah (who died in 1989), the PPSF currently is led by Samir Ghawshah. Too small to hold a seat on the PLO Executive Committee, it nevertheless has remained active in the struggle against Israel and has reflected the interests of Syria, its principal patron, in PLO councils.

---

the Arab world stemmed less from its proclivity toward violence, which tended to be counterproductive in most cases, than from its political symbolism. Since 1948 the Arab states had justified their continuing hostility toward Israel on the grounds of defending the rights of the Palestinian Arabs to return to the land whence they came. With the emergence of a grass-roots Palestinian political movement whose aim was increasingly to shoulder the burden of their own liberation, the Arab states were progressively relieved of this perceived responsibility. To the degree that the PLO demonstrated its viability and capability to mobilize the Palestinians, it was in the interest of most Arab states to support it with funds and diplomatic backing.

By 1974, only five years after assuming the chairmanship of the PLO, Yasir Arafat achieved the first stage of his quest to formulate an independent Palestinian policy. At an Arab summit conference in Rabat, Morocco, in October, the assembled Arab heads of state recognized "the right of the Palestinian people to establish an independent national authority under the command of the Palestinian Liberation Organization, the sole legitimate representative of the Palestinian people, in any Palestinian territory that is liberated." One month later, on November 13, Arafat and the PLO received international recognition when he spoke before the United Nations General Assembly, which granted the PLO observer status. The vote to admit the PLO was 105-4, with 20 abstentions. Only Israel, the United States, Bolivia, and the Dominican Republic voted against the PLO. In 1976 the PLO became the twenty-first full member of the Arab League, and by 1977 more than 100 nations had granted the PLO some form of diplomatic recognition.

The PLO's new international stature and recognition carried several implications. First, it brought into question Jordan's 1950 annexation of the West Bank, which no Arab state had ever formally recognized. Accordingly, King Hussein's efforts to negotiate a return of the territory from Israel were undercut, although the concept of a joint Jordanian-PLO negotiating posture remained a possibility. Despite his bitterness toward the PLO, with which he had engaged in a bloody war in 1970, Hussein publicly accepted the decision of the Rabat summit "without any reservations." But he did not abjure Jordanian claims to the West Bank until 1988.

Second, the new recognition produced fissures in the PLO itself. Essentially an umbrella organization of various Palestinian commando groups, each with a different political outlook, the PLO maintained its unity by incorporating the views of even its most radical members. The growing acceptance of the PLO in international affairs, however, carried with it the burden of being responsive to the basic guidelines laid down by the international community for a settlement of the Arab-Israeli conflict, namely accepting Israel, aligning with existing UN resolutions, and abandoning the struggle for the total liberation of Palestine.

Some elements of the PLO, such as George Habash's PFLP, withdrew from the PLO rather than be a party to any compromise program. Arafat, ever anxious to maintain the unity of the Palestinian movement, tried to produce a compromise approach to Israel that would be acceptable to all factions and the international community, but he was unsuccessful. He insisted that any compromise settlement should be seen only as a prelude to the total liberation of Palestine. Such a formula was obviously rejected by Israeli leaders whose experience with the PLO disposed them to perceive it primarily as a terrorist organization bent on destroying Israel. Similarly unimpressed were potential U.S. interlocutors, such as Henry Kissinger, who sought to facilitate an Arab-Israeli peace process, but only with parties willing to accept and make peace with Israel.

Israel's Position Hardens

A third implication of the enhanced international status of the PLO was a hardening of attitudes in Israel itself. Since the origins of the Zionist movement in the late nineteenth century, Zionism had been characterized by two prominent trends. The first was the socialist-labor tendency embodied in Israel's ruling Labor party. Ideological about the economic and social life of Israel, it nevertheless remained pragmatic and flexible in international relations and diplomacy. The second tendency, known as revisionist

Zionism cared little for the ideological formulations of the Labor party. Instead, it focused on the historic destiny of the Zionist movement to gain control of all Eretz Israel, composed of southern Lebanon, southern Syria, Jordan, and the territories occupied in the 1967 war. Revisionist Zionists dominated the Herut party, which had been led by Menachem Begin since 1948. They had opposed the 1947 UN partition of Palestine on the grounds that Jews could never agree to the partition of historic Israel. In the post-1967 period, the Herut party maintained that the occupied territories were parts of historic Israel that had been "redeemed." It called, therefore, for Israeli settlement of the territories and opposed any suggestion that Israel should withdraw from them.

The revisionists were supported by the Greater Land of Israel Movement, which emerged immediately following the 1967 war. The movement included many Labor party members, including then minister of defense Moshe Dayan, who favored the creation of Jewish settlements in the new territories. The intent was not necessarily to avoid returning some of the territories, but to "create facts" that would enhance Israeli security and strengthen Israel's bargaining position. Even in the summer of 1967 a number of unauthorized settlements were established in the occupied territories by various Israeli citizen groups. Menachem Begin and his supporters in the Israeli Knesset used their positions of influence to demand full government approval of the new Jewish settlements.

As time passed without movement toward an Arab-Israeli settlement, and as tensions mounted because of the continuing hostilities with the PLO, the War of Attrition, and finally the 1973 war, the view that Israel should retain most or all of the territories as the best guarantee of its security gained increasing support in Israel, especially in the military. In 1974, following the first disengagement agreements with Egypt and Syria, a new organization, Gush Emunim, made its appearance. The group was committed to creating illegal Israeli settlements near the main Arab population centers and forcing the government to accept them. Gush Emunim's efforts received behind-the-scenes support from many in the military, making it virtually impossible for the government to stop the settlements begun by the organization.

In the context of this increasingly contentious political environment, it proved impossible for Israel to consider even minor concessions to Jordan, nor did Kissinger in his efforts to facilitate the peace process try to exert pressure on the Israeli government to do so. The Arab states' presentation at this time of the PLO, rather than Jordan, as the key interlocutor with whom Israel had to reach a final settlement of the Arab-Israeli conflict could hardly draw a positive response from the increasingly militant and defensive Israeli society. Israel's concern about the implications of the PLO's growing role was apparent in the September 1975 guarantee it sought from the United States that the latter country would not "recognize or negotiate with the PLO so long as the PLO does not recognize Israel's right to exist and does not accept Security Council Resolutions 242 and 338."

Lebanese Civil War

A final implication of the international legitimization of the PLO was the impact it was to have in Lebanon. It being apparent that such legitimization would evoke no positive response in Israel, the field of PLO activity would remain Lebanon for the foreseeable future. This was a challenge to Lebanese sovereignty to which the Lebanese government, paralyzed over the issue of how to deal with the PLO, could not respond. As a result various militias, representing the different sectarian and political groups in the country, began to acquire arms, and in April 1975 the Lebanese civil war broke out.

At first the PLO avoided involvement in the conflict, but in the winter attacks on some of the vulnerable Palestinian refugee camps in Maronite Christian territory led it to enter the conflict on the side of its National Movement allies. As fighting continued during the spring, PLO involvement helped to tip the balance toward National Movement forces, which appeared to be achieving victory. In response Lebanese President Suleiman Franjieh requested Syrian intervention on behalf of his government. President Assad, apparently worried about the possibility of an Israeli intervention if he did not intervene himself, sent Syrian units into Lebanon in June 1976. The Syrian intervention on behalf of the Maronite forces was not meant to assist them in achieving victory, but rather to restore the balance. Among the forces engaged by the Syrians was the PLO, whose military units were forced back into southern and coastal Lebanon. The PLO, however, survived and suffered no loss of international stature.

Camp David Agreements

On March 26, 1979, President Sadat completed the process of normalizing relations between Egypt and Israel by signing a treaty of peace in Washington. In return for peace and the establishment of diplomatic relations, Israel agreed to withdraw completely from Sinai within a period of three years. Most of the Sinai was defined as a demilitarized zone with UN and multinational forces posted to ensure compliance with the treaty. Egypt accepted a fixed limitation on the size of the military force it was permitted to keep in a fifty-mile-wide area east of the Suez Canal. Finally, the treaty guaranteed freedom of navigation for Israeli shipping through the Strait of Tiran and the Suez Canal. *(Text, Appendix, p. 304)*

Sadat had been frustrated by the lack of progress in achieving a final agreement on Israeli withdrawal from the Sinai after the signing of the Sinai II accord in September 1975. He had concluded that only a dramatic gesture could break the psychological barrier which, in his view, made the Arab-Israeli conflict so intractable. Such a gesture seemed especially necessary following Menachem Begin's assumption of the office of Israeli prime minister in June 1977. Begin and his Likud bloc (of which the Herut party was a member) had campaigned on a promise never to return any portion of Samaria and Judea, as he referred to the lands of the West Bank. He favored accelerated Jewish settlement of all the occupied territories and referred to the PLO as a Nazi organization with whom he would never deal, even if it accepted UN Resolution 242. Moreover, Begin had adamantly opposed the concessions Israel already had made to Egypt in the two disengagement agreements.

Sadat Goes to Israel

On November 9, 1977, Sadat announced his willingness to go to Israel to discuss, directly and in person, the issue of Arab-Israeli peace with the Israeli government. Given the history of the Arab-Israeli conflict up to this time, Sadat's announcement astounded the world, although careful groundwork had been made through preparatory contacts in Morocco. Such an initiative coming from the leader of the most powerful and populous Arab state required a positive response, even by the recalcitrant and suspicious Menachem Begin.

In his address to the Israeli Knesset, after expressing his desire that Egypt and Israel live together in "permanent peace based on justice," Sadat listed the conditions he thought necessary to achieve Arab-Israeli peace. In addition to the usual references to permanent borders, mutual recognition, nonbelligerency, and settling disputes through peaceful means, he specifically called for an Israeli withdrawal from the occupied territories and the achievement of the fundamental rights of the Palestinian people, including their right to self-determination and their right to establish their own state.

In response to Sadat's initiative, Begin on December 25, 1977, visited Ismailia, Egypt, where he presented Israel's response to the Egyptian proposal. He focused primarily on points related to a settlement of issues in the Sinai but also presented his proposal for a settlement of the West Bank and Gaza issue. He proposed abolishing the military administration in these territories and replacing it with "administrative autonomy of the residents, by and for them." Security and public order were to remain the responsibility of Israel, however. Begin asserted that "Israel stands by its right and its claim of sovereignty of Judea, Samaria and the Gaza district." But he added, "In the knowledge that other claims exist, [Israel] proposes for the sake of agreement and peace, that the question of sovereignty be left open." He proposed that the status of the Holy Places and Jerusalem be considered separately in other negotiations. Begin did not address ending the Israeli occupation and granting the Palestinians the right to establish their own state.

Framework Agreements

Despite the disparity between the two positions, negotiating committees were formed to continue the dialogue. Discussion continued sporadically but unsuccessfully throughout the first half of 1978. As negotiations broke down, however, President Jimmy Carter intervened in an effort to keep the talks alive. He invited Sadat and Begin to Camp David, his presidential retreat in Maryland, for face-to-face talks, hoping to resolve their differences.

The Camp David talks, as they came to be called, convened with President Carter in attendance on September 5, 1978, and continued for thirteen days. After difficult negotiations, which apparently would have failed without the mediation of the U.S. president and his advisers, agreement was reached on September 17. The talks actually produced two agreements. Neither was a treaty, but rather an agreement to agree. Called "frameworks for peace," the first dealt with issues relating to Egypt and Israel and provided the basis for the treaty signed between the two countries in March of the following year.

The second, a "framework" for settling the future of the West Bank and Gaza, represented an agreement among Israel, Egypt, and the United States, also a signatory to the accords, on an approach for resolving this contentious aspect of the Arab-Israeli conflict. Sadat was under extreme pressure from other Arab states not to sign a separate peace treaty with Israel. He therefore was anxious to arrive at a formula that would take into account the larger Arab perspective toward Israel. Begin was annoyed by Sadat's insistence on including issues that in his view rightfully belonged to negotiations with Israel's other Arab neighbors. Nevertheless he continued pursuing a treaty that would bring peace with Egypt, thereby limiting the participation of the Arab world's most populous state in the Arab-Israeli conflict. The result was an agreement which, depending on how it was interpreted and negotiated, satisfied either Sadat's or Begin's objectives in the negotiations.

In summary, the main points of the West Bank and Gaza framework were as follows:

● Egypt, Israel, and Jordan were to agree on modalities for establishing an elected self-governing authority in the West Bank and Gaza.

● Egypt, Israel, and Jordan were to negotiate an agreement establishing the powers and responsibilities of the self-governing authority in the West Bank and Gaza.

● After agreement, Israeli armed forces were to withdraw from the West Bank and Gaza except in specified security locations.

● During a five-year transition period, Egypt, Israel, Jordan, and the West Bank-Gaza authority were to negotiate the final status of the Israeli-occupied territories.

● Israel and Jordan were to negotiate a peace agreement taking into account the agreement reached on the final status of the West Bank and Gaza.

● All negotiations were to be based on UN Security Resolution 242.

A remarkable document, it left every issue open, subject to negotiation, but it confined the debate within the boundaries of the original Palestine mandate (which included Jordan). The framework made no mention of Syria or the Golan Heights. It provided for the principle of Israeli withdrawal from occupied territory, but without specifying the extent of this withdrawal. Moreover, it left open the possibility of a variety of options on achieving a final settlement of the conflict. Among them:

● Jordanian option—a West Bank-Gaza self-governing authority under Jordanian sovereignty, or in confederation with Jordan.

● Israeli option—a West Bank-Gaza self-governing authority under Israeli sovereignty, or in confederation with Israel.

● Independent state option—possible achievement of an independent state by Arab inhabitants of the West Bank-Gaza, expressing their right of self-determination.

Other potential options also were conceivable, depending on the outcome of negotiations. Most importantly, the framework placed an emphasis on political rather than military force as the means to reach a final settlement.

Arab Response

The key to proceeding on the West Bank-Gaza framework was to secure the participation of Jordan. Although King Hussein appeared to consider seriously the possibility of joining the negotiations, he resented not having been invited to Camp David. He also had not been consulted during the talks, and he was offended at the presumption that he would follow along meekly. By agreeing to participate, he also would have implicitly accepted the premise that Jordanian sovereignty over the West Bank was negotiable. Moreover, Hussein had to take into account the attitude of his powerful neighbors—Syria, Iraq, and Saudi

Arabia—and his own large population of Palestinian citizens.

Although Hussein did not condemn Sadat's initiative, most of the rest of the Arab world did. The Arab world put intense pressure on Sadat not to go through with his plans to sign the peace treaty with Israel and subsequently on Hussein not to collaborate with it. Syria and the PLO, which perceived Egypt's withdrawal from the Arab-Israeli conflict as weakening their own positions, were especially critical of it. When Sadat did sign the treaty on March 26, 1979, nineteen members of the twenty-two-member Arab League, including Jordan, convened in Baghdad the following day and agreed to a package of political and economic sanctions against Egypt. Egypt had not been invited to attend; Oman and Sudan chose not to attend. Egypt was also expelled from the Arab League, and the league's headquarters was moved from Cairo to Tunis. All Arab League members broke diplomatic relations with Egypt, except Oman, Sudan, and notably the PLO. Egypt also was expelled from most regional political and economic institutions, such as the Organization of Arab Petroleum Exporting Countries, the Islamic Conference Organization, and the Organization of African Unity. Arab nations also endorsed a general economic boycott on trade with Egypt.

West Bank-Gaza Talks

Under these circumstances, King Hussein did not attend the first meetings in Beersheba between Sadat and Begin on May 25, 1979, concerning the West Bank-Gaza framework. The nonparticipation of Jordan in this and subsequent meetings held through May 1980 played into the hands of those Israelis who, like Prime Minister Begin, opposed Israeli withdrawal from the West Bank and Gaza. Begin used his position of leadership to encourage accelerated Jewish settlement in the territories and to develop administrative mechanisms that would strengthen the degree of Israeli authority and Jewish ownership of land in the territories. In 1977 only seventeen Jewish settlements existed on the West Bank with a combined population of about five thousand. By 1982 there were about one hundred Jewish settlements with a combined population of more than twenty thousand.

As the Begin government pursued these policies, the "autonomy talks" between Egypt and Israel stalled for a number of reasons. Israel sought to limit autonomy to the inhabitants of the territories; Egypt believed it should extend to the territory itself. Each promoted its own version of a "self-governing authority." Israel proposed an administrative council that would be subject to Israeli authority; Egypt wanted the authority to have full executive, legislative, and judicial powers. Israel wanted it to manage "areas of legitimate internal administration," with Israel to "retain those powers and functions which are essential to her defense and security." Egypt sought total Israeli withdrawal from the territories (including East Jerusalem), the dismantling of Israeli settlements, and Palestinians' right to self-determination. Israel opposed these concepts because they "would set in motion an irreversible process which would lead to the establishment of an independent Arab-Palestinian state."

Thirteen months after the talks broke down, Begin was narrowly reelected prime minister in June 1981, an election he interpreted as a mandate for his policies. After Sadat's assassination on October 6, 1981, the new Egyptian government of Hosni Mubarak proved no more amenable than Sadat to Israel's autonomy proposals. The Begin cabinet responded by moving to implement unilaterally its concept of autonomy, claiming that it fulfilled the intent of the Camp David agreement.

On November 8, 1981, the Israeli government established a new civilian administration to replace the military administration that had governed the occupied territories since 1967. This civilian administration, which nevertheless was a department of the military, began the process of constituting a "self-governing authority" in the territories. It sought to structure a system of administrative councils of the type Israel had been advocating in the Camp David talks. The civilian administration's efforts, however, were based on a reorganization of the so-called village leagues, groups of armed Palestinian informants and enforcers upon whom the military administration had relied to intimidate uncooperative Arabs.

These policies provoked strong resistance from Arabs across the territories, followed by the use of an "iron fist" policy by the army. Violence in the West Bank and Gaza escalated throughout the first six months of 1982. The Begin government believed the source of the violence was the continuing influence of the PLO among Arabs in the territories. Therefore, Israel moved in June 1982 to attack the problem at its source by invading Lebanon.

The Israeli Invasion of Lebanon

After Egypt signed a peace treaty with Israel in March 1979, the focus of the conflict turned to Israel's northern frontiers. Despite the continuing harsh anti-Israeli rhetoric emanating from Syria, the Golan front, monitored by United Nations observer forces, had been quiet since the Syrian-Israeli separation of forces agreement of 1974. The Egyptian-Israeli peace treaty diminished chances that Syria would launch an attack on Israel to regain the Golan Heights, because the Syrians could not count on Egypt to open a second front. Egypt's involvement in the Camp David process had prompted Syria to pursue parity with Israel in military capability. But Syrian leaders did not contemplate a major military action against Israel until they had substantially built up their forces. The only area where the Arab-Israeli conflict was likely to erupt, therefore, was Lebanon.

Israel's 1978 Intervention

With the entry of Syrian forces into Lebanon in June 1976 and the return of PLO units to southern Lebanon, Israel designated a "red line" in that country, which it warned Syria not to cross. At the same time it began arming a southern Lebanese militia commanded by a renegade Greek Catholic Lebanese officer, Maj. Saad Haddad. Israel hoped that this force would help it control infiltration of PLO commandos into Israel from Lebanon. Shortly after a terrorist attack by eight Fatah commandos on an Israeli beach between Haifa and Tel Aviv, however, Israel on March 14, 1978, launched a major invasion into Lebanon involving twenty thousand troops. Ostensibly undertaken as a retaliatory raid in response to the terrorist attack, the real purpose of the military operation, which had been months in the planning, was to clear an area about ten kilometers wide along Israel's northern frontier that would serve as a security zone controlled and patrolled by Haddad's Free Lebanon Militia (FLM).

Soon after the Israeli invasion, the United Nations dispatched a 6,000-troop peacekeeping force, the United Nations Interim Force in Lebanon (UNIFIL), to patrol an area in southern Lebanon separating PLO forces from the northern Israeli border. Israel and Haddad would not permit the deployment of UNIFIL into the Free Lebanon security zone, and numerous violent acts between UNIFIL and FLM units occurred during the first weeks of the United Nations mission. Despite the UNIFIL-FLM buffer, PLO units continued to find their way into Israel. More important, they made increasing use of rockets and long-range artillery to launch attacks on northern Israeli towns over the heads of the FLM and UNIFIL troops. PLO-Israeli attacks against one another became particularly violent during the last months before the signing of the Israel-Egypt peace treaty in March 1979.

In addition to sponsoring Haddad's militia, Israel in mid-1976 had begun to provide arms and training to the Maronite Lebanese Forces militia as another means of countering the PLO and its allies in Lebanon. As this relation deepened following the Lebanese civil war, Syria's President Assad feared an Israeli challenge to Syrian pre-eminence in Lebanon. Assad responded with policies aimed at securing regional hegemony to promote his new concept of "strategic parity" with Israel.

Such a policy involved combating the Lebanese Forces militia and asserting Syrian control over the PLO in Lebanon. Arguing that the Arab-Israeli conflict was an Arab problem and not simply a Palestinian one, Assad operated through Syrian-supported Palestinian groups to weaken Arafat's leadership of the PLO. In addition, he sponsored new Lebanese militia groups such as the Shi'ite organization Amal as a counterweight to the PLO and the Israeli-supported Lebanese Forces. Amal had an inherently anti-PLO bias, as its Shi'ite members had suffered greatly from the PLO-Israeli violence in southern Lebanon.

Confronted by a variety of opponents in Lebanon in the early 1980s, the PLO became increasingly isolated. It was in this context that it agreed to a cease-fire with Israel in July 1981. The cease-fire resulted from a series of negotiations mediated by U.S. Special Envoy Philip Habib.

Precursors to Invasion

In April 1981 an eruption of hostilities between the Syrians and Lebanese Forces militia in the Bekaa Valley led the Maronites to appeal for Israeli support. When Israel responded by shooting down two Syrian helicopters, Assad installed surface-to-air missiles within Lebanon near the city of Zahle. Israel's Prime Minister Begin vigorously protested the missile installations and threatened to destroy them if Syria did not remove them. The "missile crisis" prompted the United States to send Special Envoy Habib to the Middle East to negotiate a solution.

As if to demonstrate its force following Syria's installation of these missiles, Israel conducted a series of air raids on PLO targets, while the PLO retaliated with rocket barrages into northern Israel. An escalation of this violence over a three-week period in July prompted complex negotiations among Arafat, the UNIFIL commander, Saudi Arabia, Habib, and Israel that finally culminated in a PLO-Israeli cease-fire on July 24.

Despite Israeli assertions that the PLO could not adhere to a cease-fire, it did so. And the longer the cease-fire endured, the more it seemed to alarm the government of Menachem Begin in Israel. First, the cease-fire implied an indirect Israeli recognition of the PLO. Second, it gave time to the PLO to build up its forces in Lebanon in preparation for renewed conflict with Israel. Finally, it enhanced Arafat's stature as a responsible political figure who could impose discipline throughout his organization. The possibility that international pressure could build to resolve the problem of Lebanon at the expense of Israeli aspirations on the West Bank and Gaza could not be discounted. As resistance to Israeli rule in the territories increased during the spring of 1982, Israel made preparations for a major military operation against the PLO.

Expulsion of PLO from Beirut

On June 6, 1982, Israel launched its invasion of Lebanon. The publicly stated purpose of "Operation Peace for Galilee" was to clear all PLO forces from a forty-kilometer area north of Israel's border with Lebanon, thus putting northern Israel out of range of PLO artillery. As the operation developed, however, it became clear that Israel had larger objectives, including:

● The full destruction of the PLO leadership and infrastructure, thus eliminating the main perceived obstacle to Israel's consolidation of its rule over the West Bank and Gaza.

● Arrangement for the election of Bashir Gemayel as president of Lebanon. Israel hoped he could restore law and order and bring remaining Palestinians there under Lebanese government authority.

● Conclusion of a peace treaty with Lebanon.

In a rapid three-prong advance complemented by extensive naval landing operations along Lebanon's coast, PLO forces were driven back into Beirut. Israel effectively surrounded the city by June 14. In the Bekaa Valley, Israeli warplanes completely destroyed Syrian surface-to-air missile installations in a June 9 air battle. Israeli and Syrian army units on the ground engaged in heavy fighting until the two governments agreed to a cease-fire on June 11.

Israel decided to lay siege to Beirut and demand the surrender of the PLO instead of entering the city and engaging in costly urban fighting. The siege, marked by sporadic bombing and shelling of PLO centers in the city, continued through the summer until August 12, when negotiations again mediated by U.S. Special Envoy Habib finally achieved a cease-fire and an agreement allowing the PLO to evacuate southern and coastal Lebanon.

The departure of the PLO from Beirut, which was completed by September 2, deprived it of its last base in the Arab world from which to make direct attacks on Israeli territory. The organization was now scattered throughout a variety of Arab countries, none of which bordered Israel except Syria, whose policy was to not allow them autonomy of decision. It appeared that the PLO's significance to the Arab-Israeli conflict had greatly diminished. This was an illusion, however, because the strength of the PLO, although forged on the concept of armed struggle against Israel, had never rested with its military capability. The broad range of international diplomatic support the PLO had garnered over the years as the institutional symbol of Palestinian nationalism had become the principal basis of its legitimacy. In the years after the PLO's departure from Lebanon, it was this aspect of the PLO's strength that Arafat sought to husband and enhance.

Israel had achieved the key objective of its invasion of Lebanon, the expulsion of the PLO, but it found itself mired in a war it was unable to end. It opened up a second front of the Arab-Israeli conflict that was only indirectly related to the PLO or the Palestinian problem. The new conflict pitted Israel against Moslem militia groups in Lebanon that now mobilized themselves—with Syrian, Iranian, and other sources of external support—to resist the continuing Israeli occupation of southern Lebanon.

Israel's second objective of fostering a strengthened central government with which it would sign a peace treaty was shattered by the assassination of president-elect Bashir Gemayel on September 14, 1982. The Israelis succeeded in negotiating a treaty signed May 17, 1983, with the less amenable successor government of President Amin Gemayel. This treaty, however, foundered because of widespread Lebanese resistance to it and the refusal of the Syrian government to withdraw its troops from Lebanon. As it became clear that even U.S. support could not strengthen the Lebanese government sufficiently to enable it to overcome the resistance engendered by the Israel-Lebanon agreement, Israel began undertaking a series of unilateral withdrawals. By July 1985 Israel had extricated itself from Lebanon.

Israeli-Shi'ite Conflict

Israel's withdrawal from Lebanon did not end its conflict with forces in the country. As it departed, Israel left an expanded security zone in southern Lebanon controlled by its surrogate force, now called the Army of South Lebanon (ASL), commanded by Antoine Lahad, a retired Lebanese general. The purpose of the zone, as when it was first established, was to enhance the security of Israel's northern border in the absence of an Israel-Lebanon peace treaty. Israel justified the zone by pointing to the continued presence of Syrian forces in the northern parts of Lebanon and the probability of PLO reinfiltration into southern Lebanon in the absence of strong central government authority.

For the Shi'ite inhabitants of southern Lebanon, who at first welcomed the Israeli invasion but turned against it as the Israeli occupation became prolonged, the security zone was perceived as a perpetuation of the Israeli occupation and a joint effort of Israel and Lebanon's Maronite Christians to perpetuate the second-rate status Shi'ite Moslems had long held in Lebanese society. Armed and funded by Syria and Iran, two major Shi'ite militias, Amal and Hizballah (the latter inspired by the religious appeals of revolutionary Iran) continued to attack ASL and Israeli troops in the security zone. Israel often responded by arresting and imprisoning individuals who had been identified as especially strong militants.

The presence of Shi'ites in Israeli prisons provoked others to engage in acts of international terrorism to secure their release. An example was in June 1985 when three Lebanese Shi'ites hijacked a TWA airliner out of Athens, Greece. After landing in Beirut, they killed one American and held thirty-nine Americans hostage in an effort to make Israel release some seven hundred Lebanese Shi'ites imprisoned in Israel. The American hostages were freed, and Israel eventually released the Shi'ites, whom it said were previously scheduled to be released.

Although only peripherally related to the historic Arab-Israeli struggle, this new phase of the conflict inaugurated by Israel's 1982 invasion of Lebanon continued unabated through the 1980s. Supported on the Arab side mainly by Syria and Iran, this phase may be perceived as an element of the continuing Syrian conflict with Israel.

1982-1987 Diplomacy

Following the evacuation of the PLO from Beirut, the focus of the Palestinian component of the Arab-Israeli conflict tended to be on diplomacy rather than military confrontation. In September 1982 a flurry of international diplomacy provided momentum in the Arab-Israeli peace process.

The Reagan Peace Initiative

The diplomatic activity began with an American initiative proposed by President Ronald Reagan on September 1, 1982. In a nationwide telecast, Reagan outlined a new initiative to give a "fresh start" to the Camp David process. *(Text, Appendix, p. 305)*

Taking advantage of the diminished stature of the PLO, and clearly trying to appeal to King Hussein of Jordan, whose participation in the Camp David process was vital for it to achieve any meaningful success, Reagan committed U.S. policy to a "Jordanian Option." He reiterated U.S. opposition to further Israeli settlement in the West Bank or Gaza and to annexation or permanent control of the territories by Israel, while asserting that the United States would exclude the PLO from negotiations and oppose creation of an independent Palestinian state. Reagan then proposed some type of self-government by the Palestinians in the territories in association with Jordan. He further called for negotiations to decide the disposition of Jerusalem.

The Begin government immediately rejected the proposal, saying it "deviated" from Camp David in that it tended to predetermine the outcome of negotiations. On the other hand, opposition Labor leader Shimon Peres called it "a basis for dialogue with the U.S." Like Jordan's King Hussein before him, it was now Begin who resented not having been consulted. The Israeli government reminded the administration of understandings about bilateral consultations that had been agreed upon at the time of the Sinai II agreement in 1975 and at Camp David. Hussein, who had been consulted on the substance of the Reagan initiative prior to its announcement, initially indicated interest, but he noted his need to secure general Arab support and PLO approval before entering the negotiation process. Indeed the Reagan announcement was deliberately timed to precede a forthcoming Arab summit. His administration hoped that the summit would empower Hussein to respond positively to the Reagan initiative.

The Fez Summit Peace Proposal

The Arab summit, which met in Fez, Morocco, September 5-8, 1982, did not respond to the U.S. initiative as the Reagan administration had hoped. At the same time, the summit did endorse a set of principles that was the first collective Arab expression of an intent to reach a settlement of the Arab-Israeli conflict. Passed unanimously by all members present, including the PLO and Jordan (Libya had not attended because of the agenda; Egypt, no longer a member of the Arab League, also did not attend), the Fez proposal adopted a hard-line approach. Its provisions included an Israeli withdrawal from all territories occupied in 1967, the administration of the territories by the UN Security Council for a short transition period not to exceed several months, the establishment of a Palestinian state with Jerusalem as its capital, and UN Security Council guarantees to protect the peace and security of states in the region. *(Text, Appendix, p. 305)*

By continuing to designate the PLO as the sole legitimate representative of the Palestinian people and calling for the creation of an independent Palestinian state, the summit reinvigorated the PLO, so recently battered in Beirut. At the same time, it undercut any effort by King Hussein to participate in the Camp David process or indeed even to consider Jordanian sovereignty over the West Bank as legitimate.

In practical terms, the obvious incompatibility of the Fez proposal with either Israeli policy or the Camp David formula meant that no basis existed for implementing any settlement through diplomacy, a situation that actually served the interest of those Israelis who resisted compromise on the issue of the occupied territories. No negotiated settlement meant continued Israeli control of the West Bank and Gaza.

The Hussein-Arafat Initiative

Because the Reagan initiative failed to draw Jordan into the Camp David process, that process lost its momentum. The position of Israel's government remained firm. Although Shimon Perez, the head of the more accommodating Labor party, took over the prime ministership in 1984 under a coalition agreement with the rival Likud bloc, Israel was preoccupied with economic problems and the effort to withdraw Israeli forces from Lebanon. In addition Labor's Likud coalition partners did not give Peres a free hand to make any decision relating to the West Bank and Gaza that contradicted their own position.

King Hussein and Yasir Arafat held talks during late 1982 and early 1983 in an effort to find a formula that would enable Jordan to negotiate on behalf of the PLO. Two concepts dominated the dialogue: establishing a Jordanian-West Bank Palestinian confederation or creating a joint Jordanian-Palestinian delegation to participate in the Camp David process.

Arafat's efforts to reach agreement with Hussein, however, faced opposition from two sources. The first of these were PLO factions that were wedded to the concepts of armed struggle and the total liberation of Palestine. These had taken refuge mainly in Syria following the evacuation from Beirut and opposed Arafat's temptation to follow the path of diplomacy. The second source of opposition was President Assad of Syria, whose determination to dominate regional affairs, including the Palestine issue, clashed sharply with with any Jordanian or PLO effort to pursue an independent policy.

The PLO-Syrian feud reached a crisis point in May 1983, when Assad supported a mutiny against Arafat's leadership of Fatah and the PLO. Intra-PLO fighting continued in eastern and northern Lebanon throughout the summer and fall until December, when Arafat and four thousand followers once again were evacuated from Lebanon, this time from the port city of Tripoli.

To the surprise of the world, Arafat's first stop after his departure from Lebanon was Egypt, where he was received by President Mubarak. This symbolic visit marked a formal split in the PLO over management of the Arab-Israeli conflict. While Arafat moved toward reconciliation with the Camp David process (and to mold the process according to Palestinian terms), a rejectionist element of the PLO, controlled by and subordinated to Syria, held fast to an uncompromising collective Arab position. Despite sharp Israeli opposition, Mubarak lent support to the idea of developing a "new approach" that would bring Jordan and the PLO in the negotiations with Israel. So also did King Hussein, who resumed efforts with Arafat in early 1984 to seek a joint Jordanian-Palestinian policy for negotiations with Israel.

Although the two leaders shared interests in finding a common position that would secure Israeli withdrawal from the occupied territories, they did so for different reasons. For his part, Hussein was obliged to obtain a PLO mandate in order to negotiate on behalf of the Palestinian people; a 1974 Rabat summit resolution, reaffirmed at the Fez summit, had specified these terms. Meanwhile, Arafat sought to use his leverage to gain the approval of Jordan, Egypt, and ultimately the United States for the concept of an independent Palestinian state, to be achieved through the venue of an international conference, as stipulated by the Fez resolution. During 1984 Hussein reconvened the Jordanian parliament (half of whose members were West Bank Palestinians), restored diplomatic relations with Egypt in September, and sought the support of the more moderate Arab states and the United States for an enhanced Jordanian role in the peace process. Meanwhile, Arafat sought to build world support for an international peace conference and recognition of Palestinians' self-determination rights.

Because of the opposition of Syria and Syrian-based elements of the PLO that opposed his leadership, however, Arafat required reaffirmation of his role as PLO chairman before he could conclude any agreement with Hussein. Accordingly, despite Syrian threats and a boycott of Arafat's opposition, the king permitted a convocation of the Palestine National Council (PNC—equivalent to a Palestinian parliament in exile) in Jordan in November 1984. Arafat dominated its deliberations and was reelected as PLO chairman. He obtained authorization to continue his diplomatic strategy, but not to conclude any peace settlement on the basis of UN Resolution 242. Although this resolution called for Israeli withdrawal from occupied territories, it treated the Palestinian issue as a refugee problem and did not recognize the right of the Palestinian people to self-determination.

With his role as PLO chairman reconfirmed, Arafat was able to reach an agreement with Hussein on a joint diplomatic initiative, which the two signed on February 11, 1985. Its provisions included:

● An exchange of land for peace as provided for in resolutions of the United Nations, including those of the Security Council.

● The right of self-determination of the Palestinian people in the context of a Jordanian-Palestinian Arab confederation.

● The settlement of the Palestinian refugee issue in accordance with UN resolutions.

● An international peace conference in which the five permanent members of the Security Council and all parties to the conflict would participate, including the PLO.

Peace Efforts Founder

Announcement of this agreement was followed by visits to the United States by King Fahd of Saudi Arabia, President Mubarak, and King Hussein in May 1985 to solicit U.S. support for the initiative. Hussein proposed that a preliminary meeting between U.S. representatives and the joint Jordanian-Palestinian delegation, excluding PLO representatives, be held before an international con-

ference. In addition, Hussein delivered a list of Palestinians suggested by the PLO for U.S. consideration as members of the joint Jordanian-Palestinian delegation.

The United States responded cautiously to the initiative because of suspicions that hidden within the term *self-determination* lay the seeds of an independent Palestinian state. The Reagan administration reiterated its requirement for a "publicly and unequivocally" clear PLO statement that it accepted UN resolutions 242 and 338 and Israel's right to exist before the United States would meet with PLO representatives. The PNC had just as unequivocally denied Arafat the authority to make such a statement during its November meeting in Jordan. In addition, the bitter opposition of the Syrian-based PLO rejectionists constrained Arafat politically from meeting the U.S. condition unless the United States first declared its acceptance of the right of the Palestinian people to self-determination.

Deadlocked, the Hussein-Arafat initiative finally collapsed, despite the efforts of Jordan, Egypt, and the United States to maintain momentum through the summer. Two terrorist actions contributed to the demise of the diplomatic process. The first was the killing of three Israeli tourists on a yacht at Larnaca, Cyprus, on September 25, 1985, by assassins alleged to be members of Force 17, a PLO unit personally loyal to Arafat. Although Arab commentary insisted that the three Israelis were members of Mossad, the Israeli intelligence organization, and not just innocent tourists, Israel responded by bombing Arafat's PLO headquarters in Tunis on October 1.

The second terrorist action was the October 8 hijacking of the *Achille Lauro,* an Italian cruise ship, by members of the Palestine Liberation Front, a pro-Arafat group within the PLO. The hijackers' killing of Leon Klinghoffer, an American tourist confined to a wheelchair, made it impossible for moderate Arab leaders supporting Arafat to depict the PLO as a similarly moderate element suitable for inclusion in the peace process. Although the action was almost certainly sponsored by Syrian-based radical Palestinian elements opposed to Arafat and his diplomatic strategy, the continuing association of the Palestinian movement with brutal acts of terrorism against innocent civilians was gravely damaging to the Hussein-Arafat initiative.

Faced with Arafat's inability to escape his own ambiguous political situation, the Reagan administration's extreme caution, and the lack of responsiveness from a politically paralyzed Israel (despite Prime Minister Peres's efforts to keep the doors of negotiation open), King Hussein finally repudiated the agreement with Arafat in February 1986. Jordanian-PLO relations rapidly deteriorated, and in July 1986 all PLO offices in Jordan were ordered closed. In April 1987 Arafat also repudiated the accord as a first step in an attempt to effect a reconciliation with his PLO opposition.

The Peres Initiative

After the Israeli elections in 1984, the country was governed by a political coalition in which Shimon Peres, leader of the Labor party, served as prime minister for half the term of the government, until October 1986. Yitzhak Shamir, successor of Menachem Begin as leader of the Likud bloc, then assumed the office of prime minister. Unlike Shamir, who was committed to retaining the territories, Peres favored a diplomatic settlement that would leave Israel in control of territories he believed vital for its security but nevertheless would meet the demands of Jordan and the United States for the return of some of the West Bank to Jordan. Both parties of the Israeli coalition opposed the idea of an independent Palestinian state, especially one governed by the PLO, although even some Israelis were open to this option.

Peres sought to respond to the Hussein-Arafat initiative, but he was unable to make any commitment on behalf of the government because of opposition from the Likud. Peres adopted an approach that accepted the concept of an international conference under certain conditions. He said that the Soviet Union should restore diplomatic relations with Israel before such a conference and asserted that the role of the five permanent members of the Security Council should be mediatory, not coercive. The regional members of the conference—Egypt, Lebanon, Syria, Israel, and the joint Jordanian-Palestinian delegation—should all accept resolutions 242 and 338 and disavow terrorism and violence. Regarding PLO participation, his position was that any "authentic Palestinian," whether nominated by Arafat or not, was acceptable so long as the delegate did not "represent terrorism."

With the collapse of the Hussein-Arafat initiative in February 1986, Peres sought to press his formula to the diplomatic forefront. Hussein, however, would agree to return to active involvement in the peace process only after the change of government in Israel scheduled for the fall. Apparently, Hussein was convinced that nothing could be achieved with the Likud in an opposition role. Before leaving the prime minister's office, however, Peres accepted the invitation of Morocco's King Hassan to visit Rabat in July for talks about his initiative and its relationship to the principles of the Fez proposal.

After Peres had become foreign minister in April 1987, he reached an initially secret understanding with Jordan, through the mediation of the United States, to proceed with plans for calling an international peace conference under the auspices of the five permanent members of the UN Security Council. The conference was to be based on UN resolutions 242 and 338 and lead to direct negotiations between Israel and its Arab neighbors. Before further progress toward convening such a conference could be made, however, the agreement was blocked in the Israeli cabinet by Prime Minister Shamir and his fellow Likud members, who considered the idea of an international conference on the Middle East a "Soviet-inspired invention."

Jordan also faced obstacles to its participation in the conference. King Hussein was careful to avoid any appearance that he might be willing to conclude a separate peace with Israel. After he repudiated the Jordanian-PLO accord, Hussein tried to improve his relations with neighboring states, especially Syria. Moreover, President Assad had approved his efforts to facilitate the holding of an international conference. But Hussein did not yet have Syrian or general Arab approval for the specific agreement he had struck with Peres.

Accordingly, Hussein managed to convene an Arab summit conference in Amman in November 1987. The outcome was a personal triumph for the king. The conference endorsed his request to convene the international peace conference, and it placed him rather than Arafat squarely in the position of Arab leadership. It also gave leave for individual Arab countries to restore relations with Egypt, broken since the signing of the Camp David treaty, although Syrian opposition still precluded Egyptian readmission into the Arab League. Finally, the summit, with

Syrian approval, endorsed Iraq's position in the Iran-Iraq war, and Hussein was able to arrange a personal meeting between the two feuding leaders, Saddam Hussein of Iraq and Hafez Assad of Syria. (*Text of summit communiqué, Appendix, p. 307*)

The Intifada

Hussein's mandate to enter the peace process was to be short-lived, however. Within a few weeks of the summit, the outbreak of a sustained general uprising among the Arab population of the West Bank and Gaza, known as the *intifada* (literally translated as "shaking"), was to transform the Arab-Israeli conflict. The intifada shifted the focus of the conflict away from the disputes between Israel and its Arab neighbors to Israel's relations with the Arabs who lived under its occupation.

The Israeli army was unable to put down the uprising, which quickly became an established fact of life throughout the West Bank and Gaza. The sight of Palestinian children armed with rocks facing Israeli soldiers increased international sympathy for the cause of Arabs in the occupied territories. The critical problem for Israel was that the young rockthrowers, and local Palestinian leaders who emerged to explain the intifada, regarded the PLO—in particular the part led by Yasir Arafat—as the only legitimate representative of the Palestinian people. The uprising, although not directly inspired by the PLO, returned international attention to Arafat.

The intifada was a reaction to determined Israeli efforts for nearly a decade to control life in the occupied territories. The Israeli government had expropriated available land in the territories, built Jewish settlements, controlled the territories' water and electricity, destroyed houses of the families who resisted, arrested and detained Arabs arbitrarily, and in extreme cases deported Arabs engaged in anti-Israeli activity. In general the government tried to create conditions that would induce the Arabs to absolutely respect Israeli authority. The intifada represented a massive and popular upheaval against the continuing Israeli occupation. Violence and resistance to the occupation, however, were not new. What distinguished the intifada from previous violence was its universal presence throughout the territories and the inability of Israeli authorities to contain it, despite the Israeli army's use of beatings, massive arrests, curfews, and violent confrontations with the demonstrators.

Possibly inspired by the perceived success of resistance to Israel's occupation of southern Lebanon between 1982 and 1985, the intifada was also an expression of Palestinian frustration at the failure of Arab diplomacy to reach any accommodation with Israel in the years since the Camp David treaty.

In an effort to revive momentum toward a diplomatic settlement, U.S. Secretary of State George Shultz embarked on a diplomatic mission in the spring of 1988—the first official American peace initiative since the Reagan plan of 1982. The initiative laid down a tight timetable for completion of the negotiation process by the end of the year, but it was otherwise similar to the agreement reached between Foreign Minister Peres and King Hussein the previous April, and for which King Hussein now had an Arab summit mandate to pursue. Where United States mediation of that agreement had been low key due to the delicacies of negotiating an agreement with a foreign minister operating without the approval of his prime minister, the urgency of the situation now led Shultz to lend it the prestige of his personal involvement.

His mission encountered two primary obstacles, however, the opposition of Prime Minister Shamir and the noncooperation of West Bank Palestinians because of the lack of a place in his plan for the PLO. Despite initial cautious support in both Syria and Jordan, Syria eventually demanded a conference with a unified Arab delegation, and King Hussein noted that he no longer could represent either the PLO or the Palestinian people. By May it was clear that the concept of an international conference as originally conceived by Peres was no longer possible.

The changed nature of the situation was revealed at a three-day emergency Arab summit convened by Algerian President Chadli Bendjedid in Algiers June 7-9. The summit decided to withdraw from Syria, Jordan, and the PLO annual funding that previously had been allotted to confrontation countries bordering Israel. Instead, the summit endorsed general Arab support for the intifada and urged all Arab funds to be distributed to the territories through the PLO. These funds were to be allocated state by state, however, not by the Arab League as a whole. Rather than condemn the Shultz initiative, moreover, the Arab leaders reiterated their support for an international conference under UN auspices and urged the PLO to declare the establishment of an independent Palestinian state, which the Arab states proposed to designate as the principal Arab interlocutor in such a conference.

In July 1988 King Hussein—so recently authorized by the November Arab summit to seek a peace settlement with Israel—relinquished Jordan's claims to the West Bank and Gaza, which it had maintained since 1949. Hussein's action appeared designed to free Jordan, with its large Palestinian population, from the disruptive effects of the intifada and force the PLO into a more conciliatory position by making it solely responsible for representing the Arabs in the occupied territories. Although Hussein's announcement did not completely remove him from Middle East diplomacy, it was a blow to U.S. and Israeli leaders who had anticipated a prominent role for Jordan in any settlement. *(Text, Appendix, p. 309)*

As the intifada continued and the Israeli government sought to contain it with force, Arafat convened a meeting of the Palestine National Council in Algiers. On November 15, 1988, the council took the historic step of proclaiming the establishment of an independent Palestinian state and announced its recognition of UN Resolution 242, implicitly recognizing Israel. A declaration rejecting terrorism also was adopted. The council called for the convening of an international conference under sponsorship of the UN, the purpose of which would be to negotiate a resolution of the Arab-Israeli conflict. *(Text, Appendix, p. 310)*

Although the Reagan administration maintained that these initial pronouncements did not satisfy its conditions for beginning a dialogue with the PLO, Arafat on December 14 explicitly accepted resolutions 242 and 338, recognized Israel's right to exist, and renounced terrorism. The United States responded by opening talks with the PLO in Tunis despite Israeli objections. *(Text of Arafat statement, Appendix, p. 311)*

Outlook

The intifada continued and the Shamir government, returned to office in late 1988, showed no sign of responding to the new Arab consensus concerning a settlement of the Arab-Israeli conflict. Shamir made clear his total opposition to conducting direct negotiations with PLO Chairman Arafat or to accepting the principle of an independent Palestinian Arab state. Instead Shamir has advocated an election process in the West Bank and Gaza that would produce a local Palestinian delegation to carry on negotiations with Israel on implementing some type of Arab autonomy formula in accordance with the Israeli interpretation of the Camp David accords.

Difficult to resist in principle, the electoral proposal was not rejected outright by the PLO. The organization insisted, however, that before elections could take place, Israel must agree in principle to give up the occupied territories and Arab residents of East Jerusalem must be allowed to vote. Both conditions were at odds with the Israeli position and were immediately rejected.

In this manner the Arab-Israeli conflict continues. Instead of producing momentum toward settlement, the conflict tends to promote increased degrees of radicalism on both sides. Arab resistance to the very legitimacy and existence of Israel has fueled Israeli expectations that the Arabs would never make peace, leading many to justify retention of the territories occupied in 1967 for reasons of security. Mounting Israeli militancy and determination to retain and settle the territories in turn provoked the Arab radicalism symbolized by the intifada. The mounting violence associated with the intifada, meanwhile, has tended to increase the appeal of radical attitudes on both sides. It is no doubt possible that Israeli efforts to suppress the intifada will eventually succeed, but only at a terrible cost in human lives and resources.

In this environment, moderate Arab states and Arafat's PLO have continued pursuing a resolution to the Arab-Israeli conflict through diplomacy. Unable for the moment to oppose this larger Arab consensus, Syria continues to provide a haven for PLO groups opposed to the current diplomatic strategy, and Assad waits for what he regards as an inevitable rejection of this strategy by the other Arab parties owing to Israeli intransigence.

Israeli military strength, so assiduously cultivated over the decades in the interests of promoting the security of a small and vulnerable state, now seems to thwart the emergence of an Arab-Israeli settlement. Strong enough to deter any combination of regional threats arrayed against it, Israel cannot be pressured to adopt positions or enter agreements against its wishes. Although many Israelis believe otherwise, the dominant trend, as reflected in the country's most recent elections, is to reject compromise on the territories. In the absence of further compromise by both the Arabs and the Israelis, however, the resistance in the territories will continue indefinitely and a settlement of the Arab-Israeli conflict will remain a distant vision.

U.S. and Soviet Mideast Policies

3

Minutes after Israel declared its independence on May 14, 1948, the United States became the first country to recognize the Jewish state. The establishment of Israel marked the beginning of extensive U.S. political, economic, and military involvement in the Middle East. By the time of the 1967 Six-Day War, achieving peace and stability in the Middle East had become one of the most critical U.S. foreign policy concerns. During the 1970s and 1980s war between the Arabs and the Israelis, terrorism against U.S. citizens, and the continuing uncertainty about the availability and cost of Arab oil presented U.S. presidents with some of their most difficult foreign policy problems. No region seemed more volatile or produced more crises for U.S. policy makers during these decades than the Middle East.

U.S. policy in the Middle East has focused on four major objectives: ensuring the security of Israel, achieving an Arab-Israeli peace settlement, maintaining U.S. and Western access to Middle Eastern oil, and blocking Soviet expansionism in the region. The United States has also pursued several lesser policy goals that are related to its four main objectives, including combating terrorism, encouraging an end to Lebanon's civil war, preventing the spread of nuclear and chemical arms in the region, and improving economic and security ties with moderate Arab states.

These policy objectives have often conflicted with one another. In particular the special relationship between the United States and Israel has made other U.S. policy goals more difficult to achieve. For example U.S. support for Israel during the 1973 Arab-Israeli war led to an Arab oil boycott against the United States. The U.S.-Israeli relationship also has contributed to Arab resentment against the United States and a greater willingness by Arab states to seek closer ties with the Soviet Union. Nevertheless, successive U.S. administrations have agreed that all four major objectives must be pursued, and these goals have retained wide public and congressional support.

Although the Soviet Union has been less deeply involved in Middle Eastern affairs than the United States since the 1940s, it also has regarded the region as important. Soviet Middle East policy has focused on extending its influence at the expense of the United States, while avoiding a superpower military confrontation.

Only three days after the establishment of Israel, the Soviet Union recognized the Jewish state. Moscow had hoped to develop close Soviet-Israeli relations, but as Israel strengthened its ties with Western nations during the first two decades of its existence the Soviets determined that their best opportunity to expand their influence in the region was to champion the cause of Israel's Arab enemies.

Arabs in many countries, although suspicious of the military power and Communist ideology of the Soviet Union, regarded Israel as a far greater threat to their security. To counter the unflinching support of the United States for Israel, some Arab states, such as Syria and Egypt, developed close arms supply relationships with the Soviet Union. During the 1967 Six-Day War the Soviet Union severed its relations with Israel to protest the Israeli invasion of Arab countries. Moscow's continuing lack of diplomatic ties with Israel and the reluctance of the United States to include Soviet diplomats in negotiations has relegated the Soviet Union to a secondary status in the Arab-Israeli peace process. Nevertheless, the Soviet Union's vocal support for Arab causes, its arms sales to Arab countries, and its veto power in the UN Security Council have given it continued relevance to Middle East peace efforts.

Over the years Moscow has favored low-risk and low-cost methods of improving its standing with Arab states, such as treaties of friendship, arms sales, and economic cooperation. Egypt's expulsion of Soviet advisers in 1972 dealt a heavy blow to Moscow's influence in the Middle East. The Soviets adjusted to the setback by strengthening ties with Syria and the Palestine Liberation Organization. Although the Soviet Union has frequently sent advisers and arms to its Arab allies and threatened Israel and the United States during Middle East crises, it has never directly intervened militarily in the region.

Soviet Middle East policy during the 1980s was hampered by several factors. The succession of changes in leadership in the Kremlin made sustained foreign policy initiatives difficult. In addition, Soviet allies in the region, including Syria and the PLO, were often in conflict with each other. Most importantly, however, the Soviet Union's military involvement in Afghanistan cost it credibility in the Middle East, especially among moderate Arab states such as Saudi Arabia. With more than 100,000 troops in Afghanistan it was hard for Moscow to persuade states in the region that it would never threaten their security. The withdrawal of Soviet forces from Afghanistan in 1988 and 1989 and the establishment of a less threatening foreign policy posture during the late 1980s by Soviet president Mikhail Gorbachev have opened the way for improved Arab-Soviet relations. Soviet inroads into the Middle East, however, were not likely to come quickly.

Palestine Partition

President Woodrow Wilson set the framework for U.S. policy in the Middle East when he endorsed a 1917 letter from British foreign secretary Arthur Balfour to Lord Lionel Rothschild, leader of the British Zionists, pledging that Britain would support the establishment in Palestine of a "national home" for the Jewish people, on the clear understanding "that nothing shall be done which may prejudice the civil and religious rights of existing non-Jewish communities in Palestine...." The U.S. Congress adopted a resolution approving the declaration in September 1922.

Wilson also strongly influenced the post-World War I peace settlement that established national boundaries for the Middle East. He conceived the interim League of Nations mandates, which led to the formation of most of the countries that exist in the Middle East today.

Soon after World War I, the United States sent a commission (the King-Crane Commission) to the Arab regions of the old Ottoman Empire to seek their views on postwar settlements and determine which of the Western governments should act as the mandatory power, or overseeing authority, for Palestine. The commission's final report, issued in 1919, was sympathetic to the Arab cause and advised against creating a Jewish state in Palestine. However, it was never formally accepted by the Paris Peace Conference or the U.S. government.

Three years later, in July 1922, the League of Nations approved an arrangement giving Great Britain a mandate over Palestine. The mandate, which went into force September 22, 1923, included a preamble incorporating the Balfour Declaration and stressing the Jews' historical connection with Palestine. Britain was made responsible for placing the country under such "political, administrative, and economic conditions as will secure the establishment of a Jewish National Home...."

Between 1923 and 1939 more than four-hundred-thousand Jews immigrated to Palestine, causing growing resentment against the British among the Arabs. In 1939, however, Arab unrest and German and Italian attempts to improve relations with the Arabs led the British to issue a white paper that reduced the flow of Jewish immigrants to Palestine—primarily European Jews suffering from Nazi persecution—to fifteen-thousand a year for five years. After that, no more Jewish immigration was to be allowed unless agreed upon by the local Arab population. Jews denounced the restrictions and attempted to circumvent them. *(Jewish immigration, Chapter 2, p. 15)*

The United States led the effort after World War II to lift the immigration restrictions. In August 1945 President Harry S. Truman called for the free settlement of Palestine by Jews to a point consistent with the maintenance of civil peace.

Later that month he suggested in a letter to British prime minister Clement R. Attlee that an additional one-hundred-thousand Jews be allowed to enter Palestine. In December both houses of Congress adopted a resolution urging U.S. aid in opening Palestine to Jewish immigrants and in building a "democratic commonwealth."

Meanwhile in November, Britain, eager to have the United States share responsibility for its Jewish immigration policy, joined with the United States in establishing a commission to examine the problem of admitting European Jews to Palestine. Britain also agreed to permit an additional 1,500 Jews to enter Palestine each month.

In April 1946 an Anglo-American Committee of Inquiry recommended the immediate admission of one-hundred-thousand Jews into Palestine and continuation of the British mandate until a United Nations trusteeship was established. Truman immediately endorsed the proposal, but Britain stipulated that, before it would agree to continue its mandate, underground Jewish forces in Palestine would have to be disbanded.

On October 4 Truman released a communication sent to the British government in which he appealed for "substantial immigration" into Palestine "at once" and expressed support for the Zionist plan for creation of a "viable Jewish state" in part of Palestine. In response, the British government said it regretted that Truman's statement had been made public before a settlement was realized. The British feared that such an unqualified expression of American support for a Jewish state would reduce the chances of reaching a compromise between the Arabs and Israelis.

When a London conference of Arab and Zionist representatives failed to resolve the Palestine question, Britain turned to the United Nations in early 1947. The United Nations set up a committee of inquiry, which ultimately recommended that Palestine be divided into separate Arab and Jewish states, with Jerusalem becoming an international zone under permanent UN trusteeship. On November 29, 1947, the UN General Assembly ratified that decision. Britain set May 15, 1948, as the date its mandate would end.

Sporadic violence by Arab and Jewish guerrillas that had become a part of life in Palestine escalated to open civil war after the UN decision. In March 1948 the United States voiced its opposition to the forcible partitioning of Palestine and called for suspension of the plan. The Truman administration requested a special session of the UN General Assembly to reconsider the issue.

In April the Security Council adopted a U.S. resolution calling for a truce in the civil war in Palestine and a special session of the General Assembly. This effort, however, was too late to stop the division of Palestine. On May 14 the British high commissioner left Palestine, the state of Israel was proclaimed, and the General Assembly voted to send a mediator to the Holy Land to seek a truce. The United States immediately granted Israel de facto recognition. The Soviet Union recognized the new state on May 17.

Origins of Soviet Involvement

Unlike U.S. involvement, which dates to the breakup of the Ottoman empire, Soviet involvement in most of the Middle East was minimal until the mid-1950s. Before that, Moscow's interest in the region was confined primarily to the countries of the northern tier of the Middle East that shared a border with the Soviet Union: Iran, Afghanistan, and Turkey. Turkey, in particular, was important to the Soviets because it controlled the straits of the Bosporus and the Dardanelles, which provide access to the Mediterranean from the Soviet ports on the Black Sea. Before the Russian Revolution, Czarist Russia had a similar interest in the Middle East's northern tier.

Like the United States, the Soviet Union welcomed the creation of Israel in 1948. Without Soviet support the UN General Assembly might not have sanctioned the partition of Palestine. In fact, Soviet support of the young Jewish state went beyond the political and diplomatic support it gave in the UN. During the 1948 war, the Soviets supplied arms to the Yishuv, the Jewish settlement in Palestine, through Czechoslovakia.

The Soviets in their early support for the creation of the Jewish state seemed to be motivated by a number of factors. First, the Yishuv was actively opposing the British mandate and therefore opposing one of the major Western powers. Even though the Arabs also opposed the British presence, the Soviets believed the Jews of Palestine had a better chance of pushing the British out. Second, most of the leaders of the Yishuv were socialist in orientation, and Moscow believed they would be willing to establish good relations with the Soviet Union. The Israeli Mapam party platform, for example, contained Marxist elements.

Israel asserted in its declaration of independence that it would remain neutral in the superpower rivalry in the region. The Soviets saw this as a diplomatic victory that diminished Western influence there. The Soviet Union's early support for a partitioned Palestine and the fledgling Jewish state strained Soviet relations with the Arabs.

U.S. Commitment to Israel

From the moment the United States recognized Israel, U.S. commitment to the Jewish nation became a fundamental element of American Middle East policy. That commitment initially stemmed from concern for the terrible plight of Jewish refugees from Hitler's Germany and was sustained by considerable public support for a special friendship with Israel and by the politically active and influential Jewish population in the United States.

Support for Israel, however, created strong anti-American feelings in the Arab countries, subsequently opening many of them to Soviet influence and assistance. For example, the arms with which Egypt and Syria attacked Israel in 1973 were supplied by the Soviet Union. During that war, shipments of Soviet arms were countered by a massive airlift of U.S. weapons to Israel, an action that further committed the United States to guarantee the security of the Jewish nation.

The United States assumed the role of Israel's chief arms supplier with some reluctance. Throughout the 1950s and early 1960s, Washington had shunned Israeli arms requests so as not to jeopardize its friendships with moderate Arab countries or its Middle East oil interests. But with the French decision in 1967 to cut off arms to Israel, U.S. policy makers felt they had no alternative but to step into the arms supplier role to counter Soviet assistance to Israel's enemies.

The United States, however, did not conclude a formal security pact with Israel for fear that such an agreement would provide a rallying point for Arab hostility. Moreover, U.S. leaders were concerned that a treaty would encourage intransigence by Israel in any future negotiations with the Arabs.

With the United States about to become Israel's chief arms benefactor, Senate Foreign Relations Committee Chairman J. William Fulbright, D-Ark., 1945-1975, asked the State Department whether the United States had a national commitment to provide military or economic aid to Israel or any of the Arab states in the event of armed attack or internal subversion. The State Department reply, written in early August 1967, two months after Israel had decisively defeated the Arabs, stated:

> President [Lyndon B.] Johnson and his three predecessors have stated the United States' interest and concern in supporting the political independence and territorial integrity of the countries of the Near East. This is a statement of policy

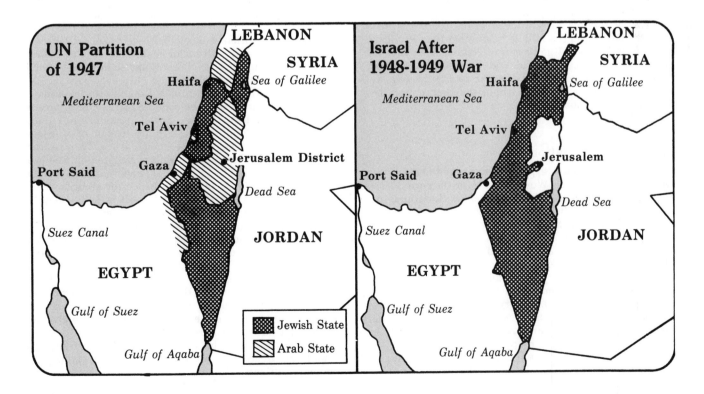

and not a commitment to take particular actions in particular circumstances.... The use of armed force in the Middle East can have especially serious consequences for international peace extending far beyond that area. We have bent our efforts to avoid a renewal of conflict there. Thus, we have stated our position in an effort to use our influence in the cause of peace.

Such references to U.S. support of the "territorial integrity of the countries of the Near East" typified the phraseology used in explaining the U.S. commitment to Israel. Although the United States clearly had become Israel's arms lifeline and its most important ally, it avoided defining exactly what that commitment entailed in an attempt to maintain the appearance of impartiality and increase its flexibility in dealing with Israel and the Arab states. The commitment to Israel, however, while not in the form of a treaty, has been reaffirmed by all U.S. administrations since Truman.

Turns in U.S. Involvement

Vast oil reserves in the Middle East and Britain's attempt to monopolize them at the end of World War I spurred U.S. interest in establishing an economic foothold in the region. Britain had moved into the oil-rich area by securing a mandate from the League of Nations to Palestine and Mesopotamia (present-day Iraq). British companies, which previously were producing less than 5 percent of the world's oil, had managed by 1919 to corner more than half of the world's known reserves.

The United States, which had provided large quantities of oil from U.S. reserves to its European allies during World War I, protested Britain's actions and asked for a share of the Middle East oil. The protests eventually paid off. In 1928 several American companies joined with a European group to operate the Turkish (later the Iraq) Petroleum Company.

Except for this early interest in oil, there was little U.S. involvement in the Middle East (other than President Wilson's influence on the League of Nations' mandates for the region) until after World War II. By 1946, however, Washington gradually was beginning to fill the role the colonial powers, particularly Britain and France, were being forced to relinquish.

Early Soviet Challenges

The United States expanded its commitments in the Middle East following World War II in response to the threat of Soviet expansionism in the region. Soviet pressure on Iran began in early 1946 when Moscow refused to withdraw troops that had been stationed in the northern part of the country since 1941. They were there under a British-Soviet wartime agreement designed to prevent Nazi influence in Iran. The agreement called for British and Soviet forces to withdraw from Iran within six months of the end of hostilities. British and American troops (which had arrived in Iran after the U.S. entry in the war to help move supplies to the Soviet Union) were evacuated, but Soviet troops remained after March 2, 1946, the date set for the departure of all foreign troops. Moscow demanded that Soviet experts remain to help administer the Iranian government.

When Iran rejected this demand, the Soviets engineered a revolt in the north through the Soviet-controlled Communist Tudeh party, which used its own forces to prevent the Iranian government from suppressing the uprising. The Soviets then established a puppet regime in the northern Iranian province of Azerbaijan with the objective of forcing the Iranian government in Tehran to recognize the new regime. President Truman, however, was determined to resist any expansion of Soviet influence in Iran. On March 5 he sent an angry note to Premier Joseph Stalin demanding the immediate withdrawal of Soviet troops and warning that U.S. forces could be moved into Iran within six weeks. Moscow avoided a confrontation by removing all its troops within two months.

Turkey had come under Soviet pressure in the summer of 1945 when Moscow demanded the cession of several Turkish districts on the Turkish-Soviet frontier and revision of the 1936 Montreux Convention providing for exclusive Turkish supervision of the Dardanelles, the strait between the Aegean Sea and the Sea of Marmara.

The Kremlin demanded joint Turkish-Soviet administration of the strait and ratification of a treaty that was similar to those between the Soviet Union and its East European satellites. Moscow also wanted to lease naval and land bases in the Dardanelles for the "joint defense" of Turkey and the Soviet Union. These demands were renewed in a Soviet note to the United States and Britain in August 1946. President Truman replied by immediately sending a naval force into the Mediterranean. Twelve days later, Britain and the United States issued a joint communiqué rejecting Moscow's demands. With the Western powers united in opposition to Soviet goals in Turkey, Moscow did not press its demands.

In Greece, Communist guerrilla forces, with aid from Albania, Bulgaria, and Yugoslavia, by early 1947 were threatening to take over the country. British troops and military assistance in 1945 had averted an earlier attempt by the Communists to gain control of the country. By 1947, however, Britain was no longer able, as a result of wartime exhaustion, to continue to fulfill its traditional role—dating from its position as a colonial power in the nineteenth century—of resisting Russian ambitions in the eastern Mediterranean. The United States moved into the vacuum, as it had in Iran and Turkey.

Faced with the threat of a Communist takeover in Greece and fearing that the collapse of the Greek government would lead to further Soviet pressure on Turkey, Truman spelled out before a joint session of Congress March 12, 1947, what became known as the Truman Doctrine. He said: "Totalitarian regimes imposed on free people, by direct or indirect aggression, undermine the foundations of international peace and hence the security of the United States." He stressed that it must be U.S. policy "to support free people who are resisting attempted subjugations by armed minorities or by outside pressure."

To bolster the sagging Greek government and that of Turkey, the president urged Congress to authorize military as well as economic aid. He also proposed that aid be given through bilateral channels, rather than through multilateral organizations such as the United Nations. Opponents argued that the Truman Doctrine would undermine the powers and prestige of the United Nations and might even provoke a clash with Moscow, but a majority in Congress supported the president. Along with the $400 million provided for Greece and Turkey went American civilian and military advisers.

U.S. Recognition of Israel

The Truman Doctrine encountered opposition from the Arab states, which did not feel threatened by the Soviet Union but were still embittered by U.S. support for the 1917 Balfour Declaration calling for the establishment in Palestine of a national home for the Jewish people. Arab hostility intensified when the United States, and the Soviet Union, voted with a two-thirds majority of the United Nations General Assembly on November 29, 1947, to partition Palestine into separate Arab and Jewish states and internationalize Jerusalem.

A majority of an eleven-nation UN special commission had recommended the partition. A minority of commission members had recommended a federal state with autonomous Arab and Jewish provinces and limits on Jewish immigration. Although the Arab countries initially insisted on absolute Arab sovereignty over Palestine, they ultimately endorsed the minority plan, while the Zionists supported the majority's approach.

The United States was the first country to extend diplomatic recognition to the new Jewish state when Zionists proclaimed the independence of Israel minutes after the twenty-five-year-old British mandate expired at midnight May 14, 1948. Arabs saw the U.S. action as a betrayal of President Franklin D. Roosevelt's promise to King Ibn Saud of Saudi Arabia in 1945 that "no decision [will] be taken with respect to the basic situation in that country [Palestine] without full consultation with both Arabs and Jews."

The day after Israel declared its independence, contingents from six Arab countries—Egypt, Transjordan, Iraq, Saudi Arabia, Syria, and Lebanon—invaded Palestine. The first of the Arab-Israeli wars had begun.

First Arab-Israeli War (1948-1949)

Although the population of the Arab states involved in the fighting was forty times larger than that of the infant Jewish state, the Arabs were torn by various rivalries and were unable to agree on common objectives. They never succeeded in placing their armies under effective joint command. Meanwhile, the outnumbered Jews profited from their greater cohesion and their paramilitary experience fighting the Palestinian Arabs during the British mandate period. Their war effort was augmented by an influx of men and aid from abroad.

The shooting war stopped January 7, 1949, and by February 24 Egypt had signed a separate armistice agreement with Israel. Lebanon signed the armistice in March, Transjordan in April, and Syria in July. Iraq refused to sign an armistice agreement and simply withdrew from Palestine.

When the fighting was over, Israel held over 30 percent more territory than had been assigned to the Jewish state under the UN partition plan. The Palestinian state envisaged by the UN plan never materialized; Arab-controlled territory was scattered in pockets within Israel and Transjordan. Israel gained about 2,500 square miles. Transjordan, which annexed territory on the West Bank of the Jordan River and transformed itself into the state of Jordan, gained 2,200 square miles. Egypt took the Gaza Strip, about 135 square miles, which it held in the status of Egyptian-controlled territory. Jerusalem was divided between Israel and Jordan. UN armistice commissions were established to police the frontiers, and several demilitarized zones were established between Israel and the bordering Arab states of Egypt, Jordan, and Syria.

The United Nations also set up the United Nations Relief Works Agency (UNRWA) to assist Palestinian Arabs who had fled or been driven from their homes. Although the number is disputed, it has been estimated that more than 700,000 Palestinian Arabs who had lived in the area taken over by Israel became refugees.

Suez Crisis

In an attempt to bring stability to the Middle East and reassure both Israel and the Arab states, the United States joined with Britain and France in issuing the Tripartite Declaration of May 1950. The three powers pledged to limit arms shipments and to oppose any attempt to alter the existing armistice lines by force. Yet the armistice lines were repeatedly violated by Arab commando raids into Israeli territory and retaliatory raids into Arab territory by Israel. The level of hostilities escalated, culminating in a second Arab-Israeli war in 1956.

Meanwhile, the United States became increasingly apprehensive about Soviet intentions. In an effort to counter Soviet pressure, the Eisenhower administration in February 1955 promoted the formation of a mutual defense treaty among Britain, Iran, Iraq, Pakistan, and Turkey. American officials participated in the defense and antisubversion committees of what became known as the Baghdad Pact, and U.S. military and economic aid was granted to members of the group. But the United States never became a signatory to the treaty. The main reason was that Iraq and Egypt were rivals for leadership of the Arab world, and the United States, hoping to persuade Egypt to join the pact, did not want to alienate Cairo by formally allying itself with Iraq. Moreover, an alliance with Iraq would have exacerbated U.S. relations with Israel.

Egypt did not join. Egypt's President Gamal Abdel Nasser denounced Iraq for allying itself with the Western powers, and in the fall of 1955 he asked the Soviet Union for military equipment. Moscow began funneling arms to Egypt through Czechoslovakia and quickly became Egypt's major arms supplier.

Soviet arms shipments to Egypt in 1955 and 1956 convinced Israel that it must prepare for a preventive war against Egypt before the military balance shifted in Cairo's favor. Israel's request for U.S. arms was rejected by President Dwight D. Eisenhower who, on March 7, 1956, warned that it could provoke an "Arab-Israeli arms race."

On July 26 Nasser, emboldened by Soviet arms shipments and the withdrawal of 80,000 British troops from the Suez Canal zone, nationalized the British-run canal and refused to guarantee the safety of Israeli shipping. Nationalization of the canal followed a U.S. refusal on July 20, 1956, to provide Egypt financing for the Aswan Dam, a mammoth project on the Upper Nile intended to furnish Egypt with cheap electricity and irrigation. The United States had been interested in the project, but it withheld assistance when Nasser moved Egypt closer to the Soviet Union and opposed the Baghdad Pact.

Nationalization of the canal directly threatened British and French interests. The British government held 44 percent of all shares in the Suez Canal Company; private French investors held more than three-quarters of the remaining shares. In addition, both nations were heavy users of the canal, which provided the shortest waterway to their oil supplies in the Persian Gulf. To them, nationalization was intolerable because Nasser could bar their vessels and

British and French investors would suffer financial losses. The two governments froze Egyptian assets and began planning for joint military action, secretly enlisting Israel's participation in the plan.

Israeli armed forces attacked Egypt October 29 and by October 31 had occupied the Sinai Peninsula to within ten miles of the Suez Canal. Britain and France began air strikes against Egyptian targets October 31, and British and French troops joined the battle November 5. By November 7 British and French forces had secured control of the canal.

Despite the close U.S. relationship with Britain and France, President Eisenhower vigorously objected to the Suez invasion. He opposed in principle the use of arms to settle the dispute and hoped to improve relations with Egypt and Arab nationalists throughout the Middle East by forcing the allies to withdraw. After intense international pressure from the United States, Britain and France withdrew their forces from Egypt in December 1956. The last Israeli units were not withdrawn from the Sinai until March 1957, and then only when the United States threatened to impose economic sanctions on Israel if it failed to do so.

The U.S. condemnation of the invasion mitigated Nasser's defeat on the battlefield, and the outcome was a severe political and moral setback for Britain and France in the Middle East. In the end, Nasser's stature in the Arab world was bolstered. Despite the U.S. efforts on behalf of Egypt, there was no significant improvement in U.S.-Egyptian relations. The Soviet Union, however, succeeded in portraying itself as a defender of the Arab cause by issuing ultimatums to the British, French, and Israelis to end the invasion after U.S. opposition had already made the allies' withdrawal inevitable.

The Suez crisis caused the Soviet Union to reevaluate its stance toward Israel. The Soviets had thought Israel could be a neutral power in the region, but after Israel's alliance with Great Britain and France Moscow concluded that the Jewish nation probably would become allied tacitly with the West. By setting itself up as a friend to the Arab states opposing Israel, the Soviet Union gained influence in the region. Nevertheless, Nasser's strong brand of Arab nationalism prevented Egypt, Moscow's closest Arab ally, from becoming a true client state.

The 1956 war did not solve the Arab-Israeli territorial conflict and only temporarily altered the military balance in the area. The Soviet Union immediately began replacing the military equipment lost by Egypt during the war. The war increased Arab hostility toward Israel, and Nasser began to successfully promote the concept of Arab unity. Arabs increasingly saw Israel as a physical barrier that split the Arab world.

Eisenhower Doctrine and CENTO

The withdrawal of the British and French after the Suez crisis created a power vacuum in the Middle East. The Eisenhower administration concluded that the U.S. commitment to resist communism in the region had to be fortified. Accordingly, on January 5, 1957, President Eisenhower went before a joint session of Congress to urge support for a declaration that was promptly dubbed the Eisenhower Doctrine. H J Res 117 (Joint Resolution to Promote Peace and Stability in the Middle East) declared that "if the President determines the necessity ... [the United States] is prepared to use armed forces to assist ...

any nation or groups of nations requesting assistance against armed aggression from any country controlled by international communism."

The resolution did not draw a precise geographical line around the area to which it was intended to apply. The Senate and House committee reports on the resolution accepted the administration's view and defined the Middle East as the area bounded by Libya on the west, Pakistan on the east, Turkey on the north, and the Sudan on the south. The Senate report said that no precise listing of nations was included in the resolution because this "would restrict the freedom of action of the United States in carrying out the purposes of the resolution."

The first test of the Eisenhower Doctrine came in 1958 following a coup in Iraq in which the pro-Western government of King Faisal II was overthrown and replaced with a regime favorable to the Soviet Union and the United Arab Republic (UAR). The new Iraqi government immediately withdrew from the Baghdad Pact.

When the government of Lebanon came under similar pressures and its president requested U.S. assistance, Eisenhower ordered U.S. Marines from the Sixth Fleet in the Mediterranean to land in that country to protect the government. Citing the Eisenhower Doctrine, the president said July 15, 1958, that Lebanon's territorial integrity and independence were "vital to United States national interests and world peace." The UAR and the Soviet Union, Eisenhower charged, were trying to overthrow the constitutional government of Lebanon and "install by violence a government which subordinates the independence of Lebanon to ... the United Arab Republic."

Iraq's withdrawal from the Baghdad Pact convinced the Eisenhower administration that the three remaining "northern tier" members of the organization needed an additional pledge of U.S. support in resisting communism. The United States initiated negotiations with Iran, Pakistan, and Turkey on defense arrangements, bringing the United States into closer cooperation with the Baghdad Pact, which was renamed the Central Treaty Organization (CENTO). Three identically worded executive agreements were signed in March 1959 between the United States and each of the three nations. Washington pledged to come to the defense of the three countries in the event of Communist aggression or subversion.

The executive agreements with Iran, Pakistan, and Turkey completed the formal commitment of the United States to resist communism in the Middle East. Throughout the 1960s, the Kennedy and Johnson administrations repeatedly pledged to uphold the territorial integrity of Israel and the Arab nations. American military assistance and arms sales provided weapons to friendly governments in the area, and limited arms sales to Israel were initiated in 1962.

USSR-Arab Nationalists Alliance

The Soviet Union saw CENTO and the Eisenhower Doctrine as a security threat, and Arab nationalists, such as Nasser, viewed it as a reintroduction of colonial power in the region. This commonality of interest gave Moscow an opening to further strengthen its ties to Nasser and like-minded Arabs.

Moscow, however, found the Arab states unwilling to become too closely allied with the Soviet Union. Many Arab nationalists were not prepared to exchange their recently won independence from colonialism for client status under the Soviet Union. Moreover, many Arabs were repelled by the atheistic ideology of communism. While most Arab nationalists were secular in their political orientation, few were atheists, and many were devout Moslems or saw Islam as an essential part of their Arab identity.

At times Moscow found Communist parties in Arab countries attacked by the same regimes that it was supporting. In Egypt, for example, Nasser considered his country's Communists a threat and suppressed them vigorously, eventually banning them. In Syria and Iraq, both allies of the Soviets, the Communist parties were viewed as a threat by the governments and suppressed.

In spite of the constant tensions, Moscow and its newly found allies still cooperated in a common effort to keep the West, the United States in particular, from solidifying and extending its power in the region. Disagreements over how local Communists should be treated and other points of contention were subordinated to their mutual opposition to the West.

The Six-Day War (1967)

Middle East tensions exploded again on June 5, 1967, when Israel began the third major Arab-Israeli war by invading its Arab neighbors. During the conflict, referred to as the Six-Day War, Israel destroyed a substantial part of the armed forces of Egypt, Jordan, and Syria. In addition, large amounts of Arab territory were captured—land that Israel did not relinquish after the fighting stopped.

Diplomatic efforts immediately preceding the war had failed to lift a blockade of the Gulf of Aqaba that Egypt's Nasser imposed on Israeli shipping May 23. The blockade followed Nasser's demand that the UN Emergency Force be removed from the Gaza Strip and the Gulf of Aqaba outpost at Sharm el-Sheikh. The United Nations relented and withdrew the Emergency Force. At the same time, Nasser moved a substantial Egyptian force into the Sinai Peninsula, raising Israel's fears of an Arab invasion.

A few hours after Israel attacked on June 5, Robert J. McCloskey, deputy assistant secretary of state for public affairs, declared that the U.S. position was "neutral in thought, word, and deed." The McCloskey statement was criticized by many members of Congress and other supporters of Israel, who pointed to the longstanding ties between the two countries. Later the same day, George Christian, President Johnson's press secretary, said the McCloskey statement was "not a formal declaration of neutrality." And at a news conference Secretary of State Dean Rusk said the term "neutral" in international law meant that the United States was not a belligerent. He said it was not "an expression of indifference."

The UN Security Council June 6 unanimously adopted a resolution calling for a cease-fire. A truce went into effect June 10, although periodic clashes continued.

Nine days later President Johnson, in his first major statement on U.S. Middle East policy since the outbreak of the war, outlined a five-point formula for peace in the Middle East. "Our country is committed—and we here reiterate that commitment today—to a peace [in the Middle East] that is based on five principles: first, the recognized right of national life; second, justice for the refugees; third, innocent maritime passage; fourth, limits on the wasteful and destructive arms race; and fifth, political independence and territorial integrity for all." Johnson also said the victorious Israeli troops "must be withdrawn" from the lands occupied during the Six-Day War. But he made it clear he would not press for a withdrawal to prewar lines in every respect.

The 1967 war substantially altered the military balance in the Middle East. Israeli planes, in their first "preemptive attack," had destroyed the bulk of the Egyptian air force while it was still on the ground. Israel's lightning move through the Sinai Peninsula broke the Egyptian blockade of the Gulf of Aqaba and once again put Israeli soldiers on the banks of the Suez Canal. In the east, Israel's forces ousted Jordanian troops from the old section of Jerusalem and seized control of all Jordanian territory west of the Jordan River. Finally, Israel captured the Golan Heights. For two decades Syria had used the heavily fortified borderland hills to harass Israel's northeastern settlements.

Israel's smashing victory stunned the Arabs and their Soviet backers and left Israel in a position of strength. In contrast to 1956, when Israeli forces were withdrawn in response to strong Washington-Moscow pressure, Tel Aviv at once announced that Israel would remain in the occupied territories until decisive progress toward a permanent settlement had been made.

The Six-Day War was an important event for Soviet influence in the area. Before the war, the Soviets had worked to create an anti-Western alliance among the Arabs and deter an Israeli attack through arms sales and encouragement of Arab defense cooperation. The Soviets thought they were partially successful when in November 1966 Syria and Egypt signed a joint defense agreement. The Soviets, however, lost prestige by not providing the Arabs with much assistance during the Six-Day War. In fact, the Soviet decision to back a cease-fire while Israel was in Arab territories angered the Arabs. The only significant measure that Moscow and its Communist allies took was severance of diplomatic ties with Israel.

Despite the Arabs' disappointment with the weak backing provided by Moscow during the fighting, in the long run the Six-Day War served to boost Soviet influence among the Arabs. Nasser, charging that U.S. aircraft had contributed to Egypt's defeat, severed diplomatic relations with Washington, as did six other Arab states. While U.S. support for Israel soured U.S. relations with the Arab states, the Soviets solidified their position as the chief benefactor and arms supplier of the Arabs. Partially to make up for its inaction during the war, Moscow rebuilt the armed forces of Egypt, Syria, and Jordan.

With the Soviet Union providing military assistance to the Arab governments, the United States moved in to fill the vacuum created by the French government's decision to end its role as chief supplier of armaments for Israel.

On November 22, 1967, the United States voted with the rest of the UN Security Council members in unanimously approving a resolution (Security Council Resolution 242) aimed at bringing peace to the Middle East. The document called for (1) withdrawal of Israeli forces from the occupied Arab areas; (2) an end to the state of belligerency between the Arab nations and Israel; (3) acknowledgment of and respect for the sovereignty, territorial integrity, and political independence of every nation in the area; (4) the establishment of "secure and recognized boundaries"; (5) a guarantee of freedom of navigation through international waterways in the area; and (6) a just settlement of the refugee problem. (Text, Appendix, p. 301)

Although UN efforts to end the Arab-Israeli conflict once again foundered, the resolution remained the basis for all subsequent UN peace initiatives. Before the 1967 war, the Arabs had insisted that Israel return all lands in excess of the territory assigned to the Jewish state by the 1947 UN partition plan. After the 1967 war, however, the Arabs gradually modified their demands and came to insist only that Israel adhere to the principles of the 1967 Security Council resolution, which they interpreted as calling for Israel to return to its pre-1967 borders.

No War, No Peace

Sporadic fighting was renewed in 1969 along the Suez Canal front after Egypt repudiated the 1967 cease-fire. During this "war of attrition" period Egypt tried to wear down the Israelis and bring about territorial withdrawals. Although frequently violated, the cease-fire technically continued on the other fronts.

In a departure from previous U.S. policy, the administration of President Richard Nixon agreed early in 1969 to a series of bilateral talks on the Middle East with the Soviet Union as well as to four-power talks including Britain and France. The talks were held throughout the year, but little progress was made.

The major elements of the U.S. diplomatic position were outlined by Secretary of State William P. Rogers on December 9, 1969. Rogers called on Israel to withdraw from Arab territories occupied in the June 1967 war in return for Arab assurances of a binding commitment to a Middle East peace. He also made public more detailed peace proposals submitted by the United States in October 1969 during talks with the Soviet Union. The proposals included a provision for Israel's withdrawal from the occupied territories in exchange for a binding peace treaty signed by the Arabs. They were rejected by both Israel and the Arab nations.

At the same time, the United States continued to support the efforts of UN envoy Gunnar V. Jarring to mediate a peace settlement. On January 25, 1970, Nixon reaffirmed U.S. support for Israel's insistence on direct peace negotiations with the Arabs. A few days later he asserted that the United States was "neither pro-Arab nor pro-Israeli. We are pro-peace."

With the situation highly volatile, and scattered border clashes continuing, Rogers in June 1970 submitted another proposal for a cease-fire and called for a resumption of UN mediation efforts aimed at implementing the 1967 Security Council resolution. Egypt and Jordan and then Israel agreed to a ninety-day cease-fire, beginning August 8, in conditionally accepting the U.S. formula for peace negotiations.

Once the agreement to seek a peace settlement was announced, however, protests arose in many parts of the Middle East. Arab guerrilla groups and the governments of Syria and Iraq rejected the peace initiative and denounced Nasser for accepting it. In Israel, six members of the Gahal minority party resigned from the cabinet of Premier Golda Meir when she announced the government's acceptance of the Nixon administration's peace formula. Palestinian commandos dramatized their opposition by carrying out a series of spectacular commercial aircraft hijackings.

Hopes for a peace settlement were dashed September 7, 1970, when Israel announced it was withdrawing from the peace talks. Its ambassador had met only once with UN mediator Jarring. Israel's decision followed charges it had made on several occasions (later validated) that Soviet missile batteries had been placed in the Suez Canal cease-fire zone in direct violation of the cease-fire agreement. These missiles later helped the Egyptian army cross the canal in the opening stages of the October 1973 war.

Soviet Troubles with Nasser, Sadat

Miltarily defeated and politically humiliated after the 1967 war, Nasser tried to improve Egyptian prestige and get Israel to pull back from the cease-fire lines. Sporadic fighting with Israel, however, yielded little and exposed Egyptian territory to Israeli air attacks. Nasser, seeking help from the Soviet Union to halt the Israeli raids, persuaded Moscow to provide an air defense system. This commitment was a departure from those of the past because it allowed the introduction of Soviet pilots and troops into Egypt to oversee the installations. This expansion of the Soviet Union's Mideast presence increased the possibility of superpower confrontation, but the Kremlin had to weigh that risk against the possibility of Nasser's downfall and a corresponding diminution of Soviet prestige in the region.

Confrontations between Soviet and Israeli pilots did occur, with Israel shooting down five planes flown by Soviet pilots. This prompted Nixon to caution the Soviets to avoid a clash that would lead to a superpower confrontation. Finally, Egypt and Israel agreed to a U.S.-proposed cease-fire in July 1970 that lasted until 1973.

President Nasser died in September 1970. In late 1971 and early 1972 the United States put forward a new proposal for indirect, U.S.-mediated peace talks between Israel and Egypt, but negotiations made little progress. This plan called for a troop pullback and the reopening of the Suez Canal.

The death of Nasser brought to office Anwar Sadat, a relatively obscure and inexperienced man whose view of Egypt's future was not widely known. Unlike Nasser, Sadat was not saddled by guilt over defeat in the 1967 war, but he believed that a no-war and no-peace situation was not in Egypt's long-range interests.

The Soviet Union soon experienced problems with Sadat that were similar to those it had with Nasser. Sadat, like Nasser, resented and opposed attempts by the Egyptian Communist party to gain control of the government. Sadat also had his own agenda for Egypt, which did not correspond perfectly with the Soviet's regional interests. He wanted and needed to rebuild Egyptian prestige and Arab pride, while the Soviet Union was more interested in limiting Western influence in the region while avoiding a direct confrontation with the United States.

Sadat asked repeatedly and unsuccessfully for increased Soviet military aid to prepare for a war with Israel. In 1971 Sadat spoke of a "year of decision" when he would plan to regain the Sinai and other territory lost in 1967. The Soviets continued to press for a peaceful solution of the conflict, repeatedly stating their support for UN Security Council Resolution 242. When the year ended with no Egyptian decision or action, the Soviets concluded Sadat's statement was a bluff to get more aid.

Differences between Moscow and Cairo worsened following a 1972 U.S.-Soviet summit conference between Nixon and Soviet Communist party chief Leonid Brezhnev. The Egyptians believed the Soviets' desire to improve relations with the United States would get in the way of their support for Egypt's goal of recapturing Israeli-occupied territory. In the joint communiqué following the summit, Nixon and Brezhnev stated their support for a peaceful resolution of the Mideast conflict according to UN Resolution 242.

As Sadat's differences with the Soviet Union became more acute, he concluded that Egyptian and Soviet goals were incompatible. Finally, on July 18, 1972, Sadat ordered all 20,000 Soviet Union military advisers out of Egypt.

Sadat's action severely damaged the Soviet position in the Middle East. Predictably, the Nixon administration was pleased by Sadat's decision, since Soviet influence in the region would be diminished. The Soviet Union then focused its attention elsewhere in the Arab world. Relations with Iraq, which already had improved sufficiently to produce a treaty of friendship, continued to get better. The Soviets also courted Syria, although that country, unlike Iraq and Egypt earlier, refused to sign a treaty of friendship. Nevertheless, Syria's President Hafez al-Assad extracted from the Soviets some of the military equipment he believed was needed to counter Israel. In addition, Moscow's relations with the Palestinian groups began to warm, and Soviet arms for the first time went directly to the Palestine Liberation Organization rather than through Arab governments.

In the summer of 1972, a group of Palestinian terrorists killed eleven Israeli athletes at the Summer Olympics in Munich, West Germany. This highly publicized terrorist action harmed the Arab diplomatic position in the West and dashed Sadat's hopes of persuading the United States to apply pressure on Israel to withdraw from the Sinai. In spite of Egypt's strained relations with the Soviet Union, Sadat won Soviet backing for his efforts to form a unified Arab front against Israel.

Fourth War (1973)

The "no-war, no-peace" stalemate held until October 1973, when Arab frustrations over the deadlock triggered the fourth Arab-Israeli war on October 6. The war broke out on Yom Kippur,* the holiest day of the Jewish calendar, when Egyptian and Syrian troops in a surprise attack broke through Israel's weakly defended forward fortifications and advanced into the Sinai Peninsula and the Golan Heights.

By seizing the initiative, the Arab forces, aided by sophisticated new Soviet weapons, were able temporarily to dictate the conditions of battle. Where Israel excelled at a "war of rapid movement and envelopment," wrote Mideast specialist Nadav Safran in the January 1974 issue of *Foreign Affairs*, the Arabs "forced the enemy to fight a set battle, where the undoubted courage of their own fighting men and their numerical superiority in manpower and equipment could be used to best effect."

This "slugging type of war," Safran went on, "turned out to be extremely costly in men and, especially, in equipment to both sides," requiring first the Soviet Union and then the United States to intervene to resupply their client states.

Despite the success of the initial Egyptian and Syrian strikes into Israeli-occupied territory, Israeli forces subsequently succeeded in breaking through the Egyptian lines as far as the western bank of the Suez Canal. On the other front, they advanced to within twenty miles of the Syrian capital of Damascus.

To avoid further defeat and humiliation of the Arabs, who had fought with conspicuously more success than in 1967, the United States and the Soviet Union joined in pressing for an end to the fighting. Following a visit by Secretary of State Henry A. Kissinger to Moscow, a joint U.S.-Soviet resolution calling for an immediate cease-fire and implementation of the 1967 UN Security Council Resolution 242 was presented to the Security Council October 21. Egypt and Israel agreed, and the cease-fire was expected to go into effect the next day.

But the fighting continued, and Egyptian president Sadat, concerned for the fate of his army, called on both the United States and the Soviet Union to send in troops to enforce the cease-fire. On the evening of October 24 Soviet General Secretary Leonid Brezhnev sent a message to President Nixon proposing joint U.S.-Soviet supervision of the truce. Brezhnev warned, "If you find it impossible to act together with us in this matter, we should be faced with the necessity urgently to consider the question of taking appropriate steps unilaterally." The proposal was rejected by the United States, which preferred a plan setting up a UN observer force without big-power participation.

In the early morning hours of October 25 U.S. armed forces were placed on worldwide alert in response to the possibility of a unilateral move by the Soviet Union to send troops to the Middle East. The crisis was defused later that day when Moscow agreed to a Security Council resolution establishing an international peacekeeping force without the participation of the five permanent members of the Security Council.

Kissinger 'Shuttle Diplomacy'

American diplomacy was instrumental in bringing about a cease-fire between Egypt and Israel and then, under the Ford and Carter administrations, a series of agreements that led finally to a peace treaty between the

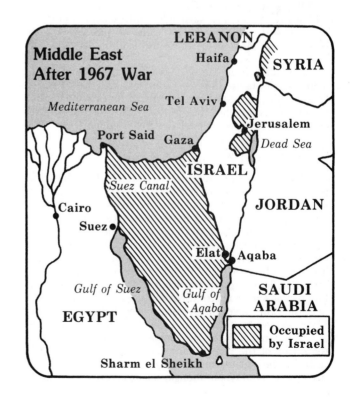

---

*The war that began on October 6, 1973, has different names. In Israel it is best known as the Yom Kippur War. The Arabs sometimes call it the War of Ramadan, since it began during their month-long period of daytime fasting.

former belligerents. Secretary Kissinger negotiated a six-point cease-fire agreement on November 11, 1973, that was signed by Egyptian and Israeli military representatives at kilometer 101 on the Cairo-to-Suez road.

On December 21, 1973, largely through Kissinger's efforts, the Geneva Conference on an Arab-Israel peace was convened in accordance with UN Security Council Resolution 338 establishing the cease-fire. The talks were attended by the Soviet Union, the United States, Israel, Egypt, and Jordan. Syria boycotted the conference.

The first round of the conference ended the following day with an agreement to begin talks on separating Israeli and Egyptian forces along the Suez Canal. Egypt and Israel signed a troop disengagement accord January 18, 1974, and the troop withdrawal was completed March 4. Meanwhile, efforts to negotiate a similar agreement between Israel and Syria were concluded May 31.

In early 1975 Kissinger sought a second-stage disengagement in the Sinai Desert, but after fifteen days of shuttling between Egypt and Israel he declared in March that his efforts had failed. After the breakdown in the talks, Egypt formally requested a resumption of the full Geneva Conference. But it became widely recognized that a propaganda battle at Geneva might degenerate into war, and the conference was indefinitely postponed.

The Soviet Union's position as cosponsor of the Geneva negotiations would mark the last time Moscow was at the center of Middle East negotiations. From the first Sinai disengagement accords to the Camp David negotiations, the Soviet Union would be locked out of the peace process. The United States proved itself to be an honest broker even with its close ties to Israel, and it was able to improve its position in many parts of the Arab world as a result.

When Kissinger returned from his shuttle talks, he and President Gerald R. Ford let it be known they were upset with Israel's negotiating position and that the United States would begin a "reassessment" of its policy in the Middle East. Consideration of Israel's request for $2.5 billion in U.S. aid was suspended until completion of the reassessment, a thinly veiled form of pressure on the Israeli government to be more forthcoming in talks with Egypt.

Excluded from the negotiations, the Soviet Union made attempts to improve relations with the PLO. It viewed this group and the Syrians as its ticket back into the negotiations. The PLO, probably the most anti-American of the Arabs, welcomed the Soviet support.

Second Sinai Accord

Negotiations began again in June 1975. President Ford met first with Sadat in Salzburg, Austria, and then with Israeli ambassador to the United States Yitzhak Rabin in Washington. The United States hoped to avoid risking a failure at another Geneva Conference. This time the talks proved to be more successful. As the culmination of Kissinger's shuttle diplomacy, a second Sinai disengagement pact was signed by Israeli and Egyptian representatives on September 1. Israel agreed to withdraw from the Sinai mountain passes and to return the Abu Rudeis oil fields to Egypt in return for Egyptian political concessions. The United States agreed to station an observation force in the Sinai.

Compared with the basic issues of recognition of Israel, the future of the Palestinians, permanent boundaries, the status of Jerusalem, and peace guarantees, the issues settled in the Sinai troop disengagement accords were minor.

In two respects, however, the accords accomplished a major breakthrough. First, they introduced Americans into the midst of the Arab-Israeli conflict. Somewhat hesitantly, Congress approved the stationing of U.S. technicians between the Israeli and Arab armies to monitor military activities. The Israeli government made it clear that its ratification of the agreement hinged on such congressional approval. Second, they established a modest basis of trust necessary to pursue more basic issues.

Journalist Edward R. F. Sheehan, who had suggested to Kissinger that he attempt to resolve the whole conflict at once, rather than pursue progress a step at a time, reported Kissinger's response: "What were the alternatives? The conflict in the Middle East has a history of decades. Only during the last two years have we produced progress. It's easy to say that what we've done is not enough, but the steps we've taken are the biggest steps so far. They were the attainable—given our prevailing domestic situation."

By the "domestic situation," Kissinger apparently had in mind the pressures applied by staunch supporters of Israel in Congress and elsewhere in the United States whenever the administration placed demands on Israel that were thought to be excessive vis-à-vis the concessions being asked of the Arabs. When Kissinger and Ford announced the "reassessment" of U.S. Middle East policy in light of the March 1975 breakdown in shuttle diplomacy and alleged Israeli intransigence, seventy-six senators wrote to the president strongly endorsing Israel's demands for "defensible" borders and additional U.S. economic and military aid.

The second disengagement agreement also resulted in considerable tension among the Arab parties to the conflict. President Assad and the PLO vigorously denounced Sadat for agreeing to what amounted, in their view, to a separate, though partial, peace with Israel. This dissension within the Arab camp became an important factor in the Lebanese civil war, which escalated the following year and became, in a sense, a civil war among Arab groups.

When Arab unity was restored at the end of 1976, a new Arab strategy began to emerge. By presenting a moderate image to the world, Sadat and most of the Arab leaders hoped to affect U.S. policy and create the conditions for resumption of the Geneva negotiations. Even the Palestine Liberation Organization began to make gestures, however ambiguous, indicating a willingness to accept the existence of Israel if the occupied territories were returned to the Palestinians.

Israeli-Egyptian Treaty

By 1977 it was widely recognized that the United States had become the key outside participant in the Middle East conflict. Aware that the Carter administration's policies would have a major impact on Middle East events—"the U.S. holds 99 percent of the cards," Sadat said repeatedly—a major effort was launched in 1977 to persuade the United States that the Arabs no longer challenged Israel's existence but did oppose its 1967 occupation of Arab lands and its refusal to recognize "Palestinian rights." In February 1977 Sadat said in an interview, "I want the American people to know ... that never before have the prospects for peace been better. Not in the last twenty-eight years—since Israel was created—have we had a better chance for a permanent settlement in the Middle

East. We must not lose the chance."

It was in this atmosphere of renewed hope for achieving a comprehensive peace settlement that President Jimmy Carter in March 1977 outlined a three-point peace plan that called for:

- Israeli withdrawal to approximately the 1967 borders.
- Creation of a "Palestinian homeland," probably in the West Bank and Gaza Strip.
- Establishment of a permanent peace between Israel and its Arab neighbors.

Although Carter was the first American president to endorse the concept of a Palestinian homeland, the details of his plan remained unclear. Moreover, Menachem Begin's election in June 1977 as prime minister of Israel further confused the situation. Not only had Begin's Likud party refused to even consider agreeing to a Palestinian homeland, it also was elected on a platform of never returning the West Bank and Gaza to Arab sovereignty.

Begin came to the United States on July 19, 1977, for two days of talks with Carter and his top Middle East advisers. Although the atmosphere was cordial, it was clear that the new American administration and the new Israeli government were far apart on many important issues.

The initial Carter strategy for achieving a comprehensive peace settlement focused on reconvening the Geneva Conference, which had met in December 1973. The Soviet Union responded favorably, and the result was a joint statement on the Middle East, issued October 1, 1977, calling for a conference "not later than December 1977" to work out a full resolution of the Arab-Israeli conflict "incorporating all parties concerned and all questions."

The Israeli and Egyptian reaction to the prospect of bringing the Soviet Union into the forefront of the peace negotiations was negative. In addition, the radical Arab governments in Algeria, Iraq, and Libya still rejected any direct negotiations with Israel. Israeli officials opposed the idea because, among other factors, they feared the Soviets might succeed in drawing the PLO into the negotiations.

The Egyptian reaction to the joint statement was equally cool. Since 1972, when Sadat had expelled Soviet military advisers from Egypt, relations between Cairo and Moscow had turned increasingly sour. A Geneva Conference cochaired by the Soviet Union was no more appealing to Sadat than it was to Israel. The unpleasant possibility that another conference might be held was seen by some observers as one reason behind Sadat's dramatic decision to visit Jerusalem and proffer his terms for peace.

Initial Peace Efforts

In addition to Sadat's desire to preempt Soviet involvement in the Middle East peace process, other reasons have been cited for his dramatic visit to Jerusalem on November 19, 1977. Analysts speculate that Sadat was motivated by his belief that if the Middle East conflict degenerated again into war the Arabs would suffer a 1967-type defeat, his fear of a radical upheaval in economically depressed Egypt, his desire to get U.S. economic aid, and his hope that a face-to-face encounter between Arabs and Israelis would do much to remove the psychological barriers that separated them.

In his address to the Israeli parliament (Knesset) November 20, the Egyptian president put forward five "principles" that he said must govern any peace settlement:

- "Ending the Israeli occupation of the Arab territories occupied in 1967;

- "Achievement of the fundamental rights of the Palestinian people and their right to self-determination, including their right to establish their own state;
- "The right of all states in the area to live in peace, within their boundaries, their secure boundaries, which will be secured and guaranteed through procedures to be agreed upon...;
- "Commitment of all states in the area to administer the relations among them in accordance with the objectives and principles of the UN Charter, particularly the principles concerning the nonresort to force and the solutions to differences among them by peaceful means;
- "Ending the state of belligerence in the region."

The Carter administration was taken by surprise by Sadat's initiative and only later gave its full support to the peace effort, in effect abandoning the comprehensive approach and supporting direct Egyptian-Israeli discussions for a separate agreement between those two nations.

Sadat's Jerusalem visit was followed by meetings between Israeli and Egyptian officials in Cairo. Then the leaders of the two nations met on December 25 in Ismailia, Egypt, where Begin presented his West Bank proposal, which offered only local "autonomy" for the Palestinians over a five-year period. Israeli troops and settlements were to remain. The plan contained no mention of eventual sovereignty for the West Bank, a critical point with Sadat.

Negotiations Break Down

The talks ended in a stalemate, and lower-level discussions over the next few months were unproductive. Although the two governments agreed to form a political committee to continue discussions on the future of the West Bank and a military committee to negotiate on the Sinai, Sadat on January 18, 1978, recalled Egyptian delegates to the political committee, stating there was "absolutely no hope" of reaching an accord.

Shortly thereafter, in February, U.S.-Israeli relations cooled with the announcement of the Carter administration's plan to sell sophisticated jet fighter airplanes to Egypt and Saudi Arabia as well as to Israel. The number of planes proposed for Israel, however, fell considerably short of the number requested by the Israeli government.

Relations between the two countries were not improved when Begin met with Carter in Washington in March. The two leaders differed sharply over territorial issues. Although the Carter administration repeated its assurances of support for Israel, the latter's settlements policy came under sharp criticism in Washington.

As negotiations broke down, the United States undertook a series of emergency attempts to rescue the situation, among them sponsoring a foreign ministers conference at Leeds Castle outside London on July 18. The meeting was attended by Secretary of State Cyrus R. Vance, Israeli foreign minister Moshe Dayan, and Egyptian foreign minister Muhammad Ibrahim Kamel. Although Vance saw some flexibility in the discussions, it failed to produce concrete results.

In August the atmosphere deteriorated, with Egypt and Israel renewing strong criticism of one another. At this point, President Carter became concerned that the impasse could jeopardize the fragile relations between the two nations and wreck any chance for peace in the Middle East. He then invited the two leaders to Camp David, the presidential retreat in Maryland, for informal face-to-face talks aimed at breaking the stalemate. No advance agenda was planned. Vance personally delivered handwritten invitations from Carter to Begin and Sadat in August. Both accepted unconditionally and immediately.

Camp David Summit

The Camp David talks were held under difficult circumstances, recalled Hermann F. Eilts, former U.S. ambassador to Saudi Arabia and Egypt, in the Winter 1980-1981 issue of *Foreign Policy:*

> Negotiations seemed to have collapsed following ... Sadat's negative reaction to the Leeds Castle foreign ministers conference ..., and Sadat became convinced that he could not do business with Israeli prime minister Begin. Thus, he arrived at Camp David wanting a confrontation with the Israeli prime minister and hoping for U.S. support. Begin, expecting to be pressured by the American negotiators, had prepared for the worst. For President Carter, the odds were long. He could not have succeeded without Sadat, who responded to Carter's plea for help, enabling him to achieve some measure of success.

Carter's decision to call the Camp David summit was widely seen as a brash gamble that paid off beyond all expectations. The announcement of the summit came in August, when the president's popularity was at a low point. In thirteen days of arduous negotiations, amid an atmosphere of gloom and mutual criticism, Carter, with the aid of Vice President Walter F. Mondale, persuaded Sadat and Begin to make compromises that led to an agreement. Both Sadat and Begin later said Carter's firmness was the key to the breakthrough.

The accords reached at Camp David essentially represented agreements to agree, rather than an actual settlement of the difficult issues dividing the two nations or the even broader disputes between Israel and other Arab nations. "This is one of those rare, bright moments of history," Carter declared as the historic accords drafted at Camp David were signed September 17 by Prime Minister Begin and President Sadat. *(Texts, Appendix, pp. 302-303)*

By the end of 1978, however, that success was threatened by a renewal of the discord. As negotiations continued and the euphoria of the Camp David summit dissipated, both Israeli and Egyptian leaders found that agreeing to the specifics of a treaty while under pressure from domestic groups who opposed a settlement was more difficult than agreeing to a "framework" in the seclusion of the presidential retreat in the Maryland mountains.

Carter repeatedly expressed frustration that Israel and Egypt would quibble over what he viewed as minor issues. But to both sides, none of the issues were minor. Israeli and Egyptian leaders were being asked to resolve longstanding disputes that had been perpetuated by years of hostility and to give up positions they considered essential to their national interests.

In return for a peace treaty, Israel was asked to give up territory that for more than eleven years had served as a buffer against one of its major enemies. Egypt was pressured by other Middle East nations not to sign a separate peace treaty with what they considered to be the Arab world's common enemy.

Highlights of Agreements

There were two agreements at Camp David, one dealing with Israeli withdrawal from the Sinai Peninsula and peace arrangements between Israel and Egypt; the other a "framework" for settling the future of the West Bank and Gaza.

The agreements centered on four categories of issues: "the nature of peace," security factors, territorial decisions, and the status of Palestine. Both documents called for Arab recognition of Israel and the establishment of normal relations between Israel and the Arab nations.

The Sinai accord between Israel and Egypt outlined security provisions, including the size and location of Egyptian forces stationed in the Sinai, the introduction of United Nations peacekeeping troops, and new monitoring stations. It also required Israel to return all Sinai territory to Egypt and to hand over the Israeli military airfields on the peninsula.

In the Gaza-West Bank accord, Israel's military presence was defined for the interim period and reduced from the existing 11,000-troop level. The accord called for negotiating the "final status" for Gaza and the West Bank, including their relationship to the Arab countries. The future of the Palestinians was treated in two ways: elected representatives from the West Bank and Gaza were to participate in negotiations on the final status of the areas and on related talks for a peace treaty between Jordan and Israel. Any agreement on the two areas was to be submitted to representatives of the residents of the areas for their approval.

To conclude a Middle East peace treaty, the Camp David negotiators recommended that talks on the future of the West Bank and Gaza follow these steps:

● The governments of Egypt and Israel ("Jordan will be invited") would plan a five-year, transitional "self-governing authority" for the two areas. Negotiations over the authority's powers and responsibilities were expected to take three months. The Arab delegations could include any Palestinian representation "as mutually agreed" upon by all parties.

● As soon as the self-governing authority, called the administrative council, had been "freely elected" by the inhabitants of the West Bank and Gaza "to provide full autonomy to the inhabitants," the Israeli military government and its civilian administration were to be withdrawn.

● Reduction of Israel's armed forces in the regions to an estimated 6,000, with such troops to be stationed in areas away from cities on the West Bank.

● Assurances of internal and external security in the areas. A "strong local police force" was to be established, and Israeli and Jordanian forces were to jointly man control posts at border points.

● Not later than the third year after the transition government took control, negotiations were to be held to determine the permanent status of the West Bank and Gaza and their relationship with their neighbors, and to conclude a peace treaty between Israel and Jordan. Two separate but related committees were to handle these talks. "The general theory for this," said a Carter administration official, "is that the negotiation of the final status of Gaza and the West Bank is intertwined with issues which will come up in the negotiation of a final peace treaty. Therefore, they can't be treated in two separate and independent tracts. They have to be treated together."

● The negotiations were to be based on all the provisions and principles in United Nations Security Council Resolution 242, which contained the basic formula for Israel to relinquish occupied territories in return for Arab recognition, peace, and security.

● The negotiations also were intended to resolve the location of boundaries and security arrangements and to foster the "legitimate rights of the Palestinian people."

Israeli Settlements, Other Issues

Compared with the long list of issues purposely ignored or vaguely addressed in the framework relating to the West Bank and Gaza, only one problem divided Israel and Egypt under the accord returning the Sinai to Egypt and establishing "normal relations" between the two countries. But it was a major one: the question of whether all the Jewish settlements in the Sinai were to be dismantled, as Sadat insisted. This issue nearly wrecked the Camp David talks as Begin also refused to give in on the matter.

The summit impasse was broken when Begin eventually consented to turn the controversy over to the Israeli Knesset for its decision. (The Knesset agreed to the dismantling on September 28.)

On other issues to be incorporated in a peace treaty, Israel and Egypt agreed to these points:

● Israel would return all of the Sinai to Egypt, including the three air bases it operated as well as the oil fields and, if the Knesset voted its approval, the territory containing the thirteen Jewish settlements.

● All Israeli forces would be withdrawn from the Sinai.

● The airfields abandoned by the Israelis would be used only for civilian purposes in the future, possibly for commercial international flights by all nations.

● The Israeli withdrawal would be accomplished in two steps, with the first major phase taking place within three to nine months after the peace treaty was signed. In that period, Israeli forces would withdraw east of a line extending from El Arish on the Mediterranean coast to Ras Muhammad at the tip of the Sinai Peninsula.

● After the interim withdrawal was completed, normal relations would be established between the two countries, including full recognition—diplomatic, economic, and cultural; termination of economic boycotts and other barriers blocking the free movement of people and goods; and protection of each nation's citizens by due process of law.

● The final withdrawal and implementation of the treaty between Israel and Egypt would take place between two and three years from the date the peace treaty was signed.

● United Nations forces would be stationed in the Sinai west of the Israeli border, and Egyptian forces would be limited east of the Gulf of Suez and the Suez Canal.

● Israeli ships would be allowed free passage through the canal.

Unresolved Problems

Shortly after the Camp David accords were signed, Secretary of State Vance optimistically predicted that a treaty could be concluded by November 19—the anniversary of Sadat's 1977 visit to Jerusalem. It soon became obvious, however, that negotiating the treaty would be a slow process. Predictions of a treaty-signing were pushed back to December 10, the date Sadat and Begin were to receive the Nobel Peace Prize, and then to December 17, the date specified in the Camp David agreement. As the end of the year approached, officials stopped predicting when the treaty would be concluded.

Even before the treaty negotiations began, disagreements developed over what actually had been said and agreed on at Camp David. Before Begin had left the United States after the Camp David summit, he and Carter locked horns over the terms of an agreement on Israeli settlements on the West Bank and Gaza. Begin said Israel could establish new settlements after a three-month moratorium, but Carter said Begin had agreed at Camp David not to establish any new settlements during the five-year transition period.

Twice, on October 25 and November 21, the Israeli cabinet approved draft treaties, each time adding reservations that made the drafts unacceptable to Egypt. Carter had to intervene personally at two early stages in drafting the treaty to prevent a breakdown in the negotiations.

While they were being pressured by the United States to reach a final agreement, both Sadat and Begin also came under intense pressure at home not to make concessions. Other Arab nations, including Jordan and Saudi Arabia, warned Sadat not to renounce Palestinian rights in the rush toward a peace treaty. In Israel Begin was sharply criticized for his apparent willingness to abandon Israeli claims to some of the territories occupied in the 1967 war.

Throughout the negotiations, the so-called Palestinian question was the key stumbling block to an agreement. Egypt wanted Israel to withdraw completely from all territories occupied in the 1967 war, including the West Bank, the Gaza Strip, and the Sinai Peninsula. Begin agreed at Camp David to return the Sinai to Egypt. He also agreed to self-rule for residents of the West Bank and Gaza.

As negotiations proceeded, the main question became whether, and to what extent, the peace treaty between Egypt and Israel would be linked to the West Bank and Gaza issues. The United States and Egypt insisted that the treaty be linked to the resolution of the occupied territories issue. Israel wanted the treaty, but did not want to include provisions dealing with the occupied territories. Begin fueled the Palestinian controversy early in the negotiations by announcing plans to expand Israeli settlements on the West Bank. Those plans were bitterly protested by Carter and Sadat and then put aside, where they simmered throughout the peace talks.

Sadat continually raised the stakes, first insisting only that the treaty be linked to the future of the occupied territories, then demanding a specific timetable for Palestinian self-rule in those territories. Sadat made those demands in part to soften criticism from fellow Arab leaders, who had accused him of deserting the Palestinians.

At a summit meeting in Baghdad November 2-5, 1978, the hard-line Arab countries charged Sadat with treason, then offered Egypt $5 billion if Sadat would cut off negotiations with Israel. Sadat refused the offer, making it clear he expected assistance from the United States instead. American officials were distressed that Saudi Arabia and Jordan, two moderate Arab nations, joined in the hard-line attacks on Egypt.

The Israeli cabinet on November 21 finally accepted a vaguely worded link between the peace treaty and the West Bank-Gaza issues, but it flatly rejected any timetable for elections. With the disagreement over a timetable unresolved, the United States early in December offered a compromise that would have put the issues in a "side letter" rather than in the treaty itself. Under that compromise, the two sides would have agreed to begin negotiations on the West Bank and Gaza within a month of ratification of the peace treaty. A target date of December 31, 1979, was proposed for elections in the territories.

Throughout the negotiations, the PLO rejected all the timetables and self-rule proposals. PLO leader Yasir Arafat said his group was the only true representative of the more than one million Palestinians on the West Bank and Gaza. He rejected Sadat's claim that the Egyptian leader was negotiating on behalf of the Palestinians.

Just as important as the PLO objection was the refusal of Jordan's King Hussein to participate in the negotiations. The West Bank had been administered by Jordan before the 1967 war, and the Camp David accords were based on the assumption that Hussein would participate in the peace settlement.

Implicit in the negotiations was the assumption that the United States would provide substantial aid to both Egypt and Israel once a peace treaty was signed. Although peace in the Middle East generally was accepted as being in the long-term interest of all parties, the short-term costs were heavy for both Israel and Egypt. Israeli officials estimated that moving its military forces from the Sinai Peninsula to the Negev Desert in southern Israel would cost approximately $3 billion over three years, a huge sum for that nation. To help pay for that move, and for other costs of peace, the Israelis asked the United States for an additional $3.3 billion over three years. At Camp David, Carter committed the United States to building two replacement military bases for Israel in the Negev.

For his part, Sadat quietly spread the word that he expected the United States to pay a major share of the cost of economic development in Egypt, possibly as much as $10 billion to $15 billion over five years. The United States had been providing Egypt $1 billion a year.

From Impasse to Treaty

After preliminary discussions between Vance, Israeli foreign minister Moshe Dayan, and Egyptian premier Mustafa Khalil in February 1979, Carter suggested that Begin and Sadat meet with him in a second round of summit talks at Camp David. The two leaders declined. Faced with the possible collapse of the treaty talks, Carter then invited Begin to meet with him alone in Washington. Begin accepted, and the talks opened March 1.

Before leaving for the United States, Begin said Israel and Egypt remained far apart and accused the Carter administration of supporting Egyptian proposals that were "totally unacceptable to us." Among the points at issue were Sadat's insistence on Israeli acceptance of Palestinian autonomy for the West Bank and Gaza within a year; deletion of a clause in the Camp David accords giving an Israeli-Egyptian peace treaty priority over Egyptian treaties with other nations; and a delay, until all other treaty issues were resolved, in discussing Israel's request that Egypt supply Israel with oil from the Sinai oil fields. On February 17 Sadat said Egypt would make no further concessions in the peace treaty negotiations and that it was "now up to the Israelis."

On March 5 Carter announced that he would press his personal mediation efforts by visiting Cairo and Jerusalem. A White House statement said: "There is certainly no guarantee of success, but . . . without a major effort such as this the prospects for failure are almost overwhelming."

Carter's Middle East trip bore fruit. After agreeing to most aspects of the compromise proposals put forward by the American president, the Israeli cabinet March 14 approved 15-0 the two remaining points that had blocked an agreement. The Egyptian cabinet approved them the next day.

Under the terms of the agreement, Israel accepted an arrangement whereby Egypt would sell it 2.5 million tons of oil a year for an "extended period." For its part, Israel agreed to submit a detailed timetable for withdrawing its forces from the Sinai.

The Israeli Knesset gave its overwhelming approval of the treaty on March 22. The vote was 95-18. Both Carter and Sadat hailed the Knesset's action. The Israeli parliament, said Carter on March 22, "spoke with a voice heard around the world today—a voice for peace."

On March 26, 1979, Israel and Egypt formally ended the state of war that had existed between them ever since Israel declared its independence in 1948. The signing of the peace treaty took place at the White House, where about sixteen-hundred guests attended the forty-five-minute ceremony. After signing three versions of the treaty—in Arabic, Hebrew, and English—the three leaders delivered speeches hailing the accord.

Calling the agreement a celebration of "a victory, not of a bloody military campaign, but of an inspiring peace campaign," Carter praised Begin and Sadat for having "conducted this campaign with all the courage, tenacity, brilliance, and inspiration of any general leading men into combat." In turn, the Israeli and Egyptian leaders had high praise for the American president. Carter, said Sadat, "performed the greatest miracle," adding that "without exaggeration what he did constituted one of the greatest achievements of our time."

Treaty Highlights

The treaty itself provided for the normalization of relations between Egypt and Israel. It implemented the "framework" for a treaty agreed on at Camp David. Specific details for further negotiations on trade, cultural, transportation and other agreements between the two countries were spelled out in Annex III. (Text of treaty, Appendix, p. 304)

Details of a phased Israeli withdrawal from the Sinai Peninsula were contained in Annex I. Basically, Israel was to withdraw eastward in stages. The most important steps were to occur in the ninth month of the withdrawal, when Israel would give up two-thirds of the Sinai, and after three years (in April 1982), when Israel would completely withdraw from the peninsula.

At the same time, Egypt and Israel were to undertake negotiations on the future of the West Bank and Gaza. The negotiations on Palestinian self-rule, to be supervised by the United States, were to begin one month after the formal exchange of treaty ratification documents and were to be completed within one year. The treaty did not mention East Jerusalem, occupied by Israel since 1967 and claimed by both Israel and Jordan. Egypt insisted that East Jerusalem was part of the West Bank and thus subject to negotiation. Israel rejected that view.

Security, Oil Agreements

Two hours after the peace treaty was signed, Secretary Vance and Foreign Minister Dayan signed a "memorandum of agreement" providing specific American assurances to Israel if the treaty fell apart. The memorandum reaffirmed, and broadened, U.S. assurances given Israel at the time of the 1975 Sinai disengagement agreement.

If the treaty were violated, the memorandum stated, the United States "will consult with the parties with regard to measures to halt or prevent the violation. . . ." And the

United States "will take such remedial measures as it deems appropriate, which may include diplomatic, economic and military measures. . . ."

Among the actions the United States pledged to carry out were:

• If Israel were attacked or its ports blockaded, the United States would consider "such measures as strengthening the United States presence in the area, the providing of emergency supplies to Israel and the exercise of maritime rights" by the United States.

• The United States would support Israel's right to navigation and airspace through and over the Strait of Tiran and the Gulf of Aqaba.

• The United States would oppose any move in the United Nations that "adversely affects" the treaty.

• With congressional approval, the United States would "endeavor to be responsive to military and economic assistance requirements of Israel."

Carter administration officials emphasized that the specific pledges would be carried out only in response to a violation of the treaty by either Israel or Egypt, and it insisted the agreement did not constitute an alliance or a mutual defense treaty with Israel.

The agreement brought a sharp protest from Egypt. In a letter to Vance, Egyptian prime minister Khalil said Egypt was "deeply disappointed to find the United States accepting to enter into an agreement we consider directed against Egypt."

The agreement "assumes that Egypt is the side liable to violate the treaty," Khalil said. He charged that Egypt was "never consulted on the substance" of the agreement. Khalil also took issue with the United States' right "to impose a military presence in the region for reasons agreed between Israel and the U.S., a matter which we cannot accept." In a second letter to Vance, Khalil said Egypt "will not recognize the legality of the memorandum and considers it null and void." In a March 28 statement, Sadat said the memorandum violated the Israeli-Egyptian accord and that it "could be construed as an eventual alliance against Egypt."

The State Department issued a response saying Khalil's complaints were "based on a misreading of the document." The agreement "does not assume that Egypt is likely to violate the pact," the response said.

Potentially one of the most controversial assurances given by Carter to Israel was the guarantee to supply oil. At the time of the September 1975 Sinai agreement, President Ford agreed to guarantee Israel an adequate oil supply for a five-year period if that nation's normal supplies were cut off. As an incentive to sign the peace treaty, Carter agreed to extend the guarantee to fifteen years. Although Congress was not asked to approve the 1975 agreement, Carter said he would ask Congress to approve the fifteen-year guarantee.

Under the agreement, the United States was to supply Israel with enough oil "to meet all its normal requirements for domestic consumption." The promise was contingent on the United States' being able to obtain enough oil "to meet its normal requirements." The United States also pledged to transport the oil to Israel, if necessary. Israel was to pay the United States "world market prices" for any oil supplied under the emergency agreement.

Even if the United States were called on to supply all of Israel's oil requirements, the result would be "hardly noticeable to us," said Vance in congressional testimony. Total Israeli oil consumption was only 165,000 barrels a day in 1979—less than 1 percent of daily U.S. consumption of nineteen million barrels.

Autonomy Talks

On May 25, 1979, in keeping with the agreed timetable, Sadat and Begin met in Beersheba to begin the Palestinian autonomy negotiations. The goal of the first stage was full autonomy for the West Bank and Gaza under a freely elected self-governing authority that would serve for a five-year transition period. Agreement on the region's final status was reserved for a second stage to begin not later than three years after the self-governing authority was inaugurated.

Several meetings were held in 1980, but little progress was made. Sadat suspended Egyptian participation in mid-August after the Knesset passed a law confirming Jerusalem's status as Israel's "eternal and undivided capital." Early in 1981 Israel requested a resumption of the talks, but the Reagan administration reacted cautiously. President Reagan's position contrasted sharply with the policies of the Carter administration, which had placed great emphasis on the negotiations and, through its special envoy, had been instrumental in keeping the negotiations alive.

More successful was the Israeli Sinai withdrawal, which had an April 1982 deadline. Under the terms of the treaty, once withdrawal was completed the United States was obligated to organize a peacekeeping force if the United Nations did not do so. Subsequently, the United Nations declined, largely because of opposition from the Soviet Union, which would have vetoed UN participation. It was expected that about one-third of the monitoring force would consist of U.S. personnel.

Normalization of relations between the two nations also went ahead as planned. "Normal relations" officially began January 26, 1980, by which time Israel had withdrawn from two-thirds of the Sinai. Borders were opened between the two countries, travel was permitted, and embassies were established.

Unified Arab Opposition

When the peace treaty was signed in March 1979, few observers expected the Arab reaction to be so universally negative. There was little doubt that the so-called hard-line Arab states—Algeria, Iraq, Libya, South Yemen, Syria, and the Palestine Liberation Organization—would indulge in virulent condemnation of the treaty between the "traitor" Sadat and the "terrorist" Begin. As the prime mover behind the treaty, the United States would be subjected to at least verbal attack as "the tool of Zionism and imperialism."

Both Egypt and the United States anticipated some criticism from traditionally pro-Western, pro-Sadat Arab nations such as Saudi Arabia, Jordan, Morocco, and the Persian Gulf states. The so-called moderates might not like the treaty, but, it was thought, they would seek to minimize any anti-Sadat—or any anti-American—measures demanded by the hard-liners.

Treaty supporters thought that conservative Arab unhappiness over Egypt's new relationship with its longtime enemy was less important than fear of radical upheaval and Soviet influence in the region.

These expectations soon proved false. A day after the Washington signing, nineteen members of the Arab League—Algeria, Bahrain, Djibouti, Iraq, Jordan, Kuwait,

Rival Arab and Israel Backers ...

The Arab-Israeli conflict is a major issue in U.S. politics. Over the last four decades the competition to influence American Middle East policy has been played out by various protagonists seeking to persuade, cajole, or coerce support from the White House and Congress. On both the Arab and Israeli sides, skilled lobbyists have vied to present their cases to policy makers in Washington. Both sides of the conflict also realize the importance of public opinion to American policy. In essence, the struggle is as much for the hearts and minds of the American people as it is for the support of policy makers.

The pro-Israel lobbies, the most prominent of which is the American Israel Public Affairs Committee (AIPAC), have risen from relative obscurity to become some of the most effective lobbying organizations in Washington. Building upon the United States' close relationship with Israel, they have helped to enhance the political, economic, and military ties between the two countries.

The Arab lobby has focused on strengthening U.S. ties with pro-Western Arab governments. It also has lobbied lawmakers to change U.S. policies toward Israel. This effort, however, has been largely unsuccessful. Congress has remained strongly supportive of Israel and has consistently exceeded presidential requests for aid to the Jewish state.

The Israel Lobby

As with almost any successful lobby group, the strength of the pro-Israel lobbies lies in the political clout of their membership. Studies indicate that the United States' six million Jews exceed the public at large in their average level of education, social status, philanthropy, and political involvement. "Two thousand years of painful experiences have forced us into round-the-clock political activity," said Thomas A. Dine, executive director of AIPAC.

The focal point of the American Jewish community where Israel is concerned is AIPAC, which evolved in 1954 out of the American Zionist Council. The group, which had a staff of about thirty and a budget of $1.3 million in 1980, grew to where in 1989 it had a staff of seventy and a budget of $7 million—all of it from American donors, according to AIPAC officials. None of the money was tax deductible because AIPAC is a registered lobbying organization. In addition, AIPAC has opened regional offices in New York, Los Angeles, and three other cities.

While other Jewish groups have multiple interests, AIPAC's sole concern has been to nurture the U.S. alliance with Israel and to prevent American relationships with Arab nations from jeopardizing Israel's security. AIPAC and other Jewish organizations are sensitive about accusations that they have a "dual loyalty." Because of this, AIPAC has been careful to frame its issues in terms of the U.S. national interest and to distance itself from the Israeli embassy, though informally the relationship is close.

AIPAC does not rate or endorse political candidates, but it does distribute records of how lawmakers vote on issues of importance to Israel. It also keeps the politically active Jewish community informed of issues before Congress. Most lawmakers have prominent constituents and campaign contributors who expect them to speak out in support of Israel.

Among AIPAC's most dramatic successes were the rapid roundup of seventy-six Senate signatures on a letter endorsing aid to Israel in 1975—a letter designed to counter the Ford administration's "reassessment" of Mideast policy—and its achievement in 1985 of persuading ninety-seven senators and an overwhelming number of House members to delay sale of sophisticated arms to Jordan until meaningful progress took place in Arab-Israeli peace talks.

AIPAC's greatest failures are usually seen as the 54-44 Senate vote in 1978 approving the Carter administration's sale of F-15 fighters to Saudi Arabia, and AIPAC's inability to block the sale of Airborne Warning and Control System (AWACS) planes to Saudi Arabia in 1981. AIPAC stalwarts, however, reject the "failure" label for the 1978 and 1981 votes, noting that Congress had never blocked an arms sale and that the close calls have made presidents gun-shy about taking on Israel's supporters. AIPAC's real successes, they say, are relatively prosaic events, such as the large amounts of U.S. aid to Israel ($3 billion a year during the late 1980s, the largest amount for any ally) in times of tight foreign aid budgets.

Leaders of most other American Jewish organizations sit on AIPAC's executive committee. This ensures that the group's reports on congressional action and its calls for grass-roots pressure go far beyond AIPAC's own membership. Many of the major Jewish organizations represented on AIPAC's board also belong to the New York-based Conference of Presidents of Major American Jewish Organizations. This is a coordinating body for debate on matters relating to Jews in other countries, especially in Israel and the Soviet Union. Thirty-four member groups and six observers participate, including groups primarily concerned with community relations, fraternal, Zionist, religious, and philanthropic activities. The Conference of Presidents was founded in 1955 to present a unified voice from the American Jewish community to the U.S. government. Its presidency is rotated among the member organizations.

Unlike AIPAC, most of these groups operate on tax-deductible donations and cannot legally devote a major portion of their resources to direct lobbying of Congress. They can, however, disseminate informa-

... Lobby for Aid and Influence

tion and alert Jews when Congress is considering an issue relevant to Israel. The organizations have wide-ranging concerns and frequently disagree deeply on religious or political questions, but support for Israel is a common and constant priority. According to one former chairman, the conference has two main purposes: to air disputes among Jewish groups and to educate American officials about pro-Israel policies.

Groups that lobby for Israel are helped by the fact that many of their constituents not only write letters but also donate freely at campaign time. A pro-Israel candidate can count on rewards.

Fund-raisers for Republicans and Democrats maintain that there is no organized, central source of "Jewish money," but most politicians known as backers of Israel have an informal network of Jewish supporters they can count on to raise money nationwide. There are also a number of political action committees (PACs) whose sole purpose is to give campaign money in key election contests to individuals who support close U.S.-Israel ties. In 1984, seventy such PACs gave $3.6 million to candidates.

The Arab Lobby

Arab lobbying efforts have lagged far behind those of pro-Israel groups, despite the putative advantages of petrodollars and oil power. The principal Arab-American organization is the National Association of Arab Americans (NAAA), which is openly modeled on AIPAC.

The NAAA's priorities include the creation of a homeland for the Palestinians (though the NAAA, unlike some Palestinian groups, supports Israel's right to exist), closer ties between the United States and Arab nations, and U.S. Middle East policies that consider Arab interests as much as Israeli interests. The NAAA is careful to couch its positions in the language of American patriotism.

NAAA's ambition is to mobilize an Arab-American constituency, an essential step if the organization is to wield significant political clout. Since the organization's founding in 1972, NAAA leaders have predicted the awakening of an Arab-American political force, but the NAAA has yet to become a major player in Washington.

NAAA's problems are inherent in the nature of the Arab immigrant community in the United States. NAAA estimates the U.S. Arab population at about three million—a diverse and fractious community largely of Lebanese, Syrian, Palestinian, and Egyptian heritage, and Moslem, Maronite Christian, Orthodox Christian, Coptic, and Druze faiths. NAAA has found it difficult to satisfy all factions.

Probably the greatest inhibiting factor to NAAA's efforts has been the continuing conflict in Lebanon. Alixa Naff of NAAA estimated that as many as 80 percent of Arab-Americans are of Lebanese background. Many of them find it hard to sympathize with the Palestine Liberation Organization (PLO) and Syria, because of their use of Lebanon as a battleground, or with the Saudis, Iraqis, and others who have contributed funds to warring factions.

The NAAA has not been able to generate the domestic financial support that would allow it to trumpet its independent status. Its budget, which stood at around $500,000 in 1981, has grown fourfold, while the staff increased from seven in 1981 to about thirty in 1989.

Most of the money, association officials confirmed, came from advertising revenue of a publication called the *Middle East Business Survey*. The magazine, which consists of articles on Arab business prospects, contains advertisements sold for up to $5,000 a page. The advertisers are primarily Arab governments, the PLO, and corporations doing business in the Middle East. Although there are no formal ties between NAAA and Arab governments, Israel's friends cite this as evidence that the NAAA is a tool of foreign regimes.

Fund raising by the NAAA's political action committee (NAAA-PAC), founded in 1984, fell far short of the money raised by NAAA's pro-Israel rivals. For the 1984 election NAAA-PAC donated only $20,000 to some forty-six candidates, almost evenly divided among Democrats and Republicans.

In addition to the NAAA, Arab-American activists have undertaken several other efforts aimed at influencing U.S. policy. One is the American Arab Anti-Defamation Committee (ADC), which organizes Arab-Americans and sympathizers—such as black groups and liberal churches—to fight what they consider to be discriminatory treatment of Arabs in the press and by the government. Another, the Arab-American Institute, seeks to elect more Arab-Americans to office through a political action committee.

Although it lacks an outspoken constituency, the pro-Arab lobby has called on American businesses, which export billions of dollars in goods and services every year to Middle East nations and depend on their oil, to present the Arab side to policy makers.

Executives of oil companies, banks, construction companies, and other international operators have access to members of Congress and cabinet officers and have sometimes used it to argue for closer U.S.-Arab relations. They have been leery, however, of pressing the Arab case in a more overt way. This is because lobbying on behalf of Arab nations might offend Jewish officers and stockholders; and multinational oil companies in particular have little interest in strengthening Arab governments that might exert more authority over them.

Lebanon, Libya, Mauritania, Morocco, the Palestine Liberation Organization, Qatar, Saudi Arabia, Somalia, Syria, Tunisia, the United Arab Emirates, the Yemen Arab Republic (North Yemen), and the Yemen People's Democratic Republic (South Yemen)—met in Baghdad and adopted a package of tough political and economic sanctions against Egypt. Of the twenty-two Arab League members, only Oman and the Sudan, close allies of Sadat, boycotted the meeting. Egypt was not invited.

On March 31 the nineteen Arab ministers for foreign affairs, economic affairs, and finance announced in Baghdad that because of the Egyptian-Israeli treaty, "the Egyptian Government has violated the rights of the Arab Nation and exposed the Nation to dangers and challenges which threaten it. It has also excommunicated itself from its national role to liberate the occupied Arab land, especially Jerusalem, as well as the restoration of full national rights of the Arab people of Palestine, including their return to their homeland and their right to self-determination and the setting up of the Palestinian state on their national soil."

Relations between the radical Arab states and Egypt had been severed before the Baghdad resolutions were announced. In early April the rest of the Baghdad participants began recalling their ambassadors from Cairo. By early May all the Arab countries except Oman and the Sudan had cut diplomatic ties with Egypt. Oman and the Sudan argued that isolating Egypt would not advance the Arab cause. Nevertheless, under pressure from other Arab nations, Sultan Qabus bin Said of Oman and President Gaafer Nimeiry of the Sudan refused to endorse the Egyptian-Israeli treaty. At the same time, Egypt was suspended from the Arab League and the forty-three-member Islamic Conference and affiliates.

Egypt also was expelled from several Arab financial institutions, including the Federation of Arab Banks, the Arab Investment Company, the Arab Bank for Economic Development in Africa, and the Arab Fund for Economic and Social Development. The Arab Civil Aviation Organization asked its members to close their airspace to Egyptian planes and to close down their offices in Cairo.

Among the most serious of the multilateral Arab measures taken against Sadat was the disbanding of the Cairo-based Arab Organization for Industrialization. The organization had been established in 1975 by Saudi Arabia, Qatar, the United Arab Emirates, and Egypt to lessen Arab dependence on imported weapons, improve the Arabs' military technology, and spur employment and aid the economy of Egypt. As a result of the shutdown, Egypt stood to lose some fifteen-hundred jobs as well as a source of technology and weapons.

Egypt also was expelled from the Organization of Arab Petroleum Exporting Countries (OAPEC) in mid-April. And the oil ministers from Saudi Arabia, Kuwait, Bahrain, the United Arab Emirates, Qatar, Iraq, Syria, Libya, and Algeria announced a ban on the sale of oil to Egypt.

Soviet Reaction, Policies

Having been excluded from any role in the Middle East peacemaking process, the Soviets reacted negatively to Sadat's 1977 visit to Jerusalem, the Camp David accords, and the resulting peace treaty between Egypt and Israel. Throughout that period, Sadat was routinely accused of betraying the Arab—particularly the Palestinian—cause and of allying himself with the "reactionary"

forces of Zionism and imperialism. The United States was denounced for encouraging an unworkable settlement to benefit only Israel and for meddling in Middle East internal affairs.

Although the Soviets were frustrated by their exclusion from the Middle East peace process, they saw the American-engineered Egyptian-Israeli peace process as an opportunity to improve their own ties with Arab opponents of a settlement. There was, on the surface at least, greater amiability between Moscow and Syria, Iraq, Libya, and the other hard-liners. Contacts between the Soviet Union and Jordan expanded, and the Jordanian media began supporting a strong Soviet Middle East peacemaking role.

During the Camp David peace process Soviet Middle East strategy had consisted of publicizing the innumerable difficulties that beset the American-mediated negotiations between Egypt and Israel. The Soviets also encouraged the hard-line Arab rejectionists to continue their opposition. Overtures were made to Jordan and even to Saudi Arabia to persuade the "moderate" Arabs to resist American pressure on them to join or support the peace process.

Soviet criticism of the Camp David accords was loud and immediate. Sadat was branded a "traitor" and a "supplicant." Moscow charged that Israel had no intention of surrendering the West Bank, Gaza, or the Golan Heights and that the United States, having broken its promise on a resumption of the Geneva Conference (proposed in 1977), was now intent upon imposing a separate solution giving its Zionist allies everything they wanted.

In October 1978 President Assad of Syria, President Houari Boumediene of Algeria, and PLO chairman Arafat all visited Moscow. During these visits, the Camp David formula was denounced, and, in return for promises of additional Soviet aid, Assad and Arafat called for a reconvening of the Geneva Conference. The Algerians, along with the Libyans and Iraqis, opposed any direct negotiations with Israel, at Geneva or elsewhere.

While heaping praise upon the policies of former antagonists Jordan and Saudi Arabia, the Soviet Union continued to denounce the "hegemonistic" plans of the United States. These denunciations were especially evident after President Carter announced in early March 1979 that he would visit Egypt and Israel to try to revive the stalled peace treaty negotiations. The Soviet media attacked Carter's trip as a typical "imperialist" effort to protect American strategic interests in the area after the revolution in Iran that ousted the Shah Mohammed Reza Pahlavi. The Soviets also warned that the treaty would encourage the United States to form Egyptian-Israeli-American "military pacts" in the region. Israel, the Soviet media argued, would receive a massive increase in U.S. arms, while Egypt would be given enough to become the "policeman" of the Middle East.

Reagan Policies

One stable factor in the search for Middle East peace has been the ability of the United States to fill the role of mediator. In spite of its close ties with Israel, the United States maintains relations with all Arab countries except Libya, and even in times of crisis U.S. diplomats gain access throughout the region. The Soviet Union, by contrast, broke its relations with Israel in 1967 and has often had poor relations with important Arab states such as

Jordan, Saudi Arabia, and Egypt.

During President Ronald Reagan's first term, the administration attempted to continue efforts toward mediating a Middle East peace. It concentrated on getting Jordan and "moderate" Palestinians into the peace process with two goals in mind: a second peace treaty between Israel and an Arab country, and an agreement giving Palestinian residents of the West Bank some form of political autonomy. Despite these goals, the Middle East policies of the administration often seemed controlled by events in the region, rather than by initiatives formulated in Washington. Some critics said the United States suffered unnecessary setbacks by following reactive rather than proactive policies and by trying to superimpose the administration's main struggle with the Soviet Union on the regional conflict in the Middle East.

American prestige and power in the region suffered badly in the early 1980s after the Reagan administration's diplomatic and military efforts failed to bring peace to wartorn Lebanon.

Other events also eroded U.S. influence and contributed to turmoil and violence. Continued hostility toward Israel by the Arab states wiped out the optimism engendered by the 1979 peace treaty between Israel and Egypt. The 1981 assassination of Egyptian president Sadat removed from the scene America's most loyal and important ally in the Arab world. The fate of the Palestinians residing in Israeli-occupied territories remained a basic cause of instability. The Iran-Iraq war that began in September 1980 escalated by 1984 to threaten shipping in the Persian Gulf, the key transportation link for much of Europe's and Japan's oil supplies.

Meanwhile, the political consensus at home on the policies the United States should pursue in the region disintegrated. As the administration shifted from diplomacy and mediation to an increased reliance on the use of American troops and large arms sales to moderate Arab states, the administration and Congress clashed repeatedly.

President Reagan brought to office a vigorous anti-Communist view of the world. In his campaign he had charged that earlier administrations were too accommodating to the Soviet Union and had allowed America's strength and reputation to decline. He identified Moscow as the source of most major international political problems, including those in the Middle East. Reagan, in contrast to

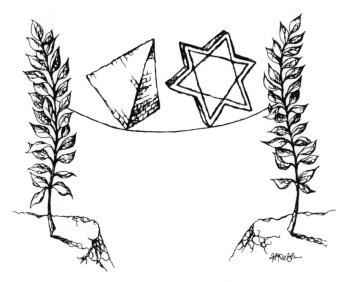

Carter, placed relatively little importance on the role of Third World nations in U.S. foreign policy. The focus of Reagan policy, rather, was on countering communism.

Reagan viewed Israel as the most reliable friend in the region, and he believed Israel's democratic system made it a natural ally for the United States. Even as governor of California, Reagan demonstrated his support of Israel at rallies and through legislation allowing Israeli bonds to be bought by savings institutions for investment purposes, the first time this was allowed by any state.

Few of Reagan's senior advisers had Middle East experience. During the first months of the administration, important Middle East policy-making posts remained vacant. An overall U.S. approach to the Middle East would not emerge until after Israel's invasion of Lebanon in June 1982. Those policies that were pursued dealt mainly with the Persian Gulf. The Arab-Israeli conflict was placed on a back burner, partly because the administration wanted to wait for the upcoming Israeli elections and partly because there was no pressing need to do otherwise.

The new administration feared that the Soviet Union might try to exploit the instability in the Persian Gulf caused by the Islamic revolution in Iran and Iran's war with Iraq. However, most nations in the region did not view the Soviets as the prime threat to stability and were unwilling to resolve intraregional disputes in order to join with the United States in this policy. Persian Gulf states, especially Saudi Arabia, were more concerned with disruption from Iran, and none of the Arab states was willing—at least openly—to put aside the dispute with Israel.

Events' Effect on Policy Decisions

Almost from its first days in office, the Reagan administration was forced by events to focus on Lebanon, a country that had suffered nearly ten years of civil war and occupation by Syrian and Israeli troops and the forces of the Palestine Liberation Organization.

The first major Reagan diplomatic effort in Lebanon came in April 1981 when intense fighting broke out between Syria and the Maronite Christian Phalange militia in the Lebanese city of Zahle. Israel, at the Phalange's urgent plea for help, shot down two Syrian helicopters, and Syria moved Soviet-supplied surface-to-air missiles into Lebanon's Bekaa Valley, where they remained until they were destroyed a year later by Israeli warplanes.

Israeli air strikes in mid-1981 against Iraq and Lebanon precipitated a temporary U.S. suspension of F-16 aircraft deliveries to Israel. The use of American-made jets in the raids raised the touchy question of whether Israel had violated a U.S. law limiting U.S. arms to defensive purposes. But beyond that, the air strikes had political repercussions in the United States, raising doubts about Israel's normally unquestioned support in Congress and in the country.

Iraqi Nuclear Plant

Using American F-16 fighter bombers escorted by F-15 fighters, Israel on June 7, 1981, attacked and quickly destroyed the Osirak nuclear reactor under construction near Baghdad, Iraq. Israeli prime minister Begin called the raid "an act of supreme, legitimate self-defense," claiming Iraq planned to use the facility to produce nuclear weapons that would threaten Israel. Critics, including many members of Congress, labeled the strike as aggression and accused Begin of launching the raid to bolster his chances in Israel's June 30 general election. The State Department condemned the raid and the administration June 10 suspended delivery of four F-16s scheduled to be shipped to Israel June 12. Not since President Dwight D. Eisenhower in the 1950s had an American president postponed aid in response to an Israeli action. Nevertheless, this demonstration of U.S. displeasure did not alter the fundamental relationship between the United States and Israel. On June 16 President Reagan said Israel appeared to have violated the defense-only legal requirements but added, "I do think one has to recognize that Israel had reason for concern in view of the past history of Iraq."

Robert C. McFarlane, State Department spokesman, said the raid had "shattered" the confidence of the United States in Israel and had "profound political implications" for the Middle East generally. The administration sought to distance itself from the Israeli action, stating that the United States was neither consulted nor advised of the raid in advance. However, neither McFarlane, Walter J. Stoessel, under secretary of state for political affairs, nor other officials suggested that American support for Israel would diminish.

There was no serious move in Congress to cut off Israel's $1.4 billion annual military aid. But Israel was chastised by many members of Congress while being defended by some. Sen. Mark Hatfield, R-Ore., called it "one of the most provocative, ill-timed, and internationally illegal actions taken" in Israel's history. Rep. Jack F. Kemp, R-N.Y., a prominent Reagan ally, said "Israel's action was not only inevitable, but justified." In the United Nations, U.S. representatives compromised with Iraq on a UN Security Council resolution that "strongly condemned" the bombing but fell far short of imposing sanctions.

Lebanon Raids

In July 1981 President Reagan broadened the suspension of F-16 aircraft deliveries to Israel amid intense clashes between Israel and the PLO in southern Lebanon. Reagan decided July 20 to suspend delivery to Israel of ten more F-16s; this was in addition to the four held up June 10. Israel already had received fifty-three of the seventy-five F-16s ordered from the United States. Reagan withheld the aircraft amid U.S. efforts to win a cease-fire along the Lebanese border, where Israel had implemented air and commando raids to quell PLO artillery and rocket fire against Israeli border settlements.

Although the attacks and counterattacks spanned nearly two weeks, the catalyst for Reagan's action was Israel's July 17 bombing of a PLO headquarters in downtown Beirut—an air strike that reportedly killed more than three-hundred persons and wounded eight-hundred. The air attack shocked U.S. officials. The State Department had been prepared that same day to announce that the four F-16s withheld after the raid on Iraq would be released.

The most direct U.S. criticism of Israel came July 23 from Deputy Secretary of State William P. Clark, who said Begin "is making it difficult for us to help Israel. Our commitments are not to Mr. Begin, but to the nation he represents." Defense Secretary Caspar W. Weinberger said Begin's actions "cannot really be described as moderate at this point."

The Beirut attack also damaged (at least temporarily) Israel's support in Congress. Many members, including some traditional Israel supporters, condemned the raid and

commended Reagan's decision. Even Israel's most ardent allies were conspicuous by their refusal to defend Israel's actions or to criticize Reagan's.

Charles H. Percy, R-Ill., chairman of the Senate Foreign Relations Committee, said at a July 20 committee session: "I favor continued suspension of the F-16 shipments to Israel." Delivery of the planes, Percy said, would be interpreted as U.S. "acquiescence" in Israel's military actions. Committee member Richard G. Lugar, R-Ind., suggested the United States should impose a "moratorium" on further military shipments to Israel "until we have a better idea of what Israel is doing."

Some supporters of Israel, such as Foreign Relations Committee member Joseph R. Biden, Jr., D-Del., openly worried that the events in Lebanon could undermine American backing for Israel. Despite congressional displeasure with Israeli behavior, there was little backing in Congress for punishing Israel by reducing U.S. assistance.

Meanwhile, the administration continued its efforts to defuse the unstable situation in the Middle East. The quest for a cease-fire and resolution of the Syrian-Israeli dispute over Syrian surface-to-air missiles in Lebanon was spearheaded by presidential envoy Philip C. Habib.

Fahd Plan

In an effort to gain favor in the United States and preempt a harder line advocated by more radical Arab states, Saudi Arabia unveiled a Middle East peace plan in August 1981, later called the Fahd plan after its author, who was then the crown prince. *(Text of plan, Appendix, p. 305)*

The Reagan administration initially had little enthusiasm for the proposal, saying only that any peace suggestions were welcome and that the Fahd plan seemed consistent with UN Resolutions 242 and 338 that the United States considered the basis for negotiations. Later, however, the administration reconsidered. It called the Fahd plan a basis for negotiation and a positive step toward peace. This change was partly an attempt to show support for the Saudis before an upcoming Arab League summit in November. It also was a response to widespread criticism of an administration plan, announced in April 1981, to sell Saudi Arabia five sophisticated Airborne Warning and Control System planes (AWACS). Critics of the AWACS sale said the planes could be used against Israel. *(AWACS details, Chapter 4, p. 76)* The administration portrayed the plan as proof that Saudi Arabia was a moderating influence in the region.

The Fahd plan, however, did not receive much support in the Middle East. The Israelis promptly rejected the proposal because it did not implicitly or explicitly recognize Israel's right to exist. Israeli officials called the Fahd plan an attempt to destroy Israel piecemeal. The November Arab summit in Fez did not reach agreement on the proposal and the meeting adjourned in the face of widening division within the Arab world.

Expanding Ties with Israel

The administration in late 1981 moved to improve relations with Israel to calm the latter's concerns over the Saudi AWACS sale and the Fahd plan re-evaluation. This effort also was propelled by Reagan's firm opinion that Israel was of strategic value to the United States and the desire of Secretary of State Alexander M. Haig, Jr., to form a "strategic consensus" to counter Soviet expansion in the region.

Israeli prime minister Begin met with President Reagan in September 1981 to discuss improved ties. The relationship between the United States and Israel traditionally rested on shared interests and values; the two nations never had a formal treaty of alliance.

At the end of November, Israeli defense minister Ariel Sharon met with Defense Secretary Weinberger to make final a "stategic memorandum of understanding." Weinberger appeared unenthusiastic about the document. He held the signing ceremony with little attention, not even allowing press photographers in the room to record the event. The memorandum of understanding was designed to counter Soviet-inspired political instability and pledged the signatories to meet threats in the Middle East "caused by the Soviet Union or Soviet-controlled forces from outside the region." It provided for military cooperation and coordination between Israel and the United States, but it did not obligate the United States to aid Israel if the Jewish state were attacked by the Arab states.

Although the agreement was hailed by the Likud party in Israel, the opposition Labor party was critical, claiming that it did nothing to ensure Israel's security and only committed Israel to defending U.S. interests in the region.

Golan Heights Law

Debate over the merits of the agreement would soon become irrelevant as U.S.-Israeli relations again became strained. On December 14, 1981, the Israeli Knesset voted 63-21 to extend Israeli law to the Golan Heights, thereby annexing the territory it had occupied since 1967. The Reagan administration strongly criticized the action and called it contrary to UN Resolutions 242 and 338. Later that week U.S. representatives supported a resolution in the UN Security Council that declared the Israeli action invalid under international law. The United States did, however, seek to head off a stronger resolution in the UN General Assembly.

In response to the annexation, Reagan ordered that the memorandum of understanding with Israel not be implemented. Begin responded sharply, accusing the administration of waging an "anti-Semitic campaign" to get Senate approval of the AWACS sale to Saudi Arabia. He added that the U.S. action amounted to cancellation of the U.S.-Israeli accord. Weinberger responded by saying that it was Israel, not the United States, that cancelled the agreement.

Period of Quiet

The diplomatic front was quiet during the first half of 1982. U.S. officials were concerned about the Israeli return of the last part of Sinai on schedule April 25, 1982, and did not want to do anything that might jeopardize the withdrawal. The administration still lacked a comprehensive policy toward the region.

Weinberger, who saw Saudi Arabia as a potential close ally, continued to push for improved ties, but on a trip there early in the year he found the Saudis unreceptive to forming a "strategic consensus" with the United States. Haig was trying to revitalize the stalled Palestinian autonomy talks between Egypt and Israel, to no avail. Administration efforts also focused on normalizing relations between Egypt and Israel.

Reagan wanted to make sure the cease-fire between Israel and the Palestine Liberation Organization negotiated the previous spring by his special Middle East envoy, Philip Habib, would hold. Israel reported numerous violations from the beginning of the cease-fire and was, the world later learned, preparing under Defense Minister Sharon to defeat the PLO militarily and politically.

Habib continued to shuttle between Middle Eastern capitals trying to keep the relative calm in place, despite continued PLO shelling of northern Israel and Israeli air raids on PLO positions in Lebanon. Rumors circulated of Israeli intentions to launch a major military operation in southern Lebanon. The Reagan administration did what it could to defuse tensions, but the efforts were to have little effect.

Israel Invades Lebanon

On June 6, 1982, Israeli armed forces invaded Lebanon with the stated purpose of creating a twenty-five-mile-wide buffer zone in southern Lebanon free of Palestinian guerrillas. Although the United States issued statements that indicated displeasure with the Israeli move, some Middle East experts have suggested that the U.S. officials gave Israel a "green light" for the invasion. Stephen Spiegel, a Middle East specialist at UCLA, suggests in his book *The Other Arab-Israeli Conflict* that "Haig declar[ed] repeatedly he was constantly cautioning Israeli officials against intervening in Lebanon; but he did not threaten sanctions or pressure if Israel acted. In this sense his warnings were similar to [President Lyndon] Johnson's before the Six-Day War and just as ineffective; Haig used a phrase similar to Johnson's, that 'Israel would be alone if it acted.' " In the initial stages of the war the United States appeared ambivalent toward the Israeli moves. Not until Israel went beyond its self-declared twenty-five-mile limit did the administration begin to voice opposition to Israeli actions.

The administration's immediate concerns were to prevent the war from expanding to include Syria. President Reagan sent Habib back into the region in an effort to prevent hostilities from expanding. On June 9 Israel and Syria fought a massive air battle over Lebanon's Bekaa Valley, in which Israel destroyed Syrian surface-to-air missiles and decimated the Syrian air force. After this crippling blow, Moscow through Syria and Washington through Israel were able to prevent Syria and Israel from engaging in an all-out ground war. On June 11 Israel and Syria signed a cease-fire, thus ending the brief encounter between the two.

Even though the administration opposed Israel's invasion it seemed to support some of its goals. U.S. officials said they would seek the withdrawal of all foreign forces from Lebanon. This expansion of the original U.S. request that Israel pull out of the country reflected Israel's goal of ending the PLO and Syrian presence in Lebanon.

In spite of Israel's original claim only to a twenty-five-mile buffer zone, its armed forces continued their advance until they reached the outskirts of Beirut and surrounded thousands of PLO guerrillas in West Beirut. Quiet opposition to Israeli actions ended when the Israelis reached Beirut. Reagan made clear that the United States did not want Israel to enter Beirut, an Arab capital.

Shultz Replaces Haig. Divisions within the Reagan administration over Middle East policy widened during the war. Although opposed to the invasion, Haig saw benefits in the Israelis' eliminating the PLO presence in Lebanon and in their pressuring the Syrians to leave. This, he thought, would change the political conditions in Lebanon, enabling the Lebanese government to regain control of the country.

Then, on June 24, 1982, Haig abruptly resigned. Most analysts suggest that internal administration conflict over Lebanon war policy was only the final in a long list of reasons for Haig's resignation.

The nomination of George P. Shultz as Haig's replacement was widely seen as portending changes in the administration's view of the Middle East. Like Weinberger, Shultz had worked for Bechtel Corp., the international engineering firm. During Reagan's presidential bid in 1980, Shultz, who had been advising Reagan on other issues, was critical of the candidate's views toward Israel. Shultz stated often that the United States should have a "balanced approach" to the Arab-Israeli conflict. During his confirmation hearings, Shultz made it clear that his approach to the Middle East would be quite different from his predecessor's. He was critical of the Israeli invasion and appeared favorably inclined toward the establishment of a Palestinian homeland.

PLO Leaves Lebanon. With the Israelis on the outskirts of Beirut, the administration tried to reassure friendly Arab states that Israel would not enter Beirut. In attempting to negotiate an end to the crisis, Philip Habib gained many cease-fire agreements, all of which were broken almost immediately. Habib eventually secured agreement for PLO forces to leave Beirut, but the evacuation did not occur until after the Israelis engaged in a day-long bombardment of the city on August 12. This Israeli action so upset Reagan that he called Begin to demand that the bombing stop.

Although the PLO had agreed in principle to leave Beirut, the final agreement was delayed while negotiators hammered out details of the evacuation and searched for a destination. President Assad of Syria refused to allow the PLO to come to his country. Jordan also refused to take the PLO because of tensions dating back to the Jordanian civil war in 1970 when factions of the PLO attempted to overthrow King Hussein.

Finally, Habib was able to get all the parties to agree to a PLO evacuation of West Beirut to various Arab countries, including Syria, that would be monitored by a multinational peacekeeping force of American, French, and Italian troops. In addition the U.S. guaranteed the safety of the Palestinians living in the refugee camps in and around Beirut.

Marines Leave, Return. The U.S. Marines in the multinational force left Lebanon September 10 after the PLO evacuation was completed. On September 14 Lebanon's president-elect, Bashir Gemayel, was assassinated. In apparent retaliation, hundreds of Palestinian civilians in the Shatila and Sabra refugee camps near Beirut were massacred during the following days by Phalange militiamen. The violence prompted Reagan to send a contingent of twelve hundred Marines back into Lebanon September 29 as part of a multinational peacekeeping force.

The president's action was criticized by members of Congress who thought Reagan was evading the requirements of the 1973 War Powers Resolution by refusing to seek congressional approval for the deployment of troops in Lebanon. The War Powers Resolution proscribed the use of U.S. forces in hostile situations for more than ninety days without congressional authorization. *(Details, facing page)*

Behind the debate over the War Powers Resolution

appeared to be concern that the United States was jeopardizing its position as a mediator by intervening militarily to prop up the existing Lebanese government. This fear was reinforced by the decision of the administration to train and equip the Lebanese army.

Reagan's Peace Initiative

In 1982 President Reagan tried to revitalize the Arab-Israeli peace process that began at Camp David in 1978. However, Reagan's Middle East peace initiative, launched in a televised speech September 1, made little headway.

Reagan said the United States would support self-government for Palestinians on the West Bank of the Jordan River and in the Gaza Strip in association with Jordan, but not in an independent state or under Israeli sovereignty. He also called upon Israel to "freeze" further Jewish settlement in the West Bank and Gaza as a prelude to resuming negotiations under the 1978 Camp David accords. He added, however, that Israel could not be expected to pull back totally from the occupied territories. *(Text, Appendix, p. 305)*

The president pledged U.S. support for the Camp David plan for an interim agreement to provide self-government for the Palestinians in the West Bank and Gaza for five years while the ultimate status of the territories was negotiated by Israel, Egypt, the United States, and Jordan. "The final status of these lands must, of course, be reached through the give and take of negotiations," Reagan said. "But it is the firm view of the United States that self-government by the Palestinians of the West Bank and Gaza in association with Jordan offers the best chance for a durable, just and lasting peace."

Reagan said the U.S. position was based on the principle "that the Arab-Israeli conflict should be resolved through negotiations involving an exchange of territory for peace," as set out in United Nations Security Council Resolution 242 in 1967. He said the resolution's call for Israel to withdraw from "territories occupied in the recent conflict" clearly applied to the West Bank and Gaza. The president took pains to reaffirm the U.S. commitment to Israel, and he urged that Israel's enemies recognize Israel's right to exist.

In a note sent to Israeli prime minister Begin, the president said the United States opposed dismantling existing settlements in the occupied territories, believed that exchange of territory should be only for real peace, and agreed that the limits to the pullback would be determined by the type of security guarantees Israel received.

"Finally," Reagan said in his television message, "we remain convinced that Jerusalem must remain undivided, but its final status should be decided through negotiations."

Nowhere in the speech did the president mention the Golan Heights or Syria. In addition he ruled out the possibility of PLO participation in the negotiations. This continued the longstanding U.S. policy of refusing to recognize or deal with the PLO until that organization repudiated violence and terrorism, accepted Israel's right to exist, and declared its support for UN Resolutions 242 and 338.

Israel promptly repudiated the Reagan plan. Jordan's King Hussein initially gave it cautious support and opened talks with PLO chairman Arafat. But Hussein failed to secure permission from the PLO to negotiate on behalf of West Bank Palestinians, and by April 1983 when the Palestine National Council meeting in Algiers rejected the plan,

Reagan Policy Foundered in Lebanon Morass

In 1982 President Reagan sought to assist peace efforts in Lebanon by sending a contingent of American Marines to Beirut. The presence of U.S. forces in Lebanon led to a near constitutional confrontation at home, the deaths of several hundred Marines at the hands of suicide bombers, and the evaporation of U.S. public support for an American role in the Lebanese morass. The president was left with little choice but to pull out the Marines and concede political influence in Lebanon to Syria.

By August 1983 the Marine contingent in Lebanon had grown to 1,800. On August 29 two Marines were killed by artillery fire from Druze Moslem forces fighting the U.S.-backed Christian government. That incident sparked a movement in Congress to force the president to invoke the War Powers Resolution. That law, passed over President Richard Nixon's veto in 1973, set a ninety-day limit on any presidential commitment of U.S. troops abroad without specific congressional authorization. Reagan, however, argued that the U.S. forces were "essential to the objective of helping to restore the territorial integrity, sovereignty, and political independence of Lebanon." It was not possible to predict how long the Marines would have to stay in that country, he said.

American participation in the conflict, however, soon expanded. On September 5 two Marines were killed by rocket fire, and on September 8 a U.S. warship fired for the first time on Moslem artillery positions believed responsible for attacking the Marines.

With a confrontation on the issue clearly building, the administration and key congressional leaders began negotiating to head off a constitutional clash between the executive and legislative branches. Congressional leaders of both parties insisted the president invoke the War Powers Resolution and acknowledge the right of Congress to share in setting the terms of the Marine deployment. With similar firmness, the president opposed any invocation of the War Powers Resolution and, like other presidents before him, questioned the law's constitutionality.

A compromise was reached in which Reagan signed a joint resolution invoking the War Powers Resolution and imposing an eighteen-month limit on the Marine deployment. In turn, the president declared in writing that he did not recognize the constitutionality of the War Powers Resolution and that he retained his constitutional authority as commander in chief to deploy U.S. forces. The joint resolution was approved by Congress September 29 and signed by Reagan October 12, 1983.

Events in Lebanon quickly diminished the relevance of the compromise. On October 23, 1983, a suicide truck bomb attack on the Marine headquarters killed 241 Americans.

The deaths of the Marines appeared to erase what support had existed for a long-term commitment of U.S. troops in Lebanon. Those who publicly continued to support the Marines' deployment said they did so only because to withdraw them after the bombing would be to encourage further terrorism.

A group calling itself the Islamic Revolutionary Movement claimed responsibility for the Marine barracks bombing. The president, however, laid much of the responsibility for the attack and Lebanon's troubles on Soviet-backed Syria, which he said had reneged on promises to withdraw its troops from Lebanon. Reagan said Syria had "become a home for seven-thousand Soviet advisers and technicians who man a massive amount of Soviet weaponry, including SS-21 ground-to-ground missiles capable of reaching vital areas of Israel." Reagan suggested that U.S. abandonment of Lebanon might lead to a Middle East "incorporated into the Soviet bloc."

Some members of Congress argued that the president appeared to be shifting his reasons for U.S. involvement in Lebanon. Sen. Patrick J. Leahy, D-Vt., said the U.S. role originally "was a peacekeeping mission" but, as explained by Reagan, had become an effort "to stop the spread of communism."

The administration position was undercut by the findings of a blue-ribbon Pentagon panel. In its December 1983 report, the panel concluded that the Marines could not perform their avowed role of neutral peacekeepers, partly because warring Lebanese factions no longer saw the Marines as "even-handed and neutral" because of the gradual involvement of U.S. military units in direct combat assistance of the Lebanese armed forces controlled by President Amin Gemayel, a Maronite Christian, who had succeeded his slain brother. The government's military force was seen by rival religious factions as an arm of the right-wing Maronite Christian "Phalange" faction in the struggle for power, the commission said.

By year's end, after other American soldiers had been killed in the first direct military clash between U.S. and Syrian forces in Lebanon, Congress was rapidly backing away from its September agreement to keep the Marines in Lebanon through mid-1985. House Democrats reached general agreement February 1, 1984, on a nonbinding resolution calling on Reagan to order the "prompt and orderly withdrawal" of the Marines, a move Senate Democrats endorsed the next day.

On February 7 Reagan announced that the 1,600 Marines in Lebanon would be moved in stages to ships offshore. In a March 30 letter to Congress, the president said he was ending all U.S. participation in the peacekeeping force in Lebanon. With the departure of the Marines and the near-collapse of the Gemayel government, Syria emerged once again as the dominant force in Lebanon.

Hussein backed away from further involvement.

The rest of the Arab world, meeting at a summit conference in Fez, Morocco, in September, a week after Reagan presented his proposal, agreed to an eight-point plan that differed only slightly from the proposal Saudi Crown Prince Fahd had offered in 1981. The administration reacted positively to the Fez proposal, stating that it was a consensus position of the Arab world closer to a peaceful resolution of the conflict. The plan, however, conflicted with Reagan's because the Arabs called for a PLO-led state in the occupied territories, demanded the complete withdrawal by Israel to pre-1967 boundaries, and did not advocate direct negotiations. In addition, it required the UN, rather than the participants in the dispute, to guarantee the peace. *(Fez proposal, Appendix, p. 305)*

Lebanon Linkage; Syria Prevails

The Reagan administration linked its initiative to a resolution of the Lebanese crisis. It viewed the possible resolution of the Lebanese situation as a first step in a broader Middle East peace.

In addition to resistance among Middle East groups, the administration found increasing opposition to its policies at home. Fears grew in Congress that the United States was getting too deeply involved in Lebanon and the lives of Marines stationed in that country were in danger. That concern grew when the U.S. embassy in Beirut was the target on April 18, 1983, of a bomb attack that killed sixty-three persons, including seventeen Americans.

The Reagan administration was intent on reducing Syrian influence in Lebanon and moving peace negotiations forward. To achieve these goals, U.S. officials sought an agreement between Lebanon and Israel and a leading role for Jordan's King Hussein in the peace process.

King Hussein met with Reagan in Washington in December 1982. During this meeting the president reportedly promised to pressure Israel to stop building new settlements in occupied territories in return for Hussein's direct negotiations with Israel. Hussein believed he needed the backing of PLO chairman Arafat before he could agree to talks because a 1974 Arab summit conference in Rabat designated the PLO as the sole representative of the Palestinians. Although Hussein and Arafat later met, the king did not get the backing he sought. After Jordan announced in April 1983 that Hussein would not enter into negotiations, the administration focused its attention on getting foreign troops out of Lebanon.

A long and difficult series of negotiations, involving top Israeli, Lebanese, and American officials, produced an agreement that in the end came to naught. The agreement, signed in Lebanon and Israel on May 17, 1983, was not called a treaty because the Lebanese were concerned about Arab reaction. Moreover, formal diplomatic relations were not to be established immediately. The agreement did, however, provide for an end to the state of war that had formally existed since 1948, a buffer security zone in south Lebanon to protect Israel, and absorption into the regular Lebanese army of the pro-Israeli militia, led by Saad Haddad, that operated in southern Lebanon. It also ensured Israeli air superiority and established in both countries semidiplomatic missions that would have immunity privileges. Lastly, the agreement provided for negotiations to reestablish normal relations between the nations.

The United States, in a separate letter to Israel, promised to guarantee the agreement, acknowledged Israel's right to retaliate against attacks from Lebanese territory, and assured the Israelis that they did not have to withdraw until Syria and the PLO pulled out.

The pact had a very short life. Even though it was signed by both parties and the Israeli Knesset ratified it, the Lebanese parliament delayed action. The Syrians, who were never part of the negotiations and who saw their influence in Lebanon being undercut, were vehemently opposed. Opponents of Amin Gemayel's administration in Lebanon also denounced the accord, fearing it would consolidate Gemayel's control with Israeli and American support and would infringe Lebanese sovereignty.

Ultimately, Syria refused to accept the agreement, which rendered it meaningless. Without a withdrawal by Syria and the PLO, the Israelis would not withdraw. Under increasing Syrian pressure, Gemayel's government abrogated the accord.

American policy in Lebanon continued to focus on preserving Gemayel's government, which was being opposed with increasing hostility from opposition forces within Lebanon. Reagan's limited use of U.S. air and naval power to support Gemayel in late 1983 and early 1984, however, drew increasing criticism from Congress. American air strikes and naval bombardments against Syrian and Lebanese Shi'ite forces appeared only to increase Lebanon's chaos, further endanger U.S. peacekeepers, and undermine the status of the United States as a mediator in the Middle East. Lawmakers, and by extension the public, pressured the administration to withdraw the Marines from Beirut and end U.S. military involvement in Lebanon. That withdrawal in 1984 concluded the American policy of trying to support Gemayel's teetering government. Syrian domination of Lebanese affairs became nearly complete. *(Reagan policy in Lebanon, box, p. 61)*

Bouts with Terrorism

Ronald Reagan entered office in 1981 just as the American hostages were being released by Iran. This humiliation to the United States had caused Reagan to promise that he would retaliate against terrorists who targeted Americans. Despite numerous terrorist attacks during the first four and a half years of Reagan's presidency, the United States had refrained from striking back at terrorists with military force.

During 1985 and 1986 a wave of Middle East terrorism against the United States and other Western nations dominated headlines, affected U.S.-Israeli relations, and pressured the Reagan administration to back up its hard-line public policies toward terrorism with action.

On June 14, 1985, Arab gunmen hijacked Trans World Airways Flight 847 from Athens to Rome with 153 people aboard. The hijackers forced the pilot to fly to Beirut where one American was killed and thirty-nine Americans were held hostage. The hijackers and their Shi'ite supporters demanded, among other things, that Israel release some 700 Shi'ite prisoners it was holding. Over the following two weeks of the crisis U.S. officials avoided both negotiating with the terrorists and publicly pressuring Israel to release the prisoners. Nevertheless, it appeared at one point as though American officials were privately pushing Israel to release its prisoners. The American hostages were released at the end of the month, and Israel began releasing its prisoners. Israeli officials, however, pointedly noted they had intended to release the Shi'ites prior to the hijacking.

A second hijacking in 1985 caused even wider international ripples. On October 14 gunmen identified as being members of the Palestine Liberation Front (PLF), a faction of the PLO, seized the Italian passenger liner the *Achille Lauro*. The gunmen surrendered to Egyptian authorities a few days later and released the hostages, but not before they killed an elderly, wheelchair-bound American passenger.

In accordance with its stern antiterrorist campaign, the United States sought to capture the hijackers. American intelligence sources soon learned that the terrorists were on an Egyptian airliner heading first toward Tunisia, where it was denied permission to land, and then to Athens. Under orders from President Reagan U.S. F-14 fighters intercepted the Egyptian airliner and forced it to land in Sicily. There Italian authorities took the hijackers into custody to await trial. Then, much to the United States' astonishment and anger, the Italians released Muhammad Abu'l Abbas, the leader of the PLF, whom the Egyptians said acted as a mediator but the United States claimed was the mastermind of the hijacking.

The interception of the aircraft infuriated Egypt. President Hosni Mubarak called it piracy. In Italy, Prime Minister Bettino Craxi's government collapsed October 16 after a coalition party withdrew on the grounds it had not been adequately consulted on the hijacking affair. Craxi resigned the following day, amid considerable bitterness over U.S. actions related to the hijacking.

Observers noted the United States had captured several hijackers but not the man U.S. officials considered the main culprit. The price for the interception was strained relations with Egypt, a key ally in the Middle East, and the embarrassment and collapse of an unusually stable Italian government that had been one of America's best friends in the Mediterranean region. To repair this damage, Reagan later in October dispatched top U.S. officials to both nations for talks.

Focus on Libya

Although Syria and Iran had been implicated in supporting terrorist activities, the Reagan administration focused its antiterrorism efforts on Libya. That nation was of less importance to American strategic interests than Iran and did not have a major role in the Arab-Israeli peace process like Syria. Moreover, the fanatical and unpredictable ideas of Libyan leader Col. Muammar Qaddafi and Libya's aggression in Africa had alienated many Arab governments and caused the Soviets to keep their Libyan allies at arm's length. Military action against Libya, therefore, was likely to involve fewer risks than action against Iran or Syria. Moreover, President Reagan appeared to be personally outraged by Qaddafi's policies and statements.

In 1985 Abu Nidal, a terrorist leader who had defected from the mainstream of the PLO, moved his base of operations from Syria to Libya. In December 1985 members of his group attacked the check-in counters of El Al airlines at the Rome and Vienna airports with automatic weapons and hand grenades. They killed eighteen persons and wounded more than one hundred.

On January 7, 1986, Reagan announced that there was "irrefutable evidence" that Libya had supported the Palestinian terrorists who carried out the attack. He ended all economic activity between the United States and Libya and ordered all American citizens to leave Libya. The next day he froze Libyan assets in the United States. The United States had little success, however, in persuading its European allies to enact similarly tough sanctions against Tripoli.

In March Reagan ordered the U.S. Navy to conduct maneuvers in the Gulf of Sidra off the coast of Libya in defiance of Qaddafi's declaration that the gulf was Libyan territorial waters. During the maneuvers Libya fired antiaircraft missiles at U.S. planes. In response, U.S. planes bombed several Libyan ships and a Libyan missile installation.

The U.S. show of strength in the Mediterranean, however, did not deter further terrorist violence. On April 2 a bomb blew a hole in the side of a TWA jet over Greece, killing four people. On April 5 a bomb exploded in a Berlin discotheque frequented by American military personnel. The blast killed two persons, including an American soldier, and wounded more than two hundred.

After intelligence indicated that Qaddafi played a role in the Berlin attack, Reagan ordered an air strike against Libya. On the night of April 14 U.S. F-111 bombers based in Britain and carrier planes in the Mediterranean staged a large-scale raid on Libya. The warplanes' targets included a naval academy, air bases, and Qaddafi's home and headquarters. The raid killed at least fifteen people, including Qaddafi's infant daughter, and injured sixty. One U.S. F-111 bomber was shot down, and its two crewmen were killed.

Reagan declared that he ordered the air strike after intercepted Libyan transmissions had proved that Libya had participated in the Berlin bombing. The attack was overwhelmingly supported by the American public and Congress. A *Washington Post*-ABC News poll showed 76 percent of Americans surveyed approved of the strike. The U.S. attack, however, did not receive the same approval overseas. The British government was the only European government to support the bombing, which was widely condemned in the Arab world. France had refused to allow U.S. bombers based in Britain to fly over its territory. Moscow cancelled a scheduled visit to Washington by Foreign Minister Eduard Shevardnadze to protest the strike.

The raid did not end terrorist attacks against the United States. Indeed, on April 17 one American and two British hostages in Lebanon were found executed in retaliation for the attack, and the same day an Arab tried unsuccessfully to smuggle a bomb on board an Israeli airliner in London. Nevertheless, the raid set the precedent that the United States would consider using military force against any state shown to be supporting terrorism, and Libyan involvement in terrorism appeared to decline during the three years after the raid.

Iran-Contra Scandal

In addition to bombings and hijackings, the Reagan administration had to contend with the kidnappings of Americans by pro-Iranian Shi'ite groups in Lebanon. During 1984 and 1985 nine Americans had been kidnapped there. Although a few had been released, the Shi'ite groups continuously held several Americans captive.

The Reagan administration was particularly concerned with the fate of William Buckley, the CIA station chief in Beirut, who was kidnapped in March 1984. Intelligence reports indicated that Buckley was being tortured to extract his knowledge of U.S. antiterrorist operations. While not of the magnitude of the 1979 Iranian hostage crisis, the plight of Buckley and the other American hostages in Lebanon frustrated the Reagan administration and led it to seek their release through methods that conflicted with the administration's policy of not dealing with terrorists.

In 1985 the Reagan administration began considering secret arms sales to Iran through Israel as a way to win the release of U.S. hostages and open a dialogue with "moderate Iranians." Reagan authorized three shipments of U.S. antitank and antiaircraft missiles from Israel to Iran in the late summer and fall. The shipments coincided with the release of one U.S. hostage in September 1985.

On January 17, 1986, President Reagan signed a secret finding authorizing a covert U.S. diplomatic initiative to Iran. The document identified three goals of the plan: "(1) establishing a more moderate government in Iran, (2) obtaining from them significant intelligence not otherwise obtainable, to determine the current Iranian Government's intentions with respect to its neighbors and with respect to terrorist acts, and (3) furthering the release of the American hostages held in Beirut and preventing additional terrorist acts by these groups." During 1986 U.S. representatives communicated with Iran through intermediaries and on one occasion traveled to Iran to seek the release of hostages in Lebanon. During these dealings the United States transferred (with Israel's assistance) additional arms and spare parts for military equipment to Iran. Although two American hostages were released during 1986, three more were kidnapped to take their place.

On November 3 a pro-Syrian Beirut magazine reported on the secret trip by U.S. representatives to Iran earlier in the year. This disclosure led to investigations in the United States that uncovered the Iranian initiative and forced Reagan to admit on November 13 that the United States had shipped arms to Iran. Although Reagan insisted that he had not traded arms for hostages, the initiative appeared to undercut the Reagan administration's policy of not negotiating with terrorists. Moreover, critics charged that Reagan had undermined U.S. standing in the Persian Gulf region, where moderate Arab nations such as Saudi Arabia had been opposing Iran in its war with Iraq.

On November 25 the Iranian initiative was further complicated by the disclosure that National Security Council officials had used some of the proceeds from the arms sales to aid the Nicaraguan contra rebels, despite a U.S. law prohibiting such assistance. This revelation transformed what had been an embarrassing and contradictory policy into a full-fledged scandal.

The Iran-contra affair deeply affected U.S. policy in the Middle East. Moderate Arab governments such as Saudi Arabia, Kuwait, and Jordan, which feared an Iranian victory in the Iran-Iraq war, felt betrayed that the United States would violate its own policy against weapons sales to Iran. The U.S. relationship with Iraq, which had established diplomatic ties with the United States in 1984, also suffered. In addition, the Reagan administration's antiterrorist policies appeared hypocritical. Reagan had urged U.S. allies to support his campaign against terrorism. The revelation that the world's leading antiterrorist had sent arms to a nation that had been implicated in terrorist activities weakened U.S. credibility and international determination to fight terrorism.

Persian Gulf Naval Escorts

In late 1986 Kuwait sought naval protection from the United States and the Soviet Union for its fleet of oil tankers, which Iran had been attacking as they passed through the Gulf. Moscow agreed to lease to Kuwait three Soviet tankers that would carry Kuwaiti oil under the Soviet flag. The Reagan administration, fearful of growing Soviet influence in the Gulf and anxious to reestablish its credibility with moderate Gulf states after its embarrassing sale of weapons to Iran, agreed to reflag eleven Kuwaiti tankers so they could receive U.S. naval protection. The naval escorts were also designed to ensure that Iran would not slow the flow of oil from the Gulf. The move represented a definite U.S. tilt toward Iraq in the Iran-Iraq war.

Critics in Congress charged that the Reagan administration was inviting disaster. They contended that the escort missions were poorly conceived and could drag the United States into the Iran-Iraq war or inspire a new wave of terrorist attacks against the United States.

Despite doubts in Congress about the reflagging, the navy began escorting Kuwaiti oil tankers on July 22, 1987. Two days later a mine explosion damaged one of the tankers, bolstering congressional opposition to the plan. Nevertheless, Reagan sent mine-sweeping helicopters to the Gulf and reaffirmed his commitment to the escorts. By October 1987 the United States had thirty-four ships in the Gulf.

The Persian Gulf naval escorts led to a number of clashes between U.S. ships and Iranian forces attempting to disrupt the flow of oil. American helicopters captured an Iranian boat that was laying mines in the Gulf in September 1987. On April 18, 1988, U.S. ships destroyed two Iranian oil platforms and sank several Iranian ships in retaliation for a mine explosion that damaged the USS *Roberts*. Nevertheless, Iran avoided open confrontations with the vastly superior U.S. naval force in the Gulf, even though it continued its attacks on vessels not under U.S. protection. Kuwaiti tankers sustained damage on several occasions, but the U.S. escorts were generally successful in protecting the Kuwaiti ships.

The U.S. presence, however, did lead to tragedy on July 3, 1988, when the USS *Vincennes* mistook an Iranian airliner for an attacking Iranian warplane and shot it down after the airliner failed to respond to several warnings. All 290 passengers were killed. President Reagan called the tragedy "understandable" but said the United States would offer compensation to the victims' families.

Later in July Reagan's high-risk policy in the Gulf was partially vindicated when Iran accepted a cease-fire in its eight-year war with Iraq. Although the U.S. naval presence in the Gulf had not been the dominant factor in pushing Iran to end the war, the escorts had helped to check Iranian aggression in the Gulf and reestablish some measure of U.S. credibility with the Gulf states. The cease-fire officially began on August 20, allowing the United States to reduce its naval force in the Gulf.

Second-Term Peace Efforts

In February 1985 Jordan's King Hussein and the PLO's Yasir Arafat provided hope that peace negotiations might move ahead. They agreed to form a joint negotiating strategy, a move consistent with the Reagan administration's opinion that a joint Jordanian-Palestinian delegation was necessary to provide legitimate representation for Palestinians. Hussein proposed that such a delegation meet with U.S. officials before formal negotiations begin. The list of Palestinians he recommended, however, included some affiliated with the PLO and therefore unacceptable to the United States, which was bound by a commitment to Israel not to negotiate with the PLO. This longstanding stumbling block temporarily stymied the Reagan administration's peace efforts.

In the fall of 1985 speeches by King Hussein and Israeli prime minister Shimon Peres before the UN General Assembly raised hopes among American policy makers that a breakthrough in the peace process was possible. Both sides seemed to be moving closer together on the issue of how to proceed with negotiations. The Reagan administration encouraged Hussein and Peres to bridge their differences and begin to negotiate. Hussein advocated an international conference under UN auspices with the permanent members of the Security Council and all parties to the conflict, including the PLO, in attendance. The United States opposed such a conference because it would bring the Soviets back into the process. Israel opposed it because the PLO would be involved and the Soviet Union did not have diplomatic relations with Israel. Although the Israelis wanted direct negotiations with Jordan, Prime Minister Peres hoped to compromise with Hussein by accepting the idea of an international conference without Soviet and PLO participation, as a first step leading eventually to direct negotiations between Israel and Jordan.

Despite U.S. encouragement, the distance between Hussein and Peres could not be bridged before October 1986, when Peres handed the post of prime minister to Likud party leader Yitzhak Shamir in accordance with the Israeli coalition government agreement of 1984. Although the Likud promised to continue efforts to begin bilateral negotiations with Jordan, Shamir was less disposed than Peres to make concessions toward achieving this end.

Intifada and the Shultz Plan

Middle East peacemaking efforts were given a new impetus in December 1987 by the Arab uprising in the West Bank and Gaza. This uprising, known as the *intifada*, differed from previous violence in the occupied territories in that it pervaded all areas of the West Bank and Gaza and became a permanent feature of life there. Palestinian youths armed with stones daily confronted Israeli soldiers. The intifada increased international sympathy for the Palestinian cause, highlighted the oppressive aspects of Israeli occupation, and created doubts both inside and outside Israel that the occupation could continue indefinitely.

In response to the intifada, Secretary of State Shultz took up Middle East peacemaking with a new urgency in early 1988. He made several trips to the Middle East, where he shuttled between capitals promoting his plan to start Arab-Israeli negotiations. His plan called for talks between Israel and a joint Palestinian-Jordanian delegation. By the fall the two sides were to agree on arrangements for local elections that would give Palestinians in the occupied territories some autonomy over their affairs for a period of three years. By December the parties were to begin talking about what and how much occupied territory Israel would eventually relinquish. The plan also called for an international peace conference attended by all five permanent members of the UN Security Council, including the Soviet Union. Shultz's plan was not greeted enthusiastically by the Israeli government, which opposed the idea of giving up occupied territory.

In July King Hussein surprised the international community and dealt a blow to Shultz's peace proposal by renouncing Jordan's claims to the West Bank and relinquishing administrative responsibility for it to the PLO. Hussein's action virtually foreclosed Jordan's participation in the peace process, which many Israeli and U.S. leaders had regarded as essential for progress toward a settlement. With Hussein out of the picture and U.S. and Israeli elections approaching in the fall, Shultz's peacemaking efforts made no progress.

U.S.-PLO Dialogue

In a 1975 memo to Israeli leaders, Secretary of State Henry Kissinger had reaffirmed the policy of three U.S. administrations that the United States would not negotiate with the PLO until it renounced terrorism, acknowledged Israel's right to exist, and accepted UN Resolutions 242 and 338. All successive administrations have abided by this approach to the PLO. Yasir Arafat and his organization refused to meet U.S. conditions, and the United States along with Israel rejected any participation by the PLO in Middle East negotiations.

In late 1988, however, Arafat was being pushed to adopt a more moderate stance toward Israel and peace negotiations by the Soviet Union, Egypt, Jordan, and other moderate Arab states. The intifada had not only raised questions about the viability of the Israeli occupation of the West Bank and Gaza but also had increased international sympathy for the Palestinian cause. The PLO determined that it could best take advantage of the intifada by being less confrontational and searching for recognition of a new Palestinian state. Meanwhile, the renunciation of Jordan's ties to the West Bank by King Hussein in July 1988 had caused the United States to take a more careful look at the prospect of negotiating with the PLO.

On November 15, 1988, in Algiers, the Palestine National Council (PNC) declared the existence of an independent Palestinian state. The PNC accepted UN Security Council resolutions 242 and 338 but issued ambiguous statements about its willingness to recognize Israel and renounce terrorism. The U.S. State Department rejected contentions by the PLO that it had satisfied U.S. conditions for a U.S.-PLO dialogue. Nevertheless, the PNC's statements led to a month of diplomatic activity in which the PLO inched its way toward meeting the U.S. conditions.

On November 26 progress toward a U.S.-PLO dialogue appeared to be scuttled when Shultz announced that he would deny Arafat a visa to enter the United States to address the United Nations. The General Assembly, however, voted overwhelmingly to hold a session in Geneva, Switzerland, so Arafat could address the body. In Arafat's UN speech on December 13 he came closer than ever before to uttering the precise words that Shultz wanted to hear, but Shultz again rejected Arafat's statement as insufficient.

Then on December 14 Arafat held a hastily arranged press conference in which he "renounced" rather than just "condemned" terrorism, accepted UN resolutions 242 and 338 without qualification, and affirmed "the right of all parties concerned in the Middle East conflict to exist in peace and security, including the states of Palestine, Israel and their neighbors." *(Text of Arafat statement, Appendix, p. 311)*

Four hours later Shultz announced that Arafat's words had finally satisfied U.S. conditions and that "the U.S. is prepared for a substantive dialogue with the PLO." Shultz instructed the U.S. ambassador in Tunisia to begin negotiations with representatives of the PLO.

Although little progress was made in the negotiations between the PLO and the United States during their first eight months, the talks significantly changed the Middle East peace process. They reaffirmed the position of the United States as the dominant outside peacemaker in the Middle East and made Palestinian nationalism more sensitive to American opinion. The meetings between Israel's closest ally and its bitterest enemy also put pressure on Israeli leaders to construct peace proposals of their own. In addition, the talks gave Yasir Arafat's Fatah branch of the PLO something to lose if it engaged in terrorist acts, since the dialogue was conditioned on a PLO renunciation of terrorism. Although rival PLO factions and individual Palestinians continued to be involved in terrorism, the mainline Fatah faction abstained from terrorist acts during the first half of 1989.

Bush Administration

Even with the opening of a dialogue with the PLO, a move the Israeli government vigorously protested, the Reagan administration's Middle East policy was characterized by its support of Israel. The election of George Bush, Reagan's two-term vice president, seemed to promise continuity in U.S.-Israeli relations and Washington's approach to achieving Middle East peace.

During the spring of 1989 the Bush administration indicated its support for Israel by warmly welcoming Prime Minister Shamir during his April visit to Washington, refusing to pressure Shamir's government to negotiate with the PLO, resisting appeals from moderate Arab leaders to agree to an international peace conference, which the Israeli government opposed, and vetoing a June 9 UN Security Council resolution that denounced Israel for violating the human rights of Palestinians in the occupied territories. In addition, the Bush administration opposed efforts to grant the PLO the status of a state in UN organizations. When the PLO petitioned for membership in the World Health Organization (WHO), an affiliated agency of the United Nations, the United States threatened to withhold its contribution to the WHO as well as to any other international organization that admitted the PLO. On May 12, 1989, the WHO voted 83-47 to delay the decision on PLO admission for another year.

Despite these actions, there were indications that Bush and his foreign policy team might be less patient with Israel than Reagan had been. At two congressional appearances in March, Secretary of State James A. Baker III said that Israel some day might have to negotiate with the PLO about the status of the occupied territories—an approach that the Israeli government had consistently rejected. Then in a May speech to the American-Israeli Public Affairs Committee, a powerful pro-Israel lobbying group, Baker said: "For Israel, now is the time to lay aside, once and for all, the unrealistic vision of a greater Israel. Israeli interests in the West Bank and Gaza—security and otherwise—can be accommodated in a [peace] settlement. Forswear annexation; stop settlement activity; allow [Arab] schools to reopen; reach out to the Palestinians as neighbors who deserve political rights."

Although Baker's comments came within a speech that was pro-Israeli and he was reiterating longstanding U.S. positions, his blunt tone angered Israeli leaders and caused staunch American supporters of Israel to worry that the Bush administration was trying to put more distance between itself and the Jewish state.

Shamir Election Plan

Rather than construct a comprehensive Middle East peace plan of its own, the Bush administration chose to move cautiously during its first months. President Bush decided to back Israeli prime minister Shamir's plan to hold elections in the occupied territories to select local Palestinians who would represent their people in peace negotiations with Israel. Many Palestinian leaders as well as conservative Israelis had rejected the idea, but Bush backed it as the best immediate option for advancing the peace process. Jordan's King Hussein gave a qualified endorsement to the proposal in April 1989.

On June 8 Ambassador Robert H. Pelletreau, Jr., the U.S. envoy to Tunisia who was holding regular talks with the PLO in Tunis, urged the PLO to accept Shamir's election plan. The PLO refused to endorse the plan but indicated some interest in it. Administration officials had hinted that if the PLO accepted the Israeli election proposal, the United States would upgrade its dialogue with the PLO to higher-ranking officials.

The right wing of Shamir's own Likud party, however, opposed the plan and maneuvered to force Shamir to accept conditions that most observers believed would make it unacceptable to any Palestinian leader. Polls showed 60 percent of Israelis favoring the plan but 55 percent of right-wing voters opposing it. On July 5, before a Likud party convention, Shamir accepted the hard-line conditions of party conservatives, which stated that Arab residents of East Jerusalem could not vote in the elections or run for office; no elections would be held until the Palestinian uprising ended; Israel would not give up any territory and no Palestinian state would ever be established; and Jewish settlements would continue to be built in the occupied territories. Because the riders were backed by a large faction of his party, Shamir could not reject them without risking a no-confidence vote from his party. The Labor party threatened to withdraw from Israel's unity government over the riders, but it did not do so, partly because the United States urged it to remain in the government.

On July 9 PLO leader Arafat announced his organization would no longer consider supporting the plan. He criticized the United States' "unconditional" support of Israel, which he said encouraged the Likud party to attach the riders to the plan. Senior Palestinian officials indicated in late July that they would endorse Shamir's election plan only if Israel agreed in principle to give up land for the creation of a Palestinian state and residents of East Jerusalem would be allowed to participate in the elections. The Israeli government rejected these conditions.

The Bush administration responded to the Likud's move by warning that if the vote plan were crippled by added conditions it might have to consider organizing an international conference to reinvigorate the Middle East peace process. Secretary of State Baker told reporters July 8, "Our calculus all along has been that if things totally bog down, if you can't make progress with this election proposal, then we would have to look a little bit more closely at the prospects for an international conference. There is an awful lot of support for that out there from other countries. We have always said that an international conference, properly structured, at the right time, might be useful." Although an international peace conference had been frequently rejected by the Likud party, it had qualified support from the Labor party.

Bush Confronts Terrorism

The first months of the Bush administration indicated that President Bush, like presidents Carter and Reagan, would face challenges from terrorists who targeted U.S. citizens and interests.

On July 28, 1989, Israeli commandos abducted Sheik Abdul Karim Obeid, a spiritual leader of the pro-Iranian Shi'ite Hizballah group that was holding several Americans and Israelis hostage in Lebanon. In response, a Shi'ite organization released a videotape that purported to show the hanging of Marine Lt. Col. William R. Higgins, a U.S. hostage held in Lebanon.

American investigators determined that the man in the video was Higgins, although they could not verify when he had been hanged. The Shi'ite group threatened to kill another hostage unless the Israelis released Obeid. The Israelis offered to trade Obeid and other Shi'ite prisoners for all Israeli and Western hostages being held by the Shi'ites. The Bush administration, while saying it would not make concessions to terrorists, explored ways to release U.S. hostages in Lebanon and welcomed an offer in August from the Iranian government to help secure their freedom.

Soviets Seek Stronger Role

After Camp David the Soviet Union continued to be shut out of the Arab-Israeli peace process despite Soviet protests. During the late 1970s and early 1980s the focus of Soviet efforts to be included in the peace process was a resumption of the Geneva Conference or the establishment of another international forum. Israel, however, strongly opposed Soviet participation in an international conference because the two nations had no relations, Moscow's harsh denunciation of the Camp David accords had angered Israel, and Israeli leaders were wary of the international pressure that such a conference might place on Israel to give up occupied territory.

The United States, meanwhile, sought to exclude the Soviets to minimize Soviet influence in the region. With the success of Camp David still fresh, neither the Carter nor the Reagan administrations felt compelled to advocate resuming the 1977 Geneva Conference with Soviet participation. Moreover, Reagan's strongly anti-Communist positions during his first term precluded virtually any dealings with the Soviet Union on regional issues.

Strategic Interests

The Reagan administration's "strategic consensus" policy, which Secretary of State Haig put forth soon after taking office, identified the Soviet Union as the primary source of instability throughout the world, including the Middle East. The United States sought the help of nations in that region to counter Soviet power. The Soviet Union, seeing a threat to its interests in this combative U.S. position, aggressively continued its policy of trying to undermine Western, particularly American, influence in the area.

The Soviets' efforts to exploit regional crises and weaken Western influence among the Arab states were hindered by several factors. Although generally considered a friend to the Arabs in their struggle against Israel, the Soviet Union proved to be an unreliable partner at times and was in no position to pressure Israel for concessions. Moreover, most Arab nations distrusted the Soviets because of their Communist ideology and atheistic philosophy. The Soviets also proved unable to forge a united front among their closest Arab allies. In particular Syria frequently feuded with Iraq and the PLO.

In December 1979 the Soviets seriously damaged their own standing in the Moslem world by invading neighboring Afghanistan to prop up a pro-Soviet Marxist government against Moslem rebels who controlled the countryside. The use of modern weapons and more than 100,000 Soviet troops against their Moslem brethren angered Arabs and called to mind Soviet pressure against Iran and Turkey after World War II. Moderate Arab governments such as Saudi Arabia, Jordan, and Kuwait took the threat of Soviet aggression more seriously. Egypt and Saudi Arabia sent aid to the rebels. The invasion also harmed Soviet relations with revolutionary Iran. That country condemned the Soviet Union as "a Great Satan" second only to the United States. In May 1983 the government disbanded the Iranian Communist Tudeh party.

Soviet problems with Arab regimes were both ideological and practical. Libya is a good example. The Libyans were a major benefactor of Soviet arms and received Soviet diplomatic support, but the two countries continued to differ on a number of issues. Libya's Muammar Qaddafi rejected the possibility of ever making peace with Israel while the Soviets repeatedly supported the permanent existence of the Jewish state. On the practical side Moscow regarded Libya's aggression in North Africa as undermining the Soviet position there. Soviet leaders were also hesitant to expand relations with Libya because of Qaddafi's unpredictable behavior and rhetoric that made him a potential target of Western enmity. After the April 1986 U.S. bombing of Libya, Moscow cancelled a trip to Washington by the Soviet foreign minister but did little else to support Libya.

In trying to enhance its own influence, undercut the U.S. position, and divide the traditionally pro-West regimes in the region, Soviet propagandists sought to tie American policy as closely as possible to Israeli policy. After Israel bombed the nearly completed Iraqi Osirak nuclear reactor in 1981, the Soviets charged that the United States, by providing the planes used by Israel, supported the attack. However, the argument failed to bring the Iraqis closer to the Soviets or to expand Soviet influence in the region. The Soviet charge was weakened when the United States sharply criticized the attack and joined in a UN resolution condemning the raid.

Israel's invasion of Lebanon in 1982 provided the Soviets with a similar opportunity to exploit the relationship of the United States and Israel. The Soviets pointed to continued U.S. support for Israel as evidence that U.S. and Israeli policies were identical. This strategy diverted attention from the Soviet occupation of Afghanistan and reinforced the view that the main threat to the region was the United States and Israel and not the Soviet Union as the Reagan administration was claiming. Moscow also opposed efforts by the United States to introduce peacekeeping troops into Lebanon and supported Syrian opposition to the U.S.-mediated accord between Lebanon and Israel.

During the early 1980s the Soviets focused on developing close relations with hard-line Arab states through arms sales and mutual cooperation agreements. Moscow carried on sustained arms sales relationships with Algeria, Iraq, Libya, and Syria during this period. Not only did these sales of highly sophisticated weapons bring needed revenue to the Soviet Union, they provided it with political influence because the Arab nations buying Soviet weapons were dependent on Moscow for maintenance and spare parts. After the Israelis decimated Syria's air force and antiaircraft missile systems at the outset of their invasion of Lebanon, the Soviets did not respond quickly, preferring to avoid a confrontation with Israel and the United States. Later, however, the Soviets gradually replaced Syria's losses.

Diplomacy under Gorbachev

The rise of a more creative and flexible diplomacy under Soviet President Mikhail Gorbachev offers the prospect that Moscow will become more involved in the peace process. Before Gorbachev came to power in March 1985 the Soviet Union had relied almost exclusively on hard-line Arab states such as Libya and Syria to promote Soviet interests in the Middle East. Gorbachev widened Soviet strategy by seeking improved relations with moderate Arab nations, pushing its hard-line allies to be more conciliatory, and opening a dialogue with Israel. His intention appeared to be to carve out a place for the Soviet Union in the Arab-Israeli peace process and build an image of the Soviet Union as a flexible, fair-minded superpower interested in resolving regional problems.

Gorbachev's efforts to improve relations with moderate Arab countries were aided by his extraction of Soviet forces from Afghanistan. In 1987 only Libya, Syria, and South Yemen refused to vote for a UN General Assembly resolution denouncing the Soviet presence in Afghanistan. As it became clear during 1987 and 1988 that the Soviets were headed toward a withdrawal, Arab attitudes softened toward Moscow.

The Soviets' acceptance of Kuwait's 1987 request for help in escorting its tankers through the Persian Gulf prompted the U.S. move to provide similar protection against Iranian harassment. Earlier in October 1985, two other Gulf states, Oman and the United Arab Emirates, had established diplomatic relations with the Soviet Union.

In 1987 the Soviets also improved their relations with Egypt by settling a dispute over Egypt's repayment of Soviet loans for military equipment. Since 1977 Egypt had refused to repay the loans and Moscow had withheld spare parts for the Soviet-made weapons in Egypt's arsenal. After the two countries agreed on terms for repayment they signed new economic agreements and Egypt allowed the Soviets to reopen their consulates in Alexandria and Port Said. In 1988 Egypt announced its support for an international Middle East peace conference in which Moscow would play a leading role.

In December 1987 King Hussein visited Moscow for the first time since 1981. His frustration at the refusal of the U.S. Congress to sanction arms sales to Jordan during the mid-1980s led him to seek Soviet weapons to supplement those Jordan bought from Great Britain.

Gorbachev has also pushed Soviet allies in the region to adopt a more conciliatory stance toward Israel. For example, Moscow reportedly pressured PLO leader Arafat to explicitly recognize Israel's right to exist and renounce terrorism in December 1988. During 1988 and 1989 the Soviet Union also quietly urged Syria to negotiate with Israel.

Improved Relations with Israel

While working to improve ties with Arab nations, Gorbachev sought to establish a dialogue with Israel and perhaps move toward a normalization of relations. In August 1986 Soviet and Israeli diplomats met in Helsinki to discuss the establishment of consulates. The meeting was the first official diplomatic contact between the two nations since relations were severed after the 1967 Six-Day War. A month later Soviet Foreign Minister Shevardnadze met with Israeli prime minister Shimon Peres at the United Nations. As a result of these meetings a Soviet consular delegation set up shop in Israel in July 1987 to look after Soviet property in Israel.

In April 1987 Gorbachev impressed the Israelis by announcing in the presence of Syria's President Hafez Assad that seeking a military solution to the Middle East conflict "has completely lost its credibility." Since then there have been many Soviet-Israeli gestures of good will. The Soviets greatly expanded the number of exit visas granted to Jews and allowed a Jewish cultural center to open in Moscow. In addition Soviet artistic groups frequently performed in Israel and Israeli medical teams flew to Armenia to treat the victims of that region's 1988 earthquake. In July 1989 the Soviet Union agreed for the first time since 1967 to allow an Israeli company to process normal Soviet tourist visas for Israeli citizens.

Many observers have speculated that the two nations will reestablish relations in the near future. Soviet spokesmen have said that Gorbachev regards the breaking of ties to Israel as a mistake. In July 1989 a Kuwaiti newspaper quoted Soviet Deputy Foreign Minister Gennadi Tarassov as saying, "A time will come when normal relations are restored [with Israel]." Nevertheless the two nations appear to be at an impasse on renewing relations: Israel has demanded that the Soviet Union reestablish ties before it will agree to Soviet participation in a Middle East peace conference, while Moscow insists that it will not restore relations until Israel agrees to such a conference.

Shevardnadze Tour

In February 1989 Shevardnadze traveled throughout the Middle East to try to establish a role for the Soviet Union in the Middle East peace process. The visit came as the new Bush administration was still putting together its foreign policy team and developing foreign policy strategies. The visit appeared designed to express the Soviets' desire to expand their role in Middle East peacemaking and their willingness to step into the temporary vacuum created by the Bush administration's slow start. The visit also appeared timed to take advantage of recently improved Arab perceptions of the Soviet Union brought on by the completion of the Soviet withdrawal from Afghanistan earlier in the month.

Shevardnadze met with Egypt's President Mubarak, Syria's President Assad, Jordan's King Hussein, the PLO's Chairman Arafat, Israel's Foreign Minister Moshe Arens, and Iran's leader Ayatollah Khomeini. Shevardnadze became the first high-level Soviet official to visit Cairo since Anwar Sadat expelled Soviet advisers from Egypt in 1972. Mubarak accepted Shevardnadze's invitation to make an official visit to Moscow later in the year. Shevardnadze also reportedly tried to heal the rift between the Soviet Union's Syrian and PLO allies that had complicated its peacemaking role.

4

Arms Sales: A Thriving Bazaar

The Arabs and the Israelis fought their first war in 1948 largely with weapons from the scrap heap of World War II—odd collections of planes, tanks, and rifles bought on the glutted world arms market. That war, and every subsequent conflict in the region, set off a scramble for newer and more powerful weapons. By the mid-1970s the quest for military security had exploded into the world's most intense and sustained regional arms race, financed on the Arab side by oil wealth and on the Israeli side by U.S. aid. While insisting they wanted restraint, the superpowers and the industrialized countries of the West were more than willing to open their arsenals to the region's competing armies.

The Middle East has led all regions of the world in arms imports ever since the end of the Vietnam War, according to the U.S. Arms Control and Disarmament Agency. Throughout the 1980s Israel, the Arab countries, and Iran together imported an annual average of more than $15 billion in foreign armaments and services—an amount far exceeding that of any other nonindustrialized region.

Although Israel was viewed widely as the region's most powerful and heavily armed country, its spending on weapons was outstripped by Arab countries with oil wealth or with close ties to the Soviet Union. Saudi Arabia, Iraq, Libya, and Syria each imported substantially more military equipment than Israel.

Beginning in 1980 the war between Iran and Iraq helped fuel Middle East arms spending during the decade. Those two countries bought billions of dollars of arms to throw at each other and heightened the horror of modern warfare by resorting to chemical weapons. Their nervous neighbors increased their arms spending to guard against a widening of the war.

The apparent end of that war in 1988—coupled with declining oil revenues—held out the prospect for at least a pause in the arms race. Several countries were considering scaling back their ambitious plans to modernize weapons systems they acquired in the 1970s. The advent of the Bush administration also generated a modest level of hope that the long-stalled "peace process" could be revived, thus diminishing the underlying tensions in the region.

History, however, argued against any sudden cooling of passions in the Middle East, and every country there continued to be concerned about its security. Both Iran and Iraq were seeking to rebuild their damaged and depleted supplies of military hardware after the war, fostering re-newed concerns among their neighbors. Moreover, outside powers continued to provide the nations of the region with advanced weapons that could damage prospects for peace and stability. One such action was the Soviet Union's sale of long-range bombers to Libya early in 1989, a sale that Israelis viewed as threatening their national security. Another adverse trend was the evident reluctance of several industrialized countries to block exports to the region of equipment and technology used for the production of chemical weapons and ballistic missiles.

Indeed, by the end of the 1980s, there were signs that the Middle East arms race could be entering a new and even more dangerous phase:

● Outside arms suppliers, especially the two superpowers, were providing increasingly sophisticated weapons throughout the region. Israel and its major Arab opponents began acquiring top-of-the-line warplanes, missiles, and tanks almost as soon as they entered service in the forces of the United States and the Soviet Union. This trend has fostered a self-generating cycle, with every country competing to match the firepower of its potential enemies.

● Every significant military power in the Middle East had obtained at least the capability to produce chemical weapons, along with missiles or bombers that could deliver the poison arms to distant targets. Israel continued to add to its nuclear arsenal, apparently regarding a strong nuclear force as the ultimate safeguard against an overwhelming Arab attack or the development of atomic weapons by hostile Arab states.

● The United States and the Soviet Union both boosted their direct military presence in the region, largely in response to the Iran-Iraq war. The most visible superpower force in the region in the late 1980s was the massive U.S. naval deployment protecting neutral shipping in the Persian Gulf. Washington started to reduce its forces after the cease-fire in the Gulf war, but the naval buildup appeared likely to leave the U.S. military presence in the region much larger than it had been before the war. The Israeli invasion of Lebanon in 1982 also led to a substantial increase in the number of Soviet military personnel stationed in Syria. In addition each superpower was enhancing its ability to project forces into the region. The United States had formal or informal access to military facilities in Oman, Kenya, Israel, Egypt, Saudi Arabia, and Bahrain. The Soviet Union had similar access in Ethiopia, South Yemen, and Syria.

● Middle Eastern countries were finding it possible to obtain arms from a wider variety of sources. If an arms request were rebuffed by one of the superpowers, a country could turn to European firms to obtain weapons of comparable quality. Latin American and Asian countries, including China, also were providing increasingly sophisticated weapons to the Middle East. To reduce their reliance on outside powers, several countries developed their own arms industries that became skilled at producing copies of foreign-built weapons. Israel, however, was the only country in the region with an arms industry able to develop original weapons systems and advanced versions of weapons produced elsewhere.

As the arms race made the Middle East a more dangerous neighborhood, diplomatic efforts made little progress toward slowing the growth of the region's arsenals. Each country worried first about its own safety; seeing the sales of weapons to other nations, it feared that falling behind could jeopardize its fundamental security.

Secretary of State George P. Shultz in 1988 echoed the sentiments of many observers from the Middle East and the international community when he warned Israel and the Arab states that their old means of obtaining security—guarded borders, heavily armed infantry forces, and sophisticated warplanes—were no longer adequate in an age of fast missiles and poison- or nuclear-tipped warheads capable of killing thousands or millions of people. Only peace treaties, signed in good faith and vigorously monitored, could provide long-term security, he said.

History of Escalation

Throughout the modern history of the Middle East, Western leaders—and some of the principal actors in the region—have decried the buildup of military forces in an area of such intense religious, political, and ethnic conflict. Periodic attempts to restrain the arms race, however, all were unsuccessful, usually victimized by war.

The Western powers actually agreed once to limit the flow of weapons into the Middle East. That was the U.S.-British-French Tripartite Declaration of May 25, 1950, responding to Israeli concerns that an arms race would threaten that country's security. The three countries declared their opposition to the "development of an arms race between the Arab states and Israel." The declaration was silent, however, on the question of arms competition among the Arab countries.

From 1950 to 1955 cooperation among the Western nations kept the Arab-Israeli arms rivalry at a low pitch. However, Britain, the major arms supplier during this period, found itself drawn into an arms race between Egypt and Iraq, longstanding rivals in the Arab world. To maintain its oil interests in Iraq and to ensure Baghdad's association with the West in the cold war, Britain furnished aircraft and training to create an Iraqi air force. To ensure's Egypt's acceptance of continued British control of the Suez Canal, Britain also helped to create an Egyptian air force. Soon, Israel, realizing that the Tripartite Declaration was breaking down, began searching for arms suppliers.

The Search for Arms

Israel's success in finding weapons was demonstrated in a February 1955 retaliatory raid into the Gaza Strip that killed more than thirty Egyptian soldiers. Egyptian president Gamal Abdel Nasser sought Western arms to restore the military balance, but he was rejected. After that refusal—coupled with the establishment of a mutual defense treaty linking Britain, Iraq, Turkey, Iran, and Pakistan—Nasser turned to the Soviet Union. He persuaded Moscow that an Egypt supplied with Soviet arms could be useful to the Kremlin's efforts to weaken Western positions in the Middle East. A September 1955 deal between Egypt and Czechoslovakia established, indirectly, a pattern of Egyptian dependence on Soviet arms that was to last for nearly twenty years.

In September 1955, after the disclosure of the Czech-Egyptian deal, Israel pressed the Eisenhower administration to provide it with arms. After a six-month delay, Israel was informed—through testimony by Secretary of State John Foster Dulles to the Senate Foreign Relations Committee—that it should rely for security not on U.S. arms but on the "collective security" of the United Nations.

Washington, eager to line up Arab allies in the cold war with the Soviet Union and to preserve its oil interests, remained reluctant until the early 1960s to become a direct arms supplier to Israel. However, the Eisenhower administration quietly encouraged its Western European allies to meet Israel's defense needs. The extent of U.S. involvement in European sales was not fully known until the disclosure in December 1964 of secret West German arms shipments to Israel, made with tacit U.S. endorsement. Egypt reacted to that disclosure by threatening to recognize East Germany—a threat that led Bonn abruptly to halt the arms flow to Israel.

Israel also had turned to Britain for arms but was advised by Prime Minister Anthony Eden to make concessions to the Arabs to avoid war. France viewed the Czech-Egyptian arms agreement in the context of its colonial war with the Moslem nationalists in Algeria. Concerned that Soviet bloc arms would find their way from Cairo to Algiers, France first sought an agreement from Nasser not to assist the Algerians. When Nasser refused, the French decided to honor Israel's request for weapons. They viewed arming Israel as a way to pin down Egypt's armed forces. France reexamined its Middle East arms sale policy in 1962 after Algeria gained its independence. Paris began discussing arms sales with Arab countries, including Jordan, Lebanon, and Egypt.

The shift in French policy, the termination of German arms, and the continued flow of Soviet arms to Arab countries forced the United States in the early 1960s to reconsider its position on supplying weapons to Israel.

The first major U.S.-Israel arms agreement came in September 1962, when Washington provided Hawk antiaircraft missiles. Three years later Israel obtained its first commitment for M-48 Patton tanks.

The aftermath of the Six-Day War in June 1967 saw the first great explosion in arms sales to the region, with all the combatants seeking to fill arsenals that were depleted in the brief but brutal conflict. Egypt, which had lost much of its air force to Israel's preemptive raids, turned to the Soviet Union; most other Arab countries shopped for arms in Western Europe; and Israel once again pressed Washington for weapons.

The United States and Israel had crossed an important threshold toward becoming strategic, as well as political, allies in 1966 when President Lyndon B. Johnson agreed for the first time to sell combat aircraft to Israel. That sale

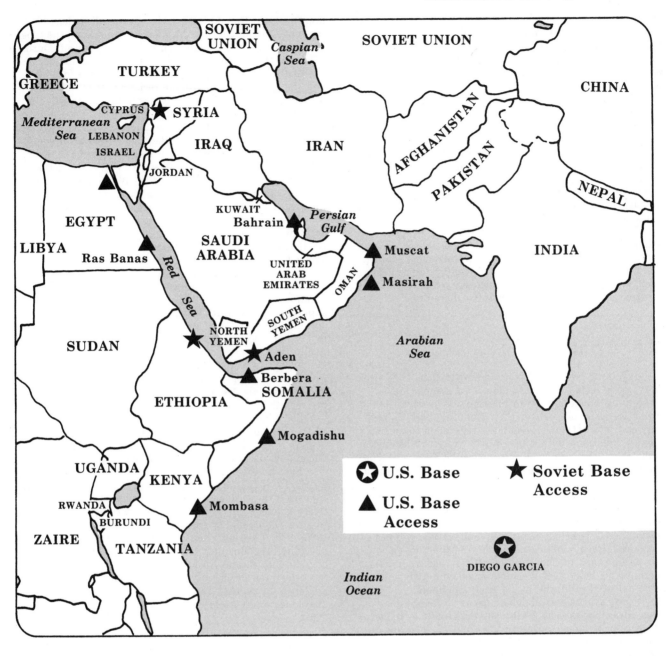

involved forty-eight A-4 Skyhawk fighter-bombers, but the planes did not arrive in Israel until 1968, a year after the Six-Day War. Perhaps more significant than the sale was Johnson's implied commitment for the United States to serve as arms supplier to Israel.

The arms buildup became much more intense after the 1973 war, which had demonstrated the serious military weaknesses of both the Israeli and Arab sides. To overcome those defects, all the major powers in the region sought increasingly sophisticated weapons.

With the oil embargo against the United States and some European countries leading to a quadrupling of oil prices, many Arab countries suddenly had the means to purchase vast new arsenals of advanced weapons. In the first year after the 1973 war, the Middle Eastern countries absorbed about 57 percent of all arms exported throughout the world. The region remained the world's most lucrative arms market through the 1970s and 1980s. In the decade between 1977 and 1986, the Middle East accounted for nearly 40 percent of the world's arms trade.

A Growing Arms Market

The Middle East accounted for the bulk of the sharp increase in U.S. arms sales beginning in the 1970s. From total overseas sales of less than $1 billion in 1970, U.S. shipments jumped nearly ninefold by 1974 and exceeded $10 billion annually through most of the 1980s.

France and Britain—the principal Western arms suppliers for the region in the 1950s and 1960s—also stepped up their sales programs after the 1973 war. France was a major source of weapons for Saudi Arabia, Iraq, Egypt, Jordan, and several of the smaller Gulf states. Britain found markets in the same countries, though its sales were far below France's. The Soviet Union, which in the 1960s was the major source of weapons for Egypt, Syria, and Iraq, began expanding its activities in the 1970s, especially after the 1973 war and Egyptian president Anwar Sadat's break with Moscow. By the early 1980s the Soviet Union was pouring nearly twice as many arms—in dollar terms—into the region as was the United States. Iraq became the major recipient of Soviet-made weapons, followed by Syria and Libya.

Israel was especially uneasy about the buildup of Soviet arms in Syria. Starting after June 1982, when Israel devastated the Syrian military during fighting in Lebanon, the Kremlin shipped hundreds of tanks and advanced warplanes to Syria. In addition, several thousand Soviet military advisers were stationed in Syria, most of them running sophisticated radar and antiaircraft systems.

Throughout the region, the quantity of weapons was matched by improvements in quality. Israel, Syria, and Saudi Arabia possessed some of the world's most sophisticated nonnuclear weapons. Israel itself produced some items of military hardware, especially electronics, that matched anything coming from U.S. laboratories.

U.S. Arms Policy

Beginning with the Nixon administration, U.S. arms sales policy rested on two fundamental assumptions:

• Helping "moderate" Arab governments modernize their armed forces would bolster their standing, both domestically and internationally, and encourage them to maintain friendly relations with the United States. Washington would then have greater influence over the actions of those governments, contributing to political and military stability in the region.

• Israel would be able, through its own resources and U.S. aid, to maintain a "qualitative" edge over any possible combination of Arab foes, even though the Arabs vastly outnumbered Israel in manpower and in many types of weaponry. Each administration in Washington elevated this assumption to the level of official policy, in effect guaranteeing Israel that Washington would not allow Israel to be defeated militarily by its Arab neighbors.

Nearly every political debate in the United States over arms sales since the late 1970s centered around a challenge by successive Israeli governments—and their staunchest American supporters—to both of those assumptions. The Israelis argued that there were no "moderate" Arab states so long as they remained technically at war. Arming the Arabs, according to this view, did nothing to encourage them toward peace and merely forced Israel to spend more on defense. Israel also has disputed the U.S. assertion that Israel's "qualitative edge" in armaments over the Arabs is sufficient to guarantee its security.

Ending, or at least slowing, the Middle East arms race was a cherished goal of Jimmy Carter when he became president in 1977. But Carter was in office for only a few months when he encountered, and agreed to, requests by Israel, Iran, and Saudi Arabia for large amounts of advanced weapons. Carter made no headway in his campaign to persuade the Soviet Union, France, Britain, and other suppliers to restrain their arms shipments to volatile regions such as the Middle East.

The Reagan administration, by contrast, tended to view arms sales not as a scourge to be ended but as a fact of life. President Ronald Reagan significantly broadened both the range of countries receiving U.S. weapons and the types of equipment that Washington was willing to sell. During his term, the Stinger portable antiaircraft missile became one of the most sought-after weapons in the Middle East, and the Pentagon had trouble resisting claims by various leaders in the region that they were vulnerable without a few of the missiles.

Partly because he was so amenable to arms sales requests, Reagan had more trouble than any of his predecessors in persuading Congress that selling weapons to moderate Arabs was appropriate policy. After an early victory in his battle to sell AWACS (Airborne Warning and Control System) radar planes to Saudi Arabia, Reagan had to negotiate with Congress over every major arms sale to Arab countries. By the middle of Reagan's second term, Congress had succeeded in blocking all sales to Jordan, effectively ending a military relationship dating from the early 1950s. Congress also halted a major Saudi request for new warplanes, causing the Saudis to turn to Europe.

The disclosure in November 1986 that the Reagan administration, with Israeli assistance, secretly had been supplying antiaircraft and antitank missiles to Iran caused a political scandal in the United States—and a sharp drop in U.S. prestige in the Middle East. Leaders of moderate Arab states appeared to be genuinely shocked that the United States would help arm the radical regime in Tehran. Doubly surprising was the strong indication that Reagan, despite his denials, was selling the weapons to secure the release of U.S. hostages held in Lebanon. The scandal widened when further investigation revealed that members of the Reagan administration had used profits from the Iranian arms sales to aid antigovernment contras rebels in Nicaragua, despite a congressional ban on such aid.

The political and diplomatic controversy far outweighed the military significance of the Iran arms sales. Iran used the U.S.-supplied TOW antitank missiles effectively against Iraq, but the numbers were not great enough to alter the course of the war. The arms sales to Iran in 1985-1986 departed from the established U.S. policy of providing weapons only to dependable pro-Western countries in the Middle East. Nevertheless the arms-for-hostages deal was consistent with the Reagan administration's tendency to quickly resort to military means or covert diplomacy when attempting to solve an international problem.

Israel

The 1967 war and the advent of the presidential campaign in 1968 combined to produce political pressure in the United States to supply Israel with the most advanced aircraft and weapons in the U.S. arsenal. Both the Republican and Democratic party platforms called for an effort to end the arms race in the Middle East, but they added that the United States should sell Israel the latest supersonic warplanes as long as other suppliers continued pouring weapons into the region.

Congress during the 1968 election year led the campaign for arms sales to Israel. The fiscal 1969 Foreign Aid Authorization Act (PL 90-554) called on the president to negotiate the sale of supersonic aircraft to Israel that would provide it with a deterrent force capable of preventing "future Arab aggression." Congress's unflinching support of arms sales to Israel was to become a familiar part of the U.S. political landscape. In October 1968, just a month before the election, President Johnson announced that he had instructed Secretary of State Dean Rusk to open negotiations for the sale of jets to Israel. The sale of fifty Phantom F-4 jets was announced by the administration in late December of that year.

The following year, in the fiscal 1970-1971 Foreign Military Sales Act, Congress called for arms control negotiations in the Middle East—but at the same time it backed President Richard Nixon's position that the United States should sell arms to Israel and other friendly nations in the region to meet threats to their security. In 1970, as part of the fiscal 1971 Defense Procurement Authorization Act, Congress expressed "grave concern" over the "deepening involvement of the Soviet Union" in the Middle East. In response to Moscow's actions, the law authorized the transfer of an unlimited amount of aircraft and supporting equipment to Israel through sales, credits, or loan guarantees.

The growing congressional backing of Israel was prompted by two factors: genuine public support and concern for Israel in the face of the vast military buildup by the Arab countries; and an increasingly sophisticated lobbying effort on Israel's behalf by Jewish organizations in the United States.

Groups such as the American-Israel Public Affairs Committee (AIPAC) increased support for Israel by portraying it as the lone democracy in a region of militaristic, authoritarian regimes.

After the 1973 war U.S. military assistance to Israel entered a new phase. Prior to that time all U.S. aid to Israel had been on either a cash sale or credit basis, with Israel required to pay market rates on its credit. Because of the magnitude of Israel's needs and the heavy toll the war had taken on the Israeli economy and military forces, Washington agreed for the first time to provide outright grants of military aid.

President Nixon on October 19, 1973, called on Congress to approve his request for $2.2 billion in military aid to Israel "to prevent the emergency of a substantial imbalance resulting from a large-scale resupply of Syria and Egypt by the Soviet Union."

The U.S. decision to resupply Israel triggered the Arab oil embargo, but this did not deter the United States. *(Oil embargo, Chapter 6, p. 112)*

By 1975 U.S. aid had enabled Israel to build its armaments to numbers in excess of what they had been at the time of the 1973 war. Supplies of tanks increased to 2,700 from 1,700, and combat aircraft to 486 from 308. The United States agreed in January 1975 to supply Israel with 200 short-range Lance missiles—a weapon not previously in the Israeli arsenal.

Not wanting to rely entirely on other countries, Israel began rapidly expanding its own arms industry, specializing in developing improved versions of weapons it bought from the United States, France, and other suppliers. A prominent example was the Kfir fighter-bomber—an advanced version of the French Mirage III. Israel also produced high-quality tanks and artillery that many military analysts regarded as superior to those purchased by Arab countries from the Soviet Union, the United States, and other countries.

Because of sustained Arab rearmament efforts, however, Israel constantly had to acquire or build more advanced weapons to maintain a "qualitative edge" over the Arabs, who collectively held a numerical advantage in weapons over Israel. Successive U.S. administrations com-

U.S. Arms Sales, 1950-1987 [a]

Saudi Arabia	$30,345,845,000
Israel	12,081,341,000
Iran	11,176,039,000
Egypt	7,512,039,000
Jordan	1,836,114,000
Kuwait	1,528,685,000
United Arab Emirates	841,208,000
Bahrain	706,041,000
Lebanon	637,565,000
North Yemen	337,723,000
Oman	89,426,000
Libya	28,249,000
Iraq	13,152,000
Qatar	3,132,000
Syria	1,000
South Yemen	0

[a] Total dollar value of defense articles and defense services purchased with cash, credit, and U.S. grants.

Source: Defense Intelligence Agency.

mitted the United States to helping Israel maintain its military superiority by ensuring, as stated by Secretary of State Shultz on September 14, 1984, "Israel's qualitative edge in armaments over any possible combination of adversaries."

To finance the Israeli buildup and bolster that country's economy, Washington by the mid-1970s was providing annually to Israel an average of nearly $2 billion in military and economic aid—half in grants and half in loans.

The Ford administration moved in 1975 to upgrade Israel's air force, agreeing to sell twenty-five of the most sophisticated planes in the U.S. arsenal: the F-15. Israel requested another twenty-five F-15s in 1978, along with one hundred fifty F-16 fighters. President Carter's Middle East arms package presented to Congress in April 1978, however, declared the administration's intention to sell Israel only fifteen F-15s and seventy-five F-16s. When Congress threatened to block the entire package because it included sixty F-16 planes for Saudi Arabia, Carter agreed to allow another twenty F-15s for Israel—putting that country's total fleet of F-15s at sixty as well. The Senate approved that arms package on May 15 after one of the earliest major battles in Congress over weapons sales to Arab countries.

Camp David. During negotiations in 1978-1979 between Israel and Egypt that led to the Camp David peace treaty, President Carter promised both countries that the United States would support their peace efforts with financial rewards and security guarantees. Carter made the following commitments to Israel, all included in side letters or other documents accompanying the March 1979 peace treaty:

● An $800 million grant to cover part of the cost of

relocating to the Negev Desert two sophisticated air bases that Israel had built in the Sinai Peninsula since the 1967 war. Israeli officials estimated the cost of building the new bases at about $4 billion. In addition the United States agreed to provide "managerial and technical assistance" for the base relocation.

• Long-term loans to enable Israel to buy $2.2 billion in arms from the United States. Purchases were to include 200 tanks, 800 armored personnel carriers, and substantial numbers of air-to-ground missiles and artillery weapons.

• Early delivery of the seventy-five F-16 planes that Israel had bought from the United States in 1978. (The delivery of fourteen of the F-16s, along with two F-15s, was held up by President Reagan in June and July 1981 following Israel's bombing of the Iraqi nuclear reactor near Baghdad and the subsequent air raid on suspected Palestine Liberation Organization headquarters in Beirut, Lebanon. Reagan lifted the freeze that August. Reagan in 1982 also held up approval of another sale of seventy-five F-16s as a protest against Israel's invasion of Lebanon; that ban was lifted in May 1983.)

• Expanded arrangements for cooperation between the United States and Israel on research and development of weapons.

In one important respect, however, the Camp David security arrangements were an economic setback for Israel. In previous years, Washington was providing half of U.S. military aid to Israel in the form of grants and half in the form of loans. Military aid was averaging about $1 billion a year in the late 1970s, before Camp David, along with slightly under $800 million a year in economic aid. To ease the strain his Camp David package would put on the U.S. budget, Carter proposed that all military aid to both Israel and Egypt be in the form of long-term loans at existing market rates. Consequently, hundreds of millions of dollars in U.S. aid to Israel was transformed from grants to loans that would have to be paid back. However, both countries would be able to defer making payments on the principal for ten years, after which they would have twenty years to pay off the balance.

Both chambers of Congress approved Carter's Camp David aid requests by overwhelming margins in May 1979. That action set in motion a significant escalation of U.S. military and economic involvement in the Middle East— and guaranteed that Israel and Egypt would continue to be the two biggest recipients of U.S. foreign aid for years to come.

After the one-time jump in military aid to about $4 billion in fiscal 1979, Israel's military aid from the United States returned to about $1 billion the following year, only to rise back to $1.4 billion in fiscal 1981 and 1982, with all of the increase in the form of grants. As part of a 1981 deal to get the Senate to approve the sale of AWACS radar planes to Saudi Arabia, President Reagan agreed to give Israel an additional $300 million annually in military aid for fiscal 1983 and 1984. Although originally intended to be temporary, this increase became permanent. Reagan proposed, and Congress approved, additional grants that increased military aid to $1.8 billion beginning in fiscal 1986. Reagan and Congress also gradually increased U.S. economic aid to Israel from an annual average of about $900 million in the late 1970s and early 1980s to $1.2 billion starting in fiscal 1985. In addition, the United States provided Israel with a one-time supplemental grant of $1.5 billion in economic aid for fiscal 1986, keyed to reforms intended to lower its inflation rate.

In actions even more important than the dollar increases, Congress and the Reagan administration gradually changed the mix of Israel's aid to emphasize grants instead of loans. By fiscal 1985 the United States had stopped lending money to Israel and was instead giving it outright grants.

'Strategic Cooperation.' On November 30, 1981, Secretary of Defense Caspar Weinberger signed the first major document establishing strategic military cooperation between Israel and the United States. Although the document did not obligate the United States to defend Israel against attacks from Arab states, it pledged the two countries to work together to meet military threats in the Middle East "caused by the Soviet Union or Soviet-controlled forces from outside the region." The Reagan administration, however, quickly withdrew that "memorandum of understanding" less than a month later, on December 18, to protest Israel's annexation of the Golan Heights, a strategic territory it had captured from Syria in the 1967 war.

Two years later, in November 1983, Reagan announced creation of the Joint Political Military Group, formalizing de facto contacts between military and diplomatic officials of the two countries. An outgrowth of that development was the U.S. declaration that Israel was a major non-NATO ally, entitled to the same privileges and concessions on military programs as the NATO countries, with which the United States had formal treaty relationships.

In March 1984 the Reagan administration renewed a Carter-era memorandum of agreement with Israel providing for cooperation in military research and development, procurement, and logistics. Under that agreement the United States in the mid-1980s bought Israeli-made radios, remotely piloted vehicles, antitank weapons, and components for F-15s and F-16s. In turn, Washington provided technology and funding for development of two major new Israeli weapons systems: the Lavi fighter plane and the Saar 5, a new class of missile attack boat.

The Lavi (Hebrew for "young lion") was to become one of the most expensive and controversial joint projects between the United States and Israel. Originally proposed in the late 1970s as a small, inexpensive fighter, the plane swiftly grew in complexity. By the time the first prototype was flown in December 1986, the cost per plane, according to some U.S. estimates, had reached $17 million—making it more expensive than the U.S. F-16 fighter.

Congress first appropriated money for the plane in 1983, earmarking $550 million of Israel's annual military aid for its development; of that amount, $400 million was for work in Israel and the remainder for purchase of components at factories in the United States.

U.S. defense industry specialists and Pentagon officials began questioning the value of the Lavi project early in 1986, and by 1987 the United States openly was pressuring Israel to drop it. Top Israeli military leaders joined in the campaign to end the Lavi program, arguing that the expense was detracting from more crucial military needs. After the expenditure of some $1.5 billion—most of it from the United States, the Israeli cabinet voted narrowly on August 20, 1987, to kill the project and divert funding into other weapons systems.

Washington offered major concessions to Israel to compensate for the hardship in the Israeli defense industry caused by the Lavi decision. These concessions included agreements to finance Israel's purchase of F-16 planes as an alternative to the Lavi and to allow the Israeli government to use U.S. aid to pay the cost of cancelling Lavi contracts. In one of its last major moves to expand military ties with Israel, the Reagan administration in June 1988 signed an agreement to fund 80 percent of the cost of developing the Arrow missile, designed to shoot down incoming ballistic missiles.

The U.S. funding was to come out of the Pentagon's budget for the Strategic Defense Initiative.

Egypt

Between the 1952 officers' coup that brought Nasser to power and the 1973 war, Egypt got most of its arms from the Soviet Union, which was seeking ways to extend its influence into the Middle East. At first, Moscow provided its weapons to Egypt through allies. That pattern was established in a September 1955 deal between Egypt and Czechoslovakia. The Czechs provided Egypt with planes, tanks, and antiaircraft guns, most of Soviet origin, and the Egyptians paid the Czechs with cotton and dates.

The Soviet Union established a lasting relationship with Egypt after the the Suez crisis of 1956, equipping all branches of the Egyptian military. After the 1967 Six-Day War the Soviets rarely used conduits to funnel their arms to Egypt, preferring instead to make direct shipments. By the early 1970s Soviet personnel essentially were running the Egyptian air defense system.

In spite of periodic improvements in U.S.-Egyptian relations—such as after President Eisenhower's intervention in the 1956 Suez crisis—neither country seemed anxious to establish an arms supply relationship. Between the 1948 war and 1975, Washington sold Egypt no weapons of any kind and provided minimal amounts of economic aid.

After the 1967 war Cairo began complaining that the Soviets were dragging their feet in resupplying Egypt with weapons lost during the 1967 war. President Anwar Sadat was especially unhappy that the Kremlin was withholding advanced weapons he had requested, such as MiG-23 fighter planes.

In July 1972, denouncing the Kremlin for "excessive caution," Sadat took the first major step toward severing his country's military relations with Moscow, ordering all of the 15,000 to 20,000 Soviet military advisers to leave the country. Even so, the Soviet Union continued providing weapons to Egypt into the mid-1970s, including MiG-23 fighters in 1975.

As relations between Egypt and the Kremlin worsened, Sadat began improving relations with the West. After talks in late 1973 between Sadat and Secretary of State Henry Kissinger, the United States and Egypt resumed diplomatic relations in February 1974. Sadat apparently hoped the United States would replace the Soviet Union as his principal arms supplier. After the signing of the Sinai disengagement pact in 1975, the Ford administration announced that Egypt could buy U.S. weapons.

Sadat was to be disappointed at first. Washington provided six C-130 transport planes in 1976 but refused to approve Sadat's requests for advanced warplanes and other items. The United States in the mid-1970s did begin extending outright financial aid to Egypt, providing nearly $1 billion a year in economic and food aid.

It was not until after Sadat's moves toward peace—highlighted by his dramatic trip to Jerusalem in November 1977—that Egypt found Washington willing to become a significant supplier of weapons. As part of his 1978 arms sale package, President Carter proposed selling Egypt fifty F-5Es, the export version of a 1960s-era short-range fighter

bomber. Congress approved the entire package after a short but harsh debate centering around the sale of sixty advanced F-15 fighters to Saudi Arabia.

As an inducement for Sadat to sign the Camp David peace treaty in March 1979, Carter offered an aid commitment that sharply boosted U.S. financial backing of Egypt. This aid was necessary in part because Saudi Arabia and some of the smaller Gulf states, which had been providing Egypt with financial support, cut off aid in response to Egypt's signing of the 1979 treaty. Carter's aid commitments to Egypt included:

- Long-term loans to enable Egypt to purchase $1.5 billion worth of arms from the United States, including F-4 fighters, destroyers, tanks, armored personnel carriers, five Hawk air-defense systems, and other equipment.
- A special $200 million economic grant and a $100 million economic loan.

In the years after Camp David, U.S. aid to Egypt gradually increased in tandem with aid to Israel. Egypt was to receive less money than Israel each year, but the formal relationship between the two countries guaranteed that Egypt would get more money whenever Israel did and would not suffer politically inspired cutbacks engineered on Capitol Hill. When Congress appropriated $1.5 billion in special economic aid for Israel in 1985, for example, Egypt received $500 million for its economy.

Egypt's aid program, pegged at about $1 billion a year

at the time of Camp David, rose to about $1.5 billion by the early 1980s and to more than $2 billion in the mid-1980s. By fiscal 1986, and for several years thereafter, Egypt was receiving $1.3 billion annually in military aid, $815 million in economic aid, and at least $200 million in U.S. food distributions—all in grants.

The U.S.-Egyptian military relationship grew along with the aid program. President Reagan in the 1980s consistently proposed major weapons sales for Egypt, all of which were approved by Congress without serious controversy. Congress in 1987 approved the single largest arms deal between the two countries—a contract for Egyptian coproduction of M-1 Abrams tanks. Although Egypt gradually switched over to U.S. weaponry, it continued to rely heavily on its old Soviet equipment through the late 1980s.

The military ties between the United States and Egypt, however, went beyond arms sales. Starting in 1980 the two countries conducted an annual combined military exercise called "Bright Star," and Egypt quietly allowed the United States to use its naval facilities for ship maintenance and for the transport of supplies to American forces stationed in the region.

Cairo did balk at one Washington request: allowing formal access to the base at Ras Banas on the Red Sea for the U.S. "rapid deployment forces" that were to respond to contingencies in the region, such as threats to shipping in the Persian Gulf.

Saudi Arabia

The United States began an arms supply relationship with Saudi Arabia in the 1950s, but it was the Nixon administration in the early 1970s that made the oil-rich kingdom one of the "two pillars" (with Iran) of U.S. policy in the Persian Gulf region.

Beginning in 1974 Saudi Arabia contracted to buy billions of dollars' worth of weapons, services, and military supplies from the United States. Within a decade, Washington had helped the Saudis acquire one of the most sophisticated armed forces in the Middle East. In dollar terms, most of the more than $30 billion that the Saudis spent was for construction and design of ultramodern air, naval, and army bases.

For the most part, the escalation of the U.S.-Saudi arms relationship went unnoticed in Washington and generated little political protest. That changed in 1978, however, when President Carter moved to bolster U.S. military ties throughout the Middle East in the wake of Egyptian President Anwar Sadat's dramatic trip to Jerusalem the previous November.

Attempting to allay fears about arming Israel's Arab neighbors, Carter assembled a gigantic arms package that combined arms sales to Egypt and Saudi Arabia with sales to Israel. The $4.8 billion package, announced in February 1978, included:

● For Israel, fifteen F-15 warplanes, in addition to twenty-five already on order. Carter also requested seventy-five F-16 fighter bombers for Israel, half of what the Israeli government wanted. The total cost for these planes was $1.5 billion.

● For Egypt, fifty F-5Es, updated versions of the standard U.S. short-range fighter-bomber dating from the 1960s. This sale—the first by the United States to Egypt in two decades—was priced at $400 million.

● For Saudi Arabia, sixty F-15 warplanes, valued at $2.5 billion. This was to be the first sale to the Saudis of the most advanced fighter in the U.S. arsenal.

The sales to Israel and Egypt generated little controversy, but Carter's proposal for a major escalation in the U.S. arms relationship with Saudi Arabia touched off a battle on Capitol Hill. Israeli's supporters in Congress argued that the sale would tip the regional balance of power away from Israel by enabling the Saudis to attack the Jewish state with sophisticated aircraft from bases hundreds of miles away.

Carter managed to win approval of the entire package only after a sustained lobbying effort in the Senate. That chamber ultimately approved the sale in May 1978 by a ten-vote margin once Carter agreed to significant concessions, such as agreeing to require that the planes be used only for "legitimate self-defense" and prohibiting the Saudis from basing them in a fashion that might threaten Israel.

Carter followed up in 1980 with a proposal to provide equipment that would enhance the range and offensive capability of the F-15s. The Saudis wanted multiple-bomb-ejection racks to increase the number of bombs the planes could carry, advanced AIM 9-L super-Sidewinder air-to-air missiles, and KC-135 tanker planes to allow midair refueling of the F-15s.

The administration justified the sale as necessary to symbolize U.S. support for moderate Arab regimes in the wake of the Soviet invasion of Afghanistan the previous December. The administration also proposed to sell the Saudis two additional F-15s, to be kept in the United States until needed to replace any of the previous sixty that might be lost or damaged beyond repair.

In a pattern that was to be repeated on several occasions during the next decade, members of Congress who supported the Israeli government's position against arms sales to Arab nations reacted swiftly against the president's proposal. Sixty-eight senators—one more than necessary to override a presidential veto—sent Carter a letter demanding that he withdraw the request. With the presidential election only months away, Carter complied, sending word that he was asking for an indefinite "delay" of the sale.

The AWACS Debate. After the outbreak of the Iran-Iraq war in October 1980, Carter took a step that was to lead to the most bruising arms sale fight ever in Congress. To help the Saudis detect Iranian planes that might threaten their oil fields, Carter sent four U.S.-manned AWACS radar planes to patrol the Persian Gulf region.

Impressed with the capabilities of the planes, the Saudis asked to buy AWACS of their own, and the incoming Reagan administration readily agreed early in 1981. In a notice to Congress that April, President Reagan said he was prepared to sell Saudi Arabia five E-3A AWACS planes, valued at $5.8 billion. Reagan also proposed selling fuel tanks, Sidewinder missiles, and tanker planes that Congress had rejected the previous year to improve the effectiveness of Saudi Arabia's F-15 fighters. However, Reagan dropped from the Saudi shopping list the multiple-bomb-ejection racks that would have allowed each F-15 to carry eighteen bombs, rather than the standard number of three.

In an attempt to soften Israeli opposition, Reagan promised Israel an extra $300 million each year in military aid for fiscal 1983 and 1984, bringing the annual amount to $1.7 billion. The $300 million increase later was to become a permanent feature of U.S. aid.

Pro-Israel lobbying organizations vigorously opposed the sale, maintaining that it would aggravate regional ten-

United States Assistance to the Middle East, 1946-1988

(U.S fiscal year — millions of dollars)

	1987	1988	Total Loans and Grants 1946-1988		1987	1988	Total Loans and Grants 1946-1988
ALGERIA				**OMAN**			
Economic	$ —	$ —	$ 203.6	Economic	$ 14.9	$ 13.0	$ 121.3
Loans	—	—	11.6	Loans	9.9	8.0	77.3
Grants	—	—	192.0	Grants	5.0	5.0	44.0
Other	—	53.7	1,098.3	Military	—	0.2	167.8
EGYPT				Loans	—	—	167.1
Economic	1,015.3	873.4	14,847.3	Grants	—	0.2	0.7
Loans	191.7	153.0	5,969.7	Other	—	—	—
Grants	823.6	720.4	8,877.6	**SAUDI ARABIA**			
Military	1,301.8	1,301.5	12,105.1	Economic	—	—	31.8
Loans	—	—	5,981.2	Loans	—	—	4.3
Grants	1,301.8	1,301.5	6,123.9	Grants	—	—	27.5
Other	—	0.3	471.3	Military	—	—	292.4
IRAN				Loans	—	—	254.2
Economic	—	—	761.8	Grants	—	—	38.2
Loans	—	—	297.6	Other	—	—	47.3
Grants	—	—	464.2	**SUDAN**			
Military	—	—	1,404.8	Economic	96.6	63.2	1,379.7
Loans	—	—	496.4	Loans	74.6	40.0	385.3
Grants	—	—	908.4	Grants	22.0	23.2	994.4
Other	—	—	128.7	Military	6.0	0.9	372.6
IRAQ				Loans	—	—	156.3
Economic	—	—	45.5	Grants	6.0	0.9	216.3
Loans	—	—	14.4	Other	—	—	41.7
Grants	—	—	31.1	**SYRIA**			
Military	—	—	50.0	Economic	—	—	353.3
Grants	—	—	50.0	Loans	—	—	274.3
Other	—	—	100.5	Grants	—	—	79.0
ISRAEL				**TUNISIA**			
Economic	1,200.0	1,200.0	15,025.6	Economic	51.7	42.0	1,134.3
Loans	—	—	2,009.9	Loans	31.6	27.0	521.8
Grants	1,200.0	1,200.0	13,015.7	Grants	20.1	15.0	612.5
Military	1,800.0	1,800.0	25,826.8	Military	34.1	28.4	695.6
Loans	—	—	11,204.2	Loans	—	—	487.4
Grants	1,800.0	1,800.0	14,622.6	Grants	34.1	28.4	209.2
Other	—	—	897.4	Other	—	—	138.3
JORDAN				**TURKEY**			
Economic	111.1	23.7	1,798.8	Economic	103.1	32.4	4,326.8
Loans	2.0	5.2	329.0	Loans	2.4	—	2,035.0
Grants	109.1	18.5	1,469.8	Grants	100.7	32.4	2,291.8
Military	41.9	28.3	1,510.9	Military	493.5	493.5	9,894.6
Loans	—	—	877.7	Loans	177.9	178.0	4,137.9
Grants	41.9	28.3	633.2	Grants	315.6	315.3	5,756.7
Other	5.7	28.2	426.5	Other	—	—	491.6
KUWAIT				**YEMEN ARAB REPUBLIC**			
Other	—	—	50.0	Economic	45.5	33.7	384.7
LEBANON				Loans	18.6	10.0	62.1
Economic	22.5	11.9	348.7	Grants	26.9	23.7	322.6
Loans	—	—	33.1	Military	2.3	2.0	41.3
Grants	22.5	11.9	315.6	Loans	—	—	14.0
Military	0.5	0.4	265.9	Grants	2.3	2.0	17.3
Loans	—	—	243.7	Other	—	—	0.6
Grants	0.5	0.4	22.2	**YEMEN, PEOPLE'S DEMOCRATIC REPUBLIC OF**			
Other	—	—	83.2	Economic	—	—	4.5
LIBYA				Grants	—	—	4.5
Economic	—	—	212.5				
Loans	—	—	7.0				
Grants	—	—	205.5				
Military	—	—	17.6				
Grants	—	—	17.6				

The cumulative figures for 1946-1988 are on a net basis, reflecting total obligations where funds obligated were not actually spent.

Economic aid totals include official development assistance, Food for Peace programs, Peace Corps, and miscellaneous programs.

Military aid includes the Foreign Assistance Act credit sales and grant programs, transfers from excess stocks, and other grants and loans.

Other includes Export-Import Bank loans often made to the private sector within a country, Agriculture Department short-term credits, OPIC direct loans, and private trade agreements under PL-480, Title I.

Source: Agency for International Development

sions. They said the Saudis did not need their own AWACS since the United States already was stationing the radar planes in the region. In addition, they said the enhancements to the F-15s would allow the Saudis to pose a threat to Israel.

The Reagan administration countered that the Saudis had become a reliable ally of the United States, whose importance was enhanced by the 1979 revolution in Iran. The October 6 assassination of Egyptian president Sadat gave the administration another argument. The loss of Washington's best Arab friend made it imperative that Congress not jeopardize U.S. ties with Saudi Arabia—or Reagan's stature—by blocking the deal at a crucial time.

Under a 1976 amendment to the Arms Export Control Act, Congress had the power to veto the sale by passing a concurrent resolution of disapproval. With the House staunchly opposed to the deal, the administration launched a high-powered campaign in the Senate for approval. Reagan met with senators (particularly Republicans) individually and in small groups in an effort to secure the fifty votes he needed to prevent the Senate from blocking the deal.

In a key move, the administration and the Saudis agreed to a series of restrictions to calm senators' fears about how the planes would be used. Reagan sent the Senate a five-page letter promising, among other things, that the United States would retain a substantial degree of control over the use of the planes and would be able to obtain any radar information gleaned by the AWACS. The president won a narrow victory on October 28, when the Senate rejected a resolution to block the sale by a dramatic 48-52 vote.

Congress in 1985 put Reagan's assurances about the AWACS into law, requiring the president to certify that several conditions had been met before the planes could be transferred to the Saudis. Reagan in 1986 officially notified Congress that the conditions had been met, and Congress, by taking no action, officially allowed the sale to proceed.

Later Battles. The AWACS battle calmed congressional concern about Saudi Arabia for the remainder of Reagan's first term. In the first two years of Reagan's second term he again proposed major arms sales to the Saudis. Unlike during his first term, however, Reagan promised the Saudis more than he could deliver on Capitol Hill. As a result, the Saudis began relying increasingly on other suppliers who placed no political conditions on arms deals and, for the right price, were willing to provide just about any weapons or equipment the Saudis requested.

In 1985 Reagan asked Congress for authority to sell the Saudis Stinger antiaircraft missiles, Harpoon antiship missiles, Blackhawk troop-carrying helicopters, and forty-two additional F-15s. He quickly withdrew the proposal, however, when both chambers voiced overwhelming opposition to the sale.

The Saudis responded by negotiating a deal with Great Britain (announced in February 1986) under which they would buy about $7 billion worth of warplanes and other items. The centerpiece of that deal was the acquisition by Saudi Arabia of seventy-two Tornado fighter-bombers built by a consortium of Britain, West Germany, and Italy. The Saudis also purchased thirty British Hawk jet trainers and thirty Pilatus PC-9 trainer planes built in Switzerland and outfitted in Britain.

The Saudi decision to turn to European suppliers represented a major setback for the longstanding U.S. policy of promoting Saudi dependence on American weapons.

Reagan administration officials also insisted that, paradoxically, Israeli and congressional opposition to the U.S. sale had jeopardized Israeli security interests. They noted that the Saudis were able to obtain the advanced Tornado planes without the restrictions on basing and offensive capabilities that Congress had imposed on earlier sales of F-15s to reduce the chance that they could be used against Israel.

In the wake of the Saudi-British deal, Reagan proposed in April 1986 a $354 million package including nearly 1,700 Sidewinder air-to-air missiles, 100 Harpoon antiship missiles, and 200 portable launchers for Stinger antiaircraft missiles, along with 600 Stingers. That package was a scaled-down version of a Saudi request that included additional F-15s, M-1 main battle tanks, and other items.

By 1986 the sale of Stingers to countries in the Middle East had become a major issue in Congress, with members arguing that the highly accurate missiles could threaten civil aviation if they fell into the hands of terrorists.

Many members of Congress also were becoming increasingly impatient with Saudi Arabia, noting that despite a moderate image it had continued to provide financial support to the radical Syrian government and the Palestine Liberation Organization (PLO). The Saudis had provoked further criticism in Congress by denouncing Reagan's April 14 bombing raid against Libya in retaliation for that country's backing of terrorism.

The House and Senate in early May both passed resolutions rejecting Reagan's arms sale proposal by overwhelming margins. That action marked the first time that both chambers had passed resolutions in an attempt to block an overseas arms sale. Under new procedures passed into law in early 1986, however, the president could veto a resolution blocking an arms sale, thus forcing Congress to override the veto to prevent the sale. The revised procedure was enacted partly in response to the Supreme Court's 1983 *Chadha* decision, which ruled "legislative vetoes" unconstitutional unless the president had a chance to participate in them. *(Details, box, p. 81)*

At the suggestion of the Saudi government, Reagan agreed to remove the controversial Stingers from the sale package. He then vetoed the congressional resolution, arguing that rejecting the deal would "damage our vital strategic, political, and economic interests in the Middle East and undermine our balanced policy in that region."

As in 1981, the House overwhelmingly opposed the sale and its fate would be determined by the Republican-controlled Senate. After heavy administration lobbying and the removal of the Stingers from the package, Reagan won by the slimmest of margins. Thirty-four senators, one more than necessary, voted to sustain the veto, thus allowing the sale to proceed.

Repeating the pattern of 1986, Congress in 1987 allowed a $1 billion arms package to Saudi Arabia—but only after twice forcing Reagan to withdraw a proposal to provide the Saudis with 1,600 Maverick antitank missiles. In both cases, a sufficient number of senators to override a presidential veto signalled their opposition to selling Mavericks to the Saudis.

Congressional opponents of the sale insisted the antitank missiles could be used to threaten the Jewish state. In addition, members complained that Saudi Arabia had refused to allow U.S. fighter planes to operate from its bases—even though the planes were protecting Saudi and other neutral ships from attack in the Persian Gulf war.

After Reagan retreated on the issue by withdrawing

the Mavericks, Congress consented to a modified package including twelve F-15 planes, electronic upgrades for the F-15s previously sold to the Saudis, artillery ammunition carriers, and modernization kits for tanks in the Saudi arsenal. Under the deal, the additional F-15s would remain in the United States and be sent to Saudi Arabia only to replace lost or worn-out planes.

Reports early in 1988 that Saudi Arabia had obtained some twenty-five Chinese long-range missiles (the CSS-2, or "Long March") produced anger and confusion in Washington. Congress voted to bar further arms sales to the Saudis unless the president certified that the missiles were not equipped with chemical weapons.

Reagan said King Fahd had sent him written assurances that the missiles would not be armed with chemical weapons. In a symbolic step to show that it also had no intention of equipping the missiles with nuclear arms, Saudi Arabia in April signed the Nuclear Nonproliferation Treaty.

Those two steps helped allay congressional unease, enabling Reagan to win approval for a sale to the Saudis of 200 Bradley fighting vehicles, TOW antitank missiles, and other items.

Despite the sales, the Saudis were unwilling to rely solely on the United States for military equipment. In July 1988 they signed a huge arms contract with Great Britain, reported to be worth at least $17 billion. Among other things, the contract provided for British work on Saudi military bases, an additional forty to fifty Tornado warplanes, sixty Hawk trainer jets, a number of Blackhawk helicopters, and six antimine ships.

Jordan

With the exception of Egypt, following the Camp David treaty, Jordan has been closer politically to Washington—and more important to U.S. hopes for advancing the peace process—than any other Arab nation. King Hussein, one of the world's most durable political figures, appeared to be the embodiment of "moderate" Arab leadership.

Beginning with the Reagan peace initiative of September 1982, Hussein also was to be the centerpiece of Washington's efforts to get the peace process moving again in accordance with the Camp David agreements. The Reagan initiative called on Hussein to agree to an "association" of Jordan and the Palestinians who lived there on the West Bank.

Despite the administration's hope that Jordan would advance the peace process, Congress from 1983 through 1986 repeatedly balked at various proposals to sell arms to Jordan. Members complained that Hussein, unlike Egypt's Sadat, refused to recognize and negotiate directly with Israel. There was a widespread perception on Capitol Hill that Hussein had given a veto to PLO Chairman Yasir Arafat over his participation in peace talks and was too timid in his efforts to get Arafat to consent to Jordan-Israel negotiations.

Frustrated by the refusal of Congress to support U.S. arms sales to Jordan, Hussein complained bitterly about the one-sidedness of U.S. policy in the Middle East and turned elsewhere, principally to Great Britain, for the weapons to modernize his military.

Congressional Opposition. Until the 1980s, the U.S.-Jordan military relationship was one of the oldest and most stable in the Middle East. The United States and Jordan signed their first military cooperation agreement in 1952. Washington helped Jordan modernize its armed forces following the 1973 war and by the early 1980s had supplied nearly $1 billion worth of weapons. Arms sales to Jordan generated little controversy on Capitol Hill, in part because larger, more visible sales to Iran and Saudi Arabia drew more attention. Strictly in dollar terms, Great Britain and France sold more weapons to Jordan—but neither of those countries went as far as the United States in coupling their sales with political considerations.

Reagan in 1983 encountered the first marked congressional resistance to a Jordanian arms sale. His failure to gain approval for these sales was especially embarrassing because his proposal was to have been secret, and its disclosure in Israel sparked the opposition on Capitol Hill.

Reagan proposed to provide Hussein financial aid and military equipment and training for a Jordanian rapid deployment force that could respond to military crises in the region. Specifically, Reagan asked for funds to equip and support two brigades of the Jordanian army with C-130 transport planes, antiaircraft and antitank missiles, communications equipment, and other supplies.

The proposal was submitted to Congress in secret, with administration officials warning that Hussein feared his standing in the Arab world would be undermined if the proposal became public. That tactic worked at first: with few members knowing about it, Congress secretly approved $220 million for the plan in the fiscal 1984 defense authorization bill passed in the fall of 1983. In mid-October, however, Israeli press reports disclosed the plan, creating an uproar in Congress and leading the House and Senate Appropriations committees to reject the funds needed to implement the plan.

The administration tried to salvage the proposal in 1984 by reducing its scope, renaming it the Joint Logistics Planning Program and dropping a controversial related proposal to sell Jordan fifty-eight portable Stinger antiaircraft missiles. Congressional opposition continued, however, and in May 1984 the administration quietly withdrew the plan.

Reagan in 1984 also suffered the first of what was to become a series of defeats in Congress on proposed arms sales intended to modernize the Jordanian army. In February he outlined a plan to sell Jordan 1,613 Stinger missiles and 315 launchers for them at a cost of $133 million. As with most arms sales it proposed for Jordan, the administration argued that the Stingers were needed to meet the military threat from neighboring Syria.

Hussein himself undermined that sale with critical comments that sparked congressional discontent that was to linger for years. In an interview published in the March 15, 1984, *New York Times*, Hussein said the United States could no longer serve as mediator between Israel and Arab countries. "You obviously have made your choice, and your choice is Israel," Hussein said. "Therefore, there is no hope of achieving anything." In subsequent interviews with U.S. television networks, Hussein refused to back down from that harsh statement, attacking Washington as a major stumbling block to peace in the Middle East. Faced with overwhelming opposition to the Stinger sale stemming from Hussein's remarks, Reagan withdrew the proposal.

A Big Gamble Lost. Hussein himself declared 1985 to be the last chance for real progress toward peace with Israel. He came to this conclusion because it was the last full year for control of Israel's shaky coalition government by the Labor party, which was more disposed to enter the peace process than the competing Likud coalition.

Partly to show U.S. support for Hussein's efforts, and also to modernize the aging Jordanian air force, Reagan in September announced plans for a major arms sale that would include advanced warplanes, Stinger and Hawk anti-aircraft missiles, and other items. The price tag was to be between $1.5 billion and $2 billion, depending on whether the U.S. Air Force decided to sell Jordan the new F-20 fighter (later scrapped for lack of sales), or a stripped-down version of General Dynamic's F-16. The warplanes were to replace many of Jordan's squadrons of U.S. F-5s and French Mirage F-1s dating from the 1960s.

With Hussein still unable to move Arafat toward participation in peace talks, congressional opposition to the proposed sale blossomed quickly. Within a few weeks, nearly three-fourths of all senators had cosponsored a resolution blocking any arms sale to Jordan until peace talks were under way.

To avert an outright defeat for the president, Richard G. Lugar, R-Ind., then chairman of the Senate Foreign Relations Committee, engineered a somewhat milder resolution deferring the Jordanian sale until March 1, 1986, unless Jordan and Israel had begun "direct and meaningful" negotiations. The Senate passed that measure overwhelmingly on October 24, the House followed suit on November 12, and Reagan withdrew the proposal.

The administration intended to propose the sale again in early 1986, hoping that Hussein finally would be able to work his way to the peace table, or at least that Congress would drop its restriction. But with elections coming up in both Israel and the United States, congressional opposition to a major Jordanian arms sale remained strong.

Secretary of State Shultz on February 3 formally notified Congress that the administration was postponing the proposed sale indefinitely—acknowledging the certainty of defeat. Testifying to a House committee two days later, Shultz charged that congressional opposition to the sale was "a major detriment to our ability to move the peace process along."

Reagan did win approval in 1985 for a supplemental $250 million aid package to bolster the Jordanian economy—but only after the Senate demanded restrictions on how the money could be spent. A year later the Reagan administration offered informally to upgrade Jordan's anti-aircraft missile system by replacing stationary Hawk missiles with a modernized, mobile version. However, the administration bowed to congressional objections and never submitted an official proposal.

Reluctantly accepting the political realities in Washington, Hussein turned to Europe for help in modernizing his armed forces. Backed with promises of Saudi financing, he signed an agreement to buy British Tornado warplanes and French Mirage 2000s.

By February 1989, Hussein was telling reporters that the U.S.-Jordanian military relationship was "minimal" and that he planned no further arms requests from Washington unless "Congress changes its attitude." However, with Jordan's economy slipping into serious trouble, in part because his Arab allies failed to follow through with promised financial aid, Hussein was reconsidering the British and French deals.

Smaller Gulf States

One of the many byproducts of the Iran-Iraq war was a heightened anxiety among the smaller nations of the Persian Gulf region. Tiny in population and land area and led by conservative royal families, the Gulf states were vulnerable to subversion and direct military attacks originating in Iran. All were heavily dependent on Saudi Arabia for protection, and each country needed foreign personnel, both for its civilian economy and its military.

Along with Saudi Arabia, the five Gulf states of Bahrain, Kuwait, Oman, Qatar, and the United Arab Emirates on May 25, 1981, formally established the Gulf Cooperation Council. The Gulf states hoped the council would enable them to coordinate their military planning.

Although each of the Gulf states turned to the United States for some weapons in the 1980s, most continued to rely heavily on European sources, particularly Britain and France. Some of the countries clearly wanted to have access to more than one major arms supplier. Kuwait, for example, bought F-18 fighter-bombers from the United States in 1988, to replace its aging fleet of A-4 Skyhawks. At the same time, Kuwait was negotiating with France to purchase Mirage 2000 fighters to replace its aging Mirage F-1s.

Except for small sales to Kuwait, the Soviet Union generally was unable to penetrate the lucrative arms market on the Arabian peninsula.

The United States had a substantial military presence in Bahrain and Oman. Until the mid-1980s, Bahrain was the home port for the U.S. Navy's Middle East task force, and it continued to keep its naval facilities open to the United States. The Carter administration in 1980 negotiated an agreement with Oman that allowed the United States to use strategically located air and naval facilities at the entrance to the Persian Gulf.

As the Gulf states began asking for larger numbers of U.S. weapons in the late 1980s, Israel began protesting sales to them as potentially threatening to Israeli security—and the pro-Israel lobby in Washington responded by opposing those arms sales.

Kuwait. The Reagan administration in 1987 agreed to protect Kuwait's eleven oil tankers by registering them as U.S. vessels—in effect, "reflagging" them—and escorting them through the Persian Gulf. Although Iraq had launched the first attacks against oil tankers, the U.S. action was widely seen as an intervention on behalf of Iraq—an ally of Kuwait's—and against Iran in the Gulf war. U.S. convoys of Kuwaiti tankers began in July 1987, in spite of criticism in Congress, and continued until after a UN-sponsored cease-fire ended the Gulf war in 1988.

To bolster the Gulf countries, the Reagan administration in 1988 persuaded Congress to allow the sale to Kuwait of forty F-18 fighter-bombers and assorted missiles for the warplanes. Kuwait previously had bought weapons from a variety of sources, including the United States. The administration hailed the sale as a decision by Kuwait to strengthen its ties with Washington.

As with similar sales to Arab countries, members of Congress who supported the Israeli government's position objected to the Kuwait sale and took action to block it. They objected in particular to Kuwait's request for 100 Maverick-D air-to-surface missiles.

Negotiations between the administration and House members produced an agreement under which Kuwait was allowed to buy, at a cost of $1.9 billion, the F-18s along with a complement of Maverick-G antiship missiles, Sidewinder air-to-air missiles, Sparrow air-to-air missiles, Harpoon antiship missiles, and cluster bombs.

The agreement included several conditions on the sale of the F-18s. Among other things, Kuwait would have to return to the United States one of its old A-4 planes in

Congressional Role in Arms Sales

The process by which Congress considers foreign arms sales became well established and embellished with ritual during the 1970s and 1980s. Although the executive branch retained control over the initiation of arms sales and Congress was rarely able to block a proposed sale entirely, lawmakers proved that they could place restrictions on sales or force the president to make compromises concerning a sale's contents and terms.

Under a 1968 arms export law the president must notify Congress of all major arms sales to foreign governments. In a 1976 amendment to that law Congress gave itself the right to veto such sales by passing a concurrent resolution within thirty days of receiving the president's notice. A concurrent resolution does not require the president's signature and therefore cannot be vetoed as can regular legislation. The 1976 law also set up procedures to guarantee rapid consideration of concurrent resolutions on arms sales.

By mutual agreement every president since 1976 gave Congress an extra twenty days of advance notice, during which the two branches frequently worked out deals on politically sensitive issues. Under the definition in use in the mid-1980s, the notice and veto provisions applied to arms sales packages totaling at least $50 million, to sales of individual weapons worth $14 million or more, and to sales of military construction services worth $200 million or more.

Supreme Court Ruling

In 1983 the Supreme Court ruled in *Immigration and Naturalization Service v. Chadha* that legislative vetoes such as the one provided for in the 1976 arms sale law were unconstitutional. If Congress wanted to veto an executive branch action, the court ruled, it must give the president a chance to veto its veto. The ruling meant that Congress no longer could block an arms sale by adopting a concurrent resolution. Instead, it had to pass a bill or a joint resolution that would be subject to a presidential veto. A veto can be overridden only by a two-thirds vote of both the Senate and House. At the end of the legislative session in December 1985, Congress responded to *Chadha* by passing legislation (PL 99-247) requiring enactment of a joint resolution—rather than a concurrent resolution—to block an arms sale.

Past Sales Battles

Although battles over arms sales to Arab countries have been regular features of the American political landscape for more than a decade, on only one occasion have both houses of Congress passed legislation aimed at blocking an arms sale. That was in 1986, when the two chambers adopted a resolution seeking to veto the sale of $354 million worth of missiles to Saudi Arabia. Congressional opponents of the sale, however, were unable to override President Ronald Reagan's veto of the resolution, and a scaled-back version of the sale went through.

The prospect of a struggle with Congress, however, forced every president from Gerald R. Ford to Reagan to make compromises on potential sales, especially those to Arab nations, or even to withdraw ones that provoked too much opposition.

In 1975-1976 Congress and President Ford wrangled over Jordan's request for advanced antiaircraft missiles. Jordan got the missiles, but at congressional insistence they were anchored in concrete to reduce the chance of their being used against Israel.

In 1977 President Jimmy Carter won approval to sell sophisticated Airborne Warning and Control System (AWACS) planes to Iran, but under strict conditions. The planes had not been delivered by the time of the 1979 revolution there. In 1978 Carter persuaded Congress to approve the sale of U.S. warplanes to Saudi Arabia and Egypt. Carter, however, agreed to place restrictions on where the Saudis could base their jets and what kinds of equipment would accompany them.

Reagan in 1981 prevailed over opposition from the pro-Israel lobby in a bruising battle over the sale of AWACS radar planes and other items to Saudi Arabia. Like his predecessors, Reagan won his battle only after agreeing to impose restrictions on their use. He promised to maintain tight U.S. control over the planes and deliver them only if Saudi Arabia had contributed to a Middle East peace.

Reagan was not so successful, however, in persuading Congress to allow various arms sales to Jordan, and by the mid-1980s Congress had forced a virtual halt in U.S. arms shipments to that country. Reagan also battled repeatedly with Congress over further sales to Saudi Arabia.

Traditions

Over the years, the executive and legislative branches developed informal rituals for the consideration of arms sales. In most cases the State and Defense departments privately informed a few key members of Congress months in advance about forthcoming arms sales. In particularly sensitive cases, however, the executive branch often tried to deflect potential opposition by giving private briefings to scores of members, arguing the merits on political, military, and diplomatic grounds.

In the early stages of an arms sale controversy, a favorite tactic by opponents was to gather as many signatures of Senate and House members as possible on letters and resolutions condemning the sale and asking the president to withdraw it. But while a large number of signatures demonstrated congressional sentiment, it did not necessarily doom a sale. In 1981 fifty senators cosponsored a resolution opposing the Saudi AWACS sale; when the vote came, seven changed their minds under intense presidential pressure.

exchange for each new F-18 it received. Kuwait also was barred from equipping the planes with extra fuel tanks that would extend their range.

Stingers in the Gulf. The Reagan administration briefly jousted with Congress in 1987 over providing hand-held Stinger antiaircraft missiles to Bahrain. Congressional opposition forced the administration to drop its plan to sell Bahrain between sixty and seventy of the missiles for about $7 million.

As the congressional session neared an end in December of that year, however, Secretary of Defense Frank C. Carlucci launched an intense lobbying campaign on behalf of the sale. Carlucci told congressional leaders in closed sessions that Bahrain was providing the United States with important facilities and services for U.S. Persian Gulf operations.

That argument proved persuasive. As part of a continuing appropriations resolution for fiscal 1988, Congress agreed to allow the sale of Stingers to Bahrain, on the condition that any unused missiles be returned within eighteen months. In the meantime, Washington was to work with Bahrain to find an alternative air defense system. State Department officials told Congress early in 1989, however, that the new Bush administration wanted Bahrain to keep the missiles. Congress in June passed legislation allowing Bahrain to retain the Stingers until October 31, 1989.

Qatar, another tiny Gulf state, secretly obtained Stinger missiles some time in 1988 but refused a U.S. request to relinquish them. Administration officials speculated that Qatar bought the missiles from one of the factions of the Afghanistan guerrillas. The CIA had started giving the Afghan rebels the missiles in 1986 to counter Soviet air attacks.

The Soviet Role

Moscow's role in the Middle East arms market has tended to mirror that of Washington's. In the 1950s and early 1960s, the Kremlin delivered weapons to the region primarily through allies, as with the 1955 deal between Egypt and Czechoslovakia. At the end of the 1967 war, however, Moscow stated its willingness to supply arms directly to Arab states if Israel refused to relinquish the West Bank and other territories it occupied during the fighting.

Although it did resupply several Arab countries after the Six-Day War, the Soviet Union in subsequent years became the primary source of weapons only for Egypt. That changed after the 1973 war, when the Arabs fully understood their vulnerability to Israel and offered to buy Soviet weapons with hard currency badly needed by the Soviets. Moscow for the first time became a major source of weapons for countries throughout the region, surpassing the European powers that once dominated the market. More important, the Soviet Union and the United States extended their overall rivalry into the volatile Middle East, each as the arms merchant and potential protector for a set of clients.

Following the break with Sadat, the Soviet Union strengthened its military and diplomatic ties with the so-called radical confrontation states—especially Syria, but also Libya and Iraq. During the 1970s, however, Moscow hesitated to sell those countries its most sophisticated

weapons, tending to allow them to buy only planes and tanks that were a generation behind those entering service with Soviet front-line forces. Washington, by contrast, began selling top-of-the line weapons to Israel and Saudi Arabia.

After Israel's invasion of Lebanon in 1982, the Soviets began allowing their clients to have more advanced weapons. Syria and Iraq were allowed to buy medium-range missiles and MiG-29 fighter bombers, which were roughly equivalent in performance to the U.S. F-16s. Early in 1989 the Soviets sold at least a dozen long-range SU-24 bombers to Libya, a step the Bush administration declared to be destabilizing to the entire Middle East.

Like Washington, Moscow also provided military advisers to its weapons customers. Syria and Libya were especially dependent on the Soviet Union for the technical expertise needed to operate the new sophisticated armaments such as air defense systems.

Syria

The Soviet Union and Syria esablished a formal military relationship in September 1972, following Sadat's expulsion of Soviet advisers from Egypt. Under that accord, Soviet forces were given access to naval facilities at Latakia and Tartus on the Mediterranean in exchange for jets and air defense missiles.

Moscow steadily built up Syrian ground and air forces after the 1973 war. In 1980 the two countries signed a twenty-year "friendship and cooperation" accord, symbolizing Syria's status as Moscow's most important ally in the Middle East.

The Soviet weapons, and the Syrians manning them, performed poorly against Israeli forces during the fierce fighting that followed Israel's invasion of Lebanon in June 1982. Israeli planes downed some ninety Syrian aircraft, and Israeli ground forces drove to within thirty kilometers of Damascus.

After those battles the Soviets began supplying Syria with weapons on a massive scale, gradually building up their arsenal of sophisticated planes, tanks, and missiles. In 1983 Syria became the first country outside the Soviet bloc to obtain medium-range SS-21 surface-to-surface missiles. The Soviets also sold Syria hundreds of modern T-62 and T-72 tanks and dozens of MiG-23 fighters. In 1987 the Soviet Union began sending its top-of-the line fighter bomber, the MiG-29, to Syria, heightening fears in Israel that its qualitative superiority in weapons over its most likely foe in a future war was eroding.

Between 1982 and 1986, the Soviet Union sold $9.6 billion worth of armaments to Syria. With the armaments came Soviet "advisers," most of them assigned to operate radar installations and Sam-5 antiaircraft missile batteries and to train Syrian pilots. By the mid-1980s, some four-thousand Soviet military personnel were stationed in Syria on a permanent basis.

Iraq

The Soviet Union and Iraq signed a fifteen-year "friendship and cooperation" treaty in 1972, but it took another ten years before the two countries established a significant military relationship. Iraq attempted to improve its ties to the West during much of the 1970s, and the Soviets tried to cultivate Iran following the 1978-1979 revolution there. As a result, relations between Moscow and Baghdad were distinctly strained during the early stages of the Iran-Iraq war.

By 1982 the Kremlin had failed in its effort to gain a foothold in Iran, and so it turned to Iraq. In subsequent years Iraq became the single most important customer for Soviet arms, buying slightly more than $15 billion worth during 1982-1986. Major items included aircraft (MiG 21s, 23s, 25s and ultimately 29s, along with Badger and Blinder bombers), attack helicopters, and several thousand tanks and armored personnel carriers.

Throughout its war with Iran, Iraq also relied heavily on the French, who were willing to sell Mirage fighters equipped with Exocet air-to-surface missiles in 1983 when Iraqi forces were gravely threatened by an Iranian offensive. Iraq used those planes and missiles against shipping in the Persian Gulf, leading the United States to escalate its military presence there. During the mid-1980s, France sold Iraq $4.5 billion worth of weapons, accounting for more than 20 percent of French arms sales worldwide.

Libya

The early years after the 1969 coup saw an uncomfortable relationship between Moscow and Libya, with Muammar Qaddafi's regime trying to keep its distance from both superpowers. Libya at that point relied heavily on the French for weapons, beginning with a purchase in 1969 of forty Mirage fighters.

After the 1973 Arab-Israeli war, however, Qaddafi began a major arms buildup—based primarily on Soviet supplies—that continued unabated throughout the 1980s. The first major Soviet-Libyan deal, in 1975, involved more than 2,000 tanks and two squadrons of MiG-23 fighters.

Qaddafi also began seeking increasingly sophisticated weapons and found the Soviet Union gradually willing to sell them. By the early 1980s the Soviets had supplied a full range of fighters, bombers, attack helicopters, tanks, and air defense systems to Libya.

In 1989 the Soviets sold Libya at least a dozen long-range SU-24 bombers capable of carrying conventional, chemical, or nuclear bombs. The planes were equipped with external fuel tanks giving them a combat radius of 800 miles, putting Israel within range.

Unlike Syria's President Hafez Assad, Qaddafi refused to grant the Soviets base-access privileges. However, he did rely on Soviet forces to operate some of the advanced weaponry he bought, especially the air defense systems. At the end of the 1980s at least 2,000 Soviet "advisers" were stationed in Libya.

Although a scourge to the United States and Israel because of its support for radical terrorist groups, Libya traditionally has posed a military threat only to its immediate neighbors, such as Chad and Egypt. Libya provided some weapons to its fellow Arab nations during the wars against Israel but could not project significant armed forces into the eastern Mediterranean. With its new Soviet-supplied long-range bombers, however, Libya's status as a parochial military power appeared to be on the verge of changing at the close of the 1980s.

Chemical Weapons

The repeated use of poison gas and other chemical weapons in the Iran-Iraq war, coupled with a flood of reports in the late 1980s that Libya and other countries were acquiring such weapons, raised world fears that the taboo on chemical warfare that had existed since the end of World War I was collapsing.

For countries in the Middle East wanting to bolster their military might, the advantages of chemical weapons are obvious. They are relatively cheap and easy to make, and the required technology is readily available on the world market. Chemical weapons and the production facilities used to make them also have the advantage of being easy to conceal. Within a matter of hours, according to experts, a chemical weapons plant can be made to appear as a production facility for pharmaceuticals or agricultural pesticides.

Most of Israel's neighbors, fearful of the Jewish state's reported nuclear arsenal and frustrated in their attempts to acquire atomic weapons, have sought to develop chemical weapons, often referred to as the "poor man's nuclear bomb." According to some U.S. sources, Israel and Egypt acquired at least the capability to produce chemical weapons in the 1960s. Syria reportedly followed in the 1970s, and other countries—such as Iran, Iraq, and Libya—entered the market in the 1980s. By the end of that decade, nearly all the major potential belligerents in a future Arab-Israeli war were able to produce militarily significant quantities of chemical weapons. At least two, Iran and Iraq, had demonstrated a willingness to use those weapons.

CIA Director William Webster testified to Congress in February 1989 that some countries in the region, particularly Iran, Iraq, Syria, and Libya, had made the acquisition of chemical weapons a "high priority." Webster said several countries in the region also were attempting to produce biological arms—weapons using living organisms that cause deadly diseases such as the plague and cholera. Worldwide concern about the chemical and biological arms race was heightened by the possibility that one or more of those Middle East countries could hand over some of the weapons to terrorist groups.

The Iran-Iraq War

Iraq opened the modern day Pandora's box of chemical weapons in 1983. Desperately trying to counter Iranian offensives in the Persian Gulf war, Iraq turned to the arsenal of mustard gas and other chemical weapons it had begun acquiring in the late 1970s from companies in the industrialized world, principally West Germany. Iraq reportedly built as many as five chemical weapons facilities, the largest of which was a facility at Samarra, northwest of Baghdad, for storage and production of nerve and mustard gas.

The first reported Iraqi use of chemical weapons was in March 1983, when Baghdad unleashed nerve gases on Iranian human-wave assaults that were threatening to overwhelm its defenses. The tactic worked militarily without causing Iraq serious political damage. Iran's offensive was halted, and Iraq received little international condemnation.

Iraq continued producing tons of chemical weapons and using them periodically through the rest of the war, killing thousands of enemy troops and civilians. Iraq, however, used these weapons less frequently in the later stages of the war when, bolstered with Soviet military supplies, it was better able to respond conventionally to Iranian advances. Iraq's last major chemical weapons attack on Iranian troops reportedly occurred in March 1988 near

Halabja. United Nations investigations, starting in 1984, confirmed Iraq's use of chemical weapons in the war. However, the world body never took formal action against Iraq.

Iran's response was predictable: It acquired its own poison arms, possibly by turning to some of the same European and Asian companies that had supplied Iraq with its production facilities. Iraq first charged that Iran was using chemical weapons in 1988, but there were unconfirmed reports that Iran experimented with poison gas on the battlefield in 1987.

Although the war-time use of the weapons received little international attention, Iraq's alleged poison gas attacks on its own Kurdish minority was vigorously condemned in several countries, especially in the United States. Iraq in 1988 reportedly began moving against Kurdish forces accused of siding with Iran. The most serious chemical weapons attacks took place in northern Iraq in mid-August, causing thousands of Kurds to flee into neighboring Turkey. According to a report issued in September by the Senate Foreign Relations Committee, the government dynamited Kurdish villages, relocated thousands of Kurds to military-controlled settlements, and made use of "terror tactics, including chemical weapons, to drive civilians out of areas to be depopulated."

Secretary of State Shultz denounced the attacks, and Congress moved to impose economic sanctions against Iraq in retaliation. Shultz's impassioned statements failed, however, to create much of a stir in world opinion, and the sanctions drive ultimately stalled in Congress.

At President Reagan's initiative, the United Nations in January 1989 sponsored an international conference on chemical weapons. The 148 nations attending condemned the chemical warfare but did not single out Iraq or any other country that actually had used the weapons.

Libya

The furor over chemical weapons might have dissipated entirely after Iraq's alleged use of them had not the U.S. government chosen in late 1988 to draw world attention to a facility in the Libyan desert. The State Department issued a statement in September that Libya was "on the verge of full-scale production" of poison gas weapons at a facility built near Rabta with the help of European and Japanese companies. Reagan heightened controversy over the issue in December by saying the United States was "discussing" with its allies the possibility of taking military action against the facility.

American officials later charged that West German businesses had provided most of the material and technology for the plant, which, once completed, would be capable of producing enormous quantities of chemical weapons. The Bonn government at first denied the involvement of any of its companies. However, after the U.S. administration leaked some of its information about the facility and news organizations began their own investigations, Bonn conceded that German companies had been major contributors to the plant. West Germany announced a series of investigations into the case and tightened its legal controls over the export of materiel and technology that could be used to make chemical weapons.

In his February 1989 testimony, CIA Director Webster said the Libya plant was "nearly ready" to produce chemical weapons. That assessment suggested that, while the plant lacked some of the necessary components, it would be only a matter of time before the Libyans could finish work on it and begin actual production of the poison weapons.

Other Countries

Other Middle Eastern countries also possessed chemical weapons or at least the capability to produce them by the late 1980s, according to U.S. government and private sources. Among them:

● Egypt reportedly acquired some chemical weapons in the 1960s, and it may have made limited use of them during its intervention in North Yemen during 1963-1967. According to some sources, Egypt was able to produce its own chemical weapons by 1973. U.S. government officials early in 1989 leaked reports that a pharmaceuticals plant under construction near Cairo was to be equipped in such a way as to permit large-scale production of poison gas. Egyptian President Hosni Mubarak heatedly denied the reports, and the Swiss engineering company that was providing equipment for the facility announced immediately that it was halting its participation.

● Israel reportedly began moving to obtain chemical weapons in the 1960s, possibly in response to Egypt's program. Israel had produced a substantial arsenal of chemical arms by the time of the 1973 war but made no use of them and denied that it had any such weapons. Unlike other countries in the region, Israel has devoted substantial resources to acquiring gas masks and protective clothing to shield its soldiers against poison gas attacks.

● Syria, like Iran, moved into the chemical weapons field relatively late—in the mid 1980s. As with its neighbors, Syria secretly obtained the necessary chemical agents and production equipment from West European firms. Within a few years, according to the CIA, it had established a substantial chemical weapons production facility and had equipped several weapons systems with nerve gas, possibly even its Soviet-supplied short-range Scud ballistic missiles.

Ballistic Missiles

Just as worrisome as the prospect of chemical weapons in the hands of terrorist groups was the proliferation of ballistic missiles in Middle Eastern countries. Poison gas weapons placed in the warheads of ballistic missiles could be carried hundreds of miles and could penetrate practically any available defensive system. In addition such missiles could be used to deliver nuclear weapons acquired by Middle East countries in the future.

Perhaps it was no coincidence that many of the same countries that acquired chemical weapons also obtained—or were trying to get—ballistic missiles capable of carrying conventional, chemical, or nuclear warheads for hundreds of miles. As with chemical weapons, some countries were not satisfied with merely purchasing ballistic missiles; they wanted to produce their own weapons to ensure that their supplies would not be cut off. The easiest way of doing that was to create new versions of missiles originally provided by the major manufacturers of ballistic missiles—the United States, Soviet Union, and China.

By the late 1980s every major country in the Middle East reportedly was equipped with at least a small arsenal of tactical missiles with ranges of a few dozen kilometers. At least three military powers—Israel, Iraq, and Saudi Arabia—also possessed intermediate range missiles that

Arms Sales to Middle East, North Africa

(millions of dollars, 1983-1987)

Recipient Nation	Total	Soviet Union	United States	France	United King- dom	West Ger- many	Italy	Czecho- slovakia	China	Bulgaria	Poland	Others
Middle East Nations	89,965	27,525	16,820	14,870	3,925	1,260	1,520	1,440	5,735	1,300	800	14,770
Bahrain	425	—	230	60	5	120	—	—	—	—	—	10
Cyprus	320	—	—	290	—	—	—	—	—	—	—	30
Egypt	7,820	340	3,400	1,600	200	60	270	—	550	—	—	1,400
Iran	8,865	100	10	NA	70	NA	NA	40	1,800	650	20	5,610
Iraq	29,895	13,900	—	4,800	40	700	370	700	3,300	625	460	5,000
Israel	4,300	—	4,300	—	—	—	—	—	—	—	—	—
Jordan	2,470	825	650	490	360	5	—	—	10	—	—	130
Kuwait	1,275	240	220	525	110	—	—	—	—	—	—	10
Lebanon	530	—	400	100	—	—	5	—	—	5	—	20
Oman	785	—	50	20	500	190	10	—	5	—	—	10
Qatar	555	—	10	525	20	—	—	—	—	—	—	—
Saudi Arabia	18,320	—	7,200	6,400	2,400	—	320	—	—	—	—	2,000
Syria	10,450	8,900	—	20	—	10	—	700	70	20	320	410
United Arab Emirates	610	20	320	—	220	—	20	—	—	—	—	30
South Yemen	1,918	1,900	—	—	—	—	—	—	—	—	—	10
North Yemen	1,435	1,300	30	—	—	5	—	—	—	—	—	100
African Nations	18,505	10,690	1,150	920	540	110	1,080	1,490	40	280	50	2,305
Algeria	3,230	2,500	240	60	160	—	40	210	—	—	—	20
Ethiopia	4,330	4,200	—	—	—	—	30	20	—	—	—	80
Kenya	80	—	40	—	40	—	—	—	—	—	—	—
Libya	7,730	3,900	—	240	—	30	600	1,200	10	200	50	1,500
Morocco	840	—	260	310	—	—	10	—	20	—	—	240
Nigeria	1,515	90	140	130	340	70	350	60	5	20	—	310
Somalia	195	—	70	10	—	—	50	—	5	—	—	150
Tunisia	585	—	400	170	—	10	—	—	—	—	—	5

Note: Totals for the Middle East include all nations in that region. Totals for Africa include only those nations listed, covering about 63 percent of arms sales on that continent. Sales to all African nations in the period covered by the chart totaled $29,295,000,000.

Source: U.S. Arms Control and Disarmament Agency, *World Military Expenditures and Arms Transfers,* 1988.

could travel several hundred kilometers and thus posed a threat to the entire region.

As with most other military technologies, Israel was at the forefront in acquiring ballistic missiles. From the United States, Israel in the late 1970s obtained an estimated 160 Lance battlefield missiles with a range of about 100 kilometers. Largely on its own, it produced a longer-range Jericho missile in two versions, both capable of carrying nuclear warheads or 500 kilograms of conventional explosives. The Jericho I reportedly had a range of 450-650 kilometers; the newer Jericho II had a range of up to 1,500 kilometers. Such a missile could attack targets throughout the Middle East and even in the southern reaches of the Soviet Union.

Israel in September 1988 also successfully launched a small satellite into orbit. The booster rocket, called the Shavit (or Comet), reportedly could be converted to a ballistic missile capable of carrying a nuclear warhead up to 7,200 kilometers—putting Moscow and all of the Middle East well within range of any base in Israel.

Israel also began work during the late 1980s on a defensive missile, the Arrow, intended to shoot down incoming ballistic missiles. The United States funded most of the research on that weapon under its Strategic Defense Initiative.

Saudi Arabia in 1988 startled the world by acquiring an estimated two dozen Chinese medium-range missiles (called the CSS-2 by the United States). Capable of carrying any type of warhead, the missile reportedly had a range of up to 2,700 kilometers. Saudi officials said the missile was intended to provide defense against Iran, but it also could threaten Israel and other targets in the region.

The Reagan administration protested the missile deal to both China and Saudi Arabia and got assurances from both countries that the weapons would not be armed with chemical or nuclear warheads. Citing those assurances and intelligence information, President George Bush in April 1989 certified to Congress that Saudi Arabia "does not possess chemical, biological, or nuclear warheads" for its missiles.

Iraq claimed to have developed two enhanced versions of a Soviet medium-range missile, the Scud-B. One Iraqi version, called the al-Husayn, was said to have a range of 650 kilometers. Iraq reportedly fired nearly 200 of them at Iran during the final stages of the Persian Gulf war. A more advanced version, the al-Abbas, reportedly had a range of some 900 kilometers.

During their war, Iran and Iraq fired hundreds of Soviet-supplied Scud-B missiles at each other, generally targeting civilian populations. For nearly two months in early 1988, the two countries attempted to demoralize each other's citizenry through the "war of the cities"—indiscriminate missile attacks that killed thousands.

Egypt, Libya, Syria, and South Yemen also were reported to possess small quantities of the Scud-B missiles, which can travel up to 280 kilometers in just five minutes. Moscow may also have supplied shorter-range SS-21 missiles to Syria and Iraq, according to some U.S. sources.

A demonstration of the internationalization of missile technology was the development of a medium-range missile jointly by Argentina, Egypt, and Iraq. An advanced version of Argentina's Condor-2, the missile was to have a range of about 800 kilometers. Argentina and Egypt were doing most of the work on the missile during the 1980s, with Iraq providing some of the financing. As of late 1989 it was not yet operational.

5

Persian Gulf: A Fragile Balance

The Persian Gulf is a strategic body of water that is home to more than half the world's oil deposits. It is fed by the two great rivers of antiquity—the Euphrates and the Tigris—and empties into the Arabian Sea through the Strait of Hormuz. Eight countries with a combined population of more than ninety million ring the Gulf: Iran, Iraq, Saudi Arabia, Kuwait, Bahrain, Qatar, the United Arab Emirates (UAE), and Oman. Iran, the only non-Arab country on the Gulf, has fifty-two million people—more than all of its Gulf neighbors combined.

From these nations, both on shore and under the Gulf waters, come millions of barrels of oil each day. Much of the petroleum is loaded on supertankers at vast but vulnerable terminals in the Gulf, and it flows in these carriers to the Indian Ocean through the narrow Strait of Hormuz. Although recent efforts throughout the region to build pipelines have reduced the Gulf nations' dependence on tanker shipments through the strait, the threat of disruption to the region's oil flow remains an international and local concern.

The effect of such a disruption on the world's economy was demonstrated by the Saudi Arabian-led 1973 Arab oil embargo. This action was a response to the Arab-Israeli war of that year and resulted in a temporary cutoff of oil from most Gulf states to the United States and a slowing of the flow to most of the rest of the world. The action contributed to a worldwide recession as the price of oil skyrocketed from less than $3 a barrel in early 1973 to about $11 a barrel in 1974.

Another round of oil price increases that began in 1979 again rocked the world's economy. That year three events occurred that raised fears in Washington and the capitals of other major industrialized nations that the Persian Gulf oil supply was vulnerable to disruption. In February the Iranian revolution resulted in the overthrow of the shah and the establishment of a fundamentalist Islamic republic under the leadership of the Ayatollah Ruhollah Khomeini. In November the seizure of the U.S. embassy in Tehran and the holding of American diplomats hostage confirmed the implacable hostility of the new government toward the West and the United States in particular. Finally, in December 1979 the Soviet Union launched a massive invasion into nearby Afghanistan to prop up the pro-Soviet government there.

The Soviet occupation raised questions about Moscow's intentions toward all of southern Asia, including the strategic Persian Gulf. Although most analysts discounted the possibility of a Soviet military move beyond Afghanistan, the Soviet invasion and the upheaval in Iran prompted President Jimmy Carter to declare in his State of the Union address on January 23, 1980, that "an attempt by any outside force to gain control of the Persian Gulf region will be regarded as an assault on the vital interests of the United States of America, and such an assault will be repelled by any means necessary, including military force." The statement came to be known as the Carter Doctrine, and it reinforced perceptions that what happened in the Persian Gulf region was of vital importance to the United States and the rest of the world.

While the 1970s had demonstrated the significance of the Gulf region, the 1980s provided evidence of its fragility. In September 1980 Iraq launched an offensive into Iran that turned into a bloody eight-year war of attrition. The war left hundreds of thousands dead, disrupted vital oil tanker traffic in the Gulf, and led to U.S. intervention in the form of naval escorts for Kuwaiti oil tankers. Meanwhile the economies of the Gulf states, all of which depend to some degree on oil, were devastated by the crash of oil prices in the mid-1980s. Plummeting oil revenues forced Gulf states to cut back severely on domestic development projects and services.

Despite these shocks the Gulf states and their governments survived. The Iran-Iraq war ended in a stalemate. Radical Islamic fundamentalism inspired by Iran did not lead to the overthrow of any Gulf government, the Soviets withdrew from Afghanistan after nine years with a deeper appreciation of the costs of direct foreign intervention, and oil prices recovered somewhat as world oil consumption began to increase. The experiences of the 1980s, however, have led Gulf states to attempt to reduce their dependence on oil income by diversifying their economies and to enhance their security through mutual cooperation.

History of the Gulf

Between A.D. 750 and 1258 maritime trading thrived in the Persian Gulf. Baghdad was the capital of the Islamic Empire and served as the hub of an extensive network of seafarers who traveled to Africa and India, supplying goods to the capital city. The fall of the Abbasid dynasty to the

Mongols in 1258, however, led to a decline in the region's trade. The political situation became increasingly unstable until 1497 when the Portuguese settled in the Gulf.

European nations—first the Portuguese and later the Dutch and British—were principally interested in controlling the trading of luxury items such as spices and silk and in securing the maritime routes to and from India; they did not want to interfere in the administrative affairs of the Gulf states. As the Portuguese empire weakened so did its influence in the Gulf. The Portuguese were followed by the Dutch, who had begun to establish trade links in the East. By the middle of the eighteenth century the Dutch began to yield to the British. With the evacuation from Kharg Island (off the coast of Iran) in 1765, the Dutch presence came to an end.

The Eighteenth and Nineteenth Centuries

The northern coastal area of Oman prospered after the al-Bu Said dynasty came to power there in 1749. The Omanis established an extensive Indian Ocean trading empire centered around the busy ports of Matrah and Muscat (the capital after 1786) on the Gulf of Oman. The Omanis extended their control as far south as the island of Zanzibar off the East African coast and as far east as Pakistan.

During the early part of the eighteenth century Kuwait and Bahrain challenged Oman's dominance in the region, especially in the northern Persian Gulf. The Utab tribe in Kuwait, under the leadership of the al-Sabah family, secured its independence from the Banu Khalid Arabs who controlled the northern part of the Arabian coast. Kuwait's location on the bay at the end of the overland route from Syria (now called the Kuwait Bay) was ideal for trading. During the 1760s a branch of the Utab tribe, the al-Khalifa, migrated from Kuwait to Qatar where they settled in 1766 at Zubara on the northern coast of the Qatari Peninsula. Later they seized from the Persians the pearl-rich archipelago of Bahrain, situated between the Qatari Peninsula and the Arabian coast. The new wealth, trading skills, and sea power of the Utab made the tribe a formidable force in the Gulf.

During the early nineteenth century, maritime warfare and pirating disrupted trade, threatened the pearl industry, and further impoverished the people of the Gulf. Unable to agree on how to stop the escalating piracy on the high seas, the Arabs allowed an outside power—the British—to assume the role of regulator of a maritime peace. The British, like the Portuguese and the Dutch, were interested in the Gulf for commercial and strategic purposes. In exchange for truces with the sheiks of the coastal tribes, the British agreed to police the Gulf. This so-called Trucial System eventually ended maritime warfare and piracy.

Britain was the major beneficiary of the Trucial System, which provided that nation with even greater freedom of trade as well as reduced expenses for naval patrols. Although the arrangement improved Arab shipping by ending sea warfare, it enabled Europe to dominate Gulf trade. Later, treaties were promulgated that gave Britain control of the foreign affairs and territorial boundaries of the Gulf sheikdoms. These treaties became the foundation of Britain's political, economic, military, and administrative hold on the Gulf that lasted for the next 150 years.

In the second half of the nineteenth century, British influence in the Gulf increased markedly. British military and economic assistance was needed to sustain the rule of the local leaders, including Oman's. After the death in 1856 of Oman's leader, Sultan Sayyid Said, his empire was partitioned between his two sons. The British, who had developed a close friendship with Said, arranged the division of the empire between his sons to end their quarrel and prevent possible civil unrest. Under the agreement Oman's southern empire centered in Zanzibar was to be controlled by one son, while the eastern empire centered in Muscat would be controlled by the other. In addition, Zanzibar was to pay Muscat a sizable annual tribute. When Zanzibar stopped paying the tribute soon after the agreement was implemented, British India began paying an equivalent sum to Muscat to support the rule of the Said family. By 1900 the British subsidy accounted for one-fifth of Muscat's revenues. Although Oman's independence was preserved, the sultans in Muscat were forced to accept increasing British control.

The Trucial States, which included Abu Dhabi, Dubai, Sharjah, Ajman, Umm al-Qaiwain, Fujairah, and Ras al-Khaimah (now the United Arab Emirates), formalized their relations with Britain in a series of agreements concluded between 1887 and 1892. The Trucial States consented to a nonalienation treaty (an agreement not to make territorial concessions). For its part, Britain agreed to defend the states against aggressors and to regulate their foreign affairs.

British influence over Bahrain, the most valuable area in the Gulf because of its lucrative pearl industry, also increased. In 1854 the Wahhabis, a highly puritanical Moslem tribe led by the Saud family in central Arabia, attacked Bahrain, and the al-Khalifa ruler sought assistance from Britain. The price of such assistance, however, was partial British control. Britain wanted Bahrain to be included in the Trucial System because it feared that an uncontrolled Bahrain would disrupt maritime peace. Despite hesitation by the al-Khalifa family, Britain did intervene to help Bahrain against the Wahhabi aggressors, and in 1880 and 1892 agreements were signed that gave Britain the responsibility for Bahrain's foreign policy and the protection of its territory.

Britain also extended its influence over Kuwait, which was formally part of the Ottoman Empire during the nineteenth century. In 1896 Mubarak al-Sabah killed his brother Mohammed, an Ottoman official who ruled Kuwait. Fearing Ottoman vengeance, Mubarak appealed to the British for protection. An agreement was concluded with Britain that provided for the nonalienation of Kuwait territory and British control over foreign affairs. In 1913 an Anglo-Ottoman agreement reaffirmed Kuwait's inclusion in the Ottoman Empire yet exempted Kuwait from Ottoman administration.

The Twentieth Century

World War I resulted in the breakup of the Ottoman Empire, which had sided with the losing Central Powers. Between World War I and World War II, Iran, Iraq, and Saudi Arabia allowed Britain to exercise influence in the Gulf. During this period the newly independent Gulf powers were preoccupied with consolidating their support, forming centralized governments, developing administrations, building armies, and modernizing their domestic economies. Britain functioned within a framework of consent by these regional states, exercising influence over the local affairs of the Gulf and protecting them from external threats.

During the period between the wars there were three

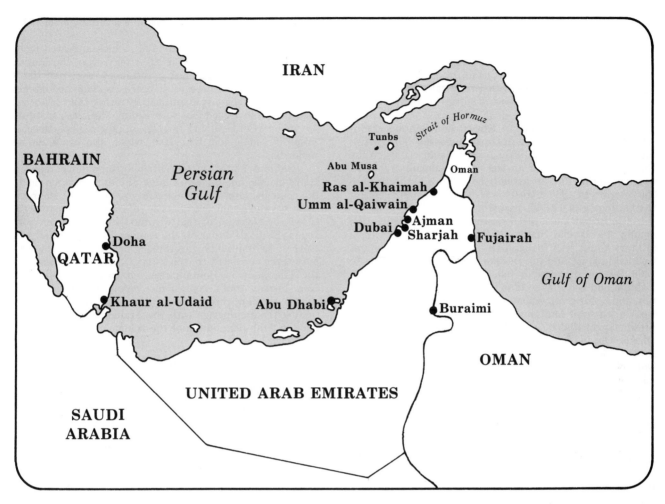

important economic developments in the region. First, oil was found in Iraq, Iran, and Bahrain, and later in Kuwait, Qatar, and Saudi Arabia. This oil bonanza brought new wealth into the area. Second, the Gulf region's isolation was reduced by the addition of roads, railways, radio communications, and airlines. Third, the rise of Japan's cultured pearl industry devastated the economies of the small Gulf states (with the exception of Bahrain because of its early oil boom).

World War II temporarily halted the development of the oil industry in the Gulf states, causing great economic hardship. Only Bahrain's oil production continued. The fear of Axis influence in Iran and Iraq led the British to intervene militarily in both countries and to install governments friendly to the Allied cause. Joint British and Soviet intervention in Iran created a corridor through which assistance was sent to the Soviet Union from the United States and other nations in the West.

After World War II, and especially after India gained independence in 1947, British interests in the Gulf materially changed. The strategic need to protect India ended, but British oil interests increased. The United States replaced Britain as the dominant outside power in Saudi Arabia before the end of the war, and British troops left Iran and Iraq in 1946 and 1947, respectively. The stationing of British troops in Oman, Sharjah (an emirate of the UAE), and Bahrain became increasingly controversial in British politics. Growing domestic disapproval of British

imperial policies led that country in 1961 to grant full independence to Kuwait. A decade later all treaty obligations with the other Gulf sheikdoms were terminated.

Britain's withdrawal from India in 1947 ended the British-Indian dominance of the Gulf economies. Europe, the United States, and Japan then became the major trading partners of the Gulf states. American influence increased in the postwar period—especially in Saudi Arabia and Iran—through economic links and the supply of arms and other assistance. The Soviet Union extended its influence in the region through gradual assistance to Iraq after 1958 and through relations with revolutionary socialist groups. The Soviets were forced to abandon an attempt to create a pro-Soviet puppet state in the northern Iranian province of Azerbaijan after World War II, however, because of angry U.S. opposition to the move.

The increase in oil production after World War II transformed the local Gulf states economically, socially, and politically. Bahrain and Kuwait changed quickly, while Oman and the Trucial States progressed more slowly. Port development began in Kuwait, Bahrain, Dubai, and Abu Dhabi. Refineries were built in Bahrain in 1937 and in Kuwait in 1949. Petrochemical, ship repairing, and food processing industries also sprang up in the postwar period. The newly acquired oil income led to a massive expansion of government activities and to a notable growth in the states' armed forces for both internal and external security.

During the 1950s and 1960s British influence in the

small Gulf states, as well as in Iran, Iraq, and Saudi Arabia, declined. After the Suez crisis of 1956, in which British, French, and Israeli forces attacked Egypt, demonstrations erupted throughout the Gulf, especially in Kuwait, which obtained independence from Britain in 1961. During this period Bahrain's relations with Britain also were hostile, although Britain retained base facilities in Bahrain until 1971.

As Britain's influence in Kuwait and Bahrain gradually declined, its influence in Oman increased. The British intervened in Oman in 1955 to resist Saudi claims to the Buraimi oasis (situated on the Saudi, Omani, and UAE border) and in 1957 to extend the sultan's authority into the interior. In 1958 a treaty was signed that provided for the stationing of British troops in Oman.

The British encouraged several measures of federation among the Trucial States. The Trucial Oman Levies, a military force, was founded in 1951, the Trucial States Council in 1952, and the Development Council in 1965. In 1968 Britain proposed a federation that would include Bahrain and Qatar as well as the Trucial States, but Bahrain and Qatar dropped out and the Trucial States became the United Arab Emirates on December 2, 1971, under the presidency of Sheik Zayed ibn Sultan al-Nahayan of Abu Dhabi. Originally the federation consisted of only six states: Abu Dhabi, Dubai, Sharjah, Ajman, Umm al-Qaiwain, and Fujairah. The seventh, Ras al-Khaimah, joined February 10, 1973.

Territorial Disputes

Britain's withdrawal from the Gulf brought regional rivalries to the forefront. For years the British had suppressed disputes instead of trying to solve them. The primary dispute between the states was territorial. Traditionally, jurisdiction over tribes in Arabia was of much greater significance than jurisdiction over territory, but with the introduction of the concept of the modern state by Europeans and the Westernization spurred on by the discovery of oil deposits, fierce territorial disputes developed in the Gulf.

Iran's Claim to Bahrain

The islands of Bahrain were wrested from Iranian control by the Utab tribe in 1783, and since then Iran has claimed the archipelago. In 1820 Great Britain concluded a treaty with Bahrain that extended it British protection. Iran was unable to challenge Britain's superior military strength, and Bahrain remained outside Iranian control.

When the British announced their intention to withdraw from the Gulf in 1968, Iran reasserted its claim to Bahrain. Iran opposed Bahrain's inclusion in a tentative plan to form a federation of Gulf states. This exacerbated shaky Arab-Iranian relations and created fear among the Gulf states of Iran's intentions.

In 1970 the shah of Iran agreed to a United Nations-supervised plebiscite in Bahrain. The UN report, drawn up after a twenty-day mission in Bahrain, stated that the Bahrainis interviewed had overwhelmingly called for a fully independent state. The report was endorsed by the UN Security Council on May 11 and was approved by the Iranian parliament three days later. This agreement, and the end of Iranian opposition to the creation of a federation

of the Trucial States, made possible a rapprochement between Iran and Saudi Arabia.

The controversy over Bahrain, which appeared to be settled in 1970, resurfaced in the aftermath of the Iranian revolution in 1979. The new government reasserted Iran's claim to Bahrain. However, it based its claim to Bahrain primarily on religious identification rather than historical tradition. Iran argued that since Shi'ite Moslems constitute the majority of Bahrain's population (about 70 percent), it properly should join with Iran, which also has a Shi'ite majority.

Bahrain and the international community rejected Iran's claims, but Bahrain's large Shi'ite population made it a principal target of Iranian subversion. In 1981 Bahraini security officials uncovered a Shi'ite Bahraini plot to overthrow the government that was thought to be inspired by Imam Hadi al-Mudarasi, an Iranian Shi'ite formerly in exile in Bahrain. The government believed that the seventy-three convicted conspirators of the Islamic Front for the Liberation of Bahrain received guerrilla training in Iran. Fear of Iran's expansionist foreign policy led Saudi Arabia to follow through with its plan to build a causeway linking the archipelago with the Arabian coast, thus confirming Arab domination of the islands.

Abu Musa and the Tunbs

In November 1971 Iran occupied the islands of Abu Musa and the Greater and Lesser Tunbs, located at the base of the Gulf, midway between Iran and the United Arab Emirates. The occupation followed three years of unproductive discussions with Britain and the emirates of Sharjah and Ras al-Khaimah, which had been given authority over the three islands by Britain. The shah's government used two arguments to justify the takeover.

First, Iran claimed that it had a historical right to the islands based on its continuous occupation of them until the end of the nineteenth century when Iran was evicted by the British. Sovereignty over the islands was illegally transferred, the Iranians contended, to Sharjah and Ras al-Khaimah. The dispute did not become a serious issue of contention until after the British announced their decision in 1968 to withdraw from the Gulf.

Second, the Iranians argued that the occupation of the islands was necessary to ensure Gulf security. The proximity of the islands to the Strait of Hormuz prompted Iran to stress their strategic location and its intention to oversee the free flow of oil and goods through the strait. The actual strategic importance of the islands, however, has been challenged by Gulf analyst Joseph Churba, who claims that control of the islands is "neither essential to block sea traffic in the Gulf, nor sufficient in itself to frustrate a determined naval power from pursuing that objective."

The current revolutionary government in Iran shows no sign of relinquishing control of the islands. Iran's occupation of Abu Musa and the Greater and Lesser Tunbs remains a contentious issue in the feud between Iran and the Arab states, despite the end of the Iran-Iraq war.

The Buraimi Oasis

The dispute over the Buraimi oasis, situated on the Saudi, Omani, and UAE border, has remained quiet since July 1974, when a bilateral agreement was signed between Saudi Arabia and the United Arab Emirates. In the years preceding the settlement, Saudi Arabia based its claim to the oasis on its historical connection to the area; the oasis was periodically occupied by Wahhabi warriors from 1800 until 1869, when Omani forces expelled them.

Abu Dhabi and Oman have a claim to the oasis based upon their shared occupation of the area since 1869. Saudi Arabia, however, reasserted its historical claim to Buraimi in August 1952, when it sent a police force to Buraimi and managed to reestablish its authority over the village of Hamasa. This development led to the Standstill Agreement of 1952, in which all parties agreed not to gain control of additional territory. In 1954 Saudi Arabia and Britain referred the dispute to an arbitration tribunal in Geneva, but the proceedings broke down after charges of bad faith on both sides. In 1955 Omani forces ejected the Saudi force from the oasis with British military assistance. In 1966 Oman and Abu Dhabi asserted their territorial claim by announcing the division of the oasis into Omani and Abu Dhabi jurisdictions.

Following Britain's announcement of its intention to withdraw from the Gulf in 1968, Saudi Arabia supported the creation of a Gulf federation, yet it continued to pursue its claim to Buraimi as well as to one-third of Abu Dhabi. In 1970, however, King Faisal of Saudi Arabia, under regional pressure to relinquish its claims, called for a resumption of talks to resolve the conflict. Bilateral negotiations between Abu Dhabi and Saudi Arabia led to a settlement in 1974. Saudi Arabia pledged to respect the claims of Abu Dhabi and Oman to the oasis in return for major concessions by Abu Dhabi on the Qatari border. Abu Dhabi agreed to give Saudi Arabia access rights to the Khuar al-Udaid inlet via a territorial corridor and pledged to share the disputed Zarara oil field. Although this agreement did not resolve many regional disputes over boundaries and water rights, it settled the central question of the oasis and led quickly to improved relations between Saudi Arabia and the UAE.

The Iranian Threat

The resurgence of Islamic fervor in the Gulf region began long before the Iranian revolution in 1979 and the outbreak of the Iran-Iraq war in 1980, but Arab fears concerning the exportation of revolution from Iran have greatly intensified since then. After the revolution, Iran's new government declared that spreading Iranian-style revolutions to other states was a primary precept of its foreign policy. Ayatollah Khomeini, Iran's spiritual leader for ten years until his death in June 1989, said it plainly: "Islam is a sacred trust from God to ourselves, and the Iranian nation must grow in power and resolution until it has vouchsafed Islam to the entire world."

According to Iran's leaders an ideal Islamic state would establish a "true Islamic government," which means that it must be ruled by antimonarchal, pro-Iranian religious leaders. It also would attain "true independence," through an anti-Western and anti-Soviet Islamic foreign policy. Finally, it would be a government of the common people, that would champion the interests of oppressed groups around the world.

Arab governments have reason to fear uprisings in their Shi'ite communities. Iran has the most people in the region, an overwhelming majority of them Shi'ites. Nearly two hundred thousand Iranians are dispersed throughout the Gulf Arab countries. Shi'ites are believed to constitute almost 70 percent of Bahrain's population and 55 percent of Iraq's. Iraq has the oldest and the most rebellious underground Shi'ite movement, known as Da'wa, in the Gulf. Although Qatar has the largest percentage of Shi'ites in the region, it has, as yet, no history of Shi'ite unrest.

Efforts to Export Revolution

In pursuit of its revolutionary goals, Iran has supported subversion and terrorism in neighboring Gulf states, as well as in nations outside the region such as Lebanon. Tehran is the headquarters of a number of revolutionary organizations, including the Islamic Revolutionary Movement of Iraq, the Islamic Revolutionary Movement of the Arabian Peninsula, and the Islamic Front for the Liberation of Bahrain. The Iranian government's precise connection with these groups is not known, although the government organized a "plan for an Islamic Front" that supposedly is under the auspices of the foreign ministry.

In 1979 Iranian cleric Ayatollah Ruhani threatened to lead a revolutionary movement to Bahrain unless Bahrain's rulers adopted "an Islamic form of government similar to the one established in Iran." Iran later denied any responsibility for the statement after strong reactions from Arab governments. Then in December 1981 Iran was accused of fomenting coups in Bahrain and other Gulf states. Although Iran again denied responsibility, Bahrain deported the Iranian chargé d'affaires for his alleged involvement in the plot. Bahraini and Saudi leaders accused Iran of training and arming more than seventy Shi'ite Arab terrorists, members of the Tehran-based Islamic Front for the Liberation of Bahrain.

Iran also was accused of instigating multiple bombings in Kuwait in December 1983. Armed terrorists allegedly entered Kuwait from Iran by boat. Western sources reported that final approval of the plot "came directly from a message carried to Kuwait by courier from Iran." The Tehran government again denied any involvement, calling the charges "a foolish and stupid lie." As a result of the bombings, Kuwait expelled more than a thousand Iranians, and other Gulf states tightened security measures.

Kuwait, however, could not insulate itself from further terrorism. In May 1985 the emir of Kuwait narrowly escaped harm when an Iraqi Shi'ite drove a car bomb into a royal procession. The Kuwait regime blamed Iran for bombings in 1986 and 1987. In April 1988 a Kuwaiti airliner was hijacked by individuals believed to belong to a pro-Iranian Shi'ite organization in Lebanon. The hijackers forced the plane to land in Iran and demanded the release of seventeen terrorists convicted in the 1983 embassy bombings in Kuwait. After refueling, the hijackers ordered the pilot to fly the plane to Cyprus, then to Algiers, where Algerian officials negotiated the release of the hostages in return for safe passage out of the country for the hijackers.

In addition to its subversive activities, Iran has attempted to export Islamic fundamentalism by proselytizing. Iran organizes and hosts international congresses for foreign religious leaders and uses the season of al-hajj, the Islamic pilgrimage to Mecca, to spread Khomeini-styled Islam to other Moslems.

In July 1987 political demonstrations by Iranian pilgrims and their attempts to take over holy shrines in Mecca during al-hajj sparked riots that resulted in the deaths of more than 400 people, 275 of whom were Iranian. The demonstrations did not appear to be ordered by the Iranian government, which had been trying to improve relations with the Saudis. Nevertheless, in the days that followed, the Tehran government accused Saudi security forces of brutality in dealing with the riots and vowed to oust the Saudi ruling family. Huge anti-Saudi riots in Tehran led to the sacking of the Saudi embassy, and two explosions at Saudi oil facilities in Saudi Arabia's eastern province were attributed to Shi'ite saboteurs.

In response to this unrest, the Saudi government strengthened its security forces and increased its military spending. It also initiated further development programs in its eastern province, which is heavily populated by Saudi Shi'ites (about 4 percent of the population), who generally harbor social, economic, and political grievances against the Sunni majority.

After Khomeini

During the first ten years after the establishment of the Islamic Republic in Iran, that government was largely unsuccessful in its attempts to export its revolution. With the exception of groups of Shi'ites in Lebanon, Iranian influence generally was rejected by Arabs, who saw Khomeini as the spokesman not for a broad-based Islamic revival, but for an Iranian, Shi'ite brand of Islam foreign to most Arab cultures. In addition, Iran's goal of destroying Iraq's government caused most Arabs to rally around their Iraqi brethren against the Iranians. The repressive aspects of the Iranian regime and its support of terrorism also cost it the support of many Arabs.

The death of Ayatollah Khomeini on June 3, 1989, was likely to affect Iran's efforts to export its Islamic revolution. There were signs that Iran's new leaders were inclined to spend a greater share of their attention and resources on economic reconstruction after the long Iran-Iraq war than on exporting revolution.

Even before Khomeini's death Iran had adopted a softer line toward revolution. During the second half of the 1980s, with all of their country's resources focused on the war with Iraq, Iranian leaders maintained that their support of Islamic revolutionaries would be primarily inspirational and rhetorical. Although Iran continued to back terrorism and subversion against neighboring governments, especially Iraq's close ally Kuwait, it was much more selective in choosing what operations it would support. Moreover, Tehran avoided aiding some foreign dissident groups, because such aid could have undermined more pressing national goals. For example, it ignored the fundamentalist Moslem Brotherhood in Syria, which opposed the regime of President Hafez Assad, because Assad's government was one of the few Arab governments to side with Iran in the Gulf war.

Iran's new president, Ali Akbar Hashemi Rafsanjani, and its new spiritual leader, Hojatolislam Ali Khamenei, have both called for a concentrated effort to rebuild Iran's economy that would include selected foreign investment. Such an effort would benefit greatly from economic links to nearby Arab neighbors. These nations, including Saudi Arabia, however, would not be inclined toward improving relations with Iran without some demonstration by Tehran that it would end its support for Shi'ite dissidents. Moreover, Iran has reason to seek accommodation with its neighbors because its oil industry is deeply affected by their production and pricing policies. Saudi Arabia's decision to increase its production in 1986 led to an oil glut that depressed prices and drastically reduced the oil revenues of producing nations, including Iran. Economic reconstruc-

tion will require that Iran maximize potential revenues from its oil industry.

The death of Khomeini has deprived Iran and some Shi'ites in the Arab world of a charismatic spiritual leader capable of inspiring them to sacrifice themselves for the cause of Islamic revolution. Nevertheless, exporting revolution remained a stated goal of the Tehran regime. Iranian leaders who rejected such action risked undermining their revolutionary credentials. The economic factors militating against an aggressive foreign policy, however, were likely to induce Iran's new government to reduce its material support for Shi'ite revolutionary groups in the Arab world.

The Iran-Iraq Rivalry

The disputes between Iran and Iraq that led to war in 1980 are rooted in historic, territorial, and ideological differences. Some analysts say the origin of enmity between Iran and Iraq goes back to the sixteenth century when the Ottoman Sunni—Persian Shi'ite struggles began. Others trace it all the way back to the Arab invasion of Persia in the seventh century and the Persians' subsequent defeat at Qadissiya. In fact, the Iraqis at times described the Gulf war as the "Second Qadissiya" or "Saddam's Qadissiya." Despite the longstanding rivalry between Iran and Iraq, their relations during the late 1970s were cordial. Then the Ayatollah Khomeini's Islamic Revolution succeeded in overthrowing the shah of Iran in 1979. This development reopened two historically contentious issues that eventually led to war: which country would control the Shatt al-Arab waterway and how much influence would the two countries exercise over the Persian Gulf region in general and the minorities in each other's country in particular.

Control of the Shatt al-Arab

Iran and Iraq have long struggled to control the Shatt al-Arab waterway, the 120-mile confluence of the Tigris and Euphrates rivers that discharges into the Gulf. *(Map, p. 97)* In 1847 the Treaty of Erzerum allocated the entire Shatt to the Ottoman Empire. This accord was later confirmed in 1911 by the Tehran Protocol. In 1913 the Constantinople Delimitation Protocol adjusted the frontier line of the Shatt al-Arab to give Iran a three-mile place of anchorage at the Iranian port of Abadan.

It was assumed that Iraq, which gained independence in 1932, would inherit the rights over the Shatt al-Arab, but Iran sought to alter the border, claiming that the treaties had been concluded at a time when Iran was weak and had no choice but to accept the terms. Border incursions by Iran occurred during the early 1930s, and in 1936 a military coup d'état in Iraq brought to power a government that was eager to make peace with Iran. Consequently, the two countries reached a new agreement on the frontier in 1937. Iraq retained control over the Shatt except for a small area near the ports of Abadan and Khorramshahr.

This treaty, however, did not end the dispute. Throughout the 1950s and 1960s Iran and Iraq accused each other of violating treaty obligations. In July 1958 a bloody coup brought a militant pan-Arabist government to power in Iraq. The following year Iraq demanded that Iran cede its offshore anchorage facilities at Khorramshahr and Abadan, excluding Iran altogether from the Shatt. Iraq asserted that the 1937 treaty had been concluded under

British pressure. Disagreements came to a head in April 1969 when Iraq demanded the withdrawal from the Shatt of all ships sailing under the Iranian flag. Iran refused and began to send naval units to accompany its ships. At one point it attempted to enforce control over the left bank of the Shatt.

On April 19, 1969, Iran unilaterally abrogated the 1937 treaty with Iraq. It expressed a desire for a new treaty—one based on the principle of international law providing for the division of the whole river along the thalweg line (the middle of the main channel of the river).

In 1971, when Iran occupied three islands in the Gulf—Abu Musa and the Greater and Lesser Tunbs—Iraq broke diplomatic relations. They were resumed in 1973 with help from Jordan and Turkey. Nevertheless, military tensions on the border escalated, prompting Iraq to protest to the UN Security Council against alleged Iranian invasions. A UN-arranged cease-fire in March 1974 remained in effect only until August when further clashes occurred. Iraqi and Iranian delegations then met in Istanbul to resolve differences, but they were unsuccessful. Tensions between the Iraqi and Iranian navies in the Shatt al-Arab continued to threaten to escalate into a full-scale war.

Relations between Iran and Iraq were complicated by Iran's support of the Kurds' fight for independence from the Iraqi government. The Kurds make up 20 percent of Iraq's population and predominate in the isolated mountains of the north. Iran had supplied the Kurds with arms and given them asylum in Iran when necessary. Iraq, in turn, backed religious and secular opponents of the shah and gave financial and military assistance to Baluchi, Kurdish, and Arab secessionist movements in Iran. Iran-Iraq relations reached a low point in 1974 when Iran, with U.S. and Israeli encouragement, began to increase aid to Iraq's Kurds. The combination of border clashes and support for rebel and dissident groups in each other's country brought Iran and Iraq close to open warfare.

By March 1975, however, tensions between Iran and Iraq began to decrease. Iraq believed it was imperative to avoid a full-scale war with Iran and to attempt to consolidate domestic power by putting an end to Iranian subversive activities. To accomplish these objectives, the shah of Iran and Saddam Hussein (then vice president of the Revolutionary Command Council) met at a session of the Organization of Petroleum Exporting Countries (OPEC) in Algiers. Assisted by the mediation efforts of the president of Algeria, the Iran-Iraq leaders issued a joint communiqué on March 6, 1975, announcing the reaffirmation of the 1913 Constantinople Protocol land boundaries but defining the thalweg line in the river as the new frontier on the Shatt al-Arab. Iran and Iraq signed a treaty on June 13, 1975, with three additional protocols concerning international borders and good neighborly relations. Each party also agreed to refrain from assisting insurgents in the other's country.

The Algiers treaty ushered in a period of friendly relations welcomed by Iran, Iraq, and neighboring Saudi Arabia. The United Arab Emirates, however, criticized Iran and Iraq for moving toward what the federation considered an organized domination of the Gulf. Iraq was scorned by some of the more radical Arab states—Syria and South Yemen—for "selling out" Arab territory. Despite the apparent rapprochement, the treaty conflicted with the Arab nationalist ideology of the Ba'ath party in Iraq. In retrospect, it is clear that the Iraqi leaders had no intention of accepting the agreement indefinitely; when Iraq was strong enough, they planned to reassert their authority over the

Shatt al-Arab.

Relations between Iraq and the shah's regime in Iran remained stable throughout the late 1970s. In July 1977 the two states signed six bilateral agreements covering trade, cultural relations, agriculture and fishing, railway linkages, freedom of movement for Iranians visiting the Shi'ite Moslem holy places in Iraq, and coordination of activities concerning the movement of "subversive elements." In October 1978 the Iraqi government complied with the nervous shah's request to evict the Ayatollah Khomeini from Najaf, Iraq, where he had been in exile since 1964 when he was forced to leave Iran.

Changes after the Iranian Revolution

The Iraqi government initially welcomed the Iranian revolution in February 1979. Hussein said of Khomeini's triumph: "A regime which does not support the enemy against us and does not intervene in our affairs ... will certainly receive our respect and appreciation." Iran broke off unofficial relations with Israel, left the Western-dominated Central Treaty Organization (CENTO), and announced that it would no longer police the Gulf. Iraq welcomed these changes. It hoped that the new government in Iran would turn inward and address domestic concerns, leaving the Gulf open to Iraqi influence.

By mid-1979 Iraqi-Iranian relations had changed dramatically. Iranian clerics had renewed Iran's claims to Bahrain and had urged Shi'ite communities in the Gulf to rebel against their ruling regimes. Shi'ites demonstrated in Saudi Arabia, Kuwait, and Bahrain. In Iraq dozens of Shi'ites were reportedly arrested in Najaf for planning demonstrations; several were executed. In response, President Hussein warned Iran: "Iraq's capabilities can be used against any side which tries to violate the sovereignty of Kuwait or

Bahrain or harm their people or land. This applies to the entire gulf." In October Iraq broke diplomatic relations with Iran, branding the revolution as "non-Islamic."

In April 1980 several incidents further harmed Iraqi-Iranian relations. On April 1 the deputy premier of Iraq, Tariq Aziz, was wounded by a hand grenade thrown by an Iranian. On April 6 Iraq cabled the United Nations to demand that Iran withdraw from Abu Musa and the Greater and Lesser Tunbs. Iran placed its border troops on alert in response. Harsh verbal attacks then followed. Khomeini called on the people of Iraq to bring down their government: "Wake up and topple this corrupt regime in your Islamic country before it is too late." Hussein responded: "Anyone who tries to put his hand on Iraq will have his hand cut off." An attack on the Iranian embassy in London by Arabs from the Iranian province of Khuzistan was widely believed to have been instigated by Iraq.

Clearly, the confrontation between Iran and Iraq had gone far beyond the dispute over the river boundary of the Shatt al-Arab. The pan-Islamic ideology of the Khomeini revolution to unite all Moslems, despite ethnic or cultural divisions, directly opposed the pan-Arab ideology of the Ba'athist government in Baghdad, Iraq's capital. Pan-Arabism is the nationalist desire to form a single nation united by language rather than religion. Khomeini and Iran's other religious leaders viewed their revolution, not only as an Iranian event, but also as the beginning of a worldwide revolution. Because of Iraq's religious composition and close proximity to Iran, it felt threatened by Iran's intentions.

Although Iraq's Shi'ites lived in poor conditions and had little influence in the Sunni-dominated government, they did not rally to the Iranian clergy's call to bring down the Iraqi regime. There are a number of reasons for this apparent paradox. First, opponents of President Hussein's rule were threatened with arrest, imprisonment, and even execution. The central figure in the Da'wa (Shi'ite) party in Iraq, Sayyid Muhammad Bakr al-Sadr, was arrested and executed in April 1980. A second reason that Iraq's Shi'ites did not rise up in great numbers against the government was that President Hussein attempted to appease the Shi'ite *ulama* (religious authorities) and population by spending funds on their mosques and other facilities and by recruiting them into the ruling Ba'ath party. Moreover, Iraq's gain in oil revenues benefited the Shi'ites. Third, some Shi'ites truly believed in pan-Arabism. Others shared the Arab distrust of Persians, and some resented Persian arrogance in affairs of religion and culture.

Despite the absence of a significant upheaval among Iraq's Shi'ites, the presence of a hostile Iranian government preaching Islamic fundamentalism and aggressively challenging Iraqi interests in the Persian Gulf was disconcerting to the Hussein regime. Even if Iran did not pose an immediate danger, its large population (almost three times the size of Iraq) made it a significant long-term military threat, and its subversive activities and intransigence on territorial issues ran counter to Iraq's regional ambitions. Given these considerations, Iraq began preparing for war in the summer of 1980.

The Gulf War

For eight years, the Iran-Iraq war threatened the stability and security of the Persian Gulf region. The war, which appeared to be lopsided in favor of Iraq when it began in 1980, turned into the longest and bloodiest war in recent Middle East history. Analysts have estimated that one million people were killed in the war, which cost the combatants hundreds of billions of dollars.

Each side possessed distinct advantages that led analysts at various points during the war to predict that it would prevail. Iraq had a more advanced arsenal of weapons and about five times as many combat aircraft as Iran. In addition, Iran's international isolation made it difficult for that country to purchase advanced weaponry and spare parts for its prewar arsenal. Iraq also enjoyed the support of most of the Arab world, including Saudi Arabia and Kuwait, which provided billions of dollars to the Iraqi war effort. In contrast, support for Iran in the Middle East was limited to Syria, Libya, and Algeria. Iran, however, had almost three times as many people as Iraq and greater territorial depth to aid defense efforts. In addition, Iranian leaders successfully portrayed the war as a religious crusade to many of the country's young fighters, who were generally more motivated than Iraqi troops through much of the war.

Neither side, however, was able to translate its advantages into victory. In the end Iran accepted a UN ceasefire after Iraqi battlefield gains in 1988. The war came to an end with both combatants in possession of about the same territory with which they started. Both societies, however, had been devastated by the war, which produced some of the most brutal tactics of the twentieth century, including rocket attacks on city centers, "human wave" assaults against fortified positions, and the use of chemical weapons.

Iraq Attacks

By mid-1980 the situation in Iran seemed to present Iraq with an ideal opportunity to end Iranian interference in the Gulf and to turn the clock back to the favorable border situation it had enjoyed until 1975. Iraq calculated that Iran was weaker militarily and more isolated internationally than ever before. Iran's central authority appeared to be disintegrating, and there was a purge in July of the remnants of the regular armed forces in Khuzistan.

On September 17, 1980, amid escalating border clashes, Iraq terminated the 1975 treaty and claimed exclusive sovereignty over the entire Shatt al-Arab. The government announced that all vessels using the estuary and waterway should fly the Iraqi flag and take on only Iraqi pilots. Iraq accused Iran of violating the 1975 agreement by supporting Kurdish rebels. In a statement published in 1979 the Iranian government said it would no longer abide by the shah's promise to stop aid to Iraqi insurgents: "The Iranian government blocked any Kurdish moves against Iraq, but the situation is different now. The Iranian government does not uphold this agreement."

On September 22 massed Iraqi forces pushed across the Iranian border east of Baghdad. In a second move the Iraqis crossed the Shatt and attacked key cities and oil installations in Khuzistan (called Arabistan and claimed by Iraq because a majority of its population is Arab and Sunni). Iraq's strategy was to destroy Iran's oil sources, refineries, and transportation routes and thus debilitate the Iranian regime. Within a month Iraq had occupied an area within Khuzistan of close to 3,500 square miles. Meanwhile Iranian jets knocked out the principal Iraqi oil installations at Kirkuk and Baghdad.

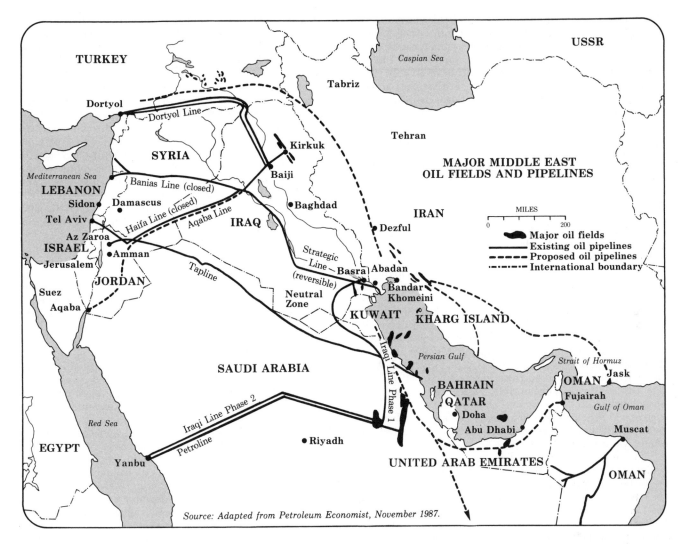

MAJOR MIDDLE EAST
OIL FIELDS AND PIPELINES

MILES
0   200

▬ Major oil fields
—— Existing oil pipelines
--- Proposed oil pipelines
–·–·– International boundary

Source: Adapted from Petroleum Economist, November 1987.

The war continued for more than a month before any significant attempts at mediation were made. All mediation efforts by the United Nations, the Islamic Conference Organization, the Palestine Liberation Organization (PLO), Pakistan, Algeria, Turkey, and others failed. The UN Security Council unanimously adopted Resolution 479 on September 28 calling upon Iran and Iraq "to refrain immediately from any further use of force and to settle their dispute by peaceful means." The resolution urged other states to refrain from "any act which may lead to a further escalation and widening of the conflict."

The Tide Turns in the War

Despite Iraq's initial success on the battlefield, it failed to achieve its ultimate objective: the fall of Khomeini's regime. The Iranian government held together. In fact, the invasion seemed to create a surge of Iranian patriotism. The war gave the Khomeini government an issue around which it could rally nationalist and religious fervor and an excuse to suppress dissent.

By November the Iranians had stopped the Iraqi offensive and were engaging the Iraqis in a war of attrition inside Iran. In the face of high casualties, the Iraqi government had expressed its willingness to negotiate, provided

Iran acknowledged Iraq's sovereignty over the Shatt al-Arab and pledged nonintervention in Iraq's affairs. Iran, however, rejected international appeals for mediation. Thus Iran's actions intensified its own isolation, while Iraq, having failed to win a quick victory, launched a diplomatic campaign to end the war.

In October 1980 the Iraqi National Assembly had appealed to parliaments around the world to urge Iran to accept peaceful means to end the war. Iraq also had sent cabinet ministers to meet leaders of Turkey, India, Saudi Arabia, Kuwait, and some European states to express "Iraq's peaceful attitude before and during the war."

The Ayatollah Khomeini, in response to all mediation attempts, repeatedly stated that Iran would fight the war until it was won. He called President Hussein "more criminal than the shah." Khomeini said his goal was "to establish an Islamic government in Iraq and to destroy the Iraqi regime in the same way as we destroyed the shah." In the late summer of 1981 Iranian forces launched heavy counterattacks designed to drive the Iraqis from Iranian territory. By April 1982 Iranian forces had recaptured the Khuzistan cities of Abadan, Dezful, and Khorramshahr. The Iraqi government decided to withdraw from the remaining Iranian territories under its control. Iran, emboldened by its military successes and driven by revolutionary zeal, was determined to strike Iraqi cities and oil fields and to break its military power. Iran planned to cut off southern Iraq from Baghdad, thus splitting Iraqi forces and creating conditions under which they hoped the large Iraqi Shi'ite population in the south would unite with Iran. In July 1982 Iranian troops entered Iraqi territory near Basra just across the Shatt al-Arab. Iraqi resistance stiffened, however, and the Iranian offensive was blunted.

In the fall, however, Iran continued attacks in the territory east of Baghdad and penetrated three miles into Iraqi territory. A large-scale Iranian offensive continued into the winter and spring of 1983. The apparent goal was to cut off Basra, Iraq's second-largest city and its main port on the Gulf. An Iranian offensive in February 1983, described as the "decisive and last," failed. It involved about 100,000 Iranian soldiers—many of whom attacked Iraqi lines in human waves. Thousands were left dead and wounded on the battlefield. Another major offensive, in April, netted Iran about twelve miles of Iraqi territory after bloody hand-to-hand fighting. Throughout the fighting Iraq's Shi'ite population generally remained loyal to the regime of President Saddam Hussein.

During the summer of 1983 Iraq embarked on a deliberate plan to internationalize the war, and to a degree it succeeded. The French sold Iraq Exocet missiles, and the Soviets increased arms sales to Baghdad. Member states of the Gulf Cooperation Council (GCC), especially Saudi Arabia and Kuwait, increased their financial support of Iraq. The United Nations, meanwhile, passed resolutions that were tougher on the Iranians than on the Iraqis. This success was primarily due to a worldwide fear of an Iranian victory in the war that seemed likely after Iran's successful offensives into Iraqi territory.

Fierce fighting continued in the spring of 1984. Iraq claimed it crushed the Iranian offensives involving as many as 400,000 troops. Iraq, however, was accused by Iran and the United States of using chemical weapons in violation of the 1925 Geneva agreement outlawing these weapons. The United States also accused Iran of throwing untrained units of teenagers against Iraqi lines to wear down the enemy before attacking with regular army units.

Tankers and Cities Attacked

In May 1984 the war entered a new and more dangerous stage. Iraq delineated a zone with a fifty-mile radius around the Iranian port of Kharg Island and began striking at tankers sailing within the zone. Baghdad justified escalating the conflict by asserting that its Gulf ports had been unusable since the beginning of the war because of shelling, while Iranian ports remained open to export oil that provided revenue to finance Iran's war effort.

Iraq hoped that the Iranian government would choose to negotiate an end to the war rather than risk having its oil exports cut off. Iran responded, however, by attacking ships calling on ports of Arab states in the Gulf that supported the Iraqi war effort. In fact, throughout 1983 Iran had declared that if it was prevented from using its own ports, it would make the entire Gulf unsafe.

The Arab Gulf states changed their previous cautious attitude and vehemently protested Iranian strikes against Gulf tankers. The Arab League also condemned Iran, and the UN Security Council adopted a similar resolution of disapproval. Despite protests, the tanker attacks continued through September 1985; by then seventy-seven ships—mostly commercial vessels not involved in the war—had been attacked in the Gulf by either Iran or Iraq.

Although both Iran and Iraq had occasionally bombed the other's cities during the first four and a half years of the war, neither had launched intensive bombing campaigns against civilians until March 1985. At that time Iraq began systematically attacking Iranian population centers in an attempt to force Iran to accept a negotiated settlement. The Iraqi attacks continued sporadically until the end of the war. The campaign against Iranian cities created many refugees and hurt Iranian morale. The Iraqis believed this campaign was the best chance they had of ending the conflict on their terms. Iran countered with surface-to-surface missile attacks on Iraqi cities. The Iranians had a limited supply of missiles, however, and their attacks inflicted much less devastation on Iraqi cities than Iraqi missiles and planes were inflicting on Tehran and other Iranian cities.

Iranian Offensives

During 1985 neither side could claim much progress in the ground war. Iran's superior numbers had not enabled it to breach the more sophisticated Iraqi defenses, but Iraq was unable to launch a counteroffensive to drive Iran from southern Iraq. Then in February 1986 Iranian forces launched a daring attack across the Shatt al-Arab that resulted in their capture of the Iraqi port city of Fao. The attack contrasted with previous Iranian offensives in that it was a well-planned military assault that relied on deception and mobility rather than on frontal assaults by poorly trained and ill-equipped Revolutionary Guards (volunteers known for their loyalty to Khomeini and their religious fervor) willing to die for the Shi'ite cause.

The attack led many observers in the Arab world and the West in mid-1986 to predict an Iranian victory. Iraq appeared to be in a tenuous position with the key city of Basra (Iraq's second largest) vulnerable to a successful Iranian offensive. All subsequent Iranian offensives failed, however. Iraqi resistance again stiffened, feuds within the Iranian government led to the dismissal of key military officers, Arab states increased their financial support of Iraq, and in the summer of 1987 the U.S. Navy began escorting Kuwaiti oil tankers in the Persian Gulf and challenging Iranian forces there. *(Tanker reflagging, Chapter 3, p. 62)*

In December 1986 Iran launched a major offensive against Basra that had been planned for a year and publicized as the final blow that would topple Saddam Hussein's regime. After two months of human wave assaults, Iran had failed to take any significant territory and had suffered huge losses of men and equipment. The failed offensive seriously damaged Iranian capabilities and morale. A UN-appointed team of observers also disclosed that Iraq had used chemical weapons on a large scale against the Iranian attackers, while Iran had employed such weapons on a smaller scale. The chemical weapon attacks may also have been a factor in the demoralization of the Iranian army.

In the late spring of 1988 the Iraqi army, supported by heavy air cover, began dislodging the weakened Iranian forces from their positions. For several months the Iraqis won major victories on the battlefield as Iranian forces retreated. Finally, in July, Iranian leaders accepted UN Security Council Resolution 598, which had called for a cease-fire in the war. The Ayatollah Khomeini, who had vowed to continue the fight until Saddam Hussein was ousted from power, called the acceptance of the cease-fire "more deadly than taking poison." The Iranian decision appeared motivated by the deteriorating situation on the battlefield, continued Iraqi air and missile attacks on Iranian cities, Iran's extreme international isolation, and a bleak economic situation caused by the war and diminished oil revenues. *(Texts of UN resolution, Iran's acceptance, Appendix, pp. 306, 308)*

The cease-fire called for in UN Resolution 598 was implemented August 20, 1988, a month after Iran accepted it. Although the cease-fire had held as of August 1989, no formal peace agreement had been signed. Neither of the exhausted combatants, however, appeared inclined to renew hostilities against the other, and debate in both countries focused on reconstruction efforts and internal politics. Nevertheless, the war did not resolve the territorial disputes and regional rivalry between the two nations, which as natural enemies could be drawn into another war in the near future.

Economic Implications

At the outbreak of the war in 1980, Iran's economic situation was very different from Iraq's. The Iranian economy was in disarray while Iraq was experiencing unparalleled growth and prosperity and possessed $40 billion in foreign assets. Ironically, the Iranian revolution had increased Iraq's prosperity by raising world oil prices, providing Iraq with the financial resources to launch an expansionist economic policy.

At the start of the war all export facilities, pipelines, and pumping stations were vulnerable targets. One week after the outbreak of fighting, major oil facilities had been attacked by both sides. The greatest damage was inflicted on Iraq. Iranian bombers hit Basra, Iraq's main oil-producing region in the south, which was responsible for approximately two-thirds of Iraq's prewar production; Mosul-Kirkuk, an important oil-producing and pipeline center; and the export terminals at Mina al-Bakr and Khor al-Amaya, which handled about two-thirds of the prewar exports. Iraq was forced to completely redirect its export flow away from the damaged and exposed Gulf outlets to overland pipelines. Iran's ally Syria, however, closed the pipeline running through its territory from Iraq to the Mediterranean Sea.

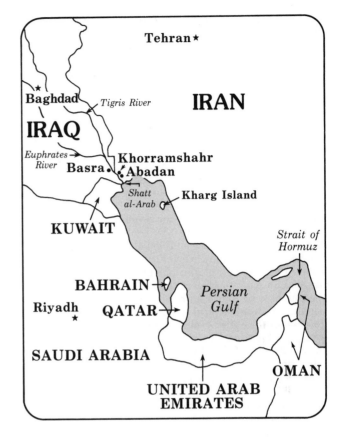

Iraq was forced to depend on just one pipeline running through neighboring Turkey to Mediterranean outlets. This pipeline facilitated the export of 1 million barrels a day, compared with Iraqi exports of 2.5 million barrels a day in 1980.

This predicament led Iraq to launch an ambitious pipeline construction program. In September 1985 Iraq opened a southern pipeline spur that joined a new trans-Saudi Arabian pipeline, thereby gaining access to export facilities at Yanbu on the Red Sea. By the end of the war Iraq's pipelines had raised its exports above 1980 levels. *(Pipelines and oil fields, map, p. 95)*

While Iraq built pipelines, Iran remained dependent on tankers to ship its oil. In the fall of 1985 Iraqi warplanes seriously damaged Iran's Kharg Island oil facility. Iraqi jets equipped with sophisticated French Exocet missiles also preyed on tankers carrying Iranian oil. As a result Iranian oil revenue fell from $14 billion in 1985 to just $5 billion in 1986, before recovering somewhat to $10 billion in 1987. This loss of oil income, upon which Iran depended to finance the war, damaged its combat capability and was a further blow to the population's morale. *(OPEC oil revenues, table, p. 117)*

Regional Implications

Disputes over territorial waters and Iran's claims to Bahrain and its annexation of three Gulf islands in 1971 have long plagued relations between the Arab states of the region and Iran. As noted earlier, Khomeini's calls for an Iranian-style revolution in the Gulf states and Iran's support for Shi'ite opponents of Gulf governments further soured relations between them and Tehran.

Fears of the Iranian expansionist threat led Gulf sheiks to align themselves with Iraq, which had itself been viewed as a threat in the past. The successful Iranian offensives in 1981 and later Iranian attacks on tankers heightened the Gulf sheiks' fears of Tehran, prompting them to provide financial help for Iraq's war effort. Gulf leaders recognized, however, that in the long term it was in the Gulf states' best interest that neither Iraq nor Iran be allowed to win a clear-cut victory that would allow the winner to dominate the Gulf. Therefore, the Arab Gulf states tried to mediate a satisfactory end to the conflict.

Saudi Arabia provided the Iraqi war effort with more than $40 billion during the course of the conflict. The Saudis also opened their ports to Iraqi shipping and began construction of the Red Sea pipeline. The Saudis feared that the spread of Iran's Islamic revolution would threaten Saudi stability and security. To contain Iranian belligerence and retain the prerevolution balance in the region, the Saudis took it upon themselves to protect the smaller Gulf states. Construction of the pipeline to the Red Sea was planned, in part, to protect the Gulf states' interests, and the purchase of American-built AWACS (Airborne Warning and Control Systems) was intended to enhance the air defenses of the entire Arabian Peninsula. Saudi Arabia also established a protective zone from the Strait of Hormuz to the Saudi port of Ras Tanura, which is located just a few miles west of Bahrain. The Saudis patrolled the area with American-built F-15 jets and naval patrol craft.

To strengthen regional security and improve economic, political, and military cooperation, Saudi Arabia, Kuwait, Bahrain, Qatar, the United Arab Emirates, and Oman formally established the Gulf Cooperation Council (GCC) in May 1981. Biannual meetings of heads of state are held, and a conference of ministers meets four times a year. The council set up a permanent secretariat in the Saudi capital of Riyadh. (Gulf Cooperation Council member states, map, p. 99)

Since its creation, the GCC has attempted to foster economic cooperation that would reduce tariffs and other barriers to trade between members. Job restrictions are being phased out, a common Gulf passport is being planned, and members have discussed unified patent legislation. The council advocates financial solidarity: the richer members would administer aid and jointly finance projects for the poorer members.

The GCC's primary purpose, however, was to enhance its members' security. The GCC established a joint military command to oversee GCC defense activities and conducted a series of joint military maneuvers—the first maneuvers ever held between Arab states—to test coordination of the six member states' Western equipment and command systems. These exercises were a visible symbol in the region that the GCC was working toward diminishing needs and pretexts for outside intervention. The GCC has also moved toward establishing a joint rapid deployment force and greater integration of members' air defense systems.

Analysts agree, however, that the GCC joint defense system could not stop an attack by a major regional power, including an Iranian strike against the Gulf states' oil installations. The Gulf states' small populations, diversity of weapons systems, and divergent domestic interests have impeded mutual defense efforts. Some of the council members have advocated close strategic ties with the United States, while others have argued for a policy balancing the superpowers. All the GCC members, however, have sought to avoid any public embrace of the United States because

of sizable American military and monetary support for Israel. Such obvious ties could have a negative effect on the Gulf regimes' relations with other Arab states and with their minority Palestinian populations.

U.S. Policy

The United States had three main objectives in the Persian Gulf war. They were to:

● prevent any disruption of Gulf oil shipments that could cause severe hardship in Western countries;

● ensure the security of the oil-producing countries in the region that have been friendly to the West;

● encourage a resolution of the conflict that did not give the Soviet Union a dominant position in either Iran or Iraq and that provided the United States with an opportunity to build relations with both countries.

Following the 1982 Iranian offensive into Iraqi territory and negative repercussions throughout the Gulf and the entire Middle East, the United States edged from its neutral stance to a slightly pro-Iraq position. In 1984 Washington reestablished ties with Iraq and began providing it with military intelligence. The official U.S. stance in the war remained neutral, however.

After the escalation of the tanker war in 1984, the Reagan administration pressed for a much more visible U.S. military presence in the Gulf. In May 1984 the United States offered to provide the Gulf states with air cover to deal with military threats. But no country took the United States up on its offer for fear that U.S. involvement would provoke Soviet intervention.

During 1985 and 1986, while the Reagan administration continued to condemn Iran's prosecution of the war and sought to internationalize its own arms embargo against that nation, official U.S. representatives tried to improve relations with Iranian moderates and secure Iranian assistance in freeing American hostages held by pro-Iranian groups in Lebanon by supplying antitank missiles and other weapons to Iran. The disclosure of the initiative in November 1986 seriously damaged U.S. credibility among the Gulf states and led to a more pronounced U.S. tilt toward Iraq in the Gulf war.

In 1987 U.S. ships began escorting reflagged Kuwaiti vessels through the Persian Gulf. The Reagan administration hoped the naval escorts would restore confidence in the United States among the Gulf states, put pressure on Iran to end the war, and ensure the flow of oil from the Gulf. The escorts brought U.S. ships and planes into direct conflict with Iranian forces on a number of occasions. American naval forces destroyed several Iranian ships and oil platforms in retaliation for Iranian attacks and minings in the Gulf. (Persian Gulf naval escorts, Chapter 3, p. 62)

While the U.S. Navy was putting military pressure on Iran, U.S. diplomats were working in the UN to build a consensus for ending the war. On July 20, 1987, the Security Council unanimously adopted Resolution 598, which called for a cease-fire. (Text, Appendix, p. 306)

Soviet Policy

The outbreak of the Iran-Iraq war in 1980 came at an inconvenient time for the Soviets. Anti-American sentiment in Iran had increased since the 1979 revolution, thus creating opportunities for the Soviets to gain influence. Iraq and the Soviet Union, however, had signed a Treaty of Friendship and Cooperation with the Soviet Union in 1972. The Soviets could not improve relations with Iran without

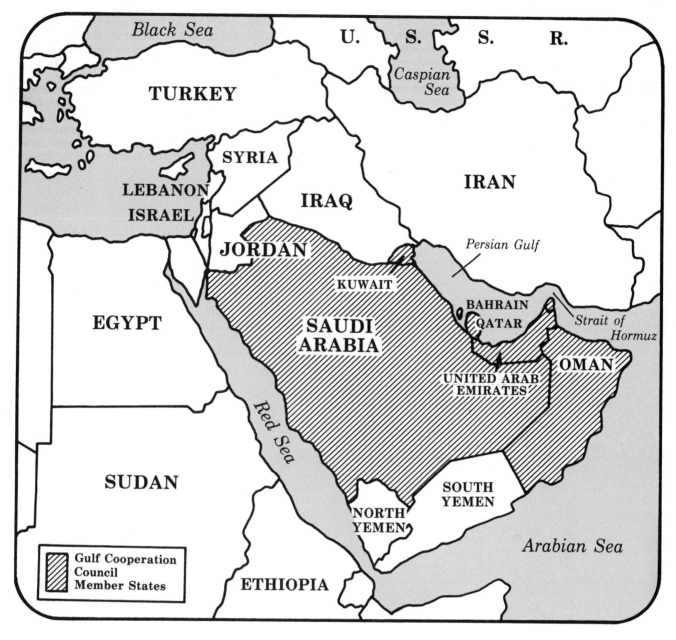

harming relations with Iraq. Although officially neutral, Soviet policy had a definite Iranian tilt.

Iran borders the Soviet Union and physically separates it from the Gulf. In the eyes of the Soviets, Iran is the real strategic prize in the region. The Soviet Union cut off arms sales to Iraq, while at the same time offering Iran major weapons systems and other forms of assistance. The Iranians rejected the Soviet offer, but Soviet arms and military supplies were provided indirectly by Libya, Syria, and Eastern European states.

Despite rebuffs, the Soviets continued to woo the Iranians in numerous ways. They pledged military, technical, and economic assistance; they offered to help the new regime deal with internal security threats; they blocked UN sanctions against Iran during the American hostage crisis in Tehran; they provided a transit route for goods bound for Iran during the U.S. economic embargo (also a result of the hostage crisis); and they even attempted to identify

with the revolutionary regime ideologically by claiming, "The liberation struggle can develop under the banner of Islam." Despite these efforts, however, the Soviets made no headway with the Iranians.

Following the Iranian offensives into Iraqi territory in 1982, the Soviets concluded new arms agreements with the Iraqis. According to Dennis Ross, executive director of the Berkeley-Stanford Program on Soviet International Behavior, this change in policy occurred for a variety of reasons. First, the Soviets had been rejected by the Iranians and were frustrated by Iranian hostility. Second, it was not necessarily in the Soviet Union's best interests to further the tide of Islamic fundamentalism and the image of an invincible Iran. The threat of a row of Iran-dominated Shi'ite states along the Soviet border must have affected the Soviet outlook. Third, the defeat of Iraq, which depended on Soviet weapons, would have embarrassed the Soviets.

During the spring of 1984, although continuing to publicly declare neutrality, the Soviets tilted further toward Iraq. In March the chairman of the State Committee for Foreign Economic Relations of the Soviet Union, Y. A. Ryabov, traveled to Baghdad and concluded important economic and technical agreements, including an agreement for Soviet construction of a nuclear reactor in Iraq. In April Iraq's deputy premier, Taha Yasin Ramadan, and Iraq's foreign minister, Tariq Aziz, visited Moscow and signed a long-term agreement expanding economic and technical cooperation between the two countries. Tariq Aziz later indicated that the Soviet Union had extended $2 billion in long-term loans with easy credit terms for Iraqi economic projects. Also it was reported that the Soviets had agreed to provide Iraq with surface-to-surface missiles and air-to-ground explosives.

For the duration of the war the Soviets continued to provide Iraq with weapons while frequently exploring opportunities to improve relations with Iran. In 1987 the Soviet Union, like the United States, agreed to escort Kuwaiti tankers through the Gulf. The Soviet naval presence, however, remained much smaller than that of the United States. In 1987 the Soviets also supported UN Security Council Resolution 598.

6

Mideast Oil: An Uncertain Future

In 1971 oil-importing nations paid about $2 a barrel for petroleum produced by the thirteen-member Organization of Petroleum Exporting Countries (OPEC). By 1981 the price of OPEC oil had jumped to an average of between $35 and $36 a barrel. This 1,700 percent increase fundamentally changed the rules that had governed international economic and political relationships. Of all known world reserves, two-thirds of the oil and one-half of the natural gas were in the Middle East. These vast supplies—monumentally surpassing any that were known in other parts of the world—meant that whatever happened in the Middle East affected the economies of countries everywhere. This was true not just of industrialized nations whose lifeblood was petroleum. It was true also of poorer developing nations that were plunged deeply into debt to meet their much simpler energy needs and then were pushed, in some cases, to the brink of economic disaster as world recession decimated the export earnings they needed to handle the debt.

At the start of the 1970s, the Western oil companies largely controlled the spigot to the oil. By the end of the decade, after two major surges in prices and a wrenching oil embargo that traumatized industrial countries, the members of OPEC had gained firm control over oil production and prices.

During the 1980s, however, OPEC lost some of its control over the oil spigot. The organization could not prevent a plummeting of international oil demand, a world oil glut, and inexorable downward pressure on petroleum prices. Religious, economic, and even military conflict among OPEC's member nations hampered the organization's ability to act with the unity required to make the cartel effective.

Nobody expected pre-1970 oil prices to return, but the 1980s showed that market supply and demand forces would have as much influence as cartel decisions on oil prices in the longer run. At the same time, the enormous Middle East petroleum reserves and the significant cost advantages in extracting oil and gas enjoyed by nations there left little doubt that OPEC nations would continue to have influence over the world's oil supply.

The impact of a seventeen-fold increase in oil prices stunned nations dependent on foreign oil, but it had equally startling consequences for the oil-rich exporting countries themselves. The most obvious and immediate effect of the two rounds of oil price increases was a redistri-

bution of wealth. While many non-Communist industrialized nations sank into economic recession, many of the thirteen oil-producing states in OPEC suddenly were gorged with money. With the transfer of wealth came a dramatic shift in political and economic power. Not only did the major oil-producing states, especially Saudi Arabia, control a vital resource, but they also had accumulated by the end of 1983 some $400 billion in foreign assets.

Supply-Demand Change

As the oil-importing economies tried to cope with the problems caused by the two rounds of oil price increases, they twice slipped into recession. The recession of 1974-1975 was the worst since World War II up to that time, but economic growth soon resumed, and with it came a steady increase in demand for imported oil, particularly from the United States. But when the industrial economies went into recession between 1980 and 1982, following the 1978-1979 round of oil price increases, world oil usage began to change. Conservation, fuel-switching, and reduced economic activity caused the demand for oil to fall in industrial and developing economies. The volume of oil exported and imported throughout the world peaked in 1979 and declined steadily until it reached about two-thirds of its 1979 level in 1983.

Despite the decline in the volume of oil traded, the price charged by oil exporting nations continued to rise. It did not peak until early 1981 when the key OPEC benchmark price—for light crude oil from Saudi Arabia—reached $34 a barrel. Even though OPEC's customers had sharply curtailed their purchases, OPEC maintained the price at that level for two more years, driving demand down farther.

The oil-exporting nations that were not members of OPEC continued to increase production. Mexico brought ever-greater amounts of oil to market from new fields in the Yucatan Peninsula, and the British and Norwegians expanded production from the North Sea.

The twin forces of sharply lower demand and escalating production from sources it did not control put increasing pressure on OPEC to lower prices as the 1980s progressed. The benchmark price of Saudi light crude could not be sustained at the record levels of 1981. OPEC production during the first quarter of 1983 averaged an abnormally low 15.5 million barrels per day (bpd), which was

considerably less than the 22.6 million barrels a day that had been produced when the Saudi benchmark price was raised to $34. In March 1983 OPEC was forced to cut the price of Saudi light by $5 to $29 a barrel and to agree upon production ceilings for its members. These measures seemed sufficient to restore equilibrium to the market temporarily. Demand remained sluggish, and a second, even more stringent, production cutback was accepted by OPEC in October 1984. Even so, more price cuts were necessary.

Because it was producing less oil at lower prices, OPEC's revenues fell. Oil-producing countries once flush with cash suddenly had to cut back their domestic development and industrialization programs. OPEC as a whole went from having a trade surplus to having a trade deficit. Saudi Arabia shouldered the largest share of the production cut. Saudi production had fallen from an average of 9.6 million bpd during 1981 to less than 3.5 bpd in 1985.

Reining in production appeared adequate to prevent further drops in oil consumption. During 1985 oil prices increased steadily, suggesting that demand was expanding. Economic recovery in the United States continued at what appeared to be a slow but sustainable pace, and the European economies also seemed to be recovering, although even more gradually. Despite the strains produced by market forces and the often bitter internal disputes between its members, OPEC continued to function as the major force propping up the price of oil.

From 1981 to 1985 OPEC's members seemed to have a willingness and ability to accept major sacrifices to support the oil price. In the 1970s observers debated whether OPEC was a true cartel, since it had never been forced to allocate production among its members. OPEC in the early 1980s began trying to do just that, imposing major production cuts that—although not perfect—effectively kept oil

prices from tumbling. The decline in oil prices had been relatively modest by late 1985 compared with the leaps upward that occurred in the 1970s. Despite severe pressures, OPEC seemed to have the discipline to prevent sharp price declines that would split it apart.

Then in 1986 the bottom fell out. In that year, oil prices plunged in a virtual free fall to under $10 a barrel. The market was dramatically communicating an important message: there was too much oil—at least in the short term. The reasons for that surplus could be traced to the internal politics of OPEC. Saudi Arabia, tired of curbing its own production to make up for the indiscipline of other OPEC members, decided to stop doing so.

Vast Reserves, Low Cost

While petroleum has been discovered in dozens of countries throughout the world, by far the largest concentrations of oil and natural gas reserves in the non-Communist world are found in the countries adjacent to the Persian Gulf.

Smaller but still important reserves are found in the Arab countries of North Africa. At the end of 1987 Middle East reserves were estimated at 470-565 billion barrels of oil and 1,084-1,167 trillion cubic feet of natural gas, representing about two-thirds of the non-Communist world's oil reserves and three-fifths of its natural gas. The countries of Abu Dhabi, Iran, Iraq, Kuwait, and Saudi Arabia each contain greater oil reserves than the still-considerable reserves found in the United States. Saudi Arabia alone has known oil reserves six times greater than the United States possesses, while Iranian gas reserves are at least twice the size of those in the United States. *("Estimated Crude Oil and Natural Gas Proved Reserves," chart, p. 105)*

The largest and most important oil fields in the Middle East, such as the giant Ghawar field in Saudi Arabia, which stretches for a hundred miles, contain oil that is easy to extract. The oil is found in formations that are well understood geologically, relatively close to the surface, and permeable enough to permit easy flow of oil to the wells. Most new oil fields being developed in other regions, such as Alaska, the North Sea, or the Gulf of Guinea, all present difficult and expensive technical challenges. Extremely expensive offshore drilling platforms or other unusual logistical support facilities, such as the trans-Alaska pipeline, add significantly to oil-production costs.

Persian Gulf Oil Advantages

The cost of producing a barrel of oil in the Persian Gulf (before royalties or taxes) has been estimated at about two dollars. Oil from most other regions is considerably more expensive to extract because of higher production and exploration costs. For the expensive frontier production areas such as Alaska the cost of each barrel of oil is on the order of $15 to $18. Consequently, major declines in world oil prices are more harmful to oil producers outside the Middle East. A price drop of $5 a barrel can make large offshore and remote projects unprofitable and force some production to be shut down.

A second advantage enjoyed by Middle East producers is that there has been relatively little exploratory and development drilling in the Middle East, compared with nations such as the United States, where oil fields have

Petroleum Supply and Disposition, 1986

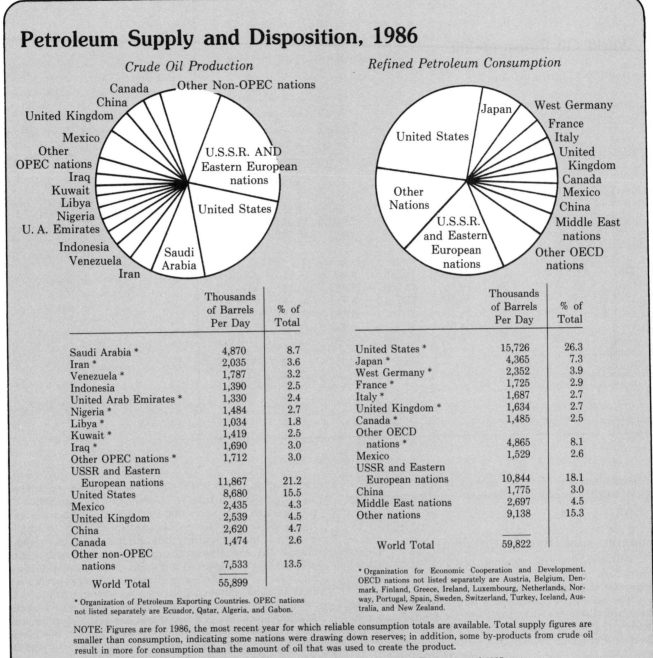

Crude Oil Production

Refined Petroleum Consumption

	Thousands of Barrels Per Day	% of Total
Saudi Arabia *	4,870	8.7
Iran *	2,035	3.6
Venezuela *	1,787	3.2
Indonesia	1,390	2.5
United Arab Emirates *	1,330	2.4
Nigeria *	1,484	2.7
Libya *	1,034	1.8
Kuwait *	1,419	2.5
Iraq *	1,690	3.0
Other OPEC nations *	1,712	3.0
USSR and Eastern European nations	11,867	21.2
United States	8,680	15.5
Mexico	2,435	4.3
United Kingdom	2,539	4.5
China	2,620	4.7
Canada	1,474	2.6
Other non-OPEC nations	7,533	13.5
World Total	55,899	

* Organization of Petroleum Exporting Countries. OPEC nations not listed separately are Ecuador, Qatar, Algeria, and Gabon.

	Thousands of Barrels Per Day	% of Total
United States *	15,726	26.3
Japan *	4,365	7.3
West Germany *	2,352	3.9
France *	1,725	2.9
Italy *	1,687	2.7
United Kingdom *	1,634	2.7
Canada *	1,485	2.5
Other OECD nations *	4,865	8.1
Mexico	1,529	2.6
USSR and Eastern European nations	10,844	18.1
China	1,775	3.0
Middle East nations	2,697	4.5
Other nations	9,138	15.3
World Total	59,822	

* Organization for Economic Cooperation and Development. OECD nations not listed separately are Austria, Belgium, Denmark, Finland, Greece, Ireland, Luxembourg, Netherlands, Norway, Portugal, Spain, Sweden, Switzerland, Turkey, Iceland, Australia, and New Zealand.

NOTE: Figures are for 1986, the most recent year for which reliable consumption totals are available. Total supply figures are smaller than consumption, indicating some nations were drawing down reserves; in addition, some by-products from crude oil result in more for consumption than the amount of oil that was used to create the product.

Source: Department of Energy, Energy Information Administration, *International Energy Annual 1987.*

been studied and explored for many years. For instance, in 1981, the year of peak oil revenues, Saudi Arabia drilled 58 exploratory wells and 160 development wells. In the United States, 90,260 exploratory and development wells were completed. Nevertheless, the Saudis outproduced the United States by nearly a million barrels a day in that year. By the 1980s the United States had already found and pumped most of the low-cost oil on its own territory, while Middle East nations were still finding large new reserves practically every time they drilled.

The magnitude of Middle East oil reserves may also be seen by comparing the Middle East's potential production rates per barrel of known oil reserves with the production rates of other producers. If the countries of the Persian Gulf tapped their oil reserves at the same rate as the United States they would produce 44 billion barrels each year, instead of the 4.2 billion actually produced. In other words, if the Middle East oil capacity were developed to its fullest extent, it could supply more than twice the total 1984 world oil production in a single year. For political and

World Oil Consumption

(thousands of barrels per day)

Year	United States	Canada	Japan	OECD Europe	Soviet Union	Other	Total
1960	9,800	840	660	4,535	2,380	3,125	21,340
1965	11,510	1,140	1,740	8,257	3,610	4,883	31,140
1970	14,700	1,149	3,850	13,580	5,300	7,891	46,470
1975	16,320	1,720	4,500	12,726	7,650	12,434	55,350
1980	17,060	1,870	4,960	13,648	8,940	16,722	63,200
1981	16,060	1,770	4,850	12,530	9,080	16,710	61,000
1982	15,300	1,580	4,580	12,069	8,950	17,141	59,620
1983	15,230	1,450	4,400	11,779	8,910	17,181	58,950
1984	15,730	1,470	4,580	11,747	8,950	17,523	60,000
1985	15,730	1,490	4,370	11,580	8,950	17,700	59,820
1986	16,280	1,510	4,390	12,030	8,980	18,170	61,360

Source: Department of Energy, Energy Information Agency, *Annual Energy Review 1988, International Energy Annual 1987.*

Consumption of oil by non-Communist nations reached a peak in 1980 and declined slightly in the following three years. A slight upturn began in 1984.

economic reasons, however, nations in this region have never tried to produce at capacity, a policy unlikely to change.

Location and Defense Problems

Although the Arab members of OPEC enjoy distinct advantages in oil production, they also must deal with important disadvantages.

The bulk of Middle Eastern oil reserves are far from the areas where the petroleum will be refined and consumed. The two principal markets for Persian Gulf oil are Western Europe and Japan. Oil destined for either region must cross thousands of miles of ocean in slow, difficult-to-defend supertankers. This oil lifeline is vulnerable to interruption at a number of points en route, but perhaps none so dangerous as the narrow Strait of Hormuz where the Gulf enters the Arabian Sea, and through which much of the world's oil passes daily. *(Persian Gulf, map, p. 89)*

The damage caused to hundreds of ships in the Persian Gulf during the Iran-Iraq war demonstrated the vulnerability of oil that must pass through the Strait of Hormuz. Early in the war, the Iraqis lost the capability to load oil for passage through the Gulf. After several unsuccessful attempts, Iraq inflicted heavy damage on the principal Iranian terminal facilities at Kharg Island. Iran threatened to close the strait if its own loading facilities were ever totally knocked out.

The 1988 Iran-Iraq cease-fire ended attacks on ships in the Gulf, but the war's effects have caused some Gulf states, particularly Iraq, to emphasize oil transportation by pipeline. Iraq may use either the Gulf or pipelines through Syria and Turkey to the Mediterranean coast to supply European markets with crude oil from its Kirkuk field. During the war Iraq's oil exports shrank to only about 800,000 bpd as Iranian attacks shut down Iraqi oil-loading facilities on the Gulf, and Syria, Iran's ally, prohibited Iraqi pipeline shipments through its territory. Iraq's only oil outlet was the Turkish pipeline ending at a port on the Mediterranean Sea. To ease these transportation problems, Iraq built a pipeline around Kuwait to join the major pipeline crossing Saudi Arabia to the Red Sea port of Yanbu, which began operating in late 1985.

Passage of goods through the Red Sea, while safer than Gulf passage, is not without risks. In late 1984 mines laid by an unknown country caused damage to many ships. Western nations and Egypt cooperated in a successful mine-sweeping operation that cleared the Red Sea. *(Pipelines and oil fields, map, p. 95)*

Natural gas transportation can be even more problematic. While oil from Algeria, on the North African coast, can be transported easily to European markets, Algeria's natural gas must be liquefied before it can be shipped across the Mediterranean to Europe and across the Atlantic to the United States. Algeria has the third-largest reserves of natural gas in the Middle East and has invested heavily in liquefying facilities, but the liquefaction project has proved expensive.

The same situation exists in much of the Middle East. Most natural gas associated with oil production is still flared (burned off), but Arab countries are beginning to use the gas in domestic development projects, either by reinjecting it into oil fields to sustain production pressure or by using it as the principal fuel for domestic industries. Some countries, notably Saudi Arabia, Kuwait, and Iran, also are trying to overcome the difficulty of transporting natural gas to distant markets by using it as the raw material for new petrochemical and fertilizer complexes. Once converted to other products, the chemicals can be transported to European markets in smaller ships able to pass through the Red Sea and Suez Canal.

Another disadvantage that Middle Eastern producers face is the difficulty of defending their production operations. For the most part, the region's oil is located in sparsely populated countries that have neither the manpower nor the topography needed to defend against a military attack by a determined aggressor.

Despite the vast spending on military weaponry by the Persian Gulf states, most of them could not withstand a military attack by a major industrial power. Yet direct intervention by outside countries has not occurred. Any unilateral hostile action in the region by an outside power would likely be opposed by other nations with an interest in the same oil supplies. Many countries, including the United States, consider continued access to Middle East oil vital to their national interests. As long as stability in the region is maintained and access to supplies is ensured, unilateral intervention seems unlikely, in part because of the deterrence provided by other powers that might fight to protect their oil supply.

The United States has long been concerned about the possibility of a Soviet military move to control Middle East oil-producing regions. To meet this perceived threat, the United States has attempted to increase its military presence in the area. Both the Carter and Reagan administrations sought access to military bases close to the Persian Gulf as support facilities for any military action that might be required to prevent Soviet intrusion into the oil fields. The key oil-producing countries of the Gulf, however, have been unwilling to permit a permanent military presence by a superpower and seem determined to avoid creating a pretext for having one forced upon them. Only Oman has granted the United States military-base rights on its territory and even that nation was under pressure from other Arab states to deny the United States access.

In an attempt to meet their security needs without involving the superpowers, six nations—Saudi Arabia, Kuwait, Qatar, Bahrain, Oman, and the United Arab Emirates—jointly formed the Gulf Cooperation Council (GCC) in 1981. Originally the organization's purpose was exchanging information about domestic threats to avoid crises that could prompt superpower intervention. Since then the GCC has taken on a more significant military role. On November 29, 1984, GCC leaders announced agreement on the creation of a GCC armed force to defend their countries, although American strategists doubt this force would be adequate to handle many foreign military threats.

Oil Price Shocks

Twice in the 1970s—in 1974-1975 and in 1978-1980—the world was made painfully aware of just how high and fast oil prices could rise. Both price leaps occurred after producing countries made a political decision to reduce supplies at a time when industrial economies were growing rapidly and inflation was gaining strength.

The first political decision came in 1973 when Arab oil-producing nations cut their production and imposed an embargo on petroleum exports to the United States and several other nations that supported Israel during the 1973 Arab-Israeli war. *(Details of embargo, this chapter, p. 112.)*

The 1978-1980 price increases came at a moment of great change in the Middle East. A revolution in Iran

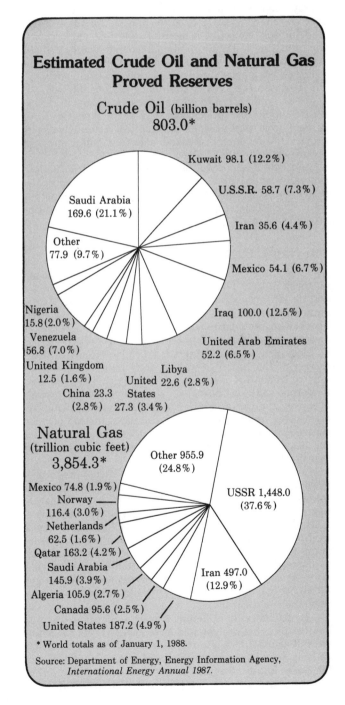

Estimated Crude Oil and Natural Gas Proved Reserves

Crude Oil (billion barrels)
803.0*

- Kuwait 98.1 (12.2%)
- U.S.S.R. 58.7 (7.3%)
- Iran 35.6 (4.4%)
- Mexico 54.1 (6.7%)
- Iraq 100.0 (12.5%)
- United Arab Emirates 52.2 (6.5%)
- Libya 22.6 (2.8%)
- United States 27.3 (3.4%)
- China 23.3 (2.8%)
- United Kingdom 12.5 (1.6%)
- Venezuela 56.8 (7.0%)
- Nigeria 15.8 (2.0%)
- Other 77.9 (9.7%)
- Saudi Arabia 169.6 (21.1%)

Natural Gas (trillion cubic feet)
3,854.3*

- Other 955.9 (24.8%)
- USSR 1,448.0 (37.6%)
- Iran 497.0 (12.9%)
- United States 187.2 (4.9%)
- Canada 95.6 (2.5%)
- Algeria 105.9 (2.7%)
- Saudi Arabia 145.9 (3.9%)
- Qatar 163.2 (4.2%)
- Netherlands 62.5 (1.6%)
- Norway 116.4 (3.0%)
- Mexico 74.8 (1.9%)

* World totals as of January 1, 1988.

Source: Department of Energy, Energy Information Agency, *International Energy Annual 1987.*

replaced the pro-Western government of Shah Mohammed Reza Pahlavi with a fundamentalist Islamic regime headed by Ayatollah Ruhollah Khomeini. Disruption in oil supplies occurred when the combined effect of turmoil and the new government's policy greatly reduced production levels. Because demand for oil does not respond quickly to changes in supply (in the vocabulary of economists it is "inelastic" in the short term), an oil shortage developed that pushed prices higher.

Because severe recessions quickly followed the major oil price increases, consuming nations had to deal with both the gloom of immediate economic downturns as well as long-range policy planning for energy production and conservation. Most countries adopted some form of domestic energy production and conservation policies designed to ease the energy crisis and better prepare for the future.

An early collective response to the first embargo was the formation of the International Energy Agency in 1974. Its initial purpose was to monitor oil allocation by the major oil companies during the supply shortfall. Although France and a few smaller consuming nations did not join, those who did agreed to create emergency plans in case of future supply disruptions. Since its early days, the IEA's primary role has been as a statistical clearinghouse to project future energy demand and to monitor progress toward common policy objectives.

For the longer term, oil-consuming industrial nations generally agreed upon a policy to reduce oil-import demand through conservation and increased production, while diversifying imported sources of oil and substituting other forms of energy for petroleum.

Varying U.S. Responses

The United States responded differently to the second oil shock in 1979-1980 than it had to the first earlier in the decade. After the first wave of price increases, both Democrats and Republicans sought to use policies and mechanisms of government to control energy prices, to encourage energy conservation, and to promote the use of other types of fuel, such as coal. After the second wave of price increases at the end of the 1970s, the U.S. government did not try to control energy prices directly. Legal price controls that were on the books were dismantled, a process begun by the Carter administration in the late 1970s but accelerated by the Reagan administration. Instead of price controls, policy makers relied on market forces to control the use of energy, allowing prices to rise as supply and demand dictated.

The first attempt at a national U.S. energy program—President Richard Nixon's 1973 Project Independence—set overly ambitious goals and relied on measures Congress found unpalatable. The program and its similar but toned-down successor devised by the Ford administration aimed to eliminate oil imports by dramatically increasing nuclear-powered electricity generation, providing greater incentives to domestic energy producers, and completely removing price controls. These programs proved impossible to get through Congress without major compromises that weakened their original intent.

In 1977 President Jimmy Carter proposed a comprehensive program designed to force energy users to switch fuels. It banned new oil- or gas-fired electricity generation and encouraging the development of synthetic and alternative fuels. Carter also attempted to promote conservation programs through tax benefits and phased-in price increases, while denying the oil companies the benefit of the higher prices through a windfall profits tax. It retained price controls on natural gas but proposed to decontrol the price of oil and gas production from newly discovered domestic resources. A "strategic petroleum reserve" of 500 million barrels was to provide protection from embargoes and other supply disruptions.

Carter's plan also met with congressional opposition, although some provisions were passed without extensive modification, including the strategic reserve, new tax credits for homeowners installing solar heating, and federal grants to schools and hospitals for energy conservation.

Upon taking office in 1981 President Ronald Reagan acted quickly to phase out oil price controls. Although this action had little immediate effect because domestic prices were about the same as foreign prices, it demonstrated Reagan's strong free-market orientation and set the tone for his energy policies. Favoring the elimination of the U.S. Department of Energy and opposing an activist government role, the Reagan administration throughout its first term was largely content to encourage market forces to bring down demand, while dismantling most of the Carter programs on conservation, mandatory fuel substitution, and alternative and synthetic fuels.

Although Reagan campaigned on the theory that this approach would stimulate increased domestic oil production, no significant increases occurred. Price decontrol instead was followed by a reduction in petroleum industry capital spending to locate new oil supplies. Indeed, much of the search for oil took place on Wall Street as companies found it cheaper to purchase other companies, and their reserves, than to discover new oil through exploration. In the surge of merger activity one of the major international oil companies, Gulf, fell victim to takeover attempts by a much smaller firm and was forced to merge with Chevron to protect itself. In other cases, major companies were forced to assume huge debts in the course of fending off takeover bids.

As oil demand fell in response to a world oil price of $34 a barrel, the quantity of oil the United States imported also dropped sharply. In 1980 the United States imported 4.3 million barrels of crude oil and products from OPEC countries; by 1984 U.S. imports from OPEC were down to only about 2 million barrels a day. The decline in U.S. imports from the Arab members of OPEC was even greater: 2.5 million barrels a day had been imported in 1980, compared with an average of 809,000 barrels a day in 1984. By 1987 imports from OPEC were back up to 3 million barrels a day and imports from Arab OPEC nations up to 1.2 million.

Push for New Fuels, Nuclear Energy

Other industrial nations placed greater emphasis on switching to other fuels and made heavy commitments to nuclear power. So strong was this trend abroad that the amount of electricity generated worldwide by atomic power increased by 33 percent between 1982 and 1984.

Nations such as Japan also made a major commitment to diversifying their sources of supply by importing liquefied natural gas. Japan increased natural gas usage by 31 percent between 1983 and 1984. Most nations, other than the United States, also increased gasoline taxes to cut petroleum consumption. At the same time, support continued for already-extensive networks of mass transportation facilities.

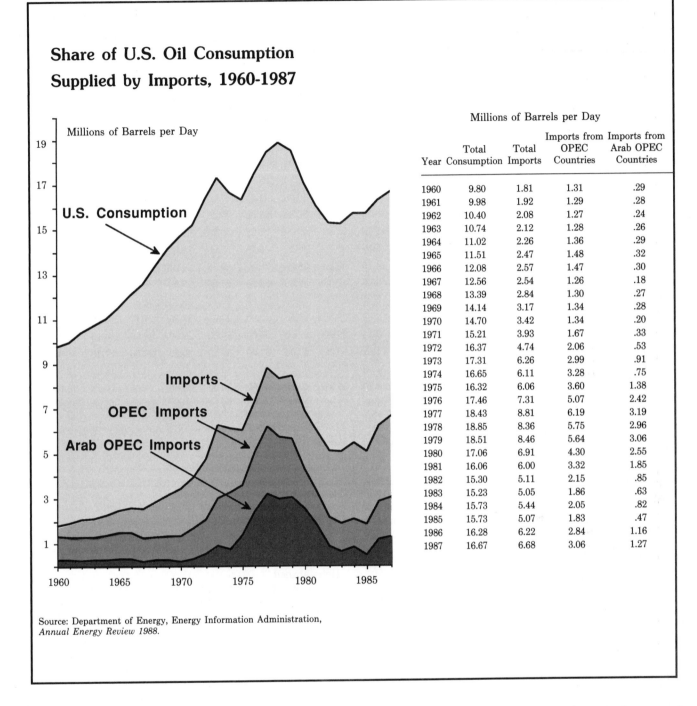

Share of U.S. Oil Consumption Supplied by Imports, 1960-1987

Millions of Barrels per Day

Millions of Barrels per Day

Year	Total Consumption	Total Imports	Imports from OPEC Countries	Imports from Arab OPEC Countries
1960	9.80	1.81	1.31	.29
1961	9.98	1.92	1.29	.28
1962	10.40	2.08	1.27	.24
1963	10.74	2.12	1.28	.26
1964	11.02	2.26	1.36	.29
1965	11.51	2.47	1.48	.32
1966	12.08	2.57	1.47	.30
1967	12.56	2.54	1.26	.18
1968	13.39	2.84	1.30	.27
1969	14.14	3.17	1.34	.28
1970	14.70	3.42	1.34	.20
1971	15.21	3.93	1.67	.33
1972	16.37	4.74	2.06	.53
1973	17.31	6.26	2.99	.91
1974	16.65	6.11	3.28	.75
1975	16.32	6.06	3.60	1.38
1976	17.46	7.31	5.07	2.42
1977	18.43	8.81	6.19	3.19
1978	18.85	8.36	5.75	2.96
1979	18.51	8.46	5.64	3.06
1980	17.06	6.91	4.30	2.55
1981	16.06	6.00	3.32	1.85
1982	15.30	5.11	2.15	.85
1983	15.23	5.05	1.86	.63
1984	15.73	5.44	2.05	.82
1985	15.73	5.07	1.83	.47
1986	16.28	6.22	2.84	1.16
1987	16.67	6.68	3.06	1.27

Source: Department of Energy, Energy Information Administration, *Annual Energy Review 1988.*

A number of nations began to exploit newly discovered oil-production areas. Britain and Norway, for example, began to reap the benefits of oil discovered in the North Sea before the embargo.

Effects of the High Dollar

From the standpoint of the United States, world oil prices had declined significantly by 1985. The official price being asked for Saudi light crude dropped from $34 to $28 a barrel between 1981 and 1985.

For most of the world, however, oil prices had not fallen by the middle of the 1980s, at least not in terms of the local currency that consumers used to pay energy bills. In fact, oil prices continued to rise even in the face of much lower demand. This occurred because the U.S. dollar rose in value compared with other currencies. Because oil payments are made in dollars, the 30 percent increase in the value of the dollar made purchase of international oil expensive for other nations.

From 1978 to the early 1980s the cost of a barrel of Saudi light for the United States slightly more than doubled, but the increase was complete by the early 1980s and declined steadily afterwards. For Germany and the United

Crude Oil Prices 1973-1988

(U.S. dollars per barrel, January 1 of selected years.)

	1973	1974	1976	1977	1979	1980	1981	1982	1984	1985	1986	1987	1988
Canada	*	*	*	*	$14.25	$26.60	$34.09	$28.86	$24.83	$24.32	$21.41	$14.03	$16.55
Mexico	*	*	$12.10	$13.35	14.10	32.00	38.50	35.00	29.00	29.00	26.21	17.00	14.83
Ecuador	$2.14	$11.29	11.45	13.00	13.03	33.50	40.06	34.25	27.50	27.50	26.15	15.86	15.46
Venezuela	2.63	10.13	11.12	12.72	13.36	25.20	32.88	32.88	27.88	27.88	27.10	16.72	15.72
Norway	*	*	*	14.33	15.10	32.50	40.00	37.25	30.25	28.50	26.61	16.86	17.60
United Kingdom	*	*	*	14.10	15.50	29.75	39.25	36.50	29.90	28.65	26.00	18.25	18.00
U.A.E.	2.47	11.75	11.92	12.50	14.10	29.56	36.56	35.50	29.56	29.31	28.15	15.55	17.92
Iran	2.40	11.04	11.62	12.81	13.45	30.37	37.00	34.20	28.00	28.00	28.05	16.14	15.55
Iraq	2.38	10.85	11.53	12.58	13.21	27.96	35.96	34.93	29.21	29.83	28.83	28.18	17.60
Kuwait	2.31	10.74	11.30	12.37	12.83	27.50	35.50	32.30	27.30	27.55	27.10	16.70	16.67
Saudi Arabia	2.41	10.84	11.51	12.09	13.34	26.00	32.00	34.00	29.00	29.00	28.00	16.15	17.52
Algeria	3.30	14.00	12.85	14.30	14.81	30.00	40.00	37.00	30.50	30.50	29.50	17.30	18.87
Libya	2.87	11.98	12.21	13.74	14.52	34.50	40.78	36.50	30.15	30.15	30.15	16.95	18.52
Nigeria	3.31	13.66	12.70	14.31	14.80	29.97	40.00	36.50	30.00	28.00	28.65	17.13	18.92
Indonesia	3.73	10.80	12.80	13.55	13.90	27.50	35.00	35.00	29.53	29.53	28.53	16.28	17.56

* No significant volume of exports.

Source: Department of Energy, Energy Information Administration, *International Energy Annual 1987.*

Kingdom the 1985 price was about three and a half times the 1978 price, while for the French and Italians the 1985 price in local currency was between four and a half to five times the 1978 level.

Recycling Oil Dollars

When oil prices soared in the 1970s, corresponding upheavals occurred in the world banking system. A vast transfer of wealth took place in less than a decade, producing unprecedented surpluses of money for oil-exporting countries, large but manageable trade deficits for industrial countries, and dangerously large trade deficits and accumulations for some developing countries.

Before the four-fold jump in oil prices between 1973 and 1974, oil exporters earned a $6 billion trade surplus. This surplus is figured on what economists call current account, which is the remaining balance after all a nation's imports of goods and services during a given period have been subtracted from its exports. By 1974 the surplus rose to $67 billion. By 1980, when oil prices again tripled, the collective surplus of oil exporters jumped to over $110 billion.

After each round of price hikes, surplus petrodollars (as international oil revenues came to be called) flooded

into OPEC bank accounts at a faster rate than they could be spent. Oil-exporting nations rapidly pushed national development programs to take advantage of the new riches, which increased spending on goods and services from nations abroad.

As oil prices and sales volumes declined by the middle of the 1980s, OPEC countries reduced their imports of goods and services, but not fast enough to prevent a deficit in their collective current account. A $15 billion deficit was incurred in both 1982 and 1983. This was still a relatively minor offset against the cumulative surplus of nearly $400 billion earned over the previous decade, but it was growing.

The flow and use of surplus petrodollars became extremely important to the world financial system as rising oil prices diverted huge amounts of money from oil-importing to oil-exporting nations. In 1983 about 37 percent of OPEC's $400 billion cumulative surplus was held as bank deposits in large industrialized countries, with 70 percent of bank deposits in dollars. About 13 percent of the surplus went into short-term government securities. Six percent of the surplus went into foreign exchange reserves such as gold and Special Drawing Rights at the International Monetary Fund. OPEC countries also made increasing investments (29 percent of the surplus by 1983) in corporate securities and agricultural and commercial real estate in industrial countries. About 15 percent was loaned to or invested in developing countries.

Until oil revenues began to decline during the 1980s the oil-producing countries of the Middle East all undertook extensive development programs. These programs later were cut back until more revenues became available, but the oil-market weakness pushed producing nations to diversify their economies.

OPEC countries always favored investment in industries related to their petroleum production, and they increasingly sought to develop refining, fertilizer, petrochemical, and oil-transportation industries. One of the most ambitious efforts was Saudi Arabia's construction of two new industrial cities at the Red Sea ports of Yanbu and Jubail. Other big projects included the $3.5 billion Iranian petrochemical complex at Bandar Khomeini, which was damaged in the war with Iraq. Kuwait also was active, purchasing refineries in Denmark and Holland, and acquiring gasoline marketing networks throughout Europe.

Early Oil Cartels, OPEC

The world's first multinational oil empire was John Rockefeller's Standard Oil Trust (predecessor of Exxon, Mobil, Amoco, Sohio, and Chevron), which by 1880 controlled more than 70 percent of the then-known supply. By 1885 at least 70 percent of Standard's business was overseas. The second worldwide oil empire was built by Marcus Samuel and his syndicate after they gained control over the Russian fields at Baku and exported oil to Western Europe and the Far East in competition with Standard. Samuel, after refusing a Rockefeller buyout offer, formed Shell Transport and Trading Company. In 1907 this company merged with Royal Dutch, which controlled Indonesian production, to form Royal Dutch Shell.

In 1906 William D'Arcy began the search for oil in the Middle East, hoping to form his own empire. However, he did not obtain the funds necessary for exploration until the eve of World War I. At that time the British government funded D'Arcy's company, Anglo Persian (predecessor of British Petroleum), in the hope of securing oil supplies for its navy. The British government took a controlling interest in the company.

Anglo Persian had earlier entered into a deal with Shell Oil and German interests to divide up the oil rights to the former Ottoman Empire. Since few of the participants in the deal knew exactly what parts of the Middle East were included, one who did, Armenian financier Calouste Gulbenkian, mapped a red line around the affected areas of what is now Turkey, Jordan, Syria, Iraq, and Saudi Arabia. The "red-line" agreement ultimately became the basis of British domination of Middle East oil. The parties were prohibited from competing with each other within the confines of the red line. Gulbenkian was awarded a 5 percent share—for which he everafter became known as Mr. Five Percent—for his part in arranging the deal. He died one of the world's wealthiest men.

In the late 1920s oil was flooding into the markets and the three rival empires engaged in intensive price competition. This competition proved short-lived, however, because representatives of the three met at Achnacarry Castle in Scotland in 1928 to form the "as-is" agreement. The agreement established principles to correct overproduction, reduce competition, and freeze individual market shares at their 1928 levels.

Even though the cartel controlled production of most oil outside the United States and the Soviet Union, and established a system for pricing oil anywhere in the world at the prevailing U.S. Gulf Coast price, it could not prevent competition from producers outside the cartel.

One of the most important challenges came from U.S. companies such as Socal, Gulf, and Texaco, which were not parties to either the red-line or as-is agreements. They had taken an active role in the search for Saudi Arabian and Kuwaiti oil but had been hindered from developing their interests by the British government. After World War II the American government insisted its companies be allowed to develop Middle East concessions. So in 1948 the red-line agreement was scrapped and the Arabian American Oil Company (ARAMCO) was formed by Esso (now Exxon), Texaco, Standard Oil of California (Socal) and Mobil to develop the Saudi concession. Huge deposits of oil were soon discovered and the American companies reaped profits by supplying low-cost oil to Europe and Japan, and later to the United States. Other American companies gained access to concessions in Kuwait, Iran, and other important Middle East oil producers.

Oil Company Control

The Middle East oil-producing nations during the first half of the twentieth century played a subservient role to the major international oil companies that had developed their oil fields. Foreign oil companies were given a free hand to exploit the oil reserves under concessions granted by the local ruler. Those agreements required the companies to pay only a nominal royalty—an average of twenty-one cents a barrel—to the oil-producing countries. In return, the oil companies were exempted from taxes and were given a blank check to determine production and pricing policy.

The oil-producing countries remained satisfied with these arrangements during times when demand was slow, prices were fluctuating or dropping, and prospects for discovering oil were uncertain. During and after World War II, however, inflation reduced the purchasing power of the fixed royalty payments given the producing countries. In other words, their share of the value of the oil being produced declined.

One of the first challenges to these arrangements came in Venezuela, where in 1945 the government demanded and received an even split in oil profits with the companies. The new rules and tax system were formulated by the Venezuelan oil minister, Juan Pablo Perez Alfonzo, later a founding father of OPEC.

In subsequent years the oil-producing countries of the Middle East, which had been getting royalties of 12.5 percent of oil profits, adopted the Venezuelan sharing plan. By the early 1950s all the producing countries had negotiated agreements providing for oil profits to be divided on a 50-50 basis with the oil company or consortium producing the oil. These agreements increased the revenues of the Middle East governments almost ten-fold between 1948 and 1960, to nearly $1.4 billion from about $150 million.

Another important development was the entry into the oil-production business in the 1950s of many new, independent companies. The original seven major corporations that had controlled the world oil market discovered that smaller, aggressive companies were eager to produce at high levels. Gulf, Texaco, Socal (now Chevron), Mobil, and Exxon were the five major American corporations, with the Royal Dutch Shell Group and the British Petroleum Company rounding out the so-called "Seven

Sisters." In the past they had reduced overseas production when the world oil market was saturated, thus preventing a drop in price.

The independents, among them Occidental, Amoco, and Getty, made it more difficult for the major companies to control prices. The smaller businesses set lower prices for gasoline and other oil products, upsetting the ordered market structure. By the end of 1957 prices were dropping. As a result, in February 1959 the major companies cut posted oil prices to reflect the lower market prices. The posted price, also known as the tax reference price, was used to establish the taxable, per-barrel profits a company was deemed to have earned on the oil produced from a particular country. The tax on this amount and a royalty payment were the producing countries' source of oil revenue. Therefore, by cutting the posted price, the oil companies reduced the royalty and tax income received by the producing nations.

The turmoil in the producing structure was felt in the United States, where producers found sales of oil from domestic wells being undercut by cheaper foreign oil. The federal government studied the situation and publicly expressed concern about dependence on foreign oil while privatelyconsidering measures to protect U.S. oil companies. The Eisenhower administration asked the suppliers of foreign oil to limit their imports voluntarily to about 12 percent. The effort failed, however, and President Dwight D. Eisenhower decided in 1959 to impose mandatory oil import quotas. Venezuela and the Arab producers suddenly found themselves unable to expand their share of the world's biggest oil market.

Producing countries were also angered by a second price cut in August 1960 by Esso, a move soon copied by the other companies. In September 1960 Iraq called a meeting of oil-producing governments to discuss the situation. Saudi Arabia, Iran, Kuwait, and Venezuela responded quickly and favorably. Leaders of the group were Perez Alfonzo of Venezuela, whose country was then the top world producer, and Sheik Abdullah Tariki, the oil minister of Saudi Arabia. The result of their session was a decision to establish OPEC. The initial goal of OPEC was to return oil prices to their earlier levels and to gain the right to consult with oil companies on future pricing decisions.

No further cuts in posted prices were made by the oil companies. Instead the United States government helped ensure that producer-nation revenues could increase without forcing the companies to raise the price. This was accomplished by an expansive interpretation of the foreign tax credit that lowered the taxes oil companies paid to the U.S. government, thereby offsetting the extra taxes they paid to producer governments. The policy proved controversial, because it appeared to permit part of the price of a barrel of oil to be considered eligible for the special tax treatment afforded payment of true foreign income taxes. Critics charged that this tax treatment amounted to a subsidy for foreign oil production.

Unified OPEC Action

During the 1960s several new nations joined OPEC. Qatar, Libya, and Indonesia were the first to join, followed by Algeria, Nigeria, Ecuador, Gabon, and the United Arab Emirates (Abu Dhabi, Dubai, and Sharjah)—bringing OPEC membership to the thirteen that belonged in 1989.

OPEC had been successful in preventing further cuts

in posted prices for oil, but it failed during the early 1960s to restore prices to their earlier levels or to agree on a formula to limit output among its members. Although individual countries continued to make progress through negotiations with particular oil companies—who during this period tried to ignore OPEC—the 50-50 split on oil profits was increasingly criticized by the producing states. Consequently, in the late 1960s OPEC began to agitate for higher revenues.

In June 1968 OPEC held a conference at its Vienna headquarters that produced a declaration of principles asserting the right of member nations to control world oil production and prices—a goal that at that time seemed unlikely to be realized. OPEC also agreed on a minimum taxation rate of 55 percent of profits, more uniform pricing practices, a general increase in the posted prices in all member countries, and elimination of allowances granted to oil companies. That same year, the Organization of Arab Petroleum Exporting Countries (OAPEC) was established.

It was the 1969 revolution in Libya that tilted the balance of power toward the producing countries, making it possible for OPEC to press for further authority. In September 1969 a group of officers headed by Muammar Qaddafi seized control of the Libyan government. He moved to force oil-production cuts and to demand, and eventually get, higher oil prices and a greater percentage of profits in the form of taxes.

It did not hurt Qaddafi's cause when in May 1970 a bulldozer accident severed the Trans-Arabian Pipeline, known as Tapline. Tapline carried Saudi oil to the Mediterranean Sea, where it was transported to Europe. With the pipeline out of operation, Libya's oil suddenly was in even greater demand, particularly by the Occidental Petroleum Company, the focus of Qaddafi's efforts. After Armand Hammer, owner of Occidental, gave in to higher prices and taxes, Qaddafi moved on to the major companies, which eventually agreed to raise their posted price by 30 cents a barrel.

The lesson was not lost on the rest of OPEC. In February 1971 the Persian Gulf states of Abu Dhabi, Iran, Iraq, Kuwait, Qatar, and Saudi Arabia met in Tehran with oil company officials. Following the precedent set by Libya, they demanded and won what was considered at the time a major price increase of thirty cents to fifty cents a barrel. The Tehran agreement also raised the minimum tax rate on oil profits from 50 to 55 percent. Two similar agreements benefiting Iraq and the Mediterranean producers followed later in the year.

The price agreements reached in 1971 were short-lived. In December 1971 the United States devalued the dollar. By January 1972 the OPEC countries were demanding adjustments to reflect their loss of buying power. The companies gave in to OPEC's demands in 1972, and did so again in June 1973 to adjust for a second devaluation in February 1973. The companies agreed to raise the posted price of crude oil immediately by 6.1 percent, making a total increase of 11.9 percent since the 1973 devaluation. The agreement, scheduled to be in effect through 1975, also set a new formula under which posted prices would reflect more fully and rapidly any changes in the dollar's value.

The OPEC countries also were increasing their power at the expense of the oil companies on another front. Algeria, long frustrated with the leftover colonial presence of the French oil company, in 1971 nationalized the French holdings. Libya took over British Petroleum's interests in its country in the same year, and it later nationalized other foreign companies. Iraq joined in 1972, nationalizing the consortium operating there. Iran, which had taken over its fields in 1951, assumed full control of the companies in 1973.

Other, less radical, countries such as Saudi Arabia wanted to have a more orderly transfer of control. In December 1972 a participation agreement was reached between various oil companies and Saudi Arabia, Kuwait, the United Arab Emirates, and Qatar. These countries agreed to accept an immediate 25 percent interest in the oil com-

U.S. Petroleum Imports From OPEC Nations, 1964-1988

(thousands of barrels per day)

Year	Saudi Arabia	Vene-zuela	Indonesia	Algeria	Nigeria	Other OPEC [a]	Total OPEC	Arab Members of OPEC [b]
1964	131	933	68	6	0	223	1,361	293
1965	158	994	63	9	15	237	1,476	324
1966	147	1,018	53	4	11	238	1,471	300
1967	92	938	66	5	5	153	1,259	177
1968	74	886	73	6	9	255	1,302	272
1969	65	875	88	2	49	256	1,336	276
1970	30	989	70	8	50	197	1,343	196
1971	128	1,020	111	15	102	296	1,673	327
1972	190	959	164	92	251	406	2,063	530
1973	486	1,135	213	136	459	564	2,993	915
1974	461	979	300	190	713	635	3,280	752
1975	715	702	390	282	762	750	3,601	1,383
1976	1,230	700	539	432	1,025	1,140	5,066	2,424
1977	1,380	690	541	559	1,143	1,880	6,193	3,185
1978	1,144	645	573	649	919	1,821	5,751	2,963
1979	1,356	690	420	636	1,080	1,456	5,637	3,056
1980	1,261	481	348	488	857	865	4,300	2,551
1981	1,129	406	366	311	620	491	3,323	1,848
1982	552	412	248	170	514	250	2,146	854
1983	337	422	338	240	302	223	1,862	632
1984	325	548	343	323	216	294	2,049	819
1985	168	605	314	187	293	264	1,830	472
1986	685	793	318	271	440	329	2,837	1,162
1987	751	804	285	295	535	390	3,060	1,274
1988 [c]	1,062	779	190	294	568	535	3,428	1,828

[a] *Includes Ecuador, Gabon, Iran, Iraq, Kuwait, Libya, Qatar, and United Arab Emirates.*
[b] *Includes Algeria, Iraq, Kuwait, Libya, Qatar, Saudi Arabia, and United Arab Emirates.*
[c] *Preliminary.*
Source: Department of Energy, Energy Information Administration, *Annual Energy Review 1988.*

panies, increasing to 51 percent by 1982. As it turned out, the countries gained a controlling share of the companies by the mid-1970s, although management for the most part remained in the hands of Westerners. The change in control meant that the share of Middle East oil owned by the international oil companies declined sharply. In 1972 the companies had an equity interest in 92 percent of the oil leaving the Middle East. By 1982 the proportion was less than 7 percent.

OPEC's Market Domination

Representatives of the major oil-exporting countries had been scheduled to meet in Vienna with officials from the world's major oil companies on October 8, 1973. The OPEC negotiators apparently were going to the October 1973 session with the aim of winning a substantial price increase. In mid-1973 they had seen the market price of oil for the first time exceed the posted price. To take advantage of this opportunity for higher oil revenues, the producing countries wanted the posted price to be higher than the market price, not just equal to it.

Many of those gathering in Vienna already were on their way to the meeting on October 6 when news came from the Middle East. An Egyptian attack on the Israeli army in the Sinai had started what became the fourth major Arab-Israeli war since 1948. For the OPEC representatives, the war served to strengthen their resolve for higher prices. They asked for $6.00 a barrel, up from the existing $3.00. The companies countered with $3.50. When OPEC officials finally offered $5.12 as their minimum acceptable price, oil company officials tried to stall, asking for a two-week recess. OPEC representatives, led by Sheik Ahmed Zaki Yamani of Saudi Arabia, rejected any delay and stood by their demand. The oil companies refused, and the meeting broke up.

OPEC then met October 16 in Kuwait. At this historic meeting the OPEC representatives agreed to set the posted oil price at $5.12 a barrel. They informed the oil companies this decision was not subject to negotiation. For the first time, the OPEC countries themselves had unilaterally set the price. In doing so they were acting in accordance with the philosophy adopted in 1968 in Vienna.

The success of OPEC's pricing decision was ensured October 17, when the Organization of Arab Petroleum Exporting Countries agreed to cut production by 5 percent each month until Israel withdrew from Arab territories occupied since the 1967 war and agreed to respect the rights of Palestinian refugees. Saudi Arabia the next day stiffened the sanction, announcing it would cut oil production by 10 percent and end all shipments to the United States if America continued to supply Israel with arms and did not modify its pro-Israel policy.

On October 19 President Nixon asked Congress for $2.2 billion in emergency military aid for Israel. Libya announced an embargo the same day. On October 20 Saudi Arabia reduced production by 25 percent and completely cut off supplies to the United States. By October 22 most other Arab producers had joined in the additional production cutback and the embargo against the United States.

The world oil market reacted frantically to these developments. Fears of inadequate supplies pushed prices upward, making even the once-shocking OPEC price of $5.12 seem reasonable. Premium oil was sold at auction for $20.00 a barrel. With renewed confidence, OPEC met again in Tehran on December 22. On December 23 the oil ministers announced a new posted price of $11.65 a barrel.

Suddenly and painfully aware of its dependence on a dozen once-obscure countries, the Western world paid the price that OPEC asked. The result of the quadrupling of world oil prices was a worldwide recession in 1974-1975 that most economists at the time labeled the worst since the Great Depression of the 1930s.

Effects of Arab Oil Embargo

Although the Arab world had tried to impose oil embargoes during previous Arab-Israeli conflicts, success did not come until 1973. In 1956 the Egyptian-Israeli war resulted in the closing of the Suez Canal, blocking the shipment of Middle East oil to Europe. But the United States was able to draw on its excess production capacity and send extra oil to Europe, thus alleviating the crisis.

In 1967, during the Six-Day War between Israel and the Arab states, the Arab oil-producing countries shut down their wells to protest support of Israel by consuming countries. But the consumers turned to the United States again and to Venezuela and Indonesia, which raised production levels to maintain the balance between supply and demand. Eventually, the Arab countries broke ranks, as shipments leaked out and eroded the effectiveness of the shutdown. The production halt had been undermined by Saudi Arabia's lack of enthusiasm for the boycott.

By 1973, however, the Arab nations were asserting a new role in the world market. They had become a significant power in the international economy, producing 37 percent of the oil consumed by the non-Communist world. In contrast, U.S. production had been falling since about 1970. The excess American oil capacity that had been called on before was gone. In addition, Saudi Arabia was a leader in the decision by OAPEC to reduce production and to place an embargo on the United States and other countries. That leadership was extremely important because the Saudis then were producing 7.6 million barrels of oil a day, or 42 percent of the Arab countries' production.

The Arabs were systematic in their embargo, with countries divided into categories. On the boycott list were nations considered to be friends of Israel. The United States was at the top. The Netherlands was included in the total boycott because the Arabs were angered by what they saw as a pro-Israel stance and reports that the Dutch had offered to aid in the transit of Soviet Jewish immigrants to Israel. In late November, Portugal, Rhodesia, and South Africa were officially placed on the embargo list. Shipments of oil to Canada were cut off because the Arabs feared the oil might be reshipped to the United States.

Exempted nations included France, Spain, other Arab and Moslem states, and—on a conditional basis—Britain. These nations were permitted to purchase the same volume of oil as they had purchased in the first nine months of 1973, but, since the fourth quarter of a year normally was a heavy buying period, these nations felt the pinch. All the remaining countries fell into the nonexempt category, which meant that they would have to divide what was left after the needs of the exempted nations had been met.

In addition to the embargo, the Arab states made monthly reductions in production. The effect of the oil squeeze was quickly felt in the consuming nations. Measures taken to cope with the oil shortage included gas rationing, bans on Sunday driving, lowered speed limits,

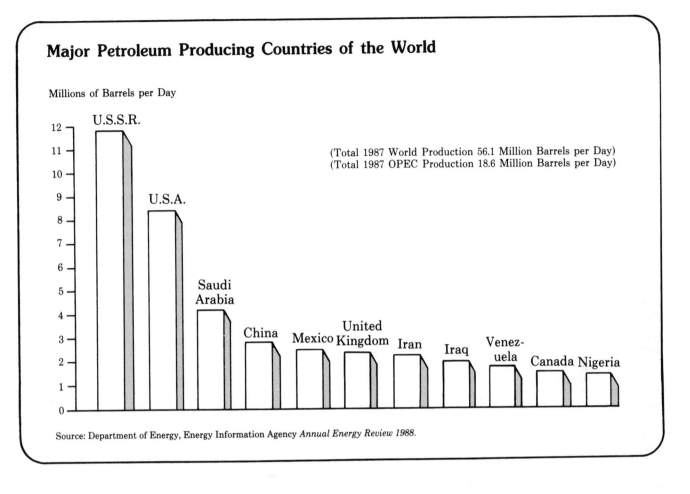

Major Petroleum Producing Countries of the World

Millions of Barrels per Day

(Total 1987 World Production 56.1 Million Barrels per Day)
(Total 1987 OPEC Production 18.6 Million Barrels per Day)

U.S.S.R.
U.S.A.
Saudi Arabia
China
Mexico
United Kingdom
Iran
Iraq
Venezuela
Canada
Nigeria

Source: Department of Energy, Energy Information Agency *Annual Energy Review 1988.*

greater use of temperature controls in public buildings, switching to alternative fuels, and the restriction of gasoline purchases to odd or even days. Most major oil-importing industrial countries joined in the formation of the International Energy Agency, which helped coordinate the allocation of supplies between nations and oversee appropriate conservation measures.

Although estimates varied, the embargo was said to have cost the United States about 2 million barrels of oil a day. A 1974 Federal Energy Administration report estimated that the five-month embargo cost 500,000 American jobs and a gross national product loss of between $10 billion and $20 billion. However, Arab oil did leak through the embargo, reportedly from Iraq and Libya. In October 1974 the United States began withholding data on its oil imports to prevent these leaks from being plugged.

Hardest hit were Japan and Western Europe, areas most dependent on foreign oil. Most of Northern Europe suffered from the embargo against the Netherlands because the Dutch port of Rotterdam was Europe's largest oil-refining and transshipment center.

Embargo as a Political Weapon

The embargo was immensely effective for the Arabs from an economic standpoint but it had a powerful political effect as well. On November 6, 1973, representatives of the European Economic Community (Common Market) meeting in Brussels, adopted a statement urging Israel and Egypt to return to the October 22 cease-fire lines that had been drawn before Israeli troops completed the encirclement of Egypt's Third Army. They called on Israel to "end the territorial occupation which it has maintained since the conflict of 1967" and declared that peace in the Middle East was incompatible with "the acquisition of territory by force." Moreover, they declared that any settlement had to take into account "the legitimate rights" of the Palestinian refugees.

Later in the month Japan followed suit. On November 22 the Japanese cabinet announced that it might reconsider its policy toward Israel. The Arabs rewarded Western Europe and Japan by exempting them from the 5 percent cut in oil production for December. On December 13 Japan appealed to Israel to withdraw to the October 22 cease-fire lines as a first step toward total withdrawal from occupied Arab territories. OAPEC made further concessions to Western Europe and Japan on December 25 by cancelling the January cutback and announcing a 10 percent oil production increase.

The United States, too, was influenced by the embargo. Although Washington officials repeatedly denounced the Arab tactics and declared that the country would not submit to such coercion, the oil squeeze undoubtedly contributed to the desire of the U.S. government and people to push for a Middle East peace.

Secretary of State Henry A. Kissinger shuttled relentlessly throughout the Middle East attempting to mediate a settlement. A series of peace missions produced the November 11, 1973, cease-fire agreement between Israel and Egypt, resumption of diplomatic relations between the United States and Egypt, the first round of Geneva peace talks, the Egyptian-Israeli disengagement accord, and a disengagement agreement between Israel and Syria.

Egyptian President Anwar Sadat led the way toward ending the boycott. On January 22, 1974, he said Arab oil states should note the "evolution" in U.S. policy toward the Middle East and later predicted that the United States would be more evenhanded in its approach to the Arab-Israeli conflict.

OAPEC's formal announcement of an end to the embargo against the United States came at a Vienna meeting on March 18, 1974. Libya and Syria, however, refused to formally end the boycott until later in the year.

Postembargo Oil Prices

After the embargo there was hope, and some expectation, among the consuming countries that OPEC would fall apart. But the OPEC nations showed their acumen by moving cautiously in 1975 when a worldwide recession depressed demand for oil. Saudi Arabia cut production sharply, from 8.5 million barrels a day in 1974 to 7.1 million barrels in 1975. Iran, Venezuela, and Kuwait also reduced production. The average OPEC price actually dropped somewhat in 1975 to $11.02 a barrel. While these cuts were undoubtedly in response to weaker oil demand during the recession, the fact that OPEC nations were willing to respond flexibly to demand rather than continue production at former levels helped keep the price from falling even further.

In October 1976, at an OPEC meeting in Bali, Indonesia, the Saudis argued that the world economy was still too fragile to risk further price increases in 1977. Although other countries were eager to add to their earnings, Saudi Arabia's rank as OPEC's leading producer gave it great influence, and it prevailed. This influence was also due to Saudi Arabia's willingness to unilaterally use its huge productive capacity to shape the world oil market.

The Saudis were less successful, however, at preserving the appearance of unity at a December 1976 OPEC session in Qatar. Unable to agree on a single price, OPEC ended up with a two-tier pricing system. Iran and ten other countries agreed to raise prices by 10 percent in January 1977 and another 5 percent that July. Saudi Arabia and the United Arab Emirates limited their total increase to 5 percent. Nevertheless, the countries that pushed for the larger increase were unable to implement it during 1977.

Price Lull Ends

During this time OPEC members were arguing among themselves about the need for more revenues, with the loudest complaints coming from Algeria, Libya, and Iraq. Inflation was shrinking their revenues, they contended, and prices had to be increased to reflect the reduced value of the dollar, the currency in which oil payments are generally made. In fact, rising inflation had had caused the price of oil to decline in real terms between 1974 and 1978.

The position of those OPEC members pushing for higher prices was enhanced in late 1978 when oil-field work stoppages and other political disruptions in Iran began to cause declines in that country's production, while Western economies were still growing vigorously. The price lull was over.

Market Takes over in 1979

In December 1978 OPEC members met in Abu Dhabi and agreed to end the eighteen-month freeze on prices. The oil ministers decided to make the 1979 increase effective in four stages, beginning January 1, 1979. By the last stage, on October 1, the price was to go up to $14.54 a barrel, for a total increase of 14.5 percent. The market, however, quickly superseded the schedule the organization had set.

Iran's output dropped in early 1979 to less than 1 million barrels a day, down from the 1978 average of 5.5 million barrels. Even though Saudi Arabia and others increased production, there still was not enough oil to meet the strong world demand. The pressure prompted OPEC to decide in March to move at once to a price of $14.54 a barrel, the level originally scheduled for October. The organization also agreed to allow countries to add surcharges to the official price, the first time it had authorized members to set prices individually.

Importers bid hungrily for oil. Spot prices, the price of oil sold in shipload lots among the web of oil traders based primarily in Rotterdam and Paris, were the first to reflect the competition for oil. Reports of oil being sold at spot prices of $25 and $30 a barrel spurred the scramble.

Evidence of the tight world oil market, and the vulnerability of importers, was particularly visible in the United States. For the first time since the winter of 1973-1974, Americans were lining up for gasoline. The lines began in California in the spring and by May had spread to the East Coast. Stations closed at midday, purchases were limited, and daily routines were thrown into disarray by the apparent lack of fuel.

Fears of instability in the Persian Gulf region contributed to rising oil prices. Iran's Shah Mohammed Reza Pahlavi had left that country on January 16, 1979. On February 1 the Ayatollah Khomeini returned triumphantly to Iran after a fifteen-year exile. He quickly moved ahead with his plans to establish an Islamic republic. The Iranian revolution had turned on the long-simmering conflict between ancient, conservative religious mores and a modern society created with oil money and protected by Western arms. The situation was not unique to Iran. Other Moslem oil-producing states facing the strains of modernization brought on by their enormous oil revenues were Saudi Arabia, Iraq, Libya, Kuwait, Qatar, and the United Arab Emirates.

Although Iran's production was back up to about 3.6 million barrels a day by the summer months, the market was still extremely tight. Nothing had happened to alleviate the fears of importers that political unrest might lead to further disruption in world supplies. The oil companies continued to buy at high levels to build their supplies.

When OPEC oil ministers met again in June 1979, they ratified the market price. Saudi Arabia, along with the United Arab Emirates and Qatar, increased prices to $18 a barrel. But the others raised prices to $20, and surcharges were authorized by OPEC so long as the contract price did not exceed $23.50.

Leaders of the United States, Japan, Canada, Italy, Britain, West Germany, and France met in Tokyo in June, and for the first time agreed to cut imports by specific amounts and to work together to increase coal use and develop alternative energy supplies.

In the past, the consuming nations had spent most of their time competing with one another for oil instead of working together. President Carter said the United States would limit future oil imports to less than 8.5 million barrels a day. The Europeans agreed to a ceiling of 10 million barrels a day.

The new cooperation came in part because Carter in April 1979 had agreed to lift price controls on domestic oil by October 1981. The Europeans had complained since the embargo that the U.S. controls were encouraging—even subsidizing—imports, thus taking oil from the rest of the world. When Ronald Reagan took office in 1981, one of his first acts was to speed up oil decontrol by abolishing price controls on January 28.

Uncertainties and Disunity

Any confidence the new accord provided consuming nations was dashed by two other events in 1979: Iran's taking of American hostages on November 4 and the Soviet invasion of Afghanistan on December 27. These events were stark reminders of the dangers of instability in the Middle East. Oil buyers assumed they were purchasing from a supply of oil that probably would get tighter in the future.

In this mood of uncertainty, OPEC was set to meet again in Caracas in December 1979. Aware of upcoming demands for major price increases by the Africans and others, Saudi Arabia and three other countries tried to head off the "price hawks" by raising prices in advance of the scheduled session. The Saudis raised their price from $18 to $24 a barrel, a one-third increase. Nevertheless, this "moderate" hike was still lower than the $26-a-barrel price that Nigeria, Algeria, and Libya already were asking, and getting, for their premium oil. So the Saudis and others raised their prices again, as did the price hard-liners. On some markets the price of oil reached $30 a barrel. The Caracas meeting ended without agreement on either a price ceiling or a price floor. For the first time OPEC had been unable to achieve even a semblance of accord, but the members thought the problem would be temporary.

By the time OPEC met again in Algiers in June 1980, the Saudis had raised their price to $28 a barrel. This time the countries were more successful in reaching general agreement. Although Saudi Arabia continued to refuse to increase its price, the other countries did. The base price, they announced, would be $32 a barrel, and the ceiling would be $37 a barrel for top quality crude oil. OPEC was still split, and Saudi Arabia had not regained control, but some order had been restored.

In December 1980 the range of allowable prices was increased again, with the base price going to $36 a barrel and the ceiling on premium oil reaching $41 a barrel. Saudi Arabia continued to lag behind, charging $32 a barrel.

Divisions within OPEC continued in the fall of 1980 and into 1981. Despite the decline in the demand for oil—accompanied by some reductions in prices—OPEC members were unable to agree on a unified pricing and production policy. Tensions within the organization were exacerbated when war broke out between Iran and Iraq in September 1980.

Eight months later, with the worldwide demand for oil still lagging, the thirteen OPEC nations convened in Geneva. A majority called for price increases as well as production cutbacks to end the world oil glut and the price downturn. (Since November 1980 the spot market price of Arabian light crude oil had dropped from about $40 a barrel to about $34-$35 a barrel.) But Saudi Arabia refused to bow to the majority demand to raise prices, arguing that they already were too high and that it was unrealistic to raise them in a situation of slackening demand. The Saudis found themselves alone; the other members voted unanimously to cut oil production a minimum of 10 percent. Iran and Iraq were exempted from the cut to allow them to return to their prewar production levels.

The Saudis announced they would maintain their oil production at a record level of 10.3 million barrels per day until the others agreed to reform the price structure. Except for the Saudis, who continued to charge $32 a barrel, OPEC members agreed on a benchmark price that ranged from $36 a barrel to the $41 charged by Algeria, Nigeria, and Libya. The two-day meeting broke up in bitterness.

Another OPEC meeting in August 1981 also ended in disunity. For the first time in the organization's twenty-one-year history, the oil ministers called on the heads of government to resolve the deadlock. Iraq offered a "compromise" that would have set the price at $35 a barrel and frozen it there through 1982. Again the Saudis, joined this time by the United Arab Emirates, rejected the proposal and said they would not support any rise beyond $34 a barrel. Iran also opposed the proposal because it would have meant lowering its price. Venezuela, Libya, and Algeria insisted on $36 a barrel.

However, the Saudis this time did agree to a million-barrel-per-day decrease in their oil production. It proved to be just one of many decreases that would be required to prop up the price of oil.

OPEC had been forced to reduce output before as the world recovered from the 1974-1975 recession. The necessary reductions then had not been that great, however, as United States demand for imported oil soon recovered. But the drop-off in world oil demand, while slow in coming, was surprisingly sharp and deep. Oil demand was relatively inelastic to changes in price in the short term, but with oil prices remaining high for several years, demand fell.

World oil production continued to decline. From a peak of 62.5 million barrels per day (bpd) in 1979 it dropped in each of the following four years—59.5 million bpd in 1980, 55.9 million in 1981, 53.5 million in 1982, and 53 million in 1983. By 1984, with the world beginning to recover from the effects of recession, it increased to an average of 54.1 million bpd. Further recovery was slow in coming, with production reaching only about 56.1 million bpd by 1987.

Production Ceilings

A cartel must be able to control the price impact of a general drop in consumption by reducing supply. Oil producers who were not members of OPEC were not, in the early 1980s, interested in reducing their output. Production from the Western Hemisphere, notably Mexico, and from the British and Norwegian sectors of the North Sea, continued to increase as world consumption declined. So OPEC was forced to implement the bulk of the necessary cutbacks in oil production itself.

OPEC was compelled for the first time ever to agree on production quotas. In March 1983 OPEC introduced a collective production ceiling of 17.5 million barrels per day and sharply reduced prices. The key grade of OPEC crude, Saudi light, fell in price from $34 a barrel to $29 a barrel.

For about fifteen months these arrangements helped maintain a rough balance in the world market. As economic activity picked up in the oil-importing countries, energy consumption increased in the first half of 1984. But economic growth slipped in the second half, and oil consumption again fell, aided by warm winter weather. Further pressure on prices developed because some OPEC members exceeded their quotas and engaged in secret price discounting.

The previous quotas eventually turned out to be too loose, so on October 23, 1984, the oil ministers of six OPEC countries, together with Mexico and Egypt, agreed in principle to a further cutback. Following emergency meetings in Geneva beginning October 29, OPEC members agreed to restrict production by a further 1.5 million bpd to defend the $29 a barrel price of Saudi light. The official price of Saudi light remained $29 a barrel until the beginning of 1985 when it was dropped to $28.

OPEC also agreed on December 20, 1984, to establish a committee to police pricing and production policies. Official responsibility for this function was assigned to OPEC's Ministerial Executive Council, chaired by Ahmed Zaki Yamani, the Saudi oil minister. The oil ministers of Venezuela, Nigeria, Indonesia, and the United Arab Emirates also sat on the council, which audited individual nations' production.

By early 1985 OPEC production had fallen 57 percent from pre-embargo levels. OPEC was producing only about 46 percent of its maximum sustainable capacity, and of this amount the greatest declines had been absorbed by OPEC's Middle East members. They had been willing to produce only 41 percent of the amount they otherwise could, while allowing the non-Arab OPEC members to produce at 65 percent of capacity.

Open Disputes

In September 1980 all pretext of unity within OPEC was shattered when two member states went to war against each other. For almost eight years Iraq and Iran remained locked in a war of attrition, with no sign of peace. Other OPEC members, while refraining from active military involvement, gave financial assistance and other logistical support to the combatants. Iran's allies included Syria and Libya, while Iraq was helped by Kuwait, Saudi Arabia, and the United Arab Emirates. Although oil was neither the cause nor sole focus of the dispute, both sides tried to destroy the other's production and loading facilities to reduce the revenues available for military purposes. Ironically, the war at first helped keep oil prices higher than they would otherwise have been: damage caused by the combat kept at least 4 million barrels of oil per day from the world market. This reduced the oversupply in a time of glut and meant that other OPEC members were able to produce more than they otherwise could.

The tensions within OPEC extended beyond the war. The Middle East members of OPEC tended to have small populations and disproportionately large oil revenues in relation to their size. When times became difficult, they were able to draw upon the credits amassed in Western banks during the years when oil prices were rocketing upward. Development projects might be scaled back but no one would go hungry. Countries such as Nigeria and Indonesia were quite different. Nigeria's 1983 gross national product per capita was $771; Indonesia's was $502. Oil revenues were crucial to each country's financial health, and even a moderate dip in revenues could mean hardship for the millions of impoverished people who depended directly or indirectly upon a high oil price. Falling oil prices caused rising political pressures against the governments of those nations. In the summer of 1985 the Nigerian government was replaced after a coup, at least in part because of dissatisfaction with falling oil revenues.

Even OPEC's richest members were having a relatively difficult time coping with the oil glut. By May 1985 Saudi Arabia's production had fallen to a twenty-year low of 2.5 million barrels per day, and it declined even further during the summer. Meanwhile, the Saudi government was running a budget deficit of at least 46 billion rials, or more than 27 percent of revenues. The ambitious Saudi domestic development program depended on the use of gas produced with oil. With oil production so low, gas production was inadequate to meet the development program's requirements. Tired of bearing the burden of holding down production while other OPEC members cheated on their quotas, Saudi Arabia in late 1985 announced that it would no longer take up all the slack between supply and demand by producing well below its own quota. It began to sell the additional quantities up to its quota limit at market rather than official prices.

The 1986 Crash

Saudi Arabia had watched its oil revenues shrink from about $110 billion in 1980 to about $26 billion in 1985, eroded less by the falling price of oil than by the kingdom's own declining production. Having cut its production repeatedly in those years in an effort to prop up prices, the Saudis in 1985 were producing as little as 1.3 million barrels a day, less than half of their OPEC quota. From 1983 to 1985 the Saudis' oil revenues dropped by nearly two thirds, forcing them to cut back development projects and imports each year and to finance budget deficits by spending cash reserves. Saudi dissatisfaction with this trend was intensified by awareness that the deficit was subsidizing non-OPEC as well as OPEC producers.

King Fahd decreed a major shift in Saudi oil policy, aimed at restoring some of the lost oil revenue by producing more and competing aggressively for a larger share of the market. The policy, first threatened at the fall 1985 OPEC meeting, went into effect that winter. Its chief tool was the "netback agreement," whereby the actual price a buyer paid for Saudi crude oil depended on the price for which the buyer could resell the refined product. With the buyer's risk limited by the built-in profit margin, Saudi Arabia's sales began booming.

The new Saudi policy was partly intended to jolt cheating OPEC members into a new respect for cartel price and production discipline. Fahd determined that his kingdom would no longer bear the burden alone and would no longer play the role of "swing producer," cutting output to support the OPEC price.

The policy was also aimed beyond OPEC. As articulated by Oil Minister Ahmed Zaki Yamani and others, its stated goal was to induce non-OPEC producers such as Britain, Norway, Mexico, and the Soviet Union to reduce their production to support the world price.

As higher oil prices had spurred energy efficiency and brought new producers into the world market, OPEC's share of the total oil production in the non-Communist world had shrunk from about 67 percent in 1973 to 42 percent in 1985. As it tried to maintain prices, OPEC tightened its belt and ratcheted production down from a high of about 31 million barrels a day in 1981 to 16 million barrels a day in 1985.

OPEC Oil Revenues, 1974-1988

(billions of U.S. dollars for selected years)

Country	1974	1979	1980	1981	1983	1985	1986	1987	1988
Saudi Arabia[a]	$22.6	$ 57.5	$102.0	$113.2	$ 46.1	$ 25.9	$ 19.3	$ 22.2	$ 20.9
Iraq	5.7	21.3	26.0	10.4	8.4	12.1	6.8	11.7	11.8
Iran	17.5	19.1	13.5	8.6	21.7	15.9	7.4	10.7	8.9
Libya	6.0	15.2	22.6	15.6	11.2	10.4	4.7	5.6	4.8
Nigeria	8.9	16.6	25.6	18.3	10.1	13.2	7.0	7.4	6.7
Kuwait	7.0	16.7	17.9	14.9	9.9	9.5	6.3	6.8	6.5
U.A.E.	5.5	12.9	19.5	18.7	12.8	12.2	6.6	8.9	7.4
Venezuela	8.7	13.5	17.6	19.9	15.0	13.1	6.8	8.3	7.3
Algeria	3.7	7.5	12.5	10.8	9.7	5.7	2.7	3.4	2.8
Indonesia	3.3	8.9	12.9	14.1	9.9	18.5	4.3	5.7	4.8
Qatar	1.6	3.6	5.4	5.3	3.0	3.1	1.6	1.9	1.5
Ecuador	—	1.0	1.4	1.5	1.1	2.0	0.9	0.7	1.2
Gabon	—	1.4	1.8	1.6	1.5	1.7	0.7	1.0	0.9
Total	$90.5	$195.2	$278.8	$252.9	$160.4	$143.3	$ 75.1	$ 94.3	$ 85.5

[a] Includes half Neutral Zone.

Sources: *Petroleum Economist,* Petroleum Finance Company.

Oil Prices Plummet

The results of the Saudi initiative were dramatic. The world's largest oil producer increased sales by underpricing oil in an already over-supplied market. There was already a glut of oil, and demand was flat. Since world crude prices had peaked in the $35-per-barrel range during 1981, they had eased down to the $28 range during the next five years. The decline from $28, still the official OPEC price, began in earnest around Thanksgiving 1985. By January 20, 1986, prices had sunk below the crucial psychological threshold of $20 a barrel. That was a ten-year low, and the lowest price even the most pessimistic forecasters had been able to imagine, but prices were still going down. Analysts used terms like "free fall" and "price war" to describe the oil market.

In the face of all this, the government of British prime minister Margaret Thatcher maintained a firm and unflappable demeanor. Britain, which had developed its North Sea oil fields within the span of a decade, had become the fifth-largest producer and the third-largest exporter, after Saudi Arabia and the Soviet Union. Britain's position would have made it a special target of the Saudi effort to gain production cuts outside OPEC, even if the Saudis had not been irked by the Thatcher government's 1985 dismantling of the state-run British National Oil Corporation, which had functioned to fix some prices above market rates. Thatcher was stoutly committed to a free-market philosophy, and she presided over a nation that was not only a major oil producer, but also a major oil consumer. As the market plunged, her government declared its determination not to tamper with North Sea production.

Sheik Yamani responded to the British hands-off declaration by warning on January 23, 1986, that without non-OPEC nations' cooperation in production cuts, "there will

be no limitation to the downward price spiral, which may bring crude prices to less than $15 a barrel, with adverse consequences for the whole world economy." His words triggered more selling and further price plunges in oil commodity markets, with futures for Britain's North Sea Brent crude losing more than $1.50 per barrel the same day, a billion-dollar hemorrhage in revenues.

Although Saudi Arabia's policy was meant to gain a larger market share for OPEC as well as for itself, it was not exactly an OPEC policy. Some OPEC nations such as Kuwait and the United Arab Emirates, still holding cash reserves and feeling the same pressures as Saudi Arabia, seemed to support the market-share strategy. But some of the poorer OPEC nations, starved for cash or burdened with debt, such as Venezuela, Nigeria, Indonesia, Iran, Algeria, and Libya, resisted it. When a five-member OPEC committee met February 3 to assess the situation, they were unable to agree on specific production goals.

News that the OPEC meeting had ended inconclusively February 4 sent oil contracts skidding down toward $15 per barrel on the New York Mercantile Exchange. "It's just about every man for himself with OPEC," observed Daniel Yergin, a Cambridge, Massachusetts, energy consultant, after the meeting.

Oil markets continued looking for a floor through the spring and summer of 1986, and finally found one in the $10-$12 range, although some prices dipped as low as $8. Oil prices, once adjusted for inflation, were almost comparable to those that had prevailed before the 1973 shock.

Action by OPEC itself finally halted the long price slide. At a meeting in early August 1986, members reached an agreement to cut combined output to 16.8 million barrels per day, about 4 million barrels less than they had been pumping earlier in the summer. Even though the agreement covered only a two-month trial period, rumors that it was coming started prices back upwards. The fever, it seemed, had broken.

A Changing Landscape

The long 1986 price slide had produced several fundamental changes within the the oil industry. Although OPEC still existed as an organization with market influence, whether it was still able to function as a classically defined cartel was open to question.

First, direct price-fixing was a thing of the past. Up until about 1983 OPEC members could export most of their oil under long-term contracts at a fixed "benchmark" price. As the market structure changed during the 1980s, however, that price could be enforced only through ever-more-strenuous cutbacks in production. Once Saudi Arabia began aggressively marketing its oil with netback agreements, other OPEC nations scrambled to do likewise, if only to keep their share of the market. The flexible netback agreements, of course, were the very antithesis of a "fixed" price. Production limits, rather than price, were becoming the main instrument of OPEC policy.

Second, less and less oil (OPEC or non-OPEC) was being sold under long-term contracts. One result was that the price of oil became more volatile. During the first half of the 1980s two new oil markets developed—the spot market and the futures market—and an increasing amount of oil was sold in them. They reflected a much more dynamic, competitive, and uncertain world oil market. In the spot market, traders buy and sell specific amounts of oil at prices that vary from day to day according to changing supply and demand. In the futures market, traders buy and sell contracts to purchase or deliver specific amounts of oil a certain number of months in the future at a specific price—a device allowing them to speculate on market trends and hedge against uncertainties.

Whether a world "free market" in oil had developed was still questionable. But the editorial page of the *Wall Street Journal*, a bastion of free-market philosophy, observing the events of January 1986, spoke of "one more sign that the world has changed, and for the better. Oil is becoming once more what it should always have been, just another commodity."

The dramatic crash had both good and bad results for the OPEC nations. Falling prices had produced circumstances that stopped the erosion of OPEC's market share. Discovery and production in many non-OPEC countries was far more costly than in most OPEC countries. As prices fell, drilling for new oil in unproven locations ceased to be profitable. In the United States there was a significant decrease in exploration drilling, and production began to fall. At the same time, in response to lower prices, consumption started to inch up again for the first time since 1979.

Nonetheless, the price drop brought serious revenue losses in the near term for most OPEC producers. OPEC Secretary General Fahdil al-Chalabi told a group of economists that reasserting its market influence had cost its members $50 billion in lost revenues during 1986. It was the inability to endure these revenue losses any longer that forced OPEC to stop its market-share offensive.

The ouster in October 1986 of Sheik Yamani, who had been Saudi Arabia's oil minister since 1962, was perhaps indicative of the changing times. He had dominated OPEC during its heyday and had become a symbol of its continu-ity. His departure signaled a break with past policies and a recognition that new strategies were needed to address new conditions. He was replaced by Hisham M. Nazer.

Recovery and Adjustment

After collapsing prices hit their bottom in August 1986, they gradually recovered during the fall of that year. OPEC members renewed their production control agreement in December. Shortly after the beginning of 1987, the world price leveled off near $18 a barrel and varied only a few dollars for most of the rest of the year.

That $18 figure also happened to the official OPEC benchmark price. The price stability of 1987 suggested that OPEC could still function effectively as a cartel. Its members agreed to abandon netback arrangements and return to the "fixed" benchmark price during most of 1987. An alternative explanation for the stability was that a relatively "free" market had found a new equilibrium point. In fact, analysts estimated that only about 20 percent of OPEC's production was being sold at the official price.

After a meeting in mid-December 1987 OPEC members virtually abandoned the benchmark price and relied on production controls instead. Despite the protests of Saudi Arabia, the main backer of the benchmark price, the postmeeting communiqué did not even mention it. To defend a fixed price, one or more members would have to stand ready to adjust their output, and Saudi Arabia was still emphatically insisting, as it had back in 1985, that it would no longer play the role of the single swing producer.

There were still serious problems with any production-based system. Cheating on production quotas, which had been a chronic problem undercutting OPEC's effectiveness during much of the 1980s, remained rampant. In August of 1987, OPEC was producing 20 percent more oil than the quotas to its individual members allowed.

One sign that the problem was not getting better was the establishment in the fall of 1987 of the "Committee of Three," a new mechanism to police production cheating. This committee, made up of OPEC's chairman (Rilwanu Lukman of Nigeria) and two member oil ministers (from Venezuela and Indonesia), was to visit the heads of state in each of the organization's thirteen countries in an effort to persuade them to stick to their quotas. The group had no actual enforcement powers beyond "jawboning."

The apparent stability of prices in 1987 was also offset by a drop of about 15 percent during the year in the value of the dollar, the currency used for most oil transactions.

As the end of the year came, 1987 seemed to offer some vindication for the Saudi market-share strategy. For the first time since oil prices had begun dropping in 1982, OPEC's annual revenues exceeded those of the year before. 1987 revenues were an estimated $93 billion or one-fifth higher than those of 1986.

Iran-Iraq War

Oddly, prices stayed relatively stable during 1987 despite the flare-up that year of naval warfare in the Persian Gulf related to the Iran-Iraq war. Ordinarily, an increased threat to Gulf tanker traffic would raise fears of shortages and push prices higher. In actuality, the 1987 flare-up seemed to exert only the most transient upward pressure on prices.

The two nations had pounded each other's oil production and shipping facilities from the war's start in 1980, removing millions of barrels per day from the export market. The oil markets, long before the 1987 attacks on Gulf shipping, had adjusted prices and taken that supply reduction into account. The grinding war itself and the sporadic attacks on tankers in 1987 became just another hazard of doing business. War jitters caused refiners to build further inventory cushions during 1987, and their tanks were full by September. This inventory surplus exerted a downward, rather than an upward push on prices.

Oil was a critical strategic variable in the grueling war of attrition between Iran and Iraq. The war pitted not only two armies against each other but also two economies, and both depended on oil for revenue to buy weapons. Iran's economy, devastated by the 1978 revolution, was especially dependent on oil.

By 1987 Saudi Arabia had provided about $40 billion in grants and loans to support Iraq's war effort, and it was oil revenues that made that aid possible. Furthermore, Saudi Arabia and Kuwait had through most of the war given Iraq 300,000 barrels of oil a day for "war relief," which Iraq could then sell for cash. The war showed that Mideast nations could use the "oil weapon" not only against Western consuming nations, but also against one another.

The Iran-Iraq war had profound effects on OPEC's internal politics. Surprisingly the cartel continued to operate by "consensus," its standard operating procedure, despite the war being fought by two of its most important members. Both continued to participate in order to pursue vital economic interests, and OPEC's internal politics increasingly became a continuation of the war by other means.

Perhaps the most important way the Saudis and other Gulf sheikdoms supported and subsidized Iraq was to wink at its cheating—first by tacitly allowing it to ignore and exceed production quotas and eventually by exempting Iraq from quotas altogether. As a result, Iraq could maximize its revenues with full-tilt production.

Iraq had long taken the position that it would not recognize any OPEC production limits until it was given a quota equal to Iran's. Finally, at a December 14, 1987, meeting when OPEC refused again to grant Iraq that parity, Iraq simply dropped out of the production agreement, and OPEC subtracted Iraq's nominal quota from its overall production limits. Iraq's demand that it be allowed greater production was resisted by Iran and non-Gulf OPEC members such as Venezuela, Nigeria, Indonesia, Ecuador, and Gabon.

Unlike Iraq, Iran sought not a sanction to produce more oil, but an increase in its price. Since Iraqi attacks had damaged Iran's shipment facilities, making it impossible for Iran to export more oil, higher prices were the only way that country could increase its revenues. Algeria and Libya were, to some degree, sympathetic to Iran's call for higher prices. Although Iran called for production cuts and higher prices in OPEC meetings, in the oil markets it cut prices to sell as much oil as possible, and it was rarely able to exceed its quota.

At the beginning of December 1987, for example, Iran's quota was 2.7 million barrels per day. Yet Iraqi attacks left Iran able to export less than 1 million bpd. Iraq, on the other hand, with an official quota of 1.6 million bpd, was producing at a rate estimated by some analysts to be as high as 2.6-2.8 million bpd and claimed production

capacity of 4 million bpd.

Iraq had acquired by 1986 the Exocet missile, deadly when used by fighter planes against tankers at sea. Once it perfected in-the-air refueling, Iraq showed it could strike Iranian oil industry targets such as Sirri Island and Larrak Island, 900 miles from its own airfields. Iran's refineries, pumping stations, shuttle tankers, and terminals all suffered damage.

To export its oil, Iran had to rely on tanker shipments from Kharg Island, which were vulnerable to Iraqi attack. Because Iran could not get credit, it had to pay for needed war supplies and food imports in cash. Since Iran was almost totally dependent on its oil exports as a source of cash, Iraqi attacks on Iranian oil targets seriously hindered Iran's war effort. Moreover, Iraqi damage to Iran's refineries forced Iran to import kerosene and heating oil for its own domestic use.

Iraq's situation was quite different from Iran's. Early in the war Iranian attacks had curtailed oil shipments from the main Iraqi terminal on the Faw Peninsula, cutting Iraqi exports from 2.5 million bpd in 1980 to 1 million bpd in 1981. The Iraqis responded over the next few years by building a network of land pipelines to transport its oil to the Red Sea through Saudi Arabia and to the Mediterranean through Turkey. Thus, Iraq reconfigured its oil transportation system so that it was largely invulnerable to Iranian attack and raised its exports above 1980 levels.

Unable to inflict further damage to Iraq's oil economy, Iran had widened its attacks to interdict the tankers of the Gulf allies, such as Kuwait, that were supporting Iraq's war effort. Iran's expanded mining of shipping lanes and positioning of new Silkworm antiship missiles along its coast in 1987 were part of this effort.

Although these threats of supply disruption exerted an upward pressure on prices in 1987, they seemed to be more than balanced by the downward push of the increased production by Iraq and others.

Saudi Arabia vs. Iran

Another key ingredient in OPEC and Persian Gulf politics was the relationship between Saudi Arabia and Iran—historically the two largest producers among OPEC nations.

A suspension of old antagonisms between Saudi Arabia and Iran in 1986 helped staunch overproduction and restore prices after the crash. Then, in late July 1987, 400 people died in Mecca during riots in which Iranian pilgrims fought Saudi police. Iran's Ayatollah Khomeini responded by calling for the overthrow of the Saudi royal family. The Saudis accused Iran of provoking the riots and called for Khomeini's removal. This hostile atmosphere spilled over to proceedings at an OPEC meeting in September.

The Saudis and Iranians, despite frequent political disagreements, had always managed to separate politics from their own economic interests. By September 1987, however, analysts were saying that the Saudi-Iranian feud and the Iran-Iraq war were beginning to overshadow economic self-interest for Persian Gulf OPEC nations.

Indeed, some analysts said that hurting Iran had been a motive for the Saudi market share offensive of 1985. Saudi policy in 1985 and 1986 had caused enormous economic damage to Iran. At the end of 1987 the prices the Saudis had helped hold up for most of the year were beginning to slip, again hurting Iran's oil revenues, and Saudi Arabia showed no signs of trying to stop the decline.

OPEC Courts NOPEC Nations

OPEC's "committee of five" oil ministers (the pricing committee) invited representatives of at least seven non-OPEC oil-producing nations (nicknamed "NOPEC") to a meeting at OPEC headquarters in Vienna on April 23, 1988. Cartel President Rilwanu Lukman of Nigeria said the meeting's purpose was to discuss "methods of cooperation"—which was presumed to mean possible production cuts. The OPEC overture was seen as acknowledgment that the thirteen cartel members were finding it difficult to exert enough control on production to keep prices from sagging.

What was significant about the April meeting was how close OPEC and non-OPEC powers came to an agreement on cutting back production. The meeting ended April 27 with an offer by six non-OPEC nations to cut their oil output by 5 percent if OPEC also cut output 5 percent. Those six were Angola, China, Egypt, Mexico, Oman, and Malaysia. Colombia attended the talks but did not endorse the proposal. Brunei was invited but did not attend. Norway sent an observer. The United Kingdom did not take part.

During the six weeks before the meeting the mere news that the meeting was to take place had set off a rally in the spot market that raised the price of one representative crude, North Sea Brent, from $14 to $17 per barrel.

The principal advocates of production cuts, as well as the opening to non-OPEC countries, were Iran, Algeria, and Libya. The leader on the other side of this debate was Saudi Arabia, joined by the United Arab Emirates, Kuwait, and Qatar.

When a full meeting of OPEC convened the next day (April 28) to consider the non-OPEC offer, it was clear that Saudi Arabia intended to block any deal. In a statement just hours before the meeting, King Fahd himself came out against it.

The Saudis' motives, according to oil-market analysts, had more to do with punishing Iran than promoting Saudi economic interests. News that OPEC had rejected the pact, of course, drove spot market crude prices lower.

The incident typified the state of OPEC and the oil market for much of 1988. After holding firm during 1987, prices in 1988 softened and the market became more volatile. It was perhaps a sign of the times that even Texas had a representative in Vienna during the meeting. He was Kent Hance, a former Democratic congressman and one of three commissioners of the Texas Railroad Commission, the body that regulates oil production in the state.

The prospect of Texas's consorting with OPEC caused a stir among the U.S. media and consumer representatives. As it turned out, Texas had no intention of striking a deal with the cartel. However, it did continue informal contacts with OPEC on the production issue, and at a subsequent OPEC meeting in November, Hance was joined by delegations from Alaska, Louisiana, and Oklahoma.

OPEC's Petroleum Industry Investments

OPEC nations adapted to the emergence of an ever-more-open and volatile oil market in the 1980s in a number of ways beyond competing for sales. Multibillion-dollar barter deals, usually involving oil-for-arms swaps, became common. There was also a growing effort by OPEC producers to acquire new positions "downstream" from the wellhead, in the refining and distribution sectors of the petroleum industry. While low prices for crude hurt the producers who pumped it from the ground, they helped refiners by widening their profit margins. It was a lesson not lost on OPEC that, during and after the price crash of 1986, earnings stayed healthy and even grew for the major oil companies. The majors were "vertically integrated"—that is, they were involved in every step of the supply process from exploration and production to petrochemicals and gasoline stations.

OPEC members wanted to hedge against price uncertainty by moving downstream as well. The most prominent example of such "downstream reintegration" was the June 1988 $1.2 billion acquisition by Saudi Arabia of 50 percent ownership of three Texaco Inc. refineries in the United States, as well as marketing access to 11,420 gas stations in twenty-three states. Kuwait had already expanded marketing of its product in Europe under the "Q-8" brand. Some Americans and Europeans were uneasy about such foreign investment by Middle East oil powers, but the deals seemed to promise greater security for consuming nations. After all, Middle East nations would only be hurting their own business if they implemented another large-scale embargo.

Peace and Parity

Iran and Iraq started moving toward a cease-fire in July of 1988 and formally agreed to one in August. Ironically, peace drove oil prices downward, even though the effects of the war had also been driving prices downward in recent years.

The market price of oil jumped higher almost reflexively for a few days when the news of imminent peace first came in late July. Some analysts saw visions of a newly unified OPEC able to cooperate on production cuts. Other analysts and traders, however, quickly predicted a longer downtrend in prices as realization deepened of what a cessation of the shooting war would mean. Production capacity in Iran and Iraq that had been put out of commission by the war, such as Iraq's export terminals at Mina al-Bakr and Khor al-Amaya on the Persian Gulf, gradually would come back on line. Both countries would have strong need for revenues to rebuild their economies and pay war debts and could be expected to produce near their capacity.

Moreover, major market fundamentals remained unchanged: inventories were high, production capacity far exceeded demand, and demand was scarcely growing at all. OPEC still controlled a minority share of the market in the non-Communist world. OPEC discipline on production quotas was getting worse as the summer of 1988 wore on, and top officials were acknowledging that it was in shambles as the world price slumped toward $13 a barrel.

By September the Saudis were increasing production further, reaching an output rate of about 5.5 million barrels a day, unabashedly violating their OPEC quota of 4.3 million barrels a day. That pushed prices for some grades of Persian Gulf crude below $10 a barrel, or about as low as they had gone during the 1986 crash. It was, in fact, a renewal of the earlier market share offensive—aimed this time more at competitors inside OPEC (namely Iran and Iraq) than those outside. Iraq's overproduction would no longer be indulged by the Saudis. They called on other OPEC members to lower output to agreed-upon quotas, generating pressure inside OPEC for a new agreement and serious discipline.

The Saudis and their close allies (Kuwait, the United Arab Emirates, and Qatar) proposed that collective OPEC

OPEC Crude Oil Production, 1979-1987

(thousands of barrels per day)

	1979	1980	1981	1982	1983	1984	1985	1986	1987[a]
Middle East OPEC									
Algeria	1,224	1,106	1,002	987	968	1,014	1,037	945	985
Iran	3,168	1,662	1,380	2,214	2,440	2,174	2,250	2,035	2,426
Iraq	3,477	2,514	1,000	1,012	1,005	1,209	1,433	1,690	2,079
Kuwait	2,500	1,656	1,125	823	1,064	1,157	1,023	1,419	1,361
Libya	2,092	1,787	1,140	1,150	1,105	1,087	1,059	1,034	972
Qatar	508	472	405	330	295	394	301	308	304
Saudi Arabia	9,532	9,900	9,815	6,483	5,086	4,663	3,388	4,870	4,186
United Arab Emirates	1,831	1,709	1,474	1,250	1,149	1,146	1,193	1,330	1,541
Subtotal	24,332	20,806	17,341	14,249	13,112	12,844	11,684	13,631	13,854
Other OPEC									
Ecuador	214	204	211	211	237	258	281	293	172
Gabon	203	175	151	156	157	157	172	166	156
Indonesia	1,591	1,577	1,605	1,339	1,343	1,412	1,325	1,390	1,311
Nigeria	2,302	2,055	1,433	1,295	1,241	1,388	1,495	1,484	1,340
Venezuela	2,356	2,168	2,102	1,895	1,801	1,798	1,677	1,787	1,751
Subtotal	6,666	6,179	5,502	4,896	4,779	5,013	4,950	5,120	4,730
Total	30,998	26,985	22,843	19,145	17,891	17,857	16,634	18,751	18,584

[a] Preliminary

Source: Department of Energy, Energy Information Administration, *International Energy Annual 1987.*

production (including Iraq's) be limited to 18.5 million bpd. Iraq's quota would be raised to 2.3 million bpd—the same as Iran's. Historically, Iraq's quota had been 1.6 million bpd, but Iraq had never followed it. Instead, Iraq had produced as much as possible, which in the fall of 1988 was about 2.7 million bpd. New pipeline capacity expected to come on line in 1989 presented the prospect of Iraq's reaching a 4 million bpd capacity. Iran argued that it deserved a higher quota because its population was three times larger than Iraq's.

At an October meeting in Madrid, Iran angrily rejected the proposal, saying it would never accept "parity" with Iraq on principle. But after intense pressure at another OPEC meeting in Vienna in late November, Iran finally gave in. Although Iran accepted parity, OPEC members allowed Iran to save face by keeping its former proportional share of overall OPEC production.

That agreement seemed to help restore some order to OPEC. Oil prices rose immediately upon news of the agreement, although the production limits did not take effect until January 1, 1989. During the first six months of 1989, the term the agreement covered, prices stayed in the $18-$22 range.

A Cloudy Future

It remained to be seen at the end of 1989 just what the 1990s held in store for OPEC. The world oil market defied prediction. In the early 1980s, after oil prices had rocketed upward to previously unmatched levels and demand was certain to fall appreciably, experts from the Department of Energy, the Congressional Budget Office, the Office of Technology Assessment, Exxon, Shell, Chevron, Texaco, and the International Energy Agency each attempted to forecast how much oil OPEC would produce in 1985. The closest projection, from the Energy Information Administration, was 45 percent above current estimates of 1985 production. Some of the worst projections were made by the oil companies, including overestimates in excess of 70 percent.

Such forecasts can only be based on a number of variables that are difficult to predict. One of the biggest of these, the 1980s demonstrated, is how consistently OPEC members can take concerted action to control the oil market.

Saudi Arabia's market share offensive and the apparent eagerness of many OPEC members to increase their individual market shares at the expense of other members, illustrated the fundamental, persistent debate that had spanned all three decades of the organization's history. OPEC has long been divided into two competing camps: the price moderates, typified by Saudi Arabia, and the price hawks such as Libya, who hope to push the price higher despite market conditions. This division has often made it difficult for OPEC to operate as an effective cartel and will continue to threaten OPEC unity.

Yet the decline of OPEC's power and resolve can be exaggerated. Although it was significant that OPEC began exceeding its own production ceiling by increasing amounts in the mid-1980s, it was perhaps even more significant that OPEC was able and willing to cut production in half and still survive. OPEC lost some control over oil prices as market forces continued to realign supply and demand, but it demonstrated market leverage when its members summoned the self-discipline and collective resolve to do so.

Cheating was chronic. OPEC, nearing the end of its third decade, still lacked any formal, institutionalized mechanism for enforcing its policies on its members. It relied on its members' perceptions of their own economic interests, and during the 1980s those interests seemed ever more divergent. One nation, Saudi Arabia, with the world's largest reserves, served as OPEC's primary enforcer. Saudi Arabia proved repeatedly in the 1980s that it alone, or perhaps joined by a small circle of Gulf allies, was big enough to dominate OPEC and to move world oil prices.

The Saudis had learned, however, that there was such a thing as too much success. OPEC's ability to drive up the price of oil in the 1970s was the source of most of its problems during the 1980s. Demand slackened as conservation, fuel-switching, inflation, and economic recession followed the price increases. New oil fields in non-OPEC countries were waiting to come on line as soon as rising prices made them profitable. This increase in world production robbed OPEC of the market power it needed to keep prices high.

During the 1990s many uncertainties outside OPEC will affect its destiny. Some of that uncertainty lies in the United States, which has debated how deeply it should commit itself to energy conservation and alternative fuels—whether conventional and abundant ones such as coal and gas or less conventional ones like solar power and methanol. Debate also rages in the United States over whether to explore for oil offshore and in wilderness areas such as the Arctic National Wildlife Refuge. A massive 1989 tanker spill in Prince William Sound, Alaska, seems likely to intensify the debate.

Other uncertainties arise over the pace of world population and economic growth, especially in the developing nations. Economic advances in these countries could greatly expand world demand for oil, but their burdens of poverty and debt make it unlikely that this will happen soon.

The 1980s produced further economic and foreign policy liberalization in China and the Soviet Union, two sleeping energy giants that had been virtually walled off from the rest of the oil market. A more complete integration of these countries into the international economy as oil exporters or importers could change the world oil market significantly.

Another global uncertainty that arose during the 1980s was the so-called greenhouse effect—climate warming caused partly by the burning of fossil fuels. Some scientists predict that the dangers of climate change will force cutbacks in petroleum consumption within the next few decades, long before underground reserves of petroleum are exhausted.

Despite such uncertainties, the importance of the Gulf states remains unquestioned. By the mid-1990s the biggest of the Gulf countries, Saudi Arabia, Iran, and Iraq, could supply 50 percent of the oil in world trade. If they cooperate with each other, as they have in the past, they could dominate the world oil market. If not, the world oil market could be subject to chaotic fluctuations in price and supply.

7

Fourteen Centuries of Islam

From Morocco on the Atlantic through North and East Africa and into sub-Saharan Africa, across the broad expanse of central and southwest Asia to the headwaters of the Indus in the lofty tableland of Tibet, and swinging southward to the far reaches of the Java Sea, the call of Islam goes forth to the world five times a day: "God is most great! I testify that there is no god but Allah. I testify that Muhammad is the messenger of Allah." This is Islam's credo and it is intoned in Arabic, the language of Islam's holy book, the Koran.

For fourteen centuries, the faith of Islam has been shaping the lives of nations and peoples that form a mosaic of nationalities, races, languages, regions, and cultures. Today, about 800 million people living in Asia, Africa, Europe, and, to a much lesser extent, the Americas profess faith in Islam.

Islam Divided

The catchall term *Islam* fails to convey the substantial differences among the many Islamic sects, races, nations, and cultures. The Islamic world is no more monolithic and homogeneous than the world of Christianity. From an anthropological point of view, there are vast differences between an Uzbek Moslem of Central Asia and a Berber from North Africa, or between a Moslem from Sumatra and a Fulani Moslem from Mali.

Political differences within the Moslem world are extensive, as evidenced by the varying ideological commitments of Moslem governments. The conservative monarchy of Saudi Arabia, the revolutionary Islamic fundamentalism of Iran, the secular socialism of the Ba'athist regimes of Syria and Iraq, and the disestablishment of Islam by the westernizing government of Turkey. This ideological diversity has promoted interstate conflict and tension. Moreover, divergent ideologies within Islamic nations have threatened to destabilize many Moslem governments.

The geographic spread of the forty or so Islamic countries (and of the approximately thirty other countries with sizable Moslem populations) has, of course, produced different societies. The cultural and historical development of Indonesia, for example, is quite distinct from that of Morocco. In the Middle East, Iran, Turkey, and Egypt are all Islamic countries, but they have little else in common.

On the theological level, Moslems also differ over interpretation of the Koran and the teachings of Muhammad. Some seventy sects and offshoots of Islam have arisen because of these doctrinal differences, which in some cases have remained irreconcilable. As in other religions, some sects of the Moslem faith are intolerant of others.

Islam as Unifier

This said, one should not overemphasize the differences and ignore the factors that unite Moslems all over the world. Islamic ideals and precepts have provided the most important element of cultural continuity and tradition in most of the Islamic countries. Although it remains largely an ideal, the notion of "the nation or community of Islam" still holds the majority of Moslems together in an informal allegiance. With the formation of the Organization of the Islamic Conference in 1972, this bond took on a more formal meaning.

A way of life as well as a religion, Islam has provided Moslems with a powerful frame of reference. Both on the conscious and subconscious levels, Moslems draw their identity, habits, and attitudes largely from Islam. This common heritage and tradition has been reinforced by most Moslem nations' shared experience of having been dominated and exploited by European colonial powers.

In spite of the ascendance of nationalism as the principal focus of political identity in modern times, in many Moslem countries the lines between national and religious identities are blurred. The two identities often overlap, so that to Arabs, Pakistanis, and Iranians, for example, national identity is largely synonymous with affiliation to Islam. Many Moslem nations expressly state in their constitutions that Islam is the official faith. In these countries Islam is more than a religion. It is a centuries-old system of values, norms, and beliefs that permeates all aspects of social, political, and cultural life.

Western Hostility

In the past the image of Islam in the West tended to be totally foreign, almost sinister. Many Moslems feel that this stereotypic image of Islam prevails in the West even today.

The negative image of Islam is due in part to ignorance about that "exotic" and "strange" religion, but it also has deep roots in history. Of all the world's religions, Islam is the closest to Christianity. Yet Christian Europe had deni-

Facts about Islam

• With about 800 million followers, Islam is the world's second-largest religion after Christianity. About forty nations have overwhelming Moslem majorities and roughly thirty other countries have sizable Moslem populations.

• Although Islam has been associated with the Middle East and the Arabs, the largest Islamic country is non-Arab—Indonesia. India, which does not have an Islamic majority, nevertheless has the second-largest Moslem population.

• Jerusalem is the third holiest place in Islam after Mecca and Medina—both in Saudi Arabia. Tradition has it that the Prophet Muhammad journeyed at night from Mecca to Jerusalem and from there ascended to heaven on a winged horse, Al-Buraq, and returned the same night.

• Most Moslem countries follow the Western (Gregorian) calendar, but a few use the lunar calendar adopted over thirteen centuries ago by Umar, second of the Rashidun caliphs. Moslem dates are referred to by the notation A. H. (Anno Hegira).

• The Moslem year has three hundred fifty-four days and twelve months. Each month begins with the new moon. Months vary between twenty-nine and thirty days and have no fixed relation to the seasons. Therefore, the months—as well as Moslem holidays—come at different times each year and may fall in different seasons. In the countries that have retained the Moslem calendar—especially Saudi Arabia—the day goes from sundown to sundown rather than from midnight to midnight. A rule of thumb is that the date of any Islamic holiday will advance eleven days from one year to the next.

grated it and ridiculed its founder, the Prophet Muhammad, throughout the medieval age and even into the modern era. Works by Dante, Voltaire, Carlyle, and other European writers, thinkers, theologians, and Orientalists attacked the Koran or Muhammad and thus influenced the attitudes of generations of Westerners.

This hostility to Islam was the result not so much of theological differences as of history and geography: it was Islam that had conquered parts of Europe and threatened much of the rest of it for several centuries. Islam's early empire expanded through conquests in the West, starting with Byzantium. The Arab armies that carried the faith to new horizons and frontiers overran Spain, Sicily, and parts of Eastern Europe and ruled them for centuries. They crossed the Pyrenees and raided France as far as Nimes. The armies of the last Islamic empire, the Ottoman, which was Turkish, not Arab, twice stood at the gates of Vienna and almost occupied the city.

Triggered by Islamic conquests in the West, the Crusades to the Holy Land by Western nations between the eleventh and thirteenth centuries deepened the hostility between the followers of the two religions and reinforced mutual suspicions and insecurities.

The legacy of alienation germinated by the Islamic conquests and counter-conquests by the West was perpetuated in literature and folk culture. Later, during the nineteenth and twentieth centuries, Western industrialization and military strength spearheaded Western hegemony in much of the Islamic Middle East. Moslems felt victimized and dehumanized, their national identities suppressed and their cultural heritage and contributions to civilization denigrated.

More recent years have witnessed a significant revival of Islamic sentiment—a product of the continuing effort of nearly all Moslem countries to shake free of the legacy of Western colonialism. For example, the overthrow of the shah of Iran and the rise to power of the Ayatollah Ruhollah Khomeini were motivated in part by the impulse of the Iranian people to establish independence from the West. The revival of Islamic sentiment, in turn, has renewed historically rooted fears in the West of the specter of "Islam on the march." Events such as the Iranian revolution of 1978-1979 and the U.S. embassy hostage crisis of 1979-1981 contributed to these fears that never had fully disappeared in Western culture. Mutual suspicions and misperceptions on both sides created hostility that still shows few signs of subsiding.

THE HISTORICAL AND CULTURAL SETTING

Alexander the Great was barely twenty-two when his Macedonian forces swept through the Middle East and India as far east as the Indus River. His goal as leader of a powerful Greek empire was to unify the Middle East into a lasting empire, which he hoped would rekindle the spirit and brilliance of "the glory that was Greece."

Alexander's imperial dream was dashed by his death in 323 B.C. His empire soon broke up into several successor states ruled by his generals. Divided and poorly led, these states warred and feuded with each other until the Romans arrived a century later and, with the exception of Mesopotamia and Iran, brought the Middle East under their tutelage.

Some eight centuries later the Roman Empire itself was ravaged by the northern Teutonic barbarians, who severed its western half in the fifth century A.D. His empire decimated, the Emperor Constantine transferred his seat of power eastward from Rome to Constantinople, giving birth to the Byzantine Empire.

The eastern Roman emperors of Byzantium controlled the Roman provinces of the Middle East, while farther east the Sasanids of Persia established a rival empire in Mesopotamia and areas of present-day Iran. The Byzantines found themselves ruling diverse peoples and cultures, including Greeks, Syrians, Phoenicians, Egyptians, Jews, several Palestinian tribes, and Arabs.

The Arabs, Semitic people who originally came from the hinterlands and shores of Arabia (present-day Saudi Arabia), had fanned out into the Middle East and established several communities and states. They were mostly pagan, but as Christianity began to spread through the Middle East in the second century A.D. many of them embraced the new religion. For example, the Arab states of Ghassanid and Lakhmid, which allied themselves with the Byzantines and the Sasanids, respectively, were Christian. Their kinsmen in Arabia, however, remained largely pagan and immune to the control of the two rival empires to the north.

Arabia: Islam's Birthplace

Arabia at the time was by no means an isolated desert removed from the civilized world or populated merely by nomads who roamed the desert. There were sedentary populations living in towns and oases scattered across Arabia and having a modicum of social order and links to the outside world. The camel had revolutionized life there by bringing city and desert together into a well-integrated system and by linking Arabia—primarily through trade—with the outside world, particularly with the prosperous and cultivated states of the Mediterranean.

The demands and prosperity of the Byzantine and Roman worlds, especially their growing appetite for spices, incense, and silk, gave a powerful impetus to trade between India and Africa, on the one hand, and the Mediterranean world, on the other. Trade had been established between them over two major routes—the Persian Gulf and the Fertile Crescent (Syria, Lebanon, Iraq, Jordan, and Palestine). But the wars between the Byzantines and the Sasanids and their Ghassanid and Lakhmid satellites made these routes increasingly risky. In time, traders shifted to new routes along the Red Sea through the rugged western part of Arabia known as the Hijaz. Soon, caravans were carrying goods from Yemen by way of the Hijaz to Syria and the Mediterranean.

The booming caravan trade worked especially to the advantage of one city in Arabia, Mecca, which was to become the largest city and most important and powerful trading center on the peninsula. Located in a long, rocky valley among bare, mountainous hills, some forty miles inland from the Red Sea, and fed by a permanent spring, Mecca first became a settlement located around a shrine called the Ka'bah (literally, cube).

The Ka'bah housed a black stone, believed by some non-Moslems to be a meteorite, which was held sacred by the Bedouins in the desert and the townsfolk of Mecca and nearby settlements. Tradition has it that the black stone was brought to earth by the archangel Gabriel and delivered to the Prophet Abraham and his son Ishmael, who encased it in the Ka'bah. The Ka'bah thus became a pilgrimage site, but pagan practices distorted its significance.

The Meccans revered Abraham as a patriarch and prophet and claimed descent from Ishmael. Later, Moslems claimed Abraham as the first Moslem, while Arabs in general claimed Ishmael as the progenitor of all Arabs.

By the sixth century A.D., when Muhammad was born, the enterprising Meccan merchants had developed into a powerful mercantile oligarchy not unlike the Italian mercantile republics of the Middle Ages. Lying in a strategic position at the crossroads of overland trade routes linking Asia and the Mediterranean by way of the Hijaz, Mecca thrived even when Constantinople and other northern centers in the eastern Mediterranean were importing more and more luxury goods from the East by way of the Black Sea and central Asia.

The prosperity of Mecca gave added prominence and power to the Quraysh, the major tribe and part of the aristocracy inhabiting the city. The Quraysh consisted of several clans and families, one of which was the family of Banu Hashim, from whom Jordan's Hashemite dynasty claims descent. It was into this family that Muhammad was born.

The Prophet Muhammad

Very little is known about the early life of Muhammad. No biography of him was written until a century after his death, and its authenticity is marred by extravagant embellishments and idealization. His date of birth generally is given as A.D. 570.

It is known that his father, Abdullah, probably died before Muhammad was born, and that his mother died when he was about six. His grandfather became his guardian and protector, and when his grandfather died the boy was left in the custody of an uncle. Without inheritance from his father, the young Muhammad had to fend for himself, and he did so by working as a caravan trader. His efficiency and honesty eventually caught the eye of a wealthy and influential widow many years his senior, who made him her business agent. Eventually, he married her and they had many children, but only four girls lived to maturity.

The Mecca in which Muhammad grew to manhood was the center of Arabia's polytheistic animism, attracting tribal pilgrims from all over the Arabian Peninsula. The Meccans at that time generally were pagan, although, as a center of trade, Mecca had come into contact with certain influences outside Arabia. These included Christianity, Judaism, and some Christian heretical and gnostic sects, some of whose adherents lived in Mecca and other Arabian towns. Zoroastrianism, a monotheistic religion practiced by Persians, also was known to some Meccans.

Through their contacts with Jews and Christians the Meccans acquired a certain awareness of monotheism and developed vague notions of a Supreme Being. They believed, however, that they could gain access to the Supreme Being only through intercessors—gods and goddesses in the form of idols. So they installed 360 such idols in the Ka'bah, which remained there until the Prophet Muhammad destroyed them and reconsecrated the Ka'bah, which subsequently became the holiest shrine of the Islamic religion.

The sect thought to have had the deepest influence on Muhammad's thinking was the Hanifis—a pious group with monotheistic leanings who were very critical of the rampant paganism and the growing commercialism and materialism of Mecca. In time Muhammad, too, became deeply troubled by the low moral fiber of Meccan society. Following ancient Middle East custom, he is said to have retreated on occasion to lonely places to think and contemplate. According to some unsubstantiated accounts, he was influenced by Christian heretics and hermits he met during his caravan trips to Syria.

Tradition has it that Muhammad chose a cave in a hillside near Mecca to meditate. His marriage had brought him material comfort, thus enabling him to stay away from work for long periods of time.

Muhammad's Revelations

It was in a cave that Muhammad, according to his seventh-century biography, experienced his first revelation. The year probably was A.D. 610, when Muhammad was about forty. He was supposed to have had a vision in which the archangel Gabriel commanded him to read a message sent from God saying that man was a creature of God and subservient to him.

Muhammad, who was believed to have been illiterate, is said to have memorized the message and repeated it to his wife and his friends, who called it a divine revelation. This first revelation was followed by others, on and off, for some twenty years, both in Mecca and Medina, another city in Arabia. These revelations became the basis of the Koran. Moslems refer to the Koran as "glorious," not holy.

Muhammad's revelations established his role as the "Prophet" and "Messenger of God" and marked the birth of Islam. The adherents of the new religion became known as Moslems.

Slowly, Muhammad began to attract believers. Most Meccans, however, spurned his teachings and ridiculed his claims of prophethood. They were outraged particularly by his audacious denunciation of Mecca's paganism and his condemnation of the Ka'bah, which gave Mecca its position of prestige and eminence in Arabia and which enjoyed the protection and sponsorship of the Meccan aristocracy.

Islam Finds a Home

The disdain of Meccan leaders eventually turned into hostility when the ruling class became aware of Muhammad's growing appeal to some segments of the population and the serious implications of his teachings. His message clearly threatened the established order and jeopardized the city's income from trade and pilgrimages. To avoid persecution Muhammad secretly fled with about seventy of his followers for Yathrib, a city to the north of Mecca, in A.D. 622. The flight from Mecca—termed the *Hegira* by Moslems—marks the beginning of the Islamic calendar.

Yathrib, later named Medina al-Manura ("City of Enlightenment") and subsequently shortened to Medina, welcomed Muhammad in the hope he would help alleviate the serious divisions and civil disorders caused by the large influx of outsiders—mostly Yemenis and Bedouins—and internal feuds among rival groups and clans. The success that Muhammad achieved in Medina was the first test for the nascent religion.

With Medina as his base, Muhammad set out to subjugate Mecca. He succeeded in A.D. 630 after years of intermittent wars. Entering Mecca in triumph, Muhammad proceeded to the Ka'bah, where he destroyed the idols of paganism.

The Islamic commonwealth now began to emerge and take shape through raids and conquests in which the Bedouin's free spirit and love for movement and booty were channeled to the call of *jihad,* meaning "striving" or "struggle"—a term often associated with the concept of religious or holy war. In fact, however, jihad has a broader meaning of striving for the common well-being of Islam and Moslems, and not necessarily by military means.

Islamized Arabs in Muhammad's lifetime carried their religion to many parts of Arabia, but the Prophet Muhammad did not live long enough to see the spectacular expansion of Islam. When he died in A.D. 632, only two years after seizing Mecca and making it the center of Islam, he had bequeathed to his followers not only a religion but also a socio-political system and even an ideology. It became the task of his followers to propagate that ideology and carry it beyond the confines of Arabia.

Islam after Muhammad

To the extent that Muhammad was God's prophet on earth, no one could succeed him. Some provision had to be adopted, however, for filling Muhammad's other roles as the spiritual and secular head of Islam. The succession question produced a major schism in Islam that has endured to this day. Some of Muhammad's followers claimed that the mantle of leadership should pass within the Prophet's family to his cousin and son-in-law, Ali, and argued that Muhammad had made this designation. Upholders of this view evolved into the Shi'ite sect of Islam. *("Schisms and Sects of Islam," box, p. 127)*

Most Moslems, however, opposed this claim and relied instead on tribal tradition, where inheritance or legal claim always had been superseded by a process of selection in which tribal elders chose a leader according to the prestige and power of his family or position in the tribal system. This view prevailed, laying the basis for the Sunni (orthodox) tradition in Islam.

Muhammad's Early Successors

Muhammad's trusted lieutenants were able to agree on one of their own, Abu Bakr, who was perhaps the first convert to Islam outside Muhammad's immediate family. He was the father of Ayshah, Muhammad's last wife. Abu Bakr thus became the first of four early *caliphs,*—a term derived from Abu Bakr's title as successor of God's messenger—who promoted the expansion of Islam. Abu Bakr's first goal was to Islamize and exert control over the rest of the Arabian Peninsula. This was accomplished by his brilliant military commander, Khalid ibn al-Walid, who conquered eastern and southern Arabia and even resubdued tribes that had revoked their allegiance to Islam after Muhammad's death. With Islam secure in Arabia, Khalid and other generals conquered the Sasanids in what is now Iraq, wrested Syria from the Byzantines, and opened all of Palestine to the Moslems.

Abu Bakr was followed as caliph by Umar ibn al-Khattab, whom Moslems sometimes call the second founder of Islam. During his ten-year reign the theocratic foundations of Islam were consolidated and Islamic conquests were pushed into new lands. Persia, central Asia, western India, and Egypt—bastions of great empires and earlier civilizations—were overrun by his Islamic forces. This expansion was driven as much by economic considerations as by religious zeal. Under Umar, the Middle East was reunified into a single, great empire, which it had not been since the age of Alexander the Great.

Umar was succeeded by the Uthman ibn 'Affan, the third of the Rashidun (rightly guided) caliphs. Like his two predecessors, Uthman had been one of Muhammad's companions, but unlike them he belonged to a powerful family, the Umayyad. It was from this family that Uthman appointed some of his senior aides as governors and generals. His most significant and historically important appointment was that of his dynamic and able cousin, Mu'awiyah ibn Abi Sufyan, as governor of Damascus. Mu'awiyah soon became the ruler of all Syria.

Schisms and Sects of Islam

About 90 percent of all Moslems are *Sunnis*—considered the orthodox sect. Of the dissident sects of Islam, the largest and most important is the *Shi'ite* sect. Shi'ah, or Shi'ism, refers to the "partisans of Ali."

When the Prophet Muhammad died without making any provisions for succession, his cousin and son-in-law, Ali ibn Abi Talib, claimed to be the Prophet's successor. But a majority of Muhammad's followers rallied around Abu Bakr, reputed to be the first person outside the Prophet's immediate family who converted to Islam.

Appointed to succeed the Prophet as the leader of the Moslem community, Abu Bakr became the first of the four *caliphs,* meaning "successors," of Muhammad.

Muhammad's son-in-law was rebuffed two more times when Moslems elected Umar ibn al-Khattab and Uthman ibn'Affan as the second and third caliphs. Eventually, twenty-three years after Muhammad's death, the caliphate passed to Ali, but the governor of Syria at the time, Mu'awiyah, and other members of a powerful tribe, the Umayyads, refused to recognize his authority. Ali ruled from Kufah, in Iraq, but his reign was marked by strife and dissension.

The first war between Moslems was waged during his reign when Ali's army defeated the rebellious forces of Mu'awiyah. Among other things, Ali was accused by his adversaries of having condoned the murder of his predecessor, Uthman, a member of the powerful Umayyad family.

In A.D. 661 Ali was assassinated by a Moslem dissident and his eldest son, Hasan, succeeded him as caliph. Challenged by the powerful Umayyad governor of Syria, Mu'awiyah, the easygoing and irresolute Hasan abdicated in favor of his rival, who was proclaimed the caliph of all Moslems, with his capital in Damascus. Before his death, Mu'awiyah designated his son, Yazid, as his successor to the caliphate. Hasan's younger brother, Husayn, rose in rebellion against Yazid but was routed and slain in Karlbala,

in Iraq, in A.D. 680. The dreadful manner in which he was tortured and killed by the Sunni followers of Yazid bred Shi'ism—the first schism in Islam.

Each year Shi'ites mark the anniversary of Husayn's martyrdom with an astounding display of emotional intensity and religious frenzy marked by breast beating and self-flagellation. The martyrdom of Husayn became the major symbol of Shi'ism.

The political dispute that gave rise to Shi'ism was reinforced later by doctrinal differences. The Shi'ites replaced the Sunni term caliphate with that of *imamate* and focused their belief on a hereditary line from Muhammad through twelve imams, beginning with Ali. The major Shi'ite sect draws its name of *Twelvers* from the twelve imams. The twelfth imam reportedly disappeared in mysterious circumstances in A.D. 878. Shi'ites disagree on how and when he died, but they agree his name was Muhammad al-Muntazar, "the expected one," and that he must reappear to complete the mission of God on earth.

Twelver Shi'ism is the state religion of Iran, the only Moslem country with an overwhelming Shi'ite majority.

Shi'ism itself has its own dissidents, those who became Isma'ilis, Alawites, and Druzes.

In the eighth century a mystical movement called *Sufism* developed in protest against the formalism and legalism of conventional Islam. The name is derived from the Arabic word for wool, *suf,* since the first Sufis wore coarse woolen garments, probably in imitation of the Christian hermits of Syria. The Sufis practiced a form of hermitic mysticism by withdrawing from the world and seeking a personal relationship and direct communion with God.

Sufism has had great influence, both within the Islamic world and beyond it. Many Sufi orders exist, each centered around different rites. Although both Sunni and Shi'ite fundamentalists reject it, Sufism retains wide appeal among those who view Islam fundamentally as a religious experience rather than as a basis for political action.

Uthman's weak leadership, and his policy of appointing many members of the Umayyad family to high office, angered other Moslems, including those who considered themselves keepers and protectors of Muhammad's legacy. Uthman eventually was murdered by rebels outraged by what they saw as his favoritism and deviation from the path set by Muhammad.

Under pressure from those rebels, Muhammad's cousin and son-in-law, Ali ibn Abi Talib, was chosen as successor to Uthman. His selection, however, was opposed by some of the powerful and influential Moslems, who accused Ali of condoning the murder of Uthman.

The Umayyad Islamic Empire

There followed an unstable period in which first Muhammad's widow and then the ruler of Syria, Mu'awiyah, challenged Ali for control of the Islamic movement. Eventually, Mu'awiyah, a member of the Umayyad family, prevailed over all his challengers, and he was proclaimed the caliph of all the Moslems in A.D. 661. Damascus then became the center of the Umayyads and their Arab empire.

The Umayyad dynasty lasted from A.D. 661 to 750 and initiated a new wave of conquests that complemented the breathtaking expansion by the first four Rashidun caliphs. The Moslem empire extended its hegemony to the fringes of India and China, overran North Africa, and, in A.D. 717, pushed across the Strait of Gibraltar. The occupation of Spain by the Moslems—given the name "Moors"—lasted until A.D. 1492. During the Umayyad dynasty Muhammad's followers gained control of an empire that surpassed in size the empire of Alexander the Great.

This was a period in which the newly conquered peoples, including the Syrians, Egyptians, and Berbers, became Arabized, adopting the faith, culture, and language of the Arabs. The Berbers retained certain local attributes, such as a native dialect, and the Persians, Turks, and some Indian groups adopted the Arabic alphabet and script but retained their own language. The Arabs themselves were exposed to a process of acculturation as the new faith acquired millions of converts among the non-Arab peoples. As a result, the Arab character of Islam became diluted.

A combination of powerful trends finally brought about the demise of the Umayyad empire that Mu'awiyah had established. The most decisive were the growing decadence of the Umayyad court in Damascus; the persistent opposition to the Umayyad dynasty by Shi'ite Moslems; the emergence of rebellious and alienated forces in Iraq and in a region of Iran known as Khurasan, once centers of great power that resented their subordinate status under the Umayyads; and the constant feuding among the Sunni tribes of Arabia.

The Abbasid Islamic Empire

About the year 740, the Abbasids, led by Abu al-Abbas, a descendant of an uncle of Muhammad, emerged as the major opposition group to Umayyad rule. They became the main rallying point of all the anti-Umayyad forces, especially the non-Arab Moslems of Khurasan. In 747 the Abbasids, led by Abu al-Abbas, openly revolted. Within three years they had defeated the Umayyads.

The Abbasids ruthlessly hunted down the Umayyad rulers. Only a few managed to escape, among them Abd al-Rahman, who fled to Spain, where he established the Umayyad caliphate of Cordoba. The Umayyads at Cordoba were threatened by internal factionalism, Berber invasions from North Africa, and resistance by Spanish Christians in the north of Spain. The regime survived these challenges, however, and then prospered under subsequent Berber/Arab dynasties that arose in North Africa. Moorish power in Spain finally came to an end in 1492 with the capture of the last Islamic stronghold at Granada by the Christian forces of King Ferdinand and Queen Isabella.

The emergence of the Abbasid Empire, with its capital in Baghdad, ushered in great changes. Non-Arab Moslems achieved greater prominence and influence than ever before. The Abbasids extended the Islamic empire to some of the Mediterranean ports in southern France and Italy and took control of Sicily and Sardinia and, in the east, part of present-day Turkey and India.

The imperial munificence and wealth of the court in Baghdad far outstripped its Umayyad predecessor in Damascus and was immortalized in the tales of *The Arabian Nights*. The arts flourished, and a great cultural movement flowered along the banks of the Tigris and Euphrates rivers. The works of the ancient Greeks, Romans, Iranians, and Hindus in philosophy, medicine, astronomy, mathematics, and science were translated into Arabic and became part of Islamic culture. A whole generation of Arab and Arabized Moslem scholars left their imprint on Western civilization.

The Abbasids leaned heavily on Persian administrators and Turkish soldiers in running their burgeoning empire, which extended almost from the borders of China to the Pyrenees. The influence of the Persians and Turks grew until the caliphs themselves became little more than figureheads of the new administrative elite.

As the power of the caliphs diminished, they became easy prey for their governors and generals, who proceeded to carve out their own principalities. Ultimately, many little dynasties and states sprouted within the Abbasid Empire, rendering it an empty shell ruled by caliphs appointed or deposed at will by the Turkish soldiers or Persian administrators. In Spain, Morocco, Tunisia, Egypt, Syria, Persia, and other areas, new self-styled caliphates and sultanates arose, maintaining a semblance of allegiance to the caliph in Baghdad. By the year 1000, the Abbasid caliph in Baghdad was rivaled by self-proclaimed independent caliphs in both Cairo and Cordoba.

The fiction of the Abbasid dynasty continued through the eleventh century, when a group of Turks, called Seljuks, captured Baghdad and won recognition from the Arab caliph there. The Seljuk rulers captured most of Anatolia (Turkey) from the Byzantines and triggered the chain of events that culminated in the Crusades.

The Ottoman Empire

The final blow to the Abbasid Empire came in 1258 when Mongols overran Baghdad. As the Middle Ages drew to a close, Moslem power shifted decisively to Anatolia, where a small Turkish tribe led by Osman began to accumulate power and territory at the expense of the Byzantine Empire. By 1453 the Ottomans, as they are called in English, had captured Byzantium. Constantinople was renamed Istanbul and became the capital of the Ottoman Turks.

The greatest of the Ottoman sultans, Suleiman the Magnificent (1520-1566), extended the frontiers of the empire to include the Middle East and North Africa as well as most of present-day Hungary and southeastern Europe. In India, another Turkish dynasty, the Moguls, established an Islamic empire that reached its height in the period between 1556 and 1658. It was during that era that the Taj Mahal was built at Agra.

The Ottoman Empire began to break up even before the European powers emerged in the nineteenth century as the new masters of the international order. The "sick man of Europe," as the tottering Ottoman rule was labeled at the turn of the century, was finally defeated in World War I, and its territories were partitioned. The remnants of the empire were centered in Turkish-populated Anatolia, which became the Turkish Republic in 1923 under the leadership of Mustafa Kemal (Ataturk).

THE DOCTRINE OF ISLAMIC FAITH

Of all the major religions, Moslems proudly point out, only Islam is named neither for its founder, as in Christianity or Buddhism, nor after the community in which it emerged, as in Judaism. They see this as proof of the uniqueness of Islam as a universal religion—neither the product of a human mind nor of a religion that is identified with a particular community.

Islam incorporates both the spiritual and temporal aspects of life into a social as well as a religious system that seeks to regulate a believer's relationship to God and relations with other persons. Its precepts and tenets, though clearly the product of a particular society and historical period, were considered to be good for all people and all times and, therefore, unalterable.

In Islam there is no separation between the religious and the secular. Almost all Islamic nations ostensibly declare their adherence to this concept. Although these nations are guided by modern, practical norms, Moslems find it necessary to seek an Islamic explanation for world events. Turkey is the only Islamic country that has made a formal separation between the religious and secular spheres. At the other extreme, Saudi Arabia and now Iran are the only countries that claim the Koran as their constitution. That, however, does not bar the Saudis from following secular practices and policies.

Islam in Arabic means "submission"—in this case, submission to the will of God. The one who submits is a Moslem. That submission is total and irrevocable. Indeed, the central theme of the Islamic faith is an uncompromising assertion of the unity, uniqueness, and sovereignty of *Allah*, the Arabic equivalent of God. Accordingly, Moslems vehemently reject the Christian doctrine of the Trinity as sinful and blasphemous.

The affirmation of the oneness of God is linked symbolically to another fundamental tenet, namely that Muhammad is the messenger, or apostle, of God and that he is the last prophet. These two affirmations constitute the *Shahadah*—the Moslem's confession of faith.

Doctrine's Sources

The Islamic doctrine has four sources: the Koran, the Hadith-Sunnah, consensus, and inference by analogy.

The Koran

The *Koran* (literally, "reading or recitation") is the primary source of Islamic teachings and doctrine. Considered the word of God, it is therefore divine, eternal and immutable. Moslems believe that the Koran is a replica of an archetype in heaven. Because the Koran was revealed to Muhammad in Arabic, Moslems are prohibited from using it liturgically in any other language.

The Koran consists of 114 chapters of varying lengths which, Moslems believe, were revealed to Muhammad piecemeal over a period of about twenty years by the archangel Gabriel. Each chapter bears the name of a person, animal, or object prominently cited in the text.

The various utterances in the Koran initially were memorized or written on parchment, leather, palm leaves, stone tablets, and other objects. They remained scattered and were not finally pieced together and collected into a standard text until well after Muhammad's death in A.D. 632. The first canonized version was set down under the caliph Uthman in the seventh century.

Islam has no priestly or clerical caste and no central body, and Muhammad has no divine attributes, but simply is considered God's messenger. Thus the Koran has an overwhelming spiritual importance in the lives of Moslems. It is the purveyor and preserver of the faith, and it exercises a powerful hold as much for its spiritual content as for the sheer majesty of its prose.

The Koran is a work of such beauty that Moslems, particularly Arabs, are sometimes transformed into a state of emotional and spiritual elation when they listen to the verses of the Koran. The verses are always chanted or intoned, perhaps to accentuate the rhythmic cadence and elegance of the text. The mutually reinforcing link between the linguistic and the spiritual importance of the Koran underlies the Moslems' deep belief in the inimitability of the holy book.

The Koran also provided a religiously sanctioned linguistic model, which protected the Arabic language from the ravages of local fragmentation and from Ottoman domination. During the Ottoman rule, Arab culture and the Arab component of Islam were diluted and nearly pushed to extinction.

Westerners, including some Orientalists, in the past applied the association of Christianity and Christ to Islam, calling it "Mohammedanism." But, unlike Christ, Muhammad ("Mohammed" still is a common Western spelling of his name) never was deified in the Koran. His attributes remained those of a prophet and messenger of God. Moslems venerate him as such and always follow his name with the phrase, "May God bless him and grant him salvation," but they do not worship him. Nevertheless, that veneration often approximates worship. It is, therefore, the Koran, not Muhammad, that is the cornerstone of Islam.

The Hadith-Sunnah

The Koran contains a wide variety of devotional regulations as well as specific rules for everyday living—rules on matters such as marriage, divorce, inheritance, and contracts. Like the testaments of other religions, however, it did not address many problems, especially those caused by the growth of the community of Islam after Muhammad's death and the twentieth-century establishment of modern secular states. The lack of comprehensive guidance in the Koran led Moslems to seek guidance elsewhere, primarily in the so-called *Hadith-Sunnah,* meaning "tradition" and "prophetic practice." *Hadith* specifically refers to Muhammad's sayings, while *Sunnah* refers to his actions or his attitude toward the actions of others. In modern usage, the two words generally are used interchangeably.

The codification of the Hadith-Sunnah did not begin until the second half of the second Islamic century (767-795), and it was not completed until the third (869-896), during the reign of the Abbasid dynasty. Since the sources of what Muhammad said and did were oral testimonies and reports handed down from one generation to another, a great deal of distortion and even spurious attributions to Muhammad slipped into the record. Sifting through the mass of oral history that had accumulated after Muhammad's death, Islamic scholars in the Abbasid era faced the formidable task of verification and compilation. Finally, the process was boiled down to six collections or compilations—the so-called Six Books.

Consensus

The third source of Islamic doctrine is *consensus,* which is practiced by leading Moslem scholars recognized as interpreters of Islamic doctrine. When the Moslem community is faced with an issue for which the Koran or the Hadith-Sunnah has no provision scholars may study the matter to determine how to deal with it. At least three scholars are required to reach a consensus on any issue.

Inference by Analogy

Inference by analogy is the fourth source of Islamic doctrine. Basically, this is the process by which judges and scholars devise a solution to a new problem or case based on solutions or principles inferred from the previous three sources. Inference by analogy corresponds to the use of precedents in the Anglo-Saxon legal tradition.

The Five Pillars of Islam

The four sources provide the system of Islamic doctrine. That doctrine entails certain obligations that are as important as faith in determining and defining the complete identity of a Moslem. The most significant obligations are the so-called Five Pillars of Islam:

I. The Confession of Faith

This is the oral declaration, "I testify that there is no God but Allah; I testify that Muhammad is God's messenger." Implicit in this testimony is commitment to belief in one true God (monotheism) and affirmation that God's revelation through the Prophet Muhammad (the Koran) is true. Islamic scholars concur that confession of the faith before witnesses is the distinction between a Moslem and a non-Moslem.

II. Prayer

Several conditions have to be met before prayers can be performed. The person must be a Moslem, decently attired, physically clean, and should turn his face toward Mecca.

Prayers should be performed five times daily: at daybreak, noon, afternoon, sunset, and evening. Kneeling and touching their foreheads to the ground, Moslems repeat ritual prayers always beginning with the declaration, "God is most great."

Moslems can perform daily prayers anywhere, and many carry a prayer rug with them. On Friday, the Sabbath, Moslems flock to mosques for what is equivalent to the Sunday mass in the Catholic church.

III. Alms

The giving of alms, like the tithe in Christianity, is obligatory for Moslems. Alms can be given to the poor or to an institution that supports the Moslem community.

IV. Fasting during Ramadan

Ramadan, the ninth month in the lunar Islamic calendar, is the month in which the Prophet Muhammad customarily retreated to fast and pray and in which the Koran was first revealed to him. In memory of the Prophet's practice and in honor of Allah's revelation, Moslems are required to fast and pray during the entire month.

Because Ramadan follows the phases of the moon, it may occur during any of the four seasons. Nothing is to be consumed between sunrise and sunset, not even water. Sexual activity and smoking are forbidden during fasting.

When the traditional cannon is fired to signal the breaking of the fast at sunset, Ramadan usually takes on a festive character in which families gather around tables laden with traditional dishes and gifts are exchanged. The month of fasting culminates in the colorful three-day holiday of *'Id al-Fitr*, one of the most important Moslem holidays.

Traditionally, the sick, the elderly, travelers, pregnant women, and nursing mothers are exempted from the rites of fasting during Ramadan.

V. Pilgrimage

The twelfth and last month of the Islamic calendar is the season of *al-hajj*, the ritual pilgrimage to Mecca. Moslem males and females of sound body and mind are required to journey to Mecca at least once in a lifetime. *("The Pilgrimage to Mecca," box, facing page)*

Articles of Faith

Moslems also adhere to a set of beliefs that can be summed up as follows:

Belief in God

Moslems are believers in one God. They pride themselves on being the only true monotheists.

Belief in God's Angels

Angels, Moslems believe, are spiritual beings created by God to carry out His orders. Angels have no independent will of their own.

Belief in God's Messengers or Prophets

These are men inspired by God to communicate His orders to mankind. The Koran speaks of a line of prophets beginning with Adam and ending with Muhammad. Both Jesus and Moses are part of this line.

Belief in God's Books

Only four books revealed to the prophets are specifically mentioned in the Koran and, therefore, recognized by Moslems: the Torah (the first five books of the Old Testament); the Psalms; the Gospel or New Testament; and the Koran. Moslems believe in the first three books to the degree that they were preserved as originally written. They contend, however, that only the Koran was so preserved, the implication being that it remains the only true book. Christians and Jews are called "People of the Book" and Moslems respect their places of worship, law codes, schools, and property.

Belief in the Day of Judgment

Both in the Koran and in the Hadith-Sunnah, man is constantly enjoined to conduct his life with awareness that

The Pilgrimage to Mecca

Once a year, Mecca—Islam's holiest city—becomes a teeming, sweltering microcosm of the Islamic world. Moslems of every race and color converge on it from all corners of the earth to perform the rites of *al-hajj* (pilgrimage). There, in Mecca's Sacred Mosque, the world of Islam comes together around the Ka'bah, the shrine rising majestically in the middle of the mosque's large open court.

The ritual of al-hajj, a Moslem ceremony known as the Fifth Pillar of Islam, is rooted in the pre-Islamic era of paganism when Arab tribesmen trekked to the Ka'bah at least once a year to worship the idols it housed. With the advent of Islam, Muhammad destroyed the idols and reconsecrated the Ka'bah as Islam's holiest shrine, thus restoring it, according to Moslems, to the temple of God built by the Prophet Abraham and his son Ishmael.

Today, the cube-like stone structure of the Ka'bah stands forty-nine feet high and is shrouded by the *kiswah,* a brocaded black cloth adorned with quotations from the Koran. The kiswah is made anew every year. The Ka'bah's focal point is a piece of rock, twelve inches in diameter, called the Black Stone. Set in silver and mounted in the east corner of the holy shrine, this sacred rock is thought by Moslems to have been delivered to Ishmael by the archangel Gabriel. It is said to be the only remaining relic from the original structure built by Abraham and Ishmael.

A Holy Ritual

Moslems of both sexes who are physically and financially able to do so are admonished by the Koran to perform the hajj at least once in their lifetime. To devout Moslems, the hajj is the crowning event of their lives. There, with thousands of other Moslems, they renew their communion with God and rededicate themselves to Islam.

The formal pilgrimage lasts only ten days, beginning on the first day of Dhul-Hijjah, the twelfth and last month of the Moslem lunar calendar. In another sense the pilgrimage begins when the Moslem leaves home for Mecca and does not end until the Moslem returns. During the whole period, the pilgrim is considered to be in a dedicated state and participating in a holy ritual.

Before entering the sacred territory around Mecca, Moslems have to be in a state of *ihram* (restriction). The men remove their clothes and don simple garments consisting of two large pieces of white fabric that cover their bodies. Nothing else is worn. The women wear their customary dress and can remain unveiled. But, unlike the men, they have to keep their heads covered. The state of ihram also requires Moslems to refrain from cutting their nails or hair, hunting, wearing jewelry, or engaging in sexual relations.

At the Sacred Mosque, tradition requires that the pilgrims perform the *tawaf,* the rite of walking around the Ka'bah seven times counterclockwise, during which they kiss or touch the Black Stone. Then comes the ceremony of *sa'y,* in which pilgrims make seven trips between the hills of Safa and Marwah, which are within the walls of the great mosque.

The ceremony is a reenactment of the desperate search by Hagar, Abraham's wife, for water when she and her son Ishmael were left alone in a desolate valley. The ordeal of Hagar and her son ended when the Well of Zamzam was revealed to them. Pilgrims ritually drink from that well.

The Final Days

On the eighth day of Dhul-Hijjah, the final days of the hajj begin. Pilgrims proceed to the village of Mina, four miles east of Mecca, where they rest, then advance the next day to the Plain of Arafat for the ritual prayers of "standing" from noon to sunset. More than a million and a half persons have been known to assemble on that sultry plain where Muhammad prayed and delivered his farewell sermon on the ninth day of Dhul-Hijjah.

On the return to Mina the pilgrims stop for the night at Muzdalifah. There they collect pebbles for the ritual stoning of Satan's three pillars in Mina that symbolize evil and temptation.

On the tenth day pilgrims celebrate 'Id al-Adha (Festival of Sacrifice) by sacrificing an animal. That ritual, which marks the end of the pilgrimage season, recalls the time when Abraham offered up his son Ishmael as a sacrifice to God, but his son was delivered when the archangel Gabriel brought a ram that was used as a sacrifice instead.

(The biblical version of the same story has Abraham offering up his son Isaac, rather than Ishmael, as a sacrifice to God.)

While the 'Id al-Adha is being celebrated at Mina, Moslems throughout the world are conducting similar ceremonies in their homes and towns. 'Id al-Adha is the highest holy day in the Islamic calendar and commemorates the sacrifice of Abraham as well as the end of the pilgrimage.

With the completion of the sacrifice ceremonies, the pilgrimage is considered completed, although many pilgrims return to the Ka'bah for final prayers and often visit the Prophet's tomb in Medina before returning home.

Moslems can go to Mecca any time of the year, but the real pilgrimage is the one performed during Dhul-Hijjah.

he will ultimately confront the day of God's judgment. For this reason, he must be attentive to Allah's commands, submit himself to them, and act with compassion and justice toward others.

According to Islamic doctrine, at the end of the world there will be a day of resurrection. All humans will be revived and come before God for judgment. The deeds of people will be assessed, and those found guilty of evil acts will be punished in hell. The righteous believer will live eternally in paradise, a green, well-watered place of ease and comfort. Believers guilty of evil will serve a certain time in hell before being restored to paradise. Eternity in hell is reserved for nonbelievers. Martyrs in the cause of Islam are believed to pass directly to paradise.

Belief in Predestination

Moslems believe that Allah is both creator and sustainer of the world, upholding its existence moment by moment. Reality is but an expression of Allah's will, and man cannot change what Allah has willed. Man nevertheless is free to accept or reject Islam, which is an expression of Allah's will. Submission to Islam implies living in harmony with God's will, which is designed to produce peace and accord among men as the natural order of things. Rejection of Islam implies rebellion against the natural order created and sustained by Allah and is responsible for the chaos and confusion that exists in the world.

Islamic Canon Law

The concept of *Islamic Law* embraces all aspects of human life and endeavor, both private and public, devotional and secular, civil and criminal. It deals with rituals as well as with matters such as commercial activities, property, marriage, divorce, inheritance, personal conduct, personal hygiene, and diet. It sets forth penalities for crimes and offenses, but in most Moslem states secular legal and penal codes are based on Western models. A few Moslem countries, notably Saudi Arabia, still apply penalties provided for in the canon law. For example, adultery can be punishable by stoning or beheading; theft by the amputation of a hand. The canon law also covers political concerns such as war and peace, relations among states, and treaties. In sum, the canon law is the most important and comprehensive representation of Islam at the practical level.

The canon law was compiled by Islamic theologians, scholars, and jurists during the first three centuries of Islam (the seventh, eighth, and ninth centuries of the Christian era), on the basis of the Koran, the Hadith-Sunnah, inference by analogy, and, significantly, *ijtihad*, individual interpretations of Islamic law.

Sunni Schools of Thought

The free exercise of analogical reasoning among Islamic scholars lent itself to several variations and systematized formulations of the canon law. These differing formulations developed into schools of thought. Four of these legalistic schools have survived within the orthodox Sunni sect of Islam to this day. They are the Hanifi, the Maliki, the Shafi'i, and the Hanbali.

Hanifi. The *Hanifi* is the official school in most of the Middle East, except in the Arabian Peninsula and Iran. It also is predominant in Turkey, Pakistan, Afghanistan, and among Moslems in India. Developed in Iraq and named after a prominent Islamic scholar, Abu Hanifa, a Persian by origin, the Hanifi school placed considerable emphasis on the role of reason and independent legal opinion in the development of Islamic doctrine and law. It is considered the most liberal and adaptable of the four schools and has the most followers.

Maliki. The oldest school, the *Maliki*, developed in Medina, emphasized the Hadith-Sunnah and the opinions of the Islamic scholars of Medina, who were thought to retain the best memory of the state and society that had existed during the lifetime of Muhammad. Today, it is followed pervasively in North and West Africa, but it has little attraction elsewhere in the Islamic world.

Shafi'i. Considered the most legally rigorous of the four schools, the *Shafi'i* originated from an attempt to reconcile the Maliki and Hanifi schools, but instead became a third school of legal doctrine. It remains influential in Egypt, the Yemens, East Africa, and Indonesia and other parts of Southeast Asia.

Hanbali. The *Hanbali*, the most conservative of the four schools, rejects all other sources of Islamic law except the Koran and the Hadith-Sunnah and emphasizes imitation of Arabian society during the lifetime of Muhammad. Today, it is the official school of law in Saudi Arabia and Qatar.

Shi'ite School of Thought

On the whole, the differences among the four majority schools are slight, and each accepts the other three as orthodox expressions of Sunni Islamic doctrine. Moslems belonging to Islam's minority Shi'ite sect, however, do not recognize them and maintain their own school, sometimes called the *Ja'afari* school.

Liberal Sunni scholars sometimes refer to this school, which is representative of Twelver Shi'ism, as a fifth school of Islamic law. Centered around certain traditions that are not accepted by the other four schools, such as Muhammad's alleged appointment of his nephew Ali as his successor, the Ja'afari school is clearly heterodox in certain of its interpretations of Islam. Nevertheless, the similarities between Sunni and Shi'ite Moslems are far greater than their differences, and neither sect denies the Islamic character of the other.

Governed by the canon law, all Moslems are required to abide by certain rules. They are forbidden to drink alcoholic beverages or engage in gambling and usury. They also have to follow dietary laws that are reminiscent of Jewish laws. The eating of pork is prohibited, and beef or lamb can be eaten only if the animal is ritually slaughtered and drained of blood.

ISLAM TODAY: A NEW ASSERTIVENESS

In many parts of the Islamic world, there are signs of a reawakened religious consciousness favoring a return to Moslem puritanism. This movement has encouraged an idealized vision of the past and an internal and global Islamic assertiveness.

In some Moslem countries, fundamentalists are challenging contemporary regimes and calling for an outright reincarnation of ancient Islamic society. In others, Moslems advocate the more moderate course of increasing the involvement of Islam in the political and social structures of the nation and re-emphasisizing Islam as a principal factor in public life. Meanwhile, more mosques are being built and younger people, in particular, are going to them in larger numbers.

Islam has been a major factor behind many recent political developments in Moslem countries. It has contributed to political power struggles, xenophobia (particularly anti-Westernism), and calls for pan-Islamic solidarity. In Afghanistan, opposition to the Soviet occupation and the Soviet-supported Afghan regime took on the character of a jihad or "holy war." Opposition groups in countries where Moslems are in the minority, such as the Philippines, India, and some African nations, have invoked Islam in their drive for greater autonomy. In a number of Islamic countries, notably Egypt, Syria, and Turkey, Islamic militants and dissidents have been quite visible and active. Islam has been used as a pretext by Libya to aid one of the major factions in Chad. In Libya itself, Col. Muammar al-Qaddafi's commitment to Islamic ideals is a major part of his worldview.

Iran is the most dramatic example of Islam's impact on recent political developments. A regime led by Islamic scholars—the closest thing to a theocracy since the dawn of Islam—took power in 1979 after bringing down one of the strongest dynasties in the Middle East. The regime succeeded in whipping up a wave of religious fervor that helped to sustain its war effort against neighboring Iraq for nine years.

The cumulative effect of these developments has clearly jolted the West, reviving a latent antipathy toward and suspicion of Islam. The literature generated in the West by references to "Islamic resurgence," "militant Islam," "the dark side of Islam," and similar phrases tended to frighten many Westerners. Islamic scholars have criticized the West for failing to comprehend the regenerative dynamics of Islam or to understand the complex political, economic, and social forces that have moved non-Western developing societies. The result, these scholars maintained, has been an alarmist perspective in the West about the meaning and potential of the contemporary wave of Islamic fervor.

The West's negative attitudes toward Islam were reinforced in 1989 by the reaction in many parts of the Islamic world to the publication of Salman Rushdie's novel *The Satanic Verses*. The book was unquestionably blasphemous from a Moslem perspective because of the doubts it raised about the authenticity of some verses of the Koran. Despite the fictional manner in which the doubts were phrased, its appearance at a time of general revival of Islamic belief and commitment was certain to make it controversial. The call for Rushdie's death by Iran's late Ayatollah Khomeini and efforts by Moslems to prevent the book's publication and distribution in the other parts of the world clashed with liberal Western traditions of freedom of speech and press. Moslems and many Western observers pointed out, however, that efforts in 1988 by some Christians in the West to prevent the showing of the film "The Last Temptation of Christ" also trampled on freedom of expression. The Rushdie affair was symptomatic of changes occurring in the Islamic world but did not necessarily constitute their essence.

Impact of Modernization

Like other countries emerging from colonial rule or discarding the old order, the modern Islamic nation-states had to borrow heavily from the West to build political and social institutions and run increasingly complex societies.

Nationalism—itself a secular European innovation—was fervently adopted by peoples whose national identity and impulses had long been suppressed by foreign rule and control. Once these peoples achieved independence, their ruling elites, many of whom were educated in the West, turned to Western ideas as a model for nation building. To a large extent, their choice of models was predetermined by the legacy of their former rulers—that is, the actual presence in their societies of European-type administrative, legal, and educational systems. These systems were too deeply entrenched to dismantle; moreover, they worked.

Direct Western influence in Islamic societies had begun to accelerate the process of modernization well before the emergence of independent nations in the Middle East. From the West came industrialization, urbanization, technology, commercialization, constitutionalism, and other notions that were powerful forces of change. The economic and political benefits of these methods and ideas heightened expectations and aspirations in the Islamic world, motivating the political elites that stepped into power to continue the process of modernization.

The effect of this acculturation was a gradual dismantling of the old order. There were limits to this process, however, that were directly related to the role of Islam in society. Given the powerful mix of politics and religion in the Middle East, where religious doctrine, cultural and behavioral patterns, and political values intersect at various levels of daily life, borrowing from the West could not proceed without some degree of religious sanction.

The exception to this proposition was Turkey, the only Islamic country formally to institute a secular system. At the other end of the spectrum, Saudi Arabia based its government and social system on a fundamentalist model. In these two nations, the role of Islam in society and government was clear. But in those Moslem states that had little experience in a governing system that separated religion from secular matters, the political elites could not ignore Islam's central role. Thus, officials sought to justify their actions in Islamic terms and to relate modern political concepts to their countries' Islamic heritage.

Working primarily through official religious organizations long accustomed to accommodating the ruling groups and sanctioning the established order, the secular officials modified and reinterpreted legal and theological aspects of Islamic doctrine. In doing so, they were drawing on the historical precedent of Islamic scholars and jurists who had adapted Islamic doctrine to current conditions. They rationalized that the Islamic canon law should not be taken literally as a fixed repository of commandments and prohibitions but rather as a model to be emulated.

Uneasy Relationship

The process of modifying Islamic doctrine to accommodate modernization and new social and political realities

Islam in the United States

There are no reliable figures on the number of Moslems living in the United States. Estimates range between two and three million—about 1 percent of the U.S. population. But their number is growing, along with American interest in Islam.

The Islamic presence in the United States dates back to just before the turn of the century when Middle Eastern Moslems, mostly from Lebanon, began to emigrate to the United States. More Moslems came after World War II, this time from other Arab, as well as non-Arab, countries. Most of the immigrants settled in large cities. Today there are a substantial number of Moslems living in the United States who have emigrated from Lebanon, Syria, Yemen, Palestine, Albania, Yugoslavia, India, Pakistan, Turkey, Egypt, Iraq, Iran, and most of the other Islamic countries.

Their Moslem identity notwithstanding, religious solidarity among Moslems in the United States is nominal. They still primarily associate with their own national and sectarian groups and rarely mix with each other. As Christians and others always have done, Moslems perpetuate their sectarian and national differences and distinctions, even after immigrating to the same foreign country.

With the growth of their population in America, leaders of the Moslem community set out to organize and create organizations to aid Moslems in practicing their faith. Today, there are mosques and Islamic centers in many American cities, and they play an important role in transmitting the cultural and religious values and teachings of Islam.

Moslem students also have set up the Moslem Students Association of the United States and Canada, which has about 200 chapters. Bookstores serving local and mail-order customers have mushroomed in many metropolitan areas.

While most Moslems living in the United States are first or second generation immigrants, black Americans who have accepted Islam constitute a visible minority of the American Moslem community. These are the Black Muslims, a movement founded in Detroit in 1930 by W. D. Fard, who was succeeded by Elijah Muhammad in Chicago. The movement was influenced by the Ahmadiyyah Movement, which was founded in India in 1879 to reinterpret Islam, but Elijah Muhammad, whose followers were drawn to Islam by its principles of social and racial equality, subverted those principles to "black supremacy." "God is black," became one of the movement's mottoes. As a result, other Moslems disassociated themselves from the Black Muslims. With the death of Elijah Muhammad, the Black Muslim movement modified its extremist position vis-à-vis the white society and, under the leadership of Elijah's son, Wallace Muhammad, began to draw closer to the mainstream of Islam.

---

has not been easy. Many traditionalists and fundamentalists have contended that Islamic doctrine—immutable and sacred—had all the answers and provided an ideal and coherent model for society that was superior to that found in the West, whose values they rejected as corrupt and debased. Consequently, they viewed departures from that ideal model as both religiously heretical and socially detrimental. Predictably, this approach was popular among the guardians of Islamic traditions, but it often was supported by other groups that felt alienated or threatened economically by modernization, including merchants and shopkeepers in the small cities and small landowners and peasants in the countryside.

Because they had to take into account these deep-seated Islamic impulses—and they themselves wished to preserve at least the essence of their traditions—the governing elites sought to reconcile traditional values and secularism. The result was a set of compromises that produced systems incorporating elements of traditionalism, modernism, secularism, socialism, and other political ideas. Not all regimes in the Islamic world subscribed to this amalgam, but most did.

This marriage of convenience worked well to a point. It began to crack under the accelerated pace of industrialization and the evolution of a new set of norms and practices brought about by materialism, individualism, a certain degree of moral laxity, a breakdown in some of the traditional Islamic codes of behavior, greater access to information and knowledge, universal education, and higher expectations of achievement.

Lack of Citizen Involvement

The resulting strains in the traditional fabric of Islamic society were compounded by economic dislocations. On the one hand, the pressures of modernization widened the gap between the rich minority and the poor majority, further impoverished the peasantry, and created a class of urban poor leading squalid lives in congested cities. On the other hand, sudden and enormous increases in wealth from oil revenues in some hitherto backward societies created acute problems as the pressures of rapid development began to unravel the old order and clash head-on with the forces of traditionalism.

Many of the systems that eventually emerged in the Middle East lacked an essential ingredient of most successful Western societies: citizen participation. The governing groups usually failed or were unwilling to create the necessary mechanisms and institutions to allow their people to participate in decisions. Colonial domination simply dissolved into variations of native repression or authoritarianism, regardless of the socialist, progressive, and democratic labels attached to them. While these modern economic and governing systems were sanctioned by most religious establishments and used Islamic symbols of identification, they failed to gain grass-roots support and popular mandates. Popular responses to the modernizing experiences buffeting Middle East societies primarily took political forms, but with an Islamic hue.

Fundamentalist Movements

The history of Islam, almost from its inception, is replete with fundamentalist attempts to reaffirm Islamic ideals or resurrect the past in the face of internal crises or external challenges. Such revivalist movements have been a common feature of Christian and Jewish histories as well. The nineteenth century, during which European power and hegemony reached its zenith in the Middle East, produced many Islamic fundamentalist movements: Mahdism in Sudan; Muhammad Abduh's *salafiyah* movement in Egypt; Jamal al-Din al-Afghani's pan-Islamism movement in Egypt; Wahhabism in Saudi Arabia, and Sanusism in Libya. Some of these fundamentalist movements were forward-looking, in that they advocated a rejuvenated and purified Islam while encouraging the assimilation of the political organization and technical advances brought by European colonial administrations.

The Islamic revolution in Iran and the Moslem Brotherhood in Egypt, Syria, Jordan, and other parts of the Arab world are the best-known fundamentalist movements in existence today. These contemporary Moslem fundamentalists actively seek a return to orthodoxy and puritanism as the path to salvation and emancipation from external threats and internal disarray. Their appeal recently has struck a chord among sectors of the population that normally have shunned fundamentalist approaches, such as the university students in Egypt and the middle class in Iran.

Iran is the only Islamic country to date in which the fundamentalist movement replaced a modernizing, though repressive, regime. The Iranian case, however, is unique and should not be seen as an example of what is likely to occur elsewhere in the region. In Iran the Shi'ite *mullas* (scholars) always had played a political role, unlike their counterparts in Sunni Moslem countries. When the shah outlawed political opposition, dissidents among the Western-educated middle class, the shopkeepers, and various leftist groups joined the only existing pocket of organized resistance in the country—the religious community, which had been a longstanding source of opposition to the government.

Unlike their counterparts in Iran, Sunni religious leaders are not self-supporting, have no priestly hierarchy, are not politically organized, and have no history of political activism. Their record generally is one of religious orientation and support of the established political order. In extreme cases, however, they may encourage dissidence.

One other country in which the religious establishment wields significant political clout is Saudi Arabia. By virtue of its descent from Shaykh Muhammad ibn 'Abd al-Wahhab, founder of the dominant Wahhabi movement in Saudi Arabia, the al-Shaykh family traditionally has assumed the religious leadership of the country.

The Saudi monarchy today has to pay close attention to what the religious establishment says, but this has not inhibited the kingdom's strides toward modernization. The religious establishment by itself does not represent a major threat to the Saudi regime. A combination of other forces—disaffected elites in the military and among the technocrats, for example—would have to coalesce to jeopardize the existing government.

The modern experiences of Iran and Saudi Arabia demonstrate that although religious considerations can play a supportive or catalytic role in politics, turmoil is more likely to derive from unfulfilled political and social expectations, lack of participation in government, and the absence of social justice.

The so-called Islamic movement represents a resurgence by Arab, African, and west Asian peoples beset by political, economic, and social crises to which they are unable to respond because they remain outside the political system—unrepresented, dispossessed, and impotent. Their turn to Islam is only one expression of their disenchantment with political leadership and the ideological alternatives over the past few decades.

Islam as a Political Force

It is difficult to visualize the emergence of a large-scale united Islamic revolutionary movement that transcends national boundaries. Recent back-to-the-roots stirrings in some parts of the Islamic world were responses primarily to local circumstances and political crises rather than a spontaneous spiritual rebirth of a messianic nature.

Leadership of the Islamic Community

As one scholar noted, an Islamic nation encompassing many present-day countries is bound to remain an ideal—a superficial goal blocked by political and economic realities. There are several reasons for this. Islam has no powerful, organized central body or hierarchy that can coordinate, mobilize, and regulate such a movement. Recently created organizations such as the Jiddah-based Islamic Conference Organization established in 1972 will probably remain *inter*national, as distinct from *trans*national, mechanisms, effective only when the interests of the individual member states coincide. Even then, their role will be exhortative, much like the United Nations.

Cairo's Al-Azhar University and Saudi Arabia's dual religious centers of Mecca and Medina have not functioned as springboards for universal Islamic action. Their role will continue to be that of supporting learning and worship. In addition, Shi'ism's limitations as a minority sect within Islam severely restrict Khomeini's successors in Iran from leading a pan-Islamic movement. The Islamic Republic in Iran also has demonstrated that a religiously run regime can be as repressive as any secular regime. Given its antiquated worldview, it is not likely to be capable of managing a complex, decentralized, and quickly changing Middle East.

Secular Influences

Almost daily, events in Islamic countries indicate that the pull of modernization and progress is equal to or greater than the pull of traditionalism. In Kuwait, for

Islam in the Soviet Union

Moslems constitute a sizable minority in the Soviet Union—some fifty million people, living primarily in five republics in Soviet central Asia and in the Volga-Ural region north of the Caspian Sea. This is the so-called Moslem Crescent comprised of Azerbaijanis, Turkmen, Uzbeks, Tadzhiks, Khirghiz, and Kazaks. All of these people share a common historical, cultural, and religious background that distinguishes them from the rest of the Soviet population.

The Moslem Crescent was first controlled by Czarist Russia some three centuries ago, and its population was subjected to a determined Russification campaign. That campaign ultimately failed.

Later efforts by the Communist regime to Sovietize the Moslems of central Asia had only limited success. Today, Moslems in the Soviet Union largely remain outside the mainstream of Soviet life and culture.

After the Bolshevik Revolution of 1917, Islamic nationalism in Central Asia erupted into struggles for independence. These temporarily were successful, but the Red Army managed to re-establish Soviet control. In the 1930s Joseph Stalin began a campaign to stamp out the ethnic character of the various Islamic groups. This campaign was reversed by his successors, Nikita Khrushchev and Leonid Brezhnev, who sought to redress the situation by rehabilitating the Moslems and allowing a substantial degree of ethnic identity. Nevertheless, the Soviet leadership's efforts to assimilate their Moslems never ceased completely.

Today, a cultural revival seems to be occurring among Soviet Moslems, although it is by no means certain that the revival has wider connotations for other nations or that it has been influenced by the Islamic upsurge in Iran, Afghanistan, and other parts of the Islamic world. Moscow recognizes that ethnic, linguistic, and religious ties exist between Soviet Moslems and the peoples of Iran, Afghanistan, and Turkey across the Soviet border. The Soviet leadership has been and remains concerned that external Islamic influences could increase nationalist sentiments in their Moslem republics that could cause internal unrest.

Several scholars point out, however, that Soviet Moslems primarily aspire to better their status within the Soviet Union, particularly their standard of living. Soviet Moslems are making headway in their modernization efforts. They are better off than many groups within the Soviet Union and many Moslems in other countries.

Another source of concern for the Soviet leadership is the rapid population growth among Soviet Moslems. Projections show that if the current birth rate continues there will be about 100 million Moslems in the Soviet Union by the year 2000. Moslems then will constitute about one-third of the population of the Soviet Union. This change in the composition of the population could force a reordering of the existing political and economic structure and strengthen the claims of the Moslem republics to greater autonomy.

example, a crisis developed in 1980 over the government's decision to ban Arab students from private Kuwaiti schools that followed non-Arab curriculums and to end the licensing of new private foreign schools. The Kuwaiti government's decision outraged the elite Arab community, Kuwaitis included, whose children attended, or were expected to attend, those schools.

In Saudi Arabia today, women are beginning to demand greater freedom and to reject their inferior role in traditional Saudi society. Many Saudi women want to join the labor force and live in a modern environment. They argue that this will lessen the country's need for foreign workers.

Iranian women have been even more forceful in pressing their views. After an initial embrace of traditional mores and customs, including the reversion to traditional garb and the veil, many modern Iranian women now are renouncing their inferior, restrictive status.

The connections between governments and religious establishments also have the potential to change. In Saudi Arabia, the government's close identification with the religious establishment poses a political threat to its power. Growing numbers of people, especially among the educated classes, resent the fact that the government has given religious leaders a large voice in the nation's affairs while denying political expression to others. This has led to talk, so far unfulfilled, of establishing a national assembly and provincial councils, and even of the need to adopt a civil, secular constitution to replace the Koran.

The obscurantism and superstition of the past have given way, in varying degrees, to the acceptance and practice of modern, pragmatic, and rational modes of thought. Fundamentalists concede that Western technology has to be acquired—but without Western culture and social norms. The dilemma for fundamentalists is whether Moslem nations can take the one without the other. Can women be educated, for example, and still be expected to accept their home-bound role? And if they are allowed to work, can they continue to be segregated from men?

Despite the arguments for economic, social, and technological modernization in Islamic countries, Islam will remain an important political force in Middle East societies. Even highly secular Moslem regimes will have to contend with the Islamic ethos of the masses and mold society and government so that it can be perceived as at least minimally compatible with Islam.

Country Profiles

Egypt   139
Iran   149
Iraq   159
Israel   167
Jordan   177
Lebanon   183
Libya   197
Persian Gulf States   205
Saudi Arabia   215
Syria   223
Yemens   231

Reclaiming Leadership in the Arab World

Egypt is again at the political center of the Arab world, which for nearly a decade shunned it for breaking ranks and signing a peace treaty with Israel in 1979. Although Egypt's emergence from its regional isolation was prepared by the patient fence mending of President Hosni Mubarak, it was hastened by developments in the Middle East in the late 1980s.

First, most Arab nations felt compelled to close ranks against Iran and the potentially subversive Islamic fundamentalism that it was attempting to export. They needed Egypt, by far the biggest Arab country, as a counterweight to Iran. Second, the Palestinian uprising in the Israeli-occupied territories elevated Egypt's status among moderate Arab governments. Suddenly, Egypt's

Hosni Mubarak

formal ties with Israel, the very thing for which Egypt was condemned a decade earlier, had become a prized asset. As the only Arab state carrying on diplomatic relations with Israel, it occupied a pivotal place between Jerusalem and the Arab capitals. Moreover, Cairo's cultivation of U.S. friendship since the 1970s, a policy that also had incurred Arab displeasure, placed Egypt in position to be the chief Arab advocate in Washington for American intervention with Israel on behalf of the Palestinians.

Although the vicissitudes of Middle East politics may account for Egypt's return to the Arab fold, much more—including geography, history, and culture—lies behind the country's traditional preeminence in the Arab world. Egypt is centrally situated in that world, which stretches westward through North Africa to the Atlantic Ocean and eastward through the Fertile Crescent and the Arabian Peninsula. Egypt is also by far the most populous Arab nation; but size alone does not account for the influence it has long exerted among its neighbors.

Unlike many Arab states that are the product of political unification in this century, Egypt has existed as a nation-state since ancient times. The Egyptian people share a nationality that predates even the Islamic conquest in the seventh century. They claim a civilization continuously recorded for more than five-thousand years, which at various times reached great heights of cultural attainment. Whatever the nature of official relations, citizens of other Arab nations are accustomed to watching Egyptian films and television programs and to listening to Egyptian singers. In addition, the Egyptian elite has strongly influenced several generations of Arab intellectuals.

Egypt has also left a large imprint on the politics of individual Arab nations and on the region as a whole. The

1952 coup in Egypt, in which Col. Gamal Abdel Nasser and his colleagues seized power and broke with colonial rule, transformed Egyptian society and had a powerful effect on the Arab world. Nasser became its chief spokesman, and he cast his spell on at least two generations of Arab political leaders. He was the model for military leaders who came to power by leading coups in North Yemen (1962), the Sudan (1969), and Libya (1969). During Nasser's years in power, his calls for pan-Arabism and socialism echoed all over the Arab world and influenced Third World nations around the globe.

Upon Nasser's death in 1970, his successor, Anwar al-Sadat, exercised Egypt's leadership in another way. After several years of military confrontation and a major war with Israel, he courted capitalism, broke the Moscow alliance Nasser had formed, sought American aid and friendship, and boldly made peace with Israel. For that audacious act, he made Egypt a pariah among Arab nations and incurred the wrath of Moslem fundamentalists. The Arab League promptly expelled Egypt from membership and adopted a package of political and economic sanctions against it. Of the twenty-one remaining league members, all but Oman, Somalia, and the Sudan severed relations. Similarly, Egypt was cast out of the Organization of Arab Petroleum Exporting Countries (OAPEC), the Organization of the Islamic Conference, and several pan-Arab financial institutions. This schism was not the first in the Arab world, but it was the first in which the leading nation became divorced from the rest.

Sadat's assassination in 1981 elevated Mubarak to the presidency. Unlike his two predecessors, the charismatic and radical Nasser and the flamboyant and impulsive Sadat, Mubarak is pragmatic and cautious—some have said plodding. He has managed, however, to return Egypt to the good graces of its Arab neighbors without reneging on the peace treaty with Israel or weakening ties to the United

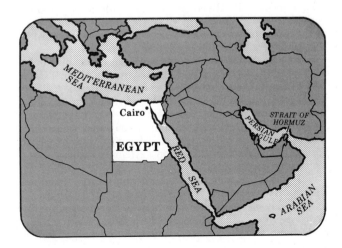

Key Facts on Egypt

Area: 386,661 square miles, including 22,500 square miles of the Sinai Peninsula.
Capital: Cairo.
Population: 53,348,000 (1988).
Religion: 94 percent Moslem (mostly Sunni), 6 percent Coptic Christian and others.
Official Language: Arabic; English and French widely known by educated Egyptians.
GNP: $36.0 billion; $710 per capita (1987).

Sources: World Bank Atlas 1988; CIA World Factbook 1988

States. Beginning in 1988, he gradually assumed a leadership role among Arab nations—just as had Nasser and Sadat at their heights of power.

Problems in a Crowded Land

Egypt's reassertion of leadership in the Arab world belies a host of internal problems. Overpopulation creates many of them and compounds others. Egypt's population, estimated at more than 53 million in 1988, has been increasing at the rate of about 2.65 percent a year. The country, which once fed itself but now must import 60 percent of its food, has one million more mouths to feed every nine months. As calculated by the Population Reference Bureau, a nongovernmental organization with headquarters in Washington, D.C., the yearly Egyptian birth rate is thirty-eight per thousand people, more than double the U.S. average. Forty percent of the people are under age fifteen.

Although Egypt has a land area of 386,661 square miles, roughly equal to the combined size of Texas and New Mexico, most of it is barren desert. Less than 4 percent of the land is arable. In a country where rainfall is only an inch or two a year, nearly all of the food that Egypt grows comes from the acreage that is within reach of irrigation from the Nile River, the source of life in Egypt since earliest recorded times. The river, the world's longest, rises in the mountains of interior Africa and flows northward to the Mediterranean, running the length of Egypt.

The Nile Valley in Egypt is never more than nine miles wide until the river branches into tributaries north of Cairo and widens into the delta. As seen from the air, the valley is but a green ribbon bisecting the brown desert for 500 miles between Cairo and the High Dam at Aswan. Lake Nasser, formed by the dam and extending 185 miles southward, some 62 miles into the Sudan, is hemmed in by geologic formations that make irrigation extremely difficult along its edges.

The Western (or Libyan) Desert, running the length of the country west of the Nile, comprises about two-thirds of present-day Egypt. It is a low plateau punctuated by depressions and basins, some of which form oases, and the great Sand Sea. This desert in Egypt and Libya itself is probably best known to the world for the extensive tank warfare conducted there in World War II. British Prime Minister Winston Churchill considered the battle of El Alamein, some seventy miles west of Alexandria, the war's turning point. There in 1942, British and Commonwealth forces turned back the hitherto victorious Afrika Korps and saved the vital Suez Canal from German capture. Stretching eastward from the Nile to the Red Sea is a sloping plateau that develops into dry, barren hills and is known as the Eastern (or Arabian) Desert. There and in the plateau- and mountain-strewn Sinai Peninsula across the Suez Canal and Red Sea, the habitation is confined chiefly to a few seaside villages and resort communities and some nomadic Bedouin groups and their flocks.

In the Nile Valley and delta are concentrated 99 percent of the people, creating some of the highest population densities on Earth. About one-fourth of the Egyptian people live in and around Cairo, the capital, making it the biggest and possibly the fastest-growing metropolis in Africa or the Middle East. Their numbers have overwhelmed many of the basic municipal services, caused massive traffic congestion, and resulted in housing shortages so severe that makeshift quarters litter the urban landscape. Untold thousands live in the city's ancient cemeteries; others make do in shacks perched atop high-rise buildings in downtown Cairo. The city has spread outward into the desert as far as the famous pyramids at Giza, twenty miles west of the Nile, and up and down the river, removing thousands of valuable acres from cultivation.

Since 1971 when the High Dam at Aswan started controlling the release of irrigation water, Egypt has put two million additional acres in cultivation, increasing its total by a third. With an adequate year-round water supply, farmers can grow as many as three crops a year. In the past, the growing season was limited principally to the season after the river's annual flooding. (It was during the flood seasons, when the peasants had no crops to tend, that the ancient pyramids were built.) The post-1971 gains in farm production, however, have not kept pace with population growth. In addition, an unintended side-effect of the dam has been to deprive the farm lands of soil-enriching silt that the flood waters left behind. Consequently, the fertility of the soil has been depleted, requiring the use of commercial fertilizers that Egypt can barely afford.

The government advocates birth control, and Moslem authorities in Egypt—where at least nine of every ten people are Moslem—have said that it does not violate Islamic doctrine. But birth control is said to be practiced almost exclusively in the cities where middle-class Egyptians find they cannot adequately support large families. Egyptian officials say rural peasants (*fellahin*) believe each family needs five or six children to assure the parents security in old age. Migratory patterns in Egypt indicate that when the children come of age, many leave their family's small plots—a legacy of Nasser's breakup of great estates into small units for the peasants—and go to the cities seeking jobs.

Unemployment and underemployment are pervasive. The government's estimate of joblessness is about one-fourth of the national work force, and it is probably much higher. For educated Egyptians, the government is the employer of last resort. Since Nasser's time, all qualifying students have been guaranteed a free education through college and then a job until retirement. Out of the large university system, thousands upon thousands of graduates have marched directly into low-paying jobs in already-bloated bureaucracies. About 30 percent of Egypt's employment is in the public sector.

Road to Reconciliation through Palestine

Some observers say that Egyptians who are unhappy with their lot may be forgiving of Mubarak because of his success in reintegrating Egypt into the Arab world and championing the Palestinian cause. However, in identifying himself with Palestinian goals, he also has raised the political stakes for himself at home as well as on the international scene. Failure could undermine his standing among his countrymen. However, the prospect of failure may be less threatening to him, and to the heads of other moderate governments, than taking no action at all. Their inaction over the Palestinian issue could cause Arab anger to turn against them in frustration. This is a risk the moderate Arab leaders apparently do not want to take.

A pivotal event on Egypt's road to reconciliation with its Arab neighbors occurred in November 1987. At that time, sixteen Arab League heads of state met in the Jordanian capital of Amman and issued a surprisingly strong-worded resolution attacking Iran for its "procrastination in accepting" a United Nations cease-fire proposal in what was then its seven-year war with Iraq. Jordan's King Hussein, the conference host, used the occasion to ask the participants—in the interest of Arab unity—to drop the league's ban on formal relations between its member countries and Egypt. They answered his appeal by declaring that a renewal of relations with Egypt would be considered "a sovereign matter to be decided by each state in accordance with its constitution and laws; and is not within the jurisdiction of the Arab League."

Jordan had already renewed relations with Cairo, and subsequently all the members did so except the hard-line states of Syria, Syrian-dominated Lebanon, and Libya. The next step was readmission to the Arab League itself. On May 23, 1989, after a ten-year absence, Egypt took its seat at an Arab League summit meeting, in Casablanca, Morocco, where Mubarak was accorded the honor of making the opening address. Egypt was instrumental in founding the league in 1945 and guiding it until 1979. In addition to newly readmitted Egypt, the 1989 membership consisted of Algeria, Bahrain, Djibouti, Iraq, Jordan, Kuwait, Lebanon, Libya, Mauritania, Morocco, Oman, the Palestine Liberation Organization (PLO), Qatar, Saudi Arabia, Somalia, Sudan, Syria, Tunisia, the United Arab Emirates, the Yemen Arab Republic (North Yemen), and the Yemen People's Republic (South Yemen). Only weeks before the Casablanca summit, OAPEC readmitted Egypt; in 1984 it had reentered the Organization of the Islamic Conference.

The 1987 Amman conference's focus on Iran had an unintended side-effect. It reportedly added to the level of frustration among the 1.5 million Palestinians living under Israeli control in the West Bank and Gaza Strip. They felt their cause had been demoted, possibly deserted by the Arab leaders. Less than a month after the conference, the Palestinian uprising (intifada) began in the occupied territories. Palestine again became the region's foremost concern, and the Iranian threat seemed to recede. In July 1988 Iran's exhaustion from years of fighting compelled the Ayatollah Ruhollah Khomeini to accept a cease-fire agreement with Iraq.

Mubarak, meanwhile, had become a leading supporter of the PLO and its leader, Yasir Arafat. "There is no war without Egypt, and there is no peace without Egypt," Arafat said in December 1988 on one of his frequent visits to Cairo. His very presence symbolized Egypt's new harmony with the PLO leadership, which in 1981 had applauded Sadat's assassination. In this new era of buried hatchets, Mubarak joined with Arafat and Arafat's old nemesis, King Hussein, in pushing for an international conference to negotiate the Palestinian demand for statehood.

Mubarak's interest in finding a solution to the Israeli-Palestinian conflict helped him improve his standing in Washington as well as the Arab capitals. In January 1988 Mubarak went to Washington and called on the Reagan administration to seek a peace settlement. "President Mubarak urged the president to send me on a mission to the Middle East," Secretary of State George P. Shultz explained February 22, 1988. Shultz carried on a "shuttle diplomacy" in the Middle East, making four trips there by mid-June to drum up support for a peace conference. He was unable, however, to persuade Israeli Prime Minister Yitzhak Shamir to negotiate on the status of the occupied territories or to enlist King Hussein as the point man for the Arabs.

Once the fate of the Shultz proposal became obvious, Hussein took the dramatic step of insulating Jordan from West Bank unrest by renouncing, on July 31, his kingdom's forty-year-old claim to that territory. He thus removed any lingering hope for the Shultz initiative, whose centerpiece was the "Jordanian option." That "option" was based on twin premises. One was that Israel's longstanding refusal to negotiate with the PLO could be overcome if Hussein headed a combined Jordanian-Palestinian negotiating team. The other was that Israel, rejecting the concept of a PLO-dominated state within or alongside its boundaries, might agree to some form of Palestinian autonomy under overall Jordanian control.

The failure of the Shultz plan, compounded by Hussein's statement, moved Egypt from a supporting to a

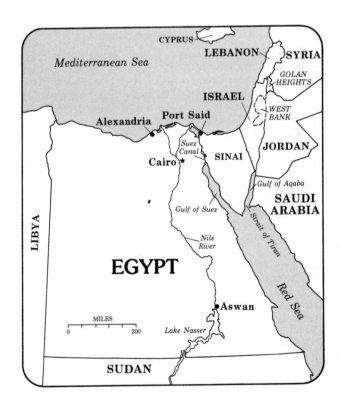

leading role in the peace movement. With Hussein out of the negotiating picture, the lead fell to Mubarak. Later that year, he implored Arafat to satisfy the U.S. government's conditions for holding talks with the PLO. In November 1988 the Palestine National Council met in Algiers and formally declared Palestinian statehood—and implicitly recognized Israel's right to exist. But Shultz demanded that Arafat explicitly renounce terrorism, accept UN Security Council Resolution 242—the basis for a Middle East peace conference—and recognize Israel's sovereignty. The resolution, adopted in the aftermath of the June 1967 Six-Day War, called for Israel's withdrawal from the territories it seized in the war—the West Bank and eastern Jerusalem from Jordan, the Gaza Strip and the Sinai Peninsula from Egypt, and the Golan Heights from Syria—in return for the Arabs' acceptance of Israel's "right to live within secure and recognized boundaries free from threats or acts of force."

After much prodding by Mubarak and a few false starts, Arafat on December 14 uttered the precise words that Shultz demanded. Within hours, the secretary of state said talks with the PLO could begin. This announcement created euphoria in the Arab world, even though the United States pointedly restated its support for Israel and withheld any backing for an independent Palestinian state. According to diplomatic sources in Cairo, Mubarak was one of several Arab and Western European leaders who urged Shultz and Reagan to accept Arafat's words as genuine.

Mubarak paid his first White House call on Reagan's successor, George Bush, in April 1989. At the conclusion of their talk President Bush told reporters: "Egypt and the United States share the goals of security for Israel, the end of the occupation, and achievement of Palestinian political rights." The statement was considered significant in that an American president was bluntly calling for something unacceptable to Israel, the end of the occupation of the West Bank and Gaza.

Nasser and the 1952 Revolution

U.S.-Egyptian relations have been subject to wild gyrations since the 1952 revolution in which Nasser and his military colleagues brought about the abdication of King Farouk and ended decades of de facto British rule. Nasser defied the West, befriended the Soviet Union, introduced socialism, and appealed to the downtrodden masses.

The revolution was at first only a bloodless coup staged by a group of self-styled "free officers" distressed by the Egyptian army's poor showing in the 1948 invasion of the newly declared state of Israel. Their initial goal was "cleaning up" the army and the state. The message they broadcast on July 23, 1952, the day of the coup—a day that became almost sacred to most Egyptians—did not go beyond their intention to "purify ourselves and to eliminate traitors and weaklings." Yet the coup developed into a genuine political, cultural, and economic revolution. As viewed by Egyptian political scientist Nazih N.M. Ayubi, these young officers were basically an urban middle-class group who "must have had a certain feeling of alienation, a feeling that Egypt was not quite Egyptian. For in spite of formal independence, the British were still there. And if the civil service was already Egyptianized, the greater part of the wealth was owned by foreigners. The problem was not simply political, economic, or administrative. It was also a cultural one—that of the search for a national identity."

From the time the last pharaoh fell to Persian invaders in 525 B.C., Egypt had been under foreign domination—either military, political, or financial—until the 1952 coup. Britain was merely the last in a long line of foreign colonial powers. In 1882 Britain sent troops into Egypt to protect its extensive financial holdings, including partial ownership (with France) of the Suez Canal. The French entrepreneur Ferdinand de Lesseps had built the canal, opening it in 1869. Six years later the Egyptian khedive Ismail (khedive is a ruler under sovereignty of the Ottoman Empire) faced bankruptcy and sold his shares in the canal to the British. They gained indirect political control of Egypt through the khedives, whom they kept in office. In 1914, at the outbreak of World War I, Britain declared Egypt a protectorate, ending the legal fiction that Ottoman sovereignty still prevailed. In 1922 it granted nominal independence, declaring Egypt a monarchy and placing Farouk's father, Faud, a compliant khedive, on the throne.

The Ottoman Turks' subjugation had lasted four and a half centuries, except for a brief interruption of French rule (1798-1801) that followed Napoleon Bonaparte's conquests in Egypt. Many scholars say the Napoleonic invasion marked the beginning of modern Egyptian history. The French brought in some liberal ideas, the printing press, and a lively interest in both modern science and Egypt's glorious but half-forgotten past.

Their short stay was followed in 1803 by the rule of Muhammad Ali, whom many consider the first Egyptian ruler to come to power on the basis of even semipopular consent. Through skill, daring, and intrigue, he rose through the military ranks to a position of power in the politically fractured Ottoman Empire, gaining virtual independence in Egypt from his nominal overlord, the sultan in Constantinople. Muhammad Ali was noted for his modernizing reforms, and notably for his efforts to create new structures of society without destroying Egyptian and Islamic traditions. The Egyptian scholar Abdel Monem Said Aly, who has written extensively on that period in Egyptian history, said Muhammad Ali's approach to reform was "successful enough to become widely employed by most of Egypt's rulers since, including Nasser, Sadat, and Mubarak."

Nasser spoke often of "Islamic socialism" even as he pushed for Egypt's modernization essentially on a secular basis. In fact, the heterogeneous group of young officers who carried out the coup included Moslem fundamentalist sympathizers as well as leftists. Their first domestic policy initiative was land reform. In September 1952 the new regime started breaking up large landholdings in an attempt to destroy the economic and political grip of wealthy, absentee owners—both foreigners and Egyptians. Soon to follow were minimum-wage decrees and reduced working hours. Meanwhile, Nasser emerged as the regime's strongman, articulating the pent-up frustrations of poor Egyptians and winning their hearts as no other ruler had done.

Foreign Policy under Nasser

In foreign policy Nasser's regime at first declared that it favored neither East nor West, but by the mid-1950s his course of nonalignment and anti-imperialism brought him into direct conflict with the West. Nasser played a prominent role in the 1955 conference of nonaligned nations in Bandung, Indonesia, and was granted equal international status with leaders such as Marshal Josip Broz Tito of

Yugoslavia, Jawaharlal Nehru of India, and Chou En-lai (Zhou Enlai) of China. That year, in response to the reluctance of Western nations to sell Egypt arms without strings attached, Nasser agreed to purchase weapons from Czechoslovakia. This action, the first Soviet-bloc arms deal with an Arab nation, was welcomed by many Arabs as a step away from traditional Western domination, but President Dwight D. Eisenhower's secretary of state, John Foster Dulles, viewed it as a step toward the Communist world—despite Nasser's clear aversion to communism and his banning of the Egyptian Communist party.

Moreover, Nasser opposed Dulles's attempts to build an anti-Communist alliance in the Middle East. On July 19, 1956, Dulles played his trump card against Nasser. He announced that the United States was withdrawing financial support for the Aswan High Dam, the centerpiece of Nasser's economic planning. Seven days later, to the roaring approval of a Cairo crowd, Nasser spat out the words: "O, America, may you choke on your fury!" Then he seized the British- and French-owned Suez Canal Company, and applied the canal's revenues to the dam project.

Egypt promised to pay off the stockholders, but Britain and France were in no mood to let it control the waterway, Europe's petroleum lifeline to the Middle East. After months of secret negotiations among Britain, France, and Israel—whose ships were barred from the canal—Israeli forces launched an attack on Egypt across the Sinai Peninsula in October 1956. Britain and France, pretending to react to a surprise threat to the safety of the canal, seized it by force. Under pressure from the United States, Soviet Union, and the United Nations, however, they were forced to withdraw, as was Israel. Eisenhower was infuriated that his two European allies had acted without consulting him, and he denied them much-needed U.S. support. By March 1957, a peacekeeping force, the United Nations Emergency Force (UNEF), was installed on the Egyptian side of the 1948 Egyptian-Israeli armistice line.

America's stand on the Suez crisis improved its relations with Nasser only slightly, and briefly. For Nasser, it was a sweet victory. He had thumbed his nose at the West and gotten away with it. Egyptian control of the Suez Canal was confirmed. When Nasser gained Soviet support for his Aswan Dam project, he made it clear that he did not need to depend on the West and that the Arab states could not be taken for granted by the Western nations. The Soviets soon assumed an important position in Egyptian foreign policy and became Egypt's major weapons supplier.

In 1958 Nasser enjoyed another triumph. He was asked by Syrian leaders to lead a union of Egypt and Syria. Nasser, who had long espoused Arab unity, found it difficult to say no, even though he was wary of an instant union. He agreed, only on the condition that the union be complete. Syrian parties were abolished, Cairo became the capital of the new United Arab Republic (U.A.R.), a new political party (the National Union) was created, and for all practical purposes Nasser ruled the new state. The union fared badly, however, and it was dissolved when Syrian antiunionists seized control of the Damascus government in 1961. The party created to be a vehicle of unification, the National Union, was replaced in Egypt by a new Nasser creation, the Arab Socialist Union.

Just as the period from 1955 to 1961 had seen the rise of Nasser's influence in the Arab world and the achievement of personal successes, the years from 1961 to his death in 1970 were marked by a series of policy failures, notably Egyptian involvement in the Yemeni civil war and the Arab defeat in the June 1967 Arab-Israeli war.

Nasser responded to a call from pro-Nasser officers in the Yemen army who overthrew the Yemeni king in September 1962. He sent troops to bolster the new government against royalist forces that retreated to the Yemeni highlands and, with Saudi Arabian aid, threatened the survival of the republican government. With as many as 80,000 Egyptian soldiers engaged in the fighting, the Yemeni war became a drain on the Egyptian treasury. The Egyptian image was tarnished by Nasser's arrogant efforts to control the Yemeni republicans and by the brutal measures Egyptian forces used against royalist villages in Yemen.

Perhaps the most damaging consequence of Egypt's involvement in the Yemeni civil war was its weakening effect on Egyptian defenses. When the 1967 war erupted, Nasser's best troops were tied down far from home. That war, a turning point in regional relations, was triggered by growing tensions between Israel and its Arab neighbors. In November 1966 Israel had destroyed a village in the West Bank (controlled by Jordan) in retaliation for Palestinian guerrilla raids across the border, and in April 1967 there were air clashes between Israel and Syria. Nasser engaged in a series of threatening steps short of war. He asked the United Nations to remove some of its peacekeeping troops from the Sinai, closed the Strait of Tiran to Israeli shipping, and signed a mutual defense treaty with Jordan.

Israel, fearing an invasion, launched a surprise attack on Egypt, Jordan, Syria, and Iraq on the morning of June 5. The air forces of the four Arab states were virtually destroyed on the ground within the first hours of the attack. Without air support the Arab armies were devastated, and by the time a cease-fire went into effect June 11, the Israelis had taken the eastern sector of Jerusalem and all of the West Bank from Jordan, seized the Golan Heights from Syria, and pushed the Egyptians out of the Gaza Strip and the whole of the Sinai Peninsula all the way to the Suez Canal.

The Egyptian army and people were again humiliated, as in 1948. Nasser publicly blamed himself for the defeat, implicitly agreeing with the verdict of history that the war resulted from his miscalculated brinksmanship. He provoked Israel in the belief that the United States would prevent the Jewish state from going to war and that the Soviet Union would come to his rescue if there were a war.

Nasser resigned as president, but a massive outpouring of support persuaded him to remain in office. The effects of the defeat were significant. Nasser withdrew Egyptian troops from Yemen, purged the top echelons of the army, and reorganized the government. Perhaps most important, Nasser's foreign policy objectives shifted. Regaining Egyptian territory held by Israel became a top priority. The quarrel with Israel was no longer only a matter of securing Palestinian rights. The return of the Sinai—approximately one-seventh of Egypt's land area—was Nasser's chief aim.

Nasser's position became more moderate after the war. He accepted UN Security Council Resolution 242 despite opposition from many Arabs, including the Syrian government and the PLO. This disagreement over the resolution foreshadowed a rift that would widen during Sadat's time. In September 1970 heavy fighting broke out in Jordan between the government of Jordan's King Hussein and the PLO. It was fitting that the chief proponent of Arab nationalism, Nasser of Egypt, should be chief mediator in the September 27, 1970, cease-fire between the two sides. The strain of the critical negotiations may have taken its toll: the following day Nasser died of a massive heart attack.

Tens of thousands of Egyptians took to the streets, passionately mourning the man who, more than any other single figure in modern Egyptian history, had redeemed the pride of Egypt and confirmed its preeminent position in the Arab world. He had been an authoritarian leader, intolerant of dissent from any quarter. He had failed to provide any genuine institutions of political participation. He had presided over the most disastrous military defeat in modern regional history. His economic policies had not produced prosperity. Yet Nasser changed the life of the average Egyptian and he was loved by the masses of lower-class Egyptians in a way that was never understood by Western political leaders.

Sadat's Leadership

As first vice president, Anwar Sadat succeeded Nasser. It was whispered that he had remained one of only two of the original Free Officers still in government because he was never a political threat to Nasser. Few would have guessed that he was destined to become a daring and powerful leader. It was widely presumed that more powerful rivals would soon divest him of power. Sadat, however, proved to be shrewder than his rivals. He outmaneuvered them, emerged from Nasser's shadow, and transformed Middle East politics in a far different way than Nasser had done. Above all else, his aim—some say his vision—was to regain the territory lost to Israel and improve Egypt's Third World standard of living. He achieved the first goal but not the second.

Training his sights on Western capitalism, Sadat introduced his "open door" economic policy in 1971. At first disguising it as a mere widening of Nasser's socialism, he set out to lure foreign investment and build a job-creating entrepreneurial class. Disillusioned with Nasser's Soviet connection, Sadat became confident enough of his power by mid-1972 to expel thousands of Soviet military advisers and civilian technicians—though without breaking diplomatic relations with Moscow—and offer Washington an olive branch. According to Alfred Leroy Atherton, Jr., a former ambassador to Cairo (1979-1983), the Nixon administration was preoccupied with a reelection campaign and the Vietnam War. President Richard Nixon did not respond promptly or fully to Sadat's overtures. So Sadat, unable to draw upon America's diplomatic clout to win back the Sinai, went to war.

Egyptian forces, better prepared than in 1967 and this time with surprise on their side, crossed the Suez Canal on October 6, 1973, and advanced deep into the Sinai. By the time a United Nations-arranged cease-fire took effect October 22, an Israeli counterattack had retaken most of the ground, and in one area held both sides of the canal. The final position of the armies, however, was less important to the Egyptian people than the enemy's initial rout.

The effect of the war on Sadat's public image in Egypt was enormous. Once viewed as a colorless, former Nasser "yes-man," Sadat achieved the title, "Hero of the Crossing" (of the canal), an epithet he treasured. The high level of Arab solidarity during the war, when an Arab oil embargo was successfully implemented against Western nations that supported Israel, was also a great boost to Sadat's standing in the Arab world.

Sadat now had Washington's attention. Secretary of State Henry Kissinger began a "shuttle diplomacy" between Jerusalem and Cairo to bring about a peace settlement. His efforts led to the first of two disengagement agreements between Egypt and Israel that went beyond the original cease-fire on January 18, 1974. That year, Egypt and the United States restored diplomatic relations, which Nasser had broken after the 1967 war. In addition, Nixon became the first president to visit Egypt since Franklin D. Roosevelt went there in November 1943, during World War II, to confer with Winston Churchill and Generalissimo Chiang Kai-shek of China. U.S. aid, cut off in the Nasser years, was resumed. The U.S. Navy helped clear the canal of wartime wreckage, permitting its reopening in 1975.

Sadat, clearly cultivating a closer relationship with the United States, envisioned it as a "full partner in Egypt's drive for peace and prosperity."

He came increasingly to view the United States as the key to resolving the Arab-Israeli conflict. Although he was often disappointed in the United States, his trust in successive administrations did not diminish publicly. When negotiations with the Israelis bore no fruit, he made his historic trip to Jerusalem in November 1977, carrying a message of peace to the heart of the enemy's country and capturing the attention of the world. It set in motion a chain of events that led to the Camp David agreements. President Jimmy Carter prevailed upon Begin and Sadat to meet at Camp David, the presidential retreat in Maryland, for twelve days in September 1978. There they hammered out two documents, "A Framework for Peace in the Middle East" and a "Framework for the Conclusion of a Peace Treaty Between Israel and Egypt." The following March 26 they returned to sign the peace treaty in a White House ceremony.

Sadat was more successful in attaining peace than prosperity. His new economic policies created a class of much-resented nouveau riche without invigorating the nation's sluggish economy. Few jobs or piasters—the small change of Egyptian currency—trickled down to the workers; average income remained below $500 a year. Part of Nasser's "social contract" with the people was that prices of food, housing, public transportation, and electricity would be subsidized by the government. In January 1977, however, Sadat was under budget-cutting pressures from Egypt's foreign creditors, and he reduced food subsidies. His action touched off weeks of rioting that threatened to undermine his ability to lead the country.

Sadat had already loosened some of the tight restrictions on political dissent that he inherited from Nasser. In 1975 he permitted three ideological groups ("platforms") to organize within the confines of the Arab Socialist Union. The following year the three were permitted some freedom to perform as political parties. The centrist "party," the Egyptian Arab Socialist Organization, became the government party, and in 1978 it was reorganized as the National Democratic party, continuing to serve as a vehicle of autocratic control and manipulation. The second "party" consisted of fundamentalists (for example, the Moslem Brotherhood, whose leaders had been freed along with other dissidents in 1973), and the third—perhaps a counterweight to the second—was made up of small leftist groups.

Sadat's political liberalization ended when the political groups outside his direct control, principally Nasserites on the left and Islamic fundamentalists on the right, began to criticize his peacemaking with Israel. Sadat did not have much more tolerance for dissent than Nasser did. Sadat cracked down repressively on dissidents—most dramatically in September 1981 when he abruptly jailed 1,500 foes, real or imagined. The stage was now set for revenge. He was assassinated the following month by Moslem extremists who wanted not a takeover of the government but simply the death of the man they regarded as a traitor to Egypt, the Arab world, and Islam.

Death came October 6, 1981, on the anniversary of the canal crossing, as Sadat reviewed a military parade commemorating the event. He was slain by soldiers who belonged to a militant Moslem faction, al-Jihad. His murder surprised Egyptians less than it did Westerners. He was remembered in the West as the instigator of the peace treaty, a corecipient (with Begin) of the 1978 Nobel Peace Prize, and the man who moved Egypt out of the Soviet orbit of influence to welcome U.S. friendship. To fellow Arabs, Sadat's difficulties with fundamentalist Moslems and other dissidents had become increasingly clear, erasing much of the popularity he enjoyed in the heady days following the October 1973 war. There was no outpouring of grief in Egypt for Sadat as there had been for Nasser. Three former American presidents, Nixon, Ford, and Carter, attended his funeral, but no Arab head of state publicly mourned the Egyptian president.

Mubarak's 'Cold Peace' with Israel

Hosni Mubarak, trying to steer a middle course in all matters, foreign and domestic, did not embrace the "partnership" with the United States with Sadat's fervor. He recognized, however, that U.S. assistance was crucial to Egypt both economically and militarily. U.S. officials generally give him high marks for trying to keep irritants in the relationship from being magnified. While continuing to maintain good relations with Washington, Mubarak has been willing to improve Soviet relations from what they were under Sadat. In February 1989, Foreign Minister Eduard Shevardnadze became the highest-ranking Soviet official to visit Egypt since the early 1970s. In Cairo on a Middle East tour, he called for a peace conference under UN Security Council sponsorship in which the Soviet Union would have a part. It was the most ambitious Soviet initiative in the Middle East in years, and it appeared to be well received by his host.

Mubarak has promoted the central tenet of Sadat's notion of peace with Israel—that the treaty with Israel meant the end of military hostilities and the establishment of a proper relationship. But it often has been a "cold peace" beset by many problems. Mubarak criticized Israel's annexation of the Golan Heights in 1981 and protested Israel's invasion of Lebanon in June 1982. That invasion was seen by the treaty's foes as confirmation that Israel could act with impunity since it no longer had to consider a military attack from Egypt.

For Mubarak, the Israeli invasion came just when Egyptian-Israeli relations seemed to be smoothing out. Egypt was still savoring the sweetest fruit of the treaty. On April 25, 1982, Israel turned over the last remaining section of the Sinai territory it had held since the 1967 war—except for a tiny beach strip called Taba, where the Israelis built a resort hotel on the Gulf of Suez. (After a seven-year dispute, Israel handed Taba over to Egypt, March 15, 1989.)

In September 1982 Mubarak recalled his ambassador from Israel to protest a massacre of Palestinians by Lebanese Christians in refugee camps outside Beirut that were guarded by Israel soldiers. The ambassador later returned to his post, but the relationship was further jolted by three shooting incidents in Cairo in 1984-1986 that left five Israeli diplomats dead and one wounded.

On another occasion, in 1985, an Egyptian military conscript killed seven Israeli tourists in the Sinai. As many as 60,000 Israeli tourists travel to Egypt annually, but only a trickle of Egyptians go to Israel; Egyptians need special permission from their government to visit Israel. Although it was reported in 1985 that Mubarak had agreed to proceed with increased tourist exchanges with Israel, little evidence was seen of it in Egypt.

On the tenth anniversary of the signing of the peace treaty, Begin said in a radio interview from his home in Jerusalem that a "full normalization of relations [with Egypt] still hasn't arrived, and we're waiting for it." For Mubarak, it is a fact of political life in Egypt that the peace treaty remains unpopular even a decade after its signing.

Questions of Internal Stability

With their characteristic touch of self-deprecatory humor, Egyptians are fond of recalling King Farouk's last words to the rebellious officers who sent him into exile: "Your task will be difficult. It is not easy to govern Egypt." Since the time of the pharoahs, successful rulers of Egypt have learned to play off one set of potential foes against another. The fact that Mubarak has never named a vice president has inspired observers to say that he exerts more political leverage by leaving the office open than choosing among leading contenders. The absence of a designated successor, however, has raised troubling questions about Egypt's political stability.

Mona Makram Ebeid, a professor of political science at American University in Cairo, speaks of "Egypt's continued experiment with democracy—we can't yet call it democracy." The press is free enough to be critical of the government and offer readers a wide range of opinion. But in December 1988, in the very month the Egyptian novelist Naguib Mahfouz was awarded the Nobel Prize in Literature, religious authorities blocked a newspaper serialization of one of his books on grounds it was "destructive of Islamic values and defamatory to Islamic prophets." The book, *Children of Gebalawi* in English translation, has long been banned in Egypt and several other Arab countries. However, all of Mahfouz's works are reported to be widely read throughout the Arab world. His Nobel award was based on other fiction works set in the wretched but lively street life of Cairo. In May 1989 it was reported that Mahfouz had received police protection in response to a threat on his life after he criticized the Ayatollah Khomeini for asking Moslems to kill Salman Rushdie, the Indian-born British author of *The Satanic Verses,* a book that many Moslems considered blasphemous and insulting to Islam.

In 1980 Egypt amended its 1971 constitution to stipulate that Islamic law, the *sharia,* is the "principal" source for legislation and the legal system. However, the governmental structure is essentially that of a Western democracy. Executive power is vested in the president, who is nominated by the national parliament, the People's Assembly, and elected for six-year terms by popular referendum. The president may appoint vice presidents, in addition to government ministers, and he may rule by decree when granted emergency powers by the People's Assembly. That is of little relevance to Mubarak, who has held emergency powers since Sadat's assassination. In addition Mubarak's own National Democratic party (NDP) holds more than three-fourths of the seats in the People's Assembly and commands the patronage system. In the last parliamentary elections, in May 1987, it won 339 of the 434 Assembly seats; it also scored a landslide victory in the 1984 parliamentary election, the only previous one that had been held since Mubarak became president.

All the opposition parties tend to be more vocally opposed to Israel than the NDP, and they advocate further liberalization of the political process. On most other issues, they split along ideological lines. "None of these parties, including the regime's NDP, has a solid social base," according to Saad Eddin Ibrahim, an Egyptian sociologist noted for his book *The New Arab Social Order*. The main opposition party, New Waft, is led by members or descendants of the upper and middle classes who opposed British rule. The original Waft was the majority party between 1922, when Egypt was accorded nominal independence, and the 1952 revolution. When Nasser came to power, he abolished it. The successor party was formed in 1978 at Sadat's behest, at the same time he created the NDP to replace Nasser's Arab Socialist Union (ASU). The NDP has performed much like the ASU. It has followed the president's lead and mobilized political strength, especially at election time.

Among the other legalized political groups is the Socialist Labor party, on the left of center, favoring a better-managed state economy, income distribution, and subsidies of basic commodities and services. Forming a coalition with another small socialist party, and opening its ranks to the Moslem Brotherhood—which is forbidden its own party—Socialist Labor won sixty Assembly seats in the 1987 election. It was another old party, outlawed by Nasser, that was permitted to start up again in 1978 "in loyal opposition" to the NDP. It was said that Sadat permitted the party's founding as a way of institutionalizing the dissent that arose over making peace with Israel.

The centrist Liberal party is similar to the Waft in its public stands but tends to represent "new money," whereas Waft draws strength from liberal-minded urban voters and what remains of the old landed gentry. At the far left is the splinter Progressive Unionist party, composed mostly of well-known Marxists. Its chairman, Khalid Mohieddin, was a leader of the 1952 revolution who lost power after disagreeing with Nasser. The party did not win a single Assembly seat in the 1984 and 1987 elections because of a requirement that any party represented there must obtain 8 percent of the votes nationwide. However, the political influence of the party's intellectuals is disproportionate to the size of its following. The Umma party, a tiny Moslem organization with headquarters in Khartoum, Sudan, won only minuscule support in the 1987 election.

Two sizable groups without legal status as political parties—Nasserites and the Moslem Brotherhood—are active in Egyptian politics. Nasserites, who dream of restoring Nasser's brand of nationalism, are reported to be well represented among military officers. But Mubarak, himself a general who once commanded the air force, has cultivated the officers' loyalty by providing them many special benefits. In what has been described the test of that loyalty, the army in 1986 answered the government's call to quell a mutiny in suburban Cairo by militia conscripts who were angered by low pay and bad living conditions.

Several members of the Moslem Brotherhood sit in the Assembly as elected representatives of officially recognized parties. The group is the strongest voice of the diffuse Islamic movement in Egypt, but there is a pronounced disagreement as to whether it represents the movement's main thrust. Since the Brotherhood's founding in 1928, it has been the embodiment of Egyptian opposition to a secular, Westernized society. Militant spinoffs from the Brotherhood have attempted to achieve that objective by violence. Nasser, the target of an assassination attempt, suppressed the Brotherhood. Partly rehabilitated by Sadat, it emerged under Mubarak as a political and economic force, attesting to the fact that Egypt shares in the religious resurgence that has swept the Islamic world during the 1980s. The Brotherhood considers Arab unification essential to the revival of Islam since the Prophet Muhammad had said, "Arabs are the first Moslems: if the Arabs are humiliated, so is Islam."

Impact of the Islamic Resurgence

The advent of Islam in the seventh century changed Egyptian life permanently. By the tenth century, Cairo had become a center of Islamic scholarship. The mosque of Al Azhar, which became Al Azhar University, remains one of the preeminent centers of Islamic learning and exerts a strong influence today on Egyptian political life. Nasser and Sadat both tried to enlist Islamic backing for their governments, although without permitting Moslem factions to achieve any real degree of control. Nasser spoke often of "Islamic socialism" even as he was pushing for Egypt's modernization essentially on a secular basis.

About 94 percent of Egyptians are Moslems, and almost all of them are of the majority Sunni branch, which generally is less fundamentalist than the Shi'ites who hold sway in Iran. Egyptians are noted for their tolerance even among Sunnis. Coptic Christians account for most of the non-Moslems in Egypt and in actual numbers form the biggest non-Moslem minority in any Arab country; estimates of the Coptic population range from three to four million. Copts comprise a larger part of the middle class and professions than their share of the population would indicate. However, many live in villages and are poor farming people. In addition to the Copts, the small remnant of Egypt's once-large Jewish population continues to attend several remaining synagogues.

Despite the relative tolerance of Egyptian Moslems, the Islamic resurgence in Egypt, as in other parts of the Middle East, has had fundamentalist aspects. The state-run airline, Egyptair, has discontinued selling alcoholic beverages, and the state-run television has purged several seamy but popular Hollywood series. Even secular-minded Egyptians often invoke the *inshallah* ("if God wills") in everyday conversation. When the muezzins issue their noontime and midafternoon calls to prayers from loudspeakers on the minarets dotting Cairo's skyline, there is a conspicuous response. Egyptians say that more than in the past, shops are likely to close and taxi drivers pull to the curb so that Moslems may unroll their prayer rugs and worship wherever they happen to be.

The Islamic revival has been troubling to the Moslem-Coptic relationship. Copts perceive demands for the complete implementation of Islamic law as a direct threat to their political, economic, and social status. Although Copts pose no direct threat to Mubarak's power, their often-strong reactions to Islamic fundamentalism sometimes fan the flames of religious hostility. On occasion, violence has erupted between Moslems and Copts.

Coptic Egyptians view themselves as the descendants of the ancient people of the Nile Valley. They embraced Christianity in the first century but broke with its orthodoxy in the fifth century over a theological question. The

Copts accepted the divinity of Christ, but they rejected the doctrine then accepted by the rest of Christendom that Christ was also fully human. The Coptic Church survived not only its break with the mainstream of Christianity but also the Islamic conquest of Egypt in the seventh century. However, over the centuries, it has suffered several persecutions at the hands of the country's Moslem majority.

Nasser attempted to improve Coptic-Moslem relations by integrating Egyptian society and by forcing members of the two faiths to live together in the same neighborhoods. The experiment seemed to increase hostility between the two groups. By the 1970s, as Islamic fundamentalism became more widespread, and demands grew for the government to implement Islamic law, several Coptic-Moslem clashes occurred. In Sadat's crackdown on dissidents shortly before his murder, he dismissed Moslem critics from their posts in the mosques and banished the Coptic pope, Shenuda, from Cairo. Moreover, Sadat banned publications that had been issued by Coptic associations and by the Moslem Brotherhood. Only after Mubarak became president did the hostilities between the government and the Copts begin to subside. In 1985 he permitted Pope Shenuda to return.

Although Egyptian authorities jailed and tried Sadat's assassins, Mubarak has quietly attempted to co-opt some religious dissent by allowing greater incorporation of Islamic principles into the political system. In trying to steer a middle course between fundamentalist and secular demands, Mubarak allowed previously banned opposition and religious newspapers to circulate, but he refused to overturn court decisions such as a 1985 ruling that abolished the 1979 women's rights laws. In response to the furor resulting from the abrogation of progressive law on women's rights, enacted with persuasion from Sadat's wife, Jihan, Mubarak took no public position. He did ensure, however, that the Assembly passed a new law that was a compromise between the position espoused by the fundamentalists and the rights guaranteed by the old law.

Mubarak has often attempted to meet some of the Islamic fundamentalists' demands halfway, but he has sometimes resorted to force when violence erupted or was threatened. In December 1988, for instance, violent clashes occurred between police and Moslem extremists in Cairo's Ein Shams slum district, resulting in five deaths and three-hundred arrests. The following April, the government cracked down on what Interior Minister Zaki Badr called "extremist groups fueling religious strife in this country." After more Moslem clashes with police, this time in the town of Fayoum southwest of Cairo, authorities attributed the violence to Islamic Jihad groups—from the movement that brought about Sadat's assassination—and arrested 1,500 persons. Some analysts have estimated that the movement has a nationwide following of no more than 20,000, and that no more than 1,000 are active militants.

Mending a Threadbare Economy

Many political analysts see a potential peril to Mubarak's government in the country's sagging economy. Egypt's inability to feed itself accounts for only part of the country's economic problems. The country has enormous foreign debts from loans secured in the early 1980s. At that time oil commanded high prices in the world market, and Egypt was cashing in on new fields along the Red Sea and the return of older ones from Israel in the Sinai. Additionally, the Middle East oil prosperity provided jobs for as many as four million Egyptians in other Arab countries. The Suez Canal's reopening, after peace with Israel, restored another important source of revenue.

Oil prices plummeted in 1986, however, affecting not only the government's royalties but also the money Egyptians were sending home from abroad. Many of them no longer had jobs. Moreover, sporadic terrorism in the Middle East crimped the tourist trade, another source of national income. Even in the "good years" early in the decade, the government was incurring annual budget deficits. Then, however, big international banks were eagerly extending credit. Now more and more of the debt incurred during that period is coming due.

United States economic aid (not including military aid) runs at about $1 billion a year and accounts for about half of the economic assistance that Egypt receives from all foreign sources. The other billion comes chiefly from the big international lending institutions, such as the World Bank and International Monetary Fund (IMF), and the governments of Western Europe and Japan. Egypt reportedly received money from Saudi Arabia and Kuwait to ease its debt problems in 1987, and there was speculation after King Fahd visited Cairo in March 1989 that more Saudi aid would be forthcoming. Whatever the Saudi aid infusions may be, they are not expected to be more than stopgap offerings.

With French credits and aid, the first section of a 26-mile subway has opened in Cairo with the intent of easing some of the world's worst traffic congestion. But the subsidized fare of about ten cents is beyond the means of many of the four million commuters; they can ride the overburdened city buses for three or four cents. The city's opulent new opera house, a much-admired gift from Japan, is an aid story with a similar twist. It has remained closed much of the time for want of money to produce operas or lure productions from abroad. Even the foreign-aid success stories tend to be short-lived. The needs of a fast-growing population, concentrated in a small area, tend to overwhelm the capacity of improvement projects.

Mubarak has faced such problems by instituting what is known as "reform by stealth." For example, he has not repealed the government's promise of a job to college graduates, but new graduates may be kept waiting several years for a job opening, and the jobs may be in undesirable places, far from the big cities. Another example concerns the price of bread. The memory of the 1977 food riots remains strong, and no political leader wants to tempt a recurrence. So the basic two-piaster loaf of bread—costing about eight-tenths of a cent—stayed on the market alongside a "new, improved" five-piaster loaf. Many consumers insist that the cheaper loaf lost its quality, forcing them to buy the more expensive one.

This approach to economic problems points to the delicate balance that the Mubarak government is trying to maintain between the conflicting demands of foreign creditors and the Egyptian people. In return for the government's pledge to stimulate production and exports, the IMF and Western creditor nations agreed in May 1987 to let Egypt reschedule $8 billion of its $44 billion in foreign debts. The repayments terms have been described by the U.S. embassy in Cairo as "more generous than had been granted to any other debtor country." The rescheduled amount included $1.2 billion of the $4.5 billion owed to the United States for military assistance before 1985, when the assistance was put on an all-grant basis.

For its part, Egypt moved to satisfy the IMF demand

by devaluing its currency 60 percent to make exports cheaper in foreign market and thus increase demand, even though Egyptian officals complained that devaluation increased the price of consumer goods and fueled inflation. During his visit with President George Bush in Washington in April 1989, Mubarak asked for further debt relief. He requested but was refused the immediate release of $230 million in U.S. economic aid that Congress froze in 1988 to pressure the Egyptian government to institute economic austerity measures.

Bush administration sources said part of the money probably would be released before summer to "facilitate" reform steps that Mubarak planned to take, the rest would follow after they were taken. Some $500 million was due to be repaid the United States by July 1, 1989, on past loans that Cairo obtained to buy American-made weapons. If it failed to do so, Egypt would be more than a year behind in its repayment schedule. That would trigger a law requiring suspension of aid. A U.S. decision to free the $230 million also could help Egypt win a new agreement from the IMF for another rescheduling of much of its $44 billion total foreign debt.

Importance of U.S. Relations

With budget deficits, huge foreign debts, and a sluggish economy, Egypt badly needs U.S. economic assistance. In addition, since Sadat kicked out the Soviets, Egypt has relied on the United States to arm and equip its armed forces, which number about 500,000 and constitute one of the largest military bodies in the Middle East. "Mubarak himself has been very careful to assure that the army has a direct stake in both his rule and the relationship to the United States, which means inevitably a continued flow of advanced weaponry," said Harvey Sicherman, who was special assistant to Secretary of State Alexander M. Haig, Shultz's predecessor, in a paper for the Washington Institute for Near East Policy.

Egypt's importance to Washington, as expressed by a former U.S. ambassador to Cairo, "is the importance of the Middle East as a whole to U.S. interests." Those interests, former ambassador Atherton wrote in a 1988 study for the Foreign Policy Institute, the Nitze School of Advanced International Studies at Johns Hopkins University, have been defined by successive administrations "in classic geopolitical terms." They are, he added, "the need for the United States and its allies to have unimpeded access to the sea and air

routes and the energy resources of the area, and for America to have political influence and presence as a counterweight to the Soviet Union and as a guarantee against Soviet domination." Without those concerns, he continued, the United States' relations with Egypt "would not be very different from its relations with many other Third World developing countries and certainly would not command so large a share of U.S. foreign assistance resources."

The 1988 Republican party platform expressed Egypt's importance to the United States in slightly different terms. Egypt, the document said, is "a catalyst in the Arab world for advancing the cause of regional peace and security." For that reason, it continued, "we believe that the United States has a significant stake in Egypt's continuing economic development and growth. As the only Arab nation to have formally made peace with Israel, it is reaping the benefits."

Only one country, Israel, receives more U.S. assistance than Egypt. That assistance, both military and economic in their various forms, has been totaling about $2.3 billion a year for Israel and $2 billion for Egypt—in line with an unwritten policy in Washington that Egypt will be given a slightly smaller amount than Israel. Because Egypt's aid is pegged to Israel's, it has risen as Israel's has gone up. This triangular relationship grew out of the Camp David accords and the 1979 peace treaty. Although both countries received U.S. aid before the treaty, the amount of aid increased dramatically after the peace was concluded. In effect, the large sums of assistance have been the cost of U.S. sponsorship of the peace between the two countries.

Since 1974, when U.S. aid to Egypt was restored after a cutoff during the Nasser era, it has amounted to $25 billion—$14.4 in economic and food aid and $10.5 billion in military aid. Aid to Egypt (but not to Israel) is explicitly conditioned on its continued observance of the Camp David agreements and, a more recent stipulation, its pursuit of economic reforms. Although economic aid has been greater than military aid over the years, military aid has accounted for a bigger share of recent aid packages. The triangular relationship provides much of America's leverage in its dealing with the two countries. The relationship, however, also involves a delicate balancing of one country's interests against the other's. Whatever the relationship's opportunities and pitfalls may be, it is clear that Egypt's enhanced role in the Middle East makes it one of the principals in bringing about any peace settlement that may be devised concerning the Palestinian question.

Charting a Course without Khomeini

The death of the Ayatollah Ruhollah Khomeini in June 1989 opened a new era in Iran. For ten years after he led the 1979 revolution that drove Shah Muhammad Reza Pahlavi from the country, Khomeini dominated Iranian society. He presided over the consolidation of power in the hands of fundamentalist Shi'ite clerics and the destruction of liberal, Communist, and intellectual opposition groups. He also refused to make peace with Iraq during a bloody eight-year war until 1988, when Iran's economic and military exhaustion and international isolation forced him to accept a cease-fire.

Khomeini's dream of creating an Islamic republic that would be imitated by other Moslem nations and inspire oppressed peoples everywhere was never realized. Because Iran was ethnically Persian and dominated by the minority Shi'ite branch of Islam, however, it was an unlikely model for Sunni Arabs. In addition, the violent excesses of the revolutionary regime, its disregard for basic human rights, its support of terrorism, and its uncompromising prosecution of the Iran-Iraq war alienated peoples and nations around the world.

Ayatollah Ali Khamenei

Yet the Islamic Republic of Iran survived, despite predictions by many analysts during the first few years of its existence that its government would collapse or be defeated by Iraq. Khomeini, who commanded great respect among most segments of Iran's population, provided an inspiring and unifying presence that overcame factionalism among Iran's leading clerics and instilled its military forces with revolutionary fervor.

As the 1990s began the new leaders of Iran were facing the problems of consolidating their own power, rebuilding Iran's broken economy, and overcoming the country's international isolation. With Khomeini gone, the potential for internal strife and division was great. If the Iranian leadership could overcome its differences, however, Iran's oil and natural gas wealth, its lack of large foreign debts, and the desire of many nations to improve relations with the post-Khomeini leadership could bring swift progress toward a recovery from the Persian Gulf war.

The Land and Its People

Iran lies on a four-thousand-foot-high plateau that is almost entirely surrounded by mountains. Where there are no mountains, vast deserts form equally impenetrable barriers. These conditions restrict internal movement by land and have contributed to the development of numerous ethnically and linguistically distinct groups.

Iran is bordered by the Soviet Union and the Caspian Sea on the north, Turkey to the northwest, Iraq to the west, the Persian Gulf and the Gulf of Oman to the south, and Pakistan and Afghanistan to the east. The Zagros Mountains, which stretch southeastward from the junction of the Turkish and Soviet borders and cover much of western Iran, have few primary roads. Villages there have remained isolated from the rest of the country. Transportation networks are only slightly better on the eastern edge of the Zagros range in central Iran. Annual rainfall averages about fifty inches in the western mountains and less than an inch in the central plateau. Iran's rural population and farms are found in its fertile mountain valleys.

Mountains and deserts also separate groups living in northern and eastern Iran. The Elburz Mountains, which run along the southern shores of the Caspian Sea, form a rugged barrier north of Tehran. Two uninhabited deserts, the Dasht-e-Lut and the Dasht-e-Kavir, cover much of eastern Iran, isolating Iranian settlements along the Afghanistan and Pakistan borders.

Oil Assets

Although Iran's topography appears to be worthless, the rugged terrain conceals large deposits of oil, Iran's most important natural resource. Most of Iran's fields are located in the southwest corner of the country in a 350-mile corridor beginning north of Dezful and running southeast almost to Bushehr. Iran also has natural gas reserves of nearly 500 trillion cubic feet, second only to the Soviet Union.

In 1987, despite attacks by Iraq on Iran's oil facilities, Iran's oil export revenues of $10.7 billion accounted for 12 percent of its gross national product. In 1988 Iran's known oil reserves of 35.6 billion barrels exceeded the oil reserves

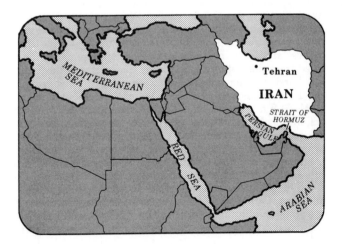

Key Facts on Iran

Area: 636,363 square miles.
Capital: Tehran.
Population: 51,924,000 (1988).
Religion: 98 percent Moslem, with great majority members of the Shi'ite sect; 5 percent of Sunni sect. Minority groups include Jews, Bahais, Zoroastrians, and Christian Armenians and Assyrians.
Official Language: Persian or Farsi. Kurdish, forms of Turkic, and Arabic are spoken by leading minorities.
GNP: $86.4 billion, $1,750 per capita (1987).

Sources: World Bank Atlas 1988; CIA World Factbook 1988

of the United States by 8.3 billion barrels. Before the Iranian revolution in 1979, Iran was producing more than 5 million barrels of oil per day, an amount greater than the production of any country but the Soviet Union, Saudi Arabia, and the United States. The upheaval caused by the Iranian revolution and the damage caused by the Iran-Iraq war, however, cut Iranian production to just 1.4 million barrels per day by 1981. Although it recovered somewhat, Iraqi bombings and the collapse of world oil prices in 1986 kept Iranian production under 2.5 million barrels per day through 1987—far below its prerevolution levels. The 1988 cease-fire with Iraq has given Iran the opportunity to restore its lost production and export capacity, although, because of the fall in oil prices, Iran will not return to the days of producing 5 million barrels per day.

Strong Local Identification

Because of Iran's geographic barriers, many Iranians have a greater allegiance to their local ethnic group than to the nation. Kurds in the Zagros Mountains have maintained their separate ethnic traditions. The rugged terrain of the northwest corner of Iran has enabled the Azerbaijanis to maintain their distance from Tehran. Turkic-speaking tribes around Mashad are isolated from the capital by the Dasht-e-Kavir, and the Baluchis, the poorest and least integrated of all Iranians, remain separated from the rest of the nation by the deserts of the east.

Farsi, the language of Iran's dominant ethnic group, the Persians, is the first language of only about half of Iran's 51.9 million people. Most Persians are urban dwellers, although they also occupy fertile mountain valleys in the central part of the country. Persians comprise the bulk of the upper class, occupy the most important bureaucratic positions, and dominate the ranks of the economic elite. Since 1502 all the rulers of Iran have been Persians.

The Kurds, numbering around 4 million, are the second largest ethnic group. Most live in northwest Iran along the Iraqi and Turkish borders. Kurds are generally Sunni Moslems, whereas most of Iran's population are Shi'ite Moslems. The Kurds' social organization is tribal.

In northern Iran, Turkic-speaking ethnic groups that entered the area around the eleventh century predominate. Like the Kurds, they are tribally organized, and some are seminomadic. The largest Turkic ethnic group is the Azerbaijanis, who live in northwest Iran between the Caspian Sea and the Turkish border. The Turkic tribes have resisted efforts by the Persians to control them.

The Bakhtiari and the Lurs, distant relatives of the Kurds, inhabit the remote mountain areas in the southeast. Sixty percent of these people are nomadic. Leadership alternates every two years between the families that head the various tribes. The leader, or *khan,* serves as a sort of ambassador to Tehran; he lives in the city and takes frequent trips to the tribal areas.

Other groups, such as the Baluchi and the Arabs (both numbering around 600,000), consider themselves as peoples distinct from the ruling Persians. They have great pride in their ancestry, and their tribal loyalties are far stronger than any national ties.

Shi'ite Moslems Predominate

The powerful unifying feature of Iran is the Islamic religion. During the second half of the seventh century, followers of Islam split into two groups: the Sunni Moslems (the majority in the Middle East) and Shi'ite Moslems (90 percent of Iran's population). The schism occurred over leadership of the Islamic community. The Shi'ites maintained that only a descendant of the Prophet Muhammad could be the rightful leader and that Ali, who had married the Prophet's daughter, was the rightful successor. In 661 Ali was assassinated. His supporters, calling themselves the followers of Ali (in Arabic, *Shiat Ali),* revolted against the Sunnis but were defeated in 680 at Karbala in Iraq; their leader, Ali's youngest son, was executed. Large numbers of Shi'ites fled to Iran. Proselytizing increased their numbers until they became the majority among Persians.

One major difference between Shi'ite and Sunni Moslem tenets is the function of the *imam,* or head of the earthly community of believers. He must be "rightly guided," one who can interpret the inner mysteries of the Holy Koran. According to Shi'ism, there have been twelve imams (Ali was the fourth), the last of them forced into hiding because of Sunni persecution. The twelfth, or "hidden Imam," is believed to have gone into occultation. He shall reappear as the *Mahdi,* or Messiah, on the day of the last divine command.

Until the return of the hidden Imam, the true faith is kept in trust by *mujtahids*—individuals who by their religious studies, understanding, and virtuous lives act as leaders of the Shi'ite community, interpreting the faith as it applies to daily life. Occasionally the mujtahids have become a clerical class with near-total authority over the community. The highest honor that can be conferred upon a mujtahid is that of *ayatollah.*

The principle of the *velavat-e-faqih* (meaning "just theologian" or "supreme jurisprudent") is very important to Shi'ite Moslems. The *faqih* is an individual or group of individuals endowed with the authority to make final decisions in matters of religious principle. The most worthy of the mujtahids select and support the faqih, who must distance himself from the daily decision-making process and intervene only to bring the government back to the "true path." The Ayatollah Khomeini served in this capacity and was succeeded by Ayatollah Ali Khamenei. As the head of the Shi'ite institutions and dominant authority in temporal affairs, the faqih wields considerable power.

A Turbulent History

Iran's history as a continuous civilization spans at least twenty-five centuries. According to the Old Testament, ancient Persia existed as a civilization even before that. However, in the sixth century B.C., Cyrus the Great established the Persian Empire, which, with his grandson Darius's subsequent conquest of Babylonia and Egypt, was extended to the Nile Valley and almost to Asia Minor.

The empire gradually shrank because of Greek and Roman conquests and its own internal decay. By the seventh century A.D. it was beset by Arab invaders who brought with them Islam and foreign rule. The Persians gradually overthrew Arab rule, but Islam remained.

Modern Iranian history begins with nationalist protests in 1905 that forced the ruler of Iran, Muhammad Ali Shah, to establish a parliament (Majlis) and grant a constitution in 1906. He was forced to abdicate in 1908 after repudiating the constitution, and he was replaced by his son Ahmad.

In 1901 the Iranians had granted William Knox D'Arcy, an Australian, a concession to search for oil. The discovery of oil in Iran in 1908 intensified the developing British-Russian rivalry over Iran. On the eve of World War I Britain purchased 51 percent of D'Arcy's company, the Anglo-Persian Oil Company (renamed the Anglo-Iranian Oil Company in 1935). Persian oil helped fuel the British fleet during World War I.

The war interrupted the sporadic growth of constitutionalism in Iran. The country was occupied by British and Russian soldiers during the war, although it officially remained neutral. In 1919 Iran concluded a trade agreement with Britain that formally affirmed Iranian independence but in fact established a British protectorate over the country. After Iran's recognition of the new Communist government in the Soviet Union, Moscow renounced the imperialistic policies of the czars toward Iran and withdrew the Soviet troops that remained there.

A second revolutionary movement, directed largely by foreigners, was initiated in 1921 by Reza Shah, an Iranian military leader and the founder of the Pahlavi dynasty. In 1925 he was placed on the throne and he proceeded to implement major domestic programs, including the establishment of a modern education system and the construction of roads and a trans-Iranian railroad. During World War II, however, his close relationship with the Germans led to another occupation in 1941 by the British and Soviets, who saw Iran as a key supply route from the West to the Soviet Union. The two powers forced him to abdicate in favor of his son, Muhammad Reza. After the war the Soviet Union attempted to establish separatist Azerbaijani and Kurdish regimes in northern Iran. This effort failed, however, after strong protests from the United States led the Soviets to withdraw their forces.

Postwar Period

The Anglo-Iranian Oil Company became a symbol of Western influence in Iran's postwar affairs and served to bolster Iranian nationalism. This consortium of British and American interests antagonized both the political right and the left in Iran. The domestic political climate was further aggravated by deteriorating economic conditions resulting from the Allied occupation in World War II. Dissatisfaction with the shah, who had tried to accommodate foreign oil interests, led in April 1951 to the election of Muhammad Mossadeq, the leader of the rightist National Front, as prime minister.

In May, with the support of the Iranian nationalist movement, Mossadeq nationalized Iran's oil industry. Iran, however, did not have the technical resources to operate its oil facilities without foreign help, and its production fell. Growing national discontent with Mossadeq led him to take repressive measures to protect his power. He dissolved the Majlis in the summer of 1953 and tried to take over the government. Muhammad Reza Shah was forced to flee the country in August. Within days, however, shah loyalists in the military, apparently with the backing of the U.S. Central Intelligence Agency (CIA), defeated military units controlled by Mossadeq, and the shah returned to power.

With Mossadeq imprisoned and his National Front allies in parliament reduced to marginal effectiveness, the shah moved to consolidate his power. He smashed the Communist Tudeh party, and hundreds of its members in the army's lower ranks were rooted out, as were its sympathizers in all significant interest groups and associations. The shah rewarded his supporters—chiefly in the officer corps—and made peace with the nationalist-minded clerical authorities.

Although Iran's oil industry remained nationalized, the shah negotiated a deal with foreign oil companies under which the companies managed Iran's oil operations for a substantial profit. In foreign affairs the shah developed close relations with the United States, which became Tehran's main arms supplier. In 1955 Iran joined the Baghdad Pact, an alliance of Britain, Iran, Iraq, Pakistan, and Turkey that was intended to deter Soviet aggression in the Middle East. Although the United States was not a member, it encouraged formation of the alliance.

In 1961, amidst growing internal criticism and the resurgence of the National Front, the shah announced the "White Revolution," an ambitious plan to stimulate eco-

nomic growth and social development. The plan promoted women's suffrage, literacy, health, the nationalization of natural resources, the sale of state-owned factories, and profit sharing for workers. The cornerstone of the White Revolution, however, was land reform. The landed classes, with allies among the Shi'ite clergy, incited violent demonstrations in June 1963 to protest the threat to their holdings. Predictably, the shah crushed this dissent. After that, reforms mollified those with moderate demands and he used repression to silence the others.

The shah used his nation's oil riches to turn Iran into a regional power. He bought billions of dollars' worth of sophisticated military equipment from the United States, which considered him a bulwark against communism. Following the 1973 war in the Middle East and the ensuing Arab oil embargo imposed on Israel's supporters, Iran's oil revenues soared. Before October 1973, Iran's oil revenues were $2.5 billion a year. By 1979 annual oil revenues had grown to $19.1 billion.

As international oil consumption grew, so did the West's dependence on Iran and its fellow Organization of Oil Exporting Countries (OPEC) members. According to CIA figures, the United States depended on Iran for 9.1 percent of its crude oil imports in August 1978, compared with 5.9 percent in September 1973. American exports to Iran increased about sevenfold from 1973 to 1978. During this five-year period, Iran bought more than $19 billion worth of military equipment from the United States. At the time of the shah's fall in 1979, Iran had a foreign debt of $7.2 billion, including $2.2 billion to U.S. banks.

The Revolution

In February 1979, after months of civil violence, a broad-based movement led by the Ayatollah Khomeini ended the thirty-seven-year reign of the shah of Iran. The Iranian revolution did not spring up with a wave of Khomeini's hand. Social, economic, and religious pressures had been building within the country for several decades. These pressures led to widespread opposition to the shah from highly diverse groups that combined their efforts to accomplish a genuine grass-roots revolution.

Revolutionary Coalition

The coalition of forces against the shah consisted of an urban-based alliance of traditionalists and modernists formed into loosely organized groups usually working independently. National religious figures close to Khomeini, who was in exile, shaped the movement inside Iran. Lesser figures among the religious hierarchy, or *ulama,* who possessed enormous local influence, particularly among the urban poor and bazaar merchants, gave the movement its strength.

On the eve of the revolution, the shah imposed price controls to curb inflation. While enforcing them, the government closed nearly two hundred fifty thousand small shops. This move obviously alienated the merchant class, many of whom were jailed or excessively fined for "profiteering." The urban poor opposed the shah mostly on moral grounds, seeing his attempts to Westernize Iranian society as attacks on revered Islamic institutions.

Modernists made up a much smaller faction within the opposition to the shah. Islamic modernists such as the

Marxist Mujaheddin-e-Khalq opposed him for his capitalist economic policies. Progressive intellectuals both religious and secular wanted a modernized Iran but no monarch. Secular modernist groups such as the Fedayin-e-Khalq and the Communist Tudeh party, both longtime opponents of the shah, were joined by the professional middle class, which viewed the shah's highly centralized control over the political and economic process as the greatest obstacle to their advancement. Estimated at between 10 and 15 percent of the population, the professionals shifted their commitment from a nationalist secular cause to an Islamic one because it was the only available means of mobilizing the masses.

Khomeini's followers mark the start of the revolution with the White Revolution riots in June 1963, when wealthy landowners and Islamic clergy joined to oppose the shah's land reform program. The ulama also opposed a new law allowing women to vote and education programs that substituted secular classes for religious instruction and permitted coeducation. The shah further alienated his people by bringing in foreigners, especially Americans, to support his programs and provide technical skills.

The shah's brutal suppression of dissent forced Khomeini and other opposition leaders into exile. During the 1960s and 1970s sentiment against the government was growing in nearly every segment of Iranian society. Middle-class Iranians who opposed the government found allies in the religious hierarchy.

The clerics were incensed not only by the secularization of the education system, which they viewed as a direct assault on their position within Iranian society, but also by the Family Protection Law that allowed women to disobey Islamic teaching and divorce their husbands. The monarchy increasingly became an anti-Islamic symbol. By relying on non-Moslem foreigners and by reducing the traditional role of the ulama in government, the shah disrupted the balance that had existed between religious and secular authority in Iran. The ulama called upon conservative elements of the Iranian population to rebel.

The opposition found its leader in the Ayatollah Khomeini. When he was exiled in 1964, Khomeini believed that the political role of the clerics was to provide moral guidance to secular forces who would manage the technical aspects of the state. Statements made by Khomeini in Paris left modernists with the impression that they would run the government once the shah was defeated.

Overthrow of the Shah

After mass demonstrations in 1976 protesting the shah's switch from the Islamic calendar to one based on the coronation of Cyrus the Great, Iran was relatively quiet for a time. Sporadic protests did occur, however in response to the repressive activities of SAVAK, the shah's hated intelligence service. These protests escalated into large-scale riots in 1978 after a government-inspired article in the Tehran newspaper *Etelaat* impugned Khomeini's character and accused him of conspiring with Communists against the shah's regime. In January Khomeini supporters protested the article in Qom, a religious center dominated by the nation's Shi'ite clergy. During the march, army troops fired into the crowd. The victims were the first of an estimated ten thousand people killed during riots in 1978. The level of violence increased as the protests became more widespread. Demonstrators rioted against the shootings, and the shah's forces put down the riots with increased fervor. The government closed Iran's universities in June, creating greater support for the demonstrators among students.

Khomeini took an active part in encouraging the increasingly frequent and intense demonstrations from Iraq. The Iraqi government, concerned with maintaining good relations with Iran, expelled Khomeini, who set up headquarters in France on October 6, 1978. In France he attracted even more worldwide attention than he had enjoyed in Iraq.

In November, Iranian workers staged strikes in sympathy with the antishah demonstrators. The most important strikes were those by oil workers, whose walkout soon produced a fuel shortage, causing serious damage to the economy of the beleaguered nation.

Once the breadth of the opposition to the shah had become apparent, he made several last-minute efforts to appease his opponents. He granted amnesty to Khomeini, but the demonstrations and strikes continued. Soon even civil servants refused to report to work.

The shah then offered to step down as head of the government, but not as the shah. He appointed Shahpur Bakhtiar as premier. Bakhtiar, a member of the National Front who had always opposed the shah, accepted the appointment and quickly moved to placate the opposition. He promised to disband the SAVAK, proclaimed that no more Iranian oil would be sold to Israel or South Africa, turned over the Israeli embassy to the Palestine Liberation Organization (PLO), and openly criticized U.S. policies supported by the shah.

These efforts, however, came too late. Bakhtiar was denounced by his own party for accepting the premiership from the shah, and rioting continued. As a last-ditch measure, the shah ordered members of his royal family to turn in their millions of dollars in Iranian holdings to the Pahlavi Foundation, a family trust and charitable organization under his absolute control, but the revolution had become irreversible.

With the end near, the shah announced, "I am going on vacation because I am feeling tired." He flew to Egypt on January 16, 1979, never to return to his country. Two weeks later on February 1 Khomeini returned triumphantly to Iran. His supporters overthrew Bakhtiar's government on February 11. Bakhtiar fled to France, and Mehdi Bazargan was installed to replace him as premier. After a public referendum overwhelmingly supported the establishment of an Islamic republic, the Islamic Republic of Iran was declared on April 1, 1979.

Role of the Intellectuals

Bazargan was part of a group of liberal intellectuals, both secular and religious, who had belonged at various times to organizations such as the underground Freedom Front and the National Front—the backbone of the nationalist coalition built by former prime minister Muhammad Mossadeq. In 1979, however, the intellectuals had no political base. Their middle-class support collapsed in the face of worsening economic conditions, political persecution, and the rising power of the clerics.

The clerics were able to neutralize and eventually prevail over other national figures, such as Ibrahim Yazdi and Sadegh Ghotbzadeh, who were among the Westernized exiles with Khomeini in France just before the overthrow of the shah. Although these men were devout Moslems, their Western education and ideas made them suspect in the eyes of the fundamentalists. Nevertheless, one of these exiles, Abolhassan Bani-Sadr, gained ascendancy in the postrevolutionary power structure in Iran. Bani-Sadr was a Sorbonne-educated economist and intellectual who became Iran's first popularly elected president in January 1980 after winning 75 percent of the vote.

Bani-Sadr, as the son of a prominent religious leader, was perhaps more acceptable to the clerics than his peer. Yet when Bani-Sadr ran for president he was opposed by the clerical leadership of the Islamic Republican party (IRP).

Consolidation of Power

After the fall of the shah's government, Iran's internal security apparatus collapsed, and bands of armed youths calling themselves Revolutionary Guards (or the *Pasdaran*) ran amok, attacking anyone associated with the former ruler. The IRP had overthrown the shah without establishing an initial domestic program of government. Civil authority was exercised by thousands of self-appointed committees (*komitehs*) that took it upon themselves to stamp passports, distribute food, set prices for goods, and police the streets—mostly without state supervision.

In this atmosphere, a struggle for power ensued between the Shi'ite clerics and secular nationalists. Although these two general groupings had cooperated with each other in overthrowing the shah, they had different goals that were likely to clash. The clerics and their Islamic Republican party sought the establishment of a conservative society based on fundamentalist Shi'ite tenets and dominated by religious leaders. The secular nationalist groups sought various forms of secular government depending on their orientation, envisioned an advisory role for religious leaders, and were generally more receptive to foreign ties and influence.

The clerics had several advantages over the secular nationalists. First the secular nationalists were merely a broad group of many organizations, including the Tudeh party, the Fedayin-e-Khalq, and the National Front, without common goals or a united leadership like that of the IRP. Second, the clerics had the support of Khomeini, who commanded enormous respect among many segments of the Iranian population. Finally, when competing for support, the clerics were able to tap the deep religious convictions of many Iranian citizens.

From 1979 to 1983 the clerics, led by Khomeini, used political maneuvering, propaganda, and terror to sweep their secular rivals aside. The liberal intelligentsia represented by President Bani-Sadr were gradually removed from positions of power. Bani-Sadr himself was crippled by the Iran-Iraq war that began on September 22, 1980, when Iraqi forces invaded Iran. As commander in chief, Bani-Sadr received blame for the military's failings, while his efforts to reorganize and reinvigorate the military led to suspicions that he was plotting to use the military to increase his own power.

Bani-Sadr survived only so long as Khomeini protected him and maintained some balance between him and the IRP. When Khomeini withdrew his support, Bani-Sadr's downfall was swift. The Majlis declared him politically incompetent and Khomeini removed him from office on June 22, 1981. Bani-Sadr fled the country in an Iranian air force jet in July. With him was Massoud Rajavi, leader of the Mujaheddin-e-Khalq. The two men were granted asylum by France.

One week after Bani-Sadr and Rajavi were forced into exile, the Mujaheddin bombed IRP headquarters, killing seventy-four of the nation's political elites, including the founder of the IRP, Ayatollah Mohammed Beheshti. The Mujaheddin espoused Islamic Marxism, arguing for a divinely integrated classless society with nationalized major industries and banks. The Mujaheddin's views on the direction of the revolution were not irreconcilable with the clerics' views, but the IRP was unwilling to share power with anyone.

In reprisal for the bombing of IRP headquarters, Khomeini turned the full force of the Revolutionary Guards against the Mujaheddin, and by the end of 1982 it was forced underground. Amnesty International estimates that between forty-five hundred and six thousand of the Mujaheddin were killed by Revolutionary Guards and thousands more were put in prison. In late 1989 the Mujaheddin was operating as an underground opposition group in Iran.

Khomeini's regime also suppressed the extreme left-wing groups such as the Iranian Communist Tudeh party and the Fedayin-e-Khalq. The Revolutionary Guards' treatment of the Fedayin-e-Khalq was so harsh that in December 1982 Khomeini publicly criticized the komitehs for their excesses. In 1983 the Khomeini faction banned the Tudeh party and jailed more than a thousand of its members.

Khomeini even attacked the merchants, or *bazaaris* who played an important role in his rise to power and remain a key element in Iran's economy. In December 1980 Khomeini, like the shah, accused them of profiteering, and in June 1981 he ordered the execution of two well-known merchants for alleged counterrevolutionary activities. When Bani-Sadr was dismissed, bazaaris distanced themselves from IRP policies.

Throughout the consolidation period the military remained loyal to the revolution. Many officers owed their positions to Khomeini's regime, and rank-and-file soldiers had demonstrated intense loyalty to Khomeini. The military also was probably reluctant to confront the disorganized but ubiquitous Revolutionary Guards, whose propensity for violence was demonstrated time and again in the urban center streets.

U.S. Embassy Hostage Crisis

An event of central importance to the Iranian power struggle was the occupation of the American embassy on November 4, 1979, by revolutionary students. The students, who soon received the support of Ayatollah Khomeini and most of the fundamentalist clerics in the government, took sixty-one Americans hostage. Nine were released within a few days, but fifty-two of the embassy staff members remained prisoners of the students.

The hostage crisis, which continued for 444 days until Iran released the diplomats on January 21, 1981, as Jimmy Carter left office and Ronald Reagan became president, was used by Iran's hard-line, anti-Western clerics to weaken the position of moderates in the Iranian government. The hard-liners pointed to the diplomatic, military, and economic measures taken by the Carter administration to obtain the release of the hostages and the admission of the shah into America for medical treatment as evidence of the malevolence of the United States. In addition, publication of documents captured by the students who took over the embassy revealed U.S. intelligence activities in Iran and confirmed the suspicions of many Iranians that the United States was interfering in their internal affairs. In this atmosphere, Iranian moderates who had had contacts with U.S. officials became suspect, while extremists in Tehran gained credibility. Moreover, the refusal of some moderate Iranian leaders to actively support the hostage taking hurt their standing and made them more vulnerable to the machinations of the hard-liners.

Government Structure under Khomeini

After the elimination of the secular nationalists and other opponents, Iran's fundamentalist clerics dominated the government. As faqih, Khomeini became the final authority in all matters of government and social policy. In 1979 he asserted that "there is not a single topic of human life for which Islam has not provided instruction and established norms." Nevertheless, he remained aloof from the everyday decision-making process, maintaining his offices in Qom rather than Tehran, the capital. Because of his eminent position, however, all important decisions had to receive his approval.

The government was presided over by a president and prime minister, who were responsible for running the ministries and executing government policy. The 270-seat Majlis, which wrote and passed new laws subject to Khomenei's approval, was led by a Speaker.

In addition to these familiar instruments of government, several councils unique to revolutionary Iran played an important role in Khomeini's government. The Council of Experts—an elected body of seventy to eighty eminent Islamic scholars—was responsible for such high matters of state as revising the 1979 constitution and selecting a successor to Khomeini. The twelve-member Council of Constitutional Guardians screened and modified all legislation from the Majlis before passing it on to Khomeini for his approval. Laws that did not meet the council's Islamic standards were sent back, often in modified form with the expectation that they would be passed and resubmitted as returned. The Revolutionary Council was in charge of the Pasdaran, or Revolutionary Guards. In addition to the council's military section, which has been responsible for most of the regime's civil violence, there were economic and political sections linked to tens of thousands of mosques. The clerics connected with the mosques functioned as local administrators. They provided food, clothing, and ration cards; ran the courts; collected taxes; and rounded up volunteers for the war against Iraq. They maintained detailed records on their flock and served as the Pasdaran's grassroots intelligence service.

During 1989 Iran was in the process of reorganizing its government. Among the expected reforms were a strengthened presidency and the elimination of the position of prime minister. Many of the elements of the government, however, were to remain unchanged.

The War with Iraq

The apparent weakness of Iran's political center encouraged Iraq to attack Iran in September 1980. Captured documents published by Iran indicated that Iraq's president, Saddam Hussein, expected that the chaos in Tehran would bring a quick victory. Instead of collapsing, however, the Iranian government responded with surprising speed, mobilizing what was left of the shah's army. Waves of untrained young zealots, some of them unarmed, threw themselves into the conflict and halted the Iraqis' advance. Even factions opposed to Khomeini's rule rallied against Iran's ancient Arab foe.

The Iranian army's counterattacks in late 1981 and 1982 forced the Iraqi army to retreat. In June 1982 Iraq began to seek peace. Saddam Hussein withdrew his troops into Iraq and unilaterally called a cease-fire. Khomeini ignored these moves and in July ordered a major attack across the border toward Basra. The Iranian force, however, had been weakened by purges of officers and shortages of equipment and was unable to sustain this offensive. The assault failed, and the war deteriorated to a standoff with the two armies inside Iraqi territory.

During the war both countries attacked the oil facilities of the other, as well as neutral tankers in the Gulf. Iranian attacks succeeded in substantially reducing Iraqi exports early in the war, although the construction of pipelines restored Iraqi export capacity by 1987. Iraqi attacks in 1984 and 1985 on Iranian refineries, oil tankers doing business with Iran, and Kharg Island, Iran's principal Gulf oil terminal, sharply reduced Iran's oil revenues. In 1983 Iran had earned $21.7 billion from its petroleum exports, but by 1985 revenues were just $15.9 billion. In 1986 the worldwide collapse of oil prices limited Iran's oil export earnings to just $7.3 billion. The loss of oil revenue further weakened an economy already suffering from poor management by inexperienced clerics and the resource drain caused by the war.

Besides economic strains, the war brought Iran increasing international isolation. Its stated goal of exporting its revolution to neighboring states and its attacks on ships in the Gulf pushed Arab nations to back Iraq financially and diplomatically. Saudi Arabia and Kuwait provided billions of dollars for the Iraqi war effort, and the Gulf states formed the Gulf Cooperation Council to coordinate their defenses against the security threat from Iran.

The war also led to military confrontations between Iran and the United States. A covert attempt by the Reagan administration to use arms sales to Iran to improve U.S. relations with Iranian moderates and obtain the release of American hostages held in Lebanon by pro-Iranian groups caused a scandal in the United States. Not only had the plan contradicted President Reagan's policies of not negotiating with terrorists and not selling arms to Iran, but investigations disclosed that administration officials had also used proceeds from the Iranian arms sales to illegally fund the contra resistance fighters in Nicaragua.

In an effort to repair its image among Gulf states and head off growing Soviet involvement in the region, the United States began escorting reflagged Kuwaiti oil tankers through the Persian Gulf. These American naval escorts fought Iranian forces on several occasions and increased the Iranians' sense of encirclement.

Iranian morale was reduced further by Iraqi air and missile attacks on Iran's largest cities, Iraq's use of chemical weapons on the battlefield, and the failure of major Iranian offensives in 1986 and 1987 to breach Iraqi defenses around Basra. In early 1988 Iraqi forces began pushing the Iranians back toward their border. By July the Iraqis had recaptured virtually all Iraqi territory and threatened to achieve significant territorial gains in Iran. Faced with this prospect, Khomeini agreed to a cease-fire, something he had vowed not to do until Iraqi leader Saddam Hussein had been driven from power. The war had resulted in the deaths of hundreds of thousands of Iranians and left the nation financially bankrupt. Much of this loss could have been prevented, because Iran could have had a permanent cease-fire in 1982 on roughly the same terms as in 1988. *(Details on the Persian Gulf war, Chapter 5, pp. 94-100)*

Iran after Khomeini

On June 6, 1989, the Ayatollah Khomeini was buried amidst a chaotic display of national grief. Hundreds of thousands of mourners showed up at the War Martyrs' Cemetery in Tehran and thousands pressed through elaborate barriers at the burial site, trying to touch Khomeini's body. The crowd overwhelmed security personnel and mourners grabbed at the corpse, causing it to fall from its wooden litter. Soldiers fought to retrieve the body as helicopters scattered the crowd. The body was airlifted away and officials were forced to delay the burial for six hours.

It seemed impossible to many Iranians that their preeminent religious and political leader was gone. For years Khomeini had defied premature predictions of death, while Western observers speculated on the government that would emerge when he was gone. Many analysts forecast that in his absence there could be a lengthy power struggle among the religious elite for control of the government. Such a power struggle had the potential to cause domestic terrorism, internal chaos, or even civil war.

In March 1989 the eighty-nine-year-old Khomeini forced Ayatollah Hussein Ali Montazeri to resign as his designated heir. The resignation of Montazeri, who was considered a moderate on social and economic issues, appeared to indicate that radical factions opposed to expansion of private enterprise and a greater opening to the West had gained ascendancy. Montazeri's ouster also confused the succession issue, increasing the possibility of a power struggle after Khomeini's death.

While the crowds at Khomeini's burial reinforced Western perceptions that Iran was out of control, the country's leadership was defying Western speculation about a power struggle by effecting an apparently smooth and peaceful transition of power. Within twenty-four hours of Khomeini's death Iran's Council of Experts had chosen outgoing president Ali Khamenei, a compromise candidate, to succeed Khomeini as supreme religious leader. Ali Akbar Hashemi Rafsanjani, the Speaker of Iran's parliament and leading candidate to succeed Khamenei as president, remarked: "We astonished the world and right now all of those wrong interpretations of power struggles and radicals versus moderates are dismissed."

In August Rafsanjani, considered by analysts to be a moderate, was overwhelmingly elected president as expected. Rafsanjani had repeatedly stated his intention to give priority to reinvigorating the economy. Although Khamenei and Rafsanjani do not have identical outlooks, they are expected to cooperate closely. They were roommates in their early revolutionary days, and Khamenei gave Rafsanjani's presidential candidacy an effusive endorsement. Moreover, few prominent hard-liners were given positions of power in the new regime, although they maintained a strong presence in the Majlis.

Despite the smooth transition, Khomeini's death created a vacuum in Iranian politics that is likely to increase elite factionalism. Neither Rafsanjani nor Khamenei command the reverence and respect of Khomeini, who served as the final arbiter of all leadership disputes. With Khomeini gone the Iranian government will be capable of greater flexibility, but it probably will be less stable.

Current Issues

Domestic Problems. The most important domestic problem facing the new leadership is rebuilding an economy seriously damaged by eight years of war with Iraq. In 1989 inflation was running close to 50 percent and unemployment was estimated to be at least 25 percent. Oil exports accounted for almost all of Iran's foreign exchange earnings, most of which were devoted to rebuilding a defense establishment weakened by the war and paying for food imports to feed the population. Many industries were producing at half capacity because of equipment shortages and power outages, and the oil industry badly needed a technological overhaul.

The Iranian people have shown increasing discontent with the country's economic conditions and having to wait in long lines for rationed food. One result of this discontent has been the expansion of a thriving black market. The nation's economic plight was so dismal that Ayatollah Khomeini approved a five-year development plan in March 1989 that allowed Iran to seek foreign loans and credits, so long as they did not threaten Iran's independence.

Adopting decisive economic policies, however, will be difficult because the regime is deeply divided over how much private sector and foreign involvement to permit. Hard-liners have argued that any foreign involvement could undermine Iranian independence and that opening up the economy to domestic private enterprise could erode Islamic values and weaken the control of religious leaders. President Rafsanjani, however, who sharply criticized Iran's economic performance, frequently stated his support for reducing state supervision of the economy and encouraging private enterprise. He has also indicated that he would welcome Western economic ties, especially technological help. Moreover, after Khomeini's death Iran signed a fifteen-year $15 billion economic reconstruction agreement with the Soviet Union. The agreement allowed Iran to incur as much as $2 billion in debt to the Soviet Union, which was to accept natural gas shipments from Iran as partial payment for the purchase of Soviet machinery, facilities, and technology.

Besides breathing life into the economy, Iran's leaders must try to pacify ethnic and political movements opposed to the regime. The establishment of an Islamic republic was intended to produce civic harmony, but it has achieved no more stability than the dictatorship of the shah. The Kurds continue to rebel, and terrorist attacks by the Mujaheddin continue to disrupt life in large cities. In March 1985 an attempt to assassinate President Ali Khamenei took the lives of an assistant and five others. Bodyguards and armor-plated limousines are status symbols of high-ranking officials. Clandestine radio stations beam antiregime programs into Iran.

Violence on the part of the regime is equally disruptive. Hundreds of followers of the Bahai faith, a mystical Islamic sect considered heretical by the Shi'ite fundamentalists, have been killed or imprisoned. The Revolutionary Guards still commit acts of violence against the populace, and the regime holds thousands of political prisoners in its jails.

Iran also suffers from a lack of governmental and technical expertise among its leadership. Although Iran's religious leaders have shown that they possess the political skills to maintain themselves in power, they may lack the skills necessary to solve the nation's domestic problems. Ministerial nominees and other officials have often been chosen according to their religious standing, rather than their experience. In February 1989, before Ayatollah Montazeri was forced to resign as Khomeini's heir, he criticized this practice and urged clerics to defer to professionals on matters of state administration. With Khomeini gone such an approach may become more acceptable.

Foreign Affairs. For eight years the war with Iraq and Iran's revolutionary goals abroad dominated its foreign policy. The desperate shape of the economy, however, may force the leadership to focus on trade relations.

President Rafsanjani has stated that he favors normalizing relations with Europe. He has even hinted that he would accept some type of dialogue with the United States. Nevertheless, many leading clerics still reject any contact with Washington. A month before Khomeini died, Rafsanjani appeared to attempt to reaffirm his revolutionary credentials by calling on Palestinians to kill Westerners, attack U.S. international interests, and hijack airplanes until Israel grants them their rights. Although Rafsanjani qualified the statement and renounced terrorism a few days later, his actions demonstrated that anti-American positions are still a key part of Iranian political culture. Ayatollah Ali Khamenei also signaled Iran's continuing opposition to the United States on August 14, 1989, by rejecting any negotiations with Washington on the fate of U.S. hostages held in Lebanon by pro-Iranian Shi'ites.

While the Iranian government remains outwardly opposed to normalizing relations with the United States, it has dramatically improved relations with the Soviet Union. During the Gulf war, Iran occasionally flirted with establishing closer relations with Moscow, particularly in the economic sphere, but it officially regarded the Soviet Union as a "Great Satan" second only to the United States. Khomeini maintained that to create purely Islamic governments the nations of the world must obtain true independence, which means they should adopt anti-Western and anti-Soviet Islamic foreign policies.

The Soviet Union took a wait-and-see position on the revolutionary regime in the hopes of gaining a political advantage in Iran, which is geopolitically important to the Soviets. In the early stages of the Iran-Iraq war Moscow even supplied arms to the Iranians. After Tehran repeatedly rejected Soviet overtures and disbanded the Communist Tudeh party in 1982 and 1983, the Kremlin realized that it was hurting Soviet-Iraqi relations without gaining anything in Iran. Moscow then reasserted its close arms supply relationship with Iraq.

The end of the Iran-Iraq war in 1988, the withdrawal of Soviet forces from Afghanistan in early 1989, and Khomeini's death later in the year helped pave the way toward improved Soviet-Iranian relations. President Mikhail Gorbachev warmly received Rafsanjani in Moscow on June 20. Negotiations between the two countries resulted in Soviet offers of military aid to Iran and a $15 billion economic development deal under which the Iranians were to purchase Soviet equipment, technology, and expertise.

Iran appeared to be headed toward a reconciliation with Western Europe in early 1989, following several months of cultivating economic contacts with Western European governments and business leaders. On February 7 Ali Akbar Velayati made the first visit to Great Britain by an Iranian foreign minister since the 1979 revolution. Then on February 14 Khomeini disrupted the thaw by calling on Moslems everywhere to kill author Salman Rushdie for writing his novel *The Satanic Verses.* The book was considered by much of the Islamic world to be blasphemous because of its unflattering portrayal of a character similar to the Prophet Muhammad and its suggestion that parts of the Koran were not the word of God. Khomeini's assassination order, which was perhaps intended to rekindle the revolutionary fervor of his own people and reassert his control over his regime's foreign policy, was immediately denounced in the West. Great Britain and the other eleven nations of the European Economic Community called diplomats home from Tehran to protest Khomeini's action. Several governments also postponed plans to offer Iran credits for reconstruction projects. Although the election of President Rafsanjani promised to lead to a warming trend in Iranian-European relations, the Rushdie incident left Western European nations wary of moving too quickly to expand economic contacts with Iran.

In the Middle East, Iran has yet to conclude a formal peace agreement with Iraq. Negotiations between the two enemies have made little progress and could remain stalemated for years.

During the 1980s Iran has had to contend with more enemies than just Iraq. The goal of the Iranian leadership to export its revolution to other states made Iran a primary security threat to Gulf nations. An Iranian-backed plot to overthrow the Bahraini government in 1981, Iran's support of Shi'ites who bombed Western embassies in Kuwait in 1983, and riots by Iranian pilgrims in Mecca for the holy pilgrimage of al-hajj in 1987, were among the most troubling instances of Iranian subversion and agitation.

In response to Iran's threat to export revolution and its attacks on Gulf shipping, Jordan, Saudi Arabia, and Kuwait openly supported Iraq financially and militarily in its war with Iran. Among Middle Eastern and North African nations, only Syria, Libya, and the People's Democratic Republic of Yemen (South Yemen) supported Iran in the war. Since the end of the war, Iran has remained a regional outcast, even though it moderated its position somewhat on the exportation of revolution.

Outlook

As of September 1989 President Rafsanjani and moderates within the Iranian government appeared to be pre-vailing on most issues, although they were proceeding very slowly with Western involvement in the economy. But fundamentalist clerics still had considerable power and were capable of frustrating government and economic reforms. Only months before Khomeini's death it appeared to many Western observers that they were in a commanding position to succeed Khomeini.

Rafsanjani must be careful not to appear too accommodating toward foreign nations. As the reaction to Rushdie's book demonstrated in February 1989, the religious fervor and anti-Western sentiment of large segments of the population can be harnessed for political purposes. Rafsanjani and Khameini are unlikely to be secure from the threat of ouster for some time, if ever.

Another factor in the continuing struggle for control of the government's direction is the potential role of Ahmad Khomeini, the son of the late ayatollah. He is reputed to have close ties to the hard-liners among Iran's religious elites, and there had been rumors that he might challenge Rafsanjani for president. Ahmad declined to run, saying that he needed time "to recover both physically and spiritually" after his father's death. His supporters, however, continued to lobby for a key position for him. More important, because he is the son of the Ayatollah Khomeini, he could become a rallying point for conservatives in any future power struggle.

In foreign affairs, the Soviet Union appears willing to expand its relations with Iran without limits. In June 1989 President Gorbachev said of his government's relations with Iran, "We are ready to go ahead as far as Iran is ready to go toward us." Iran's developing relationship with the Soviet Union should give Rafsanjani a powerful bargaining tool should the Iranian government move to improve relations with Western Europe and the United States. Any improvement in U.S.-Iranian relations, however, will likely require a willingness by Iran to help the United States free American hostages in Lebanon.

Iran has also tried to improve relations with its Arab neighbors. Tehran desires improved economic relations with Saudi Arabia and the other Gulf states and must cooperate with its fellow OPEC members if it wishes to help establish oil production and pricing policies that will benefit the whole cartel. The wounds of the eight-year Gulf war will be slow to heal, however, and Iran has not renounced its goal of spreading its Islamic revolution, although it has stated that its support for revolutionary activities would be primarily rhetorical.

Reasserting Itself in the Arab World

On September 22, 1980, President Saddam Hussein ordered Iraqi forces to invade Iran. He hoped to secure control of the long-disputed Shatt al-Arab waterway for Iraq and topple the Iranian regime of the Ayatollah Ruhollah Khomeini. After a bloody eight-year war, during which Iranian forces occupied large areas of Iraqi territory before the Iraqi army pushed the Iranians back across the border, Hussein had achieved neither of his objectives.

Yet, despite much of the population's disillusionment with the war and the potential of Iraq's majority Shi'ite population to identify with the Shi'ite government and people of Iran, Hussein kept a tight hold on power. He succeeded in building up his own personality cult and depicting the Iranians as aggressors who wanted to destroy Iraq. Many Iraqis disliked Hussein's regime, but they believed that while the war continued Iraqi security depended on President Hussein's leadership.

Saddam Hussein

Since the 1988 ceasefire there have been increasing signs of opposition to Hussein's rule. In December 1988 Iraqi army officers reportedly attempted a coup against Hussein that led to the execution of several of the conspirators and the cancellation of Iraq's annual Army Day celebration. Rumors also surfaced of an earlier army plot against Hussein in October 1988.

Perhaps in an effort to widen his support in Iraqi society now that the unifying effects of the Iranian threat had diminished, Hussein announced plans in March 1989 for political liberalization. He allowed independent candidates to run against Ba'ath party members in elections for Iraq's rubber-stamp National Assembly and called for a constitution that would guarantee democratic rule. Few analysts, however, expected Hussein to diminish significantly his power or the preeminent position of the Ba'ath party.

Hussein has also expressed his desire that Iraq become a leader of the Arab world. Toward this end, Iraq has supported the Lebanese Christians fighting Syrian troops in Lebanon and has participated in the creation of an Arab economic union with Egypt, Jordan, and North Yemen. If Hussein can maintain internal stability, Iraq's large population, experienced army, and huge oil reserves will make it a key player in Arab politics, now that it does not have to focus all of its attention on the war with Iran.

Geography

Iraq is located at the northern end of the Persian Gulf. The country's only access to the high seas is a thirty-mile coastline with two major ports, Umm Qasr on the Gulf itself and Basra, which is inland on the confluence of the Tigris and Euphrates rivers. The confluence is called the Shatt al-Arab, or "the river of the Arabs." South of Basra the Shatt al-Arab forms the international border between Iraq and Iran. When a river forms an international boundary, it is common to use the center of the main channel, or thalweg line, as the dividing line between countries. In this case, the line was drawn down the Iranian bank of the river, giving control of the Shatt al-Arab entirely to Iraq. Over the years, the placement of the boundary has been a source of dispute between the two countries, eventually contributing to the outbreak of the Iran-Iraq war in 1980.

A vast alluvial plain lies between Basra, Baghdad (the capital), and the Tigris and Euphrates rivers. This area is interlaced with irrigation canals and small lakes, and much of the land is fertile. Most of Iraq's estimated 17.6 million people live on these plains near the two cities. The area east and north of where the Shatt al-Arab begins is a large, six-thousand-square-mile marshland that extends into Iran. West of the Euphrates River lies the Syrian desert, which extends into Jordan and Saudi Arabia. The Iraqi highlands cover the region between the cities of Mosul and Kirkuk north to the Turkish and Iranian borders. Beginning as undulating hills, the land continues to rise to mountains as high as twelve thousand feet. Rainfall in this area, unlike most of the country, is sufficient to support agriculture.

Iraq's most valuable national resource is oil. The largest and most productive fields are around Mosul and Kirkuk. A series of smaller fields are located around Basra in the south. Most of Iraq's production is exported as crude oil, but refineries and petrochemical facilities process more-than-sufficient amounts of refined products to meet domestic needs. When its oil facilities are fully operational, Iraq has the capacity to produce as much as 3.5 million barrels per day (bpd) for limited periods. In 1988 Iraq's petroleum export earnings were $11.8 billion, second

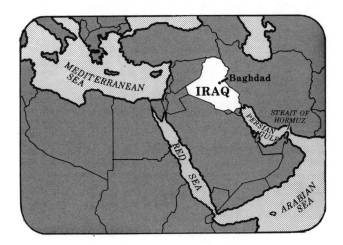

Key Facts on Iraq

Area: 172,000 square miles.
Capital: Baghdad.
Population: 17,583,000 (1988).
Religion: 96 percent Moslem, 4 percent other.
Official Language: Arabic; Kurdish minority speaks Kurdish.
GNP: $40.0 billion, $2,400 per capita (1987).

Sources: World Bank Atlas 1988; CIA World Factbook 1988

among the members of the Organization of Petroleum Exporting Countries (OPEC) to Saudi Arabia's.

Before the Gulf war, most of Iraq's oil was moved through pipelines to two oil terminals, at Khor al-Amaya and Mina al-Bakr in the Persian Gulf, where it was loaded onto tankers. Iranian attacks against these offshore terminals and other Iraqi oil facilities early in the war, however, severely reduced Iraqi oil exports. In addition, Syria reached an agreement with the government of Iran in 1982 to shut down the Banias line, a pipeline running from Iraq through Syrian territory to the Mediterranean Sea, in support of Iran's war effort. This prompted Baghdad to launch an ambitious pipeline construction program to avoid Iranian attacks and circumvent the Syrian blockade. Iraq expanded the capacity of a pipeline that runs from the Kirkuk fields to Ceyhan, a Turkish port on the Mediterranean. Iraq also built a pipeline from its southern oil fields to the Trans-Arabian Pipeline that runs to the Red Sea. A third pipeline, capable of carrying 1.6 million bpd across Saudi Arabia to the Red Sea, was under construction in 1989. *(Oil pipeline map, Chapter 5, p. 95)*

Aside from oil, Iraq has few natural resources. They include natural gas, produced at the Kirkuk fields and used domestically for power stations; limestone, which enables Iraq to export limited quantities of cement; salt; and gypsum. Iraq's potential for agricultural production is considered to be greater than that of most nations in the Middle East, but this potential has yet to be developed fully. Stone, metallic ore, timber, and other resources must be imported.

Demography

Iraq's cultural, ethnic, linguistic, and religious diversity stems in part from its history of foreign domination. Once known as Mesopotamia or "the land between rivers," Iraq served as a frontier province for the Persian, Greek, Roman, Arab, Mongol, and Turkish empires. It was the Arab invasion in the seventh century A.D. that brought Islam and the Arabic language to Iraq. *Iraq* means *to take root* in Arabic, but no invader ever succeeded in completely conquering the region, and as each empire fell it left a cultural residue that survived succeeding invasions.

One consequence of Iraq's heterogeneous population has been that some subnational groups have never been assimilated into the mainstream of Iraqi society. One-quarter of Iraq's population speaks a language other than Arabic or an Arabic dialect that is unintelligible to the rest of the population. Illiteracy, estimated to be nearly 45 percent in urban areas and as high as 75 percent in the countryside, compounds the problem.

The religious, communal, ethnic, and linguistic minorities in Iraq have a tendency to identify with their parochial communities rather than with the central governing authority. For example, the early Arab settlers successfully converted the Kurdish inhabitants of the mountainous regions to Islam, but the Kurds retained their own language and hence their ethnic identity.

Religious heresies and schisms added to the already-complex cultural makeup of the region. In the seventh century A.D. the Islamic faith split into the Sunni and Shi'ite branches. The Shi'ite movement actually began in Iraq and spread rapidly among new converts to Islam who felt excluded from the Arab-dominated faith. Shi'ites can now be found all through the Middle East, and they represent a majority of the population in Iran. Many Shi'ite martyrs are buried in Iraq, and shrines built to their memory attract large numbers of worshippers on holy days.

During Ottoman rule, which lasted from the sixteenth century until World War I, separate religious communities, called *millets*, were granted representation before the provincial Ottoman councils and were self-governing in communal matters. Because of weak or intermittent government, these groups were never forced to adapt their customs to those of the majority of the population, and they survived as coherent, nearly autonomous entities, often in conflict with the central government and with each other.

Kurds, an estimated 20 percent of the population, predominate in the isolated mountains of the north and are found in large numbers around the oil fields near Kirkuk. Arab Sunni Moslems generally live in the center of the country. Shi'ite Moslems, who make up about 60 percent of Iraq's population, are concentrated in the south around the oil fields near Basra. Recently, however, many of them have migrated to Baghdad.

Religious and Ethnic Divisions

Arab Sunni Moslems make up only about 20 percent of Iraq's population, but they occupy the country's top military and political leadership posts. Sunni control of the leadership structure is resented and often opposed by the other two major groups in Iraqi society: the Shi'ite Moslems and the Kurds.

Of these two groups the Shi'ites pose the most complex political problems for the Hussein regime. They form an impoverished and politically excluded majority of the Iraqi population. Historically, they were herders organized in tribal systems far from the settled areas. As a result, their representation in the bureaucracy and in the military has been low compared with their proportion of the whole population. Centuries of rule by the Sunni Moslem Ottoman Turks, and until 1958 by a Sunni Moslem Arab monarchy, reinforced their exclusion from the inner circles of power. The wretched living conditions in most Shi'ite villages prompted a massive urbanization of the poorest and least educated of their number and have given rise to sprawling urban slums. By the mid-1980s more than 60 percent of Iraq's population lived in urban areas, and most new arrivals in major cities came from the poorest Shi'ite districts in the south.

Iraq's Shi'ite population is highly politicized. The imposing shrines of the Shi'ite faith at Najaf and Karbala and religious ceremonies involving public processions and self-flagellation make Shi'ism a highly visible feature of life in Iraq. Because the shah of Iran, Muhammad Reza Pahlavi, tried to suppress the Shi'ites, a number of the most intractable and militant Shi'ite clerics fled to Iraq to avoid persecution. Among them was the Ayatollah Khomeini, who led the revolutionary Islamic government of Iran until his death in 1989. The Iran-Iraq war was perpetuated by Iran until 1988, in part because of Khomeini's hatred of the Hussein regime in Baghdad. This hatred stemmed from the regime's treatment of him and its attempt to maintain peace with the shah by expelling Khomeini in 1978.

The Iranian revolution of 1979 radicalized existing Shi'ite political movements. After the outbreak of war, Iran's Arabic language broadcasts referred to Iraq's most distinguished and popular Shi'ite legist, Sayyid Muhammad Bakr al-Sadr, as the "Khomeini of Iraq." In 1980 President Saddam Hussein executed him along with seven other Shi'ite leaders, six of them Iranian, who were suspected of involvement with antigovernment Shi'ite terrorist organizations.

The politicization of the Shi'ites can also be attributed to the Communist party in Iraq. On several occasions the party instigated antigovernment demonstrations among the Shi'ite communities in the major cities. In 1977 the Communists incited the Shi'ites in southern Iraq to riot. The government took stern measures to suppress them. The party was forced to go underground, and its leaders fled to Syria. The urban Shi'ites became a mob looking for a leader, and Shi'ite Moslem terrorist groups associated with the religious leadership of Iran have attempted to fill the void.

Although the Kurds, a non-Arab Moslem people, make up only about 20 percent of the population, they have also created problems for Hussein. Kurds live not only in Iraq but also in Iran and Turkey, and in smaller numbers in Syria and the Soviet Union. Kurds are Sunni Moslems but their Kurdish identity is salient. Their society was once tribal in organization, but insecurity resulting from conflict with the Iraqi, Turkish, and Iranian governments led to urbanization. Power has shifted away from the traditional feudal upper class to a growing urban intelligentsia. The emergence of this Kurdish intelligentsia has increased Kurdish national pride, which keeps hope alive for an autonomous Kurdish state.

Between 1961 and 1970 five major conflicts erupted between Kurdish tribes and Iraqi armed forces. After nearly a decade of intermittent guerrilla warfare a stalemate resulted, with the Kurds occupying the highlands and the Iraqi army holding the valleys. In 1970 Baghdad offered to grant the Kurds most of their demands in return for a promise to lay down their arms. The agreement included recognition of Kurdish nationality, five ministerial positions, and economic assistance for depressed Kurdish areas. In 1973 the central government proposed inclusion of Kurdish representatives in a national front government, along with the Communists. The Kurds distrusted the central government and did not accept the proposal. Instead they insisted that, because most of the population of Kirkuk was Kurdish, any agreement had to include a right to dispose of revenues from the Kirkuk oil fields. The Iraqi

government refused that demand and implemented the agreement unilaterally in 1974. The Kurds, who had never intended to accept less than separation from Iraq, again rejected the scheme.

By 1974 Kurdish forces had become better equipped and more numerous—an estimated hundred thousand strong. They occupied favorable terrain and had proved themselves to be excellent mountain fighters. Because of these factors they saw no reason to be accommodating. War broke out again in 1975, but this time a reequipped and retrained Iraqi army soon gained the upper hand, driving Kurdish forces to the Iranian border. The shah of Iran supplied military equipment to the Iraqi Kurds, but he was unwilling to use his armed forces against Iraq on their behalf.

In March 1975 the shah and Saddam Hussein, who was then vice president, met in Algiers and reached an agreement: the shah pledged to end his support for the Kurds while Iraq granted Iran navigational rights in the Shatt al-Arab. As a result of the agreement, the Kurds were forced to capitulate. Many were imprisoned, and more than two hundred of their leaders were executed. Thousands fled to Iran to escape further suppression by Baghdad.

When Khomeini deposed the shah in 1979, relations between Baghdad and Tehran deteriorated. The Algiers agreement collapsed and the Kurdish movement surfaced again, this time with strongly socialist overtones. The war between Iran and Iraq that began in 1980 prevented the Hussein regime from focusing its armed might against the Kurds. Soon after a cease-fire was concluded in the summer of 1988, however, Baghdad initiated a military campaign to break Kurdish resistance. This campaign drew international condemnation, in part because of evidence that the Iraqi army used poison gas against Kurdish villages and camps in northern Iraq. Thousands of Kurds fled into Turkey to escape the Iraqi army. In September 1988 the Hussein government announced an amnesty for the Kurds, an indication that it believed the Kurdish rebellion was under control.

History

Foreign influences have shaped both the modern and ancient history of Iraq. British interests wanted protection for trade routes from India and, since 1903, the Baghdad Railroad. In 1912, while Iraq was still under Ottoman domination, British, Dutch, and German entrepreneurs obtained a concession to explore for oil in the vicinity of Basra. Two years later the Ottoman Empire allied with Germany in World War I, and the British dispatched an expeditionary force to Iraq from India to maintain control. The British presence continued after the war. In 1920 the Treaty of Sevres placed Iraq and Palestine under a British mandate and Syria under the French. In 1921 the British created a constitutional monarchy in Iraq and placed at its head a Meccan prince, Faisal ibn Hussein (Faisal I), whose acceptance by the people derived from his being a descendant of the Prophet Muhammad. In 1932 Iraq became independent, but British influence over the ruling elite continued for another twenty-eight years.

The concept of nation was an alien one to most Iraqis, who identified more readily with ancient local orientations. Almost as soon as the constitutional monarchy was implanted on Iraqi soil, the process of fragmentation began. The Kurds revolted against the central government in Baghdad between 1922 and 1924. The death of King Faisal I in 1933 ended what political stability there was, and throughout the 1930s communal and tribal factions began to form around groups of European-educated intellectuals who advocated a wide variety of political solutions to Iraq's problems. The first of many coups came in 1936. It was led by anti-British army officers who advocated socialism. They, in turn, were deposed by pro-British and economically conservative officers who placed King Faisal's four-year-old grandson, Faisal II, on the throne in 1939. This last group managed to control Iraq until 1958.

During and after World War II, anti-imperialist sentiments began to grow. Opposition groups demanded the reduction of British influence in the country, the liberalization of politics, and land reform. On July 14, 1958, a group of officers led by Brig. Gen. Abdul Karim Kassim overthrew the Hashemite monarchy. King Faisal II, members of his family, and a number of persons who had assisted him in his rule were executed. The new regime reversed Iraq's international orientation and declared that Iraq was now part of the movement of nonaligned nations. Iraq's foreign policy became controlled by the drive to destroy Israel, which was regarded as the last vestige of imperialism in the Middle East.

The new Iraqi republic established relations with Communist nations and began purchasing military equipment from the Soviet Union. In March 1959 Iraq withdrew from the British-dominated Baghdad Pact, which had been formed four years before. The pact was a mutual defense treaty among Britain, Iran, Iraq, Pakistan, and Turkey. Its formation was promoted by U.S. President Dwight D. Eisenhower to counter potential Soviet aggression in the region. When Iraq withdrew, the organization moved its headquarters to Ankara, Turkey, and changed its name to the Central Treaty Organization (CENTO).

Iraq's domestic policies changed dramatically as well. The new Kassim government enacted land reform laws and greatly liberalized the political system. Previously suppressed segments within the society were granted access to the political process for the first time, and they began to press their parochial demands upon the central government. As a result, ancient local enmities increased as a factor in national politics. In March 1959 army officers from Mosul tried but failed to overthrow the Kassim regime because it was perceived as pro-Communist. In October supporters of Egypt's President Gamal Abdel Nasser unsuccessfully attempted to assassinate Kassim, because they wanted a union between Iraq and Egypt. In 1961 the Kurds launched an armed rebellion because they felt oppressed by the predominantly Arab government. Turks clashed with Kurds, Persians with Arabs, Shi'ite Moslems with Sunnis.

Out of this confusion emerged a group that eventually dominated Iraq's politics. A pan-Arab faction, opposed to the narrow nationalist policies of the Kassim government and in favor of union with Syria, formed the Arab Socialist Resurrection party, better known as the Ba'ath party. Aided by sympathetic members of Iraq's officer corps, the Ba'ath party seized power in February 1963. It lost control nine months later as the result of a coup engineered by a pro-Nasser group of officers led by Col. Abdul Salem Arif. The Ba'athists were branded "deviationists" by the Arif regime, and many were forced to flee to Syria. In 1964 Arif created a joint presidency council that was intended to hasten the union of Egypt and Iraq, scheduled to take place in 1966. Later in 1964 Arif was killed in a plane crash and was succeeded by his brother, Abdul Rahman Arif.

Although it was obvious that union with Egypt was impractical, Abdul Rahman created an officially sponsored Iraqi Arab Socialist Union, patterned after the Egyptian model. It was intended to mobilize popular support for the regime's modernization schemes and to serve as the main channel of communication between the government and the people. It failed on both counts. By 1968 the Arif government had ruined the national economy and faced serious internal opposition.

A coup in July 1968 brought the Ba'athists back to power. Officers aligned with the Ba'ath party were led by Maj. Gen. Ahmed Hassan al-Bakr, a key figure in the 1958 and 1963 coups. He assumed the presidency and set a harsh authoritarian tone for his regime by directing that "all spies for the United States, Israel, imperialism, and Zionism" be arrested. A former president, two former prime ministers, numerous high-ranking officers, and prominent members of the Shi'ite Moslem and Kurdish communities were executed. In July 1979 al-Bakr resigned because of poor health. His vice president, Saddam Hussein, succeeded him.

Almost from the beginning of the Ba'ath party rule, Saddam Hussein served as the regime's leading policy maker on national and international issues. He negotiated with Iran the 1975 Treaty of International Boundaries and Good Neighborliness, which settled longstanding border disputes. Many experts credit him with the expansion of Iraq's commercial ties to Western markets in the early 1970s.

Ba'athism

Ba'athism is first and foremost a pan-Arab movement with broad appeal to the diverse sectarian interests in Iraq. The party regards existing national borders as West-imposed artificial barriers that must one day be eliminated if Arab unity is to be achieved. During the 1970s this viewpoint led to poor relations with some conservative Arab states, whose leaders were reluctant to relinquish their national identity for unity in an all-Arab federation presumably led by either Egypt or Iraq.

The philosophy of the Ba'ath party is central to Iraq's

political organization and policies. Ba'ath socialism emerged during the 1940s when European policies toward Middle Eastern nations were particularly oppressive and when Jewish immigration to Palestine was a major Arab concern. The party's founders were three Paris-educated, middle-class Syrians—one a Sunni Moslem, one a Greek Orthodox Christian, and one a member of an extremist Shi'ite sect. Its basic tenets were pan-Arab, secular, and socialist. They rejected communism as contrary to pan-Arabism and lacking in the spiritual qualities essential to the Arab way of life. Their national socialist approach was meant to include all Arabs as a single indivisible political unit; that is, the Arab nation.

The Ba'ath party maintains that ethnic and linguistic modes of identity should be suppressed. Socialism is upheld as the only way to destroy the traditional Arab aristocracy and extend economic benefits to the lower classes. Private ownership of homes, businesses, and agricultural plots is permitted, but the renting of buildings and tenant farming is not.

A major factor in the Iraqi Ba'ath party's survival has been its capacity to control all the important functions of organized society. At each echelon of the state structure, beginning with local governments, there is a functionally parallel party organization that oversees the performance of the bureaucracy, sometimes even performing the bureaucratic service itself. Party links to the national level provide a line of vertical communication parallel to but distinct from that of the state. The heads of important bureaucracies are frequently high-ranking party members. At lower levels, the second in charge of an office often is a high-ranking party member who reports on his superior's performance and loyalty. Even Iraqi embassies have Ba'ath party cells, and Iraq's ambassador may not be the highest-ranking party member on the embassy's staff.

Party membership is selective and usually requires a long period of apprenticeship. There are only an estimated twenty-five thousand full party members, less than 0.2 percent of the population. If a member's behavior is judged by party leaders to be disloyal, scandalous, or imprudent, that member can be expelled from the party, imprisoned, or even executed.

During the early 1960s the Syrian and Iraqi Ba'ath parties were united, but in 1966 they split over differences concerning international issues and party leadership. Decision making in Iraq is centralized in the Ba'ath party's fifteen-member Revolutionary Command Council chaired by President Hussein. This council serves both as the nation's legislature and executive branch. Since 1982 several of the fifteen positions have remained unfilled. Hussein—as president, commander in chief of the armed forces, and head of the Ba'ath party—exerts nearly total control over Iraq's political system.

The Gulf War

The war with Iran overshadowed all other issues in Iraq from September 22, 1980, when Iraq attacked Iran, until Iran agreed to a cease-fire on July 18, 1988. Saddam Hussein's objective was to regain total control over the Shatt al-Arab. In addition, he hoped that an Iranian military defeat would cause the fall of the Ayatollah Khomeini. At the time of the Iraqi attack the Iranian government appeared to be vulnerable. Eighteen months after the revolution in Iran, individuals and groups were still struggling for influence within the government, and the military was in

total disarray following the purges of officers who had supported the shah.

A year after the war began, however, it became obvious that the Iraqi government had miscalculated. Initial success quickly turned to failure as a combination of poor strategy and equally bad tactical execution brought the invasion to a halt. By June 1982 Iran had driven the Iraqi army back to its own borders. President Hussein announced a unilateral cease-fire and expressed a willingness to negotiate through the Saudi Arabian government. Iran ignored the proposals and in July 1982 launched an attack across the border toward Basra. The Iranian offensive was stopped by the Iraqi army and the war degenerated into a stalemate.

In the first years of the war, Iraq had few international supporters. The Ba'ath party's repressive treatment of the Communists in 1977 and the greater geopolitical importance the Soviet Union placed on Iran led Moscow to suspend the delivery of military weapons to Iraq. Soon after the war began, Syria, Libya, and North Korea began supplying Iran with Soviet military equipment, apparently with Moscow's blessings. The Soviet Union did not resume arms shipments to Iraq until late 1983. The conservative Arab nations on the Persian Gulf initially hedged their support for Iraq out of concern that Iran might retaliate against them. At first the only Western nation that supported Iraq's war effort was France.

As the war dragged on, however, and as Iran's foreign policy became more aggressive, the Arab states and some nations in the West backed Iraq in the conflict. Although hesitant initially, Jordan, Kuwait, and Saudi Arabia expedited the transport of consumer goods through their ports to compensate for Iraq's closing of Iraq's port facilities. Moreover, Saudi Arabia, Kuwait, and other Gulf states had extended Iraq tens of billions of dollars in aid and interest-free loans. To compensate for Iraq's loss of oil revenues, Saudi Arabia and Kuwait agreed to sell three hundred thousand barrels a day of their own oil to Iraq's customers, with the understanding that Iraq would pay it back at some future time.

Fearing the consequences of an Iranian victory, Western and most Arab nations continued supporting Iraq, despite internal repression by the Hussein regime, Iraq's attacks on neutral ships doing business with Iran, and Iraq's use of brutal tactics, including air strikes against Iranian cities and poison gas attacks against Iranian troops. After several Iranian offensives in 1986 and 1987 failed to capture Basra, Iraqi forces pushed the Iranians back across the border in the spring and summer of 1988, causing an exhausted Iran finally to accept a cease-fire.

Current Issues

Although the cease-fire has held, Iraq and Iran have failed to conclude a formal peace agreement. Foremost among the issues that must be resolved is who controls the Shatt al-Arab waterway. Iraq wants to renegotiate the 1975 Algiers accord, which designated the center of the main channel of the river as the boundary. Iran, however, wants to preserve the 1975 agreement. Iran also wants Iraq to pay it reparations for starting the war, and both governments want the other to pledge not to support dissident movements within their countries. As of August 1989 little progress had been made on these issues. Peace negotiations potentially could drag on for years without a settlement. In the meantime, a 350-troop UN peacekeeping force patrols the 740-mile frontier between the belligerents, watching for cease-fire violations.

Economy. The war seriously damaged Iraq's economy by reducing oil exports and forcing huge expenditures on defense. To pay for the war Iraq built up a $60 billion foreign debt and liberally injected new currency into its economy. The resulting inflation reduced the value of the Iraqi dinar and squeezed most workers who had to be content with prewar salaries. Foreign goods are difficult for most Iraqis to buy and there have been shortages of some consumer goods in major cities.

In the long term, however, the war may give a boost to the Iraqi economy. It forced Hussein to abandon some of the Ba'ath party's socialist tenets and to expand the role of the private sector while streamlining the central bureaucracy. Privatization has increased productivity and relieved shortages of many agricultural products. In addition, Iraq's oil pipeline construction projects, undertaken to insulate its oil exports from Iranian bombings, have boosted its export capacity above prewar levels. Finally, rail and highway networks, including overland routes to Kuwait, Jordan, and Turkey, were expanded after Iranian forces sealed off access to the ports of Basra and Umm Qasr in the Persian Gulf.

Antiregime Movements. Saddam Hussein's regime faces opposition from several sources. A number of Shi'ite underground movements, all of which are to some degree in contact with the Iranian government, persistently harass the government. The most prominent of these movements are the Party of the Islamic Call (*Da'wa* for short) and the Moslem Warriors or Mujaheddin. The Da'wa, first reported as being involved in antiregime activities in the 1960s, has the most extensive popular support. Da'wa has been responsible for terrorist incidents in recent years, including the attempted assassination of high-level government and Ba'ath party officials.

The Mujaheddin formed in 1978 or 1979 around a group of young, deeply religious graduates of secular schools. Although the Mujaheddin are not so well organized and numerous as the Da'wa, they are believed to be the more violent of the two. Both draw their supporters from the slums of Baghdad and their political orientation from Muhammad Bakr al-Sadr, who became a martyr figure when he was executed by the Ba'athists in April 1980. Like the Da'wa, the Mujaheddin were radicalized by the 1979 Iranian revolution. It was in that year that the Mujaheddin began to resort to terrorist attacks on police outposts and Ba'ath party offices.

Although the Iraqi army's 1988 campaign against the Kurds in northern Iraq dealt a heavy blow to the Kurdish resistance movement, the Kurds were unlikely to give up their fight for political rights and greater autonomy.

The gravest threat to Saddam Hussein's regime, however, is the military itself. Hussein has attempted to maintain the predominance of the civilian wing of the Ba'ath party by placing trusted allies and members of his family in key command and intelligence positions within the military establishment. Nevertheless, Hussein must constantly guard against coup attempts by the military, such as the one reported to have occurred in December 1988. Peace may cause military officers who built up reputations during the war to become politically ambitious.

Foreign Relations. Iraq has been at odds with at least one of its neighbors since it gained independence in 1932. Before the 1958 coup, Iraq was the only Arab member of the Baghdad Pact and thus was at odds with the anti-

Western, pan-Arab policies of Syria and Egypt. After the coup, Iraq reversed its position and aggressively pursued pan-Arab socialism, which made it the ideological enemy of the conservative Arab states. In 1961 Iraq claimed that Kuwait was historically part of Iraq; only the presence of a British military force dissuaded President Qasim from invading Kuwait. In 1973 Baghdad pressed a similar claim on two small Kuwaiti islands off Umm Qasr. There also have been boundary disputes with Saudi Arabia, and before the 1970s both Saudi Arabia and Oman accused Iraq of supporting dissident movements in their countries.

The Gulf war, however, caused most Arab nations to rally around Iraq. Only Syria, Libya, and South Yemen supported Iran. The Arab states believed that if Iran won the war they would be vulnerable to Iranian subversion or even invasion. And an Iranian victory was likely to encourage unrest among their Shi'ite populations.

Another reason for Iraq's better position in the Middle East is the effort it has made to improve relations with fellow Arab nations. In 1976 Iraq became a major contributor to the Arab Fund for Economic and Social Development and the Islamic Development Fund. About the same time, it began providing bilateral aid to support imports of oil by nations of the Middle East and Africa, committing more than $1 billion to that effort by 1979. By the start of the war with Iran, Iraq had given nearly $9 million toward Egypt's balance of payments deficits, and Jordan had received more economic assistance from Iraq than from either Saudi Arabia or the United States. Iraq extended interest-free loans totaling more than $200 million to developing nations caught in the oil price rises of 1979.

Shortly after he became president and before the beginning of the war, Saddam Hussein demonstrated to the leaders of nearly all the conservative Arab states that he wished to establish close relations. During the winter of 1979 he was in constant contact with the leaders of Saudi Arabia and Jordan, and his visit to Saudi Arabia in August 1980 was the first by an Iraqi president in twenty-two years. In addition, high-ranking officials of the Ba'ath party and members of the cabinet communicated with their counterparts in most of the Arab states on the Persian Gulf and Jordan.

Since the war Iraq has continued to seek good relations with its Arab neighbors. In March 1989 King Fahd became the first Saudi king to visit Iraq since the Ba'athists seized power in 1968. Iraq also took a leading role in the creation of the Arab Cooperation Council, a loose economic union that Iraq, Egypt, Jordan, and North Yemen established in 1989.

Syria, however, remains a bitter Iraqi enemy, and Hussein is not likely to soon forgive Syria's President Hafez Assad for backing Iran in the Gulf war. Iraq expressed its enmity for Syria and its desire to be a major Middle East power broker by supplying military equipment in 1989 to Christian militia forces in Lebanon fighting to expel Syrian troops from their country.

Iraq's relations with the United States have been rocky since November 26, 1984, when Saddam Hussein announced the resumption of full diplomatic relations, which Iraq had severed because of U.S. support for Israel in the June 1967 Arab-Israeli war. In 1986 the renewed U.S.-Iraqi relationship was hurt by the disclosure that the administration of President Ronald Reagan had sold arms to Iran in an effort to build contacts among Iranian moderates and win the release of American hostages held in Lebanon. Iraq also accused the United States of providing it with false intelligence information. In May 1987 an Iraqi jet mistakenly fired a missile at the USS *Stark,* killing thirty-seven crew members. The United States accepted Iraq's explanation that the attack was an accident. The relationship improved that summer when the United States began naval patrols in the Persian Gulf to halt Iranian attacks on Kuwaiti ships. But another setback came in 1988, when the Reagan administration vigorously condemned Iraq for using chemical weapons against Kurdish rebels and civilians.

Outlook

Iraq's participation in the Arab Cooperation Council and its military aid to Lebanese Christians have demonstrated Saddam Hussein's intention to assert Iraqi influence in the Arab world now that the Gulf war is over. If Hussein can build his stature as a statesman he may be able to portray himself as indispensable to Iraq's standing in the Arab world, just as he portrayed himself as indispensable to Iraq's survival during the war. Given Iraq's military power, economic potential, and indebtedness to other Arab states, Arab leaders are likely to pursue closer relations with Baghdad. Syria, however, will remain Iraq's rival.

The possibility of economic recovery in Iraq is excellent. Its enormous oil reserves, second in size only to Saudi Arabia's, will provide it with substantial income for the foreseeable future. It also has more agricultural potential than any country in the Middle East and is expending large sums to develop its food production industries. Having lived through the deprivation caused by eight years of war, the Iraqi people have high expectations that the economy will improve swiftly. Failure to deliver on economic promises could create unrest among all ethnic and religious groups.

Despite Hussein's calls for political liberalization, his regime is likely to continue to dominate the political system through repression and stringent organizational control. Iran's appeal for an Islamic revolution in Iraq did not stir the Shi'ite masses to rebel, and the Da'wa and the Mujaheddin remain small groups. Yet Hussein's rule is in perpetual danger of a coup by the military.

Should Hussein be removed from power for any reason, the pervasiveness of the Ba'ath party in Iraqi society offers the possibility for a smooth transfer of political power to his successor. Exactly who that might be is shrouded in secrecy.

However, an orderly transition is contingent upon general agreement within the party concerning who the successor should be. If that agreement is absent, it is likely that the religious, communal, ethnic, and linguistic rivalries that have caused so much violence for centuries will resurface, and instability once again will dominate Iraq's political scene.

Can the Status Quo Endure?

In the spring of 1989 Israel faced a triple challenge. The more than one million Palestinians living in the occupied West Bank and Gaza Strip continued to defy Israeli rule through persistent violent and nonviolent acts. This uprising, or "intifada," in turn pushed the Palestine Liberation Organization (PLO) leadership to engage Israel in a diplomatic process aimed at effecting its withdrawal from the territories captured in the 1967 Arab-Israeli war.

Added to these tests was the continuing problem of Israel's underperforming economy, where increasing unemployment and the shakiness of major industrial and agricultural enterprises continued to command attention.

Yitzhak Shamir

Since its creation in 1948, Israel has fought five wars with its Arab neighbors—in 1948, 1956, 1967, 1973, and 1982—as well as a continuous war against Palestinian nationalism and its political manifestation—the PLO. In its early years Israel commanded the admiration of much of the world. This state of approximately three million (which has since swelled to more than four million) was widely perceived in the West as the underdog struggling to survive against a host of fanatical Arab enemies. Its intention to rebuild the Jewish people and establish an egalitarian society won the admiration of both East and West.

Today, however, Israel's continuing hostile occupation of territories seized in 1967 and the Palestinian uprising it has produced have begun to shift popular perceptions of Israel from that of victim to one of victimizer. Many foreign observers and some Israelis have questioned Israel's ability to maintain the political status quo given its economic problems, the difficulties of controlling the intifada, and international pressures to trade land for peace.

The Land and Its People

A small country about the size of New Jersey, Israel is sandwiched between the Mediterranean Sea and a crescent of Arab nations: Lebanon to the north, Syria to the northeast, Jordan and the West Bank to the east, and Egypt to the southwest. Egypt is the only neighbor with which Israel has signed a formal peace treaty, although the borders with Jordan and Syria have been quiet for more than a decade. On the Syrian-Israeli border in the Golan Heights, United Nations peacekeepers are interposed between the two antagonists.

Despite its size, Israel contains three disparate geographical regions: the coastal plain where most of the population resides, running from Haifa south to Tel Aviv; the Galilee region in the north, hilly and lush, and dominated by the Sea of Galilee; and the Negev Desert in the south, lacking both material and natural resources.

Most of the country enjoys a temperate climate, except for the Negev, which is hot and dry throughout the year. Water is an important commodity in the country because of the small amount of rainfall: twenty-eight inches annually in the north, nineteen to twenty-one inches in the central regions, and only one to eight inches in the Negev. Large investments have been made on desalinization, irrigation, and water conservation projects and water has been a prominent feature of Israel's disputes with Syria, Jordan, and Palestinians on the West Bank.

Almost totally devoid of natural resources of commercial value, Israel in its early years concentrated on agricultural production. Chemical manufacturing, diamond cutting and polishing, and developing high technology products with commercial and military applications have surpassed agriculture as the most important areas of Israel's modern economy. One out of four Israeli workers today is employed directly or indirectly by the arms industry. Even the kibbutz, the Socialist agricultural cooperatives that were the most prominent expression of the Jews' "Return to the Land," now earn more of their income through manufacturing than agricultural production.

A Nation of Immigrants

What Israel lacks in natural resources, it makes up for in the human talent of a culturally diverse population. Israel, like the United States, is a nation of immigrants. Israelis originate from more than one hundred countries. Among Israel's Jewish population, 57 percent are native born, 24 percent hail from Europe and the Western hemisphere, and 19 percent were born in Asia and Africa. Those of Western origin—the original Zionist "pioneers" and ideologues—are called Ashkenazim. Jews from Eastern lands, including

Key Facts on Israel

Area: 7,993 square miles.

Capital: Jerusalem; Tel Aviv is the diplomatic capital recognized by the United States.

Population: 4,297,000 (1988).

Religion: Predominantly Judaism; Arab minority is largely Moslem; also Christian Arabs who are chiefly Greek Catholic and Greek Orthodox.

Official Language: Hebrew. Arabic is used by 15 percent of the population. English is widely spoken.

GNP: $29.8 billion; $6,810 per capita (1987).

Sources: World Bank Atlas 1988; CIA World Factbook 1988

Spain, Turkey, Greece, Iraq, and Morocco, are called Sephardim. Sephardim and their native offspring now comprise 60 percent of the Jewish population. Israel's Arab population is approximately 15 percent of the total.

The creation of the state of Israel in 1948 brought about significant demographic changes. During the course of hostilities, more than 500,000 Palestinian Arabs living in what was to become the Jewish state fled or were expelled, ensuring an overwhelming Jewish majority of approximately 85 percent in the new nation.

Both the aftermath of the Holocaust and the formation of the Jewish state created conditions for a large scale "ingathering" of Jews in Israel. In 1948, 100,000 Jews languishing in European "displaced persons'" camps emigrated to Israel. The next year saw a massive influx of Jewish immigrants, including 250,000 from Turkey, Libya, Poland, Romania, and almost 50,000 from Yemen alone. From May 1950 to December 1951, Israel organized the emigration of 113,000 Iraqi Jews.

As a result of this influx, by 1951 Israel's 1948 Jewish population of 650,000 had more than doubled to 1.4 million. Not surprisingly, the population boom strained the resources of the young country. Many new immigrants, especially the largely poor, illiterate masses of Sephardim, were forced to live in shantytowns far from the established Jewish settlements along the coastal plain, breeding a resentment of Israel's Labor party establishment that contributed to the party's ouster in the 1977 elections and that continues today.

Zionism: A Search for a Home

Since the Roman destruction of Jerusalem's Second Temple in A.D. 70, the suppression of the Bar Kochba revolt sixty-five years later, and subsequent expulsion of Jews, the return to Zion has been a leitmotif of the Jewish people. The Old Testament proclaims the great religious significance of the Jews' return to Jerusalem: "If I forget thee O Jerusalem, let my right hand forget her cunning. If I do not remember thee, let my tongue cleave to the roof of my mouth: if I prefer not Jerusalem above my chief joy."

Not until the mid-nineteenth century did the confluence of political emancipation, racially based theories of nationalism, and state-sponsored anti-Semitism through-

out Europe create the conditions for an organized effort to reestablish Jewish sovereignty in Palestine. Early Zionist thinkers such as Moshe Hess, an associate of Karl Marx and author of *Rome and Jerusalem,* the first Zionist tract, Leo Pinsker, who in 1882 at the outset of the Russian pogroms wrote *Autoemancipation,* and Theodor Herzl, author of the seminal *Jewish State,* argued that the immutability of anti-Semitism and the "otherness" of Jews in nations created as expressions of non-Jewish cultural and racial purity required that Jews too create their own nation.

Creating a Jewish State

From 1882 to 1914 more than 2.5 million Jews emigrated from Eastern Europe, the heart of Ashkenazi Jewry. The overwhelming majority, however, emigrated to countries in the West. Only small numbers of ideologically committed Zionists emigrated to Palestine, where they established a variety of communal and capitalistic agricultural settlements. To gain popular support for his idea of a Jewish state, the indefatigable Herzl convened the First Zionist Congress in Basel, Switzerland, in 1897. The World Zionist Organization was established at this conference as part of a program that stated, "The aim of Zionism is to create for the Jewish people a home in Palestine secured by public law. . . ."

While Herzl and his successors tried to win diplomatic recognition of Zionist enterprise from the European and Ottoman powers, from 1910 onward the exponents of "practical Zionism," notably Chaim Weizmann, worked to create a new reality in Palestine by fostering Jewish settlement that would be difficult to uproot.

The exigencies of World War I prompted Britain to issue the Balfour Declaration on November 2, 1917, which promised British support for "the establishment in Palestine of a national home for the Jewish people." The statement was designed to gain Jewish support for the British war effort and ensure British control over Palestine if the shaky Ottoman Empire collapsed. British support for a Jewish national home was, however, to be conditioned upon an understanding that "nothing shall be done which may prejudice the civil and religious rights of existing non-Jewish communities in Palestine." This policy established the contradictory impulses that were to affect British actions toward Palestine until Jewish independence.

Upon the defeat of the Ottoman Empire in World War I, Britain and France collaborated to divide its Middle Eastern holdings. Palestine was placed under a new form of colonial supervision—British mandatory authority. The British mandate in Palestine was legitimized in 1920 by the League of Nations.

While the growing Jewish community in Palestine, known as the *Yishuv,* viewed the British mandate as an opportunity to expand Jewish control in Palestine, Palestinian Arabs saw British rule as a threat to Arab sovereignty and an obstacle to independence such as that granted or promised to Egypt, Iraq, Syria, and Lebanon. The Yishuv therefore adopted a strategy of cooperation with the British authorities and under its protection constructed the administrative, economic, and military building blocks of Jewish sovereignty. Arab efforts, organized around clan-based political parties, were far less successful in achieving the Arab aim of an end to British control and the creation of an Arab state in Palestine.

In 1947 an exhausted and overextended Britain announced that it would terminate its mandate over Palestine and withdraw on May 15, 1948. The fledgling United Nations was entrusted with the problem of determining the successor to the mandate. On November 29, 1947, the UN General Assembly proposed the partition of Palestine into separate Arab and Jewish states and the internationalization of Jerusalem. The Zionist leadership supported the UN·decision and prepared for statehood. Leaders of the Palestinian Arabs and the Arab League, a federation of seven Arab states formed in 1944, rejected partition.

In the succeeding months scattered warfare between Palestinian and Jewish irregulars occurred throughout Palestine. On May 14, 1948, David Ben-Gurion, the head of the Zionist Executive, the leadership body of the Yishuv, declared the establishment of the state of Israel and became the country's first prime minister and defense minister. From May until January 1949, when separate armistice agreements were initialed, armies from Egypt, Iraq, Syria, Jordan, and Lebanon fought unsuccessfully to abort Jewish statehood and, in Egypt's case, to prevent the expansion of Transjordan into most of the region earmarked for Palestinian Arab independence. Armistice agreements signed between the warring parties confirmed the viability of Jewish statehood, but they failed to fix permanent boundaries or to establish contractual peace between the new state and its neighbors.

Religion and Politics

Since the first days of their nation's creation, Israelis have debated the proper role of religion in the Jewish state. Although similar to secular democracies in its parliamentary form of government, Israel is unique in its foundation as a specifically constituted religious state in which Jews anywhere are automatically entitled to Israeli citizenship and privileged treatment by the government. This privileged position for Jews is the raison d'etre of the state, and its ramifications are a source of never-ending debate in Israel.

All issues of religious identification, marriage, birth certification, and divorce are the province of religious authorities, who, while supported by the state, exercise their authority relatively independently. There is, for example, no institution for secular marriage or divorce, which continues to be the province of Moslem, Christian, or Jewish religious authorities. For Jews in such cases, only the Orthodox Jewish establishment (as opposed to reform or conservative trends) is recognized as legitimate.

The continuing power and authority of religious institutions in a modern democracy is a function of political expediency as well as the undeniable influence of Jewish religious tradition on the modern ideology of Zionism. Every Israeli government formed since the state's birth has included the vital participation of religious parties as part of the governing parliamentary coalition. As a price for their political support, these parties have exacted commitments—until 1977 from the Mapai and its successor, the Labor alignment, and since then from the Likud—that provide for the continuing and expanding role of orthodox religious principles in various aspects of public and private life, from divorce law to the playing of soccer on the Sabbath.

Arab-Israeli Wars

The issues left unresolved after the first Arab-Israeli war have been a source of constant confrontation in succeeding decades. On four occasions—1956, 1967, 1973, and 1982—this endemic conflict erupted into full-scale military hostilities. *(For a detailed description of the five Arab-Israeli wars, see Chapter 3.)*

In October 1956 Israel, in coordination with France and Great Britain, launched an invasion into the Sinai aimed at toppling Egyptian leader Gamal Abdel Nasser, opening the port of Eilat to maritime commerce and neutralizing Palestinian fedayeen (guerrilla) attacks mounted from the Gaza Strip. The invasion did succeed in opening the port of Eilat to international commerce, but it boosted rather than deflated Nasser's prestige, and it brought unprecedented Soviet-American pressure upon Israel to withdraw to the preinvasion boundaries. From this episode Israel learned the importance of gaining U.S. support for its military ventures. It would never again begin a major military operation without first receiving what it considered to be a "green light" from Washington.

In June 1967 Israel launched a successful preemptive attack against the Egyptian and Syrian air forces. In the following days the Israeli Defense Force (IDF) gained control of Syria's Golan Heights, the Jordanian West Bank, including East Jerusalem, the Egyptian-administered Gaza Strip, and Egypt's Sinai Peninsula bordering the strategic Suez Canal. Israel thus gained control of the entire post-1921 mandatary Palestine. Israeli analysts contended that the addition of territory on three vulnerable fronts gave Israel the "strategic depth" necessary to defend its borders that pre-1967 Israel lacked.

Egypt and Syria, however, were determined to avenge their defeat. In the absence of any diplomatic progress, the two countries launched a coordinated, surprise offensive on October 6, 1973. Both Syria and Egypt had limited territorial objectives, aimed at recovering territories lost in June 1967.

The initial Syrian and Egyptian offensives startled Israel, which had grown complacent and disdainful of Arab capabilities after the relatively easy 1967 victory. In the Sinai, Israel's vaunted Bar-Lev Line was breached, while in the Golan civilians were hurriedly evacuated from Jewish settlements constructed after 1967 as the Syrians advanced early in the fighting. These outposts proved to be an obstacle to rather than a vehicle for Israel's defense of the Golan.

Within days, Israel, aided by timely U.S. resupply, had turned back the Arab assault and gained the military advantage. In negotiations following a cease-fire, Israel and Syria reached a detailed disengagement agreement that has been scrupulously maintained. Egyptian-Israeli talks resulted in an interim agreement on the Sinai, which opened the way to a complete Israeli withdrawal from occupied Egyptian territory and the Israeli-Egyptian peace treaty of 1979.

In June 1982 Israel launched an invasion of Lebanon. The Israelis hoped to decimate the political as well as the military power of the PLO, which had successfully frustrated Israeli efforts to win Palestinian acquiescence to permanent Israeli rule in the occupied West Bank and Gaza Strip. Israel also wanted to establish a new political order in Lebanon based on the rule of the Christian Phalange party led by its military leader, Bashir Gemayel. Finally, the Israelis aimed to humiliate Syria and remove it from its historical position of influence over Lebanese affairs. The war failed in each of these objectives and brought an ignominious end to the tenure of Menachem Begin, Israel's longest-serving prime minister, in 1983. The controversial nature of Israel's "war of choice" created divisions among the Israeli people that have yet to heal.

Parliamentary Government

Israel has a parliamentary form of government: the prime minister is the head of government and the president is the head of state. The powers of the president are very limited; it is the prime minister who is responsible for maintaining a ruling coalition and for running the government. The Knesset, Israel's unicameral parliament, has 120 members. To form a government, a party must win a 61-seat majority, a feat that has yet to be accomplished, or form a coalition with one or more minority parties.

Unlike members of the U.S. Congress or British Parliament, Israel's legislators do not stand for election as representatives from a geographic district. Consequently, the primary allegiance of members is to their party, and party discipline is exacting. Candidates selected by the party apparatus run on a single slate. Voters therefore do not cast their vote for a particular candidate but for a single party. Each party can present a complete list of 120 candidates, although in practice only the two major parties make such an effort. The first name on each party list is that party's choice for prime minister.

The number of seats allocated to each party is determined by the percentage of votes it receives. To qualify for a Knesset seat a party must gain at least 1 percent of the valid votes cast. The total number of valid votes for all eligible parties is then divided by 120 to determine the minimum number of votes required for each seat. Each party is given the largest number of seats possible. Any seats not distributed in this fashion are awarded to those parties with the largest number of remaining votes. If any seats still remain unassigned, they are given to the parties with the largest number of seats.

This method of proportional representation has all but guaranteed a faction-ridden parliament and created a situation where never in Israel's short history has a single party commanded a Knesset majority, forcing the creation of a succession of coalition governments. In the current Knesset formed in 1988, for example, fifteen different parties are represented.

When no single party controls a majority of Knesset seats, it must join with smaller parties to gain the confidence of the Knesset in a coalition government. After the election the president, in his most important role, consults with the leaders of all parties to determine which has the greatest likelihood of forming a government. He then asks the leader of that party to form a government within a specified period, which under certain circumstances can be extended.

1977 Elections

The victory of Menachem Begin's Likud party was a political earthquake of the first order. For the first time since the establishment of the state the political embodiment of Israel's pioneering and state-building generation, the Labor party, had been forced from power. This landmark election had important ideological and political consequences. The Likud was unambiguous in its view that the West Bank—Judea and Samaria in its vocabulary—was an inseparable part of the "Land of Israel" promised by God to the Jewish people. It replaced the Labor alignment's security rationale for remaining permanently in the occupied territories with one based upon divine right.

Unfettered by Labor's desire to maintain a negotiating posture that did not rule out some degree of withdrawal from the territories as part of a peace settlement, the Likud embarked upon an ambitious settlement drive throughout the West Bank and Gaza, expanding the areas Labor had marked for eventual annexation. The Likud settlement program attempted to create a new reality of more than one hundred Jewish settlements and hundreds of thousands of Jewish settlers in the territories. Likud leaders believed such a settlement program would subvert any attempt to trade territory for peace as outlined in UN Security Council resolutions 242 and 338 adopted after the 1967 war.

The philosophy of the Herut (freedom) party, the dominant element of the Likud bloc, is rooted in the thinking of Vladamir Jabotinsky, a prestate Zionist leader who broke with Labor and Liberal Zionists over the means necessary to achieve Jewish sovereignty. Jabotinsky advocated a plan of militant resistance against both the British and the Arabs, best expressed in his theory that the Jewish community should erect an "Iron Wall" of Jewish sovereignty throughout the Land of Israel, against which the Arab world would eventually become reconciled. He and his followers, among them Menachem Begin and Yitzhak Shamir, rejected any partition of the biblical Land of Israel and called for Jewish settlement on both sides of the Jordan River.

1981 Elections

Israel's worsening economic condition, highlighted by a November 1980 announcement of an annual inflation rate of 200 percent, set the stage for the 1981 election contest.

Labor fielded a team headed by Shimon Peres, the party leader since 1977, and Yitzhak Rabin, the former prime minister and perennial challenger to Peres's leadership. Peres prevailed once again over Rabin in preelection party wrangling, but his victory represented less an ideological victory than an acknowledgement of Peres's ability to manage the petty factionalism engulfing the party. Indeed, its election platform regarding the occupied territories was described by party elder Israel Galili as aimed at "refuti[ing] the Likud's false assertions that if the Alignment comes to power it will guide the ship of state weak kneed back to the June 4, 1967 lines."

Begin, however, made Labor's ostensible "softness" on the issue of the territories the centerpiece of his electoral campaign. Begin labeled Peres a "Husseinist" for his advocacy of territorial compromise. The economy, too, enjoyed a temporary upsurge. A new finance minister manipulated fiscal and tax regulations to put more cash in the hands of Israeli voters. The destruction of Iraq's nuclear reactor by a daring Israeli air attack only weeks before the election also increased the popularity of Begin and his party. Peres, on the other hand, was pelted with tomatoes and prevented from addressing the annual festival of Moroccan Jews in Jerusalem. Sephardic antipathy toward Labor, the product of a generation of discrimination and neglect by Labor's Ashkenazi leadership, had yet to subside.

Labor and the Likud each won forty-eight seats in the Knesset balloting. The preference of the religious parties for the Likud led to a coalition government headed by Begin and marked Labor's second consecutive defeat.

Sephardim and Ashkenazim

Israeli can be said to be composed of three major ethnic groups. Ashkenazi Jews and their offspring are approximately 35 percent of the population, Palestinian Arabs inside Israel proper comprise about 15 percent, and Sephardic Jews make up almost 50 percent. If the population of the West Bank, Gaza Strip, and Golan Heights is included, the Jewish majority in the region between the Mediterranean Sea and Jordan River shrinks from 85 percent to about 60 percent of the total. Demographers estimate that parity between the two groups will be reached early in the twenty-first century.

Much has been made of the antagonisms that exist within the Jewish community between Ashkenazim and Sephardim. These differences are as much the product of the economic gulf dividing the two communities as any cultural dissimilarities. The Ashkenazis are Israel's founders. Political Zionism is a European creed; the institutions of the state—the Knesset, the kibbutz economy, and most significantly the army—are Ashkenazi creations, to which the Sephardic majority has come late and the Arab minority hardly at all.

The waves of Sephardi immigration were welcomed by Israel's leadership in the 1950s, but the key to their integration into Israeli life was predicated on their adoption of the dominant Ashkenazi culture. Israeli society was European and reflected the traditions of Ashkenazi Jews, who viewed their coreligionists from Yemen and Iraq with disdain and not a little chauvinism. This kind of assimilation proved impossible for Sephardim, who possessed a varied and vibrant heritage of their own. In addition, their comparatively large families, lack of education, and meager financial resources put them at additional disadvantage. Begin's Likud capitalized on this growing sense of discrimination beginning in 1977.

The disparities dividing the two Jewish communities remain. In educational and economic achievement and political representation, the Sephardic majority still has not overcome structural barriers established in previous generations. Particularly in a period of economic recession, such as the one Israel was experiencing in the late 1980s, the poor Jewish residents of the inner city and development towns, along with Israeli Arabs, feel the brunt of retrenchment and cutbacks in state services.

The Labor party has not been popular with the Sephardic majority living in development towns and poorer urban areas. It has lacked the populist appeal—hawkishness on foreign policy and the antiestablishment rhetoric of the have-nots on economic matters—that the Likud has exploited so successfully.

Israel's Arab minority are ostensibly full members of Israel's political culture. They vote, and Arab politicans are present in the Knesset. As a community, however, they suffer as non-Jews in a Jewish state. This prejudiced condition is apparent in economic development and government assistance, education, employment, and housing—all sectors where state-supported discrimination exists and is supported by law.

1984 Elections

The 1984 elections occurred against a background of military stagnation in Lebanon and growing economic problems. Begin, stunned by the death of his wife and traumatized by Israel's failure to end the PLO's political challenge to Israeli hegemony in the occupied territories, resigned the premiership in August 1983. His successor, Yitzhak Shamir, a veteran of the Jewish underground and the Mossad, Israel's CIA, was initially viewed as a caretaker whose tenure would not disrupt the ambitions of the Likud's second generation: Moshe Arens, David Levy, and Ariel Sharon. In the months following his appointment, Shamir wrestled with exploding inflation and dwindling foreign currency reserves, a crisis in Israel's Lebanon policy that portended a controversial, indefinite occupation of parts of that country, and incipient challenges to his leadership by the Likud's young guard. His continued tenure as party leader was a measure of his political acumen.

The results of the July 1984 elections resulted in a national unity coalition government unique in Israeli history. The willingness of Israel's two major political blocs to rule together suggested that the issues separating them were more apparent than real. There had been one unity government previously, formed in the months before the June 1967 war under Labor's leadership. The 1984 coalition agreement, however, called for an unprecedented rotation of the premiership between Shamir and Labor party leader Shimon Peres. Each man would serve as prime minister for two years while the other was foreign minister, and both major parties would be awarded an equal number of cabinet portfolios.

It was widely anticipated that such a "two-headed" government was a prescription for disaster. The government confounded these expectations, however. Inflation was tamed without a significant increase in unemployment or decreases in purchasing power, postponing if not solving the country's economic problems. A compromise withdrawal of the IDF from Lebanon was effected, reestablishing the security zone run by the surrogate South Lebanese Army with IDF logistical and military support.

Colonization efforts in the occupied territories continued uninterrupted, albeit at a slower pace, during the stewardship of both Peres and Shamir.

"All the forces operative on the ground since Begin assumed power in 1977," wrote Israeli analyst Meron Benvenisti in 1986, "have continued to operate with tremendous drive under Peres. In the last two years the government has spent $300 million in order to advance Israeli interests in the territories. In comparison to cuts in other development budgets, the relative proportion of investments in the West Bank has even risen." Yet, even as investment remained steady, the number of Jewish settlers dwindled. In 1985, for example, only 4,800 Jews moved to the West Bank, down from 15,000 in 1983.

Policy in the occupied territories was managed during the government's entire four-year tenure by Labor's Yitzhak Rabin. It was during this period that a new chapter in the "Iron Fist," a series of tough, repressive measures against a restive Palestinian population, emboldened by economic hardship and the continuation of the status quo, was put into effect. Deportation and administrative detention of Palestinian suspects, two measures that had fallen into relative disuse during the Begin era, were resurrected by Rabin as he attempted to quell the growing number of violent confrontations.

Intifada

What has become known as the Palestinian uprising or intifada was sparked by a series of incidents in the Gaza Strip in the second week of December 1987. Violent confrontation between Palestinians of all ages and the IDF and Jewish settlers has become a constant feature of life in the territories since then. Almost five-hundred Palestinians and approximately twenty-five Israeli Jews have been killed within two years, undermining the assumptions upon which a generation of Israeli occupation policy has been based.

Israel's response to massive Palestinian protests, involving, for the first time in the history of the occupation, the sustained participation of all sectors of the Palestinian community, was grounded in its longstanding determination to crush any manifestation of opposition to Israeli rule. As far as Israelis and Palestinians were concerned, a state of war existed between the two antagonists.

"A political solution," Prime Minister Shamir explained, "is not always what puts an end to the opposition of one's enemy to one's existence. First of all, one must repel the dangers and then think about peace, if that is possible." Palestinian political demands, aimed at undermining the policies of de facto annexation and Israel's refusal to negotiate with the PLO, were ignored.

Instead, Defense Minister Rabin described Israeli policy on January 21, 1988, as one of "force, might, and blows." By the end of February, 80 Palestinians had been killed and 650 wounded in almost 5,000 recorded violent confrontations. A U.S. organization, Physicians for Human Rights, issued a report after a delegation visited the occupied territories. It charged the Israeli government with implementing "an essentially uncontrolled epidemic of violence by soldiers and police in the West Bank and Gaza Strip, on a scale and degree of severity that poses the most serious medical, ethical, and legal problems."

In January 1989, Amnesty International charged that the methods Israel has employed in its unsuccessful effort to end the revolt "show that the Israeli Government is apparently not willing to enforce international human rights standards."

The intifada is coordinated by the National Command of the Uprising, a clandestine committee in the territories composed of representatives of the Palestinian resistance organizations. The command's exhortations—for strikes, protests, and boycotts of Israeli goods and the services provided by the military government—are implemented by semiautonomous "strike forces," organized from the street to the regional level. The absence of any single organizational center has enabled the various strike forces to function despite arrests and detentions numbering over 20,000. Popular Committees, also formed on the street and neighborhood level, coexist and support the strike forces. The committees' purpose is to implement the Palestinian strategy of self-reliance in the wake of the vacuum created by the virtual paralysis of local administrative and educational institutions and to mobilize the community to boycott institutions of the military administration.

The IDF has failed to impose a military solution on the uprising, which continues as a communal challenge to Israeli rule. Indeed, one officer, when asked why the army simply didn't arrest the revolt's leaders, replied, "We do not want to have more detainees than inhabitants." Nonetheless, proponents of a military solution to the uprising remain in the ascendancy in the Israeli government.

The political program of the uprising has always noted the allegiance of Palestinians in the occupied territories to the leadership of the PLO. The decision of the Palestine National Council to recognize Israel and endorse UN Resolutions 242 and 338 in November 1988 was seen as a victory for Palestinians under occupation, who have long urged the PLO to adopt a realistic diplomatic posture toward Israel.

The intifada is seen as a vital complement to the PLO's diplomatic strategy aimed at winning an Israeli withdrawal from the occupied territories and the realization of Palestinian sovereignty. It has failed, however, to move Israelis to adopt a political program based on a territorial rather than a functional (the granting of autonomy) solution to the twenty-two-year-old occupation.

1988 Elections

The National Unity Government established after the 1984 elections served a full four-year term, which in itself was an achievement. The 1988 elections were in large measure a public referendum on the record of this unique form of political accommodation. The election, conducted against a background of political and economic crisis, continued the drift of the Israeli electorate toward the religious, chauvinist right and confirmed continuing popular support for hard-line policies against the Palestinian uprising. Labor, led by Shimon Peres, won 39 seats in the 120-member Knesset. Shamir's Likud also won 39 seats.

The 1988 election underscored several important political trends. Israel's Arab voters emerged as the most significant electoral obstacle to the creation of a decisive right-wing majority. Small right-wing parties, and particularly anti-Zionist religious parties, emerged as key players in subsequent coalition negotiations. Labor, in contrast, was preoccupied with recriminations, directed primarily at Peres, who had failed to lead Labor to an electoral victory in four straight elections.

In one of the many commentaries about the demise of Labor, noted Israeli historian Ze'ev Sternhal observed, "[Labor's] base of support declined gradually and it has lost its grip in all sectors of society. The process is uniform and constant in the big cities and in the farming areas, in the local councils and development towns. The 'new faces' did not help, nor the efforts of internal democratization. . . .

The Labor Party no longer appeals to the Israeli. It is hard to point to any social group that votes for it with pleasure and faith."

The U.S. decision to begin a "substantive dialogue" with the PLO in December 1988 contributed to the decision of Labor and Likud to reestablish the National Unity Government, if only to present Washington with a wall-to-wall coalition opposed to including the PLO in the diplomatic process. This new unity government, unlike its predecessor, would function under the unchallenged leadership of the Likud. The terms of this power-sharing agreement placed Yitzhak Shamir as prime minister for the life of the government. Labor's Yitzhak Rabin remained in the pivotal post of defense minister, the second most powerful position in Israel. Shimon Peres accepted the finance portfolio, a measure of Labor's preeminent concern to safeguard the future of its ailing kibbutz and industrial establishments, and also of Peres's eclipse as a political force.

Foreign Policy

Israel's foreign policy is defined by its role as a protagonist in the conflict with its Arab neighbors and its de facto alliance with the United States, which has guaranteed Israel's military superiority over its enemies. Despite their differences, Israel's major parties have defined a national consensus supporting permanent Israeli hegemony in the area between the Mediterranean Sea and the Jordan River, the annexation of the Golan Heights won from Syria in the 1967 war, and the central importance of maintaining close military and political ties with the United States.

Israel and the United States have maintained good ties since Israel's creation in 1948, when the United States was the first country to grant Israel de facto recognition. Israel is the largest single recipient of U.S. foreign aid, currently amounting to $3 billion annually ($1.8 billion for military aid, $1.2 billion for economic aid) in outright grant assistance. Israel also has had the support of the Democratic and Republican parties, as well as the AFL-CIO. Israel has been the staunchest U.S. ally in the United Nations, voting with the United States more than any other country.

An important symbol of U.S.-Israel cooperation is the Joint Memorandum on Strategic Cooperation, agreed to by the Reagan administration, which has established a variety of institutional mechanisms between the defense establishments of both countries for military and intelligence coordination. Also during the Reagan administration, Israel became a key player in Washington's covert efforts to reestablish ties with and sell arms to the Iranian government, to support the Christian parties in Lebanon, and to fund the contra rebels in Nicaragua.

While no issue has challenged the essential comity of interests upon which U.S.-Israeli relations are based, there have been occasions when the two nations have clashed over goals, actions, and priorities. Israeli collaboration with the joint French-British invasion of Egypt in 1956 is the most notable instance of such conflict. More recent examples include the "agonizing reappraisal" of U.S.-Israeli relations undertaken by President Gerald R. Ford before the signing of the second Israeli-Egyptian disengagement agreement in 1975, Washington's temporary interruption of military deliveries after Israel's destruction of the Iraqi nuclear reactor and the bombing of PLO headquarters in Beirut, and the arrest of Jonathan Pollard, who passed U.S. secrets to Israel. Israel also opposed the 1982 Reagan peace plan and Secretary of State George P. Shultz's "territory

for peace" suggestions formulated in the wake of the intifada as well as the inauguration of a dialogue with the PLO. Prime Minister Shamir has derided the Bush administration's opposition to Greater Israel and continued Jewish settlement in the occupied territories as "useless."

While both Labor and Likud share the commitment to maintaining U.S. support and assistance, the Likud has historically been less committed than Labor to maintaining the atmospherics of amity so important when Labor ruled. Similarly, because its rationale for continuing occupation is often formulated in terms of divine and not diplomatic or military necessity, the Likud is seen by American policy makers as a more strident and difficult, albeit more authentic, representative of Israel's point of view.

Even though all Arab League member nations are in a formal state of war with Israel, Israel's policies toward them are not uniform. Syria poses the most serious threat to Israel because of its modern military arsenal and because of the country's formidable president Hafez al-Assad and his determination to reach "strategic parity" with Israel as a precondition to any diplomacy.

Jordan and Lebanon pose a qualitatively different degree of threat. Lebanon has never posed a military danger to Israel although its destruction has resulted in the use of its sovereign territory by irregular forces hostile to Israel. In military terms Israel considers Lebanon an extension of its hostile border with Syria and, as the 1982 invasion demonstrated, an arena of potential Israeli-Syrian military confrontation. In recent years the vacuum of central authority has enabled both Israel and Syria to employ Lebanon as an arena for creating buffer zones and competing spheres of influence. Israel has established a "security zone" in Lebanese territory administered by the IDF-supported South Lebanese Army.

Nonbelligerency has characterized relations with Jordan in recent years. In the wake of Jordan's loss of the West Bank in 1967, both countries established a number of informal arrangements aimed at preserving a measure of Jordanian influence in the occupied territories and maintaining vital commercial, family, and trade links between the two banks of the Jordan. This "functional compromise" was complemented by Labor's "Jordanian option," which called for Israel's annexation of approximately 30 percent of the West Bank, with the remainder to be returned to Jordanian sovereignty. The increasing importance of the PLO after 1973 made this strategy increasingly problematic. King Hussein's dramatic August 1988 announcement severing Jordan's links with the West Bank has forced Labor to reappraise Jordan's utility as a potential negotiating partner.

The Likud has adopted a more aggressive attitude toward Jordan, consistent with its view of Jordan as a Palestinian state. A Likud leadership might be less disposed to preserve Hashemite rule than was Labor, which during Hussein's battle with Syrian-backed PLO forces in September 1970 acted as a counterweight to Syrian intervention.

Although the Israel-Egypt peace treaty is ten years old, the two countries' long history of hostility and enmity remains a vital component of their new relationship. Their "cold peace" is a product of the continuing stalemate over the occupied territories, Egypt's anger about Israel's invasion of Lebanon in 1982, and Israel's disappointment at the absence of significant trade, cultural, and tourism ties. Both nations, however, have faithfully implemented the central elements of their peace treaty. The long-simmering border dispute at Taba on the Gulf of Aqaba has been settled in Egypt's favor, and Egypt has removed itself from the alignment of Arab nations ranged hostilely against Israel.

Economic Problems

Israel's economic development has been shaped by its isolation from the markets and resources of neighboring countries and the requirements of maintaining extraordinary expenditures on defense. Lacking almost entirely in natural resources, denied local export markets, and tied by tradition, education, and foreign policy to Europe and the United States, Israel has built an economy that remains a captive to these forces.

The conclusions of a November 1984 U.S. Senate Foreign Relations Committee staff report have remained relevant through the 1980s: "The economic crisis gripping Israel today, if not swiftly and effectively addressed by the new unity government, could pose as serious a threat to the security of Israel as any hostile neighbor in the region."

During its first twenty years of existence, Israel had an annual average inflation rate of 7 percent. The tremendous costs of financing the October 1973 war, however, pushed inflation to nearly 40 percent by 1976. By the end of the decade annual rates were running at 130 percent. But the disruptive effects of such a spiral were almost completely offset by a complex scheme of indexation which ensured that the purchasing power of wage earners did not suffer.

The economic stimulation program implemented by a Likud government in the early part of the 1980s, combined with the expenditures required by the invasion of Lebanon, pushed Israel's inflation rate to almost 400 percent by 1984. A new currency, the third in less than a decade, was created. Unemployment, traditionally a rarity in Israel's full-employment economy, rose to 5.9 percent. Even so, Israel's economy has proved remarkably resilient. Its per capita gross domestic product is almost $8,000, by far the highest in the region, and its standard of living approaches that of Greece or Spain. Almost 20 percent of Israel's budget of $25 billion (fiscal 1988) is covered by foreign grants and loans, including an annual grant of $3 billion from the United States, and approximately $500 million in grants from the world Jewish community.

Israel spends a sizable 22 percent of its gross national product on defense. An additional 46 percent of GNP is devoted to servicing Israel's $26 billion debt. Since the prestate era, Israel has invested a large segment of its national resources in creating a national arms industry, primarily to ensure a reliable source of supply. Since the 1970s, however, the maintenance and expansion of a defense industry producing top-of-the-line weapons systems for the IDF required Israel to join the international competition for foreign arms sales. Israel is today one of the world's leading arms exporters, with annual sales of military equipment and related electronics estimated in excess of $1 billion. Israel's military-industrial complex—which includes the kibbutz sector—and diamond cutting now dominate industrial production and export sales, a significant change from the era when citrus and agricultural products were the country's most significant earners of foreign currency and its most popular international symbols.

Israel's weapons industry is taking part in the U.S. Strategic Defense Initiative program, most notably in the development of an antitactical ballistic missile defense.

The Likud has been committed to reducing the presence of the state in the national economy, a legacy of Labor's leadership. After more than a decade in power, however, the Likud presides over a state budget that accounts for more than 75 percent of GNP, and many subsidy and indexation programs remain intact.

The central mandate the National Unity Government established after the 1984 elections was to find a way out of Israel's plunging economic fortunes. According to the Commerce Department's report on Israel, the government's Economic Stabilization Program "produced marked successes through 1986 and early 1987." Hyperinflation was reduced to 16 percent; foreign exchange reserves increased to $5.3 billion; the budget was balanced in 1986 and showed a small deficit ($700 million) in 1987; and GNP, which had grown annually by 7 to 9 percent until the late 1960s, and which had stagnated by the early 1980s, grew in the 1985-1987 period by approximately 5.5 percent annually. Yet the Commerce Department survey warned that "without further reform, the improvements brought about by stability are not permanent."

The Palestinian uprising further complicated Israeli efforts to get its economic house in order. Increased expenditures by the defense, justice, and police ministries; the increase in reserve days of military service Israeli Jewish men are required to serve; depressed exports to the territories; decreased tourism; and an erratic labor supply from the occupied territories were prominent features of this additional burden upon the Israeli economy.

In March 1989 Israel's unemployment rate reached 8.2 percent. Particularly hard hit have been development towns in the north and south of the country. Major industrial enterprises such as the Koor conglomerate have been forced to retrench, resulting in widespread layoffs.

Outlook

The continuing vitality of the concept of a national unity government, expressed, for example, in a May 1989 cabinet endorsement of Prime Minister Shamir's plan to hold elections in the West Bank and Gaza Strip, is important in three respects. First, the concept symbolizes the compact between Israel's two major parties supporting a solution to the status of the occupied areas based upon a restrictive autonomy under permanent Israeli control rather than withdrawal and Palestinian independence. Second, it is an enduring testament to the absence of politically significant conflict between Israel's two major, and ostensibly antagonistic, political parties. Finally, it confirms the ascendancy of the Likud, and the concomitant decline of Labor, as Israel's most authentic political voice.

The U.S. decision to begin a "substantive dialogue" with the PLO in late 1988 also served to unify Labor and Likud. Both parties agree in their assessment that this initiative presents a dangerous challenge to longstanding American-Israeli collaboration in support of the territorial status quo.

"For the PLO," explained Prime Minister Shamir, "a Palestinian state is the minimum. Therefore, anyone who engages in negotiations with it in effect accepts this principle. What else can one talk about with the PLO, if not about a Palestinian state?"

The idea for autonomy, articulated in the Camp David accords but out of fashion in the diplomacy of the eighties, has been resurrected by the new government as Israel's response to the twin challenge posed by the intifada and the U.S.-PLO rapprochement. Israel has apparently received a vital U.S. endorsement for its strategy to move diplomacy away from the question of withdrawal (and thus consideration of demands for sovereignty presented by the PLO) and toward a reconsideration of autonomy, which Israel sees as a means to remain permanently in the contested territories.

Maintaining its presence in the territories, while sustaining key American economic, military, and diplomatic support, is the central element of current Israeli foreign policy.

Israel's economy presents an equal, if not greater, challenge. Past economic failures and the challenges offered by the Free Trade Agreement with the United States, the creation of a unified market in Europe, and the contraction of demand in the international arms market will require far-reaching structural economic changes if Israel is to build a stable foundation for future development.

JORDAN

Freed of Central Role in Arab-Israeli Crisis

Since its origins in the aftermath of World War I, Jordan has been challenged by its stronger and wealthier neighbors. Its Hashemite kings have been the target of innumerable assassination attempts. The current king, Hussein ibn Talal, was present when his grandfather was killed on the steps of the Al-Aqsa Mosque in Jerusalem in 1951 by a young Palestinian. Sixteen-year-old Hussein survived that day only because the bullet intended for him was deflected off a medal on his tunic. The challenges to the rule of the Hashemites have not diminished in the intervening years.

Hussein ibn Talal

Jordan is a poor nation surrounded by regionally powerful states. Most of the attention and aid Jordan has received since 1948 from the great powers and from other Arab states have been given because of Jordan's pivotal position in the Arab-Israeli conflict. King Hussein, who claimed to represent the West Bank and had extensive ties to the Palestinian population there, was viewed by many nations since he became king in 1953 as one of the most important players in the Arab-Israeli conflict. With his own kingdom comprising a population that is about 60 percent Palestinian, Hussein has struggled to preserve its integrity and his leadership and to achieve the kind of resolution to Arab-Israeli and inter-Arab conflicts that would be conducive to a peaceful, prosperous Jordan.

This shrewd tactician and master of cautious flexibility weathered the conflicts between Arabs and Israelis and between Arabs and Arabs for thirty-five years before removing himself, in effect, from the heart of the Arab-Israeli dispute by giving up all claims and legal connections to the Israeli-occupied West Bank in July 1988. This important decision freed him from his continuous rivalry with the Palestine Liberation Organization (PLO) and others for leadership of the Palestinians. The move will allow Hussein to devote greater attention to the demanding problems of Jordan itself, but it also diminished his, and Jordan's, importance to other Arab states and to the great powers concerned with the region. It is likely that Hussein would not have taken such a step unless he believed that failure to do so would have jeopardized his own kingdom. The political, demographic, and economic challenges facing King Hussein are formidable, but he brings years of political experience to bear upon them.

Geography

Jordan is bounded on the north by Syria, the east by Iraq and Saudi Arabia, the south by Saudi Arabia, and the west by Israel and the Israeli-occupied West Bank. Jordan's only port is located on the Gulf of Aqaba in a narrow crescent of coastline between Israel and Saudi Arabia.

About the size of Indiana, Jordan covers a territory of 35,466 square miles. Only a small percentage of the land (under 10 percent) is arable. Virtually all the rest is steppe or desert primarily suitable for nomadic grazing and periodic pasturage. A small forested region in the northwest near Ajlun covers about 1 percent of Jordan's territory.

The Jordan River Valley and the Wadi al-Araba (officially the Wadi al-Jayb) are an extension of the great rift that begins in East Africa and continues up the Red Sea into Jordan. The Jordan River, which rises in Lebanon and Syria, descends from an elevation of 9,842 feet to Earth's deepest land-surface depression at the Dead Sea, some 1,400 feet below sea level. The East Bank of the Jordan River rises precipitously to form a sharp escarpment cut by numerous valleys and gorges. From the top of the plateau, the extremely arid land (receiving less than twelve inches of rain a year) extends to the east as part of the Great Syrian Desert. The land near the East Bank tributaries of the Jordan River is the only area to receive sufficient rainfall for intensive cultivation.

Jordan's main crops are fruits and vegetables. Although various other crops are grown, the country must import foodstuffs to meet its needs. Jordan has developed several light industries and prosperous phosphate mining operations located at the Dead Sea. With the demise of many banks and commercial enterprises in Beirut caused by Lebanon's civil war, Amman, the capital of Jordan, has attracted a number of these concerns because of the economic stability of the country and active governmental support.

During the early 1980s as many as 400,000 Jordanians—many of them Palestinians with Jordanian passports—lived and worked outside the country. Many of

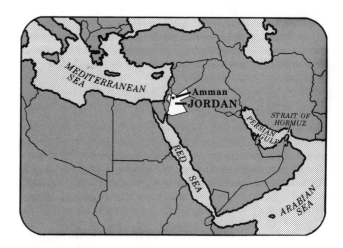

Key Facts on Jordan

Area: 35,466 square miles.
Capital: Amman.
Population: 2,850,000 (1988).
Religion: 95 percent Sunni Moslem, 5 percent Christian.
Official Language: Arabic.
GNP: $4.4 billion; $1,540 per capita (1987).

Sources: World Bank Atlas 1988; CIA World Factbook 1988

them remitted a portion of their income to family members in Jordan, thereby gaining for Jordan a significant source of potential development funds. Remittances were estimated to be running at $1.3 billion a year in the mid-1980s, but they fell sharply later in the decade.

Demography

In 1988 Jordan's population was estimated to be about 2,850,000. The average annual growth rate of Jordan's population is 3.6 percent. Ethnically, 98 percent of the population is Arab with Arabic the official language, although English is widely spoken and understood. Nearly 95 percent of the population are Moslems, nearly all of whom are Sunnis; most of the remaining Jordanians are Christians. Jordanian authorities proudly claim more than 70 percent of the population is literate, which is indicative of the government's emphasis on education and the degree to which education is viewed as a key to social mobility.

Hashemite leadership in Jordan is built upon the political support of the numerically small Bedouin tribes—only 6 to 8 percent of the population. Abdullah ibn Hussein, who became emir of Transjordan in 1921, developed a special relationship with these groups during the early 1920s. This relationship has been strengthened and institutionalized by his grandson King Hussein. The Bedouins constitute the core of Jordan's army, which is the power source of the existing monarchy. Hussein, like his grandfather, has an intense personal interest in the welfare of these tribesmen and continues to spend considerable time visiting and socializing with them. Originally a martial, desert people, the Bedouins of today are more sedentary and their political influence has diminished somewhat. Bedouins, however, still occupy key positions in the military, and they remain committed to Hussein and the Hashemite regime.

An estimated 60 percent of Jordan's population is ethnic Palestinian. Many of the Palestinians who arrived in Jordan during the late 1940s and the early 1950s were better educated than the native population, and they tended to prosper economically. Palestinians who settled in Jordan during the 1960s, however, brought with them considerably fewer skills and resources. Many of them simply moved from refugee settlements on the West Bank to similar ones on the East Bank. Estimates in the late 1980s indicate that well over 250,000 Palestinians reside in camps

in Jordan. It is clear, however, that most Palestinians in Jordan share the hope of returning to Palestine.

The ingestion of a large Palestinian population into Jordan has resulted in serious dislocation. The problem of absorbing hundreds of thousands of displaced persons, coupled with the more traditional and conservative orientation of the East Bank social and political elites, has led to mutual suspicion and distrust between Jordanians and Palestinians. Palestinian support for military action against Israel has resulted in numerous confrontations with Jordan's leadership. The most serious and potentially catastrophic of these conflicts occurred in September 1970 when the PLO challenged Hussein's political leadership throughout the country. In a series of bloody skirmishes, the Jordanian military was able to defeat the PLO forces and preserve Hashemite rule. Since that time Hussein has made a concerted effort to integrate more Palestinians into the mainstream of Jordanian society, thereby enhancing his kingdom's political stability.

History

The Old Testament recounts the settlement of present-day Jordan by Gilead, Ammon, Moab, Edom, and Joshua. Others such as the Nabataeans, Greeks, Romans, Arabs, and European crusaders held sway at various times until the Ottoman Empire extended its domination over much of the Arabian Peninsula, including Jordan, in the early 1500s.

The British and their Arab allies in 1918 ousted the Ottomans from Palestine and Transjordan (which would later be named Jordan), and the area was briefly ruled by Prince Faisal as part of the Hashemite Kingdom of Syria. Faisal's ejection by the French in 1920 placed Transjordan under the loose administration of Britain. The territory comprising Palestine, Transjordan, and Iraq was awarded to Britain under the League of Nations mandate and the provisions of secret agreements concluded during World War I.

Hussein ibn Ali, the king of Hijaz , and his sons, Faisal and Abdullah, opposed the creation of the mandates, arguing that independence had been promised to the Arabs if they sided with the Allies against the Ottomans during the war. Although the Allies balked at granting independence, Faisal and Abdullah were allowed to set up partially autonomous kingdoms for themselves in Iraq and Transjordan, respectively. In May 1923 Britain recognized the independence of Transjordan within informal parameters established by the British.

Abdullah sought to meld the disparate Bedouin tribes into a cohesive group capable of maintaining Arab rule in the face of increasing Western encroachment. To maintain his rule, Abdullah accepted financial assistance from Britain and agreed to accept advice on financial and foreign affairs. It was during this period that the fabled Arab Legion—British officered but staffed with Bedouin troops—was established as the cornerstone of the regime. The British mandate over Transjordan ended May 22, 1946. Three days later Abdullah was proclaimed king of the newly independent state of Transjordan.

The British abdicated their Palestinian mandate on May 14, 1948, and Jewish leaders proclaimed the state of Israel the next day. Transjordan joined its Arab neighbors in attacking the new Jewish state. When the fighting ended in 1949, Transjordan controlled central Palestine (the West Bank) and East Jerusalem. In April of that year the regime in Amman announced that Transjordan would henceforth be known as Jordan. Nearly 500,000 Palestinian Arabs who had fled the fighting found that they could not return to their homes and were forced to remain refugees in Jordan.

Abdullah, seeking to use his occupation of the West Bank as a steppingstone to the creation of a Hashemite-led Greater Syria, annexed the West Bank in 1950. He conducted a number of discussions with the Israelis in an attempt to resolve some of the Arab grievances against Israel. On July 20, 1951, a Palestinian assassinated King Abdullah for his hostility to Palestinian nationalist aspirations.

Abdullah's eldest son, Talal, was proclaimed his successor on September 5, 1951, but mental illness led to his forced abdication in favor of a regency for Talal's eldest son, Hussein. The new king, away at the Sandhurst Military Academy in Britain, returned to be crowned king on his eighteenth birthday, May 2, 1953.

The next two decades were difficult times for the young monarch. In 1955 and 1956 anti-Western, pro-Egyptian sentiments made Jordan's ties to Britain a serious political liability. To calm the political turmoil, Hussein relieved the British commander of the Arab Legion, Gen. John Glubb (popularly known during his twenty years of service in Jordan as Glubb Pasha), of his post and severed Jordan's mutual defense pact with Britain. Hussein also refused to join the pro-Western Baghdad Pact, even though he had been involved in its creation. Hashemite rule in Jordan under Hussein barely survived a military plot uncovered in 1957 and a number of assassination attempts—including one effort by the Egyptian air force to shoot down Hussein's plane. Hussein was able to stay in power because the army continued to back him in his efforts to curb domestic unrest and foreign meddling.

To withstand the forces arrayed against him, Hussein sought to form a union with his uncle, King Faisal of Iraq. The Iraqi revolution and the killing of Faisal in July 1958, however, destroyed that avenue of assistance. The revolution emboldened anti-Hashemite elements in Jordan to defy the king and his government. Hussein, fearing a concerted anti-Hashemite campaign directed by Egypt's president, Gamal Abdel Nasser, requested British and American assistance. In response, the British stationed troops in Jordan from July 17 to November 2, 1958, and the United States greatly increased its economic assistance to the kingdom.

In the years immediately following this successsful defense of his crown, Hussein kept a low profile in inter-Arab politics while attempting to ameliorate domestic tensions within his country. The more-or-less tolerable state of peace between Israel and Jordan was broken on June 5, 1967, by the Israeli surprise attack against Arab states that opened the Six-Day War. Israeli warplanes destroyed almost the entire air forces of Egypt, Syria, and Jordan during the first few hours of the war, leaving Jordan's forces vulnerable to air attack and with almost no chance to stop the Israeli advance. After a spirited defense of East Jerusalem, Jordanian units were forced to withdraw from the entire length of the West Bank with sizable casualties and loss of equipment.

After the war guerrilla commandos of the Palestinian resistance movement—better known as the fedayeen—expanded their organizational and recruitment activities in Jordan, Syria, and Egypt and used these countries as bases for their assaults. Their attacks against Israeli targets captured the imagination of the Arab world. In particular,

Palestinian expatriates saw in these fighters hope for regaining their homeland from Israeli control. Hashemite claims to the West Bank had never been supported by most Palestinians or the other Arab states, and the military debacle of the Arab governments in the 1967 Arab-Israeli war destroyed any lingering Palestinian support for the Jordanian position.

In the immediate aftermath of the 1967 war, Hussein permitted the PLO to organize and strike at Israel from Jordanian territory in the hope that he would be able to have some degree of influence over their operations. By 1970 these hopes had been dashed as the PLO sought to establish its political dominance within the Palestinian refugee community in Jordan and ultimately in all of Jordan.

By September 1970 the rising tensions had escalated into a full-scale civil war in Jordan. Ostensibly, the Popular Front for the Liberation of Palestine triggered the war by hijacking three commercial airplanes belonging to American, British, and Swiss airlines. The hijackers held 400 passengers hostage on a deserted airstrip in Jordan. Hussein viewed the hijacking and stand-off in the desert as the beginning of a power struggle for control of Jordan. He decided to hurl his army against the Palestinian resistance movement in an effort to save his throne.

Intense fighting erupted between the Jordanian army and the PLO in Amman and in a string of villages and towns near the Syrian border. Syrian armored units, camouflaged to look like Palestine Liberation Organization units, charged across the Jordanian border on September 20, 1970. After consultations with the Americans to see how they might support him, Hussein decided to throw his small air force against the invading Syrian armor. Syrian air force commander Hafez al-Assad, noting Israel's mobilization along the Jordanian and Syrian border, decided not to support the Syrian tanks with air cover, thereby allowing

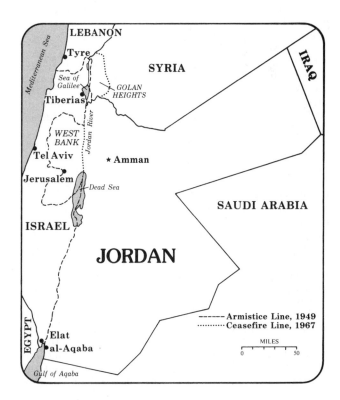

Jordanian air power to pummel the nearly defenseless tanks as they retreated back into Syria. The lightly armed PLO guerrilla forces were no match for the artillery, tanks, and aircraft of the Jordanian army and lost ground everywhere.

Foreign ministers of surrounding Arab states met in Cairo on September 22, 1970, to try to resolve the conflict. King Hussein and PLO leader Yasir Arafat signed an agreement calling for substantial concessions by the fedayeen. Nevertheless, tensions continued. In July 1971 the Jordanian army crushed the last PLO positions in the pine forest above the northwestern Jordanian village of Ajlun. The fighting was reported to have been so bitter that many PLO fighters sought to swim the Jordan River and surrender to the Israelis rather than face the Jordanian army.

Although Hashemite rule was preserved in Jordan, the regime was forced to bear an onerous political burden. Jordan had come to be viewed as the enemy of the Palestinian movement, and the PLO swore revenge. The first of many casualties of this shadowy war was Jordan's prime minister, Wasfi al-Tal, who was assassinated in Cairo in November 1971.

In October 1974 at the Rabat Arab summit conference, the PLO was declared the officially recognized representative of the Palestinian people, the objections of King Hussein notwithstanding. Hussein argued that the PLO would never be able to wrest Palestine from the Israelis militarily or to effect a political settlement. Grudgingly, he acquiesced to the Rabat decision. At the same time, however, cautious Hussein maintained his options by strengthening his contacts with the Palestinian community on the West Bank, cooperating more with Syrian authorities, and intimating that he remained open to discussions with Israel on a wide range of issues.

Jordan's performance during the 1973 October war did not increase its political standing with other Arab countries. Hussein did not opt to enter the war until it was well into its final stages and then only by sending armored units to fight in the Syrian Golan Heights. The border between Israel and Jordan remained quiet during the entire war.

The civil war in Lebanon that began in 1975 gave Jordan an opportunity to decrease its political isolation. Hussein watched the Arab consensus that had formed after the October war and the Rabat summit come unglued, thereby increasing his maneuvering room. Beginning in 1977 an uneasy reconciliation took place between Hussein and PLO chairman Arafat.

Egyptian president Anwar Sadat's 1977 visit to Jerusalem was followed in 1979 by the Camp David peace treaty between Egypt and Israel. The agreement visualized a role for Jordan in a future settlement of the Palestinian issue, raising considerable skepticism in Amman. To Hussein, Sadat seemed to be opting out of the struggle for Palestinian national rights and bypassing the truly difficult issues—the political nature of the Palestinian entity on the West Bank, the level of Israel's official presence there, and the future of Jerusalem. Hussein believed that if Egypt, with all of the support of the United States behind it at Camp David, could not coax a viable compromise out of the Israelis, then he had little chance of doing so. The role envisaged for Jordan in the Camp David accords was nothing but a recipe for disaster, he feared.

Without the outline of a settlement in sight that at least addressed most of the issues critical to the Palestinians, Hussein resolved not to move too far ahead of the Arab consensus. Influential members of the Likud party in

Israel emphatically suggested that Jordan really was the Palestinian state. Such assertions angered King Hussein.

From late 1982, after the PLO was pushed temporarily out of Lebanon by the Israeli army, until early 1986, King Hussein sought to co-opt and to subordinate PLO leader Arafat by negotiating with him on the formation of a joint Palestinian-Jordanian position, and possibly, negotiating team. Arafat, politically weakened in the wake of his defeat in Lebanon, agreed in February 1985 to an accord for political coordination with Hussein, although the details were unclear. Hussein continued to try to obtain Arafat's agreement on PLO acceptance of UN Resolution 242, but Arafat, whose leadership of the PLO had been rendered tenuous by more radical elements within the organization, refused. In February 1986 King Hussein broke off the dialogue with the PLO, and his relations with the organization returned to their normal coolness.

Unsuccessful in his negotiations with Arafat and stung by the refusal of the U.S. Congress in 1985 to sell Jordan mobile I-Hawk air defense missiles, F-16 aircraft, and Stinger missiles, Hussein focused his attention on relations with other Arab states. The Iran-Iraq war and the attacks on shipping in the Persian Gulf by both combatants had pushed the Palestinian issue lower on the agenda of the Arab nations and the international community in general. King Hussein worked hard to achieve reconciliation among the Arab states, especially to gain acceptance of Egypt's return to the Arab fold. Although his main attention was now on the Arab world, he quietly made several gestures aimed at cultivating a moderate, non-PLO leadership on the West Bank, including announcement of an ambitious $1.3 billion West Bank development plan in mid-1986.

In April 1987 King Hussein secretly met with Israeli Labor party leader Shimon Peres in London and reached an agreement to work for a five-power international peace conference. This attempt at advancing negotiations foundered when Peres failed to secure the support of the Israeli cabinet for the initiative.

Jordan's relations with Iraq, Egypt, and Saudi Arabia were good, and its relations with Syria—very hostile because of Jordanian support of Iraq and Syria's support of Iran during the Gulf War—had begun to improve slightly in late 1985. Hussein tried assiduously to bring Syria together with Iraq. Saudi Arabia and the conservative Arab states of the Gulf also put pressure on Syria, especially after the Iranian threat to the Arab states of the Gulf was manifested in the Mecca riots by Iranian pilgrims in August 1987.

The high point of King Hussein's diplomatic efforts in the Arab world came in November 1987 when he hosted an Arab League summit in Amman. Through relentless diplomacy, Hussein secured unanimous agreement among Arab states on two contentious issues. First, Iran's ally, Syria, agreed to join a resolution condemning Iran for holding Iraqi territory and for failing to accept a UN-sponsored cease-fire. Second, although Syria still did not agree that Egypt could rejoin the Arab League, Syrian president Hafez al-Assad agreed to a resolution explicitly permitting Arab League states to restore diplomatic relations with Egypt. Most important for King Hussein, Arafat and the PLO received little attention at the summit. The Palestinian issue—so often the main topic of Arab summits—was clearly secondary to the Iran-Iraq war.

The popular Palestinian uprising on the West Bank and Gaza that began in December 1987 transformed Jordan's diplomatic position and had serious consequences for its domestic situation. Unlike the other Arab countries abutting Israel, Jordan faces more than a foreign policy matter in the Palestinian problem. Hussein feared that the uprising could spill over and affect the Palestinians of the East Bank, who had become more or less integrated into the Jordanian polity since the Jordanian-Palestinian war of 1970. Moreover, the intifada threatened to diminish his role in the Middle East peace process relative to the PLO, which, although it had not started and did not control the uprising, still commanded the allegiance of most West Bank and Gaza Palestinians. Hussein pinned his hopes on international efforts to restart the peace process; the United States and moderate factions in Israel remained firmly committed to a key role for Jordan in the process and outcome of any Arab-Israeli negotiations. Although Hussein could not agree to the proposals of U.S. Secretary of State George P. Shultz in March 1988 because they went too far in front of Arab consensus on the conflict, he was cordial to U.S. attempts to restart negotiations, knowing that he would be a key player in any American effort.

Arafat, meanwhile took advantage of the uprising to strengthen his leadership role. The PLO leader succeeded in assembling an extraordinary conference of the Arab League in June 1988. There the Arab heads of state (minus Egypt, which had still not been permitted to rejoin) gave their full attention to the Palestinian issue. The Jordanian king could not prevent the summit from adopting Arafat's proposal to give the PLO full financial control over support to the Palestinians in the occupied territories. In an even more threatening proposal, Arafat suggested that, as leader of the PLO, he should be the sole legal representative of all Palestinians everywhere. The summit did not adopt this stand, but it was affirmed by the Palestine National Council in November 1988. This proposal was an insult and a threat to the king of Jordan, whose population is 60 percent Palestinian.

Renunciation of West Bank Claims

In response to these events, and perhaps hoping to insulate his kingdom from the continuing violence in the occupied territories, King Hussein severed his connections to the West Bank on July 31, 1988. This bold move renounced Jordanian claims to the area that had existed since 1950, and it called on the PLO to take responsibility for the Palestinians in the occupied territories that it had long claimed. Hussein quickly implemented this decision by severing all legal and administrative ties to the area: he dissolved the Jordanian parliament (half of whose members represented the West Bank); he ordered the Jordanian passports held by West Bank Palestinians to be changed into two-year travel documents; and he cut off salaries to West Bank residents who were being paid by Jordan to administer the West Bank but who had not been able to perform their jobs since 1967 because of the Israeli occupation.

This surprising change in Jordanian policy profoundly altered the situation in the Middle East. Pressure grew on the PLO to act like a proclaimed state-in-exile, and by the end of 1988 the PLO had proclaimed the independence of Palestine (which King Hussein recognized immediately), accepted UN Security Council Resolution 242, recognized the existence of Israel in a formula acceptable to the United States, and moved into formal dialogue with the latter.

The United States and moderate Israeli leaders were unhappy with the king's announcement, having hoped for a long time to avoid the establishment of a Palestinian state by some arrangement with the kingdom of Jordan. Both the United States and Israel had viewed Hussein as the Arab leader around whom a solution to the Arab-Israeli conflict could be most likely constructed, but neither had given him much help in his efforts to maintain his leadership of the West Bank. The United States had provided Jordan with considerable economic assistance over the years, but recent U.S. administrations had found Congress mistrustful of Jordan and unwilling to sell King Hussein the weapons he regarded as essential.

Current Issues

King Hussein has never been able to sit easily on his throne. Even before becoming king, he was made aware of the fragility of the Jordanian kingdom and especially of Hashemite rule there by events such as the assassination of his grandfather. Although attempts on his life have become less frequent over the years, he has had to deal with the complicated tensions of the Arab world and maintain his links with the leaders of the moderate, oil-rich Arab countries with whom he is most comfortable and whose support is essential to him. The eight-year Iraq-Iran war afforded him an opportunity to prove his value to these Arab states by providing aid to Iraq, by working for inter-Arab unity, and especially by helping Egypt to come back into the Arab mainstream. Hussein's link to the West Bank up until July 1988, though it was costly and created complications for him, also enhanced his kingdom's strategic importance and attracted aid. He now faces a set of internal and external problems that have been given new dimensions by his decision to abdicate his claims to authority over the West Bank.

Domestically, there are renewed concerns about the loyalty of the Palestinian Jordanians. Although most fears of Palestinian disloyalty were laid to rest when few of the Palestinian soldiers in the Jordanian army sided with the PLO in the 1970 war, the electrifying events in the occupied territories have intensified the common bond between East Bank Palestinians and their fellow Palestinians in the West Bank and Gaza Strip. The inevitable tension caused by the presence of Jordan's overwhelming Palestinian majority, coupled with the monarchy's dependence on the Bedouins and the army, remains a problem.

A second domestic problem—which is related to the first—is the decreased political freedom in Jordan. With the 1988 dissolving of the parliament (which had little power in any case), even the opportunity to vent political grievances has diminished. Although Jordan does not compare with some of the truly repressive Arab regimes, such as neighboring Syria and Iraq, there is an increasing unease in Jordan over restraints on political openness. A student uprising at Yarmuk University in May 1986, for example, officially was said to be caused by dissatisfaction over increased tuition and the expulsion of thirty-one students for academic reasons. Yet at least three, and possibly as many as thirty, students were killed in the confrontation with security forces, and the students were reported to be more in defiance of Jordanian foreign policy than the university's academic policies or tuition rates. Given the lack of a mechanism for political expression, it is difficult to know how deep support for King Hussein runs within the Palestinian population.

The loyalty of the army remains quite strong and the

Jordanian army and security forces are large and efficient. The extent of their intrusion into the nation's political life, however, has become a matter of concern for many Jordanians. A general amnesty for prison inmates was announced in March 1989 and an obvious effort by the king to reach out to the population through public appearances give hope that political freedoms will be expanded if the domestic situation remains stable.

A third domestic problem—also related somewhat to Jordan's severed ties to the West Bank—is the Jordanian economy. The danger to Hussein's government posed by Jordan's weak economy was demonstrated in April 1989 when rioting broke out in several Jordanian cities in reaction to price increases on cigarettes, gasoline, and many other nonfood consumer items. The price increases had been imposed as part of a deal with the International Monetary Fund whereby Jordan would receive a new loan and be allowed to reschedule its debts. The rioting forced Hussein to abruptly return to Jordan during a foreign tour and led to the resignation of his prime minister, Zaid al-Rifai.

Jordan labors under $6 billion of external debt, with about $1 billion due in payments in 1989. Unemployment is also high, especially among the best-educated Jordanians. In addition, lowered oil prices have caused remittances from Jordanians working in the Persian Gulf states to decrease (in 1986, for example, remittances fell by $1.2 billion). Meanwhile, capital flight, especially from Jordanian Palestinians who control much of the wealth in the economy and who are uncertain about their situation in light of the recent events, has resulted in destabilization and depreciation of the Jordanian currency and a dramatic drop in reserves of foreign exchange. Although the oil-producing Arab states in 1978 pledged an annual payment of about $1.25 billion to Jordan as a frontline country in the Arab-Israeli conflict, in fact only the Saudis made the payments. The Saudi subsidy, which supplied Jordan with about one-third of its revenues, was due to end in 1989. A new Saudi aid commitment, however, was almost a certainty.

The Jordanian government clearly hopes that a 1989 economic alliance with Egypt, Iraq, and North Yemen will provide an economic boost in the form of a regional export market (similar to the European Common Market), and perhaps a moderate political axis supported by Saudi Arabia.

The foreign policy implications of Jordan's broken ties with the West Bank are not entirely clear yet. While the decision will allow Hussein to better focus his attention on domestic problems, he has lost some control over events across Jordan's borders and must accept his diminished importance in the Arab world. Adding to this is the reduced scope of Jordanian diplomacy since the cease-fire in the Iraq-Iran war. King Hussein surely hopes that his steadfast support of Iraq and his efforts to help Egypt return to the Arab camp will not be forgotten now that the war has ended and Egypt has been accepted by most Arab states and readmitted to the Arab League.

A foreign policy issue that predates the July 1988 decision on the West Bank is Jordan's important relationship with the United States. Since the ebbing of British influence in the Middle East after World War II, the United States has had close relations with Jordan. American economic and military support have been important to King Hussein and the relationship remained strong despite strains over Hussein's rejection of the Camp David formula for Middle East peace. Jordan was the centerpiece of American plans for an Arab-Israeli settlement through several administrations. In October 1983 the Reagan administration considered training and equipping an elite Jordanian force of 8,000 troops for rapid insertion into the Persian Gulf to support moderate Arab governments there. The uproar in the U.S. Congress when this plan was revealed, and Congress's refusal in 1985 to provide Jordan with Stinger missiles that had been provided to Israel, Saudi Arabia, and ultimately even the guerrilla forces in Afghanistan were the first signs of a serious erosion in the American-Jordanian relationship.

The American rejection of Jordanian military requests has opened the door for the Soviets to become suppliers of air defense equipment and some other military hardware that the United States had refused to provide. Although an enthusiastic embrace of the Soviet Union is extremely unlikely, and Jordan's ties with the United States are still friendly, Jordan is likely to take the path of its financial supporter, Saudi Arabia, which has turned to European arms sources in the face of American rejection.

Although Jordan's role in the Arab-Israeli conflict is now diminished, it is not irrelevant. Israel strongly prefers to negotiate with King Hussein over the West Bank rather than to have any contact with the PLO, as the Israeli foreign minister informed Washington in March 1989. Although that option is foreclosed as far as King Hussein is concerned, Israel will continue to try to invigorate the Jordanian role in any peace conference.

Outlook

King Hussein has, by his July 1988 decision, substantially freed himself and Jordan from the volatile events in the Israeli-occupied territories, but at the cost of decreasing Jordan's influence in the region and its strategic importance to states outside the Middle East. Despite the American and Israeli preference for Jordanian involvement in any settlement of the Palestinian issue, it is unlikely that the king will renege on his decision.

In addition Saudi Arabia is unlikely to let economic problems destabilize the friendly Jordanian monarchy, especially when the Saudi subsidy—though large and important to Jordan—is relatively insignificant to the Saudis, even in the face of lowered oil prices. Saudi Arabia has been willing to provide financial aid to Arab states for causes they believe to be in their own interests, including the ongoing Syrian involvement in Lebanon and the Iraqi war effort against Iran during the 1980s. Saudi Arabia will unquestionably be willing to pay a price indefinitely to keep a moderate monarch with close ties to the West in power in neighboring Jordan, especially if the alternative is some form of Palestinian rule.

The king of Jordan, unlike some of the authoritarian rulers in the region, has never seemed comfortable with repressive methods of governing. It is likely that he will loosen up domestic politics as it becomes clear that the unsettling events of 1986-1988 are not going to destabilize his rule. He may even schedule new parliamentary elections. There are sharp limits, however, to any political liberalization on Hussein's part. He has never encouraged genuine and far-reaching democratization that might result in any dilution of his power, and he could clamp down, perhaps more severely than ever before, if he believes that Palestinian agitation, whether from the West Bank or from Palestinians in Jordan, threatens his kingdom or his power.

Restive Survivor of Relentless Strife

Fourteen years after Lebanon's devastating civil war in 1975-1976, the country remains torn by sectarian conflict and factional rivalry. The inability of the Lebanese parliament in September 1988 to select a new president seemed to lead the country even farther down the road toward national disintegration. Outgoing president Amin Gemayel's last-minute appointment of Gen. Michel Aoun, commander of the Lebanese armed forces, as acting prime minister, coupled with the refusal of the former government headed by Prime Minister Selim al-Hoss to step aside, seemed to foreshadow a de facto partition of the country. In addition, the two competing governmental structures continued their institutional development. The fiction of a Lebanese state continued to linger, however, and hope for a rebirth was kept alive by the idea that the parliament might meet any day and, in a classic Lebanese compromise, settle on a new president to symbolize the unity of the country.

In the absence of a settlement or a strong central government, sectarian militias, political warlords, terrorist groups, and criminal elements dominated different parts of the country—areas sometimes no bigger than a local neighborhood. Significant Western assistance was deterred by small militant groups, believed to be mainly Lebanese Shi-'ites, who held Western hostages and made Lebanon an unsafe place for foreigners to reside. Syria's continued occupation of large parts of the country, and Israel's support for its surrogate South Lebanon Army, demonstrated the impotence of Lebanon's central government in fulfilling its national security mission. Lacking a credible central authority, Lebanese of all persuasions continued to rely on local, sectarian, or independent political leaders as the best guarantee of their personal and communal security.

Efforts by General Aoun in the spring of 1989 to assert the hegemony of government forces over local militias, including the Maronite Lebanese Forces militia, and to rally the country against Syrian occupation were courageous moves designed to end the strife in Lebanon. Initially, however, they led to an intensification of warfare.

The support provided to different Lebanese groups by competing regional powers—most notably Syria, Iraq, Iran, Israel, and Libya—virtually guaranteed that the process of restoring national authority would be just as violent and bloody as the country's original descent into political anarchy in the mid-1970s. So Lebanon, long the local battleground for wider regional rivalries, once again found its domestic problems hostage to at least partial settlements of wider regional disputes, including the Arab-Israeli conflict and Iraq's disagreements with Iran and Syria. As a result, any prospect for a near-term settlement in Lebanon seemed remote.

Geography: Vulnerable Location

Lebanon is a small country of 4,015 square miles (smaller than the state of Connecticut) located on the eastern edge of the Mediterranean Sea. From north to south it has a maximum length of 135 miles, and its average width from west to east is less than 35 miles. It shares a two-hundred-mile internationally recognized border with Syria to the north and east. To the south its forty-five-mile border with Israel marks the United Nations-sponsored cease-fire line agreed upon by Lebanon and Israel in 1949. During the 1967 Arab-Israeli war, however, Israel abrogated this agreement. Then, in the Israel-Lebanon agreement of May 17, 1983, it was accepted again as the permanent boundary. Less than a year later, in March 1984, the government of Lebanon, at Syria's urging, abrogated the agreement. Lebanon's southern border with Israel therefore remained unsettled and legally undefined in terms of international law.

Lebanon's geographical position jeopardizes its security. Its only two neighbors, Syria and Israel, remain hostile to one another, and each has attempted to exploit the underlying diversity and disunity of Lebanon to pursue its own strategic advantage. Both countries are far stronger than even a politically unified Lebanon could aspire to be, and they have vested security interests in the outcome of the continuing Lebanese crisis.

Within its compact land area, Lebanon is divided into four distinct, parallel geographical regions: (1) a narrow coastal plain that runs the full length of the 130-mile Mediterranean coast, where the major port cities of Tripoli, Beirut, Sidon, and Tyre are located; (2) a coastal mountain range (known as Mount Lebanon), where the country's principal non-Sunni Moslem religious communities (Maronite Christians, Druze, and Shi'ite Moslems) have their roots; (3) the fertile, grain-producing Bekaa Valley, which varies from five to eight miles in width; and (4) a lower, interior mountain range (called the anti-Lebanon), through which runs the border with Syria. Each of these regions has a different climate, soil, water supply, density of settlement, life style, and history.

Within the main Mount Lebanon range, deep valleys stretch back several miles from the coast and divide the

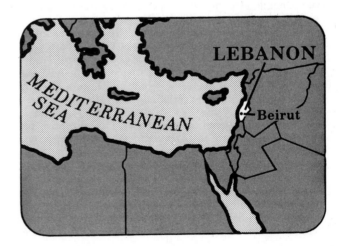

Key Facts on Lebanon

Area: 4,015 square miles.
Capital: Beirut.
Population: 2,674,000 (1988).
Religion: 55 percent Christian, 44 percent Moslem and Druze (based on 1932 official census); by the mid-1970s, Moslems believed to constitute a slight majority.
Official Language: Arabic; French and English are widely spoken.
GNP: Not available.

Sources: World Bank Atlas 1988; CIA World Factbook 1988

mountains into a number of distinct districts that give the Jbaylis, Kisrawanis, Metnis, Shufis, and other Lebanese living in them a strong sense of local identity. Most Lebanese define themselves according to their town, city, district, or region, as well as to their clan and religious community. Deeply rooted in historical tradition, such loyalties provide the Lebanese with a source of security during troubled times. The local, tribal, and religious identifications of the people, however, clash with their similarly strong sense of national identity. Although often conquered by foreign powers, Lebanon continues to resist the rule of outsiders.

The climate of the country's coastal plain, where more than half the population lives, is typically Mediterranean—hot and humid with little rain during the long nine-month summer, and quite rainy but with almost no snow during the short three-month winter. The climate of coastal Lebanon contrasts sharply with the climate of the mountains, where heavy snows fall in the winter, the summers remain cool and invigorating, and the four seasons are distinct.

Economy: Severe Deterioration

Aside from its largely self-subsistent agricultural base, Lebanon is poor in natural resources. As a result, its modern economic structure developed around trade, banking, and tourism. Before the 1975-1976 civil war, two-thirds of the country's gross national product (GNP) was based on these service industries. The routing of most Middle Eastern trade with the West through the port of Beirut gradually transformed that city into the major commercial and financial entrepôt of the region. Sidon and Tripoli, the sites of two major oil pipeline terminals and refining facilities, also profited.

Lebanon's economic growth, boosted by enterprise and a laissez-faire approach to government interference, was spectacular but uneven. Although Beirut became a glittering center of international trade, some parts of Lebanon, such as the Shi'ite-inhabited southern regions and the northern Bekaa, remained primitive and undeveloped. The attraction of Beirut led to the haphazard development of housing that quickly deteriorated into massive slums, particularly in the southern suburbs. There large numbers of

rural poor, especially Shi'ite Moslems and Palestinian refugees, settled to seek work in the city.

As a result of the civil war, which was mainly an urban conflict fought in Beirut, the entire structure of the Lebanese economy changed. The commercial center of the city—where most of Lebanon's banks, hotels, and international businesses were located—was almost totally destroyed and remains in shambles. Nevertheless, some Lebanese entrepreneurs, businessmen, and traders continued to function through a number of militia-controlled "illegal" ports that sprang up along the Lebanese coast. Only in the wake of Israel's 1982 invasion of Lebanon did serious economic deterioration set in, signaled by the sharp decline in the value of the Lebanese lira during 1984 and 1985. Since that time, the economy has deteriorated drastically.

Demography: A Nation of Minorities

Historically, Lebanon has been a haven for religious, ethnic, and political minorities. Canaanite (Phoenician) in biblical times and largely Christianized prior to the rise of Islam, Lebanon later became a country where Christian and non-Sunni Moslem minorities could maintain a relatively autonomous communal existence. This was particularly true in the Mount Lebanon region. Its northern end was occupied by Maronite Christians, its central portion by the Druze, and its southern end by Shi'ite Moslems. These three sects are the principal religious communities of Mount Lebanon, around which the unique historical development of the country has turned. Fiercely independent, they have alternately banded together to resist external control and battled one another to keep any one group from becoming dominant.

The major cities along the coast—Tripoli, Beirut, and Sidon—existed apart from Mount Lebanon for centuries and became populated by Sunni Moslems. The few Christians who lived in these towns were usually Greek Orthodox. Only in the mid-nineteenth century did large numbers of Maronites, Druze, and Shi'ites begin to settle in the coastal towns, and then primarily in Beirut. Tyre, the main coastal city in southern Lebanon, has long been inhabited principally by Shi'ite Moslems.

The Bekaa Valley and its neighboring anti-Lebanon mountains did not share the special heritage of Mount Lebanon as a political or ideological refuge. These regions historically served as arenas of contest between the prevailing powers in Mount Lebanon and the Syrian interior. Nevertheless, the Bekaa is characterized by sectarian diversity: in the north, Shi'ite Moslems; in the central valley, Sunni Moslems, Greek Orthodox, and Greek Catholics (Greek Orthodox who adhered to Rome in the late eighteenth century); and in the south, Druze.

In 1920 France created *Grand Liban,* or "greater Lebanon," the current Lebanese state. To make the new state more economically and demographically viable, it expanded the boundaries of traditional Mount Lebanon, and in so doing joined disparate groups under a single political authority. In creating Lebanon, France was acting on behalf of the Maronite Christian community, which in the nineteenth century had become a virtual French client. Expansion of Lebanon's demographic base enabled Maronite political leaders to gain power. They cultivated the allegiance of more politically passive groups, especially the Sunni Moslem community of coastal Lebanon, as a means of dominating the Druze and Shi'ite Moslems, who fiercely resented Maronite control of the new Lebanese state.

Lebanon was granted its independence from the French in 1941, and three years later it reinstituted constitutional procedures based on sectarian politics. A national census in 1932 had determined that the ratio of Christians to Moslems was six to five. This gave rise to the formula for apportioning parliamentary representation. The census defined the Maronite and the Sunni Moslem communities as the two largest sectarian groups (30 percent and 20 percent of the population, respectively), and on this basis agreement was reached that the president of Lebanon would be a Maronite and the prime minister a Sunni Moslem. The agreement was called the National Covenant of 1943, and it remained the formula, however obsolete, upon which the weak and ineffective Lebanese government was structured in the 1980s.

In fact, the formula was fragile from the beginning because it represented an agreement between the political leaders of only two of Lebanon's many sectarian communities. It also reinforced the notion that sectarian affiliation was politically significant, thereby hindering the development of national unity. The chief weakness of the National Covenant, however, was its rigidity and inability to anticipate socioeconomic and demographic changes. Its implicit assumption of Maronite-Sunni Moslem collaboration in governing Lebanon was flawed. Despite this fundamental weakness, the formula worked with a reasonable degree of effectiveness for more than thirty years, in part because the Lebanese feared the consequences of its failure.

By 1975, however, many questioned the validity of the National Covenant. Lower birthrates and higher rates of emigration among the more prosperous Christian communities—combined with higher birthrates and less emigration among the more disadvantaged Moslem and Druze communities—greatly changed the country's demographic makeup. Tens of thousands of deaths during the civil war and massive emigration in response to new flareups of violence have further distorted the country's demographic picture. Some analysts believe the Christian-Moslem ratio in Lebanon has reversed, although this is difficult to verify because no official census has been taken since 1932.

Lebanon has a population of between 2.5 million and 3.0 million persons, roughly 93 percent of which is Arab. Hundreds of thousands of Palestinian refugees flocked to Lebanon following the 1948 Arab-Israeli war and Jordan's civil war in 1970. Although there were one hundred eighty-two thousand Palestinians officially registered in Lebanon in December 1971, estimates of their numbers during the 1980s were as high as three hundred fifty thousand.

The Ottoman Period, 1516-1918

Mount Lebanon became incorporated into the vast Ottoman Empire as a result of Istanbul's conquest of Syria in 1516. Nevertheless, for most of the Ottoman period it remained an autonomous political entity under the rule of an indigenous emir who recognized the sovereignty of the Ottoman sultan. These emirs (the Maan dynasty followed in 1697 by the Chehab dynasty) were Druze, but they governed on behalf of all the inhabitants of the mountain, providing them with a sense of unique political identity within the empire. The Lebanese emirate began to be undermined, however, during the first half of the nineteenth century.

In 1826, in an effort to revive its rapidly declining

power, the Ottoman central government embarked on a program of reform, known as the *Tanzimat*. One aim of the program was to break down centers of local authority and impose a centralized system of administration throughout the empire. Another factor that weakened the emirate was the steady growth of the Maronite Christian population in northern Lebanon. Maronites expanded gradually into the Druze-inhabited area of central Lebanon, provoking Druze hostility while making the Maronites the principal champions of Lebanese autonomy. As noted earlier, France forged close commercial, religious, and cultural ties with the Maronite community. Faced with the centralization policies of the Ottoman government, the Maronites viewed French protection as the best guarantee of political autonomy.

International Commission

In 1860—after nearly thirty years of mounting unrest, Druze massacres of Maronite Christians in central Lebanon, and the spread of sectarian conflict to Damascus—an international commission headquartered in Beirut was established to resolve the crisis. Its members represented the five principal European powers (Great Britain, France, Austria, Prussia, and Russia) plus the Ottoman government.

The regime imposed on Lebanon by the commission did not resolve conflicting sectarian interests, but it did restore general order and security. The six-power, international treaty of June 9, 1861, served as a kind of constitution for Mount Lebanon for the next fifty years, until its abrogation by Turkey during World War I. Ottoman ambitions to administer the country were satisfied by making

the governor or *mutasarrif* of Lebanon an Ottoman appointee. French and Maronite concerns were met by a provision that the governor be a non-Lebanese Ottoman Christian acceptable to the European powers.

The treaty created a twelve-member central administrative council with representatives from the principal religious communities in the country: two Maronites, two Druze, two Greek Orthodox, two Greek Catholics, two Shi'ite Moslems, and two Sunni Moslems. The council had the authority to assess taxes, manage the budget, and give advice on questions submitted to it by the governor. This system of *confessional representation* (political participation based on quotas allotted to different religious sects) later characterized the independent Lebanese government.

Growth and Development

As time passed, the Ottoman-appointed governor became more of a figurehead, and the authority of the central administrative council increased. The period of the *mutasarrifiyyah* (1860-1914) proved to be a time of great social and economic development. Roads and railroads opened up not only Lebanon but also the whole Syrian interior to international commerce. Beirut began to flourish as a commercial center and to attract many immigrants from the countryside, gradually transforming the traditional, largely Sunni Moslem town into a thriving multisectarian and cosmopolitan city. This was also the time of the so-called Arab renaissance in learning and culture. The Syrian Protestant College, later renamed the American University of Beirut, was established by American missionaries in Beirut in 1866, and French Jesuits established the Université de St. Joseph in Beirut in 1875.

By the end of the nineteenth century Lebanon had emerged as one of the most tranquil, prosperous, and highly developed regions of the Ottoman Empire. Many former Maronite and Druze peasants acquired real estate and became prosperous landowners. In the larger mountain towns, artisans and tradesmen prospered, and in the coastal cities of Tripoli, Beirut, and Sidon, trading families rose to positions of great wealth.

The political impact of these developments was the emergence of a strong sense of Lebanese identity among the people of Mount Lebanon, especially among the Maronites, who tended to perceive themselves as the vanguard of progress in the country, partly because of their closer links with the West, particularly France. Even more important was Lebanese leadership of the Arab nationalist movement against Turkish rule. The despotic policies of Sultan Abdul Hamid (1876-1909), and of the Young Turk regime (1908-1918) that deposed him several months after it took power, led Christians and Moslems throughout Syria, Lebanon, and Palestine to organize into clandestine political opposition groups. The end of Turkish rule, however, was less the result of Arab nationalist activity than of the Allied armies' victory over the Turks in World War I. The Allied powers, France and Britain in particular, had an agenda of their own for that region of the world—one that did not include the immediate independence of any new state.

French Mandate, 1918-1943

Following World War I, France was granted a League of Nations mandate to oversee the political development of Syria and Lebanon, and its first action on September 1, 1920, expanded the frontiers of the traditional Ottoman Mount Lebanon *mutasarrifiyyah* to include the major coastal towns, part of the Akkar plain to the north of Mount Lebanon, the Bekaa and portions of the anti-Lebanon range, and the largely Shi'ite Moslem-inhabited Jabal Amil, the extension of the Mount Lebanon range south of the Litani River.

On May 26, 1926, an elected Lebanese representative council, the direct descendant of the Ottoman central administrative council, adopted a constitution that transformed the expanded Lebanon into the Lebanese Republic. Although amended many times by successive governments, this constitution has remained the fundamental document outlining the organization of the Lebanese government and defining its powers.

The constitution provided for equitable representation of the various sectarian communities in Lebanon, but it did not establish a fixed ratio for such proportional representation, nor did it reserve specific government positions for members of different communities. These matters were left to be resolved by representatives of the various groups.

Constitutional amendments in 1927 and 1929 transformed the originally bicameral legislature into a unicameral body and extended the renewable three-year term of the president to a nonrenewable six-year term. Both these reforms became permanent features of Lebanon's government. Although members of parliament were popularly elected from established electoral districts, the president was elected by parliament rather than by popular vote—a provision that provided a degree of stability in turbulent times. Because of the civil war of 1975-1976 and subsequent turmoil in the country, the current parliament has not stood for reelection since 1972. Presidential elections, however, were successfully conducted in 1976 and 1982.

The first president of Lebanon, elected in 1926, was not a Maronite Christian, as later became customary, but a prominent Greek Orthodox lawyer and journalist. In 1932 a prominent Sunni Moslem jurist ran for president, but when it appeared that he would win, the French high commissioner temporarily suspended the constitution. France's interests in both Syria and Lebanon and its ties with the Maronite Christian community precluded the election of a Sunni Moslem as president.

The most significant problem of the French mandate era was conflict between Maronite Christians, who generally supported the concept of an independent Lebanon, and Sunni Moslems, who opposed the creation of greater Lebanon and favored the reincorporation, with Syria, of those regions that France had annexed to Mount Lebanon in 1920. The conflict continued until an alliance was formed between an increasingly powerful Maronite party, led by Bishara al-Khoury, who favored Lebanese independence on the basis of cooperation with the Sunni Moslem community, and a Sunni Moslem bloc, led by Riyad al-Solh, who favored an independent Lebanon and cooperation with the Maronites as a means to end the French mandate.

The principal catalyst in cementing this alliance was British, and later American, support for Lebanese and Syrian independence following the Allied reoccupation of Lebanon and the deposition of the Vichy-appointed high commissioner in 1941. Although Free French officials continued to administer Lebanese affairs for two years following the 1941 proclamation of independence, British support enabled the Khoury-Solh coalition to lead the movement for Lebanese sovereignty. With the restoration of the constitution in 1943, Bishara al-Khoury was elected the first president of the newly independent state, and he immediately named Riyad al-Solh as his first prime minister. Even so, the Maronite-Sunni coalition was fragile from the beginning and had many opponents who opposed Lebanese independence.

Lebanese Politics, 1943-1975

After Lebanon gained independence in 1943, a strong presidency proved to be the principal stabilizing element in an otherwise chaotic political environment. Not surprisingly, the most profound political crises occurred at the time of presidential elections in 1952, 1958, 1976, and 1982, although there have been countless subplots in the drama of Lebanese politics. In general, however, a consensus prevailed that no one party or power should predominate and thus destabilize the delicate political status quo established in 1943. In 1975 this consensus was breached, and order has yet to be reestablished in the country.

Lebanese politics from 1943 to 1975 were based almost exclusively on family networks and patron-client relationships between the country's dominant political figures and less central actors. All of Lebanon's major sectarian communities had leading families who dominated the country's politics: the Khourys, Eddes, Chamouns, Chehabs, Franjiehs, and Gemayels among the Maronites; the Solhs, Salams, Yafis, and Karamis among the Sunnis; the Jumblatts and Arslans among the Druze; and the Assads and Hamadahs among the Shi'ites. Below this tier were other families, closely associated with the premier families, who were counted among the Lebanese "aristocracy" but had not yet attained a position of dominance. Through a combination of wealth and political influence these families were able to build powerful patron-client relationships in the mountain districts or urban quarters that served as the principal base of their national political influence. The political parties that did exist tended to be the creations of the leading families, who thus controlled voting blocs in parliament. Political status generally passed from father to son, and with certain exceptions members of the families who dominated Lebanon at the time of independence remained key political figures into the 1980s.

The dynamics of the Lebanese political system flowed from the National Covenant of 1943. That agreement stipulated that Lebanon's president should be a Maronite Christian, while its prime minister should be a Sunni Moslem. This arrangement spurred competition among leading Maronite political figures. Candidates allied with other leading sectarian politicians to form parliamentary blocs strong enough to capture a majority vote. Sunni Moslems also vied with one another to become prime minister.

Khoury and Chamoun

Lebanon's first president, Bishara al-Khoury (1943-1952), governed effectively during the first four years of his six-year term. In 1947, however, he was charged with influencing elections to secure a parliament that would amend the constitution and thus enable him to extend his term in office. When parliament did extend his term, his protégé Camille Chamoun turned against him. Chamoun, Kataeb party leader Pierre Gemayel, Druze leader Kamal

Jumblatt, and others formed an alliance known as the Socialist Front, which called for an end to sectarianism and the corruption and favoritism they accused the regime of fostering. The death of Prime Minister Riyad al-Solh in 1951 increased the president's political vulnerability. In the summer of 1952 the Socialist Front successfully organized a countrywide general strike to force al-Khoury to resign. Following his capitulation, the Lebanese parliament on September 23 elected Chamoun president.

Like his predecessor, Chamoun governed with reasonable effectiveness during the first years of his term (1952-1958). Unlike al-Khoury, however, who had based his power on a strong alliance with his Sunni Moslem prime minister, Chamoun sought to dominate the Moslem community by changing prime ministers regularly and by playing Sunni politicians off against each other. To weaken the political strength of his Maronite rivals and to improve his own popularity, Chamoun presented himself as a populist leader of all Lebanese citizens. Charges of election fraud, however, eroded his support.

Chamoun, like al-Khoury in 1947, was accused of fraudulently influencing parliamentary elections in 1957 and of seeking a constitutional amendment that would enable him to be reelected. Unable to resist effectively through constitutional procedures, his opponents turned to violence and terrorism following the parliamentary elections. Unlike the 1952 crisis, the absence of a rival Maronite candidate for president made the conflict appear as a distinctly sectarian clash, although Chamoun had many Moslem supporters and Maronite detractors.

Regional developments again played an important role in aggravating the domestic crisis. During the mid-1950s Egyptian president Gamal Abdel Nasser had emerged as a charismatic champion of Arab nationalism. At a time when Chamoun was perceived as undermining the Moslem role in Lebanese politics, Nasser's appeal was strong. Chamoun believed the growth of pan-Arab sentiment in Lebanon, inflamed and supported by Egyptian influence, threatened Lebanon's independence, and he looked to the West for support. In March 1957, in spite of strong Moslem opposition, the Lebanese government accepted the so-called Eisenhower Doctrine—a resolution the U.S. Congress passed in January 1957 declaring that "if the President determines the necessity ... [the United States] is prepared to use armed forces to assist ... any nation or groups of nations requesting assistance against armed aggression from any country controlled by international communism."

Rise of Chehabism

Dramatic regional developments in the spring and summer of 1958 fueled the Lebanese domestic crisis. The formation of the United Arab Republic (UAR) in February by a union of Egypt and Syria was viewed enthusiastically by many Lebanese Moslems, who demonstrated in favor of Lebanon's joining the UAR. In May an anti-Chamoun journalist was assassinated. This transformed the general tension into open violence that quickly spread to all non-Maronite districts. The armed capability of the rebels was seen as evidence that men, arms, and ammunition were being infiltrated into Lebanon by pan-Arab forces in Syria. President Chamoun ordered Gen. Fuad Chehab, the commander of the Lebanese army, to crush the revolt, but Chehab refused, arguing that the army's role was to deter external aggression, not to resolve domestic political disputes.

Principal Armies, Militias, Factions,...

Lebanese Armed Forces

The army of the government of Lebanon. Commanded during 1988 and 1989 by Gen. Michel Aoun, the Maronite leader designated in 1988 by then president Amin Gemayel as acting prime minister. Aoun attempted to use the armed forces, which are composed of both Moslems and Christians, to end fighting between rival militias and to expel Syrian troops. His efforts led in 1989 to intensified combat between Syrians and Lebanese armed forces.

Maronite Groups

Kataeb (Phalange) Party. Right-wing party organized by Pierre Gemayel in 1936. Modeled after European Fascist parties. Characterized by centralized decision making, rigid discipline, and a paramilitary wing. Became the dominant Maronite party during the 1975-1976 civil war. Captured the presidency in the 1982 elections. Eclipsed by the Lebanese Forces in 1988.

Lebanese Forces. Military arm of the Lebanese Front, a coalition of Maronite parties. Created by Bashir Gemayel, leader of the Kataeb party militia, during the civil war as a personal army to enable him to dominate other Maronite militias. Composed of Kataeb and non-Kataeb members. Incorporated all remaining members of the Kataeb militia under the leadership of Samir Jaja in October 1988 after the end of Amin Gemayel's presidency.

National Liberal Party. A primarily Maronite following of former president Camille Chamoun. Its Tiger militia was crushed and liquidated by the Lebanese Forces in 1980.

Zghorta Liberation Army/Marada (Giants). Militia of the Franjieh family in northern Mount Lebanon. Not a part of the Lebanese Forces and opposed to the Kataeb party. Supported by Syria.

Leftist Groups

Lebanese National Movement (LNM). Broad coalition of left-wing parties formed in 1969 and led by Druze leader Kamal Jumblatt and later by his son Walid Jumblatt. Advocated elimination of allocation of political positions to religious groups, as well as political and economic reforms. Defunct after the Israeli invasion of Lebanon in 1982.

Lebanese National Resistance Front (LNRF). Successor coalition to the Lebanese National movement. Organized to conduct armed resistance to the Israeli occupation of Lebanon. Much more covert than the LNM. Supported by Syria and Libya.

Progressive Socialist Party (PSP). Founded in 1949 by Druze leader Kamal Jumblatt as a means of linking his political power to an ideological platform. Based on a Druze following, but with adherents from other sects. Enabled Jumblatt to organize and assume leadership of the LNM in 1969.

Finally, the outbreak of a bloody pro-Egypt military coup d'état in Iraq on July 14 raised general expectations throughout the Arab world that the long-awaited day of Arab political unity, inspired by Nasser, was at hand. Fearful not only for the independence of Lebanon but also for his life, and having already presented to the United Nations Security Council a formal complaint accusing the UAR of interference in domestic Lebanese politics, President Chamoun invoked the Eisenhower Doctrine and called upon the United States to send troops to Lebanon.

By the evening of July 15, 1958, the first of approximately fifteen thousand U.S. Marines had landed without armed opposition in Lebanon. The American action deterred any other foreign intervention and provided a security umbrella for a U.S. negotiator, Under Secretary of State Robert Murphy, to mediate among the country's competing politicians. President Chamoun assured his rivals that he planned to leave office on the last day of his term, September 22, 1958. Sunni Moslem leaders made it known that they considered General Chehab, who had gained their favor by refusing to deploy the army against them, the only acceptable Maronite to replace Chamoun as president. Duly elected by the parliament on July 31, Chehab did not take office until September 23, the day

after Chamoun stepped down. With the transition of power accomplished, the U.S. Marines withdrew from Lebanon between October 4 and 25.

Fuad Chehab, a descendant of Lebanon's former ruling Druze family, which had converted to Maronite Christianity in the nineteenth century, was the quintessence of Lebanese aristocracy. He had served as commander of the Lebanese army since 1945. Not a professional politician, Chehab sought to cultivate the image of a statesman who was above the hurly-burly of daily politics. Using the formula "no victor, no vanquished" as his slogan for resolving the 1958 crisis, he reestablished political stability by drawing pro- and anti-Chamoun politicians into his government. The old political system based on powerful regional leaders, which Chamoun had tried to suppress, reemerged under Chehab's seemingly aloof and yet dominating rule. Like Bishara al-Khoury, Chehab cultivated a close Maronite-Sunni relationship by sharing power primarily with a single prime minister, Rashid Karami, the dominant Sunni politician of Tripoli. Karami continued to serve under Chehab's successor, Charles Helou (1964-1970).

Chehab pursued a deliberately neutralist foreign policy that sought to be inoffensive to neighboring Arab regimes, especially Egypt, yet acceptable to the West. Ac-

...and Parties in Lebanon

Jumblatt was assassinated in 1977, probably upon orders from Syria. His son Walid currently heads the PSP.

Syrian Socialist Nationalist Party (SSNP). Strongly secular-nationalist party that advocates the union of all of greater Syria under a socialist regime. Mostly Greek Orthodox and Sunni Moslem membership. A leading participant in the LNM and later the LNRF.

Lebanese Communist Party. Oldest Communist party in the Arab world. Founded in the 1920s as an arm of the French Communists. Following drawn mainly from Greek Orthodox and Shi'ite Moslem communities.

Communist Action Organization (CAO). Separate Communist party that emerged in the 1960s as a Lebanese wing of the Democratic Front for the Liberation of Palestine (DFLP). Separated from the DFLP in 1969. Membership drawn mainly from Shi'ite Moslem community.

Murabitun. A largely Sunni Moslem militia centered in Beirut. The military wing of the "independent Nasserist" movement. Composed of individuals faithful to the Arab nationalist principles inspired by President Gamal Abdel Nasser of Egypt in the 1950s and 1960s. An important party in the LNM prior to 1982, but now largely defunct. Counterpart in Tripoli is the October 24 movement; and in Sidon, the Popular Nasserist organization.

Syrian Ba'ath Party, Lebanese Wing. The Ba'ath party of Lebanon, supported by and affiliated with the Ba'ath party of Syria.

Shi'ite Groups

Amal. Founded in the early 1970s as the militia of the Imam Musa Sadr's populist Shi'ite "movement of the deprived." Gained strength following the Iranian revolution in 1979. Supported by Syria.

Islamic Amal. A militant group that split from Amal, led by Hussein Musawi, following the Israeli invasion of Lebanon in 1982. Based upon Shi'ites in the Bekaa Valley. More closely associated with Hizballah than with Amal.

Hizballah (Party of God). Third split among Lebanon's Shi'ite community. Calls for the transformation of Lebanon into an Islamic state, based on the Iranian model. A rival of Amal for Shi'ite loyalties.

South Lebanon Army (SLA)

Israeli-supported force with the mission of maintaining security in the enclave along Lebanon's southern border with Israel. Established in 1978, following Israel's 1978 invasion of southern Lebanon, as the Free Lebanon Militia (FLM) under the command of Lebanese major Saad Haddad. Now headed by Lebanese general Antoine Lahad. Primarily a Christian militia, but with some Shi'ite participation.

---

cording to his political philosophy, later called Chehabism, the government should serve Christians and Moslems equally. He relied on the army's Deuxième Bureau (military intelligence) to monitor and report on domestic political developments, a policy that made his presidency akin to a military regime.

In addition, Chehab concentrated on infrastructure development throughout the country, including the areas outside of Mount Lebanon that had been largely neglected by al-Khoury and Chamoun. Chehab brought considerable stability to Lebanon. Elitist rather than populist (like Chamoun), or more traditionally patrimonial (like Khoury), Chehab gained many adherents, and Chehabism continues to have numerous partisans in contemporary Lebanon.

Chehab Successor

As his predecessors had done, Chehab considered seeking a second term, but when opposition emerged he gave his support to Charles Helou, who was elected president in 1964, rather than risk destabilizing the country. A former banker, journalist, and diplomat, Helou was an able and accomplished individual. Because Helou had no personal base of power except for the Chehabist-controlled government and parliament, Chehab appointees continued to run Lebanon during his term of office. Helou lacked the political authority either to control his own government or to deal effectively with the country's other powerful politicians.

Under these circumstances, following the 1967 Arab-Israeli war, Lebanese politics became increasingly polarized over regional issues. Although Lebanon had avoided becoming a combatant in the war, it could not avoid involvement in the ongoing Arab-Israeli conflict after the war. The gradual emergence of the Palestine Liberation Organization (PLO) as an autonomous political and military force in the late 1960s strongly affected Jordan and Lebanon because of their large concentrations of Palestinian refugees (in Lebanon's case, about 10 percent of the resident population). The PLO and its cause became a divisive political issue that ultimately provoked Lebanon's civil war.

Maronite politicians looked for a way that would enable Lebanon to support the Palestinian cause yet oppose the armed activities of the PLO in Lebanon. Moslem politicians, however, also seeking to reflect the will of their constituencies, generally supported the PLO. President Helou was unable to act decisively because of powerful political pressures from both sides. His use of the Deuxième Bureau to monitor developments and to try to control them provoked serious resentment.

The Civil War

Although it was sparked by a specific event—the April 13, 1975, attack by unknown gunmen on Maronite worshipers at a Sunday church service in the Beirut suburb of Ayn Rummaneh—the Lebanese civil war had deeper causes that were years in the making. The polarization of the Lebanese public over government policy toward the PLO could be seen as early December 1968, when an Israeli commando raid on Beirut International Airport destroyed thirteen Lebanese civilian aircraft. Undertaken in retaliation for airplane hijackings and commando raids by the PLO, this Israeli raid paralyzed the Lebanese government and rapidly radicalized public opinion.

Further Israeli attacks in southern Lebanon in response to PLO guerrilla operations led to the collapse of the Lebanese government in May 1969; Prime Minister Karami resigned rather than sanction Lebanese military actions against the PLO. Unable to form a new cabinet with another Sunni prime minister, President Helou resolved the crisis by acceding to the Egyptian-sponsored Cairo agreement in November 1969. This agreement confined the PLO armed presence to certain localities in southern Lebanon.

The Syrian Socialist Nationalist party (SSNP), the Lebanese Communist party (LCP), the Lebanese branch of the Syrian Ba'ath party, and other new ideological parties, often closely affiliated with the PLO, attracted more and more adherents during the late 1960s. Many of these parties were disillusioned with established Moslem politicians who used their influence to protect the PLO but failed to actively support it. The result was the formation of the multi-party Lebanese National Movement (LNM) in 1969. Its leader was Kamal Jumblatt, the powerful head of Lebanon's Druze community, who since 1949 had organized his own political followers into the Progressive Socialist party (PSP).

Franjieh's Victory

In the August 1970 presidential election, Suleiman Franjieh, a Maronite politician from Zghorta in northern Mount Lebanon, defeated his Chehabist rival, Elias Sarkis, just before King Hussein's war against the PLO in Jordan. Franjieh's election was generally perceived as a victory for those who sought to crush the PLO's growing strength in Lebanon. The parliamentary vote electing him, however, had been only 50-49, and the decisive vote had been cast by LNM leader Jumblatt, who in siding with Franjieh was really voting against continued Chehabist control of the government. Owing his election at least partly to the LNM, Franjieh began his presidency as a radical reformer, seeking to co-opt the LNM's opposition by trying to implement needed changes in government administration. Entrenched political interests, however, stymied the reforms, and he soon abandoned the effort. After 1972 Franjieh's rule was increasingly based on personal control of the government bureaucracy and defense of the established political system. The LNM, angered by this reversal of policy, tried to mobilize public opinion against the government. One significant reform Franjieh had been able to make, however, was the liquidation of the Chehabist-controlled Deuxième Bureau. This deprived the government of an effective intelligence service at a time of increasing disorder and tension in the country.

Following the defeat of the PLO in Jordan in 1970-1971, Lebanon became the last center of armed Palestinian resistance against Israel in the Arab world. Israeli retaliatory raids against Palestinian guerrilla bases located in Lebanese border villages produced a steady exodus of Shi'ite Moslems from southern Lebanon to Beirut. Shantytowns sprang up, usually in and around the long-established Palestinian refugee camps that ringed Beirut. Disillusioned with their political leaders, who had failed to protect their homes and land from either the PLO or Israel, these restless and impoverished Shi'ite Moslems provided ready recruits to the militias of the LNM. At this time a populist Shi'ite organization called Amal (meaning "hope") was established. It sought a larger role for the Shi'ite community in the Lebanese political system. Rampant inflation during the early 1970s, partly due to the growing flow of Arab oil money into Lebanon's thriving banking sector and to the absence of controls over the country's freewheeling economy, accentuated the gap between rich and poor and increasingly associated the political conflict in Lebanon with class distinctions.

During the 1972 parliamentary elections (the last such elections to be held in Lebanon), the LNM pressed hard to elect antiestablishment candidates, but the outcome demonstrated the traditional leaders' powerful hold over the electoral process. To those who sought radical transformation in Lebanon, revolutionary violence seemed the only available route. Nevertheless, the election of a few radical deputies—especially the overwhelming victory of a pro-Nasserist candidate over an established conservative rival in Beirut—sent tremors through the conservative political establishment.

In April 1973 Israeli commandos raided the heart of Beirut, killing three top PLO leaders. The LNM organized mass demonstrations against the government to protest its passivity toward Israeli aggression. President Franjieh and other Maronite leaders, however, decided the government could not delay longer in moving against the PLO. Heavy fighting on May 2 between the army and PLO fighters in the Burj al-Barajina refugee camp quickly spread to other parts of the country. But the government policy provoked powerful opposition and Maronite leaders, as yet unprepared to carry on alone the fight against the PLO, had to back down. The May 18, 1973, settlement at Melkart basically reaffirmed the provisions of the Cairo agreement of 1969, but it did not resolve the fundamental issue that had provoked the fighting. Further showdowns were inevitable. In the months that followed, the Maronite leaders, the parties of the LNM, and the PLO intensified recruitment efforts and searched worldwide for the arms and funds necessary to meet the challenge that awaited them.

War among Militias

The Lebanese civil war that finally erupted in April 1975 was not so much a conflict between Christians and Moslems, as widely reported in the Western press, as it was a battle between the militias of the dominant Maronite leaders of the established political order and the various militias of the LNM, whose leaders sought to overthrow the traditional political system. Indeed, the vast majority of

Lebanese were victims rather than active participants in the conflict. The fighting could continue only because of the army's political incapacity to intervene. The established Moslem politicians refused to countenance army intervention so long as the conflict remained a fundamentally domestic one. But the army did intervene when the PLO, which at first had held back from the fighting, entered the fray in late 1975 to shore up the sagging fortunes of the LNM militiamen in Beirut's hotel district.

The army became an enemy of the joint PLO-LNM forces and a tacit ally of the Maronite militias. Sensing impending victory, the Maronites undertook a massive destruction and depopulation campaign against Palestinian and Shi'ite Moslem refugee camps on the east side of Beirut. This action brought the PLO fully into the conflict and prompted retaliatory attacks against strategically located Maronite towns in areas otherwise controlled by the joint PLO-LNM forces. As these campaigns continued during January 1976, morale within Lebanon's multi-confessional army could not be sustained. By early February the army had totally collapsed, and many of its soldiers took sides with one or another of the fighting militias. Lebanon plunged into full-scale civil war.

Syrian Intervention

Unlike 1958, when U.S. intervention played a role in stabilizing Lebanon, in 1975 Lebanon's president had no relatively disinterested external party to turn to for help in stemming the political chaos. To Lebanese nationalists, particularly Maronites, independence primarily meant independence from Syria. Yet in 1975-1976 only Syria had the vital interest in the outcome of the Lebanese crisis to expend the political, military, and financial resources necessary to bring it under control. It was strategically important that Lebanon not become either a base or a corridor for an Israeli invasion of Syria.

Assad's Fear of Radical Regime

Prior to 1975 Syria had strongly supported the PLO and the LNM in Lebanon. By late March 1976 a PLO-LNM victory seemed imminent. Syrian president Hafez al-Assad became convinced that such a victory would lead to Israeli intervention—an action that he wanted to preempt. At the same time, Lebanon's Maronite leaders and their Moslem political colleagues also feared the possible results of a PLO-LNM victory. Consequently, Assad began to seek—and the Maronite leaders began to accept—the principle of a primary role for neighboring Syria in resolving the Lebanese conflict.

Syrian forces dispatched to Lebanon defended the presidential palace in Baabda in March 1976, provided security for the presidential elections held in May, and in June forcibly restored the pre-April 1975 political status quo. But fighting, primarily between Syrian and PLO-LNM forces, continued throughout the summer. The better-trained Syrian units gradually managed to achieve strategic superiority. In October representatives of the various warring parties concluded a generally accepted cease-fire agreement in Riyadh, Saudi Arabia.

A summit of the Arab League, which then included all the Arab states, ratified the Riyadh agreement in Cairo on October 25. A key provision was the establishment of the Arab Deterrent Force (ADF), which was to provide security throughout the country while a process of national reconciliation was undertaken. Placed technically under the authority of the newly elected Lebanese president, Elias Sarkis (the Chehabist rival of President Franjieh, who was favored by Syria in the May elections), the ADF was to be composed of units from several Arab countries. It was tacitly understood, however, that Syrian elements would form the main body of the force. By this means, Syria's role in Lebanon gained legitimacy. As various units from other Arab countries were recalled in the months that followed, the ADF became a completely Syrian force, albeit supported and at least partially financed by the multinational Arab League.

Syrian intervention in Lebanon's civil war temporarily restored order to most of the country, but, because the intervention did not resolve the fundamental problems, the peace was short-lived. Conflict and violence, often in the form of terrorist bombings and attacks, soon dominated Lebanese political life once again.

Although Syria had intervened on behalf of Lebanon's Maronite leaders against the PLO and LNM, it had not put an end to PLO activity in Lebanon. Indeed, the Riyadh agreement specifically affirmed the 1969 Cairo agreement. The terms of the Cairo agreement, however, had never been accepted by the non-Chehabist Maronite leadership. Thus, the honeymoon between Syria and these leaders—grouped together as the Lebanese Front—was brief. In May 1977, only days after Menachem Begin was elected prime minister of Israel, the front issued a statement declaring that the Cairo agreement was null and void and that the Maronite militias would remain armed as long as the PLO did.

Even during the civil war, the Maronite leaders had entered into covert arms deals with Israel's Labor government. With the coming to power of Menachem Begin, who openly supported the Lebanese Front, the Maronite leaders dared to challenge Syria directly with assurances of Israeli support, making confrontation between Syria and the Maronite militias inevitable.

Under the terms of the Riyadh agreement, PLO fighters returned to southern Lebanon in spite of warnings by Israel that it would not tolerate a resumption of commando activity in the region. As the PLO returned, Israel responded by arming and helping to organize a local, predominately Christian militia commanded by Maj. Saad Haddad, a renegade Lebanese officer who sought to counter and contain PLO and LNM expansion into the border area.

Israel's higher profile in Lebanon following the civil war was closely linked to Syria's presence there. After Syrian forces entered Lebanon in 1976, Israel announced the existence of an undefined "red line" somewhere in southern Lebanon, beyond which it would not tolerate Syrian troops.

The line was generally considered to be in the vicinity of the Litani River. Syria never seriously challenged this Israeli condition, and southern Lebanon, historically one of Lebanon's most neglected and underdeveloped areas, became a virtual no man's land where neither Lebanese, Syrian, nor even Israeli authority extended. Bloody conflict among the supporters of Saad Haddad, the PLO, the LNM militias, and the predominately Shi'ite population that lived in the area poisoned the political atmosphere elsewhere in Lebanon, where every group in the south had its supporters.

Divide-and-Rule Strategy

Syria's conservatism in dealing with security problems also escalated tensions. Syria sought to mediate agreements among Lebanon's various militias and political parties, but it did not seriously try to disarm them even though it was authorized to do so by the Riyadh agreement. As a result, the militias remained armed, and Lebanon continued to live on the edge of violence and renewed civil war. Syria's policy for containing conflict was to move in with sufficient strength to crush violence when it erupted. Such a policy, although it produced respect, also produced resentment, and it did little to halt the growing number of terrorist acts used by the various militias. As a result of its divide-and-rule strategy—tolerating every group but really supporting none—Syria was increasingly perceived by most Lebanese as serving no particular interest except its own.

Disenchantment with the PLO also grew during the late 1970s, especially among Lebanon's southern Shi'ites, who previously had perceived themselves as sharing a common plight with the Palestinians. Three events in 1978 and early 1979 helped to rally support for the populist Amal organization: Israel's invasion of southern Lebanon in March, the unexplained disappearance of Amal leader Musa Sadr while on a visit to Libya in September, and the successful example of a Shi'ite revolution in Iran. The escalating conflict in the south between the Shi'ite Moslem population and the PLO laid the basis for the Shi'ites' popular reception of Israeli armed forces during their summer 1982 invasion of Lebanon. The sectarian solidarity of the community, however, also laid the basis for the ultimate failure of Israeli policy in Lebanon.

Israeli Invasions of 1978, 1982

Israel's invasions of southern Lebanon in March 1978 and June 1982, although allegedly provoked by Palestinian terrorist incidents, were aimed at achieving broader policy goals. The principal result of the 1978 invasion was the clearing of an area several kilometers wide along Israel's northern frontier to serve as a security zone under the control of Maj. Saad Haddad's Free Lebanon Militia (FLM). The inability of the FLM to achieve this mission was the chief factor necessitating Israel's military intervention.

In spite of the operation's success, PLO groups continued to find ways to cross the frontier and to conduct terrorist operations in northern Israel. The presence in southern Lebanon of some six thousand soldiers of the United Nations Interim Force in Lebanon (UNIFIL) undoubtedly ameliorated the problem, but UNIFIL failed to deploy in the security zone because of Israeli opposition and its own inability to control all Palestinian movements in southern Lebanon. Moreover, various PLO groups acquired long-range artillery and multiple-rocket launchers capable of firing over the heads of both UNIFIL and the FLM. This created a new danger that led Begin's government to devise strategies for dealing with the threat to northern Israel.

Other developments in Lebanon in 1980-1981 had a significant impact on how the 1982 invasion was eventually carried out. The Maronite militias (except for that of former president Franjieh) joined together under the leadership of Bashir Gemayel, son of Maronite Kataeb party leader Pierre Gemayel. This made Bashir the principal Maronite wielding military power and thus a viable presidential candidate in the 1982 elections. For him to be elected, however, Syrian opposition to his candidacy had to be neutralized. Militantly opposed to the PLO and Syrian presence in Lebanon, Bashir favored decisive action to end the vicious cycle of violence that had killed so many. Like the Israelis, Amal followers, and a growing number of ordinary Lebanese citizens, Bashir Gemayel largely attributed violence to the PLO's continuing presence in Lebanon. Increasingly isolated, the PLO found it advantageous on July 24, 1981, to enter into a cease-fire agreement with Israel that had been negotiated by U.S. special envoy Philip C. Habib. The isolation of the PLO also cleared the way for Israel to launch a full-scale invasion of Lebanon in June 1982 targeted at the PLO. *(Israeli invasion of Lebanon, Chapter 2, p. 33)*

As a result of that invasion, the PLO was formally expelled from Beirut and southern Lebanon in August. Lebanon's Maronite leaders understandably interpreted this as a victory for their cause and particularly for Bashir Gemayel, who was duly elected president. Although Bashir was assassinated before he could take office, his brother Amin was quickly elected to take his place.

The victory claimed by the Maronites over the PLO, however, was illusory. It had been achieved by Israeli military strength, not the Maronite militias. The continuing occupation of Lebanon by both Israeli and Syrian forces transformed the domestic conflict into a regional one in which Lebanon remained the principal arena of death and destruction.

U.S. Involvement, 1982-1984

In September 1982 the United States, France, Italy, and the United Kingdom dispatched a five-thousand-man multinational peacekeeping force (MNF) to Beirut to bolster the confidence of the new Lebanese government. At the same time, U.S. diplomats sought to broker agreements that would lead to the full withdrawal of Syrian, PLO, and Israeli forces, provide for the security of Israel's northern border, and strengthen the Lebanese government's authority. Unresolved conflict between Syria and Israel in other areas, especially regarding the status of the Golan Heights, which Israel had effectively annexed in December 1981, made even indirect negotiations between these two countries impossible.

After receiving assurances from Syria that it would leave Lebanon if Israel unconditionally withdrew, the United States sought to mediate a withdrawal agreement between Israel and Lebanon. On May 17, 1983, representatives of Israel, Lebanon, and the United States initialed such an agreement. It contained guarantees that Israel would withdraw its forces completely from Lebanon in return for Lebanese political, economic, and military concessions that Israel considered necessary for the security of its northern frontier. After the initialing of the document, however, Israel tied full implementation to a similar commitment by Syria to withdraw its forces from Lebanon.

Syria immediately asserted that its forces would not withdraw unless the agreement was abrogated. Damascus objected to the agreement's establishment of special security zones in southern Lebanon and a joint Lebanese-Israeli committee that would hold ultimate authority over matters of security within these zones. These and other provisions were perceived by Syria as placing unacceptable restrictions on Lebanese sovereignty, in effect partitioning the country into zones of Israeli and Syrian influence and increasing the Israeli threat to Syria.

The agreement was rejected by most Lebanese political factions, which had leagued together as the National Salvation Front to resist it. Moreover, Syrian forces, from their strategically dominant position in the hills overlooking Beirut, supported Lebanese groups opposing the agreement and intimidated the Maronite community with shellfire and threats. Meanwhile, the high cost of sustaining the Israeli occupation, the increasingly heavy Israeli casualties from Lebanese resistance, and the September 1982 massacres at the Sabra and Shatila refugee camps, in which hundreds of Palestinians were killed by Maronite militiamen under the nose of the Israeli army, had begun to erode support at home for Israel's involvement in Lebanon.

Militia groups virtually crushed by Israel's invasion in 1982 regrouped with Syrian support during the summer of 1983. Events climaxed in September 1983 when Israel undertook a partial, unilateral withdrawal from its forward positions along the Beirut-Damascus highway to more defensible positions below the Awali River short of Sidon. Fighting erupted throughout the Shuf region in central Lebanon between Druze militias, supported by PLO and Shi'ite elements on the one hand, and the Lebanese armed forces and Maronite militia forces on the other. Druze forces prevailed, causing a mass flight of Maronite Christians from their villages in the region and enabling Walid Jumblatt (who had become Druze leader after pro-Syrian forces assassinated his father, Kamal, in March 1977) to consolidate his authority throughout the Shuf, although the Lebanese army succeeded in maintaining control over militias in West Beirut.

On October 23, 1983, a terrorist bombing of the American Marine barracks in Beirut killed 241 servicemen. This attack and the earlier April 18, 1983, bombing of the U.S. embassy in Beirut, which had killed 63 persons, diminished U.S. public support for a military role in Lebanon.

Following the collapse of Lebanese government authority in West Beirut in early February 1984, the United States announced its decision to withdraw its MNF contingent. The last U.S. Marines were evacuated in March. Italy, Britain, and France also withdrew their forces during early 1984.

Revived Syrian Hegemony

With the departure of Western troops from Lebanon, Syria reemerged as the dominant external power influencing affairs in Lebanon. Lebanese\president Amin Gemayel moved quickly to restore relations with Damascus, and on March 5, 1984, the Lebanese government announced its abrogation of the May 17, 1983, Lebanon-Israel agreement. Following further discussions between Syrian representatives and Lebanese political leaders, a government of "national unity" was formed in April, and a security plan aimed at restoring government authority throughout the country was agreed upon.

Implementation of the plan proved impossible, however, because of sectarian conflict, particularly over the continuing Israeli occupation of southern Lebanon. Shi'ite, Druze, and other militia groups there refused to disarm so long as Israeli forces still occupied the region. Attacks against Israeli forces escalated, even as Israel's new government elected in 1984 adopted an "iron fist" policy in an attempt to contain them.

Turmoil in Southern Lebanon

With the disintegration of its previous policy objectives in Lebanon, Israel in the spring of 1985 began a graduated, unilateral withdrawal from Lebanon. As it did so, however, it left in place an expanded security zone under the control of a surrogate militia, the South Lebanon Army (SLA), now commanded by retired Lebanese general Antoine Lahad. Although the zone was designed to promote the security of Israel's northern border and was controlled ultimately by Israel—which had armed, funded, and advised the SLA—the zone's presence provoked continuing resistance on the part of the mainly Shi'ite inhabitants of southern Lebanon. The Shi'ite resistance to the SLA was split into two rival factions. The first, more closely linked with Syria, was the Amal organization, which sought to demonstrate to Israel its capability and determination to control the PLO in Lebanon and thus remove any pretext for Israel to maintain the security zone. In May 1985 Amal's efforts to control PLO activities by maintaining a siege around Palestinian camps in Beirut and southern Lebanon erupted into open warfare. The Shi'ite-Palestinian "camp wars" continued until January 1988, when Amal leader Nabih Berri lifted the siege of the camps following the outbreak of the Palestinian intifada in the Israeli-occupied West Bank and Gaza.

The rival Shi'ite faction to Amal was the Hizballah (party of God) movement, which received inspiration and support from revolutionary Iran. Unlike Amal, which sought a stronger Shi'ite role in Lebanon's multi-sectarian political system, the partisans of Hizballah favored the establishment of Lebanon as a fully Islamic state. Imbued with fanatical determination, the Hizballahis competed with Amal for Shi'ite attention and loyalty by conducting spectacular suicidal attacks against SLA and Israeli patrols in southern Lebanon. In addition, they preferred to collaborate with Palestinian guerrillas in their struggle against Israel and opposed Amal's efforts to contain Palestinian military activity. These different approaches occasionally provoked intra-Shi'ite conflict and violence.

Another tactic used by some groups (believed in most cases to be associated with Hizballah) was the taking of Western hostages. Beginning in early 1984, soon after the withdrawal of the U.S. Marines from Lebanon, isolated kidnappings of Americans and later French, British, West German, Saudi, and even South Korean nationals began to occur. Among other motives, the kidnappers sought to win the release of Shi'ite prisoners in Kuwaiti, Israeli, or Western jails and to enhance their influence in local Lebanese and regional affairs. The kidnappings greatly reduced the Western presence in Lebanon and consequently the ability of Western nations to exert influence in that country or to react forcibly because of the potential danger to the hostages.

Israel's efforts to contain Shi'ite and Palestinian guerrilla activity in southern Lebanon through commando raids, air strikes, artillery shelling, and the capture and arrest of guerrilla leaders, meanwhile, intensified the region's turmoil and provoked retaliation. An example was the hijacking of TWA Flight 847 in June 1985 by three Lebanese Shi'ites who killed one American serviceman and held thirty-nine people hostage in an effort to force Israel to release some seven hundred Lebanese Shi'ites imprisoned in Israel. The eventual arrest and trial of one of these hijackers, Muhammad Ali Hamadai, in West Germany provoked yet another round of kidnappings of West German citizens in Lebanon by a group, probably centered around relatives of Hamadai, called the Organization of the Oppressed of the Earth.

Tripartite Agreement

While southern Lebanon remained in turmoil and resistant to the reestablishment of central Lebanese government authority, efforts of the Gemayel government to reconcile with Syria in 1984 prompted elements of the militant Maronite Christian Lebanese Forces militia in northern Lebanon headed by Samir Jaja to revolt in early 1985 against central government authority. The Lebanese Forces regarded Gemayel's accommodation toward Syria as evidence that the government was caving in to Syrian efforts to establish hegemony.

Syria in December 1985, working with Sunni prime minister Rashid Karami but not with President Gemayel, managed to forge a "tripartite agreement" among Elie Hubayka, representing a counterfaction of the Lebanese Forces; Druze leader Walid Jumblatt; and Amal leader Nabih Berri. The agreement was aimed at reaching a compromise settlement of the Lebanese conflict, centered around the principal militias rather than the traditional politicians. To be implemented, it required Hubayka and Berri to assert control over the more radical factions of their respective communities. Despite increased Syrian support, neither proved able to do so, and fierce intra-Maronite and intra-Shi'ite conflict occurred during the spring and summer of 1986.

Continued deterioration of the security situation throughout the country finally led Syria in August 1986 to reintroduce about seven hundred troops into Beirut. In February 1987 President Assad increased his commitment by sending into Lebanon an additional seven thousand troops supported by tanks and heavy artillery. With the reimposition of Syrian military control in West Beirut and central Lebanon, Damascus began slow but deliberate efforts to strengthen Amal at the expense of Hizballah and PLO elements remaining in Beirut and southern Lebanon. Syrian leaders, however, were careful to avoid jeopardizing relations with Iran, whose alliance with Syria against Iraq took priority over any heavy-handed effort to crush the Hizballah movement entirely. Anti-Syrian resistance was growing, symbolized by the emergence during 1987 of a new terrorist group, the Lebanese Liberation Front, which assassinated Syrian officials and soldiers in Syrian-controlled areas of Lebanon. Nevertheless, the Syrian influence in Lebanon by the summer of 1988 was sufficiently strong to have a decisive bearing on Lebanese presidential elections, which constitutionally had to occur before September 23.

Syrian-Maronite Conflict

To help counter Syrian efforts to dictate the outcome of the electoral process, the Lebanese Forces found a willing ally in Iraqi president Saddam Hussein, who, having achieved a cease-fire in his war with Iran in August, looked for ways to retaliate against Syria for supporting Iran. Iraqi arms began reaching Lebanon in October, and the Lebanese Forces led a movement to block the election of presidential candidates favored by Syria. As a result, no presidential election could take place. Just before his term of office expired, President Gemayel appointed Lebanese armed forces commander Michel Aoun as acting Maronite prime minister to preside over an interim military government until elections could be held. When the government of Sunni Moslem prime minister Selim al-Hoss refused to step down and recognize the new government of General Aoun, Lebanon found itself with two acting governments, one recognized as legitimate by Syria and its Moslem allies and the other by the Lebanese Forces and most of the Maronite community.

Efforts by the Arab League in late January 1989 to mediate the impasse led Aoun in mid-February to assert the authority of his government and armed forces over the various independent militias in Lebanon. Beginning with the Lebanese Forces, which at first resisted his offensive against them in a series of bloody clashes, Aoun ordered the army to take over militia headquarters and barracks in the greater Beirut area and to bring all illegal militia-controlled ports under the control of the army. As this operation succeeded, he extended the order in early March to include illegal ports controlled by the Druze and Moslem militias and attempted to impose a naval blockade on them. Druze and Moslem militias countered Aoun by shelling Maronite areas. Aoun considered these attacks to be inspired by Syria. Consequently, he responded to Druze and Moslem shelling by targeting mainly Syrian military positions, although many of these were located in heavily populated residential areas of Beirut. At the same time, he sought to appeal to increasingly widespread anti-Syrian sentiment in all sectors of the Lebanese population by calling for a general uprising against the Syrian occupation and a liberation of Lebanon from Syrian control.

The support received by Aoun from Iraq, and reportedly from Israel as well, virtually guaranteed that Syria would determinedly resist Aoun's efforts to weaken its position in Lebanon. At the same time, Aoun could not expect to dislodge the Syrian occupation by force alone, and he hoped for eventual international intervention and mediation on behalf of continued Lebanese sovereignty and independence. Arab League efforts in late April did result in a cease-fire agreement, and Aoun lifted his blockade of Druze and Moslem ports. Continued efforts by Aoun and the Lebanese Forces, however, to receive military supplies through ports along the Maronite portion of the Lebanese coast prompted Syria to shell the ports and to blockade ships serving them. Continued retaliatory shelling by Aoun's army and the Lebanese Forces against Syrian military positions made the cease-fire agreement a dead letter and the summer of 1989 one of the bloodiest and most violent seasons in Lebanon's fourteen-year conflict.

Outlook

No end of civil disorder and violence can yet be foreseen in Lebanon, although events in late 1989 seemed to be pushing the continuing Lebanese crisis toward some kind of climax. The time probably has passed when the Lebanese state—admitted as a founding member of the United Nations in 1945—can be reconstituted on the basis of some new formula for national reconciliation.

The future remains unclear for the land called Lebanon and its people, whose identity as Lebanese seems to have grown stronger during the long years of civil violence and foreign intervention.

Neither a formal partition of Lebanon into ministates (reflecting the country's de facto partition) nor a formal annexation of large parts of the country by Syria and Israel (which some posit as the ultimate solution to the conflict) carries any guarantee that the pattern of conflict and violence associated with Lebanon will cease. Indeed, the Lebanese problem has become so complex that many observers consider it a microcosm of the larger conflicts of the Middle East. In Lebanon the Arab-Israeli conflict in both its Syrian and Palestinian dimensions continues to be fought; Iraqi battles with both Iran and Syria continue to be waged; the revolutionary potential of Islamic fundamentalism continues to be tested; and cold war clients of the Soviet Union face off against traditional friends and clients of the United States. Many argue that Lebanon has become the hostage of these larger conflicts and that any resolution of the crisis in Lebanon will require significant movement toward settlement of the larger issues, especially the Arab-Israeli conflict. It is true that Lebanon fuels the conflict by accepting external sources of support to pursue its own parochial goals, but most Lebanese are victims rather than perpetrators of the seemingly unending violence that has come to characterize the country. In a proper set of circumstances, many will rally in support of a formula that restores general security and relative fairness to the social order.

It is perhaps in the new U.S.-Soviet relationship that a glimmer of hope can be perceived for Lebanon. With the apparent abatement in the late 1980s of the traditional U.S.-Soviet rivalry and the creation of significant joint efforts to resolve a number of longstanding regional conflicts around the world, the possibility has arisen for the exertion of superpower pressure on traditional clients to resolve a number of outstanding Middle Eastern issues. No doubt General Aoun's initiative in the spring of 1989 was taken in light of perceived changes in the overall international climate.

Both the United States and the Soviet Union, along with the general international community, continue to recognize the independence and territorial sovereignty of a state called Lebanon. The moment may soon be approaching, however, when the international community, led by its principal powers, will have to decide whether Lebanon can be salvaged and, if so, what pressures will have to be applied to preserve it.

Maverick of the Arab World

The September 1969 coup d'etat that replaced King Idris I with a Revolutionary Command Council (RCC) headed by Muammar al-Qaddafi ushered in one of the most dramatic social and political transformations to occur in the Arab world during the modern era. The West, especially the United States, has watched with alarm Qaddafi's transformation of Libya and the radicalization of its foreign policy. By the 1980s many Westerners regarded Qaddafi as a madman. To the Reagan administration in particular he was seen as a diabolical nemesis of the West because of his radical foreign policy, support of foreign terrorists and subversive groups, and assassinations of Libyan dissidents abroad.

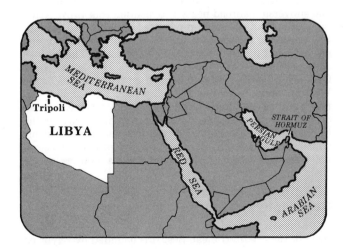

Muammar al-Qaddafi

As long as Qaddafi could use Libya's huge oil profits to improve Libya's standard of living, the small Libyan population tolerated his foreign adventures, and he enjoyed considerable popularity. Falling oil prices during the 1980s, however, led to economic disruption. Libya's declining economic fortunes, Qaddafi's domestic repression, and the disorder resulting from his sometimes bizarre political and economic policies dramatically eroded the Libyan leader's support among his people. By the end of the 1980s what popularity Qaddafi had enjoyed during the heyday of oil revenues in the 1970s had dissipated, leaving him in control of Libya largely by virtue of his command of the military and security forces.

Moreover, the Libyan military—on which Qaddafi had showered as much as $1 billion a year in advanced Soviet equipment—had performed poorly during the late 1980s. Libyan forces were beaten in several clashes with the United States (most notably the 1986 American bombing raid of Libya), and the Libyan army was defeated in Chad by the ragtag Chadian army (with French assistance). These developments cast doubt on Qaddafi's ability to hold on to power, despite his twenty-year tenure as Libyan leader and his control of the elements of force.

Three aspects of Qaddafi's foreign policy remained more or less unchanged in the two decades that followed the 1969 coup: his ardent desire for Arab unity through mergers with other Arab nations, his staunch opposition to outside nations—especially Western—seeking to affect the course of events in the Middle East, and his hostility to Israel, which he views as the major manifestation of Western imperialism in the region. Other Qaddafi policies emerged over time or changed after his accession to power: his own brand of Islamic fundamentalism, his unique political theories, his willingness to support domestic subversive groups in other countries and international terrorist groups whose goals seem to match his own, and his pragmatic relationship with the Soviet Union.

During the early 1970s U.S. policy toward the new Libyan leader was somewhat ambivalent because anticommunism was an early hallmark of Qaddafi's regime. During the 1970s, however, as Qaddafi and Egyptian president Anwar Sadat became increasingly estranged because of Egypt's U.S.-sponsored reconciliation with Israel, the American perception of Qaddafi as a threat to U.S. interests grew. The more Sadat moved toward an agreement with Israel after the October 1973 Arab-Israeli war, the more Qaddafi moved into the forefront of the Arab "rejectionist" group that repudiated Sadat's policies. The closer American interests became identified with Sadat and his policies toward Israel, the closer Qaddafi edged toward the Soviet Union. As the Soviets' military assistance to Libya increased, American suspicions of Qaddafi increased.

In the decade of the 1980s, another element of strain was added to the already-hostile relationship between the United States and Libya: Libyan support (mostly financial, sometimes logistical) of international terrorists who attacked American citizens and interests. The Reagan administration responded first with economic sanctions, and then with military provocations and confrontation. On April 14, 1986, Reagan ordered a coordinated air strike against Libya in response to evidence that Qaddafi had supported terrorist activities. The U.S. raid destroyed several military targets and killed dozens of Libyan military personnel and civilians, including Qaddafi's daughter.

Qaddafi's radicalism appears linked to his conscious desire to follow the early policies of his hero, Gamal Abdel Nasser of Egypt. Qaddafi was profoundly influenced by the broadcasts of Radio Cairo to which he listened while growing up during the height of Nasser's influence. Like several other military coups in the Arab world, the 1969 coup in Libya was a clear emulation of Nasser's 1952 revolution. As

197

Key Facts on Libya

Area: 679,536 square miles.
Capital: Tripoli
Population: 3,956,000 (1988).
Religion: 97 percent Moslem.
Official Language: Arabic.
GNP: $22.3 billion; $5,500 per capita (1987).

Sources: World Bank Atlas 1988; CIA World Factbook 1988

chairman of Libya's Revolutionary Command Council, Qaddafi seems to have wanted to go beyond Nasser in his devotion to Arab unity, his hostility toward Israel, and his leadership of Arab and African nations.

Like Nasser, Qaddafi has not been content simply to rule; he has tried to formulate a philosophy of government to be implemented in his own nation and exported abroad. He has been a leader in the Arab rejectionist movement—those nations that refused to participate in any peace process with Israel and that cut ties with Egypt for doing so. But while many other rejectionist nations (and the Palestine Liberation Organization) have renewed formal ties with Egypt and occasionally taken a conciliatory stand toward Israel, Qaddafi has remained steadfastly hostile to both countries.

The attention focused on Qaddafi's support of Iran in the Iran-Iraq war, of radical factions of the PLO (especially the extremist Abu Nidal organization that has concentrated its attacks on American targets), and of subversive groups outside the Middle East (including the Irish Republican Army) has accentuated the image of Libya's power in the region. Although Qaddafi has used Libya's financial resources to back up his foreign policy and has purchased an impressive arsenal of Soviet weapons, he has not made major attempts to use Libyan military muscle except in Chad, where he intervened militarily in 1973, 1980, 1983, and 1987 and whose northernmost Aouzou strip he has annexed. Indeed, many discussions of Libyan radicalism and subversion abroad neglect to mention that Libya's tiny population and its single-product economy, based on rapidly depleting oil resources, make this large desert nation an unlikely candidate for regional leadership. The nations of the Middle East and North Africa do not consider Qaddafi to be the madman he is often portrayed as in the Western press, and they generally have backed him pro forma in his military confrontations with the United States. Nevertheless, they do not trust him and are willing to deal with him (and sometimes join yet another of his ephemeral merger schemes) for their own practical reasons, not necessarily because they support his policies or his goals.

Geography

Libya is located in the center of the North African coast of the Mediterranean Sea. It is bounded by Egypt on

the east, Sudan on the southeast, Tunisia and Algeria on the west, and Niger and Chad on the south. Except for those bordering Tunisia and Egypt, the areas of Libya adjacent to its neighbors are inhabited very sparsely, if at all.

With an area of 679,536 square miles (about two and a half times the size of Texas), Libya is the fourth-largest country in Africa and the fifteenth largest in the world. Most of the country is desert, and more than 90 percent of its people live in less than 10 percent of the country, primarily in the fertile areas along the 1,100-mile Mediterranean coast. The coastal strip has a Mediterranean climate of warm summers, mild winters, and scant rainfall, but most of Libya has arid, desert weather with no rainfall and no permanent rivers. There are two small areas of hills and mountains in the northeast and northwest regions and another zone of hills and mountains in the Sahara in the south and southwest.

Libya is made up of three distinct regions that, until independence in 1951, were relatively unrelated to one another. Tripolitania—about 16 percent of the nation's land area—extends from the center of the Libyan coast westward to Tunisia and has been linked with the Maghreb, a term used historically to denote Tunisia, Algeria, and Morocco. Directly to the south of Tripolitania is the region called Fezzan—33 percent of the nation and mostly desert. The entire eastern part of Libya, from the Mediterranean to the border with Chad, is Cyrenaica, which comprises 51 percent of Libya's land area. This region has been more closely associated with the Arab states of the East than with the Maghreb.

Oil and the Libyan Economy

Petroleum production dominates Libyan economic life. In addition to oil, Libya's mineral resources include large iron deposits, salt beds, and construction materials (gypsum, limestone, cement rock, and building stone). Other than some cement and gypsum, these nonpetroleum mineral resources have only begun to be exploited.

After oil was discovered in Algeria in the early 1950s, exploration began in Libya under the rule of King Idris I. The first oil was found in 1957 in western Fezzan and the first major strike occurred in 1959 in Cyrenaica. By 1961 oil was being exported by Esso. Although there are dozens of major and minor oil fields (including some offshore), the major strikes of the late 1950s and early 1960s were in Sirtica, an arid zone in the center of Libya's coastal area, and this remained the source of most of Libya's oil exports. Unlike other Middle Eastern oil-producing states that granted rights to develop their oil to a single company, Libya gave oil concessions to many petroleum companies in the United States, Great Britain, West Germany, and other nations.

Several factors have made Libyan oil particularly marketable. First, Libyan light crude has a low sulphur content, which makes it more attractive for engine use because it burns more cleanly, thereby producing less air pollution. Second, because of its proximity to the coastline, most Libyan oil can be piped directly from the well to the tanker. A third factor is the proximity of Libya to major European oil-importing nations. Libyan tankers need not go through the Suez Canal or around Africa to reach European ports, as is the case with almost all Persian Gulf oil. Finally, Libya's late start in the petroleum export business proved to be beneficial. The expertise already acquired in other Middle Eastern and North African oil fields made Libyan oil operations more efficient.

The overthrow of King Idris I in 1969 brought changes in Libyan oil policy. Although Libya had joined the Organization of Petroleum Exporting Countries (OPEC) in 1962, it encouraged foreign competition for oil exploration and provided concessionary terms for foreign companies. After Qaddafi came to power, however, oil policy became increasingly attuned to political objectives. Soon efforts were under way to "Libyanize" employment, increase posted oil prices, establish Libyan government control over the rate of oil production, and increase government ownership of the oil companies. The government demanded that foreign oil companies agree to Libyan participation or be nationalized. In September 1973 Libya nationalized 51 percent of the assets of all foreign oil companies, and six months later the government completely nationalized the Libyan holdings of three American corporations: Texaco, California-Asiatic (a subsidiary of Standard Oil of California), and Libyan-American (a subsidiary of Atlantic-Richfield). After nationalizing foreign oil interests, Libya began a policy of joint production instead of simply granting concessions to foreign concerns.

Libya's domestic energy needs are still quite limited, and very little oil is refined in Libya. Although Libyan petroleum reserves (including both oil and natural gas) are substantial, experts have estimated that they will last no more than about thirty years, depending on the rate of production.

Demography

Although it has one of the highest growth rates in the world, the Libyan population is still quite small, estimated in 1988 at just under four million. Because of the country's underpopulation, the government has encouraged a high birth rate and has imported many foreign workers to fill essential jobs in the economy. There may be as many as half a million foreigners working in Libya, most of them in the major cities of Tripoli and Benghazi.

Well over 90 percent of the Libyan people are Arabic-speaking Sunni Moslems who are ethnically a mixture of Arab and Berber stock. The rest are mainly pure Berbers, Tuareg tribes people (Moslem nomads of the central and western Sahara), black Africans, or members of various foreign communities of longstanding residence (Greek or Maltese). The Arabic dialect of the western parts of Libya in Tripolitania and Fezzan is similar to those of the other Maghreb nations to the west, while the Arab dialect prevalent in Cyrenaica is closer to that of Egypt. Although Libya is steadly becoming more urbanized, there are still nomadic and seminomadic Bedouin tribes in the desert and adjacent areas. Qaddafi himself is from one such tribe.

History

The term *Libya* was used historically—especially by the Greeks—to denote most of North Africa, and the modern nation-state of Libya is not equivalent to the area denoted by the ancient name. In fact, unlike Egypt, for example, Libya has no history as an identifiable nation before independence in 1951. Its history is that of several regions, groups, and tribes out of which the modern state of Libya was formed. The Libyans' identification with a region—either Cyrenaica, Tripolitania, or Fezzan—persisted well after independence united the three zones. Just

as in ancient times the people of Tripolitania came in contact with Phoenician civilizations further west along the coast and the inhabitants of Cyrenaica had ties with the Greeks, so also in modern times the two regions of Libya—separated by the desert of the Sirtica Basin—have tended to be oriented to the adjacent areas of North Africa. Triploitania has had close ties with the Maghreb, while Cyrenaica has identified with Egypt and the Arab world. Fezzan has maintained contacts with the coastal areas but also has ties to the African nations in the Sahel to its south: Chad, Niger, and to a lesser extent Mali.

The coastal zone appears to have been inhabited since neolithic times. Although the origin of the indigenous Berber people is still unknown, some scholars conjecture that they migrated from southwestern Asia beginning around 3000 B.C. The coast of what is now Libya was once the site of Phoenician, Greek, and Roman settlements.

Undoubtedly the most important single phenomenon of Libya's history was the advent of Islam in the middle of the seventh century. Only a little more than a decade after the death of the Prophet Muhammad in 632, Arab Moslem armies took control of Cyrenaica and overcame fierce resistance from Berbers in Tripolitania. By 663 they controlled Fezzan, and by 715 Andalusia in present-day Spain also had come under Arab Moslem rule. North Africa, like most of the great Arab empire, was ruled by caliphs (successors to the Prophet Muhammad), governing first from Damascus and later from Baghdad and then Cairo. Tripolitania lay within the realm of the semiautonomous Maghrebi dynasties that ruled most of Morocco and Algeria, while Cyrenaica was controlled by the rulers of Cairo. After a brief period of Spanish rule in Tripolitania, Ottoman authority was established, at least nominally, and by the end of the sixteenth century even Fezzan had been brought under Ottoman authority.

Early in the eighteenth century a local Turkish officer began a dynasty in Tripolitania that extended into parts of Cyrenaica. The piracy supported by the rulers in Tripoli was feared by European merchants, and in 1799 the United States, like many European states, paid tribute to Tripoli to prevent attacks against its vessels. When the United

States did not quickly meet Tripoli's demand for an increase in its payment in 1801, the American consulate was attacked and the consul expelled from Tripoli. Only after a small-scale naval war with the United States was peace restored. Political turmoil and economic problems in Tripolitania prompted reimposition of direct Ottoman rule in 1835.

In 1879 Cyrenaica was separated administratively from the rest of the country. The Ottomans exercised limited control over the more inaccessible parts of Cyrenaica and Fezzan, and in the coastal areas where the Ottomans retained control their rule was repressive, corrupt, and unpopular.

Also during the nineteenth century an Islamic religious sect began to change the lives of the people of Cyrenaica. Muhammad bin Ali al Sanusi, a native of what is now Algeria, settled in Cyrenaica in the 1840s and attracted Bedouins and town dwellers to a new approach to Islam, one that combined the mysticism of Sufi Moslems and the rationalism of orthodox Sunnis. He was soon venerated by tribal adherents, although such sainthood is abhorrent to orthodox Islam. His descendants increased the following of what became known as the Sanusi order, and by the beginning of the twentieth century it had the allegiance of virtually all Cyrenaican Bedouins as well as followers in Egypt, the Sudan, and even Arabia.

Italy was a latecomer in the European colonial rivalry in the Middle East and Africa, but by 1912 it had wrested what is now Libya from the weakened Ottoman Empire. The Italian government, however, had great difficulty subduing its new domain. Members of the Sanusi order inflicted heavy losses on Italian troops in Libya's hinterland. Nevertheless, Italy maintained control of much of Libya.

By 1916 leadership of the Sanusis was in the hands of young Muhammad Idris al Sanusi (who would become King Idris of Libya). Although the United Kingdom and Italy recognized Idris as emir (prince) of the Cyrenaican hinterland and granted him substantial autonomy over his realm, the victorious allies of World War I recognized Italy's sovereignty over Libya as a whole. The nationalists of Tripolitania, who wanted independence from Italy, were badly divided by personalities and tribal affiliations. They apparently realized that agreement on one of their own number was impossible and that a united front against the Italians was needed. Consequently, they offered Idris in 1922 the title of emir of Tripolitania and thus the leadership of their region. Idris did not aspire to authority in Tripolitania, where he had few followers, but accepted the role within a few months. This resulted in a split with the Italians, who by then were convinced that Idris threatened their control. In late 1922 Idris fled to Egypt, where he continued to guide his followers from exile.

Following Prime Minister Benito Mussolini's accession to power in 1922, Italy again attempted to subjugate its Libyan possessions. By 1931, through a brutal campaign, it finally succeeded despite strong resistance from Libyan nationalists. The Italian government exploited Libya's resources and encouraged colonization of its North African holdings aimed at relieving unemployment and overpopulation at home. More than 100,000 Italian colonists settled in Libya during the 1930s. In 1939 Libya was formally annexed to Italy. Although Italian colonial rule brought some economic progress, the life of the indigenous population was little improved in the cities and became worse in the countryside, where grazing land was confiscated for distribution to Italian settlers. The leaders of the Sanusi

sect remained for the most part outside of the country.

World War II provided Libyan nationalists with the opportunity to oust the Italians by cooperating with the British, in the hope that Britain would support Libyan independence when the war was won. Despite serious disagreements between the nationalists from Cyrenaica and Tripolitania, the two regions agreed to accept the leadership of Idris, the leader of the Sanusi sect, and to provide volunteers to the British forces. The Libyan Arab Force fought alongside the Allies under British command until the Axis forces were driven out of Libya in February 1943.

Cyrenaica and Tripolitania were administered by the British, and Fezzan by the French, from 1943 until 1951. Although the Libyan people enthusiastically welcomed Idris back into Libya, and the British allowed him to form an independent Sanusi emirate in Cyrenaica, the European powers did not believe Libya was ready for independence. Various transitional plans were devised during the late 1940s, but the Europeans were slow to reach a consensus on how to administer the former Italian colonies.

In some ways, Libya was indeed unready for independence, although a majority of its inhabitants apparently favored it. United as a single entity only since 1939, Cyrenaica and Tripolitania continued to be very different socially and politically. Tripolitanians demanded a republic, and Cyrenaicans called for a Sanusi monarchy, fearing domination by the larger and more sophisticated Tripolitanian population. Fezzan, a tribal society like Cyrenaica, had its own leading family. The economic situation was profoundly unpromising: Libya had no known natural resources and depended heavily on external aid.

Finally, a United Nations resolution was agreed upon that called for establishment of an independent, unified Libyan state by the beginning of 1952. An international council (including Libyans from each of the three regions) was set up to assist in establishing a government. A National Constituent Assembly began deliberations in late 1950 and, despite some dissent, decided upon a federal system with Idris as the monarch. On December 24, 1951, King Idris I formally declared Libya an independent state.

Although there was a legislature, the king held most of the political power. His rule was conservative and pro-Western. Occasionally the regions challenged the central government's power, and political parties were banned when they showed signs of dissent, but Idris's eighteen-year reign was generally stable. He quickly established close ties with the British and with the Americans, who were granted military base rights in exchange for economic assistance. Idris changed the constitution in 1963 in an effort to bring greater centralization to the federal form of government established in 1951. He hoped that the change would help to unify Libya and erode the regionalism that was pervasive throughout Libya's history.

Under the conservative monarchy of King Idris, Libya enjoyed particularly good relations with other conservative Arab and African nations such as Saudi Arabia and Ethiopia. Libya also remained somewhat removed from the Arab-Israeli conflict.

The low literacy rate and rising prosperity because of oil revenues might have enabled Idris to insulate his country from external conflicts and upheavals if it had not been for two related factors. First, the growing influence of Egypt's President Nasser permeated Libya as Egyptian broadcasts carried his speeches throughout the Arab world. Second, the June 1967 Arab-Israeli war, and the attendant humiliation of the Arab nations, galvanized Libyans as it did Arabs everywhere. Young people and workers began to rally to the call of Arab nationalism.

Idris did not succeed in creating a Libyan nation united around the institution of the monarchy. After nearly two decades as ruler, he was still mistrusted by Tripolitanians. Support for the monarchy eroded as many Libyans in urban areas became disillusioned with the failure of the king to spread the benefits of oil income to all segments of the population. Although Idris supported subsidies to the "front line" Arab states of Egypt and Jordan, he generally continued to pursue policies that favored the West at a time when anti-Western sentiments were becoming more pronounced throughout the Arab world. In September 1969 King Idris was overthrown by a coup launched by army units in Benghazi.

Qaddafi's Regime

Although the names of the twelve members of the Revolutionary Command Council that seized power on September 1, 1969, were not released until the following year, a week after the coup one of the RCC members, Capt. Muammar al-Qaddafi, was promoted to colonel and named commander in chief. He was just twenty-seven years old. Since then Qaddafi has been the predominant force in Libyan politics. His ideas and policies have been implemented. His Bedouin background, his education in Moslem schools, and his adolescence during the height of anti-imperialism and Nasserism all influenced his thinking. Scholars have traced his puritanical personal life, his aversion to both capitalism and communism, and his inclination to egalitarianism to his early life and upbringing.

The new government quickly championed Arab unity, the Palestinian cause, and an Arab-Islamic style of socialism. It was clear from the beginning that Qaddafi and the Free Officers' movement, a group of young reformist military men who had carried out the coup, looked to Nasser's Egypt as the model for their new government. The slogans about socialism and Arab unity, the titles (the Free Officers' movement, the Revolutionary Command Council), and the organizations (the Arab Socialist Union as the political party) all were an expression of Qaddafi's hero worship of Nasser. Nasser himself had learned, by 1969, to temper his political objectives according to prevailing political realities, but Qaddafi was ready immediately to pursue all the goals that his new government espoused. A few weeks after the coup, Qaddafi's deputy, Abdel Sallem Jalloud, traveled to Egypt and the Sudan to propose unification of the three nations. Qaddafi repeatedly demonstrated an obsession with achieving Arab unity through schemes to unify profoundly different political systems.

After the coup the new regime sought to mollify foreign friends of the deposed king by declaring that Libya would adhere to its treaty obligations. Despite such assurances, the United States and the United Kingdom—each with ties to Idris—were soon disillusioned. The new regime prosecuted (mostly in absentia) former officials and expelled many Jews and Italians. Libya's relations with the West deteriorated. Even before Qaddafi seized power, the United States had agreed to leave Wheelus Air Force Base in Libya. A national holiday was declared on the day the U.S. evacuation was completed in June 1970.

In the mid-1970s Qaddafi began to move closer to the Soviet Union and its allies, principally through arms transfer agreements. Nevertheless, Qaddafi has never reneged on his denunciation of communism as a form of atheism and has never permitted the establishment of a Communist (or indeed any other nongovernment) party in Libya.

Observers of Libyan internal politics have been puzzled by Qaddafi's disappearance from public view in 1972 and again in 1974. In both instances, Qaddafi left his administrative duties in the hands of his trusted second-in-command, Jalloud, who was appointed prime minister in 1972. On both occasions Qaddafi retained the post of commander in chief of the armed forces. Qaddafi's brief withdrawals from politics in 1972 and 1974 are now viewed by analysts as periods in which he devoted himself to political reflection and the formulation of his ideology. These "retreats" do not appear to have resulted in a diminution of Qaddafi's power.

Qaddafi's political philosophy has developed through several stages. In 1973 he introduced a "cultural revolution" reminiscent of China's in the mid-1960s. Castigating the Libyan people for their lack of revolutionary fervor, Qaddafi ordered the annulment of all pre-1969 laws and the repression not only of communism but also of capitalism, the Moslem Brotherhood (a militant Sunni group), and any manifestation of atheism. He rejected all "non-Islamic thinking" and established "people's committees" throughout the country and at every level of the government. He declared that this program marked the beginning of a return to the true Islamic heritage of decision making by consultation.

The next stage in Qaddafi's political thinking resulted from his 1974 retreat. The following year he reorganized the party he had created after the coup—the Arab Socialist Union—into people's congresses. People's congresses are large gatherings of Libyans that operate, in Qaddafi's view, as manifestations of direct democracy. At a people's congress, individuals are technically free to express their views openly. In practice, these meetings often tend to be little more than rallies to back government policy. Despite Qaddafi's condemnation of representation, congresses at lower levels do send people to the General People's Congress. This apparent contradiction has never been explained by the government.

In 1977 the General People's Congress became the main organ of government in Libya, and the country's name was changed to the Socialist People's Libyan Arab Jamahiriya (an invented word meaning roughly "state of the masses"). Although power still rests securely in Qaddafi's hands, neither he nor any of his former RCC colleagues has formally held office in Libya since 1977.

During Qaddafi's 1974 retreat he assembled his political philosophy into a book. His *Green Book, Part I*, which is entitled *The Solution of the Problem of Democracy*, was published in 1976. This was followed in 1978 by *The Green Book, Part II: The Solution of the Economic Problem— Socialism*. In Part I he declared that representation is an inherently undemocratic concept. He explicitly rejected not only representational democracy but also parliaments, referendums, majoritarian electoral systems, and multiparty and single-party systems. In Part II of the *Green Book* Qaddafi proclaimed his belief that every man has the right to a house, an income, and a vehicle. While mandating rights to private ownership of one house (and no more), Qaddafi urged the abolition of business, and in 1978 he encouraged the takeover by people's committees of many business establishments, especially retailing operations. Qaddafi's fundamental theory, what he calls the "Third International Theory," rejects capitalism and communism and claims to establish in Libya true, direct democracy.

The implementation of Qaddafi's eccentric ideas has wrought havoc with daily life in Libya. Some schemes have been merely expensive, such as the plane in the late 1980s to move the capital and transfer the government ministries to scattered locations around the nation or the building of the "great man-made river"—an extraordinarily costly water pipeline from aquifers deep in the desert to the coastal area. Other actions have damaged the economy severely in the interest of Qaddafi's utopian notions of equality, such as the abolition of retail trade, the seizure of bank accounts and businesses, the destruction of land tenure records, and a proposal for the abolition of money.

Domestic Issues

The two key domestic issues in Libya are the chaotic state of the economy and political repression. As long as Qaddafi kept the standard of living of the population high and had the money for projects, such as water wells, schools, and housing, that directly benefited the Libyan people, there was a general tolerance for his bizarre political theories, his foreign adventurism, and even his dictatorial powers at home. The world oil glut of the early 1980s dramatically lowered Libya's oil earnings from about $22 billion in 1980 to less than half that amount in 1985. A year later they were almost halved again. Foreign exchange reserves dropped by 80 percent in the same period.

Unlike many developing nations, Libya has not taken out significant loans from foreign countries and banks. Nevertheless its unpaid bills to foreign businesses for purchases of industrial equipment and other items and services may amount to as much as $4 billion, and it owes at least that much to the Soviet Union for military equipment. There are shortages of food and consumer goods, due to bureaucratic inefficiency and unpaid bills abroad. Inflation is only partially disguised by price controls. Almost three-quarters of the labor force is employed by the government, and sudden salary cuts and dismissals of personnel without university educations have created insecurity among workers. Travel restrictions have been imposed both by the Libyan government and by Western governments and opportunities for study abroad have been curtailed as well.

In addition to these troubling economic conditions, Libyans must contend with a politically repressive regime. Reports indicate that hundreds of Libyans have been executed over the two decades of Qaddafi's rule and thousands of political prisoners are in his jails. There is no mechanism for political activity other than that sanctioned—and controlled—by the government. All political parties are banned and membership in them, or in fundamentalist Moslem groups, is a capital crime.

Qaddafi remains in power by balancing the agents of his repression. Like most military dictators, he fears the army most of all. He has relied on three principal groups to stay in power—and has played them off against one another to prevent any of the three from gaining ascendency: his old colleagues from the RCC (especially his second-in-command, Jalloud); relatives from his own Qadadfa tribe; and his "Revolutionary Guards"—small detachments of young men established all over the country, even in the military itself. The latter, although under the command of Jalloud, seem to be intensely loyal to Qaddafi personally. They were involved in the assassination of Libyan dissidents abroad; they "kept order" in the capital after a major dissident attack in May 1984; and they maintain a watchful and sometimes violent vigilance over the population at large. Experts disagree on the relative power of each of these three groups, and of the regular military, in recent years. Qaddafi himself seems finally to have perceived the popular resentment of the Revolutionary Guards and, as part of a limited liberalization of the political atmosphere in September 1988, he criticized the Guards' "excesses," such as the arbitrary arrests that had terrorized the population. He also loosened travel restrictions and reopened borders with some of the neighboring states.

Foreign Policy Issues

Qaddafi's principal foreign policy problem is his isolation. None of the governments of Libya's neighboring states likes or trusts him, for good reasons. Each of them has been the target of verbal abuse and, in several cases, subversion or attack. Their relations with Tripoli change according to several factors: Qaddafi's own interest in reaching accommodation with them, their own need for funds or aid from Libya, the degree of polarization in the Arab world, and their desire to see diminished Libyan aid to their own dissident groups or external enemies. Not since the earliest days of his regime have any neighboring states dealt with Qaddafi on the basis of ideology or common principles. To take only one recent example, Morocco's King Hassan agreed to a bizarre unification of his country with Libya in 1984 to end Libyan aid to the Polisario guerrillas who are fighting in the Western Sahara to prevent Morocco from annexing their land. The unification agreement, which was signed but never implemented, was renounced in the wake of Qaddafi's criticism of the king's meeting in July 1986 with Israeli Prime Minister Shimon Peres. Attempts at unity with Egypt, Sudan, and Syria (beginning in 1970), with Tunisia (1974), and with Syria (1980) also ended in acrimony.

Libya's isolation in the Arab world was accentuated by political developments in the late 1980s. The end of the Iraq-Iran war (in which Qaddafi had backed non-Arab Iran), Egypt's reentry into the Arab fold, and the PLO's moderated stance and dialogue with the United States all undermined Qaddafi's unquenched ambition to play a leading role in a radicalized, rejectionist Arab world. His policy of opposition to any negotiations with Israel and his support of extremist splinter groups of the PLO are less relevant since Yasir Arafat's acceptance of UN Resolution 242 and recognition of Israel.

Relations with the Soviet Union have also been somewhat strained. Although the Soviets denounced the 1986 American bombing of Libya and promised to make up the equipment lost in the confrontation with the United States, Qaddafi criticized them for failing to prevent the attack. The Soviets agreed to provide new, advanced military aircraft in early 1989, but it was unclear whether the Soviet Union would continue to maintain close relations with Libya given Mikhail Gorbachev's strategy of improving relations with the West.

Libya's relations with the United States remain extremely bad. There is no official contact between the two nations, and American economic sanctions, first imposed in 1981, remain in effect. In late 1988 and early 1989 the United States sought international condemnation and sanctions against Libya for constructing what the United States claimed was a factory capable of producing chemical weapons. The possibility of continued small military confrontations between American naval forces and Libya in the Mediterranean remains, although such clashes have became less likely since President Ronald Reagan, who seemed to have a personal obsession with the Libyan leader, left office.

Although the West Europeans did enact sanctions against Libya in 1986, and Great Britain severed its relations with Libya in 1988 following a terrorist incident at the Libyan embassy in London, the Europeans retain economic ties with Libya. Several thousand West Europeans live in Libya, and Libya has outstanding debts to businesses in Italy and West Germany. France, West Germany, Great Britain, and Spain also still have investments in Libya. Despite the sanctions, most West European governments believe the Reagan administration went too far in its confrontations with Libya and wish to retain a relationship not only because of Libyan oil supplies, but also to prevent Qaddafi from moving closer to the Soviet Union.

The next most serious foreign policy issue for Qaddafi is the failure of the Libyan army in Chad. Twice in 1987 Chadian forces, equipped and supported by the French and Americans, routed invading Libyan troops, who reportedly lost three thousand (out of ten thousand) men and $1 billion of equipment. This embarrassing defeat of Qaddafi's costly military machine in its only substantial conflict was not reported by the official Libyan news media, but it became known widely in the country nonetheless.

Qaddafi's isolation may cause him to focus his attention on the home front, as he began to do with his limited political liberalization program in late 1988. The freedom in foreign policy afforded him by Libya's oil wealth of the 1970s has ended, although it took Qaddafi some time to realize the depth of the domestic problems facing him. Nevertheless, he is unlikely to change many of his extreme foreign policy positions—on Israel, on the United States, on peacemaking—because such changes would force him to deny his own ideology and back down from frequently stated policy goals.

He can also be expected to continue to press his claim to the Aouzou strip in Chad, because it is a sovereignty issue (and is believed to have deposits of uranium), and to seek mergers with Arab states as he has in the past. A closer embrace of the Soviet Union or the offering of a base such as Tobruk to the Soviets remains unlikely because Qaddafi remains essentially anti-Communist, despite his tactical alliance with the Soviet Union. In addition, if relations continue to improve between the Soviet Union and the United States, the Soviets may reduce aid to the unpredictable Libyan ruler as a concession to the West.

Even if Qaddafi increased his attention to domestic politics he might not be able to prevent his eventual downfall. There were coup conspiracies and other challenges to Qaddafi's rule by dissident forces throughout the 1980s. A major uprising seemed unlikely, despite the unpopularity of the regime, but such forces as Islamic fundamentalism could provide a rallying point of opposition against Qaddafi. He retained firm control of the clergy, but some of his policies, such as putting women in the military, making divorce easier for women to obtain, and discouraging polygamy, alienated many devout Moslems. Although Qaddafi himself claims to be a devout Moslem, and leads a rather ascetic life, his religious views and policies are quite unorthodox.

Qaddafi has demonstrated over the last twenty years that he has the political skill necessary to remain in power. Nevertheless, a military coup, whether by pro-Soviet, Islamic fundamentalist, or pragmatic officers, remains a real possibility. In a closed society such as Libya there is often little sign of a dramatic change until the moment it occurs. If Qaddafi is removed from power, the event is likely to be as much of a surprise as was Qaddafi's own coup d'etat in 1969.

Economies Diversify after Oil Crash

Not long ago the desert sheikdoms that dot the western and southern shores of the Persian Gulf were remote and backward lands peopled by camel herders and pearl harvesters. The world was barely conscious of places such as Kuwait, Bahrain, Abu Dhabi, Dubai, Oman, and Qatar.

But that was before the dramatic increase in demand for oil, coupled with price hikes by the Organization of Petroleum Exporting Countries (OPEC). Since 1973-1974, when oil prices began increasing sharply, the Persian Gulf states have become significant forces in the world economy, with Kuwait, Abu Dhabi, and Qatar enjoying per capita incomes exceeding those of many Western industrialized nations. Oil revenues produced substantial funds for domestic development projects and investments overseas.

The oil glut of the mid-1980s, however, sent oil prices plummeting and seriously reduced the oil revenues of the Persian Gulf states. Their leaders were forced to cut back on spending for social services, construction, economic development, and defense. While oil is still their main source of income, and oil prices recovered somewhat in the late 1980s, the Gulf states are trying to create diversified economies that would insulate them from falling oil prices and continue to provide a high standard of living after oil reserves have been depleted. Bahrain, which is closest to exhausting its oil reserves, and Qatar have been the most active in developing alternative industries.

The Gulf states are dependent to varying degrees on Saudi Arabia for policy guidance and security, yet all are determined to avoid Saudi domination. In response to the threats posed by the Iran-Iraq war, the states of Bahrain, Kuwait, Qatar, the United Arab Emirates (UAE), Oman, and Saudi Arabia joined to create the Gulf Cooperation Council (GCC) in 1981. The organization's purpose is to enhance regional security and prosperity through greater military, economic, and political coordination.

During the 1980s area leaders were preoccupied with the Gulf war and the growing threat of Shi'ite unrest within the largely Sunni-dominated Gulf states. Although the war

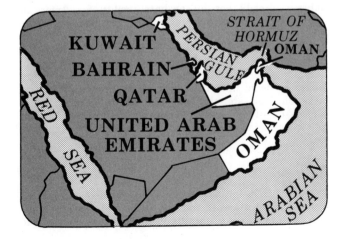

has ended, the conservative societies of the Gulf states will continue to be vulnerable to terrorism and internal strife.

Bahrain

Area: 260 square miles.
Capital: Manama.
Population: 480,000.
Religion: Moslem; 70 percent Shi'ite.
Official language: Arabic; English is widely spoken.
GNP: $4.0 billion; $8,330 per capita.

Bahrain, the smallest of the Persian Gulf states, was the first to export oil in the 1930s. It established the foundations for a modern, industrialized economy earlier than its neighbors, enabling it to become a regional banking and service center during the oil boom of the 1970s.

During the 1980s Bahrain faced a number of challenges to its political and economic stability. Soon after the Ayatollah Khomeini seized power in Iran, Bahrain's Shi'ite population became the focus of Tehran's efforts to incite a fundamentalist revolution in the Gulf. The depression of the oil market in the mid-1980s further aggravated social tensions and complicated the government's development plans. With rapidly diminishing oil resources, Bahrain became more dependent on the aid of its Gulf neighbors.

Although the end of the Iran-Iraq war is likely to lead to greater stability in the Gulf, the Bahraini regime continues to be challenged by a politically disenfranchised Shi'ite majority and a domestic economy that will soon become the first in the Gulf to enter the postpetroleum era.

Geography

Bahrain, meaning "two seas," is an archipelago of about thirty-five islands, six of which are inhabited. Al-Bahrain—the largest island and the location of the capital, Manama—is also the country's namesake. Situated in the Persian Gulf, Bahrain lies between the Saudi Arabian coast and the Qatari Peninsula. Its total land mass is one-fifth the size of Rhode Island. Al-Muharraq, connected to Manama by a causeway, is the second principal island and the location of Bahrain's international airport. Bahrain's climate is hot and humid most of the year with daytime temperatures often exceeding 100 degrees Fahrenheit. Oil and gas are the country's only natural resources, and they are expected to last only ten and thirty years, respectively. Pearling, a traditional industry, has almost ceased to exist.

Demography

The vast majority of the approximately 480,000 Bahrainis are Moslems. Bahrain has a higher proportion of native citizens to resident aliens than many Gulf countries. The immigrant residents, nearly one-third of the inhabitants, are mostly non-Arab Asians from India, Iran, and Pakistan. Bahrain is also the only Gulf country besides Iran and Iraq where Shi'ite Moslems outnumber Sunnis. Seventy percent of Bahrain's population is Shi'ite, although the ruling al-Khalifa family is Sunni. Shi'ites do not hold wealth and power in proportion to their numbers. Arabic is the official language, but Persian is often spoken among the Iranian-descended Bahrainis. By Gulf standards, Bahrain has a sophisticated population, noted for its intellectual tradition and articulate labor force.

History

Bahrain was the site of the ancient civilization of Dilmun, which flourished as a trading center from 2000 to 1800 B.C. Portuguese sailors captured the strategically important islands from local Arab tribes in A.D. 1521 and ruled until 1602. The islands were then alternately controlled by Arab and Persian forces until the Arabian Utub tribe expelled the Persians in 1783. The members of the al-Khalifa family established themselves as sheiks in 1782 and have ruled ever since.

British interests in the Persian Gulf developed in the early nineteenth century as London sought safe passage for its ships to India, Iraq, and Iran. By 1820 the British established hegemony over the islands, taking over the responsibility of defense and foreign affairs. The al-Khalifa family claimed suzerainty over neighboring Qatar until 1868, when at the request of Qatari notables the British opposed Bahraini claims.

Bahrain's special relationship with Britain continued until 1971. British interference in Bahraini domestic affairs was minimal and both countries enjoyed the support of the other. After World War II, Britain moved its regional ambassador from Iran to Bahrain.

In 1968 the United Kingdom announced its intention to end its treaty obligations to the Persian Gulf sheikdoms by 1971. Bahrain then joined Qatar and the Trucial States (now called the United Arab Emirates) in negotiations aimed at forming a confederation. Plans for a union failed, and in 1971 Bahrain became an independent state.

Current Issues

Bahrain is officially a constitutional monarchy under the dynastic rule of the al-Khalifa family. A thirty-seat national assembly elected in 1973 was dissolved in August 1975 after alleged subversive activity by some assembly members. Emir Isa bin Sulman al-Khalifa, who ascended to the throne on November 2, 1961, at the age of twenty-eight, now rules through an appointed cabinet. All major ministerial posts are held by members of the al-Khalifa family. The traditional administrative system of *majlis,* whereby residents directly present petitions to the emir, remains.

Bahrain's modest petroleum reserves provided steadily decreasing revenues in the 1980s. Most of Bahrain's income comes from refining Saudi and local crude. The country also has an aluminum industry, a ship repair center, and offshore banking services that are largely free from regulation or taxation. The advantages of this banking environment have prompted more than a hundred international banks to open offices in Bahrain. At the height of the oil boom, Bahrain became the region's financial and banking capital, surpassing Hong Kong in total assets. However, the collapse of world oil prices in the mid-1980s hurt Bahrain's oil and banking industries. The resulting decline in revenues severely depressed the economy and necessitated reductions in government spending.

Tensions created by the economic slowdown and religious divisions have threatened to rally the politically disenfranchised in Bahrain. Of principal concern to the al-Khalifa regime has been the potential for domestic unrest among its majority Shi'ite population. Shortly after the Ayatollah Khomeini seized power in Iran in 1979, unrest increased among Bahrain's Shi'ites. In 1981 security officials uncovered an attempted coup by Shi'ite Bahrainis that was thought to be directed by Imam Hadi al-Mudarasi, an Iranian Shi'ite formerly in exile in Bahrain. The government believed that all seventy-three convicted conspirators, representing the Islamic Front for the Liberation of Bahrain, received guerrilla training in Iran. In February 1984 an arms cache discovered in Bahrain's Shi'ite section was attributed to Iran. Another plot to overthrow the government was discovered in 1985, and a plan to sabotage Bahrain's petroleum refinery was disclosed in December 1987.

The al-Khalifa regime has made considerable efforts to conciliate the Shi'ite community. While strengthening its internal security forces, the government has shown leniency to Shi'ite dissidents. It chose to waive the death penalty for the perpetrators of the aborted 1981 coup. The regime has also increased Shi'ite representation in the cabinet and bureaucracy and has shown greater respect for Shi'ite religious rituals and traditions. Since the mid-1980s the level of support for the Iranian government has diminished, as most Bahraini Shi'ites became disenchanted with the direction of Iran's revolution and the Iran-Iraq war. Still, disaffection among the Shi'ite citizenry will likely remain a problem for the regime as long as the Shi'ites are less well off than Sunni citizens and feel they are inadequately represented in the government.

Of equal concern to the Bahraini regime are issues of regional security. Because of Bahrain's small size and important strategic position it is particularly vulnerable to instability in the Gulf and depends heavily on collective defense arrangements. In 1981 Bahrain signed a bilateral defense pact with Saudi Arabia and joined five other Gulf states in forming the Gulf Cooperation Council. In 1984 Bahrain received funds from the GCC for improvement of its defenses and participated with Qatar and other Gulf states in the GCC's "peninsula shield" military exercises. By the end of the Gulf war Bahrain also bought four F-16s from the United States and began constructing an air base. Bahrain already has an onshore facility for American forces, and there is a large U.S. Navy presence in the country.

The maintenance of safe merchant transport in the Persian Gulf is especially important to Bahrain, as the Bahraini economy relies heavily on its oil refining and tanker-servicing industries. During the Iran-Iraq war attacks on Gulf shipping led Bahrain to take a bolder stance—openly expressing support for Iraq and for Kuwait's decision to seek international protection for oil tankers.

Outlook

The conclusion of the Iran-Iraq war and the gradual increase in oil prices in the late 1980s bode well for Bahrain's future. Greater stability in the Gulf may also enable

Bahrain to regain its position as the trade and service center in the region. If the oil market continues to improve, Bahrain will be well situated to reap the benefits of the Gulf's economic revival.

Although the Bahraini banking industry was scaled down in the mid-1980s due to declining oil revenues and competition from Kuwaiti and Saudi banks, Bahrain is still a preferred location for business in the region, because of its first-rate communications, permissive banking laws, tolerance of Western social customs, and time zone, which allows dealers to trade with Tokyo and Singapore in the morning and London and New York in the afternoon. The country's early economic diversification efforts and well-educated population provide Bahrain with a strong industrial base as well.

Bahrain's future will rest heavily on its oil-rich neighbors. As its oil reserves continue to diminish, Bahrain will become increasingly dependent on its income from peripheral industries servicing the better-endowed Gulf countries. Joint industrial projects undertaken by the GCC have become more important to Bahrain's prosperity, as has the construction of the King Fahd Causeway, a twenty-five-kilometer link between Bahrain and Saudi Arabia that has provided new channels for trade and tourism between Bahrain and the other Gulf states.

Bahrain will still remain highly vulnerable to the uncertainties in the oil market and instability in the region. Future downturns in oil prices would jeopardize Bahrain's extensive industrial projects and expanding financial markets. The resumption of hostilities in the Gulf could threaten the Bahraini economy by destroying international business confidence and place the country's own security at risk. Because of Bahrain's small size and limited security forces the country continues to be open to threats of outside aggression and foreign intrigue.

As the only Arab Gulf state with a Shi'ite majority, Bahrain is likely to remain susceptible to Iranian subversion. Tehran still maintains an eighteenth-century territorial claim to Bahrain and has been persistent in its desire to gain control of the island. The Shi'ites in Bahrain continue to be an unpredictable force in Bahraini politics. While the appeal of the Iranian revolution has died down, the traditionally vocal Shi'ite community is likely to demand greater political and economic equality. Another potential source of domestic unrest arises from Bahrain's young educated class. The al-Khalifa regime has been under pressure from this class for some time to reconvene the national assembly—which has been dissolved since 1975—and to move in the direction of a more modern democratic form of government.

Kuwait

Area: 6,880 square miles.
Capital: Kuwait City.
Population: 1,938,000.
Religion: Nearly all Moslem; majority are Sunni with about 30 percent Shi'ite.
Official language: Arabic; English is widely spoken.
GNP: $27.3 billion; $14,870 per capita.

Before 1935 life in Kuwait revolved around pearl div-ing, fishing, and trade with India and Africa. Most of the inhabitants were Bedouin nomads. Today, as a result of the discovery and exploitation of vast oil reserves four decades ago, Kuwait is one of the world's richest countries.

While Kuwait has enjoyed forty years of economic prosperity, it has been vulnerable to both internal and external threats to its security. Positioned at the vortex of the Iran-Iraq war through the 1980s, Kuwait was forced to weather military threats from Iran and occasional Iranian attacks on its shipping. Although the July 1988 cease-fire between Iran and Iraq decreased the direct military threat from Iran, Kuwait's ruling al-Sabah family is still threatened by militants bent on ousting the country's moderate leadership in favor of a fundamentalist Islamic government.

Geography

Kuwait—meaning "little hut"—lies at the head of the Persian Gulf, bordering Iraq and Saudi Arabia. Roughly the size of New Jersey, the country covers 6,880 square miles. Nearly two-thirds of Kuwait's inhabitants live in Kuwait City, the capital. The oil towns of Ahmadi, Jahra, Hawalli, and Fahaheel are the other principal cities.

As a result of the 1922 Treaty of Uqayr, ending hostilities between Kuwait and Saudi Arabia, there is a 2,200-square-mile neutral zone south of Kuwait. Kuwait and Saudi Arabia each administer half of the zone, and oil revenues from the entire area are shared equally.

Kuwait's terrain is mainly flat desert with few oases. Blazing summer temperatures often reach well into the hundreds, with cooler winters bringing frequent dust storms. Petroleum-based products are the only financially exploitable resources, with significant oil reserves estimated to last for more than a century.

Demography

The people of Kuwait are primarily Arab in origin, but only 40 percent are indigenous to Kuwait. Many expatriated Arabs have taken up residency, drawn by the employment opportunities of the oil boom. Kuwait also has sizable Iranian and Indian communities. Fears of internal unrest and terrorism related to Islamic fundamentalism and the quest for a Palestinian homeland have prompted the Kuwaiti government to quietly work toward changing the composition of the country's work force from one dominated by Arabs and Iranians to one that relies more on workers from India, Pakistan, and other parts of Asia.

Kuwaiti citizens are entitled to a wide array of free services, but immigrant workers' benefits are limited. This situation has led to hostility between the minority native Kuwaiti population and the majority immigrant population. Only persons meeting stringent conditions can become Kuwaiti citizens, largely because of the generous benefits that come with citizenship. About 70 percent of Kuwaitis are Sunni Moslems while 30 percent are Shi'ite. The ruling al-Sabah family is Sunni.

History

Kuwait's modern history dates from the founding of the city of Kuwait by a sect of the Anaiza tribe at the beginning of the eighteenth century. The ruling Sabah dynasty was founded in the middle of that century, when settlers decided to appoint a sheik to administer their affairs, provide them with services, and represent them in dealings with the Ottoman Empire.

During the latter half of the nineteenth century, Kuwait looked to Britain as a counterbalance to Ottoman dominance in the region. In 1899 Mubarak al-Sabah "the Great" signed an agreement with the United Kingdom, effectively establishing Kuwait as a British protectorate. This arrangement, in which Britain handled Kuwait's foreign affairs and security, lasted until 1961. On two occasions, the British intervened on Kuwait's behalf. The first action repelled attacks from the Wahhabis, a tribe from central Arabia. The 1922 Treaty of Uqayr settled the conflict and established a neutral zone south of Kuwait. In 1961, at the time of independence, Iraq proclaimed its sovereignty over Kuwait based on old Ottoman records. When Baghdad threatened to invade, Kuwait asked for and received British military assistance, deterring Iraqi action. An Arab League peacekeeping force soon replaced the British, and Iraq recognized Kuwait's independence in 1963. That same year Kuwait was admitted into the United Nations.

Current Issues

Kuwait is a constitutional monarchy ruled by an emir. The current emir, Sheik Jaber al-Ahmad al-Sabah, succeeded to the throne December 31, 1977. The 1962 constitution contains provisions on the powers and relationships of the branches of government and on the rights of citizens. Upon the death of an emir, the crown prince assumes his position. A new crown prince is then selected by members of the Sabah family.

The constitution also established the fifty-member National Assembly. As a result of strict eligibility requirements, however, no more than 5 percent of Kuwaitis qualify to vote in assembly elections. Women, immigrants, and persons who are illiterate or under twenty-one years old are excluded. The assembly was suspended from 1976 to 1981 because the ruling emirs feared its increasingly vocal debates could contribute to instability. The assembly was again suspended in July 1986 after it reverted to a forum for inter-Arab and domestic disputes.

Of all the Gulf nations, Kuwait has been the most vulnerable to regional disruption. The threat of Iranian-sponsored Islamic fanaticism is keenly felt and terrorists have struck Kuwait many times. The next-door Iran-Iraq war had a profound effect on Kuwait, as Kuwaiti territory and shipping were an occasional target of Iranian military aggression. Beginning in May 1984 Iran began bombing Kuwaiti oil tankers in the Persian Gulf. The bombings were perceived as warnings to Kuwait to reduce its support for Iraq in the Gulf war.

In early 1987 Kuwait sought protection for its oil tankers from both the United States and the Soviet Union. The development of increased Iranian military power deployed to threaten Gulf shipping and a desire to prevent the Soviet Union from gaining influence in the Gulf region led the United States to accept Kuwait's request for assistance. In May 1987 eleven Kuwaiti tankers were put under American registration (reflagged), entitling them to U.S. naval protection. The Soviet Union concurrently registered three Kuwaiti tankers for Soviet protection. Since the July 1988 cease-fire reduced the military threat to its shipping, Kuwait has begun sailing several of the reflagged tankers under Kuwaiti colors.

Despite the cease-fire, the danger of Iranian-sponsored terrorist acts by Iranians living in Kuwait and Kuwait's own Shi'ite population remains. In late 1983 and early 1984 car bombs wracked Western embassies and Kuwaiti military installations. In response to the increasing terrorism, the government deported thousands of Iranians and increased restrictions on free passage through Kuwait.

In May 1985 an Iraqi member of the banned Voice of Islam organization tried to assassinate the emir by driving a car bomb into a royal procession. The attack was seen as a reaction to Kuwait's refusal to release seventeen convicted terrorists involved in 1983 car bombings of Western embassies. In April 1988 a Kuwait Airways Boeing 747 was hijacked by a group believed to be part of a pro-Iranian Shi'ite organization in Lebanon. After landing in Iran the group demanded the release of the seventeen terrorists. The fifteen-day hijacking ordeal, in which two Kuwaitis were killed, eventually ended in Algeria where the plane had been forced to land. The Algerian government negotiated the release of the hostages in exchange for safe passage out of the country for the hijackers. Fundamentalist Shi'ite groups committed other terrorist acts against Kuwait in 1988, signaling a continued threat of terrorism in the country.

For many years Kuwait's economic situation has been the envy of many developing nations. Its vast oil resources have brought an era of great prosperity, and its per capita income is one of the highest in the world. Kuwait has developed a generous welfare state in which Kuwaiti citizens do not pay taxes but are entitled to a wide range of services including free education, free medical care, and virtually free housing.

The onset of the oil glut of the 1980s, however, inflicted some serious financial difficulties on Kuwait. In September 1982 its Soukh al-Mankh stock exchange collapsed, leading to a prolonged financial crisis. Lower oil prices have resulted in the government's first budget deficits, but the country's economic difficulties have not become so severe that they have diminished the quality of life for most Kuwaitis.

Outlook

The cease-fire between Iran and Iraq has meant that Kuwait is no longer threatened by a potential widening of that war and its shipping is no longer imperiled by bombing raids in the Persian Gulf. The American reflagging of Kuwaiti tankers put the U.S.-Kuwait relationship on firm ground after it had been shaken in the mid-1980s by the U.S. sale of weapons to Iran and Washington's refusal to sell Kuwait Stinger antiaircraft missiles. What effect the death of Iran's Ayatollah Ruhollah Khomeini in June 1989 will have on Islamic fundamentalism in Kuwait and elsewhere in the Middle East remains to be seen. Given Kuwait's recent experience with Iran-sponsored or -encouraged Islamic fundamentalist terrorism, however, the Kuwaiti leadership will surely continue to make internal security a high priority.

Despite recent financial setbacks, Kuwait's economic outlook is more promising than problematic. With the cessation of the Iran-Iraq war and the return of relative calm to Persian Gulf shipping, Kuwait can expect to regain its prehostilities trading position in the oil market. The government has also taken steps to reduce spending and diversify its economy somewhat, attempting to reduce the effects of lower oil revenues.

One potential cloud over Kuwait's economic future is

the country's rapid population growth, which is slightly greater than 3.7 percent. An expanding Kuwaiti population with its attendant entitlement expectations may force an uncomfortably finer slicing of the economic pie. Nevertheless, possession of the world's second-largest oil reserves by such a small country guarantees a sound economy for the foreseeable future.

Oman

Area: 82,030 square miles.
Capital: Muscat.
Population: 1,345,000.
Religion: Moslem; majority are Ibadhi sect, and approximately 20 percent, Sunni.
Official language: Arabic; Persian, Urdu are also spoken.
GNP: $7.8 billion; per capita $5,780.

The sultanate of Oman has long been considered the political maverick of the Persian Gulf. Most notable is its independent foreign policy and strong commitment to the West, especially the United States. A *New York Times* article in 1985 aptly dubbed Oman as America's "most reliable ally in the Persian Gulf." It was the only Gulf nation to endorse the Camp David accords and refuse to sever relations with Egypt because it made peace with Israel.

Formerly known as the sultanate of Muscat and Oman, the country changed its name in 1970 after the current sultan, Qaboos bin Said, gained power. Inner Oman and the coastal strip where Muscat is situated traditionally have been at odds over religious and political matters. The name change signaled an effort to unite the country in its attempt to modernize.

Relations with the United States date back to 1833 when the two countries established formal diplomatic relations. During the 1970s the United States eclipsed Great Britain's traditional role of protector and trusted ally. Since then, Oman has become increasingly involved in U.S. strategic plans for establishing a rapid deployment force in the Middle East.

Oman stands out among the other Gulf states not only for its markedly warm relations with the West, but also for its relatively long and independent history as a free nation.

Geography

Oman stretches for 1,000 miles from the mouth of the Persian Gulf around the southeast coast of the Arabian Peninsula to the People's Democratic Republic of Yemen (South Yemen). The country has four distinct regions: the Musandam Peninsula, a noncontiguous province that juts into the Persian Gulf at the strategic Strait of Hormuz; the Batinah, a fertile and prosperous coastal plain that lies northwest of Muscat, the capital; Inner Oman, which is located between the Jabal al-Akhdar (Green Mountains), where heights reach 9,900 feet, and the Rub al-Khali (Empty Quarter) desert; and the Dhofar region that stretches along the southern coast to South Yemen.

A fertile country, Oman receives the tail end of the Indian monsoon rains from June to September. During most of the year Oman's desert climate is hot and exceptionally humid. The coastal area of Dhofar, however, is more tropical with less extreme temperatures.

Demography

Although no official census has ever been conducted in Oman, the population is estimated to be slightly more than one and a quarter million people. Nearly half of all Omanis live in the central hill region of Inner Oman; the most densely populated area is the Batinah Plain where about one-third of Oman's people live. The Dhofar province has approximately sixty thousand inhabitants. The al-Shahouh tribes dwell in the Musandam Peninsula and number about fifteen thousand.

Most Omanis are Ibadhi Moslems, a small Islamic sect that believes in a nonhereditary caliphate, or temporal ruler. About 20 percent of the population are Sunni. Expatriate labor in Oman is rapidly increasing, numbering at least two-hundred-thousand workers. Most come from India, Pakistan, Bangladesh, and Sri Lanka.

History

Oman's early history is obscure. Converted to Islam in the seventh century A.D., native Omanis embraced Ibadhism, which traces its roots to the Kharijite movement, an early Islamic offshoot. European influence began in 1508 when Portugal replaced Oman as the dominant power of the Arabian Sea. Seventeenth-century Portuguese fortifications on the Omani coast still stand in and around Muscat.

The Portuguese were ousted in 1650 as an Omani renaissance began. Elected Ibadhi imams of the central hill region and hereditary sultans situated in Muscat became the political leaders of the region. Divisions between the coast and interior of the country were exacerbated in 1786 when the capital moved from Rostaq to coastal Muscat. The Muscat rulers were responsible for extending Oman's control to Zanzibar (near Tanzania), a large part of the Arabian Peninsula, and the Makran coast (Pakistan). By the early nineteenth century Omani power was unchallenged in southern Arabia and East Africa.

Oman has remained independent since 1650 except for a brief period of Persian rule from 1741 to 1744. Ahmad ibn Said defeated the Persians and shortly thereafter founded the al-Bu Said dynasty, which is still in power today.

Oman's regional power began to decline during the latter half of the nineteenth century when it was forced to relinquish control of its East African colonies. In 1958 Oman sold its last colonial possession, Gwadur, to Pakistan for three million pounds.

Ibadhi Moslems in the interior pressed for greater independence from Muscat around the beginning of the twentieth century. Two rebellions flared up in 1950 when the people of Inner Oman, under their own elected imam, resisted the efforts of Sultan Said bin Taimur to extend his control into the interior. With the aid of the British, the insurgents were defeated in 1959. Later the sultan invalidated the office of the elected imam.

The government of Sultan Said was regarded as one of the most traditional and conservative in the Arab world. Slavery was still common, and social and economic development was completely ignored, despite growing oil revenues. In 1964 a major tribal revolt occurred in the southern province of Dhofar. The rebels operated from bases in neighboring South Yemen, conducting a war of attrition against Sultan Said and his successor for more than ten years.

In a palace coup Sultan Qaboos overthrew his father's stifling rule in 1970 and embarked on a program of modernization. Although Oman's economic progress partially stemmed the insurgents' rebellion, fighting nevertheless continued. In 1974 rebel forces formed the People's Front for the Liberation of Oman (PFLO). In December 1975, after a rebel offensive was overcome, Sultan Qaboos declared complete victory.

The rebellion flared up again in June 1978 when exiles from South Yemen reported renewed support of the PFLO by Cuba. This development caused the Omani government to close its border with South Yemen in June 1981 and put its defense forces on full alert. Tensions then receded, and in October 1982 Oman and South Yemen reestablished diplomatic relations and signed an agreement ending the conflict. According to official Omani sources, the PFLO is now defunct. Even with the achievement of relative stability, however, relations between Oman and South Yemen remain uneasy.

Current Issues

Oman is an absolute monarchy dominated by the sultan. No constitution or parliament exists because the sultan legislates by decree. He acts as the premier, foreign minister, defense minister, and finance minister. In 1981, however, the sultan established the State Consultative Council. The council's fifty-five members are appointed government officials, selected merchants and business leaders, and approved tribal leaders from politically sensitive regions. Chaired by the sultan himself, the council has no legislative powers. Nevertheless, it performs a valuable advisory function for the sultan on important matters such as conceiving economic priorities and articulating development goals.

Sultan Qaboos is particularly noted for his strong leanings toward the West. About twenty of his closest advisers are either Britons, Americans, or Arabs who have encouraged the sultan to maintain close relations with Western states. A 1980 agreement with Oman grants the United States access to Omani military installations, emergency landing rights, and the authority to preposition military hardware at Omani storage facilities. The Musandam Peninsula facility, an Omani military base near the Strait of Hormuz to which the United States has access, is a valuable listening post for monitoring activity in Iran and a strategic focal point from which the United States can prepare for the defense of Gulf oil-producing nations.

In recent years, however, Oman has exhibited a sensitivity to global and regional politics and has adhered to an independent and nonaligned political agenda. In 1987 the Omanis attempted to bring more balance to their foreign policy by upgrading diplomatic relations with the Soviet Union to the ambassadorial level, following the example of Kuwait and the United Arab Emirates.

Establishing diplomatic relations with the Soviet Union helped pave the way for improved relations with South Yemen, a Soviet ally. On the heels of the move to strengthen Soviet-Omani relations, Oman announced it would open an embassy in South Yemen in 1988. Further indication of progress that year appeared when a skirmish between Omani and South Yemeni border patrols, in which eight South Yemenis were killed, was dismissed as a "mis-

understanding." In another sign of improving relations, South Yemen's president paid his first visit ever to the sultan in Muscat in late 1988.

Oman also exhibited its political independence by agreeing to exchange ambassadors and open embassies with Syria in 1988. Closer to home, Oman maintained relations with Iran throughout the Iran-Iraq war, again breaking ranks with most other Arab states. In 1987 Omani and Iranian defense ministers exchanged visits.

The Omani economy is almost wholly dependent on the oil industry, which provides the government with most of its revenues. Compared with other Gulf states, Oman's oil reserves are of moderate size. They are expected to last only another twenty years. Oman is not a member of the Organization of Petroleum Exporting Countries (OPEC) or the Organization of Arab Petroleum Exporting Countries (OAPEC) and hence does not abide by their quota system. This has enabled Muscat to weather the world oil glut by adjusting its output to maintain a steady flow of petroleum revenues—to a point.

Even Oman's freedom from OPEC could not insulate its economy from the volatile oil prices of the late 1980s. Its capacity to pump is restricted by its relatively small and inaccessible fields. As a result, falling prices have led to falling government revenues and budget slashing. Numerous development projects have been delayed or discontinued and the Omani riyal has been devalued. Recently, the sultan had to cancel the purchase of eight advanced Tornado fighter-bombers from Britain—a sacrifice that confirms the severity of Oman's financial situation.

Outlook

Sultan Qaboos has given the al-Bu Said dynasty new direction, and since his defeat of the insurgents in the Dhofar province in 1975, his rule has gained greater legitimacy. His reforms have reversed the stagnant social and economic conditions that prevailed under his father.

The sultan enjoys broad support and the public generally approves of his foreign and domestic policies. Throughout Oman, no significant political opposition or abuse of human rights exists. As Oman's development continues, however, the sultan will have to meet the growing expectations of his increasingly well educated population. If Oman's long-term growth or the state's paternal distribution of wealth is ever disturbed, perhaps the sultan's staunch commitment to the principle of monarchal rule, with no popular representation, will become less tolerable to Omanis.

To prevent this scenario, the sultan has encouraged the "Omanization" of the country. This general policy is designed to reduce the number of foreigners in the public sector, thereby creating new opportunities to absorb the growing number of educated Omanis. Without an heir, Sultan Qaboos (unmarried and fifty years old in 1989) has left the question of the form of Oman's future government open for speculation.

Qatar

Area: 4,247 square miles.
Capital: Doha.

Population: 328,000.
Religion: Mostly Sunni Moslem of the Wahhabi sect.
Official language: Arabic; some English is spoken.
GNP: $4.1 billion; $12,360 per capita.

Qatar has gone through a profound period of social transformation since oil production began in that small country in 1947. Before then Qatar (KAH-tar) was one of the poorest and least developed countries of eastern Arabia. The economy depended heavily on fishing and pearling. Petroleum production and export rapidly converted a nomadic population into a mostly urban and settled people, with one of the highest per capita incomes in the world.

The ruling al-Thani family is one of the largest families in the region, numbering in the thousands. Its members dominate all important government functions and all major ministries—interior, defense, and foreign affairs. Qatari society is staunchly religious and conservative, with strong ties to Saudi Wahhabism.

Qatar has been relatively unfazed it by the economic recession and regional instability that rocked the Gulf in the 1980s. The government's conservative development policies have enabled the country to maintain a stable economy despite declining oil revenues. Although its shipping was threatened by nearby attacks during the Gulf war, Qatar was not seriously challenged during the 1980s by foreign intrigue or domestic unrest. The royal family prefers to keep a low international profile, and it plays a limited role in regional politics. However, Qatar is a strong supporter of the GCC and other Arab causes.

Geography

Qatar occupies a thumb-shaped desert peninsula, about the size of Connecticut, that stretches north into the Persian Gulf. In the south it borders the United Arab Emirates and Saudi Arabia. The peninsula is a low, flat, barren plain, consisting mostly of sand-covered limestone. The climate is hot and humid. One-half of Qatar's water supply is provided by sea-water desalinization.

On the west coast is a chain of hills, the Dikhan Anticline, beneath which lie important oil reserves. Off the northeast Qatari coast lies one of the world's largest concentrations of natural gas not associated with oil. Qatar has known reserves of 163 trillion cubic feet of high-quality natural gas, more than 4 percent of worldwide reserves.

Demography

The population is composed of Qataris, Arabs from neighboring states, and Iranian, Pakistani, and Indian immigrants. Only about one-quarter of Qatar's 328,000 inhabitants are native born. Most Qataris adhere to the Wahhabi school of Sunni Islam. Approximately 16 percent of the population, composed primarily of expatriates, is Shi'ite. More than 80 percent of all Qatar's inhabitants reside near the capital city of Doha.

The ruling family is divided into three main branches, each quite independent of the other: Bani Hamad, Bani Ali, and Bani Khalid. The current emir, Sheik Khalifa bin Hamad al-Thani, comes from the Bani Hamad.

History

Qatar was formerly dominated by Bahrain's ruling al-Khalifa family, which regarded Qatar as its own, errant province. Rising to prominence in the nineteenth century, the al-Thani family established its own dynasty in Qatar, gaining independence and legitimacy through successive agreements with Great Britain. At the request of leading Qatari families, the British in 1868 opposed the Bahraini claim in exchange for a larger British role in Qatar's protection.

The British-Qatari relationship was interrupted in 1872 when the Ottoman Turks occupied Qatar. After the Ottomans evacuated the peninsula in the beginning of World War I, however, the al-Thani dynasty entered into treaty obligations with Great Britain and became a formal British protectorate in 1916. A 1934 treaty gave Britain a more extensive role in Qatari affairs. Oil was discovered in 1940, but exploitation was delayed by World War II. During the 1950s and 1960s, gradually increasing oil revenues brought prosperity, rapid immigration, and social progress.

From 1947 to 1960 Qatar was led by Emir Ali, who was forced from his throne by his son Ahmad with the help of a British gunboat in Doha harbor. Ahmad's profligate and venal rule, however, was ended by a 1972 bloodless coup by his cousin Khalifa bin Hamad al-Thani, the current emir.

Qatar declared its independence on September 1, 1971, after attempts to form a union with neighboring Gulf emirates (Bahrain and the Trucial States) failed. Later that year British forces concluded their withdrawal from the region.

Current Issues

Emir Khalifa holds absolute authority to enact all laws, appoint members to the advisory council (a consultative assembly), and amend the provisional 1970 constitution. Qatar's constitution or "basic law" is officially designated as a provisional document to be replaced by a final constitution following a transitional period. However, there is no indication that a new constitution is forthcoming. Currently, no popularly elected governmental body exists.

Emir Khalifa rules under the guidance of strict Islamic law. On major decisions he seeks a family consensus. The Qatari throne is hereditary within the al-Thani family, but it is not automatically passed from father to son. Instead the ruler is designated by the consensus of leading family members.

The emir's rule is constrained by rival families and by the conservative religious establishment. The al-'Atiyyah family continuously vies with the al-Thanis for predominance within Qatar's economy and armed forces. Other family clans also have challenged the al-Thanis.

Qatar is less puritanical than Saudi Arabia. It allows movie theaters and women drivers, but it prohibits the importation, manufacturing, and consumption of alcohol. Qatar provides free education and medical services to all its citizens.

Qatari society constituted one of the most ethnically homogeneous communities among all Gulf states until petroleum production began in the late 1940s. Today foreign workers—principally from Iran, Pakistan, and India—constitute approximately 80 percent of Qatar's work force. Detailed rules closely govern their entrance into the country and their political rights. In the summer of 1980 about 250 Indian and Pakistani laborers were arrested for irregular immigration activities. In 1985 new laws were passed restricting the industrial and commercial activities of non-Qataris. Foreign workers are usually content to forgo civil liberties in exchange for high wages.

The successful integration of Qatar's growing population is due primarily to the enormous revenues generated by the emirate's principal export, petroleum. Oil accounts for about 90 percent of Qatar's national income. However, Qatar's relatively small petroleum reserves—3.2 billion barrels in early 1988—are expected to last only another thirty years. Production cuts brought on by the world oil glut in the mid-eighties have led to attempts to consolidate alternative sources of revenue.

The focus of the government's economic diversification effort has been the development of its North Field project, designed to exploit Qatar's large offshore natural gas resources. In 1987 the government initiated the first phase of the project—which includes the construction of offshore production facilities linked to the shore by submerged pipelines—at a cost of $1.3 billion. With proven natural gas reserves estimated at 150 trillion cubic feet, the North Field is expected to become a valuable source of energy and income for Qatar for the next hundred years.

Emir Khalifa has traditionally favored a moderate foreign policy. He signed a bilateral defense agreement in 1982 with Saudi Arabia and generally follows its lead in policy matters. Qatar supported Iraq throughout the Iran-Iraq war and joined the Gulf Cooperation Council in 1981.

While remaining strongly pro-Western, Qatar's relationship with the United States was strained in March 1988 when Washington learned that Qatar had secretly acquired thirteen American-made Stinger antiaircraft missiles. After Qatar refused to reveal where they got the missiles, the U.S. Senate voted to prohibit weapons sales to Qatar. Later in 1988 Qatar became the fourth Gulf state to establish diplomatic relations with the People's Republic of China and the Soviet Union.

Qatar continues to be engaged in long-running border disputes with Bahrain. In April 1986 Qatar raided the island of Fasht ad-Dibal, which had been reclaimed from an underlying coral reef by the Bahraini government. The Qatari forces seized twenty-nine foreign workers who were building a Bahraini coast guard station on the island. The dispute was finally resolved in May when Bahrain and Qatar agreed to destroy the island and to submit future disputes to international arbitration. In addition to Fasht ad-Dibal, Qatar and Bahrain have each claimed the town of Zubara on the mainland of Qatar and Hawar Islands off the coast of Qatar.

Outlook

Qatar continues to be one of the most politically and economically stable countries in the Gulf. Calls for radical changes or greater participation in the government are few. Foreign workers seem content to reap the benefits of Qatar's oil economy despite the constraints placed upon them. The ruling family has sufficiently shared the oil wealth with the country's meager population to avoid popular discontent. There is little reason to expect a change in the political climate as long as national revenues are maintained and indigenous workers remain quiescent.

Qatar's most pressing problem is the lack of sufficient employment opportunities for its increasingly educated population. Despite the rapid pace of development, Qatari society has been unable to adequately absorb the more than 2,000 secondary school and college graduates that enter the work force each year. At the same time few Qataris are able or willing to fill the technical and laboring jobs that are critical to the economy. Such inconsistencies

in the labor market are likely to cause increasing frustration among Qatar's native population, while making it more difficult for the government to reduce the number of foreign workers in the country.

Despite the recession of the 1980s Qatar's economic future remains promising. In the short term the country's oil reserves are expected to support its conservative economic path, and the development of the North Field natural gas project promises continued prosperity in the postoil era. Still, as a small state, Qatar has interests that are tied closely to the fortunes of OPEC and the regional security provided by the GCC. One potential threat to Qatar's future economic prospects is an Iranian claim to a substantial portion of the North Field gas reservoir. While Tehran's claim does not affect the first stage of Qatar's development program scheduled for completion in 1991, the dispute could evolve into a major political or even military confrontation.

The United Arab Emirates

Area: 32,280 square miles.
Capital: Abu Dhabi.
Population: 1,980,000.
Religion: Moslem; 16 percent Shi'ite.
Official language: Arabic.
GNP: $22.83 billion; $15,680 per capita.

The United Arab Emirates (UAE), formerly known as the Trucial States, is the only federation of states in the Middle East. By 1972 seven disparate emirates ruled by individual tribal sheiks had merged to create a federal framework within which they could preserve their local autonomy and avoid being dominated by their two large neighbors, Saudi Arabia and Iran.

Commercial development of petroleum resources, which began in the late 1950s, stimulated population growth and development in the emirates. The combined population of the emirates increased from 180,000 in 1968 to more than one million by 1980, largely because of immigration. Development among the emirates proceeded unevenly, however, and the smaller emirates that lacked oil were left almost untouched by petroleum riches.

Inequalities persist in size, population, development, and wealth. Abu Dhabi and Dubai stand out among the other emirates for their vast oil revenues, large populations, and expansive territory. More than 1.5 million of the 1.9 million people in the UAE live in Abu Dhabi, Dubai, or Sharjah, a latecomer to oil production. Tiny Ajman, with 100 square miles and just 60,000 inhabitants, is the smallest emirate.

All the states fiercely compete with each other for development funds and projects, often at the expense of national unity and economic planning. Because of the absence of a strong centralized government, duplication of many facilities, such as international airports and harbors, has occurred throughout the country.

The Seven Emirates

Abu Dhabi, the largest, most populous, and influential of the seven emirates, is the federal capital. With the advent of petroleum production, Abu Dhabi became a classic example of a traditional society transformed almost overnight by tremendous oil wealth. The UAE's largest oil producer, the emirate has proven reserves of 31 billion barrels and accounts for more than 60 percent of the federation's GNP.

Dubai, second only to Abu Dhabi in oil riches, has a long tradition of entrepôt trading. Dubai boasts one of the Gulf's most important deepwater ports, Jebel Ali, and has close trade links with Iran and the Indian subcontinent. Dubai's free trade zones have become the center of nonpetroleum industry in the UAE.

After oil production began in Sharjah in 1974, it joined Abu Dhabi and Dubai to form an elite group of oil producers within the federation. Sharjah's economy, however, continues to be saddled with a large debt burden caused by financial mismanagement.

Ras al-Khaimah entered the federation in February 1972 after its fruitless efforts to recapture the two Tunb islands and the islet of Abu Musa, which Iran overran on March 30, 1971. Comparatively large and fertile, Ras al-Khaimah contains only minor offshore oil reserves, which were discovered in 1983. Fujairah, Ajman, and Umm al-Qaiwan are subordinate to the wealthier emirates and rely on their largess for development programs and to overcome economic and social disparities.

Geography

The UAE extends for 746 miles along the southern rim of the Persian Gulf, where six of the emirates are located. Fujairah faces the Gulf of Oman, a part of the Arabian Sea. Sharjah also has additional, noncontiguous territory along the coast with Fujairah.

About the size of South Carolina, the UAE has approximately 32,000 square miles of mostly barren flat land. Temperatures sometimes soar to 140 degrees Fahrenheit. Its undefined southern border with Saudi Arabia merges into the great, virtually uninhabited wasteland of the Rub al-Khali (Empty Quarter). In the east along the Omani border lie the Western Hajar Mountains.

The UAE's major natural resources are oil and natural gas. Its proven published reserves in 1988 were estimated at 50 billion barrels of petroleum, the bulk of which is located in Abu Dhabi. Abu Dhabi also possesses most of the UAE's 200 trillion cubic feet of natural gas reserves.

Demography

Indigenous inhabitants of the seven emirates account for less than 20 percent of the federation's nearly two million people. Most of the immigrant residents are Indian, Pakistani, and Iranian. Among the expatriate Arab population are Omanis, Palestinians, Jordanians, Egyptians, and Yemenis. About 80 percent of the labor force is foreign.

The country is overwhelmingly Sunni, with about 16 percent following the Shi'ite branch of Islam. Hindus and Christians reside in the foreign communities; few are granted citizenship rights. Bedouin nomads, comprising 5 to 10 percent of the population, live around oases and are slowly settling towns or migrating to urban areas.

History

During the early nineteenth century the Qawasim tribe was the dominant Arab power in the lower Gulf coast. After Wahhabi warriors from the Arabian Peninsula overran their territory in 1805, the tribe turned from sea trading to piracy. These armed outlaws made the sea perilous for British maritime traders. To secure the lower Gulf for safe trading, Britain negotiated a peace treaty in 1820 with what was then known as the Pirate Coast and thereafter as the Trucial Coast. The local sheiks signed with Great Britain a perpetual maritime truce in 1853 and an exclusive agreement in 1892 that gave Britain control over the Trucial States' foreign policy.

Britain supported Abu Dhabi in a 1955 dispute with Saudi Arabia over the Buraimi Oasis and other territories in the south. The oasis is now shared by Abu Dhabi and Oman. The border between the UAE and Saudi Arabia remains undemarcated. Minor boundary differences still persist with Oman.

After Britain announced in 1968 its intention to withdraw from the Gulf by the end of 1971, Qatar, Bahrain, and the Trucial States initiated plans to form a confederation. Qatar and Bahrain, however, decided in favor of independent sovereign status.

On December 2, 1971, the UAE proclaimed its independence and immediately entered into a treaty of friendship with Britain. Originally only six emirates signed the act of confederation, but after two months Ras al-Khaimah accepted membership.

Current Issues

Sheik Zayed ibn Sultan al-Nahayan of Abu Dhabi has ruled as president of the UAE since its inception. He heads the highest body in the country, the Supreme Council of the Union (SCU), which is comprised of the rulers of the federation's seven member states. The SCU is responsible for the election of the president and vice president, for general federal policy, and for the ratification of federal laws. Abu Dhabi and Dubai have veto power over all federal matters.

The Council of Ministers is responsible for operating the bureaucracy, drafting laws, and planning the annual budget. Its members are appointed by the SCU. The forty-member Federal National Council functions primarily as a consultative assembly and forum for debate. Members are chosen by each emir.

The government of the UAE is based on a provisional constitution promulgated in 1971, which has been renewed at five-year intervals. The establishment of a permanent constitution has been delayed by the reluctance of individual emirates to relinquish their autonomy—particularly in the areas of natural resources and defense. Contributions to the federal budget have also been a source of dispute, as Abu Dhabi has become increasingly reluctant to continue contributing more than 80 percent of the total budget.

Family rivalries also have influenced interemirate politics. In June 1987 Abdul Aziz, the older brother of Sheik Sultan of Sharjah, tried to replace his younger brother as ruler of the emirate. Abu Dhabi favored Abdul in the power struggle, while Dubai supported Sheik Sultan. Finally after days of uncertainty the other members of the GCC stepped in to help negotiate a compromise in which Sheik Sultan regained power while Abdul Aziz was made crown prince.

The reduction in oil revenues due to the world oil glut put considerable strain on the UAE's federal budget. In 1982 the government began running budget deficits for the first time in its history; a number of development projects were postponed, canceled, or scaled down. When oil prices collapsed in 1986, oil revenues fell 40 percent below those of 1984, leading to a dramatic decline in gross national product. Government austerity measures enabled the country to maintain a surplus in its balance of payments, but the oil market led the emirates to place greater emphasis on economic diversification. The development of industry and trade continues to be a high priority, despite the modest upturn in oil prices in the late 1980s.

Regional stability is also of prime importance to the UAE. The federation attempted to steer a neutral course during the Iran-Iraq war. While joining with the other Arab Gulf states to form the GCC in 1981 and entering into a bilateral defense agreement with Saudi Arabia in 1982, the UAE maintained stable relations with Iran and served as the major transshipment point for goods going into Iran. The UAE's relations with the Tehran government enabled Sheik Zayed to play a mediating role as the Gulf war escalated in the mid-1980s. The federation has also tried to maintain balanced relations in the broader international arena. In October 1984 it opened diplomatic relations with China. In November 1985 it became the third Gulf state to the Soviet Union.

Outlook

Nearly two decades after attaining independence, the UAE has developed into a functional unified state. Despite tribal rivalries and economic disparities, the seven emirates and their leaders appear to be more committed to the success of the UAE federation than when the experiment began. But a number of obstacles to the full integration of the emirates remain. Cooperation among them on economic policy continues to be limited. Each state devises its own oil policies and pursues separate development plans, which often result in the duplication of basic services. In foreign affairs as well, individual emirates do not always adopt identical stands.

The issue of political succession is also of major concern. Sheik Zayed, who was elected for his fourth term in 1986, is in his seventies; and Sheik Rashid, the UAE's prime minister and emir of Dubai, has been incapacitated by serious illness since 1981. While both leaders have designated their eldest sons as heirs, their offspring lack their experience and commitment to the federation.

The end of the Gulf war and the improvement in oil prices in 1988 has raised hopes for the UAE's economy. The stabilization of the oil market has been a particular boon to Abu Dhabi, which produces 75 percent of the UAE's petroluem exports and has relied on its immense oil revenues to preserve its preeminent position within the UAE. Although the federation will remain heavily dependent on oil for the foreseeable future, economic diversification efforts are expected to become increasingly important. Abu Dhabi has begun to widen its industrial base and Dubai has continued to expand its transportation and export trade. Such hopeful forecasts for the UAE's economy are conditioned, however, on the continued stability of the postwar oil markets and peripheral industries.

Among the UAE's domestic political concerns is its heavy reliance on foreign labor. Although the federal government has stepped up efforts to "nationalize" employment, the small size of the country's native labor force and its strong commitment to industrial development have given the federation no option but to retain a large number of foreign workers. Although the expatriates have remained relatively quiescent compared with those in other Gulf states, the large foreign majority may threaten the emirates' conservative culture and political system..

In foreign affairs, the UAE is likely to continue to maintain close ties with the conservative, pro-Western group of GCC states, while seeking to develop a balanced relationship with both Iran and Iraq. Preventing a shift in the regional balance of power is of primary importance to the UAE, as it to all GCC states.

Reasserting Influence in the Gulf

During the 1980s—a tumultuous decade marked by political unrest, regional instability, and economic recession—the Kingdom of Saudi Arabia demonstrated remarkable stability and resilience.

Despite a siege of the Grand Mosque in Mecca by Moslem extremists in 1979 and the disruption of the annual pilgrimage to Mecca by Iranian-inspired riots in 1987, the kingdom was able to withstand the wave of Islamic fundamentalism that swept the Middle East after the Iranian revolution and indeed strengthen its reputation as the protector of conservative Islamic values.

Saudi Arabia also prevented the Iran-Iraq war from threatening its security by unifying its allies, building a massive defense arsenal, and participating in naval patrols in the Persian Gulf. Although the collapse of oil prices forced the government to scale back its ambitious development plans, Riyadh averted serious social and economic dislocations by drawing on its vast foreign reserves.

In 1988 the Saudi regime succeeded in pressuring Organization of Petroleum Exporting Countries (OPEC) states to agree to a new production quota agreement for the first time in five years, contributing to a modest recovery in oil prices. The kingdom also demonstrated new flexibility in its relations with the superpowers by initiating contacts with the Soviet Union and negotiating an arms deal with China that may enable Saudi Arabia to become more independent from the United States.

Nevertheless, the Saudis are confronted with many significant problems. Despite the recent upturn, oil prices remain far below the levels of the late 1970s. With drastically reduced revenues, the Saudi government will have difficulty supporting the high standards of living to which its citizens have become accustomed, especially given the significant diminution of Saudi financial reserves.

The rapid pace of economic development in Saudi Arabia also poses a threat to the stability of the regime. King Fahd ibn Abdul Aziz has encouraged gradual modernization while preserving the country's conservative Islamic culture, but this balance is hard to maintain. The government must deal with conflicting domestic pressures for new reform and for a return to more traditional values.

Fahd ibn Abdul Aziz

Geography and People

Saudi Arabia extends over four-fifths of the Arabian Peninsula and is in a strategic location stretching from the Persian Gulf to the Red Sea and the Gulf of Aqaba. The country—approximately 873,000 square miles or about one-third the size of the continental United States—shares borders with Jordan, Iraq, Kuwait, Bahrain, Qatar, the United Arab Emirates, Oman, the Yemen Arab Republic, and the People's Democratic Republic of Yemen. Several of these borders in desert areas are undefined. To the east, Saudi Arabia faces Iran across the Persian Gulf, and, to the west, Egypt, the Sudan, and Ethiopia across the Red Sea. It also sits opposite the Sinai Peninsula, across the Gulf of Aqaba.

Saudi Arabia's 1,560-mile coastline provides the only access to water for an otherwise arid wasteland. Recently built dams have trapped floodwaters for irrigation and urban needs, and the country has made agricultural advances, particularly in the production of wheat, which doubled in 1982 and again in 1983.

Saudi Arabia has five major regions. Adjoining the Red Sea is the Hijaz region, which includes the holy cities of Islam—Mecca and Medina—plus the diplomatic capital, Jiddah. The mountainous Asir region, where peaks rise above nine-thousand feet, lies to the south along the Red Sea. The province of Najd occupies the central part of the country where the capital city, Riyadh, is located. The eastern province, known as the al-Hasa, contains Saudi Arabia's rich oil fields. The main feature of the rugged northern provinces is the trans-Arabian pipeline that crosses that area, Jordan, Syria, and Lebanon en route to the Mediterranean Sea.

The Syrian desert in the north extends southward into the 22,000 square miles of the Al-Nufud desert. In the south, the vast Rub al-Khali (empty quarter) extends over 250,000 square miles of nearly uninhabited desert.

Most of the peninsula is desert. Saudi Arabia is the largest country in the world without a river. Rainfall is erratic, averaging about two to four inches a year, except in the mountainous Asir region, which receives periodic monsoon rains and averages nearly twenty inches of annual

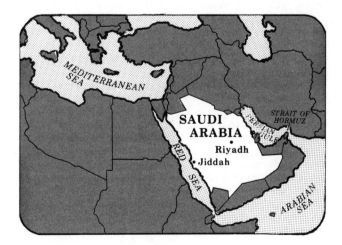

Key Facts on Saudi Arabia

Area: 873,000 square miles; some borders undefined.

Capital: Riyadh; diplomatic capital located at Jiddah.

Population: 15,452,000 (1988).

Religion: 99 percent Sunni Moslem.

Official Language: Arabic.

GNP: $83.3 billion, $6,930 per capita (1986).

Sources: World Bank Atlas 1988; CIA World Factbook 1988

---

rainfall. Heat is intense during the summer months, frequently exceeding 110 degrees Fahrenheit in the interior. Snow and ice are rare in winter, although the temperature occasionally dips below freezing.

No recent official census figures are available, but Saudi Arabia's population was estimated in 1988 at about 15.5 million persons. The government assumes an annual growth rate of 3.5 percent. The problem in gaining more precise figures is primarily due to the difficulty of estimating the number of foreigners in the country. Prior to the meteoric growth of the oil industry, nearly all Saudis were nomadic or seminomadic. Today, however, only about 20 percent of the population can be so classified.

Ethnically, Saudis are Arabs, although there are a few small groups of non-Arab Moslems. These minorities are Turks, Iranians, Indonesians, Indians, and Africans who came on pilgrimages and remained in the Hijaz region. Since Saudis make no distinctions based on race, mixed racial strains are common.

Nearly all Saudis are Moslems, and most are Sunni Moslems following the puritanical doctrines of Muhammad ibn Abd al-Wahhab, an eighteenth-century revivalist whose philosophy gained favor with the founder of the Saud dynasty. Wahhabi Moslems, who belong to the Hanbali school of thought, seek a return to Islamic fundamentals and condemn modern religious practices begun since the time of the Prophet Muhammad. A small minority of Saudi Moslems belong to the Shi'ite sect, which is viewed with some trepidation by the government. Most of the Shi'ites live near the oil-rich eastern province.

Because of its small population, Saudi Arabia has had to rely on foreign workers to develop the country's industrial base. As many as 3.5 million foreigners work in Saudi Arabia, including North Yemenis, Egyptians, Pakistanis, Koreans, and Filipinos, as well as American advisers. Their presence has long been viewed as a threat to the country's traditional Islamic society. The Saudi government frequently has declared its intention to curtail the influx of workers, but several factors have hampered its ability to do so. The country's traditionalism limits the use of women in the work force. Saudis also have shown disdain for what they consider menial jobs, which in turn must be filled with foreign labor.

Foreign labor, for all its short-run advantages, presents the kingdom with several problems. First, it creates a dependence on other countries; foreign managers administer new projects, and their support staff carry out the day-to-day work. Second, the massive influx of foreigners could help stir internal unrest. The Saudis are particularly sensitive to Iranian calls for a fundamentalist Shi'ite revolution in the Gulf.

The reduction of the kingdom's dependence on foreign labor was a key feature of the government's five-year development plan for 1985-1990. The Saudi leadership planned to send home 600,000 foreigners by 1990 and thereby increase the Saudi share of the work force from 40.2 percent to 51.2 percent. Plans were also made to double enrollments in the country's vocational training programs and to increase the number of women in the educational system.

The combination of the government's vigorous efforts to restrict the number of expatriates and the reduced demand for labor created by the economic recession has already led to a significant decline in the number of foreigners in Saudi Arabia. Approximately 1.1 million people were reported to have left the country between October 1984 and April 1986, far exceeding the objectives of the 1985 economic plan.

Early Saudi History

Saudi Arabia takes its name from the Saud family, which first established its rule in the mid-1700s, aided by the leaders of the Wahhabi Islamic movement. In the early 1800s the Ottoman sultan became concerned by the expansion of the Saudi kingdom and ordered the leader of the Ottoman Empire in Egypt to invade the Arabian Peninsula. Egyptian forces remained there from 1818 until 1840, when internal problems forced Egypt to abandon its conquest. During the Egyptian occupation the power of the Rashid family grew at the expense of its rival, the Saud family. The Rashids ruled much of Arabia during the late 1800s and forced the Saudi royal family into exile.

Abd al-Aziz, a Saudi leader also known as Ibn Saud, returned to Arabia in 1902 to reconquer what he considered to be his rightful lands. He waged a thirty-year campaign that brought him control of the inner Arabian Peninsula.

On the eve of World War I Ibn Saud conquered what is now known as the eastern province, a move that led to closer contact with Great Britain. In 1915 he signed an agreement that placed Saudi lands under a British protectorate. Another treaty, signed in 1927, canceled the protectorate and declared the country's independence.

The final part of Ibn Saud's goal of unifying the Arabian Peninsula under his leadership was realized in 1926 when he ousted Hashemite leader Sherif Hussein, his chief Arab rival, from the Hijaz. Shortly after the victory he proclaimed himself king of the Hijaz in the Great Hall of Mecca.

Ibn Saud was surprisingly evenhanded toward the peoples conquered by his armies, and he took a mildly favorable view of modernization. These developments stirred unrest among some of his conservative Wahhabi Moslem followers, who rejected Western ways and technology. In 1929 leaders of the armies he had led to victory turned against him, launching attacks against Saudi tribes. The short civil war ended in 1930, when British forces captured the rebel leaders in Kuwait and delivered them to Ibn Saud.

The modern kingdom of Saudi Arabia dates from September 24, 1932, when Ibn Saud issued a royal decree unifying the kingdoms of Hijaz and Najd plus their dependencies. Since 1934 the kingdom has known only peace.

During World War II Saudi Arabia retained a neutral stance, but its preference for the Allied cause was apparent. In 1945 Ibn Saud nominally declared war on Germany, a move that ensured Saudi Arabia's charter membership in the United Nations. The importance of the country's oil and strategic geographic location was not lost on Franklin D. Roosevelt, who met with Ibn Saud in 1945 on board an American warship in the Mediterranean. The same year Saudi Arabia joined the Arab League, but the country's religious conservatism limited its interaction with other Arab states.

Postwar Developments

Ibn Saud's death in 1953 placed his eldest son, Saud, on the Saudi throne, and the second son, Faisal, became the heir apparent. The dissimilarity between the approaches of the two brothers—Saud's traditional views and Faisal's penchant for modernization—kept them at odds. Faisal was granted executive powers in March 1958, and on November 2, 1964, Saud was deposed by the ruling family, and Faisal claimed the throne.

Saudi Arabia's relationships with its Arab neighbors, as well as domestic politics, tested the growing nation. In 1961 Saudi Arabia responded to a request from Kuwait by sending troops to that country to deter an Iraqi threat. Iraq had just undergone a revolution, and the new government sought territorial rights over Kuwait, which had just received its independence from Great Britain. Saudi troops remained in Kuwait until 1972.

Hostility between Saudi leaders and Egyptian president Gamal Abdel Nasser dominated Saudi-Egyptian relations during Nasser's tenure from 1954 to 1970. In 1958 Nasser accused King Saud of plotting to assassinate him. Thereafter, Egyptian propaganda vehemently attacked the Saudi royal family and the country's monarchal form of government. Tensions flared in 1962 when Egypt and Saudi Arabia backed opposing sides in the Yemeni civil war.

The United States became an important influence in Saudi Arabia during the postwar era, although it has refrained from involvement in Saudi internal affairs. Between 1952 and 1962 the United States maintained an air base at Dhahran on the Persian Gulf. The arrangement was not renewed in 1961, due partly to Saudi Arabia's opposition to U.S. support of Israel. Both King Saud and King Faisal, however, took strong stands against communism, warning against its influence in Arab and Moslem countries.

Saudi Arabia supported the Arab cause in the Six-Day War in 1967 but did not participate militarily. When Egypt closed the Suez Canal, Saudi Arabia joined other Arab allies in briefly suspending oil shipments to Great Britain and the United States, although the Saudis retained diplomatic relations with both countries. Egypt's defeat at the hands of Israel during the Six-Day War apparently did not disappoint King Faisal because the defeat weakened Nasser considerably, and the Saudis gained influence from the episode.

1973 Oil Embargo

Political and economic developments during the 1970s catapulted Saudi Arabia to the forefront of world politics. On October 17, 1973, during the Arab-Israeli October war, the kingdom joined with ten other oil-producing Arab nations in reducing by 5 percent each month the amount of oil sold to "unfriendly" countries. On October 18 Saudi Arabia independently cut oil production by 10 percent to bring direct pressure on the United States. Two days later, after President Richard Nixon unveiled plans for additional U.S. aid to Israel, Riyadh announced a total halt in oil exports to the United States. Other members of the Organization of Arab Petroleum Exporting Countries (OAPEC) joined the embargo.

The embargo triggered serious discussions in the United States about using military force to keep the oil flowing, but force was not used to resolve the crisis. At a meeting in Vienna on March 18, 1974, Saudi Arabia lifted the five-month-old embargo against the United States. It was joined by Algeria, Egypt, Kuwait, Abu Dhabi, Bahrain, and Qatar; only OAPEC members Libya and Iraq dissented. Saudi oil minister Ahmed Zaki Yamani then announced that Saudi Arabia would increase its oil output by one million barrels a day and sell the increase to the United States.

After 1974 Saudi Arabia continued to oppose large OPEC price rises, insisting that the stability of the West's financial system could be severely undermined. In December 1976 Saudi refusal to go along with the full amount of an OPEC price rise resulted in a two-tier pricing system and increases in Saudi Arabia's oil production.

Government and Politics

Saudi Arabia's government is a monarchy, headed by a king and a crown prince chosen as the heir apparent. There is no constitution in the Western sense. Instead, the Koran, the basis of Islamic law, serves as the constitution and limits the authority of the king, as do unwritten tribal laws and customs. Major decisions are usually made by consensus of members of the royal family, who consult closely with religious leaders. Since 1953 the Council of Ministers, appointed by the king, has advised Saudi rulers on policy

and on administration of the growing bureaucracy. Although the monarchy has promised to establish a national consultative assembly to increase political participation, no legislative body had been created by 1989.

Fahd ascended the throne in 1982 at the age of sixty after the death of his sixty-nine-year-old half-brother, King Khalid. The current heir apparent is Crown Prince Abdullah, a half-brother of Fahd, who also serves as first deputy prime minister and commander of the National Guard, the Saudi internal security force.

Fahd served in top government posts for two decades before taking the throne. During King Faisal's reign (1964-1975) he served as minister of the interior. As crown prince and heir apparent under the fragile King Khalid, Fahd ran many of the day-to-day operations of the government. Considered a moderate among Middle East Arabs, Fahd as king has maintained a pro-Western stance and has shown a willingness to involve Saudi Arabia as a mediator in regional disputes.

Not all of Saudi Arabia's estimated four-thousand princes play a major role in the government, but at least a few hundred do. The Saud family always has been careful to cultivate its bonds with the two other great families in the country, the Sudeiris and the al-Shaykh, who helped the Saud family gain control of most of the Arabian Peninsula between 1750 and 1926.

Legislation is enacted by royal decree and must follow the tenets of the Koran and the *Hadith-Sunnah,* the chronicled teachings and examples of the Prophet Muhammad. Judges appointed by the senior religious leaders, called the *ulama,* head a system of religious courts. The king serves as the highest court of appeal and has the right to issue pardons.

The country is divided into fourteen provinces with individual governments. Saudi princes or close relatives of the royal family direct policy in the major provinces. The king appoints all governors.

For more than fifty years the Saudi citizenry has accepted the rule of the royal family with little resistance. The monarchy has enjoyed wide popular support by relying on Islamic traditions and by dramatically increasing government services. Well-established traditions permit male citizens to petition the king directly, thus allowing the average man to believe that he has a participatory role in the government. Top Saudi leaders also recognize that they must rule by consensus of the royal family and in consultation with religious leaders.

The Saudi government provides free education, medicine, and health care services to all Saudi citizens. The Saudis' version of Social Security provides pensions to widows, orphans, the elderly, and the permanently disabled. Social aid helps victims of natural disasters and persons who are temporarily disabled. The government also supplies interest-free loans for home mortgages, construction, small business, and agricultural development.

In recent years the Saudi regime has faced two major tests of its authority. The first occurred in November 1979 when the Grand Mosque in Mecca was occupied by about 250 armed followers of a Sunni Moslem extremist. The rebels held the mosque, Islam's holiest shrine, for two weeks until the army, National Guard, and police units received the approval of the nation's top religious leaders to storm the site. One hundred three insurgents and 127 Saudi troops were killed in the battle to secure the huge, sprawling mosque. The insurgents were mostly Saudis, but there were also some Egyptians, South Yemenis, and Ku-

waitis. Most were opposed to modernization and had hoped to eliminate the royal family and return Saudi Arabia to stricter adherence to the Islamic faith.

The second major challenge to the Saudi regime took place in July 1987 when Iranian pilgrims clashed with Saudi security forces during al-hajj (the annual pilgrimage of Moslems to the Islamic holy city of Mecca). With more than 150,000 Iranians present, a political demonstration of Iranian pilgrims sparked violent riots, resulting in the deaths of 402 people, 275 of whom were Iranian. In the following days, mass demonstrations took place in Tehran; the Saudi embassy was sacked and Iranian leaders vowed to avenge the pilgrims' deaths by overthrowing the Saudi ruling family. Shortly afterward, two powerful explosions were reported at Saudi oil installations in the eastern province. The explosions were widely believed to be acts of sabotage by Shi'ite workers with connections to Iran.

Such outbreaks of political unrest pose a threat to the stability of the Saudi regime. Attacks on the holy city of Mecca imperil the legitimacy of the Saudi ruling family as the "protector of the holy places," while attempts by Iran to exploit al-hajj to its own political advantage threaten to spread internal dissension within the kingdom and to increase regional hostilities in the Gulf.

The Saudi regime responded to these threats to its Islamic legitimacy by expanding the influence of the religious authorities in the affairs of state, calling more often upon the religious leaders to sanction government actions. In 1986 King Fahd further emphasized the special Islamic character of his rule by adopting the official title "Servant of the Holy Places."

To stem the tide of unrest by the Shi'ite Moslem community in the oil-rich eastern province, the Saudi government bolstered its security forces and accelerated government-funded development in the area. The regime also sought to grant greater social and religious equality to the Shi'ites. Having been oppressed by the Wahhabi sect of Sunni Islam for two centuries, the Shi'ite population has received considerably more attention from the government in the 1980s.

The more pressing threat of military confrontation with Iran was addressed by an increased commitment of resources to defense. In 1987 the government allocated 35.7 percent of its budget to the military, by far its largest budget item. During the 1980s the monarchy undertook a number of major arms purchases including AWACS (Airborne Warning and Control System) aircraft from the United States, Tornado fighter-bombers and Hawk trainer aircraft from the United Kingdom, and a number of CSS-2 medium-range missiles from China.

Saudi Arabia has also strengthened its defensive capabilities by developing an extensive "peace shield" program, which includes the development of a computerized command, control, and communications system for all its air defenses, and the establishment of industrial plants to produce avionics and telecommunications equipment.

Other threats to the stability of the Saudi regime include the sizable foreign labor force, rivalries within the royal family, rapid modernization, and the gap between rich and poor within Saudi society. These potential sources of instability, however, are balanced by other factors that have contributed to the durability of the regime—the lack of organized political opposition, the tribal connections of the monarchy, and its strong ties to the country's religious establishment. Also helping to stabilize the government are the use of consultation councils, the control of the armed forces through familial appointments, and the informal assembly of princes that has restricted internal quarrels within the royal family.

The strength of the Saudi regime is evidenced by the failure of the neo-fundamentalist movement and Khomeini-inspired organizations to gain wider appeal within the kingdom or to pose a more significant challenge to the regime as they have in some other Arab and Moslem countries.

The Economy

The most important industry in Saudi Arabia is the production of crude petroleum and petroleum products. Saudi Arabia has the capacity to pump more than ten million barrels per day (bpd), although the oil glut that developed in the mid-1980s prompted significant production cuts. With reserves estimated at 166,600 million barrels, Saudi Arabia can expect to have more than ninety years of production at 1987 levels.

In recent years the country's vast oil wealth has been both a boon and a disappointment, depending on the conditions of the market. The dramatic oil price increases beginning in 1973 inundated the kingdom with massive amounts of new wealth. Government petroleum revenues jumped from $1.2 billion in 1970 to $22.6 billion in 1974. The economy expanded rapidly, permitting the government to initiate ambitious development plans for the expansion of services, improvement of education, and diversification of industry. Until 1983 oil accounted for about 90 percent of government revenues.

As a result of the government's intensive industrialization program, Saudi Arabia dramatically improved its petroleum refining capacities to 64,000 bpd by 1985. The country can now produce its own fuel oil, kerosene, and other products rather than send its crude oil to foreign refineries and then import refined products.

Since 1981 the Saudis have also tapped the country's natural gas resources to fuel industrial complexes and generate electric power. In addition the government is cooperating with the United States to develop solar power.

During the 1970s oil revenues accumulated faster than the country's capacity to spend them. Past surpluses have generated high levels of foreign currency reserves, largely invested in Europe, Japan, and the United States. Saudi Arabian foreign assets grew from about $4.3 billion in 1973 to more than $120 billion in 1982.

In 1970 the country began a series of five-year development projects. The first program, modest in nature, committed $80 million to developing a basic infrastructure and improving government services. Under the second plan (1975-1980), the government spent $149 billion, much of it on new construction around the kingdom. The results of the initial plans were impressive: the length of paved highways tripled, power generation increased twenty-eight times, and the capacity of the country's seaports grew tenfold.

The government's third plan (1980-1985) was aimed at developing a varied economy less reliant on oil revenue. Particular emphasis was placed on agriculture to reduce the country's dependence on imported foodstuffs. The plan also stressed the need for worker training, reducing the reliance on foreign labor, and encouraging private Saudi investors to play a more active role in the economy.

The results of the third plan were mixed. The nonoil sector showed steady growth and accounted for 24.2 per-cent of government revenue in 1983. There was also a sharp increase in production of cement, chemical fertilizers, and many agricultural crops, particularly wheat. Led by the oil industry, Saudi exports totaled $45.9 billion in 1983. Total imports were $43 billion.

But oil production tumbled after 1981. As world demand for oil declined, Saudi production fell from a high of 10 million bpd in 1980 to an estimated 2.5 million bpd by 1985. The slowdown was felt by all sectors of the economy. Early in 1985 the government stopped work on two refineries, even though orders were already taken and engineering work was nearly complete.

The Saudis tried to balance their budget by cutting back government spending. The regime reduced expenditures by 20 percent in 1984. The Saudis were able to weather the drop in oil revenues by drawing upon their enormous financial reserves.

The five-year plan released in the spring of 1985 contained the Saudi government's sobering recognition that its expansion period had come to a close: "The expansive environment of the last decade has ended, and now the Saudi Arabian private sector faces normal world conditions where business success will depend on tight financial controls, high standards of product quality and service, and efficient and well planned marketing strategies."

The 1985-1990 plan focused on improving the efficiency of existing resources, expanding nonoil revenue-generating activities (particularly in manufacturing, agriculture, and financial services), promoting private-sector initiatives, and developing a better-trained work force to reduce dependence on foreign labor.

Declining oil prices further reduced revenues in 1986, but by 1988 the fourth development plan appeared to be leading the Saudi economy toward a modest recovery. According to the Saudi Ministry of Finance, the country achieved a real growth rate of 3.2 percent in 1988, compared with 0.8 percent in 1987 and 2.3 percent in 1985. The industrial sector was reported to have risen by 4.7 percent, compared with only 1.9 percent in 1987. Industrial growth was led by the petrochemical and refining industries, which nearly doubled their profits in the first half of 1988. The agricultural sector grew an unprecedented 10.8 percent.

The Saudi economy received an additional boost from the rise in crude oil prices that followed the achievement of a new quota agreement among the members of OPEC in December 1988. Yet as oil prices and production remain far below levels set during the boom years in the late seventies, the country is still expected to register significant budget deficits. In 1989 the deficit was projected to range between $6 billion and $8 billion. Saudi Arabia's vast foreign reserves adequately cover its deficits. However, as reserves have declined from $114 billion in 1985 to an estimated $75 billion in 1989, the government has become more reluctant to draw upon them, for fear of diminishing future investment income.

Continued growth of the nonoil sector is believed to be the key to the long-term expansion of the Saudi economy. Government policy objectives call for the industrial sector to account for about 15 percent of Saudi Arabia's gross domestic product (GDP) by the early 1990s, up from 10 percent in 1986. Although the Saudi economy will remain heavily dependent on oil, the country will continue to seek a more varied economic base to generate some of the revenue lost due to decreased prices and production levels of crude and to provide a hedge against the volatility of the energy industry.

Development of Oil Wealth

Oil was discovered in Saudi Arabia during the 1930s, but exploitation of the rich fields did not begin in earnest until after World War II. In 1933 Standard Oil of California (now Chevron) was granted a sixty-six-year concession to develop and exploit Saudi Arabia'a oil reserves under the operating name Arabian-American Oil Company (Aramco). Other U.S. oil companies acquired shares in Aramco until Standard Oil of California, Standard Oil of New Jersey, and Texaco each owned 30 percent of the company and Mobil Oil owned 10 percent. In 1949 Pacific Western Oil Company (later Getty Oil) received a concession in the Saudi Arabian-Kuwait neutral zone.

Two developments in 1950 heightened the importance of Saudi oil. First, a 753-mile oil pipeline was opened across Jordan and Syria to the Mediterranean, where Saudi oil could be shipped abroad easily. Second, Saudi Arabia and Aramco signed an agreement to share Aramco's profits on a 50-50 basis, greatly increasing Saudi Arabia's oil revenues. Other oil-rich Middle East nations would later make similar 50-50 deals with foreign oil companies.

Oil production expanded rapidly in the early 1970s in response to rising world demand. In 1969 oil flowed at 3 million bpd. Five years later that figure had nearly tripled to 8.48 million bpd. When the revolution in Iran halted that country's production in early 1979, Saudi Arabia increased its output to 10 million bpd to make up for the shortfall. Saudi production also made up for a shortfall in 1980 when the Iran-Iraq war disrupted oil production. That year the Saudi government completely nationalized Aramco, culminating a gradual process begun in 1973 of acquiring ownership of its oil production facilities. Continued high production levels, combined with rising petroleum prices, pushed Saudi oil revenues to a record $103 billion in 1981.

Policies Toward OPEC

As the OPEC nation with the largest oil reserves, Saudi Arabia is in a position to influence the organization's pricing and production policies. During much of the late 1970s the Saudis kept their prices down and their production levels high, which forced other countries to hold the line on prices. This kept the world market relatively stable. Saudi light crude, at $32 a barrel, was the cheapest in OPEC in 1981. Prices by other organization members ranged as high as $41 a barrel.

The Saudi position during the 1970s and early 1980s seemed to be that excessive price hikes would reduce world oil consumption and encourage investment in alternative sources of energy—two developments that would lower OPEC's long-term income. To force other OPEC members to reduce their prices, the Saudis pumped 10 million bpd in the spring of 1981 and vowed to continue until other countries lowered prices. Despite the Saudi efforts, prices remained high, causing an oil glut.

Oil production in the non-Communist world outside OPEC jumped 25 percent from 1979 to 1984. At the same time, world demand for oil dropped 15 percent because of energy conservation and permanent shifts to natural gas and coal.

To avoid a collapse of prices, OPEC countries slashed production. In 1982 the Saudis alone cut production by about 7 million bpd. Together the thirteen OPEC members produced about 16 million bpd in 1984, down from 31.6 million bpd in 1979 and 23.5 million in 1981. Prices had

fallen to a benchmark price in 1985 of $28 a barrel for Saudi light crude.

Saudi Arabia bore the brunt of the production cuts because poorer OPEC countries—those that relied almost exclusively on oil income—suffered more from the price slowdown. Some of those same countries, however, offered secret discounts to Western suppliers to keep the oil dollars flowing, a factor that undercut OPEC's—and Saudi Arabia's—price and production scheme.

In October 1984 Saudi Arabia agreed to become OPEC's "swing producer," cutting its own production to keep prices and production levels as high as possible for other OPEC nations. At the time, the Saudis could make this sacrifice because the country had a cash surplus of more than $100 billion.

By mid-1985, however, the kingdom's economic situation had deteriorated. Saudi production dropped off sharply and the country's oil revenues rapidly declined. Under significant domestic pressure, King Fahd finally decided to abandon Saudi Arabia's role as swing producer and to substantially increase production. The government's intention was to force the price of oil to decline in an effort to discipline OPEC members into limiting their production and coerce non-OPEC countries into limiting their production, thereby enabling Saudi Arabia to regain its "fair share of the market."

The strategy resulted in the collapse of oil prices during the first half of 1986. As Saudi Arabia increased its production to 5.7 million bpd, other OPEC members refused to rein in their production to accommodate the extra Saudi output. The corresponding oil glut led prices to tumble below $10 a barrel (about one-third the level of the early 1980s). The Saudi oil industry was therefore generating only a fraction of the revenue that it had made a year earlier. In desperation, the kingdom abandoned its "fair-share" policy in October, and it dismissed long-time oil minister Ahmed Zaki Yamani, who had designed the plan.

In December 1986 OPEC agreed to a new Saudi proposal that established a target price of $18 a barrel, supported by strictly enforced restrictions on output. Under the agreement, Saudi Arabia was alloted a nominal quota, again effectively making it a "swing producer."

Saudi Arabia sought to sustain the $18 target in 1987 through a series of threats of price cutting and hints of production concessions to encourage the rest of OPEC to curb its output. When Kuwait and the United Arab Emirates failed to oblige, the Saudis resorted to full quota production and price cutting.

Overproduction, however, only caused oil prices to decline further, falling to below $12 in September 1988. In response, the Saudis again placed its own economy and its prestige at risk by independently boosting oil production. Such a gross violation of the quota agreement was intended to shock OPEC members into respecting their own output targets. This time the tactic proved effective. In late November 1988 OPEC reached a new quota agreement for the first time since 1983, and oil prices began to recover by the end of the year.

Foreign Affairs

During the 1980s Saudi Arabia's main foreign policy objectives were to maintain its security and to promote greater stability in the region. The country sought to develop a unified front with its allies to meet the challenge of the Iran-Iraq war and to promote solidarity within the Arab world. While remaining strongly pro-Western, the

Saudi government also exercised greater flexibility in its relations with the United States and the Communist world.

The Gulf Corporation Council. The Saudis were the driving force behind the creation of the Gulf Cooperation Council (GCC) in 1981. The six members of the group are Saudi Arabia, Kuwait, Bahrain, the United Arab Emirates, Qatar, and Oman.

Although the Saudi government initially emphasized that the GCC was created to promote economic and industrial cooperation, security concerns appeared to be the primary motivation for the formation of the council. The rise of Ayatollah Khomeini in Iran in 1979 and the outbreak of the Iran-Iraq war in 1980 gave Saudi Arabia and the smaller Persian Gulf countries significant cause for alarm. The preservation of oil transport routes—as well as concern for internal security—led to the coordination of economic, political, and defense policies through the GCC.

Subsequent attacks on Gulf oil tankers by Iran and Iraq spurred the young alliance into action. The council provided more than $2 billion (with Saudi Arabia contributing the largest share) to help Bahrain and Oman upgrade their armed forces, and GCC members participated in joint military exercises. Saudi Arabia and Kuwait also shared data gathered by Saudi AWACS in hopes of limiting attacks on Gulf shipping. In November 1984 the council agreed to create a rapid deployment force of 10,000 to 13,000 soldiers to defend member nations against external military threats. Saudi Arabia contributes the largest share of troops and equipment to the rapid deployment force.

In addition to its coordinated security efforts, the GCC has made significant progress towards economic integration. Since 1981 the six member countries have laid the foundation for a potential "Gulf Arab common market," in which goods and workers will move freely across borders. Tariffs and job restrictions between members are being phased out and heads of government and ministers have met regularly to develop policy. Richer members have offered direct aid and jointly financed industrial projects to poor members.

The Iran-Iraq War. Perhaps the most pressing problem confronting the Saudis during the 1980s was the Iran-Iraq war. Faced with continued instability in the Gulf from September 1980 to August 1988, Saudi Arabia struggled to contain Iranian belligerence without placing its own security at risk.

The Saudis supported Iraq throughout the war, providing tens of billions of dollars to the Iraqi cause. Oil revenues obtained from the neutral zone shared by Saudi Arabia and Kuwait provided Baghdad with an additional $30 billion to compensate for its loss of oil capacity during the war.

As the tanker war escalated during 1984, the kingdom appeared to be on the verge of becoming directly involved. On June 4 Iranian F-4 fighter planes flew over Saudi territorial waters, presumably seeking naval targets. They were intercepted by Saudi F-15s and shot down. Neither Saudi Arabia nor Iran escalated tensions further. Many American observers believed that the incident proved to the Iranians that the Saudis would not be intimidated by aggression in the Gulf.

Saudi Arabia came close to a confrontation with Iran again in 1987, following the July 31 clashes between Iranian pilgrims and Saudi security forces in Mecca. As the level of hostility rose between Riyadh and Tehran, Iranian leaders threatened armed retaliation for the deaths of the pilgrims. Eventually the tense situation culminated in Saudi Arabia's April 1988 decision to sever diplomatic relations with Iran.

Despite the threatened disruption of tanker traffic in the Gulf during the latter half of the Iran-Iraq war, the Saudis were opposed to intervention by the United States to safeguard the region. Concerned about Arab reaction abroad and anti-American sentiment at home, Saudi Arabia refused to give the United States access to military facilities on its territory. Yet the Saudis did countenance the U.S. decision to escort reflagged Kuwaiti tankers in the Gulf in June 1987, when they provided essential cooperation in clearing mines and extending surveillance operations to the area.

In November 1987 Saudi Arabia joined the other members of the Arab League in unanimously condemning Iran for prolonging the Gulf war, deploring its occupation of Iraqi territory, and urging it to accept without preconditions UN Security Council Resolution 598, which called for an end to the war. *(Text of Resolution 598, Appendix, p. 306)*

Relations with Arab Neighbors. Within the Arab world, Saudi Arabia is considered a moderate. Although it provides financial support to some of the region's more radical elements, the country charts its foreign policy carefully. The Saudis retain close ties to the United States—often to the consternation of other Arab leaders—and place a high price on regional stability to help ensure long-term prosperity. As a peacemaker, the Saudis act cautiously, seeking a collective Arab approach to diplomatic efforts.

In September 1983 Saudi diplomats launched a major effort to reach a cease-fire in war-torn Lebanon, hoping for withdrawal of all foreign forces. Several months of talks led to a cease-fire between Syria and Lebanese guerrilla units in Lebanon, a move that spurred national reconciliation talks. The country also played a role in talks between the Palestine Liberation Organization (PLO) and Syria and in pushing for withdrawal of Israeli troops from Lebanon.

On most regional issues Saudi Arabia has been cautious not to break away from the standard Arab line, preferring to work behind the scenes to reach a consensus. The country's leaders support Arab insistence that Israel must withdraw from all Arab territories occupied in June 1967, including East Jerusalem, and have called for the creation of a Palestinian state.

Saudi Arabia has provided financial aid to the PLO as well as to countries that border Israel. Some U.S. observers have criticized the monarchy for not using its financial influence to force policy changes, saying that the Saudis have remained too cautious in dealing with their Arab partners, particularly in negotiations on the Palestinian question.

Saudi Arabia has had limited success in its efforts to achieve a comprehensive peace settlement in the Middle East. The monarchy opposed the Camp David accords negotiated in 1979 between Egypt and Israel. Then in 1981 Saudi Crown Prince Fahd announced a wide-ranging peace initiative that implied acceptance of Israel's right to exist. But Arab consensus on the issue did not come until September 1982, when a new peace plan was put forward at an Arab League summit in Morocco; it was immediately rejected by Israel. *(Text, Appendix, p. 305)*

Saudi diplomats had more success in the North African region of the Arab world. In May 1987 King Fahd was instrumental in bringing together the rulers of Morocco and Algeria to discuss their differences over the Polisario, the Saharan people's independence movement. In November 1987 Saudi Arabia helped to further the cause of Arab unity by resuming full diplomatic relations with Egypt, nine years after relations had been broken off over its signing of the Camp David accords. The Saudis' action followed a decision by the Arab League that permitted member states to restore relations with Egypt at their own discretion.

Relations with the United States. The relationship between Saudi Arabia and the United States has been driven by Saudi Arabia's oil resources, its strategic location in the Middle East, and the Saudi family's stern anti-Communist policies. Saudi Arabia has maintained close ties with the United States since 1940, when formal diplomatic relations were established. Since the fall of the shah of Iran in 1979, the United States has increasingly relied on Saudi Arabia as its major strategic ally in the Persian Gulf.

During the early 1980s the cooperation of Saudi Arabia was considered critical to the Reagan administration's "strategic consensus" policy that sought to mobilize the anti-Communist states of the Middle East to counter threats of Soviet encroachment in the region. Maintaining that the Soviet Union, and not the Arab-Israeli conflict, was the main threat to regional security and oil supplies to the West, the White House supported the sale of sophisticated military equipment to the Saudis, often over Israel's objections.

Washington also sought Saudi assistance in dealing with the Middle East peace question. In 1983, when President Reagan called for a partial Israeli withdrawal from the occupied territories and self-rule for West Bank Palestinians, he asked the Saudis to pressure the PLO to allow Jordan's King Hussein to speak for the Palestinians.

In the mid-1980s a common interest in containing the spread of Iranian revolutionary activity and securing free shipping in the Gulf provided additional areas for cooperation between Saudi Arabia and the United States. In 1986 Washington finally delivered sophisticated AWACS surveillance planes that the Saudis had purchased in 1981, and Riyadh provided essential aid to the U.S. naval convoys, which began escorting reflagged Kuwaiti tankers through the Gulf in June 1987. Nevertheless, Riyadh refused to allow U.S. access to its military facilities there.

Differences over the Arab-Israeli conflict, however, continued to strain relations between Washington and Riyadh. American support for Israel led to restrictions on U.S. military sales to Saudi Arabia and made Saudi leaders less willing to support U.S. policies in the region. The kingdom's reluctance to pressure its Arab neighbors toward a peace settlement has frustrated some American leaders.

In early 1987 congressional opposition to supplying sophisticated weapons to an Arab country forced the Reagan administration to withdraw its proposal to sell the Saudis Stinger missiles, F-15 planes, and Maverick anti-tank missiles. In frustration, the Saudis vastly increased their purchase of weapons from the United Kingdom, ultimately leading the British to displace the United States as the Saudis' main supplier of arms.

In March 1988 the disclosure that Riyadh had secretly purchased an unspecified number of CSS-2 medium-range missiles from China led to a diplomatic confrontation between Washington and Riyadh. The missiles had a range of 2,600 kilometers and were capable of carrying nuclear weapons. Stunned that the Saudis had acquired the missiles and had kept the deal hidden from the United States for more than two years, Washington protested strongly to King Fahd. The king responded by requesting that the American ambassador who had delivered the protest be replaced. Later the Saudis even shed some of their customary distrust of the Soviet Union by welcoming a visit by Soviet officials to Riyadh for the first time in fifty years, signaling the possibility of reviving relations with Moscow.

Still, Saudi Arabia and the United States remain allies. Although the Saudi regime has displayed a greater willingness to assert its independence from Washington in recent years, the Saudis continue to depend on the United States to provide valuable military and technological assistance and to ensure its regional security. Saudi oil exports remain critical to the United States and American prosperity continues to be essential to Saudi Arabia's long-term trade and investments.

In regional affairs Saudi Arabia is also firmly in the Western camp. The Saudis continue to be suspicious of Soviet intentions toward the Middle East. These suspicions were intensified by the Soviet invasion of Afghanistan in 1979. Saudi Arabia provided financial support for the rebels fighting the Soviets in Afghanistan during the nine-year Soviet occupation of that country. The Saudis have also been uneasy about the presence of a Soviet ally, South Yemen, on its southwestern frontier.

Outlook

The early 1990s will be an important period of transition for Saudi Arabia. Following nearly a decade of war and declining oil revenues, the Saudis' economic future will be determined by their ability to live within their means while promoting diversification away from oil exports. Having begun to show greater assertiveness in OPEC, Saudi Arabia will have to continue exerting its leadership within the organization to help maintain stable oil prices."

The challenge of maintaining the pace of modernization while sustaining the country's conservative Islamic foundation is also likely to become more acute. As the Saudi middle class becomes more powerful, King Fahd may come under greater pressure to honor his promise for increased political participation, which has been strongly opposed by religious authorities. Moreover, despite the government's desire to curtail the number of expatriates in the kingdom, further reductions of foreign workers are likely to cause disruptions within the economy and inhibit the infusion of high-technology foreign investment and expertise that the economy needs.

In foreign affairs, the conclusion of the Iran-Iraq war has created a new set of priorities for the Saudi regime. Many observers predict that the Saudis will try to improve relations with Iran while maintaining close ties to Iraq. This would require Riyadh to restore relations with Iran. Cooperation with Tehran will be particularly important to maintaining unity within OPEC. Economic issues will likely take precedence over security concerns in Saudi Arabia's interactions with the GCC countries as well.

U.S.-Saudi relations may also experience some changes. Having established contact with Chinese and Soviet leaders, the Saudi regime has indicated a greater willingness to assert its independence from Washington. In the aftermath of the Soviets' withdrawal from Afghanistan it is possible that the kingdom will go as far as restoring formal diplomatic relations with Moscow. Such diplomatic moves, however, are unlikely to create any permanent damage to U.S.-Saudi ties. Common economic and strategic interests will ensure continued—if somewhat less cordial—cooperation between Washington and Riyadh.

Playing a Major Role in the Region

Syria has had stable rule for almost two decades under President Hafez al-Assad. This period of relative calm follows years of tumult. Syria experienced more than a dozen coups and attempted coups between 1946, when the departure of French soldiers left Syria independent, and 1970, when Assad seized power. Under his rule, Syria not only achieved domestic stability but it also gained a leading role in regional politics.

Assad suffered several serious foreign policy setbacks in 1988 and 1989. In war-torn Lebanon, he was unable to force the remnants of the Lebanese government to accept the pro-Syrian candidate for the presidency, despite the presence of more than forty thousand Syrian troops in the country. In early 1989 these troops were fighting the decimated Lebanese army. The focus of the Arab struggle against Israel moved dramatically away from Syria with the ongoing uprising in the Israeli-occupied territories and the decision by Yasir Arafat of the Palestine Liberation Organization (PLO) to recognize Israel and accept UN Security Council resolutions 242 and 338. Syria's leading position in the Arab world also was eroded by the cease-fire in the Iraq-Iran war, which enabled Syria's bitterest Arab rival, Iraq, to increase its involvement in inter-Arab affairs. More serious for Syrian leadership in the Arab world, by 1989 Egypt had emerged fully from the isolation imposed on it by most of the Arab states after its 1979 peace treaty with Israel. Under pressure from Saudi Arabia, Assad agreed not to block Egypt's return to the Arab League.

Hafez al-Assad

The Syrian president was also concerned about Soviet leader Mikhail Gorbachev's more moderate stance toward the Middle East. Even Syrian relations with Iran, which had been close through most of the Iraq-Iran war, were undermined as rival groups in Lebanon associated with Syria and Iran struggled for dominance of the local Shi'ite community.

What is extraordinary about the role of Syria and Assad in the Middle East is that, despite these setbacks, Syria remains a key player throughout the region: Syria is still the single strongest force in fragmented Lebanon; no permanent solution to the Arab-Israeli conflict can be achieved without Syria's active participation; Syria remains a pivotal player in inter-Arab politics; and, while the Soviet Union regards Syria as its most important client in the Middle East, Syria also has managed to begin a dialogue with the United States.

Assad's success in achieving domestic stability and regional influence however, has been extremely costly. The expense of maintaining Syrian troops in Lebanon has burdened Syria's economy, and Assad's rule has remained repressive. His apparently successful suppression of the Moslem Brotherhood uprising of 1982 came at the cost of severe military measures and thousands of lives. Although Assad is one of the shrewdest politicians ever to appear on the Middle East stage and analysts are reluctant ever to underestimate his staying power, several factors threaten to undermine his leadership: the concentration of power in his hands; his ambivalence about a possible successor; his poor health (one or more heart attacks or strokes in 1983 and 1984); his brutal suppression of Islamic fundamentalists; the continuing weakness of the Syrian economy; and his failure to regain the Golan Heights lost in the 1967 Arab-Israeli war and subsequently annexed by Israel.

Geography

Syria is located at the eastern end of the Mediterranean Sea and shares borders with Turkey to the north, Iraq to the east, Jordan to the south, Israel to the southwest, and Lebanon to the west. It has a land area of approximately 71,498 square miles (including the 500 square miles of the Golan Heights, which is currently occupied by Israel).

Syria is geographically divided into an inland plateau in the east and a much smaller coastal zone in which two mountain ranges enclose a fertile lowland. A chain of low mountains crosses the inland plateau diagonally, extending from the mountainous Jebel Druze area in the southwest corner of Syria to the Euphrates River that flows from the mountains of Turkey diagonally across Syria to Iraq. South of these mountains, along the eastern portion of the Syrian-Jordanian border and the southern portion of the Syrian-Iraqi border, is the Hamad desert region. The largest fertile area of Syria is known as the Jazirah "island," which is northeast of the Euphrates.

About 50 percent of Syria's land is arable, but only about 31 percent is under cultivation. Syria is one of the

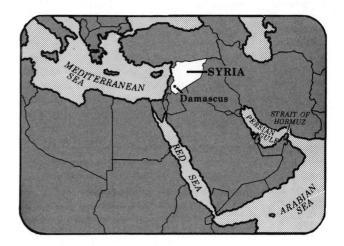

Key Facts on Syria

Area: 71,498 square miles, including about 500 square miles occupied by Israel.

Capital: Damascus.

Population: 11,570,000 (1988).

Religion: 74 percent Sunni Moslem; 16 percent Alawite, Druze, and other Moslem sects; 10 percent Christian.

Official Language: Arabic; Kurdish, Armenian, French, and English are also spoken.

GNP: $20.4 billion; $1,820 per capita (1987).

Sources: World Bank Atlas 1988; CIA World Factbook 1988

few nations of the Middle East that still have unexploited arable land. Most of Syria's water is supplied by its rivers (80 percent from the Euphrates alone) and underground reservoirs.

Syria's largest cities are located in fertile areas: Latakia (a major port) is in the coastal plain, and Damascus, Aleppo, Hamah, and Homs are in fertile river plains. All of these cities except Latakia are inland of the coastal mountain ranges and have been traditional centers of trade.

The climate of Syria is varied. The coastal zone receives fairly plentiful rainfall as the mountain ranges catch precipitation blown from the Mediterranean. The barren desert regions of the southeast receive little rain. The 75 percent of the country that lies between these two regions has a semiarid climate; the rivers there supply most of the water.

Arable land is Syria's most important resource, although there are relatively small oil and gas deposits. Otherwise Syria's only natural resources are low-grade phosphate deposits and small amounts of natural asphalt, rock salt, and construction materials (sand, stone, gravel, and gypsum). Syria's oil and gas deposits are quite small by regional standards and were late in being exploited. Oil was discovered in 1956 but production did not begin until 1968. Oil and gas production provided the Syrian economy with a small but important boost during the 1970s and 1980s. Syria also profits from the petroleum pipelines that cross its territory transporting petroleum products to the Mediterranean Sea from the oil-producing states bordering the Persian Gulf.

Demography

In Syria, like neighboring Lebanon, demography has had a powerful effect on the country's political situation. About 90 percent of the population are Arabs, and at least 65 percent of the population are Sunni Moslems. Ethnic minorities include Kurds (about 5 to 7 percent of the population), Armenians (about 3 percent), and much smaller numbers of Turkomans, Circassians, Assyrians, and Jews. Major religious minorities include several small Islamic sects (the two most important being the Alawis and the Druze), as well as Greek Orthodox Christians and various other Christian sects.

Religious and ethnic identification in Syria is usually

accompanied by certain regional, social, and economic characteristics. Although Alawis comprise less than 15 percent of the population as a whole, they represent a majority in the coastal province of Latakia and are mostly poor farmers. Druze, who comprise perhaps 3 percent of the population, are located primarily in the Jebel Druze in the southwest corner of Syria, the Golan Heights, and Damascus. Traditionally denied political influence by the Sunni majority and lacking means of advancement other than free military training, the Alawis and Druze flocked to the military and to the secular Ba'ath party. With the advent to power of the Ba'ath party, these two minority groups gained political influence disproportionately greater than their numbers or economic clout. Because President Assad is a member of the Alawi minority and supports secular rule, Moslem fundamentalists—especially the Sunni Moslem Brotherhood—have often opposed his leadership.

The Alawi and Druze sects are offshoots of Shi'ite Islam, the religion of Iran, rather than the orthodox Sunni sect. The theologies of Alawis and Druze diverge sharply from orthodox Sunni Islam, and even from Shi'ite Islam. They are considered heretical by most Sunnis and Shi'ites. This compounds Assad's difficulties, not only in dealing with Sunni fundamentalism at home, but also with his support of Shi'ite Iran and Shi'ite elements in Lebanon.

History

The modern nation of Syria did not come into existence until the twentieth century. The name Syria, used first by the Greeks, historically denoted the region at the eastern end of the Mediterranean lying between Egypt and Asia Minor. This larger region—generally called Greater Syria to distinguish it from the nation-state that bears the name today—has a rich history. Containing some fertile farmland and located at the crossroads of three continents, Greater Syria was the invasion route of armies, the battleground of adjacent empires, and an arena of conflict for centuries. The waves of migration and invasion in ancient times and the ever-changing religious and political leaders left Greater Syria a mosaic of ethnic and religious groups.

Because no single indigenous power has ever been able to control all of Greater Syria, people in the area have closely identified with their city or region. This has left its mark on the modern nation of Syria, where religious and ethnic differences are often reinforced by differences of region. Geography has been a fragmenting influence; the two distinctive zones separated by mountains (the coastal plain and the interior plateau) and the lack of navigable rivers have reinforced Syrians' historical identification with their own region and group.

Damascus, one of the oldest continuously inhabited cities in the world, may have been settled as early as 2500 B.C. It was dominated by various civilizations over the centuries: Aramean, Assyrian, Babylonian, Persian, Greek, Roman, Nabatean, and Byzantine. In A.D. 636, Damascus came under Moslem rule. The city rose to its peak of power as the capital of the Umayyad Empire, which stretched from India to Spain and lasted from 661 to 750.

After the downfall of the Umayyads, Greater Syria became the prey of powerful neighboring states and empires in Mesopotamia, Anatolia, and Egypt. Religious conflict is an integral part of the history of this area. The Fatimid rulers of Egypt did much to spread Islam in Greater Syria, often by force. When the Christian crusaders came to the area to fight the Moslems, some local

Christian groups provided aid, thereby creating bonds between Levantine and European Christians and encouraging hostility between Moslem and Christian inhabitants of Greater Syria. Damascus was a provincial capital of the Mameluke Empire from 1260 until 1516 when the rule of the Ottoman Turks began.

The 400 years of Ottoman rule strongly influenced what would one day become the nation-state of Syria. The Ottoman Empire was extraordinarily heterogeneous, including most of the lands of the eastern and southern Mediterranean coast. The Ottoman system provided substantial autonomy not only to provincial governors but also to different religious groups, as long as taxes were paid to the Ottoman government. The system allowed each recognized religious community, or millet, to run its own system of personal law and perform certain civil functions. This accentuated the localism and communal separatism that resulted from the presence of so many different groups. The people continued to identify with their own city or region rather than with a larger political entity.

By the nineteenth century the Ottoman Empire had weakened and European nations had begun to develop direct ties with minority groups in Greater Syria: the French with the Catholics, especially the Maronites of Mount Lebanon (the mountains near the coast of what is now Lebanon); the Russians with the Orthodox; the British with the Protestants and the Druze.

Shortly after the turn of the twentieth century, Ottoman authorities, fearing the growth of Arab nationalism, clamped down on Greater Syria. Ottoman repression, however, did not succeed in quelling the Arab independence movement. Many Syrians supported Sherif Hussein, the leader of Mecca in the Arabian Peninsula, in his efforts to break away from Ottoman control. Sherif Hussein and Arab nationalists throughout the area believed that the British would support the establishment of independent Arab states in the eastern Mediterranean after the end of World War I. In 1918 Prince Faisal, son of Sherif Hussein, gained control of Damascus. By the time the Ottoman Empire collapsed at the end of the war, there was already an Arab administration in Damascus and in the interior areas of what is now Syria. The British controlled Palestine and the French controlled the Syrian coastal areas.

The victorious Europeans made conflicting promises, however, concerning the future of the region. In 1915 Britain assured Sherif Hussein that independent Arab entities would be established in parts of the former Ottoman Empire. The 1916 Sykes-Picot Agreement between Britain and France (kept secret until 1917 when it was revealed by the revolutionary government of Russia) divided Greater Syria between the British and French, and the 1917 Balfour Declaration promised British support for the establishment of a Jewish homeland in Palestine.

Although Syrian nationalists called for an independent nation with Faisal as king in 1919, the 1920 San Remo Conference of the victorious allies placed the area that is now Syria and Lebanon under French control. French troops entered Damascus, and in 1922 the League of Nations formally recognized France's mandate over the area.

French rule was oppressive and divisive. The French divided the mandated area into regions that roughly corresponded to religious and ethnic groupings, undoubtedly to discourage unified opposition to French rule. Mount Lebanon was the major location of the Maronite Christians, a group with strong historic ties to France, and this district was enlarged by adding the coastal cities and the Bekaa

Valley to the east. This had the effect of increasing the area dominated by Maronites but at the same time diluting Maronite strength in the region as Druze from the mountains and Moslems from the adjacent areas were added. Other areas of the mandate were also administered by the local dominant groups: Latakia (Alawis), Alexandretta (Turks), Jebel Druze (Druze), Aleppo and Damascus (Sunni Moslems).

French control was not imposed easily. The inhabitants of the French mandate as well as other European nations pressured France to discuss the future independence of the area, and negotiations between the French and local Arab nationalists were held throughout the late 1920s. A major point of disagreement was the links between Mount Lebanon, Jebel Druze, Alexandretta, and the rest of the region. Arab nationalists insisted that the entire area under French control become independent as one nation, while the French were intent on protecting the autonomy of certain minority groups, especially the Maronites of Mount Lebanon. Local nationalists were further alienated from France when it granted the area around Alexandretta to Turkey in 1939.

Not until World War II did Syria achieve independence. When the Free French took over Syria from the Vichy government representatives in 1941, they promised independence to gain local support. Formal de jure independence was granted in late 1941, and an elected government under President Shukri al-Kuwatly took power in 1943, the same year that neighboring Lebanon achieved independence. The last French soldiers were not withdrawn, however, until 1946, and even then the French were reluctant to leave.

Early Independence

The first twenty-five years of Syrian independence were characterized by political instability. Syria developed a reputation as the Arab state that was most prone to military coups. The civilian government of al-Kuwatly was overthrown in March 1949 in a bloodless coup by the army chief of staff, Col. Husni al-Zayim. Syria's poor military showing in the first Arab-Israeli war in 1948, bickering among the members of the civilian government, and a weak

economy prompted the insurrection.

This first military coup was the beginning of more than twenty years of instability and military involvement in political affairs. This phenomenon not only has given minority groups that are disproportionately represented in the army greater power than the majority Sunnis but also has politicized the Syrian army, with harmful effects on its combat capability.

The first military regime was toppled only four and a half months later by another military group, which was itself overthrown in December 1949. The new regime, led by Lt. Col. Adib al-Shishakli, seemed relatively liberal in its first two years in power: a constitution was enacted in 1950 and a parliament was elected that permitted free speech within limits. Rising opposition, however, triggered repressive measures beginning in late 1951, and these steps resulted in Shishakli's overthrow in February 1954.

The next four years of democratic government saw frequent cabinet changes and the rapid growth of political parties with strong ideological bases, most importantly the Arab Socialist Resurrection party (the Ba'ath party). The Ba'ath party was the result of a merger in 1953 of two political groups with two distinctive ideological objectives. From one group the Ba'athists inherited a socialist orientation, although they explicitly rejected Marxism. From the other they received an emphasis on Arab unity. Although the party recognizes the connection between Arabism and Islam, it is not based on Islamic solidarity. Ba'athism has broad appeal in other Arab countries and ultimately came to be the ruling ideology in Iraq as well, although a factional split between Ba'athists in Syria and Iraq has been a divisive factor in Syrian-Iraqi relations for many years.

The Syrian Ba'athists worked assiduously to build party support within the army. The secular ideology of the party attracted many young officers of minority religious groups. Two other parties with strong ideological orientations, the Syrian Communist party and the Syrian National party, also actively sought to increase their power during the 1954-1958 period. The Ba'athists were represented in the cabinet for the first time in 1956 and soon began to accrue power disproportionate to their numbers.

By late 1957 the Ba'athists feared that the Communist party was overtaking them in their efforts to control policy in Damascus. The appeal of the political left in Syria grew not only because of the ineptitude of the democratic governments but also because of the wave of anti-Western feeling that had swept the Arab countries in the late 1940s and the 1950s. The creation of Israel in 1948 and the 1956 Suez crisis accelerated opposition to the West. Egyptian President Gamal Abdel Nasser's appeals for Arab nationalism gave the Ba'athists the opportunity to salvage their threatened domestic situation by asking the Egyptian leader to form a union with Syria. Nasser had cracked down severely on Communists in Egypt and could be expected to do the same in Syria if a union were established. Although the Ba'athists knew that their own party would be restricted as well, they favored a union because they believed it would eliminate the threat from the far left. Although Nasser was reluctant initially, the United Arab Republic was announced in February 1958.

The three and one-half years of Syrian union with Egypt were not pleasant for Syrian politicians. Nasser insisted that he would accept only a complete merger, not a federation, and the much smaller Syrian nation was submerged in the union. Although the religious leaders, landowners, and wealthy business people who made up the traditional political elite in Syria most strongly opposed the union, the Ba'athists as well soon regretted their plea for union with Egypt. In 1961 Nasser began to emphasize socialism, and Syria suffered a drought and an economic downturn. These may have been the last straws for disaffected Syrians, and the coup of September 1961 brought to power in Damascus traditional political figures who immediately brought about Syria's secession from the union.

The coup of September 1961 ushered in another period of confusion and instability in Syrian politics. Government succeeded government, and popular discontent grew as the traditional Sunni politicians, both inside and outside the military, proved incapable of providing stable leadership.

In March 1963 the Ba'ath party assumed power following another coup, and since then elements of the party have ruled Syria. The party itself became the arena of political conflict, and until Hafez Assad took power in 1970 the leftists and the centrists of the Ba'ath party leadership contested for power.

Syria Under Assad

In July 1963 an attempted coup by pro-Nasser officers was violently suppressed by the Ba'ath regime. This marked a change in the relatively peaceful pattern of coups in Syria up to that point. Lt. Gen. Amin al-Hafez became president and ruled for the next two and one-half years. In February 1966 a coup by Alawi officers ushered in a period of civilian Ba'athist rule, although Gen. Salah Jadid was clearly the final arbiter of Syrian politics. Between 1966 and 1970 tension grew between the more radical civilian wing of the Ba'ath party and the more pragmatic military wing. The civilian leaders of the country were ardent supporters of pan-Arabism and the PLO, while the military group led by Hafez al-Assad, a forty-year-old Alawi air force lieutenant general, represented greater support of Syrian national objectives. In November 1970 a coup brought Assad to power.

During the first five years of his rule, Assad consolidated power domestically and strengthened ties abroad. Gradually Syria began to emerge from the isolation imposed by years of domestic instability. Although Assad was careful to place loyal Alawi officers in key positions, especially in intelligence, he broadened the base of his regime by bringing various leftist elements into the government. As early as 1973 Sunnis demonstrated against the regime, but objections to the political domination of the Sunni majority by an Alawi minority did not become politically significant until the latter part of the 1970s, perhaps because most Syrians were relieved at the stability the new regime offered and the relatively liberalized political atmosphere established by Assad in his early years in power.

The foreign policy of Assad's first five years achieved friendly relations with most of the Arab states, improved relations with the Soviet Union after some strain in late 1970, and even renewed diplomatic relations with several Western nations (Great Britain in 1973, the United States and West Germany in 1974). Assad's cooperation with other Arab states reached its peak in the close coordination with Egypt that led to the October 1973 Arab-Israeli war. Despite Syria's failure to retake the Golan Heights from Israel, the war was regarded by Syrians as a success because their troops performed well during the fighting.

By the mid-1970s, however, serious domestic and foreign problems began to plague Assad's regime. Political dissent, especially from disaffected Sunnis, became more violent, and the civil war in Lebanon put Assad in the difficult position of reconciling his support of Arab nationalism and the Palestinians with Syrian national interests.

Syrian Involvement in Lebanon

The involvement of Syrian troops since 1976 in the Lebanese civil war has complicated every aspect of Syria's foreign policy. Syrian troops have supported virtually every faction in the Lebanese war at one time or another, and Syrian activities in Lebanon are impossible to understand without a clear grasp both of the conflicting goals of Syrian foreign policy and of specific Syrian objectives in Lebanon.

Since the beginning of Ba'athist domination of Syria in 1963, there has been a contradiction between the concepts of Syrian nationalism and Arab nationalism. Ba'athist ideology focuses enormous attention on Arab nationalism. Although Assad's 1970 coup represented the victory of the less radical, more pragmatic wing of the party, Syria remained committed to the concept of an Arab nation. At the heart of Arab nationalism lies the Palestinian conflict with Israel, and so the Syrian commitment to Arab nationalism implies strong support of the PLO. On the other hand, Syrian national interests have often been in conflict with general Arab objectives. Syria's intervention in Lebanon has highlighted the contradiction between these two threads of Syrian foreign policy and has vastly complicated Assad's desire to maintain good relations with his fellow Arab leaders and to play a leading role in the Arab world.

Syrian objectives in Lebanon are rooted in the history of Syria and Lebanon before their independence. In 1920 the French added areas with Moslem majorities to the predominantly Maronite Christian Mount Lebanon region and ruled this area separately from the rest of its mandate. Syrian nationalists viewed French policy as an unjustified division of one national entity, and Syrian governments never openly accepted the legitimacy of a separate Lebanon. Despite the close ties between the two states, Syria has never had diplomatic relations with Lebanon.

Throughout Syria's history migration, trade, and other forms of contact with Lebanon have continued. Some of the minority groups that make up the fractured Lebanese polity are also found in Syria.

Given these close connections and the fragility of the Lebanese government, Syria has always sought to influence events in Lebanon. Some Syrians even have advocated annexing Lebanon to Syria outright, but Assad has never aspired to do so. He appears to favor a compliant Lebanese government in which Syrian influence plays a strong hand. Annexation of Lebanon, with its quarreling factions and bitter religious-political differences, might destabilize Syria itself. In addition, for many years the Druze of Syria competed with the Alawis for influence in the Ba'ath party, and Assad is unlikely to want to add some 200,000 Lebanese Druze (with an armed and combat-ready militia) to his own country.

Assad's objective in Lebanon appears to be the creation of a peaceful, prosperous climate with a weak, politically moderate central government dependent upon Syria for its survival. This goal helps explain the shifts in Syrian support for the various Lebanese factions.

After the 1970 Jordanian-Palestinian war, most PLO troops were displaced to Lebanon, the one Arab state adjacent to Israel where they could operate without being threatened by a strong government. The arrival of PLO troops upset the fragile balance of the Lebanese political system and in April 1975 triggered civil war. At first Syria played a constructive role, receiving praise from other Arab states, as well as the United States and France, for its attempts to reconcile warring factions.

By mid-1976, however, it appeared that an alliance of the PLO and the Lebanese left was about to triumph over the conservative Christian Maronites and their allies. The prospect of a radical government in Beirut and a PLO unresponsive to Syrian control prompted Assad to send his troops into Lebanon in June 1976 to prevent the collapse of the Maronite coalition. With the aid of Syrian forces, the Maronites were able to avoid defeat.

The Arab states were appalled at the sight of Syria troops attacking the PLO and participating in the Maronite assault on Palestinian refugee camps. In response some Arab states broke their ties with Syria. By the end of 1976 a temporary halt in the fighting had been achieved. Saudi Arabia helped to mediate a compromise: an Arab peacekeeping force would patrol Lebanon to prevent violence, and the Syrian forces already present would make up the majority of these peacekeepers. Saudi Arabia and other Arab oil producers agreed to pay most of the expenses incurred by the presence of Syrian troops in Lebanon.

This compromise allowed Syrian rapprochement with some of its Arab critics, but in 1977 the disagreement between Assad and President Anwar Sadat of Egypt over policy toward Israel became an open quarrel. Although Assad had agreed to a U.S.-sponsored disengagement agreement with Israel in May 1974, he had opposed Sadat's growing rapprochement with the United States. He condemned Sadat's November 1977 trip to Jerusalem and became a leader of the Arab states that rejected the 1979 Camp David peace treaty and any other compromises with Israel.

Violence in Lebanon continued, despite the 1976 compromise. By 1978 the Maronites had begun to turn to Israel for external aid, while Syria had shifted its support to the alliance between the left and the Palestinians, which it considered more likely to further Syrian interests.

When Israel invaded Lebanon in June 1982, Syrian forces in Lebanon's Bekaa Valley suffered serious losses. Although the Soviet Union has since replaced weapons and military equipment lost during the fighting, the damage to Syrian military prestige was substantial and underlined Syria's inability to use military means to reverse Israel's annexation of the Golan Heights. Although Assad had recouped much stature in the Arab world by his support of the Palestinians and the Lebanese left since 1978, the poor showing of his military in 1982 as the Israelis fought their way to Beirut and bombarded the city caused analysts to predict a gloomy political future for him. Assad's foreign policy problems were compounded by political dissent at home, which he violently suppressed.

As usual, however, Assad rebounded from the lackluster performance of his troops in Lebanon in 1982. Taking the lead of the diverse and mutually suspicious factions that shared only an opposition to Israel, for three years Assad worked to push the Israelis out of Lebanon and reassert his influence over that country. By 1985 a May 1983 U.S.-brokered agreement between Israel and Lebanon, which Assad opposed, had been abandoned by the powerless government of Amin Gemayel; the American marine force had been withdrawn in disarray following the 1983 bombing of its barracks; and in June 1985 Israel withdrew the bulk of its forces, leaving few units to aid the pro-Israeli Lebanon militia in southern Lebanon.

This resurgence of Syrian power in Lebanon, however, was soon challenged. Israeli influence had been removed except from the areas adjacent to the border, but soon Assad was again in conflict with the PLO and even with pro-Iranian segments of the Shi'ite community. In early 1987 Syria increased its military contingent in Lebanon and attempted once again to control Beirut. Although Syria controls one of the small factions within the PLO, it has failed in its efforts to exercise decisive influence over Arafat and the organization as a whole. In early 1988 Syria tried to get the PLO out of Beirut by pushing Amal, the Shi'ite militia allied with Syria, to lay siege to the Palestinian refugee camps where the PLO held sway. After weeks of fighting, Amal lifted the siege and the PLO moved to the predominantly Sunni town of Sidon on the southern coast of Lebanon. There remains bitterness between the PLO and Assad and between pro-Iranian and pro-Syrian factions within the Shi'ite community.

Syrian conflict with the most important Maronite militia, the Lebanese Forces, is more straightforward. For Assad, the Lebanese Forces are reactionary, pro-Israeli diehards who stand in the way of his domination of Lebanon. The Lebanese Forces regard Assad as a relentless enemy who wants to take over Lebanon and destroy the Maronite community, politically if not physically. The Syrian attempt failed in the fall of 1988 to force the rump Lebanese parliament to select as president pro-Syrian Maronite and former president Suleiman Franjieh. Assad was also unsuccessful in having another pro-Syrian Maronite, Michel Daher, elected in September. The deadlock ended with President Amin Gemayel stepping down at the end of his term and naming the Christian commander of the armed forces, Michel Aoun, as head of government. Syria and those factions allied with it have refused to accept this and view Gemayel's last prime minister, Selim Hoss, as the head of government. In early 1989 Aoun, after attempting to unify the Christian militias, challenged the Syrians directly by calling for the evacuation of all foreign forces from Lebanon. In response, the Syrians bombarded Christian sections of Beirut and areas outside the capital. Sporadic fighting has continued between Syria and the Christian militias.

The prospects for Syrian withdrawal from Lebanon are remote. The situation there remains complex, the more so because Syria's major Arab rival, Iraq, has again become involved since its cease-fire with Iran. Iraqi support of Syria's foremost Lebanese enemy—the Christian Lebanese Forces—reinforced Iran's links with the Lebanon's Shi'ite Hizballah organization. In addition, the presence of the Israelis in the south and the PLO in the Palestinian refugee camps makes Syria's efforts to achieve its goals in Lebanon unlikely to succeed. Nevertheless, although Syria may not be able to bring about the establishment of a weak, pro-Syrian central government in Lebanon, it can prevent the success of any resolution to the conflict in the foreseeable future that does not conform with Syrian interests.

Current Issues

Assad's ability to hold on to power has surpassed all predictions, and his continuing importance in regional politics despite formidable obstacles still confounds those who prophesied his demise. The problems facing him, however, are serious, and perhaps more pressing than ever before. Domestically, Assad faces major questions about the stability of his government and who will succeed him, as well as a weak economy that is weighed down by the costs of Syrian involvement in Lebanon.

Economic problems, especially since 1982, include low productivity, a massive trade deficit, a sizable brain drain, inflation, hard currency shortages, and low economic growth. Hard currency remittances from Syrians working in the oil-producing Arab countries have diminished with lowered oil prices of the 1980s, and Syria remains relatively resource-poor.

Despite these conditions, Assad has chosen to field a large standing army of more than four hundred thousand troops, the second largest force in the Arab world next to Egypt. Defense expenditures have averaged over half of the nation's operating budget. It has not been possible to attain and maintain the strategic parity with Israel that Assad wants and simultaneously meet the demands of industrialization and agricultural expansion.

As a result, Syria remains heavily reliant on foreign aid, especially from Saudi Arabia and Kuwait. The drop in oil prices not only reduced remittances but it also reduced aid from the Arab oil-producing states. In response to these problems, Assad began to take tough measures in 1986, restricting imports, cutting the budget, and publicly rebuking ministers charged with economic and financial policies.

Economic problems, however, are not Assad's most serious domestic issue. Assad crushed a rebellion by the fundamentalist Moslem Brotherhood in 1982 by leveling large parts of the city of Hamah and killing thousands. Since then, other than a brief spate of antigovernment terrorism in early 1986, there have been few indications of the strength of anti-Assad forces. The growth of the Islamic revival movement in other Arab countries, however, suggests that the Moslem Brotherhood may be increasing its numbers covertly. The viability of a regime whose head and whose key personnel are members of a minority sect viewed as heretical by the Moslem Brothers and other Sunnis remains questionable. Another domestic political issue is who will succeed Assad, a matter on which he remains ambivalent. Although Assad has not experienced periods of illness since 1984, he does not enjoy robust health.

Involvement in Lebanon and the Arab-Israeli conflict remain the most critical foreign issues for Syria. Although foreign aid—presumably from Saudi Arabia—supports much of the Syrian military presence in Lebanon, the conflict there remains a drain on Syria economically and politically. In the past Syrian involvement in Lebanon has complicated its relations with the other Arab states and even with the Soviet Union, which was reportedly much displeased with Syria's 1976 intervention. Assad's objectives in Lebanon—a peaceful and prosperous Lebanon under a weak, pro-Syrian government—have required extraordinary maneuvers to balance the changing power equations over the past fifteen years and some of his actions—intervention on behalf of the Maronites in 1976, support of anti-Arafat rebels in the struggle for power within the PLO, and the use of the Shi'ite Amal militia against the PLO in the refugee camps in 1985—have earned for Assad the vilification of much of the Arab world. The very tenacity of Syria's involvement in Lebanon at these high costs, however, demonstrates its pivotal importance to Assad.

Related to its policy in Lebanon is Syria's position in the Arab-Israeli conflict. Assad continues to try to prevent any resolution of the conflict in which he is not centrally involved. He is especially keen to prevent any Israeli-Palestinian accord that might result from the moderation of the PLO stance toward Israel that occurred in late 1988. Assad fears that such an accord might resolve the conflict without providing for Israel's return of the Golan Heights to Syria.

There had been hopes of a reconciliation between Assad and Yasir Arafat following an April 1988 meeting between the two leaders, but Arafat's agreement in December 1988 to recognize Israel and accept the relevant UN Security Council resolutions angered Assad. To derail the U.S.-PLO dialogue and to keep Arafat off balance, Assad has reportedly encouraged radical PLO factions to raid northern Israel through Lebanon. Assad has openly compared Arafat's new stance to Sadat's agreement to the Camp David accords—which Assad continues to reject.

In early 1989, however, Assad was apparently finding it hard to control his allies among the Palestinian guerrilla groups. The Popular Front for the Liberation of Palestine—General Command (PFLP-GC) is headquartered in Damascus. This group, which was reponsible for several raids on Israel by way of neighboring states, was, according to some reports, likely to be linked with the bombing of the Pan American jet over Scotland in December 1988, and it was becoming a liability to Assad in his relations with the United States and Western Europe. If investigators proved the PFLP-GC was responsible for the bombing of the airliner, Syrian relations with the West would probably decline dramatically. Assad was reportedly trying to get the PFLP-GC to move to Libya, but without success.

The Syrian position in the Arab world and its relations with the superpowers are two other important foreign policy issues. Syria has been the major client state of the Soviet Union in the Middle East since 1972, and Moscow has demonstrated clearly its commitment to Syria, especially by rearming the Syrian military after its losses to Israel in the early 1980s. Gorbachev's policies, however, make Assad nervous. The Syrian leader must worry about the continued Soviet commitment to the PLO, Soviet attempts to improve relations with moderate and conservative Arab regimes, and Moscow's tentative moves toward renewal of diplomatic relations with Israel. The possibility that the Soviets will reach an accord on the Middle East with the United States without Syrian involvement also threatens Assad. Soviets have attempted to reassure him with official visits. For example, Damascus was the first Middle East stop in Soviet Foreign Minister Eduard Shevardnadze's tour of the area in early 1989.

Relations with the United States have been mercurial, but the continued efforts of the United States to improve ties with Assad despite his links to some terrorist groups demonstrates the degree to which the U.S. government regards Assad as essential to any resolution of the Arab-Israeli or Lebanese conflicts. Former secretary of state George P. Shultz stopped in Damascus in February 1988,

although his initiative was unsuccessful. During the early stages of the Bush administration, what was termed a "high-level" dialogue with Syria was maintained through the American ambassador in Damascus. There continued to be hope in Washington that Assad would, as he presumably had done before, use his influence on the Lebanese group Amal to get other Shi'ite groups to free American hostages held in Lebanon.

Outlook

In late 1989 observers were once again forecasting difficulties for Assad, especially in his efforts to retain his position of power within the region. Described by analysts and observers as "shrewd," "tenacious," and by one observer as "far and away the most intelligent and Machiavellian Arab leader," Assad's influence should not be discounted. He is pragmatic and ruthless as well as shrewd, and these qualities have enabled him to propel a nation that is ethnically heterogenous, possessing limited natural resources, to a position of great regional power.

It is unlikely that Syria will make great progress economically in the near future, especially if it continues to spend a large share of its resources on its military. Syria's relatively small petroleum deposits, however, have given its economy a boost as Syrian imports of oil have been dramatically reduced by domestic production.

It is also unlikely that Syrian troops will be returning soon from Lebanon. That bitter conflict appears no closer to resolution than it did a decade ago, and Syrian influence there is so important to Assad that he will not withdraw his forces until a resolution satisfactory to him has been reached.

Although Assad's position within the Arab world in the late 1980s has been eclipsed by the resurgence of both Egypt and Iraq, it is too soon to demote Assad to secondary status. The other Arab states are aware that he can scuttle any resolution of the Arab-Israeli conflict or the Lebanese civil war. Saudi Arabia remains a key financial backer of both Syria and the divided Lebanese government, and yet even the Saudi leadership does not give orders to Assad. When the Saudis want Assad's support—such as for the readmission of Egypt to the Arab League—they negotiate and compromise with him. This is unlikely to change so long as Assad remains in power.

Syrian influence in the region will continue to go through cycles of strength and weakness. The key factor remains Assad himself. The stability he has brought to his nation—even at the cost of repression and austerity—is the precondition for Syrian influence in the Middle East. While Assad appears to be in relative good health and in firm command of the army—the key to power in Syria—his health and the succession issue remain the critical questions in Syrian politics.

Oil Brightens Prospects as a Fragile Peace Continues

On September 26, 1962, a military coup in North Yemen put an end to the Rassid dynasty—one of the oldest and most enduring in history—and proclaimed the Yemen Arab Republic. Established in about A.D. 897, the Rassid dynasty claimed descent from the Prophet Muhammad and produced 111 imams (kings and religious leaders) before it was uprooted by the 1962 revolution.

To the south, where the other Yemen still was under British colonial rule, the coup was a great inspiration to underground groups agitating for political freedom. By 1967 the largest of these—the Marxist-oriented National Front for the Liberation of South Yemen (NLF)—had crushed its rivals and wrested independence from Britain. The People's Democratic Republic of Yemen, the name chosen by the Front, was born.

Divided since the early 1700s, the two Yemens have publicly committed themselves to the principle of unification, yet the two remain far apart politically. In February 1979 tension between them led to a border war that had international ramifications. Fearful that South Yemen's military assaults on its neighbor's borders were Soviet-inspired, Saudi Arabia agreed to underwrite the sale by the United States of $390 million worth of modern weapons to North Yemen. The delivery of the arms was suspended when a cease-fire was arranged March 17, 1979.

Shortly after the cease-fire, North and South Yemen pledged to renew efforts to establish a union. With North Yemen opposed to the Marxist doctrine of the regime in the south, however, unity has remained elusive.

History

The area covered by the Yemens was known to the ancient Arabs as Al-Yaman, but it was divided into kingdoms and enclaves of various sizes. Strategically poised at the junction of major trading routes between Africa and India and endowed with an abundance of fertile land, Yemen's ancient kingdoms grew prosperous and powerful. Among Yemen's centers of civilization was the fabled Kingdom of Saba ruled by the Queen of Sheba of biblical fame.

In about 1000 B.C. the Kingdom of Saba was a great trading state with a major agricultural base supported by a sophisticated system of irrigation, at the heart of which was the Marib dam, a regional wonder. In the north of Yemen the kingdom of the Mineans arose, coexisting with Saba and maintaining trading colonies as far away as Syria. During the first century B.C., the Kingdom of Himyar was established, reaching its greatest extent and power in the fifth century A.D. Both Christian and Jewish kings were among its leaders.

Developments in the Roman Empire were largely responsible for the decline of pre-Islamic civilization in Yemen. New trade routes bypassed the old caravan trails, and Christian Romans did not need the frankincense used in pagan funeral rituals. By the sixth century A.D. the Marib dam had collapsed, symbolizing a process of political dis-

integration in southern Arabia that helped pave the way for Islam.

When followers of the Islamic Shi'ite sect split off from the mainstream Sunni religion in what is today Iran and Iraq, many persecuted Shi'ites fled during the eighth and ninth centuries to the highlands of northern Yemen. Claiming descent from the Prophet Muhammad, one of their leaders proclaimed himself imam and established the Rassid dynasty, which espoused a sect of Shi'ite Islam called Zaydism.

Zaydism dominated the tribes of the northern and eastern mountains, but the Sunni doctrine prevailed in the coastal plain and in other parts of Yemen. The religious division was to dominate Yemeni politics for generations.

In the sixteenth century the Ottoman Turks captured the Yemeni plains and the port of Aden, but a young Zaydi imam led a successful resistance, forcing the Ottomans to conclude a truce and eventually leave Yemen in 1636. One of his successors unified the mountains and plains into a single state extending to Aden, with the northern city of Sanaa as its capital. But war and chaos soon returned to Yemen. In 1728 the sultan of the southern province broke away from the Zaydi regime and forced the division between north and south that exists today.

The Ottoman sultan in Istanbul continued to claim suzerainty over Yemen, but his control was tenuous. In the meantime, the British, jointly with the Dutch at first, had established a trading post in Yemen's coffee-rich area of Mocha and by 1770 had become major coffee traders. After Napoleon's seizure of Egypt in 1798, Britain took control of Aden to protect its routes to India via the Suez.

A small Turkish military presence in Yemen came to an end after Turkey's defeat in World War I. The Zaydi Imam Yahya was left in control of the area evacuated by the Turks. He subsequently tried to consolidate his control over Yemen, but his efforts were opposed by the British and their local protégés in the south and by the Saudis in

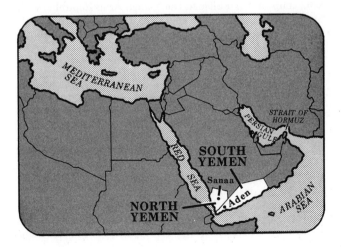

Key Facts on North Yemen

Area: 75,290 square miles.
Capital: Sanaa.
Population: 6,732,000 (1988).
Religion: Moslem.
Official Language: Arabic.
GNP: $4.9 billion, $580 per capita (1987).

Sources: World Bank Atlas 1988; CIA World Factbook 1988

the north. War ensued, ending in a humiliating defeat for Yahya in 1934, although he remained in control of part of Yemen.

After the opening of the Suez Canal and the development of large steamships in the nineteenth century, the port of Aden had gradually become a major international fueling and bunkering station between Europe, South Asia, and the Far East. In 1937 the British made Aden a crown colony and divided the hinterland sultanates in the south into the Western and Eastern Aden Protectorates.

The British further developed the port facilities in Aden in the 1950s and built an oil refinery. Consequently, Aden became the dominant economic center in southern Arabia—a densely populated urban area with a rapidly growing working class.

Yahya, whose isolationism and despotism had alienated a large number of Yemenis, was assassinated in an attempted coup in 1948. His son, Ahmad, succeeded him. Growing nationalism among the Arab countries after World War II, exemplified by the rise of Egypt's Gamal Abdel Nasser as a genuine pan-Arab leader, as well as improving communications and the emergence of Arab oil wealth, forced Ahmad to abandon the isolationist policies of his father. He joined Egypt and Syria in the ill-fated United Arab Republic in 1958 and sought aid from Communist and capitalist nations alike.

The Yemeni Republics

Ahmad's repressive domestic policies touched off the 1962 coup that established the Yemen Arab Republic, with Sanaa as its capital. The coup invigorated Arab nationalism in southern Yemen and elsewhere on the peninsula.

This nationalism combined with severe urban problems in congested Aden to create an unstable situation in southern Yemen. The British, hoping to withdraw gracefully from the area while protecting their interests, persuaded the sultans in the Western and Eastern Protectorates to join Aden in the Federation of South Arabia in 1963, which was to be the nucleus of a future independent state.

Arab opponents of the British plan mounted a campaign of sabotage, bombings, and armed resistance. Britain, failing to persuade the various opposing factions to agree on a constitutional design for a new independent state, announced early in 1966 that it would withdraw its military forces from Aden and southern Arabia by the end of 1968. (Britain had signed a treaty in 1959 guaranteeing

full independence to the region by 1968.)

London's announcement turned the anti-British campaign of terror into one of interfactional competition. The National Front for the Liberation of South Yemen, backed by the British-trained South Arabian army, emerged as the victor among the various factions, and on November 30, 1967, Aden and southern Arabia became an independent state under the name of the People's Republic of Southern Yemen (later changed to the People's Democratic Republic of Yemen). The NLF leader, Qahtan al-Sha'bi, became the republic's first president.

North Yemen

Alternately called North Yemen or the Yemen Arab Republic (YAR), the country lies in the southwestern corner of the Arabian Peninsula, bordered by the Red Sea on the west, Saudi Arabia on the north and northeast, and the People's Democratic Republic of Yemen on the south and southeast.

The fact that some of the YAR's borders have never been clearly defined has caused armed conflict with Saudi Arabia, and previously with Britain when it controlled southern Arabia. The 1934 Saudi-Yemeni treaty of friendship settled part of the border dispute, but a large section of the border with Saudi Arabia remains undefined. Britain's rejection of North Yemen's claim to southern Yemen led to intermittent border clashes until the 1934 Treaty of Sanaa sought to settle the border issue. Differing interpretations of the treaty led to further conflict, and efforts to demarcate the borders have not succeeded.

Geographically, the YAR is divided into a semidesert coastal plain, called the Tihama, that stretches for about 260 miles along the Red Sea and extends 40 miles inland to the chain of interior highlands and mountains that make up the other part of the YAR. Abundant rainfall makes the interior highlands one of the most important agricultural areas of the Arabian Peninsula.

Economy

North Yemen's economy rests on the twin pillars of workers' remittances and revenue from its oil and gas exports. North Yemen's human resources are greatly underdeveloped. Even though North Yemen has been modernizing since the 1962 revolution, most of its people have remained poor, uneducated, and agriculturally oriented. Education and health services are insufficient and confined to North Yemen's three urban centers: Sanaa (the capital), Ta'izz, and Hudaydah.

The country's economic growth has been hindered by a decline in coffee production (once its main export and principal source of foreign exchange), limited natural resources (other than oil), and enormous development problems. The lack of raw materials and a low level of industrial development have made North Yemen dependent on imports for virtually all of its essential needs.

Most of North Yemen's estimated 6.7 million citizens are scattered over the country's mountainous terrain in approximately 50,000 different rural settlements. About 75 percent of North Yemen's work force is engaged in agriculture. Most of the remaining work force is providing unskilled labor to the labor-poor, capital-rich countries of the Arabian peninsula such as Saudi Arabia and the United

Arab Emirates. Throughout the 1970s and the 1980s the wages paid to these workers provided a steady capital inflow that, along with foreign aid, has been vital to the country's economic stability.

Remittances from abroad, however, have been a mixed blessing. In the past, they created income disparities and sparked a strong demand for consumer goods that was hard to meet after the downturn in oil prices in the early 1980s. Moreover, the exodus of workers has made it difficult for North Yemen to develop its own large-scale agriculture and industrial base. North Yemen now finds itself in the ironic position of having to import foreign labor.

For years North Yemen has been dependent on foreign aid. Assistance has come from Communist countries, particularly the Soviet Union, China, and East Germany, and from Western nations, including the United States. Other major sources of aid have been Saudi Arabia, Kuwait, and the World Bank. As with remittances, this external aid often brings undesired consequences. Dependence on foreign loans and grants has made North Yemen's economy vulnerable to the capriciousness of the world economy and foreign governments. During the early and mid-1980s North Yemen's economy suffered because funding from previous Arab donors was diverted to sustain Iraq's war effort, and a global recession diminished other external sources of finance.

In addition, Yemen's economy has been hampered by the widespread social habit of qat chewing. The mildly narcotic leaves of the qat shrub are chewed daily by men and women of all social classes. Qat chewing encourages lethargy, and North Yemenis tend to spend inordinate portions of their meager incomes on the leaves. A portion of North Yemen's indigenous wealth and labor productivity is literally chewed away.

Qat has also affected North Yemen's agricultural industry. Most experts agree that for a farmer a qat bush is easy to grow, tolerates frequent cropping, and provides instant cash returns. Many fields that previously grew edible and exportable crops have been converted into qat fields. Some analysts argue that qat growing has saved the rural economy by returning money to the villages from the urban consumers. After centuries of food self-sufficiency, however, North Yemen has been transformed into an import-dependent country whose agricultural base has been slow to recover from the impact of prolonged droughts, civil strife, and qat growing.

Government efforts to discourage qat production have largely foundered. Recently, the government appears to have accepted qat's prevalence and importance in Yemeni culture. Instead of attempting to limit its production, the authorities have tried to tax it.

The discovery of oil in the early 1980s in the eastern part of the country near Marib promises to transform North Yemen's economy. Although the fields are modest in size compared with those of North Yemen's Persian Gulf neighbors, North Yemen should be able to satisfy its own energy requirements and export a significant amount of oil.

In 1985 and 1986 Yemen Hunt Oil, a subsidiary of Hunt Oil of the United States, announced the discovery of several fields whose yield was eventually estimated to total one billion barrels. By late 1988 North Yemen's oil production was targeted at 200,000 barrels a day. Hunt's initial discoveries have spurred great interest among other international oil companies to explore in North Yemen.

North Yemen's oil revenues will benefit the country in many ways. They will help offset the decline in worker remittances, decrease costly imports, and support an increase in domestic demand for energy. Oil revenues can also help construct a modern infrastructure that is necessary before North Yemen can establish even a rudimentary industrial base and market.

In addition, the prospect of steady oil revenues has prompted investment by the World Bank and other development agencies. Increased independence from workers' remittances will give North Yemen far greater leverage in its relations with Saudi Arabia, where many North Yemenis work. Thus oil promises to enrich and strengthen the state and confer upon it greater political independence.

Religious Factionalism

The North Yemenis fall into two principal Islamic groups of almost equal size: the Zaydis and the Shafi'is. The Zaydis, belonging to a Shi'ite sect, inhabit the northern, central, and eastern areas of the country. The Shafi'is, who are Sunnis, live mainly in the south and southwest.

The Zaydi-Shafi'i division has plagued North Yemen throughout its history and continues to be a major obstacle to the country's political development. The built-in tension between the two sects has been caused primarily by the political and military dominance of the Zaydis.

Civil war raged in Yemen for eight years after the establishment of the Yemen Arab Republic. When the last monarch, al-Badr, fled Sanaa after the 1962 coup, he mustered loyal tribal warriors and waged war against the republican government. Aid from Saudi Arabia and Jordan helped to sustain his resistance movement. In response, the

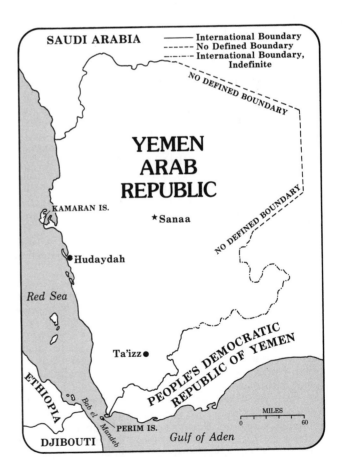

new president, Col. Abdullah al-Sallal, turned to Nasser, who sent a military force to support the new republic.

Hostilities continued on and off until 1967 when Arab-Israeli tensions made it imperative for Egypt to withdraw its forces from North Yemen. In the meantime, fighting broke out among the republican leaders themselves, and President al-Sallal was removed from office. Moderate republicans, led by Gen. Hasan al-Amri, seized power and managed to push back a serious monarchist offensive against Sanaa. After the withdrawal of Egyptian forces, Saudi Arabia began to reduce its commitment to al-Badr's followers, and in 1970 it recognized the Yemeni republic after the monarchists agreed to drop their claims and cooperate with the republican regime.

Government, Foreign Relations

The republic has been run by a succession of military and civilian governments, and dissension continues. During the early 1970s the formation of a three-person republican council headed by Judge Abd al-Rahman al-Iryani seemed to have produced stability. During that period, Saudi Arabia became a major provider of foreign aid, perhaps to forestall greater Communist aid to Sanaa and to counter the growing Marxist orientation of South Yemen. Relations between the two Yemens deteriorated and flared into border fighting, pushing North Yemen closer to Saudi Arabia.

In 1976 Col. Ibrahim al-Hamdi ousted the civilian government of al-Iryani and embarked on a major program of healing old factional and religious wounds. Though a popular leader, al-Hamdi was assassinated in 1977. His successor, Ahmad al-Ghashmi, was assassinated in 1978. Lt. Col. Ali Abdullah Salih then took over and remained in power as of late 1989.

Under Salih's rule North Yemen continued to be beset by turmoil, much of it resulting from tensions between the two Yemens that erupted in the 1979 border war. Salih actively sought arms from the Soviet Union, and in mid-1979 Sanaa concluded a new arms agreement with Moscow. The agreement was partly spurred by the Saudis' anger over the March 1979 announcement of merger plans between North and South Yemen and by the Saudis' subsequent decision to scale down military aid to North Yemen.

Early in 1979, during the border war between the two Yemens, Saudi Arabia had considered direct military intervention in support of North Yemen and had been willing to underwrite U.S. arms sales to Sanaa. But in late 1979 and early 1980 Saudi Arabia suspended military and economic aid to its neighbor, and the U.S. arms program was terminated.

Salih's government sought to reassure Saudi Arabia that it was not abandoning North Yemen's traditional policy of nonalignment, and that its proposed merger with South Yemen did not mean the emergence of a Soviet-oriented alliance.

Since well before the establishment of the republic, North Yemen has maintained relations with and received economic and technical assistance from both the Soviet Union and the People's Republic of China. While North Yemen might like to expand the scope of its relations with the United States, the U.S. government has been careful not to encroach on Saudi prerogatives. This has created a difficult triangular relationship between the United States, North Yemen, and Saudi Arabia.

The major threat to the Salih government has come from the National Democratic Front (NDF), a coalition of opponents engaged in political and military action against the government. The National Democratic Front is backed by South Yemen. By the fall of 1981 the NDF occupied much of the southern part of North Yemen and seemed on the point of winning a war of attrition. Over the next few months, however, Salih turned the menacing situation around through vigorous military action and an astute political compromise reached in May 1982 with South Yemen leader Ali Nasser Muhammad. Muhammad agreed to halt support for the NDF if amnesty for and political incorporation of NDF elements were forthcoming. This agreement led to a gradual normalization of the situation in North Yemen and strengthened Muhammad against his hard-line opponents in Aden, who wanted to support NDF military operations vigorously.

Outlook

Although early in his presidency Salih seemed to be a young political novice struggling to survive, after 1982 he was able to consolidate his political power. With his defeat of the NDF rebellion, Salih succeeded in cementing his political legitimacy and encouraging his regime's stability. Salih has expanded the scope of the YAR's rudimentary representative political organizations, especially the General People's Congress, and the ability of North Yemen's tribes to flout and subvert the authority of the central government may be declining.

In 1985 Yemeni citizens (farmers, merchants, businessmen, and some women) were encouraged to vote for the newly created Local Council for Cooperative Development, which became responsible for the administration of village development projects. This extension of the state bureaucracy to remote areas was an attempt, somewhat successful, to diminish the entrenched power of the local tribal leaders. Despite these efforts, smuggling persists and the government's control over some northern tribes is still weak.

In 1988 Salih permitted elections to establish a long-promised Consultative Assembly. In the voting 1.2 million Yemenis chose twelve-hundred delegates to the assembly, which is not authorized to initiate legislation but is permitted to amend or critique it. One of its first official acts was to name Salih as head of state de jure. His landslide victory illustrated the public's general approval of (and resignation to) Salih's political ambitions.

These trends toward democratic and representational government in North Yemen embody the current regime's efforts to placate tribal interests while retaining ultimate power. If Salih can maintain this balance and achieve central authority with a national consensus, solving other problems might be easier. Tribal loyalties could complicate north-south unification, because estranged tribal interests can be easily manipulated to thwart diplomatic efforts and spark armed conflicts.

A significant part of North Yemen's foreign relations remains independent of its internal politics. Salih's willingness to shelter the deposed South Yemeni president Muhammad and his supporters has strained relations with the current South Yemen government. Muhammad's denunciations of the south from his asylum in the north has complicated Salih's encouragement of Yemeni unification and reconciliation between Muhammad and his successors.

Perhaps North Yemen's new oil wealth can facilitate these two goals. North Yemen has pushed for joint exploration with the south in a disputed border zone that has proceeded smoothly thus far. If significant amounts of oil are found, however, the prospects of joint and fair exploitation appear less hopeful. In addition, North Yemen may choose to spend some of its newly acquired wealth on the capital-starved south to expedite the unification process. Much of this depends on the price of oil and the amounts produced and whether Salih will choose to give North Yemen's foreign policy or internal development goals priority.

South Yemen

The country alternately called South Yemen or the People's Democratic Republic of Yemen (PDRY) encompasses the southern end of the Arabian Peninsula, stretching along the coastal line from the Bab al-Mandab Strait at the entrance to the Red Sea to Oman on the east. Somewhat confusingly, North Yemen extends as far south as South Yemen, and South Yemen extends farther north.

The small, strategic island of Perim in the Bab al-Mandab Strait and the much larger island of Socotra in the Gulf of Aden belong to South Yemen. Kamaran, an island off the northern coast of North Yemen, continues to be claimed by South Yemen, though it is currently occupied by North Yemen.

The narrow coastal plane (Tihama) that runs along North Yemen's Red Sea coast continues along the Arabian Sea coast of South Yemen, eventually terminating at the Musandam Peninsula at the entrance to the Persian Gulf. Similarly, the mountain chain that runs through North Yemen continues eastward along the Arabian Peninsula's southern flank, gradually sloping into the great sandy desert of the Empty Quarter (Rub al-Khali). The mix of heat and humidity makes the coast uncomfortable, and in the interior summer temperatures soar to about 130 degrees Fahrenheit. Indian Ocean monsoons provide scanty and irregular rainfall, although in 1982 and 1989 there was severe spring flooding in the western part of South Yemen.

The infrequent rainfall and difficult terrain severely limit agriculture in South Yemen. Fishing has always been an important industry. Recent oil strikes may alleviate the country's grinding poverty; the per capita annual income is estimated at about $420.

South Yemen's population is about 2.4 million and is growing at a rate of almost 3.2 percent annually. The people pride themselves on being primarily Qahtani or southern Arabs, those with the most ancient roots, as opposed to Adnani or northern Arabs. Life expectancy is about forty-five years and literacy is roughly 32 percent. Aden, with about 250,000 residents, is the only major city in a country with a largely rural and sedentary population. Slightly less than half the work force is engaged in fishing or agriculture.

Unlike North Yemen's population, which is evenly divided between Shi'ites and Sunnis, South Yemen's population is almost entirely Sunni. Arabic is spoken nearly everywhere, although a few people in the extreme eastern part of the country continue to speak a pre-Arabic dialect.

Economy

South Yemen remains one of the poorest Arab countries. Its economic policies of collectivization and state control have never effectively stimulated economic growth. Efforts to redistribute land have had limited success, and the collectivization policies have encountered resistance from tribal farming communities that cling to traditional patterns of ownership and cultivation.

Malnutrition and poverty are rampant in the hinterland, where the lack of basic services and facilities, the dispersion of the small population, and a hostile terrain have hindered development. Food shortages and high levels of disease and infant mortality persist.

The port of the city of Aden has traditionally been the center of economic activity in South Yemen. In the past, this port serviced thousands of oil tankers and its refineries competed favorably with those of other Gulf oil states. However, as political instability and extremism wracked South Yemen and oil tankers increased their range and depended less on refueling ports, Aden's port activity waned. This decline enhanced the importance of agriculture and fishing, but these sectors have not been able to generate sufficient income for the fast-growing population.

Recently, the government has applied Soviet and other foreign assistance to the renovation of Aden's port facilities. Saudi Arabia, Kuwait, and Abu Dhabi have made generous contributions, indicating that South Yemen may seek closer economic ties with conservative Arab states without completely abandoning its traditional patron, the Soviet Union.

In 1987 South Yemen began producing oil and by 1989 it began to export oil in significant quantities. South Ye-

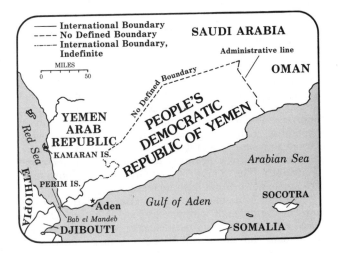

men's oil income is small compared with that of most Gulf states, but depending on the price of oil and the success of joint North-South Yemen development of the oil-rich Marib/Jauf border region, the increased revenues could help Aden finance its infrastructural, technological, educational, and health service needs.

Government, Foreign Relations

Since its independence in 1967 as the People's Republic of Southern Yemen, South Yemen has had a socialist orientation. The ruling party, the National Front for the Liberation of South Yemen, preached "scientific socialism" with a Marxist flavor. President Qahtan al-Sha'bi sought closer ties with the Soviet Union and China as well as with the more radical Arab regimes.

Al-Sha'bi's orientation, however, was not radical enough for some elements of the NLF. In 1969 he was overthrown by a group of militants led by Salim Rubayyi' Ali, and in 1970 the country was renamed the People's Democratic Republic of Yemen. The new regime took extreme steps, including repression and exile, to break traditional patterns of tribalism and religion and eliminate the vestiges of the bourgeoisie and familial elites.

Externally, relations between Aden and Sanaa were rocked by political and ideological differences despite mutual advocacy of Yemeni reunification. Saudi Arabia joined with North Yemen in actively opposing South Yemen's Marxist regime and backing opposition efforts in the south.

Salim Rubayyi' Ali had a powerful rival in the person of Abd al-Fattah Isma'il, secretary general of the NLF (renamed the National Front). Ali was considered a Maoist with pro-China sympathies, while Isma'il was thought of as a pragmatic Marxist loyal to Moscow. In June 1978 Isma'il seized power and executed Ali. He reorganized the National Front into the Yemeni Socialist party (YSP), became chairman of the Presidium of the People's Supreme Assembly, and named Ali Nasser Muhammad prime minister. In October 1979 Isma'il signed a friendship and cooperation treaty with the Soviet Union.

Isma'il, however, was unable to hold on to power. In April 1980 he relinquished his posts as Presidium chairman and YSP secretary general. The party indicated that he had resigned because of poor health, but it appeared that Isma'il had lost a power struggle, in part because of his foreign policy positions. The YSP Central Committee named Ali Nasser Muhammad, a leading rival of Isma'il, to take his place. Isma'il had intended to further cement ties with the Soviet Union and Eastern Europe, and on this point there was agreement between him and Muhammad. The latter, however, also wanted to improve relations with Saudi Arabia and other Gulf countries to end South Yemen's isolation in the Arab world, secure new sources of foreign aid, and facilitate union between the two Yemens.

Muhammad began his tenure with visits to the Soviet Union, Saudi Arabia, North Yemen, and other neighboring countries. He signed agreements on economic and technical cooperation with the Soviets, and in late 1980 he agreed to a friendship and cooperation treaty with East Germany. The Soviet military presence in South Yemen increased significantly. The number of East German and Cuban military personnel in Aden also increased in 1980.

Overall, Muhammad's regime attempted to pursue a more moderate path, cultivating economic ties with the West, achieving political reconciliation with North Yemen and Oman, and moderating between as many tribal rival-

ries as possible. But in the fall of 1985 Isma'il, Muhammad's predecessor, precipitated a power struggle by returning from his self-imposed exile in the Soviet Union.

In January 1986 a bloody coup attempt by supporters of Isma'il escalated to civil war. Pitched tank battles and anarchy broke out in Aden as Muhammad was driven from power and forced to flee the country. Some ten-thousand people died during twelve days of fighting and thousands more fled the country.

Ironically, Isma'il himself disappeared during the fighting and was presumed dead. Haider Abu Bakr al-Attas, the prime minister in Muhammad's government who happened to be out of the country during the conflict, returned to Aden January 25 and was named provisional president. In October 1986 he was elected president for a full term. His government also has followed a local brand of "pragmatic Marxism." It has pursued a close relationship with the Soviet Union, discussed unification with North Yemen, and supported mainstream Arab causes. South Yemen restored diplomatic relations with Egypt in 1988 and considered reestablishing ties with the United States.

Local ethnic differences and tribal loyalties—as opposed to competing ideologies— seem to be at the root of many of the enduring power struggles of South Yemen. Even during the 1986 coup, Isma'il's forces were said to have been extremely fragmented, united only in their animosity against the president. Within the military, bitter rivalry between tribes is easy to ignite and difficult to extinguish. Political obervers cite such rivalries as the principal obstacle blocking national unity.

Although President Attas offered amnesty after the 1986 coup for some select political exiles, reconciliation has remained incomplete. The incumbent government tried 142 former government officials—including the former president and some of his cohorts in absentia—for treason. Their trial resulted in numerous death sentences and five actual executions at the end of 1987, a decision that has only hardened the resolve of Muhammad to return to power through violence.

Outlook

South Yemen has a long upward climb to achieve the economic progress and political stability that many of its neighbors on the peninsula enjoy. Clearly, the authority of the state is accepted only when it converges with more powerful and immediate tribal interests.

Unfortunately for South Yemen, its Marxist disposition and revolutionary ideology continue to estrange many of its richer, fellow Arab states whose assistance South Yemen could use. Moreover, if the Soviet Union continues to seek improved relations with the West and moderate Arab nations, South Yemen may receive less Soviet attention and aid.

Thus, economic imperatives might begin to reshape Aden's policies. The discovery of oil in 1987 with exporting potential has attracted Western capital. In addition, Saudi Arabia, Kuwait, and Abu Dhabi have contributed to projects to upgrade and modernize the port of Aden and provide relief to an area devastated by a flood that left tens of thousands of South Yemenis homeless in early 1989. If Attas can control tribal rivalries, strengthen central authority, and maintain the peaceful status quo with North Yemen and Oman, then perhaps South Yemen can begin to concentrate on building a sound economic base worthy of foreign investment.

Appendix

Sketches of Middle East Leaders   239
Major Events, 1900-1944   247
Chronology of Events, 1945-1989   249
Documents   301

Sketches of Middle East Leaders

Following are biographical sketches of some of the leading twentieth-century political figures in the Middle East.

Abd-ul-Ilah (1913-1958). Regent of Iraq (1939-1953); crown prince (1953-1958). Educated at Victoria College, Alexandria. Became regent when his cousin King Faisal II succeeded to the throne at age three. Known for his loyalty to the boy king, his opposition to violent nationalism, and his cooperation with the West. Relinquished power to Faisal II when he reached majority in 1953. Assassinated with the king in Baghdad uprising July 14, 1958.

Abdullah ibn Hussein (1882-1951). Emir of Transjordan (1921-1946); Hashemite king of Jordan (1946-1951). Born in Mecca, second son of Hussein ibn Ali (later king of Hijaz). Played major role in Arab revolt against Turkey during World War I. In 1920 boldly occupied Transjordan; recognized as emir by the British, who held a mandate over the region. Established Transjordan as an entity separate from Palestine, extracting a pledge from British that Jews would not settle in his emirate.

In World War II sent his army, the Arab Legion, to assist British troops in Iraq and Syria. In 1946 rewarded with independence by Britain, renamed country Jordan, and became king. After the partition of Palestine in the 1948 Arab-Israeli war, Abdullah's army captured Old Jerusalem and held central Palestine for Arabs. When Jordan annexed these territories, Abdullah angered Egypt, Saudi Arabia, and Syria, which supported an independent Arab Palestine. Accused of betraying the Palestinian cause by negotiating with Israel and attempting to settle Palestinian refugees in Jordan. Assassinated in Aqsa Mosque, Jerusalem, July 20, 1951, by a young Palestinian Arab.

Abdullah al-Salem al-Sabah (1895-1965). Emir of Kuwait in 1961 when British withdrew protection over the emirate and recognized Kuwait's independence. When Iraq threatened to make Kuwait a province, Abdullah deterred Iraqi action by obtaining British aid. Modernized the country by using vast oil wealth; shared riches with people to give Kuwait one of the world's highest standards of living.

Aoun, Michel (born 1936). Commander of Maronite Christian brigades of the Lebanese army. Head of the provisional military government appointed by outgoing president Amin Gemayel in December 1988. Became prime minister of East Beirut Christian military government, although his premiership was not accepted by Lebanon's Moslem community. Led Christian opposition to Syrian presence in Lebanon in 1989.

Arafat, Yasir (born 1929). Head of the Palestine Liberation Organization (PLO) since 1968. Trained as a guerrilla fighter, founded Al Fatah, a militantly nationalist Palestine organization, in 1957. Addressed the UN General Assembly in November 1974. Condemned the separate peace treaty between Egypt and Israel that was signed March 26, 1979. Evicted from Beirut September 1982 following the Israeli bombardment and set up new headquarters in Tunis.

In November 1988 became president of the newly formed Palestinian government in exile. Gained U.S. recognition of the PLO in December 1988 after explicitly renouncing terrorism and accepting UN resolutions 242 and 338.

Arens, Moshe (born 1925). Israeli foreign minister. Born in Lithuania; emigrated to the United States in 1939, then to Israel in 1948. Elected to the Israeli Knesset in 1977 as a member of the Herut party. Ambassador to Washington (1982-1983), until appointed minister of defense when Ariel Sharon resigned in 1983.

Became minister without portfolio in the national unity government in 1984. Placed in charge of Arab affairs in 1986. Became foreign minister in the 1988 national unity government.

Arif, Abdul Rahman (born 1916). Ba'ath party leader, president of Iraq (1966-1968). Became president when his brother, President Abdul Salem Arif, was killed in a helicopter crash April 13, 1966. Abdul Rahman Arif made attempts to end the Kurdish revolt in northeast Iraq. During the 1967 Arab-Israeli war, sent troops to the Sinai and Jordan; cut off oil supplies to the West; severed diplomatic relations with the United States, Britain, and West Germany. The Arab defeat, Kurdish troubles, and economic problems led to his overthrow in a bloodless coup July 17, 1968; living in exile.

Arif, Abdul Salem (1921-1966). Headed the Ba'athist army coup that overthrew Iraqi dictator Abdul Karim Kassim, making Arif the Iraqi president in 1963. Improved relations with oil companies; dropped Iraqi claims to Kuwait. Killed in a helicopter crash near Basra April 13, 1966.

al-Assad, Hafez (born 1928). President of Syria since 1971. Became defense minister in 1965; headed Nationalist faction of Ba'ath party, which favored weaker ties to Soviet Union. After an unsuccessful February 1969 coup, led a successful coup in November 1970, deposing President Nureddin. Assumed the presidency March 1971. Improved relations with Saudi Arabia and other conservative Arab states as well as with Egypt. Launched war against Israel on the Golan Heights in October 1973 but agreed to troop disengagement with the Jewish state in 1974. U.S.-Syrian relations, broken off in 1967, were resumed in 1974. Accepted massive Soviet military aid and Soviet advisers in Syria during the 1970s and 1980s. Took Syria into the Lebanese conflict in mid-1976. Supported Iran in the Iran-Iraq war. Reelected president in 1985 for a third seven-year term.

al-Atasi, Louai (born 1926). Syrian army officer and statesman. In March 1963 led the pro-Nasser military faction that seized control of the Syrian government. Commander in chief of Syria's armed forces and president of the Revolutionary Council (March 1963-July 1963). Helped establish Ba'ath party predominance, ending its twenty-year clandestine existence. Resigned in 1963; in exile in Egypt since 1969.

al-Atasi, Nureddin (born 1929). Syrian medical doctor and government official. Led the Progressive faction of the Ba'ath party, favoring strong ties to the Soviet Union and a Marxist economy. Became president in 1966; deposed by Hafez al-Assad in a November 1970 bloodless coup.

al-Attas, Haider Abu Bakr (born 1939). President of South Yemen since 1986. Appointed to the cabinet in 1969. Elevated in 1972 to the Yemen Socialist party central committee. Became prime minister and politburo member in 1985. Appointed provisional head of a new Marxist coalition government following a January 1986 coup that took place while he was out of the country. Formally elected president later in 1986.

Bakhtiar, Shahpur (born 1914). Iranian prime minister and opposition leader. Appointed by the shah in January 1979 to form a new civilian government just before the monarch left the country; expelled from membership in the National Front opposition coalition upon assuming the premiership. Resigned on February 12, 1979, when forces loyal to the Moslem leader Ayatollah Khomeini took over the government. Bakhtiar fled to France, where he is active in opposition to the Islamic Republic.

al-Bakr, Ahmed Hassan (1912-1982). President of Iraq (1968-1979). Seized power in a bloodless coup on July 17, 1968, and assumed the presidency and premiership. Under his regime Iraq sought to end the Kurdish revolt by granting Kurds a measure of autonomy; but after Iraq settled differences with Iran, which had armed the Kurds, al-Bakr ordered the military to crush the revolt in March 1975. In June 1973 his regime defeated an attempted military coup, resulting in the execution of thirty-six officers. In April 1972 signed a fifteen-year friendship treaty with the Soviet Union; in June 1972 nationalized the Iraq Petroleum Co. Resigned for health reasons July 1979.

Bani-Sadr, Abolhassan (born 1932). Opponent of the shah of Iran, exiled to France where he became a leader of antishah students abroad. In direct contact with the exiled Ayatollah Khomeini after 1972. Following the shah's downfall, elected in January 1980 as first president of the Islamic Republic. In a victory for Iranian extremists, dismissed by Khomeini as president in June 1981. Fled to France in July 1981.

al-Barzani, Mustafa (1904-1979). General and leader of the Kurdish revolt against Iraq. Declared war on the Baghdad government in 1974 after turning down an offer of limited autonomy. Iraqi armed forces crushed the revolt in March 1975; Barzani fled into exile in Iran.

Bazargan, Mehdi (born 1905). Iranian prime minister appointed by Ayatollah Khomeini in February 1979 to head postrevolutionary government. Resigned November 6, 1979, over Khomeini's support for detention of American hostages. Leader of Liberation Movement, the only opposition party legalized by the Islamic Republic.

Begin, Menachem (born 1913). Prime minister of Israel (1977-1983). Commander of Irgun Jewish underground organization (1943-1948), which launched a series of attacks against the British mandate authorities. In 1948 founded Herut opposition party. Became prime minister of Israel in June 1977 as leader of the conservative Likud bloc. His surprise election victory cast doubt over Israel's willingness to compromise on the Palestinian question and on the West Bank and Gaza Strip territories. Signed Camp David peace treaty with Egypt on March 26, 1979, at the White House in Washington, D.C. Reelected in June 1981. Resigned from office August 1983.

Ben-Gurion, David (1886-1973). Zionist leader and Israel's first prime minister. Born in Poland; went to Palestine in 1906 as a laborer. Founded the Labor party. During World War I was expelled from Palestine by the Turks; went to New York, where he formed the Zionist Labor party. Joined the Jewish Legion, part of British forces in Palestine. From 1918, lived in Tel Aviv and headed the Labor party.

Founded the underground Haganah organization in 1920 as a fighting force to defend the Jewish community in Palestine. At Tel Aviv May 14, 1948, read the public declaration of Israel's independence. Became prime minister and defense minister of the new state, holding both posts until 1963 except for one interlude. Sent troops into the Suez Canal conflict of 1956. Resigned as premier in June 1963 but remained a member of the Knesset until 1970.

Ben-Zvi, Isaac (1884-1963). Second president of Israel (1952-1963). Went to Palestine in 1907 and helped found the Hashomer, a Jewish self-defense organization. After his exile by the Turks in 1915, went to New York and, with David Ben-Gurion, established the Hechalutz (Pioneer) movement and the Jewish Legion. Founder and chairman of the Vaad Leumi (National Council of Palestine Jews). Signed the Israeli declaration of independence. Elected to the Knesset in 1949 and the presidency on December 8, 1952, after Chaim Weizmann's death.

Berri, Nabih (born 1938). Leader of the Amal Shi'ite movement and the principal Shi'ite politician in Lebanon. Joined the Shi'ite movement known as the Movement of the Dispossessed shortly after it was founded by Imam Musa Sadr. In 1975, when Amal was created as the military wing of Imam Sadr's movement, became a member of its politburo. Elected to head Amal in 1980; reelected in 1986. Considered a moderate in Shi'ite politics and an ally of the Syrians; has had difficulty controlling radical factions within Amal and rival Shi'ite movement Hizballah. Became a minister under Amin Gemayel but remained for the most part an opponent of the government. Became minister of justice in national unity government formed in 1984; reappointed to the position by Lebanese Moslem government created in 1988.

al-Bitar, Salah (1912-1980). Syrian prime minister. Helped create the socialist Ba'ath party, which became Syria's ruling party, and the short-lived United Arab Republic, a union between Syria and Egypt. Led a pro-Nasser coup in Syria that on March 8, 1963, resulted in Bitar's becoming premier. Held that post intermittently until 1966. Killed in Paris in 1980 by assassins allegedly under Syrian orders.

Chamoun, Camille (1900-1987). President of Lebanon (1952-1958) and prominent Maronite politician. In 1958 his pro-Western policies led to open Moslem revolt. At his request President Dwight D. Eisenhower sent U.S. Marines into Lebanon in July 1958 to help restore order. In July 1975 became defense and foreign minister in "rescue cabinet" formed to end bloody Moslem-Christian clashes over Palestinian refugee issue in Lebanon. Headed the National Liberal party (1958-1986). From 1984 until his death, served as Lebanese finance minister.

Chehab, Fuad (1903-1973). President of Lebanon (1958-1964). Served as commander in chief of the Lebanese army, prime minister, interior minister, and defense minister. As president, pursued a neutralist policy acceptable to Arabs and the West. Put down an attempt to overthrow his government by the Syrian Popular party, which sought Lebanese union with Syria.

Dayan, Moshe (1915-1981). Israeli military commander and political leader. Member of Jewish police force (1936-1939). Lost eye from a sniper's bullet during an Allied operation against French Vichy forces in Lebanon. Chief of staff for all Israeli forces (1953-1958); prepared plans for the invasion of the Sinai Peninsula during the 1956 Suez crisis. Elected to the Knesset in 1959 on the Labor party ticket. Appointed defense minister in 1966 and became a hero of the 1967 Six-Day War. Quit the cabinet in 1974 after criticism over the army's lack of preparedness during the 1973 Arab-Israeli war. In 1977 defected from the Labor party to become foreign minister to Menachem Begin's government. Resigned as foreign minister in October 1979 in protest of Israel's hard-line settlements policy.

Eban, Abba (born 1915). Israeli diplomat and member of the Knesset. Deputy prime minister of Israel (1963-1966); foreign minister (1966-1974). Worked to maintain strong U.S.-Israeli ties; architect of several Middle East peace plans. Appointed chairman of Knesset Foreign Affairs and Security Committee in 1984.

Eshkol, Levi (1895-1969). Finance minister of Israel when David Ben-Gurion resigned the premiership in 1963; succeeded him as prime minister (1963-1969). Under his leadership, Israel defeated the Arab states in the Six-Day War of 1967.

Fadlallah, Muhammad Hussein (born 1939). Spiritual leader of the Shi'ite Hizballah organization in Lebanon, a radical fundamentalist group with ties to Iran. Thought to maintain some influence over Islamic Jihad and other radical fundamentalist groups in Lebanon.

Fahd ibn Abdul Aziz (born 1922). Succeeded Khalid as king of Saudi Arabia in June 1982. As crown prince after King Faisal's death in 1975 and later as king, Fahd has been regarded as the most important figure in shaping Saudi foreign policy. Wrote the first Middle East peace initiative sponsored by Saudi Arabia in 1981.

Faisal ibn Abdul Aziz al-Saud (1906-1975). King of Saudi Arabia (1964-1975). Became crown prince when his brother, King Saud, ascended to the throne in 1953. Served as prime minister, foreign minister, defense minister, and finance minister. Became king in March 1964 when Saud was legally deposed. Supported pan-Arab and pan-Islam solidarity. Pressed for economic and educational advances.

A Moslem ascetic and anti-Communist, Faisal called for Israel to evacuate Islamic holy places in Jerusalem and all occupied Arab territory. Fostered ties with United States and supported conservative Arab regimes. During 1973 Arab-Israeli war, enforced the Arab oil embargo and price hike against the United States, Western Europe, and Japan. Assassinated by a nephew March 25, 1975, in Riyadh.

Faisal I (Faisal ibn Hussein) (1885-1933). King of Iraq (1921-1933). Horrified by Turkish anti-Arab actions, led an Arab revolt, assisted by T. E. Lawrence (Lawrence of Arabia) and the British against the Ottomans in World War I. To consolidate an Arab state in Syria, served briefly as king of Syria in 1920 until expelled by the French, who held a mandate for Syria. With British help, elected in 1921 to a second throne in Baghdad. Worked to strengthen and liberate his kingdom.

Faisal II (1936-1958). King of Iraq (1939-1958). Inherited the throne at age three upon the accidental death of King Ghazi. Crowned May 2, 1953. During his five-year reign, Iraq pursued an anti-Communist course, culminating in the 1955 Baghdad Pact in which Britain, Iran, Iraq, Pakistan, and Turkey pledged to thwart possible Soviet intrusion into the Middle East. Assassinated July 14, 1958, with most members of the royal family in Baghdad revolution, which resulted in Iraq's being declared a republic.

Farouk I (1920-1965). King of Egypt (1936-1952). Reign marked by his quarrel with the dominant Wafd party and with the British over the Sudan. The disastrous campaign against Israel in 1948 and charges of corruption connected with arms purchases damaged his public standing. Forced to abdicate after a military coup in July 1952. Died in exile in Italy.

Franjieh, Suleiman (born 1910). President of Lebanon (1970-1976). Maronite Christian and strong supporter of Syria. During the crisis of 1975 between rightist Christians and leftist Moslems, could not develop a formula for a government placating all sides. Refused to leave the presidency, even after a petition from parliament and a military assault on his residence, until his term of office expired in September 1976. His staunch support of Syria alienated leaders of Maronite Lebanese Forces. Backed by Syrians for president in 1988 but received little support.

Fuad I (1868-1936). King of Egypt (1922-1936). Proclaimed king when Britain relinquished its protectorate over Egypt in 1922. Fuad's reign was marked by a struggle between the Wafd party and palace parties centering around the king. Interested in education and charitable causes; prime mover in establishing the first Western-style Egyptian university, the Fuad I (now Cairo) University, in 1925.

Gemayel, Amin (born 1942). President of Lebanon (1982-1988). Son of Pierre Gemayel. Elected September 1982 to succeed his slain brother, Bashir. Although Amin was a Phalangist deputy, Phalange extremist groups refused to recognize him as their leader. His pro-American policies also antagonized other sects. Retained only nominal control of the country amidst continued civil unrest. His six-year term ended without the election of a successor. Appointed Michel Aoun as the head of an interim military government in the last minutes of his presidency.

Gemayel, Bashir (1947-1982). Son of Pierre Gemayel and brother of Amin Gemayel. Commander of Phalange militia. Elected August 1982 as president of Lebanon with Israeli support and pressure. Once elected, Gemayel tried to adopt a more neutral stance. Killed by a bomb while speaking at Phalange party headquarters in East Beirut September 1982.

Gemayel, Pierre (1905-1984). Leader of the Phalange party in Lebanon. Became member of parliament in 1960 and held office in most Lebanese governments. Ran for the presidency in 1970 but withdrew in favor of neutral candidate Suleiman Franjieh.

Habash, George (born 1925). Palestinian leader of "rejection front" that refuses to consider coexistence with Israel. In 1970 his Popular Front for the Liberation of Palestine (PFLP) became known for its hijacking of foreign planes. The PFLP was held responsible for triggering the Jordanian civil war in 1970 and for helping spark the Lebanese civil war in 1975.

Hassan ibn Talal (born 1947). Crown Prince of Jordan. Educated in England at the Harrow School and Oxford. Brother of King Hussein and heir to the throne. Appointed crown prince in 1965. Ombudsman for National Development since 1971; founder of the Royal Scientific Society in Jordan.

Helou, Charles (born 1911). President of Lebanon (1964-1970). Former banker, journalist, and diplomat who was a compromise choice for president in 1964. Steered a neutralist course between the West and neighboring Arab countries.

Herzog, Chaim (born 1918). President of Israel since 1983. Previously a member of the Knesset and Israel's ambassador to the United Nations (1975). Military governor of the West Bank (1967) and Israel's first chief of military intelligence.

Hoveida, Amir Abbas (1919-1979). Iranian prime minister (1965-1977). Former general managing director of National Iranian Oil. Replaced as prime minister by Jamshid Amuzegar in August 1977. Executed April 7, 1979, during revolutionary trials.

Hussein ibn Ali (Sherif Hussein) (1854-1931). Emir of Mecca (1908-1916); king of Hijaz, now part of Saudi Arabia, (1916-1924). During World War I his negotiations with the British led to Arab revolt against Turkey. Opposed mandatory regimes imposed on Syria, Palestine, and Iraq by the Versailles Treaty. Hijaz kingdom attacked by Ibn Saud of the Wahhabi sect; Hussein forced to abdicate in 1924. Ibn Saud later was proclaimed king of Saudi Arabia and exiled Hussein to Cyprus. Hussein's son Ali was king of Hijaz briefly; another son, Abdullah, became king of Jordan; a third son became King Faisal I of Iraq.

Hussein, Saddam (born 1937). President of Iraq since July 1979. Succeeded Ahmed Hassam al-Bakr, who resigned for health reasons. Former vice chairman of the Revolutionary Command Council. Helped bring about détente with Iran in 1975, but as president launched an invasion of that country September 1980 that developed into a costly eight-year war. Moved away from alliance with the Soviet Union and toward a closer relationship with moderate Arab states during the war. Restored diplomatic relations with the United States 1984. Concluded a cease-fire with Iran August 20, 1988. Allegedly ordered the use of chemical weapons against Kurdish population in northern Iraq in the late 1980s.

Hussein ibn Talal (born 1935). King of Jordan since 1953. Educated at Royal Military Academy, Sandhurst, England. Crowned May 2, 1953, after his father, King Talal, was declared mentally ill. In 1956 abrogated Jordan's treaty with Britain. Accepted U.S. economic aid.

Supported Nasser in Egypt's 1967 war against Israel. After losing half his kingdom (West Bank of the Jordan River), tried to deal indirectly with Israel to recover lost lands. Crushed Palestinian guerrilla enclaves during 1970 civil war between his army and Palestinians. At Rabat summit conference of the Arab League in 1974, the right to negotiate for return of the West Bank was taken from Hussein and given to the Palestine Liberation Organization. Hussein denounced the Egyptian-Israeli peace treaty signed in March 1979 and broke off relations with Egypt. Restored diplomatic ties with Egypt September 1984. Surrendered Jordan's claim to the West Bank in favor of the PLO and announced the breaking of all legal and administrative ties to the Israeli-occupied territory in August 1988.

Ibn Saud (1880-1953). First king of Saudi Arabia (1932-1953). Made war on King Hussein of Hijaz, forcing him to abdicate and leading to the merger of the Hijaz and Najd kingdoms into Saudi Arabia in 1932. Worked to consolidate his realm and improve relations with his enemies in other Arab states.

In 1933 granted a sixty-year oil concession to a U.S. oil company that became Aramco. Oil royalties greatly enriched his treasury. During the 1940s launched a social and economic revolution in Saudi Arabia. In 1945 helped form the Arab League.

Idris I (1890-1983). King of Libya (1951-1969). As emir of Cyrenaica, fought Italian occupation of Libya. Was declared constitutional monarch when Libya was made an independent state in 1951. Deposed September 1, 1969, by a coup led by Col. Muammar al-Qaddafi, who declared Libya a Socialist republic. Lived in exile in Egypt until his death in May 1983.

Isa bin Sulman al-Khalifa (born 1933). Emir of Bahrain. Declared Bahrain's independence after Britain quit the Persian Gulf in 1971. Rejected a proposed federation of Bahrain with neighboring Qatar and United Arab Emirates.

Isma'il, Abd al-Fattah (1939-1986). President of South Yemen (1978-1980). Pro-Soviet politician, served as secretary general of the National Liberation Front (1971-1978). Following coup against Rubayi Ali in 1978 became general secretary of the reorganized Yemen Socialist party and was elected head of state. Resigned from both positions and moved to Moscow in 1980, presumably because of an internal power struggle. Returned to South Yemen in

1985 and was elected to the politburo. His return precipitated January 1986 coup and subsequent civil war. Wounded during the fighting and presumed dead.

Jumblatt, Kamal (1917-1977). Father of Walid Jumblatt. Leader of leftist forces in Lebanese civil war. Strong supporter of the Palestinian cause and of secular reforms that would change the age-old practice in Lebanon of distributing public offices among the country's religious factions. Assassinated in March 1977.

Jumblatt, Walid (born 1949). In 1977 succeeded his father, Kamal, as leader of Lebanon's Druze-dominated Progressive Socialist party, which maintains a close political-military relationship with Syria. A leader of the revolt against Amin Gemayel in 1983. Druze military victories established him as an influential politician. Subsequently joined the cabinet but remained one of Gemayel's most vociferous opponents. Minister of public works, transport, and tourism in the Moslem government created in 1988.

Kamel, Muhammad Ibrahim (born 1927). Egyptian foreign minister (1977-1978). Appointed foreign minister by President Anwar Sadat in December 1977 to replace Ismail Fahmy, who resigned over Sadat's trip to Israel. Kamel was involved in peace talks with Israel but resigned September 18, 1978, in protest of the Camp David accords. Retained in foreign service with ambassadorial rank.

Karami, Rashid (1921-1987). Four-time prime minister of Lebanon and influential Sunni politician. Born in Tripoli; educated in Cairo. Served as prime minister under Camille Chamoun (1955-1956) but resigned after a dispute with Chamoun. Served as prime minister again under Fuad Chehab and Charles Helou (1958-1969) until resigning in 1969 to protest the violent suppression of a pro-Palestinian demonstration. Reappointed prime minister by Suleiman Franjieh during the civil war (1975-1976). Held the office for a fourth time beginning in 1984 under Amin Gemayel, with whom he had a strained relationship. Made numerous unsuccessful attempts to promote national reconciliation. Resigned May 1984, but his resignation was not accepted. Assassinated in June 1987.

Kassim, Abdul Karim (1914-1963). Iraqi dictator (1958-1963). As an army general, led July 14, 1958, military revolution that killed young King Faisal II and most of the royal family. After the revolution a republic was proclaimed and Kassim was named prime minister. Withdrew Iraq from the Baghdad Pact and improved relations with the Soviet Union and China. Escaped an attempted assassination in October 1959; thirteen former officials and army officers were executed.

Crushed a Kurdish revolt in 1962. Laid claim to Kuwait after its independence in 1961, but British sent troops to Kuwait's aid, deterring any Iraqi action. Executed after a coup by "free officers" of Ba'ath party in 1963.

Khalaf, Salah (born 1933). PLO security chief. Born in Jaffa. Educated at University of Cairo, where he joined Yasir Arafat in the Palestinian Student's Union. In 1970 took part in Black September Palestinian fighting in Jordan. Member of the Palestine Central Council since 1973.

Khalid ibn Abdul Aziz (1913-1982). King of Saudi Arabia (1975-1982). Represented Saudi Arabia at various international conferences. Became vice president of the Council of Ministers, 1962; elevated to crown prince, 1965; succeeded to throne when King Faisal was assassinated in March 1975. Died of a heart attack in June 1982.

Khalifa bin Hamad al-Thani (born 1937). Emir of Qatar. Assumed power after deposing his cousin, Emir Ahmad bin Ali bin Abdullah al-Thani, in a bloodless coup February 22, 1972. Headed a program of social and economic improvements made possible by oil revenues. Joined in the Arab oil embargo against the West in 1973.

Khamenei, Ayatollah Ali (born 1939). Succeeded Ayatollah Ruhollah Khomeini as Iran's spiritual leader. A disciple of Khomeini in Qom, Khamenei was one of the most active Shi'ite clerics in the Iranian revolution. Imprisoned twice for opposition to the shah. Cofounded the Islamic Republic party in 1978. Elected as third president of the Islamic Republic in October 1981. Reelected to a second presidential term 1985. Appointed as spiritual leader of Iran upon Khomeini's death June 1989.

Khomeini, Ayatollah Ruhollah (1902-1989). Shi'ite Moslem leader of Iran (1979-1989) who established the Islamic Republic. Educated in the theological center in Qom. Led political protests against the shah's social reforms (1962-1963), resulting in his exile to Turkey in 1963, then Iraq a year later. During his fifteen-year exile, Khomeini issued statements guiding the antishah protests of clerics in Iran. Expelled from Iraq in 1978 for conducting political agitation. Lived in France until the overthrow of the shah, returning to Iran on February 1, 1979.

Khomeini forces formed Council of the Islamic Revolution to replace the shah-appointed Bakhtiar government. In March 1981 he ordered a national referendum to seek support for the new Islamic Republic. Decided to accept a cease-fire of the eight-year Iran-Iraq war July 1988, reversing his unflinching commitment to overthrow Iraq's President Saddam Hussein. Died in Tehran June 3, 1989.

al-Khoury, Bishara (1860-1964). Elected president of Lebanon in 1943 while the country was controlled by the Free French. After the French arrested Khoury and other government officials, an insurrection led to restoration of the Lebanese government.

In 1946 France relinquished its Lebanese mandate and Lebanon became independent. During Khoury's presidency, Beirut grew rapidly and became a trade and financial center. Khoury's abuses of power angered the public and he was deposed by a popular movement in 1952.

Kuwatly, Shukri (1891-1967). Twice Syrian president. During 1920s and 1930s emerged as a nationalist leader opposed to the French mandate. Elected president in 1943 while Syria was controlled by the Free French; secured the withdrawal of the French and attainment of Syrian independence in 1946. Overthrown by a 1949 coup. Returned from exile in 1954 and advocated a broad Arab union led by Egypt. Elected president again in 1955, serving until 1958, when United Arab Republic of Egypt and Syria was inaugurated.

Mansour, Hassan Ali (died 1965). Iranian prime minister (1963-1965). Helped form the New Iran party from centrist groups in 1963. Died from gunshot wounds inflicted by a student January 21, 1965.

Meir, Golda (1898-1978). Israeli prime minister (1969-1974). Also served as ambassador to the Soviet Union, minister of labor, and minister of foreign affairs. A native of Kiev, Russia, Meir was brought to the United States in 1906; she emigrated to Palestine in 1921. Active in labor movement, World Zionist Organization, and Haganah movement to establish a Jewish state.

While prime minister maintained an inflexible policy vis-à-vis Arab states. Her government received criticism for lack of preparedness for the 1973 Arab-Israeli war. Unable to form a new government after several tries, she relinquished premiership in 1974.

Montazeri, Ayatollah Hussein Ali (born 1922). Iranian religious leader. Studied theology in Isfahan, then went to Qom where he met Ayatollah Khomeini. Entered politics in the early sixties, assuming leadership of a sit-in protest against the shah. After the Islamic revolution, elected to the Council of Experts, later becoming its Speaker. Considered a moderate on domestic issues, but backed efforts to export Iran's Islamic revolution. Khomeini designated him as his successor in November 1985. Lost favor with Khomeini and resigned under pressure in March 1989 amidst turmoil within Iran's political leadership.

Mossadeq, Muhammad (1880-1967). Iranian prime minister. Largely responsible for nationalizing the Anglo-Iranian Oil Company in 1951. His efforts to obtain more political power led to strained relations with the shah. Overthrown by the military in April 1953; later sentenced to a three-year prison term for treason.

Mousavi, Mir Hossein (born 1941). Iranian prime minister (1981-1989). Educated as an architect. Founded the Islamic Society of Students in Iran. Arrested in 1973 for opposing the monarchy. Elected prime minister in November 1981; reelected in 1985 and 1988. Involved mainly in domestic issues. Believed to be an advocate of strong government control of industry and trade. Lost post in July 1989 when office of prime minister was abolished by a constitutional referendum.

Mubarak, Hosni (born 1928). Elected president of Egypt following the assassination of Anwar al-Sadat on October 6, 1981. Appointed air force chief of staff 1969; became its commander in 1972; credited with air force's successful performance in the early days of the October 1973 war with Israel. Appointed vice president in 1975. Presided over cabinet meetings and attended most international discussions on Middle East policy. Considered to be Sadat's closest adviser. Reelected for a second six-year term October 1987. Focused mainly on domestic economic issues, while gradually repairing relations with the Arab world damaged by the Camp David agreements.

Muhammad, Ali Nasser (born 1939). President of South Yemen (1980-1986). Served as prime minister (1971-1978); assumed positions of president and party head in 1980. His attempt in January 1986 to have his enemies in the politburo assassinated touched off a bloody civil war and led to his overthrow. Living in exile in Ethiopia since 1986.

Naguib, Muhammad (1901-1984). President of Egypt when it was declared a republic in 1953. Leader of the Free Officer junta that opposed King Farouk. Ousted after a power struggle with Nasser in 1954.

Nasser, Gamal Abdel (1918-1970). Egyptian president (1954-1970). As head of the Revolutionary Command Council, Nasser led a revolt that deposed King Farouk and established a republic on June 18, 1953. Became president after a power struggle with President Naguib.

Negotiated the withdrawal of British troops from the Suez Canal zone in 1954 and nationalized the canal in 1956, prompting Anglo-French-Israeli military intervention. Af-

ter the United States forced allies to withdraw, Nasser's prestige grew in the Arab world. Created the United Arab Republic, a union between Egypt and Syria, in 1958 and served as its president until Syria seceded in 1961.

Israel's defeat of Egypt in 1967 led to détente between Nasser and conservative Arab states that had distrusted his revolutionary goals. Received revenues from Saudi Arabia and Kuwait and arms from the Soviet Union. At home, pursued a course of social justice, redistribution of land, improved medical care, and education. Construction of the Aswan Dam symbolized his achievements. Died of a heart attack following the September 1970 conference in Cairo that ended the Jordanian civil war.

Navon, Yitzhak (born 1921). President of Israel (1978-1983). Member of the Knesset (1965-1978). Reelected to the Knesset July 1984.

Pahlavi, Muhammad Reza (1919-1980). Shah of Iran (1941-1979). Became shah upon the abdication of his father, Reza Shah Pahlavi. Established a close alliance with the United States. Staged a counter-coup in 1953 to regain control of the government from prime minister Mossadeq. Launched a land and social reform program known as the White Revolution in the 1960s. The shah's thirty-seven-year reign as monarch ended January 16, 1979, when he left Iran for an "extended vacation," a few weeks before Moslem leader Ayatollah Khomeini returned from exile to set up the new Islamic Republic. In 1980 Iranians demanded return of the shah for trial as a condition for release of American hostages. Died in Cairo after bout with cancer July 27, 1980.

Pahlavi, Reza Shah (1878-1944). Shah of Iran (1925-1941). Gained the throne after a coup deposed Ahmad Shah. Autocratic ruler who ignored constitutional safeguards. Built Trans-Iranian Railway; developed road system. Sought machinery and technicians from Germany, which led to the World War II occupation of Iran by British and Soviet troops. Forced to abdicate by the British and the Soviets in 1941 in favor of his son, Muhammad Reza Pahlavi, after he refused to expel German expatriates.

Peres, Shimon (born 1923). Prime minister of Israel for twenty-five months (1984-1986). Rotated out of the premiership in accordance with a coalition agreement between the Labor and Likud parties. Served as foreign minister for the remainder (1986-1988) of the coalition's fifty-one-month term. Became finance minister under the coalition government formed in December 1988.

Leader of the Israeli Labor party; became acting prime minister in April 1977 when Yitzhak Rabin resigned because of a scandal. Considered a hard-liner within the Labor party. Designated as Labor's choice for prime minister in 1977 and 1981, but was defeated by Menachem Begin's conservative Likud party.

While prime minister, was instrumental in bringing about the withdrawal of the Israeli army from Lebanon. Also made efforts to improve relations with Egypt and to promote negotiations with Jordan; sponsored an unsuccessful plan for a peace conference between Israel and a Palestinian-Jordanian delegation under UN sponsorship.

Qaboos bin Said (born 1942). Sultan and absolute ruler of Oman since 1970 when he overthrew his father, Sultan Said bin Taimur, one of century's most tyrannical despots. Educated in Britain, Qaboos embarked on an ambitious program of social and economic development after assuming power. Defeated Dhofari rebels after a military offensive in 1975. Also improved relations with his Arab neighbors; particularly members of the Gulf Cooperation Council. Established relations with the Soviet Union in 1985, while maintaining close ties with the United States.

al-Qaddafi, Muammar (born 1942). Chairman of the Revolutionary Command Council of Libya since 1969 when he led a coup that overthrew King Idris. Educated at the University of Libya and the Libyan Military Academy. Evicted the United States and Britain from Libyan military bases and nationalized Libya's oil industry. Tried unsuccessfully to extend his influence and achieve Arab unity through merger schemes with Egypt and Tunisia.

Known for his implacable enmity toward Israel and the United States. Strong supporter of Palestinian "rejectionist front" and other radical Arab movements. The United States bombed Libyan targets in 1986 in retaliation for Qaddafi's support of terrorism. Built modern army from Soviet-supplied weapons but suffered military defeats in Chad after Libya invaded that country in 1987.

Rabin, Yitzhak (born 1922). Prime minister of Israel (1974-1977). Chief of staff of the Israeli army; credited with planning Israel's overwhelming victory in the 1967 war. Served as ambassador to Washington (1982-1983). Became prime minister when Golda Meir retired in 1974. Adopted hard-line position in peace negotiations. After a scandal involving an illegal bank account held in Washington by his wife, Rabin resigned as prime minister in April 1977, just one month before the Israeli election. Became defense minister in 1984 and retained the post in 1988 coalition government.

Rafsanjani, Ali Akbar Hashemi (born 1934). President of Iran since 1989. Studied under Khomeini in Qom, organized opposition movements in Iran leading to the 1979 revolution. In 1980 elected to Majlis (parliament) as a member from Tehran and elected Speaker later the same year. Was Khomeini's representative on the Supreme Defense Council. In June 1988 appointed acting commander in chief of Iranian armed forces. Elected president in July 1989 following Khomeini's death. Generally considered to be a pragmatic politician.

al-Rifai, Zaid Samir (born 1936). Jordanian prime minister (1985-1989). Diplomat since 1957, serving in Cairo, Beirut, and at the UN. In 1972 became a political adviser to King Hussein and was later appointed minister of defense and minister of foreign affairs (1974-1976). Accused by the Black September organization in Jordan of playing a leading role in the Jordanian effort to liquidate the Palestinian resistance during the 1970-1971 struggles. Became prime minister upon the resignation of Ahmad Ubeidat April 1985. Resigned April 1989 amidst public protests against government price hikes and accusations of corruption.

al-Sabah, Jaber Al-Ahmed (born 1920). Emir of Kuwait. Ruled Kuwait since the 1977 death of Sabah al-Salem al-Sabah. In 1980 revived the National Assembly, which had been suspended since 1976. Suspended assembly again in July 1986 amid acrimonious debates on foreign affairs and internal matters.

al-Sadat, Anwar (1918-1981). President of Egypt (1970-1981). Educated at Military College, Cairo. Deputy to President Nasser in organizing the secret revolutionary brotherhood that overthrew the monarchy. Speaker of the National Assembly and twice vice president. Became president when Nasser died in 1970.

In 1972 ordered twenty thousand Soviet military advisers out of Egypt. Became Arab hero in the 1973 war with Israel when Egypt won initial victories. Agreed to troop disengagement accords in the Sinai in 1975. Moved his country away from the radical socialism of Nasser to attract Western capital.

In June 1975 reopened the Suez Canal after an eight-year closure. In March 1979 signed the Camp David peace accords with Israel, incurring the wrath of Egypt's Arab neighbors. Assassinated October 6, 1981, by Moslem extremists.

Salam, Saeb (born 1905). Lebanese foreign affairs minister, defense minister, prime minister (1952, 1953, 1960-1961, 1973). Resigned as prime minister for the final time during the 1973 crisis over Israeli raids on Palestinian commando groups in Beirut and Saida. Living in Geneva since 1984.

Salih, Ali Abdullah (born 1942). President of North Yemen since 1978. Rose rapidly through army ranks to become chief of staff. Elected president in July 1978 following the assassination of President Ahmed ibn Hussein al-Ghashmi.

Sarkis, Elias (1924-1986). President of Lebanon (1976-1982). Assumed office September 1976 during civil war, succeeding Suleiman Franjieh. Supported by Syrians over Raymond Edde. Died in exile in Paris June 1986.

Saud ibn Faisal (born 1941). Foreign minister of Saudi Arabia since 1975. Saudi prince; fourth of the eight sons of the late King Faisal. Educated at Princeton University. Possible future king.

Saud IV (1902-1969). King of Saudi Arabia (1953-1964). Succeeded his father, Ibn Saud. Expanded his father's modernization program, with emphasis on educational and medical services. In foreign affairs, continued friendship with the United States and all Arab nations. Suspicious of communism and firmly opposed to Israel. Abdicated in 1964 after the royal family effectively transferred power to his brother, who became King Faisal.

Shah of Iran (See Muhammad Reza Pahlavi.)

Shamir, Yitzhak (born 1915). Prime minister of Israel in the national coalition government formed in December 1988. Born in Poland, emigrated to Palestine in 1935 and studied law in Jerusalem. Member of Irgun underground resistance organization (1937-1940). Later joined the Stern Gang, a more radical underground organization, becoming its leader in 1942. Israeli intelligence operative abroad 1948-1965.

Elected to the Knesset in 1973 on the Herut party list, serving as parliamentary Speaker 1977-1980. Foreign minister (1980-1983); then appointed prime minister after Begin's resignation in 1983. In 1984 Shamir's Likud party concluded a coalition agreement with the Labor party that provided for a rotating premiership. Shamir served as foreign minister (1984-1986), then as prime minister (1986-1988). After the 1988 elections another coalition government was formed, in which Shamir was to hold the premiership throughout the coalition's four-year term.

Sharon, Ariel (born 1928). Defense minister during Israel's invasion of Lebanon. Served as military officer in 1967 and 1973 wars. Elected to the Knesset in 1973 on the Likud party ticket; resigned in 1974. Appointed minister of defense in second Begin government in 1981. Planned January 1982 invasion of Lebanon. Personally involved in all stages of the Lebanese war; frequently charged with concealing his moves from the prime minister. Forced to resign as defense minister after the massacres at the Sabra and Shatilla refugee camps, but remained in the cabinet as minister without portfolio. Appointed minister of industry and trade in the National Unity government of 1984 and reappointed by the coalition government of 1988.

al-Solh, Rashid (born 1926). Lebanese premier (1973-1975). Resigned amid criticism of his handling of the bloody Christian-Moslem riots that put Lebanon on the brink of civil war. Deputy in parliament during the 1980s.

al-Tal, Wasfi (1920-1971). Prime minister of Jordan five times between 1962 and 1971. Assassinated in Cairo November 1971 by Black September, a Palestinian terrorist organization, in reprisal for the Jordanian government's crushing of Palestinian strongholds in Jordan.

Talal (1909-1972). King of Jordan (1951-1952). Deposed in 1952 after being declared mentally ill by the Jordanian parliament. Spent rest of his life in a mental institution in Turkey. Succeeded by his son, King Hussein.

Velayati, Ali Akbar (born 1945). Iranian foreign minister since 1981. Born in Tehran, graduated from Tehran University with medical degree, studied for six months in the United States. Elected to Majlis (parliament) in 1980 and became foreign minister in December 1981. Considered a moderate. Promoted Iranian involvement in international organizations and expansion of bilateral relations with Islamic, European, and Third World nations.

Wazir, Khalil (1933-1988). Former military chief of the Palestine Liberation Organization. Also known as Abu Jihad. After June 1967 War, became responsible for Palestinian military operations launched against Israel from Jordan, Syria, and Lebanon. Served as commander in chief of PLO in Yasir Arafat's absence. Became a close associate of Arafat and enjoyed wide prestige within the PLO. Assassinated April 1988 at his home in Tunis by a commando unit suspected to have been dispatched from Israel.

Weizman, Ezer (born 1924). Commander of Israeli air force (1958-1966), army deputy chief of staff (1966-1969), and businessman until appointed defense minister in 1977. Played major role in negotiating Egypt-Israel peace treaty. Resigned May 1980 to protest government's settlement policy in occupied territories.

Weizmann, Chaim (1874-1952). First president of Israel (1948-1952). Born in Russia; educated in Germany. Taught chemistry at University of Manchester, England. Headed British Admiralty Laboratories that created synthetic acetene for explosives in World War I. Rewarded with Balfour Declaration, a British white paper that called for creation of a homeland for Jews in Palestine. President of the World Zionist Organization (1920-1931). In 1947 headed the Jewish Agency delegation to the United Nations.

Yamani, Ahmed Zaki (born 1930). Saudi Arabia's minister of petroleum and mineral resources (1962-1986). A commoner descended from desert tribesmen; educated at the University of Cairo, New York University, and Harvard. Leader in formulating participation agreements with oil companies in Arab states, in devising 1973-1974 oil embargo against the West, and in setting Organization of Petroleum Exporting Countries (OPEC) oil prices. Dismissed in 1986 because of disagreements with the Saudi leadership over future oil policies.

Zayed ibn Sultan al-Nahayan (born circa 1916). Emir of Abu Dhabi, president of the federation of the United Arab Emirates since its formation in December 1971. Used vast oil wealth to modernize his sheikdom and provide social programs for its people.

Major Events, 1900-1944

Following is a chronological listing of major events in Middle Eastern history from the beginning of the twentieth century through 1944. A more detailed chronology of important events from 1945 through September 1989 is provided in the next section, which begins on p. 249.

1900. Russia lends Persia funds to secure Russian commercial and political influence throughout the region.

1901. Fifth Zionist Congress begins collections for the Jewish National Fund to purchase land in Palestine. May, Iran grants William D'Arcy a concession to search for oil.

1902. First Aswan Dam opens, greatly expanding irrigation and food production in Egypt. Ibn Saud makes successful raid on Riyadh against Ottoman forces.

1903. August 22, Zionist Congress opens at Basel, Switzerland.

1904. April, Anglo-French Entente Cordiale ends contest for control of Egypt.

1905. Death of Muhammad Abduh, leader of Egyptian Islamic modernist movement opposed to foreigners and imperialist occupation. December, prominent Iranian business and religious leaders protest shah's corruption and demand "House of Justice" for safe expression of views opposing the government.

1906. May 13, Sinai Peninsula officially becomes part of Egypt after the British force the Ottomans to withdraw from Taba. December, Iranian revolution erupts in response to British and Russian intervention and local corruption; shah is forced to grant constitution.

1907. January 4, Muzaffar Ali Shah, Persian monarch, dies. August 31, Anglo-Russian agreement divides Iranian territory into separate spheres of influence.

1908. May 26, first major oil strike in Iran is made at Masjed Soleyman. July, Muhammad Ali Shah is forced to abdicate in Iran. July 21, after uniting under Committee of Union and Progress, Young Turk movements demand the sultan's immediate restoration of Ottoman constitution.

1909. Anglo-Persian Oil Company is formed to exploit the D'Arcy concession in Iran. April, Ottoman counterrevolt quashes the Ottoman Third Army and deposes Abdulhamid II.

1910. February 10, Premier Butros Ghali of Egypt is assassinated.

1911. The Italian army invades Libya and defeats the Ottoman forces. Lord Herbert Kitchener takes power in Egypt.

1912. Ottomans cede Libya to Italy. Ibn Saud establishes his army of Ikhwan (brothers) from Wahhabi soldiery.

1913. January, Committee of Union and Progress takes direct control of Ottoman government. June, Arab Congress convenes in Paris supporting an Ottoman government in which every nation under its rule would have equal rights and obligations.

1914. August, Ottomans enter World War I on the side of Germany. November, British declare war on the Ottomans, annex Cyprus, and land troops in lower Iraq. December 18, British declare protectorate over Egypt.

1915. February, Ottoman forces attack the Suez Canal. April 25, allied troops mount an amphibious operation at Gallipoli designed to knock the Ottoman Empire out of the war by seizing Istanbul, the imperial capital; the British fail to capture the Dardanelles. November 16, Sir Henry MacMahon promises Hussein ibn Ali, the emir of Mecca, that Britain will support Arab independence if the Hashemites rebel against Ottoman rule.

1916. Arab revolt against Turks begins; British appoint T. E. Lawrence as political and liaison officer to Faisal's (Hussein's son's) army. May, Britain, France, and Russia conclude the Sykes-Picot Agreement outlining the future division of Ottoman lands. July 19, second Ottoman campaign against the Suez begins. December 15, British recognize Hussein as king only of Hijaz.

1917. November 2, Britain issues Balfour Declaration calling for "support of the establishment in Palestine of a national home for the Jewish people." December 9, Turks surrender Jerusalem to Gen. Edmund Allenby.

1918. June, Emir Faisal ibn Hussein and Zionist leader Chaim Weizmann meet in Transjordan to discuss future cooperation between the Arab and Jewish national movements. October, British and Arabs capture Damascus, then Aleppo.

1919. March, Egyptians rebel against British after the deportation of nationalist leader Saad Zaghlul. June, King-Crane commission, appointed by Paris peace conference, arrives in Syria to determine wishes of the population concerning the future of Palestine and Syria. August, proposed Anglo-Persian treaty stirs national opposition in Iran and is never ratified by Persian Majlis (parliament).

1920. March, Syrian National Congress proclaims Faisal king of Syria and Palestine. April 24, through League of Nations' San Remo Agreement, Britain is awarded mandates over Iraq and Palestine, and France over Syria and Lebanon. July, French forces evict Faisal from the throne in Damascus and Faisal's brother Abdullah is offered the throne in Baghdad, causing large-scale riots in Palestine and Iraq. August, French high commissioner creates Greater (modern) Lebanon in an attempt to utilize religious differences, particularly between Christians and Moslems, to ease the task of French administration.

1921. February, Reza Khan seizes power in Iran. March, organized by the British under Winston Churchill, the Cairo Conference names Faisal ibn Hussein king of Iraq and Abdullah ibn Hussein emir of Transjordan (which was carved out of Palestine).

1922. February 28, Britain unilaterally terminates its rule over Egypt while retaining control over communications vital to the empire, foreign interests, the Sudan, and minority rights in a policy known as the Four Reserved Points. March, Fuad takes title of king of Egypt. July 22, Council of the League of Nations confirms mandate allocations made to Britain and France two years earlier. October 10, Anglo-Iraqi Treaty signed. November, Mustafa Kemal abolishes the Ottoman sultanate.

1923. April, Egypt drafts constitution and holds elections. May 15, Britain recognizes Transjordan as a self-governing state. October, Kemal officially proclaims Turkish republic and begins his fifteen years as president.

1924. Ibn Saud takes Hijaz from Hashemites. March, Kemal abolishes the caliphate. November, Sir Lee Stack, governor-general of Sudan, is murdered in Egypt.

1925. April, Hebrew University in Jerusalem opens. December 12, Iranian Majlis approves Reza Khan's establishment of Pahlavi dynasty; he becomes Reza Shah Pahlavi.

1926. January 8, Ibn Saud is proclaimed king of the Hijaz. May 26, Lebanese constitution adopted.

1927. May, British recognize Ibn Saud as king of the Najd and Hijaz.

1928. April, Turkey is declared a secular state and adopts the Latin alphabet.

1929. August, prolonged Arab-Jewish riots spring from conflict over claims that the Jews were seeking control of the Temple Mount; the riots eventually lead to a pro-Arab turn in British policies.

1930. October 20, Britain issues Passfield White Paper, limiting Jewish immigration to "economic absorptive capacity" and restricting land sales to Jews.

1931. February, Responding to Jewish criticism of Passfield White Paper, Prime Minister Ramsay MacDonald sends letter assuring Chaim Weizmann that Britain will promote a national Jewish home in Palestine in accordance with its mandate.

1932. June 1, oil is discovered in Bahrain. September 24, Ibn Saud issues royal decree unifying the kingdoms of Hijaz and Najd into Saudi Arabia. October 3, Britain grants Iraq independence but retains military bases and oil interests.

1933. August, Assyrian uprising in Iraq suppressed. September 8, King Faisal of Iraq dies.

1934. Kuwait grants first oil concession, for seventy-four years, to the Kuwait Oil Company.

1935. March, Iran becomes the official name for Persia. October, Italians invade Ethiopia.

1936. April-October, Arab general strike is mounted in Palestine. July, Montreux Convention gives Turkey control of Straits of Dardanelles.

1937. Sa'dabad Treaty is concluded among Afghanistan, Iran, Iraq, and Turkey, implicitly designed to block Soviet expansion. July, Peel commission calls for partition of Palestine.

1938. Oil discovered at al Burqan just south of Kuwait City. Saudi Arabian oil exports begin. November, Woodhead commission declares partition plan for Palestine unworkable.

1939. February, Anglo-Arab Conference on Palestine held in London. May 17, British publish white paper limiting Jewish immigration into Palestine. September, most independent Middle East countries declare their neutrality as World War II begins.

1940. September 12, Italian forces in Libya invade Egypt. November 25, French freighter *Patria,* holding eighteen hundred illegal Jewish immigrants who were prevented from entering Palestine by British authorities, explodes and sinks in Haifa harbor. December 27, British announce no quota for Jewish immigration to Palestine will be set for October 1930 to March 1941.

1941. June, a nationalist coup d'état in Iraq, led by military commanders sympathetic to Germany, prompts Britain to invade Baghdad and Basra areas, then occupy Syria and Lebanon. August 26, British and Soviet forces invade Iran. September 16, Reza Shah is forced to abdicate in favor of his son, Muhammad Reza Pahlavi.

1942. January, Britain and the Soviet Union sign treaty guaranteeing Iranian independence and securing vital communications between Soviet and Allied forces in the Middle East. February, British force King Farouk to appoint pro-Allied cabinet. May, Zionists issue Biltmore Program. July, Allies halt German advance in Egypt. October 23, Allied forces begin decisive assault against German lines at El Alamein in Egypt.

1943. November, Lebanon declares its independence; its Christians and Moslems adopt their "National Pact." December, Syrian state absorbs Jebel Druze.

1944. February 3, the Arabian-American Oil Company (Aramco) announces plans to build a refinery in Saudi Arabia. October 8, Syria, Transjordan, Iraq, Lebanon, and Egypt sign a protocol providing for establishment of the Arab League. November 6, Jewish "Stern Gang" assassinates Lord Moyne, the British resident minister in the Middle East.

Chronology of Events, 1945-1989

1945

March 22. *Arab League Established.* The Arab League is founded in Cairo. Members are Egypt, Iraq, Lebanon, Syria, Saudi Arabia, and Transjordan.

August 16. *Truman on Palestine.* President Harry S Truman calls for free settlement of Palestine by Jews to the point consistent with the maintenance of civil peace.

November 13. *Committee of Inquiry Created.* President Truman in Washington and British Foreign Secretary Ernest Bevin in London announce agreement on creation of the Anglo-American Committee of Inquiry to examine the problems of European Jews and Palestine. The committee holds opening session in Washington January 7, 1946.

December 12. *Congress on Palestine.* The Senate Foreign Relations Committee approves, 17 to 1, a resolution urging U.S. aid in opening Palestine to Jews and in building a "democratic commonwealth." The resolution is adopted by the Senate December 17 and the House December 19.

1946

February 25. *Soviets to Keep Troops in Iran.* Moscow tells Tehran it will retain some troops in Iran after the March 2 deadline for foreign troop withdrawal set by the 1942 Anglo-Soviet-Iranian Treaty.

March 2. *Arab League on Palestine.* The Arab League asks the Anglo-American Committee of Inquiry to support an Arab Palestinian state and says the league will oppose creation of a Jewish state in Palestine.

March 5. *Truman Protests Troops in Iran.* The United States protests Soviet retention of troops in Iran. President Truman warns Moscow that U.S. forces will be sent to Iran if the Soviets do not withdraw.

March 22. *Transjordan Mandate Ends.* Britain and Transjordan sign a treaty ending the British mandate in that country.

April 5. *Soviet Troops Leave Iran.* The Soviet Union and Iran reach agreement on a Soviet troop withdrawal. Soviet forces leave Iran May 6.

April 30. *Recommendations on Palestine.* The An-glo-American Committee of Inquiry recommends the immediate admission of 100,000 Jews into Palestine and continuation of the British mandate until establishment of a United Nations trusteeship. The Arab League protests the report May 2, and the Arab Higher Committee warns Britain that the "national struggle" will be resumed if the committee's recommendations are adopted.

July 25. *Tripartite Partition Recommended.* The Anglo-American Committee of Inquiry in London proposes a tripartite partition of Palestine into Jewish, Arab, and British-controlled districts.

October 4. *Truman Backs Jewish State.* On the Jewish holiday of Yom Kippur, President Truman makes public a message sent to Britain appealing for "substantial immigration" into Palestine "at once" and expressing support for the Zionist plan to create a "viable Jewish state" in part of Palestine. The British government expresses regret that Truman released the statement because it might jeopardize a settlement between Arabs and Jews.

1947

February 14. *Conference Is Unsuccessful.* The London conference on Palestine attended by Arab delegates and Zionist observers closes after a two-and-a-half-week session without an agreement on a plan for Palestine. The conference is informed of Britain's decision to refer the Palestine question to the United Nations.

April 28. *UN Session on Palestine Opens.* The UN General Assembly opens a special session convened to study the Palestine question. The UN Special Committee on Palestine (UNSCOP) is established May 13.

May 14. *Soviets for Division of Palestine.* Andrei A. Gromyko, Soviet delegate to the United Nations, proposes that Palestine be divided into two independent states, if the Arabs and Jews cannot agree on formation of an Arab-Jewish state.

August 31. *Committee Backs Palestine Division.* The UN Special Committee on Palestine issues a majority report recommending Palestine be divided into two separate Arab and Jewish states by September 1, 1949, with Jerusalem and vicinity maintained as an international zone under permanent UN trusteeship. A minority report calls for a federated Arab-Jewish state in three years. Zionist leaders approve the majority plan of UNSCOP; the Arab Higher Committee denounces the plan and threatens military action. The British cabinet announces acceptance of the UNSCOP majority report September 20.

October 9. *Military Preparations.* The Arab League recommends member nations station troops along Palestine's borders to prepare for action if British troops evacuate. The league pledges December 8 to help Palestine Arabs resist any move to partition Palestine.

October 11. *U.S. Endorses Partition.* The U.S. representative to UNSCOP endorses the proposal to partition Palestine. The Soviet Union endorses the plan October 13.

November 29. *UN Votes for Partition.* The UN General Assembly votes, 33 to 13, with ten abstentions, to partition Palestine into separate, independent Jewish and Arab states, effective October 1, 1948, with the enclave of Jerusalem to be administered by the UN Trusteeship Council. Arab members denounce the decision and walk out.

December 5. *Arms Embargo.* The United States embargoes arms shipments to the Middle East because of fighting and violent disorders that followed the UN decision.

1948

March 19. *U.S. Urges Suspension of Plan.* The United States proposes to the UN Security Council suspension of the plan to partition Palestine and urges a special session of the General Assembly to restudy issue.

April 1. *Council Adopts Resolution.* The UN Security Council adopts a U.S. resolution calling for a truce and a special session of the General Assembly to reconsider the Palestine question.

May 13. *Arab League Proclaims War.* The Arab League proclaims the existence of a state of war between league members and Palestinian Jews.

May 14. *Israel Proclaimed.* The state of Israel is proclaimed in the afternoon. Israel comes into existence when the proclamation goes into effect at midnight. The British mandate for Palestine ends as the British high commissioner sails from Haifa.

May 15. *U.S. Recognizes Israel; Arabs Invade.* President Truman recognizes Israel at 12:11 a.m. (6:11 p.m. in Washington), eleven minutes after its independence. Simultaneously, five Arab states—Transjordan, Egypt, Iraq, Syria, and Lebanon—invade Israel. Egyptian planes bomb Tel Aviv. The Soviet Union recognizes Israel May 17.

May 25. *Israel Asks for Loan.* Israel's President Chaim Weizmann visits President Truman and appeals for a $90 million to $100 million loan to arm Israel and assist immigration. Truman says May 27 that Israel's loan application should be sent to the World Bank and the U.S. Export-Import Bank.

June 11. *Arab-Israeli Truce.* A four-week Arab-Israeli truce goes into effect. Arabs refuse to extend the truce July 8 but agree to an extension July 18.

September 17. *UN Mediator Assassinated.* UN mediator Count Folke Bernadotte is assassinated, allegedly by Jewish terrorists; Ralph J. Bunche is named to succeed him.

September 20. *Arab Government Announced.* The Arab League announces establishment of an Arab government for Palestine—a move denounced by Transjordan

and Iraq as amounting to recognition of Palestine's partition.

October 22. *Israel, Egypt Again Halt Fighting.* Israel and Egypt agree to halt renewed fighting and comply with a cease-fire order by the UN Security Council October 19. The truce does not hold, however, and fighting continues into the new year.

December 11. *New UN Commission.* The UN General Assembly sets up a new Palestine Conciliation Commission.

1949

January 6. *Cease-Fire Announced.* Israel and Egypt agree to a final cease-fire on all fronts to begin January 7. Israel withdraws its troops from Egypt January 10.

January 25. *First Israeli Election.* In the first Israeli election, Prime Minister David Ben-Gurion's Labor party wins the largest number of seats in the Knesset.

January 31. *U.S. Extends Full Recognition.* The United States extends full diplomatic recognition to Israel and Transjordan following a flurry of diplomatic activity during which a number of Western nations including France on January 24 and Britain January 29 recognize Israel.

February 1. *Israel Incorporates Jerusalem.* Ending its military governorship of Jerusalem, Israel formally incorporates the city as part of the new state.

March 7. *Suez Canal Agreement.* Egypt signs an agreement on the Suez Canal with the British-owned Suez Canal Company calling for 80-90 percent of the company's jobs to be held by Egyptians and for Egypt to receive 7 percent of its profits.

March 11. *Transjordan-Israel Cease-Fire.* Transjordan and Israel sign a "complete and enduring" cease-fire agreement to be binding even if they fail to reach agreement on other points.

March 21. *UN Palestine Council Meets.* The first meeting of the UN Palestine Council Commission to settle the question of Arab refugees opens in Beirut, Lebanon.

April 5. *Israeli-Syrian Talks Break Down.* Armistice talks between Israel and Syria run aground because of Israel's refusal to negotiate with representatives of Syria's new military government, which took over the country in a coup March 30.

April 26. *Transjordan to Be Called "Jordan."* Transjordan announces that the correct name of the country is Jordan, or Hashemite Jordan Kingdom.

April 26. *Syria Closes Jordanian Border.* In response to Jordan's statement on April 7 that a "greater" Jordan may evolve, Syria closes its Jordanian border and warns against attempts to annex its territory.

April 28. *Israel Blocks Return of Refugees.* The Israeli government rejects a proposal to allow Arab refugees to return to their homes inside Israel's borders.

May 11. *Israel Admitted to UN.* Israel is admitted to the United Nations after a vote of 36 to 12 in the General Assembly. Great Britain abstained from voting. Six Arab delegates walk out to protest the vote.

July 20. *Syria and Israel Sign Armistice.* Syria and Israel sign an armistice agreement setting up demilitarized zones and calling for both countries to keep their forces behind the frontiers.

July 27. *Mediator Says War Has Ended.* UN Middle

East mediator Ralph Bunche reports that "the military phase of the Palestine conflict is ended."

September 13. *UN Drafts Jerusalem Proposal.* The UN Palestine Conciliation Commission issues a draft statute whereby the United Nations would control Jerusalem, neither Israel nor the Arab states could have government offices there, and neither would control the city except for local administration of areas where their citizens lived. Holy places would be under permanent international supervision. Israel rejects the statute November 15.

December 16. *Jerusalem to Become Capital.* Israeli Prime Minister Ben-Gurion announces that Jerusalem will become the country's capital January 1, 1950. Transfer of government offices from Tel Aviv to Jerusalem's New City is already under way.

1950

March 9. *Turkey, Iran Recognize Israel.* Turkey becomes the first Moslem state to recognize Israel. Iran recognizes Israel March 15.

April 1. *Israel Rejects Arab League Terms.* The Arab League Council votes to expel any member making a separate peace with Israel. Israel rejects Arab League terms for peace negotiations April 13, which include a return to 1947 UN partition boundaries. The Arab League secretary condemns Anglo-American policy in the Middle East April 20 and urges Arab states to turn to Moscow.

April 24. *Jordan Annexes Eastern Palestine.* Jordan formally annexes Jordan-occupied eastern Palestine, including the Old City of Jerusalem. Britain recognizes the Jordan-Palestine merger April 27 and changes its recognition of Israel from de facto to full recognition.

May 25. *Western Nations Agree on Arms Sales.* Truman discloses an agreement with France and Britain, reached at the London foreign ministers' conference, to sell arms to Mideast states, including Israel, on a basis of parity between Israel and Arab countries if purchasers promise there will be no renewal of the Palestine war. The Arab League pledges June 21 not to use new arms purchases for aggressive purposes.

November 21. *Britain Refuses to Leave Canal.* In response to Egyptian demands for Britain's immediate withdrawal from the Suez Canal Zone and the Anglo-Egyptian Sudan, British Foreign Secretary Bevin tells Parliament that British troops will remain in Egypt until the 1936 Anglo-Egyptian treaty is altered "by mutual consent."

1951

March 7. *Iranian Premier Assassinated.* Gen. Ali Razmara, Iranian premier since June 26, 1950, is assassinated by a religious fanatic belonging to a group favoring the nationalization of Iran's oil industry. Razmara had angered members of that group by supporting U.S.-suggested economic reforms. He is succeeded March 11 by Hussein Ala, a strongly pro-West official who had served as a former ambassador to the United States.

April 28. *Iran Nationalizes Oil Company.* The Iranian parliament votes unanimously to sanction government expropriation of the British-owned Anglo-Iranian Oil Company. With favorable Senate action April 30, the oil nation-

alization bill becomes law.

May 18. *UN Protests Israeli Project.* The UN Security Council adopts a resolution calling on Israel to halt the Huleh border zone drainage project that has set off boundary clashes between Israel and Syria. Criticizing Israeli aerial attacks on Syria, the resolution denounces the use of force by both countries to settle their differences. Israel halts work on the drainage project June 6.

July 5. *Iran Proceeds with Nationalization.* The International Court of Justice at The Hague hands down a 10 to 2 decision calling for Iran to reinstate the Anglo-Iranian Oil Company to full control of its assets and operations. Iran's ambassador to Britain says his country will "ignore" the recommendations and proceed with the nationalization of the oil company. Disclaiming all previous obligations, Iran opens sales of its oil July 14 on an equal basis to old and new clients of the Anglo-Iranian Oil Company.

July 20. *King Abdullah Assassinated.* Jordan's King Abdullah is assassinated, reportedly by a member of a faction opposing his annexation of parts of Palestine. The king's son, Prince Talal, is crowned king September 6 in Amman.

July 24. *Britain and Iran to Negotiate.* Secret plans for Iranian-British negotiations over nationalization of the Anglo-Iranian Oil Company are sent to London after formulation during eight days of talks between Iranian officials and W. Averell Harriman, a U.S. envoy sent to Iran by President Truman. Britain and Iran formally agree August 2 to begin negotiations aimed at settling the dispute.

September 1. *Egypt Urged to End Blockade.* The UN Security Council calls on Egypt to end its three-year-old blockade of the Suez Canal to ships carrying cargoes bound for Israel. Egypt refuses September 2 to comply until Israel obeys previous UN resolutions dealing with the partition of Palestine, repatriation and compensation of Arab refugees, and internationalization of Jerusalem.

September 13. *UN Conference Opens.* The UN Palestine Conciliation Conference with Israeli and Arab delegates opens in Paris.

September 21. *Israel Willing to Sign Pacts.* Israel agrees to sign nonagression pacts with each of its four Arab neighbors but warns that peace negotiations should not continue if Arabs will not meet in the same room with Israeli delegates. Israel offers to compensate Arab refugees and to make contributions to their resettlement in Arab countries, but it is unwilling to accept repatriation of the refugees in Israel.

September 25. *Iran Expels British Oil Workers.* Iran orders the last British oil technicians to leave the country by October 4. Britain's remaining three-hundred oil employees depart October 3.

October 8. *Egypt Announces Canal Aims.* Egypt announces plans to expel British troops from the Suez Canal and to assume full control of the jointly administered Anglo-Egyptian Sudan. The next day, Britain declares it will neither vacate the Suez Canal nor withdraw its administrators from the Sudan.

October 16. *British and Egyptians Fight.* Tension builds in the Suez Canal zone as eight persons are killed and seventy-four wounded during fighting between British troops and Egyptian rioters. A three-day state of emergency is proclaimed throughout Egypt. Meanwhile, the Egyptian parliament approves the change of King Farouk's title to "king of Egypt and the Sudan" and extends the Egyptian constitution to apply to the Sudan.

October 27. *Egypt Renounces British Alliance.*

Egypt formally notifies Britain that the 1936 Treaty of Alliance and the 1889 agreement on joint administration of the Sudan are both considered broken. In the Sudan, the legislature rejects the decision to place the country under the Egyptian crown.

November 15. *British Plan for the Sudan.* Britain proposes self-rule for the Sudan, with the voters of that country deciding in a year or two whether to unite with Egypt.

November 21. *UN Commission Ends Efforts.* Citing the "rigid positions" on both sides, the UN Palestine Conciliation Commission ends mediation efforts between Israel and the Arab states.

December 2. *Coup in Syria.* Following a bloodless military coup in Syria, the army chief of staff, Col. Adib al-Shishakli, becomes president, after the resignation of President al-Atassi. Col. Fawzi Silo is appointed premier December 3.

December 10. *Iran Ends Boycott of Court.* Reportedly in response to President Truman's appeals, Iran ends a six-month boycott of the International Court of Justice's proceedings on nationalization of the Anglo-Iranian Oil Company and agrees to contest the court's ruling.

December 24. *Libya Gains Independence.* The Federation of Libya, an Arab kingdom created with the endorsement of the United Nations, becomes independent. By agreement, Britain and the United States will retain their military bases in the country.

1952

January 18. *Egyptians Fight British Troops.* British troops and Egyptian guerrillas battle for four hours at Port Said. British troops disarm Egyptian police in Ismailia January 25. Fighting breaks out, killing forty-two persons. Martial law is imposed January 26 in Egypt following widespread rioting and burning in Cairo. Extensive damage to American, British, and French property is estimated to total over $10 million.

April 2. *New Sudanese Constitution.* Britain's submission of a new constitution for the Sudan, during renewed British-Egyptian talks on the Sudan, brings an immediate Egyptian protest. The Sudanese parliament welcomes the new constitution April 23 and asks for an amendment allowing the Sudanese to determine whether they wish union with Britain, Egypt, or neither.

May 3. *Britain Offers to Withdraw Troops.* Britain, proposing a solution to the dispute with Egypt over the Suez Canal and the Sudan, offers to evacuate British troops from the base in the Suez Canal, but it denies recognition of King Farouk as ruler of the Sudan until the Sudanese people are consulted.

July 22. *Court Cancels Anglo-Iranian Ruling.* Canceling its year-old decision calling for restoration of property to the British-owned Anglo-Iranian Oil Company, the International Court of Justice at The Hague rules it has no jurisdiction in the dispute over Iranian nationalization of the oil company.

July 23. *King Farouk Abdicates.* Egyptian King Farouk flees the country following a military coup that empowers Maher Pasha as premier. Farouk abdicates July 26 and goes into exile in Italy. The king's infant son, King Fuad II, is proclaimed ruler of Egypt and the Sudan by the cabinet.

August 11. *Hussein Crowned King.* Declaring that King Talal, suffering from mental disorders, is unfit to rule, the Jordanian parliament proclaims Crown Prince Hussein the new king.

August 11. *Mossadeq Given Dictatorial Power.* Iranian Premier Mossadeq is granted full dictatorial powers by the Senate. The chamber of deputies had approved the dictatorial powers August 3.

September 18. *Lebanese President Resigns.* Ending a nine-year rule, Lebanon's President el-Khoury resigns in the face of general strikes to protest political corruption. The parliament elects Foreign Minister Camille Chamoun president September 23.

October 7. *Iran Severs Ties with Britain.* Iranian Premier Mossadeq demands $1 billion from Britain before talks can resume on the question of nationalizing the Anglo-Iranian Oil Company. Iran severs diplomatic ties with Britain October 22 after Britain's rejection October 14 of Iran's demand.

November 7. *Israeli President Weizmann Dies.* Israel's first president, Chaim Weizmann, dies. The Israeli Knesset December 8 names Isaac Ben-Zvi to succeed him.

1953

February 12. *Britain, Egypt Sign Agreement.* British and Egyptian officials sign an agreement in Cairo establishing immediate self-government in the Anglo-Egyptian Sudan and calling for self-determination by the Sudanese people within three years. The Sudanese may choose to unite with Egypt, become independent, or follow another path.

May 2. *Iraq Crowns King Faisal II.* King Faisal II of Iraq is crowned on his eighteenth birthday, thus ending the regency of his uncle, Emir Abd-ul-Ilah.

August 16. *Shah Flees to Iraq.* The shah of Iran seeks sanctuary in Iraq after his unsuccessful attempt to dismiss dictator Premier Mossadeq.

August 19. *Iranian Royalists Oust Mossadeq.* A revolt by Iranian royalists and troops loyal to the shah ousts Premier Mossadeq. Announcing plans to return to Iran, the shah names Maj. Gen. Gazollah Zahedi as premier. The shah returns August 22.

November 29. *Sudanese Favor Union with Egypt.* The Sudan's first general elections yield a decisive victory to forces seeking union with Egypt.

December 21. *Court Convicts Mossadeq.* An Iranian military court convicts former premier Mossadeq of attempted rebellion. Instead of the death penalty, the court imposes a three-year solitary confinement sentence after the shah requests clemency.

1954

February 26. *Syrian President Ousted.* A Syrian army revolt ousts President Shishakli. Former president Hashim Atassi succeeds him February 28.

April 18. *Nasser Named Premier.* Egyptian Col. Gamal Abdel Nasser, a leader of the revolt against King Farouk, replaces Mohammed Naguib as premier of the government. Naguib retains the largely ceremonial post of president.

July 27. *Egypt and Britain Sign Agreement.* Egypt and Britain sign an agreement ending the dispute over the Suez Canal. Britain will remove its forces from the area within twenty months, but it will retain the right to use the canal base in the event of aggression against an Arab state or Turkey.

November 2. *Jordan Protests River Diversion.* Jordan summons the ambassadors of Britain, France, and the United States to ask their governments to halt Israel's unilateral diversion of the Jordan River.

November 14. *Naguib Deposed.* Egypt's ruling military junta deposes President Mohammed Naguib. Gamal Abdel Nasser, who has held most executive power since he became premier April 18, is named president.

1955

February 24. *Iraq and Turkey Sign Pact.* Iraq signs a mutual defense treaty (Baghdad Pact) with Turkey despite Egyptian protests. Britain joins Baghdad Pact April 4. Pakistan joins September 23.

August 16. *Sudan Calls for Troop Evacuation.* The Sudanese parliament unanimously calls for the evacuation of British and Egyptian troops from the Sudan within ninety days.

October 20. *Egypt and Syria Sign Pact.* Egypt and Syria sign a mutual defense treaty, triggering Israeli requests for an Israeli-American security pact. Israel also cites recent Egyptian arms purchases from Czechoslovakia.

November 3. *Iran Joins Baghdad Pact.* Iran joins Baghdad Pact despite Soviet warning October 12 that such a move by Iran would be "incompatible" with peace in the Middle East.

November 22. *New Baghdad Pact Organization.* The five Baghdad Pact countries announce the establishment of a permanent political, military, and economic organization, the Middle East Treaty Organization, to be based in Baghdad. Members are Britain, Iran, Iraq, Pakistan, and Turkey.

1956

January 30. *Israel Appeals for Arms.* Israel urges the United States and Britain to allow it to buy arms. Secretary of State John Foster Dulles, not excluding "the possibility of arms sales to Israel," suggests February 6 that Israel look for security in the United Nations and the 1950 Anglo-American-French Three-Power agreement.

February 16. *U.S. Providing Tanks to Saudis.* It is disclosed that the United States is sending tanks to Saudi Arabia, an action Israel calls "regrettable" to the balance of power in the Mideast.

March 3. *Jordan Grants Bases to Britain.* Agreeing to honor the 1948 treaty of friendship with Britain, Jordan announces it will grant Britain bases in Jordan.

March 10. *Jordan Launches Raids.* Ending a two-year period of relative quiet on their border, Jordan stages raids on Israel.

April 18. *U.S. Joins Baghdad Pact Committee.* The United States, which has not joined the Baghdad Pact in deference to Israel, becomes a full member of the pact's Economic Committee. The next day the United States

agrees to set up a military liaison office at the headquarters of the Baghdad Pact.

May 9. *U.S. Rejects Arms Sales to Israel.* Secretary of State Dulles states that the United States will refrain from selling arms to Israel because he fears confrontation in the Middle East. On May 12 the United States confirms its sale of arms to Saudi Arabia and twelve jets arrive in Israel from France in a deal that has tacit U.S. approval.

June 13. *Britain Ends Occupation of Canal.* Britain turns over full responsibility for the defense of the Suez Canal to Egypt. On June 18 Britain declares its occupation of the canal ended.

June 24. *Nasser Becomes President of Egypt.* After an uncontested election, Gamal Abdel Nasser becomes Egypt's first elected president, having received 99 percent of the vote.

July 20. *U.S. Refuses Egypt Aswan Dam Loan.* Following disputes over funding the Aswan Dam, the United States refuses to lend Egypt funds for the project and Britain withdraws its offer to supplement the American loan. Egyptian officials are surprised and angered by the move.

July 27. *Nasser Nationalizes Suez Canal.* Egyptian President Nasser nationalizes the Suez Canal and imposes martial law there in retaliation for American and British withdrawal of support for the financing of the Aswan Dam. Income from the canal will be used to build the dam. Britain freezes assets of Egypt and the Suez Canal held in Britain July 28.

August 14. *U.S. Creates Oil Committee.* The United States creates a Middle East Emergency Committee to supply U.S. oil to Western Europe if shipments from the Middle East are discontinued during the current crisis.

August 16. *Suez Crisis Meeting.* In London, twenty-two nations open a conference on the Suez Canal crisis. Eighteen nations agree August 23 to ask Egypt to negotiate for international operation of the Suez Canal. On August 28 Nasser agrees to meet with a five-nation delegation.

September 11. *Economic Pressure on Egypt.* After initial efforts at negotiations fail, Britain and France agree to apply economic pressure to force Egypt to accept international control of the Suez Canal. The United States rejects the plan "under present circumstances."

September 21. *Suez Conference Concludes.* The Suez Conference in London concludes with a draft plan for a Suez Canal Users' Association. The following day, Britain issues invitations to eighteen nations for another conference on the Suez Canal situation.

October 8. *Canal Proposal Rejected.* Egypt and the Soviet Union reject proposals for international supervision of the Suez Canal.

October 29. *Israel Attacks Egypt.* After secretly conspiring with Britain and France to strike a coordinated blow against Egypt, Israel attacks Egyptian forces in the Sinai. The Israeli attack is intended to provide Britain and France with a justification for using military force to seize the Suez Canal. Israeli troops drive to within twenty-five miles of the Suez Canal on the first day of fighting. Israel claims the attack was designed to eliminate Egyptian commando bases in the Sinai that had been used to stage raids against Israel.

October 30. *British-French Ultimatum.* Britain and France warn that troops will be sent to the Suez unless Egyptian and Israeli troops cease fighting and withdraw ten miles from the canal. Israel accepts the ultimatum on the condition that Egypt also agrees; Egyptian President

Nasser rejects the ultimatum. British and French forces on Cyprus are readied for an attack on Egypt. President Dwight D. Eisenhower appeals to the allies to refrain from military intervention. Britain and France veto a U.S.-sponsored UN Security Council resolution calling for a halt to all military action in the area and an Israeli withdrawal.

October 31. *British-French Air Attacks.* British and French aircraft attack Egypt as Israel continues its drive in the Sinai. Israel reaches the banks of the Suez Canal before withdrawing to the ten-mile limit demanded by the British-French ultimatum. Israeli forces continue operations in the Sinai and the Gaza Strip, which is captured November 3.

November 1. *Egypt Breaks Ties.* Egypt breaks off diplomatic relations with Britain and France and seizes their property in Egypt as bombing of military targets continues. Jordan also severs ties with France and tells Britain that it will no longer be allowed to use ground or air bases in Jordan for further attacks on Egypt. Britain and France reject the UN's call for a cease-fire.

November 5. *British and French Troops Attack.* British and French paratroopers enter the fight against Egypt; allied commandos are landed by sea November 6. The Soviet Union warns that it is prepared to use force "including rockets" to restore the Mideast peace. The Soviets call for joint Soviet-American action against "aggressors," a proposal the United States rejects as "unthinkable."

November 6. *Cease-Fire.* British and French troops capture the Egyptian city of Port Said. Under heavy U.S. pressure, France and Britain agree to a cease-fire in Egypt at midnight.

November 7. *UN Calls for Withdrawal.* The UN General Assembly calls on Britain, France, and Israel to withdraw their forces from Egypt. The UN also decides to send a peacekeeping force to the area. Britain and France say they welcome creation of the peacekeeping force and will withdraw. President Eisenhower in a personal note to Prime Minister Ben-Gurion says Israeli rejection of the UN appeal would "impair friendly cooperation between our two countries." Israel agrees November 8 to withdraw from the Sinai.

November 9. *Iraq Breaks Ties with French.* Iraq breaks off ties with France and announces it will boycott any future meeting of the Baghdad Pact attended by Britain.

November 10. *Volunteer Force Threatened.* The Soviet Union calls for the withdrawal of British, French, and Israeli troops from Egypt and warns that Soviet volunteers will be allowed to join Egyptian forces unless the withdrawal takes place. On November 14 President Eisenhower says the United States would oppose any such Soviet intervention.

November 15. *UN Force Arrives in Egypt.* The UN Emergency Force lands in Egypt. UN troops begin monitoring the truce at positions near Port Said November 20.

November 21. *Withdrawal from Egypt Begins.* British, French, and Israeli troop withdrawals from Egypt begin. Eisenhower, according to sources, is reported to have sent private messages to the British and French governments urging complete troop withdrawal from the area. The last British and French troops leave Egypt December 22.

December 26. *Dulles on Soviet Expansion.* Secretary of State Dulles says the United States has a "major responsibility" to prevent Soviet expansion in the Middle East. The same day, the Syrian ambassador to the United States says that Syria and other Arab states will not welcome American protection against the Soviets.

1957

January 4. *Suez Canal Opens.* The Suez Canal opens halfway, for medium-sized shipping.

January 5. *Eisenhower Doctrine Announced.* President Eisenhower addresses a joint session of Congress to urge support for a declaration, dubbed the Eisenhower Doctrine, calling for American action to counter Communist actions in the Middle East. Turkey, Pakistan, Iran, and Iraq, the four Moslem nations of the Baghdad Pact, endorse the doctrine January 21. Saudi Arabian King Saud states his approval during a meeting in Washington with Eisenhower February 6.

January 15. *Nasser Begins "Egyptianization."* Egyptian President Nasser undertakes an "Egyptianization" process. Only natural citizens may hold shares of Egyptian-based companies. British and French banks and insurance companies are nationalized.

March 1. *Israelis Withdraw from Gaza.* Israel agrees to withdraw its troops from the Gaza Strip and the Gulf of Aqaba on "assumptions" that the UN Emergency Force will administer Gaza until a peace settlement is reached and that free navigation of the gulf will continue. The last Israeli forces withdraw from Egyptian territory March 7.

March 13. *Jordan and Britain End Alliance.* Jordan and Britain cancel their 1948 treaty of alliance. British troops are to withdraw within six months.

March 14. *Egyptian Administrators to Gaza.* In violation of UN resolutions, Egypt sends civil administrators into Gaza and on March 15 announces that Israel would not be permitted to use the Suez Canal. Saudi Arabia halts Israeli use of the Gulf of Aqaba March 15.

March 22. *U.S. Joins Military Committee.* The United States announces it will join the Military Committee of the Baghdad Pact.

April 24. *U.S. Backs Jordan.* As internal political turmoil continues in Jordan, a U.S. statement, authorized by President Eisenhower and Secretary of State Dulles, warns that the United States regards "the independence and integrity of Jordan as vital." On April 25 the United States orders the Sixth Fleet into the Eastern Mediterranean. The United States extends $10 million in military supplies and services June 29.

May 5. *Hussein Defeats Leftists.* King Hussein announces that the government's battle against leftist elements in Jordan has succeeded.

June 10. *Jordanian-Egyptian Rift.* A rift arises in Jordanian-Egyptian relations as Jordan charges that an Egyptian military attaché is plotting against Jordanian officials. His recall is requested. Egypt complies.

July 19. *British Troops Clash with Rebels.* British-led forces step in to suppress a tribal revolt in Muscat and Oman on the Arabian Peninsula. On July 24 British planes attack military targets controlled by rebel tribesmen in Oman after the rebels refuse to heed a British warning. British troops withdraw from Oman August 20, following rebel recognition August 11 of the sultan of Oman's authority.

August 13. *Syria Ousts American Diplomats.* Following Syrian accusations of U.S. efforts to overthrow that government, Syria ousts three American embassy officials. On August 14 the United States expels Syrian diplomats.

September 5. *U.S. Announces Arms Shipments.* The United States announces plans to send arms to Jordan, Lebanon, Turkey, and Iraq. Affirming his doctrine on the Middle East, President Eisenhower says September 7 that the United States will take action to protect pro-West Middle East countries if they are threatened by Syria.

November 12. *Shah Seeks Bahrain.* The shah of Iran instructs his cabinet to present a bill to parliament to bring Bahrain, a British oil protectorate, under Iranian jurisdiction.

1958

January 30. *Dulles Affirms U.S. Commitment.* Secretary of State Dulles, addressing the Baghdad Pact countries meeting in Ankara, Turkey, tells the delegates that the Eisenhower Doctrine commits the United States to the Mideast as effectively as would membership in the Baghdad Pact.

February 1. *Egypt and Syria Form U.A.R.* Egypt and Syria merge into the United Arab Republic. Citizens of the two countries approve the merger, nearly unanimously, in plebiscites February 21. Yemen agrees to federation with the U.A.R. February 11.

February 14. *Iraq and Jordan Form Federation.* Iraq and Jordan form the Arab Federation, with Iraqi King Faisal II serving as head of the two-state federal union. King Hussein retains sovereignty in Jordan. The federation is approved February 17 by the Iraqi parliament and by the Jordanian parliament February 18.

March 24. *Faisal Receives Power.* King Saud of Saudi Arabia transfers some of his absolute power to his brother Crown Prince Faisal. Faisal is granted full power to lay down the state's internal, external, and financial policies, and to oversee their implementation.

May 24. *UN Debates Lebanon.* the UN Security Council meets to discuss Lebanon's complaint that the U.A.R. has caused continuing antigovernment rioting that started May 10.

June 11. *UN Troops to Lebanon.* The UN Security Council votes 10-0 to send UN observers to Lebanon to guard against the smuggling of arms or troops into that country.

July 4. *Lebanon Expels U.A.R. Diplomats.* Lebanon orders the departure of six U.A.R. diplomats accused of inciting the Lebanese revolt and financing the fighting.

July 14. *Coup in Iraq.* Revolutionaries seize Baghdad, overthrow the Iraqi government, kill King Faisal and Premier as-Said, and proclaim a republic. Brig. Gen. Abdul Karim Kassim is named premier. In reaction to the coup, King Hussein of Jordan announces his assumption of power as head of the Arab Federation of Iraq and Jordan. Hussein and Lebanese President Chamoun each appeal for U.S. military assistance because of the Iraqi coup. Martial law is declared in Iraq July 15.

July 15. *U.S. Troops to Lebanon.* President Eisenhower dispatches 5,000 Marines to Lebanon. He asserts that the troops will protect American lives and help defend Lebanon's sovereignty and independence. At a meeting of the UN Security Council, the United States says its troops will remain in Lebanon until UN forces can guarantee Lebanese "continued independence."

July 17. *British Troops to Jordan.* British paratroopers land in Jordan at the request of King Hussein.

July 19. *U.A.R.-Iraqi Pact.* The U.A.R and the new Iraqi regime sign a mutual defense treaty. Jordan severs relations with the U.A.R. July 20, because of its recognition of the new Iraqi regime. Iraq and the U.A.R. set up committees July 24 to enhance cooperation between those countries in political, economic, military, and educational fields.

July 19. *British Land in Libya.* British commandos land in Libya in support of the government when rumors surface of an Egyptian plan to overthrow it.

July 31. *Chehab Elected President.* General Fuad Chehab, sympathetic to the Lebanese rebels, is elected president of Lebanon by parliament over the strong objections of Premier Said.

August 2. *Jordan and Iraq Split.* Iraq says it has not renounced the Baghdad Pact, nor will it buy arms from the Soviet Union at this time. Jordan announces the formal dismemberment of the Arab Union of Jordan and Iraq, in light of the new regime in Iraq. The United States recognizes the new Iraqi government.

August 13. *Eisenhower Peace Plan.* President Eisenhower presents the UN General Assembly with a "framework of a plan of peace" in the Middle East. It includes provisions for a UN peacekeeping force in the region and for an "Arab development institution on a regional basis, governed by the Arab states themselves." U.S. forces began withdrawing from Lebanon August 12 to demonstrate to the UN that the United States was not trying to build up its forces in that country. The last U.S. troops leave Lebanon October 25.

August 21. *UN Urges Early Withdrawal.* The UN General Assembly unanimously adopts an Arab resolution calling on Secretary General Dag Hammarskjöld to take the necessary steps to restore order in Jordan and Lebanon and thereby "facilitate the early withdrawal" of foreign troops. In the next few days, tension in the Mideast appears to lessen.

September 22. *Karami Becomes Premier.* Lebanon's pro-Western cabinet resigns. Rashid Karami, a rebel leader, becomes premier September 24. The United States September 27 assures Karami of continued U.S. support.

1959

January 17. *Suez Pact Signed.* Egypt and Britain sign the British-Egyptian Suez Pact, which resolves their two-year dispute generated by the Suez crisis in 1956. The agreement includes provisions requiring the British release of frozen Egyptian assets in Britain and Egyptian payments for British property it had nationalized.

March 5. *Mutual Defense Pacts Signed.* Iran signs a bilateral defense treaty with the United States despite Soviet protests. Turkey and Pakistan also sign mutual defense treaties with the United States that are described by the Eisenhower administration as extensions of its policy to resist Soviet expansion into the Middle East.

March 20. *Nasser Attacks Soviet Interference.* U.A.R. President Nasser denounces Soviet interference in Arab affairs and protests Soviet Premier Nikita Khrushchev's remark the day before that Nasser's hostility toward Iraq was "hot-headed." Nasser on March 11 had accused Iraq and foreign Communist agents of attempting to divide the Arab world.

March 24. *Iraq Leaves Baghdad Pact.* Iraq withdraws from the Baghdad Pact, which is left with four members—Britain, Turkey, Iran, and Pakistan. The United States announces June 1 the termination of U.S.-Iraqi military assistance agreements.

July 13. *Upheaval in Iraq.* Communist demonstrations in Kirkuk, an Iraqi oil center, nearly erupt into civil war. After the Iraqi army bombs the rebels, the government regains control.

August 18. *Baghdad Pact Renamed CENTO.* With the departure of Iraq from the Baghdad Pact, the organization is renamed the Central Treaty Organization (CENTO), with Britain, Iran, Pakistan, and Turkey remaining as members. The United States supports the organization, participates in certain committees, but is not an official member.

September 4. *U.A.R.-Saudi Arabia Talks.* After four days of talks, U.A.R. President Nasser and Saudi Arabian King Saud agree to resume relations with Britain and to seek to end Communist penetration in Iraq.

December 1. *Britain and U.A.R. Reestablish Ties.* Britain and the U.A.R. reestablish diplomatic relations after a three-year break.

1960

January 18. *Soviet Support for Dam.* The U.A.R. announces that the Soviet Union will finance the second stage of the Aswan Dam.

February 11. *Nasser Threatens Israel.* Jordanian Foreign Minister Musa Nasir says the Arab states are "completely united" on a "declaration of war" against Israel if Israel attempts to divert the Jordan River to irrigate the Negev Desert.

April 8. *Suez Canal Seizures.* UN Secretary General Hammarskjöld protests U.A.R. seizure of ships carrying Israeli supplies and products through the Suez Canal. Hammarskjöld says he will renew persuasive efforts to end such actions.

July 23. *Iran Recognizes Israel.* Iran announces recognition of Israel. The new diplomatic ties cause the U.A.R. to break relations with Iran July 27 and impose an economic boycott of Iran July 28.

September 15. *OPEC Established.* At the end of a five-day conference in Baghdad, representatives of Iraq, Iran, Kuwait, Venezuela, and Saudi Arabia agree to form the Organization of Petroleum Exporting Countries (OPEC). The permanent organization is intended to help member nations unify their oil policies. Other oil exporting nations may join if all the charter members approve.

November 17. *Jordan and Iraq to Restore Ties.* Jordan and Iraq agree to resume diplomatic ties in December. Relations had been cut off in July 1958, following the Iraqi revolution.

December 21. *Prince Faisal Resigns.* Saudi Arabian Prince Faisal resigns as premier, returning complete control of the government to his brother, King Saud. Saud had relinquished executive power to Faisal early in 1958.

1961

March 16. *U.S.-Saudi Pact Expires.* It is disclosed that a U.S.-Saudi Arabian pact of 1957, which called for the setting up of a U.S. military base at Dhahran, will not be renewed. On April 11 Saudi Arabian King Saud explains that the decision was partially due to American aid to Israel.

June 19. *Kuwait Gains Independence.* Great Britain grants independence to Kuwait and signs a treaty with the new nation assuring British protection if requested. Kuwaiti Sheik Abdullah al-Salem al-Sabah says June 26 he will fight to maintain Kuwait's independence after Iraq claims that Kuwait is an "integral part" of Iraq.

July 20. *Kuwait Joins Arab League.* The Arab League unanimously admits Kuwait to membership. Iraq walks out of the meeting, accusing the league of aiding "British imperialism." British protective forces in Kuwait are replaced September 19 by Arab League troops sent to ensure Kuwait's sovereignty against Iraqi claims.

September 29. *Syria Breaks with U.A.R.* Following a coup September 28 by dissident Syrian army units, the revolutionary command sets up a civilian government for Syria and announces independence from the U.A.R. Jordan and Turkey recognize the new Syrian government. President Nasser announces October 1 in Cairo that the U.A.R. has broken ties with Jordan and Turkey for their recognition of the new Syrian government. Syria is reseated at the United Nations October 13, regaining the seat it gave up when it merged with the U.A.R. The new Syrian government is recognized by the Soviet Union October 7 and by the United States October 10.

December 26. *Nasser Ends Union with Yemen.* U.A.R. President Nasser dissolves his country's union with Yemen, formed in 1958, thus reducing the United Arab Republic to only the state of Egypt.

1962

March 28. *Syrian Army Ousts Government.* Syrian army leaders oust the new Syrian government, which was elected after the break with Egypt in the fall of 1961. The Syrian army leaders declare their intentions to work closely with Egypt and Iraq.

April 13. *Syrian President Returns to Office.* Syrian President Nazem el-Kodsi, ousted by an army coup March 28, is reported returned to office. Kodsi tells Syrians April 14 that he will seek a union of "liberated Arab states, beginning with Egypt."

August 29. *Saudi-Jordanian Agreement.* Saudi Arabian King Saud and Jordanian King Hussein agree to merge military troops and economic policies.

September 26. *Military Revolt in Yemen.* Yemen's Imam Badr, only days after assuming power, is driven from Sanaa (the capital) in a military revolt led by Col. Abdallah al-Sallal. Al-Sallal received political support from U.A.R. President Nasser, who later sent Egyptian military forces to Yemen.

November 6. *Saudis Break Ties with U.A.R.* Saudi Arabia breaks off diplomatic ties with the U.A.R. following charges that U.A.R. planes bombed Saudi Arabian villages near the Yemen border. The U.A.R. is reportedly cooperating with the revolutionary government in Yemen.

1963

February 8. *Iraqi Coup.* The Iraqi air force overthrows the government of Premier Kassim. Kassim is killed by a firing squad. A Nasserite and conspirator in the coup, Col. Abdul Salem Arif, is appointed provisional president.

March 8. *Syrian Coup.* A coup by pro-Nasser and Ba'ath party followers ousts the Syrian government. The U.A.R. and Iraq governments threaten war if other nations interfere in the Syrian revolt.

March 12. *Syrian Premier Advocates Federation.* Syria's new premier, Salah el-Bitar, voices hopes of a federation of Syria, Iraq, and Egypt under one president.

April 10. *Federation Plan Outlined.* U.A.R. Prime Minister Aly Sabry outlines plans for a new federation between the U.A.R., Syria, and Iraq. Later it is announced that the federation proposal will be submitted to national plebiscites to be held September 27, 1963. Street demonstrations break out in Jordan April 20 in support of Jordan's joining the new U.A.R. federation.

May 21. *U.A.R. Troops Remain in Yemen.* In violation of an agreement reached in April, U.A.R. President Nasser declares that U.A.R. troops will not leave Yemen until royalist factions have been put down.

July 22. *Nasser Renounces Unification.* U.A.R. President Nasser renounces an agreement to unite Egypt, Syria, and Iraq and denounces the Syrian Ba'ath party.

August 21. *Arab League Meets.* The Arab League meets to consider a unified stance in support of Syria against Israel as fighting breaks out near the Sea of Galilee. Iraqi forces are placed "at the disposal of" Syria. U.A.R. troops are on alert for possible support of Syria. Israel and Syria agree to a UN-mediated cease-fire August 23.

August 25. *Israel-Jordan Clash.* Israeli and Jordanian troops clash in Jerusalem before the UN truce observers persuade both sides to agree to a cease-fire.

November 12. *Syrian Premier Resigns.* Syrian Premier el-Bitar resigns and a new Syrian government is set up with Maj. Gen. Amin el-Hafez as the president of the Revolutionary Council.

November 18. *Iraqi Coup.* Iraq's President Arif announces that his forces have overthrown the civilian Ba'athist government. Arif becomes president and chief of staff of the army. The new government announces November 21 that it will seek to fulfill the April agreement between Iraq, Syria, and Egypt on the formation of a union and offers November 22 to settle differences with "the Kurds, our brothers."

1964

February 10. *Iraqi-Kurdish Cease-Fire.* Iraq's President Arif announces a cease-fire agreement with Iraqi Kurds, apparently concluding the Kurds' struggle for autonomy within Iraq.

March 28. *Faisal Gains Power.* Saudi Arabian King Saud turns over his powers to his half-brother Crown Prince Faisal. Faisal's maneuverings to gain power were backed by a council composed of members of the royal family and religious and tribal leaders who recommended that Saud be deposed. Instead the council accepts the recommendation of Prince Faisal to retain Saud as a figurehead monarch.

April 14. *Hussein-Johnson Talks.* In talks with President Lyndon B. Johnson in Washington, Jordanian King Hussein stands firm on Arab intentions to dam two tributaries of the Jordan River and block Israel's plans to divert the Jordan for irrigation purposes.

May 3. *Iraqi Constitution Backs Union.* Iraqi President Arif introduces a new provisional constitution May 3 that has as its main goal the union of Iraq with the U.A.R. The two countries sign an agreement May 26 providing for joint command of their troops in time of war.

August 22. *U.S., Britain to Leave Bases.* Libyan Premier Mahmud Mutasser announces that both the United States and Great Britain have agreed to give up their military bases in Libya.

September 11. *Arab Heads Urge Water Projects.* After seven days of talks, chiefs of state of thirteen Arab nations issue a final communiqué urging immediate Arab efforts on water projects to cut off the Jordan River from Israel and thwart its plans to dam the Jordan for irrigation.

November 2. *Prince Faisal Crowned.* The Saudi Arabian cabinet and consultative counsel proclaim Crown Prince Faisal the king of Saudi Arabia, thus dethroning King Saud.

1965

January 3. *Syria Nationalizes Industries.* Syria nationalizes, in whole or part, 107 principal industries, reportedly to stem the flow of capital from the country.

January 12. *Israel's Allies Warned.* After four days of talks in Cairo, the premiers of thirteen Arab nations issue a communiqué saying they will take joint action against nations henceforth recognizing Israel or aiding in her "aggressive military efforts." The statement is regarded as directed primarily at West Germany, which had shipped arms to Israel the previous month.

January 26. *Iranian Premier Dies of Wounds.* Premier Hassan Ali Mansour of Iran dies of gunshot wounds inflicted by a student January 21.

February 10. *Bonn Halts Military Aid to Israel.* West Germany temporarily halts military aid to Israel in the face of Arab threats to recognize the East German government if the military aid continues. Israel's parliament February 15 denounces West Germany's "surrender to blackmail."

February 17. *U.S. Approval Disclosed.* The State Department acknowledges that the United States had secretly approved the West German-Israeli military aid agreement that sent U.S.-made tanks to Israel in December 1964.

February 24. *Ulbricht Promises Aid to U.A.R.* After East German leader Walter Ulbricht arrives in Cairo despite West German protests, West Germany suspends its economic assistance to the U.A.R. and cancels its program of guarantees for private investment there. During his seven-day visit, Ulbricht agrees to provide the U.A.R. with $100 million in economic aid.

March 4. *Syria Nationalizes Oil Companies.* Syria nationalizes nine oil companies: six Syrian, two U.S. affiliates, and one joint British-Dutch company.

March 16. *Nasser Reelected.* U.A.R. President Nasser is elected to another six-year term.

April 21. *Tunisian Peace Proposal.* Tunisian President Habib Bourguiba criticizes Arab policy toward Israel and proposes broad terms to end the Arab-Israeli conflict. He calls for the opening of direct negotiations between Israel and the Palestinian Arabs on the basis of the 1947 United Nations plan for partition of Palestine into Jewish and Arab states, and for cession of one-third of Israel's territory for a Palestine Arab nation. Israel rejects Bourguiba's plan April 25. The U.A.R. rejects the proposal April 27 and "strongly denounces the issuance of such a proposal from the head of an Arab state."

May 12. *Israeli-West German Ties Established.* Israel and West Germany establish full diplomatic relations. The U.A.R. breaks diplomatic ties with West Germany. Nine other Arab states later also break ties with Bonn.

August 23. *Syrian Legislature Formed.* The Arab Socialist Ba'ath party in Syria establishes a National Council (legislature) to consolidate the party's political control. The new provisional legislature reelects Hafez as chairman of the Presidency Council, September 2.

August 24. *Agreement on Yemen.* Saudi Arabian King Faisal and U.A.R. President Nasser sign an agreement aimed at stopping the fighting in Yemen. The accord calls for an immediate halt to hostilities, for Saudi Arabia to end military aid to the royalists, and for the U.A.R. to withdraw its troop support of the revolutionary republicans. Representatives of the opposing factions had agreed August 13 to end the three-year civil war.

November 24. *Kuwaiti Emir Dies.* Kuwait's Emir al-Sabah dies and his younger brother Sabah al-Salem al-Sabah is proclaimed the new ruler.

1966

February 25. *Coup in Syria.* Following a coup February 23 by left wings of the military and of the Ba'ath party, Syria announces that the military junta in power has named Nureddin Atassi chief of state. Atassi had been ousted from office by a coup in December 1965.

April 13. *Iraqi President Killed.* Iraqi President Abdul Salem Arif dies in a helicopter crash. Maj. Gen. Abdul Rahman Arif is elected April 16 by a joint session of the cabinet and the national defense council to succeed his brother as president.

May 19. *U.S. Sells Jets to Israel.* It is reported in Washington that the United States agreed in February to sell several tactical jet bombers to Israel. This is the first such weapons sale to be disclosed.

May 25. *Hussein Begins Dam Construction.* Jordanian King Hussein lays the first stone of the Mokheiba Dam. The dam is part of an Arab effort to divert the Jordan River from Israel.

November 4. *Syria-U.A.R. Treaty.* Syria and the U.A.R. sign a mutual defense treaty that provides for joint command of their armed forces.

November 29. *Hussein Accuses Soviets.* Jordan's King Hussein charges Soviet fomentation of tension in the Middle East following a week of antigovernment demonstrations and riots.

December 7. *Syrian Calls for Hussein's Ouster.* Syrian Chief of State Atassi calls on Jordanians and Palestine Arabs to overthrow Jordan's King Hussein and offers them arms.

1967

February 19. *Iran Buys Soviet Arms.* Iran and the Soviet Union sign an agreement whereby Iran will purchase $110 million in arms and supplies.

April 20. *Iraq and Kuwait Battle.* Iraq and Kuwait call home their ambassadors as fighting erupts along their common border.

May 15. *Military Alert.* The U.A.R. alerts its military forces because of mounting tension with Israel. Syria also announces that its military forces are ready for action.

May 19. *UN Peacekeepers Withdraw.* The UN Emergency Force in the Middle East ends its patrols in the Gaza Strip and at Sharm el Sheikh at the mouth of the Gulf of Aqaba at the request of the U.A.R., ending a ten-year peacekeeping mission. The U.A.R. declares May 20 that a state of emergency exists along the Gaza Strip.

May 22. *U.A.R. Blockades Israel.* The U.A.R. closes the Strait of Tiran at the entrance to the Gulf of Aqaba to Israeli ships and to ships carrying strategic cargo bound for Israel. The United States and Israel issue warnings May 23 against the blockade. President Johnson orders the Sixth Fleet to the eastern Mediterranean. May 24 reports disclose Egypt has mined the Strait of Tiran. Egyptian and Israeli troops skirmish in the Gaza Strip, May 29.

May 23. *Jordan Closes Syrian Embassy.* Following the explosion of a bomb on the Jordan-Syria border, Jordan orders the closing of the Syrian embassy and the departure of Syria's ambassador to Jordan.

May 30. *Jordan-U.A.R. Pact.* Jordan and the U.A.R. sign a mutual defense pact.

June 5. *Six-Day War Begins.* Israeli warplanes carry out early morning surprise attacks that almost entirely destroy the air forces of Egypt, Syria, and Jordan. Israeli troops drive deep into the Sinai and engage Arab troops in Jerusalem on the first day of fighting. The UN Security Council adopts a resolution calling for an immediate cease-fire in the Middle East.

June 6-7. *Arab Responses.* In response to the Israeli attack, the U.A.R., Syria, Iraq, Sudan, Algeria, and Yemen sever diplomatic relations with the United States; Kuwait and Iraq cut off oil supplies to the United States and Britain; and the U.A.R. closes the Suez Canal, charging that U.S. and British planes are aiding Israel. The United States strongly rejects the charges.

June 7. *Israelis Capture Territory.* In a sweeping seizure of territory, Israel breaks the blockade of the Gulf of Aqaba and takes over the Old City of Jerusalem, Bethlehem in Jordan, the Sinai Peninsula between the Negev Desert and the Suez Canal, and the Gaza Strip. Israel announces it will accept the UN cease-fire resolution if the Arab states do. The cease-fire is quickly accepted by Jordan, June 7. The U.A.R. accepts the cease-fire June 8.

June 8. *U.S. Ship Attacked.* Israeli planes attack the American electronics ship *Liberty* in the Mediterranean, killing at least thirty-four. Tel Aviv says its forces mistook the *Liberty* for an Egyptian vessel, but a U.S. Navy inquiry issued July 28 says Israeli forces "had ample opportunity to identify the *Liberty* correctly." Israel apologizes and later pays the United States $3 million for the families of the dead sailors.

June 9. *Nasser's Resignation Refused.* Claiming sole responsibility for Egypt's defeat, President Nasser resigns. The National Assembly rejects his resignation.

June 10. *Soviets Cut Ties with Israel.* The Soviet Union severs diplomatic ties with Israel, pledging assistance to Arab states if Israel refuses to withdraw from conquered territory.

June 10. *Israel Captures Golan Heights.* Israeli air attacks force the Syrian army to withdraw from the strategic Golan Heights on the sixth day of the war. Israel and

Syria sign a cease-fire agreement that goes into effect that evening, bringing the war to an end.

June 12. *Israel Refuses to Withdraw.* Israel announces that it will not withdraw to the 1949 armistice boundaries and calls for direct negotiations between Israel and Arab nations.

June 19. *Johnson Peace Plan.* President Johnson, in a nationally televised speech, sets forth five points for peace in the Middle East: right of each country's national existence, fair and just treatment of Arab refugees, freedom of innocent maritime passage, limitation of arms buildup, and guaranteed territorial integrity for each Middle East country. Meanwhile at the UN, Soviet Premier Aleksei N. Kosygin calls for the condemnation of Israel, the withdrawal of Israeli forces from occupied Arab lands, and Israeli reparations to Syria, Jordan, and the U.A.R. for damages incurred during the war.

June 23. *Glassboro Summit.* President Johnson and Soviet Premier Kosygin meet for five and one-half hours at Glassboro State College in New Jersey to discuss the Middle East, Vietnam, and arms control. They meet again for more than four hours June 25, but later Johnson says that "no agreement is readily in sight on the Middle East crisis." Kosygin, at a televised news conference, says the first step to peace in the Middle East is Israel's withdrawal to 1949 armistice lines.

June 28. *Jerusalem Unified under Israelis.* Israel proclaims the merger of all of Jerusalem under Israeli rule. The action ends the de facto division of the city that had existed since the 1948 Arab-Israeli war and defies demands from other countries that the city be internationalized.

July 4. *Suez Cease-Fire.* UN Secretary General U Thant asks Israel and the U.A.R. to accept UN supervision of the cease-fire in the Suez Canal zone. The U.A.R. agrees July 10 and Israel accepts July 11.

July 17. *Israeli Conditions for Talks.* Israel tells the General Assembly that the Arab states must recognize Israel's "statehood, sovereignty, and international rights" before peace talks can begin.

September 1. *Nonmilitary Means Endorsed.* Arab heads of state, meeting in Khartoum, agree to seek a nonmilitary solution to the tensions with Israel.

September 24. *Israeli Announces Settlements.* Israel announces it will move settlers into occupied Syria and the captured Jordanian sector of Jerusalem. The United States expresses its "disappointment" with that decision September 26.

September 27. *Israeli Proposals.* Israeli foreign minister Abba Eban suggests economic cooperation between Israel, Lebanon, and Jordan, the demilitarization of the Sinai, and the establishment of a "universal status" for the "holy places" of Jerusalem.

October 22. *Israel Announces Pipeline.* Israel announces plans to build an oil pipeline between Elat on the Gulf of Aqaba and Ashdod on the Mediterranean to circumvent the Suez Canal.

November 5. *Hussein Ready to Recognize Israel.* Jordan's King Hussein tells an American television audience that his country is ready to recognize Israel's right to exist.

November 22. *Resolution 242 Adopted.* The UN Security Council unanimously adopts a British proposal (Resolution 242) for bringing peace to the Middle East. Under the plan, Israel would withdraw from conquered territory, each country would agree to recognize the territory of the other states, and free navigation through inter-

national waterways would be ensured. *(Text, Appendix, p. 301)*

November 23. *Nasser on Israel.* U.A.R. President Nasser says he will continue to deny Israeli ships access through the Suez Canal and that Israeli withdrawal from occupied lands is not open to negotiation.

November 28. *South Yemen Independence.* Britain declares the independence of South Arabia, which is renamed the People's Republic of South Yemen. British troops complete their evacuation of Aden November 29. The country had been a British colony since 1839. The new government announces the dismissal of all remaining British military and administrative officers February 27, 1968.

1968

February 15. *Israel and Jordan Battle.* Significant fighting between Jordan and Israel erupts along their common border. U.S. embassies in both states are successful in negotiating a cease-fire after eight hours of fighting. The next day, Jordan's King Hussein calls for an end to terrorist activities originating within Jordan against Israel because, he says, such raids prompt Israeli retaliation.

April 10. *Support for Palestinians.* U.A.R. President Nasser says his country is "fully prepared to support and arm the Palestine resistance movement" in its fight against Israel. Iraq April 13 announces the formation of a committee to raise funds for the Arab guerrillas.

June 1. *Martial Law in Beirut.* Martial law is proclaimed in Beirut following an unsuccessful assassination attempt on Lebanese President Chamoun.

July 5. *Israel Rejects UN Force.* Israel rejects plans for a UN peacekeeping force in the Israeli-occupied Sinai Peninsula, endorsed the day before by the U.A.R. Israeli leaders again call for direct negotiations on a peace settlement with Arab states.

July 10. *Palestine National Council Meets.* The Palestine National Council holds its first meeting, in Cairo.

July 17. *Iraqi Coup.* The fourth coup in ten years deposes Iraq's government. Ahmed Hassan al-Bakr is named president and premier July 31.

August 11. *U.A.R. Proposals.* Easing its position on a Middle East settlement, the U.A.R. says it will agree to a demilitarization of the Sinai, lift demands for the return of Arab refugees to their homeland, accept internationalization of the Gaza Strip, and grant Israeli cargoes on non-Israeli ships passage through the Suez Canal and Israeli vessels passage through the Strait of Tiran.

October 8. *Israeli Peace Plan.* Israeli Foreign Minister Eban offers a nine-point peace plan at the United Nations. The proposal calls for Israeli withdrawal from occupied territory following the establishment of "permanent" boundaries between the Arab states and Israel. The U.A.R. rejects the plan October 9 but agrees October 10 to accept a UN timetable for implementing UN Security Council Resolution 242.

December 2. *Jordan and Israel Battle.* Jordanian and Israeli troops clash in heavy fighting. After a predawn Jordanian artillery attack December 3, Israeli jets strike Jordanian targets.

December 5. *Hussein Calls for Arab Unity.* Jordan's King Hussein sends messages to the U.A.R., Saudi Arabia, Iran, Kuwait, and Lebanon calling for unified action to liberate Arab lands.

December 9. *Scranton Statement.* President-elect Richard Nixon's special envoy to the Middle East, William Scranton, tells reporters that he believes U.S. policy in the area should be more "even-handed."

December 28. *Israelis Destroy Planes.* In retaliation for an attack by two Arabs on a loaded Israeli airliner December 26 at the Athens airport that resulted in the death of one passenger, an Israeli task force attacks the Beirut International Airport, destroying thirteen unoccupied Arab airliners. On December 31 the UN Security Council unanimously condemns Israel for the attack.

1969

February 2. *Nasser Interview. Newsweek* magazine publishes an exclusive interview with U.A.R. President Nasser who suggests a five-point peace plan for the Middle East: "a declaration of non-belligerence; the recognition of the right of each country to live in peace; the territorial integrity of all countries in the Middle East, including Israel, within recognized and secure borders; freedom of navigation on international waterways; a just solution to the Palestinian refugee problem." Israel rejects Nasser's plan February 4.

February 26. *Eshkol Dies.* Prime Minister Levi Eshkol of Israel dies following a heart attack. Foreign Minister Golda Meir accepts election as leader of the Labor party March 7 and thereby becomes premier.

April 10. *Hussein Peace Plan.* In Washington for talks with President Nixon, Jordan's King Hussein addresses the National Press Club and sets forth a six-point peace plan that he says has U.A.R. President Nasser's approval. Similar to UN Resolution 242, the plan is contingent upon Israeli withdrawal from occupied lands. Israel rejects the plan the following day as propaganda.

April 22. *Israeli-Egyptian Conflict.* UN Secretary General U Thant says that Israel and Egypt are engaged in "a virtual state of active war" and declares that the UN cease-fire has become "totally ineffective in the Suez Canal sector." The U.A.R. April 23 repudiates the UN cease-fire, contending that Israeli forces had not advanced to their present position on the eastern bank of the canal when the cease-fire was adopted in 1967.

July 20. *Israeli Air Attacks.* After two weeks of sporadic fighting along the Suez Canal, Israeli jets attack U.A.R. ground installations.

August 3. *Israel to Keep Territory.* Israel announces that to protect its security it will retain the Golan Heights, the Gaza Strip, and part of the Sinai Peninsula.

August 21. *Al Aqsa Mosque Fire.* A fire damages the Al Aqsa Mosque in Jerusalem, one of Islam's holiest shrines. Israeli authorities arrest Michael Rohan, an Australian tourist, and charge him with setting the blaze. Arabs in the occupied territories discount the arrest and hold a general strike August 23 to protest Israel's failure to prevent the fire. The same day U.A.R. President Nasser charges Israel with responsibility for the fire and calls for an all-out war with Israel to restore Arab control over Jerusalem and its holy sites. The mosque reopens September 19 after repairs are completed. Rohan pleads guilty at his arson trial in Israel October 7.

August 31. *TWA Hijacking.* Arab hijackers blow up a TWA airliner after diverting it to Damascus following takeoff from Rome. The hijackers demand imprisonment

of all the Israeli passengers, but Syria releases all but six Israelis August 30. Those six are held hostage for the release of Syrian prisoners of war in Israel.

September 1. *Idris Overthrown.* Libya's King Idris is overthrown by a revolutionary council. The council, on September 2, says it will honor existing agreements with oil companies. Muammar al-Qaddafi, head of the Revolutionary Command Council, emerges as leader of the regime.

September 18. *Nixon Proposes Arms Curb.* President Nixon addresses the UN General Assembly, suggesting an arms curb in the Middle East by the big powers. The Soviet Union rebuffs the suggestion September 19.

October 22. *Gulf Federation Established.* The nine-nation Federation of Persian Gulf Emirates is established with Zayed ibn Sultan al-Nahayan of Abu Dhabi as president.

October 28. *Libya Orders U.S. Withdrawal.* The new military regime in Libya notifies the United States that Wheelus Air Base, near Tripoli, must be evacuated by December 24, 1970. The United States formally relinquishes the base on June 11, 1970.

December 9. *U.S. Peace Proposal.* Secretary of State William Rogers discloses a previously secret U.S. proposal for Middle East peace, including a provision for Israel's withdrawal from occupied lands in exchange for a binding peace treaty signed by the Arabs. Israeli Premier Golda Meir says December 12 that the plan is an attempt by the United States to "moralize."

1970

January 16. *Qaddafi Becomes Premier.* Muammar al-Qaddafi, leader of the Revolutionary Command Council, becomes premier and defense minister of Libya, succeeding Mahmoud Soliman al-Maghreby.

January 21. *Arabs and Israelis Battle.* Israel, launching its largest ground operation since June 1967, captures the Egyptian island of Shadwan at the entrance of the Gulf of Suez. The heaviest fighting between Israel and Syria since the June 1967 war breaks out in the Golan Heights February 2.

April 14. *Yemen War Ends.* The civil war in Yemen between republican and royalist forces ends. Saudi Arabia signs an agreement with the republican regime, pledging to discontinue the arms and funds it has supplied to royalist rebels since the outbreak of hostilities in 1962.

May 9. *Israeli Warning.* Responding to an apparent infusion of Soviet troops and antiaircraft missiles into Egypt, Israel warns that the installation of Soviet SAM-3 missiles along the Suez Canal will not be permitted. It threatens to attack Soviet planes if they interfere with Israeli attacks on Egyptian bases.

June 24. *Soviets Flying Combat Missions.* Foreign intelligence reports received in Washington indicate that Soviet pilots have taken over the air defense of Egypt against Israel and are flying combat missions south of the Suez Canal.

June 25. *Cease-Fire Proposal.* Secretary of State Rogers tells a news conference in Washington of a broad-based diplomatic effort to encourage Arab and Israeli representatives "to stop shooting and start talking" under UN supervision. The heart of the proposal is a ninety-day cease-fire tied to withdrawal of Israeli forces from territory occupied during the June 1967 war. Israeli Prime Minister

Meir rejects the plan June 29.

July 5. *Libya Nationalizes Oil Distributors.* Libya's Revolutionary Command Council announces nationalization of that country's four oil distributing companies.

July 23. *U.A.R. Accepts Cease-Fire.* The U.A.R. accepts a U.S. proposal calling for a ninety-day cease-fire in the Middle East. Jordan accepts the proposal July 26. One of the terms of the cease-fire requires Jordan to control guerrilla activities organized within its borders. Yasir Arafat, head of the Palestine Liberation Organization (PLO), rejects a cease-fire and all other compromise solutions to the conflict with Israel July 31.

August 4. *Israel Accepts Cease-Fire.* Israel formally accepts the Middle East cease-fire. Israeli Prime Minister Meir tells the Israeli parliament that she agreed to accept the proposal after assurances of military and political support from President Nixon. The cease-fire goes into effect August 7.

September 1. *Hussein Escapes Assassination.* The motorcade of Jordan's King Hussein is fired upon by unidentified gunmen in Amman. The assailants escape and the king is not injured. The attack follows several days of hostilities between Jordanian army troops and Palestinian guerrillas and causes the fighting to intensify.

September 6. *PFLP Hijackings.* Members of the Popular Front for the Liberation of Palestine (PFLP), a member organization of the PLO, are successful in three of four attempts to hijack commercial jets. A Pan Am 747 is forced to land in Cairo, passengers are disembarked, and the plane is blown up. A Swissair jet and a TWA jet are forced to land at a desert airstrip in Jordan controlled by the PFLP. The use of the Jordanian airstrip is regarded as a direct challenge to King Hussein's authority by the Palestinian hijackers. The next day, the PFLP releases nearly half of the passengers from the planes brought down in the desert. It demands the release of Arab guerrillas held in Israel and Western Europe in exchange for the remaining hostages. The seizure of a fourth plane, an Israeli passenger jet bound from Amsterdam to New York, was thwarted by security guards aboard the aircraft.

September 9. *Hijacking Continues.* Members of the PFLP seize a fifth plane, a British BOAC jet, and hijack it to Jordan to join the two other planes in the desert. Hostages total nearly 300. The PFLP releases all but 54 of its hostages September 12 and blows up the three empty airplanes. Britain announces it will release an Arab commando seized in an aborted hijack effort September 6.

September 16. *Hussein Proclaims Martial Law.* Jordanian King Hussein proclaims martial law and installs a military government in response to continued fighting between his army and Palestinian guerrillas. The move precipitates open civil war between Jordanian troops and Palestinian forces. Thousands of military and civilian casualties are reported during the following weeks. In Amman, where the fighting is heaviest, the government enforces an around-the-clock curfew that leaves many residents without food or water. President Nixon indicates September 17 that the United States would intervene if the Jordanian government were threatened by outside powers.

September 18. *Meir-Nixon Meeting.* Israeli Prime Minister Meir meets with President Nixon in Washington and says Israel will not participate in the UN peace talks until Egypt removes new missile installations along the Suez Canal.

September 19. *Jordanian Civil War.* A Syrian column enters northern Jordan September 19 in support of the Palestinian guerrillas. With Syrian help the guerrillas gain control of much of northern Lebanon by September 21. U.S. forces in the Mediterranean are reinforced September 20 in preparation for a possible intervention. The U.S. government reports September 22 that the Soviet Union has said it has asked Syria to withdraw its forces from Jordan. Jordanian tanks and planes push Syrian tanks out of northern Jordan September 23.

September 25. *Cease-Fire.* The Jordanian government and the leaders of the Palestinian guerrillas agree to a cease-fire. Sporadic fighting continues in Amman, but the cease-fire effectively ends fighting between major units. King Hussein appoints a new civilian-military government to replace the military government appointed September 16.

September 27. *Jordanian-Palestinian Pact.* A fourteen-point agreement is signed in Cairo by Arab heads of state—including Jordan's King Hussein and PLO leader Yasir Arafat—to end hostilities in Jordan. The agreement calls for King Hussein to remain on the throne, but for a three-member committee, headed by Tunisian Premier Ladgham, to supervise the government until conditions are normalized. Arab leaders also pledge to support the Palestinian struggle against Israel.

September 28. *Nasser Dies.* U.A.R. President Gamal Abdel Nasser, 52, dies suddenly of a heart attack. Anwar Sadat is sworn in as president of the U.A.R. October 17, following an October 15 election in which he receives 90 percent of the vote.

September 29. *Hostages Released.* Palestinian commandos release the last hostages held since several planes were hijacked earlier in the month. Forty-eight others had been released September 25. Switzerland announces that a total of nineteen Arabs will be released by Britain, West Germany, Switzerland, and Israel.

November 4. *Cease-Fire Extended.* The UN General Assembly votes for a ninety-day extension of the Middle East cease-fire and for unconditional resumption of the peace talks between Arab states and Israel.

November 13. *Syrian Coup.* Syrian President and Premier Nureddin al-Atassi is reported to have been placed under house arrest. "Provisional leadership" will guide the government until a national congress can elect permanent leaders.

1971

January 15. *Aswan Dam Dedicated.* U.A.R. President Sadat and Soviet President Nikolai V. Podgornyi dedicate the Aswan Dam.

March 12. *Israeli Position.* Golda Meir, stating Israel's position on a Middle East settlement, calls for demilitarization of the Sinai, Israeli possession of Jerusalem, and Israeli retention of Sharm el Sheik, Israel's sole land link with East Africa and Asia.

March 13. *Assad Becomes President.* Premier Hafez al-Assad is proclaimed president of Syria.

April 3. *Fighting in Jordan Continues.* Amid continued Palestinian guerrilla activity in Jordan, King Hussein says the guerrillas must remove their weapons from Amman within two days. The commandos have said they will stay in Amman and continue their fight to overthrow Hussein and to use Jordan as a base for operations against Israel.

April 17. *Federation Agreement Signed.* Egypt, Syria, and Libya sign an agreement to form the Federation of Arab Republics. Plebiscites will be held September 1 in the three countries to gain popular approval for the union.

May 27. *U.A.R.-Soviet Treaty.* U.A.R. President Sadat and Soviet President Podgornyi sign a fifteen-year treaty of friendship and cooperation. The U.A.R. and the Soviet Union issue a joint communiqué July 4, declaring that the Suez Canal will be opened only after Israel withdraws all of its forces from Arab territory.

August 12. *Syria-Jordan Rift.* Syria breaks off diplomatic relations with Jordan following clashes on their common border.

August 14. *Jordanian Demand.* Jordan demands the end of economic pressures exerted by other Arab states as a condition for Jordan's efforts to resolve hostilities between its army and Palestinian commandos.

September 2. *Citizens Favor Federation.* Citizens of Egypt, Libya, and Syria vote almost unanimously in favor of the proposed Federation of Arab Republics that is intended to provide a solid front against Israel.

October 4. *Sadat Chosen Federation President.* Egyptian President Sadat is selected as the first president of the Federation of Arab Republics.

October 4. *U.S. Peace Plan.* Secretary of State Rogers presents a detailed account of the U.S. position on the Middle East. He calls on Israel and Egypt to agree to open the Suez Canal as a first step toward peace in the area. Egypt rejects the proposal October 6, lacking assurances of Israeli withdrawal from Arab lands.

November 1. *Israel Links Jets to Talks.* Israel says it will not agree to the U.S. proposal for indirect talks with Egypt without U.S. guarantees of a continuing supply of Phantom jets.

November 28. *Wasfi al-Tal Assassinated.* Jordanian premier Wasfi al-Tal is assassinated while visiting Cairo. Ahmed al-Lawzi succeeds him as premier November 29. The Jordanian government December 17 formally charges the Palestinian guerrilla group Al Fatah with responsibility for the slaying.

November 30. *Iranians Occupy Islands.* Iranian troops occupy the Iraqi territory of Abu Musa, Greater Tunb, and Lesser Tunb, all in Persian Gulf waters near the Strait of Hormuz. Iraq severs relations with Iran and Britain as a result.

December 2. *U.A.E. Proclaims Independence.* The United Arab Emirates proclaims its independence. Zayed ibn Sultan al-Nahayan of Abu Dhabi is named president of the union, which consists of six Persian Gulf sheikdoms. Ras al-Khaimah becomes the seventh sheikdom to join the union February 11.

1972

January 5. *Bahrain Base Agreement.* The United States announces an agreement with Bahrain for the establishment of a U.S. naval base in the Persian Gulf.

March 15. *Hussein Plan.* Jordanian King Hussein unveils his plan to make Jordan a federated state comprised of two autonomous regions on the East and West Bank of the Jordan River. Hussein proposes Jerusalem as the capital of the West Bank, or Palestine, region. Israel, the same day, denounces the plan. The Federation of Arab Republics denounces the plan March 18 and calls on all

Arab governments to similarly reject it. Egypt severs diplomatic relations with Jordan April 6, criticizing Hussein's proposal.

May 8. *Hijacked Jet Rescued.* Four Palestinians, later identified as members of the Black September organization, seize a Belgian airliner after leaving Vienna en route to Tel Aviv. Israeli troops break into the plane at Lod Airport in Tel Aviv May 9, killing two of four Palestinian commandos and rescuing all ninety passengers and ten crew members.

May 30. *Lod Airport Massacre.* Three left-wing Japanese terrorists attack the Lod International Airport near Tel Aviv with hand grenades and automatic weapons. They kill twenty-six people and wound at least seventy-five others. Two of the three terrorists are killed and the third is captured. The Popular Front for the Liberation of Palestine headquartered in Beirut says it recruited the killers and takes responsibility for the attack.

June 1. *Iraq Petroleum Nationalized.* Iraq nationalizes the Iraq Petroleum Company, owned jointly by American, British, French, and Dutch oil companies. The company produces 10 percent of Middle East oil.

July 18. *Sadat Expels Soviets.* Egyptian President Sadat orders all Soviet military advisers out of his country and places all Soviet bases and equipment under Egyptian control. Sadat says July 24 during a four-hour speech that the Soviet Union's "excessive caution" as an ally led him to his decision.

August 2. *Libyan-Egyptian Unity.* Libyan leader Qaddafi and Egyptian President Sadat jointly declare their intention to establish "unified political leadership."

September 5. *Olympic Hostage Crisis.* Eight Arab commandos of the Black September organization seize a building housing the Israeli team at the Olympic Games in Munich, West Germany. Two Israelis are killed immediately, and nine are taken hostage. After day-long negotiations, the Arabs and their hostages are flown by helicopter to a Munich airport, where West German police engage the Arabs in a gun battle. All nine of the Israeli hostages, five of the Arabs, and one West German police officer are killed. The remaining three Arabs are wounded and captured. In response Israel launches September 8 the most extensive air raids on Arab guerrilla bases in Syria and Lebanon since the June 1967 war.

September 13. *Soviet-Syrian Agreement.* Syria and the Soviet Union agree to security arrangements. The Soviets will improve naval facilities in two Syrian ports for Soviet use and Syria will receive jet fighters and air defense missiles.

September 18. *Unification Progress.* Egyptian President Sadat and Libyan leader Qaddafi, taking a step toward unification, agree to make Cairo the capital of their projected unified state, to popularly elect one president, and to allow one political party.

September 19. *Terrorist Attacks.* A letter bomb, believed to have been sent by the Black September organization, explodes in the Israeli embassy in London, killing the Israeli agricultural counselor. Similar terrorist activities in the next two days are blamed on the Black September group.

October 15. *Israel Launches Attack.* Israel, launching its first unprovoked attack on Palestinian guerrilla bases in Syria and Lebanon, says "we are no longer waiting for them to hit first."

October 28. *Yemen Accord.* Ending several weeks of heavy fighting, Yemen and South Yemen sign an accord in

Cairo calling for their merger.

October 29. *Hijacking of West German Plane.* Two Arab guerrillas of the Black September organization hijack a West German airliner, forcing the release of three commandos held in the September 5 murder of eleven Israeli athletes at the Olympic Games. Israel protests the German action, calling it "capitulation to terrorists."

November 1. *Soviets to Restore Missiles.* It is reported that the Soviet Union will restore missiles to Egypt's air defense system that were removed when the Soviets were ousted by the government in July.

November 27. *Hussein Confirms Coup Attempt.* Jordanian King Hussein confirms reports of an aborted coup to overthrow him, planned by Libyan leader Muammar Qaddafi, PLO leader Yasir Arafat, and other Palestinians.

1973

February 21. *Israel Downs Airliner.* A Libyan passenger airliner, reportedly failing to heed Israeli instructions to land after straying over Israeli-occupied Sinai, is fired upon and crashes, killing 106 persons. Israel assumes no responsibility for the crash and instead blames the airline pilot for not landing and Cairo air controllers for misguidance.

March 14. *Israeli Shrine Offer.* Golda Meir offers Jordan guardianship of the Islamic shrines in the Old City of Jerusalem.

July 20. *Japan Air Lines Hijacking.* Arab and Japanese hijackers seize a Japan Air Lines jet and demand the release of a Japanese man serving a life sentence for taking part in the May 1972 massacre of twenty-six persons at the Tel Aviv airport. The hijackers blow up the plane July 24 at Libya's Benghazi airport after the passengers and crew are evacuated. The hijackers are arrested by Libyan officials.

August 5. *Athens Attack.* Two Black September guerrillas kill three persons and wound another fifty-five after firing machine guns and hurling grenades in the Athens airport.

August 11. *Israelis Divert Plane.* Israel forces a Middle East Airlines jet, flying over Lebanon, to land in Israel. Israel announces it diverted the wrong plane in its search for the leader of the Popular Front for the Liberation of Palestine, the group held responsible by Israel for the slayings in the Athens airport.

August 29. *Libya, Egypt Pursue Gradual Unity.* Libyan leader Qaddafi and Egyptian President Sadat announce the "birth of a new unified Arab state" and a gradual approach to unification of their countries. Egypt had insisted on gradual unification instead of completion of the union by September 1, 1973, as originally agreed.

October 6. *Arab-Israeli War Begins.* War breaks out on the Jewish holy day of Yom Kippur. Egyptian forces cross the Suez Canal and establish a bridgehead on the Israeli-held eastern bank. Syria attacks Israeli positions in the Golan Heights. UN observers report that the Egyptian and Syrian armies initiated the hostilities.

October 7. *Fighting Continues.* Israeli forces counterattack in the Sinai and on the Golan Heights. Fierce fighting leaves hundreds of Arab and Israeli soldiers dead. Iraq nationalizes the American-owned Mobil Oil and Exxon corporations in retaliation for U.S. support of Israel.

October 8. *Arab Support.* Tunisia, the Sudan, and Iraq pledge support of Egyptian and Syrian forces battling Israel.

October 10. *Israeli Retreat.* Israel acknowledges it has abandoned its Bar-Lev defense line near the Suez Canal. The Egyptian offensive has forced the Israelis to withdraw about ten miles from the canal. Israel also says its forces in the Golan Heights have turned back the Syrian advance and crossed the 1967 cease-fire line.

October 12. *Israelis Advance in Syria.* Israeli forces advance to within eighteen miles of Damascus.

October 13. *Jordan, Saudi Arabia Join Fight.* Jordan announces it will join Egypt and Syria in the war against Israel. Saudi Arabian troops also participate after urging by Egyptian President Sadat. The same day, Israel claims to have nearly eliminated an Iraqi division in Syria.

October 15. *U.S. Resupply Effort.* The United States announces it is resupplying Israel with military equipment to counterbalance a "massive airlift" to Egypt by the Soviet Union. In the Sinai, Israeli detachments cross to the western bank of the canal and establish a bridgehead while the main Egyptian and Israeli forces continue to fight on the eastern side of the canal.

October 17. *Sadat Proposes Cease-Fire.* Egyptian President Sadat, in an open letter to President Nixon, proposes an immediate cease-fire on the condition that Israel withdraws to pre-1967 boundaries. The same day, foreign ministers of four Arab states meet in Washington with President Nixon and Secretary of State Henry Kissinger to present a similar peace proposal. Meanwhile, a major battle erupts between Egyptian and Israeli tank units on both sides of the Suez Canal.

October 18. *Arab Oil Strategy.* Saudi Arabia announces a 10 percent cut in oil production and pledges to cut off all U.S. oil shipments if American support of Israel continues. The day before, OPEC ministers meeting in Kuwait agreed to reduce oil production by 5 percent each month until Israel withdraws from the occupied territories and agrees to respect the rights of the Palestinians.

October 19. *Nixon Asks for Aid to Israel.* President Nixon asks Congress to appropriate $2.2 billion for emergency military aid for Israel. Libya cuts off all oil exports to the United States and raises the price of oil from $4.90 to $8.92 per barrel. Saudi Arabia halts oil exports to the United States October 20.

October 20. *Kissinger-Brezhnev Talks.* Secretary of State Kissinger arrives in Moscow for talks with Soviet Communist party chief Leonid I. Brezhnev on restoring peace to the Middle East.

October 21. *Arab Oil Embargo.* Kuwait, Qatar, Bahrain, and Dubai announce suspension of all oil exports to the United States, theoretically marking the total cutoff of all oil from Arab states to the United States.

October 21. *UN Cease-Fire Resolution.* The United States and the Soviet Union present a joint resolution to the UN Security Council calling for a cease-fire in the Middle East and Israeli withdrawal from lands occupied since the 1967 war. The proposal, known as Resolution 338, was formulated during Kissinger's trip to Moscow. It is, adopted by the Security Council early October 22. That day a cease-fire takes effect on the Egyptian-Israeli front, but fighting continues nonetheless. Jordan accepts the U.S.-Soviet cease-fire proposal. Iraq and the Palestinian Liberation Organization reject it.

October 23. *Egyptian III Corps Cut Off.* Egypt and Israel accuse each other of cease-fire violations as heavy fighting resumes on the canal front. Israeli forces on the canal's western bank push south to cut off both the city of Suez and the 20,000-troop Egyptian III Corps on the eastern bank. The UN Security Council votes to reaffirm the Middle East cease-fire, asks Egypt and Israel to return to the cease-fire line established the day before, and asks that UN observers be stationed along the Israeli-Egyptian cease-fire line.

October 24. *Sadat Appeal.* President Sadat appeals for the United States and the Soviet Union to send troops to supervise the cease-fire. The White House announces it will not send forces.

October 25. *U.S. Military Alert.* President Nixon orders a worldwide U.S. military alert as tension mounts over whether the Soviet Union may intervene in the Middle East crisis. Kissinger says there are "ambiguous" indications of that action. To avert a U.S.-Soviet confrontation in the Middle East, the UN Security Council votes to establish an emergency supervisory force to observe the cease-fire. The force would exclude troops from the permanent Security Council members, particularly the United States and the Soviet Union.

October 27. *Egypt and Israel to Talk.* The United States announces that Egypt and Israel have agreed to negotiate directly on implementing the cease-fire.

October 28. *III Corps Receives Supplies.* The trapped Egyptian III Corps receives food, water, and medical supplies after Israel agrees to allow a supply convoy to pass through Israeli lines. It is reported that Israel yielded following U.S. warnings that the Soviet Union threatened to rescue the troops. Israeli sources concede that on October 23 their units drove to the port of Adabiya to isolate the III Corps.

October 29. *Syria Accepts Cease-Fire.* Syrian President Assad says Syria has accepted the cease-fire after receiving Soviet guarantees of Israel's withdrawal from all occupied territory and recognition of Palestinian rights.

October 31. *Meir in Washington.* Israeli Prime Minister Golda Meir arrives in Washington for talks with President Nixon on her country's concern over U.S. pressure to make concessions. The same day, Egyptian President Sadat warns that his country will take up the fight again if Israel does not withdraw to the cease-fire lines of October 22, 1973. Meir says November 1 that she has been assured of continued U.S. support.

November 7. *U.S., Egypt Agree to Restore Ties.* After talks between Kissinger and Sadat, it is announced that Egypt and the United States will resume diplomatic relations. Ties are resumed February 28, 1974.

November 11. *Cease-Fire Signed.* Israel and Egypt sign a cease-fire accord, drawn up by Kissinger and Sadat. The six-point plan calls for: both sides to observe the cease-fire; immediate discussions on returning to the October 22 cease-fire lines; immediate food and medical supplies for Suez City; immediate nonmilitary supplies to the stranded Egyptian III Corps on the eastern bank of the Suez Canal; replacement of Israeli troops along the Suez by UN forces; and exchange of all prisoners of war. The cease-fire is the first important document signed by the two parties since the 1949 armistice agreement. The first planeloads of Egyptian and Israeli POWs are exchanged November 15.

November 18. *Arabs Cancel Output Cut.* The Organization of Arab Petroleum Exporting Countries (OAPEC) cancels its 5 percent output cut slated for December in a conciliatory gesture to most West European nations. The embargo against the Netherlands and the United States

continues because of their pro-Israeli stance. Saudi Arabia threatens November 22 to cut oil production by 80 percent if the United States retaliates for Arab oil cuts or embargoes.

November 26. *Arab Conference.* A conference of Arab heads of state opens in Algeria. Fifteen Arab leaders declare November 28 that Middle East peace is conditional on Israeli withdrawal from "all occupied Arab territories."

December 21. *Geneva Conference.* The first Arab-Israeli peace conference opens in Geneva. Israel, Egypt, Jordan, the United States, the Soviet Union, and the United Nations are represented. Syria boycotts the conference.

December 25. *Oil Production Increase.* The Saudi Arabian oil minister, speaking for the OAPEC countries, announces the cancellation of a further 5 percent oil production cut and instead discloses a 10 percent production increase. The U.S. oil embargo will continue, however.

December 31. *Israeli Election.* Israel holds general elections, resulting in a loss of parliamentary seats for Prime Minister Meir's Labor-led coalition. A governmental crisis begins that extends into the spring of 1974 as Meir seeks unsuccessfully to form a government.

1974

January 17. *Suez Disengagement.* Secretary of State Kissinger's "shuttle diplomacy" results in announcement of accords on Suez disengagement. The accords are signed January 18. The chief provisions are: Israel is to abandon its western bank bridgehead and to withdraw on the eastern bank about twenty miles from the canal; Egypt is to keep a limited force on the eastern bank; a UN truce force is to patrol the buffer zone between the two; the pullback is to be completed in forty days. Sadat says he will press Syria to open talks with Israel. Israeli forces begin the Suez pullback January 25. By January 28 the withdrawal lifts the siege of the city of Suez and ends the isolation of the Egyptian III Corps.

February 28. *U.S., Egypt Renew Ties.* The United States and Egypt renew full diplomatic relations after a seven-year break. President Sadat announces he has invited President Nixon to visit Egypt.

March 4. *Israel Completes Pullback.* Israel completes its Suez front pullback, restoring to Egypt control of both banks of the canal for the first time since the 1967 war.

March 10. *Israeli Cabinet Formed.* A nine-week political crisis ends in Israel with the formation of a new cabinet, including Moshe Dayan as defense minister. He had wanted the right-wing Likud party included in the coalition, a move repeatedly rejected by Prime Minister Meir.

March 18. *Arabs Lift Oil Embargo.* After a joint meeting in Vienna, Saudi Arabia, Algeria, Egypt, Kuwait, Abu Dhabi, Bahrain, and Qatar lift a five-month oil embargo against the United States. Libya and Syria refuse to join in the decision.

April 10. *Meir Resigns as Prime Minister.* Golda Meir quits the Israel premiership in an intraparty squabble over where to put the blame for military shortcomings in the October war.

April 23. *Rabin Asked to Form Government.* Labor party leader Yitzhak Rabin is asked to form a new Israeli government by President Ephraim Katzir.

April 29. *Kissinger Diplomacy.* Meeting in Geneva, Secretary of State Kissinger and Foreign Minister Gromyko pledge U.S.-Soviet cooperation in seeking a troop separation accord on the Syrian-Israeli front. The next day Kissinger in Cairo begins a month-long quest to end the Golan Heights confrontation.

May 15. *Maalot Crisis.* In a schoolhouse battle at the Israeli town of Maalot, sixteen teen-agers are killed and seventy are wounded after three Arab guerrillas seize the school and demand the release of twenty-three prisoners held by Israel. The Arabs are slain when Israeli soldiers attack the school. Israel initiates a week-long series of raids May 16 in reply to the Maalot tragedy. Planes and gunboats hit Palestinian camps and hideouts in Lebanon, killing at least sixty-one persons.

May 29. *Israeli-Syrian Disengagement.* Syria and Israel agree on a disengagement. The accords, achieved by Kissinger in his latest round of "shuttle diplomacy," are signed in Geneva May 31. Israel and Syria accept a separation of forces, a UN-policed buffer zone, and a gradual reduction of forces. Israel returns 382 Arab prisoners June 6 to Syria, which hands over 56 Israeli POWs. Israeli withdrawal from the buffer zone is completed June 23.

June 12-18. *Nixon Middle East Tour.* During a Middle East tour, President Nixon signs a friendship accord with Egyptian President Sadat June 14. The United States promises Egypt nuclear technology for peaceful purposes. In Damascus June 16, Syrian President Assad and Nixon restore full U.S.-Syrian diplomatic relations that were broken in the 1967 war. In Israel June 17 Nixon says the United States and Israel will cooperate in nuclear energy, and the United States will supply nuclear fuel "under agreed safeguards."

August 7. *Sadat-Qaddafi Dispute.* Egyptian President Sadat blames Libyan President Qaddafi for plots against Sadat and for the recall of Libya's Mirage jets loaned to Egypt. The two leaders meet August 18 in an attempt to settle the dispute.

September 21. *PLO Declared Sole Representative.* Meeting in Cairo, the Palestine Liberation Organization, Egypt, and Syria declare the PLO to be the sole representative of the Palestinian people.

October 12. *Israelis Demonstrate.* About eight thousand Israelis in Jerusalem demonstrate in opposition to the surrender of any West Bank land to Jordan as Kissinger arrives on a new Middle East peace-seeking mission.

October 13. *Kissinger-Faisal Talks.* After talks with King Faisal, Kissinger tells reporters he has assurances that Saudi Arabia will take "constructive steps" to lower the world price of oil.

October 14. *PLO Invited to UN Debate.* The UN General Assembly overwhelmingly passes a resolution inviting the PLO to take part in its debate on the Palestine question. Israel denounces the UN vote October 15.

October 28. *Rabat Summit.* The twenty Arab League heads of state in a summit meeting at Rabat, Morocco, unanimously recognize the PLO as the "sole legitimate representative of the Palestinian people on any liberated Palestinian territory." Jordan's King Hussein agrees to honor the PLO's claim to negotiate for the West Bank.

November 4. *Hussein on West Bank.* King Hussein says Jordan will rewrite its constitution to exclude the West Bank from Jordan and that it is "totally inconceivable" that Jordan and a Palestinian state could form a federation.

November 13. *Arafat at UN.* Addressing the UN General Assembly, Yasir Arafat says the PLO's goal is "one democratic [Palestinian] state where Christian, Jew, and Moslem live in justice, equality, and fraternity." In rebuttal, Israeli delegate Yosef Tekoah asserts the Arafat proposal would mean the destruction of Israel and its replacement by an Arab state.

November 20. *UNESCO Cuts Off Aid to Israel.* The United Nations Educational, Scientific, and Cultural Organization (UNESCO) votes 64-27 in Paris to cut off annual financial aid to Israel because of its "persistence in altering the historical features of Jerusalem."

November 22. *UN Resolution on the PLO.* The UN General Assembly approves a resolution recognizing the right of the Palestinian people to independence and sovereignty and giving the PLO observer status at the UN.

December 1. *Katzir on Atomic Weapons.* Israeli President Ephraim Katzir says Israel has the capacity to produce atomic weapons and will do so if needed.

December 31. *Libyan Embargo Ends.* The *Times* (London) reports Libya has quietly ended its fourteen-month-old oil embargo against the United States.

1975

January 2. *Kissinger Interview.* In a *Business Week* interview, Kissinger warns that the United States might use force in the Middle East "to prevent the strangulation of the industrialized world" by Arab oil producers. His remarks arouse angry world reaction.

January 6. *Lebanon Charges Israeli Aggression.* At the UN, Lebanon charges Israel with 423 acts of aggression in the past month. These include border crossings made by Israel to wipe out guerrilla forces in southern Lebanon.

January 23. *Israelis Buy Missiles.* The Pentagon announces the Israeli purchase of two hundred Lance missiles, to be armed with conventional warheads but capable of carrying nuclear ones. Israel also asks for $2 billion in U.S. military and economic aid.

February 18. *Shah Offers Oil to Israel.* The shah of Iran says he will send additional oil to Israel if Israel cedes Abu Rudeis oil fields to Egypt in a general peace settlement. His offer comes after a meeting with Kissinger, who visited several Middle East countries seeking "a framework for new negotiations."

February 21. *UN Commission Condemns Israel.* The UN Commission on Human Rights adopts resolutions condemning Israel for carrying out the "deliberate destruction" of Quenitra, a Syrian city in the Golan Heights, and for "desecrating" Moslem and Christian shrines.

March 5. *Palestinians Seize Hotel.* Eighteen persons, including six non-Israeli tourists, are slain when eight Palestinian guerrillas seize a shorefront hotel in Tel Aviv. Israeli troops kill seven attackers and capture the other.

March 5. *Iran-Iraq Agreement.* Iraq and Iran agree to end their longstanding dispute over frontiers, navigational claims, and Iranian supply of the Kurdish rebellion in northern Iraq. Two days later Baghdad launches a major military offensive against the Kurds, who seek total autonomy.

March 22. *Kissinger Suspends Peace Efforts.* Kissinger suspends his efforts to draw Israel and Egypt into new accords, calling the breakdown "a sad day for America."

March 22. *Kurdish Rebellion Fails.* The Kurdish rebellion collapses in Iraq. Rebel leader Mustafa al-Barzani flees to Iran.

March 25. *Faisal Assassinated.* Saudi King Faisal is shot to death by his nephew, Prince Faisal ibn Musaed. Crown Prince Khalid becomes king. Prince Fahd is named heir apparent. The royal family claims the assassin is deranged and acted alone. Prince Faisal is beheaded June 18.

May 28. *Karami Becomes Premier.* Rashid Karami is appointed Lebanese premier May 28, promising to end the bloody Christian-Moslem strife over the Palestinian refugee question. Karami replaces Rashid al-Solh, who resigned under criticism of his handling of riots in April.

June 2. *Ford-Sadat Meeting.* President Gerald R. Ford holds a two-day conference with Egyptian President Sadat in Salzburg, Austria. During the parley, Israel orders a partial withdrawal of its forces in the Sinai in response to a reopening of the Suez Canal. Sadat cautiously hails the Israeli gesture as a step toward peace.

June 5. *Suez Canal Reopens.* The Suez Canal reopens after an eight-year closure to commercial shipping. President Sadat leads a ceremonial convoy of ships through the waterway to mark the opening.

June 11. *Rabin in Washington.* Israeli Premier Yitzhak Rabin begins five days of talks in Washington with President Ford and Secretary of State Kissinger. They agree on renewing efforts to negotiate another limited Israeli-Egyptian accord in the Sinai.

July 1. *Beirut Truce.* After ten days of fighting in Beirut, during which at least 280 persons are killed, a truce is proclaimed. Premier Rashid Karami forms a "rescue cabinet," which includes all major Moslem and Christian groups except the warring Moslem Progressive Socialists and Christian Phalangists.

July 7. *Sadat Releases Prisoners.* President Sadat releases two thousand prisoners convicted of trying to overthrow the late president Nasser, as a wave of anti-Nasser commentary runs through the Egyptian press.

August 21. *Shuttle Diplomacy.* Secretary of State Kissinger arrives in Israel to begin a new round of shuttle diplomacy. His arrival sparks nationwide demonstrations by Israelis who dislike his brand of diplomacy and are skeptical of agreements with the Arabs. At Tel Aviv airport, Kissinger says that "the gap in negotiations has been substantially narrowed by concessions on both sides."

August 22. *Hussein Visits Syria.* Jordan's King Hussein ends a five-day visit to Syria and both countries announce a "supreme command" to coordinate foreign policy, information, and military affairs.

August 28. *Progress on Sinai Accord.* A senior official with the Kissinger party in Jerusalem says implementation of a new Sinai agreement hinges on approval by Congress of the use of American civilian technicians to man Sinai monitoring posts.

September 1. *Sinai Pact Concluded.* In separate ceremonies in Jerusalem and Alexandria, Israeli and Egyptian leaders initial a new Sinai pact. Israel withdraws from Sinai mountain passes and returns the Abu Rudeis oil fields to Egypt in return for modest Egyptian political concessions. Secretary of State Kissinger initials provisions for stationing U.S. technicians in the Sinai. President Ford asks that Congress approve the new U.S. Middle East role. Egyptian and Israeli representatives sign the agreement in Geneva September 4. Syria calls the Sinai pact "strange and shameful," while Zuhayr Muhsin of the PLO calls Sadat a "traitor and conspirator" for signing the accord.

September 26. *U.S. Open to Egyptian Arms Sales.* The White House announces the United States will now consider Egypt's request to purchase limited types of arms.

October 28. *Sadat Urges U.S.-PLO Dialogue.* Sadat urges Washington to open a dialogue with the PLO while Egypt and the United States sign four economic and cultural exchange agreements.

November 10. *UN Resolution on Zionism.* The UN General Assembly adopts a resolution defining Zionism as "a form of racism or racial discrimination" on a 72-35 vote with thirty-two abstentions and three absences. U.S. Ambassador Daniel Patrick Moynihan says, "The United States . . . does not acknowledge, it will not abide by, it will never acquiesce in this infamous act." A second resolution recognizes Palestinians' right to self-determination and to attend any UN Middle East negotiation. The Israeli Knesset rejects the UN resolution on Zionism and indicates Israel will not participate in the Geneva talks if the PLO is invited.

December 4. *PLO Invited to UN Debate.* After Israeli jets attack Palestinian refugee camps in Lebanon, killing seventy-four persons, the UN Security Council votes 9-3 with three abstentions to invite the PLO to participate in debate about the air attacks. The PLO is granted speaking privileges of a member nation.

December 5. *General Assembly Resolution.* The UN General Assembly by an 84-17 vote with twenty-seven abstentions adopts a resolution condemning Israel's occupation of Arab territories and calling upon all states to refrain from aiding Israel.

December 22. *Pope on Palestinians.* Pope Paul VI appeals to Israel to "recognize the rights and legitimate aspirations" of the Palestinians.

1976

January 12. *Security Council Vote.* The UN Security Council opens its Middle East debate by voting 11-1 with three abstentions to allow the PLO to participate with the speaking rights of a member.

January 28. *Rabin Visits Washington.* Prime Minister Rabin rules out any negotiations with the PLO in an address to a joint meeting of the U.S. Congress. Rabin and President Ford end talks January 29, reportedly with the understanding that the United States would promote the convening of the Geneva conference without the PLO.

February 13. *UN Human Rights Commission Vote.* The UN Commission on Human Rights votes 23-1 with eight abstentions for a resolution accusing Israel of having committed "war crimes" in the occupied Arab territories. The United States casts the lone "no" vote.

February 22. *Sinai Accord Implemented.* The final step in the previous September's Sinai accord is carried out, with UN personnel turning over the final eighty-nine square miles to Egyptian forces.

March 2. *Ford Proposes Ending Egypt Embargo.* The Ford administration informs key congressional leaders it wants to lift the arms embargo against Egypt by selling six C-130 military transport planes.

March 13. *Franjieh Refuses to Resign.* Lebanese President Suleiman Franjieh is presented with a petition signed by two-thirds of parliament asking him to resign, but he refuses.

March 14. *Israeli Nuclear Capacity.* Senior CIA officials estimate Israel has ten to twenty nuclear weapons "ready and available for use." Israel says April 5 that it is not a nuclear power and will not be the first to introduce nuclear weapons into the Middle East conflict.

March 23. *U.S. Position on Settlements.* U.S. Ambassador to the UN William Scranton tells the Security Council the United States considers the presence of Israeli settlements in the occupied territories to be "an obstacle to the success of the negotiations for a just and final peace."

March 25. *Security Council Vote.* The Security Council votes 14-1, with the United States vetoing the action, to deplore Israel's efforts to change the status of Jerusalem, to call on Israel to refrain from measures harming the inhabitants of the occupied territories, and to call for an end to Israeli settlements in the occupied territories.

April 18. *Israeli West Bank Demonstration.* About thirty-thousand Israelis march for two days through the West Bank under the leadership of Gush Emunim. Arab counter demonstrations in Nablus and Ramallah are broken up. Prime Minister Rabin tours Jordan Valley settlements April 20 and assures settlers in new villages that they are "here to stay for a long time."

May 8. *Sarkis Elected President.* Elias Sarkis is elected president of Lebanon. Backers of Raymond Edde boycott the election, protesting interference by Syria.

May 26. *Security Council Statement.* The Security Council at the end of a Middle East debate presents a majority statement deploring Israeli measures altering the demographic character of the occupied territories. The United States disassociates itself from the statement.

May 31. *Syrians Advance into Lebanon.* Syrian troops numbering five-thousand begin advancing into Lebanon's Akkar Valley in the north. Large numbers of additional Syrian troops enter Lebanon a week later.

June 16. *U.S. Diplomats Killed.* U.S. Ambassador Francis Meloy and Economic Counselor Robert Waring are shot to death on their way to a meeting with President Sarkis in Beirut. The State Department strongly urges June 19 that all American citizens leave Lebanon. The United States evacuates 263 Americans and foreign nationals from Lebanon by sea with the help of the PLO.

June 21. *Arab Peacekeepers Arrive in Lebanon.* About a thousand Syrian and Libyan troops, the vanguard of an Arab League peacekeeping force, arrive in Lebanon.

June 27. *Entebbe Hijacking.* A jetliner on its way from Tel Aviv to Paris is hijacked in Athens and taken to Entebbe airport in Uganda the following day. Israeli commandos stage a raid at the Entebbe airport July 4, freeing the 103 passengers held hostage.

July 16. *Beirut Embassy Closes.* The U.S. embassy in Beirut announces closure of all consular services and urges all Americans to leave Lebanon. The United States evacuates 308 more American and foreign nationals from Beirut July 27, again with the PLO helping to provide security.

September 6. *PLO Admitted to Arab League.* The PLO is unanimously granted full voting membership in the Arab League.

September 17. *Allon Article.* Israeli Foreign Minister Yigal Allon publishes an article in *Foreign Affairs* advocating Israeli withdrawal from most occupied Arab territory and creation of a demilitarized joint Jordanian-Palestinian entity in the West Bank and Gaza Strip.

September 17. *Sadat Elected to Second Term.* President Sadat of Egypt receives over 99 percent approval for a second six-year term as president. He is sworn into office October 16.

September 23. *Sarkis Inaugurated.* Elias Sarkis is inaugurated as president of Lebanon before sixty-seven members of the National Assembly.

September 28. *Arafat Appeals for Help.* With his PLO units in Lebanon under attack from Syrian troops, Yasir Arafat sends an urgent appeal to all Arab heads of state asking for immediate intervention to prevent Syria from "liquidating the Palestinian resistance."

October 18. *Riyadh Peace Plan.* Arab leaders of Saudi Arabia, Kuwait, Syria, Egypt, Lebanon, and the PLO, meeting in Riyadh, sign a Lebanon peace plan calling for a cease-fire and a thirty-thousand-troop peacekeeping force under the command of Lebanese President Sarkis. In Cairo October 25, all members of the Arab League, except Iraq and Libya, approve the Riyadh agreement.

November 11. *Security Council on Settlements.* The UN Security Council, in a consensus statement, deplores the establishment of Israeli settlements in occupied Arab territories and declares "invalid" the annexation of eastern Jerusalem by Israel.

November 15. *Syrian Forces in Beirut.* Syrian peacekeeping forces take up positions in both Christian and Moslem sections of Beirut.

November 23. *UN Votes Against Resettlement.* The General Assembly of the UN votes 118-2 with two abstentions for a resolution calling on Israel to halt resettlement of Palestinian refugees in Gaza and to return all refugees to their camps.

November 23. *Israeli Deployment.* Israeli forces are deployed along the Lebanese border following reported movements of Syrian peacekeeping forces toward the border.

November 24. *UN Supports Palestinian Rights.* UN General Assembly approves by 90-16 with thirty abstentions the report of the Committee on the Inalienable Rights of the Palestinian People proclaiming the right of Palestinian Arab refugees to establish their own state and reclaim former properties in Israel.

December 19. *Israeli Elections Called.* Rabin ousts the National Religious party from his coalition government five days after the NRP abstained on a vote of no-confidence in the Knesset. Rabin resigns December 20 and new elections are called.

1977

January 18. *Egyptian Demonstrations.* Thousands of Egyptian workers demonstrate against price rises. President Sadat cancels the price increases January 19. At least sixty-five persons are reported killed in clashes with police. Sadat bans demonstrations and strikes January 26. In a February 10 referendum on Sadat's decree outlawing demonstrations and strikes, 99 percent vote to approve, according to the government. About four-hundred students demonstrate in Cairo February 12 against the new law banning such protests.

February 15. *UN Commission Accuses Israel.* The UN Human Rights Commission accuses Israel of practicing "torture" and "pillaging of archeological and cultural property" in occupied Arab territories.

February 22. *Rabin Wins Labor Nomination.* By a vote of 1,445 to 1,404 the Israeli Labor party selects Yitzhak Rabin over Shimon Peres as its candidate for prime minister. In exchange for a real peace agreement, the

Israeli Labor party platform adopted February 25 calls for return of some West Bank territory to Jordan.

March 6. *PFLP Position.* George Habash tells reporters that the Popular Front for the Liberation of Palestine (PFLP) and three other "rejectionist" groups will break from the PLO if the Palestine National Council decides to participate in a Geneva peace conference or to recognize Israel.

March 9. *Arafat-Hussein Meet.* In Cairo Yasir Arafat and King Hussein meet publicly for the first time since "Black September" in 1970.

March 12. *Palestine National Council Opens.* The Palestine National Council opens in Cairo and President Sadat pledges that Egypt "will not cede a single inch of Arab land."

March 15. *Rabin Bank Account Disclosed.* The Israeli newspaper *Ha'aretz* reports that Prime Minister Rabin's wife has an illegal bank account in Washington.

March 16. *Carter Endorses Idea of Homeland.* At a Clinton, Massachusetts, town meeting President Jimmy Carter—the first American president ever to do so—endorses the idea of a Palestinian "homeland."

March 16. *Jumblatt Assassinated.* Leftist leader Kamal Jumblatt is assassinated near Beirut.

April 4. *Sadat Visits Washington.* President Sadat visits Washington and tells President Carter that the Palestinian question is the "core and crux" of the Arab-Israeli dispute. U.S. officials report April 8 that Sadat said Egyptian-Israeli relations could be normalized within five years.

April 7. *Rabin Withdraws.* Prime Minister Rabin withdraws from the top spot on the Israeli Labor party ticket with elections only six weeks away. Shimon Peres is selected to replace him April 10. Rabin's wife, Leah Rabin, pleads guilty to maintaining an illegal bank account April 17 and is fined $27,000. Rabin is fined $1,500 for his role in maintaining the illegal account.

April 16. *Egypt Accuses Libya.* Egypt delivers to the Arab League a note accusing Libya of plotting against the Sudan, seizing portions of Chad, and harboring "international criminals." Moscow accuses Egypt April 27 of attempting to provoke armed clashes between Egypt and Libya. Libya reportedly is planning to expel some of the 200,000 Egyptians working in Libya.

May 9. *Carter-Assad Meeting.* President Carter and Syrian President Assad meet in Geneva to discuss Middle East peace prospects. The same day Saudi Crown Prince Fahd says the PLO would be likely to recognize Israel in the context of an overall peace settlement.

May 12. *Carter on Middle East.* President Carter pledges "special treatment" for Israel in regard to arms requests and coproduction of advanced U.S. weaponry. Carter again calls for a Palestinian homeland and says, "There's a chance that the Palestinians might make moves to recognize the right of Israel to exist."

May 17. *Likud Victory.* Menachem Begin's right-wing Likud party unexpectedly wins a plurality in the Israeli election. President Katzir officially asks Begin June 7 to form Israel's next government.

May 19. *Begin Calls for Settlements.* Begin calls for many new Jewish settlements in the Israeli-occupied territories.

May 20. *Rabin Admission.* Prime Minister Rabin admits that he maintained an illegal Washington bank account with his wife.

May 25. *Dayan Accepts Foreign Ministership.* Moshe Dayan agrees to serve in a Begin government as

foreign minister. He resigns from the Labor party May 27 because of the resultant furor over his acceptance.

June 17. *U.S. Peace Plan.* U.S. Vice President Walter F. Mondale delivers a major speech on the Middle East that outlines the Carter administration's views and emphasizes a three-point peace plan: return to approximately the 1967 borders, creation of a Palestinian homeland probably linked to Jordan, and establishment of complete peace and normal relations between the countries in the area.

June 21. *Begin Becomes Prime Minister.* Menachem Begin officially becomes prime minister of Israel after winning a 63-53 vote of confidence in the new Knesset. Begin delivers his first major speech as prime minister June 23. He announces that Israel will not "under any circumstances" relinquish the West Bank or allow the creation of a Palestinian state west of the Jordan River.

June 27. *U.S. on Negotiations.* The U.S. State Department issues a statement on the Middle East warning that "no territories, including the West Bank, are automatically excluded from the items to be negotiated." Israel's government is infuriated by the timing of this statement, coming just weeks before Prime Minister Begin's scheduled visit to Washington.

June 29. *EEC Endorses Palestinian Homeland.* The nine members of the European Economic Community issue a statement endorsing the idea of a Palestinian "homeland."

July 10. *Jordan-Palestinian Link.* King Hussein and President Sadat agree in Cairo to an "explicit link" between Jordan and the Palestinians. President Carter notes his personal preference July 12 "that the Palestinian entity . . . should be tied in with Jordan and not independent."

July 13. *Assassination Threat.* A spokesman for the Palestinian "rejection front" threatens with assassination any Arab leader who signs a peace agreement with Israel.

July 13. *Sadat on Egyptian-Israeli Relations.* President Sadat, speaking to members of the U.S. Congress, expresses Egypt's willingness to establish diplomatic and trade relations with Israel within five years of signing a peace agreement.

July 20. *Carter and Begin Meet.* Israeli Prime Minister Begin visits Washington and confers with President Carter, who after their meeting states, "I believe that we've laid the groundwork now that will lead to the Geneva Conference in October." At a news conference telecast live to Israel from Washington, Begin discloses his "peace plan," which is loudly criticized by all Arab parties.

July 22. *PLO Joins ECOSOC.* The PLO becomes the first nonstate to have full membership in any UN body when it is accepted as a member of the Economic Commission for Western Asia of the UN Economic and Social Council.

July 28. *Carter Proposes PLO Discussions.* President Carter states at a press conference that "the major stumbling block" to reconvening the Geneva Conference "is the participation by the Palestinian representative." He offers to discuss this matter with the PLO and to possibly advocate a Palestinian role at Geneva if the PLO will agree to recognize Israel and to negotiate on the basis of UN Resolutions 242 and 338.

August 1. *Sadat Proposes Pre-Geneva Meeting.* Secretary of State Cyrus Vance confers with President Sadat in Cairo to push resumption of the Geneva Peace Conference on the Middle East. Sadat proposes a pre-Geneva meeting of Egyptian and Israeli foreign ministers. Prime Minister Begin endorses Sadat's proposal August 3.

August 2. *Carter Suspends Iran AWACS Sale.* The Carter administration announces the suspension of the proposed sale to Iran of seven Airborne Warning and Control Systems (AWACS) planes because of congressional opposition to the deal.

August 10. *Vance on Middle East Peace.* Secretary Vance officially ends a Middle East peace mission with a round of talks with Israeli officials. Leaving Tel Aviv, Vance says both sides remain far apart on the basic issues that have to be resolved before the Geneva talks can resume.

August 14. *Arab Rights in Occupied Lands.* The Israeli government announces it will extend "equal rights, the same as those enjoyed by residents of Israel," to Arabs in the occupied West Bank and Gaza Strip. Prime Minister Begin denies the move is the beginning of "annexation" of the territories.

August 17. *New West Bank Settlements.* The Israeli government approves plans for three new settlements in the West Bank. In an August 23 news conference, President Carter reiterates the administration's position that Israel's plan for new settlements in the West Bank are "illegal" and "an unnecessary obstacle to peace."

August 25-26. *PLO Denounces U.S. Efforts.* The Central Council of the PLO meets in Damascus, Syria, and denounces U.S. peace efforts in the Middle East. The PLO underscores its objection to Resolution 242 as the basis for a settlement, calling for an agreement that recognizes the Palestinian people's right to independence and sovereignty.

September 12. *New U.S. Policy.* The U.S. State Department unveils a new policy emphasizing that "the Palestinians must be involved in the peace-making process." Palestinians and Egyptians praise the U.S. statement September 13. Cairo says the policy offers "a new chance for the PLO to put their trust in the U.S. peace effort."

September 18. *Documents on* Liberty *Attack.* The American Palestine Committee releases CIA documents suggesting Israel deliberately attacked the U.S. Navy ship *Liberty* during the 1967 Arab-Israeli war. Thirty-four Americans died in the attack. A CIA spokesman calls the documents "unevaluated information."

September 19. *Israeli Peace Proposal.* Israeli Foreign Minister Moshe Dayan submits his country's proposal for a Middle East peace agreement during White House talks with President Carter and U.S. officials. The proposal contains provisions for internal autonomy and self-government for Arabs in the occupied West Bank.

September 21. *Carter, Vance Meet with Fahmy.* President Carter and Secretary of State Vance meet with Egyptian Foreign Minister Ismail Fahmy as part of the pre-Geneva peace talks. Fahmy reports Arab countries are prepared "for the first time to accept Israel as a Middle East country to live in peace . . . in secure borders."

September 25. *Israel Endorses U.S. Plan.* Israel accepts U.S. plan for reconvening the Geneva peace conference. The plan calls for a unified Arab delegation, including Palestinians, at the talks. Egypt, Syria, and Jordan also approve the plan but reject Israel's conditions limiting Palestinian participation.

September 26. *Cease-Fire in Southern Lebanon.* Heavy fighting ends in southern Lebanon as a U.S.-arranged cease-fire goes into effect. Key elements of the truce include withdrawal of Palestinian guerrillas six miles from the Israeli border and their replacement with Lebanese troops.

September 26. *Carter Backs PLO Involvement.* President Carter tells a news conference he favors PLO involvement in a Middle East settlement but does not consider the organization "the exclusive representative of the Palestinians."

October 1. *U.S.-Soviet Declaration.* The United States and the Soviet Union issue a joint declaration on the Geneva peace conference suggesting that talks guarantee "the legitimate rights of the Palestinian people." Israel rejects the joint statement October 2 as "unacceptable."

October 5. *U.S., Israel Agree on Procedures.* The United States and Israel announce agreement on procedures for reconvening the Geneva conference following talks between President Carter and Foreign Minister Moshe Dayan in New York. PLO leaders in Beirut reject the U.S.-Israeli plan October 16.

October 5. *Lebanese Fighting Resumes.* The U.S.-arranged cease-fire in southern Lebanon breaks down as serious fighting resumes between Christian and Palestinian forces.

October 26. *Egypt Suspends Soviet Payment.* Egypt announces it will suspend payment on its $4 billion military debt to the Soviet Union because of Moscow's refusal to continue arms sales to Egypt.

November 6. *Arafat Rejects Lebanon Pullout.* PLO leader Yasir Arafat says Palestinian guerrilla forces will not pull out of southern Lebanon in accordance with the U.S.-arranged truce agreement.

November 9. *Israelis Bomb Guerrillas.* Israeli jets bomb Palestinian guerrilla enclaves in southern Lebanon. The Lebanese government reports more than 100 people are killed.

November 9. *Sadat Willing to Go to Israel.* In a major speech, Egyptian President Sadat urges an all-out effort to reconvene the peace talks in Geneva. He says "I am ready to go to the Israeli Parliament itself to discuss [peace]."

November 11. *Begin Welcomes Sadat Proposal.* Israeli Prime Minister Begin is receptive to a visit from President Sadat and states, "I, for my part, will, of course, come to your capital, Cairo, for the same purpose: no more wars—peace, a real peace and forever."

November 15. *Begin Invites Sadat.* Prime Minister Begin extends a formal invitation to President Sadat to address the Israeli Knesset, at the same time offering an informal invitation to other Arab leaders to come to Israel for diplomatic discussions.

November 17. *Sadat Accepts Invitation.* President Sadat accepts the invitation of the Begin government. Egyptian Foreign Minister Ismail Fahmy resigns in apparent disagreement over Sadat's decision to go to Israel. Other Arab leaders, fearing Sadat will negotiate a separate settlement with Israel, also protest his plans.

November 19. *Sadat in Israel.* President Sadat arrives in Israel, the first Arab leader to visit that nation since it was established in 1948. In a historic address to the Israeli Knesset in Jerusalem November 20, he says that "we welcome you among us with all security and safety." Sadat and Begin hold a joint news conference November 21 and express their desire for peace and the hope that the Geneva peace conference will reconvene soon. At Sadat's departure Begin calls his visit "a great moral achievement."

November 22. *Sadat Visit Reaction.* The Egyptian delegate to the UN walks out on a speech by the Syrian delegate after the Syrian called Sadat's visit to Israel "a stab in the back of the Arab people." The European Community adopts a resolution praising Sadat's visit and "his courageous initiative."

November 26. *Cairo Conference Invitation.* Sadat invites all parties in the Middle East conflict to a pre-Geneva preparatory meeting in Cairo to resolve procedural differences. The United States and Israel announce they will accept but Syria, Lebanon, Jordan, and the Soviet Union reject Sadat's offer.

December 5. *Egypt Splits with Arab Nations.* Egypt severs diplomatic relations with Syria, Iraq, Libya, Algeria, and South Yemen, citing attempts by the hard-line Arab states to disrupt Sadat's recent peace efforts. The action follows conclusion of a December 2 meeting in Tripoli, Libya, where the Arab states declared a new "front for resistance and opposition" to thwart Egypt's peace initiatives. Egypt also closes several Soviet and Soviet-bloc cultural centers and consulates in Cairo because of Moscow's endorsement of the Tripoli Declaration.

December 14. *Cairo Conference.* The Cairo conference to discuss procedures for reconvening the Geneva peace talks opens. Representatives from Egypt, Israel, the United States, and the United Nations participate.

December 15. *Carter on PLO.* President Carter declares that the PLO has removed itself from "serious consideration" as a participant in the Middle East peace talks because of its refusal to recognize Israel.

December 25. *Begin and Sadat Meet.* Begin and Sadat hold a summit in Ismailia, Egypt, to draft guidelines for establishing peace in the Middle East. Talks conclude with no substantive agreement on any major issue.

1978

January 4. *Hammani Killed.* Said Hammani, chief representative of the PLO in Britain, is killed in London by an unknown assassin. Hammani had strained relations with other PLO representatives because of his moderate stance on coexistence with Israel and his opposition to terrorism.

January 9. *Shah Backs Sadat's Peace Moves.* In a meeting with President Sadat in Aswan, Egypt, the shah of Iran endorses Egypt's peace initiatives.

January 11. *Soviet-Syrian Arms Deal.* Syria and the Soviet Union sign an arms deal under which Damascus will begin receiving shipments of Soviet planes, tanks, and advanced air-defense missiles.

January 18. *Sadat Recalls Delegation.* Meetings in Jerusalem of the Israeli-Egyptian Political Committee end abruptly following Egypt's recall of its delegation. President Sadat blames the breakdown on Israel's "aim at deadlocking the situation and submitting partial solutions."

January 26. *Egypt-Israeli Talks.* Egypt and Israel hold private talks in a move to reopen peace negotiations. The Egyptian-Israeli Military Committee resumes talks January 31 in Cairo on arranging a technical agreement for Israel's return of the Sinai Peninsula to Egypt.

February 3. *Sadat in U.S., Europe.* President Sadat visits the United States to press his plans for peace in the Middle East and to seek American arms assistance. Sadat leaves the United States for Europe February 9 to continue his campaign for his peace initiatives.

February 14. *Middle East Arms Package.* The Carter administration announces a $4.8 billion arms package for Egypt, Saudi Arabia, and Israel that will include advanced warplanes. Secretary of State Vance says February

24 that the sale must be a "package deal." The administration plans to void the deal if Congress tries to veto any part of it.

February 18. *Sebai Killed; Hostages Taken.* Two Palestinian gunmen assassinate Youssef el-Sebai, an Egyptian newspaper editor and confidant of Anwar Sadat, in a hotel lobby in Nicosia, Cyprus. After killing Sebai, the terrorists seize thirty hostages and demand safe conduct to the Larnaca airport. Seventy-four Egyptian commandos land at the airport February 19 with orders to free the hostages, who are now being held aboard a Cypriot jet by the two Palestinians. Cypriot national guard troops intercept the commandos and fifteen Egyptians are killed in an exchange of gunfire. Following the fighting the Palestinians release their hostages and surrender. Egypt cuts diplomatic ties with Cyprus February 22 in anger over the attack by Cypriot troops on Egyptian commandos.

February 27. *Egypt Action on Palestinians.* Egypt announces it is revoking special privileges granted to the 30,000 Palestinians living in Egypt because of the assassination of Youssef el-Sebai by two Palestinians in Cyprus.

March 4. *Begin 242 Interpretation.* Prime Minister Begin informs President Carter that his government does not interpret UN Security Council Resolution 242 as saying that Israel is specifically obligated to withdraw from the occupied West Bank and Gaza Strip. Carter reiterates the U.S. position that the resolution mandates an Israeli withdrawal "from all three fronts."

March 14. *Israel Occupies Lebanese Territory.* Israel launches an all-out attack on Palestinian bases in Lebanon in retaliation for a terrorist raid March 11 that killed thirty Israeli civilians. Israeli troops occupy a six-mile deep "security belt" on Lebanese territory along the Israeli border. Egyptian, Syrian, and Lebanese leaders denounce Israel's actions in southern Lebanon March 15. Israel declares a unilateral truce in southern Lebanon March 21 and UN troops move into the region to enforce the cease-fire. Israel begins a two-phase withdrawal from its positions in southern Lebanon April 11. The withdrawal is completed June 13.

March 23. *Begin-Carter Talks.* President Carter and Prime Minister Begin conclude two days of talks in Washington after failing to reach agreement on any of the major points blocking progress in the Middle East peace negotiations.

April 1. *Rally in Israel.* An estimated twenty-five-thousand Israelis rally in Tel Aviv, calling on Prime Minister Begin to soften his stance on relinquishing Israeli-occupied territory in the West Bank and Gaza Strip.

May 15. *Senate Supports Arms Package.* The U.S. Senate votes to support the Carter administration's plan to sell warplanes to Israel, Egypt, and Saudi Arabia.

June 6. *Sadat Speaks to Troops.* In a speech to Egyptian troops President Sadat warns that if Israel "continues not to understand" what is behind his peace initiative, Egypt's armed forces would have "no alternative but to complete the battle of liberation."

June 24. *Assassination in North Yemen.* North Yemen President Ahmed Hussein al-Ghashni is slain in Sanaa. He is succeeded by Lt. Col. Ali Abdullah Salih.

June 26. *Ali Deposed in South Yemen.* South Yemen President Salim Rubayyi' Ali is deposed and executed in Aden. Ali, a Maoist with pro-China sympathies, is replaced by Abd al-Fattah Isma'il, who has close ties to Moscow.

July 1. *Syrians, Christian Militia Battle.* Syrian troops of the Arab League peacekeeping force in Lebanon attack Christian militia in Beirut. At least 200 people are killed in the worst fighting since the 1975-1976 civil war.

July 5. *Egyptian Peace Plan.* Egypt formally announces its plan for peace in the Middle East. Under the proposal Israel will withdraw from occupied territories over a five-year period and the Arab residents of the West Bank and Gaza Strip "will be able to determine their own future." The Israeli cabinet rejects the Egyptian peace plan July 9.

July 22. *Sadat Criticizes Begin.* President Sadat calls Prime Minister Begin an "obstacle" to peace in a speech at a political rally.

August 8. *Camp David Talks Announced.* U.S. authorities announce that President Sadat and Prime Minister Begin will meet with President Carter in September at Camp David, Maryland, to explore ways to resolve the Middle East deadlock.

August 13. *Explosion in Beirut.* Two hundred people die in an explosion that levels a nine-story building in Beirut. The building housed the headquarters of the pro-Iraqi Palestine Liberation Front and the rival Al Fatah faction of the PLO.

September 5-17. *Camp David Agreements.* President Carter, Prime Minister Begin, and President Sadat hold peace talks at Camp David, Maryland. On September 17 they sign two historic documents: "A Framework for Peace in the Middle East" and a "Framework for the Conclusion of a Peace Treaty Between Israel and Egypt." The Egyptian cabinet unanimously approves the Camp David agreements September 19. The Israeli cabinet approves the accords September 24. The Israeli Knesset gives its approval September 28 by an 84-19 vote.

September 8. *Iranian Demonstrations.* Hundreds of Iranian demonstrators are killed when government troops open fire during an antigovernment march in Tehran. In a September 10 White House statement President Carter assures the shah of Iran of continued U.S. support for his regime.

September 24. *Arabs Break Egyptian Ties.* Syria, Algeria, South Yemen, Libya, and the PLO break off all political and economic relations with Egypt because of the Camp David accords.

September 28. *Lebanese Crisis.* President Carter calls for an international conference to end the hostilities between Moslems and Christians in Lebanon. Syria declares a unilateral cease-fire in Beirut October 7 after a week of heavy fighting with Christian militia forces.

October 12-21. *Draft Treaty Negotiations.* Negotiations on a U.S. draft treaty between representatives of Egypt and Israel are held in Washington. President Carter intervenes to head off a breakdown in the talks after Israel announces its delegation will be called home for consultations. As a result, Israeli and Egyptian negotiators reach agreement on main elements of a peace treaty.

October 25. *Cabinet Acts on Draft Treaty.* The Israeli cabinet approves the draft treaty "in principle" but adds amendments drafted by Prime Minister Begin dealing with linkage between the treaty and the future of the West Bank and the Gaza Strip. The cabinet submits the treaty to the Knesset for approval.

October 26. *Dispute over Settlements.* President Carter sends a message to Prime Minister Begin expressing concern over Israel's decision to enlarge West Bank settlements. Egypt says its negotiators may be recalled in protest. Sadat decides October 28 not to call his chief negotiators home after a personal plea from Carter.

October 27. *Nobel Prize Announced.* The Norwegian Nobel Prize Committee announces that the 1978 Peace Prize will be awarded to President Sadat and Prime Minister Begin for their contributions to peace in the Middle East. The prizes are awarded December 10.

October 31. *Iranian Oil Strike; Martial Law.* Forty thousand Iranian petroleum workers go on strike in the largest single antigovernment move to date. The strike drastically reduces Iranian oil production and exports. The shah of Iran imposes martial law November 6 in an effort to quell violent antigovernment riots that have shaken the country since January. By November 13 government pressure has caused most oil workers to return to their jobs.

November 2-5. *Arab Meeting.* Arab nations, minus Egypt and six other moderate nations, meet in Baghdad and vow to impose an economic and political boycott on Egypt if President Sadat signs a separate treaty with Israel. Sadat refuses to meet with a delegation from the Baghdad summit November 4.

November 3. *Vance on Negotiations.* Secretary of State Vance announces progress on negotiations between Israel and Egypt saying, "We have now resolved almost all the substantive issues." The Israeli cabinet, however, objects to a preamble to the draft treaty that links a peace settlement with Egypt to resolution of the Palestinian problem.

November 11. *Sanjabi Arrested.* Iranian National Front leader Karim Sanjabi is arrested in Tehran while attempting to hold a news conference. Sanjabi has just returned from two weeks in Paris where he consulted with exiled religious leader Ayatollah Khomeini.

November 12. *Peace Negotiations Continue.* Secretary of State Vance and Israeli Foreign Minister Moshe Dayan reach a tentative agreement on a new formula for satisfying Egypt's concerns about the Palestinian issue. Vance presents the latest U.S. compromise plan to Prime Minister Begin. Administration officials say President Carter gave no secret guarantees or commitments to Sadat on the West Bank, Gaza, or Jerusalem. The Israeli cabinet, meeting without Begin, Dayan, or Defense Minister Ezer Weizman, rejects Egypt's demands for linking a treaty to a timetable for transferring power to the Palestinians.

November 21. *Israeli Cabinet Vote.* The Israeli cabinet votes 15-2 to accept a U.S.-proposed draft of a peace treaty that contains a generalized commitment to negotiate toward a settlement on the West Bank and the Gaza Strip. But the cabinet rejects Egypt's demands that a treaty be linked to a timetable for Palestinian autonomy. Egypt announces the recall of its chief negotiator from Washington in an apparent expression of displeasure.

December 1. *Carter Meets with Khalil.* Carter meets with Egyptian Prime Minister Mustafa Khalil, who presents President Sadat's latest proposals. They agree that peace talks should be renewed.

December 4. *Iranian Oil Strike.* Thousands of antigovernment workers renew their strike in Iran, reducing oil output by 30 percent.

December 7. *Carter on Peace Treaty.* President Carter pressures Israel and Egypt to meet the original December 17 deadline for completing a peace treaty. He says failure to meet that date would "cast doubt on whether the Egyptians and Israelis would carry out the difficult terms" of the treaty. He also says establishment of new Israeli settlements in the West Bank would violate the Camp David accords.

December 11. *Isfahan Riot; Oil Strike.* Fifty Iranians die and 500 are wounded in an antigovernment riot in Isfahan, Iran's second largest city. The United States begins evacuation of American dependents. Seventy percent of Iran's petroleum workers stay off the job December 12 in response to exiled Moslem leader Ayatollah Khomeini's calls for continuance of the strike. Oil production there drops to near-record lows. Widespread antigovernment demonstrations in Iran December 14-21 result in hundreds of deaths and injuries.

December 12. *U.S. Treaty Proposal.* President Sadat accepts U.S.-proposed side letters aimed at resolving the outstanding issues blocking conclusion of a peace treaty. Prime Minister Begin, however, raises strong objections November 13 to proposed treaty side letters: one explaining Egypt's legal commitment to other Arab nations and a second letter that sets a "target" date, rather than a timetable, for talks on Palestinian self-rule.

December 15. *Cabinet Backs Begin.* The Israeli cabinet backs Prime Minister Begin's rejection of the latest draft. Begin says Egypt bears "total responsibility" for the failure of negotiators to settle on a treaty by the December 17 deadline. President Carter says the decision on future negotiations "is primarily in the hands now of the Israeli cabinet."

December 17. *OPEC Price Increases.* OPEC ends an eighteen-month price freeze by adopting a phased-in increase plan that would raise crude oil prices 14.5 percent by October 1, 1979.

December 29. *Shah Appoints Bakhtiar.* The shah of Iran appoints Shahpur Bakhtiar, a member of the opposition National Front, to head a new civilian government. The shah had earlier established a military government in an attempt to bring the uprising against the monarchy under control.

December 31. *Israel Willing to Negotiate.* Prime Minister Begin says Israel is willing to discuss Egypt's proposals for the exchange of letters on the status of the West Bank and Gaza Strip.

1979

January 6. *New Iranian Government.* The shah of Iran officially installs a new civilian government headed by Shahpur Bakhtiar. A crowd of 100,000 Iranians demonstrates in a rally denouncing the new government. The shah announces he will leave the country soon for a vacation. A nine-member regency council is formed January 13 in Iran to carry out the duties of the shah after he leaves.

January 16. *Shah Leaves Iran.* Shah Mohammed Reza Pahlavi leaves Iran for a "vacation" abroad. Foreign observers agree the monarch will probably remain in permanent exile, ending his thirty-seven-year rule. Exiled religious leader Ayatollah Khomeini, from his home near Paris, hails the shah's departure, calling it "the first step" toward ending the reign of the Pahlavi dynasty.

January 16-27. *U.S. Diplomatic Efforts.* U.S. Special Ambassador Alfred Atherton meets with Israeli officials in Jerusalem, and then with Egyptian officials in Cairo, but fails to make substantial progress toward a treaty.

January 26. *Khomeini's Return Blocked.* Ayatollah Khomeini plans to return to Iran from Paris, then postpones his trip after Iranian officials close the nation's airports. Iranian army troops open fire on a crowd of demonstrators in Tehran, killing more than sixty people. The United States orders the evacuation of all dependents and nonessential American officials from Iran.

February 1. *Khomeini Returns.* Ayatollah Khomeini returns to Iran after fifteen years in exile and threatens to arrest Premier Shahpur Bakhtiar if he does not resign. Speaking to a crowd of his followers, Khomeini says, "The parliament and the government are illegal. I will appoint a government with the support of the Iranian people." In the first step of a plan to establish an Islamic republic in Iran, Khomeini appoints Mehdi Bazargan February 5 to head a proposed "provisional government."

February 11. *Bakhtiar Overthrown.* Armed revolutionaries and army sympathizers overthrow the government of Premier Shahpur Bakhtiar in Iran. A provisional government formed by religious leader Ayatollah Khomeini takes power.

February 14. *U.S. Embassy Occupied.* Leftist guerrillas storm the U.S. embassy in Tehran and hold more than 100 employees hostage. The embassy personnel are later freed by armed supporters of the Ayatollah Khomeini.

February 18. *Arafat in Tehran.* In Tehran, PLO leader Yasir Arafat meets with Khomeini and Prime Minister Bazargan. Arafat says the Iranian revolution "turned upside down" the balance of forces in the Middle East. The new Iranian government executes the former head of the Iranian secret police and three former army generals.

February 23. *Fahd Cancels U.S. Trip.* Saudi Arabian Crown Prince Fahd cancels a scheduled visit to the United States. Sources say he did not want his visit to be linked to the impending Israeli-Egyptian peace agreement.

February 27. *Iranian Oil Price Hike.* Iran's revolutionary government announces it will resume exports of crude oil, at a price 30 percent higher than the level set by OPEC in December 1978.

March 1-4. *Carter-Begin Talks.* Prime Minister Begin arrives in Washington for new talks with President Carter. In a strongly worded statement, Begin says the Egyptian-Israeli talks are "in a state of deep crisis." Carter and Begin fail to make progress toward resolving remaining issues. Carter announces March 4 he will fly to Egypt and Israel in the hope of breaking the impasse blocking a peace treaty between the two nations.

March 5. *Israeli Cabinet Approves Plan.* After more than five hours of closed-door debate, the Israeli cabinet approves President Carter's latest Middle East treaty proposals. The proposals were kept secret to give Egypt time to study them. After the cabinet's action, Carter announces that he will travel to the Middle East to continue his peacemaking efforts.

March 8. *Carter in the Middle East.* President Carter arrives in Cairo March 8 for talks with President Sadat. Sadat says Egypt and Israel are "on the verge of an agreement." Carter travels to Jerusalem March 10 where he meets with Prime Minister Begin and members of the Israeli cabinet.

March 12. *Treaty Issues Still Unresolved.* President Carter appears to have failed to resolve the issues blocking a treaty. White House officials announce the president will return to Washington without an accord and with no agreed procedure for continuing the talks.

March 13. *Cairo Airport Announcement.* Before returning to the United States from Israel, President Carter flies to Cairo for a final meeting with President Sadat. In a dramatic announcement at the Cairo airport Carter says Sadat has approved all outstanding points of a proposed treaty. Carter says Begin has agreed to submit to his cabinet "the few remaining issues" that Israel has yet to endorse. In Jerusalem, Begin says that if the Knesset rejects the compromise, his "government will have to resign."

March 14. *Cabinet Approves Proposals.* The Israeli cabinet approves the compromise proposals by a 15-0 vote, making approval of the entire treaty by the Knesset likely. Carter returns to the United States and tells congressional leaders of his plans to provide an additional $4 billion in aid to Egypt and Israel over three years.

March 15. *Egyptian Cabinet Approves Treaty.* The Egyptian cabinet votes unanimously to approve the peace treaty.

March 19-21. *Israel Approves Treaty.* The Israeli cabinet approves the treaty by a 15-2 vote. On March 21 after two days of debate the Israeli Knesset votes 95-18 in favor of the treaty.

March 26. *Begin and Sadat Sign Treaty.* Prime Minister Begin and President Sadat sign the peace treaty at a White House ceremony witnessed by President Carter. The treaty formally ends the state of war between Egypt and Israel.

March 31. *Arabs Isolate Egypt.* In response to the Israeli-Egyptian peace treaty, the foreign ministers of eighteen Arab League countries and a PLO representative vote to impose a total economic boycott on Egypt and exclude it from the league. The ministers also announce the immediate withdrawal of their ambassadors from Cairo and recommend that all Arab League members break diplomatic ties with Egypt within one month.

April 1. *Khomeini Proclaims Republic.* After Iranian voters approve the formation of an Islamic republic in a national referendum during the previous two days, Ayatollah Khomeini proclaims the establishment of the regime calling it "the first day of a government of God."

April 10. *Egyptian Assembly Ratifies Pact.* The Egyptian People's Assembly (parliament) ratifies the Egyptian-Israeli pact. The treaty is also overwhelmingly approved in a nationwide Egyptian referendum April 19.

April 18. *Christians Declare Strip Independent.* Leaders of the Christian militia in southern Lebanon declare a six-mile wide strip of land there "independent" of Beirut's control. Militiamen say the "independent area" will return to Lebanese control only after all Palestinian and Syrian troops have left Lebanon.

April 22-27. *Arabs Break Egypt Ties.* Kuwait, Saudi Arabia, Morocco, and Tunisia sever diplomatic relations with Egypt, making a total of fifteen Arab states that have cut ties with Cairo.

April 25. *Ratification Documents Exchanged.* The Egyptian-Israeli peace treaty formally goes into effect as the two nations exchange ratification documents. Israeli and Egyptian military officers begin talks April 29 on the details of Israel's withdrawal from the Sinai.

May 1. *Sadat Accuses Saudis.* President Sadat at a May Day rally accuses Saudi Arabia of pressuring other Arab countries to break diplomatic ties with Egypt.

May 9. *Egypt Expelled.* Egypt is expelled from the forty-three-member Conference of Islamic States during a five-day meeting in Fez, Morocco, because of its peace treaty with Israel.

May 9. *Israel Raids Lebanon.* Israeli ground troops follow up air and naval strikes by staging a retaliatory raid in southern Lebanon against Palestinian guerrillas.

May 16. *Lebanese Premier Resigns.* Lebanese President Elias Sarkis accepts the resignation of Premier Selim al-Hoss and his ministers in an effort to resolve disunity between warring Christian and Moslem factions.

May 25. *Israel Begins Withdrawal.* Israel begins withdrawing from the Sinai Peninsula and returns El Arish, capital of the Sinai, to Egypt in accordance with the peace treaty. Both countries open talks in Beersheba on granting Palestinian autonomy in the West Bank.

May 27. *Border Opened Early.* Egypt and Israel announce the opening of borders between the two countries, agreeing not to wait until January 1980 as planned.

June 6. *PLO to Withdraw from Southern Lebanon.* The Palestine Liberation Organization and its leader, Yasir Arafat, promise to withdraw forces from southern Lebanon and to close PLO headquarters in Tyre.

June 6. *Travel Pact Concluded.* The foreign ministers of Egypt and Israel conclude a pact allowing their citizens to travel freely between both countries by air and sea, but not overland through the Sinai Peninsula.

June 11. *Begin on Territories Policy.* Prime Minister Begin defends Israel's right to establish settlements in the West Bank and Gaza Strip. He pledges to implement the autonomy plan for residents of the occupied territories as agreed to in the September 1978 Camp David accords.

June 20. *Court Blocks Israeli Settlement.* The Israeli Supreme Court, in response to a suit by Arab landowners, orders a halt to work on the controversial West Bank settlement of Elon Moreh. Arabs in the West Bank city of Nablus continue riots and demonstrations protesting the settlement.

June 21. *Khalil Sworn In.* Prime Minister Mustafa Khalil and his cabinet are sworn into office in Cairo. President Sadat's National Democratic party won a large majority in parliamentary elections held June 7 and 14, the first multiparty elections since the 1952 revolution in Egypt.

June 24. *Weizman Removed as Negotiator.* Israeli Defense Minister Weizman is removed from the team negotiating with Egypt and the United States on Arab self-rule in the West Bank and Gaza. Weizman had earlier opposed establishment of the Israeli Elon Moreh settlement near Nablus.

June 28. *OPEC Meeting.* At the end of a three-day meeting in Geneva, OPEC ministers agree to raise the average price of oil 16 percent, making the price hike for the first six months of 1979 more than 50 percent. Leaders of the seven major western powers agree June 29 to set specific, country-by-country limits on their oil imports through 1985.

July 6-24. *Israeli Attacks.* Israeli jet fighters and ground troops attack Palestinian guerrillas in southern Lebanon. The heaviest raids occur July 22 when Israeli planes bomb a twenty-one-mile stretch south of Beirut, killing approximately twenty persons and wounding fifty, according to Beirut radio.

July 15. *Carter Energy Plan.* In a nationally televised address, President Carter presents a six-point energy package designed to reduce U.S. dependence on foreign oil.

July 16. *Hussein Named President.* Iraqi President Ahmed Hassan al-Bakr resigns, naming Gen. Saddam Hussein as his successor.

July 24. *UN Peacekeeping Plan.* The UN Security Council allows the term of the United Nations Emergency Force (UNEF), which separated Egyptian and Israeli forces in the Sinai, to expire. The council agrees to a U.S.-Soviet plan to use an expanded United Nations Truce Supervision Organization (UNTSO) force in the area to monitor the Israeli withdrawal.

August 12-14. *Tehran Riots.* Supporters and foes of Ayatollah Khomeini clash in Tehran in the most serious rioting since the overthrow of the shah in February.

August 15. *Young Resigns.* Andrew Young resigns as U.S. ambassador to the United Nations because of his unauthorized contacts with the PLO.

September 1. *Latakia Riots.* The Syrian government sends 1,400 troops to the port of Latakia to quell rioting by members of the Alawite Moslem sect.

September 4. *Iran Expels Journalists.* Iran expells four Associated Press correspondents, bringing to fourteen the number of foreign journalists ousted since the Islamic revolution in February.

September 4-6. *Begin-Sadat Meeting.* President Sadat and Prime Minister Begin, meeting in Haifa, Israel, agree to joint Israeli-Egyptian patrols of the Sinai in the wake of UNEF's withdrawal.

September 16. *Israel Rescinds Law.* Despite opposition from the United States and Egypt, Israel lifts the 1967 law preventing Israeli citizens and businesses from buying Arab-owned land in the occupied West Bank and Gaza Strip.

September 19. *Monitoring Agreement Reached.* After two days of negotiations U.S., Egyptian, and Israeli officials reach a tentative agreement for monitoring the Israeli-Egyptian peace pact in the Sinai.

September 24. *Syrian-Israeli Air Battles.* Syrian warplanes challenge Israeli fighters over southern Lebanon. Israel claims its pilots downed four Syrian MiG-21 fighters. Syria acknowledges the losses but claims that Israel also lost two jets.

September 27. *Turkey Recognizes the PLO.* Turkey recognizes the Palestinian Liberation Organization, becoming the first NATO member to grant the PLO full diplomatic status.

October 9-18. *Oil Price Hikes.* Kuwait, Libya, Iran, and Iraq raise oil prices, threatening the stability of the $23.50-a-barrel price ceiling established by OPEC in June.

October 21. *Dayan Resigns.* Moshe Dayan resigns as foreign minister of Israel. He reportedly favored a more moderate stand on the Palestinian autonomy question than other leaders in the Begin government.

October 22. *Court Bans Israeli Settlement.* The Israeli Supreme Court bans the controversial settlement of Elon Moreh, near Nablus on the West Bank.

October 24. *Shah Has Surgery in New York.* Shah Mohammed Reza Pahlavi, who arrived in New York for surgery two days earlier, has his gallbladder and several gallstones removed at New York Hospital-Cornell Medical Center. Doctors report November 5 that the shah will receive radiation therapy for cancer.

October 25. *South Yemen—Soviet Pact.* Representatives of the Soviet Union and South Yemen sign a twenty-year friendship pact in Moscow.

November 4. *Hostage Crisis Begins.* Demanding the return of the shah, Iranian students seize the U.S. embassy in Tehran and take sixty-three Americans hostage. On November 6, Ayatollah Khomeini accepts the resignation of Premier Bazargan, who opposes the hostage taking, and orders the Revolutionary Council to run the country.

November 9. *Carter Responses.* In response to the hostage crisis President Carter blocks delivery of $300 million in military equipment and spare parts to Iran. The next day he orders the deportation of Iranian students residing illegally in the United States.

November 11. *Iranians Assault Beirut Embassy.* About fifty Iranian students break into the grounds of the U.S. embassy in Beirut. They lower the American flag and burn it before being dispersed by Syrian troops.

November 12. *Additional U.S. Sanctions.* The Carter administration suspends Iranian oil imports. Iran had cut oil deliveries to the United States, Great Britain, and Japan by 5 percent retroactive to October 1. President Carter issues an executive order November 14 freezing Iranian assets in the United States. The freeze affects an estimated $8 billion, according to the U.S. Treasury.

November 19-20. *Some Hostages Freed.* Iranians free thirteen American hostages—five women and eight blacks.

November 20. *Grand Mosque Seized.* Three hundred armed Islamic militants seize control of the Grand Mosque in Mecca. Iranian radio broadcasts accuse the United States and Israel of involvement in the takeover of Islam's most sacred shrine. These rumors precipitate an attack on the U.S. embassy in Pakistan in which two Americans are killed. Pakistani troops help embassy staff escape.

November 29. *UN Vote.* By a 75-33 vote, the UN General Assembly adopts a resolution declaring that the 1978 Egyptian-Israeli peace treaty has no validity for the Palestinian people.

December 2. *Libyan Embassy Attacked.* A mob of 2,000 Libyans attacks the U.S. embassy in Tripoli. The demonstrators heavily damage the building but no Americans are injured.

December 4 *Saudis Gain Control of Mosque.* Saudi troops regain full control of the Grand Mosque in Mecca from Islamic militants who seized it November 20. Nearly 130 people are killed during the fighting, including 60 Saudi troops and many civilian hostages.

December 4. *Security Council on Hostages.* The UN Security Council unanimously adopts a resolution calling for the release of the hostages in Tehran.

December 6. *Libya Pressures PLO.* Libyan troops surround the PLO office in Tripoli as part of an effort to induce the organization to adopt a more radical stance toward Israel. Libyan leader Col. Muammar Qaddafi accuses the PLO of accommodation with Israel on the question of Palestinian autonomy and expels the top PLO official in Libya December 9.

December 15. *Shah Goes to Panama.* The shah flies to Panama after his treatment for cancer in New York.

December 17-20. *OPEC Abandons Pricing System.* At a meeting in Caracas, Venezuela, OPEC ministers abandon their collective pricing system, causing oil prices to soar. Prices for a barrel of oil range from Saudi Arabia's $24 to Libya's $30.

December 22. *Libya Cuts Ties with PLO.* Libya severs relations with the PLO. Qaddafi questions PLO leader Arafat's commitment to the Palestinian cause.

December 24-27. *Soviets Invade Afghanistan.* The Soviet Union launches a massive invasion of Afghanistan to prop up the pro-Soviet Marxist regime in Kabul.

1980

January 9. *Saudi Executions.* Saudi Arabia executes sixty-three militants involved in the Grand Mosque takeover of November 1979.

January 13. *Iran Resolution Vetoed.* A U.S.-proposed UN Security Council resolution urging economic sanctions against Iran is vetoed by the Soviet Union. Moscow justifies its vote by saying that sanctions would have "dealt a blow to the Iranian revolution."

January 23. *Carter Doctrine.* In his State of the Union address, President Carter warns that "An attempt by any outside force to gain control of the Persian Gulf region will be regarded as an assault on the vital interests of the United States of America, and such an assault will be repelled by any means necessary, including military force." This statement comes to be known as the "Carter Doctrine" and is regarded as being aimed primarily at the Soviet Union.

January 26. *Border Opened.* Ceremonies mark the formal opening of the Egyptian-Israeli border. The day before, Israel completed its withdrawal from two-thirds of the Sinai.

January 28. *Bani-Sadr Elected President.* Abolhassan Bani-Sadr, a former foreign minister, is elected president of Iran.

January 28. *Egypt Cuts Soviet Embassy Staff.* Egyptian President Sadat denounces the Soviet invasion of Afghanistan and cuts the Soviet embassy's staff in Cairo from fifty persons to seven.

January 29. *Canadians Aid U.S. Personnel.* Canada announces that six Americans from the U.S. embassy in Tehran, who had been secretly sheltered by Canadian embassy personnel since the November takeover, were flown out of Iran January 28.

February 11. *Conditions for Hostage Release.* President Bani-Sadr sets conditions for the hostages' release: the United States must acknowledge "past crimes," promise not to interfere in Iran's internal affairs, and recognize Iran's right to extradite the former shah and take control of his fortune.

February 25. *U.S. Offers Egypt Advanced Jets.* The United States agrees to sell Egypt F-15 and F-16 fighter planes. Egypt decides to purchase only F-16s.

February 26. *Ambassadors Exchanged.* Egypt and Israel exchange ambassadors in another step toward normalization of diplomatic relations.

March 1. *U.S. Reversal on Settlements Vote.* The UN Security Council unanimously adopts a resolution calling on Israel to dismantle its West Bank and Gaza Strip settlements. On March 3 President Carter disavows U.S. chief delegate Donald McHenry's vote for the resolution and explains that the action "does not represent a change in our position regarding Israeli settlements... nor regarding the status of Jerusalem." On March 4 Secretary of State Cyrus Vance accepts responsibility for the communications failure.

March 10. *Shamir Becomes Foreign Minister.* The Israeli cabinet approves Yitzhak Shamir as foreign minister, replacing Moshe Dayan, who resigned in October 1979.

March 24. *Shah Given Asylum in Egypt.* The former shah of Iran flies from Panama to Egypt, where he is offered permanent asylum.

April 7. *Tension in the Gulf.* The border dispute between Iraq and Iran worsens as Iraq expels 7,000 Iranians and both countries place their armies on full alert.

April 7. *Israel Responds to Raid.* Palestinians attack the Israeli kibbutz Misgav Am near the Lebanese border. In response Israeli soldiers push five miles into southern Lebanon April 9. Israeli troops withdraw from the area April 14.

April 7. *Carter Breaks Ties with Iran.* President Carter severs diplomatic relations with Iran. All Iranian diplomatic employees still in the United States are ordered to leave by April 8. Carter imposes an embargo on American exports, except food and medicine, to Iran.

April 8. *Khomeini Calls for Hussein's Ouster.* Iran's Ayatollah Khomeini appeals to the Iraqi army and people to overthrow the government of President Saddam Hussein. Baghdad permits armed Iranian exiles to organize against Khomeini's government.

April 17. *More U.S. Actions against Iran.* President Carter bans all imports from Iran and prohibits travel there by American citizens. U.S. military equipment previously purchased by Iran and impounded after the embassy takeover is made available for sale to other nations. Carter also asks Congress to use frozen Iranian assets to pay reparations to the hostages.

April 23. *South Yemen President Resigns.* Abd al-Fattah Isma'il resigns as president of South Yemen and secretary general of the ruling Yemeni Socialist party. His premier, Ali Nasser Muhammad, replaces him.

April 25. *Rescue Mission Fails.* A hostage rescue mission undertaken by a U.S. commando team is aborted in the Iranian desert because of equipment failure. Eight Americans are killed in a helicopter-airplane accident that occurs as the rescue team is about to leave the area. Secretary of State Vance resigns in protest against the rescue mission April 28. The Senate confirms Vance's successor, Sen. Edmund S. Muskie, D-Maine, May 7.

May 5. *London Hostage Crisis.* British commandos storm the Iranian embassy in London and free nineteen persons held hostage since April 30 by Arab Iranian terrorists. Two hostages reportedly were killed before the attack. The terrorists had demanded that the Iranian government release ninety-one prisoners being held in Iran's Arab-speaking Khuzistan province and grant the province greater autonomy.

May 15. *Sadat Reorganizes Government.* President Sadat carries out a major reshuffling of Egypt's cabinet. He assumes the additional post of premier in an attempt to take full personal control of Egyptian internal affairs. Egyptian voters approve major changes in the nation's 1971 constitution May 22.

May 25. *Weizman Resigns.* Ezer Weizman resigns as Israeli defense minister because of disagreements with Prime Minister Begin over defense budget cuts. Under Israeli law Begin automatically assumes the post.

June 2. *Bombings Target West Bank Arabs.* Bombing attacks in four West Bank cities injure two Arab mayors. Israeli Jewish extremists are believed to be responsible.

June 9-10. *OPEC Sets $32 Base Price.* OPEC ministers in Algiers set a $32-a-barrel base price for crude oil and a ceiling price of $37. Saudi Arabia and the United Arab Emirates call the base price excessive and vote against it.

June 13. *EC on Palestinians.* At the end of a two-day summit in Venice, the European Community urges full self-determination for the Palestinian people and suggests that the PLO be "associated with" Middle East peace negotiations.

June 22. *Jerusalem Move.* The Israeli government announces the transfer of Prime Minister Begin's office and the cabinet's conference room from West Jerusalem to East Jerusalem. On June 30 the UN Security Council votes against Israeli actions to make the whole of Jerusalem the capital of Israel.

July 7-8. *Fighting in Lebanon.* The Phalangist party emerges as the dominant Christian armed force in Lebanon after decisively defeating National Liberal party forces in and around Beirut. Fighting kills an estimated 320 people.

July 11. *Hostage Released.* Iran releases hostage Richard I. Queen, a vice consul, because of an illness later diagnosed as multiple sclerosis.

July 21. *Oil Prices Decline.* The average price of OPEC crude oil drops to $32.97 a barrel from $33.40 a week earlier. A developing world oil glut resulting from conservation efforts by industrialized nations and the continued high production of Saudi Arabia causes the drop.

July 27. *Shah Dies.* The deposed shah of Iran dies in Cairo of cancer.

July 30. *Knesset Reaffirms Jerusalem Claim.* The Israeli Knesset adopts a law reaffirming its claim to all of Jerusalem. Egypt protests the move August 3 by asking for a temporary suspension of talks on Palestinian autonomy. President Sadat informs Prime Minister Begin in a letter August 9 that Egypt regards the new law and the establishment of additional Israeli settlements in the occupied territories as obstacles to the resumption of the talks.

August 20. *Security Council Jerusalem Vote.* The UN Security Council adopts, 14-0, a resolution condemning Israel's claim to all of Jerusalem. The United States abstains.

September 3. *Egypt, Israel to Resume Talks.* U.S. special envoy Sol Linowitz announces in Alexandria, Egypt, that Israel and Egypt have agreed to resume suspended talks on Palestinian autonomy.

September 4. *Saudis Complete Takeover.* The Saudi government completes its takeover of assets of the Arabian American Oil Co. (Aramco), which accounts for about 97 percent of Saudi oil output.

September 10. *Merger Agreement.* Libya and Syria sign an agreement to merge the two countries into a unified Arab state. The proclamation announcing the merger urges other Arab states to join the union.

September 12. *Khomeini's Release Terms.* Ayatollah Khomeini sets terms for release of the hostages: the United States must relinquish the property and assets of the shah, cancel all financial claims against Iran, release Iran's frozen assets, and promise not to interfere in Iran's internal affairs.

September 17. *Iran-Iraq Border Clashes.* Iraqi President Saddam Hussein declares a 1975 border agreement with Iran void. Frontier clashes between the two countries intensify.

September 22. *Iran-Iraq War.* The Iran-Iraq dispute escalates into full-scale war. Both sides bomb oil fields. Iraq invades Iran and threatens to block the strategic Strait of Hormuz. President Carter says an oil cutoff from Iran and Iraq poses no current danger of shortages for the United States, but he warns that "a total suspension of oil exports from the other nations who ship through the Persian Gulf would create a serious threat to the world's supplies." The United States and the Soviet Union pledge neutrality in the conflict September 23. The UN Security Council unanimously approves a resolution September 28 calling on Iran and Iraq to "refrain immediately from the further use of force." Iraq conditionally accepts the UN resolution September 29, but Iran rejects it October 1.

October 5. *Yamani on Oil Production.* Saudi Arabia's oil minister, Sheik Ahmed Zaki Yamani, says major Persian Gulf oil producers will step up oil exports to offset losses caused by the Iran-Iraq war.

October 7. *Syria Declares Support for Iran.* Syria becomes the first Arab state to side with Iran in its war against Iraq.

October 8. *Soviet-Syrian Pact.* Representatives of the Soviet Union and Syria sign a twenty-year friendship pact in Moscow.

November 13. *Israel Backs Nuclear Arms Ban.* Israel submits a proposal to the UN General Assembly to abolish nuclear weapons in the Middle East; the plan officially ends Israel's opposition to such a ban.

November 25-27. *Arab League Summit.* Syria, Libya, Algeria, Lebanon, South Yemen, and the PLO boycott the eleventh summit meeting of the Arab League in Amman, Jordan. Deteriorating relations caused by the Iran-Iraq war keep league members away. At the summit Jordan's King Hussein assails Syria's support for non-Arab Iran in the war with Iraq.

December 9. *Oil Imports Reduced.* Representatives of the world's largest oil-consuming countries agree to reduce oil imports in the first three months of 1981 by 10 percent in the hope of preventing further OPEC price hikes. Oil stocks of the twenty-one members of the International Energy Agency remain adequate despite the ten-week war in the Persian Gulf. IEA officials in Paris say world oil production dropped 2 million barrels a day as a result of the conflict.

December 16-18. *Syria and Libya Slow Merger.* Syria and Libya disagree on details of their proposed merger at talks in Benghazi, Libya. The countries decide instead to establish a "revolutionary leadership for unionist action until the time the merger is fulfilled."

December 18-31. *Fighting in Lebanon.* Israelis, Lebanese Christians, Syrians, and PLO guerrillas clash in southern Lebanon. Israel downs two Syrian jets December 31.

December 28. *U.S. Hostage Proposal.* The United States proposes a three-stage process for the return of the hostages. If the Iranians simultaneously released the hostages, the United States would: transfer $2.5 billion of Iranian assets on deposit with the Federal Reserve to an escrow account in Bonn or London, unblock approximately $3 billion of the estimated $4.8 billion in Iranian assets held by American banks abroad, and establish an international claims commission to decide the disposition of Iran's remaining assets. The proposal is delivered by Algerian intermediaries to the Iranians on January 3, 1981.

1981

January 6. *Libya, Chad Merge.* At the end of a four-day visit to Libya by Chadian President Goukouni Oueddei, Libya announces a merger with Chad and the opening of the Chad-Libya border. France condemns the agreement, saying that the merger defies an earlier international agreement that scheduled free elections in Chad in 1982 to decide that country's future.

January 15. *Hostage Agreement Close.* Behzad Nabavi, the chief Iranian negotiator in the American hostage crisis, says Iran is close to agreement with the United States on releasing the hostages but demands the transfer of Iranian frozen assets held in U.S. overseas bank branches to an escrow account before Iran pays off its loans to those banks. After transfer, part of the money would be put aside to repay the loans those American banks made to Iran.

January 18. *Hostage Agreement Announced.* Iranian negotiator Nabavi announces that the United States and Iran have "reached agreement on resolving the issue of the hostages."

January 19. *Hostage Release Delayed.* Shortly before 5:00 a.m., President Carter announces resolution of the hostage crisis. When Iranian negotiator Nabavi objects to an appendix to the agreement dealing with Iran's ability to recover assets, the hostages' release is delayed.

January 20. *Hostages Released, Reagan Sworn In.* Iranian and American negotiators in Algiers agree on the disputed appendix. Soon afterward the United States transfers $8 billion in frozen assets to the Bank of England. The hostages board two Algerian planes at 12:25 p.m. (EST), minutes after Ronald Reagan succeeds Jimmy Carter as president of the United States. The Algerian government notifies the Algerian central bank when the planes clear Iranian air space. The bank then notifies the Bank of England that it may transfer assets to Iran.

February 1. *Iran Breaks Ties.* Iran severs diplomatic ties with Morocco and Jordan because of their support for Iraq in its war with Iran.

February 18. *Reagan to Observe Agreement.* The Reagan administration formally announces that it will observe the terms of the hostage agreement with Iran negotiated by the Carter administration.

March 6. *Saudi Arms Sale.* The Reagan administration announces plans to sell Saudi Arabia air-to-air missiles and fuel tanks that would enhance the combat capability of its F-15 jet fighters. Israel and some members of Congress object to the sale.

March 24. *Assad to Permit PLO Bases.* Syrian President Hafez Assad says he will permit PLO guerrillas to use his country's territory to mount attacks against Israel. Assad criticizes King Hussein's refusal to let the PLO establish bases in Jordan.

April 2. *Fighting in Lebanon.* Lebanese Christian militia and Syrian troops clash in Beirut in the most violent fighting since the 1976 civil war. Thirty-seven persons are killed. Lebanese President Elias Sarkis issues a cease-fire order April 8.

April 4-8. *Haig Middle East Tour.* Secretary of State Alexander M. Haig, Jr., confers with Egyptian president Sadat, Israeli prime minister Begin, Jordanian king Hussein, and Saudi crown prince Fahd during his first Middle East tour.

April 10-12. *U.S.-Iraqi Initiative.* Deputy Assistant Secretary of State Morris Draper confers in Baghdad with Iraqi leaders to explore the possible resumption of diplomatic ties between the two countries. Earlier in the month the Reagan administration approved the sale of five new Boeing jetliners to the Iraqi national airline.

April 19. *Yamani Disclosure on Oil Glut.* Saudi oil minister Yamani on "Meet the Press" confirms that Saudis engineered the current oil glut and pledges that his country will maintain its record production levels until other OPEC members agree to a long-term price strategy.

April 21. *AWACS Sale Announced.* The Reagan administration announces a massive arms sale package for Saudi Arabia, including five controversial AWACS radar defense planes. Israel vigorously protests the sale. Saudi oil minister Yamani says Israel, not the Soviet Union, is the chief danger to his country. On April 26 Reagan delays submitting the arms package for congressional approval until later in the year.

April 28. *Israel Joins Battle in Lebanon.* For the first time Israel intervenes in fighting between Syrian and Lebanese Christian militia forces near Beirut. Israeli jets shoot down two Syrian helicopters. The Israeli government says that it "cannot acquiesce in the attempt of the Syrians to conquer Lebanon and liquidate the Christians in that country." Syria says it will continue its policy of seeking "national reconciliation" in Syria.

April 29. *Syria Installs Missiles.* Syria moves SAM-6 surface-to-air missiles into Lebanon's Bekaa Valley April 29 in response to the Israeli attack the day before. The move precipitates a diplomatic crisis. Israel demands that the missiles be removed and contends that the Syrian action violates an agreement concluded with Syria in 1976 that such missiles would not be introduced in Lebanon. Syria contends that the missiles are necessary to defend against Israeli air attacks.

May 6. *U.S. Closes Libyan Mission.* The United States orders Libya to close its diplomatic mission in Washington because of Libya's support for international terrorists and its sanctioning of assassination attempts on Libyans living abroad.

May 7-13. *Habib Diplomatic Efforts.* U.S. special envoy Philip Habib shuttles between Beirut, Damascus, and Jerusalem seeking a settlement to the Israeli-Syrian missile dispute. The Soviets reportedly also advise the Syrians to take action to cool the crisis. Syrian forces fire at Israeli reconnaissance planes over Lebanon May 12. The Syrians claim they downed one Israeli jet.

May 14. *Missile Crisis Deepens.* Syrian missiles down an Israeli reconnaissance drone over Lebanon's Bekaa Valley. Israel confirms the incident. This is the first time Israel acknowledges the loss of an Israeli aircraft since the Syrians moved missiles into Lebanon in late April. Israel acknowledges the loss of two more drones by May 25. Prime Minister Begin demands May 21 that Syria not only remove its missiles from Lebanon, but also those on Syrian territory near Lebanon.

May 24. *Begin Claims Soviets in Lebanon.* Israeli Prime Minister Begin alleges that Soviet military advisers have accompanied Syrian troops into Lebanon. The Soviets deny the charge and the U.S. State Department says that it has "no knowledge of any Soviet advisers in Lebanon."

May 25. *Gulf Cooperation Council Established.* At a meeting in Abu Dhabi, the heads of state of Saudi Arabia, Kuwait, Oman, Qatar, Bahrain, and the United Arab Emirates sign a pact formally establishing the Gulf Cooperation Council.

May 26. *OPEC Meeting.* Meeting in Geneva, OPEC ministers freeze oil prices between $36 and $41 per barrel and cut oil production by a minimum of 10 percent. Iran and Iraq are exempted from the new production levels. Saudi Arabia opts to maintain its high production (10.3 million barrels a day) and keep its crude oil prices at $32 a barrel. The Saudis resist pressure to increase their price of oil or lower production in a continuing effort to win support for a unified OPEC price strategy.

June 4. *Sadat-Begin Meeting.* Egyptian president Sadat and Israeli prime minister Begin, meeting at Sharm el Sheik in the Israeli-occupied part of the Sinai, hold their first high-level meeting since January 1980. Talks focus on the situation in Lebanon. Sadat supports the withdrawal of Syrian forces but criticizes Israel's attacks on PLO bases in Lebanon.

June 7. *Israel Bombs Iraqi Reactor.* Israeli warplanes bomb and destroy the Osirak nuclear reactor near Baghdad, Iraq. The United States, the Soviet Union, and other foreign nations, including France—which sold the Osirak reactor to Iraq— condemn the raid. At a news conference

June 9 Israeli Prime Minister Begin rejects international criticism and defends the attack as an action meant to prevent another Holocaust. The United States suspends delivery June 10 of four F-16 fighters ordered by Israel. On June 11, however, President Reagan tells Israeli Ambassador Ephraim Evron that, despite U.S. opposition to the raid, no "fundamental reevaluation" of the U.S.-Israeli relationship is planned.

June 19. *Security Council Condemns Raid.* The UN Security Council unanimously condemns the Israeli raid on the Iraqi nuclear plant. U.S. Ambassador Jeane Kirkpatrick and Iraqi Foreign Minister Saadun Hamadi had worked out the compromise resolution in private negotiations June 17-18.

June 22. *Bani-Sadr Dismissed.* In a victory for extremists, Ayatollah Khomeini dismisses Abolhassan Bani-Sadr as president of Iran. Bani-Sadr had been dismissed as commander in chief June 10. Violent clashes between supporters and opponents of Bani-Sadr occur June 20 in Tehran. The government carries out mass executions of "counterrevolutionaries" involved in the violence.

June 24. *Saudis Cut Oil Production.* Saudi Arabia reduces oil production to 9.8 million barrels a day from a record level of 10.3 million barrels. The cutback still keeps daily production well above the official ceiling of 8.5 million barrels, in effect since July 1979. The reduction in output is considered too small to end the world oil glut.

June 28. *Tehran Bombing.* An explosion at the Tehran offices of the Islamic Republican party kills seventy-two people, including Chief Justice Ayatollah Beheshti, four cabinet ministers, and more than twenty members of the parliament. No group claims responsibility for the bombing.

June 30. *Syria Lifts Siege of Christians.* Syria agrees to lift its three-month siege of the Lebanese city of Zahle, where a Christian militia force had been holding out. The Syrian action is seen as a first step toward resolving the Lebanese missile crisis.

June 30. *Likud Wins Narrow Victory.* The Likud party led by Prime Minister Begin wins 48 seats in the 120-member Israeli Knesset and is expected to take the lead in forming a coalition government. The rival Labor party wins 47 seats.

July 5. *Bani-Sadr Verdict.* Iran's revolutionary court calls for the execution of former president Bani-Sadr, who is hiding in the Kurdistan region under the protection of Kurdish tribes. Iranian authorities announce July 6 that 27 "counterrevolutionaries" had been executed overnight, bringing to 130 the estimated number of persons killed since clashes erupted between supporters and opponents of Bani-Sadr.

July 10-16. *Israeli Raids.* The Israeli air force bombs Palestinian positions in southern Lebanon, killing about 50 people. Deaths caused by Israeli bombings total 160 since January 1981.

July 16. *Saudis to Fund Reactor.* Saudi Arabia announces it will fund the rebuilding of the Osirak nuclear reactor destroyed by Israeli jets June 7.

July 17. *Downtown Beirut Bombed.* After a week of Israeli air raids against Palestinian positions in southern Lebanon, Israeli jets attack the headquarters of the PLO in downtown Beirut. Bombs falling on the heavily populated area kill three-hundred persons, mostly Lebanese civilians. The United States on July 20 indefinitely suspends delivery of six F-16s to Israel but declines to link the action to the July 17 Israeli bombing raid.

July 24. *Israel-PLO Cease-Fire.* Israel and the PLO endorse separate cease-fire agreements to end the fighting along the Lebanese-Israeli border. The agreement had been mediated by Saudi Arabia and the United States.

July 29. *France Grants Asylum to Bani-Sadr.* Former Iranian president Bani-Sadr receives asylum in France.

August 3. *Israeli-Egyptian Agreement.* Israel and Egypt sign an agreement establishing a 2,500-member international peacekeeping force in the Sinai by April 25, 1982, the day Israel is to complete its withdrawal from the peninsula.

August 5. *Begin Establishes Government.* Israeli Prime Minister Begin wins approval for his four-party coalition government of 61 seats in a vote of confidence in the 120-seat Knesset.

August 5-6. *Sadat in Washington.* Egyptian President Sadat visits President Reagan in Washington. They discuss plans for Israeli-Egyptian talks on Palestinian autonomy. Sadat urges Reagan to establish contacts with the PLO but says "the PLO isn't the sole representative of the Palestinians."

August 7. *Saudi Peace Plan.* Saudi Prince Fahd offers an eight-point peace plan that recognizes Israel's right to exist. Israeli Prime Minister Begin rejects the plan while PLO leader Yasir Arafat states August 16 that it could lead to peace.

August 11. *Reagan Holds Back More Fighters.* The Reagan administration suspends the delivery of four more F-16 and two F-15 fighter planes to Israel. Resumption of deliveries is said to depend on the success of the June 24 cease-fire between Israel and the PLO. The ban on delivery of the planes is lifted August 17.

August 19. *Libyan Jets Downed.* Two U.S. Navy F-14 jets down two attacking Soviet-built Libyan SU-22s about sixty miles from the Libyan coast in the northern part of the Gulf of Sidra. The confrontation occurs during U.S. naval maneuvers. Libya claims the Gulf of Sidra as part of its territorial waters, but the United States regards it as international waters.

August 24. *AWACS Sale Announced.* The Reagan administration formally notifies Congress of its plan to sell Saudia Arabia five sophisticated Airborne Warning and Control System (AWACS) planes. The sale had originally been announced April 21, 1981.

August 26. *Begin, Sadat Meet.* Egyptian President Sadat and Israeli Prime Minister Begin meet in Alexandria, Egypt. They agree to resume stalled Palestinian autonomy talks September 23.

August 30. *Bombing in Tehran.* A bomb explosion in the prime ministry building in Tehran kills Iranian President Mohammed Ali Rajai and Premier Mohammed Jad Bahonar.

September 3-4. *Egyptian Arrests.* The Egyptian government arrests more than 1,500 critics of the regime, including religious leaders, journalists, and political opponents. The crackdown is the severest during Sadat's eleven years in power.

September 8. *Iran Cancels Oil Contracts.* The Iranian government cancels all contracts signed with multinational oil companies before the 1979 Islamic revolution.

September 15. *Egypt Expels Soviets.* Egypt expels Soviet Ambassador Vladimir Polyakov, six embassy aides, and two Soviet correspondents accused of fomenting religious unrest.

October 1. *Reagan Gulf Policy.* In a news conference

President Reagan says that the United States will not permit Saudi Arabia to become another Iran and pledges military action if the Persian Gulf oil supply is threatened.

October 6. *Sadat Assassinated.* Men in military uniform assassinate Egyptian President Sadat as he watches a military parade commemorating the 1973 war with Israel. Vice President Hosni Mubarak assumes control of the armed forces and reaffirms Egypt's commitment to the Camp David accords and other international treaties. Sadat is buried with full military honors September 10. Former U.S. presidents Nixon, Ford, and Carter, Israeli Prime Minister Begin, and other leaders from more than eighty nations attend the funeral. President Reagan and Vice President George Bush stay away for security reasons.

October 13. *Mubarak Elected.* Vice President Mubarak, the National Democratic party candidate, is elected president of Egypt.

October 28. *Senate Approves AWACS Sale.* After President Reagan certifies to the U.S. Senate that the Saudi government agreed not to use AWACS against Israel, the Senate approves the AWACS sale, 52-48. The House opposed the deal by an overwhelming margin, but by law a majority of both chambers had to vote against the arms sale to block it.

October 29. *Reagan on Saudi Plan.* In remarks to reporters President Reagan indicates that the Saudi peace plan announced in August was a significant step toward Middle East peace because it "recognized Israel as a nation to be negotiated with." Previously the administration had dismissed the plan. Reagan's comments stir new interest in the eight-point plan. Israel, however, denounces the plan and expresses its regret over Reagan's statements. The State Department says October 30 that the administration does not support all provisions of the plan and remains committed to the Camp David peace process, which was not mentioned by the Saudi proposal.

November 9. *Sharon Threatens Military Action.* Israeli Defense Minister Ariel Sharon accuses the PLO of repeatedly violating the July cease-fire agreement. He says the continued presence of Syrian surface-to-air missiles in Lebanon is preventing Israeli reconnaissance flights. He indicates that Israel may take military action against the missiles if they are not withdrawn.

November 12. *Autonomy Talks Fail.* Israel and Egypt end two days of talks on Palestinian autonomy without making progress toward an agreement. Since November 1, Arabs in the occupied territories had held numerous demonstrations, some of which resulted in clashes with Israeli soldiers.

November 25. *Arab League Summit.* Arab heads of state meet in Fez, Morocco, to discuss the Saudi peace plan and construct a unified Arab position on establishing peace in the Middle East. Only thirteen of twenty-one leaders show up, however, and the meeting breaks down without progress after only six hours.

November 30. *U.S.-Israeli Strategic Pact.* The United States and Israel sign a strategic memorandum of understanding in Washington that establishes joint measures to meet threats in the Middle East "caused by the Soviet Union or Soviet-controlled forces from outside the region." The agreement does not provide for joint U.S.-Israeli maneuvers or pledge the United States to aid Israel if the Jewish state is attacked.

December 14. *Israel Annexes Golan Heights.* The Israeli Knesset passes a bill supported by Prime Minister Begin that annexes the strategically important Golan Heights. Syria declares the action to be a "declaration of war." The United States immediately denounces the annexation, and Egyptian President Hosni Mubarak says the move violates the Camp David accords and is a "direct blow" to Middle East peace. The UN Security Council December 17 unanimously calls the annexation illegal and threatens sanctions.

December 18. *U.S. Suspends Agreement.* The United States suspends the strategic pact concluded with Israel November 30 in response to Israel's surprise annexation of the Golan Heights. Prime Minister Begin harshly denounces the U.S. action, saying Washington is treating Israel like a "vassal state."

1982

January 19. *Begin on Lebanon.* Israeli Prime Minister Begin, reacting to U.S. speculation, assures Washington that Israel will not attack Lebanon unless provoked by Palestinian guerrillas or Syria.

January 20. *U.S. Vetoes Resolution.* The United States vetoes a UN Security Council Resolution calling for punishment of Israel for annexing the Golan Heights.

February 2. *Mubarak Visit.* Hosni Mubarak arrives in Washington on his first official visit to the United States as president of Egypt. Mubarak tells President Reagan February 3 that solving the Palestinian problem is the "key to peace and stability" in the Middle East.

February 2. *Syrian Uprising.* An uprising by Moslem fundamentalist rebels in the Syrian city of Hama leads to heavy fighting between the rebels and Syrian troops. The two sides engage in artillery battles that destroy parts of the city. Reports from Damascus February 18 indicate that thousands of Syrians have died in the fighting and hundreds of rebels have been executed by Syrian troops who gradually gain control over the city. Syrian authorities admit for the first time February 22 that the Hama confrontation was a major uprising.

February 26. *Iraq Removed from Terrorism List.* The U.S. government takes Iraq off a list of nations that support terrorism, thereby paving the way for an easing of trade restrictions against Iraq.

February 28. *Israeli Conditions for Visit.* The Israeli government says Egyptian President Hosni Mubarak will not be invited to Israel if he refuses to visit Jerusalem. Prime Minister Begin vows March 2 not to go to Egypt until Mubarak agrees to visit Jerusalem. Mubarak postpones his scheduled trip to Israel March 15.

March 22. *Iranian Offensive.* Iran launches a major spring offensive that forces Iraqi troops to retreat from long-held positions inside Iran.

March 23. *No-Confidence Votes.* Israeli Prime Minister Begin submits his government's resignation after three motions of no confidence in the Knesset result in 58-58 votes. The tie votes do not require the government to resign, and Begin agrees to remain in office after the Israeli cabinet rejects his resignation, 12-6. The no-confidence votes are a response by the opposition parties to the government's handling of disorder on the West Bank, where Israeli security forces had engaged protesters in violent clashes.

April 6. *Egyptian Peace Plan.* At a conference of nonaligned nations in Kuwait, Egypt proposes a new peace plan that does not mention the Camp David accords. The plan calls for "an end to Israeli occupation of Arab territories" and is regarded as representing a tougher stance on the issue of Palestinian autonomy.

April 11. *Dome of the Rock Shooting.* Alan Harry Goodman, an American-born Israeli soldier, kills two Arabs and wounds many in a shooting spree at the Dome of the Rock mosque in Jerusalem. Israeli police arrest Goodman in the mosque minutes afterward. The incident sparks demonstrations in Arab countries and the occupied territories.

April 15. *Sadat's Killers Executed.* Five Moslem militants convicted of assassinating President Sadat are executed in Egypt.

April 25. *Israel Returns Territory.* Israel returns the final portions of the Sinai Peninsula to Egypt under the terms of the 1979 peace treaty. Mubarak commends Israel's "enthusiasm for peace" April 26.

May 2. *Begin Abandons Settlement Law.* Prime Minister Begin, reacting to weak support, drops a proposal for legislation that would have prevented future Israeli governments from dismantling Israeli settlements in the occupied territories as part of any future peace agreement.

May 9. *Israeli Raids.* Israeli jets strike PLO bases near Beirut. Israel claims the raids were retaliation for the PLO's repeated violations of the 1981 cease-fire agreement. PLO forces respond by shelling northern Israel.

May 26. *Israeli Arms to Iran.* Israeli Defense Minister Ariel Sharon confirms that Israel has supplied Iran with arms in its war with Iraq.

June 3. *Attempted Assassination.* Shlomo Argov, the Israeli ambassador to Britain, is shot and severely wounded in London. Israel accuses the PLO of responsibility and retaliates by launching air strikes against PLO targets in Lebanon that kill 45 and wound 150. The PLO responds with more artillery attacks against northern Israel.

June 6. *Israel Invades Lebanon.* Israel launches a three-pronged armored assault across the Lebanese border supported by air strikes. Israeli forces penetrate all the way to Sidon thirty miles north of the border on the first day of the invasion. Prime Minister Begin informs President Reagan that the purpose of the assault is to establish a twenty-five-mile security zone in southern Lebanon that will ensure the security of northern Israeli towns from Palestinian artillery attacks. The UN Security Council unanimously calls on Israel to withdraw from Lebanon.

June 7. *Reaction to Invasion.* The Reagan administration refuses to condemn the Israeli invasion of Lebanon but issues a statement saying, "Israel will have to withdraw its forces from Lebanon, and the Palestinians will have to stop using Lebanon as a launching pad for attacks on Israel." U.S. envoy Philip Habib travels to Israel to discuss ending hostilities. The Soviet Union and Arab states condemn the invasion, and Egypt labels it "a blatant violation of international law."

June 9. *Syrian Missiles Destroyed.* In a massive air battle Israeli pilots destroy Syrian surface-to-air missiles in Lebanon's Bekaa Valley. Israel claims that Syria lost twenty-two planes while all ninety of Israel's jets returned unharmed. Syria admits losing sixteen planes but claims nineteen Israeli jets were downed. Israeli forces advance to within sight of Beirut. The UN Security Council demands an immediate Israeli withdrawal.

June 10. *Israel Threatens Beirut.* Israeli warplanes repeatedly bomb targets in and around Beirut and drop leaflets warning Syrians to evacuate the city in advance of an Israeli assault upon it. The Reagan administration re-

portedly warns Israel against trying to capture the city.

June 11. *Israeli-Syrian Cease-fire.* Israel declares a unilateral cease-fire that is quickly joined by Syria. Israel and the PLO announce a cease-fire June 12 that breaks down the following day.

June 13. *Israel Sets Conditions for Pullout.* Israeli leaders tell U.S. envoy Philip Habib that they would withdraw from Lebanon if Syrian forces left the country and a demilitarized zone were created in southern Lebanon that would be patrolled by an international peacekeeping force not controlled by the UN.

June 13. *Fahd Becomes King.* King Khalid of Saudi Arabia dies of a heart attack and is succeeded by his half-brother, Crown Prince Fahd. Fahd chooses Prince Abdullah ibn Abdul Aziz to be crown prince.

June 14. *Egypt Suspends Talks.* Egypt suspends autonomy talks with Israel because of Israel's invasion of Lebanon. Israeli forces cut off West Beirut, trapping PLO leaders.

June 16. *Israeli Beirut Intentions.* U.S. officials claim Israel has assured them Israeli forces will not seize Beirut.

June 21. *Begin Meets with Reagan.* Prime Minister Begin and President Reagan, meeting in Washington, agree that all foreign forces should be removed from Lebanon. In comments after the meeting Reagan emphasizes the common long-term interests of the United States and Israel and says that Israel "must not be subjected to violence from the north."

June 24. *U.S. Closes Embassy.* The United States closes its embassy in Lebanon. Hundreds of Americans, Europeans, and Lebanese are evacuated from the country by the U.S. Sixth Fleet. Israel June 25 begins its heaviest bombing of Beirut since June 6. It announces June 26 that it is observing a cease-fire.

June 27. *Israeli Peace Plan.* Israel promises to guarantee safe passage to Syria to Palestinians in Lebanon who lay down their weapons. Israel says it would then open negotiations on establishing the territorial integrity of Lebanon and achieving the withdrawal of all foreign forces from that country. PLO leader Yasir Arafat agrees in principle to accept the Israeli proposal.

July 6. *Reagan Offers U.S. Forces.* President Reagan agrees to contribute a small contingent of U.S. Marines to a multinational peacekeeping force that would oversee the withdrawal of PLO forces from West Beirut. The Soviet Union July 7 warns the United States against sending troops to Lebanon. The United States announces it will not reconsider its offer. France announces July 10 that it will also send peacekeeping troops to Lebanon.

July 9. *Syria Rejects Plan.* Syria says that it will not allow PLO forces to be evacuated to Syria. The Syrian rejection prompts weeks of international negotiations on how and where to evacuate the PLO.

July 13. *PLO on Israeli Recognition.* In Paris, Issam Sartawi, a high PLO official, proclaims that the PLO would recognize Israel "on a reciprocal basis" and calls on the United States to deal with the PLO directly. The U.S. State Department says July 14 that Sartawi's statement did not qualify as official PLO recognition of Israel's right to exist.

July 16. *U.S. Stops Sale of Shells to Israel.* The United States suspends further sales of cluster artillery shells to Israel pending review of their use in Lebanon. Israel asserts July 18 that it did not violate the agreement governing their use. President Reagan bans the sale of the shells indefinitely July 27.

July 22. *Cease-Fire Broken.* Israeli jets attack Palestinian and Syrian forces in Lebanon in retaliation for alleged violations of a ten-day-old cease-fire. The cease-fire is restored July 28 after several days of fighting and Israeli bombing raids.

August 4. *Israel Enters West Beirut.* Under cover of heavy artillery fire, Israeli armored units enter West Beirut. The UN Security Council adopts a resolution calling for an immediate cease-fire, withdrawal of Israeli forces to the positions of August 1, and a reprimand of Israel for not complying with earlier UN resolutions. Despite pleas from the United States, Israel refuses August 5 to withdraw its troops.

August 6. *PLO Agrees to U.S.-Mediated Plan.* The PLO agrees to all major points of a U.S. plan for PLO withdrawal from Beirut. Syria and several other Arab countries agree to accept PLO fighters.

August 9. *U.S. Presents Plan to Israel.* The United States formally presents Israel with a plan calling for the evacuation of the PLO from Beirut with the aid of UN forces. Israel accepts the plan in principle August 10 but insists on the departure of PLO forces before UN troops arrive.

August 12. *Israeli Bombing Raids.* Israeli jets bomb Beirut for eleven hours. President Reagan telephones Begin to express U.S. "outrage" and demand an end to the attacks. Israel's cabinet votes to stop the bombing, and Begin calls Reagan to announce that a "complete" cease-fire has been ordered.

August 15. *Israel Accepts Peacekeeping Force.* Israel accepts U.S. envoy Philip Habib's plan for deploying an international peacekeeping force in Beirut. Lebanon approves the plan August 25.

August 19. *PLO Withdrawal Pact Concluded.* The Israeli cabinet unanimously accepts a U.S. plan that provides for the withdrawal of PLO forces from Lebanon. The Lebanese government and the PLO had approved the pact the day before. President Reagan orders 800 Marines to participate in the peacekeeping force overseeing the withdrawal. The Marines arrive in Lebanon August 25.

August 21. *PLO Withdrawal Begins.* French paratroopers arrive in Lebanon to participate in the international peacekeeping force. The first group of 397 PLO guerrillas then departs Lebanon for Cyprus, beginning the two-week pullout. Yasir Arafat leaves Beirut for Greece August 30.

August 23. *Bashir Gemayel Elected.* Bashir Gemayel, Christian Phalangist leader, is elected president of Lebanon.

September 1. *Reagan Peace Plan.* President Reagan, in a major address, presents his "initiative" for peace in the Middle East. It calls for "self-government by the Palestinians of the West Bank and Gaza in association with Jordan," a "freeze" on Israeli settlements in the occupied territories, and an "undivided" Jerusalem with final status to be decided in negotiations. The Israeli cabinet unanimously rejects the plan September 2.

September 1. *PLO Withdrawal Completed.* The last of 15,000 PLO and Syrian troops leave Beirut. Lebanese forces take full control of the city the following day.

September 5. *Israel to Build Settlements.* Israel allocates funds for three new West Bank settlements and approves plans for seven more. The United States denounces the move.

September 9. *Fez Summit Peace Plan.* The Arab League summit in Fez, Morocco, announces an eight-point plan calling for an Israeli withdrawal to pre-1967 borders, the creation of a Palestinian state, and UN guarantees of peace among "all states of the region." U.S. Secretary of State George Shultz sees a chance for a "breakthrough" in light of the Arab League proposal, but Israel rejects the plan.

September 14. *Gemayel Assassinated.* Lebanese president-elect Bashir Gemayel is killed by a bomb blast at Phalange party headquarters in East Beirut.

September 15. *Israelis Occupy West Beirut.* Israeli troops and tanks reenter West Beirut in a move the Israeli government describes as a "police action." Israeli leaders contend the presence of Israeli troops is necessary to keep order after the assassination of Bashir Gemayel. The United States September 16 calls on Israel to withdraw from the city.

September 15. *Arafat Meets Pope.* PLO leader Yasir Arafat meets with Pope John Paul II at the Vatican. Israel condemns the meeting.

September 15. *Soviet Middle East Position.* Soviet leader Leonid Brezhnev summarizes the Soviets' position on a Middle East settlement in a six-point plan he says is "not at variance" with the Arab League plan of September 9.

September 18. *Sabra and Shatila Massacre.* Reports emerge of the massacre of hundreds of Palestinian civilians in the Sabra and Shatila refugee camps outside Beirut by Lebanese Christian militiamen permitted into the area by Israeli authorities September 15-18. President Reagan expresses "outrage and revulsion" and demands an immediate Israeli withdrawal from West Beirut. Israeli Labor party leader Shimon Peres September 19 calls for the resignation of Prime Minister Begin and Defense Minister Ariel Sharon.

September 20. *Peacekeepers Requested.* Lebanese leaders request the return of an international peacekeeping force to Beirut. Italy, France, and the United States agree to again provide troops, but Reagan stipulates that Israel must give permission and pull back its forces in the area. Israel agrees September 21.

September 20. *Amin Gemayel Elected.* Amin Gemayel is elected president of Lebanon to succeed his slain brother Bashir. He is sworn in September 23 for a six-year term.

September 22. *Sharon Disclosure.* Israeli Defense Minister Ariel Sharon acknowledges that Israel coordinated the entry of the Lebanese Phalangist forces into the refugee camps where the massacre occurred. Sharon says Israeli military commanders had emphasized to their Phalangist counterparts that the refugee camp operation was to be directed only at terrorists.

September 26. *Begin Requests Commission.* Prime Minister Begin requests the establishment of a judicial commission of inquiry to investigate Israel's role in the Beirut massacre. The panel is established September 28.

October 9-10. *Arafat and Hussein Meet.* Yasir Arafat and King Hussein meet in Jordan to discuss proposals for resolving the Palestinian problem. They say the Reagan plan is insufficient because it does not recognize the PLO as the "sole legitimate representative of the Palestinians."

October 10. *Israeli Terms for Withdrawal.* Israel announces that its troops will not withdraw from Lebanon until the Lebanese government signs a security agreement with Israel and all Israeli prisoners are returned.

November 8. *Begin Testifies.* Prime Minister Begin tells the commission investigating the September Beirut massacre that he was not aware of the army's plan to send Lebanese militiamen into the refugee camps where the killings took place.

November 29. *Peacekeeping Force Expanded.* Lebanon requests an expansion of the international peacekeeping force. The United States agrees December 1 to double its troop strength in Lebanon.

December 14. *Jordan, PLO Agreement.* After two days of talks Jordan and the PLO agree to a "special and distinctive relationship" in which the two closely coordinate their international political moves.

December 21. *Hussein, Reagan Meet.* Jordan's King Hussein meets with President Reagan in Washington and expresses sympathy for Reagan's peace initiative, but he says Jordan will not represent Palestinians in peace negotiations with Israel unless the PLO and other Arab states approve of such an arrangement.

December 28. *Israeli-Lebanese Talks Begin.* Negotiations between Lebanon and Israel begin in Khalde, Lebanon, on withdrawal of foreign forces from Lebanon.

1983

January 17. *Palestinian Groups Meet.* Hard-line Palestinian factions meeting in Tripoli, Libya, reject the Reagan plan and other peace proposals. They call for continued armed struggle against Israel. Their position is seen as a challenge to the authority of PLO leader Yasir Arafat.

February 2. *U.S.-Israeli Confrontation.* A U.S. Marine draws his pistol in an effort to force three Israeli tanks to retreat from an American guard post in Beirut. The incident is the latest in a series of provocative confrontations between U.S. peacekeeping troops and Israeli forces in Beirut.

February 8. *Commission Findings.* The Israeli commission of inquiry investigating the September 1982 massacre near Beirut recommends the dismissal of several officers for neglect of duty, including Defense Minister Ariel Sharon. The cabinet accepts the commission's findings February 11. Sharon resigns the same day but accepts Prime Minister Begin's offer to remain in the government as a minister without portfolio. Former ambassador to the United States Moshe Arens is named to succeed Sharon as Israeli defense minister February 14.

February 15. *Army Moves into East Beirut.* Christian militia forces withdraw from East Beirut and are replaced by Lebanese regular army units.

March 14. *OPEC Price Cut.* OPEC members agree to establish national production quotas and cut their benchmark crude oil prices from $34 a barrel to $29 a barrel. The price cut, brought on by the developing world oil glut, is the first in OPEC's history.

March 21. *Cabinet Announces New Settlements.* The Israeli cabinet announces plans to build twenty-three additional Jewish settlements in the West Bank during the next two years.

March 31. *Reagan Delays Shipment of F-16s.* President Reagan says that the United States will not ship F-16 jets to Israel, until that country withdraws from Lebanon. The White House had delayed the delivery of seventy-five F-16s after the Israelis invaded Lebanon in June 1982.

April 10. *PLO, Jordan Break on Talks.* Jordan's King Hussein and PLO leader Yasir Arafat fail to agree on an approach to peace negotiations under the Reagan plan. Jordan withdraws from efforts to implement Reagan's plan and accuses the PLO of reneging on recent pledges regarding their joint participation in the peace process.

April 10. *Sartawi Assassinated.* Issam Sartawi, a close adviser to PLO leader Yasir Arafat and an advocate of mutual Israel-PLO recognition, is assassinated in Lisbon, Portugal. The Revolutionary Council of the Fatah, a radical Palestinian faction, claims responsibility.

April 18. *Beirut Embassy Bombed.* A car bomb attack partially destroys the U.S. embassy in Beirut, killing 63 persons and wounding more than 100. A pro-Iranian group, the Islamic Jihad, claims responsibility. President Reagan says the attack "will not deter us from our goals of peace in the region."

May 4. *Israeli-Lebanese Pact.* The Lebanese government accepts a U.S.-mediated draft agreement on withdrawal of Israeli troops from Lebanon. The accord calls for an end to the state of war between Israel and Lebanon, the withdrawal of Israeli troops in eight to twelve weeks if Syrian and PLO forces also leave, and limitations on the Lebanese military's presence near the Israeli border. The Israeli Knesset and the Lebanese parliament approve the pact May 16. Representatives of the two countries sign the agreement May 17. Syria rejects the agreement May 13 and closes land routes and communication channels between Beirut and Syrian-held areas of Lebanon May 17.

May 4. *Iran Breaks Up Communist Party.* Iran disbands the Communist Tudeh party, charging it with spying for the Soviet Union. Tehran also expels eighteen Soviet diplomats it accuses of espionage and subversion.

May 20. *Reagan Ends Embargo.* President Reagan lifts the ban on the sale of seventy-five F-16 fighters to Israel imposed after the invasion of Lebanon.

June 1. *PLO Rebellion.* More than twenty leading members of Yasir Arafat's Al Fatah wing of the PLO announce their support for an ongoing rebellion within the PLO against Arafat's leadership. Arafat supporters and Al Fatah rebels engage in heavy battles in Lebanon's Bekaa Valley. Arafat accuses Libyan leader Muammar Qaddafi June 7 of supporting the rebels.

June 24. *Syria Expels Arafat.* Syria's President Hafez Assad expels PLO leader Arafat from Syria. The day before Arafat had accused Syria of aiding PLO rebels in their fight against Arafat. Syrian tanks had reportedly supported rebel PLO attacks on Arafat's forces in the Bekaa Valley during the previous week.

July 5. *PLO Rebellion Unresolved.* A PLO mediation team fails to negotiate an end to the rebellion against Arafat. A cease-fire was established before the meeting began July 2.

July 20. *Israeli Redeployment.* The Israeli cabinet unanimously approves a plan to redeploy Israeli troops in Lebanon south of the Awali River in a more defensible security zone.

July 24. *PLO Fighting.* Heavy fighting breaks out in Lebanon between PLO rebels and Arafat loyalists, ending a three-week-old cease-fire. The rebels reportedly drive Arafat's forces from several positions in the Bekaa Valley.

August 1. *Syrian Withdrawal Talks.* New U.S. envoy Robert C. McFarlane arrives in Beirut to begin talks on a Syrian withdrawal from Lebanon. He meets with President Assad August 7. McFarlane's ongoing efforts yield no progress during August. Meanwhile, fighting between local factions in Lebanon intensifies.

August 4. *U.S. Aid to Chad.* President Reagan increases U.S. military aid to Chad from $10 million to $25 million in response to growing U.S. concern over Libyan backing of Chadian rebels.

August 18. *French Troops to Chad.* Reacting to the massing of Libyan forces in northern Chad, Paris sends planes and 450 additional troops to Chad. The reinforcements build French troop strength in the country to 2,000. The French presence is credited with deterring further Libyan advances.

August 28. *Begin to Resign.* Menachem Begin announces his intention to resign as Israeli prime minister for personal reasons.

August 29. *Fighting Spreads to Beirut.* Two U.S. Marines are killed and fourteen wounded in Beirut as units of the Lebanese army and Moslem militia clash. Reagan September 1 orders 2,000 Marines to be stationed in ships off Beirut in case troops in Lebanon should need to be reinforced. Four French peacekeepers are killed August 31.

September 3. *Israeli Redeployment.* Israeli troops begin a redeployment from the Shouf Mountains south of Beirut to more defensible positions in southern Lebanon. Druze forces take control of the area after the Israeli pullout.

September 12. *New Israeli Government.* Six parties of Begin's governing coalition agree to form a new government under Foreign Minister Shamir. Shamir's government wins the Knesset's endorsement October 10.

September 13. *Marines to Return Fire.* U.S. Marine peacekeeping forces are authorized to call in naval gunfire and air strikes to defend themselves against artillery attacks.

September 16-19. *U.S. Begins Shelling.* For the first time U.S. naval guns fire on targets in Syrian-controlled Lebanon. President Reagan defends the action as essential to the safety of American peacekeepers. French planes attack antigovernment positions east of Beirut in response to the shelling of the French peacekeeping headquarters.

September 25. *Lebanese Cease-Fire.* A cease-fire is announced between warring factions in Lebanon. The agreement takes effect September 26.

September 29. *War Powers Compromise.* Congress authorizes Marines to remain in Lebanon for eighteen more months. President Reagan indicates that he will sign the law.

October 11. *French Jets Arrive in Iraq.* Several French Super Etendard fighter-bombers arrive in Iraq. Iran had threatened to cut off oil traffic through the Persian Gulf if the French sold the planes to Iraq. President Reagan says October 19 that he will not allow the flow of oil from the Gulf to be stopped.

October 23. *Marine Barracks Bombed.* A suicide truck-bomb attack on the barracks of U.S. peacekeeping forces in Beirut kills 241 Marines and Navy personnel. An almost simultaneous attack against the French compound kills 58. President Reagan reaffirms the U.S. commitment to the peacekeeping effort.

October 31. *Lebanese Talks.* Lebanese national reconciliation talks convene in Geneva. The talks adjourn November 11 with no progress reported.

November 3. *PLO Rebels Attack Arafat Forces.* Syrian-backed PLO rebels attack positions held by forces loyal to PLO leader Yasir Arafat outside Tripoli, Lebanon.

November 4. *Israeli Headquarters Bombed.* The Israeli headquarters in Tyre, Lebanon, is destroyed by a suicide truck bomb. Sixty Israeli soldiers and Arab prisoners are killed. In retaliation, Israeli jets hit Palestinian positions in the mountains east of Beirut.

November 13. *Assad Illness.* Syrian President Hafez Assad reportedly suffers a heart attack. The Syrian press agency claims the illness is appendicitis.

November 16. *Arafat Stronghold Captured.* PLO rebels overrun the Beddawi refugee camp, a stronghold of forces loyal to Yasir Arafat. Arafat sets up headquarters in Tripoli and vows November 17 to "fight to the end."

November 23. *PLO Cease-Fire.* PLO factions in Damascus accept a Saudi-sponsored cease-fire to allow Yasir Arafat and his troops to evacuate Tripoli.

November 24. *Prisoner Exchange.* Israel trades 4,500 Palestinian and Lebanese guerrilla prisoners for six Israeli soldiers held by the PLO.

December 3. *Evacuation Plan.* UN Secretary General Javier Pérez de Cuéllar agrees to allow Yasir Arafat's PLO forces to evacuate Tripoli under the UN flag. The UN Security Council unanimously agrees to the plan.

December 4. *U.S. Air Strikes.* U.S. planes attack Syrian positions in Lebanon in response to Syrian attacks on unarmed American reconnaissance planes December 3. Two U.S. planes are shot down; one pilot is killed and the other captured. The same day eight U.S. Marines are killed by artillery fire from Druze militia near Beirut.

December 9-19. *Israeli Ships Shell PLO.* Israeli gunboats continually shell PLO positions in Tripoli, forcing a delay in the evacuation of forces loyal to Yasir Arafat. The United States publicly urges Israel to allow the evacuation December 19.

December 20. *Arafat Forces Evacuated.* Yasir Arafat and 4,000 of his PLO troops are evacuated from Tripoli by Greek ships flying UN flags. The convoy is escorted out of Tripoli harbor by French warships and sails for Tunis.

December 22. *Arafat, Mubarak Meeting.* Yasir Arafat meets in Cairo with Egyptian President Mubarak. They announce resumption of relations broken off after the signing of the Egyptian-Israeli peace treaty.

1984

January 3. *Goodman Released.* In response to a visit by the Rev. Jesse L. Jackson, Syria releases U.S. Navy Lt. Robert Goodman, Jr., who had been captured when his plane was shot down December 3. Jackson and Goodman return to the United States January 4.

January 9. *Jordanian Parliament Meets.* King Hussein convenes the Jordanian parliament for the first time in nearly seven years. It approves plans to hold elections in the East Bank while Israel continues to control the West Bank.

January 19. *Islamic Conference Admits Egypt.* The Islamic Conference Organization, convening in Casablanca, votes to reinstate Egypt, which had been expelled after signing the 1979 peace treaty with Israel. Egypt formally rejoins the conference April 2.

January 23. *Iran Named Terrorist Supporter.* The United States declares Iran to be a supporter of international terrorism and tightens controls on Iran's purchase of American goods.

February 5. *Government Resigns.* Under pressure from Moslem factions, the Lebanese government of Amin

Gemayel resigns. Gemayel himself remains president and calls for national reconciliation.

February 6. *Moslem Militia Routs Army.* After a week of heavy fighting, Moslem militia forces drive the Lebanese army from West Beirut.

February 7. *Peacekeepers Withdraw.* President Reagan orders U.S. peacekeeping troops to redeploy to ships off the Lebanese coast. Britain and Italy also announce they will withdraw their peacekeepers from Lebanon. The British pullout begins February 8; the Italians leave February 20. The U.S. redeployment begins February 21 and is completed February 26. Reagan reaffirms U.S. support for the Gemayel government February 22 and says the Marines will return to Beirut if necessary.

February 8. *Naval Bombardment.* In accordance with new rules of engagement that allow U.S. commanders to respond to artillery attacks on Beirut whether or not U.S. soldiers are threatened, the battleship *New Jersey* fires more than 250 one-ton shells from 16-inch guns into positions southeast of Beirut.

February 22. *Shultz Confirms PLO Contacts.* Secretary of State Shultz confirms a *New York Times* report of February 18 that the Reagan administration held secret talks with the PLO through an intermediary from August 1981 to May 1982.

February 27. *Iraq Blockades Kharg Island.* Iraq announces a blockade of the Iranian oil facilities on Kharg Island. Baghdad says the blockade will continue until Iran agrees to end the war.

March 5. *Lebanon Cancels Israeli Accord.* the Lebanese government breaks the May 1983 troop withdrawal agreement with Israel. The move paves the way for reconciliation talks between warring Lebanese factions.

March 5. *U.S. Accuses Iraq.* The United States accuses Iraq of using chemical weapons in its war against Iran. The Red Cross March 7 supports the U.S. claim after examining Iranian victims.

March 12. *Reconciliation Talks.* Lebanese President Amin Gemayel opens talks in Lausanne, Switzerland, with leaders of factions fighting in Lebanon. They agree on a nationwide cease-fire March 13. Druze and Shi'ite leaders offer a plan March 14 for collective leadership and greater Moslem participation in the government. The conference ends March 20 without agreement.

March 12. *Jordanian Elections.* For the first time since 1967, Jordan holds elections for vacancies in its sixty-member Council of Delegates.

March 14. *Hussein Interview.* In a *New York Times* interview Jordan's King Hussein precludes Jordanian participation in peace talks with Israel. He says U.S. support for Israel has compromised the credibility of the United States as a mediator of the Middle East peace process.

March 21. *Stinger Sale Dropped.* In response to strong congressional opposition, President Reagan cancels proposed sales of Stinger antiaircraft missiles to Jordan and Saudi Arabia.

March 24. *French Troops Leave Lebanon.* France announces it will withdraw its peacekeeping force from Lebanon. The French pullout is completed March 31.

March 30. *Fleet Leaves Lebanese Coast.* U.S. ships leave the waters near the Lebanese coast, ending American participation in the international peacekeeping effort.

April 12. *Bus Hijacking.* Four Palestinians hijack an Israeli bus carrying thirty-five persons. All four hijackers and one hostage are killed when police storm the bus April 13. Press reports assert one of the hijackers was captured

alive and later beaten to death by police.

April 17. *Britain-Libya Embassy Incident.* A hail of gunfire from inside the Libyan embassy in London kills a British policewoman and wounds ten Libyan exiles demonstrating outside. British police surround the embassy after the shooting and demand the right to search it. In response, Libyan troops surround the British embassy in Tripoli. Britain breaks diplomatic ties to Libya April 22. The Libyan government agrees April 24 to a mutual exchange of diplomats. British and Libyan diplomats return to their respective countries April 27.

April 19. *Egypt, Soviet Union Restore Ties.* Egypt and the Soviet Union agree to restore diplomatic relations after a three-year break.

April 19-20. *Assad, Gemayel Meet.* Syrian President Assad and Lebanese President Gemayel meet in Damascus and reach agreement on the basics of a power-sharing accord among warring Lebanese factions.

April 29. *Jewish Terrorist Attack Prevented.* Israel says that it has uncovered a plot by a Jewish underground organization to blow up Arab buses in Israel. Twenty-one persons are arrested.

May 10. *New Lebanese Cabinet Meets.* A new unity cabinet that includes top Moslem and Christian leaders meets for the first time in Lebanon.

May 27. *Egyptian Elections.* President Mubarak's National Democratic party wins 73 percent of the popular vote and 391 of 448 contested parliamentary seats.

May 28. *Bus Hijackers Beaten to Death.* The Israeli Ministry of Defense admits that two of four bus hijackers killed April 13 were captured alive and beaten to death by police. The government promises to charge those responsible.

May 29. *Stingers to Saudi Arabia.* President Reagan authorizes the sale of 400 Stinger antiaircraft missiles to Saudi Arabia in the face of increasing attacks on Persian Gulf shipping by Iran and Iraq. During the past weeks Iran had attacked Saudi and Kuwaiti tankers in retaliation for Iraq's attacks on Iranian ships. The sale did not require congressional approval because Reagan certified that U.S. national security demanded an immediate transfer of the weapons.

June 5. *Saudis Down Iranian Jets.* Guided by U.S. surveillance planes, Saudi Arabian F-15s reportedly shoot down two Iranian warplanes as they approach protected shipping lanes off the Saudi coast. The United States says June 12 that only one Iranian plane was downed.

June 23. *Lebanese Unity Plan.* The Lebanese cabinet approves a plan to restructure the army to provide more equal representation between rival Moslem and Christian factions and bring unity to the country.

July 4-7. *Lebanese Army in Beirut.* A reconstituted Lebanese army assumes control of Beirut from militias and begins the destruction of the Green Line wall dividing Moslem and Christian sectors. An agreement approved by the Lebanese cabinet June 23 restructured the army to provide more equal representation between rival Moslem and Christian factions.

July 23. *Israeli Elections.* In Israeli elections, the Labor party wins 44 seats in the 120-seat Knesset. The Likud party wins 41 seats. President Chaim Herzog asks Labor leader Shimon Peres August 5 to form a new government.

July 31. *Red Sea Explosions.* The pro-Iranian Islamic Jihad claims responsibility for numerous mine explosions that have damaged ships in the Red Sea during June.

The United States, France, and Britain send minesweeping units to the Red Sea in August. Iran radio hails the explosions August 7, but the Ayatollah Khomeini August 9 denounces the mining.

August 15. *Soviet-Kuwait Arms Sale.* Kuwait announces a purchase of surface-to-surface and surface-to-air missiles from the Soviet Union reportedly worth $327 million. Soviet advisers are to accompany the missiles to Kuwait to instruct Kuwaiti personnel in their use.

September 13. *Coalition Government Formed.* Labor party leader Shimon Peres and Likud party head Yitzhak Shamir agree to form a coalition government in which they will exchange the posts of prime minister and defense minister in 1986 at the midpoint of the coalition's fifty-one-month term. Peres will serve as prime minister first. The Knesset approves the agreement September 14.

September 20. *U.S. Embassy Attacked.* A suicide car-bomb damages the U.S. embassy building outside Beirut, killing eight. The Islamic Jihad claims responsibilty.

September 25. *Libyans, French Leave Chad.* Libya and France begin a mutual troop withdrawal from Chad under a September 17 understanding.

September 25. *Jordan to Establish Egypt Ties.* Jordan announces it will reestablish diplomatic relations with Egypt. Of the seventeen Arab countries that broke ties with Egypt after Egypt signed the 1979 peace treaty with Israel, Jordan is the first to reestablish relations.

October 31. *Israeli-Lebanese Talks.* Israel and Lebanon agree to begin new talks on an Israeli withdrawal from Lebanon. Syria approves of the negotiations but will not participate. The talks begin November 8.

November 22-29. *PLO National Council Meets.* The PLO National Council meets in Amman despite a boycott by Syrian-supported factions. The council reaffirms its support for PLO leader Yasir Arafat. Jordan's King Hussein addresses the meeting November 22 and calls for a joint PLO-Jordanian peace initiative based on UN Resolution 242.

November 26. *U.S., Iraq Establish Ties.* The United States and Iraq resume diplomatic relations after a seventeen-year split.

December 4. *Kuwaiti Airliner Hijacked.* Four Arabs hijack a Kuwaiti passenger jet carrying 161 people and divert it to Tehran. The hijackers demand the release of 17 Arabs in Kuwaiti prisons for attacks on American and French missions. One American hostage is killed December 4 and another December 6. Iranian police storm the aircraft and free the hostages December 9. The United States December 11 accuses Iran of backing the hijackers and demands that they be extradited. Iran refuses the extradition request December 12 and says the hijackers will be tried in Iran.

1985

January 5. *Jordan Buys Soviet Arms.* Jordan announces that it has purchased Soviet arms, including shoulder-fired antiaircraft missiles.

January 14. *Israeli Withdrawal Plan.* The Israeli cabinet endorses a three-stage plan to withdraw Israeli forces from Lebanon during the next six to nine months. Israel begins the initial phase of the pullout January 20. Israeli troops leave Sidon February 16.

February 11. *Assad Reelected.* Syrian President Assad is reelected to another seven-year term after receiving 99.97 percent of the votes, according to the Syrian news agency.

February 14. *Hostage Escapes.* Jeremy Levin, an American journalist held almost a year in Lebanon, escapes and seeks help at a Syrian army post. The Syrians transport Levin to the U.S. embassy in Damascus. Middle East analysts speculate that Levin's captors allowed him to escape.

February 22. *Jordan-PLO Plan.* Jordan makes public the text of a February 11 agreement on the Middle East peace process between King Hussein and Yasir Arafat. The plan calls for a total Israeli withdrawal from occupied territories, the right of self-determination for Palestinians within the context of a Jordan-Palestine confederation, and peace negotiations under UN auspices with the five permanent Security Council members and all parties to the conflict, including the PLO within a joint Palestinian-Jordanian delegation. Arafat says March 1 that the PLO is holding talks with Hussein to "clarify" their agreement and would continue to do so until Jordan agrees to accept PLO ammendments.

February 24-27. *Egyptian-Israeli Talks.* Egypt and Israel exchange high-level representatives who engage in talks aimed at invigorating the Middle East peace process.

March 17. *Heavy Fighting in Iraq.* Iran and Iraq fight for control of the Baghdad-to-Basra highway in what is reported to be the heaviest fighting of the war to date. Egypt's President Mubarak and Jordan's King Hussein visit Baghdad March 18 to show Arab support for Iraq.

March 21. *Camera Crew Killed in Lebanon.* Two Lebanese members of a CBS News camera crew are killed in their car by a shell fired from an Israeli tank. The crew was filming an Israeli military operation near Sidon. Israel says the journalists were in a dangerous area during a battle and their deaths were accidental. Other journalists charge that the Israeli tank fired deliberately at the CBS car, which was well marked.

March 21. *Reagan on the Middle East.* In a televised news conference, President Reagan says the United States is willing to meet with a Jordanian-Palestinian delegation that does not include PLO members. Israeli Prime Minister Peres rejects the idea March 24.

April 9. *De Cuéllar Diplomatic Effort.* After a three-day diplomatic tour of Iran and Iraq, UN Secretary General Javier Pérez de Cuéllar says the gap between Tehran and Baghdad is "as wide as ever." Iraqi officials told de Cuellar April 8 that they are ready to discuss a comprehensive settlement to the war, but Iran rejects any halt to the fighting until Iraqi president Saddam Hussein is ousted.

April 12. *Qaddafi Assassination Attempts.* The *Washington Post* reports that conservative Libyan army officers recently made two attempts to assassinate Muammar Qaddafi and that he retaliated by executing as many as seventy-five officers.

April 17. *Lebanese Cabinet Resigns.* After heavy fighting between rival Moslem militias in West Beirut, the one-year-old Lebanese unity cabinet resigns.

April 24. *Israeli Withdrawal.* The Israeli army begins withdrawing from eastern and central Lebanon as part of the second phase of the Israeli troop withdrawal. This phase is completed April 29.

April 30. *U.S. Aid.* The Reagan administration, responding to an urgent request from Israeli Prime Minister Peres, agrees to grant Israel $1.5 billion in additional economic aid. In keeping with U.S. policy, Egypt will receive

$500 million in additional aid.

May 8. *PLO Positions.* PLO officials assert that only declared PLO members can participate in talks with U.S. officials. PLO leader Yasir Arafat says May 13 that he is determined to pursue both negotiation and "armed resistance" to end Israeli occupation of Arab territories.

May 19. *Palestinians Battle Shi'ites.* Heavy fighting breaks out between Palestinians living in refugee camps near Beirut and the Amal Shi'ite militia. Amal, aided by a Shi'ite brigade of the Lebanese army, establishes partial control over the camps by May 30. The Shi'ites were trying to prevent the PLO from reestablishing a presence in southern Lebanon that would invite Israeli reprisals. Members of PLO factions that had fought each other in 1983 reportedly united against the threat from the Shi'ites.

May 20. *Prisoner Exchange.* Israel frees 1,150 Palestinians and other prisoners in exchange for 3 Israeli prisoners of war still in Palestinian hands. The exchange is the largest since November 1983.

May 25. *Assassination Attempt.* Kuwaiti emir Sheikh Jaber al-Ahmed al-Sabah narrowly escapes harm when a bomb-laden car rams his motorcade. The assassin and three other people are killed by the blast.

May 29. *Hussein on Talks.* During a visit to Washington, Jordan's King Hussein says the PLO would agree to hold peace talks with Israel under the "umbrella" of an international conference.

June 10. *Israeli Withdrawal Completed.* The Israeli army completes its withdrawal from Lebanon.

June 11. *Jordanian Airliner Hijacked.* Shi'ite gunmen in Beirut hijack a Jordanian airliner carrying seventy-four passengers. The hijackers demand that all Palestinian guerrillas leave Lebanon. After forcing the plane to fly to Cyprus and Sicily June 12, the hijackers order the plane back to Beirut, where they release the hostages and blow up the plane.

June 14. *TWA Hijacking.* Trans World Airways Flight 847 carrying 153 passengers and crew, including 104 Americans, from Athens to Rome is hijacked and forced to land at Beirut, where 19 passengers are freed, mostly women and children. The plane then flies to Algiers, where 18 more passengers are released and the hijackers threaten to execute the remaining passengers unless Israel releases Moslem prisoners captured in Lebanon. The plane returns early June 15 to Beirut, where passenger Robert D. Stethem, a U.S. Navy diver, is shot and killed. The two or three hijackers claim to be members of the Islamic Jihad group. The jet is forced to return later that day to Algiers, where about 70 more passengers are released. The plane returns early June 16 to Beirut, where Shi'ite Amal militia leader Nabih Berri assumes negotiations on behalf of the hijackers. Several passengers with "Jewish sounding names" are removed from the plane but are kept hostage elsewhere. The remaining 30 passengers are removed June 17 but also are not freed. The pilot and 2 crew members remain hostage aboard the plane. Berri says the former passengers are being held "somewhere in Beirut." The Amal militia allows Western journalists to hold a news conference with the hostages June 20.

June 18. *Reagan News Conference.* President Reagan vows at a news conference that the United States would never give in to terrorists or ask any other government to do so. However, administration officials say June 20 that if the 40 American hostages from TWA Flight 847 were freed, Israel would later release more than 700 Lebanese Moslem prisoners. Israel says June 23 that it will release 31 Shi'ite

prisoners but that the move is "not linked whatsoever" to the demands of the hijackers. Amal says it has no plans to release the American hostages.

June 24. *Hostage Negotiations Continue.* Nabih Berri sets a new demand for release of the hijack victims: withdrawal of U.S. warships from positions near the Lebanese coast. The White House warns June 25 of economic and military reprisals against Lebanon unless the hostages are released in the "next few days." One hostage is released June 26.

June 30. *Hostages Freed.* Thirty-nine U.S. hostages from Flight 847 are freed and driven to Damascus. They arrive in West Germany July 1. The Syrian government reportedly was instrumental in negotiating their release. The Reagan administration made no direct concessions to the hijackers, but it assured Syria that Israel would release 735 Lebanese Moslem prisoners in stages soon after the Americans were freed. Israel releases 300 of the prisoners July 3.

July 1. *Israeli Austerity Measures.* Israel declares a state of economic emergency and announces new austerity measures. These include an 18.8 percent devaluation of the shekel, sharp cuts in government subsidies of basic commodities, and a three-month wage and price freeze.

July 25. *OPEC Cuts Prices.* At the end of a contentious four-day meeting, OPEC agrees to small price cuts. Iran, Libya, and Algeria vote against the measure. Saudi Arabia indicates July 31 that it is planning to double its production rate.

August 9. *Beirut Fighting.* Artillery and gun battles between Christian and Moslem militias break out in Beirut. Dozens of civilians are killed.

August 15. *Iraq Raids Kharg Island.* Iraq claims to have destroyed Iran's oil export terminal at Kharg Island, but neutral observers say it is still partially functional. The raid comes amidst continuing attacks by both sides on ships in the Persian Gulf.

September 14. *Hostage Released.* The Rev. Benjamin Weir, one of seven Americans held hostage in Lebanon by Shi'ite militia, is released after sixteen months in captivity. The Reagan administration confirms his release September 18.

September 15. *Saudi-British Arms Deal.* Great Britain announces that Saudi Arabia will purchase between $3 billion and $4 billion worth of British combat aircraft, including forty-eight British Tornado fighter bombers. The Saudis approached the British after being frustrated in their efforts to buy U.S. F-15 fighters. The sale is concluded September 26.

September 25. *Palestinians Attack Yacht.* Palestinian gunmen storm a small private yacht in Cyprus, killing three Israelis. Before surrendering to police, they demand the release of twenty Palestinians held by Israel.

September 27. *Jordanian Arms Sale.* President Reagan notifies Congress of his intention to sell Jordan between $1.5 billion and $1.9 billion in arms, including forty F-20 or F-16 fighters, seventy-two Stinger missiles, and thirty-two Bradley fighting vehicles.

September 27. *Hussein at UN.* King Hussein tells the UN General Assembly that consultation on the Middle East between the United States and the Soviet Union is "both necessary and positive." He says he is ready to negotiate with Israel at a UN-sponsored international conference that includes PLO representation.

October 1. *Israel Bombs PLO Headquarters.* Israeli planes destroy the PLO headquarters in Tunis in retaliation for the killing of three Israelis by Palestinians in Cyprus six days earlier. Leaders throughout the Arab world condemn the bombing, which kills more than seventy persons. The United States calls the attack "a legitimate response" to terrorism. On October 2, however, it revises its position, saying the attack was "understandable" but that it "cannot be condoned."

October 7. *Achille Lauro Hijacking.* Heavily armed gunmen hijack the Italian cruise ship *Achille Lauro* with more than 400 people on board. They demand that Israel release 50 Palestinian prisoners. Yasir Arafat denies PLO involvement. Israeli officials say they have proof a wing of the PLO is behind the hijacking.

October 9. *Hijackers Surrender.* The four hijackers of the *Achille Lauro* surrender in Egypt after gaining assurances of safe passage to an undisclosed location. Italy later reports that Leon Klinghoffer, a wheelchair-bound New Yorker, is missing and is believed to have been slain and his body thrown overboard. Egypt later confirms the report.

October 10. *Hijackers Intercepted.* U.S. warplanes intercept an Egyptian plane carrying the hijackers of the *Achille Lauro* and force it to land in Sicily. An Italian public prosecutor October 11 charges the four Palestinians with murder and kidnapping. Egyptian President Hosni Mubarak October 12 condemns the U.S. interception of the hijackers and says the action has strained U.S.-Egyptian relations.

October 14. *British Cancel Meeting.* Britain calls off a meeting with a Palestinian-Jordanian delegation. Foreign Secretary Geoffrey Howe says the Palestinian members of the delegation refused to sign a statement supporting a peaceful settlement of the Arab-Israeli conflict that would recognize Israel's right to exist within pre-1967 borders.

October 14. *UN Withdraws Arafat Invitation.* The UN General Assembly declines to invite Yasir Arafat to attend ceremonies marking the UN's fortieth anniversary after the United States threatens to boycott the ceremonies if he attends.

October 21. *Peres on Middle East Peace.* In an address to the UN General Assembly October 21, Israeli Prime Minister Shimon Peres says that he is willing to travel to Jordan before the end of the year and that he would participate in an "international forum" on Middle East peace. Peres concludes by calling for an end to the state of war between Israel and Jordan. King Hussein praises the "spirit" of Peres's speech October 23.

October 23. *Jordan Arms Sale Postponed.* Congressional opposition to the Reagan administration's proposed arms sale to Jordan prompts Reagan to delay the deal until March 1, unless Jordan and Israel begin "direct and meaningful" peace negotiations before then.

October 23. *Abbas Implicated in Hijacking.* One of the *Achille Lauro* hijackers reportedly tells Italian investigators that Muhammad Abu'l Abbas, leader of the Palestine National Front, was the mastermind behind the operation. Italy allowed Abbas to leave Italy October 21 despite American requests for his detention.

October 31. *Israeli Government Rift.* Two conservative Israeli government officials, Ariel Sharon and Yuval Neeman, accuse Prime Minister Peres of holding secret negotiations with King Hussein of Jordan. Peres denies the accusations.

November 10. *Peres-Hussein Agreement.* The *New York Times* reports that Israeli Prime Minister Peres and Jordan's King Hussein have reached an informal agreement, through U.S. mediation, on holding a Middle East peace conference. Peres pledged that Israel would attend if Jordan agreed to bring only Palestinians acceptable to Israel.

November 15. *Government Collapse Prevented.* Israeli officials avert the collapse of the National Unity Government. Prime Minister Peres had threatened to fire Minister of Industry and Commerce Ariel Sharon for publicly insulting him and attacking his peace initiatives toward Jordan. Peres withdraws his threat after Sharon apologizes.

November 21. *Pollard Arrested.* Jonathan Jay Pollard, a civilian employee of the U.S. Naval Intelligence Service in Suitland, Maryland, is arrested outside the Israeli embassy in Washington while attempting to seek political asylum. He is charged with selling classified information to Israel over the previous eighteen months. Pollard's wife, Anne Henderson-Pollard, is arrested November 22 and charged with unauthorized possession of classified U.S. documents. The Israeli government denies knowledge of the spy operation November 24 but says it will investigate the allegations.

November 23. *Montazeri Named Successor.* The eighty-three-man Council of Experts formally designates Ayatollah Hussein Ali Montazeri as the eventual successor to Ayatollah Ruhollah Khomeini as leader of Iran. Montazeri is said to be Khomeini's personal choice.

November 23. *Egyptian Airliner Hijacked.* Egyptair Flight 648 from Athens to Cairo is hijacked. The airplane is the same one intercepted October 10 while transporting the *Achille Lauro* hijackers out of Egypt. A hijacker and an Egyptian security agent are killed in a midair gun battle. Stray bullets pierce the fuselage, depressurizing the cabin and forcing the plane to land on Malta. There the hijackers release eleven female passengers and demand fuel. When their request is not granted, they begin shooting Israeli and American passengers and throwing them from the plane. Three of the five passengers who are shot, however, do not receive fatal wounds.

November 24. *Rescue Attempt.* Egyptian special forces storm the hijacked Egyptair plane after dark. The hijackers shoot at the passengers and toss three incendiary grenades that set the cabin on fire. Fifty-nine of the original ninety-eight passengers and crew are killed during the hijacking. Only one hijacker survives. The hijackers are reported to be pro-Libyan followers of Mazen Sabry al-Banna, alias Abu Nidal, who heads a Palestinian group opposed to PLO chairman Yasir Arafat. Egyptian officials accuse Libya of backing the hijacking. Libya denies any involvement. Before the rescue attempt Egypt had declared a state of emergency along its border with Libya and it had reinforced troops in western Egypt.

November 25. *Hassan Agrees to Meet Peres.* King Hassan II of Morocco agrees to meet Israeli Prime Minister Shimon Peres if Peres has serious proposals for Middle East peace. Peres says he would meet with the king. Israel declares November 26 that it will seek clarification of conflicting accounts of Hassan's offer to meet with Peres after Hassan is quoted as setting conditions on his purported invitation.

December 1. *Peres Apologizes* Prime Minister Shimon Peres apologizes to the United States for Israeli espionage exposed by the Pollard spy case. Peres says Israel will dismantle the unit involved if allegations are proven true. Secretary of State George Shultz says the United States is "satisfied" with the statement.

December 8. *OPEC Meeting.* OPEC oil ministers

agree to abandon their official pricing structure in an effort to gain a larger share of the world's oil market. Although many OPEC members had been selling oil below OPEC prices, the formal announcement causes oil prices to drop 10 percent amidst predictions of an oil price war. Saudi Arabia, which in the past had cut its output to support world prices, says it will not produce below its quota.

December 8. *Mubarak on PLO.* Egyptian President Hosni Mubarak strongly endorses the need for the PLO to play a major role in the Middle East peace process and accuses the United States of trying to exclude the PLO. He says, "The PLO is the sole representative of the Palestinians, whether we like it or not."

December 27. *Airport Attacks.* Palestinian gunmen attack crowds of travelers at El Al Israeli Airlines check-in counters in Rome and Vienna, throwing grenades and firing submachine guns. The gunmen kill 18 people and wound 111. Four terrorists are killed and 3 others are wounded and captured. One surviving terrorist identifies himself as a member of the Fatah Revolutionary Council, a renegade Palestinian group led by Abu Nidal. A note found in the terrorist's pocket claims the assault was in retaliation for the October 1 Israeli air raid on PLO headquarters in Tunis. The PLO condemns the airport attacks. Austrian authorities December 29 absolve Yasir Arafat's faction of the PLO, Al Fatah, of responsibility in the attack at the Vienna airport.

December 28. *Lebanese Pact Signed.* Leaders of Lebanon's rival militia forces sign a pact in Syria to end fighting in Lebanon. The agreement has two sections, one containing a mechanism to end the civil war, and another describing a new political power-sharing arrangement between Christians and Moslems.

1986

January 7. *U.S. Sanctions against Libya.* President Reagan asserts there is "irrefutable evidence" of Libyan support for Abu Nidal, who is believed to be behind the December 27, 1985, airport attacks in Rome and Vienna. Reagan ends all trade and economic activity between the United States and Libya and calls for the one thousand to fifteen hundred Americans working in Libya to leave the country. He signs an executive order January 8 freezing Libyan assets in the United States. The State Department issues a report highlighting Libyan involvement in international terrorism, but most European nations say they will not join in a trade boycott against Libya. During January, however, several countries, including Canada, Italy, Great Britain, West Germany, and France, impose limited sanctions against Libya.

January 13. *Civil War in South Yemen.* An attempt by President Ali Nasser Muhammad to have rival politburo members assassinated precipitates a coup against his rule in South Yemen. Fierce battles between loyal government forces and supporters of the coup erupt in and around Aden. Both sides declare their allegiance to Moscow. British and Soviet ships evacuate thousands of foreigners. The rebel forces claim victory January 19. Western sources estimate that as many as ten thousand South Yemenis may have been killed. Prime Minister Haider Abu Bakr al-

Attas, who was out of the country when the fighting erupted, returns to Aden January 25 and is named provisional president in a Marxist coalition government. Ali Nasser Muhammad reportedly flees the country.

January 15. *Christians Fight in Lebanon.* Phalangist party forces loyal to President Amin Gemayel defeat the Lebanese Forces militia, commanded by Elie Hobeika, in a two-day battle that leaves more than two hundred dead. Hobeika is captured and forced to resign as leader of the Lebanese Forces. His defeat collapses a December 1985 Syrian-brokered peace accord signed by Christian and Moslem militia leaders.

January 31. *Reagan Halts Jordan Arms Sales.* President Reagan indefinitely postpones plans to sell $1.9 billion in U.S. arms to Jordan, because of overwhelming congressional opposition.

February 4. *Israelis Intercept Libyan Jet.* Israeli warplanes intercept a Libyan civilian jet on its way from Tripoli to Damascus and force it to land in Israel. The Israelis suspect that Palestinian terrorists are aboard, but they find none. The United States February 6 vetoes a UN Security Council resolution condemning Israel's action.

February 11. *Iranians Capture Fao.* Iranian forces capture Fao, an Iraqi oil port near Kuwait, in one of the most daring offensives in the five-and-a-half-year Persian Gulf war.

February 17. *Israelis Raid Lebanon.* Lebanese Moslem guerrillas capture two Israeli soldiers near the Israeli border in southern Lebanon. Israel launches a large-scale land, sea, and air operation to search for its men. In Beirut the Islamic Resistance Front claims responsibility February 18 for seizing the Israelis. An anonymous caller February 19 tells news services in Beirut that one Israeli soldier has already been executed.

February 19. *Hussein Speech.* In a televised speech Jordan's King Hussein declares that he is ending a year-long joint effort with the PLO to revitalize the Arab-Israeli peace process. He accuses Arafat of failing to cooperate by rejecting UN Security Council resolutions 242 and 338, despite major U.S. diplomatic concessions secured by Jordan. Hussein nevertheless reaffirms his support of the 1974 Arab League designation of the PLO as the sole legitimate representative of the Palestinian people.

February 25-March 2. *Violence in Egypt.* Thousands of Egyptian security police conscripts mutiny after false rumors spread that their tour of duty will be extended. They destroy major tourist hotels near the Pyramids. Violence spreads to Cairo and other cities before the revolt is quashed by army troops. The fighting is the most serious unrest in Egypt since Hosni Mubarak became president. It is suspected that Islamic militants opposed to the government were instrumental in the insurgence.

March 11. *Reagan Announces Saudi Arms Sale.* The Reagan administration notifies Congress of its intention to sell $354 million in advanced missiles to Saudi Arabia because of concern over the escalation of the Iran-Iraq war. Delivery is scheduled for 1989.

March 23-27. *U.S. Mediterranean Maneuvers.* The U.S. Navy's Sixth Fleet begins "freedom of navigation maneuvers" in the disputed Gulf of Sidra near Libya. Libya fires antiaircraft missiles at U.S. warplanes March 24, prompting U.S. air strikes against Libyan ships and a Libyan missile installation later that day. The U.S. fleet leaves the area March 27.

April 2. *Explosion on TWA Jet.* A bomb explodes on a Trans World Airlines passenger jet en route from Rome

to Athens killing four, all Americans, and injuring nine. The bodies are sucked out through a hole torn in the side of the plane. The flight lands safely in Athens. An anonymous caller in Beirut claims the group responsible is the Ezzedine Kassam unit of the Arab Revolutionary Cells, believed to be a faction associated with Abu Nidal.

April 5. *Bomb Explodes in Berlin Disco.* A bomb explodes in a Berlin discothèque, killing an American soldier and a Turkish woman, and injuring more than two hundred, including sixty-four Americans. The United States says it suspects Libyan participation. In a televised news conference April 9 Reagan says the United States will respond militarily if it finds evidence that Libya was involved in the Berlin bombing.

April 14. *U.S. Attacks Libya.* American planes attack targets in Libya, including the home and headquarters of Muammar Qaddafi, a naval academy, and air bases in Benghazi. A residential neighborhood in Tripoli is inadvertently hit. The raid kills at least fifteen people and injures sixty. Qaddafi's infant daughter is among the dead. One U.S. F-111 bomber is shot down and its two crewman are killed. All Arab nations condemn the air strike and most Western European nations criticize the action. France refused to permit U.S. planes based in Britain to fly over its territory. Reagan says he ordered the strike after receiving "irrefutable evidence," through interception of Libyan transmissions, that Qaddafi was involved in the April 5 terrorist bombing in West Berlin. On April 15 Libya fires two missiles at a U.S. Coast Guard installation on the Italian island of Lampedusa, but they fall harmlessly in the sea. The Soviet Union cancels Foreign Minister Eduard Shevardnadze's May 14-16 visit to Washington to protest the attack. The United States, Britain, and France April 21 veto a UN Security Council resolution condemning the raid.

April 17. *Hostages Shot.* One American hostage, Peter Kilburn, and two British hostages, Leigh Douglas and Philip Padfield, are found shot to death near Beirut. Two days earlier Abu Nidal's pro-Libyan terrorist group had warned that his forces would strike against the United States and countries that cooperated with it. A note found with the bodies threatens more violence in retaliation for the air raid on Libya.

April 17. *Bomb Found at Heathrow.* Security guards of El Al Israeli Airlines find a bomb in a pregnant woman's luggage at London's Heathrow airport. Anne-Marie Murphy is believed to be the innocent dupe of her Jordanian boyfriend, Nezar Hindawi, who had given her the bag. Hindawi is charged April 22 with conspiring to murder the flight's passengers.

April 21. *Europeans Curb Libyan Missions.* Twelve European countries impose restrictions on the size and activities of Libyan diplomatic missions to demonstrate their displeasure with Qaddafi's involvement in international terrorism.

May 5. *Assad Meets Hussein.* President Hafez Assad of Syria arrives in Amman for talks with Jordan's King Hussein on regional and bilateral issues. It is Assad's first trip to Jordan in nine years. They discuss their different approaches to negotiations with Israel and their opposing loyalties in the Iran-Iraq war.

May 7. *Congress Rejects Saudi Arms Deal.* The U.S. House of Representatives, in a 356-62 vote, adopts a resolution rejecting the $354 million arms deal with Saudi Arabia. The Senate had rejected the sale 73-22 May 5. President Reagan vetoes the resolution May 21.

May 24. *Thatcher Visits Israel.* Margaret Thatcher arrives in Jerusalem, becoming the first British prime minister to go to Israel. During Thatcher's three-day visit, she meets with senior Israeli officials and with leading Moslem and Christian Arabs from the Israeli-occupied West Bank and Gaza Strip.

May 25. *Secret U.S. Mission to Tehran.* Former U.S. national security adviser Robert McFarlane, National Security Council staff member Lt. Col. Oliver North, and several other American officials arrive in Tehran on a secret diplomatic mission aimed at freeing U.S. hostages in Lebanon. Their plane also carries a pallet of Hawk missile spare parts, which had been loaded in Israel. They meet officials in the Iranian prime minister's office. McFarlane demands May 27 that U.S. hostages in Lebanon be released the next day. On May 28 McFarlane is told the Iranians think they can get two hostages out now and the remaining two after delivery of the missile parts. McFarlane rejects the offer and the delegation leaves Tehran, but not before the Iranians take the missile parts from the aircraft. McFarlane reports May 29 directly to President Reagan on his trip to Tehran and suggests that the arms-for-hostages initiative be discontinued.

June 1. *Israelis Remove Attorney General.* The Israeli government replaces Attorney General Yitzhak Zamir for defying the government's wishes in ordering a criminal investigation of Avraham Shalom, the head of Shin Beth, the internal security organization. Zamir asserted that Shalom had tried to cover up information on the deaths of two Palestinians who hijacked a civilian bus in April 1984. Israeli press reports indicate July 2 that Foreign Minister Yitzhak Shamir may have participated in the alleged cover-up.

June 4. *Pollard Pleads Guilty to Spying.* Jonathan Jay Pollard pleads guilty to spying on the U.S. government for Israel. The Justice Department names four Israelis as unindicted conspirators. The guilty plea is part of an agreement to avoid a trial that might further strain U.S.-Israeli relations.

June 5. *Saudi Arms Deal Allowed.* Thirty-four senators vote to approve President Reagan's proposed arms sale to Saudi Arabia, sustaining Reagan's veto of a congressional resolution blocking the deal. Compromise reductions in the arms package and the president's lobbying win over enough senators to uphold the veto.

June 8. Achille Lauro *Report.* An Italian report says the Arab terrorist group that hijacked the *Achille Lauro* cruise ship was selected and directed by Palestinian leader Muhammad Abu'l Abbas and trained in one of his camps in Algeria.

June 25. *Shin Beth Affair.* Avraham Shalom, the head of Shin Beth, Israel's internal security agency, resigns in exchange for immunity from prosecution. He had been accused of ordering and then covering up the killings of two Palestinian bus hijackers in 1984. Members of the Israeli Labor party demand that Prime Minister Shimon Peres order a commission of inquiry to investigate the involvement of political leaders in the Shin Beth affair. Foreign Minister Shamir opposes any further inquiry. A leading Labor party minister calls for Shamir's resignation, June 29. After a month of silence, Shamir July 3 denies approving the killings of the bus hijackers or the subsequent cover-up. The Israeli cabinet decides July 14 not to form a commission of inquiry. The attorney general then announces that he is ordering an investigation of the scandal. The Israeli Justice Ministry December 28 clears Shamir of any wrongdoing in the killings or the cover-up.

June 30. *OPEC Fails to Reach Agreement.* OPEC ends a six-day conference without agreeing on a strategy to cut production. The world oil glut has forced prices as low as $12 a barrel.

July 10. Achille Lauro *Hijackers Convicted.* An Italian jury convicts eleven of the fifteen men charged with participating in the *Achille Lauro* hijacking. Three of the defendants receive sentences of between fifteen and thirty years. Muhammad Abu'l Abbas and two other fugitives—tried in absentia—are given life sentences for organizing the hijacking.

July 22. *Peres Meets Hassan.* Prime Minister Peres of Israel and King Hassan II of Morocco meet in Ifrane, Morocco. In reaction Syria breaks all diplomatic ties with Morocco. Other hard-line Arab countries and the PLO denounce the meeting as a betrayal of the Arab cause. Egypt's President Mubarak hails the talks as a "good initiative." Peres calls the meetings a success. Hassan stresses that Israel must accept the PLO and evacuate all of the occupied territories before a peace settlement can be achieved. Hassan resigns as chairman of the Arab League July 28 because of Arab criticism.

July 26. *Jenco Released.* The Rev. Lawrence Jenco, who had been kidnapped January 8, 1985, is released in Lebanon.

August 4. *OPEC Agreement.* The ministers of OPEC reach a unanimous tentative agreement on an Iranian proposal to limit oil production to bolster prices. The agreement aims at cutting production from 20.5 to 16.0 million barrels a day, raising prices from below $12 to $15-$19 a barrel, and ending the year-long price war in the cartel.

August 18. *Soviet-Israeli Talks.* Soviet and Israeli diplomats meet in Helsinki to discuss the establishment of consulates. The talks are the first formal diplomatic contact between the two countries in nineteen years. The Soviets say the move does not signify any basic change in policy toward Israel.

September 6. *Istanbul Synagogue Attack.* Two Arabs attack Jewish worshippers in an Istanbul synagogue with automatic weapons and grenades. Twenty-one Jews are killed. The assailants kill themselves after being trapped in the synagogue by police. Israeli trade minister Ariel Sharon causes a furor when he claims the attack was the result of Prime Minister Peres's peace initiatives. After refusing one retraction, Peres accepts Sharon's second letter of apology September 8.

September 9. *Kidnappings in Beirut.* Frank Herbert Reed, the American director of the Lebanese International School in West Beirut, is kidnapped. Joseph J. Cicippio, acting comptroller at the American University of Beirut, is kidnapped September 12. American author and book salesman Edward Austin Tracy is kidnapped October 21.

September 11-12. *Egyptian-Israeli Summit.* In the first talks between leaders of Egypt and Israel in five years, President Mubarak meets with Prime Minister Peres in Alexandria, Egypt. On September 10 representatives of the two nations prevented the summit from being delayed by agreeing on terms for submitting their border dispute over the resort city of Taba for arbitration.

October 5. *Israeli Nuclear Arsenal Report.* The *Sunday Times* of London reports that, according to former Israeli nuclear technician Mordechai Vanunu, Israel has been manufacturing nuclear weapons for twenty years at a secret underground factory near its Dimona nuclear research plant. Vanunu maintains that Israel had built be-

tween one hundred and two hundred atomic bombs and has the capability to produce thermonuclear weapons. Israel confirms November 9 that it has arrested Vanunu. He is charged with espionage November 28.

October 20. *Shamir Becomes Prime Minister.* Israeli leaders Yitzhak Shamir and Shimon Peres trade jobs in accordance with a power-sharing agreement concluded between the Likud and Labor parties after the 1984 election. Shamir takes over as prime minister, while Peres becomes foreign minister.

October 24. *Britain Breaks Syrian Ties.* After a British jury convicts a Palestinian with links to Syria of attempting to smuggle a bomb on an Israeli airliner taking off from London April 17, the British government severs relations with Syria. European Community nations (except Greece) agree November 10 to jointly impose sanctions against Syria for its part in the plot.

October 29. *Yamani Dismissed.* Saudi Arabia's King Fahd dismisses Ahmed Zaki Yamani from his post as Saudi oil minister.

November 2. *Jacobsen Released.* Hostage David P. Jacobsen, who had been kidnapped May 28, 1985, is released in Beirut.

November 3. *Magazine Reports McFarlane Visit.* A pro-Syrian Beirut weekly magazine, *Al-Shiraa*, discloses Robert McFarlane's secret trip to Tehran in May. The magazine says that the information was leaked through the office of Ayatollah Hussein Ali Montazeri, the designated heir to Iranian leader Khomeini. During a bill-signing ceremony, President Reagan tells reporters November 6 that stories about McFarlane traveling to Tehran have "no foundation."

November 13. *Reagan's Speech.* In a televised speech from the White House, President Reagan admits that his administration sent arms to Iran but says that the shipments were not ransom payments for hostages but were good-faith gestures intended to open a "dialogue" with moderates there. The president's speech is the first official acknowledgment that the United States directly shipped military equipment to Iran.

November 19. *Reagan Press Conference.* President Reagan says in a news conference that he has ruled out future arms sales to Iran. He insists that the covert operation was not a mistake. Reagan denies that Israel was involved in the Iran initiative, but after the press conference the White House issues a statement acknowledging that a third country was involved.

November 25. *Diversion Disclosed.* In a hastily called news conference, President Reagan says that he had not been "fully informed" about the Iran arms deals. Attorney General Edwin Meese III discloses that members of the administration may have helped divert an estimated $10 million to $30 million from the Iran arms sales to support the Nicaraguan contra rebels. Reagan admits in a radio address December 6 that "mistakes were made" in the Iran initiative.

December 11. *Libyan Troops Attack Chad.* Libya launches a major offensive against Chad. France and the United States send aid to Chad's government, but France says its troops in that country will not enter the battle unless Libyan forces cross the sixteenth parallel.

December 11-20. *OPEC Production Cuts.* OPEC ministers meeting in Geneva agree to reduce their combined oil production by about 6 percent effective January 1, 1987. They also agree to establish a fixed price of $18 a barrel rather than let market forces determine the price.

1987

January 12. *Iraq Condemns United States.* Iraq's first deputy prime minister, Taha Yasin Ramadan, accuses the United States of having supplied Iraq with faulty intelligence information that resulted in the deaths of thousands of Iraqi soldiers. Ramadan's condemnation, reported in the January 13 *Wall Street Journal,* comes amidst allegations that the United States had passed false information to both Iran and Iraq, which the CIA denies.

January 13. *Hamadai Arrested.* West German authorities arrest Muhammad Ali Hamadai at the Frankfurt airport after they discover a powerful liquid explosive in his possession. Hamadai is one of four men indicted by the United States for the hijacking of a TWA jet in June 1985. The United States January 15 asks West Germany to extradite him.

January 20. *Waite Disappears.* Anglican church emissary Terry Waite, on his fifth mission to Lebanon to negotiate the release of hostages, is last seen on his way to a meeting with a Shi'ite group. Moslem militia officials January 30 confirm reports that he has been taken hostage.

January 24. *Four Kidnapped in Lebanon.* In the largest single kidnapping of American citizens in Beirut, terrorists disguised as Lebanese police abduct three Americans and one Indian from the Beirut University campus. The three Americans are Alann Steen, Jesse Jonathan Turner, and Robert Polhill, all professors at the university. Mithileshwar Singh, chairman of the business school, is an Indian citizen who is a permanent resident of the United States. The Reagan administration January 28 bars most Americans from traveling to Lebanon and gives Americans living in Lebanon thirty days to leave.

January 31. *U.S. Reporter Detained.* A *Wall Street Journal* reporter, Gerald F. Seib, is detained by Iranian police. Seib was among more than fifty Western journalists invited to Iran to observe Iran's war efforts against Iraq. Iran calls Seib "a spy for the Zionist regime." Seib is released February 6.

February 14-15. *Food Reaches Palestinians.* Trucks carrying food enter a Palestinian refugee camp in Lebanon that had been under siege by Shi'ite Amal militia forces since November 1985. International pressure aroused by fears that Palestinians would soon begin to starve to death led Amal leaders to allow the convoy to pass.

February 15. *Beirut Factions Battle.* Heavy fighting in West Beirut between Shi'ite Amal militia forces and a Druze-led leftist coalition leaves three hundred dead. Lebanese Moslem leaders request February 20 that Syria send troops to halt the fighting. Thousands of Syrian troops enter West Beirut February 22-23. Outbursts of factional fighting continue, but the Syrians gain control of the city.

February 17. *Shamir in United States.* During a ten-day visit to the United States Israeli prime minister Shamir voices his opposition to an international Middle East peace conference. He tells U.S. congressional leaders February 18 that he will provide written accounts of Israeli involvement in the transfer of arms to Iran, if U.S. officials drop their attempts to seek the testimony of Israeli citizens.

February 27. *Peres-Meguid Communiqué.* After two days of meetings, foreign ministers Shimon Peres of Israel and Esmat Abdel Meguid of Egypt issue a joint communiqué calling for an international peace conference in 1987 that would lead to direct Arab-Israeli talks. Israel's Prime Minister Shamir denounces the communiqué at a March 1 cabinet meeting, and Peres does not press his plan.

March 11. *Israel Investigates Pollard Affair.* Prime Minister Shamir appoints a commission in Israel to conduct an inquiry into the Pollard spy case. The commission May 26 criticizes the government's role in the affair but declares top Israeli officials innocent of involvement.

March 23. *U.S. Offers Tanker Protection.* The United States offers to protect Kuwaiti oil tankers sailing in international waters in the Persian Gulf. Kuwait announces it favors both U.S. and Soviet escorts, but the Reagan administration declines to participate with the Soviets. Kuwait April 6 proposes reflagging some of its tankers as U.S. ships. Moscow announces April 14 that it will lease three tankers to Kuwait that may be escorted by Soviet warships.

March 27. *Libyan Retreat.* Libyan troops withdraw from Faya-Largeau, a strategic town in northern Chad, after Chadian battlefield victories imperiled the Libyan stronghold. The withdrawal is seen as a major setback for Libyan leader Muammar Qaddafi's ambitions in Chad.

April 20-26. *PLO Reunites.* At a convention of the Palestine National Council in Algiers, Yasir Arafat is reelected head of the PLO. To gain the support of PLO radicals, Arafat pledges to adopt a harder line toward Israel. The meeting ends with a declaration of unity.

April 23. *Assad and Gorbachev Meet.* Soviet leader Mikhail Gorbachev hosts Syrian president Assad in Moscow. Gorbachev promises Assad arms and debt rescheduling if Syria will support a unified PLO and an international Middle East peace conference.

May 4. *Karami Resigns.* Lebanese prime minister Rashid Karami announces his resignation, citing criticism of his leadership and the inability of Lebanon's divided cabinet to function. He agrees to serve until a successor is named.

May 17. *Iraqi Missile Hits U.S. Ship.* An Iraqi warplane fires a missile that seriously damages the U.S. frigate *Stark,* killing thirty-seven crew members and wounding twenty-one others. The ship is struck eighty-five miles from its final destination of Bahrain in the Persian Gulf. The Iraqi government calls the attack a tragic error.

May 19. *U.S.-Kuwaiti Agreement.* The United States announces an agreement with Kuwait to reflag eleven Kuwaiti tankers that will receive U.S. naval protection while in the Persian Gulf. The Reagan administration May 28 delays the reflagging operation until late June or July, after the Senate votes 91-5 on May 21 to require the administration to submit a report on security measures and rules of engagement to be employed by the U.S. task force.

June 1. *Lebanese Prime Minister Killed.* Rashid Karami, awaiting appointment of his successor as Lebanon's prime minister, is killed when a bomb explodes in his helicopter. No group takes responsibility for the assassination. Selim al-Hoss is appointed acting premier. Christians and Moslems mourn Karami's death and stage a general strike to observe his funeral.

June 11. *Saudi Missile Sale Delayed.* President Reagan announces that he is temporarily withdrawing a plan to sell sixteen hundred air-to-ground missiles to Saudi Arabia because of congressional opposition. Reagan cancels the missile sale October 8 as part of a compromise that allows $1 billion in other arms to be sold to Saudi Arabia.

July 12. *Soviets Arrive in Israel.* The first Soviet consular delegation to visit Israel since the 1967 Six-Day War arrives in Tel Aviv.

July 17. *France Breaks Iranian Ties.* France severs diplomatic relations with Iran because of a dispute over an Iranian sought for questioning about terrorist bombings who took refuge in the Iranian embassy in Paris. Iran accuses a French diplomat in Tehran of espionage and blockades the French embassy in retaliation.

July 20. *UN Resolution 598.* The UN Security Council unanimously adopts a resolution calling for a cease-fire between Iran and Iraq. The United States says it would support sanctions and an arms embargo against either nation if it refused to accept Resolution 598. Iraq accepts the resolution July 21, but Iran rejects it, declaring it will pursue its goal of toppling Saddam Hussein's regime.

July 22. *Escorts Begin.* American ships escort the first two Kuwaiti tankers to receive American protection into the Persian Gulf. The reflagged Kuwaiti tanker *Bridgeton* sustains minor damage after hitting an underwater mine July 24. Subsequently the United States and other Western nations send minesweeping equipment to the Persian Gulf.

July 31. *Mecca Riots.* Protests by thousands of Iranian pilgrims near the Grand Mosque in Mecca lead to a riot in which more than 400 people, including 275 Iranian pilgrims, are killed. The Saudi government claims its security forces did not fire on the crowd, and that most of the victims were killed by a stampede of Iranian pilgrims near the Grand Mosque. Iran accuses Saudi Arabia of slaughtering Iranian pilgrims with automatic weapons. Iranians rioters sack the Saudi and Kuwaiti embassies in Tehran August 1.

August 18. *Hostage Escapes.* American journalist Charles Glass escapes from his captors in Beirut amid speculation that he was allowed to escape because of Syrian efforts to secure his release. He had been kidnapped June 17.

August 29. *Tanker War Resumes.* Iraq attacks Iranian ships and oil installations, breaking a forty-five-day pause in the tanker war in the Persian Gulf. Iran responds with attacks against Arab tankers. By September 3 as many as twenty ships are damaged.

September 4. *Missile Hits Kuwait.* A long-range surface-to-surface missile strikes Kuwait, damaging houses and industrial facilities. Kuwait accuses Iran of firing the missile and expels five Iranian diplomats.

September 11-15. *De Cuéllar Diplomacy.* United Nations Secretary General Javier Pérez de Cuéllar travels to Iraq and Iran in an effort to negotiate an end to the Gulf war. Iran announces September 13 that it would accept a cease-fire if the UN identified Iraq as the aggressor in the war.

September 21. *U.S. Actions in the Gulf.* American helicopters disable an Iranian ship reportedly laying mines in the Persian Gulf. The ship and its surviving crew members are captured September 22 by U.S. forces. Ten contact mines are found aboard. American helicopters attack four more Iranian gunboats October 8 after a U.S. surveillance helicopter is attacked. One Iranian ship is sunk and two are captured.

October 16. *U.S.-Flagged Tanker Attacked.* The Kuwaiti tanker *Sea Isle City* is hit by an Iranian Silkworm missile within Kuwaiti territorial waters, where Kuwait is responsible for defending the U.S.-flagged ships. The attack wounds eighteen crew members. The Ayatollah Kho-

meini congratulates the Revolutionary Guards "for their heroic deed." In retaliation U.S. destroyers bombard an Iranian oil platform in the Persian Gulf. The oil platform, described by Pentagon sources as a fortified outpost, housed radar and communications equipment and served as a base for launching small boat attacks against Gulf shipping. The Iranians aboard the platform had been warned of the attack and allowed to flee. A platform six miles away that also had been evacuated is investigated by naval commandoes, who destroy its radar and communications equipment.

October 26. *United States Embargoes Iran.* President Reagan orders the embargoing of all imports of Iranian products and prohibits the exportation of fourteen types of "militarily useful" items to Iran. Reagan states that the action was taken in response to Iran's hostile actions toward the United States in the Gulf and its refusal to accept UN Security Council Resolution 598.

November 8-11. *Arab Summit.* At an emergency Arab League summit hosted by King Hussein in Amman, Arab leaders focus on the Gulf war while largely ignoring the Arab-Israeli conflict. Members unanimously condemn Iran's "aggression," express support for Iraq, and call on the international community to "adopt the necessary measures to make the Iranian regime respond to the peace calls." The league votes November 10 to allow members to reestablish relations with Egypt at their own discretion. Within six weeks nine Arab nations restore ties with Egypt.

November 25. *Hang Glider Attack.* Two Palestinians fly motorized hang gliders over the Israeli-Lebanese border. One penetrates an Israeli army base and kills five soldiers before he himself is shot.

November 29. *Embassy Sieges End.* France and Iran agree to allow each other's diplomats in the Tehran and Paris embassies to return home. Each nation had besieged the embassy of the other after an Iranian official in Paris took refuge in the Iranian embassy to avoid being questioned by French officials about a series of terrorist bombings. France also announces that it will begin negotiations with Iran concerning repayment of money owed by France to Iran. Earlier, on November 27, two French hostages in Lebanon had been released. American and British officials criticize the French for apparently striking a deal with Iran in return for the release of the hostages.

December 9. *Palestinian Uprising.* Palestinians in the Gaza Strip confront Israeli soldiers with rocks and molotov cocktails in response to an accident involving an Israeli army truck the day before that killed four Arabs. Israel soldiers kill one Palestinian, mortally wound another, and wound fifteen. The unrest spreads quickly to the West Bank. Israeli efforts to suppress protests in the occupied territories fail, as the sudden explosion of Palestinian anger turns into a sustained uprising. By December 18, Israeli soldiers kill at least seventeen Palestinians.

December 21. *Palestinian General Strike.* As the Palestinian death toll rises and protests continue, Palestinians residing in Israel hold a general strike in support of the uprising in the occupied territories.

December 22. *Security Council Faults Israel.* With the United States abstaining, the UN Security Council unanimously approves a resolution that "strongly deplores" Israel's handling of the Palestinian protests and its "excessive use of live ammunition." Israel announces December 25 that its troops have incarcerated nearly a thousand Palestinian suspects from the territories.

1988

January 3. *Israel Deports Arabs.* Israel announces that it will deport nine Palestinians accused of inciting riots in the occupied territories. The United States and the other members of the UN Security Council January 5 unanimously call on Israel to halt the deportations. Israel deports four of the nine Palestinians January 13.

January 19. *Israeli Policy Criticized.* Israeli defense minister Rabin announces that Israeli forces will combat the Palestinian uprising *(intifada)* with "force, might, and beatings" in an effort to reduce the number of Palestinians being killed.

Thirty-eight Palestinians had been shot to death during the first six weeks of the uprising. The new tactic is criticized by Britain and the United States, and thirty thousand Israeli demonstrators march on Tel Aviv to protest the policy. In response to the criticism, the Israeli army January 24 issues guidelines designed to reduce indiscriminate beatings.

February 15. *Palestinians Buried Alive.* Israeli news agencies confirm that the army arrested two soldiers for allegedly burying four Palestinian protesters alive in the West Bank town of Salim. According to witnesses the soldiers ordered a bulldozer to dump a load of dirt on the Palestinians. After the soldiers left, Arab residents uncovered the protesters. All four were injured but survived. Israeli defense minister Rabin expresses horror at the transgression and vows to investigate the charges.

February 17. *American Officer Abducted.* While serving as a UN observer in southern Lebanon, U.S. Marine Lt. Col. William R. Higgins is taken captive near Tyre. The Organization of the Oppressed on Earth, a shadowy Shi'ite movement with close ties to Hizballah, claims responsibility and charges Higgins with spying for the CIA.

February 25. *Shultz's Shuttle Diplomacy.* U.S. Secretary of State Shultz arrives in Israel to begin a week-long diplomatic offensive that includes stops in Jordan, Syria, and Egypt. Shultz is unable to garner much support among Middle East leaders for a U.S. peace initiative that calls for local elections to achieve limited Arab autonomy in the occupied territories.

February 29. *War of the Cities.* After Iraq bombs an Iranian oil refinery near Tehran February 27, Iran hits Baghdad with two long-range missiles. For the next several months the two sides fire missiles at each other's major cities almost daily, although Iraq launches many more missiles than Iran. These missile exchanges become known as the "war of the cities" and cause heavy damage and casualties.

March 2. *UN Condemns PLO Office Closure Plan.* The UN General Assembly adopts two resolutions opposing the U.S. move to close the PLO's New York office. The resolutions call for the International Court of Justice (the World Court) to issue an advisory opinion and accuse the United States of breaching its 1947 treaty with the United Nations.

Congress had mandated that the PLO office be closed despite the State Department's opposition to the move. Attorney General Meese March 11 formally orders the office to close within ten days. When the PLO refuses to obey the order, the Justice Department files suit March 22 to have the office closed.

March 6. *Soviet Embassy in Tehran Attacked.* An Iranian mob, angered by Soviet sales of missiles to Iraq that are being used against Iranian cities, attacks the Soviet embassy in Tehran with rocks and molotov cocktails. No Soviet personnel are killed, but the incident damages Soviet-Iranian relations.

March 10-12. *Arab Police Resign.* After Palestinian leaders issue leaflets calling on Arab members of police forces in the occupied territories to quit or risk being considered collaborators with Israel, nearly half of the one thousand police officers in the territories resign.

March 14-17. *Shamir Visits the U.S.* During a four-day visit to Washington, Prime Minister Shamir of Israel meets with President Reagan and Secretary of State Shultz. Shamir expresses his dissatisfaction with most of the important elements of Shultz's Middle East peace plan.

March 16. *Iraqi Chemical Attack.* The Iraqi army reportedly bombs the Kurdish town of Halabja in northeastern Iraq with chemical weapons after it is captured by the Iranian army. Iran claims that nearly five thousand Kurds died. Iran allows Western journalists to survey the destruction. A UN investigative team says April 26 that chemical weapons were used, but its report makes no conclusions about who used them.

March 19. *Saudis Purchase Chinese Missiles.* Saudi Arabia confirms reports that it has purchased from China a number of CSS-2 ballistic missiles with a range of about sixteen hundred miles. The United States criticizes the sale but warns Israel against attempting to destroy the missiles in a preemptive strike. To ease U.S. concerns about the missiles, Saudi Arabia announces April 25 that it will sign the multinational Nuclear Nonproliferation Treaty concluded in 1968.

March 28. *Israel Seals Off Territories.* In response to demonstrations planned by Palestinians for March 30, the Israeli army announces that it will seal off the occupied territories March 29-31. Under the plan Palestinians are not allowed to travel between the territories and Israel, journalists are not allowed into the territories without a military escort, and strict curfews are imposed.

April 5. *Kuwaiti Airliner Hijacked.* Shi'ite hijackers seize a Kuwaiti airliner en route from Bangkok to Kuwait and force it to land in Mashad, Iran. The hijackers demand that Kuwait release seventeen Shi'ites convicted of terrorist bombings. Iran refuels the plane April 8 after the hijackers fire warning shots and throw a grenade from plane. The jet then flies to Beirut but is prevented from landing by Lebanese air controllers and is diverted to Cyprus. There, two Kuwaiti passengers are killed before hijackers force the plane to fly to Algiers April 13. Algerian officials obtain the release of the remaining thirty-one hostages April 20 in return for guaranteeing the hijackers free passage out of country.

April 14. *Frigate Strikes Mine in Gulf.* Ten U.S. sailors are wounded when the frigate *Samuel B. Roberts* strikes a mine in the Persian Gulf near Bahrain. In retaliation, U.S. warships April 18 shell two Iranian oil platforms believed to be used as radar stations. Later that day U.S. ships clash with Iranian gunboats in the southern Gulf. Six Iranian ships are sunk or crippled.

April 16. *Wazir Assassinated.* Khalil Wazir (also known as Abu Jihad), the PLO's military chief and the second-ranking official of the PLO's Fatah faction, is killed in his home in Tunisia by a commando team presumed to have been sent by Israel. The Israeli government refuses to confirm or deny responsibility for the action.

April 18. *Iraq Recaptures Fao.* Iraq recaptures the Fao Peninsula from Iran in a surprise attack that began April 17.

April 25. *Arafat, Assad Meet.* In Damascus, PLO Chairman Yasir Arafat meets with Syrian president Hafez Assad for the first time since 1983.

April 26. *Saudi Arabia Breaks Iran Ties.* The Saudi government breaks off diplomatic relations with Iran because of its actions regarding the 1987 riots in Mecca by Iranian pilgrims and its continuing attacks on Gulf shipping.

May 2. *Israeli Operation.* As many as two thousand Israeli troops cross into Israel's self-declared security zone in southern Lebanon to search for Palestinian guerrillas who have stepped up their raids across the border. The Israelis find no Palestinians, but they engage Shi'ite militia forces May 4 near the town of Maidun north of the security zone. Forty Shi'ites and two Israelis are reported killed.

May 4. *French Hostages Freed.* Four days before French elections, France's remaining hostages in Lebanon are released after the government agrees to repay Iran about $300 million in old debts. In announcing the release, Prime Minister Jacques Chirac publicly thanks the Iranian government and Syria's President Assad for helping to secure the hostages' freedom. France announces May 18 that it is ready to reestablish diplomatic relations with Iran and pay an outstanding balance on a $1 billion loan.

May 6. *Rival Shi'ite Militias Clash.* Syrian-backed Amal troops battle Iranian-backed Hizballah forces in southern Lebanon and West Beirut. Fighting continues despite Iranian and Syrian officials' attempts to impose a cease-fire. Syria and Iran agree May 26 to a plan that sends Syrian troops into the area to restore order. Syrian deployments May 27-28 end the three-week battle, which has killed more than three hundred people.

May 25. *Qaddafi Recognizes Chad.* Libyan leader Muammar Qaddafi announces that Libya will end its armed conflict with Chad and recognize the Chadian government of President Hissene Habra. The two countries formally restore diplomatic relations October 3.

June 7-9. *Arab Summit on Uprising.* In an emergency meeting in Algiers, members of the Arab League adopt a resolution to "support by all possible means" the Palestinian uprising, but they do not respond to PLO requests for a specific commitment of financial aid. The summit also declines to designate the PLO as the sole distributor of financial aid to the uprising.

June 16. *French-Iranian Ties Restored.* After several weeks of negotiations France and Iran restore diplomatic relations broken in August 1987.

June 29. *PLO Office Closure Blocked.* A U.S. District Court judge rules that the United States may not close the PLO's UN observer mission in New York City because such an action would violate U.S. obligations as the host country under the UN charter. The Justice Department announces August 29 that it will not appeal the decision.

July 3. *U.S. Downs Iranian Airliner.* The American cruiser *Vincennes,* after a clash in the Persian Gulf with several Iranian gunboats, shoots down an Iranian passenger airliner, killing all two hundred ninety people aboard. The captain of the ship claims to have mistaken the airliner for an Iranian F-14 fighter. The ship warned the plane several times but received no response. President Reagan calls the incident "an understandable accident." Reagan announces July 11 that the United States will offer compensation to the victims' families.

July 8. *Saudi-British Arms Deal.* Great Britain announces that it has concluded an arms sale to Saudi Arabia worth $12 billion to $30 billion. The sale includes fifty advanced Tornado fighter planes. Saudi officials indicate that they sought the huge arms deal because of the difficulty of obtaining U.S. congressional approval to purchase American arms.

July 18. *Iran Accepts Cease-Fire.* Iranian president Ali Khamenei accepts UN Security Council Resolution 598, which calls for a cease-fire in the eight-year Gulf war. The Ayatollah Khomeini says July 19 that the decision to accept the cease-fire was "more deadly than taking poison." Iraq expresses skepticism about Iran's intentions and continues its attacks against Iranian positions. United Nations officials arrive in Tehran to negotiate a cease-fire July 23. Iraqi forces penetrate into Iran before ending offensive operations July 24. Iraq announces July 25 that it will withdraw from Iranian territory occupied during the previous week.

July 31. *Jordan Renounces West Bank Claim.* Jordan's King Hussein surrenders Jordan's claim to the West Bank in favor of the PLO and says he will cut all legal and administrative ties to the occupied territories. The move is seen as a blow to U.S. peace efforts, which had envisioned a major role for Jordan in settling the issue of the occupied territories. On August 4 Jordan says that it will stop paying the salaries of twenty-one thousand Palestinian civil servants on the West Bank.

August 8. *Cease-Fire.* After two weeks of mediation, UN Secretary General Javier Pérez de Cuéllar announces a cease-fire agreement between Iran and Iraq that will go into effect August 20. The cease-fire begins on schedule as a three-hundred-fifty-member UN peacekeeping force commences patrols along the Iran-Iraq border August 20. Talks on achieving a broader peace agreement begin August 25 in Geneva, but they stall the following day over Iraq's insistence that it control the entire Shatt al-Arab waterway. The negotiations recess September 13 without progress.

August 30. *Turkey Opens Borders to Kurds.* Turkey officially opens its borders to tens of thousands of Iraqi Kurds fleeing Iraqi government attacks. The government's offensive, designed to defeat Kurdish resistance groups, began July 30 after a de facto cease-fire had been achieved in the war with Iran. Since that time as many as one hundred thousand Iraqi Kurds are reported to have fled into Turkey. Many Kurdish refugees say Iraqi attacks have included the use of poison gas. The U.S. government says that intercepted Iraqi military communications and interviews with Kurds in Turkey have confirmed Iraq used chemical weapons.

September 22. *Rival Governments Formed.* After the Lebanese parliament fails to elect a successor to him, President Amin Gemayel, whose term expires at midnight, appoints Gen. Michel Aoun, a Maronite Christian, as acting premier of a provisional military government. On September 23 Moslems refuse to recognize Aoun's government and form a rival government around Selim al-Hoss, who had been acting premier under Gemayel. Before Gemayel's term expired, the United States and Syria tried unsuccessfully to find a presidential candidate acceptable to all major factions.

September 29. *Egypt Awarded Taba.* An international arbitration panel awards Egypt control of the Sinai resort of Taba. The area was claimed by Egypt but had been occupied by Israel since the 1967 Six-Day War. The two countries agreed in 1986 to settle the dispute through binding arbitration. Egypt takes possession of Taba March 15, 1989.

October 3. *Indian Hostage Released.* Mitheleshwar Singh is freed by his Islamic Jihad captors. Singh, an Indian citizen with permanent resident-alien status in the United States, was kidnapped in Beirut in January 1987.

October 19. *Car Bombing in Southern Lebanon.* After a suicide car bomb kills seven Israeli soldiers in southern Lebanon, Israeli jets attack Lebanese targets October 21, killing as many as fifteen people.

November 1. *Israeli Elections.* The Likud party claims victory after it wins thirty-nine parliament seats, compared with thirty-eight for the Labor party. Likud's chances of leading a ruling coalition are increased by the strong showing of Israel's small, right-wing religious parties, which win a total of eighteen seats—six more than in 1984. Likud leader Yitzhak Shamir says November 2 that his party will be able to form a coalition with the religious parties. President Chaim Herzog November 14 asks Shamir to form a government.

November 15. *Palestinian State Declared.* At the end of a four-day meeting in Algiers, the Palestine National Council (PNC) proclaims an independent Palestinian state in Gaza and the West Bank. On November 14 the PNC had voted to accept UN Security Council resolutions 242 and 338, an action that implicitly recognized Israel's right to exist. The United States rejected the declaration of independence and said that the PNC's actions did not satisfy U.S. conditions for opening a dialogue with the PLO.

November 26. *Arafat Denied Visa.* Secretary of State Shultz denies PLO leader Yasir Arafat an entry visa into the United States to address a special session of the UN General Assembly. Shultz says he acted because the PLO has engaged in terrorism. The General Assembly December 2 votes 154-2 to move the meeting to Geneva so Arafat can speak.

December 6-7. *Arafat Meets American Jews.* The Swedish foreign minister and a delegation of five American Jews meet with Arafat in Stockholm to discuss Middle East peace. They issue a statement December 7 to clarify the positions taken by the PNC in November. It says the council recognized Israel "as a state in the region" and "declared its rejection and condemnation of terrorism in all its forms, including state terrorism."

December 13. *Arafat Addresses UN in Geneva.* Yasir Arafat calls on Israel to join peace talks and reiterates the PNC's acceptance of UN resolutions 242 and 338 and rejection of terrorism.

December 14. *U.S. Opens Dialogue with PLO.* At a press conference in Geneva, Arafat explicitly renounces terrorism and accepts both Israel's right to exist and UN resolutions 242 and 338. Hours later the United States announces that Arafat has finally met its conditions for opening a U.S.-PLO dialogue. The State Department instructs Ambassador Robert H. Pelletreau to begin the dialogue with PLO representatives in Tunisia.

December 19. *Israeli Coalition Formed.* Israel's Likud and Labor parties agree to form a coalition government. Likud leader Shamir is designated as prime minister for the duration of the government. The U.S.-PLO dialogue and the reluctance of either party to accept the right-wing religious parties as coalition partners led to the decision to form another unity government.

December 21. *Reagan on Libyan Plant.* President Reagan says in a television interview that the United States and its allies are concerned about a chemical plant under construction in Rabta, Libya. Reagan maintains the plant is capable of producing large quantities of chemical weapons. He refuses to rule out a military strike aimed at destroying the facility. Libya claims the plant will produce only pharmaceuticals. News reports disclose December 31 that the United States has determined that Imhausen-Chemie, a West German company, aided Libya in the construction of the plant.

December 21. *Lockerbie Crash.* A Pan Am airliner breaks apart during a flight from London to New York and crashes in Lockerbie, Scotland. All 259 people aboard the jet and at least 11 people on the ground are killed. British investigators determine December 28 that a bomb caused the crash. No group claims responsibility for the bombing, but Middle East-based terrorist organizations are suspected.

1989

January 1. *Israel Deports Palestinians.* In renewed efforts to stem the year-long uprising in the occupied territories, Israeli authorities deport thirteen Palestinians suspected of leading the resistance.

January 2. *Arafat Threat.* During a radio broadcast, PLO leader Yasir Arafat reputedly threatens Arabs standing in the way of the Palestinian uprising. After U.S. officials January 4 characterize Arafat's remark as inconsistent with his renunciation of terrorism, the PLO insists that the remark had been taken out of context.

The United States, which had obtained a tape recording of Arafat's statement, maintained that his remarks translated into English were, "Whoever thinks of stopping the intifada before it achieves its goals, I will give him ten bullets in the chest."

January 4. *Mediterranean Dogfight.* Two U.S. Navy warplanes down two Libyan fighters in international waters near Libya. The United States contends that its pilots were on a routine training exercise and fired in self-defense.

Libya says its planes were unarmed, but the U.S. Defense Department releases videotape January 5 showing that the Libyan planes were carrying what appeared to be air-to-air missiles. The United States, Britain, and France January 11 veto a UN Security Council resolution deploring the downing of the Libyan planes.

January 5. *Soviet-Iran Thaw.* Soviet officials receive an Iranian diplomatic delegation in Moscow. In a letter delivered to Mikhail Gorbachev, the Ayatollah Khomeini asks the Soviet leader to abandon communism and study Islam.

January 11. *Chemical Weapons Conference.* A 149-nation conference in Paris condemns the use of chemical weapons but fails to single out any nation for violating the 1925 Geneva Protocol that prohibits their use. The outcome is seen as a victory for Iraq, which had recently been criticized for using chemical weapons against its Kurdish minority and Iranian troops.

January 30. *Shi'ite Truce.* After a month of fighting, the rival Amal and Hizballah Shi'ite Lebanese militias conclude a truce sponsored by Iran and Syria.

February 1. *Shamir Proposes Withdrawal.* Israeli

prime minister Shamir says that he is ready to pull troops out of some of the main population centers of the occupied territories whenever the Palestinian residents agree to accept political autonomy as the first stage of a Middle East peace settlement.

February 8. *Israel Condemns Report.* The Israeli government condemn as "harsh" and "one-sided" the annual U.S. State Department human rights report, which criticized Israel for frequently using gunfire against Palestinian protesters.

February 14. *Khomeini Calls for Author's Death.* Ayatollah Khomeini calls on Moslems everywhere to kill Indian-born British author Salman Rushdie for writing *The Satanic Verses.* Khomeini also urges the assassination of persons involved in publishing the novel. The book, which many Moslems considered blasphemous because of its irreverent portrayal of a character resembling Muhammad and its insinuation that the Koran might not be the word of God, had recently been protested in many Islamic nations. Iranian president Ali Khamenei suggests February 17 that the death decree might be lifted if Rushdie apologizes. Rushdie, who had gone into hiding in Britain, issues an apology February 18, but Khomeini rejects it February 19, saying the death sentence could not be withdrawn.

February 18-27. *Shevardnadze Tours Middle East.* Soviet foreign minister Eduard Shevardnadze visits Syria, Jordan, Egypt, Iraq, and Iran during a ten-day visit to the Middle East. At separate meetings in Cairo February 22, he confers with Israeli foreign minister Moshe Arens and PLO leader Yasir Arafat. Shevardnadze's trip is seen as an effort by Moscow to improve relations with Middle Eastern states following completion of the Soviet troop withdrawal from Afghanistan earlier in the year. During the trip Shevardnadze reiterates Soviet support for a UN-sponsored Middle East peace conference.

February 20. *Europeans Recall Diplomats.* The twelve member states of the European Economic Community vote unanimously to recall their ambassadors from Tehran to protest Khomeini's call for Salman Rushdie's death. West Germany announces February 22 that it is withdrawing an offer to guarantee credits for West German exporters doing business with Iran.

February 23. *Mubarak, Hussein Meet Bush.* Egypt's President Hosni Mubarak and Jordan's King Hussein at separate meetings in Tokyo ask President Bush to support an international Middle East peace conference. The leaders are in Japan for the funeral of Emperor Hirohito.

March 7. *Iran Breaks British Ties.* Iran breaks diplomatic relations with Britain after the British government refuses to denounce Salman Rushdie and his novel *The Satanic Verses.*

March 13. *Baker-Arens Meeting.* Secretary of State James A. Baker III meets with Israeli foreign minister Arens in Washington. Baker proposes that Israel take several steps to reduce tensions in the occupied territories while the United States presses the PLO to discourage violent protests among Palestinians and to end raids from Lebanon into Israel. Arens emphasizes that his government has no intention of talking to the PLO but says it will try to reduce tensions.

March 14. *Conflict in Lebanon.* The heaviest artillery exchange between Moslem and Christian forces in Lebanon in several years kills forty people. Afterwards Maronite Christian leader Michel Aoun declares "a campaign of liberation against the Syrian presence in this country." During the next several months the Lebanese army under his command carries on an artillery duel with Syrian forces and Moslem militias that devastates Beirut and the surrounding area.

March 18. *Kuwait Suppresses Shi'ites.* The Kuwaiti government orders a crackdown on its Moslem Shi'ite minority. The action is a response to continued concern over Iran-inspired terrorism.

March 21. *Christians Isolated in Lebanon.* Moslem militia and Syrian troops block all routes to Lebanon's Christian heartland, thereby imposing a blockade on the region controlled by forces under Aoun.

March 27. *King Fahd Visits Egypt.* Saudi Arabia's King Fahd makes his first trip to Egypt since Anwar Sadat signed a peace treaty with Israel in 1979.

March 28. *Khomeini's Heir Resigns.* The Ayatollah Hussein Ali Montazeri, appointed heir of Iranian spiritual leader Ayatollah Khomeini, announces his resignation after Khomeini asks him to step down. Montazeri had recently come into disfavor for criticizing the regime's policies.

April 6. *Shamir Election Plan.* Israeli prime minister Shamir discusses a new election plan with President George Bush in Washington during a ten-day trip to the United States. Shamir's plan is similar to the formula for achieving Palestinian autonomy agreed upon in the Camp David accords. Under the plan Palestinians would elect local representatives, who would then negotiate with Israel on establishing Palestinian autonomy in the occupied territories. Later the two sides would hold talks on a permanent peace. Bush expresses his support for the plan.

April 18. *Riots in Jordan.* Riots break out in Jordan over an increase in food prices. The government imposes tight security measures to stop the riots, but they continue until April 22. King Hussein, who had been in the United States, cancels a planned stop in Britain April 21 and returns to Jordan April 23. Hussein accepts the resignation of Prime Minister Zaid Samir al-Rifai April 24 and appoints an interim government that is to stay in power until elections can be held. Demonstrators had accused Rifai of economic mismanagement and corruption.

April 20. *Hussein on Shamir Plan.* Jordan's King Hussein gives a qualified endorsement to Israeli prime minister Shamir's plan to allow Palestinians in the West Bank and Gaza Strip to elect representatives to negotiate with Israel. Hussein's statement comes after a meeting with U.S. Secretary of State Baker in Washington.

April 26. *Palestinians Reject Shamir Plan.* More than eighty local Palestinians representing East Jerusalem, the West Bank, and the Gaza Strip issue a statement rejecting Prime Minister Shamir's plan to hold elections in the occupied territories. They call the plan "nothing more than a maneuver for the media to save Israel from its international isolation."

May 3. *Arafat Reaffirms Stand on Charter.* PLO leader Arafat reaffirms that the declaration of Palestinian independence adopted in November by the Palestinian National Council ended the PLO's challenge to Israel's right to exist. Arafat says the Palestinian charter, which calls for Israel's destruction, is "null and void."

May 5. *Rafsanjani Advocates Killings.* Speaker Ali Akbar Hashemi Rafsanjani of the Iranian parliament urges Palestinians to kill Americans and other Westerners in retaliation for Israel's handling of the uprising in the occupied territories. PLO leader Arafat May 7 denounces Rafsanjani's statement. Rafsanjani recants his call to kill Westerners May 10, saying, "I really do not advise this and consider it a weak point."

American Hostages in Lebanon[1]

Name	Position	Date Kidnapped	Status as of September 1989
David Dodge	President, American University of Beirut	July 19, 1982	Released July 20, 1983
Frank Reiger	Department head, American University of Beirut	February 10, 1984	Released April 15, 1984
Jeremy Levin	Bureau chief, Cable News Network	March 7, 1984	Released February 14, 1985
William Buckley	Station chief, Central Intelligence Agency	March 16, 1984	Died June 3, 1985 [a]
Benjamin F. Weir	Presbyterian minister	May 8, 1984	Released September 15, 1985
Peter Kilburn	Librarian, American University of Beirut	December 3, 1984	Killed April 14, 1986 [b]
Lawrence M. Jenco	Director, Catholic Relief Services	January 8, 1985	Released July 26, 1986
Terry A. Anderson	Chief Middle East correspondent, Associated Press	May 16, 1985	Still held
David P. Jacobsen	Director, American University of Beirut hospital	May 28, 1985	Released November 2, 1986
Thomas Sutherland	Acting dean of agriculture, American University of Beirut	June 9, 1985	Still held
Frank H. Reed	Director, Lebanese International School	September 9, 1986	Still held
Joseph J. Cicippio	Acting comptroller, American University of Beirut	September 12, 1986	Still held
Edward A. Tracy	Writer	October 21, 1986	Still held
Alann Steen	Professor, Beirut University College	January 24, 1987	Still held
Jesse J. Turner	Assistant professor, Beirut University College	January 24, 1987	Still held
Robert Polhill	Professor, Beirut University College	January 24, 1987	Still held
Charles Glass	Journalist	June 17, 1987	Escaped August 18, 1987 [c]
William R. Higgins	Lt. Col., USMC UN observer	February 17, 1988	Killed on or before July 31, 1989 [d]

[1] As of October 20, 1989
[a] Died in captivity, probably on this date.
[b] Murdered, possibly in retaliation for U.S. attack on Libya.
[c] There was some speculation that Glass was allowed to escape.
[d] A videotape was released July 31, 1989, supposedly showing Higgins hanging, but forensic experts believe he died earlier. His body has not been released.

May 12. *UN Agency Defers PLO Application.* The UN's World Health Organization defers until 1990 consideration of a PLO application for admission as a member state. The United States had vigorously opposed PLO admission and had threatened to withhold its contribution to any international organization granting the PLO membership.

May 22. *Baker on Territories.* Secretary of State Baker, speaking bluntly to the American Israel Public Affairs Committee in Washington, calls on Israel to renounce "the unrealistic vision of a greater Israel" that would incorporate the occupied territories. He says, "Israeli interests in the West Bank and Gaza—security and otherwise—can be accommodated in a settlement." Prime Minister Shamir rejects Baker's approach as "useless."

May 22. *Egypt Rejoins Arab League.* Arab leaders formally welcome Egypt back into the Arab League, after a ten-year suspension resulting from Egypt's peace treaty with Israel.

June 3. *Khomeini Dies.* The Ayatollah Ruhollah Khomeini, Iran's top spiritual and political leader, dies in a Tehran hospital, reportedly after suffering a heart attack earlier in the day. Iran's Council of Experts names President Ali Khamenei to replace Khomeini June 4. Khomeini had undergone surgery May 23 to stop internal bleeding. His body is taken June 6 to the War Martyrs' Cemetery in Tehran where hundreds of thousands of Iranians gather. A mob of mourners rushes the corpse in an attempt to touch it before it is buried, causing it to spill from its wooden litter. After troops retrieve the body with a helicopter, the burial is carried out later in the day.

June 20. *Shamir Heckled by Settlers.* At the funeral of an Israeli stabbed to death in the West Bank, right-wing Jewish settlers shout down Prime Minister Shamir as he tries to deliver a eulogy. Later a few settlers try to physically assault him, but they are blocked by security officers. Many settlers in the crowd of about one thousand maintain that Shamir had not been tough enough with Palestinians in the occupied territories.

June 20-23. *Rafsanjani in Moscow.* Iranian parliament speaker Rafsanjani is warmly received in Moscow, where he holds several meetings with President Gorbachev. The two leaders sign a multibillion-dollar economic cooperation agreement and declare that Soviet-Iranian relations have entered "a new stage."

July 5. *Shamir Accepts Hard-Line Conditions.* Under pressure from the right wing of his Likud party, Prime Minister Shamir accepts conditions on his West Bank and Gaza election plan, in return for the party's endorsement of it. The conditions—which include the barring of Arab residents of East Jerusalem from participation, the postponement of any elections until the Palestinian uprising ends, and the continuation of Jewish settlements—appear to ensure that the plan would be unacceptable to Palestinians. Shamir could not disregard the conditions without risking a no-confidence vote from his own party. On July 6 the PLO says that the move has ended further Palestinian consideration of the plan.

July 10. *Israeli Coalition in Jeopardy.* The executive bureau of the Israeli Labor party recommends July 10 that Labor withdraw from the coalition government because of conditions placed on Shamir's peace initiative by the Likud. On July 23, however, the Israeli cabinet affirms that the Likud's conditions did not change government policy toward the peace initiative. Labor leaders indicate after this compromise that the party's central committee will

vote to stay in the coalition.

July 12. *West Bank Schools to Reopen.* The Israeli government announces that it will gradually reopen schools on the West Bank. The schools had been closed as part of Israel's campaign to stop the Palestinian uprising.

July 24. *Shamir Talks with Palestinians.* Prime Minister Shamir's office confirms that he had discussed his election proposal with Arab leaders from the West Bank. Jamil Tarifi, a prominent West Bank lawyer with ties to the PLO, admits July 25 that he had met Shamir. The prime minister is criticized by right-wing Israeli leaders, who regard the talks as indirect negotiations with the PLO.

July 28. *Israelis Abduct Hizballah Leader.* Israeli commandos abduct Sheik Abdul Karim Obeid, a spiritual leader of the pro-Iranian Shi'ite Hizballah group, from his home in southern Lebanon. Israel says Obeid was "arrested" because he had encouraged and helped to plan kidnappings and terrorist attacks.

July 31. *Shi'ite Group Claims It Killed Hostage.* After Israeli authorities refuse to release Sheik Obeid, the Organization of the Oppressed on Earth releases a videotape that it claims shows the hanging of U.S. Marine Corps Lt. Col. William Higgins, a hostage held in Lebanon since February 1988. President Bush condemns the "brutal murder" of Higgins but refrains from ordering military retaliation. Israeli officials acknowledge that they originally had hoped to trade Obeid for three Israeli hostages held in Lebanon. The Israelis widen their position on a hostage swap by offering to release all Shi'ite prisoners in Israel in exchange for the freedom of all Western hostages held by Shi'ite groups in Lebanon. The FBI says August 7 that its forensic experts determined it was likely that Higgins was the person in the videotape, but that he probably was already dead when the tape was made.

August 3. *Kidnappers Suspend Death Threat.* The Revolutionary Justice Council, a Shi'ite group holding U.S. hostages in Lebanon, says it has suspended its plan to kill American hostage Joseph Cicippio. The group had threatened to kill Cicippio if Israel did not release Sheik Abdul Karim Obeid.

August 13. *Syrian Ground Offensive.* Syrian troops and their Moslem allies in Lebanon attack Christian positions with infantry and tanks. Fighting continues despite a call for a cease-fire by the UN Security Council on August 15. Since March, fighting in Lebanon had been confined almost exclusively to artillery barrages. The shelling had killed about seven hundred people, according to local police.

August 14. *Khamenei Rejects U.S. Talks.* The Ayatollah Ali Khamenei, Iran's top spiritual leader, rejects negotiations with the United States on American hostages being held by pro-Iranian Shi'ites in Lebanon. During the previous two weeks the Iranian government and press had hinted that Iran might be willing to work for the release of the hostages.

August 17. *Rafsanjani Inaugural.* Iranian president Ali Akbar Hashemi Rafsanjani takes the oath of office in Tehran. In his inaugural address he criticizes the failures of the revolution and says that it is time to concentrate on economic reconstruction. Rafsanjani names a twenty-two-member cabinet August 19 that excludes prominent hardliners. In a sweeping endorsement of Rafsanjani, Iran's parliament approves all twenty-two nominees August 29.

August 18. *Israeli Permits Introduced.* Israeli officials issue new work and identification permits to Palestinian workers from the territories. Palestinian leaders condemn the permits as a device aimed at controlling the uprising and call for a twelve-day general strike. On the first day, however, six thousand of the usual ten thousand workers report for work.

September 4. *Palestinians Executed for Spying.* The Fatah Revolutionary Council, a radical Palestinian group led by Abu Nidal, states that it has killed fifteen Palestinians for espionage against Palestinian guerrilla groups in Lebanon. Many of those put to death are alleged to have worked for Israeli, American, Iraqi, Jordanian, Egyptian, or Lebanese intelligence services.

September 6. *Beirut Embassy Evacuated.* The skeleton staff of the U.S. embassy in Beirut, headed by Ambassador John McCarthy, shreds sensitive documents and boards helicopters to Cyprus in response to threats from the Lebanese army commander, General Aoun. Seeking greater U.S. involvement in Lebanon's civil war, Aoun told the French newspaper *Figaro* that perhaps he should "take twenty American hostages." Following this report, nearly one thousand Christian Lebanese supporters of Aoun blocked the entrances to the U.S. ambassador's residence, claiming that personnel would enter and exit at their own risk until the United States increased its involvement in Lebanon. The Bush administration warns Syria that the embassy staff's withdrawal does not give Syria license to do whatever it wants in Lebanon.

Documents

Following is a compilation of major documents about Middle East political issues. They include United Nations Security Council resolutions 242 and 338, the Israeli-Egyptian Peace Treaty, and various peace plans proposed by Arabs, Israelis, and the United States. The selection also includes the text of UN Security Council Resolution 598, which formed the basis of the 1988 Iran-Iraq cease-fire, and former Iranian president Ali Khamenei's letter accepting the resolution.

TEXT OF UN SECURITY COUNCIL RESOLUTION 242

Following the Six-Day War, the UN Security Council on November 22, 1967, unanimously approved Resolution 242 aimed at bringing peace to the Middle East.

November 22, 1967

The Security Council,
Expressing its continued concern with the grave situation in the Middle East,
Emphasizing the inadmissibility of the acquisition of territory by war and the need to work for a just and lasting peace in which every State in the area can live in security,
Emphasizing further that all Member States in their acceptance of the Charter of the United Nations have undertaken a commitment to act in accordance with Article 2 of the Charter
1. *Affirms* that the fulfilment of Charter principles requires the establishment of a just and lasting peace in the Middle East which should include the application of both the following principles:
    (i) Withdrawal of Israel armed forces from territories occupied in the recent conflict;
    (ii) Termination of all claims or states of belligerency and respect for the acknowledgement of the sovereignty, territorial integrity and political independence of every State in the area and their right to live in peace within secure and recognized boundaries free from threats or acts of force.
2. *Affirms further* the necessity
    (a) For guaranteeing freedom of navigation through international waterways in the area;
    (b) For achieving a just settlement of the refugee problem;
    (c) For guaranteeing the territorial inviolability and politi-

cal independence of every State in the area, through measures including the establishment of demilitarized zones:
3. *Requests* the Secretary-General to designate a Special Representative to proceed to the Middle East to establish and maintain contacts with the States concerned in order to promote agreement and assist efforts to achieve a peaceful and accepted settlement in accordance with the provisions and principles in this resolution;
4. *Requests* the Secretary-General to report to the Security Council on the progress of the efforts of the Special Representative as soon as possible.

TEXT OF UN SECURITY COUNCIL RESOLUTION 338

Between 1967 and 1973 the UN Security Council reaffirmed Resolution 242. Attempting to end the October war of 1973, the Security Council passed Resolution 338.

October 22, 1973

The Security Council,
1. *Calls upon* all parties to the present fighting to cease all firing and terminate all military activity immediately, not later than 12 hours after the moment of the adoption of the decision, in the positions they now occupy;
2. *Calls upon* the parties concerned to start immediately after the ceasefire the implementation of Security Council Resolution 242 (1967) in all of its parts;
3. *Decides that,* immediately and concurrently with the ceasefire negotiations start between the parties concerned under appropriate auspices aimed at establishing a just and durable peace in the Middle East.

RESOLUTION OF ARAB HEADS OF STATE

In Rabat, Morocco, on October 28, 1974, Arab heads of state declared the Palestine Liberation Organization the sole represen-

tative of the Palestinian people, removing this title from King Hussein of Jordan.

Rabat, October 28, 1974

The Conference of the Arab Heads of State:

1. *Affirms* the right of the Palestinian people to return to their homeland and to self-determination.

2. *Affirms* the right of the Palestinian people to establish an independent national authority, under the leadership of the PLO in its capacity as the sole legitimate representative of the Palestine people, over all liberated territory. The Arab States are pledged to uphold this authority, when it is established, in all spheres and at all levels.

3. *Supports* the PLO in the exercise of its national and international responsibilities, within the context of the principle of Arab solidarity.

4. *Invites* the kingdoms of Jordan, Syria and Egypt to formalize their relations in the light of these decisions and in order that they be implemented.

5. *Affirms* the obligation of all Arab States to preserve Palestinian unity and not to interfere in Palestinian internal affairs.

Peace Treaty Documents

On March 26, 1979, the state of war that had existed between Egypt and Israel since Israel's creation was formally ended with the signing in Washington of a peace treaty between the two countries. The treaty provided for the normalization of relations and implemented the framework for peace that had been agreed upon at Camp David, Maryland, in a historic meeting there in the fall of 1978 between President Jimmy Carter, Israeli Prime Minister Menachem Begin, and Egyptian President Anwar Sadat.

A FRAMEWORK FOR PEACE IN THE MIDDLE EAST

Following is the text of the Camp David accord, "A Framework for Peace in the Middle East Agreed to at Camp David," as signed by President Jimmy Carter, President Anwar Sadat of Egypt, and Prime Minister Menachem Begin of Israel at the White House on September 17, 1978:

Muhammad Anwar al-Sadat, President of the Arab Republic of Egypt, and Menachem Begin, Prime Minister of Israel, met with Jimmy Carter, President of the United States of America, at Camp David from September 5 to September 17, 1978, and have agreed on the following framework for peace in the Middle East. They invite other parties to the Arab-Israeli conflict to adhere to it.

Preamble

The search for peace in the Middle East must be guided by the following:

The agreed basis for a peaceful settlement of the conflict between Israel and its neighbors is United Nations Security Council Resolution 242, in all its parts.

After four wars during 30 years, despite intensive human efforts, the Middle East, which is the cradle of civilization and the birthplace of three great religions, does not yet enjoy the blessings of peace. The people of the Middle East yearn for peace so that the vast human and natural resources of the region can be turned to the pursuits of peace and so that this area can become a model for coexistence and cooperation among nations.

The historic initiative of President Sadat in visiting Jerusalem and the reception accorded to him by the Parliament, government and people of Israel, and the reciprocal visit of Prime Minister Begin to Ismailia, the peace proposals made by both leaders, as well as the warm reception of these missions by the peoples of both countries, have created an unprecedented opportunity for peace which must not be lost if this generation and future generations are to be spared the tragedies of war.

The provisions of the Charter of the United Nations and the other accepted norms of international law and legitimacy now provide accepted standards for the conduct of relations among all states.

To achieve a relationship of peace, in the spirit of Article 2 of the United Nations Charter, future negotiations between Israel and any neighbor prepared to negotiate peace and security with it, are necessary for the purpose of carrying out all the provisions and principles of Resolutions 242 and 338.

Peace requires respect for the sovereignty, territorial integrity and political independence of every state in the area and their right to live in peace within secure and recognized boundaries free from threats or acts of force. Progress toward that goal can accelerate movement toward a new era of reconciliation in the Middle East marked by cooperation in promoting economic development, in maintaining stability, and in assuring security.

Security is enhanced by a relationship of peace and by cooperation between nations which enjoy normal relations. In addition, under the terms of peace treaties, the parties can, on the basis of reciprocity, agree to special security arrangements such as demilitarized zones, limited armaments areas, early warning stations, the presence of international forces, liaison, agreed measures for monitoring, and other arrangements that they agreed are useful.

Framework

Taking these factors into account, the parties are determined to reach a just, comprehensive, and durable settlement of the Middle East conflict through the conclusion of peace treaties based on Security Council Resolutions 242 and 338 in all their parts. Their purpose is to achieve peace and good neighborly relations. They recognize that, for peace to endure, it must involve all those who have been most deeply affected by the conflict. They therefore agree that this framework as appropriate is intended by them to constitute a basis for peace not only between Egypt and Israel, but also between Israel and each of its other neighbors which is prepared to negotiate peace with Israel on this basis. With that objective in mind, they have agreed to proceed as follows:

A. West Bank and Gaza

1. Egypt, Israel, Jordan and the representatives of the Palestinian people should participate in negotiations on the resolution of the Palestinian problem in all its aspects. To achieve that objective, negotiations relating to the West Bank and Gaza should proceed in three stages:

(a) Egypt and Israel agree that, in order to ensure a peaceful and orderly transfer of authority, and taking into account the security concerns of all the parties, there should be transitional arrangements for the West Bank and Gaza for a period not exceeding five years. In order to provide full autonomy to the inhabitants, under these arrangements the Israeli military government and its civilian administration will be withdrawn as soon as a self-governing authority has been freely elected by the inhabitants of these areas to replace the existing military government. To negotiate the details of a transitional arrangement, the Government of Jordan will be invited to join the negotiations on the basis of the framework. These new arrangements should give due consideration both to the principle of self-government by the inhabitants of these territories and to the legitimate security concerns of the parties involved.

(b) Egypt, Israel, and Jordan will agree on the modalities for establishing the elected self-governing authority in the West

Bank and Gaza. The delegations of Egypt and Jordan may include Palestinians from the West Bank and Gaza or other Palestinians as mutually agreed. The parties will negotiate an agreement which will define the powers and responsibilities of the self-governing authority to be exercised in the West Bank and Gaza. A withdrawal of Israeli armed forces will take place and there will be a redeployment of the remaining Israeli forces into specified security locations. The agreement will also include arrangements for assuring internal and external security and public order. A strong local police force will be established, which may include Jordanian citizens. In addition, Israeli and Jordanian forces will participate in joint patrols and in the manning of control posts to assure the security of the borders.

(c) When the self-governing authority (administrative council) in the West Bank and Gaza is established and inaugurated, the transitional period of five years will begin. As soon as possible, but not later than the third year after the beginning of the transitional period, negotiations will take place to determine the final status of the West Bank and Gaza and its relationship with its neighbors, and to conclude a peace treaty between Israel and Jordan by the end of the transitional period. These negotiations will be conducted among Egypt, Israel, Jordan, and the elected representatives of the inhabitants of the West Bank and Gaza. Two separate but related committees will be convened, one committee, consisting of representatives of the four parties which will negotiate and agree on the final status of the West Bank and Gaza, and its relationship with its neighbors, and the second committee, consisting of representatives of Israel and representatives of Jordan to be joined by the elected representatives of the inhabitants of the West Bank and Gaza, to negotiate the peace treaty between Israel and Jordan, taking into account the agreement reached on the final status of the West Bank and Gaza. The negotiations shall be based on all the provisions and principles of UN Security Council Resolution 242. The negotiations will resolve, among other matters, the location of the boundaries and the nature of the security arrangements. The solution from the negotiations must also recognize the legitimate rights of the Palestinian people and their just requirements. In this way, the Palestinians will participate in the determination of their own future through:

1) The negotiations among Egypt, Israel, Jordan and the representatives of the inhabitants of the West Bank and Gaza to agree on the final status of the West Bank and Gaza and other outstanding issues by the end of the transitional period.

2) Submitting their agreement to a vote by the elected representatives of the inhabitants of the West Bank and Gaza.

3) Providing for the elected representatives of the inhabitants of the West Bank and Gaza to decide how they shall govern themselves consistent with the provisions of their agreement.

4) Participating as stated above in the work of the committee negotiating the peace treaty between Israel and Jordan.

2. All necessary measures will be taken and provisions made to assure the security of Israel and its neighbors during the transitional period and beyond. To assist in providing such security, a strong local police force will be constituted by the self-governing authority. It will be composed of inhabitants of the West Bank and Gaza. The police will maintain continuing liaison on internal security matters with the designated Israeli, Jordanian, and Egyptian officers.

3. During the transitional period, representatives of Egypt, Israel, Jordan, and the self-governing authority will constitute a continuing committee to decide by agreement on the modalities of admission of persons displaced from the West Bank and Gaza in 1967, together with necessary measures to prevent disruption and disorder. Other matters of common concern may also be dealt with by this committee.

4. Egypt and Israel will work with each other and with other interested parties to establish agreed procedures for a prompt, just and permanent implementation of the resolution of the refugee problem.

B. Egypt-Israel

1. Egypt and Israel undertake not to resort to the threat or the use of force to settle disputes. Any disputes shall be settled by peaceful means in accordance with the provisions of Article 33 of the Charter of the United Nations.

2. In order to achieve peace between them, the parties agree to negotiate in good faith with a goal of concluding within three months from the signing of this Framework a peace treaty between them, while inviting the other parties to the conflict to proceed simultaneously to negotiate and conclude similar peace treaties with a view to achieving a comprehensive peace in the area. The Framework for the Conclusion of a Peace Treaty between Egypt and Israel will govern the peace negotiations between them. The parties will agree on the modalities and the timetable for the implementation of their obligations under the treaty.

C. Associated Principles

1. Egypt and Israel state that the principles and provisions described below should apply to peace treaties between Israel and each of its neighbors — Egypt, Jordan, Syria and Lebanon.

2. Signatories shall establish among themselves relations normal to states at peace with one another. To this end, they should undertake to abide by all the provisions of the Charter of the United Nations. Steps to be taken in this respect include:

    (a) full recognition;

    (b) abolishing economic boycotts;

    (c) guaranteeing that under their jurisdiction the citizens of the other parties shall enjoy the protection of the due process of law.

3. Signatories should explore possibilities for economic development in the context of final peace treaties, with the objective of contributing to the atmosphere of peace, cooperation and friendship which is their common goal.

4. Claims Commissions may be established for the mutual settlement of all financial claims.

5. The United States shall be invited to participate in the talks on matters related to the modalities of the implementation of the agreements and working out the timetable for the carrying out of the obligations of the parties.

6. The United Nations Security Council shall be requested to endorse the peace treaties and ensure that their provisions shall not be violated. The permanent members of the Security Council shall be requested to underwrite the peace treaties and ensure respect for their provisions. They shall also be requested to conform their policies and actions with the undertakings contained in this Framework.

For the Government of the
Arab Republic of Egypt: Al-Sadat
For the Government of Israel: M. Begin
Witnessed by: Jimmy Carter, President of the
United States of America

FRAMEWORK FOR AN EGYPTIAN-ISRAELI TREATY

Following is the text of the Camp David accord, "A Framework for the Conclusion of a Peace Treaty Between Egypt and Israel," as signed by President Jimmy Carter, President Anwar Sadat of Egypt, and Prime Minister Menachem Begin of Israel at the White House on September 17, 1978:

In order to achieve peace between them, Israel and Egypt agree to negotiate in good faith with a goal of concluding within three months of the signing of this framework a peace treaty between them.

It is agreed that:

The site of the negotiations will be under a United Nations flag at a location or locations to be mutually agreed.

All of the principles of U.N. Resolution 242 will apply in this resolution of the dispute between Israel and Egypt.

Unless otherwise mutually agreed, terms of the peace treaty will be implemented between two and three years after the peace treaty is signed.

The following matters are agreed between the parties:

(a) the full exercise of Egyptian sovereignty up to the internationally recognized border between Egypt and mandated Palestine;

(b) the withdrawal of Israeli armed forces from the Sinai;

(c) the use of airfields left by the Israelis near El Arish, Rafah, Ras en Naqb, and Sharm el Sheikh for civilian purposes only, including possible commercial use by all nations;

(d) the right of free passage of ships of Israel through the Gulf of Suez and the Suez Canal on the basis of the Constantinople Convention of 1888 applying to all nations; the Strait of Tiran and the Gulf of Aqaba are international waterways to be open to all nations for unimpeded and nonsuspendable freedom of navigation and overflight;

(e) the construction of a highway between the Sinai and Jordan near Elat with guaranteed free and peaceful passage by Egypt and Jordan; and

(f) the stationing of military forces listed below.

Stationing of Forces

A. No more than one division (mechanized or infantry) of Egyptian armed forces will be stationed within an area lying approximately 50 kilometers (km) east of the Gulf of Suez and the Suez Canal.

B. Only United Nations forces and civil police equipped with light weapons to perform normal police functions will be stationed within an area lying west of the international border and the Gulf of Aqaba, varying in width from 20 km to 40 km.

C. In the area within 3 km east of the international border there will be Israeli limited military forces not to exceed four infantry battalions and United Nations observers.

D. Border patrol units, not to exceed three batallions, will supplement the civil police in maintaining order in the area not included above.

The exact demarcation of the above areas will be decided during the peace negotiations.

Early warning stations may exist to insure compliance with the terms of the agreement.

United Nations forces will be stationed: (a) in part of the area in the Sinai lying within about 20 km of the Mediterranean Sea and adjacent to the international border, and (b) in the Sharm el Sheikh area to ensure freedom of passage through the Strait of Tiran; and these forces will not be removed unless such removal is approved by the Security Council of the United Nations with a unanimous vote of the five permanent members.

After a peace treaty is signed, and after the interim withdrawal is complete, normal relations will be established between Egypt and Israel, including: full recognition, including diplomatic, economic and cultural relations; termination of economic boycotts and barriers to the free movement of goods and people; and mutual protection of citizens by the due process of law.

Interim Withdrawal

Between three months and nine months after the signing of the peace treaty, all Israeli forces will withdraw east of a line extending from a point east of El Arish to Ras Muhammad, the exact location of this line to be determined by mutual agreement.

For the Government of the
Arab Republic of Egypt: A. Sadat
For the Government of Israel: M. Begin
Witnessed by: Jimmy Carter, President of the
                                        United States of America

EGYPTIAN-ISRAELI TREATY OF PEACE

Following is the text of the Treaty of Peace Between the Arab Republic of Egypt and the State of Israel, signed in Washington March 26, 1979, by President Anwar Sadat of Egypt and Prime Minister Menachem Begin of Israel and witnessed by President Jimmy Carter of the United States:

The Government of the Arab Republic of Egypt and the Government of the State of Israel;

Preamble

Convinced of the urgent necessity of the establishment of a just, comprehensive and lasting peace in the Middle East in accordance with Security Council Resolutions 242 and 338;

Reaffirming their adherence to the "Framework for Peace in the Middle East Agreed at Camp David," dated September 17, 1978;

Noting that the aforementioned Framework as appropriate is intended to constitute a basis for peace not only between Egypt and Israel but also between Israel and each of the other Arab neighbors which is prepared to negotiate peace with it on this basis;

Desiring to bring to an end the state of war between them and to establish a peace in which every state in the area can live in security;

Convinced that the conclusion of a Treaty of Peace between Egypt and Israel is an important step in the search for comprehensive peace in the area and for the attainment of the settlement of the Arab-Israeli conflict in all its aspects;

Inviting the other Arab parties to this dispute to join the peace process with Israel guided by and based on the principles of the aforementioned Framework;

Desiring as well to develop friendly relations and cooperation between themselves in accordance with the United Nations Charter and the principles of international law governing international relations in times of peace;

Agree to the following provisions in the free exercise of their sovereignty, in order to implement the "Framework for the Conclusion of a Peace Treaty between Egypt and Israel":

Article I

1. The state of war between the Parties will be terminated and peace will be established between them upon the exchange of instruments of ratification of this Treaty.

2. Israel will withdraw all its armed forces and civilians from the Sinai behind the international boundary between Egypt and mandated Palestine, as provided in the annexed protocol (Annex I), and Egypt will resume the exercise of its full sovereignty over the Sinai.

3. Upon completion of the interim withdrawal provided for in Annex I, the Parties will establish normal and friendly relations, in accordance with Article III (3).

Article II

The permanent boundary between Egypt and Israel is the recognized international boundary between Egypt and the former mandated territory of Palestine as shown on the map at Annex II, without prejudice to the issue of the status of the Gaza Strip. The Parties recognize this boundary as inviolable. Each will respect the territorial integrity of the other, including their territorial waters and airspace.

Article III

1. The Parties will apply between them the provisions of the Charter of the United Nations and the principles of international law governing relations among states in times of peace. In particular:

    a. They recognize and will respect each other's sovereignty, territorial integrity and political independence;

    b. They recognize and will respect each other's right to live in peace within their secure and recognized boundaries;

    c. They will refrain from the threat or use of force, directly or indirectly, against each other and will settle all disputes between them by peaceful means;

2. Each Party undertakes to ensure that acts or threats of belligerency, hostility or violence do not originate from and are not committed from within its territory, or by any forces subject to its control or by any other forces stationed on its territory, against the population, citizens or property of the other Party. Each Party also undertakes to refrain from organizing, instigating, inciting, assisting or participating in acts or threats of belligerency, hostility, subversion or violence against the other Party, anywhere, and undertakes to insure that perpetrators of such acts are brought to justice.

3. The Parties agree that the normal relationship established between them will include full recognition, diplomatic, economic and cultural relations, termination of economic boycotts and discriminatory barriers to the free movement of people and goods, and will guarantee the mutual enjoyment by citizens of the due process of law. The process by which they undertake to achieve such a relationship parallel to the implementation of other provisions of this Treaty is set out in the annexed protocol (Annex III).

Article IV

1. In order to provide maximum security for both Parties on the basis of reciprocity, agreed security arrangements will be established including limited force zones in Egyptian and Israeli territory, and United Nations forces and observers, described in detail as to nature and timing in Annex I, and other security arrangements the Parties may agree upon.

2. The Parties agree to the stationing of United Nations personnel in areas described in Annex I. The Parties agree not to request withdrawal of the United Nations personnel and that these personnel will not be removed unless such removal is approved by the Security Council of the United Nations, with the affirmative vote of the five Permanent Members, unless the Parties otherwise agree.

3. A Joint Commission will be established to facilitate the implementation of the Treaty, as provided for in Annex I.

4. The security arrangements provided for in paragraphs 1 and 2 of this Article may at the request of either party be reviewed and amended by mutual agreement of the Parties.

Article V

1. Ships of Israel, and cargoes destined for or coming from Israel, shall enjoy the right of free passage through the Suez Canal and its approaches through the Gulf of Suez and the Mediterranean Sea on the basis of the Constantinople Convention of 1888, applying to all nations. Israeli nationals, vessels and cargoes, as well as persons, vessels and cargoes destined for or coming from Israel, shall be accorded non-discriminatory treatment in all matters connected with usage of the canal.

2. The Parties consider the Strait of Tiran and the Gulf of Aqaba to be international waterways open to all nations for unimpeded and non-suspendable freedom of navigation and overflight. The Parties will respect each other's right to navigation and overflight for access to either country through the Strait of Tiran and the Gulf of Aqaba.

Article VI

1. This Treaty does not affect and shall not be interpreted as affecting in any way the rights and obligations of the Parties under the Charter of the United Nations.

2. The Parties undertake to fulfill in good faith their obligations under this Treaty, without regard to action or inaction of any other party and independently of any instrument external to this Treaty.

3. They further undertake to take all the necessary measures for the application in their relations of the provisions of the multilateral conventions to which they are parties, including the submission of appropriate notification to the Secretary General of the United Nations and other depositories of such conventions.

4. The parties undertake not to enter into any obligation in conflict with this Treaty.

5. Subject to Article 103 of the United Nations Charter, in the event of a conflict between the obligations of the Parties under the present Treaty and any of their other obligations, the obligations under this Treaty will be binding and implemented.

Article VII

1. Disputes arising out of the application or interpretation of this Treaty shall be resolved by negotiations.

2. Any such disputes which cannot be settled by negotiations shall be resolved by conciliation or submitted to arbitration.

Article VIII

The Parties agree to establish a claims commission for the mutual settlement of all financial claims.

Article IX

1. This Treaty shall enter into force upon exchange of instruments of ratification.

2. This Treaty supersedes the agreement between Egypt and Israel of September, 1975.

3. All protocols, annexes and maps attached to this Treaty shall be regarded as an integral part hereof.

4. The Treaty shall be communicated to the Secretary General of the United Nations for registration in accordance with the provisions of Article 102 of the Charter of the United Nations.

Done at Washington, D.C. this 26th day of March, 1979, in triplicate in the English, Arabic, and Hebrew languages, each text being equally authentic. In case of any divergence of interpretation, the English text shall prevail.

For the Government of the Arab Republic of Egypt: A. Sadat
For the Government of Israel: M. Begin
Witnessed by: Jimmy Carter, President of the United States of America

Other Documents

THE FAHD PLAN

Crown Prince Fahd of Saudi Arabia presented an eight-point peace plan in August 1981. Some Arab states supported the plan, but disagreements over its details contributed to the breakup of the Fez Arab Summit in November.

1. Israel to withdraw from all Arab territory occupied in 1967, including Arab Jerusalem.
2. Israeli settlements built on Arab land after 1967 to be dismantled.
3. A guarantee of freedom of worship for all religions in holy places.
4. An affirmation of the right of the Palestinian Arab people to return to their homes, and compensation for those who do not wish to return.
5. The West Bank and Gaza Strip to have a transitional period under the auspices of the United Nations for a period not exceeding several months.
6. An independent Palestinian state should be set up with Jerusalem as its capital.
7. All States in the region should be able to live in peace.
8. The U.N. or member-states of the U.N. to guarantee carrying-out of these principles.

THE REAGAN PEACE INITIATIVE

Following the Israeli invasion of Lebanon in June 1982, the United States attempted to continue the Camp David peace process. On September 1, 1982, President Ronald Reagan presented the following proposal:

First, as outlined in the Camp David accords, there must be a period of time during which the Palestinian inhabitants of the West Bank and Gaza will have full autonomy over their own affairs. Due consideration must be given to the principle of self-government by the inhabitants of the territories and to the legitimate security concerns of the parties involved.

The purpose of the 5-year period of transition, which would begin after free elections for a self-governing Palestinian authority, is to prove to the Palestinians that they can run their own affairs and that such Palestinian autonomy poses no threat to Israel's security.

The United States will not support the use of any additional land for the purpose of settlements during the transition period. Indeed, the immediate adoption of a settlement freeze by Israel, more than any other action, could create the confidence needed for wider participation in these talks. Further settlement activity is in no way necessary for the security of Israel and only diminishes the confidence of the Arabs that a final outcome can be freely and fairly negotiated.

I want to make the American position well understood: The purpose of this transition period is the peaceful and orderly transfer of authority from Israel to the Palestinian inhabitants of the West Bank and Gaza. At the same time, such a transfer must not interfere with Israel's security requirements.

Beyond the transition period, as we look to the future of the West Bank and Gaza, it is clear to me that peace cannot be achieved by the formation of an independent Palestinian state in those territories. Nor is it achievable on the basis of Israeli sovereignty or permanent control over the West Bank and Gaza.

So the United States will not support the establishment of an independent Palestinian state in the West Bank and we will not support annexation or permanent control by Israel.

There is, however, another way to peace. The final status of these lands must, of course, be reached through the give-and-take of negotiations. But it is the firm view of the United States that self-government by the Palestinians of the West Bank and Gaza in association with Jordan offers the best chance for a durable, just and lasting peace.

We base our approach squarely on the principle that the Arab-Israeli conflict should be resolved through negotiations involving an exchange of territory for peace. This exchange is enshrined in U.N. Security Council Resolution 242, which is, in turn, incorporated in all its parts in the Camp David agreements. U.N. Resolution 242 remains wholly valid as the foundation stone of America's Middle East peace effort.

It is the United States' position that — in return for peace — the withdrawal provision of Resolution 242 applies to all fronts, including the West Bank and Gaza.

When the border is negotiated between Jordan and Israel, our view on the extent to which Israel should be asked to give up territory will be heavily affected by the extent of true peace and normalization and the security arrangements offered in return.

Finally, we remain convinced that Jerusalem must remain undivided, but its final status should be decided through negotiations.

In the course of the negotiations to come, the United States will support positions that seem to us fair and reasonable compromises and likely to promote a sound agreement. We will also put forward our own detailed proposals when we believe they can be helpful. And, make no mistake, the United States will oppose any proposal — from any party and at any point in the negotiating process — that threatens the security of Israel. American's commitment to the security of Israel is ironclad. And, I might add, so is mine.

FEZ SUMMIT PEACE PROPOSAL

An Arab summit was held in Fez, Morocco, in September 1982 in response to the Israeli invasion of Lebanon and President Reagan's September initiative. The following eight-point plan came from that summit.

1. The withdrawal of Israel from all Arab territories occupied in 1967 including Arab Al Qods (East Jerusalem).
2. The dismantling of settlements established by Israel on the Arab territories after 1967.
3. The guarantee of freedom of worship and practice of religious rites for all religions in the holy shrine.
4. The reaffirmation of the Palestinian people's right to self-determination and the exercise of its imprescriptible and inalienable national rights under the leadership of the Palestine Liberation Organization (PLO), its sole and legitimate representative, and the indemnification of all those who do not desire to return.
5. Placing the West Bank and Gaza Strip under the control of the United Nations for a transitory period not exceeding a few months.
6. The establishment of an independent Palestinian state with Al Qods as its capital.
7. The Security Council guarantees peace among all states of

the region including the independent Palestinian state.

8. The Security Council guarantees the respect of these principles.

UN SECURITY COUNCIL RESOLUTION 598

The UN Security Council on July 20, 1987, unanimously approved Resolution 598, which called for an end to the war between Iran and Iraq.

The Security Council,

Reaffirming its resolution 582 (1986),

Deeply concerned that, despite its calls for a cease-fire, the conflict between Iran and Iraq continues unabated, with further heavy loss of human life and material destruction,

Deploring the initiation and continuation of the conflict,

Deploring also the bombing of purely civilian population centres, attacks on neutral shipping or civilian aircraft, the violation of international humanitarian law and other laws of armed conflict, and, in particular, the use of chemical weapons contrary to obligations under the 1925 Geneva Protocol,

Deeply concerned that further escalation and widening of the conflict may take place,

Determined to bring to an end all military actions between Iran and Iraq,

Convinced that a comprehensive, just, honourable and durable settlement should be achieved between Iran and Iraq,

Recalling the provisions of the Charter of the United Nations, and in particular the obligation of all Member States to settle their international disputes by peaceful means in such a manner that international peace and security and justice are not endangered,

Determining that there exists a breach of the peace as regards the conflict between Iran and Iraq,

Acting under Articles 39 and 40 of the Charter of the United Nations,

1. *Demands* that, as a first step towards a negotiated settlement, Iran and Iraq observe an immediate cease-fire, discontinue all military actions on land, at sea and in the air, and withdraw all forces to the internationally recognized boundaries without delay;

2. *Requests* the Secretary-General to dispatch a team of United Nations Observers to verify, confirm and supervise the cease-fire and withdrawal and further requests the Secretary-General to make the necessary arrangements in consultation with the Parties and to submit a report thereon to the Security Council;

3. *Urges* that prisoners-of-war be released and repatriated without delay after the cessation of active hostilities in accordance with the Third Geneva Convention of 12 August 1949;

4. *Calls upon* Iran and Iraq to co-operate with the Secretary-General in implementing this resolution and in mediation efforts to achieve a comprehensive, just and honourable settlement, acceptable to both sides, of all outstanding issues, in accordance with the principles contained in the Charter of the United Nations;

5. *Calls upon* all other States to exercise the utmost restraint and to refrain from any act which may lead to further escalation and widening of the conflict, and thus to facilitate the implementation of the present resolution;

6. *Requests* the Secretary-General to explore, in consultation with Iran and Iraq, the question of entrusting an impartial body with inquiring into responsibility for the conflict and to report to the Security Council as soon as possible;

7. *Recognizes* the magnitude of the damage inflicted during the conflict and the need for reconstruction efforts, with appropriate international assistance, once the conflict is ended and, in this regard, requests the Secretary-General to assign a team of experts to study the question of reconstruction and to report to the Security Council;

8. *Further requests* the Secretary-General to examine, in consultation with Iran and Iraq and with other States of the region, measures to enhance the security and stability of the region;

9. *Requests* the Secretary-General to keep the Security Council informed on the implementation of this resolution;

10. *Decides* to meet again as necessary to consider further steps to ensure compliance with this resolution.

ARAB LEAGUE SUMMIT COMMUNIQUE

In Amman, Jordan, on November 11, 1987, the Arab League issued a communiqué condemning Iran for not accepting UN Security Council Resolution 598 and declaring that members could reestablish diplomatic relations with Egypt at their own discretion.

Pursuant to the will of the Arab countries' leaders expressed in the resolution the Arab League Council adopted in its extraordinary session which resumed in Tunis on 26 Muharram 1408 Hegira, corresponding to September 20, 1987, and in response to an invitation from His Majesty King Hussein Bin Talal, King of the Hashemite Kingdom of Jordan, the Jordanian capital of Amman hosted an extraordinary session of the Arab summit which convened from 17-20 Rabi' Al-Awwal 1408, corresponding to November 8-11, 1987.

From the premise of our historical responsibility and pan-Arab principles; based on the relations of brotherhood and the interconnection of security, political, and economic interests and the interconnection of history and civilization; out of an awareness of the sensitive and difficult stage the Arab homeland is experiencing and of the challenges against the Arab homeland's present and future which pose a threat to its existence; and realizing that the state of division and fragmentation causes a weakness that dissipates the Arab nation's resources and exhausts its potentialities, the issue of Arab solidarity has been the focus of the Arab leaders' attention. They discussed its various aspects, and pinpointed its weak and strong points. They stressed the need to support and enhance it, and allotted it priority. Their viewpoints were in agreement on this issue, and they agreed that Arab solidarity is the only means to achieve the Arab nation's dignity and pride and to ward off danger and harm from it. The leaders unanimously agreed to overcome differences and to eliminate the causes of weakness and the factors of dismemberment and division. From the premise of their loyalty to their homeland and their genuine affiliation to their nationalism, they decided to adopt Arab solidarity as a basis for a joint Arab action whose objective is to embody the unity of their stand, build the capabilities of the Arab nation, and provide it with factors of strength and impregnability.

After listening to His Majesty King Hussein's speech at the first closed session of the summit, the leaders decided to consider the speech in which His Majesty launched the slogan of reconciliation and accord as the title of the summit and an official document of the summit. They reiterated their abidance by the need to support Arab-African cooperation. They condemned the terrorism and racial discrimination which the racist regime in South Africa is carrying out. They also reiterated their support for the struggle of the people in South Africa and Namibia.

In adherence to the Arab League Charter, the Collective Arab Defense Pact, and the Arab Solidarity Charter; to emphasize the determination to protect pan-Arab security and to safeguard the Arab territory; and in an atmosphere filled with the spirit of fraternity and love which prevailed at the Amman summit, the Iraq-Iran war and the situation in the gulf region topped the summit agenda. The leaders expressed their concern over the continuation of the war and expressed their dissatisfaction with the Iranian regime's insistence on continuing it and on going too far in provoking and threatening the Arabian Gulf states. The conference condemned Iran for occupying part of the Iraqi territory and its procrastination in accepting UN Security Council Resolution Number 598. The conferees called on Iran to accept and fully implement this resolution in accordance with the sequence of its clauses. They appealed to the international community to assume its responsibilities, exert effective efforts, and adopt the necessary measures to make the Iranian regime respond to the peace calls. The conference also announced its solidarity with Iraq and its appreciation for its acceptance of Security Council Resolution Number 598 and its response to all peace initiatives. It also stressed its solidarity with and support for Iraq in protecting its territory and waters, and in defending its legitimate rights.

The leaders reviewed the developments in the gulf area and the serious consequences resulting from Iranian threats, provocations and aggressions. The conference announced its solidarity with Kuwait in confronting the Iranian regime's aggression. It also denounced the bloody criminal incidents perpetrated by Iranians in the Holy Mosque of Mecca. The conference affirmed its support for Kuwait in all of the measures it has taken to protect its territory and waters, and to guarantee its security and stability. The conference announced its support for Kuwait in confronting the Iranian regime's threats and aggressions.

The conference also affirmed its complete support for Saudi Arabia and its full support for the measures taken by Saudi Arabia to provide a suitable atmosphere so that the pilgrims can perform pilgrimage rites in peace and humility, and to prevent any encroachment on the sanctity of the Holy Mosque and Muslims' feelings. The leaders affirmed their rejection of any riotous acts in the holy places that would violate pilgrims' security and safety and encroach on the sovereignty of Saudi Arabia. The conference calls on the Islamic countries and governments to adopt this stand and to stand against the incorrect practices which contradict Islamic teachings.

The conference also discussed the Arab-Israeli conflict and reviewed its developments in the Arab and international areas. The conference reiterated that the Palestinian question is the essence and basis of the conflict, and that peace in the Middle East can only be achieved through regaining all occupied Arab territory, particularly Jerusalem; through restoring the Palestinian peoples' national, inalienable rights; and through resolving the Palestinian issue in all its aspects.

The summit announces that reinforcing the Arabs' capability, building their intrinsic strength, entrenching their solidarity, and embodying the unity of their stands are essential factors to confront the Israeli danger threatening the entire Arab nation and exposing its existence and future to harm and danger. Within the framework of supporting peaceful efforts and attempts to achieve a just, permanent peace in the Middle East within international legitimacy and UN resolutions on the basis of regaining all the occupied Arab and Palestinian territories and the Palestinian people's national inalienable rights, the leaders support the convocation of an international peace conference under UN auspices and the participation of all the concerned parties, including the PLO, the Palestinian people's sole, legitimate representative, on an equal footing, as well as the permanent Security Council members. This is because the international conference is the only appropriate means to resolve the Arab-Israeli conflict in a peaceful, just and comprehensive settlement.

The leaders express deep admiration and appreciation to the Palestinian people in the occupied Arab territories and praise their steadfastness, struggle, and their adherence to their land, and renew their commitment to support them.

The leaders discussed the Lebanese crisis and its tragic complications for the fraternal Arab Lebanese people. The leaders emphasize their concern for Lebanon's national unity, its Arabism, and unity of territory. They also affirm endeavors to help Lebanon overcome its crisis and restore its sovereignty and welfare.

The leaders discussed the issue of international terrorism. They voice condemnation of all forms of international terrorism regardless of its origin. They affirm their conviction of the justice of the peoples' struggle to achieve independence and sovereignty,

and restore their freedom and legitimate rights. The leaders believe that the prerequisites, demands and conditions of pan-Arab security cannot be realized except through full solidarity that covers the entire Arab homeland and enables the mobilization of the Arab nation's capabilities and resources to achieve pan-Arab objectives. The leaders also believe in the unity of hope, aspirations and common views regarding the dangers threatening Arab existence and future in terms of evil and hostile intentions. Thus, the leaders decided that diplomatic relations between any Arab League member state and the Arab Republic of Egypt is a sovereign act decided by each state in accordance with its constitution and laws.

The summit reviewed the historical relations between the two divine religions, Islam and Christianity, embodied in Jerusalem, the symbol of peace. The summit also reviewed Israel's practices and its exposed attempts at blackmail. The summit calls on the member states to intensify dialogue with the Vatican in order to gain its support. The summit also calls on His Majesty King Hussein, the summit's chairman, to undertake contacts with the Vatican on behalf of the Arab leaders.

The leaders express their gratitude to the generous Jordanian people and their great king for their warm hospitality, reception, and perfect preparations. They also express appreciation for His Majesty's King Hussein's wise leadership, which created a clear, brotherly climate for the summit and facilitated its success. Thank you.

IRAN'S ACCEPTANCE OF RESOLUTION 598

President Ali Khamenei accepted UN Resolution 598 on behalf of Iran in a July 18, 1988, letter to UN Secretary General Javier Pérez de Cuéllar. The letter was the first step in establishing a truce in the Iran-Iraq war.

In the name of God, the Compassionate, the Merciful.
Excellency,
Please accept my warm greetings with best wishes for Your Excellency's success in efforts to establish peace and justice.

As you are well aware, the fire of the war which was started by the Iraqi regime on 22 September 1980 through an aggression against the territorial integrity of the Islamic Republic of Iran has now gained unprecedented dimensions, bringing other countries into the war and even engulfing innocent civilians.

The killing of 290 innocent human beings, caused by the shooting down of an Airbus aircraft of the Islamic Republic of Iran by one of America's warships in the Persian Gulf is a clear manifestation of this contention.

Under these circumstances, Your Excellency's effort for the implementation of Resolution 598 is of particular importance. The Islamic Republic of Iran has always provided you with its assistance and support to achieve this objective. In this context, we have decided to officially declare that the Islamic Republic of Iran—because of the importance it attaches to saving the lives of human beings and the establishment of justice and regional and international peace and security—accepts Security Council Resolution 598.

We hope that the official declaration of this position by the Islamic Republic of Iran would assist you in continuing your efforts, which has always received our support and appreciation.

HUSSEIN'S RENUNCIATION OF CLAIM TO WEST BANK

In a July 31, 1988, speech King Hussein of Jordan renounced his nation's claims to the West Bank and severed all legal and administrative links with it.

In the name of God, the compassionate, the merciful and peace be upon his faithful Arab messenger

Brother citizens.... [W]e have initiated, after seeking God's assistance, and in light of a thorough and extensive study, a series of measures with the aim of enhancing the Palestinian national orientation, and highlighting the Palestinian identity. Our objective is the benefit of the Palestinian cause and the Arab Palestinian people.

Our decision, as you know, comes after thirty-eight years of the unity of the two banks, and fourteen years after the Rabat Summit Resolution, designating the Palestine Liberation Organization (PLO) as the sole legitimate representative of the Palestinian people. It also comes six years after the Fez [Morocco] Summit Resolution of an independent Palestinian state in the occupied West Bank and the Gaza Strip....

The considerations leading to the search to identify the relationship between the West Bank and the Hashemite Kingdom of Jordan, against the background of the PLO's call for the establishment of an independent Palestinian state, are twofold:

I. The principle of Arab unity, this being a national objective to which all the Arab peoples aspire, and which they all seek to realize.
II. The political reality of the scope of benefit to the Palestinian struggle that accrues from maintaining the legal relationship between the two banks of the kingdom....

... We respect the wish of the PLO, the sole legitimate representative of the Palestinian people, to secede from us in an independent Palestinian state. We say this in all understanding. Nevertheless, Jordan will remain the proud bearer of the message of the great Arab revolt; faithful to its principles; believing in the common Arab destiny; and committed to joint Arab action.

Regarding the political factor, it has been our belief, since the Israeli aggression of June 1967, that our first priority should be to liberate the land and holy places from Israeli occupation.

Accordingly, as is well known, we have concentrated all our efforts during the twenty-one years since the occupation towards this goal. We had never imagined that the preservation of the legal and administrative links between the two banks could constitute an obstacle to the liberation of the occupied Palestinian land....

Lately, it has transpired that there is a general Palestinian and Arab orientation towards highlighting the Palestinian identity in a complete manner.... It is also viewed that these [Jordanian-West Bank] links hamper the Palestinian struggle to gain international support for the Palestinian cause, as the national cause of a people struggling against foreign occupation....

... [T]here is a general conviction that the struggle to liberate the occupied Palestinian land could be enhanced by dismantling the legal and administrative links between the two banks, we have to fulfill our duty, and do what is required of us. At the Rabat Summit of 1974 we responded to the Arab leaders' appeal to us to continue our interaction with the occupied West Bank through the Jordanian institutions, to support the steadfastness of our brothers there. Today we respond to the wish of the Palestine Liberation Organization, the sole legitimate representative of the Palestinian people, and to the Arab orientation to affirm the Palestinian identity in all its aspects....

Brother citizens.... We cannot continue in this state of suspension, which can neither serve Jordan nor the Palestinian cause. We had to leave the labyrinth of fears and doubts, towards clearer horizons where mutual trust, understanding, and cooperation can prevail, to the benefit of the Palestinian cause and Arab unity. This unity will remain a goal which all the Arab peoples cherish and seek to realize.

At the same time, it has to be understood in all clarity, and without any ambiguity or equivocation, that our measures regarding the West Bank, concern only the occupied Palestinian land and its people. They naturally do not relate in any way to the Jordanian citizens of Palestinian origin in the Hashemite Kingdom of Jordan. They all have the full rights of citizenship and all its obligations, the same as any other citizen irrespective of his origin. They are an integral part of the Jordanian state. They belong to it, they live on its land, and they participate in its life and all its activities. Jordan is not Palestine; and the independent Palestinian state will be established on the occupied Palestinian land after its liberation, God willing. There the Palestinian identity will be embodied, and there the Palestinian struggle shall come to fruition, as confirmed by the glorious uprising of the Palestinian people under occupation.

National unity is precious in any country; but in Jordan it is more than that. It is the basis of our stability, and the springboard of our development and prosperity. It is the foundation of our national security and the source of our faith in the future. It is the living embodiment of the principles of the great Arab revolt, which we inherited, and whose banner we proudly bear. It is a living example of constructive plurality, and a sound nucleus for wider Arab unity.

Based on that, safeguarding national unity is a sacred duty that will not be compromised. Any attempt to undermine it, under any pretext, would only help the enemy carry out his policy of expansion at the expense of Palestine and Jordan alike. Consequently, true nationalism lies in bolstering and fortifying national unity. Moreover, the responsibility to safeguard it falls on every one of you, leaving no place in our midst for sedition or treachery. With God's help, we shall be as always, a united cohesive family, whose members are joined by bonds of brotherhood, affection, awareness, and common national objectives....

The constructive plurality which Jordan has lived since its foundation, and through which it has witnessed progress and prosperity in all aspects of life, emanates not only from our faith in the sanctity of national unity, but also in the importance of Jordan's Pan-Arab role. Jordan presents itself as the living example of the merger of various Arab groups on its soil, within the framework of good citizenship, and one Jordanian people. This paradigm that we live on our soil gives us faith in the inevitability of attaining Arab unity, God willing....

Citizens, Palestinian brothers in the occupied Palestinian lands, to dispel any doubts that may arise out of our measures, we assure you that these measures do not mean the abandonment of our national duty, either towards the Arab-Israeli conflict, or towards the Palestinian cause.... Jordan will continue its support for the steadfastness of the Palestinian people, and their courageous uprising in the occupied Palestinian land, within its capabilities. I have to mention, that when we decided to cancel the Jordanian Development Plan in the occupied territories, we contacted, at the same time, various friendly governments and international institutions, which had expressed their wish to contribute to the plan, urging them to continue financing development projects in the occupied Palestinian lands, through the relevant Palestinian quarters.

... No one outside Palestine has had, nor can have, an attachment to Palestine, or its cause, firmer than that of Jordan or of my family. Moreover, Jordan is a confrontation state, whose borders with Israel are longer than those of any other Arab state, longer even than the combined borders of the West Bank and Gaza with Israel.

In addition, Jordan will not give up its commitment to take part in the peace process. We have contributed to the peace process until it reached the stage of a consensus to convene an international peace conference on the Middle East. The purpose of the conference would be to achieve a just and comprehensive peace settlement to the Arab-Israeli conflict, and the settlement of the Palestinian problem in all its aspects....

Jordan, dear brothers, is a principal party to the Arab-Israeli conflict, and to the peace process. It shoulders its national responsibilities on that basis.

I thank you and salute you, and reiterate my heartfelt wishes to you, praying God the almighty to grant us assistance and guidance, and to grant our Palestinian brothers victory and success.

May God's peace, mercy, and blessings be upon you.

DECLARATION OF PALESTINIAN STATE

The Palestine National Council declared the establishment of an independent Palestinian state at a November 15, 1988, meeting in Algiers.

Palestine, the land of the three monotheistic faiths, is where the Palestinian Arab people was born, on which it grew, developed and excelled. The Palestinian people was never separated from or diminished in its integral bonds with Palestine. Thus the Palestinian Arab people ensured for itself an everlasting union between itself, its land and its history....

Despite the historical injustice inflicted on the Palestinian Arab people resulting in their dispersion and depriving them of their right to self-determinination, following upon U.N. General Assembly Resolution 181 (1947), which partitioned Palestine into two states, one Arab, one Jewish, yet it is this Resolution that still provides those conditions of international legitimacy that ensure the right of the Palestinian Arab people to sovereignty.

By stages, the occupation of Palestine and parts of other Arab territories by Israeli forces, the willed dispossession and expulsion from their ancestral homes of the majority of Palestine's civilian inhabitants, was achieved by organized terror; those Palestinians who remained, as a vestige subjugated in its homeland, were persecuted and forced to endure the destruction of their national life.

Thus were principles of international legitimacy violated. Thus were the Charter of the United Nations and its Resolutions disfigured, for they had recognized the Palestinian Arab people's national rights, including the right of Return, the right to independence, the right to sovereignty over territory and homeland.

... [F]rom out of the long years of trial in evermounting struggle, the Palestinian political identity emerged further consolidated and confirmed. And the collective Palestinian national will forged for itself a political embodiment, the Palestine Liberation Organization, its sole, legitimate representative recognized by the world community as a whole.... And so Palestinian resistance was clarified and raised into the forefront of Arab and world awareness, as the struggle of the Palestinian Arab people achieved unique prominence among the world's liberation movements in the modern era.

The massive national uprising, the *intifada,* now intensifying in cumulative scope and power on occupied Palestinian territories, as well as the unflinching resistance of the refugee camps outside the homeland, have elevated awareness of the Palestinian truth and right into still higher realms of comprehension and actuality. Now at last the curtain has been dropped around a whole epoch of prevarication and negation. The *intifada* has set siege to the mind of official Israel, which has for too long relied exclusively upon myth and terror to deny Palestinian existence altogether. Because of the *intifada* and its revolutionary irreversible impulse, the history of Palestine has therefore arrived at a decisive juncture.

Whereas the Palestinian people reaffirms most definitively its inalienable rights in the land of its patrimony:

Now by virtue of natural, historical and legal rights, and the sacrifices of successive generations who gave of themselves in defense of the freedom and independence of their homeland;

In pursuance of Resolutions adopted by Arab Summit Conferences and relying on the authority bestowed by international legitimacy as embodied in the Resolutions of the United Nations Organizations since 1947;

And in exercise by the Palestinian Arab people of its rights to self-determination, political independence and sovereignty over its territory,

The Palestine National Council, in the name of God, and in the name of the Palestinian Arab people, hereby proclaims the establishment of the State of Palestine on our Palestinian territory with its capital Jerusalem (Al-Quds Ash-Sharif).

The State of Palestine is the state of Palestinians wherever they may be. The state is for them to enjoy in it their collective national and cultural identity, theirs to pursue in it a complete equality of rights. In it will be safeguarded their political and religious convictions and their human dignity by means of a parliamentary democratic system of governance, itself based on freedom of expression and the freedom to form parties. The rights of minorities will duly be respected by the majority, as minorities must abide by decisions of the majority. Governance will be based on principles of social justice, equality and non-discrimination in public rights of men or women, on grounds of race, religion, color or sex, under the aegis of a constitution which ensures the rule of law and an independent judiciary. Thus shall these principles allow no departure from Palestine's age-old spiritual and civilizational heritage of tolerance and religious coexistence.

The State of Palestine is an Arab state, an integral and indivisible part of the Arab nation, at one with that nation in heritage and civilization, with it also in its aspiration for liberation, progress, democracy and unity. The State of Palestine affirms its obligation to abide by the Charter of the League of Arab States, whereby the coordination of the Arab states with each other shall be strengthened. It calls upon Arab compatriots to consolidate and enhance the emergence in reality of our state, to mobilize potential, and to intensify efforts whose goal is to end Israeli occupation.

The State of Palestine proclaims its commitment to the principles and purposes of the United Nations, and to the Universal Declaration of Human Rights. It proclaims its commitment as well to the principles and policies of the Non-Aligned Movement.

It further announces itself to be a peace-loving State, in adherence to the principles of peaceful co-existence....

In the context of its struggle for peace in the land of Love and Peace, the State of Palestine calls upon the United Nations to bear special responsibility for the Palestinian Arab people and its homeland. It calls upon all peace- and freedom-loving peoples and states to assist it in the attainment of its objectives, to provide it with security, to alleviate the tragedy of its people, and to help it terminate Israel's occupation of the Palestinian territories.

The State of Palestine herewith declares that it believes in the settlement of regional and international disputes by peaceful means, in accordance with the U.N. Charter and resolutions. Without prejudice to its natural right to defend its territorial integrity and independence, it therefore rejects the threat or use of force, violence and terrorism against its territorial integrity or political independence, as it also rejects their use against the territorial integrity of other states. Therefore, on this day unlike all others, November 15, 1988, as we stand at the threshold of a new dawn, in all honor and modesty we humbly bow to the sacred spirits of our fallen ones, Palestinian and Arab, by the purity of whose sacrifice for the homeland our sky has been illuminated and our Land given life....

Therefore, we call upon our great people to rally to the banner of Palestine, to cherish and defend it, so that it may forever be the symbol of our freedom and dignity in that homeland, which is a homeland for the free, now and always.

ARAFAT STATEMENT ON ISRAEL, TERRORISM

At a December 14, 1988, press conference in Geneva, Palestine Liberation Organization leader Yasir Arafat explicitly recognized Israel's right to exist, renounced terrorism, and accepted UN Security Council resolutions 242 and 338. Arafat's statement prompted the United States to open a dialogue with the PLO. Following is the text of Arafat's statement as recorded by Reuters.

Let me highlight my views before you. Our desire for peace is a strategy and not an interim tactic. We are bent on peace come what may, come what may.

Our statehood provides salvation to the Palestinians and peace to both Palestinians and Israelis.

Self-determination means survival for the Palestinians and our survival does not destroy the survival of the Israelis as their rulers claim.

Yesterday in my speech I made reference to United Nations Resolution 181 as the basis for Palestinian independence. I also made reference to our acceptance of Resolution 242 and 338 as the basis for negotiations with Israel within the framework of the international conference. These three resolutions were endorsed by our Palestine National Council session in Algiers.

In my speech also yesterday, it was clear that we mean our people's rights to freedom and national independence, according to Resolution 181, and the right of all parties concerned in the Middle East conflict to exist in peace and security, and, as I have mentioned, including the state of Palestine, Israel and other neighbors, according to Resolution 242 and 338.

As for terrorism, I renounced it yesterday in no uncertain terms, and yet, I repeat for the record. I repeat for the record that we totally and absolutely renounce all forms of terrorism, including individual, group and state terrorism.

Between Geneva and Algiers, we have made our position crystal clear. Any more talk such as "The Palestinians should give more"—you remember this slogan?—or "It is not enough" or "The Palestinians are engaging in propaganda games, and public-relations exercises" will be damaging and counterproductive.

Enough is enough. Enough is enough. Enough is enough. All remaining matters should be discussed around the table and within the international conference.

Let it be absolutely clear that neither Arafat, nor any for that matter, can stop the intifada, the uprising. The intifada will come to an end only when practical and tangible steps have been taken towards the achievement of our national aims and establishment of our independent Palestinian state.

In this context, I expect the E.E.C. to play a more effective role in promoting peace in our region. They have a political responsibility, they have a moral responsibility, and they can deal with it.

Finally, I declare before you and I ask you to kindly quote me on that: We want peace. We want peace. We are committed to peace. We are committed to peace. We want to live in our Palestinian state, and let live. Thank you.

Supplement:
The Persian Gulf Crisis

The Persian Gulf Crisis 315

Chronology of the Gulf Crisis 355

Documents on the Gulf Crisis 369

The Persian Gulf Crisis

During 1989 and early 1990, the Middle East was commanding less of the world's attention than it had in recent years. Compared to the monumental changes taking place in Germany, the Soviet Union, and Eastern Europe, events in the Middle East seemed less central to world affairs than they had in the past. The region also appeared less turbulent. The Iran-Iraq war had ended in 1988 with an inconclusive but stable cease-fire. After the death of the Ayatollah Ruhollah Khomeini in 1989, Iran's leaders moderated their efforts to export their brand of Islamic fundamentalism and focused their energies on domestic reconstruction. The Palestinian *intifada* (uprising) against Israeli control of the occupied territories continued unabated, but it had neither yielded significant progress toward a peace settlement nor threatened to escalate into another Arab-Israeli war. Although Lebanon remained an unpredictable hot spot, in most areas of the Middle East the status quo was prevailing in 1989 and the first half of 1990.

This apparent lull in the turbulence of the Middle East was misleading. Middle East specialist William Quandt of the Brookings Institution observed in *Foreign Affairs* at the beginning of 1991: "The apparently frozen landscape of the Middle East—no progress toward Arab-Israeli peace, no economic success stories, no impressive strides toward democratization, no new and inspiring leaders—may have given a false illusion of stability; in fact it merely masked political currents with explosive potential."

On August 2, 1990, any illusions that the Middle East had become more stable or predictable were shattered when Iraqi troops stormed into neighboring Kuwait. The invasion and subsequent annexation of Kuwait by Iraqi president Saddam Hussein set in motion a crisis that would remain at the forefront of the international agenda for more than seven months. By early March 1991, a U.S.-led coalition force had driven the Iraqi army from Kuwait and occupied much of southern Iraq. Virtually every target of military significance in Iraq had been bombed, and Hussein's regime was fighting for its life against an array of domestic rebel forces emboldened by the coalition's defeat of the Iraqi military.

No Middle Eastern nation was unaffected by the seven-month crisis. Egypt and Syria sent tens of thousands of troops to Saudi Arabia to join the multinational coalition opposing Iraq. Saudi Arabia, which had long tried to insulate itself from outside influences, allowed its eastern prov-inces to be transformed into a huge military base housing hundreds of thousands of foreigners. Israel became the target of Iraqi missile attacks. United Nations economic sanctions against Iraq unraveled the economy of Jordan, Iraq's largest trading partner. Many Palestinian, Egyptian, and Yemeni workers living in Kuwait, Iraq, and Saudi Arabia lost their jobs, and hundreds of thousands of Arabs became refugees.

The effects of the Gulf crisis were felt far beyond the Middle East, as well. Nearly forty nations contributed combat forces, transport assistance, medical teams, or financial aid to the coalition effort attempting to force Iraq from Kuwait. Even in nations that did not send forces to Saudi Arabia, such as Japan and West Germany, the Gulf crisis became an important political issue. One antiwar rally in Germany drew as many as 250,000 people. The Gulf crisis also became a test of the effectiveness of the United Nations Security Council to confront international aggression in the post-Cold War era.

The most widely felt consequence of the crisis, however, was the dramatic rise in the price of oil. After the invasion of Kuwait and the subsequent imposition of an international economic embargo against Iraq, oil prices skyrocketed in response to the marketplace's loss of Iraqi and Kuwaiti oil and fears that war would damage Saudi oil facilities. The price increases affected peoples and economies throughout the world, but developing economies dependent on oil were especially hard hit.

Three factors distinguished the Iraqi invasion of Kuwait as a situation that demanded an international response. First, Kuwait's importance to the international economy is far beyond its size. It sits atop the fourth largest oil reserve in the world. If Saddam Hussein could have added Kuwait's oil resources to Iraq's and used his superior military might to bully Saudi Arabia and the smaller Gulf oil states into supporting Iraq's positions in the Organization of Petroleum Exporting Countries (OPEC), he could have dominated oil production and pricing policies. Oil prices still would have been tied to supply and demand, but Hussein would have been in a position to push prices up, thereby straining the world economy. Second, Iraq's efforts to acquire nuclear weapons and its existing conventional, chemical, and biological weapons capabilities made that country a long-term military threat to the entire Middle East and perhaps beyond. Third, Iraq's government had demonstrated an appetite for military con-

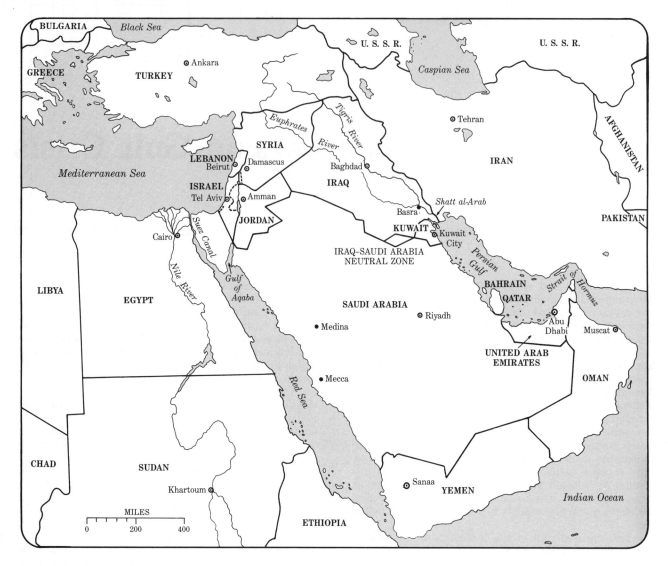

quest and a capacity for brutality. Since 1980, Iraq had invaded Iran, resorted to the use of chemical weapons against Iranian soldiers and ballistic missiles against Iranian citizens, and used poison gas against its own Kurdish population during a campaign to snuff out the Kurdish resistance movement.

Because much of the Arab world and the international community during the 1980s considered Iraq to be a counterweight to a more threatening Iran, world reaction to Iraqi behavior had been restrained. But the invasion of Kuwait revealed an unmistakable pattern of Iraqi aggression. It demonstrated that the Iraqi regime considered military power to be its primary foreign policy tool, and it would probably continue to use force until it was checked by greater military power. Thus, the Iraqi regime represented a more ominous threat than other similarly aggressive regimes.

The multinational coalition destroyed Iraq's offensive military capacity, at least for the short term. However, the war left many political and economic questions concerning the Middle East unanswered. By forcing Middle East countries to choose sides in an expanding conflict, Iraq's act of aggression inflamed regional problems seemingly unrelated

to the invasion. The crisis demonstrated that peace and stability in the Middle East would remain elusive until such time as the nations of that region and the entire international community dealt with the Arab-Israeli conflict, the regional arms race, the disparities in wealth between Middle Eastern countries, and other contentious issues.

Road to Aggression

Iraq's aggression against Kuwait grew out of Iraqi economic problems produced by the Iran-Iraq war. The war had left Iraq $80 billion in debt. Almost half of this was owed to Saudi Arabia, Kuwait, and the Gulf states. Iraqi leaders believed that debts to Arab nations related to the war with Iran should be forgiven. They reasoned that Iraq had served as a shield against Iran, which threatened all Arabs, especially those on the Persian Gulf. During the eight years of war, Iraq had paid a steep price—hundreds of thousands of Iraqi's had been killed or maimed and the country was left with few funds for reconstruction, despite its huge oil reserves. Given these circumstances, Saddam Hussein regarded the refusal of his Arab brothers to forgive Iraq's debts as an injustice. Moreover, he maintained that forgiving Iraqi debts was in his creditors' self-interest because Iraq's economic health remained crucial to the security of the Arab world. If Iraq were weakened, Iran might be tempted to resume the war. Arguments that Iraq had started the war against Iran in pursuit of its own objectives, not as a defensive action to block Iranian aggression toward the Arab world, had little persuasive power in Baghdad.

During the spring and summer of 1990, Kuwait became the focus of Iraqi resentment against its Arab creditors. Not only did Kuwait refuse to write off Iraqi war debts, it was exceeding its oil production quota set by OPEC, thereby contributing to low international oil prices. Iraqi reconstruction could only be based upon revenues from its oil resources. But the low price of oil limited the cash Iraq could earn through oil sales. Iraq blamed quota violators—specifically, Kuwait and the United Arab Emirates—for the depressed prices. According to Saddam Hussein, the overproduction by his Arab brothers amounted to economic warfare that threatened his country's security and prosperity. That Iraq, like most other OPEC members, also had engaged in overproduction made little difference to Hussein. He had problems, and he believed he could profit by blaming Kuwait and the United Arab Emirates.

In a speech in Baghdad on July 17, Saddam Hussein threatened to use force against unnamed Arab oil-producing states if they did not cut back their production. The following day a letter from Iraqi foreign minister Tariq Aziz to the Arab League was made public. It named Kuwait and the United Arab Emirates as the quota busters, accusing them of being part of an "imperialist-Zionist" conspiracy to keep oil prices low. Iraq also charged that Kuwait had pumped $2.4 billion worth of oil that rightfully belonged to Iraq from the Rumaila oilfield, only a small part of which lies under Kuwaiti territory. These communications alarmed other Arab leaders who feared that Iraq was not bluffing about its intention to force changes in the oil production policies of Kuwait and the United Arab Emirates. Indeed, the Iraqis had already begun to move tens of thousands of troops south toward the Kuwaiti border.

On July 25 tensions eased somewhat. Egyptian president Hosni Mubarak, who had been the focus of Arab efforts to mediate the dispute, announced that Iraq and Kuwait had agreed to hold talks in Jiddah, Saudi Arabia, on August 1 to discuss their differences. Mubarak also said that Saddam Hussein had assured him that Iraq did not plan to attack Kuwait. Meanwhile, a critical OPEC meeting had begun in Geneva. Iraq called for increasing the OPEC target price for crude oil from $18 a barrel to $25 a barrel. Kuwait supported leaving the price where it was. OPEC oil ministers dismissed the idea that OPEC could engineer a seven-dollar increase in the price of oil given prevailing oil supply and demand realities. But on July 27 they endorsed the Iraqi strategy of following stricter production quotas aimed at achieving a price increase. The ministers settled on a target price of $21 a barrel, which was considered a victory for Iraq—a move that decreased the chances that it would use force against Kuwait.

The talks in Jiddah on August 1 lasted only two hours before they broke down. The following day Iraqi army units invaded Kuwait. Given that Iraqi intimidation tactics appeared to be working (or, at least, were far from being proven ineffective) the quick Iraqi resort to military force following a token attempt at direct negotiations with Ku-

wait appeared premeditated. It is almost certain that Iraq planned before the Jiddah talks to invade Kuwait.

Although Kuwait's oil production policies contributed to the Iraqi regime's aggressive posture toward Kuwait, it is possible that even if Kuwait had appeased Iraq fully by agreeing to cut oil production, write off Iraq's debts, and compensate Iraq for oil taken from the Rumaila oilfield, Saddam Hussein would still have found a pretext to invade the country. Iraq's invasion was more than a response to its neighbor's oil production policies. It was an attempt to provide a quick fix to Iraq's severe economic problems and to obtain funding for continued expansion of Iraqi military capabilities by seizing Kuwait's immense wealth. The invasion also was intended to improve Iraq's access to the Persian Gulf and to redraw colonial borders to which Iraq had long objected. Iraqi schools had taught that Kuwait was part of Iraq until the British split it off. Indeed, like most Middle East nations, Iraqi and Kuwaiti borders had been established by colonial rulers. In 1922 Sir Percy Cox, the British high commissioner of Iraq, had drawn lines on a map that would become the borders of Saudi Arabia, Iraq, and Kuwait. After Kuwait received full independence from Great Britain in 1961, Baghdad claimed Kuwait on the basis of records from the Ottoman Empire. Iraqi forces penetrated into Kuwait, but withdrew when the British sent forces to Kuwait at the request of the Kuwaiti government. In 1963, Iraq recognized Kuwait's independence, but Baghdad continued to maintain that the separation of Kuwait from Iraq was a colonial injustice.

Invasion and Occupation of Kuwait

Before dawn on August 2, 1990, Iraqi armored divisions drove into Kuwait. The well-equipped, battle-hardened Iraqi army, led by elite Republican Guard troops, quickly seized control of the country. The Iraqis attacked during the heat of August when many Kuwaiti government and business leaders were vacationing in cooler countries. Kuwait's ruler, Sheik Jaber Ahmed al-Sabah, had fled Kuwait by car shortly before Iraqi forces arrived at his palace in Kuwait City. Most members of the al-Sabah family who were in Kuwait at the time of the invasion were able to escape.

Saddam Hussein claimed that his forces were responding to a call for help from Kuwaiti revolutionaries who had overthrown the al-Sabah regime. Iraq's government indicated the day after the invasion that it planned to withdraw from Kuwait by August 5. In actuality there was no revolution, and Iraq had no intention of withdrawing. On August 8 Baghdad ended the pretense by announcing that it was annexing Kuwait, which would become Iraq's "nineteenth province."

The invasion had caught Kuwait by surprise. In the days leading up to the attack, Kuwaiti military officials had pressed the government to allow them to call a partial or complete military alert. The Kuwaiti regime, however, believed that such a move could give Iraq a pretext for an invasion. Consequently, when the assault did occur, as many as three-quarters of the Kuwaiti armed forces personnel were on leave or away from their military posts. Kuwaiti military leaders have asserted that had they been able to prepare their forces, they could have slowed the Iraqi invasion force for several days.

The attack also surprised the international community. A limited Iraqi incursion into Kuwait to bolster the intimidation value of Iraqi troops on the Kuwaiti border had been recognized as a possibility, but a massive invasion of a fellow Arab nation that had provided significant financial and diplomatic support to Iraq during the Iran-Iraq war seemed unthinkable.

International outrage at Iraq's aggression and duplicity was compounded by stories of Iraqi atrocities told by people who had fled Kuwait. The behavior of Iraqi troops and commanders revealed a deep-seated resentment among many Iraqis of Kuwait's wealth and superciliousness. The occupation was deliberately bloody, destructive, and vindictive; much of the damage done had no strategic or military purpose or benefit. Refugees described torture and summary executions of Kuwaiti citizens and widespread looting by Iraqi troops. The invasion force appeared to be systematically stripping Kuwait of everything of value. Troops carted off furniture, computers, food stuffs, traffic signals, hospital equipment, and other items. Animals from the Kuwait City Zoo were shot, set free to roam city streets, or shipped to Baghdad for display.

Descriptions provided by refugees of individual atrocities committed in the days after the invasion were especially horrifying. Witnesses claimed to have seen Iraqi soldiers taking patients off life-support systems and removing babies from their incubators. The Iraqis also reportedly had conducted executions in front of the victims' families. Throughout its occupation of Kuwait, Baghdad refused to allow journalists or Red Cross observers to visit Kuwait to investigate human rights abuses.

While robbing Kuwait of its wealth, Iraq initiated a campaign to depopulate it and replace its citizens with Iraqis. An early objective of Iraqi troops had been the Ministry of the Interior, where Kuwaiti birth records were kept. By altering these records, Baghdad could more easily lay claim to Kuwait. Iraqis were being moved into Kuwait, and Kuwaitis who were allowed to leave the country had their identity papers and passports confiscated. Kuwaitis who were out of the country at the time of the invasion were barred from returning. Some Kuwaitis were forcibly deported to Iraq. By October intelligence reports estimated that only 240,000 of Kuwait's 600,000 citizens remained in the country.

American and Saudi Response

Like much of the world, the Bush administration and the U.S. intelligence community were caught off guard by the Iraqi invasion. Although the massing of Iraqi forces on the Kuwait border had caused U.S. leaders concern, few officials or analysts believed that Saddam Hussein was audacious enough to invade Kuwait.

In his first comments on the invasion August 2, President Bush indicated that he and his advisers were not discussing the use of military force. After a previously scheduled meeting with British prime minister Margaret Thatcher later in the day, however, Bush refused to rule out any option. He quickly froze Iraqi and Kuwaiti assets in the United States and urged Saudi Arabia and Turkey to close Iraqi oil pipelines, which they soon did. Secretary of State Baker, who was in Moscow, joined with Soviet foreign minister Eduard Shevardnadze in denouncing the invasion and calling for an international embargo on the sale of arms to Iraq.

The tough attitude adopted by the Bush administration sharply contrasted to its pre-invasion policy of seeking

King Fahd ibn Abdul Aziz of Saudi Arabia broke with past Saudi policy on August 6 when he invited U.S. military forces into his kingdom.

better relations with Hussein's government. On July 25, April Glaspie, the U.S. ambassador to Baghdad, had met with Saddam Hussein to discuss the massing of Iraqi forces near the Kuwait border. A transcript of the meeting released by Iraq in September revealed that Glaspie had expressed U.S. concern with the Iraqi deployments, but continued the Bush policy of conciliation toward Iraq. Iraq had released the transcript with the intention of showing that it had little reason to believe that the United States would respond forcefully to the invasion of Kuwait. At one point the transcript quotes her as saying: "I know you need funds. We understand that and our opinion is that you should have the opportunity to rebuild your country. But we have no opinion on the Arab-Arab conflicts, like your border disagreement with Kuwait." The State Department refused to comment officially on the accuracy of the Iraqi transcript, leading to speculation that it was essentially correct. In testimony before the Senate Foreign Relations Committee in March 1991, however, Glaspie called the transcript a "fabrication" and claimed to have used tough language in warning Hussein not to take aggressive action against Kuwait. *(Hussein-Glaspie meeting, documents, p. 375)*

Bush's primary concern in the days after the invasion was deterring an Iraqi attack on Saudi Arabia. The Saudi's massive oil reserves were vital to the world's economy. An Iraqi move against them or the Saudi government would force the United States to take military action, almost regardless of the circumstances or the relative strength of American and Iraqi troops in the region at the time.

Bush pressed the Saudi Arabian government to allow American soldiers to be stationed in that country. Although the Saudis maintained a close relationship with and bought most of their military equipment from the United States, they had never sought or consented to an American military presence in Saudi Arabia. Because of U.S. support for Israel, most Arab countries were wary of accommodating American troops. The Saudi government, as the guardian of the Islamic holy places in Mecca and Medina, also could expose itself to criticism that it was allowing the holy places to be defiled by the presence of a large non-Islamic army.

In the early days of August, however, Saudi officials considered the threat from Iraq to be much greater than the damage an American military presence might do to Saudi Arabia's domestic stability and standing within the Moslem community. After U.S. defense secretary Dick Cheney on August 6 showed King Fahd ibn Abdul Aziz satellite intelligence of Iraqi missiles pointed at Saudi Arabia and Iraqi forces massing near the Saudi border, the king threw his lot in with the United States. American forces began arriving in Saudi Arabia the next day.

Without outside assistance, Saudi Arabia was vulnerable to a large-scale Iraqi attack—despite spending at least $200 billion on defense during the 1980s. The Saudi royal family had inhibited the development of a strong, independent military establishment because it feared that the loyalty of the military could not be ensured. In other Middle Eastern countries, including Egypt, Iraq, Yemen, and Syria, a ruling monarch had been ousted by the military. The Saudi royal family attempted to avoid this fate by playing the various branches of the Saudi military off one another and placing family members in military leadership posts. The military objective of defending the nation against a foreign threat was secondary to the objective of protecting the regime.

The royal family also tried to reduce the threat from its own military by keeping it small. Saudi Arabia's defense forces numbered only about 66,000 troops. By comparison, the Iraqi military, drawn from a population only slightly larger than Saudi Arabia's, numbered about a million. Few Saudi citizens considered the military to be an avenue of social advancement. To compensate for the small size of its military, the Saudi regime had purchased the latest military technology that the United States, Great Britain, and others would sell it. But without foreign military assistance, Saudi Arabian forces would have been overwhelmed by Iraq's huge and experienced army had Iraq elected to launch an all-out blitz.

During the initial stages of the deployment, American forces and their Saudi allies were outnumbered greatly by Iraqi forces in Kuwait and southern Iraq. By the end of the third week in August, however, the threat of an Iraqi offensive had diminished as the United States, Great Britain, and several other nations assembled formidable air and naval forces in the Gulf region. Meanwhile the United States continued its deployments of ground forces. They were joined in August by troops from Great Britain, France, Egypt, Syria, Morocco, Pakistan, and a number of other countries.

Anti-Iraq Coalition

The United States encouraged broad international participation in the military effort to defend Saudi Arabia and enforce UN sanctions. The U.S. presence in Saudi Arabia would be far more acceptable to the Arab world if Arab nations besides Saudi Arabia and Kuwait contributed to the effort against Iraq. The United States also welcomed support from Western nations, remembering its experience in the Vietnam War, when its allies came to denounce American involvement in that conflict.

The Bush administration succeeded in building a broad multinational coalition that proved to be enduring and resilient. More than two dozen nations contributed combat forces to the defense of Saudi Arabia and the eventual liberation of Kuwait. Other nations provided medical teams, transport assistance, or financial aid to the coalition.

Aside from Saudi Arabia, Egypt and Syria were the most important Arab members of the coalition. Egypt's president Hosni Mubarak led Arab opposition to the Iraqi invasion. By January 1991 Egypt had deployed 30,000 troops in the region. Syria long had denounced U.S. patronage of Israel, and the United States had declared Syria to be a supporter of international terrorists, but both temporarily set aside their differences to pursue their common interest of forcing Iraq out of Kuwait. President Hafez al-Assad sent 19,000 troops to Saudi Arabia. Combat forces from the Arab states of Morocco, Bahrain, Oman, Qatar, the United Arab Emirates, and Kuwait also participated in the coalition under Saudi command. The Bush administration placed a high value on the continuing participation of the Arab members of the coalition. The presence in Saudi Arabia of troops from a variety of Arab countries weakened Iraqi claims that the United States and its Western allies were waging a war of aggression against Arab nations and peoples.

Throughout the Gulf crisis, Great Britain was the staunchest Western ally of the United States. It contributed 35,000 troops—the largest Western contingent to the multinational force next to the United States—and it provided unswerving support for American initiatives. The level of British participation in the coalition reflected Britain's close alliance with the United States and the Conservative government's determination to play an important international role, especially in the Middle East, where Great Britain was a dominant power until the 1950s. The British also felt some responsibility for Kuwait, which had been under British protection until it received its full independence in 1961.

With 17,000 troops committed to the coalition, France also made a sizable contribution. Italy and Canada provided warplanes to the effort and many other Western nations sent combat ships to the region. Pakistan and Bangladesh each sent several thousand troops to Saudi Arabia, and Turkey maintained an imposing military presence on Iraq's northern border that both guarded against an Iraqi attack and forced Iraq to keep several divisions near its northern border.

Although the Soviet Union declined to send significant forces to the region (it did have ships in the Gulf) and sometimes pursued its own agenda during the crisis, Moscow backed the United States in every important vote in the United Nations Security Council, including the votes imposing a total economic embargo against Iraq and authorizing coalition forces to go to war.

Although the coalition arrayed against Iraq was impressive by the standards of recent history, it was clearly an American-led operation. No other Western nation possessed military forces large enough to form the core of an

Contributions to the Multinational Coalition

Argentina—100 troops, 2 transport planes, and 2 warships.

Australia—2 warships and 1 supply ship.

Bangladesh—6,000 troops.

Belgium—2 minesweepers, 1 supply ship, 3 other ships, and 6 transport planes.

Bulgaria—Medical personnel.

Canada—2 warships, 1 supply ship, 18 combat aircraft, and 12 other planes.

Czechoslovakia—200 chemical defense troops and 150 medical personnel.

Denmark—1 ship.

Egypt—30,000 troops and 400 tanks.

France—17,000 troops, 350 tanks, 38 combat aircraft, and 14 ships.

Germany—5 minesweepers and 3 other ships in the eastern Mediterranean and 18 warplanes in Turkey as part of a defensive NATO deployment.

Great Britain—35,000 troops, 120 tanks, 60 combat aircraft, and 18 ships.

Greece—1 ship.

Gulf Cooperation Council (Saudi Arabia, Bahrain, Oman, United Arab Emirates, Qatar, and Kuwait)—Combined force of 10,000 frontline troops. Each country also made individual contributions of planes and ships.

Kuwait—7,000 frontline troops, 34 combat aircraft.

Italy—4 minesweepers, 6 other ships, and 8 combat aircraft.

Morocco—2,000 troops.

Netherlands—3 warships and 18 combat aircraft.

New Zealand—2 transport planes and medical personnel.

Niger—480 troops.

Norway—1 support ship.

Pakistan—2,000 troops in Saudi Arabia and 3,000 troops in the United Arab Emirates.

Poland—Medical personnel and 1 hospital ship.

Portugal—1 transport ship.

Saudi Arabia—66,000 troops (20,000 serving at the front lines), 550 tanks, 300 planes (about 135 of which are modern combat aircraft), and 8 ships.

Senegal—500 troops.

Soviet Union—4 ships on patrol in the region but not involved in coalition operations.

Spain—3 warships.

Sweden—Medical personnel.

Syria—19,000 troops deployed in Saudi Arabia, 50,000 deployed along the Iraqi-Syrian border, and 270 tanks.

Turkey—100,000 troops deployed along the Iraqi-Turkish border, 2 warships in the Persian Gulf, 7 ships in the eastern Mediterranean.

United States—430,000 troops, approximately 2,000 tanks, 1,800 combat aircraft, and more than 100 ships (including 6 aircraft carriers).

Note: Figures are as of January 15, 1991, and include ships stationed in the Red Sea and eastern Mediterranean.

Sources: Associated Press; Center for Defense Information; *The Economist; New York Times; Time; Washington Post.*

---

anti-Iraq coalition. Had the United States sat on the sidelines, an international military force would not have been deployed in Saudi Arabia and economic sanctions might not have been strictly enforced.

Despite U.S. satisfaction at the participation of many nations, there was much grumbling in Congress and elsewhere that the U.S. burden in the crisis, particularly if war came, would be disproportionately heavy. Most of the unhappiness was directed at the lack of action by Japan and West Germany.

The constitutions of both nations contained provisions restricting foreign deployment of troops. The West German government was prohibited from sending troops outside the territory of members of the North Atlantic Treaty Organization (NATO) alliance, while the Japanese government was prohibited from sending troops to any foreign country. Although observers suggested that it might be possible to get around these provisions or that the constitutions could be quickly amended to allow for deployment of troops participating in UN-sanctioned operations, there was little support in either nation for sending troops to the Gulf. A Japanese government proposal to send noncombat support troops to Saudi Arabia was harshly criticized and

defeated in Japan. The German government did send ships to the eastern Mediterranean and eighteen warplanes to NATO member Turkey as part of a NATO deployment in January, but Chancellor Helmut Kohl firmly rejected the idea of sending German combat forces to the Gulf.

In the past, the Japanese have displayed little interest in what went on in the Gulf, despite their heavy reliance on oil from the region. They adopted the attitude that whichever nation controlled the Gulf's huge oil reserves would be willing to sell. In addition, in an effort to reduce its dependence on oil, Japan has pursued a long-term energy policy that makes increasing use of nuclear power. But the Gulf crisis forced Japan to react because it intensified international perceptions (especially perceptions in the United States) that Japan was an economic superpower that refused to carry its share of international political and military burdens. The Japanese did not want to be seen as taking advantage of the crisis by sitting on the sidelines while their major industrial competitors and trade partners committed huge resources to defending Saudi Arabia and liberating Kuwait.

Consequently, the Japanese government pledged financial aid instead of troop deployments. On August 23 it announced that it would contribute $1 billion to the Gulf effort, but none of it was earmarked for direct military purposes. This pledge did little to quiet criticism that Japan was not doing its share. On September 14 Tokyo responded to the criticism by announcing that it would provide $3 billion more in financial aid. By early 1991, Japan had pledged a total of almost $11 billion to the United States and $3 billion to Middle East nations.

Like Japan, Germany was criticized for failing to make a Gulf contribution that was proportional to its national wealth, international standing, and dependence on Gulf oil. Resentment among the Americans, British, and French was driven in part by perceptions that Germany owed the West a huge favor for supporting rapid German unification. Bonn claimed that its capacity to fund the coalition was limited by the high cost of achieving unification. Nevertheless, it pledged $2 billion to the Gulf effort on September 15 and later increased its total contribution to almost $8 billion, $6.5 billion of which would go to the United States.

The biggest financial contributors to the military effort against Iraq, however, were Saudi Arabia and Kuwait, both of which pledged more than $16 billion. Virtually the entire cost of the U.S. military deployment in the Gulf through March 31, 1991—estimated at $53.5 billion— would be covered by foreign financial pledges, if those pledges were kept.

United Nations Sanctions

In tandem with the U.S. military effort to defend Saudi Arabia, the Bush administration launched a diplomatic campaign to create an anti-Iraq consensus within the international community. The United Nations Security Council became the focus of this campaign.

The Security Council is composed of fifteen members—five permanent memberships (the United States, Soviet Union, Great Britain, France, and China) and ten memberships distributed on a rotating basis between the other members of the United Nations. Since 1945, when the United Nations was founded, the Security Council had rarely played an active role in settling world conflicts. Because the permanent members of the body could veto any resolution, the Soviet Union had been able to obstruct any attempts by the council to take action sponsored by the United States and, conversely, the United States had been able to block resolutions backed by the Soviet Union and its allies. The one notable exception to this pattern was the Security Council's call for members to support South Korea against the North Korean invasion in 1950. The Security Council was able to take the action because the Soviet Union was boycotting it at the time (and China was not yet a permanent member of the Security Council).

The end of the Cold War between the United States and the Soviet Union, however, reinvigorated the Security Council. The struggling Soviet economy, ethnic upheavals, and other severe internal problems had forced the Soviet government to focus its energies on domestic affairs and reduce its financial and military commitments abroad. The Soviet veto in the Security Council, however, gave the Soviet Union equal status in that body with the United States and the other three permanent members. Moscow regarded the body as a low-cost means through which it could exercise international influence. Consequently, a So-

viet veto of a U.S. initiative was no longer a certainty. Because American and European assistance had become critical to Soviet economic revitalization, the Soviet Union was inclined to support Western initiatives, such as confronting Iraq's aggression against Kuwait.

On August 2, the same day as Iraq's invasion, the UN Security Council met in emergency session and unanimously passed Resolution 660, which condemned the invasion and called for an immediate Iraqi withdrawal. Four days later the Security Council passed Resolution 661, which established an almost total embargo on Iraqi commerce. Only twice before had the UN Security Council established mandatory economic sanctions against a nation. In 1967 the Security Council had imposed sanctions against Rhodesia that were in effect for thirteen years, and beginning in 1977 sanctions were imposed against South Africa. The embargo was to include all imports going to and exports coming from Iraq, except for humanitarian shipments of medicine and some food. Iraq was particularly vulnerable to a complete economic embargo because it depended almost completely on oil exports for foreign earnings and it imported about 75 percent of its food. Iraqi oil could only be exported through the Persian Gulf sea route and through pipelines running across Saudi Arabia to the Red Sea and across Turkey to the Mediterranean. All three avenues of export were quickly cut off by the embargo, depriving Iraq of hard currency earnings. (*Resolutions 660 and 661, documents, p. 369*)

The embargo was designed to cause economic hardship in Iraq that would compel the Iraqi government to withdraw from Kuwait. It also was intended to weaken Iraq militarily by creating shortages of spare parts, munitions, and fuel and by stalling further progress on its chemical weapons and ballistic missile industries and its pursuit of nuclear weapons. Finally, the United States and its allies hoped that the embargo might foment enough discontent within Iraq to cause the ouster of the Hussein regime. Few strategists, however, believed that this outcome could be accomplished by sanctions alone.

Resolution 661 only called on UN member states to observe the embargo. It provided no explicit authorization of a military blockade to enforce the sanctions. During the weeks following the passage of Resolution 661, members of the Security Council were split over enforcement of its provisions. The United States insisted that it had the right to use military force to prevent circumvention of the embargo. On August 16 U.S. naval forces in the Persian Gulf began interdicting ships carrying cargoes to or from Iraq. The British concurred in this judgment, but the other three permanent members of the council, the French, Chinese, and Soviets, claimed that a new resolution was necessary if military force were to be used to prevent leakage through the embargo.

On August 25, after much lobbying by the United States, the Security Council passed Resolution 665, specifically authorizing the use of force necessary to ensure compliance with the embargo against Iraq. Any commerce between Iraq and the rest of the world would have to occur over land. While circumvention of the embargo by traders operating out of Jordan (and to a lesser extent, Turkey and Iran) would help keep Iraq supplied with foods and certain other goods, its economy would be crippled by the embargo. The UN blockade quickly succeeded in cutting off virtually all of Iraq's exports and, by some estimates, 90 percent of its imports. (*Resolution 665, documents, p. 372*)

UN Security Council Resolutions on Iraq

August 2—Resolution 660 Condemns Iraq's invasion of Kuwait. Demands an unconditional and immediate withdrawal. *Vote:* 14 for, 0 against, 1 abstention (Yemen).

August 6—Resolution 661 Imposes mandatory economic sanctions against Iraq that include a complete trade embargo. Only food and medicine "in humanitarian circumstances" are exempted. *Vote:* 13 for, 2 abstentions (Yemen and Cuba).

August 9—Resolution 662 Declares Iraq's annexation of Kuwait null and void. *Vote:* Unanimous (15-0).

August 18—Resolution 664 Condemns Iraq for holding foreign nationals hostage and demands their immediate release. Demands that Iraq refrain from closing diplomatic and consular missions in Kuwait. *Vote:* Unanimous (15-0).

August 25—Resolution 665 Authorizes coalition warships to use force if necessary to prevent circumvention of the trade embargo against Iraq. *Vote:* 13 for, 2 abstentions (Yemen and Cuba).

September 13—Resolution 666 Establishes guidelines for humanitarian food aid to Iraq and occupied Kuwait. Reaffirms that medical supplies are exempt from the embargo. *Vote:* 13 for, 2 against (Yemen and Cuba).

September 16—Resolution 667 Condemns Iraq for violence against foreign embassies and diplomats in Kuwait. Demands protection for diplomatic and consular personnel. *Vote:* Unanimous (15-0).

September 24—Resolution 669 Agrees to consider exceptions to Resolution 661 for shipment of humanitarian supplies to Iraq and authorizes the examination of requests by states for economic assistance under Article 50. *Vote:* Unanimous (15-0).

September 25—Resolution 670 Tightens the embargo on air traffic to and from Iraq and authorizes the detention of Iraq's merchant fleet. *Vote:* Unanimous (15-0).

October 29—Resolution 674 Holds Iraq responsible for all financial losses resulting from its invasion of Kuwait and calls on UN members to gather evidence of human rights abuses by Iraqi troops in Kuwait. Demands that Iraq release third-country nationals and provide food to those being held against their will. Reiterates demand that diplomatic missions in Kuwait be protected. *Vote:* 13 for, 2 abstentions (Yemen and Cuba).

November 28—Resolution 677 Condemns Iraqi attempts to alter the demographic composition of Kuwait and to destroy the civil records maintained by the legitimate government of Kuwait. Mandates the UN secretary general to take custody of a copy of the Kuwaiti population register. *Vote:* Unanimous (15-0).

November 29—Resolution 678 Authorizes "member states cooperating with the government of Kuwait" to use "all necessary means" to uphold the above resolutions if Iraq has not complied with them by January 15, 1991. *Vote:* 12 for, 2 against (Yemen and Cuba), 1 abstention (China).

Hostages

When it became obvious that the United States and other Western nations were going to oppose the invasion of Kuwait with military deployments and severe economic sanctions, the Iraqi regime moved to play one of the cards in its hand—Westerners stranded in Iraq and Kuwait. On August 9 Iraq announced that it was sealing its borders and allowing only diplomatic personnel to leave. Four days later, Iraqi officials confirmed that foreigners would not be allowed to leave Iraq (or Kuwait) until the crisis was over. Iraq avoided calling the foreigners hostages, referring to them instead as "guests." In late August the Iraqi government began rounding up Westerners in Iraq and Kuwait, many of whom had gone into hiding, for the purpose of holding them at strategic military sites throughout Iraq. The Iraqis primarily used American and British citizens as "human shields," but citizens of a number of European nations and Japan were detained at military sites as well.

Iraq's detention of Westerners was intended to deter a coalition air attack against military targets inside Iraq and Kuwait, stimulate peace movements in Western countries, and paralyze governments that might otherwise vigorously oppose Iraq. But by holding hostages, Iraq was taking a big propaganda risk. Only hard-core Iraqi supporters in a few Arab countries would condone the use of innocent civilians as hostages and human shields. Western leaders repeatedly pointed to the hostage taking as another example of Saddam Hussein's brutality, and UN Security Council votes included provisions calling for the release of the hostages.

Saddam Hussein's incomplete understanding of how his holding of hostages would be perceived was demonstrated by a bizarre meeting between Hussein and a group of British hostages August 23. Iraqi television broadcast a forty-minute videotape of the meeting, which was intended to portray Hussein as a benign, patriarchal leader concerned for the welfare of his "guests." Images of the Iraqi leader smiling as he spoke with tense Britons through an interpreter, posing with the hostages for a group photograph, and patting the head of distrusting young boy reinforced Hussein's reputation in the West as manipulative and maniacal.

Sensing that holding the hostages could backfire, the Iraqis announced August 28 that it would release foreign women and children. By September 22 all Western and

Japanese women and children who wanted to leave Iraq and Kuwait had been flown out on chartered Iraqi flights, for which their governments had to pay Iraq hard currency. The Iraqi's, however, held on to most male adult hostages, continuing to house many of them at strategic locations.

Arab Politics

The Iraqi invasion of Kuwait forced Arab governments to choose sides in a conflict that was fraught with dangers for the individual countries of the Middle East and the region as a whole. Saudi Arabia was directly and immediately threatened by Iraqi forces, and was therefore willing to join the United States in opposing Baghdad. On August 6, after reviewing U.S. satellite intelligence of the Iraqi buildup on the Saudi border, King Fahd invited the United States to deploy troops in Saudi Arabia. Other Arab nations, however, were left to sort out competing loyalties, values, and objectives.

Almost every Arab state regarded Saddam Hussein's annexation of Kuwait as unlawful. Fourteen of twenty-one Arab League nations condemned Iraq's invasion of Kuwait the day after it happened. Like Kuwait, the boundaries of most Middle East countries had been created arbitrarily during colonial times. Hussein's argument that his invasion of Kuwait merely was an effort to redress past colonial injustices threatened to set the precedent that all Middle East boundaries could be subject to reinterpretation.

Arab leaders also understood that Hussein's ambitions, which stretched far beyond Kuwait, could place their own regimes in jeopardy. However, they were hesitant to abandon the myth of Arab unity or take a position that could place them on the side of a Western military intervention against a fraternal Arab state, especially one with menacing military strength.

After a week of indecision in the Arab world, President Mubarak of Egypt called an emergency meeting of the Arab League that was held in Cairo August 10. Mubarak announced that the meeting would attempt to find an "Arab solution" to the crisis in an effort to avert outside intervention. Iraq, however, refused to make any concessions on Kuwait. Its delegation to the Cairo summit even asserted that Baghdad's August 8 annexation of Kuwait gave it the right to control Kuwait's seat at the meeting. The summit ended with twelve of the twenty-one Arab League members voting to send troops to Saudi Arabia to defend it against Iraq. Arab troops were to operate under Saudi command, distinct from Western contingents that might also be deployed in Saudi Arabia. The twelve Arab nations opposing Iraq were: Bahrain, Djibouti, Egypt, Kuwait, Lebanon, Morocco, Oman, Qatar, Saudi Arabia, Somalia, Syria, and the United Arab Emirates. Iraq, Libya, and the Palestine Liberation Organization (PLO) voted against the measure. Jordan, Mauritania, and Sudan voted for it "with reservations." Algeria and Yemen abstained, and Tunisia did not attend the meeting.

Arab governments made their decision according to their own perceived self-interests, not according to their feelings toward Kuwait or their desire to preserve Arab unity. The wealthy Gulf states, which had the most to fear from Iraq, followed Saudi Arabia's leadership and joined with the West in opposing Iraq. Egypt, which received $2.3 billion a year in aid from the United States and which has traditionally been an Iraqi rival for Arab leadership, also sided with Saudi Arabia and the West. President Assad of Syria joined the coalition despite longstanding differences with the United States. His personal enmity toward Saddam Hussein and his ambitions for Damascus to eclipse Baghdad as a power center in the Arab world made an Iraqi defeat a tantalizing prospect. He also was anxious to improve relations with the wealthy Gulf states who could replace dwindling Soviet financial support.

In contrast, poorer Arab nations tended to side with Hussein or declare their neutrality. As the leader of a militarily powerful Arab nation confronting the oil-rich Gulf Arabs, Israel, and the West, Saddam Hussein had a strong appeal among poorer segments of the Arab population. Jordanians and Palestinians in particular rallied to support Hussein, but pro-Iraq demonstrations also were common in Yemen, Lebanon, Algeria, Libya, Tunisia, and the Sudan. Demonstrations of support for Iraq also were reported in some nations whose governments joined the coalition, including Egypt, Syria, and Morocco.

Limits of Pan-Arabism

The Iraqi invasion of Kuwait and the willingness of Arab governments to pursue their own interests, even if it meant allying themselves with foreign troops, demonstrated that the notion of pan-Arabism did not reflect the realities of the Arab world. Pan-Arabism was the concept that all Arabs in the Middle East could unite to form a single Arab nation. That Iraq could invade its Arab neighbor and subject Kuwaiti citizens to torture was powerful evidence that pan-Arabism could not be taken seriously.

Although Arab states share common linguistic, religious, historical, and cultural roots, and have sought to limit outside influence in the Middle East, they have evolved into independent nations with widely different needs and objectives since the Ottoman Empire was fragmented after World War I. The twenty-one members of the Arab League, an organization founded in 1945 on pan-Arabist principles, were divided by their ties to foreign powers, sectarian and ethnic compositions, levels of wealth, and other factors. Yet despite the obvious limits of Pan-Arabism in the modern Middle East, the concept has a strong appeal among poorer Arabs who have seen their individual countries dominated by Western powers and militarily threatened by Israel and Persian Iran. Pan-Arabism has held out the hope of achieving Arab military strength, economic independence from the West, and a more equal distribution of oil wealth among the Arab people. Saddam Hussein sought to take advantage of the pan-Arabist romanticism of many poor Arabs. Ironically, he portrayed his invasion of Kuwait as a first step toward a broader Arab union that would restore the Arab world's glorious past. Hussein attempted to create an image of himself as a strong Arab nationalist who would defend the rights of poor Arabs against Israel and the wealthy Gulf rulers.

Hussein's march into Kuwait and his lonely stand against the West appealed to longstanding Arab resentments and frustrations. To Arabs who hated their colonial past, his confronting a coalition that included the United States, Great Britain, France, and other Western nations signaled the beginning of a new era of Arab independence. To Arabs frustrated by several military defeats at the hands of Israel, the apparent might of Hussein's army proved that Arab states were not necessarily doomed to military inferiority. To poverty-stricken Arabs the sight

The Many Incarnations...

During his career, Saddam Hussein has transformed himself into numerous expedient political persona, including a Ba'athist revolutionary, a party henchman, an Iraqi and regional strongman, a devout Moslem, and a Pan-Arabist messiah. His mercurial ruthlessness, combined with his domestic terror tactics, his xenophobia, and his political acumen have enabled him to become the absolute ruler of Iraq and a hero to many dispossessed Arabs outside his country. Yet his willingness to sacrifice his people for his ambitions and causes has left his oil-rich nation impoverished, divided, isolated, and devastated.

Saddam, whose name literally means "he who confronts," was born in a village near Tikrit in northern Iraq on April 28, 1937. His childhood was marked by mistreatment, poverty, and ignorance. He was reportedly beaten and abused by his stepfather in his early youth. He did not enter primary school until he was nine years old.

Kairallah Talfah, a charismatic uncle who participated in an unsuccessful revolt against the British-supported Iraqi monarchy in 1941, raised Saddam from the age of ten. Talfah's ardent anti-Semitism and pro-Nazi leanings helped mold young Saddam's view of the world. He indoctrinated his nephew with a hatred of British colonialism, which eventually ripened into scorn for all foreign influences in the Middle East.

As a teenager, Hussein led a gun-toting street gang of young Tikritis. In 1955, he entered the al-Karkh secondary school in Baghdad, a hotbed of the Iraqi student nationalist movement; it was here that Hussein joined the Ba'ath party. One year later, Hussein was involved in an abortive coup attempt against Iraq's King Faisal II and his prime minister. Although the effort failed, Hussein gained the attention of Ba'ath party leaders.

In 1959 Hussein was selected, along with nine other Ba'ath zealots, to assassinate Prime Minister Abdul Karim Kassem, who had led a successful military coup against the pro-British monarchy in 1958. The ambush of Kassem failed, and most of the plotters were arrested. Though wounded in the leg, Hussein escaped. Legend has it that he excised the bullet with a pen-knife and escaped incognito across the

Reuters/Bettmann

Saddam Hussein

desert on a donkey, arriving in Syria to begin his exile.

Egyptian president Gamal Abdel Nasser purportedly sponsored Hussein and arranged for safe passage to Cairo. Nasser's influence on Hussein cannot be underestimated. Hussein's political dream to be leader of a pan-Arabist union and his rhetoric trace to Nasser. His conduct in the Kuwait conflict—as a lone Arab battling the arrayed forces of the West—is reminiscent of the late Egyptian leader.

Hussein returned to Iraq in 1963 after a Ba'ath government temporarily came to power. Hussein reportedly was in charge of a torture operation in Baghdad, until the regime was overthrown later that

of Kuwait's elite being transformed from wealthy oil barons with extravagant lifestyles into refugees was satisfying. When Saddam Hussein promised an equal distribution of oil wealth among the Arab people, he was seen as a modern day Robin Hood, whose brutal means could be justified by his goals. He also was compared to Saladin, the twelfth-century Moslem military leader who defeated European Crusaders and liberated Jerusalem.

Although Hussein was hailed in the streets of Amman,

the villages of the West Bank, and in many other parts of the Arab world, the fact remained that most Arab governments opposed him. Moreover, the three most powerful and influential Arab nations besides Iraq—Egypt, Saudi Arabia, and Syria—all were deploying sizable military forces on the Saudi-Kuwaiti border. Eight Arab nations had refused to sanction military deployments against Iraq, but the twelve that did contained 60 percent of the people living in Arab countries and a much larger percentage of

...of Saddam Hussein

year and he was returned to exile. As an Iraqi expatriate, Hussein moved among Ba'ath party leadership circles in Egypt and Syria. He finished his secondary education and began to study law in Cairo.

When the Ba'athists recaptured power in Iraq in 1968, Hussein had consolidated his influence within the party. Ahmed Hassan al-Bakr became president of Iraq, but many analysts have theorized that the driving force behind the regime was al-Bakr's second in command and distant cousin, Saddam Hussein. Hussein's organization of a secret police force had been an important factor in the relatively easy Ba'ath seizure of power.

Hussein began to enhance his personal position through contacts outside the party. His ties to the military resulted in his amassing supreme military rank and honors and even obtaining advanced degrees in military science. Hussein was able to gain the loyalty of key officers, in part by sponsoring a military buildup unparalleled in the Arab world.

Authoritarianism soon became the norm inside Iraq. Party and nonparty purges were routine. Hussein had experience in these matters; he allegedly had served as a Ba'ath party executioner in his early days and reportedly killed his brother-in-law because of his Communist party activities. The first serious challenge to the al-Bakr-Hussein regime occurred in 1973, when Iraq's internal security chief headed a plot to assassinate the two leaders. Many of the plotters were executed. Since that time, Hussein has been careful to maintain control of his security apparatus through placement of Tikriti loyalists in key positions.

In 1979 Hussein eliminated all pretenses of power by placing al-Bakr under arrest and assuming the presidency himself. Hussein then embarked on a campaign to establish his own cult. Young Iraqis were taught Ba'ath party doctrine, and Hussein was extolled in literature, music, and film. Thirty-foot portraits of Hussein were erected in every city and village. His media image was carefully orchestrated to display him in various ethnic garb and in nearly every station of life.

Hussein burst upon the world scene with his invasion of Iran in 1980. Casualties from the eight-year conflict reached an estimated 120,000 Iraqi dead and 300,000 wounded. Despite the stalemate that resulted, Hussein achieved a three-fold aim: his power within Iraq was unquestioned, he had gained political stature in the Arab world for blunting the perceived advance of the Iranian revolution, and Iraq had emerged as the premier regional military power.

Hussein's thirst for advanced military technology grew during the war. Israel's preemptive destruction of Iraq's nuclear reactor in 1981 reinforced Hussein's desire to build the most powerful military machine in the Middle East. To this end, Hussein launched an aggressive campaign to acquire Western military technology and nuclear weapons.

His repression of the Kurdish minority in Iraq was well known for years, but his chemical attack on the unarmed village of Halabja in 1988 brought worldwide media attention and international condemnation. The gassing reportedly killed thousands. The Halabja attack and Hussein's reputation as a violator of human rights within Iraq were foremost on the minds of many when he invaded Kuwait in August 1990. Prior to the invasion, he had openly complained about the lack of repayment of war debts by his Gulf neighbors. As a prelude to war, he revived the idea of a border dispute with Kuwait and spurned his political courtship of conservative Gulf states.

Perhaps the most revealing aspect of the Kuwait invasion was Hussein's limited experience with the West. Because of the American tilt toward Iraq in the war with Iran, he was rumored to believe that the United States would not resist the invasion of his oil-rich neighbor. His public references to Vietnam indicate that Hussein also may have been convinced that the United States lacked the will to contest his annexation of Kuwait.

Little is known about Saddam Hussein's personal life. He has been married since 1963 to Sajida Khayrallah, a first cousin to whom he was betrothed at age four. Sajida is renowned in Iraq for her extravagance, some of which has rubbed off on Hussein himself. They have five children. Hussein's wife and several other family members are rumored to have escaped to Mauritania to avoid the allied bombing of Iraq.

Arab wealth. With this level of Arab participation in the multinational coalition, Hussein would find it difficult to convince Arabs not already inclined to support him that he was fighting a holy war against invaders.

Linking Kuwait and the Palestinian Issue

Despite their differences, most Arab states had been able to agree on one thing over the years: their opposition to Israel. Enemies as devout as Syria and Iraq were united in their hostility toward the Jewish state. Although Egypt had broken from the Arab ranks to make peace with the Jewish state in 1979, Cairo continued to oppose Israel's hold on the occupied territories and its refusal to allow Palestinians to establish a state of their own there. If Saddam Hussein were going to attempt to splinter the Arab states from the coalition facing him, focusing on Israel as the common enemy of all Arabs was his best strategy. Hussein therefore attempted to link his occupation of Kuwait to Israel's continuing occupation of the West Bank and Gaza Strip and its annexation of the Golan Heights and East Jerusalem.

Hussein first attempted to connect the two issues in an August 12 speech in Baghdad. He proposed that "all cases of occupation, and those cases that have been portrayed as occupation" be resolved through "an immediate and unconditional Israeli withdrawal from occupied Arab lands in Palestine, Syria, and Lebanon; a Syrian withdrawal from Lebanon; mutual withdrawals by Iraq and Iran; and arrangement for the situation in Kuwait." Later Baghdad scaled back its demands, saying that it might consider a withdrawal from Kuwait if the United States and its allies agreed to convene an international conference on the Middle East—an event that the Israeli government refused to consider. Arab leaders long had called for such a conference as a means to push Israel toward a negotiated settlement of the Palestinian issue that would involve an Israeli withdrawal from the occupied territories in exchange for Arab recognition of Israel's right to exist and international security guarantees. Several Western allies, including France, already supported such a conference. The Bush administration's established policy was that it would back a Middle East peace conference under certain circumstances. But Bush refused to link U.S. support for a Middle East peace conference to an Iraqi withdrawal, saying that the United States would not make any concession that would reward Iraq's aggression.

Throughout the crisis, the Iraqis accused the United States and other Western nations of a double standard with regard to foreign occupations in the Middle East. The United States, Baghdad said, was willing to send hundreds of thousands of troops to Saudi Arabia and enforce severe economic sanctions against Iraq in an effort to reverse Iraq's occupation of Kuwait, but it did nothing to force Israel out of the occupied territories. Baghdad noted that the embargo of Iraq and the coalition troop deployments in Saudi Arabia were based on UN Security Council resolutions, but the international community had taken no similar actions to implement UN Security Council Resolutions 242 and 338, which called for Israel to withdraw from the occupied territories. *(Resolutions 242 and 338, documents, p. 301)*

The United States countered that Hussein did not invade, plunder, and annex Kuwait in an effort to secure Palestinian rights. Even Hussein's supporters did not believe that he ordered the invasion of Kuwait to further the Palestinian cause. But the Iraqi leader certainly understood before the invasion that he would be able to accuse those nations who might denounce his action of a double standard. By linking Kuwait to the Palestinian issue, Hussein hoped to weaken support for the coalition among Arab governments, who would not wish to be seen as fighting on the side of Israel or standing in the way of an attempt to secure a homeland for the Palestinians. He also expected that being a champion of Palestinian rights would increase his popularity in the Arab world, thereby intensifying pressure on opposing Arab governments to soften their policies toward Iraq and perhaps end their support for the U.S.-led coalition.

On October 8, events in East Jerusalem played into Hussein's hands. According to news reports, thousands of Palestinians had assembled to oppose a group of conservative Jews who planned to lay the cornerstone of a new Jewish temple that the conservative Jews wanted built on the Haram al-Sharif (known to Jews as the Temple Mount), one of Islam's holiest sites. The Palestinians began showering Jewish worshipers at the nearby Western Wall with stones. The Israeli worshipers, a few dozen of whom were injured, and a relatively small contingent of Israeli security police withdrew out of range of the stones.

After the police contingent was reinforced, it charged the Haram al-Sharif to break up the riot. The police opened fire with live ammunition (tear gas and rubber bullets had not dispersed the crowd), killing between nineteen and twenty-one Palestinians and wounding about 150. The clash was the bloodiest single incident in the three-year history of the intifada.

The Jerusalem killings presented Saddam Hussein with an opportunity to undermine Arab support for the coalition. The Bush administration was dismayed that the Israeli government had allowed the violent confrontation to occur during such a sensitive period. The United States quickly moved to sponsor Security Council Resolution 672, which condemned Israel for the deaths of the Palestinians and provided for a fact-finding mission to be sent to Jerusalem. The United States, which had not joined a vote against Israel since 1982 after Israel invaded Lebanon, hoped to preempt an attempt by the PLO and Arab states to introduce a harsher resolution that the United States might be compelled to veto. Such a veto would lend credence to Iraq's claims that the United States was working in tandem with Israel and would always back Israel against the Arabs.

The passage of Resolution 672 infuriated Israel, and the PLO was infuriated by the Security Council's unwillingness to take tougher action against Israel. American-Israeli relations were cooler than they had been in years, with Israel claiming that it had been betrayed by the United States, and the United States complaining that Israel was insensitive to the delicacy of the U.S. position and the necessity of maintaining the anti-Iraq coalition. On October 24 the United States again joined in a unanimous Security Council vote on Resolution 673, which condemned Israel for refusing to receive the UN fact-finding mission. *(Resolutions 672 and 673, documents, p. 379)*

The United States had fervently maintained that Iraq's invasion of Kuwait and the Arab-Israeli conflict were two separate issues. Its own frantic diplomacy at the United Nations demonstrated what was obvious: few issues in the Middle East, especially Iraq's aggression against Kuwait, could be separated entirely from the Arab-Israeli conflict. Nevertheless, the Bush administration remained firm in its refusal to reward Iraq in any way for its aggression against Kuwait. Despite their opposition to Israel, Arab members of the coalition remained focused on stopping the more immediate threat from Iraq.

Palestinian Support for Iraq

The Iraqi invasion of Kuwait placed the PLO leadership in the difficult position of having to choose between backing Iraq and thereby alienating Western and Arab countries supporting the coalition or ignoring strong support among Palestinians for Saddam Hussein. To ignore the groundswell of Palestinian support for Iraq would have undermined PLO leader Yasir Arafat's claim of being the voice of the Palestinian people, but to support Hussein the PLO would have to align itself with an isolated dictator whose aggression against a small neighbor was receiving almost universal condemnation from the international community, including Saudi Arabia and other Gulf Arab states that had contributed large sums to the Palestinian cause in the past.

The Palestinians' enthusiasm for Saddam Hussein was rooted in that people's perceptions of their own plight. Since the late 1940s, their attempts to gain a homeland had been frustrated. Among the reasons Palestinians cite for their continuing stateless condition are Israeli military power and political intransigence, lukewarm support (and occasionally open hostility) from some Arab leaders, and insensitivity to their plight by the international community. Many Palestinians remarked during the crisis that they would support anyone who would stand up to Israel and act as an advocate for them. It did not matter to most Palestinians that Iraq's invasion of Kuwait was motivated by factors other than Palestinian rights. That many Palestinians working in Kuwait were deprived of their livelihoods by the invasion was accepted by most Palestinians as a necessary sacrifice. What was important was that Saddam Hussein was willing to challenge Israel and the West with military force and champion the Palestinian cause. By doing so, Iraq demonstrated that an Arab nation did not have to be militarily weak. The Palestinians, who had witnessed many frustrating Arab defeats at the hands of the Israeli military, were as impressed with Hussein's military strength as they were encouraged by his advocacy of Palestinian rights. If Hussein could confront an international coalition led by a superpower, he also was strong enough to take on Israel.

In contrast, neither Cairo, which had made peace with Israel in 1979, nor Damascus, which had avoided military conflict with Israel since the Jewish state inflicted a beating on Syria in 1982, was willing to challenge Israel. Egypt, Syria, and other Arab countries continued to lobby for Palestinian rights in world forums, but only Iraq appeared committed to forcing the Palestinian issue to the top of the international agenda.

In addition, recent events had made the Palestinians more desperate for a champion. The intifada, begun in December 1987, had given Palestinian's hope that they finally had found a political tool that would earn them international support and pressure Israel into making concessions that could lead to a Palestinian homeland in the occupied territories. By 1990, however, the intifada had produced few results. The one major diplomatic breakthrough the PLO had achieved during the period—the U.S. decision in 1988 to open a dialogue with it—had been lost in June 1990, when President Bush suspended the dialogue in response to the PLO's refusal to denounce an attack on Israel by Palestinian guerrillas.

Moreover, the political power of Israeli conservatives who opposed trading occupied lands for peace appeared to be growing. Several prominent members of the right wing had received important cabinet posts in the new Israeli government formed in June 1990, and the conservative coalition led by the Likud party appeared to be more secure than recent coalition governments. Finally, as part of Moscow's new lenient policy toward Jewish emigration, hundreds of thousands of Soviet Jews were pouring into Israel. Palestinians feared that the Israeli government would begin settling large numbers of Soviet Jews in the occupied territories to further solidify Israel's hold on these lands. Amidst these developments, few Palestinians could resist the appeal of Saddam Hussein's anti-Israeli rhetoric and calls for a Middle East peace conference at which the Palestinian plight would be discussed.

After some initial wavering, Yasir Arafat and the PLO leadership chose to accept the will of the majority of their constituents and back Saddam Hussein. The PLO joined Libya and Iraq in voting against the August 10 Arab League resolution providing for Arab forces to be sent to Saudi Arabia to oppose the Iraqi military in Kuwait. On several occasions during the crisis Arafat was warmly received by Saddam Hussein in Baghdad.

The PLO's embrace of Iraq tarnished its international image, changed the views of some officials in the West who believed the PLO could become a moderate force for peace, and hardened the attitudes of many Israelis toward the issue of the occupied territories. The Israeli government pointed to the crowds of Palestinians cheering Saddam Hussein's invasion of Kuwait and threats against Israel as evidence that the PLO could not be trusted to respect Israel's security or refrain from terrorist activities. In December 1988, Yasir Arafat had renounced terrorism and recognized Israel's right to exist. But the PLO's support for Saddam Hussein was at odds with both positions, because Iraq was known to be a base for terrorists and had threatened to attack Israel with chemical weapons.

Perhaps most damaging to the PLO, however, were the perceptions of Gulf Arabs that they had been betrayed by the Palestinians. For many years, Saudi Arabia, Kuwait, and the other Gulf states had provided the PLO with substantial financial aid. The Gulf Arabs reasoned that if Arafat and the PLO could applaud the destruction of Kuwait, which had given it billions of dollars and was home to hundreds of thousands of Palestinians who sent their earnings back to relatives in Jordan and the occupied territories, then the PLO was capable of treachery against any Gulf state. In fact, many Palestinians deeply resented the Kuwaitis for their affluence and for regulations that denied to Palestinians living in Kuwait citizenship and full legal rights. But to Saudi Arabia and other Gulf states threatened by Hussein's military power, nothing could justify PLO support for Iraq.

Jordan's Predicament

No third party was damaged more by the Iraqi invasion of Kuwait than Jordan. Like Yasir Arafat, Jordan's King Hussein ibn Talal was forced to choose between opposing Iraq to maintain good relations with the West and the Gulf Arab states or supporting Iraq, as most of his people did. Jordan had long been considered one of the most moderate and pro-Western Arab states. King Hussein had cultivated good relations with the West and had relied on Western nations for economic and military aid. But the vast majority of Jordanians, 60 percent of whom were Palestinian, passionately supported Saddam Hussein and condemned the United States for sending troops to Saudi Arabia. If the king sided with the coalition, he risked alienating his people and losing control of his country. Like Arafat, he chose to back Iraq.

King Hussein, however, attempted to finesse his predicament by tilting heavily toward Iraq, while officially declaring that Jordan would remain neutral in the conflict. He continued to recognize Kuwait's government-in-exile and announced that Jordan would abide by UN sanctions imposed against Iraq. But by almost every measure Jordan became a noncombatant ally of Iraq. King Hussein refused to join fully in the August 10 Arab League decision that sent Arab forces to Saudi Arabia, voting in favor of the measure but with "reservations." Despite Jordan's pledge

An Egyptian worker who fled Iraq sits amidst the suitcases of his fellow refugees after reaching Jordan.

Reuters/Bettmann

to observe the UN embargo against Iraq, diplomats and journalists in Iraq and Jordan reported a flow of commerce between the two nations that the Jordanian government was making no effort to stop. During late 1990 Jordan reportedly helped Iraq stockpile military supplies and smuggle crucial chemicals used to purify water and refine jet fuel. Jordan also announced that it would consider any Israeli use of Jordanian airspace an act of war—even if Israel was responding to an Iraqi missile attack. On February 6, 1991, in the midst of the coalition's air war against Iraq, King Hussein delivered an angry televised address stating his unequivocal support of Saddam Hussein.

Throughout the crisis, King Hussein was condemned in the West for his pro-Iraqi stance, but given the sentiments of his people, he would have risked riots against his government had he aligned his nation with the coalition. Hussein's decision to cast his lot with Iraq was therefore an exercise in personal survival, and his support of Saddam Hussein caused his popularity among Jordanians to rise substantially.

Regardless of how King Hussein responded to Iraq's invasion of Kuwait, the Gulf crisis created enormous economic problems for Jordan. Iraq was Jordan's largest trading partner, and even if Jordan did not comply fully with the UN embargo against Iraq, the sanctions diminished Jordanian-Iraqi commerce. In addition, the crisis brought a flood of refugees to Jordan who had fled economic hardship and potential war in Kuwait and Iraq. Jordan, a poor country, was not equipped to handle this sudden onslaught of refugees. Western governments and Japan pledged several billion dollars in aid to Middle East nations (principally Egypt, Turkey, and Jordan) whose economies were hard hit by the UN embargo of Iraq, but Gulf leaders, who had provided aid to Jordan in the past were generally unsympathetic. The Saudi government, with which King Hussein had always had close ties, was especially vindictive over Jordan's stand during the crisis. In September Riyadh suspended deliveries of oil to Jordan and expelled twenty Jordanian diplomats in retaliation for King Hussein's position.

Toward War in the Gulf

Once U.S. and allied military deployments in Saudi Arabia had ended the possibility that Iraq could launch an offensive that could threaten Saudi Arabia and its oilfields, the Bush administration had to decide on a strategy for dealing with Saddam Hussein's occupation of Kuwait. There was broad consensus among Americans and members of Congress that Hussein should be opposed and Saudi Arabia should be protected. The public's support for a possible U.S.-led military action against Iraq was less certain.

On November 8, two days after midterm congressional elections in the United States, President Bush announced that he was reinforcing the 230,000 U.S. troops already in the Gulf participating in what was known as "Operation Desert Shield." He provided no specific total of how many troops would be sent, but Pentagon sources said that approximately 200,000 more troops would be deployed in the region. Secretary of Defense Dick Cheney announced the following day that the United States no longer planned to rotate troops into and out of the Gulf. *(Bush increases forces, documents, p. 379)*

The new deployments to Saudi Arabia and the end of troop rotation plans alarmed critics in Congress, who complained that the administration's policies shortened the time economic sanctions would have to take effect and force Iraq out of Kuwait. Military experts agreed that the United States could not sustain such a large force in an inhospitable desert environment indefinitely, and the new deployments would force the administration to choose between withdrawing part of the force, which would be perceived as a moral victory for Saddam Hussein, or going to war.

Bush Administration Strategy

The massive military buildup in Saudi Arabia reflected a change in President Bush's strategy. He appeared to be rejecting the long-term approach of relying on economic sanctions to force Iraq out of Kuwait. In announcing the deployments on November 8 Bush said that the additional forces being sent to Saudi Arabia were intended to "insure that the coalition has an adequate offensive military option should that be necessary to achieve our common goals." Bush believed that his best chance to force Iraq out of Kuwait peacefully was to present Baghdad with a coalition force capable of inflicting terrible damage on Iraqi forces. Until such a coalition force was in place, Bush did not believe that the threat of attack would be credible. The new buildup, therefore, was a high stakes gamble. It increased the pressure on Hussein to withdraw, but greatly heightened the likelihood of war if he did not.

Saddam Hussein was believed to be a ruthless tyrant willing to sacrifice many lives for his purposes, but he also was seen as a leader who could be counted on to act in his self interest. Sanctions might not force Hussein out of Kuwait, even if faced with a complete embargo imposed over a number of years. But if he could be made to see that his armies, upon which he depended for his personal power and prestige, would be destroyed in a war with the United States and its coalition partners, Bush and his advisers believed that Hussein would find a face-saving way to withdraw from Kuwait.

The Bush administration also took this approach because the perceived fragility of the anti-Iraq coalition created a sense of urgency. It was feared that unrest motivated by support for Iraq within Arab countries supporting the coalition could topple friendly governments or weaken the resolve of these governments to remain in the coalition. In addition, the October 8 killings of as many as twenty-one Palestinians in Jerusalem by Israeli security policy demonstrated that events in the occupied territories or any provocative Israeli military strike could cause Arabs to reconsider their opposition to a fraternal Arab nation that was militarily strong enough to be a counterweight to Israel. Not everyone agreed, however, that moving toward war was a remedy for the pressures on the cohesiveness of the coalition. These sentiments were expressed by former chairman of the Joint Chiefs of Staff Admiral William Crowe. He said in testimony to the Senate Armed Services committee on November 28, "I cannot understand why some consider our international alliance strong enough to conduct intense hostilities but too fragile to hold together while we attempt a peaceful solution."

The timing of an offensive, if one became necessary, was an additional consideration. After the middle of March, extreme desert heat would return to the Gulf region, and this would favor the defenders. Also, the Moslem holy month of Ramadan would begin in March, complicating Arab participation in the coalition. These factors weighed heavily on the side of employing the military option sooner instead of later. Perhaps the most important factor in the Bush administration's decision, however, was that many officials at the Pentagon and the White House and their Arab counterparts feared an Iraqi withdrawal from Kuwait almost as much as a war. A pullout would have left the formidable Iraqi military (as well as its nuclear research facilities and its chemical and biological weapons industries) intact and capable of threatening its neighbors, including Saudi Arabia and Kuwait. Even if the international community agreed to impose indefinite restrictions on sales of arms and technologies with military uses to Iraq, Baghdad would already be in possession of military power that none of its neighbors could match. Consequently, President Bush stated that if Iraq withdrew, an international peace-keeping force would be needed on the ground and U.S. naval forces in the Persian Gulf would need to be strengthened.

Meanwhile, seeking to prove that his withdrawal from Kuwait was not an act of cowardice or betrayal of the cause of poor Arabs, Saddam Hussein would be tempted to pursue other aggressive policies, particularly against Israel. Such conditions would heighten Arab-Israeli tensions and dramatically increase the possibility of another Arab-Israeli war. Israel already had hinted that it could not allow Iraq to make further progress toward developing accurate missiles and atomic weapons. Its air attack against the Iraqi Osirak nuclear reactor in 1981 had demonstrated that Israel was quite willing to use military force against Iraq without a direct Iraqi military provocation. If Iraq threw its military weight behind an Arab attack against Israel, the conflagration would far exceed previous Arab-Israeli wars. The military threat posed by Iraq, especially its chemical and biological weapons, might even induce Israel to use nuclear weapons against Iraq. Consequently, the Bush administration regarded peace based on an Iraqi withdrawal as an outcome nearly as dangerous as a war. The official U.S. policy objectives continued to be the ouster of Iraq from Kuwait through economic sanctions and the threat of military force, but implicit in Bush's willingness to make the military threat was an underlying belief that war might be the wise option. The liberation of Kuwait was an important goal of the Bush administration, but it also was seen as the means through which the Iraqi military threat might be destroyed.

Constitutional Debate

The deployment of large numbers of American forces in Saudi Arabia triggered a constitutional debate on the division of war powers between the executive and legislative branches in the United States. The war power issue had been debated since the Constitution was written, but the argument had become especially intense since the Vietnam War, when the executive branch was perceived to have pulled the country into a long undeclared conflict. After the Vietnam War, Congress had overridden a veto by President Richard Nixon and passed the War Powers Act, which attempted to expand and clarify Congress' responsibility for deciding when the nation should go to war and remain at war. Most U.S. military actions since the Vietnam War, including the invasion of Grenada in 1983 and the deployment of troops in Lebanon from 1982 to 1984, brought complaints from Congress that the president had not adequately consulted with it in accordance with the War Powers Act.

With the increase of U.S. forces in Saudi Arabia, Congress became concerned that a president was again pushing the nation toward war without seeking congressional approval. Most lawmakers asserted that because the responsibility to declare war rested with the Congress, the president did not have the power to launch a military offensive against Iraq without prior congressional approval—unless Iraq attacked U.S. forces. The administration disputed this assertion, claiming that the president's role as commander in chief empowered him to order offensive actions against Iraq.

The president, however, promised to consult closely with Congress with regard to his Gulf policy. In January, when war became likely and Bush appeared to have enough votes in Congress to win approval for the war option, he sought to unite the government and the country behind his policies by asking Congress to authorize an attack against Iraq if one became necessary in his judgment. The request satisfied most members of Congress that their war-making role had not been usurped by the president.

UN Deadline

After announcing the new military deployments to Saudi Arabia, the Bush administration began pursuing the possibility of a UN Security Council sanction for the use of force against Iraq. On November 29 the UN Security Council voted 12-2 (with Yemen and Cuba dissenting) to implicitly authorize coalition nations to use force to expel Iraq from Kuwait. Security Council Resolution 678, however, allowed for a month and a half of diplomacy by authorizing force only after January 15. The United States had pressed for a January 1 deadline, but compromised with the Soviet Union, which had wanted the January 15 deadline to allow diplomacy more time to work. Diplomats would have forty-seven days to persuade Iraq to withdraw from Kuwait peacefully or to construct a compromise. *(Resolution 678, documents, p. 380)*

China had voted for each of the previous eleven UN Security Council resolutions related to the Iraqi invasion of Kuwait, but it abstained from the vote to approve military force, saying that the council should avoid "hasty actions" that could lead to war. Nevertheless, the Chinese refrained from vetoing the resolution. Secretary of State Baker, who chaired the Security Council meeting when the vote was taken, declared the vote to be "a watershed in the history of the United Nations." Any U.S.-led military action taken after January 15 to oust Iraq from Kuwait now had international legitimacy.

Release of Foreign Hostages

During October and November a parade of foreign luminaries visited Baghdad to discuss the Gulf crisis and plea for the release of hostages. Hussein made a practice of releasing a token number of hostages to these visitors. Many of Hussein's callers were former leaders of nations opposed to Iraq's occupation of Kuwait, including former prime minister Yasuhiro Nakesone of Japan, former chancellor Willy Brandt of West Germany, and former prime minister Edward Heath of Great Britain.

On December 6, a week after the UN Security Council passed a resolution authorizing the coalition to use military force against Iraq after January 15, Saddam Hussein informed the Iraqi National Assembly that all foreign hostages would be released. Some observers were surprised that Hussein gave up these potentially valuable pawns. He had indicated that his strategy in a war would be to break the will of the Americans and their Western allies to fight by inflicting unacceptable numbers of Western casualties. By releasing the hostages, he had greatly reduced the number of Westerners who would be killed if the coalition decided on war. But in his statement announcing the impending release of the hostages, Hussein said that during the time foreigners had been held to prevent coalition attacks, Iraq had completed its fortification of Kuwait. He claimed, "We have now reached the time when, with God's care, our blessed force has become fully prepared." Hussein may have believed that his army, now well dug in in Kuwait, would be able to inflict more than enough coalition casualties to achieve his purpose. In effect, Hussein regarded coalition infantry troops as his ultimate hostages. *(Hussein message freeing hostages,*

documents, p. 381)

Western observers speculated that the Iraqi leadership also may have come to believe that the hostages would not deter a coalition attack, and might even provoke one. Therefore, for propaganda purposes, Iraq released hostages it no longer wanted to hold. At the time of Hussein's announcement, about 900 Americans and 1,200 Britons were stranded in Iraq or Kuwait, with about 100 Americans and 350 Britons being used as human shields at strategic locations.

Diplomacy

For almost four months diplomats and leaders of Arab and Western nations had attempted to find a nonmilitary solution to the crisis. The UN Security Council's November 29 decision to authorize force against Iraq if it had not withdrawn from Kuwait by January 15 brought new urgency to their endeavors.

President Bush made the first significant diplomatic initiative himself. On November 30 he invited Iraqi foreign minister Tariq Aziz to visit Washington in mid-December. Secretary of State Baker would then travel to Baghdad sometime before the January 15 deadline. Bush insisted that the purpose of these talks would not be to negotiate, but instead to provide an opportunity to confront the Iraqis with U.S. resolve and convince them to leave Kuwait.

The Iraqis accepted the exchange of foreign ministers in principle December 1 and called for a December 17 meeting in Washington between Bush and Aziz. But they also said that Saddam Hussein could not meet with Baker in Baghdad until January 12. The official reason given by Iraq for the late meeting date was that Saddam Hussein's schedule was too busy to accommodate a meeting with Baker. Bush scoffed at the excuse. On December 14 he declared, "It simply is not credible that he cannot, over a two-week period, make a couple of hours available for the secretary of state, unless, of course, he is seeking to circumvent the United Nations deadline." Both sides announced that they would not go ahead with a Bush-Aziz meeting until the issue of the meeting in Baghdad was settled. The United States called on the Iraqi government to agree to hold a Baker-Hussein meeting no later than January 3. The Bush administration considered the proposed January 12 meeting date to be an attempt by Iraq to render the January 15 UN deadline meaningless by drawing out diplomatic activity well past the deadline. The Iraqis seemed to believe that it would be politically impossible for the United States to initiate an attack while diplomatic efforts to end the crisis were still alive. Once the deadline had passed, momentum for an attack could be stunted. Bush was determined to be in a position to launch an attack on Iraq any time after January 15.

During the last half of December, both sides continued their mutual recriminations without any breakthrough on scheduling talks. As the year ended, members of Congress stepped up pressure on the administration to compromise with Iraq on a meeting date, and independent peace initiatives were launched by France and the European Community (EC). On January 3, in an effort to reassert leadership over the peace process, Bush set aside the idea of a foreign minister exchange and proposed a meeting between Baker and Aziz to take place January 7, 8, or 9 in Geneva. Such a meeting did not serve the original purpose behind Bush's proposal of the Baghdad meeting—to allow Baker the opportunity to meet Hussein face to face in an effort to convince him that the United States was willing to use

Foreign Minister Tariq Aziz and Secretary of State James Baker shake hands January 9, 1991, at the beginning of their meeting in Geneva.

Reuters/Bettmann

overwhelming force against Iraq to drive it from Kuwait. But with the deadline quickly approaching, the Baker-Aziz meeting was a reasonable alternative. The following day Iraq accepted Bush's proposal, saying it would send Aziz to Geneva January 9.

The Baker-Aziz meeting appeared to be the last chance to avoid war. The negotiations began amidst general pessimism that neither the Americans nor the Iraqis would make compromises necessary to avoid war. But as the talks dragged on during the day, journalists in Geneva speculated that the two diplomats might be making progress toward a compromise solution. The most likely scenario seemed to be that Aziz had proposed an Iraqi withdrawal in return for concessions by the coalition. Baker's telephone call to President Bush during a break in the meeting heightened speculation that the Iraqis had presented U.S. negotiators with a deal, either as a genuine attempt to find a face-saving way out of Kuwait or as a propaganda ploy.

After six and a half hours, however, Baker and Aziz emerged from their meeting and reported that neither side had budged from their original position. Aziz had refused even to accept a letter written by Bush to Saddam Hussein, saying the letter's language was "not compatible with the language that should be used in correspondence between heads of state." American officials said the letter called on Hussein to withdraw from Kuwait and described the military capability of the international force arrayed against him. Bush later called Aziz's performance at the meeting "a total stiff-arm, a total rebuff." The Iraqi foreign minister's intransigence at the Geneva meeting had the unintended effect of solidifying support among some members of Congress for the president's threat to use force if Iraq did not withdraw from Kuwait. *(Baker and Aziz Geneva statements, documents, p. 382; Bush letter to Hussein, documents, p. 383)*

With the failure of the U.S.-Iraqi talks, other international diplomats began last-ditch efforts to preempt the war. With U.S. support, United Nations Secretary General Javier Pérez de Cuéllar traveled to Baghdad for talks on January 13 with Saddam Hussein. Pérez de Cuéllar reportedly offered to guarantee that the coalition would not attack Iraq or its troops if Hussein agreed to an immediate withdrawal

from Kuwait. The secretary general also told Hussein that he would work to arrange an international peace conference on the Arab-Israeli conflict at an early date after the Gulf crisis was over. According to Pérez de Cuéllar, the Iraqi leader was not interested in any formula for peace that involved his unconditional withdrawal from Kuwait.

On January 14 the French government surprised its coalition partners by proposing that the Security Council agree to hold an international conference on the Israeli-Palestinian conflict if Hussein withdrew from Kuwait. The United States angrily reiterated that it was unwilling to link the two issues and would not reward Iraq in any way for its invasion of Kuwait. The French dropped the proposal January 15 after the British and the Soviet Union also criticized it and the Iraqis showed no interest.

Before the French announcement on January 14, the European Community had decided against sending a representative to Baghdad after General Secretary Pérez de Cuéllar told a meeting of EC leaders in Paris that Saddam Hussein had been completely intransigent during their meeting in Baghdad the day before. Pérez de Cuéllar said, "Unfortunately, I don't see any more reasons to be optimistic. I don't see any reason to have real hope."

On January 15 Pérez de Cuéllar issued one last call for peace. He told Iraq again that it would not be attacked if it withdrew from Kuwait and that UN observers would be made available to supervise the withdrawal. As he had in Baghdad two days before, he pledged his commitment to resolving the Israeli-Palestinian issue by saying, "I have every assurance, once again from the highest levels of government, that with the resolution of the present crisis, every effort will be made to address, in a comprehensive manner, the Arab-Israeli conflict, including the Palestinian question. I pledge my every effort to this end." He received no response from Iraq.

The American War Decision

The Gulf war was unique in American history in that it began after the expiration of a previously set deadline. When the deadline passed at midnight EST January 15,

The Gulf Crisis and Its Effects...

When Iraq invaded and annexed Kuwait in August 1990, a long-feared international economic nightmare threatened to come true: a belligerent military power was in a position to dominate the oil reserves of the Persian Gulf. The invasion sent shock waves through international oil markets, raising questions about how oil traders would respond to this sudden military disruption of the status quo.

In times of peace and normalcy, oil prices are established primarily by the balance of world supply and demand. In times of conflict and uncertainty, future expectations of the availability of oil exert their own powerful and unpredictable pressures on oil prices. The Persian Gulf crisis of 1990 is notable for the degree to which these secondary factors overshadowed the laws of supply and demand in the international oil markets.

The Iraqi invasion marked the beginning of a tumultuous season of oil trading, distinguished by several contradictory pressures that pulled the market in opposite directions. Daily news broadcasts and events formed the future expectations of buyers and sellers. These expectations forced prices up or down regardless of the prevailing long-term supply and demand equations.

Pressures on Oil Prices

During the first two and a half months of the crisis, fear of war and oil shortages created a strong upward trend in oil prices. Saddam Hussein's seizure of Kuwait's oil facilities represented both a long-term and an immediate threat to stable oil prices and therefore to the world's economy. The addition of Kuwait's oil reserves to Iraq's gave Baghdad control of more than 20 percent of the world's known oil reserves—about the same amount as that of Saudi Arabia. At some time in the future, Hussein could attempt to drive prices up (an Iraqi goal throughout early 1990) by drastically cutting production. By controlling the Kuwaiti wells, Hussein could affect the market by himself. Even more ominous was the prospect that Iraq could use its huge army to make a grab for Saudi Arabia's oilfields or coerce Saudi rulers into following Baghdad's lead in oil production and pricing policies.

Scenarios like these created panic in the oil markets—especially because the United States was trying to fend off a recession, which would be exacerbated by a dramatic rise in oil prices. Higher oil prices would lead to inflation, larger budget deficits, and decreased purchasing power for consumers. In addition, the United States had become more dependent upon foreign oil imports than at any other time in history. In July 1990 the United States was importing more than 50 percent of its oil from abroad, and nearly half of its imports came from the Middle East.

During August, fears that Iraq might invade Saudi Arabia were reduced by the forceful response to the invasion by the United States, but the imposition August 6 of a total embargo on Iraqi imports and exports by the UN Security Council effectively removed all Iraqi and Kuwaiti oil from the marketplace. Traders' worries that demand would exceed supply without oil from Iraq and Kuwait drove prices up. The upward trend in prices was reinforced by traders' expectations that consumers would respond to fears of a shortage by topping off their supplies as quickly as possible.

Soon after the embargo was announced, however, Saudi Arabia assured the industrialized nations that it would increase production to meet world oil needs. In general, Saudi production increases exerted downward pressure on oil prices. However, because of doubts that the Saudis could activate spare and idle wells in time to fill the demand for winter heating, the downward pressure was not as strong as might have been expected.

In the months following the invasion, as the United States committed more troops to the Gulf, Saudi Arabia's proximity to where a Gulf war would be fought was a source of anxiety to oil traders and politicians. Fear of war and what it might do to hamper, slow, or arrest production from the largest and most accessible oil reserves in the world sent prices upward whenever the likelihood of war seemed to increase. For example, on October 3, 1990, Hussein visited Kuwait for the first time since the invasion. Traders perceived the visit as a signal that he was unlikely to withdraw from Kuwait quickly or easily, and therefore that the chances of war were great. This perception caused the price of oil to jump 10 percent.

These fears produced the setting in which traders justified an inflated price for oil throughout most of the crisis. However, a constant abundant supply of oil on the world market prevented prices from rising uncontrollably. Venezuela and Nigeria joined Saudi Arabia in increasing their production to make up for lost Iraqi and Kuwaiti supplies. Furthermore, higher prices had reduced world consumption through informal conservation efforts and greater reliance on alternative energy sources. In addition, the United States and other nations had large stockpiles of oil. Prior to the invasion, the U.S. Strategic Petroleum Reserve contained 5.9 billion barrels of oil. This reserve was available to regulate supply to match demand and to prevent prices from rising too high too fast. Thus, supply and demand realities caused oil prices to drop on days when events indicated that a peaceful resolution to the crisis might be achieved. One of the largest price drops occurred on October 22, 1990, after Saudi defense minister Prince Sultan

...on International Oil Markets

Abdel Aziz hinted that Saudi Arabia was willing to allow Iraq to keep strategic areas of Kuwait if the Iraqis withdrew unconditionally from the rest. Oil traders (like many political observers) saw this statement as an indication that a negotiated peace was possible. Prince Sultan's remarks signaled the beginning of a long, downward slide from $32.40 to $26.75 a barrel because traders felt that the market would not sustain such high prices.

Some events produced an unpredictable spin on oil prices. For example, in late September, President Bush announced that the United States would sell 5 million barrels from the U.S. Strategic Petroleum Reserve. The administration wanted to demonstrate through this token use of the reserve that the United States had plenty of oil stored that could be released to the market to stabilize oil prices, if necessary. Analysis of trading patterns after the announcement revealed that the market took notice of Bush's action immediately; the price of oil began to fall in expectation that the extra oil on the market would produce a short-term glut. However, minutes later, the price of oil began to rise, because traders reasoned that Bush would not have released the oil unless the administration expected further price increases.

War and Its Aftermath

After the allied bombing campaign began, the oil market generally stabilized. News that the war had begun in the evening hours of January 16 EST brought a sharp but brief rise in oil prices on markets that were open. A few hours later, however, as highly optimistic reports of the bombing reached traders, oil prices went into a steep decline. This result belied the predictions of some veteran oil traders that war could cause oil prices to jump above $50 a barrel. The enormous air superiority of the allied forces and the success of the initial raids resulted January 17 in the biggest one-day drop (almost $11) in oil prices ever on the New York Mercantile Exchange. At the end of trading, oil prices closed at $21.44, ten cents lower than the price on August 1, 1990, the day before Iraq invaded Kuwait. The failure of Iraq to respond to the air attacks with either a counterattack or effective defensive measures convinced oil traders that the coalition probably would succeed in forcing Iraq out of Kuwait, and the Iraqi air force did not present a major threat to Saudi oil facilities. Although the war was not over, and many uncertainties remained, analysts acknowledged that fears of war and hopes for peace were no longer to exert the same influence over market prices as they had since early August.

The Gulf crisis underscored the vulnerability of the traders' psyche to fears surrounding Persian Gulf politics and consumer behavior. Although other oil-producing countries were able to compensate for Kuwaiti and Iraqi supplies and the United States had strategic reserves to unleash as a regulatory force on the market, these downward pressures could not compensate for the fear, and the fear of fear, among consumers and producers in the market place. The price of oil rose to a high of $40 a barrel in October, and during most of the crisis oil was nearly $10 a barrel higher than supply and demand probably would have dictated.

Now that the war is over, most members of the Organization of Petroleum Exporting Countries will support cuts in production to achieve higher prices. In early March 1991, Saudi Arabia was hinting that it would press other producers to stabilize prices at slightly higher levels. Significant price increases, however, will be difficult to achieve during the next few years. Demand for oil is down because the economies in the West are weak and they have cut consumption in response to the temporary price increase resulting from the war. When Iraq and Kuwait are able to resume pumping, they will do so to recoup a steady source of income to pay for reconstruction. Saudi Arabia also will need as much oil revenue as possible to refill its cash reserves, which were depleted to help pay for the war effort. Given these factors, experts are speculating that oil prices are unlikely to rise much higher than $20 a barrel for years to come.

Weekly Averages of West Texas Intermediate Oil, July 1990-March 1991

Week Starting	Price (U.S. $)	Week Starting	Price (U.S. $)
July 2	$16.84	November 12	$32.27
July 9	$17.21	November 19	$30.53
July 16	$18.67	November 26	$32.55
July 23	$19.64	December 3	$28.31
July 30	$21.19	December 10	$26.28
August 6	$26.72	December 17	$27.47
August 13	$26.78	December 26	$27.32
August 20	$29.86	January 2	$26.81
August 27	$27.88	January 7	$26.93
September 4	$29.52	January 14	$28.13
September 10	$30.78	January 21	$22.92
September 17	$33.34	January 28	$22.01
September 24	$38.46	February 4	$21.21
October 1	$36.76	February 11	$22.33
October 8	$39.48	February 18	$20.10
October 15	$37.87	February 25	$18.44
October 22	$31.42	March 4	$19.82
October 29	$34.61	March 11	$19.71
November 5	$33.95	March 18	$19.82

Source: *Platt's Oilgram.*

the world braced for a war that could begin at any time. The start of this war would not take the country by surprise, as during World War II, nor would U.S. forces slide gradually into combat, as in Vietnam. The situation played out like an old western movie, with the U.S.-led coalition giving the Iraqi outlaw forty-seven days to get out of town, or else.

That month and a half pause before the deadline brought an intensification of the debate on whether to reverse Iraq's occupation of Kuwait by launching a massive attack. Few Americans did not have an opinion on the issue. Judgments about whether to go to war depended not only on one's expectation of how the battle for Kuwait would turn out, but also on the war's long term effect on Middle East and international security and prosperity. The latter outcome was more difficult to predict than the outcome of the fighting. Even a relatively swift and decisive allied victory over Iraq could lead to a violent backlash across the Arab world that would threaten moderate Arab governments, greatly expand international terrorism, and inflame the Arab-Israeli conflict.

Question of Vital Interests

For at least two months before Bush announced that troop strength in Saudi Arabia would be dramatically increased, members of Congress and large segments of the American public questioned if the United States had sufficient interests in liberating Kuwait to use military force. Facing a recession and hoping to reap the benefits of a "peace dividend" that would follow the end of the Cold War, Americans worried that the Gulf mission would undermine the U.S. economy. After witnessing the diminishment of the Soviet military threat, they also had hoped that the world was entering a safer, less confrontational era.

Most Americans backed Bush's initial deployments of troops to Saudi Arabia. As the crisis continued, however, support among Americans for Bush's strategy weakened as fears of a recession and a long stalemate in the desert increased. A *New York Times*/CBS News public opinion poll taken October 8-10 showed that 57 percent of Americans supported the president's Gulf policies, as compared with 75 percent in early August.

Perceptions that a war fought to liberate Kuwait would in reality be a war fought for American access to cheap oil created cynicism among some segments of the American public. The rallying cry of many opponents to the military buildup in Saudi Arabia became "no blood for oil." Other Americans accepted the proposition that Saddam Hussein should be stopped, but questioned why it was up to U.S. soldiers to do it.

Most journalists, politicians, and scholars who closely followed the administration's explanations of its policies commented that Bush had failed to make a coherent case for the need to use force if Iraq refused to withdraw from Kuwait. The difficulty the Bush administration was having in explaining its actions stemmed partly from the nature of the Iraqi threat and partly from the administration's haphazard presentation of the motivations behind its policy.

Saddam Hussein's invasion of Kuwait certainly did not threaten American shores. Instead, it threatened U.S. interests overseas, the international economy, and principles of international law. No single reason for going to war against Iraq was entirely compelling by itself. The Iraqi invasion required citizens to weigh a complex balance sheet of variables for and against the use of force, instead of responding to a ringing cry to arms in the interest of national defense. Moreover, for Americans who saw Iraq as a threat but had doubts about the wisdom of war, continuing a policy of enforcing severe economic sanctions against Iraq offered a compromise option through which a person could oppose both the barbarous acts of Saddam Hussein and the launching of what might be a very bloody war in the desert.

In a November 15 interview with the Cable News Network (CNN), Bush admitted that he needed to explain more clearly the reasons behind his policies in the Persian Gulf. In his August 8 speech announcing the first deployment of U.S. forces in Saudi Arabia, President Bush declared:

> Four simple principles guide our policy.
> First, we seek the immediate, unconditional, and complete withdrawal of all Iraqi forces from Kuwait.
> Second, Kuwait's legitimate government must be restored to replace the puppet regime.
> And third, my administration, as has been the case with every president from President [Franklin D.] Roosevelt to President [Ronald] Reagan, is committed to the security and stability of the Persian Gulf.
> And fourth, I am determined to protect the lives of American citizens abroad.

Subsequently, the Bush administration gave several more reasons for the president's strong response to Iraq's invasion of Kuwait and the possible necessity of using military force to reverse it. Often the justifications were moral. Bush announced that the United States would not stand for Iraq's brutal aggression against Kuwait. The administration cited Iraq's duplicity before the invasion; Kuwait's peaceful history; reports of atrocities by Iraqi troops; and Iraqi efforts to depopulate Kuwait, strip it of its valuables, and annex it to Iraq. Bush stressed that the Iraqi invasion was an opportunity to establish a "new world order" in which collective action would deter and combat aggression and uphold international law.

As the crisis wore on, the Bush administration cited other factors behind its forceful response to Iraq's invasion of Kuwait, depending on what was happening in the crisis and the mood of the American people, as indicated by public opinion polls. In mid-November growing concerns among Americans about the economy led the Bush administration to emphasize the importance of liberating Kuwait to the economic health of the nation. Secretary of State Baker said November 13 that the administration policy in the Gulf was motivated by economic concerns: "If you want to sum it up in one word, it's jobs. Because an economic recession worldwide, caused by the control of one nation—one dictator, if you will—of the West's economic lifeline [oil], will result in the loss of jobs for American citizens."

Similarly, when public opinion polls in late November showed that Americans were more concerned about Iraq's potential for developing nuclear weapons than any other aspect of the Gulf crisis, administration officials focused on the Iraqi nuclear threat. Administration officials noted that Iraq's aggressive nuclear research program could succeed in developing rudimentary nuclear weapons within several years. Some experts disputed that Iraq could build nuclear weapons that quickly, but the prospect of a nuclear-armed Iraq sometime in the future was a potent argument for going to war against Iraq. Nevertheless, many Americans, even some who supported the president, had serious doubts that U.S. vital interests were at stake in the Gulf.

Munich and Vietnam

The debate in the United States over what strategy to pursue in the Gulf was deeply affected by two twentieth-century foreign policy experiences: the appeasement of Adolph Hitler at Munich in 1938 and the Vietnam War. President Bush and many advocates of military force compared Saddam Hussein to Hitler. They contended that Hussein, like Hitler, was an ruthless military dictator with an insatiable appetite for power. He had to be stopped before he developed military capabilities that would make an inevitable future war much bloodier.

Many supporters of a nonmilitary solution to the Gulf crisis compared the U.S. military deployments in the Persian Gulf to the slippery slope of military escalation in Vietnam. They maintained that the liberation of Kuwait—like the defense of South Vietnam—was not a vital interest of the United States that demanded military action. Opponents of using force also said that the United States was helping a tyrant, comparing the nondemocratic Kuwaiti government led by Sheik Jaber to the generally corrupt South Vietnamese government. Finally, opponents of the buildup worried that the United States was headed toward another protracted, Vietnam-style war against an opponent in the developing world.

Both the Vietnam War and the appeasement of Hitler held valuable lessons for American foreign policy. Yet the circumstances of the Gulf crisis were unique, and only imperfect parallels could be drawn from either. The threat to the world from Hussein was not of the same magnitude as the threat from Hitler. Moreover, the survival of Iraq's military establishment did not make a wider war inevitable. Some analysts argued that Saddam Hussein's invasion of Kuwait had finally convinced most nations that he was a serious threat, thereby making Iraq's long-term isolation and containment an easy task.

At the same time, a coalition attack in the Gulf was not likely to lead to a protracted war in the Middle East that the United States could not win. The battle for Kuwait would be a battle for territory in the open desert, whereas the Vietnam War had been a battle of attrition in a thick jungle where U.S. air superiority could not be fully utilized. In addition, although the al-Sabah government was indeed undemocratic, most Kuwaitis supported it. Finally, whereas much of the world opposed U.S. involvement in Vietnam and the Vietnamese Communists were being resupplied by the Soviet Union and China, the Gulf crisis pitted Iraq against a broad U.S.-led international coalition that had the support of the Soviet Union. The UN embargo against Iraq assured that it would not receive any significant outside military aid.

The conventional wisdom emanating from the American media, Congress, and even administration officials was that the American public might withdraw its support for a war if it dragged on too long. This was a lesson drawn from the Vietnam War. But the erosion of public support for that war was a reaction to more than just its length. The American public questioned Vietnam's strategic importance, the morality of supporting a corrupt regime in a civil war, the tactical restraints placed on the military by the civilian leadership, the military's overly optimistic assessments of how the war was going, and many other factors. The American public might well support a lengthy war if it were confident that the cause for which U.S. troops were fighting was just and vital to American interests, that the military's strategy was effective and minimized the loss of lives, and that indisputable progress was being made toward victory.

Debate on Effectiveness of Sanctions

The final decision whether to go to war against Iraq depended greatly on estimates of the effectiveness of the economic sanctions being imposed against Iraq by the United Nations. If the sanctions were hurting Iraq, the arguments of those opposed to the war option would be strengthened. In the U.S. Congress a significant part of the debate begun January 10, 1991, on a resolution authorizing the president to use force against Iraq focused on estimates of the sanctions' effectiveness. The vast majority of members agreed that Saddam Hussein must not be allowed to keep Kuwait or profit from aggression, but many thought sanctions should be given more time to work and objected to the strategy of going to war shortly after January 15.

Supporters of the sanctions option cited intelligence reports claiming that Iraq's economy had been devastated by the United Nations embargo. They emphasized that even though the Bush administration's top intelligence official, CIA director William Webster, had testified that sanctions alone were not guaranteed to produce an Iraqi withdrawal, he also estimated that "more than 90 percent of imports and 97 percent of exports have been shut off." Many members of Congress believed that if the embargo had so completely isolated Iraq economically, it would eventually create internal discontent that could topple the Hussein regime. *(Webster testimony on sanctions, documents, p. 380)*

They argued that even if sanctions ultimately failed to cause the downfall of Saddam Hussein or force him to withdraw his army from Kuwait, it was wise to give sanctions more time because they were degrading the Iraqi army's effectiveness with every passing day. In response to the argument that delaying war in favor of continuing indefinitely with sanctions would give the Iraqis more time to build up their defenses in Kuwait, Senate Majority Leader George J. Mitchell (D-Maine) said at the beginning of the congressional debate, "Time to fortify Iraq's defenses will do little good if some of Iraq's planes can't fly for lack of spare parts, if some of its tanks can't move for lack of lubricants, if its infrastructure and ability to wage war have been weakened. If it eventually becomes necessary for the United States to wage war, our troops will have benefited from the additional time given the sanctions to degrade Iraq's military capabilities."

Advocates of sanctions admitted that war might eventually be necessary, but they argued that a war's cost in lives demanded that all options be exhausted before resorting to force.

Proponents of authorizing military force expressed their doubts that sanctions could squeeze Iraq out of Kuwait within an acceptable time period. They cited the poor record of past international sanctions efforts to force recalcitrant regimes to alter their political behavior. In Iraq's case, evidence showed that while weapons and large industrial equipment were being effectively interdicted, imported consumer goods were reaching stores. Western diplomats and journalists inside Iraq reported that most consumer goods were plentiful, although the price of everything had risen dramatically. Iraqi citizens who were interviewed said they were having no problems buying food, clothing, and most household goods. Even beer was readily available in Baghdad shops. The level of deprivation was far from what might be expected to foment unrest in a disciplined, war-hardened society. Given such conditions, starving the Iraqi people into overthrowing their government could take years if it were possible at all.

Advocates of the military force option questioned whether the world community would be willing to deprive the Iraqi people of food over the long run. Even the UN Security Council resolutions provided for "humanitarian" exceptions to the UN embargo. They also observed that Iraq would surely use what supplies it did have to meet the needs of its army in the field first, even if ordinary Iraqis had to go without. Sen. John McCain (R-Ariz.) argued, "Who are the ones who would suffer as a result of sanctions? ... [I]t is the innocent civilians and children and others that Saddam Hussein would view as nonessential to his war effort. I don't think we as a nation are prepared to watch films of children suffering from malnutrition...." The people who were likely to suffer most were the Kuwaitis remaining in Kuwait, many of whom reportedly had taken trips to Iraq to buy consumer goods.

The assertion that time was on the side of the international coalition was disputed by advocates of force. They cited the difficulty in holding together for many months or perhaps years a multinational coalition composed of countries with divergent interests. Under pressure of a long stalemate in the desert, allied Arab regimes would be in as much danger from assassination attempts and unrest as would the Iraqi regime.

Advocates of force emphasized that the sanctions approach assumed that creating hardships for the Iraqi people could compel Saddam Hussein to order a withdrawal from Kuwait. Most observers, however, believed that Hussein would neither be moved by the economic suffering of the Iraqi people nor easily overthrown.

Finally, advocates of force observed that the United States had deployed so many troops to the Gulf in preparation for war that adopting a long-term sanctions approach probably would have required a reduction in those forces to allow for troop rotation. A drawing down of U.S. military power in the Gulf, even one that was explained as a strategic decision to allow sanctions time to operate, would have been seen as a retreat from the threat to use military force against Iraq. Such a retreat would have alarmed some allies committed to military force, while confirming Saddam Hussein's suspicions that the United States did not have the stomach for a potentially bloody war. It also would have been a resounding political victory for Saddam Hussein within the Arab world that could have emboldened pro-Iraqi opponents of Arab governments supporting the coalition and enhanced Hussein's reputation among many Arabs.

Congressional Approval

Both houses of Congress concluded their debates and voted January 12 to empower the president to use force to drive Iraq from Kuwait. The vote was 250-183 in the House and 52-47 in the Senate. Bush had claimed the authority as commander in chief to order an attack against Iraq regardless of congressional action, but the vote strengthened his domestic position. Most members of Congress who had voted against authorizing war accepted the decision of the body and closed ranks behind the president. The coalition would go to war unless Iraq took steps to withdraw from Kuwait by January 15. *(Congressional resolution authorizing force, documents, p. 384)*

That neither the president nor the country was taking action alone made the war much easier for the American public to support. Congressional approval of the resolution authorizing the president to launch an offensive against Iraq was given after careful consideration and long debate. This was not a Tonkin Gulf Resolution—a measure passed almost unanimously in 1964 that gave President Lyndon B. Johnson broad authority to wage war in Vietnam and that subsequently was used by the president to justify his escalation of American military involvement in that country. Congress understood the consequences of its Persian Gulf vote. Equally important, most members of Congress who voted against the resolution said that now that Congress had expressed its will, they would support the president and U.S. troops. Lawmakers were deeply divided over the strategy and wisdom of going to war, but once at war they would not attempt to divide the nation.

Americans also were comforted by the UN Security Council authorization of war and the presence of troops from many foreign countries in Saudi Arabia. Americans had fought alone in Vietnam under international pressure (even from close allies) to quit the war. It was important to Americans still haunted by the memories of Vietnam to be part of a coalition and to have American military efforts in the Gulf appreciated in most parts of the world. The lead editorial in the January 17, 1991, edition of the *Washington Post* noted:

> President Bush submitted his choices to two separate but worthy partners in policy, two exacting boards of review. He went to the United Nations: particularly since Vietnam, there has been in this country and abroad a palpable craving to test diplomatic options and then if military action is deemed necessary, to conduct it with international blessing. Then he went to the forum that necessarily counts most in the American system, Congress. In the two places, not his every tactic but nonetheless the thrust of his policy was explored, weighed and finally approved.

Saddam Hussein's War Decision

American policy toward Iraq during the forty-seven-day "grace period" focused on convincing Iraq—and Saddam Hussein in particular—that the United States and its allies were serious about waging war and that if war came, Iraq would lose. American policy makers thought that Hussein's instinct for survival would lead him to withdraw from Kuwait if he believed he and his army were threatened. If he refused to pull his army out, they reasoned, it was only because he grossly overestimated his army's capabilities or believed that the United States was bluffing.

There is evidence that suggests Saddam Hussein was not convinced that the United States would go to war against him, especially if the war was likely to be a long one. According to the Iraqi transcript of the July 25, 1990, meeting in Baghdad between Hussein and U.S. ambassador April Glaspie, he remarked, "Yours is a society which cannot accept 10,000 dead in one battle." Arab, European, and American diplomats who had dealt with him in the past had reported that U.S. behavior during the Vietnam War had greatly influenced his opinions about the United States. Hussein's strategy seemed to be to present the United States with the prospect of a very bloody war by heavily fortifying Kuwait. If U.S. leaders perceived that

Iraq's Major Weapons Suppliers

Following is a summary of the major weapons in Iraq's arsenal before the beginning of the Gulf crisis. Most were obtained from the Soviet Union, but China, France, the United States, and other nations also had sold weapons to Iraq.

WEAPON	TOTAL	TYPES
Main battle tanks	5,530	1,500 Soviet T-54/55/M-77; 1,500 Chinese T-59/69; 1,500 Soviet T-62; 1,000 Soviet T-72; 30 British Chieftain
Light tanks	100	Soviet PT-76
Infantry fighting vehicles	1,500	Soviet BMP
Armored personnel carriers	6,000	Soviet BTR-50/60/152 and MTLB; Czech OT-62-64; Chinese YW-531; French Panhard M-3; Brazilian EE-11; U.S. M-113A1/A2
Self-propelled artillery	500	122-mm: Soviet 2S1; 155-mm: 100 U.S. M-109, 85 French AUF-1 GCT; 152-mm: Soviet 2S3
Towed artillery	3,000	105-mm: Yugoslav M-56; 122-mm: Soviet D-74, D-30, M-1938; 130-mm: Soviet M-46; 152-mm: M-1937, M-1943; 155-mm: U.S. M-114
Multiple rocket launchers	200	122-mm: Soviet BM-21; 127-mm: Brazilian ASTROS II; 132-mm: Soviet BM 13/16; 180-mm: ASTROS SS-30; 262-mm: Iraqi Ababeel 50; 300-mm: ASTROS SS-60
Surface-to-air missile launchers	710	160 Soviet SA-2; 150 SA-3; 300 SA-6/8/9/14, SA-7/14; 100 French-German Roland
Air defense guns	4,000	23-mm: Soviet ZSU-23-4; 37-mm: Soviet M-1939; 57-mm: ZSU-57-2
Surface-to-surface missile launchers	118	50 Soviet Frog-7; 32 Soviet Scud-B (fixed); at least 36 Soviet Scud-B (mobile); Iraq also possessed at least 500 Scud missiles.
Attack helicopters	159	56 Spanish Bo-105; 40 Soviet Mi-24; 20 French SA-342; 30 SA-316; 13 SA-321
Ground attack fighters	360	90 Soviet MiG-23; 64 French Mirage EQ5/200; 30 Soviet Su-7; 70 Su-20; 60 Su-25; 30 Chinese J-6; 16 Su-24
Air superiority fighters	275	25 Soviet MiG-25; 150 MiG-21; 30 MiG-29; 40 Chinese J-7; 30 French Mirage F-1EQ

Sources: *Armed Forces Journal International,* October 1990; The International Institute for Strategic Studies, *The Military Balance 1990-1991,* 1990.

coalition casualties would be high, they would be unlikely to order an attack. *(Hussein-Glaspie meeting, documents, p. 375)*

If the coalition did attack, Hussein hoped that by inflicting heavy casualties, Iraqi forces might cause American public backing for the war to erode, as it had during the Vietnam War. Such an erosion of support could force the Bush administration to seek a negotiated peace on terms favorable to Iraq. Iraq's experience in the Iran-Iraq war, during which well-fortified Iraqi defenders had inflicted appalling casualties on Iranian attackers, may have colored Hussein's judgment about how the battle would proceed. The Iraqi military's concentration of its forces in Kuwait also suggests that Hussein and his commanders believed that, for political reasons, coalition ground troops would not be permitted to enter Iraq. Thus, even if Hussein understood that he was outmatched on the battlefield (and most analysts believed that he did), he may have thought that Iraqi forces were capable of winning the war by pushing the number of enemy casualties beyond the level that the American people and the world community would accept. Meanwhile, Iraq, hardened by eight years of war, would absorb all the firepower the coalition could deliver.

A Second Nasser

It is possible, however, that Hussein accepted the impending war with the U.S.-led coalition even though he understood that by not leaving Kuwait he was subjecting his forces to an attack, probably with devastating results. In adopting this suicidal strategy, Hussein would have been seeking an outcome to war like those achieved by President Gamal Abdel Nasser, ruler of Egypt from 1954 to 1970. Nasser, an early hero of Saddam Hussein, had manufactured political victories out of two military defeats: the 1956 Suez crisis and the 1967 Six-Day War with Israel. During the Suez crisis British, French, and Israeli forces occupied the Sinai Peninsula and captured the Suez Canal; they later withdrew under pressure from President Dwight D. Eisenhower. During the Six-Day War, Israel easily crushed Egyptian forces and again captured the Sinai. Yet in both cases, Nasser's regime survived and his reputation was strengthened. By taking on Israel and presenting himself as the leader of pan-Arabists, Nasser's prestige remained unmatched in the Arab world.

Hussein's confrontation of a coalition made up of the United States, former European colonial powers, wealthy Gulf Arab states, and others already had made him the most popular leader in many areas of the Arab world. If his forces could give the coalition a good fight and strike a few blows against Israel, Hussein would become a legend among dispossessed Arabs frustrated by Arab military weakness and passivity. Through military defeat, Hussein, like Nasser, could solidify his reputation as the only Arab leader willing to go to war to defend Arab rights and interests. In the process, he could weaken pro-Western Arab regimes that had sided with the coalition.

Half-Hearted Efforts to Avoid War

The theory that Saddam Hussein invited war is supported by his half-hearted efforts to avoid it. During the crisis Arab and Western officials put forward numerous diplomatic plans that were designed to allow the Iraqis to save face. None of them were seized with sufficient vigor or flexibility by Hussein and his diplomats to achieve a negotiated settlement. Hussein even rebuffed two last-minute diplomatic initiatives by the French and by UN Secretary General Javier Pérez de Cuéllar, when a positive response could have yielded substantial propaganda benefits. The French offer, announced January 14, was especially tempting to Iraq because it linked an Iraqi withdrawal from Kuwait to an international peace conference on the Middle East—a condition demanded by Iraq but rejected by the United States. Had Hussein responded positively to either of these gestures, he might have delayed a coalition attack or, at the very least, placed the United States in the position of pressing for an attack against the objections of some of the more hesitant allies. But Hussein rejected both as if he were resigned to war.

Moreover, Hussein was not dependent upon outside peace initiatives. Many observers noted that he probably could have saved his army, retained his position as the champion of the Arab masses, and gained a valuable piece of Kuwait by executing a partial withdrawal from Kuwait. American policy makers were so worried about this possibility that it had become known in the Bush administration as the "nightmare scenario." A partial Iraqi withdrawal from Kuwait could have left Baghdad in control of northern Kuwait, including the Kuwaiti portion of the

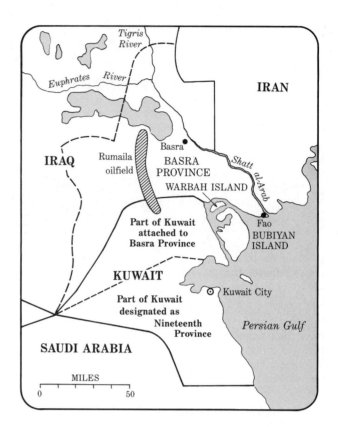

After annexing Kuwait, the Iraqi Ministry of Information produced maps showing Kuwait as part of Iraq. Saddam Hussein had declared Kuwait to be Iraq's "nineteenth province." However, on the new Iraqi maps, the northern part of Kuwait, including the Bubiyan and Warbah Islands and land containing the Rumaila oilfield, was attached to Iraq's Basra Province. Only the southern two-thirds of Kuwait were designated as a new province. Some Western analysts suggested that the map provided a clue to Saddam Hussein's ultimate bargaining position. They speculated that if Iraq were allowed to control the northern part of Kuwait, Hussein would be willing to withdraw from the rest of it.

disputed Rumaila oilfield and Warbah and Bubiyan Islands. With U.S. and world public opinion divided over going to war to liberate Kuwait, it was questionable whether the Bush administration could rally support for a war to expel Iraq from a thin slice of desert in northern Kuwait. But if the United States excepted this partial solution, U.S. credibility and the efficacy of the collective action against Iraq would be undermined. Iraq would gain a financial windfall from its possession of northern Kuwait that would aid its efforts to continue improving its arsenal. It also would achieve its longstanding goal of improving its access to the Persian Gulf.

Hussein could have arranged for PLO leader Yasir Arafat, Jordan's King Hussein, or some other sympathetic Arab leader to publicly plead with him to accept a partial withdrawal in the interest of keeping his army intact as a counterweight to Israel. Under this type of diplomatic cover, and with Iraqi forces retaining control of northern Kuwait, Hussein would hardly have been perceived by most Arabs as having lost face. Hussein's failure to take advantage of the nightmare scenario or respond to diplomatic initiatives with more positive responses that could have delayed an attack or weakened coalition unity was perplexing given his reputation for political cunning and self-preservation.

Many observers have suggested that Hussein's sense of honor did not allow him to withdraw from any part of Kuwait without a fight. Hussein certainly is a man driven by a code of honor that frowns on retreat and compromise, but he had demonstrated in his dealings with Iran that he was capable of realpolitik moves that would preserve Iraqi security until the confrontation could be renewed at a time better suited to Iraq. In 1975 he had negotiated an agreement with Iran in which Iraq recognized Iranian control of the eastern half of the Shatt al-Arab waterway in return for an Iranian pledge to end its support for Iraqi's Kurdish rebels. In 1980, when Hussein had the Kurds under control and Iran appeared disorganized and militarily weak following its revolution, he declared the 1975 agreement null and void and attacked Iran. In August 1990, when it became apparent that Iraq's annexation of Kuwait was going to be opposed by a U.S.-led coalition, Hussein offered Tehran a final peace to the Iran-Iraq war on Iranian terms so that he could move troops from the Iranian border to the Kuwait theater. Hussein's action amounted to capitulation to a hated enemy with whom Iraq had concluded a bloody eight-year war only two years before. *(Iran-Iraq war, p. 94)*

Yet Hussein seemed unwilling to swallow his pride over Kuwait, perhaps because he faced a coalition reminiscent of colonial times. He also had repeatedly claimed that Iraq would never relinquish any of Kuwait. Given his fear of losing face, his expectation that Iraqi forces could bloody the U.S.-led coalition, his intention to break up the coalition by drawing Israel into the war, and his heroic recollections of Nasser, it is less surprising that Hussein and his regime chose war over a pullout.

Air War

On the morning of Tuesday, January 15, President Bush signed an executive order in Washington, D.C., authorizing an aerial offensive against Iraq that would begin the following night unless a diplomatic breakthrough occurred before the deadline passed at midnight EST January 15. Wednesday afternoon Secretary of Defense Cheney ordered the U.S. commander in Saudi Arabia, Gen. H. Norman Schwarzkopf, to launch the attack. The coalition's strategy was to wage an extended air campaign against strategic targets in Iraq and Kuwait. Coalition military leaders were confident that they could quickly establish air supremacy over the badly outmatched Iraqi air force. Coalition warplanes could then methodically destroy Saddam Hussein's military machine and soften Iraqi defenses, so that when a ground offensive was launched, fewer coalition casualties would be suffered.

Initial Bombing Raids

The first coalition planes left Saudi airfields at 12:50 a.m. Saudi time September 17 (4:50 p.m. EST September 16)—less than seventeen hours after the UN deadline passed. At about the same time U.S. warships in the Persian Gulf launched a barrage of Tomahawk cruise missiles,

which fly at subsonic speeds close to the ground toward their targets.

The world learned that the air campaign (known as "Operation Desert Storm") had begun at 2:35 a.m. Saudi time when reporters in Baghdad in the Al-Rashid Hotel reported thunderous bomb explosions amidst a torrent of antiaircraft fire from Iraqi soldiers. During the first night of bombardment in Baghdad, CNN reporters Peter Arnett, John Holliman, and Bernard Shaw avoided being sent to the bomb shelter underneath the hotel with other Western reporters and thus were able to keep a phone line open. Although unable to transmit pictures, they provided a running description of what they could see of the bombing from their hotel room.

Shortly after 7:00 p.m. EST (3:00 a.m. Iraqi time), White House press secretary Marlin Fitzwater announced, "The liberation of Kuwait has begun." Two hours later, President Bush addressed the nation from the Oval Office. He said Saddam Hussein's intransigence left "no choice but to drive Saddam from Kuwait by force. We will not fail." *(Bush announces war, documents, p. 385)*

One hour before bombs began falling on Baghdad, the United States took the unprecedented step of informing the Soviet Union of its plans. Secretary of State Baker called Soviet foreign minister Aleksandr Bessmertnykh to inform him of the pending attack. Bessmertnykh asked Washington to postpone the assault to give President Gorbachev one last chance to persuade Saddam Hussein to relent, but the planes were already on their way. After the initial raids on Iraq by coalition aircraft, Gorbachev blamed Saddam Hussein for the war. The Soviet president emphasized that the USSR had done its best to convince Hussein to pull out of Kuwait. The Soviet president declared, however, that his country's support for the war would not extend to the complete destruction of Iraq.

American, British, Saudi, and Kuwaiti warplanes participated in the first wave of bombing. They were soon joined by French and Italian aircraft. The coalition had assembled more than 2,000 planes in the Persian Gulf theater. During an intense bombardment campaign by the United States during the Vietnam War known as "Rolling Thunder," U.S. pilots flew about 3,150 "sorties" (one round-trip mission by one plane) a week. Coalition air forces would average about 2,000 sorties per day during Desert Storm.

Much of the world greeted news of the attack with resigned support. But within a first few hours after the bombardment began positive reports on the bombing created a euphoria in the United States and elsewhere in the international community, raising hopes that the chore of driving Iraq from Kuwait might be less costly in lives and wealth than previously imagined. This confidence resulted from the seeming inability of the Iraqi military to defend itself against air attacks or to take any significant offensive action against coalition forces.

Public euphoria also was fueled by false or overly enthusiastic news reports. Reporters quoted anonymous military sources as saying that all of Iraq's Scud surface-to-surface missile launchers had been destroyed and that the Iraqi Republican Guard troops (Hussein's best, numbering about 110,000) had been "decimated." In fact, neither account was true.

The first wave of bombing had been enormously successful, however. It had disrupted Iraqi command, control, and communications abilities, severely damaged Iraq's nuclear, chemical, and biological weapons facilities; destroyed

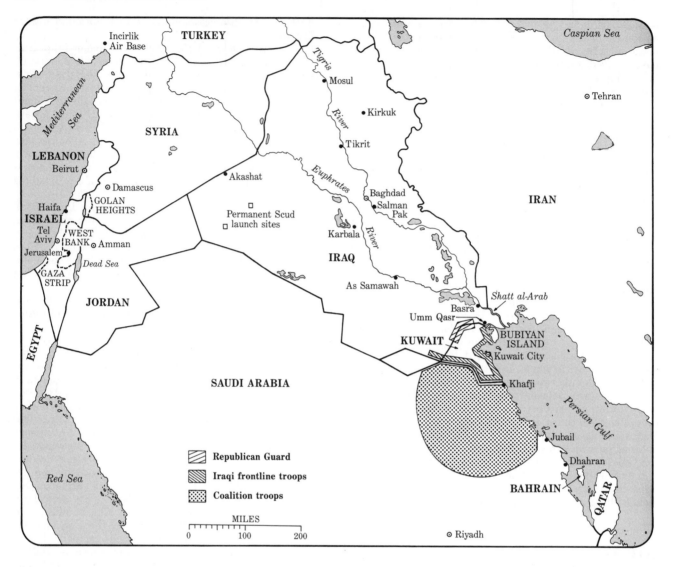

Before the Gulf war began on January 17, 1991, coalition ground forces were concentrated opposite Iraqi fortifications along the Saudi-Kuwaiti border. Iraqi commanders hoped to bloody the attackers as they tried to breach frontline minefields and obstacles. Republican Guard units were stationed behind Iraqi lines with the mission of responding to coalition breakthroughs. The Iraqis intended to draw Israel into the conflict by firing Scud surface-to-surface missiles at the Jewish state from fixed launch sites and mobile missile launchers positioned in Western Iraq. After the bombing campaign began, the coalition secretly moved much of its attacking ground forces west to positions along the Saudi-Iraqi border, which Iraq had left almost undefended.

most of Iraq's fixed Scud missile launch sites; suppressed many Iraqi antiaircraft radars and weapons; and grounded most of the Iraqi air force by damaging major air fields. Despite their knowledge that an attack could be imminent, the Iraqi military appeared to have been surprised. At the very least, it had underestimated the firepower that a coalition attack could deliver and the difficulty of defending against a sophisticated air assault.

Scud Attacks

Early on January 18, the Iraqis struck back amid the unrelenting allied bombing campaign by launching a salvo of Soviet-made Scud missiles armed with conventional high explosive warheads at Israel. Eight Scuds struck the Jewish

state in and around the cities of Tel Aviv and Haifa. The Scuds injured more than a dozen people, but no one was killed. Later in the day the Iraqis launched a Scud missile at Saudi Arabia. A U.S. Patriot antimissile missile intercepted and destroyed the Scud before it reached the ground. During the coming weeks, Iraq would fire dozens of Scuds at Israel and Saudi Arabia.

The Scud missile was a Soviet-made surface-to-surface weapon designed to deliver nuclear weapons over a short distance. The Soviets had sold hundreds of them to Iraq during the 1980s and Iraq had used them during the Iran-Iraq war to terrorize the population of Tehran with conventional warheads. Iran had fired its own Scuds at Baghdad in a dual that became known as "the war of the cities." Iraq had modified the Soviet Scuds, which had an original range of about 175 miles, so that they could travel increased distances. The Iraqis named their modified Scud missiles the Al-Hussein, which had a range of almost 400 miles, and the Al-Abbas, which could travel approximately 540 miles. To enable the small missiles to fly the longer distances necessary to reach Israel, Iraqi engineers had to reduce the payloads. As a result, the thirty-seven-foot modified Iraqi Scuds could carry at most the equivalent of a 1,100 pound bomb—half the explosive power that the unmodified shorter-range Scud could carry and only a fraction of what one U.S. fighter-bomber could deliver.

Because of their small payloads and inaccuracy, the Scuds had negligible strategic value. Iraq could not use them to destroy coalition military targets. They did, however, demonstrate to the Iraqi people and Saddam Hussein's supporters outside Iraq that the Iraqi military could strike back in some fashion against the coalition. More important, Saddam Hussein hoped that these missile attacks against Israel would draw the Jewish state into the war.

Keeping Israel Out of the War

Israel's military reputation in the Middle East is based on its consistent retaliation for attacks against the Jewish state and its citizens and on its use of superior technology to defeat its opponents. The Iraqi missile attacks created enormous frustration in Israel, because political realities called for restraint and the Israeli Defense Force's high technology arsenal could do little to stop the missiles.

Hussein was counting on Israel behaving as it had in the past. If Israel retaliated against Iraq in response to Scud attacks, Arab members of the coalition would be placed in the uncomfortable position of fighting on the same side as Israel. Even if the Arabs did not back out of the coalition in response to an Israeli counterattack, Israeli participation in the war would increase sympathy for Iraq in the Arab world and thereby intensify the domestic political problems of Arab leaders supporting the anti-Iraq effort.

After the initial Scud attacks against Israel, the Israeli leadership came under extreme pressure from some cabinet members and citizens to strike back. The domestic pressure to retaliate was largely emotional, however. Most Israelis understood that if their government could resist the temptation to attack Iraq, the coalition would be stronger and better able to destroy Iraq's military quickly. They also knew that restraint on the part of their government could yield substantial political benefits and financial aid when the war was over.

In addition, an Israeli attack against Iraq would have only marginal strategic value. Iraq was already undergoing saturation bombing by the huge coalition air forces. A proportional response to the Scuds by Israel, including air sorties, missile attacks, or commando raids, would not have contributed much to Iraq's defeat. American military officials worried that, because Israel was not part of the coordinated coalition air campaign, any Israeli warplanes in Iraqi skies would create a serious battle management problem that could result in confusion, collisions, or dogfights between coalition and Israeli aircraft.

The primary worry of Israeli officials was that Iraq would place chemical weapons on their Scuds. Although Iraq had substantial experience delivering chemical weapons with artillery and warplanes, delivering chemical weapons effectively on missiles traveling hundreds of miles was

The U.S. Patriot missile, which had never been used in combat before the Gulf war, destroyed a high percentage of Iraqi Scud missiles fired at Saudi Arabia and Israel.

a technically difficult task. The Iraqis had never placed chemical weapons on missiles during the Iran-Iraq war. A chemical weapons attack against Israel may have been only marginally more dangerous to Israeli citizens than a conventional weapons attack, but poison gas used against Israelis would call up memories of the Holocaust, during which millions of Jews died in Nazi gas chambers. The Israeli government promised retaliation if Iraq used its Scuds to deliver chemical weapons against Israel.

An Israeli entry into the war against Iraq could conceivably have unraveled President Bush's careful diplomacy and splintered the anti-Iraq coalition. Regardless of their attitude toward Iraq, Arab states were united in their opposition to and distrust of Israel. No Arab leader would want to be perceived by his people as fighting alongside Israel against an Arab country. Nevertheless, Kuwait and Saudi Arabia appeared committed to the coalition regardless of whether the Israelis chose to retaliate. President Mubarak of Egypt said before the attack on Iraq that he would not withdraw his support for the coalition in response to Israeli retaliation for missile attacks. The Syrian government indicated after the first few Scud attacks on Israel that it also might not withdraw its forces from Saudi Arabia if Israel launched a limited retaliatory attack. Consequently, a proportional Israeli retaliation would not have necessarily caused the coalition to fall apart as some analysts worried. Nevertheless, an Israeli attack against Iraq could have placed leaders of Arab nations participating in the coalition, especially Hosni Mubarak, in a difficult position domestically.

The Bush administration was especially concerned that an Israeli attack against Iraq could lead to an Israeli-Jordanian conflict. If Israel used aircraft to launch a retaliatory strike against Iraq, it would have to fly over Jordan or take a long circuitous route through Saudi Arabia that would require refueling. King Hussein had promised that Jordan would regard any Israeli violation of its airspace as an act of war. If Jordan fired upon Israeli jets, or if Israel destroyed Jordan's Hawk surface-to-air missile batteries, Jordan could be drawn into the war on the side of Iraq, and

Arab coalition partners would be more likely to abandon the coalition or qualify their support for it.

Consequently, the Bush administration vigorously pressed the Israeli government to stay out of the war. Bush promised Israeli leaders that mobile Scud missile batteries in Western Iraq would be a top priority target of U.S. pilots. He also dispatched Patriot antimissile missile batteries and their U.S. crews to Israel. This deployment represented the first time that U.S. combat forces had ever been stationed in Israel. The Israeli government declared that the U.S. troops would remain only until Israeli units could be trained to operate the Patriot batteries. As in Saudi Arabia, the Patriot missiles successfully shot down most Scuds targeted against Israel. A few Scuds continued to get through, however.

Israeli leaders understood that, because Saddam Hussein's purpose in attacking Israel was to draw Israel into the war, an Israeli retaliation would be playing into his hands. Ironically, the most effective way for Israel to punish Iraq for the missile strikes was by not attacking; in this way Israel would avoid creating strains within the anti-Iraq coalition and, in turn, would weaken Hussein's claim that his invasion of Kuwait was an extension of the Arab-Israeli conflict.

This logic, combined with the Patriot deployments and the Bush administration's entreaties, persuaded the Israeli government to abandon its usual policy of retaliation. Because the circumstances of the Iraqi attacks were unique, by declining to retaliate Israel was not likely to weaken the effect of its long-term deterrence strategy. Israeli officials continually hinted that they might retaliate, but despite frequent Scud attacks, Israel stayed out of the war.

Three Phases of the Air Campaign

The coalition bombing campaign proceeded in three phases. The initial phase sought to destroy the ability of the highly centralized Iraqi command structure to communicate effectively with its troops. It also sought to obliterate Iraq's nuclear, biological, and chemical weapons research and production facilities and destroy or disable Iraq's ability to launch Scud missiles. This phase was also aimed at gaining air superiority so that allied pilots could bomb their targets with minimal risk of being shot down by Iraq's air force or antiaircraft weapons.

The second phase of the bombing focused on isolating Iraqi forces in Kuwait and southern Iraq from the rest of the country. To achieve this, allied warplanes bombed bridges, roads, rail lines, and truck convoys throughout Iraq. They also continued hitting communications facilities. Although the Iraqis had stockpiled large amounts of food and ammunition with their troops in Kuwait, like any army, the Iraqis were in need of resupply. The allied bombing campaign reduced the flow of supplies south to a trickle, while simultaneously destroying many of the supplies that had been stockpiled. Coalition commanders believed that Iraqi soldiers would be less disposed to fight if they were running short of food, water, and ammunition.

The final phase of the bombing campaign focused on destroying Iraqi forces themselves and "shaping" the battlefield for a ground attack. Allied planes targeted artillery pieces and tanks with precision-guided munitions, and huge B-52s carpet bombed Iraqi troop concentrations and frontline fortifications.

The bombing campaign did not move neatly from phase to phase. Many targets, especially airfields, roads, and communications facilities had to be hit repeatedly throughout the bombing campaign because they could be repaired. Although Iraq's fixed Scud missile launch sites were destroyed early in the bombing, Iraq's easily concealed mobile Scud missile launchers remained a target during the entire campaign.

Saddam Hussein's best equipped and trained forces, the Republican Guard, were targeted from the beginning. This 110,000-troop force was the heart of Hussein's army. They were stationed behind the front lines, near the Iraq-Kuwait border, and were assigned the task of responding to any allied breakthrough or flanking maneuver. Perhaps more important, they were the troops that ensured the loyalty of the rest of the Iraqi army. Deserting or fleeing soldiers and units from the front line would have to pass the Republican Guard to get back to Iraq. Pentagon analysts theorized that if the Republican Guard could be seriously weakened or destroyed, the rest of the army would not put up much of a fight.

The air campaign was an unqualified success, given the minimal number of aircraft lost by the coalition and the destruction inflicted upon the Iraqi military, defense industries, and weapons research facilities. In a January 23 briefing, Colin Powell, chairman of the Joint Chiefs of Staff, declared that the coalition had achieved air superiority. Iraqi frustrations with the continuing air war were demonstrated by a futile armored attack by three Iraqi battalions against the deserted Saudi border town of Khafji on January 29. The Iraqis succeeded in capturing Khafji, but after two days of fighting coalition forces recaptured the town and more than 400 Iraqi prisoners.

Iraqi warplanes had been so ineffective that during late January the Iraqi leadership had sent more than a hundred of its best planes to the safety of airfields in Iran. At first the motivation for the exodus was unclear. Analysts speculated that large numbers of pilots simply were defecting. But the organized fashion of the retreat indicated that it was a premeditated scheme. The few Iraqi warplanes that had challenged coalition aircraft or attempted to penetrate air defenses in Saudi Arabia and the Persian Gulf had been shot down. Meanwhile, allied air attacks were destroying many of Iraq's hardened aircraft shelters, presumably concealing warplanes inside them. Little would be left of the Iraqi air force if it tried to wait out the bombing in Iraq. Therefore, planes were sent to Iran in the hope they could be recovered after the war, or perhaps later in the present conflict. Iran, however, declared that it would return the planes to Iraq only after the war was over. Thus, dozens of Iraqi warplanes, many of which only two and a half years before had been bombing Iranian targets, sat out the fighting on Iranian airfields. After the war, Iran announced that it would keep the Iraqi planes.

As the bombing progressed the international community became increasingly uncomfortable with the level of destruction inflicted upon Iraq. American military leaders emphasized that coalition pilots were taking extreme risks to avoid hitting civilian targets, while Iraq countered with film of bombed houses and apartment buildings and civilian corpses. The propaganda struggle climaxed on February 13 when U.S. warplanes destroyed a building containing an underground bomb shelter that was occupied by hundreds of civilians. Iraq claimed that the attack had been deliberate and resulted in the deaths of more than 400 Iraqis. The United States maintained that the building was an Iraqi military communications center and suggested that the Iraqis sent civilians to the shelter knowing that it was a potential military target.

Despite the destruction experienced by Iraq, the coalition air war had not forced an Iraqi capitulation as some military analysts had speculated might be possible. Nor had it triggered an internal Iraqi uprising against Saddam Hussein's regime. If coalition forces were going to reclaim Kuwait, they would have to do it on the ground.

Ground War

The international community feared the beginning of the ground campaign almost as much as it had feared the opening of hostilities. Although coalition losses during the air war were much lighter than expected, military experts had predicted that the larger and more sophisticated coalition air force would gain air superiority soon after the beginning of the war. The Iraqi army, however, appeared to be much more formidable than the Iraqi air force, and Saddam Hussein had pinned his hopes of bloodying the attackers on the ground phase of the battle.

The coalition almost certainly would be able to defeat the battered Iraqis in a ground war with air power and superior armor, but the Iraqi force in the Kuwait theater was estimated at approximately 540,000 troops (after the war, U.S. military officers with access to revised intelligence reports of Iraqi troop strength said that the number of Iraqis in the Kuwait theater might actually have been as few as 350,000). Any force this large had the potential to inflict thousands of coalition casualties, even if it had been bombed for five and half weeks. The coalition had assembled nearly 700,000 troops in and around Saudi Arabia, but fewer than 400,000 would be directly involved in the attack against the Iraqis. Commentators pointed out that many Iraqi soldiers had gained extensive experience during the eight-year Iran-Iraq war, while most coalition forces would be seeing combat for the first time. The Iraqis also had the advantage of defending heavily fortified positions. Finally, the Iraqis were almost certain to use their stocks of chemical weapons against the attackers as they had done effectively during the Iran-Iraq war. Coalition forces were equipped with high quality protective gear and were very mobile, but chemical attacks were dangerous and would slow the pace of any battle.

Battle Plan

The official goal of the coalition offensive against Iraq had been the liberation of Kuwait. But President Bush and other coalition leaders hoped to destroy Hussein's army in the process, so he would be unable to threaten his neighbors in the near future. The coalition battle plan, therefore, sought not only to drive Iraqi forces from Kuwait, but also to cut off and destroy retreating Iraqi units. In his January 23 briefing, Gen. Powell had declared bluntly, "Our strategy to go after this army is very, very simple. First, we're going to cut it off, and then we're going to kill it." The air war had succeeded in isolating Iraqi forces in Kuwait and southern Iraq. The battle plan for the ground campaign was designed to maximize the destruction of Iraqi military equipment.

The battle plan included two major deceptions. First, naval and amphibious maneuvers were held before the ground offensive to make the Iraqis think that the coalition

Chairman of the Joint Chiefs of Staff Colin Powell, one of the architects of the successful coalition battle plan, briefs the Senate Foreign Relations Committee December 3, 1990, on the Gulf crisis.

was preparing to attack the Kuwaiti coastline. Coalition commanders deployed 18,000 Marines on ships off the Kuwaiti coast to reinforce this impression, and once the ground campaign had begun, U.S. marines faked a helicopter assault against Iraqi coastline defenses. As a result, Iraq committed 125,000 troops to defend against a coastal attack that would never happen. Second, before the air campaign began, coalition forces had concentrated along the Saudi-Kuwaiti border to give the Iraqis the impression that the attack would be confined to that area. After American warplanes achieved air superiority, preventing Iraqi aircraft from flying surveillance missions, approximately 270,000 American, British, and French troops, along with their heavy equipment and sixty days of supplies, were moved far to the west along the Saudi-Iraqi border. These forces were in a position to launch an attack around the Western flank of the Iraqi army in Kuwait. Even if Iraqi military leaders had known about the massive coalition force in the West, they could have done little about it because any column of troops or tanks sent west to reinforce the few Iraqi units facing the coalition army would have been vulnerable to air attacks.

The battle plan called for the coalition forces in the west to encircle the Iraqi army by sweeping around the Iraqis' right flank all the way to the Euphrates River. Republican Guard armored units would be forced to come out of their dug-in positions, making them vulnerable to attack from the air. Other coalition units would punch holes in the Iraqi defensive positions in Kuwait and drive on to Kuwait City. Meanwhile, the bombardment of Iraq and Kuwait by coalition warplanes would be intensified to give ground units as much air support as possible.

Soviet Peace Initiative

As the ground war approached, and Iraqi losses from the coalition air campaign mounted, Baghdad showed interest in a negotiated settlement to the conflict. The Iraqi regime announced February 15 that it was willing to withdraw from Kuwait, but attached numerous conditions to the withdrawal offer. President Bush and other coalition leaders immediately rejected the proposal.

Iraqi officials then turned for mediation assistance to the Soviet Union, their longtime patron, which had been urging them since August to withdraw peacefully from Kuwait. President Gorbachev presented a Soviet withdrawal plan to Foreign Minister Aziz on February 18. President Bush, who had been informed of the contents of the proposal, told Gorbachev the following day that it was inadequate. On February 21, the Soviets announced that Iraq had accepted a modified Soviet plan that called for a "full and unconditional Iraqi withdrawal" from Kuwait. The six-point proposal, however, failed to meet a growing list of U.S. conditions for an end to the war, including Iraqi willingness to pay reparations to Kuwait, disclose the location of all mines, and abide by all UN Security Council resolutions related to the Gulf war. The Bush administration also insisted that Iraqi forces withdraw from Kuwait within one week so that they would be unable to take all of their equipment with them. The Soviet plan allowed the Iraqis three weeks to leave. *(Iraqi response to Soviet peace plan, documents, p. 387)*

Increasingly confident that a coalition ground campaign (which was ready to be launched) would be successful, President Bush moved to head off further Iraqi peace proposals that he feared could divide the coalition by offering terms that came close to, but fell short of meeting all coalition demands. On February 22, he announced that Saddam Hussein had until noon EST February 23 to begin a withdrawal and accept "publicly and authoritatively" all coalition requirements for a cease-fire. The U.S. conditions appeared designed to allow Hussein no room to save face if he accepted them. They mandated a swift and humiliating retreat that the Bush administration hoped would disgrace Hussein in the eyes of his supporters in Iraq and the Arab world. Reports that Iraqi troops had begun committing systematic atrocities in Kuwait and setting Kuwaiti oil wells ablaze stiffened coalition resolve to go to war immediately if Hussein did not agree to Bush's terms. The February 23 deadline passed without signs of an Iraqi withdrawal, and Bush ordered the offensive to proceed. *(U.S. conditions for ending the war, documents, p. 386)*

One Hundred Hours

At 4:00 a.m. Saudi time February 24 the coalition launched its coordinated ground offensive, code-named "Operation Desert Saber." The assault would last exactly one hundred hours. The huge American, British, and French force to the west penetrated deep into Iraq at a blitzkrieg pace. With French forces guarding their left flank, American troops reached the Euphrates River during the evening of February 25. Because allied bombers had destroyed bridges over the Euphrates, Iraqi units could not escape the coalition envelopment. Meanwhile American, Saudi, Egyptian, Syrian, Kuwaiti, and other Arab forces quickly breached Iraq's supposedly formidable frontline fortifications, consisting of barbed wire, sand berms, bunkers, minefields, and trenches filled with oil that could be ignited. These forces pushed toward Kuwait City, taking tens of thousands of Iraqi prisoners along the way.

With his army collapsing, Saddam Hussein delivered a radio speech on February 26 announcing an Iraqi withdrawal from Kuwait. Hussein maintained a defiant tone, suggesting that the Iraqi retreat was a strategic withdrawal and telling Iraqis that "Kuwait is part of your country and

was carved from it in the past." Most Iraqi forces were already engaged in a disorganized retreat by the time the speech was broadcast. With most Iraqi troops giving up without a fight, coalition troops suffering unbelievably light casualties, and domestic public opinion strongly in favor of pressing the advantage to ensure that Saddam Hussein would not soon be able to threaten his neighbors, Bush was not inclined to call off the attack unless Iraq agreed to severe terms. He responded to Hussein's speech later on February 26 by saying that the withdrawal did not meet his terms for a cease-fire and that the coalition would continue its offensive. *(Hussein announces withdrawal, documents, p. 388; Bush response to Hussein, documents, p. 389)*

The American and British forces that had penetrated deep into Iraq in the west drove eastward February 26 toward Republican Guard divisions and other Iraqi forces trapped below the Euphrates. In the ensuing battles, most Iraqi tanks, artillery pieces, and military vehicles in the Kuwaiti theater that had escaped the air campaign were destroyed. The most intense fighting occurred February 27 when coalition armored units destroyed several Republican Guard divisions that were attempting to shield other Iraqi troops retreating from Kuwait. More than 200 Iraqi tanks were destroyed in the battle without the loss of a single coalition tank.

American Marines and Arab coalition troops marched into Kuwait City February 27 after fighting several pitched battles on the outskirts of the city. They found that all but a few stranded Iraqis had fled the capital the previous day. Kuwaiti resistance fighters and citizens welcomed home Kuwaiti troops who led the coalition march into the city.

At 9:00 p.m. EST February 27, President Bush declared in a televised address, "Kuwait is liberated. Iraq's army is defeated. Our military objectives are met." He announced that coalition forces would cease offensive operations three hours later at midnight EST (8:00 a.m. February 28 in the battle zone). Bush said a permanent cease-fire would require the Iraqis to accept all UN Security Council resolutions pertaining to the Gulf crisis, release all prisoners of war and Kuwaiti hostages, and disclose the locations of mines. Iraqi commanders also were required to meet with coalition military leaders within forty-eight hours to work out the military details of the cease-fire. Earlier on February 27, a letter from Foreign Minister Aziz to the UN Security Council had declared Iraq's willingness to observe all UN Security Council resolutions. On March 3, Gen. Schwarzkopf met with Iraq military representatives, who agreed to abide by all coalition conditions for the military cease-fire. By March 5 Iraq had released all coalition prisoners of war. *(Bush announces cease-fire, documents, p. 390)*

Throughout the ground campaign, many Iraqi soldiers surrendered as soon as they encountered coalition troops or after giving only token resistance. Thirty-eight days of coalition bombing had destroyed many units' equipment and supplies and cut their communications with their military commanders. Some Iraqi soldiers did not even have water.

The war weariness of Iraqi troops, the technological superiority of coalition weapons, the lack of Iraqi air cover, and an efficient U.S. battle plan led to coalition casualty levels that Lt. Gen. Sir Peter de la Billiere, the commander of British forces in Saudi Arabia, called "the smallest number for the size of the campaign in the history of warfare." As of March 22, the United States reported that 125 Amer-

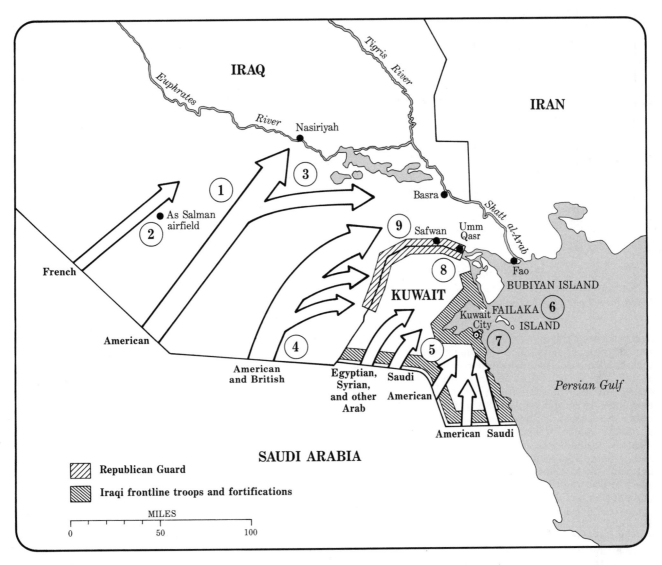

The coalition ground attack that liberated Kuwait began at 4:00 a.m. Saudi time February 24 and lasted one hundred hours until 8:00 a.m. February 28, when the cease-fire declared by President Bush went into effect.

1. American special forces landed deep behind Iraqi lines before the attack to provide strategic reconnaissance.

2. A French division supported by an American brigade destroyed an Iraqi division near As Salman airfield and established defensive positions to guard the western flank of attacking coalition forces.

3. The U.S. Army's Eighteenth Airborne Corps (containing three and a half divisions) launched a lightning attack toward the Euphrates River city of Nasiriyah. By the evening of February 25, American forces had reached the river and severed the main highway leading north to Baghdad, effectively cutting off the Iraqi army in Kuwait and southern Iraq.

4. The U.S. Army's Seventh Corps (containing five divisions) and the First British Armored Division drove into Iraq and turned toward Kuwait and the Basra region.

5. Saudi, Egyptian, Syrian, Kuwaiti, and other Arab forces, along with two U.S. Marine divisions and a U.S. Army brigade, breached Iraqi frontline defenses along the Saudi-Kuwaiti border and converged on Kuwait City.

6. An 18,000-troop U.S. Marine force remained in naval vessels positioned off Kuwait. The Marines feigned a helicopter-borne assault on the Kuwaiti coast to convince Iraqi coastline defenders that an amphibious landing was imminent. Approximately 125,000 Iraqis defending Kuwaiti beaches waited for an attack that would never come.

7. Saudi and Kuwaiti troops supported by U.S. Marines entered Kuwait City on February 27. Most Iraqi troops had abandoned the city the day before. Coalition forces found Kuwaiti resistance fighters in control of much of the capital.

8. Iraqi troops attempting to flee Kuwait were attacked by coalition pilots who jammed roads by bombing vehicles at the front and rear of Iraqi convoys headed north. Coalition air attacks on February 26 reportedly left more than a thousand Iraqi vehicles destroyed or disabled on the main highway north of Kuwait City.

9. In the climax to the ground offensive, American and British forces engaged Iraqi Republican Guard units in a massive tank battle along a wide front west of Basra February 27-28.

To guard against Iraqi chemical weapons attacks, U.S. troops taking part in the ground offensive were outfitted with heavy protective suits.

icans had been killed in combat during the entire six-week war. Of these, 28 were killed by a single Iraqi Scud missile that struck a barracks in Dhahran, Saudi Arabia, on February 25. The total number of American soldiers killed in action was less than the 202 American soldiers who had been killed in accidents related to operations in the Middle East since August 2. Only 4 American soldiers were killed in ground combat during the first two days of the land offensive. In addition, 357 Americans had been wounded and 21 were listed as missing in action. The percentage of battle deaths to American military personnel involved was lower in Iraq than it had been in the operation to depose Panamanian dictator Manuel Noriega in 1989, where U.S. troops faced just a few thousand Panamanian troops. There 23 U.S. soldiers were killed in hostilities involving 27,000 Americans. In Kuwait and Iraq, the ground war involved about 300,000 U.S. combat soldiers. Other coalition nations also reported light casualties. As of February 28, 15 Britons and 44 Saudis reportedly were killed.

One of the mysteries of the ground battle was why the Iraqis had not used chemical weapons. Iraqi chemical warheads have a shelf-life of only thirty to forty-five days. One explanation is that the destruction of chemical weapons production and storage facilities in the first days of the bombing campaign may have disrupted the supply of fresh chemical shells to the front. Gen. Schwarzkopf cited the effectiveness of coalition aircraft in destroying Iraqi artillery and grounding the Iraqi air force as a reason why Iraq may not have been able to deliver chemical warheads. Other military officers and analysts suggested that disruptions of Iraq's command and control capabilities prevented the use of chemical weapons because front-line soldiers would not use them without being directed to do so by their superiors. Other observers suggested that the Iraqis were deterred from using them by the threat of nuclear or chemical retaliation (the United States did not bring chemical weapons to the Gulf, but could have transported them there from the United States within half a day) or by allied declarations that Iraqi commanders ordering their use would be considered war criminals. Finally, the weather may have played a role because winds on the initial day of the ground attack were blowing from the south. Iraqi gun-

ners firing chemical shells at coalition troops would have risked having the gas blown back at their own forces. Captured Iraqis claimed that many Iraqi units were vulnerable to chemical attack because they were not adequately equipped with gas masks and protective suits.

The coalition attack left the Iraqi army in disarray. Approximately 63,000 Iraqis were taken prisoner and between 25,000 and 100,000 were killed or wounded, according to widely varying unofficial coalition estimates. Tens of thousands of others were reported to have deserted before or shortly after the coalition ground campaign. Gen. Schwarzkopf estimated that as many as 30 percent of Iraqi troops in the Kuwait theater had deserted before the ground battle began. More important to the weakening of Iraq's offensive military potential was the destruction of most of its heavy equipment. British military officials estimated February 28 that Iraq lost about 3,500 of its 4,200 tanks in Kuwait and southern Iraq, 2,000 of its 3,000 artillery pieces, and 2,000 of its 2,700 troop carriers. American estimates of Iraqi equipment losses were slightly higher. These losses, along with the destruction of more than 100 Iraqi warplanes and 70 Iraqi naval vessels, crippled Iraq's ability to wage war against its neighbors in the short run. Iraq retained a large army—more than 300,000 troops and about 1,000 tanks stationed near the Turkish and Iranian borders and around Baghdad were not involved in the ground war. But the loss of such a high percentage of its best troops and equipment would limit the Iraqi military's offensive capability for a long time to come.

The Middle East After the War

By most measures the U.S.-led coalition's war against Iraq was enormously successful. Kuwait was liberated and the legitimate Kuwaiti government was restored to power; coalition forces sustained fewer casualties than almost anyone predicted; Iraq's offensive military potential and nuclear weapons research facilities were destroyed; and the wave of terrorism that Saddam Hussein had threatened to loose upon his enemies had not appeared.

The Middle East remains a region of multiple, interconnected dangers. In stopping the threat at hand—Iraq's military might and aggressiveness—the coalition created or exacerbated other problems. The defeat of Iraq's military opened the way for Iran and perhaps Syria to reexert their regional ambitions. The destruction of much of Iraq's arsenal did nothing to stem the impulse of other Middle Eastern nations to acquire more sophisticated and destructive weapons. Hussein's defeat made Palestinians even more desperate for a remedy to their situation, while many Israelis saw Iraq's hostility toward Israel and aggression toward Kuwait as definitive confirmation that the Arabs could not be trusted. In addition, the Iraqi army unleashed devastating ecological terrorism upon the region by setting fire to approximately 600 Kuwaiti oil wells and creating a huge oil slick in the Persian Gulf by opening the valves at a Kuwaiti refinery complex.

Nevertheless, the aftermath of the war did bring some hope that the crisis had created conditions that would further progress toward peace and stability in the Middle East. The destruction and loss of life brought on by the crisis demonstrated the urgency of addressing the region's economic, political, and military problems. In addition, collective action had been shown to be effective in stopping an aggressor nation. Middle East nations might be more willing in the future to take risks for peace if they could rely on the United Nations and individual states in the region to come to their aid.

Iraq

President Bush and other coalition leaders had hoped that the humiliating defeat in Kuwait and the destruction of Iraq's military machine would lead to Hussein's ouster. He clung tenaciously to power, however. His repression of dissent, frequent purges of the military and his Ba'ath party, and efforts to prevent anyone from accumulating too much power had blocked the emergence of rival centers of power in Baghdad that could lead a coup against him. Hussein did have to contend with factional rebellion, however.

Soon after the cease-fire with the U.S.-led coalition forces was declared, Iraq was torn by civil violence. Realizing that much of the Iraqi military's best equipment had been destroyed and many troops had been killed, Kurdish resistance fighters in northern Iraq and Shi'ite Moslem rebels in southern Iraq began waging open warfare against Iraqi troops loyal to Hussein.

The two rebel movements had divergent goals. The Kurds, an estimated 20 percent of Iraq's population, had fought Baghdad's rulers for decades in pursuit of greater autonomy. The Iraqi Kurdistan Front, a coalition of the two largest Kurdish parties, wanted to establish an independent Kurdish state in northern Iraq. The Shi'ites, who comprise a majority of Iraq's population (Saddam Hussein is a Sunni Moslem), hoped to overthrow Hussein and establish a Shi'ite government in Baghdad. They were less organized than the Kurds, but they were receiving support from Iran's Shi'ite government.

With the war for Kuwait over, Saddam Hussein ordered what was left of his military to put down the rebellions. The Kurds routed Hussein's troops and established temporary control of a wide region of mountainous northern Iraq, including Kirkuk, a city 150 miles north of Baghdad with a population of one million people.

In the south, however, Hussein's forces, including some Republican Guard units that had escaped from Kuwait, were using tank and helicopter assaults to break the Shi'ite rebellion. Shi'ite sources claimed that as many as 20,000 people had been killed by Iraqi troops in the fighting in southern Iraq. As of late March, sporadic fighting continued between Shi'ite rebels and Iraqi government forces, but Hussein's troops appeared to have gained the upper hand. Some military equipment had been transferred north to bolster troops fighting the Kurds.

Throughout this period coalition troops retained control of a large section of Iraq northwest of Kuwait. American warplanes shot down two Iraqi jets flying missions against the rebels. U.S. officials claimed that this action was taken because the Iraqis were prohibited from flying fixed-wing aircraft by one of the conditions of the Gulf war cease-fire. President Bush declared that the United States would not intervene in the Iraqi civil war, saying, "I think it would be better if everybody stayed out and let the Iraqi people decide what they want to do." He maintained that coalition troops would be withdrawn from Iraq soon after Baghdad agreed to a permanent cease-fire accord based on a new UN Security Council resolution.

The fighting in Iraq was greeted with mixed emotion in much of the Middle East and the Western world. Even though Arab nations that had supported the coalition wanted Hussein removed from power, they did not want to see the disintegration of Iraq. Commentators warned that Iraq could go the way of Lebanon—a splintered nation where regions were controlled by warring factions based on nationalist and religious loyalties. Kurdish strength in the north and Shi'ite strength in the south made this a possibility for Iraq after the end of the Gulf war. The Gulf Arabs, in particular, were concerned that a fractured Iraq would open the way for Iran to dominate the Persian Gulf region—a scenario that had led the Gulf states to closely cooperate with Iraq during the eight-year Iran-Iraq war.

The factions fighting against Hussein have attempted to coordinate their activities. Leaders from Kurdish, Shi'ite, and smaller opposition groups such as the Communists and Arab nationalists met in Damascus and pledged to cooperate in their efforts to overthrow Hussein. They also stated their intention to preserve the territorial integrity of Iraq and establish a democratic unity government if they were successful in ousting Hussein's. Toward this end they moved to establish an opposition council within Iraqi territory controlled by the Kurds. Middle East analysts, however, have expressed doubts that groups with such divergent goals and ideologies could create a unity government. Once Hussein had been removed, the opposition groups would be without a unifying goal. Yet no single group appeared strong enough to seize power over all of Iraq or diverse enough to command or bargain for the loyalty of most of the other opposition groups.

It is unlikely that Saddam Hussein will be able to pacify the rebellions against his rule and completely reestablish control of the entire country, but his regime may be able to survive from its power center in Baghdad. If Hussein remains in power, Iraq's severe economic problems are likely to multiply, because the UN embargo on imports and exports (excluding food and medicine) will almost certainly remain in effect. Iraq still possesses the second largest oil reserves in the world, however. If the Hussein government is overthrown and relations with the international community are normalized, Iraq does have the resources to rebuild itself.

Iran

No Middle Eastern nation is more likely to benefit from the Gulf war than Iran. The fighting was an Iranian dream come true. It pitted Iran's two most recent and hated antagonists, Iraq and the United States, against one another in a war that promised to destroy much of Iraq's military might while increasing opposition to the United States in some parts of the Middle East.

Even before the fighting began, Iran derived significant benefits from the crisis. Saddam Hussein, seeking to prevent the possibility of having to fight a two-front war, capitulated to Iranian terms for a resolution to the Iran-Iraq war, which had ended in August 1988 without a permanent cease-fire. On August 15, 1990, he offered to return Iranian territory still occupied by Iraq and recognize Iranian control of the eastern half of the Shatt al-Arab waterway. The two countries also began exchanging prisoners of war, and on September 10, 1990, they agreed to reestablish diplomatic relations. Economically, Iran reaped extra profits from the higher oil prices brought on by the Gulf crisis.

Despite declaring its neutrality in the conflict, Iranian interests were threatened by Iraq's annexation of Kuwait. Permanent Iraqi control of Kuwait would have substantially strengthened Iran's primary rival in the region. An Iraq bolstered by the oil reserves of Kuwait and possessing an excellent port and a wide outlet to the Persian Gulf would be in a position to launch another war against Iran, or at least to severely restrict Iranian influence in the Persian Gulf region.

It is certain that the Iranian leadership wanted Iraq out of Kuwait and the Iraqi military destroyed, both as retribution for the war Iraq unleashed upon Iran in 1980 and because Iraq has been the most important Arab counterweight to Iranian regional influence. Iran therefore condemned the Iraqi invasion of Kuwait and pledged its cooperation with the UN embargo against Iraq. The strong coalition response to the invasion allowed Iran to sit out the conflict, as sanctions and then coalition military power weakened Iraq and forced it from Kuwait. Throughout the crisis, Iran presented itself as a responsible mediator that denounced all military aggression and foreign military deployments (including the coalition's) in the region.

After the war started, Iran agreed to receive Iraqi aircraft that Baghdad wished to shelter from allied air attacks. A total of 137 Iraqi warplanes, many of them among Iraq's best, were sent to Iranian airfields. Iran assured the coalition that it would not return the aircraft until the fighting was over.

After the coalition drove the Iraqis from Kuwait and destroyed a large part of Hussein's military power, Iran adopted a harder line toward Baghdad. Tehran informed the Hussein regime that it would keep the Iraqi warplanes, thereby substantially boosting the strength of the Iranian air force. In addition, Iran began supporting the Shi'ite rebellion in southern Iraq. It gave rebels sanctuary in Iranian territory and supplied them with weapons and supplies. Iran also has provided weapons to Kurdish groups in northern Iraq, who have had close relations with Iran in the past.

Tehran would like to see Saddam Hussein overthrown and replaced by a Shi'ite government or a coalition government made up of Shi'ites and Kurdish nationalists. Tehran has called for free elections in Iraq, where the majority Shi'ite population would likely choose a government that would cooperate closely with Iran. Hussein's forces were successful in protecting the regime during March 1991, but the Kurds, Shi'ites, and other opposition groups are unlikely to give up their fight against Baghdad.

With Iraq's influence in the region greatly diminished as a result of the destruction of Hussein's military, Iran is in a much stronger position to pursue regional ambitions that extend far beyond Iraq. Yet the Islamic government of President Ali Akbar Hashemi Rafsanjani and the Iranian people have remained focused on the goal of reconstructing their war-torn economy, which has made only minor progress toward a recovery since the Iran-Iraq war ended. Iran does not want to commit its few assets to far-flung revolutionary endeavors or become embroiled in another war with Saddam Hussein. Radicals in favor of making the wholesale export of Iranian fundamentalism a high priority, as it was under the spiritual leadership of the Ayatollah Ruhollah Khomeini, who died in 1989, have lost ground to Rafsanjani and other advocates of an opportunistic but cautious foreign policy.

While pursuing the downfall of Saddam Hussein through substantial aid to Iraqi rebels, Iran has attempted to build bridges to the Gulf states, Egypt, and the West. Tehran has focused especially on improving relations with Saudi Arabia, primarily because the Saudis have the great-

est influence over OPEC policies. Iran favors using stricter OPEC oil production quotas to elevate prices and needs Saudi cooperation to achieve this goal. The two nations formally reestablished relations on March 26, 1991. Ties had been broken in 1987 after several hundred Iranian pilgrims in Mecca were killed in confrontations with Saudi security police. Iran also has reestablished ties with Great Britain, and is expanding economic relations with several Western nations, especially Germany. Although the United States and Iran have not restored diplomatic relations, Washington did lift a ban on Iranian oil imports.

Kuwait

The occupation of Kuwait and the war for its liberation turned the once sparkling emirate into a ravaged nation that will take years to rebuild. Kuwait's oil production capacity has been badly damaged. Before they fled, Iraqi soldiers set fire to more than 600 Kuwaiti oil wells, creating an economic and environmental disaster. According to Kuwaiti authorities, the damaged wells consume $1.2 million worth of oil each day. Experts estimate that it will take at least two years to extinguish all the fires and rebuild Kuwait's oil industry to the point where it can resume production at pre-August 1990 levels. Because more than 90 percent of Kuwait's noninvestment income comes from oil exports, restoring these facilities will be a top priority. Kuwait's other economic asset, its overseas investments, will be significantly depleted during the next few years in order to pay for reconstruction and the country's share of the war effort. Allied bombing and the Iraqi occupation caused at least $25 billion worth of damage to Kuwait's infrastructure and service sector. Most of Kuwait's government buildings, desalinization plants, and harbor facilities have to be rebuilt.

As Kuwaitis devote their energies to reconstruction, they also must address the political future of their country. The invasion of Kuwait has created a new political environment that will complicate a return to the old system of autocratic rule by Sheik Jaber al-Ahmed al-Sabah and the al-Sabah family. Before the invasion, there were many Kuwaitis who were unhappy with the form and substance of the al-Sabahs' rule. The ruling family has occasionally loosened its grip on power and allowed its citizens to dabble with various constitutional and parliamentarian reforms, but these reforms have never endured. During the early 1980s, Kuwait's elected assembly was noted in the Arab world for its vigorous debates on foreign aid, the Palestinian issue, nationalization of oil, citizenship, the status of women, and other pressing matters. In 1986, however, the emir dissolved the assembly and suspended certain articles of the constitution, declaring that he would rule by decree.

Many Kuwaitis who endured Iraqi atrocities felt empowered to demand change. With the royal family in exile, the invasion provided fertile ground for the Kuwaiti resistance movement to organize and gain strength and purpose. A new willingness to challenge the old order was manifested by the claims of some Kuwaitis that the resistance movement did not receive the material and financial assistance it needed to be effective from the Kuwaiti government-in-exile because the royal family did not want the movement to pose a threat after liberation. There also is sentiment among some Kuwaitis that, had the emir instituted more astute foreign and economic policies, he could have prevented the Iraqi invasion. These sentiments may translate into broader public support for the opposition.

In October, the exiled ruling family rejected opposition demands for a new cabinet-in-exile that would include opposition leaders. As a compromise, the emir agreed to appoint a committee of opposition figures to monitor government decision making. It is unlikely that this compromise will fully satisfy the opposition. After Iraq's defeat, the al-Sabahs declared martial law for security reasons, delaying formal debate on the future of the country. In addition, the government took control of broadcasting and publishing facilities in Kuwait.

While many Kuwaitis are clamoring for more democratic freedoms and a stronger voice in the country's decision making, there are many others who believe the al-Sabahs need to unify the country under their rule. After the trauma of the Iraqi invasion, many Kuwaitis do not want divisive domestic political debates to invite subversion or foreign aggression. These supporters of the royal family and the royal family itself may be intolerant of any challenge to the old order from below. Days after the country was liberated, a well-known former member of the Kuwaiti parliament and critic of the royal family was shot, sending a clear signal to other dissidents that democratic change will not come easily to Kuwait.

The Iraqi invasion created great tensions between Kuwaitis and Kuwait's Palestinian population. Kuwaitis regarded enthusiasm for Saddam Hussein among Palestinians in Jordan and the occupied territories as a betrayal. The cooperation given to Iraqi troops by some Palestinians in Kuwait turned all Palestinians into suspected collaborators in the eyes of Kuwaitis. In the wake of Kuwait's liberation, Palestinians who fled Kuwait were denied reentry. Those who remained in Kuwait (about 170,000 out of a preinvasion Palestinian population of 350,000) have been harassed and, according to some reports, tortured. Middle East Watch, a human rights monitoring group, claimed several weeks after liberation that Kuwaiti security forces and freelance gangs had detained and tortured approximately 2,000 Palestinian residents of Kuwait who were suspected of collaborating with Iraqi troops. Many Palestinians complained of abuse and said that Kuwaiti authorities were not providing as much food and water to Palestinians as they were to other residents of Kuwait.

It appears, however, that Sheik Jaber has not completely abandoned the cause of the Palestinians and their struggle for a homeland. Kuwait's prime minister has said that Kuwait will continue to provide financial and moral backing for a Palestinian homeland despite "deep anger" over Palestinian support for Hussein. Other foreign policy questions will hinge on developments in Iraq and the region as a whole, but Kuwait will likely strengthen its already close ties to Saudi Arabia, Egypt, and the United States. The United States and its Western coalition partners are likely to press for democratic political reforms in Kuwait. As early as September 1990, Washington hinted that a return to the status quo in Kuwait would not be acceptable. Given the continuing threat to Kuwaiti security from Iraq and Iran, the Western powers will surely retain some leverage with the al-Sabah regime.

Coalition Arabs

On March 10, 1991, the foreign ministers of Egypt, Syria, Saudi Arabia, and the five small Persian Gulf states met in Riyadh with Secretary of State Baker. The gathering endorsed a plan under which the eight Arab nations would work with the United States to ensure the security of the Persian Gulf region. The plan called for the formation of a sizable peacekeeping force consisting of Egyptian, Syrian, and Gulf Arab troops. This force was to be backed by enhanced U.S. naval deployments in the Persian Gulf. The plan also called for frequent joint maneuvers on the Arabian peninsula involving Arab and American troops and the storage of large stocks of U.S. military equipment in Saudi Arabia that would allow a division or more of U.S. troops to be rapidly deployed to the Gulf in the event of a crisis.

The developing security cooperation between Egypt, Syria, Saudi Arabia, and the Gulf Arabs signaled the emergence of a moderate Arab bloc that had the potential to dominate Arab politics. The strength of such a bloc would be in its merging of the wealth of Saudi Arabia and the Gulf states with the large populations and military strength of Egypt and Syria.

The main interest of the Gulf Arabs in the creation of a moderate Arab alliance is security. As the Gulf crisis proved, Saudi Arabia, Kuwait, and the other Gulf states could not defend themselves without outside assistance. Alliance with the large armies of Egypt and Syria could provide protection from future threats from Iran or Iraq without forcing the Gulf Arabs to lean too heavily on the United States. Although Gulf rulers favor greater military cooperation with the United States, they want to limit the presence of American forces in their countries to avoid disruptions in their conservative societies and charges that they are sponsoring Western colonialism.

Egypt's primary interest in a closer alliance with the Gulf states is economic. Egypt has a chronically depressed economy that is laboring under 20 percent unemployment and massive foreign debt. In addition, the Gulf crisis weakened three of the four pillars of the Egyptian economy. Egyptian oil revenues went up temporarily, but these gains were more than offset by the depression in Egypt's tourist industry brought on by fears of traveling in the Middle East, the loss of remittances from the 500,000 Egyptian workers who fled the Gulf region, and the dwindling of Suez Canal revenues as fewer commercial ships chose to sail in Middle East waters. The U.S. government's forgiveness of $7 billion in Egyptian military debts eased Cairo's financial situation, but the Egyptian economy requires long-term investment. President Hosni Mubarak hopes Egypt's efforts to contribute to Gulf security will bring such investment from Saudi Arabia and the other Gulf states. Like the United States, Saudi Arabia has already forgiven billions of dollars in Egyptian debt as a reward for Cairo's support during the Gulf crisis. Mubarak also expects that Saudi Arabia will hire many Egyptian workers who lost their jobs in Iraq. Because hundreds of thousands of Yemenis who worked in Saudi Arabia left the kingdom under pressure from the Saudi government, which was angered by Yemen's tilt toward Iraq, Saudi Arabia has a need for Egyptian workers.

Syria's apparent move toward the moderate Arab camp has surprised some observers. For many years, Syria has been one of the most radical Arab states. President Hafez al-Assad has taken a hard line toward Israel, supported terrorist activities, and maneuvered to dominate Lebanon. Assad is not likely to significantly moderate his policies toward Lebanon or his iron-fisted rule of his own nation, but changes in Soviet foreign policy have forced him to reassess Syria's foreign policy position. Moscow's domestic economic problems and its new emphasis on cooperation with the West have made continued Soviet financial backing of Syria uncertain. The Gulf crisis presented Syria with an opportunity to improve relations with the wealthy Gulf states, which could provide Syria financing to make up for expected cuts in Soviet aid. Politically, an alliance with Egypt and the Gulf states is an opportunity for Syria to increase its influence within the Arab world and perhaps gain greater leverage in possible peace talks with Israel.

Israeli-Palestinian Conflict

Saddam Hussein's confrontation with the U.S.-led coalition has achieved one of his stated goals: increasing international pressure for a settlement to the Palestinian issue. During the summer of 1990 the Palestinian intifada was commanding fewer headlines and the United States had broken off its dialogue with the PLO. Iraq's invasion of Kuwait and the subsequent crisis refocused international attention on the Palestinian issue. Ironically, although the Palestinians' enthusiasm for Saddam Hussein cost them much credibility (especially in the United States, in the Arab nations that supported the anti-Iraq coalition, and among Israeli liberals), the Gulf war strengthened the international commitment to achieve a negotiated settlement to the Palestinian issue, because it demonstrated the urgency of achieving peace and stability in the Middle East.

In his speech before a joint session of Congress on March 6, 1991, President Bush proclaimed, "By now it should be plain to all parties that peacemaking in the Middle East requires compromise.... A comprehensive peace must be grounded in United Nations Security Council Resolutions 242 and 338 and the principle of territory for peace." Bush claimed that "no one will work harder for a stable peace in the region than we will." European governments also expressed their desire to move quickly toward a solution to the Palestinian issue.

Achieving peace in the Middle East, however, ultimately depends on the parties involved in the Arab-Israeli dispute, not outside powers. Neither the Palestinians, the Arab states, nor Israel had indicated any major change in their positions. Without major concessions by one or more of the parties involved, progress toward a negotiated settlement to the Palestinian issue and the Arab-Israeli conflict would be impossible.

The Israeli government showed no signs of being ready to offer major compromises, even though it recognized that the outcome of the Gulf war had strengthened its position in relation to its Arab neighbors. Throughout the Gulf crisis, Prime Minister Yitzhak Shamir and other Israeli leaders maintained that Saddam Hussein's military machine must be destroyed. Despite Hussein's threats to respond to a coalition offensive by attacking the Jewish state, most Israelis were convinced that peace was more dangerous than war. Israel preferred the threat of being struck by Iraqi missiles with conventional or even chemical warheads at a time when Iraq faced a powerful international coalition, to the threat of being attacked several years in the future with nuclear missiles at a time chosen by Iraq.

The Iraqi invasion of Kuwait, therefore, had unintentionally served Israeli purposes. It had split the Arab world and placed Israel's most powerful and belligerent adversary in jeopardy of being destroyed by an international coalition with the sanction of the United Nations. The Israelis greatest fear during the crisis was that Hussein would accept a face-saving way out of Kuwait that would preserve his military machine.

The subsequent damage done to Hussein's army and the destruction of his nuclear weapons facilities eliminated the one Arab military threat that worried Israeli military planners. With Iraq's offensive military capacity crippled, no combination of Arab forces could soon threaten Israeli security.

Diplomatically, however, the Israeli government viewed the Gulf crisis as a mixed blessing. The restraint Israel had shown by not attacking Iraq after Saddam Hussein fired Scud missiles into the Jewish state had won Israel international praise. The attacks also lent credence to Israel's claims that Arab hostility necessitated extraordinary measures to safeguard Israeli security. But Shamir's government has expressed apprehension that the momentum to achieve peace in the Middle East in the wake of the Gulf war could lead to strong pressure on Israel to make concessions to the Palestinians that it does not want to make.

The focus of much Israeli concern is the United States. As the provider of more than $3 billion in annual aid to Israel, the United States is in a position to exert substantial pressure on Israel to trade all or part of the occupied territories for a peace settlement. While the United States is indebted to Israel for not retaliating against Iraq during the Gulf war, Washington is equally indebted to the Arab members of the coalition, who support a Palestinian homeland in the occupied territories. Israelis worried that the experience of the Gulf crisis and the increasingly close ties developing between Washington, Riyadh, and Cairo would cause the United States to refocus its Middle East policy away from Israel toward greater cooperation with moderate Arab states that were essential to the security of the economically vital Persian Gulf region. This worry was reinforced by the Bush administration's backing of four votes of condemnation against Israel in the UN Security Council between October 1990 and January 1991 and proposals for multibillion dollar U.S. arms sales to Saudi Arabia and Egypt.

No matter how much pressure the United States might eventually exert on Israel, progress toward a negotiated settlement of the Palestinian issue is unlikely unless the Israeli government moderates its stand on trading land for peace. The Shamir government has never endorsed the idea that Israel should give up the occupied territories to the Palestinians in return for Palestinian and Arab recognition of Israel's right to exist. Shamir also has ruled out talks with the PLO or Israeli participation in an international peace conference on the Middle East. He has continued to promote the idea of Palestinian elections in the occupied territories that would lead to some form of limited Palestinian autonomy. In addition, Iraqi missiles and Palestinian support for Saddam Hussein have caused many Israelis who had favored a land for peace deal to take a harder line toward the Palestinian question. Domestic pressure on the Israeli government to make concessions, therefore, has weakened considerably.

Meanwhile, the Gulf crisis has inflamed the Palestinians in the occupied territories. Israeli security forces have responded with strict curfews and administrative detentions of Palestinian leaders, which have been denounced by the United States and many other Western governments. But acts of violence between Israelis and Palestinians intensified during the Gulf war and have continued in its aftermath. Many Palestinians, frustrated with Iraq's defeat and their own sense of hopelessness, have begun to debate a

A Palestinian boy waves an outlawed PLO flag as other Palestinians flee Israeli security forces during a street demonstration in the Gaza Strip. Palestinian desperation in the wake of Saddam Hussein's defeat may intensify unrest in the occupied territories.

change of strategy from the street demonstrations of the intifada to armed struggle.

The U.S.-led military campaign against Iraq also increased Palestinian distrust of the West. Palestinians saw the Gulf war as the latest in a series of actions by the Western powers (especially the United States) designed to suppress the development of power centers in the Arab world and control the economic assets of the Middle East.

The current environment appears to offer little hope for progress toward a peace settlement. President Bush has proposed a "dual track" negotiating strategy that advocates separate talks between Israel and its Arab neighbors and Israel and Palestinian representatives. This general approach has been endorsed by Egypt, Saudi Arabia, and Syria, and the Israeli government has expressed interest in it. But even if such talks are launched the chasms of disagreement between Israel and the Arabs will be difficult to bridge anytime soon.

Soviet Union

In the days after Iraq's invasion of Kuwait, Soviet leaders were outwardly angered that Saddam Hussein had deceived them about his intentions toward Kuwait. Soviet leaders appeared to have been manipulated, and they suffered the additional embarrassment of having been Iraq's main arms supplier.

The government of President Mikhail S. Gorbachev responded with support for the U.S.-led coalition. Moscow immediately suspended arms shipments to its Arab client and demanded an unconditional Iraqi withdrawal from Kuwait. On August 6 it joined in the UN Security Council vote that established a trade embargo against Iraq. In November the Soviet Union voted with the majority of UN Security Council members to authorize the use of force against Iraq to drive it from Kuwait.

Despite its support for the U.S.-led coalition, Moscow did not send troops to the Gulf. The trauma of the Afghanistan war remained fresh in the minds of the Soviet public. Another deployment of Soviet troops in a war zone, even as part of an international coalition, was not likely to be popular. In addition, the use of Soviet troops against Iraq, a recent Soviet client, would have angered many Soviet conservatives and military leaders. Gorbachev also was trying to respond to a deepening domestic economic crisis. The Soviet Union itself had become a recipient of billions of dollars of foreign aid. For Moscow to incur expenses associated with sending troops to Saudi Arabia would have further strained the Soviet economy. Because the Soviet Union's conduct in supporting the coalition's effort was seen as extraordinary compared with its past obstructionist behavior and because Soviet participation could limit the coalition's freedom of action during the crisis, the Bush administration did not press Gorbachev to commit forces. Moscow would not have derived much additional international benefit from supplying troops to the coalition, but such a move could have damaged a Soviet regime already beset by domestic criticism.

The Gorbachev government did not regard its interests in the Middle East as identical to those of the United States. Throughout the fall, the Soviet Union continued its support of the coalition while launching independent diplomatic initiatives. Gorbachev adviser and Middle East expert Yevgenii Primakov was dispatched to Baghdad on several occasions in an attempt to convince Saddam Hussein to make concessions that could lead to a peaceful resolution of the crisis. Primakov's diplomacy met with little success. After the war had begun Moscow continued to advocate a negotiated settlement. The Soviet Union became the focus of last-minute diplomatic efforts to avoid a ground war. The Iraqis sought Soviet mediation to construct a proposal that would allow them a face-saving retreat out of Kuwait. In cooperation with Baghdad, Moscow developed such a proposal, but the Bush administration rejected it, declaring that the plan contained too many unacceptable conditions. *(Iraqi response to Soviet peace plan, documents, p. 387; U.S. conditions for ending the war, documents, p. 386)*

Gorbachev wanted to play a mediation role that would strengthen his international image, demonstrate that the Soviet Union still had an independent foreign policy, preserve Iraqi security, and placate Soviet conservatives and military leaders who objected to Soviet support for the United States. Gorbachev, however, did not want to be perceived as tilting toward Iraq, for fear of alienating the West (which was much more important to Soviet long-term interests than Iraq) or squandering the good will that had been built up among moderate Arab nations by Soviet backing of UN Security Council resolutions against Iraq.

Moscow's support for the U.S.-led coalition was determined in part by the Soviets' need for Western financial aid and cooperation in rejuvenating their economy and by their desire for a continuing détente with the West. But it also was motivated by the Kremlin's desire to broaden its relations in the Middle East. Since Gorbachev has come to power, the Soviets have gradually moved away from basing their influence in the region solely on support for unpredictable radical Arab states, such as Iraq and Syria. They have sought to improve relations with moderate Arabs and Israel. Soviet backing of the anti-Iraq effort led to dramatic improvements in the Saudi-Soviet relationship. Saudi Arabia and the smaller Persian Gulf states announced November 29, 1990, that they would offer Moscow as much as $4 billion in financial aid and loans.

Because economic reconstruction is Gorbachev's top priority, his courting of wealthy Gulf states and other moderate Arab nations will continue. The Soviets also will continue to promote collective action by the UN Security Council as the best means through which to deal with Middle East problems. Because the Soviet Union has a veto in the council, it can do much to shape council policy. The Security Council, therefore, offers the Soviets a low-cost way to protect its interests in the region and exert diplomatic influence.

New Order in the Middle East?

In his January 29, 1991, State of the Union address, President Bush said that the success of the coalition in forcing Iraq out of Kuwait would be "an enduring warning to any dictator or despot, present or future, who contemplates outlaw aggression. The world can therefore seize this opportunity to fulfill the long-held promise of a new world order—where brutality will go unrewarded and aggression will meet collective resistance." Indeed, throughout the crisis, Bush maintained that one of his goals in opposing the Iraqi annexation of Kuwait was to uphold international law and demonstrate that a new world order that would use collective action to combat aggression in the Middle East and elsewhere was possible. He believed that if the coalition succeeded in removing Iraq from Kuwait, an international precedent would be set that would deter future aggressions around the world.

Saddam Hussein's invasion of Kuwait created a threat that tested how the post-Cold War world would react to aggression. Existing institutions, especially the UN Security Council, were used to respond to the Iraqi invasion. Under U.S. leadership, the international community as-sembled a formidable coalition that blockaded Iraq and that eventually used military force to drive Iraq from Kuwait. But collective action depended on three factors that might not always be present in future crises.

First, with the notable exception of many poorer Arabs who regarded Saddam Hussein as a savior, most of the world community agreed that Hussein must be stopped from controlling Persian Gulf oil and committing further acts of aggression. Not every country agreed that military force should have been used, but most nations supported the imposition of severe economic sanctions against Iraq, in part because Hussein's invasion threatened one of the world's most vital resources.

Hypothetically, one could ask (as many opponents of military force did) whether the United States and the world community would have come to the rescue of Kuwait had that country not possessed vast oil reserves. The likely answer is no. Many other small countries have been overrun, threatened, or terrorized by a larger neighboring nation without receiving significant international aid. The American and international response to the invasion of Kuwait demonstrated that nations are likely to intervene on behalf of a victim of aggression only when it is in their vital interests. Expelling Iraq from Kuwait was judged by the Bush administration and leaders of other coalition nations to be in their vital interests primarily because Iraq could not be allowed to control Kuwait's oil assets or threaten those of Saudi Arabia.

The second factor that made collective action possible was that Saddam Hussein was judged by most nations to be operating far outside the norms of international behavior. Saddam Hussein's ambition appeared so insatiable and his military so strong, relative to his neighbors, that Bush and his advisers came to believe that the Middle East of 1990 was analogous to Europe of 1938. Even outside the Bush administration, Hussein was regarded by some as a Middle East version of Adolph Hitler who would bully and threaten and invade his neighbors until someone stopped him. Iraq's aggressive nuclear weapons research program also created a sense of urgency. If Hussein acquired even a rudimentary nuclear force, facing him down in the future would be far more risky.

As the crisis progressed, the actions of Saddam Hussein and his army seemed to confirm Bush's contention that he was an outlaw dictator in charge of an immoral regime that would use any means to achieve its purposes. Iraqi soldiers committed many documented atrocities in Kuwait and systematically plundered the country. Hussein held civilian hostages for months as human shields at military sites in violation of the Geneva convention, forced the closure of foreign embassies in Kuwait, and threatened to use chemical weapons against coalition troops and Israel. After the war started he displayed beaten prisoners of war; ordered oil pumped into the Persian Gulf, creating the largest oil spill in history; and launched Scud missiles into population centers in Israel and Saudi Arabia. Finally as Iraqi soldiers scrambled to leave Kuwait, they took thousands of Kuwaiti civilians hostage and set hundreds of Kuwaiti oil wells on fire.

In short, Saddam Hussein's brutality offended almost everyone's sense of morality. The next aggressive dictator who surfaces in the Middle East or elsewhere will likely be more morally ambiguous.

A final factor that made collective action work was the developing international cooperation between the United States and the Soviet Union. For more than forty years the

United States had been prevented from taking military action against Soviet client states for fear that a conflict would escalate into a superpower confrontation. If the Soviet Union's foreign policy had not changed from what it was in the early 1980s, the United States would not have been able to assemble an international coalition against Iraq. Nor is it likely that it would have risked going to war for the liberation of Kuwait. In addition, without Soviet support, the UN Security Council could not have been used to organize and legitimize the international response to Iraq's invasion.

Bush's new world order, therefore, is dependent on the continuing cooperation of the Soviet Union. If the Soviets perceive themselves as having been burned by the U.S. decision to go to war, they will be far less willing to side with the United States in future efforts to curb aggression. Also, no guarantee exists, given the uncertain state of Soviet internal politics, that a regime that seeks cooperation with the West will remain in power.

The outcome of the Persian Gulf crisis will cause leaders who may contemplate military aggression against their neighbors to carefully consider the risk of prompting a collective international response. It also probably will enhance the role of the United Nations in Middle East peacekeeping. But the Gulf crisis does not signal the beginning of a new world order, especially in the Middle East, where alliances shift frequently. President Bush's coalition came together because its members had a mutual interest in opposing Iraq's invasion of Kuwait. A future aggression will not necessarily provoke a similar collective response.

Chronology of the Gulf Crisis

JULY 1990

July 17. *Hussein Speech.* Iraqi president Saddam Hussein accuses unnamed Gulf leaders of plotting with the United States to keep oil prices low through overproduction. He says in a speech marking Iraq's Revolution Day that artificially low oil prices have damaged the Iraqi economy, and he threatens to use force to stop noncompliance with production quotas. Observers agree that his accusation is aimed at Kuwait and the United Arab Emirates (UAE).

July 18. *Iraqi Letter Names Kuwait, UAE.* Iraq discloses the contents of a letter written by Iraqi foreign minister Tariq Aziz to the Arab League. The letter charges that Kuwait and the United Arab Emirates are part of an "imperialist-Zionist" conspiracy to hold down oil prices. The letter also charges Kuwait with pumping $2.4 billion worth of Iraqi oil out of the Rumaila oilfield, a small part of which extends into Kuwait. Aziz says Iraq's Arab creditors should forgive the debt incurred by Iraq during the war with Iran.

July 23. *Iraq Deploys Troops on Border.* Arab and U.S. officials report that Iraq is massing tens of thousands of troops on Kuwait's border. The United States discloses July 25 that Iraqi deployments have reached 100,000 troops.

July 24. *U.S.-UAE Maneuvers.* The United States announces that American ships and refueling planes are participating in joint maneuvers with forces from the United Arab Emirates. The maneuvers are intended to demonstrate U.S. commitment to defending friendly Gulf nations and the free flow of oil from the Gulf. The following day UAE officials deny that their country is holding special maneuvers with the United States, saying the two nations merely are engaging in routine training.

July 25. *Mubarak Diplomacy.* After four days of talks with Arab leaders in Egypt, Iraq, Saudi Arabia, and Kuwait, Egyptian president Hosni Mubarak announces that Iraq and Kuwait have agreed to discuss their differences in talks to be held in Jiddah, Saudi Arabia. Mubarak says Saddam Hussein has told him that Iraq has "no intention" of invading Kuwait.

July 25. *Glaspie Meets Hussein.* The American ambassador to Iraq, April Glaspie, meets with Saddam Hussein in Baghdad. She expresses concern about the massing of Iraqi forces on the Kuwaiti border, but emphasizes that the United States wants better relations with Iraq. According to an Iraqi transcript of the meeting released in September, she tells him that the United States has "no opinion on the Arab-Arab conflicts, like your border disagreement with Kuwait." Hussein reportedly tells Glaspie that Iraq does not wish a confrontation with the United States and that Iraq's forces on the Kuwaiti frontier have not been deployed for the purpose of invasion.

July 25-27. *OPEC Raises Target Price.* The Organization of Petroleum Exporting Countries (OPEC) holds a meeting in Geneva amid the brewing crisis in the Gulf. On July 27 the oil ministers announce a $3 increase to $21 a barrel in OPEC's target price for oil. Iraq had demanded that the target price be raised to $25 a barrel. Kuwait had favored leaving the target price at $18. The increase is seen as a victory for Iraq. Most members of OPEC had supported a price increase and stricter production quotas, but wanted to implement them more gradually than Iraq.

AUGUST

August 1. *Jiddah Talks Fail.* After just two hours, Saudi-mediated talks between Iraq and Kuwait held in the Red Sea city of Jiddah break down.

August 2. *Iraq Invades Kuwait.* Iraqi forces massed on the border of Kuwait invade the sheikdom and quickly seize control of most strategic locations. The Iraqis face little initial resistance, although pockets of the surprised Kuwaiti armed forces fight tenaciously before being overwhelmed. Kuwait's ruler, Sheik Jaber al-Ahmed al-Sabah, flees to Saudi Arabia. President Hussein claims Iraq was responding to appeals for help from Kuwaiti revolutionaries who had overthrown the government. By the end of the day Iraqi troops are in firm control of the country, although isolated incidents of armed resistance by Kuwaitis continue. U.S. president George Bush denounces the invasion and imposes economic sanctions against Iraq. He initially says that he is not planning to intervene militarily, but after a previously scheduled meeting with British prime minister Margaret Thatcher later in the day in Aspen, Colorado, Bush says, "We're not ruling any options in, but we're not ruling any options out." The governments of the United States, Great Britain, and France freeze Iraqi and Kuwaiti assets in their countries. The Soviet Union cuts off arms deliveries to Iraq. The UN Security Council votes 14-0 (with Yemen abstaining) to condemn the invasion and threatens to impose mandatory economic sanctions if Iraq does not withdraw immediately from Kuwait.

August 3. *Aftermath of the Invasion.* Soviet foreign minister Eduard Shevardnadze and U.S. secretary of state James A. Baker III issue a joint statement in Moscow condemning the Iraqi invasion of Kuwait and calling for an international arms embargo against Iraq. Fourteen of twenty-one Arab League members vote to condemn Iraq's "aggression." Japan, Canada, and many European nations follow the lead of the United States, Great Britain, and France by freezing Kuwaiti assets to protect them from the Iraqis. The European Community (EC) August 4 announces broad economic sanctions against Iraq, including an arms embargo, a freeze on Iraqi assets, and a ban on imports of Iraqi and Kuwaiti oil. Japan announces similar economic sanctions August 5.

August 6. *UN Imposes Sanctions.* The UN Security Council passes Resolution 661, imposing mandatory economic sanctions on Iraq. All members of the security council voted for the resolution except Yemen and Cuba, both of which abstained. The resolution calls on UN members to end all economic intercourse with Iraq, including trade. Food and medicine are exempted from the embargo "in strictly humanitarian circumstances."

August 6. *Saudis Request U.S. Forces.* Responding to an Iraqi buildup in southern Kuwait near the Saudi border, King Fahd ibn Abdul Aziz of Saudi Arabia requests that U.S. forces be stationed in his country. The request followed a meeting between King Fahd and U.S. secretary of defense Dick Cheney, at which Cheney showed the king satellite photographs of the Iraqi buildup. That evening, President Bush orders U.S. forces to Saudi Arabia. The deployment begins the morning of August 7, but is not formally announced until August 8. It includes F-15 fighters, F-111 and B-52 bombers, numerous warships, and 2,300 paratroopers. Prime Minister Thatcher orders British naval and air forces to Saudi Arabia August 8.

August 8. *Iraq Annexes Kuwait.* Despite a statement August 3 that it would withdraw its forces from Kuwait, Baghdad announces that it has annexed Kuwait. The UN Security Council August 9 votes 15-0 for a resolution declaring the annexation "null and void."

August 8. *Bush Address.* In a televised address from the White House, President Bush emphasizes the defensive nature of U.S. military deployments to Saudi Arabia. He says U.S. policy toward the Gulf crisis is based on "four simple principles": Iraq's unconditional and complete withdrawal from Kuwait, the restoration of Kuwait's legitimate government, Persian Gulf security and stability, and the protection of Americans abroad.

August 9. *King Fahd Denounces Iraq.* In his first public statement since Iraq invaded Kuwait, King Fahd calls the invasion "the most sinister aggression witnessed by the Arab nation in its modern history."

August 9. *Iraq Seals Its Borders.* Baghdad announces that it is sealing its borders and only foreign diplomats will be permitted to leave the country. The move is regarded in the West as an indication that Iraq is preparing to use Westerners in Kuwait and Iraq as hostages.

August 10. *Arab League Votes to Commit Troops.* At a closed meeting of the Arab League in Cairo, twelve Arab League members vote for a resolution backing Arab troop deployments to Saudi Arabia to oppose Iraq. Iraq, Libya, and the Palestinian Liberation Organization (PLO)

vote against the resolution. Jordan, Sudan, and Mauritania vote for the measure with reservations. Algeria and Yemen abstain, and Tunisia did not attend. Shortly before the vote, Saddam Hussein had called on all Arabs and Moslems to begin a "holy war" against foreign armies and "corrupt" Arab rulers. The first Egyptian and Moroccan troops land in Saudi Arabia August 11. Syrian forces begin arriving August 14.

August 10. *Iraq Orders Embassies in Kuwait Closed.* The Iraqi government orders foreign governments with embassies in Kuwait to shut those embassies and transfer their diplomatic personnel to Baghdad within two weeks.

August 12. *Hussein Links Iraqi Pullout to Israel.* President Hussein says Iraq might withdraw from Kuwait if Israel withdraws from "the Arab-occupied territories in Palestine, Syria, and Lebanon."

August 13. *Iraq Uses Westerners as Hostages.* Iraqi officials announce that thousands of Westerners stranded in Iraq and Kuwait will not be allowed to leave until the crisis is over. Iraq avoids calling the Westerners "hostages" and instead refers to them as "guests."

August 15. *Hussein Offers Settlement to Iran.* Faced with a growing coalition opposing his occupation of Kuwait, President Hussein offers Iran a favorable peace settlement to the Iran-Iraq war. (The fighting had ended in August 1988 without a formal peace being concluded.) Hussein's proposal amounts to an acceptance of Iranian terms. He offers to return Iranian territory still occupied by Iraqi troops, recognize Iranian control of the eastern half of the Shatt al-Arab waterway, and begin a prisoner exchange. Iran accepts the proposal enthusiastically. Iraqi troops begin withdrawing from Iranian territory August 18 and complete their withdrawal August 21, according to Baghdad.

August 16. *Bush Meets King Hussein.* President Bush meets with Jordan's King Hussein ibn Talal in Kennebunkport, Maine. King Hussein had met with Saddam Hussein three days earlier, but he brings no peace initiative to Bush, as some observers had predicted. The king says he intends to observe UN sanctions against Iraq.

August 16. *U.S. Begins Blockade.* Responding to an order issued by President Bush August 12, U.S. naval forces begin forcibly "interdicting" ships headed to or from Iraq with commercial or military cargoes. The British government indicated earlier that its ships also would use force if necessary to implement the UN sanctions. The Soviet Union, France, and China, as well as UN Secretary General Javier Pérez de Cuéllar, criticize the de facto blockade. They maintain that the use of force to uphold economic sanctions must be authorized by the Security Council.

August 16. *Americans, Britons Ordered to Report.* Iraqi military authorities order U.S. and British citizens in Kuwait to assemble at two hotels. The U.S. embassy tells Americans to decide for themselves if they want to comply.

August 17. *Iraq Places Hostages at Key Sites.* The speaker of Iraq's parliament, Saadi Mahdi Saleh says Iraq will house American and other Western citizens at important military and industrial installations. The move is seen as an attempt to deter air attacks against Iraq. On August 18 the Bush administration condemns the action, and the UN Security Council calls for the release of all foreigners held in Iraq. Baghdad announces August 20 that it has begun moving Westerners to key facilities.

August 19. *All Westerners Ordered to Report.* Iraq orders all Westerners in Kuwait to present themselves to Iraqi authorities at three designated hotels in Kuwait City. In response to Iraq's effort to round up French citizens, the

French government authorizes its ships to use force to uphold UN economic sanctions.

August 22. *Bush Calls Up Reservists.* President Bush orders a limited mobilization of reservists as U.S. military deployments to Saudi Arabia continue.

August 22. *Iraq Threatens Embassies.* Iraq warns that any embassy in Kuwait still operating after August 24 will be forcibly closed and its personnel will be taken into custody.

August 23. *Hussein Meets with Hostages.* Iraqi television shows President Hussein chatting with a group of tense British hostages. Hussein's attempt to portray himself as a benign host concerned for the welfare of his "guests" is regarded in the West to have been a clumsy and counterproductive attempt at propaganda. British foreign secretary Douglas Hurd calls it "the most sickening thing I've seen for a long time."

August 23. *Japan Pledges $1 Billion.* The Japanese government announces that it will provide $1 billion in aid to Arab governments hurt by the UN embargo of Iraq. The Japanese government had been criticized for not doing more to support the coalition effort.

August 24. *Troops Surround Embassies in Kuwait.* Iraqi troops surround several foreign embassies in Kuwait, including those of the United States, Britain, and France, which are operating with skeleton staffs. In an apparent effort to force the closure of the embassies without a confrontation that could lead to war, the troops begin cutting off the embassies' electricity and water. At least twenty-seven nations have kept their embassies in Kuwait open despite Iraqi demands that they be shut.

August 25. *Security Council Backs Use of Navies.* The UN Security Council votes 13-0 (with Yemen and Cuba abstaining) to allow U.S. and allied ships to use force if necessary to ensure compliance with the sanctions against Iraq.

August 27. *U.S. Expels Iraqis.* In response to Iraq's invasion of Kuwait, its taking of hostages, and its siege of the American embassy in Kuwait, the U.S. government orders thirty-six personnel of the Iraqi embassy in Washington, D.C., to leave the country.

August 28. *Iraq Releases Women and Children.* Iraqi television reports that President Hussein will allow Western women and children detained in Iraq to leave.

August 28. *Iraq Declares Kuwait a Province.* An Iraqi presidential decree declares Kuwait to be Iraq's nineteenth province. It also changes the name of Kuwait City to Kadhima.

August 29. *OPEC to Increase Production.* At a meeting in Vienna, ten of thirteen OPEC members support an increase in oil production to make up for the shortfall created by the Persian Gulf crisis. Saudi Arabia and Venezuela had previously increased their production in response to the crisis and had told other members that they would make up for the loss of Iraqi and Kuwaiti oil by themselves if necessary. Libya and Iraq boycott the meeting. Iran attends but opposes any production increase. OPEC is expected to increase its production by 4 million barrels per day.

August 30. *Bush Calls for Burden Sharing.* At a news conference, President Bush says the United States will seek contributions from its allies to help pay for the military buildup in the Gulf region and to aid nations that have suffered economic losses because of the embargo on Iraq, principally Egypt, Turkey, and Jordan. Bush explains that the financial burden of Operation Desert Shield should be "shared by those being defended and those who benefit from the free flow of oil." Bush announces that he is dispatching Secretary of State Baker and Treasury Secretary Nicholas Brady to solicit contributions in selected countries.

August 30-September 1. *Arab League Meeting.* Thirteen Arab League foreign ministers meet in Cairo and pass a series of anti-Iraqi resolutions. The resolutions demand that Iraq withdraw from Kuwait, release all hostages, permit foreign embassies in Kuwait to operate, and pay war reparations. Eight Arab states boycott the meeting. Libya attends, but votes against the resolutions.

SEPTEMBER

September 1. *Hostages Begin Leaving Iraq.* The first hostages released by Iraq, a group of sixty-eight Japanese women and children, leave Baghdad. In the days that follow, many other foreign women and children are allowed to leave.

September 2. *Pérez de Cuéllar on Aziz Talks.* After meeting with Foreign Minister Aziz August 31-September 1 in Amman, Secretary General Pérez de Cuéllar says Aziz gave no indication that Iraq might be willing to release foreign male hostages or make concessions toward a settlement that could produce an Iraqi withdrawal from Kuwait.

September 5. *Hussein Television Message.* A spokesman reads a message from Saddam Hussein on Iraqi television charging that the "the children of Iraq are dying because they're being deprived of their milk and their food and their medicine." Hussein calls for the ouster of President Mubarak and King Fahd and reiterates an earlier call for Moslems to launch a holy war to drive U.S. forces from the Gulf region.

September 6. *Saudis, Kuwaitis Pledge Billions.* The Saudi government pledges to contribute about $500 million a month to help defray the costs of the U.S. military deployments to Saudi Arabia. The Saudis also pledge $4 billion a year in financial aid to states whose economies have been damaged by the crisis. The Saudi contribution follows a meeting between Secretary of State Baker and King Fahd in Jiddah. Baker meets with the exiled emir of Kuwait September 7 in Taif, Saudi Arabia. The emir pledges $2.5 billion in 1990 to help pay for U.S. military operations in the Gulf region and another $2.5 billion to help struggling Middle East economies. The exiled Kuwaiti government says September 21 that it is prepared to provide even more aid in support of the effort to liberate its country.

September 7. *European Community Aid.* After a meeting of foreign ministers in Rome, the twelve-member European Community pledges $2 billion in aid to Jordan, Egypt, and Turkey through 1991. The foreign ministers oppose providing aid to the U.S. military effort in the Gulf, however.

September 9. *Helsinki Summit.* President Bush and Soviet president Mikhail S. Gorbachev discuss the Gulf crisis at a summit in Helsinki. They issue a joint statement condemning Iraq's invasion of Kuwait and calling for an immediate withdrawal. The statement also recognizes that the Soviet Union should be an important player in the Arab-Israeli peace process. Gorbachev says his country has no plans to send forces to Saudi Arabia. The summit was announced September 1.

September 10. *Iran, Iraq Agree to Restore Ties.* After two days of talks in Tehran, Foreign Minister Aziz and Iranian foreign minister Ali Akbar Velayati announce that their nations have agreed to restore diplomatic relations. Iran and Iraq open their embassies October 14 in Baghdad and Tehran.

September 11. *Bush Addresses Congress.* In a televised speech to a joint session of Congress, President Bush explains his reasons for deploying American forces in Saudi Arabia. He says Iraq must not be allowed to annex Kuwait or dominate the vital Persian Gulf oil reserves. Bush also says that U.S. policy in the Gulf seeks "to curb the proliferation of chemical, biological, ballistic-missile and, above all, nuclear technologies." He reemphasizes that military action might be necessary if UN sanctions do not force Iraq from Kuwait and that Iraq's holding of Western hostages would not change American policy.

September 12. *Khamenei Says War Is Justified.* Despite reiterating Iran's support for UN sanctions against Iraq, Ayatollah Ali Khamenei, Iran's top spiritual leader, says an Islamic holy war is justified to oppose the U.S. military buildup in the Gulf. Khamenei implies that U.S. forces could become the target of Islamic terrorist attacks.

September 14-15. *France, Britain Increase Forces.* French president Francois Mitterand announces September 15 that France is increasing its troop strength in Saudi Arabia in response to Iraqi aggression against its embassy. He says 4,000 more troops (bringing the total number of French forces to 13,000) and additional warplanes, helicopters, and tanks will be sent to the Gulf. On September 14 Iraqi troops in Kuwait had searched the ambassadors' residences of France, Belgium, the Netherlands, and Canada. The Iraqis removed four French citizens from the French mission. They released one, but took into custody the other three, who had sought refuge at the mission. Great Britain announced September 14 that it was sending additional warplanes and its Seventh Armored Brigade, consisting of 8,000 troops and 120 tanks, to bolster its forces already in Saudi Arabia. Canada and Italy also announce September 14 that they are sending warplanes to the Gulf.

September 14-15. *Japan, Germany Announce Aid.* Responding to international criticism, especially from the United States, the Japanese government announces that it will provide an additional $3 billion in aid to the Gulf effort (it had previously pledged $1 billion); $2 billion of this would be economic aid to Egypt, Jordan, and Turkey. The West German government announces a $2 billion aid package September 15.

September 15. *Iraq Opens Kuwait-Saudi Border.* The Iraqi military, which previously had tightly controlled Kuwait's borders, allows thousands of Kuwaitis to cross into Saudi Arabia after taking their passports and other papers. Western officials speculate that the move is intended to help strengthen Iraq's control of and claim on Kuwait by reducing the Kuwaiti population. On September 17, Iraqi border guards begin detaining military-age Kuwaiti men who attempt to leave, causing the flow of Kuwaiti refugees to dwindle. Kuwaitis who reach Saudi Arabia claim that the Iraqi army is engaging in widespread torture and looting in Kuwait.

September 16. *Iraqi TV Shows Bush Video.* An eight-minute, unedited speech by President Bush is broadcast on Iraqi state-run television at 7:00 p.m. local time. On September 6, the Iraqi government had offered Bush the chance to speak on Iraqi television after the Bush administration complained that Saddam Hussein was getting extensive exposure on American television. Bush declined to be interviewed by an Iraqi film crew, but the White House

produced the videotaped speech and sent it to Baghdad. In his speech, Bush tells the Iraqi people that a broad international coalition, including most Arab states, opposes Iraq and that "there is no way Iraq can win." Bush says the United States has no quarrel with the Iraqi people, but that the Iraqi leadership has moved the Middle East to the brink of war. Bush's speech, which is broadcast unannounced, is followed immediately by an Iraqi rebuttal. Saddam Hussein replies to Bush in his own seventy-five-minute video, which is intended to be shown on American television networks. The Cable News Network airs it in full at 1:00 a.m. September 26. Other networks show only limited excerpts from it.

September 17. *Cheney Fires Dugan.* Air Force Chief of Staff Michael J. Dugan is fired by Secretary of Defense Cheney for poor judgment in discussing U.S. strategy for an attack on Iraq. Dugan had told *Washington Post* and *Los Angeles Times* reporters that the U.S. military had a contingency plan to "decapitate" the Iraqi leadership, including Saddam Hussein, and that the Israelis had advised the United States that the "best way to hurt Saddam" was by targeting him, his family, his mistress, and the soldiers that guarded him. Dugan also said the United States had plans to heavily bombard Baghdad in an effort to demoralize the Iraqis. Cheney and President Bush, who reportedly concurred in Cheney's decision, were concerned that Dugan's remarks about bombing Baghdad and targeting specific individuals would weaken international support for the American military effort in the Gulf. Bush administration officials emphasize that Dugan, the highest ranking officer to be relieved of duty since President Harry S Truman removed Gen. Douglas MacArthur in 1951, was not in the chain of command for Gulf operations.

September 17. *Saudi Arabia, USSR Restore Ties.* Saudi Arabia and the Soviet Union announce that they will restore diplomatic relations, which had been severed since 1938.

September 20. *Saudi Actions Against Jordan.* The Saudi government cuts off oil shipments to Jordan, citing Jordan's support for Iraq and its failure to pay for recent oil shipments. The Saudis also expel twenty Jordanian diplomats September 22. On September 19, the Jordanian government had appealed to the world community for more financial aid, saying the embargo against Iraq and Kuwait and the burden of receiving hundreds of thousands of refugees from Kuwait and Iraq could cause its economy to collapse.

September 22. *Final Hostage Flight Leaves Iraq.* The last flight carrying Western women and children who had chosen to leave Iraq and Kuwait arrives in London.

September 23. *Hussein Threatens Israel, Oilfields.* Saddam Hussein issues a statement threatening to attack Israel and the oilfields in Saudi Arabia and other Gulf states if Iraqis "are being strangled" by the UN economic embargo.

September 24. *Mitterand UN Speech.* President Mitterand tells the UN General Assembly that if Iraq withdrew from Kuwait and freed its foreign hostages "everything would be possible." He outlines a plan to achieve peace in the Middle East after an Iraqi withdrawal that includes international guarantees of "democratic expression" in Kuwait, regional arms control measures, and "an integrated approach" to settle the Arab-Israeli conflict and the Lebanese civil war.

September 25. *Shevardnadze UN Speech.* Foreign Minister Shevardnadze tells the UN General Assembly that his government would back military action sanctioned by the United Nations to force Iraq's withdrawal from Kuwait, if Iraq refused to leave peacefully.

September 25. *Security Council Extends Blockade.* The UN Security Council votes 14-1 to embargo air traffic to and from Iraq. Cuba casts the dissenting vote. The resolution says cargoes verified by inspectors to be humanitarian in nature are exempt from the embargo. Passenger flights by airlines other than Iraqi Airways also are exempt.

September 26. *Bush Taps Strategic Oil.* President Bush announces that in response to rising oil prices, he has approved the release of 5 million barrels of oil from the 590-million barrel U.S. Strategic Petroleum Reserve. The release was expected to have a minimal effect on the oil supply, but it was intended to demonstrate to speculators and the public that the United States was not in danger of experiencing an oil shortage.

September 27. *Emir Addresses General Assembly.* Speaking to the UN General Assembly, Sheik Jaber al-Ahmed al-Sabah condemns the brutality of the Iraqi occupation of Kuwait and asks the world community "not to waver" in efforts to force Iraq out of his country. He also claims that, counter to Iraqi propaganda, Kuwait devoted a higher percentage of its gross national product to foreign aid than any nation in the world. The emir discusses the Iraqi occupation and depopulation of his country with President Bush at the White House September 28. President Bush's national security adviser Brent Scowcroft says after the meeting that Iraq's "systematic destruction" of Kuwait is affecting the president's estimation of how long he could rely on the UN embargo to force an Iraqi withdrawal before resorting to a military offensive.

OCTOBER

October 1. *Bush Addresses General Assembly.* President Bush tells the UN General Assembly that he seeks a peaceful resolution to the Gulf crisis. During the speech he implies a willingness to link a settlement of the Gulf crisis to efforts to resolve the Arab-Israeli conflict. He says if Iraq withdrew from Kuwait, "I truly believe there may be opportunities . . . for all the states and the peoples of the region to settle the conflicts that divide the Arabs and the Israelis." At a news conference following the speech, however, Bush rejects any linkage between the two issues.

October 2. *Congress Supports Bush Policy.* The Senate votes 96-3 for a joint resolution supporting President Bush's Persian Gulf policy to date. The House had passed the resolution 380-29 the day before. Members of both houses emphasize that the votes in no way sanction future presidential actions or offensive military operations against Iraq.

October 3. *Hussein Visits Kuwait.* During his first known visit to Kuwait since the invasion, Saddam Hussein discounts coalition military strength and declares, "There will be no compromise. Iraq will never give up one inch of this land now called Province Nineteen."

October 5. *Primakov Meets Hussein.* On the second day of a visit to Baghdad, Yevgenii Primakov, a Middle East expert and adviser to President Gorbachev, meets with Saddam Hussein. Primakov gives Hussein a message from Gorbachev urging the Iraqi leader to comply with the UN resolutions. Primakov also seeks and receives assurances from Hussein that 5,000 Soviet citizens in Iraq will be allowed to leave.

October 5. *Iraqi Offers No Concession at the UN.* In his address to the UN General Assembly, Iraq's deputy UN representative, Sabah Talat Kadrat, condemns the United States and its allies for practicing imperialism. Western officials had speculated that the Iraqis might use the speech to put forward a diplomatic initiative.

October 7. *Israelis to Receive Gas Masks.* The Israeli government begins distributing gas masks to its entire population in preparation for a possible gas attack by Iraq.

October 8. *Israeli Police Kill Palestinians.* Israeli police respond with automatic weapons fire to an attack in Jerusalem by thousands of Palestinian stone throwers. Between nineteen and twenty-one Palestinians are reported killed (the highest number of casualties in any single incident since the beginning of the Palestinian intifada in 1987) and as many as 150 are injured. Some twenty to thirty Israelis are injured by the stones. Israeli and Palestinian accounts of the hour-long clash and its results differ widely. Western press reports state that Palestinians on the Haram al-Sharif (known to Jews as the Temple Mount) pelted Jewish worshipers and Israeli police with rocks at the Western Wall. The worshipers withdrew from the area while the police were reinforced. Then the police stormed the Haram al-Sharif, firing upon the crowd to break up the riot. The Israeli government says the police acted in self defense and accuses Palestinian leaders of inciting the riot. Palestinians claim that the use of deadly force by the police was unnecessary and indiscriminate. Many nations, including the United States, criticize Israel for using excessive force. Saddam Hussein reacts to the killings by threatening October 9 to attack Israel with long-range missiles.

October 9. *U.S. Proposes Resolution.* The United States proposes a UN Security Council resolution condemning Israel for the shootings in Jerusalem the day before. Bush administration officials hope the resolution will preempt efforts by other nations to propose a tougher resolution that it might have to veto. They fear that such a veto would alienate the Arab members of the anti-Iraq coalition.

October 10. *Shamir Appoints Commission.* Prime Minister Yitzhak Shamir appoints a three-person independent commission to investigate the October 8 clash between Palestinians and Israeli police in Jerusalem. The commission is not given the power of subpoena.

October 12. *Resolution 672 Passes.* The UN Security Council votes 15-0 in favor of a resolution drafted by the United States condemning Israel. The vote follows four days of furious diplomacy by U.S. officials to prevent a resolution supported by the PLO from being brought to a vote. Resolution 672 criticizes both the Israeli security police and the Palestinian rioters, but "condemns especially the acts of violence" committed by the police. The resolution also provides for a fact-finding mission to be sent to Israel to investigate the Jerusalem clash. It is the first UN resolution condemning Israel that receives U.S. backing since 1982, when Israel invaded Lebanon. The Israeli cabinet votes unanimously October 14 not to cooperate with the UN investigative mission.

October 13. *Aoun Abandons Struggle.* Lebanese Christian leader Gen. Michel Aoun ends his fight against Syrian forces and the Lebanese government and takes refuge in the French embassy in Beirut following heavy Syrian-led attacks against his army. For more than two years, Aoun and his supporters had refused to submit to the rule of the Syrian-backed Lebanese government. Aoun's defeat is a blow to Iraq, which had provided the general's forces with weapons as a means of opposing Syrian goals in Lebanon and punishing President Hafez al-Assad for his support of Iran during the Iran-Iraq war.

October 14. *Soviets on Possible Settlement.* The Soviet *Novosti* press agency maintains that, during talks with Soviet envoy Yevgenii Primakov, Saddam Hussein had indicated a willingness to withdraw from Kuwait if Iraq received control of the Rumaila oilfield and Bubiyan and Warbah islands. The official Iraqi news agency denies that Iraq would accept such a deal. Secretary of State Baker says October 16 that Iraq must completely and unconditionally withdraw from Kuwait before talks on any other issues can begin.

October 15. *Kuwaitis Call for Liberation.* A conference of one thousand Kuwaiti exiles in Saudi Arabia calls on the UN Security Council to liberate their country. The gathering also denounces the PLO for its pro-Iraqi stand during the crisis. The crown prince of Kuwait, Sheik Saad al Abdullah al-Sabah, told the conference October 13 that after liberation, the Kuwaiti parliament would be restored, free parliamentary elections would be held, and the role of women in society would be enhanced.

October 18. *Arab League Defeats PLO Resolution.* At a meeting in Tunis, the Arab League votes 11-10 to defeat a resolution written by the PLO condemning U.S. policy toward Palestinians. After the vote the PLO and its supporters in the Arab League walk out of the meeting in symbolic protest. Later the Arab League passes a resolution condemning only Israel.

October 19. *Iraq Rations Gasoline.* The Iraqi government announces that it will begin rationing gasoline. On October 28 Saddam Hussein rescinds the rationing plan and fires his oil minister. Western observers speculate that the Iraqi leadership may have adopted the rationing to convince the coalition that its sanctions were working, thereby decreasing the chances that the coalition would decide to go to war. Under this scenario, a change of strategy or domestic discontent that reportedly surfaced because of the rationing may have caused Hussein to reverse the decision.

October 20. *Antiwar Protests.* Opponents to the U.S. military buildup in the Persian Gulf gather in numerous U.S. cities for the first organized nationwide antiwar protest since the crisis began. Crowds number in the hundreds in most cities, but in New York City the protest draws at least 5,000 and perhaps as many as 20,000 marchers.

October 21. *Palestinian Kills Three Israelis.* In an apparent reprisal for the killing of twenty-one Palestinians by Israeli police October 8, a Palestinian stabs to death three Israelis in West Jerusalem before being wounded and captured. A spokesman for Prime Minister Shamir says the UN Security Council condemnation of Israel had a role in inciting the attack. After the October 8 clash, Israeli-Palestinian violence had escalated throughout the occupied territories.

October 21. *Saudis Act Against Yemenis.* In response to Yemen's support for Iraq, the Saudi government revokes the residency privileges of Yemenis. The move leads to an acceleration of the Yemeni exodus from Saudi Arabia (350,000 Yemenis already had returned home).

October 22. *Saudi Hints of Compromise.* Saudi defense minister Prince Sultan ibn Abdul Aziz Al Saud is reported to have told Arab journalists "The Arab countries are ready to give Iraq all its rights." He cites previous Saudi territorial settlements with Iraq and the United Arab Emirates as evidence that Arab nations can work out their disputes peacefully. However, Prince Sultan rejects any settlement that does not provide for Iraq's unconditional withdrawal from Kuwait and the restoration of the Kuwaiti government. The comments, which were made October 21, create speculation that the Saudis favor a negotiated settlement with Saddam Hussein. Saudi officials assure the United States that Prince Sultan's comments do not reflect Saudi government policy. President Bush October 23 rejects any compromise that would reward Iraqi aggression. King Fahd October 26 prohibits Saudi government and military officials from making conciliatory statements toward Iraq.

October 24. *UN Casts Second Vote Against Israel.* The UN Security Council votes 15-0 to deplore Israel's refusal to accept a UN mission intended to investigate the October 8 killing of as many as twenty-one Palestinians by Israeli police. The United States joins in the vote after Prime Minister Shamir refuses President Bush's personal request that Israel cooperate with the mission.

October 25. *Soviets Pessimistic on Diplomacy.* Soviet representatives tell nonaligned Security Council members that Soviet envoy Yevgenii Primakov has detected no sign that Saddam Hussein is interested in a diplomatic settlement to the Gulf crisis that would require him to give up any of Kuwait.

October 26. *Israeli Commission Issues Report.* An Israeli government commission concludes that Israeli police were justified in firing upon Arab rioters on the Temple Mount in Jerusalem October 8. The commission's report blames the violence on the Palestinian rioters and the political and religious leaders who it says incited them. The report exonerates the police, but criticizes two police commanders for ignoring intelligence reports predicting the clash and failing to have enough officers on the scene. The commission also cites "the immediate need to develop alternatives to the use of live ammunition." The Israeli cabinet endorses the report October 28. The United States says October 30 that it still believes the Israeli police used excessive force. One of the police commanders criticized by the report, Aryeh Bibi, is promoted November 12.

October 28. *Soviet Diplomacy.* Soviet envoy Yevgenii Primakov meets with Saddam Hussein in Baghdad. President Gorbachev announces October 29 that Primakov had reported some flexibility in Hussein's position. In Moscow October 31, Primakov says he believes Hussein has become more willing to seek a diplomatic solution to the Gulf crisis.

October 29. *Security Council Passes Resolution.* The UN Security Council votes 13-0 (Cuba and Yemen abstain) in favor of a resolution declaring Iraq liable for damages, injuries, and financial losses caused by its aggression against Kuwait. The measure tells UN members to collect information on their claims and on Iraqi war crimes. The resolution also demands that Iraq release all foreigners and end its siege of embassies in Kuwait.

October 30. *Two Embassies Hold Out in Kuwait.* France evacuates its last diplomatic personnel from Kuwait, leaving only the besieged British and American embassies in operation.

NOVEMBER

November 1. *Bush Softens Comments.* On a campaign trip to Orlando, Florida, President Bush says that he wants "a peaceful resolution" to the Gulf crisis and that he is "prepared to give sanctions time to work." During the previous week Bush and Secretary of State Baker had engaged in scathing anti-Iraqi rhetoric that caused observers to speculate that the administration was preparing the nation for war.

November 3. *Baker Trip.* Secretary of State Baker begins an eight-day trip to solidify international support for the U.S.-led coalition opposing Iraq. After visiting with U.S. troops in the Gulf, he shuttles to Bahrain, Saudi Arabia, Egypt, Turkey, the Soviet Union, Great Britain, and France. While in Cairo, Baker meets with Chinese foreign minister Qian Qichen, who indicates that China would not veto a Security Council resolution authorizing the use of force to drive Iraq from Kuwait.

November 5. *U.S.-Saudi Military Command Agreement.* King Fahd and Secretary of State Baker agree on a military command and control agreement during talks in Saudi Arabia. The plan provides for overall Saudi command of the defense of Saudi Arabia, but overall U.S. command if the coalition forces launch an offensive against Iraq. Any attack against Iraq would have to be approved by both the United States and Saudi Arabia.

November 8. *Bush Announces Deployments.* President Bush announces that he is ordering a huge increase in U.S. military forces in the Persian Gulf region "to insure that the coalition has an adequate offensive military option should that be necessary to achieve our common goals." Neither Bush nor Secretary of Defense Cheney say how many troops will be sent, but reports indicate it will be close to 200,000 more troops, bringing the total number of U.S. forces in the region to approximately 430,000 by early 1991. Cheney says November 9 that the Pentagon has dropped a troop rotation plan that would have shifted fresh troops into Saudi Arabia, allowing others to return home after a designated period.

November 11. *Congressional Response to Plan.* Senate Armed Services Committee Chairman Sam Nunn (D-Ga.) says the administration's new troop deployments and its cancellation of troop rotation plans could force the United States into a war before sanctions have had a chance to work. House Armed Services Committee Chairman Les Aspin (D-Wis.), however, expresses his support for the president's plan. During the following week, several leading lawmakers, including Richard G. Lugar (R-Ind.) and Edward M. Kennedy (D-Mass.), call for a special session of Congress to debate the administration's Gulf strategy. President Bush meets with a bipartisan group of members of Congress November 14. He tells them that he has not made a decision to go to war against Iraq and that he will consult closely with Congress on the issue.

November 15. *Hussein Interview.* In an interview with ABC News' Peter Jennings, Saddam Hussein says he is ready for negotiations with the nations that oppose him, but he rejects an unconditional Iraqi withdrawal from Kuwait as a precondition to talks.

November 18. *Hussein Hostage Offer.* Saddam Hussein offers to release all foreigners between December 25 and March 25, 1991. Analysts say the offer appears to be intended to forestall a coalition attack during the winter months when cooler weather would provide more favorable conditions for an offensive. The Bush administration calls for the immediate release of all hostages.

November 19. *Iraqi Troop Deployments.* Iraq claims that it will deploy as many as 250,000 more troops in Kuwait and southern Iraq. U.S. military officials say that most of the additional troops Iraq could deploy in the region are poorly trained reservists.

November 21-22. *Bush Visits Saudi Arabia.* President Bush travels to Saudi Arabia to spend Thanksgiving with U.S. troops. He meets on November 21 with King Fahd and Sheik Jaber al-Ahmed al-Sabah in Jiddah before touring four U.S. military posts November 22.

November 23. *Bush, Assad Meet.* President Bush meets with President Assad in Geneva to discuss the coalition's effort against Iraq. Bush's willingness to meet with Assad is criticized by some observers because of evidence that Assad has supported terrorists in the past. Bush says he would "work with" any country that opposes Iraq.

November 27-29. *Senate Armed Services Hearings.* Several prominent officials from previous administrations testify before the Senate Armed Services Committee that the United States should not rush into a war with Iraq. James Schlesinger, former defense secretary and CIA director, says he believes the chances of the sanctions forcing Iraq out of Kuwait are "very, very high." Former chairmen of the Joint Chiefs of Staff, retired Gen. David Jones and retired Adm. William Crowe, Jr., testify November 28 that the United States should give sanctions more time to work before launching an offensive. The same day, however, former secretary of state Henry Kissinger testifies that only military force can drive Iraq from Kuwait. Former assistant secretary of defense Richard Perle agrees with Kissinger November 29.

November 29. *Security Council Authorizes Force.* The UN Security Council passes Resolution 678 by a 12-2 vote. It authorizes coalition forces in the Persian Gulf region to use "all necessary means" to expel Iraq from Kuwait if Iraq does not withdraw by January 15. Yemen and Cuba vote against the resolution. China (which, as a permanent member of the Security Council, could have vetoed the resolution) abstains. The resolution is the first UN authorization to wage war against a member nation since 1950, when the Security Council called on members to help defend South Korea against the North Korean invasion.

November 30. *Bush Offers Talks.* Armed with the Security Council's approval of the use of force against Iraq, President Bush proposes at a White House news conference that Foreign Minister Aziz come to Washington in mid-December and Secretary of State Baker go to Baghdad "between December 15 and January 15" in an effort to achieve a peaceful resolution to the Gulf crisis. Bush says he will continue to demand Iraq's unconditional withdrawal from Kuwait, but says he wants to "go the extra mile for peace." The president also insists that if war comes, it will not be like the Vietnam War. American soldiers, he says, "will have enough force . . . to win, and then get out as soon as possible, as soon as the UN objectives have been achieved. I will never, ever agree to a halfway effort." On December 1, Iraq accepts in principle Bush's call for an exchange of foreign ministers.

DECEMBER

December 4. *Iraq Permits Soviets to Leave.* After Moscow reportedly threatens to use military force against Iraq, the Iraqi government announces that the more than 3,000 Soviet citizens still in Iraq may leave if the USSR will compensate Iraq for financial losses resulting from the departure of Soviet workers under contract. Moscow says

December 5 that it is willing to discuss the issue.

December 5. *Levy Warns of Israeli Attack.* Israeli foreign minister David Levy says the threat of Iraqi military capabilities might force Israel to attack Iraq if the anti-Iraq coalition does not.

December 5. *Webster Testifies.* William Webster, director of the Central Intelligence Agency, testifies before the House Armed Services Committee on the progress of sanctions being employed against Iraq. He says that the embargo is hurting the Iraqi economy and that the lack of spare parts and other supplies would begin to degrade the Iraqi air force's capabilities after three months and the Iraqi army's capabilities after nine months. He cautions, however, that "economic hardships" cannot guarantee that Hussein will change his policies.

December 6. *Hussein to Release All Hostages.* Saddam Hussein informs the Iraqi National Assembly that all foreigners held by Iraq will be freed. Hostages begin leaving Iraq December 8 on special Iraqi Airways flights chartered by Western nations. Middle East analysts speculate that Hussein freed the hostages in a bid to soften world opinion toward Iraq and because he was convinced that keeping the hostages might provoke instead of deter a coalition attack.

December 7. *Kuwait Embassy to Be Evacuated.* The State Department announces that all diplomatic personnel will be evacuated from the U.S. Embassy in Kuwait after Americans who want to leave the country have gone.

December 8. *Iraq Proposes Late Meeting Date.* The Iraqi government announces that Foreign Minister Aziz is ready to visit Washington December 17 and invites Secretary of State Baker to meet with Saddam Hussein in Baghdad January 12. Hussein's busy schedule is cited as the reason for the late date offered for the Baghdad meeting. The Bush administration December 9 objects to the date, insisting that any meeting take place by January 3. White House officials say that a January 12 meeting would not allow enough time for Iraq to completely withdraw from Kuwait by January 15. They also scorn the excuse that Hussein cannot find time to meet with Baker.

December 11. *Bush, Shamir Meet.* President Bush and Prime Minister Shamir meet in Washington to repair damage done to the U.S.-Israeli relationship by Israel's policies toward the occupied territories and U.S. support for UN Security Council resolutions condemning Israel. After the meeting, Shamir says he received Bush's assurances that the United States would not support an international conference on the Arab-Israeli issue or other concessions to the Palestinians in return for an Iraqi pullout from Kuwait. Shamir meets December 12 with Foreign Minister Shevardnadze, who is in Washington.

December 12. *Hussein Replaces Defense Minister.* Saddam Hussein fires his defense minister, Gen. Abdel Jabar Khalil Shanshal, and replaces him with Maj. Gen. Saadi Tuma Abbas, who had distinguished himself by commanding forces defending Basra during the Iran-Iraq war.

December 13. *Last Hostage Flight Leaves Iraq.* The last U.S.-chartered flight carrying Americans and other Westerners from Iraq flies to Frankfurt, Germany. Among the passengers are the five remaining members of the U.S. embassy staff in Kuwait, including Ambassador W. Nathaniel Howell III. Great Britain evacuated its embassy staff December 12. The State Department said December 11 that more than 500 Americans, some with dual citizenship, decided to remain in Iraq or Kuwait.

December 14. *U.S., Iraq Spar over Meeting Date.* The Iraqi government announces that Foreign Minister Aziz will not go to Washington until the United States and Iraq agree on a date for a meeting in Baghdad between Secretary of State Baker and Saddam Hussein. That same day President Bush backs away from a meeting with Aziz unless Baghdad agrees to receive Baker by January 3. Bush ridicules Iraq's excuse that Hussein is too busy to see Baker by listing the foreign visitors that Hussein has received recently: "Saddam Hussein is not too busy to see ... Kurt Waldheim, Willy Brandt, Muhammad Ali, Ted Heath, John Connally, Ramsey Clark and many, many others on very short notice."

December 18. *EC Cancels Meeting.* The foreign ministers of the European Community vote to cancel a meeting between Italian foreign minister Gianni De Michelis, the current EC president, and Foreign Minister Aziz. The action is intended to present Iraq with a united front in the wake of the refusal by Iraq to schedule talks with the United States before January 3. France, Greece, Italy, and Spain vote in favor of holding the De Michelis-Aziz meeting.

December 19. *Allied Readiness Questioned.* The deputy commander of American forces in the Gulf, Lt. Gen. Calvin A. H. Waller, tells reporters that there is a "distinct possibility that every unit will not be fully combat-ready until some time after February 1." Waller says that troops might not be matched up with their equipment and in position at the front until as late as mid-February. Administration officials later discount the general's assessment, saying that the coalition forces will be ready to launch an attack anytime after the January 15 deadline passes. The administration is concerned that Waller's statements had undermined their strategy of convincing Saddam Hussein that he must have all his forces out of Kuwait by the deadline or face imminent attack.

December 20. *Shevardnadze Resigns.* In a speech to the Congress of People's Deputies, Soviet foreign minister Eduard Shevardnadze warns against the growing threat of tyranny in the Soviet Union and announces his surprise resignation. Shevardnadze had been a strong supporter of the UN efforts against Iraq.

December 20. *U.S. Joins Third Vote Against Israel.* The United States votes in favor of a UN Security Council resolution condemning Israeli treatment of Arabs in the occupied West Bank and Gaza Strip and calling for the secretary general to monitor the safety of Arabs there. The resolution, which referred to the occupied territories as "Palestinian territories," was introduced by nonaligned countries for the PLO. The United States had worked to soften the resolution and had been successful in deleting a statement supporting an international conference on the Middle East.

December 22. *U.S. Sailors Die When Ferry Sinks.* Twenty U.S. sailors drown when a ferry carrying more than a hundred sailors back to the aircraft carrier *Saratoga* from a shore leave in Haifa, Israel, sinks in rough waters. The carrier was stationed in the eastern Mediterranean as part of operations in the Persian Gulf region. From August to the beginning of hostilities in January, nearly one hundred U.S. military personnel are killed in accidents related to Operation Desert Shield.

December 28. *U.S. Announces Inoculations.* The Defense Department announces that some U.S. troops in Saudi Arabia will be vaccinated against possible attack by Iraqi biological weapons.

December 31. *Israeli Air Force Targets PLO.* Israeli

warplanes bomb a PLO stronghold in Lebanon, reportedly killing twelve members of Yasir Arafat's Fatah faction. It is the twenty-first time in 1990 that Israel has attacked targets in Lebanon.

JANUARY 1991

January 2. *NATO Sends Jets to Turkey.* The North Atlantic Treaty Organization (NATO) announces that it will send forty-two warplanes to alliance member Turkey to strengthen 100,000 Turkish troops on the Iraqi frontier. Among the NATO warplanes are eighteen German jets. They are the first military forces in post-World War II history that Bonn has deployed outside Germany. During January, Turkey reinforces its border with an additional 80,000 troops. Iraq reportedly has 120,000 troops facing Turkey in northern Iraq.

January 3. *Bush Proposes Meeting.* After weeks of diplomatic stalemate, President Bush proposes that Secretary of State Baker and Foreign Minister Aziz meet in Geneva in an effort to settle the Gulf crisis. He leaves open the possibility that Baker might then travel to Baghdad afterwards to meet with Saddam Hussein. On January 4, Iraq accepts Bush's offer of talks in Geneva, which then are scheduled for January 9. Bush, however, rules out the possibility that Baker might go on to Baghdad for talks with Saddam Hussein. Administration officials say the president believes a Baghdad meeting would be used by Iraq to stall for time.

January 4. *U.S. Delays Saudi Arms Sale.* The Bush administration postpones a proposed $13 billion arms sale to Saudi Arabia until after the Persian Gulf crisis is over. The administration sought to avoid a devisive debate in Congress over the sale. Some members of Congress had complained that weapons involved in the sale would not arrive in time to be used in a conflict with Iraq, but could be used against Israel in the future. Saudi officials concurred in the decision to delay consideration of the sale.

January 4. *Security Council Condemns Israel.* The United States joins with other Security Council members in condemning Israel for its treatment of the Palestinians. The unanimous vote is a response to Israel's use of force during increasingly violent confrontations between Israeli security police and soldiers and Palestinian protesters. The Security Council resolution is the fourth condemning Israel since October.

January 8. *Bush Asks Congress to Back Force.* In a letter to congressional leaders, President Bush asks Congress to pass a resolution authorizing him to use military force to expel Iraqi forces from Kuwait.

January 8. *Aspin Predicts Victory.* House Armed Services Committee Chairman Aspin tells a news conference that coalition forces would likely defeat Iraqi forces in less than a month and with relatively few casualties. Aspin says the offensive would begin with a massive bombing campaign that would soften up Iraqi forces before a ground assault would finish the task. He predicts 3,000 to 5,000 American casualties, with 500 to 1,000 dead.

January 9. *Baker and Aziz Meet.* Secretary of State Baker and Foreign Minister Aziz meet in Geneva to seek a resolution to the Gulf crisis. The two diplomats meet for six and a half hours before emerging to tell a huge press corps that no progress had been made. At the beginning of the meeting Aziz refuses to accept a letter from President Bush to Saddam Hussein. He says after the meeting that it was not "compatible with the language which should be used in corresponding between heads of state." Aziz also says after the meeting that Iraq would definitely attack Israel if coalition forces attack Iraq.

January 12. *Congress Authorizes Force.* Following three days of intense debate, the U.S. Congress votes to give President Bush the authority to wage war against Iraq. The Senate passes the measure 52-47 to approve the use of "all means necessary" to expel Iraq from Kuwait. The House passes it 250-183. President Bush praises the action, saying it demonstrates U.S. resolve.

January 12. *Iraqi Diplomats Expelled.* All but four of Iraq's diplomats working at the Iraqi embassy in Washington, D.C. are expelled from the country. The State Department claims that the action was taken "to reduce Iraq's ability to orchestrate terrorism."

January 13. *Pérez de Cuéllar Unsuccessful.* Secretary General Javier Pérez de Cuéllar meets for two and a half hours with Saddam Hussein in Baghdad in a last-ditch effort to convince him to withdraw his forces from Kuwait. Pérez de Cuéllar reports that Hussein is determined not to budge. Hussein tells a group of Arab newspaper editors that "any last-minute chances for peace must come from them, not us." UN officials later disclose that Hussein had made Pérez de Cuéllar wait for six hours before seeing him.

January 14. *Iraqi Assembly Calls for Holy War.* The National Assembly, Iraq's rubber-stamp parliament, votes unanimously to support President Saddam Hussein in the Gulf crisis. It calls for a "holy war" in defense of Kuwait.

January 14. *French Peace Proposal.* France puts forward an eleventh-hour peace proposal calling for an immediate, unconditional Iraqi withdrawal to be followed by an international peace conference on the Middle East. The proposal is supported by many Arab and European nations, but the United States and Great Britain reject it as linking an Iraqi pullout to the Arab-Israeli issue. Iraq ignores the French proposal.

January 14. *PLO Officials Assassinated.* Two high-ranking PLO officials of the mainline Fatah faction headed by Yasir Arafat are assassinated in Tunis by one of their bodyguards. The PLO initially blames Israel, which denies any involvement in the slayings. The assassin is subsequently revealed to have had ties with a rival faction of the PLO headed by Abu Nidal.

January 15. *Bush Issues Order for Attack.* During a morning meeting with his advisers, President Bush signs an executive order authorizing an attack on Iraq unless last-minute diplomatic progress is made.

January 15-16. *British, French Back War.* The House of Commons votes 534-57 to endorse the British government's policy of joining the international coalition in using force to compel Iraq to leave Kuwait. The French National Assembly January 16 approves the use of force against Iraq 523-43.

January 16. *Deadline Passes.* At 8:00 a.m. in Saudi Arabia (12:00 midnight EST January 15) the deadline for Iraq to withdraw from Kuwait passes.

January 17. *Coalition Forces Attack.* At 12:50 a.m. in Saudi Arabia (4:50 p.m. EST January 16) the first wave of allied warplanes takes off from Saudi airfields on their way to targets in Iraq and Kuwait. In addition, cruise missiles are launched from American ships in the Persian Gulf and Red Sea. At 2:35 a.m. Western television reporters in Baghdad report that the city is under attack. A half hour later the White House announces that coalition forces have begun the process of liberating Kuwait. Early military reports from Saudi Arabia are overwhelmingly positive. More than 1,000 sorties are flown in the first fourteen hours of the operation. During that time, just four allied planes—one American, one Kuwaiti, and two British—are downed by Iraqi antiaircraft guns or surface-to-air missiles. Only a handful of Iraqi warplanes reach the skies, either because of bombed airfields or because Iraqi commanders hold them back. Coalition warplanes strike Iraqi power stations, radar installations, communications centers, nuclear research facilities, chemical and biological weapons plants, antiaircraft weapons, Scud missile sites, air bases, and other targets. President Bush explains his decision to go to war in a nationally televised address from the Oval Office at 9:00 p.m. EST January 16, two and a half hours after the bombs began to fall. He says, "The United States, together with the United Nations, exhausted every means at our disposal to bring this crisis to a peaceful end." On Wall Street, the morning after the attack, the Dow Jones industrial average rises 115 points—the second biggest point gain in the history of the index. Meanwhile oil prices, which had been expected to skyrocket once a war was launched, fell almost $11.00, the largest drop in a single day ever, to $21.44 on the New York Mercantile Exchange. The surprising plunge is a reaction to the stunning success of the initial coalition bombing raids and a realization by traders that the Iraqi military would probably not be able to inflict damage upon Saudi Arabia's vast oil facilities.

January 18. *Iraq Hits Israel with Scuds.* At 2:15 a.m. (7:15 p.m. EST January 17) Iraq launches a salvo of eight Scud missiles armed with conventional high explosive warheads at Tel Aviv and Haifa. Original reports that at least one of the missiles carried chemical weapons prove false. Three of the missiles fall harmlessly in open areas, but five cause damage. Fifteen Israelis are injured, but no one is killed by the Scuds. The improper use of gas masks, however, reportedly causes the suffocation of four Israelis. Israel does not retaliate against Iraq, but Israeli officials say they may do so. President Bush urges Israel not to retaliate and promises that coalition forces would mount "the darnedest search and destroy mission that's ever been undertaken" against the remaining mobile Scud missile launchers in Western Iraq. Iraq also launches one Scud missile at Saudi Arabia in the early hours of January 18. It is intercepted and destroyed by a U.S. Army Patriot antimissile missile.

January 18. *U.S. Planes Strike Iraq from Turkey.* American warplanes based at Turkey's Incirlik air base begin bombing Iraqi targets. At the urging of President Turgut Ozal, Turkey's parliament January 17 had authorized the United States to launch air attacks against Iraq from its territory.

January 18. *Riyadh Briefing.* Gen. H. Norman Schwarzkopf, commander of all coalition forces, and Lt. Gen. Charles A. Horner, commander of the U.S. Air Force in the Persian Gulf, brief reporters in Riyadh on the progress of the air war. They say seven coalition aircraft have been downed. Horner shows film of successful laser-guided bombing runs against Iraqi targets, including the headquarters of the Iraqi Air Force.

January 19. *Patriots Sent to Israel.* After four more Scud missiles strike Israel at dawn, American Patriot antimissile missiles and their army crews arrive in the Jewish state. These U.S. forces are the first combat personnel ever deployed in Israel. President Bush had offered the Israeli government the Patriots as part of his effort to avert Israeli

retaliation for Iraqi Scud missile attacks on the Jewish state. Deputy Secretary of State Lawrence Eagleburger meets with Prime Minister Shamir in Jerusalem January 21. Shamir pledges to consult with the United States before launching any retaliation against Iraq for its missile attacks.

January 19. *Americans React to the War.* Protesters in San Francisco and Washington, D.C., stage the biggest antiwar rallies since U.S. military deployments to Saudi Arabia began. The crowd in Washington is estimated at 25,000, while the gathering in San Francisco reportedly draws 35,000. Another antiwar rally in Washington January 26 draws 75,000 people, according to police estimates. Organizers of the rally say more than 200,000 people attended. In a *New York Times*/CBS News poll taken January 17-20 and published January 22, 82 percent of Americans who were surveyed approved of the way President Bush has handled the Gulf crisis and 75 percent approved of his decision to begin a war against Iraq.

January 20. *Hussein Address.* Saddam Hussein says in a radio address that Iraq has used only a fraction of its military arsenal against the coalition. Hussein's speech and the absence of Iraqi warplanes from the conflict lead many observers to speculate that Hussein is saving his combat aircraft until a ground war begins.

January 20. *Iraq Displays Prisoners.* Iraqi television broadcasts interviews with seven prisoners (three of whom are Americans) identified as coalition pilots. The prisoners, who denounce the war against Iraq, appear dazed and have bruises on their faces. The Iraqi government January 21 declares that captured pilots will be housed at strategic military and scientific sites that might be coalition bombing targets. The same day, President Bush denounces Iraq's "brutal parading of allied pilots." Iraq broadcasts videotape of two more U.S. prisoners January 22.

January 21. *Arabs on Israeli Retaliation.* In interviews with reporters, Egyptian and Saudi officials indicate that they would not leave the anti-Iraq coalition if Israel retaliated in proper proportion for Iraqi missile attacks against Israeli cities. The Arab officials, however, express their hope that Israel would not take such action.

January 21-23. *Patriots Knock Down Scuds.* During a three-day period, Iraq launches twenty-one Scud missiles at Saudi Arabia. American Patriot missiles destroy seventeen of the Scuds. The other four land in open areas or the Persian Gulf, resulting in no casualties.

January 22. *Deadly Scud Attack on Israel.* An Iraqi Scud missile strikes a residential area in Tel Aviv, reportedly killing three people and wounding more than sixty. A Patriot missile had struck the incoming Scud but failed to destroy it.

January 22. *Israel Requests Aid.* During a meeting with Deputy Secretary of State Eagleburger, Israeli finance minister Yitzhak Modai says that because of expenses related to the Persian Gulf crisis and the settlement of hundreds of thousands of Jewish immigrants from the Soviet Union, Israel needs $13 billion in additional aid from the United States.

January 23. *Powell Briefing.* At a Pentagon briefing, chairman of the Joint Chiefs of Staff Gen. Colin Powell claims that the coalition has achieved "air superiority." He also says that Iraq's nuclear reactors have been completely destroyed and no Iraqi warplane has attacked a single coalition ground target. Powell describes the coalition plan to defeat the Iraqi army in Kuwait: "First, we're going to cut it off, then we're going to kill it."

January 24. *Air War Continues without Pause.* A Saudi F-15 fighter destroys two Iraqi jets armed with Exocet antiship missiles on their way to attack coalition warships in the Persian Gulf. French planes bomb targets inside Iraq for the first time (previously the French government had allowed its planes to strike targets only in occupied Kuwait). Canadian warplanes fly their first combat missions of the conflict. Qatari warplanes had flown their first missions January 22.

January 24. *Kaifu Proposes Aid.* Japanese premier Toshiki Kaifu proposes that Japan contribute an additional $9 billion to the Gulf war effort. Japan had already pledged $4 billion.

January 25. *U.S. Accuses Iraq of Spilling Oil.* The United States accuses Iraq of "environmental terrorism," saying that Iraq has created the largest oil spill in history by deliberately leaking oil into the Persian Gulf. Officials say satellite photographs indicate the oil spill began January 23. Iraq claims the spill was caused by coalition bombing attacks against Iraqi tankers. In angry statements to reporters, President Bush asserts the spill would give Iraq "no military advantage whatsoever." American military officials, however, say it could complicate an amphibious landing in Kuwait. Gen. Schwarzkopf states January 26 that Iraq had created the spill by releasing oil from Iraqi supertankers and from a Kuwaiti refinery complex. On January 27 U.S. warplanes bomb parts of the complex, successfully cutting off the flow of oil into the sea. The spill, which covers an estimated 350 square miles, threatens Persian Gulf wildlife and desalinization plants in Saudi Arabia.

January 26. *Iraqi Planes Flee to Iran.* The Pentagon says at least twenty-four Iraqi planes have fled to the safety of Iran. On January 30 Gen. Schwarzkopf says the number of Iraqi aircraft seeking shelter in Iran had risen to eighty-nine. American military officials claim Saddam Hussein is trying to save his best planes from coalition raids against Iraqi airfields and hardened aircraft shelters. Tehran maintains that the planes will not be returned to Iraq until the war is over. At the end of the war, a total of 137 Iraqi aircraft had fled to Iran.

January 29. *Baker-Bessmertnykh Statement.* At the end of a four-day meeting in Washington, D.C., Secretary of State Baker and Soviet foreign minister Aleksandr Bessmertnykh issue a joint statement that appears to link an Iraqi withdrawal from Kuwait to U.S. and Soviet efforts to promote an Arab-Israeli peace settlement. Though Bessmertnykh claims the statement is "important," the White House denies any change in President Bush's demand that Iraq withdraw from Kuwait unconditionally. Baker and Bessmertnykh announced January 28 that they had agreed to postpone a summit meeting between President Bush and President Gorbachev scheduled for February 11-13 in Moscow. The two sides said the meeting has been delayed until sometime later in the "first half" of 1991 because of the Gulf war and the failure of U.S.-Soviet talks to produce a final treaty on strategic nuclear weapons reductions. Neither side mentioned U.S. concerns about Moscow's recent crackdown on Baltic pro-independence demonstrators.

January 29. *Battle of Khafji.* In the first major ground engagement of the war, three Iraqi tank battalions cross the Saudi border and occupy the deserted town of Khafji. The attack coincides with other smaller Iraqi incursions along the Saudi-Kuwaiti border. Iraq portrays the campaign as a major victory. By the evening of January 31,

however, Saudi, Qatari, and U.S. forces retake the town. Eighteen Saudis and eleven U.S. Marines are reported killed in the fighting. An investigation subsequently reveals that seven of the Marines were killed when an American warplane accidently fired upon their armored vehicle. The coalition reports capturing 500 Iraqi prisoners and destroying 42 Iraqi tanks in the battle. Gen. Schwarzkopf says January 31 that the clash was "as significant as a mosquito on an elephant."

January 29. *Germany Pledges More Aid.* The German government pledges an additional $5.5 billion in aid for the Gulf war effort. Previously Bonn had pledged about $3.5 billion in aid to the coalition and Arab states whose economies were damaged by the UN embargo of Iraq. Germany also announces that it is sending to Turkey new air defense systems and 580 troops to operate them.

January 29. *Israel Arrests Nusseibeh.* Israeli authorities arrest prominent West Bank Palestinian leader Sari Nusseibeh for allegedly providing Iraq information on the location of its Scud missile strikes in Israel. He is sentenced to six months of administrative detention without a trial. A judge later reduces his sentence to three months. Nusseibeh is among thousands of Palestinians detained by Israel during the Gulf war.

FEBRUARY

February 3. *Demonstrations in Morocco.* In Rabat, Morocco, 300,000 to 500,000 demonstrators gather to protest Morocco's participation in the coalition and to express support for Saddam Hussein and Yasir Arafat. American, British, French, and Israeli flags are burned, and Egyptian and Saudi leaders are denounced.

February 4. *Iranian Diplomacy Rejected.* Iranian president Ali Akbar Hashemi Rafsanjani announces his willingness to mediate a peaceful resolution to the war, but the Bush administration and Iraqi diplomats both reject the offer.

February 6. *King Hussein Allies with Iraq.* In a speech broadcast on Jordanian television, King Hussein abandons Jordan's officially neutral posture and states in unequivocal terms his country's new alliance with Iraq. He condemns the coalition's air campaign against Iraq and claims it is a war "against all Arabs and Moslems." He does not, however, offer Iraq any military aid. President Bush says the king "made a mistake." The State Department announces that it is reassessing Jordan's aid package for fiscal year 1992.

February 6. *Baker on Postwar Middle East.* Testifying before the House Foreign Affairs Committee, Secretary of State Baker outlines the administration's postwar goals in the Middle East. He says policy after the conflict should be based on five points: a new security arrangement between Gulf nations; an arms control agreement that would constrain Iraq's ability to rebuild its nuclear, chemical, and biological weapons programs; an economic reconstruction program that would ease tensions between wealthy and poor Middle East nations; a new diplomatic effort to end the Arab-Israeli dispute; and a campaign to reduce U.S. dependence on imported oil.

February 7. *Iraqi Civilian Casualty Reports.* Secretary General Pérez de Cuéllar says Iraqi civilian casualties from the coalition bombardment appear to number in the thousands. Since the bombing began, Iraqi officials had taken Western reporters on several visits to damaged hospitals and residential areas. President Bush claimed February 5 that the coalition was doing everything possible to minimize civilian casualties and that Iraq had moved some military assets to civilian areas to escape bombing.

February 8. *Cheney and Powell in Saudi Arabia.* Gen. Powell and Defense Secretary Cheney arrive in Saudi Arabia, where they are to assess the progress of the air war and plan for a possible ground offensive against Iraqi forces. Cheney and Powell leave for the United States February 10.

February 11. *Iraq to Draft Seventeen-Year-Olds.* The Iraqi government announces that it will begin calling up seventeen-year-olds for military service.

February 11. *Bush Says Air War Will Continue.* After meeting with Defense Secretary Cheney and Gen. Powell, who had returned from the Persian Gulf the previous day, President Bush deflates speculation that a ground offensive is imminent by saying the air war would continue "for a while." Reports from the Persian Gulf indicated that coalition forces had recently increased the frequency of bombing raids and artillery barrages against Iraqi targets.

February 12. *Hussein Meets Soviet Envoy.* At a meeting in Baghdad, Soviet envoy Yevgenii Primakov urges Saddam Hussein to comply with UN resolutions and withdraw his forces from Kuwait unconditionally. After the meeting, Baghdad radio reports that Iraq is willing to cooperate with the Soviet Union. In Moscow February 13 Primakov says he is optimistic about the chances for progress toward a negotiated settlement and announces that Foreign Minister Aziz will come to Moscow the following week for talks with Soviet officials.

February 13. *Attack Kills Hundreds of Iraqis.* More than 400 Iraqi civilians are killed when a U.S. Stealth F-117A bomber drops two laser-guided, 2,000-pound bombs on a building housing an underground bomb shelter in Baghdad. Iraqi officials maintain the shelter was deliberately targeted, calling the raid "a well-planned crime." The Bush administration and the Pentagon deny any knowledge that the reinforced building was being used as a civilian shelter and insist that it was a military communications center. The United States accuses the Iraqi government of endangering innocent civilians by sheltering them in the facility. Allied air raids continue unabated. The attack generates protests against the United States in Jordan and other locations in the Arab world.

February 15. *Iraq Offers Conditional Withdrawal.* Iraq's Revolutionary Command Council (a ruling body headed by Saddam Hussein) announces that it is prepared to withdraw Iraqi forces from Kuwait. Initial response from world leaders is optimistic, but hope fades as Iraq reveals numerous conditions for its withdrawal. These conditions include the abolition of all UN resolutions pertaining to the Persian Gulf, the application of the same UN resolutions against Israel if it refuses to withdraw from the occupied territories, the removal of all foreign military bases from the region, and the forgiveness of Iraqi debts to coalition nations. Bush denounces the proposal as a "cruel hoax" and vows to continue the war. He also urges the Iraqi people to remove Hussein from power. Other leaders of coalition nations call on Iraq to withdraw from Kuwait immediately and unconditionally.

February 18. *Soviets Propose Peace Plan.* President Gorbachev presents a peace plan to Foreign Minister Aziz during a meeting in Moscow. Aziz returns to Baghdad, where the Revolutionary Command Council is to consider

the plan on February 20. After being informed of the plan's contents, President Bush says February 19 that it "falls well short" of coalition requirements to end the war. The same day the Pentagon says it is prepared to launch a ground offensive.

February 20. *U.S. Troops Take Iraqi POWs.* In fierce ground clashes on the Saudi-Kuwaiti border that are seen as a prelude to an offensive, U.S. troops and helicopters attack Iraqi positions and capture more than 450 Iraqi soldiers, while incurring minimal casualties.

February 21. *Iraq Backs Soviet Plan.* Soviet officials announce that Iraq has agreed to withdraw unconditionally from Kuwait under the terms of a Soviet six-point plan. The plan calls for a gradual unconditional Iraqi withdrawal from Kuwait, the lifting of sanctions against Iraq when the withdrawal is two-thirds completed, and the repeal of all UN resolutions directed at Iraq when all Iraqi forces have left Kuwait. Foreign Minister Aziz, who has returned to Moscow, says Saddam Hussein has given the plan a "positive response." The White House announces President Bush told President Gorbachev that he had "serious concerns" about the plan. The Bush administration begins consultations with its coalition allies on the plan, while the war effort continues.

February 21. *Hussein Delivers Fiery Speech.* Saddam Hussein delivers a speech over Baghdad radio that contrasts with Foreign Minister Aziz's acceptance of the Soviet peace proposal. Hussein denounces "Zionism and U.S. imperialism," Arab leaders who sided with the coalition, and the Western media. He says coalition leaders have waged a cowardly air war against Iraqi civilians, because they are afraid of the consequences of a ground war against Iraqi forces.

February 22. *Bush Sets Deadline.* President Bush announces that to end the war and avoid a ground offensive, Saddam Hussein must accept coalition terms "publicly and authoritatively" and Iraq must begin an unconditional withdrawal from Kuwait by noon EST February 23. Bush says the deadline is necessary because Iraq has begun burning Kuwaiti oil wells in what he describes as a "scorched-earth policy." White House Press Secretary Marlin Fitzwater enumerates several other U.S. demands, including Iraq's agreement to pay reparations to Kuwait, its disclosure of all mines, its release of all prisoners of war and Kuwaiti detainees, and its complete withdrawal from Kuwait within seven days. American officials indicate that the Soviet peace plan was deemed inadequate because it permitted UN resolutions to go out of force and gave Iraqi troops three weeks to withdraw, which would have allowed them to take all their heavy military equipment back to Iraq.

February 23. *Iraq Ignores Ultimatum.* Foreign Minister Aziz issues a statement in Moscow reiterating his government's acceptance of the Soviet peace proposal. As President Bush's deadline passes, however, Iraq makes no moves to withdraw from Kuwait. Bush declares that there is "no alternative to war."

February 24. *Coalition Launches Ground War.* At 4:00 a.m. Saudi time, eight hours after Bush's deadline passes, coalition ground forces launch a massive offensive against Iraqi defenses in Kuwait and Iraq. President Bush announces the offensive in a televised address delivered two hours later (10:00 p.m. EST February 23). Coalition troops quickly breach Iraqi fortifications on the Saudi-Kuwaiti border without encountering chemical weapons attacks. Meanwhile a huge coalition force secretly deployed on the Saudi-Iraqi border to the west penetrates deep into Iraq against light opposition. Coalition troops find that many Iraqi units have been severely weakened by bombing attacks and desertions. Thousands of Iraqi troops surrender without a fight. By the end of the ground offensive an estimated 63,000 Iraqis are taken prisoner.

February 25. *Scud Hits U.S. Barracks.* An Iraqi Scud missile strikes a U.S. Army reservist barracks in Dhahran, Saudi Arabia. Twenty-eight soldiers, including three women, are killed, and at least eighty-nine others are wounded.

February 25. *U.S. Forces Reach Euphrates.* American troops leading the assault into southern Iraq reach the Euphrates River valley late in the evening, severing the main escape route between Kuwait and Baghdad.

February 26. *Iraqis Abandon Kuwait City.* As coalition forces press toward Kuwait City, Iraqi troops abandon the capital, taking thousands of Kuwaitis with them as hostages. Coalition warplanes create a massive traffic jam of Iraqi vehicles on the road running north out of Kuwait City by destroying vehicles at the front and rear of the fleeing Iraqi convoy. For hours coalition pilots bomb the stalled convoy, destroying more than a thousand Iraqi vehicles. Kuwaiti resistance fighters take control of Kuwait City and begin hunting the few Iraqis who had stayed behind. From Saudi Arabia, the emir of Kuwait, Sheik Jaber, declares that the country will remain under martial law for three months. Kuwaiti, Saudi, and U.S. troops march into the city in the early morning hours of February 27.

February 26. *Hussein Announces Withdrawal.* Saddam Hussein delivers a defiant speech over Baghdad radio announcing the withdrawal of Iraqi troops from Kuwait, although most Iraqi forces already are in full retreat. President Bush angrily responds to Hussein's speech, saying that the war will continue because Hussein's announcement failed to meet the coalition's conditions for a cease-fire.

February 27. *Schwarzkopf Briefing on War.* Gen. Schwarzkopf explains the strategy behind the coalition's ground offensive in a detailed one-hour briefing in Riyadh. Schwarzkopf says that coalition air supremacy prevented the Iraqis from detecting a massive redeployment of troops and equipment westward along the Saudi-Iraqi border. When the ground war began, these forces quickly outflanked Iraqi troops and cut off their escape routes out of Kuwait. He belittles Saddam Hussein's military leadership ability and says that U.S. forces could have marched to Baghdad "unopposed for all intents and purposes." Schwarzkopf calls the low number of casualties suffered by the coalition "miraculous" and says he cannot positively explain why the Iraqis did not use chemical weapons as they had threatened. He declines to estimate how many Iraqi troops were killed in the fighting, but American military analysts say between 25,000 and 50,000 Iraqis were probably killed during the war. Saudi officials estimate between 85,000 and 100,000 Iraqis were killed.

February 27. *Tank Duel with the Republican Guard.* American and British forces engage several divisions of Iraq's elite Republican Guard troops in a furious tank battle west of Basra. The clash is the largest tank battle since World War II. More than 200 Iraqi tanks are destroyed without the loss of a single coalition tank. The battle continues until 8:00 a.m. February 28 Saudi time when a cease-fire goes into effect.

February 27. *Aziz Letter Accepts UN Resolutions.* Foreign Minister Aziz notifies the United Nations by letter that Iraq will accept the twelve Security Council resolutions related to Iraq's invasion of Kuwait.

February 27. *Bush Announces a Cease-fire.* In a televised address delivered at 9:00 p.m. EST from the White House, President Bush declares that the coalition's military objectives have been met and announces a cease-fire that will begin at 12:00 midnight EST (8:00 a.m. February 28 Saudi time). The ground war lasts exactly one hundred hours. Baghdad radio announces the cease-fire soon afterward. Bush also enumerates the conditions that Iraq must meet to achieve a permanent cease-fire. He says Iraq must accept all UN resolutions pertaining to its invasion of Kuwait, release all prisoners of war and Kuwaitis taken hostage during the retreat from Kuwait, disclose the locations of mines, and agree to a quick meeting with coalition military leaders to formalize the military details of the cease-fire.

February 28. *Iraq Accepts Cease-fire.* The Iraqi government says it will accept a cease-fire and send military officers to meet with coalition commanders to arrange the specifics of the cease-fire. The White House announces coalition troops will remain in Iraqi territory until Iraq complies fully with all terms of the cease-fire.

MARCH

March 1. *King Hussein Speech.* In a televised speech, King Hussein announces he is in favor of repairing Jordan's relations with Arab and Western members of the anti-Iraq coalition.

March 1. *Civil Unrest in Iraq.* Reports from refugees and other sources indicate Basra has degenerated into chaos, as mobs openly defy government authorities. On March 3 Shi'ite Moslem rebels claim to have taken control of the city. By March 5, fighting spreads to numerous other southern Iraqi cities. However, forces loyal to Hussein are effectively counterattacking Shi'ite rebels and disaffected Iraqi soldiers who had joined them. Leaders of the Kurdish resistance movement based in northern Iraq announce March 6 that they have begun a large-scale offensive against Iraqi government troops and have taken control of many areas.

March 2. *Cease-fire Broken.* Unaware of a cease-fire, Iraqi tank units southwest of Basra fire upon U.S. forces. American helicopters and tanks attack the Iraqi forces, destroying sixty vehicles before the Iraqis surrender. No Americans are killed in the fight.

March 3. *Iraqis Accept Allied Terms.* Gen. Schwarzkopf meets with high-ranking Iraqi military leaders near the southern Iraq town of Safwan. The Iraqis accept all allied terms for formally ending the Gulf war. The Iraqis promise to release promptly all prisoners of war and Kuwaiti civilians, provide locations of all mines, avoid further skirmishes, pay Kuwait for war damages, and comply with all UN resolutions pertaining to Iraq's invasion of Kuwait.

March 4-5. *Iraq Frees Prisoners of War.* Iraqi authorities, who claim to hold forty-five coalition prisoners of war, release ten on March 4 and the remaining thirty-five on March 5. A few coalition troops remain listed as missing in action, but U.S. officials say they believe Iraq has released all the prisoners of war they captured. Iraq begins freeing its Kuwaiti civilian hostages March 7.

March 5. *Iraq Voids Annexation of Kuwait.* Baghdad radio reports that the Iraqi government has voided its annexation of Kuwait and promised to return Kuwaiti assets seized during the occupation.

March 6. *Bush Victory Speech.* In a victory address to a joint session of Congress, President Bush announces U.S. forces in the Persian Gulf will be brought home as soon as possible. He expresses his intent to translate the coalition military victory into progress toward a solution to the Palestinian issue and the Arab-Israeli conflict. Bush announces a Middle East policy that contains four points: a collective security arrangement for the Persian Gulf; an economic development program; arms control agreements to stop the spread of weapons of mass destruction; and the opening of talks between Israel and the Arab states and Israel and the Palestinians that are intended to achieve a comprehensive peace "grounded in United Nations Security Council Resolutions 242 and 338 and the principle of territory for peace."

March 6. *Hussein Appoints New Interior Minister.* Saddam Hussein appoints Ali Hassan Majid, who reportedly was responsible for ordering the use of chemical weapons against Kurdish rebels in 1988, as his new interior minister. The appointment and the expulsion of foreign journalists the same day are seen as indications that Hussein intends to brutally suppress the Kurdish and Shi'ite uprisings.

March 7. *Baker to the Middle East.* Secretary of State Baker departs for a seven-day tour of Middle East capitals. He advocates a gradual, dual-track peace process under which Israel and the Arab states would take steps to moderate their positions toward one another, while Israel and the Palestinians engage in direct negotiations.

March 8. *Rafsanjani Says Hussein Should Resign.* President Rafsanjani calls on Saddam Hussein to "submit to the will of the people" and resign. Rafsanjani's statement marks a renewal of hostility between the governments of Iran and Iraq. Many sources report that the Iranian government has been aiding the Shi'ite and Kurdish uprisings against Hussein's rule, but Rafsanjani denies any involvement.

March 9. *U.S. to Bomb Iraq if It Uses Poison Gas.* The Bush administration announces that it will bomb Iraqi government forces if they use chemical weapons against Iraqi rebels. American officials say that U.S. intelligence had intercepted a March 7 communication from the Iraqi government to troops in the field directing them to initiate a chemical weapons attack against a specific rebel target. Later that day the State Department issues a strong warning to Iraq to refrain from using poison gas.

March 9. *Kuwait-Leader Promises a Parliament.* During a meeting with Secretary of State Baker, Prince Saad al-Abdullah al-Sabah, Kuwait's prime minister, tells reporters the Kuwaiti government will soon reinstitute the Kuwaiti parliament that had been dissolved in 1986.

March 10. *Coalition Arabs Endorse Security Plan.* Foreign ministers from Saudi Arabia, Egypt, Syria, Kuwait, Oman, Qatar, Bahrain, and the United Arab Emirates meet with Secretary of State Baker in Riyadh. They agree that a Persian Gulf security structure should include an Arab peacekeeping force consisting of troops from the eight Arab nations, an enhanced U.S. naval presence in the Persian Gulf, the storage of U.S. military equipment in Saudi Arabia, and frequent U.S.-Arab joint military maneuvers. The Arab foreign ministers also praise President Bush's four-point policy toward the Middle East announced March 6. The Arabs, however, state their support for an international peace conference on the Middle East, while Baker says "this is not the appropriate time" for such a conference.

March 12. *Baker in Israel.* During talks with Prime Minister Shamir in Israel, Secretary of State Baker urges him to make concessions to Arab states that could lead to productive Arab-Israeli negotiations. Baker later meets with ten Palestinian leaders from the occupied territories.

March 13. *Iraqi Uprising Continues.* For the first time since the Iraqi uprising began, the regime of Saddam Hussein admits its troops are engaged in a war with rebel groups. Kurdish resistance leaders claim to be in control of most of the Kurdish region of Iraq. Several sources report large Shi'ite demonstrations in Baghdad. At the end of a three-day conference in Beirut, leaders of twenty-three Iraqi opposition groups appeal for outside assistance and announce they will cooperate to topple the Hussein regime.

March 14. *Emir Returns to Kuwait.* Sheik Jaber returns to Kuwait for the first time since the Iraqi invasion of his nation. His return coincides with statements of concern by U.S. officials about the deportation from Kuwait of Palestinians and other Arabs suspected of collaborating with Iraqi troops. Many of the deported Palestinians charge that they were tortured by Kuwaiti police or vigilantes.

March 16. *Hussein Promises Reforms.* In a televised speech, Saddam Hussein appeals for the support of Iraqis by promising democratic reforms as soon as the antigovernment rebellions have been put down. The reforms are to include a multiparty system and a referendum on a new constitution. He claims that the insurrection in the south was the work of foreigners and traitors and that it has been broken. He admits that fighting continues in the north.

Documents on the Gulf Crisis

Following are texts of selected documents, speeches, and letters associated with the Persian Gulf crisis. The texts are arranged in chronological order.

UN SECURITY COUNCIL RESOLUTION 660

In response to Iraq's August 2 invasion of Kuwait, the UN Security Council later that day passed Resolution 660, condemning the invasion and demanding an Iraqi withdrawal. The vote was 14-0 with 1 abstention.

The Security Council,
Alarmed by the invasion of Kuwait on 2 August 1990 by the military forces of Iraq,
Determining that there exists a breach of international peace and security as regards the Iraqi invasion of Kuwait,
Acting under Articles 39 and 40 of the Charter of the United Nations,
1. *Condemns* the Iraqi invasion of Kuwait;
2. *Demands* that Iraq withdraw immediately and unconditionally all its forces to the positions in which they were located on 1 August 1990;
3. *Calls upon* Iraq and Kuwait to begin immediately intensive negotiations for the resolution of their differences and supports all efforts in this regard, and especially those of the League of Arab States;
4. *Decides* to meet again as necessary to consider further steps to ensure compliance with the present resolution.

UN SECURITY COUNCIL RESOLUTION 661

On August 6, 1990, the UN Security Council passed Resolution 661, which imposed severe economic sanctions against Iraq. The vote was 13-2.

The Security Council,
Reaffirming its resolution 660 (1990) of 2 August 1990,

Deeply concerned that the resolution has not been implemented and that the invasion by Iraq of Kuwait continues with further loss of human life and material destruction,
Determined to bring the invasion and occupation of Kuwait by Iraq to an end and to restore the sovereignty, independence and territorial integrity of Kuwait,
Noting that the legitimate Government of Kuwait has expressed its readiness to comply with resolution 660 (1990),
Mindful of its responsibilities under the Charter of the United Nations for the maintenance of international peace and security,
Affirming the inherent right of individual or collective self-defence, in response to the armed attack by Iraq against Kuwait, in accordance with Article 51 of the Charter,
Acting under Chapter VII of the Charter of the United Nations,
1. *Determines* that Iraq so far has failed to comply with paragraph 2 of resolution 660 (1990) and has usurped the authority of the legitimate Government of Kuwait;
2. *Decides,* as a consequence, to take the following measures to secure compliance of Iraq with paragraph 2 of resolution 660 (1990) and to restore the authority of the legitimate Government of Kuwait;
3. *Decides* that all States shall prevent:
(a) The import into their territories of all commodities and products originating in Iraq or Kuwait exported therefrom after the date of the present resolution;
(b) Any activities by their nationals or in their territories which would promote or are calculated to promote the export or trans-shipment of any commodities or products from Iraq or Kuwait; and any dealings by their nationals or their flag vessels or in their territories in any commodities or products originating in Iraq or Kuwait and exported therefrom after the date of the present resolution, including in particular any transfer of funds to Iraq or Kuwait for the purposes of such activities or dealings;
(c) The sale or supply by their nationals or from their territories or using their flag vessels of any commodities or products, including weapons or any other military equipment, whether or not originating in their territories but not including supplies intended strictly for medical purposes, and, in humanitarian circumstances, foodstuffs, to any person or body in Iraq or Kuwait or to any person or body for the purposes of any business carried on in or operated from Iraq or Kuwait, and any activities by their nationals or in their territories which promote or are calculated to promote such sale or supply of such commodities or products;
4. *Decides* that all States shall not make available to the Government of Iraq or to any commercial, industrial or public utility undertaking in Iraq or Kuwait, any funds or any other financial or economic resources and shall prevent their nationals and any persons within their territories from removing from their territories or otherwise making available to that Government or to

any such undertaking any such funds or resources and from remitting any other funds to persons or bodies within Iraq or Kuwait, except payments exclusively for strictly medical or humanitarian purposes and, in humanitarian circumstances, foodstuffs;

5. *Calls upon* all States, including States non-members of the United Nations, to act strictly in accordance with the provisions of the present resolution notwithstanding any contract entered into or license granted before the date of the present resolution;

6. *Decides* to establish, in accordance with rule 28 of the provisional rules of procedure of the Security Council, a Committee of the Security Council consisting of all the members of the Council, to undertake the following tasks and to report on its work to the Council with its observations and recommendations:

(a) To examine the reports on the progress of the implementation of the present resolution which will be submitted by the Secretary-General;

(b) To seek from all States further information regarding the action taken by them concerning the effective implementation of the provisions laid down in the present resolution;

7. *Calls upon* all States to co-operate fully with the Committee in the fulfillment of its task, including supplying such information as may be sought by the Committee in pursuance of the present resolution;

8. *Requests* the Secretary-General to provide all necessary assistance to the Committee and to make the necessary arrangements in the Secretariat for the purpose;

9. *Decides* that, notwithstanding paragraphs 4 through 8 above, nothing in the present resolution shall prohibit assistance to the legitimate Government of Kuwait, and *calls upon* all States:

(a) To take appropriate measures to protect assets of the legitimate Government of Kuwait and its agencies;

(b) Not to recognize any regime set up by the occupying Power;

10. *Requests* the Secretary-General to report to the Council on the progress of the implementation of the present resolution, the first report to be submitted within thirty days;

11. *Decides* to keep this item on its agenda and to continue its efforts to put an early end to the invasion by Iraq.

BUSH ANNOUNCES TROOP DEPLOYMENTS

On August 8, 1990, President Bush delivered a televised address from the Oval Office on his decision to send U.S. military forces to Saudi Arabia to help it defend itself against possible aggressive actions by Iraq.

In the life of a nation, we're called upon to define who we are and what we believe. Sometimes, these choices are not easy. But today, as president, I ask for your support in a decision I've made to stand up for what's right and condemn what's wrong, all in the cause of peace.

At my direction, elements of the 82nd Airborne Division, as well as key units of the United States Air Force, are arriving today to take up defensive positions in Saudi Arabia. I took this action to assist the Saudi Arabian government in the defense of its homeland. No one commits American armed forces to a dangerous mission lightly, but after perhaps unparalleled international consultation and exhausting every alternative, it became necessary to take this action.

Let me tell you why. Less than a week ago in the early morning hours of August 2, Iraqi armed forces, without provocation or warning, invaded a peaceful Kuwait. Facing negligible resistance from its much smaller neighbor, Iraq's tanks stormed in blitzkrieg fashion through Kuwait in a few short hours. With more than 100,000 troops, along with tanks, artillery, and surface-to-surface missiles, Iraq now occupies Kuwait.

This aggression came just hours after [Iraqi President] Saddam Hussein specifically assured numerous countries in the area that there would be no invasion. There is no justification whatsoever for this outrageous and brutal act of aggression.

A puppet regime, imposed from the outside, is unacceptable. The acquisition of territory by force is unacceptable.

No one, friend or foe, should doubt our desire for peace, and no one should underestimate our determination to confront aggression.

Four simple principles guide our policy.

First, we seek the immediate, unconditional, and complete withdrawal of all Iraqi forces from Kuwait.

Second, Kuwait's legitimate government must be restored to replace the puppet regime.

And third, my administration, as has been the case with every president from President [Franklin D.] Roosevelt to President [Ronald] Reagan, is committed to the security and stability of the Persian Gulf.

And fourth, I am determined to protect the lives of American citizens abroad.

Immediately after the Iraqi invasion, I ordered an embargo of all trade with Iraq, and, together with many other nations, announced sanctions that both froze all Iraqi assets in this country and protected Kuwait's assets.

The stakes are high. Iraq is already a rich and powerful country that possesses the world's second-largest reserves of oil and over a million men under arms. It's the fourth largest military in the world.

Our country now imports nearly half the oil it consumes and could face a major threat to its economic independence. Much of the world is even more dependent on imported oil and is even more vulnerable to Iraqi threats.

We succeeded in the struggle for freedom in Europe because we and our allies remain stalwart. Keeping the peace in the Middle East will require no less.

We're beginning a new era. This new era can be full of promise, an age of freedom, a time of peace for all peoples. But if history teaches us anything, it is that we must resist aggression, or it will destroy our freedoms.

Appeasement does not work. As was the case in the 1930s, we see in Saddam Hussein an aggressive dictator threatening his neighbors. Only fourteen days ago, Saddam Hussein promised his friends he would not invade Kuwait. And four days ago, he promised the world he would withdraw. And twice we have seen what his promises mean. His promises mean nothing.

In the last few days I've spoken with political leaders from the Middle East, Europe, Asia, the Americas, and I've met with [British] Prime Minister [Margaret] Thatcher, [Canadian] Prime Minister [Brian] Mulroney, and NATO Secretary General [Manfred] Wöerner. And all agree that Iraq cannot be allowed to benefit from its invasion of Kuwait.

We agree that this is not an American problem or a European problem or a Middle East problem. It is the world's problem, and that's why soon after the Iraqi invasion, the United Nations Security Council, without dissent, condemned Iraq, calling for the immediate and unconditional withdrawal of its troops from Kuwait.

The Arab world, through both the Arab League and the Gulf Cooperation Council, courageously announced its opposition to Iraqi aggression. Japan, the United Kingdom, and France, and other governments around the world have imposed severe sanctions.

The Soviet Union and China ended all arms sales to Iraq, and this past Monday, the United Nations Security Council approved for the first time in twenty-three years mandatory sanctions under Chapter VII of the United Nations Charter.

These sanctions, now enshrined in international law, have the potential to deny Iraq the fruits of aggression, while sharply limiting its ability to either import or export anything of value, especially oil.

I pledge here today that the United States will do its part to see that these sanctions are effective and to induce Iraq to withdraw without delay from Kuwait. But we must recognize that Iraq may not stop using force to advance its ambitions.

Iraq has massed an enormous war machine on the Saudi border, capable of initiating hostilities with little or no additional preparation. Given the Iraqi government's history of aggression against its own citizens as well as its neighbors, to assume Iraq will not attack again would be unwise and unrealistic. And therefore, after consulting with [Saudi] King Fahd, I sent Secretary of Defense Dick Cheney to discuss cooperative measures we could take.

Following those meetings, the Saudi government requested our help and I responded to that request by ordering U.S. air and ground forces to deploy to the kingdom of Saudi Arabia.

Let me be clear: The sovereign independence of Saudi Arabia is of vital interest to the United States. This decision, which I shared with the congressional leadership, grows out of the long-standing friendship and security relationship between the United States and Saudi Arabia. U.S. forces will work together with those of Saudi Arabia and other nations to preserve the integrity of Saudi Arabia and to deter further Iraqi aggression.

Through the presence, as well as through their training and exercises, these multinational forces will enhance the overall capability of Saudi armed forces to defend the kingdom.

I want to be clear about what we are doing and why. America does not seek conflict, nor do we seek to chart the destiny of other nations. But America will stand by her friends. The mission of our troops is wholly defensive. Hopefully, they will not be needed long.

They will not initiate hostilities, but they will defend themselves, the kingdom of Saudi Arabia, and other friends in the Persian Gulf.

We are working around the clock to deter Iraqi aggression and to enforce UN sanctions. I'm continuing my conversations with world leaders. Secretary of Defense Cheney has just returned from valuable consultations with President [Hosni] Mubarak of Egypt and King Hassan of Morocco. Secretary of State [James A.] Baker [III] has consulted with his counterparts in many nations, including the Soviet Union. And today he heads for Europe to consult with President [Turgut] Ozal of Turkey, a staunch friend of the United States. And he'll then consult with the NATO foreign ministers.

I will ask oil-producing nations to do what they can to increase production in order to minimize any impact that oil-flow reductions will have on the world economy. And I will explore whether we and our allies should draw down our strategic petroleum reserves.

Conservation measures can also help. Americans everywhere must do their part.

And one more thing: I'm asking the oil companies to do their fair share. They should show restraint and not abuse today's uncertainties to raise prices. Standing up for our principles will not come easy. It may take time and possibly cost a great deal, but we are asking no more of anyone than of the brave young men and women of our armed forces and their families, and I ask that—and the churches around the country—prayers be said for those who are committed to protect and defend America's interests.

Standing up for our principles is an American tradition. As it has so many times before, it may take time and tremendous effort, but most of all, it will take unity of purpose. As I've witnessed throughout my life in both war and peace, America has never wavered when her purpose is driven by principle, and on this August day, at home and abroad, I know she will do no less.

Thank you, and God bless the United States of America.

FAHD SPEECH ON GULF CRISIS

Following is King Fahd ibn Abdul Aziz's speech to the Saudi Arabian people on the Iraqi threat, as translated by the Saudi government from his broadcast August 9, 1990:

In the name of God, the Merciful, the Compassionate. Thanks be to God, Master of the Universe and Prayers of Peace be upon the last of Prophets Mohamad and all his kinfolk and companions.

Dear brother citizens, May God's peace and mercy be upon you.

You realize, no doubt, through following up the course of the regrettable events in the Arab Gulf region during the last few days the gravity of the situation the Arab Nation faces in the current circumstances. You undoubtedly know that the government of the Kingdom of Saudi Arabia has exerted all possible efforts with the governments of the Iraqi Republic and the State of Kuwait to contain the dispute between the two countries.

In this context, I made numerous telephone calls and held fraternal talks with the brothers. As a result, a bilateral meeting was held between the Iraqi and Kuwaiti delegations in Saudi Arabia with the aim of bridging the gap and narrowing differences to avert any further escalation.

A number of brotherly Arab kings and presidents contributed, thankfully, in these efforts based on their belief in the unity of the Arab Nation and the cohesion of its solidarity and cooperation to achieve success in serving its fateful causes.

However, regrettably enough, events took an adverse course, to our endeavors and the aspirations of the Peoples of the Islamic and Arab nation, as well as all peace-loving countries.

Nevertheless, these painful and regrettable events started in the pre-dawn hours of Thursday 11 Muharram 1411H., corresponding to 2nd August A.D. 1990. They took the whole world by surprise when the Iraqi forces stormed the brotherly state of Kuwait in the most sinister aggression witnessed by the Arab nation in its modern history. Such an invasion inflicted painful suffering on the Kuwaitis and rendered them homeless.

While expressing its deep displeasure at this aggression on the brotherly neighbor Kuwait, the Kingdom of Saudi Arabia declares its categorical rejection of all ensuing measures and declarations that followed that aggression, which were rejected by all the statements issued by Arab leaderships, the Arab League, the Islamic Conference Organization, and the Gulf Cooperation Council, as well as all Arab and international bodies and organizations.

The Kingdom of Saudi Arabia reaffirms its demand to restore the situation in the brotherly state of Kuwait to its original status before the Iraqi storming as well as the return of the ruling family headed by H.H. [His Highness] Sheik Jaber al-Ahmed al-Sabah, the Emir of Kuwait and his government.

We hope that the emergency Arab summit called by H.E. [His Excellency] President Mohamad Hosni Mubarak of sisterly Egypt will lead to the achievement of the results that realize the aspirations of the Arab nation and bolster its march towards solidarity and unity of opinion.

In the aftermath of this regrettable event, Iraq massed huge forces on the borders of the Kingdom of Saudi Arabia. In view of these bitter realities and out of the eagerness of the Kingdom to safeguard its territory and protect its vital and economic potentials, and its wish to bolster its defensive capabilities and to raise the level of training of its armed forces—in addition to the keenness of the government of the Kingdom to resort to peace and non-recourse to force to solve disputes—the Kingdom of Saudi Arabia expressed its wish for the participation of fraternal Arab forces and other friendly forces.

Thus, the governments of the United States, Britain and other nations took the initiative, based on the friendly relations that link the Kingdom of Saudi Arabia and these countries, to dispatch air and land forces to sustain the Saudi armed forces in performing their duty to defend the homeland and the citizens against any aggression with the full emphasis that this measure is not addressed to anybody. It is merely and purely for defensive purposes, imposed by the current circumstances faced by the Kingdom of Saudi Arabia.

It is worth mentioning in this context that the forces which will participate in the joint training exercises with the Saudi armed forces are of a temporary nature. They will leave the Saudi territory immediately at the request of the Kingdom.

We pray to Almighty God to culminate our steps towards everything in which lie the good of our religion and safety of our homeland, and to guide us on the right path.

May God's peace and blessing be upon you.

UN SECURITY COUNCIL RESOLUTION 665

On August 25, 1990, the UN Security Council passed Resolution 665, which authorized the use of naval forces to ensure compliance with the UN embargo against Iraq. The vote was 13-0 with 2 abstentions.

The Security Council,

Recalling its Resolutions 660 (1990), 661 (1990), 662 (1990) and 664 (1990) and demanding their full and immediate implementation;

Having decided to impose sanctions in accordance with Chapter VII of the Charter of the United Nations;

Determined to bring an end to the occupation of Kuwait by Iraq, which imperils the existence of a member state, and to restore the legitimate authority and the sovereignty, independence and territorial integrity of Kuwait, which requires the speedy implementation of the above resolutions;

Deploring the loss of innocent life stemming from the Iraqi invasion of Kuwait and determined to prevent further such losses:

Gravely alarmed that Iraq continues to refuse to comply with Resolutions 660 (1990), 661 (1990), 662 (1990) and 664 (1990) and in particular at the conduct of the Government of Iraq in using Iraqi flag vessels to export oil;

1. *Calls upon* those member states cooperating with the Government of Kuwait which are deploying maritime forces to the area to use such measures commensurate to the specific circumstances as may be necessary under the authority of the Security Council to halt all inward and outward maritime shipping in order to inspect and verify their cargoes and destinations and to ensure strict implementation of the provisions related to such shipping laid down in Resolution 661 (1990);

2. *Invites* member states accordingly to cooperate as may be necessary to ensure compliance with the provisions of Resolution 661 (1990) with maximum use of political and diplomatic measures, in accordance with paragraph 1 above;

3. *Requests* all states to provide in accordance with the Charter such assistance as may be required by the states referred to in paragraph 1 of this resolution;

4. *Further requests* the states concerned to coordinate their actions in pursuit of the above paragraphs of this resolution using as appropriate mechanisms of the Military Staff Committee and after consultation with the Secretary General to submit reports to the Security Council and its committee established under Resolution 661 (1990) to facilitate the monitoring of the implementation of this resolution;

5. *Decides* to remain actively seized of the matter.

BUSH, GORBACHEV SUMMIT STATEMENT

On September 9, 1990, after their summit meeting in Helsinki, Finland, U.S. president George Bush and Soviet president Mikhail S. Gorbachev issued a joint statement on the Gulf crisis.

We are united in the belief that Iraq's aggression must not be tolerated. No peaceful international order is possible if larger states can devour their smaller neighbors.

We reaffirm the joint statement of our foreign ministers of Aug. 3, 1990, and our support for United Nations Security Council Resolutions 660, 661, 662, 664 and 665. [These resolutions condemned Iraq's invasion of Kuwait, called for Iraq's immediate withdrawal, and imposed an economic embargo on the country.]

Today, we once again call upon the government of Iraq to withdraw unconditionally from Kuwait, to allow the restoration of Kuwait's legitimate government and to free all hostages now held in Iraq and Kuwait.

Nothing short of the complete implementation of the United Nations Security Council resolutions is acceptable.

Nothing short of a return to the pre-Aug. 2 status of Kuwait can end Iraq's isolation.

We call upon the entire world community to adhere to the sanctions mandated by the United Nations, and we pledge to work, individually and in concert, to ensure full compliance with the sanctions.

At the same time, the United States and the Soviet Union recognize that UN Security Council Resolution 661 permits, in humanitarian circumstances, the importation into Iraq and Kuwait of food. The Sanctions Committee will make recommendations to the Security Council on what would constitute humanitarian circumstances.

The United States and the Soviet Union further agree that any such imports must be strictly monitored by the appropriate international agencies to ensure that food reaches only those for whom it is intended, with special priority being given to meeting the needs of children.

Our preference is to resolve the crisis peacefully, and we will be united against Iraq's aggression as long as the crisis exists.

However, we are determined to see this aggression end, and if the current steps fail to end it, we are prepared to consider additional ones consistent with the UN Charter. We must demonstrate beyond any doubt that aggression cannot and will not pay.

As soon as the objectives mandated by the UN Security Council resolutions mentioned above have been achieved, and we have demonstrated that aggression does not pay, the presidents direct their foreign ministers to work with countries in the region and outside it to develop regional security structures and measures to promote peace and stability.

It is essential to work actively to resolve all remaining conflicts in the Middle East and Persian Gulf. Both sides will continue to consult each other and initiate measures to pursue these broader objectives at the proper time.

BUSH SPEECH TO CONGRESS

On September 11, 1990, President Bush addressed a joint session of Congress on the U.S. response to Iraq's invasion of Kuwait.

Mr. President, Mr. Speaker, members of the Congress, distinguished guests, fellow Americans, thank you very much for that warm welcome.

We gather tonight witness to events in the Persian Gulf as significant as they are tragic. In the early morning hours of August 2, following negotiations and promises by Iraq's dictator Saddam Hussein not to use force, a powerful Iraqi army invaded its trusting and much weaker neighbor, Kuwait. Within three days, 120,000 Iraqi troops with 850 tanks had poured into Kuwait and moved south to threaten Saudi Arabia. It was then I decided to act to check that aggression.

At this moment, our brave servicemen and women stand watch in that distant desert and on distant seas, side by side with the forces of more than twenty other nations. They are some of the finest men and women of the United States of America, and they're doing one terrific job.

These valiant Americans were ready at a moment's notice to leave their spouses, their children, to serve on the front line halfway around the world. And they remind us who keeps America strong—they do.

In the trying circumstances of the Gulf, the morale of our servicemen and women is excellent. In the face of danger, they are brave, they're well-trained and dedicated.

A soldier, Pfc. Wade Merritt of Knoxville, Tennessee, now stationed in Saudi Arabia, wrote his parents of his worries, his love of family, and his hopes for peace. But Wade also wrote: "I am proud of my country and its firm stand against inhumane aggression. I am proud of my army and its men. I am proud to serve my country."

Well, let me just say, Wade, America is proud of you and is grateful to every soldier, sailor, marine, and airman serving the cause of peace in the Persian Gulf.

I also want to thank the chairman of the Joint Chiefs of Staff, Gen. [Colin L.] Powell [Jr.], the chiefs here tonight, our commander in the Persian Gulf, Gen. [H. Norman] Schwarzkopf, and the men and women of the Department of Defense. What a magnificent job you all are doing, and thank you very, very much from a grateful country.

I wish I could say that their work is done, but we all know it is not. So if ever there was a time to put country before self and patriotism before party, the time is now. And let me thank all Americans, especially those here in this chamber tonight, for your support for our armed forces and their mission. That support will be even more important in the days to come.

So tonight, I want to talk to you about what's at stake, what we must do together to defend civilized values around the world and maintain our economic strength at home. Our objectives in the Persian Gulf are clear, our goals defined and familiar: Iraq must withdraw from Kuwait completely, immediately and without condition.

Kuwait's legitimate government must be restored. The security and stability of the Persian Gulf must be assured, and American citizens abroad must be protected.

These goals are not ours alone. They've been endorsed by the United Nations Security Council five times in as many weeks. Most countries share our concern for principle. And many have a stake in the stability of the Persian Gulf. This is not, as Saddam Hussein would have it, the United States against Iraq. It is Iraq against the world.

As you know, I've just returned from a very productive meeting with Soviet President [Mikhail S.] Gorbachev. And I am pleased that we are working together to build a new relationship. In Helsinki, [Finland], our joint statement affirmed to the world our shared resolve to counter Iraq's threat to peace. Let me quote: "We are united in the belief that Iraq's aggression must not be tolerated. No peaceful international order is possible if larger states can devour their smaller neighbors. Clearly, no longer can a dictator count on East-West confrontation to stymie concerted United Nations action against aggression."

A new partnership of nations has begun, and we stand today at a unique and extraordinary moment. The crisis in the Persian Gulf, as grave as it is, also offers a rare opportunity to move toward an historic period of cooperation. Out of these troubled times, our fifth objective—a new world order—can emerge: a new era—freer from the threat of terror, stronger in the pursuit of justice, and more secure in the quest for peace, an era in which the nations of the world, East and West, North and South, can prosper and live in harmony.

A hundred generations have searched for this elusive path to peace, while a thousand wars raged across the span of human endeavor. And today that new world is struggling to be born, a world quite different from the one we've known, a world where the rule of law supplants the rule of the jungle, a world in which nations recognize the shared responsibility for freedom and justice,

a world where the strong respect the rights of the weak. This is the vision I shared with President Gorbachev in Helsinki. He, and other leaders from Europe, the Gulf and around the world, understand that how we manage this crisis today could shape the future for generations to come.

The test we face is great and so are the stakes. This is the first assault on the new world that we seek, the first test of our mettle. Had we not responded to this first provocation with clarity of purpose, if we do not continue to demonstrate our determination, it would be a signal to actual and potential despots around the world.

America and the world must defend common vital interests, and we will.

America and the world must support the rule of law, and we will.

America and the world must stand up to aggression. And we will.

And one thing more—in the pursuit of these goals—America will not be intimidated.

Vital issues of principle are at stake. Saddam Hussein is literally trying to wipe a country off the face of the Earth. We do not exaggerate. Nor do we exaggerate when we say Saddam Hussein will fail.

Vital economic interests are at risk as well. Iraq itself controls some 10 percent of the world's proven oil reserves. Iraq plus Kuwait controls twice that.

An Iraq permitted to swallow Kuwait would have the economic and military power, as well as the arrogance, to intimidate and coerce its neighbors, neighbors who control the lion's share of the world's remaining oil reserves. We cannot permit a resource so vital to be dominated by one so ruthless—and we won't.

Recent events have surely proven that there is no substitute for American leadership. In the face of tyranny, let no one doubt American credibility and reliability.

Let no one doubt our staying power. We will stand by our friends. One way or another, the leader of Iraq must learn this fundamental truth.

From the outset, acting hand in hand with others, we've sought to fashion the broadest possible international response to Iraq's aggression. The level of world cooperation and condemnation of Iraq is unprecedented. Armed forces from countries spanning four continents are there at the request of King Fahd of Saudi Arabia to deter and, if need be, to defend against attack. Muslims and non-Muslims, Arabs and non-Arabs, soldiers from many nations stand shoulder to shoulder, resolute against Saddam Hussein's ambitions.

And we can now point to five United Nations Security Council resolutions that condemn Iraq's aggression. They call for Iraq's immediate and unconditional withdrawal, the restoration of Kuwait's legitimate government, and categorically reject Iraq's cynical and self-serving attempt to annex Kuwait.

Finally, the United Nations has demanded the release of all foreign nationals held hostage against their will and in contravention of international law. It is a mockery of human decency to call these people "guests." They are hostages, and the whole world knows it.

[British] Prime Minister Margaret Thatcher, our dependable ally, said it all: "We do not bargain over hostages. We will not stoop to the level of using human beings as bargaining chips—ever."

Of course—of course our hearts go out to the hostages and their families. But our policy cannot change. And it will not change. America and the world will not be blackmailed by this ruthless policy.

We're now in sight of a United Nations that performs as envisioned by its founders. We owe much to the outstanding leadership of Secretary General Javier Pérez de Cuéllar. The United Nations is backing up its words with action. The Security Council has imposed mandatory economic sanctions on Iraq, designed to force Iraq to relinquish the spoils of its illegal conquest. The Security Council has also taken the decisive step of authorizing the use of all means necessary to ensure compliance with these sanctions.

Together with our friends and allies, ships of the United States Navy are today patrolling Mideast waters, and they've already intercepted more than 700 ships to enforce the sanctions.

Three regional leaders I spoke with just yesterday told me that these sanctions are working. Iraq is feeling the heat. We continue to hope that Iraq's leaders will recalculate just what their aggression has cost them. They are cut off from world trade, unable to sell their oil, and only a tiny fraction of goods gets through.

The communiqué with President Gorbachev made mention of what happens when the embargo is so effective that children of Iraq literally need milk or the sick truly need medicine. Then, under strict international supervision that guarantees the proper destination, then food will be permitted.

At home, the material cost of our leadership can be steep. And that's why Secretary of State [James A.] Baker [III] and Treasury Secretary [Nicholas F.] Brady have met with many world leaders to underscore that the burden of this collective effort must be shared.

We are prepared to do our share and more to help carry the load; we insist others do their share as well.

The response of most of our friends and allies has been good. To help defray costs, the leaders of Saudi Arabia, Kuwait, and the UAE, the United Arab Emirates, have pledged to provide our deployed troops with all the food and fuel they need. And generous assistance will also be provided to stalwart front-line nations, such as Turkey and Egypt.

And I'm also heartened to report that this international response extends to the neediest victims of this conflict—those refugees. For our part, we have contributed $28 million for relief efforts. And this is but a portion of what is needed. I commend, in particular, Saudi Arabia, Japan, and several European nations who have joined us in this purely humanitarian effort.

There's an energy-related cost to be borne as well. Oil-producing nations are already replacing lost Iraqi and Kuwaiti output. More than half of what was lost has been made up, and we're getting superb cooperation.

If producers, including the United States, continue steps to expand oil and gas production, we can stabilize prices and guarantee against hardship. Additionally, we and several of our allies always have the option to extract oil from our Strategic Petroleum Reserves, if conditions warrant. As I've pointed out before, conservation efforts are essential to keep our energy needs as low as possible.

And we must then take advantage of our energy sources across the board: coal, natural gas, hydro, and nuclear. Our failure to do these things has made us more dependent on foreign oil than ever before.

And finally, let no one even contemplate profiteering from this crisis. We will not have it.

And I cannot predict just how long it will take to convince Iraq to withdraw from Kuwait. Sanctions will take time to have their full intended effect. We will continue to review all options with our allies, but let it be clear: We will not let this aggression stand.

Our interest—our interest, our involvement in the Gulf, is not transitory. It predated Saddam Hussein's aggression and will survive it. Long after all our troops come home—and we all hope it's soon, very soon—there will be a lasting role for the United States in assisting the nations of the Persian Gulf. Our role then, is to deter future aggression. Our role is to help our friends in their own self-defense and something else: to curb the proliferation of chemical, biological, ballistic missiles, and, above all, nuclear technologies.

And let me also make clear that the United States has no quarrel with the Iraqi people. Our quarrel is with Iraq's dictator and with his aggression. Iraq will not be permitted to annex Kuwait. And that's not a threat, it's not a boast—it's just the way it's going to be.

Our ability to function effectively as a great power abroad depends on how we conduct ourselves at home. Our economy, our armed forces, our energy dependence, and our cohesion all determine whether we can help our friends and stand up to our foes. For

America to lead, America must remain strong and vital. Our world leadership and domestic strength are mutual and reinforcing; a woven piece, strongly bound as Old Glory. To revitalize our leadership capacity, we must address our budget deficit—not after Election Day or next year, but now.

Higher oil prices slow our growth, and higher defense costs would only make our fiscal deficit problem worse. That deficit was already greater than it should have been—a projected $232 billion for the coming year. It must—it will—be reduced.

To my friends in Congress: Together we must act this very month, before the next fiscal year begins on October 1, to get America's economic house in order. The Gulf situation helps us realize we are more economically vulnerable than we ever should be. Americans must never again enter any crisis, economic or military, with an excessive dependence on foreign oil and an excessive burden of federal debt.

Most Americans are sick and tired of endless battles in the Congress and between the branches over budget matters. It is high time we pulled together—and get the job done right. It is up to us to straighten this out.

And the job has four basic parts. First, the Congress should this month, within a budget agreement, enact growth-oriented tax measures to help avoid recession in the short term and to increase savings, investment, productivity, and competitiveness for the longer term.

These measures include extending incentives for research and experimentation; expanding the use of IRAs [Individual Retirement Accounts] for new homeowners; establishing tax-deferred family savings accounts; creating incentives for the creation of enterprise zones and initiatives to encourage more domestic drilling; and, yes, reducing the tax rate on capital gains.

Second, the Congress should this month enact a prudent multi-year defense program, one that reflects not only the improvement in East-West relations, but our broader responsibilities to deal with the continuing risks of outlaw action and regional conflict. Even with our obligations in the Gulf, a sound defense budget can have some reduction in real terms, and we are prepared to accept that. But to go beyond—to go beyond such levels, where cutting defense would threaten our vital margin of safety, is something I will never accept.

The world is still dangerous. Surely that is now clear. Stability is not secure. American interests are far-reaching. Interdependence has increased. The consequences of regional instability can be global. This is no time to risk America's capacity to protect her vital interests.

And third, the Congress should this month enact measures to increase domestic energy production and energy conservation in order to reduce dependence on foreign oil.

These measures should include my proposals to increase incentives for domestic oil and gas exploration, fuel-switching, and to accelerate the development of the Alaskan energy resources—without damage to wildlife.

As you know, when the oil embargo was imposed in the early 1970s, the United States imported almost 6 million barrels of oil a day. This year, before the Iraqi invasion, U.S. imports had risen to nearly 8 million barrels per day. We had moved in the wrong direction. And now we must act to correct that trend.

And, fourth, the Congress should this month enact a five-year program to reduce the projected debt and deficits by $500 billion—that is, by half a trillion dollars. And if, with the Congress, we can develop a satisfactory program by the end of the month, we can avoid the ax of sequester—deep across-the-board cuts that would threaten our military capacity and risk substantial domestic disruption.

I want to be able to tell the American people that we have truly solved the deficit problem. And for me to do that, a budget agreement must meet these tests:

● It must include the measures I've recommended to increase economic growth and reduce dependence on foreign oil.

● It must be fair. All should contribute, but the burden should not be excessive for any one group of programs or people.

● It must address the growth of government's hidden liabilities.

● It must reform the budget process, and, further, it must be real.

I urge Congress to provide a comprehensive five-year deficit-reduction program to me as a complete legislative package—with measures to assure that it can be fully enforced. America is tired of phony deficit reduction, or promise-now save-later plans.

Enough is enough. It is time for a program that is credible and real.

● And, finally, to the extent that the deficit-reduction program includes new revenue measures, it must avoid any measure that would threaten economic growth or turn us back toward the days of punishing income tax rates.

That is one path we should not head down again.

I have been pleased with recent progress, although it has not always seemed so smooth. But now it's time to produce. I hope we can work out a responsible plan. But with or without agreement from the budget summit, I ask both Houses of the Congress to allow a straight up-or-down vote on a complete $500 billion deficit-reduction package—not later than September 28.

And if the Congress cannot get me a budget, then Americans will have to face a tough, mandated sequester.

I am hopeful—in fact I am confident—the Congress will do what it should. And I can assure you that we in the executive branch will do our part.

In the final analysis, our ability to meet our responsibilities abroad depends upon political will and consensus at home.

This is never easy in democracies, where we govern only with the consent of the governed. And although free people in a free society are bound to have their differences, Americans traditionally come together in times of adversity and challenge.

Once again, Americans have stepped forward to share a tearful goodbye with their families before leaving for a strange and distant shore. At this very moment, they serve together with Arabs, Europeans, Asians and Africans in defense of principle and the dream of a new world order. And that's why they sweat and toil in the sand and the heat and the sun.

And if they can come together under such adversity; if old adversaries like the Soviet Union and the United States can work in common cause; then surely we who are so fortunate to be in this great—Republicans, liberals, conservatives—can come together to fulfill our responsibilities here.

Thank you, good night, and God bless the United States of America.

IRAQI TRANSCRIPT OF HUSSEIN-GLASPIE MEETING

On September 11, 1990, an ABC News program quoted a transcript released by the Iraqi government of a meeting in Baghdad July 25, 1990, between President Saddam Hussein and April Glaspie, U.S. ambassador to Iraq. Iraqi foreign minister Tariq Aziz also was present. After the program, excerpts from the transcript appeared in British and American newspapers. The Iraqi government released the transcript as evidence that the United States had led Iraq to believe that it would not take forceful action if Iraq invaded Kuwait. The U.S. State Department declined to comment on the accuracy of the Iraqi document, but in testimony before a Senate committee March 20, 1991, Glaspie called it a "fabrication." Following are excerpts from the Iraqi transcript, as translated by ABC News:

SADDAM HUSSEIN: I have summoned you today to hold comprehensive political discussions with you. This is a message to President Bush.

You know that we did not have relations with the U.S. until 1984 and you know the circumstances and reasons which caused them to be severed. The decision to establish relations with the U.S. were taken in 1980 during the two months prior to the war between us and Iran.

When the war started, and to avoid misinterpretation, we postponed the establishment of relations hoping that the war would end soon.

But because the war lasted for a long time, and to emphasize the fact that we are a nonaligned country, it was important to re-establish relations with the U.S. And we choose to do this in 1984.

It is natural to say that the U.S. is not like Britain, for example, with the latter's historic relations with Middle Eastern countries, including Iraq. In addition, there were no relations between Iraq and the U.S. between 1967 and 1984. One can conclude it would be difficult for the U.S. to have a full understanding of many matters in Iraq. When relations were re-established we hoped for a better understanding and for better cooperation because we too do not understand the background of many American decisions. . . .

We had hoped for a better common understanding and a better chance of cooperation to benefit both our peoples and the rest of the Arab nations.

But these better relations have suffered from various rifts. The worst of these was in 1986, only two years after establishing relations, with what was known as Irangate, which happened during the year that Iran occupied the Fao peninsula. . . .

[We] accepted the apology, via his envoy, of the American President regarding Irangate, and we wiped the slate clean. And we shouldn't unearth the past except when new events remind us that old mistakes were not just a matter of coincidence.

Our suspicions increased after we liberated the Fao peninsula. The media began to involve itself in our politics. And our suspicions began to surface anew, because we began to question whether the U.S. felt uneasy with the outcome of the war when we liberated our land.

It was clear to us that certain parties in the United States—and I don't say the President himself—but certain parties who had links with the intelligence community and with the State Department—and I don't say the Secretary of State [James A. Baker III] himself—I say that these parties did not like the fact that we liberated our land. Some parties began to prepare studies entitled, "Who will succeed Saddam Hussein?" They began to contact gulf states to make them fear Iraq, to persuade them not to give Iraq economic aid. And we have evidence of these activities.

Iraq came out of the war burdened with $40 billion debts, excluding the aid given by Arab states, some of whom consider that to be a debt although they knew—and you knew too—that without Iraq they would not have had these sums and the future of the region would have been entirely different.

We began to face the policy of the drop in the price of oil. Then we saw the United States, which always talks of democracy but which has no time for the other point of view. Then the media campaign against Saddam Hussein was started by the official American media. The United States thought that the situation in Iraq was like Poland, Romania or Czechoslovakia. We were disturbed by this campaign but we were not disturbed too much because we had hoped that, in a few months, those who are decision makers in America would have a chance to find the facts and see whether this media campaign had had any effect on the lives of Iraqis. We had hoped that soon the American authorities would make the correct decision regarding their relations with Iraq. Those with good relations can sometimes afford to disagree.

But when planned and deliberate policy forces the price of oil down without good commercial reasons, then that means another war against Iraq. Because military war kills people by bleeding them, and economic war kills their humanity by depriving them of their chance to have a good standard of living. As you know, we gave rivers of blood in a war that lasted eight years, but we did not lose our humanity. Iraqis have a right to live proudly. We do not accept that anyone could injure Iraqi pride or the Iraqi right to have high standards of living.

Kuwait and the U.A.E. [United Arab Emirates] were at the front of this policy aimed at lowering Iraq's position and depriving its people of higher economic standards. And you know that our relations with the Emirates and Kuwait had been good. On top of all that, while we were busy at war, the state of Kuwait began to expand at the expense of our territory.

You may say this is propaganda, but I would direct you to one document, the Military Patrol Line, which is the borderline endorsed by the Arab League in 1951 for military patrols not to cross the Iraq-Kuwait border.

But go and look for yourselves. You will see the Kuwaiti border patrols, the Kuwaiti farms, the Kuwaiti oil installations— all built as closely as possible to this line to establish that land as Kuwaiti territory....

I have read the American statements speaking of friends in the area. Of course, it is the right of everyone to choose their friends. We can have no objections. But you know you are not the ones who protected your friends during the war with Iran. I assure you, had the Iranians overrun the region, the American troops would not have stopped them, except by the use of nuclear weapons.

I do not belittle you. But I hold this view by looking at the geography and nature of American society into account. Yours is a society which cannot accept 10,000 dead in one battle.

You know that Iran agreed to the cease-fire not because the United States had bombed one of the oil platforms after the liberation of the Fao. Is this Iraq's reward for its role in securing the stability of the region and for protecting it from an unknown flood?

So what can it mean when America says it will now protect its friends? It can only mean prejudice against Iraq. This stance plus maneuvers and statements which have been made has encouraged the U.A.E. and Kuwait to disregard Iraqi rights.

...We are not the kind of people who will relinquish their rights. There is no historic right, or legitimacy, or need, for the U.A.E. and Kuwait to deprive us of our rights. If they are needy, we too are needy.

The United States must have a better understanding of the situation and declare who it wants to have relations with and who its enemies are. But it should not make enemies simply because others have different points of view regarding the Arab-Israeli conflict.

We clearly understand America's statement that it wants an easy flow of oil. We understand America saying that it seeks friendship with the states in the region, and to encourage their joint interests. But we cannot understand the attempt to encourage some parties to harm Iraq's interests.

The United States wants to secure the flow of oil. This is understandable and known. But it must not deploy methods which the United States says it disapproves of—flexing muscles and pressure.

If you use pressure, we will deploy pressure and force. We know that you can harm us although we do not threaten you. But we too can harm you. Everyone can cause harm according to their ability and their size. We cannot come all the way to you in the United States, but individual Arabs may reach you.

You can come to Iraq with aircraft and missiles but do not push us to the point where we cease to care. And when we feel that you want to injure our pride and take away the Iraqis' chance of a high standard of living then we will cease to care and death will be the choice for us. Then we would not care if you fired 100 missiles for each missile we fired. Because without pride life would have no value.

It is not reasonable to ask our people to bleed rivers of blood for eight years then to tell them, "Now you have to accept aggression from Kuwait, the U.A.E. or from the U.S. or from Israel."

We do not put all these countries in the same boat. First, we are hurt and upset that such disagreement is taking place between us and Kuwait and the U.A.E. The solution must be found within an Arab framework and through direct bilateral relations. We do not place America among the enemies. We place it where we want our friends to be and we try to be friends. But repeated American statements last year made it apparent that America did not regard us as friends....

We consider the others' interests while we look after our own. And we expect the others to consider our interests while they are dealing with their own. What does it mean when the Zionist war

minister is summoned to the United States now? What do they mean, these fiery statements coming out of Israel during the past few days and the talk of war being expected now more than at any other time?

I do not believe that anyone would lose by making friends with Iraq. In my opinion, the American President has not made mistakes regarding the Arabs, although his decision to freeze dialogue with the P.L.O. was wrong. But it appears that this decision was made to appease the Zionist lobby or as a piece of strategy to cool the Zionist anger, before trying again. I hope that our latter conclusion is the correct one. But we will carry on saying it was the wrong decision.

You are appeasing the usurper in so many ways—economically, politically and militarily as well as in the media. When will the time come when, for every three appeasements to the usurper, you praise the Arabs just once?

APRIL GLASPIE: I thank you, Mr. President, and it is a great pleasure for a diplomat to meet and talk directly with the President. I clearly understand your message. We studied history at school. They taught us to say freedom or death. I think you know well that we as a people have our experience with the colonialists.

Mr. President, you mentioned many things during this meeting which I cannot comment on on behalf of my Government. But with your permission, I will comment on two points. You spoke of friendship and I believe it was clear from the letters sent by our President to you on the occasion of your National Day that he emphasizes—

HUSSEIN: He was kind and his expressions met with our regard and respect.

GLASPIE: As you know, he directed the United States Administration to reject the suggestion of implementing trade sanctions.

HUSSEIN: There is nothing left for us to buy from America. Only wheat. Because every time we want to buy something, they say it is forbidden. I am afraid that one day you will say, "You are going to make gunpowder out of wheat."

GLASPIE: I have a direct instruction from the President to seek better relations with Iraq.

HUSSEIN: But how? We too have this desire. But matters are running contrary to this desire.

GLASPIE: This is less likely to happen the more we talk. For example, you mentioned the issue of the article published by the American Information Agency and that was sad. And a formal apology was presented.

HUSSEIN: Your stance is generous. We are Arabs. It is enough for us that someone says, "I am sorry, I made a mistake." Then we carry on. But the media campaign continued. And it is full of stories. If the stories were true, no one would get upset. But we understand from its continuation that there is a determination.

GLASPIE: I saw the Diane Sawyer program on ABC. And what happened in that program was cheap and unjust. And this is a real picture of what happens in the American media—even to American politicians themselves. These are the methods the Western media employs. I am pleased that you add your voice to the diplomats who stand up to the media. Because your appearance in the media, even for five minutes, would help us to make the American people understand Iraq. This would increase mutual understanding. If the American President had control of the media, his job would be much easier.

Mr. President, not only do I want to say that President Bush wanted better and deeper relations with Iraq, but he also wants an Iraqi contribution to peace and prosperity in the Middle East. President Bush is an intelligent man. He is not going to declare an economic war against Iraq.

You are right. It is true what you say that we do not want higher prices for oil. But I would ask you to examine the possibility of not charging too high a price for oil.

HUSSEIN: We do not want too high prices for oil. And I remind you that in 1974 I gave Tariq Aziz the idea for an article he wrote which criticized the policy of keeping oil prices high. It was the first Arab article which expressed this view.

TARIQ AZIZ: Our policy in OPEC [Organization of Petroleum Exporting Countries] opposes sudden jumps in oil prices.

HUSSEIN: Twenty-five dollars a barrel is not a high price.

GLASPIE: We have many Americans who would like to see the price go above $25 because they come from oil-producing states.

HUSSEIN: The price at one stage had dropped to $12 a barrel and a reduction in the modest Iraqi budget of $6 billion to $7 billion is a disaster.

GLASPIE: I think I understand this. I have lived here for years. I admire your extraordinary efforts to rebuild your country. I know you need funds. We understand that and our opinion is that you should have the opportunity to rebuild your country. But we have no opinion on the Arab-Arab conflicts, like your border disagreement with Kuwait.

I was in the American Embassy in Kuwait during the late 60's. The instruction we had during this period was that we should express no opinion on this issue and that the issue is not associated with America. James Baker has directed our official spokesmen to emphasize this instruction. . . . All that we hope is that these issues are solved quickly. With regard to all of this, can I ask you to see how the issue appears to us?

My assessment after 25 years' service in this area is that your objective must have strong backing from your Arab brothers. I now speak of oil. But you, Mr. President, have fought through a horrific and painful war. Frankly, we can only see that you have deployed massive troops in the south. Normally that would not be any of our business. But when this happens in the context of what you said on your national day, then when we read the details in the two letters of the Foreign Minister, then when we see the Iraqi point of view that the measures taken by the U.A.E. and Kuwait is, in the final analysis, parallel to military aggression against Iraq, then it would be reasonable for me to be concerned. And for this reason, I received an instruction to ask you, in the spirit of friendship—not in the spirit of confrontation—regarding your intentions.

I simply describe the concern of my Government. And I do not mean that the situation is a simple situation. But our concern is a simple one.

HUSSEIN: We do not ask people not to be concerned when peace is at issue. This is a noble human feeling which we all feel. It is natural for you as a superpower to be concerned. But what we ask is not to express your concern in a way that would make an aggressor believe that he is getting support for his aggression.

We want to find a just solution which will give us our rights but not deprive others of their rights. But at the same time, we want the others to know that our patience is running out regarding their action, which is harming even the milk our children drink and the pensions of the widow who lost her husband during the war, and the pensions of the orphans who lost their parents.

As a country, we have the right to prosper. We lost so many opportunities, and the others should value the Iraqi role in their protection. Even this Iraqi [the President points to the interpreter] feels bitter like all other Iraqis. We are not aggressors but we do not accept aggression either. We sent them envoys and handwritten letters. We tried everything. We asked the Servant of the Two Shrines—King Fahd [of Saudi Arabia]—to hold a four-member summit, but he suggested a meeting between the Oil Ministers. We agreed. And as you know, the meeting took place in Jiddah. They reached an agreement which did not express what we wanted, but we agreed.

Only two days after the meeting, the Kuwaiti Oil Minister made a statement that contradicted the agreement. We also discussed the issue during the Baghdad summit. I told the Arab Kings and Presidents that some brothers are fighting an economic war against us. Because if the capability of our army is lowered then, if Iran renewed the war, it could achieve goals which it could not achieve before. And if we lowered the standard of our defenses, then this could encourage Israel to attack us. I said that before the Arab Kings and Presidents. Only I did not mention Kuwait and U.A.E. by name, because they were my guests.

Before this, I had sent them envoys reminding them that our war had included their defense. Therefore the aid they gave us should not be regarded as a debt. We did no more than the United States would have done against someone who attacked its interests. . . .

GLASPIE: I spent four beautiful years in Egypt.

HUSSEIN: The Egyptian people are kind and good and ancient. The oil people are supposed to help the Egyptian people, but they are mean beyond belief. It is painful to admit it, but some of them are disliked by Arabs because of their greed.

GLASPIE: Mr. President, it would be helpful if you could give us an assessment of the effort made by your Arab brothers and whether they have achieved anything.

HUSSEIN: On this subject, we agreed with [Egyptian] President Mubarak that the Prime Minister of Kuwait would meet with the deputy chairman of the Revolution Command Council in Saudi Arabia, because the Saudis initiated contact with us, aided by President Mubarak's efforts. He just telephoned me a short while ago to say the Kuwaitis have agreed to that suggestion.

GLASPIE: Congratulations.

HUSSEIN: A protocol meeting will be held in Saudi Arabia. Then the meeting will be transferred to Baghdad for deeper discussion directly between Kuwait and Iraq. We hope we will reach some result. We hope that the long-term view and the real interests will overcome Kuwaiti greed.

GLASPIE: May I ask you when you expect [Kuwaiti prime minister] Sheik Saad to come to Baghdad?

HUSSEIN: I suppose it would be on Saturday or Monday at the latest. I told brother Mubarak that the agreement should be in Baghdad Saturday or Sunday. You know that brother Mubarak's visits have always been a good omen.

GLASPIE: This is good news. Congratulations.

HUSSEIN: Brother President Mubarak told me they were scared. They said troops were only 20 kilometers north of the Arab League line. I said to him that regardless of what is there, whether they are police, border guards or army, and regardless of how many are there, and what they are doing, assure the Kuwaitis and give them our word that we are not going to do anything until we meet with them. When we meet and when we see that there is hope, then nothing will happen. But if we are unable to find a solution, then it will be natural that Iraq will not accept death, even though wisdom is above everything else. There you have good news.

AZIZ: This is a journalistic exclusive.

GLASPIE: I am planning to go to the United States next Monday. I hope I will meet with President Bush in Washington next week. I thought to postpone my trip because of the difficulties we are facing. But now I will fly on Monday.

SHEIK JABER UN ADDRESS

On September 27, 1990, Sheik Jaber al-Ahmed al-Sabah, the exiled emir of Kuwait, addressed the UN General Assembly. Following are excerpts from the speech as translated by the Kuwaiti government in exile:

. . . I speak from this rostrum today as my peaceful country is passing through extremely harsh circumstances that have given rise to an unprecedented crisis in the history of the United Nations, which, since its inception, has sought to uphold justice on the basis of international law. Indeed, the Security Council has demonstrated that role by recently adopting a series of firm resolutions in the face of naked and brutal aggression against the State of Kuwait.

There is no doubt that the key role played by the Security Council is indeed a propitious one under the prevailing grave circumstances in Kuwait, and, in fact, in the world at large. It is our earnest hope that this role will continue to grow without waning and gain momentum without setbacks, in order to consolidate the rule of international law.

Today, I bring to you the message of a peace-loving nation. A nation that has consistently worked for peace; a nation that reached out with a helping hand to all those who truly needed help; a nation that sought mediation and reconciliation among adversaries. It is this very nation whose security and stability have been trampled upon as a result of its abiding belief in lofty principles inspired by our true Moslem faith and echoed in universal charters, pacts and codes of morality.

Today, I plead before you the cause of a people whose land, until so recently, was a beacon for peaceful co-existence and genuine brotherhood among the family of nations. A people whose national territory was a gathering place for individuals from various peaceful nations who sought a decent and dignified life through constructive work. Some of these people have now been made homeless, wanderers living only on hope in their banishment, while others have become prisoners or fighters refusing, even at the risk of their own lives, to surrender or yield to occupation with all its violence and brutality....

The crisis of Kuwait is a manifold tragedy, whose dire consequences affect not only Kuwaitis but other peoples as well. In fact, it has jeopardized stability in the world, especially in the Gulf region.

And so, I come to this forum, which is the focal point of international collective action, in order to acknowledge the overwhelming global solidarity that has been shown to us in a multitude of Security Council resolutions that have been passed in an unprecedented fashion. This demonstrates rock-solid international rejection of the assassination of the norms of international law, rules of good neighbourly relations and established customs and practices at the hands of armed military invaders whose tanks rolled over and crushed all those concepts. Indeed, this is what makes the Iraqi aggression against the State of Kuwait quite a peculiar case. For we have never seen in contemporary post-World War II history a country that overran a sovereign independent state, a member of the United Nations, and then sought not only to annex it by brutal force but also to erase its name and entire entity from the world political map and wipe out the parameters of its national identity as defined by its institutions and its political, economic, and social structures. All of this, Mr. President, has taken place as we approach the end of the twentieth century!

I came here to tell you of the horrors and suffering we are enduring both inside and outside our occupied homeland, and to put before you our just case. Now, the fate of a people, of a nation, is in your hands....

The aggression by the Iraqi regime against the State of Kuwait which resulted in occupation of the Iraqi vicious attempts to annex Kuwait in flagrant violation of all charters, norms of conduct and treaties, including those legal instruments concluded between the two countries and deposited right here with the United Nations, is not an ordinary conflict between two states over a piece of land. Rather, the Iraqi aggression was the culmination of a premeditated scheme to occupy and seize the entire state by force of arms. This aggression, alas, was perpetrated by a country with which we have several internationally recognized treaties and agreements within the League of Arab States, the Organization of the Islamic Conference, the United Nations and other international organizations.

This Iraqi regime has invented false pretexts and untenable claims against my peaceful and peace-loving country. In response to them, and despite our firm conviction that those claims were totally unfounded, we proposed the constitution of a mutually acceptable, neutral Arab arbitration panel to which both parties would submit their differences. However, Iraq turned down that offer out of hand. Our last attempt at a peaceful resolution of our problems with Iraq was the bilateral round of talks in Jiddah, Kingdom of Saudi Arabia, in the course of which Kuwait stressed the need to resolve its outstanding problems with Iraq within an Arab context. But Iraq's plans were not anchored in any legal framework or based on any formal legal instruments. In fact, Iraq was bent on sweeping through the entire territory of Kuwait, violating its sovereignty and violating the sanctity of Kuwaiti citizens' lives and property. As a consequence, rape, destruction,

terror, and torture are now the rule of the day in the once peaceful and tranquil land of Kuwait. Hundreds of thousands of Kuwaiti citizens along with nationals of various other countries who were our guests have been made homeless and many of them have had their life savings robbed. Hundreds have lost their lives. Others have been held hostage. Indeed, at this very moment, an intense campaign of terror, torture, and humiliation continues unabated in that dear land. We receive daily reports of massacres and continuing systematic armed looting and destruction of state assets and individual property.

This has prompted the forces of rightness, justice, and peace in the world to try to acquaint themselves with the calamity of those innocents. In accordance with its responsibilities derived from the Fourth Geneva Convention of 1949 on the protection of civilians in times of war, the International Committee of the Red Cross has attempted to dispatch a team that would have reported on their conditions. But the aggressor, persisting in his inhumane conduct, declined to allow this international committee to send representatives to Kuwait in order to carry out their tasks. He also refused to let envoys of the United Nations Secretary-General visit Kuwait to stand on the conditions of its population.

Such conduct constitutes yet another violation by the aggressor of international and humanitarian covenants, thus demanding a resolute stand against it.

Against all these odds, an enormous source of solace to us has been the position taken by virtually all countries of the world in support of Kuwait's rights. Hence, the League of Arab States, the Conference of the Foreign Ministers of the Islamic Countries and the United Nations Security Council all took appropriate decisions condemning the Iraqi aggression and calling for the annulment of the Annexation Act and the immediate and unconditional withdrawal of the invading Iraqi forces to the border that existed prior to the aggression. Thus, the legitimate government of Kuwait would be able to exercise its functions and responsibilities as it used to before the invasion....

Two years have now elapsed since I made an initiative from this rostrum calling for the cancellation of foreign debts under the burden of which numerous countries suffer enormously. In point of fact, these countries have fallen victim to a host of factors that not only thwarted any prospect for their economic prosperity but also generated mounting pressure on them. Though some measure of progress has indeed been made in this area, the magnitude and scope of the problem continue to pose a grave threat to the lives of millions of human beings, a threat that in all likelihood may undermine world peace and stability. The longstanding academic argument that economic stability and political stability are closely interlinked is perhaps as valid and timely now as it has ever been. Along these lines, it would be advisable for us all to review the conclusions of the United Nations-sponsored Conference on the Problems of the Least Developed Countries, held in Paris earlier this month, in order to appreciate better the weight of the problem and the urgency it has assumed with a view to making tangible headway toward an effective remedy in the interest of all mankind. In this spirit, Kuwait, for its part, has decided, in line with our previous proposal regarding this issue, to write off all interests on its loans. In addition, Kuwait will consider with the poorest nations arrangements regarding the principal of its loans with a view to easing the burden of their debts....

From the early years of independence, my country has been privileged to be in the forefront of states that gave development aid to other countries. Kuwait's contributions represent the highest rate in the world in terms of gross national product, amounting to 8.3 percent of its GNP [gross national product]. This highlights Kuwait's genuine desire to contribute toward raising the standard of living in the developing nations. It also proves that Kuwait has been a leader in the efforts to improve the economic infrastructure of other countries....

In closing, may I take this opportunity, Mr. President, to address a few words to my people, my kinsfolk, the loyal sons and daughters of Kuwait, from this august forum, a forum for justice and fairness, a forum for guidance and hope, to assure each and every one of you that Allah, the Almighty, will ultimately secure triumph for us, thanks to your struggle and resolve, thanks to the gracious role of the United Nations, thanks to the support lent to us by our brethren and friends along with all people of good conscience throughout the world. The withdrawal of the invaders is, God willing, undoubtedly imminent. We shall return to our Kuwait, the oasis of safety and peace, which embraces all Kuwaitis and foreigners living in our midst as brothers. Together, we will join hands in concert and harmony to secure our development and progress. This will be a fulfillment of God's promise as rendered in the following verse:

> "O ye who believe,
> If you will aid (the cause of)
> Allah, He will aid you,
> And plant your feet firmly."

> (Surah 47, *Mohammad*, Verse 7.)

And whose word can be truer than Allah's?

Thank you and may Allah, our Lord, bring you all peace and grace.

UN SECURITY COUNCIL RESOLUTIONS 672 AND 673

On October 12, 1990, the UN Security Council unanimously passed Resolution 672, which condemned Israel for the violent response of its security forces to an October 8 attack by Palestinian stone throwers in Jerusalem. As many as 21 Palestinians were killed and approximately 150 were injured. The United States sponsored Resolution 672 in an effort to avoid having to veto a more severe resolution. After the Israeli government refused to receive a UN investigative mission, the UN Security Council on October 24 unanimously passed Resolution 673, deploring Israel's refusal to comply with Resolution 672.

RESOLUTION 672

The Security Council,

Recalling its resolutions 476 (1980) and 478 (1980),

Reaffirming that a just and lasting solution to the Arab-Israeli conflict must be based on its resolutions 242 (1967) and 338 (1973) through an active negotiating process which takes into account the right to security for all States in the region, including Israel, as well as the legitimate political rights of the Palestinian people.

Taking into consideration the statement of the Secretary-General relative to the purpose of the mission he is sending to the region and conveyed to the Council by the President on 12 October 1990.

1. *Expresses* alarm at the violence which took place on 8 October at the Al Haram Al Shareef and other Holy Places of Jerusalem resulting in over 20 Palestinian deaths and the injury of more than 150 people, including Palestinian civilians and innocent worshippers;

2. *Condemns* especially the acts of violence committed by the Israeli security forces resulting in injuries and loss of human life;

3. *Calls* upon Israel, the occupying Power, to abide scrupulously by its legal obligations and responsibilities under the Fourth Geneva Convention, which is applicable to all the territories occupied by Israel since 1967;

4. *Requests,* in connection with the decision of the Secretary-General to send a mission to the region, which the Council welcomes, that he submit a report to it before the end of October 1990 containing his findings and conclusions and that he use as appropriate all of the resources of the United Nations in the region in carrying out the mission.

RESOLUTION 673

The Security Council,

Reaffirming the obligations of Member States under the United Nations Charter,

Reaffirming also its resolution 672 (1990),

Having been briefed by the Secretary-General on 19 October 1990,

Expressing alarm at the rejection of Security Council resolution 672 (1990) by the Israeli Government, and its refusal to accept the mission of the Secretary-General,

Taking into consideration the statement of the Secretary-General relative to the purpose of the mission he is sending to the region and conveyed to the Council by the President on 12 October 1990,

Gravely concerned at the continued deterioration of the situation in the occupied territories,

1. *Deplores* the refusal of the Israeli Government to receive the mission of the Secretary-General to the region;

2. *Urges* the Israeli Government to reconsider its decision and insists that it comply fully with resolution 672 (1990) and to permit the mission of the Secretary-General to proceed in keeping with its purpose;

3. *Requests* the Secretary-General to submit to the Council the report requested in resolution 672 (1990);

4. *Affirms* its determination to give full and expeditious consideration to the report.

BUSH INCREASES FORCES IN SAUDI ARABIA

On November 8, 1990, President George Bush announced at a White House news conference that he was sending additional U.S. forces to Saudi Arabia to establish an "adequate offensive military option." Following is Bush's opening statement announcing the additional deployments:

On August 6th, in response to the unprovoked Iraqi invasion of Kuwait, I ordered the deployment of U.S. military forces to Saudi Arabia and the Persian Gulf to deter further Iraqi aggression and to protect our interests in the region. What we've done is right, and I'm happy to say that most members of Congress and the majority of Americans agree.

Before the invasion in August, we had succeeded in the struggle for freedom in Eastern Europe, and we'd hopefully have begun a new era that offered the promise of peace. Following the invasion, I stated that if history had taught us any lesson, it was that we must resist aggression or it would destroy our freedom.

Just ask the people of Kuwait. And the foreign nationals in hiding there. And the staffs of the remaining embassies who have experienced the horrors of Iraq's illegal occupation, its systematic dismantling of Kuwait, and its abuse of Kuwaitis and other citizens.

The world community also must prevent an individual clearly bent on regional domination from establishing a chokehold on the world's economic lifeline. We're seeing global economic stability and growth already at risk as, each day, countries around the world pay dearly for Saddam Hussein's aggression.

From the very beginning, we and our coalition partners have shared common political goals: the immediate, complete, and unconditional withdrawal of Iraqi forces from Kuwait, restoration of Kuwait's legitimate government, protection of the lives of citizens held hostage by Iraq both in Kuwait and Iraq, and restoration of security and stability in the Persian Gulf region.

To achieve these goals, we and our allies have forged a strong diplomatic, economic, and military strategy to force Iraq to comply with these objectives. The framework of this strategy is laid out in ten UN resolutions, overwhelmingly supported by the UN Security Council. In three months, the U.S. troop contribution to the multinational force in Saudi Arabia has gone from 10,000 to 230,000 as part of Operation Desert Shield. Gen. [H. Norman] Schwarzkopf [commanding general, U.S. forces in Saudi Arabia] reports that our forces, in conjunction with other coalition forces, now have the capability to defend successfully against any further Iraqi aggression.

After consultation with King Fahd and our other allies, I have today directed the Secretary of Defense to increase the size of U.S. forces committed to Desert Shield to ensure that the coalition has an adequate offensive military option should that be necessary to achieve our common goals. Toward this end, we will continue to discuss the possibility of both additional allied force contributions and appropriate UN actions.

Iraq's brutality, aggression, and violations of international law cannot be allowed to succeed. Secretary Baker has been consulting with our key partners in the coalition. He's met with the emirs of Bahrain and Kuwait, King Fahd, President Mubarak, as well as the Chinese Foreign Minister, President Ozal, Foreign Minister Shevardnadze, President Gorbachev. He also will be meeting with Prime Minister Thatcher and President Mitterrand. I've been heartened by Jim's appraisal of the strong international solidarity and determination to ensure that Iraq's aggression does not stand and is not rewarded.

But right now Kuwait is struggling for survival. And along with many other nations, we've been called upon to help. The consequences of our not doing so would be incalculable because Iraq's aggression is not just a challenge to the security of Kuwait and other gulf nations, but to the better world that we all have hoped to build in the wake of the Cold War. And, therefore, we and our allies cannot and will not shirk our responsibilities. The state of Kuwait must be restored or no nation will be safe, and the promising future we anticipate will, indeed, be jeopardized.

Let me conclude with a word to the young American GIs deployed in the gulf. We are proud of each and every one of you. I know you miss your loved ones and want to know when you'll be coming home. We won't leave you there any longer than necessary. I want every single soldier out of there as soon as possible. And we're all grateful for your continued sacrifice and your commitment.

UN SECURITY COUNCIL RESOLUTION 678

On November 29, 1990, the UN Security Council passed Resolution 678. It authorized member nations to use "all necessary means" after January 15, 1991, to force Iraq to withdraw from Kuwait and comply with all UN Security Council resolutions related to its aggression. The vote was 12-2 with 1 abstention.

The Security Council,
Recalling and reaffirming its resolutions 660 (1990), 661 (1990), 662 (1990), 664 (1990), 665 (1990), 666 (1990), 667 (1990), 669 (1990), 670 (1990) and 674 (1990),
Noting that, despite all efforts by the United Nations, Iraq refuses to comply with its obligation to implement resolution 660 (1990) and the above subsequent relevant resolutions, in flagrant contempt of the Council,
Mindful of its duties and responsibilities under the Charter of the United Nations for the maintenance and preservation of international peace and security,

Determined to secure full compliance with its decisions,
Acting under Chapter VII of the Charter of the United Nations,
1. *Demands* that Iraq comply fully with resolution 660 (1990) and all subsequent relevant resolutions and decides, while maintaining all its decisions, to allow Iraq one final opportunity, as a pause of goodwill, to do so;
2. *Authorizes* Member States cooperating with the Government of Kuwait, unless Iraq on or before 15 January 1991 fully implements, as set forth in paragraph 1 above, the foregoing resolutions, to use all necessary means to uphold and implement Security Council resolution 660 (1990) and all subsequent relevant resolutions and to restore international peace and security in the area;
3. *Requests* all States to provide appropriate support for the actions undertaken in pursuance of paragraph 2 of this resolution;
4. *Requests* the States concerned to keep the Council regularly informed on the progress of actions undertaken pursuant to paragraph 2 and 3 of this resolution;
5. *Decides* to remain seized of the matter.

WEBSTER TESTIMONY ON SANCTIONS

On December 5, 1990, CIA director William H. Webster testified before the House Armed Services Committee regarding the Persian Gulf crisis. He provided an assessment of the effectiveness of economic sanctions imposed against Iraq. Following are excerpts from his testimony:

. . . At the technical level, economic sanctions and the embargo against Iraq have put Saddam Hussein on notice that he is isolated from the world community and have dealt a serious blow to the Iraqi economy. More than one hundred countries are supporting the UN resolutions that impose economic sanctions on Iraq.

Coupled with the U.S. government's increased ability to detect and follow up on attempts to circumvent the blockade, the sanctions have all but shut off Iraq's exports and reduced imports to less than 10 percent of their pre-invasion level.

All sectors of the Iraq economy are feeling the pinch of sanctions, and many industries have largely shut down. Most importantly, the blockade has eliminated any hope Baghdad had of cashing in on higher oil prices or its seizure of Kuwaiti oil fields.

Despite mounting disruptions and hardships resulting from sanctions, Saddam apparently believes that he can outlast international resolve to maintain those sanctions. We see no indication that Saddam is concerned at this point that domestic discontent is growing to levels that may threaten his regime or that problems resulting from the sanctions are causing him to rethink his policy on Kuwait.

The Iraqi people have experienced considerable deprivation in the past. Given the brutal nature of the Iraqi security services, the population is not likely to oppose Saddam openly. Our judgment has been and continues to be that there is no assurance or guarantee that economic hardships will compel Saddam to change his policies or lead to internal unrest that would threaten his regime. . . .

The blockade and embargo have worked more effectively than Saddam probably expected. More than 90 percent of imports and 97 percent of exports have been shut off. Although there is smuggling across Iraq's borders, it is extremely small relative to Iraq's pre-crisis trade.

Iraqi efforts to break sanctions have thus far been largely unsuccessful. What little leakage has occurred is due largely to a relatively small number of private firms acting independently, and we believe that countries are actively enforcing the sanctions and plan to continue doing so.

Industry appears to be the hardest hit so far. Many firms are finding it difficult to cope with the departure of foreign workers and with the cutoff of imported industrial inputs, which [made up] nearly 60 percent of Iraq's total imports prior to the invasion.

These shortages have either shut down or severely curtailed production by a variety of industries, including many light industrial and assembly plants, as well as the country's only tire manufacturing plant.

Despite these shutdowns, the most vital industries, including electric power generation and refining, do not yet appear to be threatened. We believe they will be able to function for some time, because domestic consumption has been reduced, because Iraqi and Kuwaiti facilities have been cannibalized and because some stockpiles and surpluses already existed.

The cutoff of Iraq's oil exports and the success of sanctions have also choked off Baghdad's financial resources. This, too, has been more effective and more complete than Saddam probably expected. In fact, we believe that a lack of foreign exchange will, in time, be Iraq's greatest economic difficulty. The embargo has deprived Baghdad of roughly $1.5 billion of foreign exchange earnings monthly. . . .

We believe Baghdad's actions to forestall shortages of food stocks, including rationing, encouraging smuggling and promoting agricultural production, are adequate for the next several months. The full harvest of fruits and vegetables is injecting new supplies into the market and will provide a psychological as well as tangible respite from mounting pressures.

The Iraqi population in general has access to sufficient staple foods. Other foodstuffs, still not rationed, also remain available. However, the variety is diminishing, and prices are sharply inflated. For example, sugar purchased on the open market at the official exchange rate went from $32 per 50-kilogram bag in August to $580 per bag last month. . . .

Looking ahead, the economic picture changes somewhat. We expect Baghdad's foreign exchange reserves to become extremely tight, leaving it little cash with which to entice potential sanctions busters. At current rates of depletion, we estimate Iraq will have nearly depleted its available foreign exchange reserves by next spring.

Able to obtain even a few key imports, Iraq's economic problems will begin to multiply as Baghdad is forced to gradually shut down growing numbers of facilities in order to keep critical activities functioning as long as possible. Economic conditions will be noticeably worse, and Baghdad will find allocating scarce resources a significantly more difficult task.

Probably only energy-related and some military industries will still be functioning by next spring. This will almost certainly be the case by next summer. Baghdad will try to keep basic services such as electric power from deteriorating. . . . The regime will also try to insulate critical military industries to prevent an erosion of military preparedness. Nonetheless, reduced rations, coupled with rapid inflation and little additional support from the government, will compound the economic pressures facing most Iraqis.

By next spring, Iraqis will have made major changes in their diets. Poultry, which is a staple of the Iraqi diet, will not be available. Unless Iraq receives humanitarian food aid, or unless smuggling increases, some critical commodities such as sugar and edible oils will be in short supply.

Distribution problems are likely to create localized shortages. But we expect that Baghdad will be able to maintain grain consumption, mainly wheat, barley, and rice, at about two-thirds of last year's level until the next harvest in May. The spring grain and vegetable harvest will again augment food stocks, although only temporarily. To boost next year's food production, Baghdad has raised prices paid to farmers for their produce and decreed that farmers must cultivate all available land. Nonetheless, Iraq does not have the capability to become self-sufficient in food production by next year. . . .

Although sanctions are hurting Iraq's civilian economy, they are affecting Iraq's military only at the margins. Iraq's fairly static defensive posture will reduce wear and tear on the military equipment and, as a result, extend the life of its inventory of spare parts and maintenance items.

Under non-combat conditions, Iraq ground and air forces can probably maintain near current levels of readiness for as long as nine months. We expect the Iraqi air force to feel the effects of sanctions more quickly and to a greater degree than the Iraqi ground forces because of its greater reliance on high technology and foreign equipment and technicians.

Major repairs to sophisticated aircraft like the F-1 will be achieved with significant difficulty, if at all, because of the exodus of foreign technicians. Iraqi technicians, however, should be able to maintain current levels of aircraft sorties for three to six months.

The Iraqi ground forces are more immune to sanctions. Before the invasion, Baghdad maintained large inventories of basic military supplies, such as ammunition, and supplies probably remain adequate.

The embargo will eventually hurt Iraqi armor by preventing the replacement of old fire-control systems and creating shortages of additives for various critical lubricants. . . .

While we can look ahead several months and predict the gradual deterioration of the Iraqi economy, it is more difficult to assess how or when these conditions will cause Saddam to modify his behavior. At present, Saddam almost certainly assumes that he is coping effectively with the sanctions. . . .

Saddam's willingness to sit tight and try to outlast the sanctions, or in the alternative, to avoid war by withdrawing from Kuwait, will be determined by his total assessment of the political, economic, and military pressures arrayed against him.

HUSSEIN MESSAGE FREEING HOSTAGES

On December 6, 1990, Baghdad radio broadcast a message from Iraqi president Saddam Hussein to the Iraqi National Assembly, Iraq's rubber-stamp parliament, asking the assembly to approve the release of all foreigners held in Iraq. Following is the text of Hussein's message as translated by the Foreign Broadcast Information Service:

In the name of God, the merciful, the compassionate. Mr. National Assembly Speaker, members:

Peace be upon you. Under difficult conditions, the strength of the believers' affiliation and loyalty is put to the test. Their action in the service of principles is also put to the test. Iraqis in general, and you among them, have proved that on very dark nights, the spark of faith glows in a much nicer way than on ordinary nights. Adherence to the supreme principles governing the relation between man and his Creator and his duty toward Him, as well as the relation between the Iraqis with all peoples, becomes even stronger in the more difficult circumstances.

And, just as the continued endeavor is required on earth, the correct answers to the continuous test are also required, without making the test or success in it dependent on a certain phrase and time.

On the basis of these principles and what we desire—that the influence of the believers expands, and that the knowledge of mankind in general expands with the believers' principles and the truth of their mission—we believe that, this time, the National Assembly is asked to make a decisive and final decision concerning a humanitarian issue, which you, and the whole world, know about.

National Assembly members, the thing that worries the faithful struggler, the honorable struggler, and the brave fighter—who has the values of the chivalrous believer—most is when the trenches in the battle arena get mixed and when some people, who do not want to fight and who are not among the evildoers, get trapped in the space between the two trenches. This worry becomes deep grief when that kind of people are harmed because of the level and type of the conflict.

The foreigners who were prevented from traveling are among those people in the battle between right, led by Iraq's great people and valiant armed forces, and evil, whose failing mass is led by Bush, the enemy of God. As you and my brothers in the leadership know, I realize that despite what they had to put up with, denying those people the freedom to travel has rendered a great service to the cause of peace. And because God has taught us that forbidden things should never be resorted to except in very urgent cases and without any excesses, we must not keep these emergency measures, especially this measure, any longer.

The days, weeks, and months through which our people and nation have passed have been such that our options, even those concerning the nature and form of defense, were not open or without limits in every area and all conditions. For instance, our valiant forces did not have the chance to complete their concentrations in order to confront the possibilities of military aggression against them in the Kuwaiti governorate. So any measure that was taken to delay the war may not have been correct from the humanitarian and practical standpoints and under established norms, but it has provided an opportunity for us to prepare for any eventuality.

We have now reached the time when, with God's care, our blessed force has become fully prepared, if God wills that we should fight in defense of his values and ideals against the infidels, profligates, and traitors, and also in defense of the great national, pan-Arab, and humanitarian gains.

Gentlemen: Good people, men and women of different nationalities and political trends have come to Iraq. Dear brothers from Jordan, Yemen, Palestine, Sudan, and the Arab Maghereb have also consulted with us on this issue, as on others. We have felt, guided by our humanitarian feelings, that the time has come to make a firm decision on this subject. We had considered a timing different from the present one; namely, the occasion of Christmas and New Year, which are of special significance to Christians in the world, including Christians in the West.

However, the appeal by some brothers, the decision of the Democratic majority in the U.S. Senate, and the European Parliament's invitation to our Foreign Minister for dialogue; all these have encouraged us to respond to these good, positive changes—changes that will have a major impact on world public opinion in general, and U.S. public opinion in particular, in restraining the evil ones who are seeking and pushing for war as the option they have chosen out of their evil tendencies and premeditated intentions to do harm.

In view of all of this, we have found that exigencies that permitted the impermissible, and thus prevented the travel of foreigners, have weakened and have been replaced by something stronger; namely, this positive change in public opinion, including the change in U.S. public opinion, which will constitute a restraint on the intentions and decisions or the evil ones, who are led in their evil intentions and steps by the enemy of God, Bush.

Therefore, I call on you, brothers, to make your just decision and allow all foreigners on whom restrictions were placed to enjoy the freedom of travel and to lift these restrictions, without our apologies for any harm done to anyone of them. God, the Almighty, grants forgiveness.

Brothers, I ask you, and through you I ask the Iraqi people and our brave armed forces, to maintain your alertness and vigil because the armies of aggression are still on our holy lands, in the Arabian Peninsula, and the evil ones are talking of war. Bush's invitation for talks, as far as we can discern, has continued to bear the possibilities or the inclination toward aggression and war. The buildup is growing.

Therefore, the steadfast believers, both on the level of the public and on the level of our armed forces, should not fall in the trap in which some have fallen in the past.

May God protect you and protect our people and nation, steer humanity from what God hates, help the faithful to carry out what

God wishes, and smite the infidels and traitors after exposing them and their shameful deeds. He is the best supporter and backer. God is great, accursed by the infidels and traitors, who gave the oppressors and infidels the opportunity to invade the holy land.

Glory and greatness to the mujahedeen of the occupied land and all the steadfast mujahedeen and fighters of our great Arab nation.

BAKER AND AZIZ GENEVA STATEMENTS

On January 9, 1991, U.S. secretary of state James A. Baker III and Iraqi foreign minister Tariq Aziz met in Geneva for six and a half hours to seek a peaceful resolution to the Gulf crisis. After their meeting, at which neither side made concessions, Baker and Aziz held consecutive press conferences to explain their positions and give their appraisals of the meeting. Baker appeared first. Following are the opening statements of Baker and Aziz to reporters:

BAKER STATEMENT

I have just given President Bush a full report of our meeting today. I told him that Minister Aziz and I had completed a serious and extended diplomatic conversation in an effort to find a political solution to the crisis in the gulf. I met with Minister Aziz today not to negotiate, as we had made clear we would not do, that is, negotiate backwards from United Nations Security Council resolutions, but I met with him today to communicate. And "communicate" means listening as well as talking. And we did that, both of us.

The message that I conveyed from President Bush and our coalition partners was that Iraq must either comply with the will of the international community and withdraw peacefully from Kuwait or be expelled by force.

Regrettably, ladies and gentlemen, I heard nothing today that—in over six hours I heard nothing that suggested to me any Iraqi flexibility whatsoever on complying with the United Nations Security Council resolutions.

There have been too many Iraqi miscalculations. The Iraqi Government miscalculated the international response to the invasion of Kuwait, expecting the world community to stand idly by while Iraqi forces systematically pillaged a peaceful neighbor. It miscalculated the response, I think, to the barbaric policy of holding thousands of foreign hostages, thinking that somehow cynically doling them out a few at a time would somehow win political advantage, and it miscalculated that it could divide the international community and gain something thereby from its aggression.

So let us hope that Iraq does not miscalculate again. The Iraqi leadership must have no doubt that the twenty-eight nations which have deployed forces to the gulf in support of the United Nations have both the power and will to evict Iraq from Kuwait.

If it should choose—and the choice is Iraq's—if it should chose to continue its brutal occupation of Kuwait, Iraq will be choosing a military confrontation which it cannot win, and which will have devastating consequences for Iraq.

I made these points with Minister Aziz not to threaten but to inform, and I did so with no sense of satisfaction. For we genuinely desire a peaceful outcome, and as both President Bush and I have said on many occasions, the people of the United States have no quarrel with the people of Iraq.

I simply wanted to leave as little room as possible for yet another tragic miscalculation by the Iraqi leadership. And I would suggest to you, ladies and gentlemen, that this is still a confrontation that Iraq can avoid.

The path of peace remains open, and that path is laid out very clearly in twelve United Nations Security Council resolutions adopted over a period of over five months. But now the choice lies with the Iraqi leadership. The choice really is theirs to make. And let us all hope that that leadership will have the wisdom to choose the path of peace.

AZIZ STATEMENT

If we had an earlier opportunity, several months ago, I told the Secretary that we might have been able to remove a lot of misunderstandings between us—there was a chance, or there is a chance, for that. Because he spoke at length about his government's assumptions of miscalculations by Iraq—and when I came to that point, I made it clear to him that we have not made miscalculations. We are very well aware of the situation. We have been very well aware of the situation from the very beginning.

And I told him that we have heard a lot of talk on his side and on the side of President Bush that the Iraqis have not got the message, they don't know what's going around them. . . . I told him if we had met several months ago, I would have told you that we do know everything. We know what the deployment of your forces in the region mean [sic]; we know what the resolutions you imposed on the Security Council mean; and we know all the facts about the situation—the political facts, the military facts, and the other facts. So talking about miscalculation is incorrect.

I hear Secretary Baker describing our meeting in form and I say also that from the professional point of view, it was a serious meeting. We both listened to each other very carefully. We both gave each other enough time to explaining [sic] the views we wanted to explain—to convey the information we wanted to convey. From this aspect, about this aspect of the talks, I am satisfied.

But we had grave, or big differences about the issues we addressed. Mr. Baker reiterated the very well-known American position. He is interested in one question only; that's the situation in the Gulf, and the Security Council resolutions about that situation. I told him very clearly, and I repeated my idea and explained it at length, that what is at stake in our region is peace, security, and stability. What's at stake is the fate of the whole region . . . which has been suffering from wars, instabilities, hardships, for several decades.

If you are ready to bring about peace to the region—comprehensive, lasting, just peace to the whole region of the Middle East—we are ready to cooperate. I told him I have no problem with the international legality. I have no problem with the principles of justice and fairness.

Concerning the new world order, or the international world order, I said I have no problem with that order. And we would love to be partners in that order. But that order has to be implemented justly, and in all cases, not using that order in a single manner, in a selective manner, impose it on a certain case . . . and neglect the other issues and not show sincerity and seriousness about implementing it on other issues.

He said that he does not believe that what happened on the 2d of August and later was for the cause of the Palestinian question, or to help the Palestinians. I explained to him the history of Iraq's interest in the Palestinian question. I explained to him that the Palestinian question is a matter of national security to Iraq. If the Palestinian question is not resolved, we do not feel secure in our country.

And I told him that the United States actually implemented embargo on Iraq before the 2d of August. We had dealings with the United States in the field of foodstuffs; we used to buy more than a billion dollars of American products. And we were faithful and accurate in our dealing with the American relative institutions. Early in 1990, the American administration suspended that deal, which was profitable to both sides. And we were denied food from the United States.

Then the United States government decided to deny Iraq the purchase of a very large list of items. That was done also by the British government and other Western governments. So the boycott was there before the 2d of August. The threat to the security of Iraq was there before the 2d of August. The threat to the Palestinians was there before that date. The threat to the security of Jordan was there before that date.

If the matter is the implementation or the respect of . . . Security Council resolutions, we have a number of resolutions about the Palestinian question. They have been neglected for decades. The last two important resolutions, 242 and 338. The first was adopted in 1967, the other in 1973, and they are not yet implemented. And the United States and members of the coalition . . . have not sent troops to impose the implementation of those resolutions. They have not taken measures against Israel.

On the contrary, the United States Government has covered the Israeli position, protected it politically at the Security Council and that's very well known to everybody. And the United States Government still supplies Israel with military and financial means to stick to its intransigence. So if the matter is respect of international law, Security Council resolutions, we would like you to show the same attention to all Security Council resolutions. And if you do that, a lot of differences between us will be removed.

Concerning the threats—or no threats, which the Secretary referred to and has addressed to you—the tone of his language was diplomatic and polite. I reciprocated. But the substance was full of threats. And I told him, also in substance, that we will not yield to threats. We would like to have genuine constructive dialogue . . . in order to make peace in the region and between our two nations.

You hear that I declined to receive the letter from President Bush to my president. At the beginning of the meeting, Secretary Baker told me that he carries a letter from his president to my president, and he handed over a copy to me. I told him I want to read this letter first. And I read it . . . carefully and slowly, and I knew what it was about. I told him I am sorry, I cannot receive this letter.

And the reason is that the language in this letter is not compatible with the language that should be used in correspondence between heads of state. I have no objection that Mr. Bush would state his position very clearly. But when a head of state writes to another head of state a letter, and if he really intends to make peace with that head of state or reach genuine understanding, he should use a polite language. Therefore, because the language of the letter was contrary to the traditions of correspondence between heads of state, I declined to receive it.

BUSH LETTER TO HUSSEIN

Following is the text of a letter from U.S. president George Bush to Iraqi president Saddam Hussein. Secretary of State James A. Baker III of the United States handed the letter to Foreign Minister Tariq Aziz of Iraq at their meeting on January 9, 1991, in Geneva. Aziz refused to accept the letter, saying its language was "contrary to the traditions of correspondence between heads of state."

Mr. President:

We stand today at the brink of war between Iraq and the world. This is a war that began with your invasion of Kuwait; this is a war that can be ended only by Iraq's full and unconditional compliance with UN Security Council Resolution 678.

I am writing you now, directly, because what is at stake demands that no opportunity be lost to avoid what would be a certain calamity for the people of Iraq. I am writing, as well, because it is said by some that you do not understand just how isolated Iraq is and what Iraq faces as a result.

I am not in a position to judge whether this impression is correct; what I can do, though, is try in the letter to reinforce what Secretary of State [James A.] Baker [III] told your Foreign Minister and eliminate any uncertainty or ambiguity that might exist in your mind about where we stand and what we are prepared to do.

The international community is united in its call for Iraq to leave all of Kuwait without condition and without further delay. This is not simply the policy of the United States; it is the position of the world community as expressed in no less than 12 Security Council resolutions.

We prefer a peaceful outcome. However, anything less than full compliance with UN Security Council Resolution 678 and its predecessors is unacceptable.

There can be no reward for aggression. Nor will there be any negotiation. Principle cannot be compromised. However, by its full compliance, Iraq will gain the opportunity to rejoin the international community.

More immediately, the Iraqi military establishment will escape destruction. But unless you withdraw from Kuwait completely and without condition, you will lose more than Kuwait.

What is at issue here is not the future of Kuwait—it will be free, its government will be restored—but rather the future of Iraq. This choice is yours to make.

The United States will not be separated from its coalition partners. Twelve Security Council resolutions, 28 countries providing military units to enforce them, more than 100 governments complying with sanctions—all highlight the fact that it is not Iraq against the United States, but Iraq against the world.

That most Arab and Muslim countries are arrayed against you as well should reinforce what I am saying. Iraq cannot and will not be able to hold on to Kuwait or exact a price for leaving.

You may be tempted to find solace in the diversity of opinion that is American democracy. You should resist any such temptation. Diversity ought not to be confused with division. Nor should you underestimate, as others have before you, America's will.

Iraq is already feeling the effects of the sanctions mandated by the United Nations. Should war come, it will be a far greater tragedy for you and your country.

Let me state, too, that the United States will not tolerate the use of chemical or biological weapons or the destruction of Kuwait's oil fields and installations. Further, you will be held directly responsible for terrorist actions against any member of the coalition.

The American people would demand the strongest possible response. You and your country will pay a terrible price if you order unconscionable acts of this sort.

I write this letter not to threaten, but to inform. I do so with no sense of satisfaction, for the people of the United States have no quarrel with the people of Iraq.

Mr. President, UN Security Council Resolution 678 establishes the period before Jan. 15 of this year as a 'pause of good will' so that this crisis may end without further violence.

Whether this pause is used as intended, or merely becomes a prelude to further violence, is in your hands, and yours alone. I hope you weigh your choice carefully and choose wisely, for much will depend upon it.

George Bush

CONGRESS AUTHORIZES USE OF FORCE

On January 12, 1991, Congress adopted H J Res 77, which authorized the use of military force against Iraq. The House

approved the resolution by a vote of 250-183. The Senate approved the measure (originally introduced as S J Res 2) by a vote of 52-47.

To authorize the use of United States Armed Forces pursuant to United Nations Security Council resolution 678.

Whereas the Government of Iraq without provocation invaded and occupied the territory of Kuwait on August 2, 1990; and

Whereas both the House of Representatives (in HJ Res. 658 of the 101st Congress) and the Senate (in S Con Res 147 of the 101st Congress) have condemned Iraq's invasion of Kuwait and declared their support for international action to reverse Iraq's aggression; and

Whereas, Iraq's conventional, chemical, biological, and nuclear weapons and ballistic missile programs and its demonstrated willingness to use weapons of mass destruction pose a grave threat to world peace; and

Whereas the international community has demanded that Iraq withdraw unconditionally and immediately from Kuwait and that Kuwait's independence and legitimate government be restored; and

Whereas the UN Security Council repeatedly affirmed the inherent right of individual or collective self-defense in response to the armed attack by Iraq against Kuwait in accordance with Article 51 of the UN Charter; and

Whereas, in the absence of full compliance by Iraq with its resolutions, the UN Security Council in Resolution 678 has authorized member states of the United Nations to use all necessary means, after January 15, 1991, to uphold and implement all relevant Security Council resolutions and to restore international peace and security in the area; and

Whereas Iraq has persisted in its illegal occupation of, and brutal aggression against, Kuwait: Now, therefore be it

Resolved by the Senate and House of Representatives of the United States of America in Congress assembled,

Section 1. Short Title. This joint resolution may be cited as the "Authorization for Use of Military Force Against Iraq Resolution."

Section 2. Authorization for Use of United States Armed Forces

(a) AUTHORIZATION. The President is authorized, subject to subsection (b), to use United States Armed Forces pursuant to United Nations Security Council Resolution 678 (1990) in order to achieve implementation of Security Council Resolutions 660, 661, 662, 664, 665, 666, 667, 669, 670, 674, and 677.

(b) REQUIREMENT FOR DETERMINATION THAT USE OF MILITARY FORCE IS NECESSARY. Before exercising the authority granted in subsection (a), the President shall make available to the Speaker of the House of Representatives and the President pro tempore of the Senate his determination that (1) the United States has used all appropriate diplomatic and other peaceful means to obtain compliance by Iraq with the United Nations Security Council resolutions cited in subsection (a); and

(2) that those efforts have not been successful in obtaining such compliance.

(c) WAR POWERS RESOLUTION REQUIREMENTS.

(1) SPECIFIC STATUTORY AUTHORIZATION. Consistent with section 8(a)(1) of the War Powers Resolution, the Congress declares that this section is intended to constitute specific statutory authorization within the meaning of section 5(b) of the War Powers Resolution.

(2) APPLICABILITY OF OTHER REQUIREMENTS. Nothing in this resolution supersedes any requirement of the War Powers Resolution.

Section 4. REPORTS TO CONGRESS.

At least once every 60 days, the President shall submit to the Congress a summary on the status of efforts to obtain compliance by Iraq with the resolutions adopted by the United Nations Security council in response to Iraq's aggression.

BUSH ANNOUNCES WAR ON IRAQ

On January 16, 1991, President Bush addressed the nation from the Oval Office at 9:00 p.m. EST, a few hours after the beginning of a multinational bombing campaign against Iraq and Iraqi forces in Kuwait. The bombing was the first phase of the military plan developed by the United States and its coalition allies to expel Iraq from Kuwait.

Just two hours ago, allied air forces began an attack on military targets in Iraq and Kuwait. These attacks continue as I speak. Ground forces are not engaged.

This conflict started August 2 when the dictator of Iraq invaded a small and helpless neighbor. Kuwait, a member of the Arab League and a member of the United Nations, was crushed, its people brutalized.

Five months ago, Saddam Hussein started this cruel war against Kuwait. Tonight the battle has been joined.

This military action, taken in accord with United Nations resolutions and with the consent of the United States Congress, follows months of constant and virtually endless diplomatic activity on the part of the United Nations, the United States, and many, many other countries.

Arab leaders sought what became known as an Arab solution, only to conclude that Saddam Hussein was unwilling to leave Kuwait. Others traveled to Baghdad in a variety of efforts to restore peace and justice.

Our Secretary of State James [A.] Baker [III] held an historic meeting in Geneva, only to be totally rebuffed.

This past weekend, in a last ditch effort, the secretary-general of the United Nations went to the Middle East with peace in his heart—his second such mission. And he came back from Baghdad with no progress at all in getting Saddam Hussein to withdraw from Kuwait.

Now, the twenty-eight countries with forces in the Gulf area have exhausted all reasonable efforts to reach a peaceful resolution [and] have no choice but to drive Saddam from Kuwait by force. We will not fail.

As I report to you, air attacks are under way against military targets in Iraq. We are determined to knock out Saddam Hussein's nuclear bomb potential. We will also destroy his chemical weapons facilities. Much of Saddam's artillery and tanks will be destroyed. Our operations are designed to best protect the lives of all the coalition forces by targeting Saddam's vast military arsenal.

Initial reports from General [H. Norman] Schwarzkopf are that our operations are proceeding according to plan. Our objectives are clear: Saddam Hussein's forces will leave Kuwait, the legitimate government of Kuwait will be restored to its rightful place, and Kuwait will once again be free.

Iraq will eventually comply with all relevant United Nations resolutions, and then, when peace is restored, it is our hope that Iraq will live as a peaceful and cooperative member of the family of nations, thus enhancing the security and stability of the Gulf.

Some may ask, why act now? Why not wait? The answer is clear. The world could wait no longer. Sanctions, though having some effect, showed no signs of accomplishing their objective. Sanctions were tried for well over five months, and we and our allies concluded that sanctions alone would not force Saddam from Kuwait.

While the world waited, Saddam Hussein systematically raped, pillaged, and plundered a tiny nation, no threat to his own. He subjected the people of Kuwait to unspeakable atrocities, and among those maimed and murdered, innocent children.

While the world waited, Saddam sought to add to the chemical weapons arsenal he now possesses an infinitely more dangerous weapon of mass destruction, a nuclear weapon. And while the world waited, while the world talked peace and withdrawal, Saddam Hussein dug in and moved massive forces into Kuwait. While the world waited, while Saddam stalled, more damage was being done to the fragile economies of the Third World, the emerging democracies of Eastern Europe, to the entire world, including to our own economy. The United States, together with the United Nations, exhausted every means at our disposal to bring this crisis to a peaceful end. However, Saddam clearly felt that by stalling and threatening and defying the United Nations, he could weaken the forces arrayed against him. While the world waited, Saddam Hussein met every overture of peace with open contempt. While the world prayed for peace, Saddam prepared for war.

I had hoped that when the United States Congress, in historic debate, took its resolute action, Saddam would realize he could not prevail and would move out of Kuwait in accord with the United Nations resolutions. He did not do that. Instead, he remained intransigent, certain that time was on his side. Saddam was warned over and over again to comply with the will of the United Nations, leave Kuwait or be driven out. Saddam has arrogantly rejected all warnings. Instead he tried to make this a dispute between Iraq and the United States of America. Well, he failed.

Tonight twenty-eight nations, countries from five continents—Europe and Asia, Africa, and the Arab League—have forces in the Gulf area, standing shoulder to shoulder against Saddam Hussein. These countries had hoped the use of force could be avoided. Regrettably, we now believe that only force will make him leave.

Prior to ordering our forces into battle, I instructed our military commanders to take every necessary step to prevail as quickly as possible and with the greatest degree of protection possible for American and allied servicemen and women.

I've told the American people before that this will not be another Vietnam, and I repeat this here tonight. Our troops will have the best possible support in the entire world, and they will not be asked to fight with one hand tied behind their back.

I'm hopeful that this fighting will not go on for long and that casualties will be held to an absolute minimum. This is an historic moment. We have in this past year made great progress in ending the long era of conflict and cold war. We have before us the opportunity to forge for ourselves and for future generations a new world order, a world where the rule of law, not the law of the jungle, governs the conduct of nations.

When we are successful—and we will be—we have a real chance at this new world order, an order in which a credible United Nations can use its peacekeeping role to fulfill the promise envisioned of the UN's founders. We have no argument with the people of Iraq; indeed, for the innocents caught in this conflict, I pray for their safety. Our goal is not the conquest of Iraq; it is the liberation of Kuwait. It is my hope that somehow the Iraqi people can even now convince their dictator that he must lay down his arms, leave Kuwait and let Iraq itself rejoin the family of peace-loving nations.

Thomas Paine wrote many years ago, "These are the times that try men's souls." Those well-known words are so very true today, but even as planes of the multinational forces attack Iraq, I prefer to think of peace, not war. I am convinced not only that we will prevail, but that out of the horror of combat will come the recognition that no nation can stand against a world united, no nation will be permitted to brutally assault its neighbor.

No president can easily commit our sons and daughters to war. They are the nation's finest. Ours is an all-volunteer force, magnificently trained, highly motivated. The troops know why they're there, and listen to what they say, for they've said it better than any president or prime minister ever could. Listen to Hollywood Huddleston, Marine lance corporal. He says: "Let's free these people so we can go home and be free again."

He's right. The terrible crimes and tortures committed by Saddam's henchmen against the innocent people of Kuwait are an affront to mankind and a challenge to the freedom of all.

Listen to one of our great officers out there, Marine Lt. Gen. Walter Boomer. He said: "There are things worth fighting for. A world in which brutality and lawlessness are allowed to go unchecked isn't the kind of world we're going to want to live in."

Listen to Master Sgt. J. P. Kendall of the 82nd Airborne: "We're here for more than just the price of a gallon of gas. What we're doing is going to chart the future of the world for the next 100 years. It's better to deal with this guy now than five years from now."

And finally we should all sit up and listen to Jackie Jones, an Army lieutenant, when she says: "If we let him get away with this, who knows what's going to be next."

I have called upon Hollywood and Walter and J. P. and Jackie and all their courageous comrades in arms to do what must be done. Tonight, America and the world are deeply grateful to them and to their families. And let me say to everyone listening or watching tonight, when the troops we've sent in finish their work, I am determined to bring them home as soon as possible.

Tonight, as our forces fight, they and their families are in our prayers. May God bless each and every one of them, and the coalition forces at our side in the Gulf, and may he continue to bless our nation, the United States of America.

U.S.-SOVIET STATEMENT ON MIDDLE EAST

On January 29, 1991, Secretary of State James A. Baker III and Foreign Minister Aleksandr A. Bessmertnykh of the Soviet Union issued a joint statement on the Gulf Crisis and other Middle East issues.

In the course of the discussions held in Washington on January 26-29, 1991, USSR Minister of Foreign Affairs Bessmertnykh and U.S. Secretary of State James Baker devoted considerable attention to the situation in the Persian Gulf.

The ministers reiterated the commitment of their countries to the UN Security Council resolutions adopted in connection with Iraq's aggression against Kuwait. They expressed regret that numerous efforts of the United Nations, other international organizations, individual countries, and envoys were all rebuffed by Iraq. The military actions authorized by the United Nations have been provoked by the refusal of the Iraqi leadership to comply with the clear and lawful demands of the international community for withdrawal from Kuwait.

Secretary of State Baker emphasized that the United States and its coalition partners are seeking the liberation of Kuwait, not the destruction of Iraq. He stressed that the United States has no quarrel with the people of Iraq, and poses no threat to Iraq's territorial integrity. Secretary Baker reiterated that the United States is doing its utmost to avoid casualties among the civilian population, and is not interested in expanding the conflict. Minister of Foreign Affairs Bessmertnykh took note of the American position and agreed that Iraq's withdrawal from Kuwait must remain the goal of the international community. Both sides believe that everything possible should be done to avoid further escalation of the war and expansion of its scale.

The ministers continue to believe that a cessation of hostilities would be possible if Iraq would make an unequivocal commitment to withdraw from Kuwait. They also believe that such a commitment must be backed by immediate, concrete steps leading to full compliance with the Security Council resolutions.

The Iraqi leadership has to respect the will of the international community. By doing so, it has it within its power to stop the violence and bloodshed.

The ministers agreed that establishing enduring stability and peace in the region after the conflict, on the basis of effective security arrangements, will be a high priority of our two governments. Working to reduce the risk of war and miscalculation will be essential, particularly because a spiraling arms race in this volatile region can only generate greater violence and extremism. In addition, dealing with the causes of instability and the sources of conflict, including the Arab-Israeli conflict, will be especially important. Indeed, both ministers agreed that without a meaningful peace process—one which promotes a just peace, security, and a real reconciliation for Israel, Arab states, and Palestinians—it will not be possible to deal with the sources of conflict and instability in the region. Both ministers, therefore, agreed that in the aftermath of the crisis in the Persian Gulf, mutual U.S.-Soviet efforts to promote Arab-Israeli peace and regional stability, in consultation with other parties in the region, will be greatly facilitated and enhanced.

The two ministers are confident that the United States and the Soviet Union, as demonstrated in various other regional conflicts, can make a substantial contribution to the achievement of a comprehensive settlement in the Middle East.

U.S. CONDITIONS FOR ENDING THE WAR

On February 22, 1991, in response to indications that Iraq would formally accept a Soviet peace plan calling for a conditional Iraqi withdrawal from Kuwait, President George Bush announced that, in order to end the war, Iraq would have to withdraw in accordance with terms set by the U.S.-led coalition. He said Saddam Hussein must accept the terms "publicly and authoritatively" before noon EST February 23. After Bush's statement, White House Press Secretary Marlin Fitzwater outlined the terms that Iraq would have to meet to end the war. Following are the statements of Bush and Fitzwater:

BUSH'S STATEMENT

Good morning. The United States and its coalition allies are committed to enforcing the United Nations resolutions that call for Saddam Hussein to immediately and unconditionally leave Kuwait.

In view of the Soviet initiative, which very frankly we appreciate, we want to set forth this morning the specific criteria that will ensure Saddam Hussein complies with the United Nations mandate.

Within the last twenty-four hours alone, we have heard a defiant, uncompromising address by Saddam Hussein, followed less than ten hours later by a statement in Moscow that on the face of it appears more reasonable.

I say "on the face of it" because the statement promised unconditional Iraqi withdrawal from Kuwait, only to set forth a number of conditions, and, needless to say, any conditions would be unacceptable to the international coalition and would not be in compliance with the United Nations Security Council Resolution 660's demand for immediate and unconditional withdrawal.

More importantly and more urgently, we learned this morning that Saddam has now launched a scorched-earth policy against Kuwait, anticipating perhaps that he will now be forced to leave. He is wantonly setting fires to and destroying the oil wells, the oil tanks, the export terminals and other installations of that small country. Indeed, they are destroying the entire oil-production system of Kuwait. And at the same time that the Moscow press conference was going on and Iraq's foreign minister was talking peace, Saddam Hussein was launching Scud missiles.

After examining the Moscow statement and discussing it with my senior advisers here late last evening and this morning, and after extensive consultation with our coalition partners, I have decided that the time has come to make public with specificity just exactly what is required of Iraq if a ground war is to be avoided.

Most important, the coalition will give Saddam Hussein until noon Saturday to do what he must do—begin his immediate and unconditional withdrawal from Kuwait. We must hear publicly and authoritatively his acceptance of these terms.

The statement to be released, as you will see, does just this, and informs Saddam Hussein that he risks subjecting the Iraqi people to further hardship unless the Iraqi Government complies fully with the terms of the statement. We will put that statement out soon. It will be in considerable detail, and that's all I'll have to say about it right now. Thank you very much.

FITZWATER'S STATEMENT

The Soviet announcement yesterday represents a serious and useful effort, which is appreciated. But major obstacles remain.

The coalition for many months has sought a peaceful resolution to this crisis in keeping with the UN resolutions. As President Bush pointed out to President Gorbachev, the steps the Iraqis are considering would constitute a conditional withdrawal, and would also prevent the full implementation of relevant UN Security Council resolutions.

Also, there is no indication that Iraq is prepared to withdraw immediately.

Full compliance with the Security Council resolutions has been a consistent and necessary demand of the international community. The world must make sure that Iraq has, in fact renounced its claim to Kuwait and accepted all relevant UN Security Council resolutions.

Indeed, only the Security Council can agree to lift sanctions against Iraq, and the world needs to be assured in concrete terms of Iraq's peaceful intentions before such action can be taken.

In a situation where sanctions have been lifted, Saddam Hussein could simply revert to using his oil resources once again—not to provide for the well-being of his people, but instead, to rearm.

So, in a final effort to obtain Iraqi compliance with the will of the international community, the United States, after consulting with the government of Kuwait and our other coalition partners, declares that a ground campaign will not be initiated against Iraqi forces if prior to noon Saturday, February 23, New York time, Iraq publicly accepts the following terms, and authoritatively communicates that acceptance to the United Nations.

First, Iraq must begin large-scale withdrawal from Kuwait by noon New York time, Saturday, February 23. Iraq must complete military withdrawal from Kuwait in one week. Given the fact that Iraq invaded and occupied Kuwait in a matter of hours, anything longer than this, from the initiation of the withdrawal, would not meet Resolution 660's requirement of immediacy.

Within the first forty-eight hours, Iraq must remove all its forces from Kuwait City and allow for the prompt return of the legitimate government of Kuwait.

It must withdraw from all prepared defenses along the Saudi-Kuwait and Saudi-Iraq borders, from Bubiyan and Warba Islands, and from Kuwait's Rumaila oilfield.

Within the one week specified above, Iraq must return all its forces to their positions of August 1 in accordance with Resolution 660.

In cooperation with the International Red Cross, Iraq must release all prisoners of war and third-country civilians being held against their will and return the remains of killed and deceased servicemen.

This action must commence immediately with the initiation of the withdrawal and must be completed within forty-eight hours.

Iraq must remove all explosives or booby traps, including those on Kuwaiti oil installations, and designate Iraqi military liaison officers to work with Kuwaiti and other coalition forces on the operational details related to Iraq's withdrawal.

To conclude, the provision of—to include the provision of all data on the location and nature of any land or sea mines.

Iraq must cease combat air fire, aircraft flights over Iraq and Kuwait, except for transport aircraft carrying troops out of Kuwait, and allow coalition aircraft exclusive control over and use of all Kuwaiti airspace.

It must cease all destructive actions against Kuwaiti citizens and property and release all Kuwaiti detainees.

The United States and its coalition partners reiterate that their forces will not attack retreating Iraqi forces, and further will exercise restraint so long as withdrawal proceeds in accordance with the above guidelines and there are not attacks on other countries.

Any breach of these terms will bring an instant and sharp response from coalition forces in accordance with United Nations Security Council [Resolution] 678.

That's the conclusion of our prepared statement.

Let me just add a couple of points.

First of all, that a copy of this document was provided to Iraqi diplomats here in Washington about noon today. President Bush and Secretary Baker spoke with President Gorbachev for over an hour and fifteen minutes this morning to discuss the situation.

Secretary Baker spoke with Soviet Foreign Ministry officials both yesterday and today, and we have consulted with all of our allies and coalition partners last night or this morning. The coalition remains strong and united.

IRAQI RESPONSE TO SOVIET PEACE PLAN

On the morning of February 23, 1991, Iraqi foreign minister Tariq Aziz issued a statement in Moscow reiterating his government's acceptance of a Soviet peace proposal that provided for a conditional Iraqi withdrawal from Kuwait.

Last evening, the Soviet Government declared a proposal about the situation in the gulf region and in order to achieve a peaceful settlement to that situation in accordance with the UN resolutions.

You are familiar with the points in that declaration, but anyhow, I am going to reiterate those points in English.

First, Iraq agrees to comply with Resolution 660 and therefore to withdraw immediately and unconditionally all its forces from Kuwait to the positions in which they were located on the first of August 1990.

Second, the withdrawal of the forces shall begin on the day following the cease-fire and the cessation of all military operations on land, at sea and in the air.

Third, the withdrawal shall be completed within a period of 21 days, including the withdrawal from the city of Kuwait within the first four days of the said period.

Four, immediately upon the completion of the withdrawal of the troops from Kuwait, the grounds for which all the other resolutions of the Security Council were adopted will have been removed, and thereby those resolutions will cease to operate.

Five, all prisoners of war shall be released and repatriated within three days of the cease-fire and the cessation of all military operations.

The last point, the sixth, the cease-fire and withdrawal shall be confirmed, verified and supervised by observers and/or a peace-keeping force as determined by the Security Council.

These are the points of the plan, or the initiative that was declared by the Soviet Government last evening. I am here to tell you that the Iraqi Government fully endorses this plan and fully supports it.

Last night the Revolution Command Council issued a statement saying that Iraq supports the Soviet initiative and it appreciates the Soviets' efforts to reach a peaceful settlement to the situation. And we particularly appreciate the efforts of His Excellency, President Mikhail Gorbachev and his Government in this regard.

The second point I would like to address is the allegations made by the American Government yesterday that Iraq has created a new ecological situation in Kuwait, and you are aware of those allegations.

My Government has strongly denied those allegations in the statement made last night. And the Iraqi Government asks the Security Council to establish immediately a committee to investigate the situation in Kuwait. If the American authorities would like to use this pretext to justify their aggressive position, such a pretext has no grounds.

HUSSEIN ANNOUNCES WITHDRAWAL

On February 26, 1991, Iraqi president Saddam Hussein delivered a defiant speech over Baghdad radio announcing the withdrawal of Iraqi troops from Kuwait. Most Iraqi forces already were in full retreat when the announcement was broadcast. Following is the text of the speech as translated by the Foreign Broadcast Information Service:

In the name of God, the merciful, the compassionate.

O great people; O stalwart men in the forces of holy war and faith, glorious men of the mother of battles; O zealous, faithful and sincere people in our glorious nations, and among all Muslims and all virtuous people in the world; O glorious Iraqi women:

In such circumstances and times, it is difficult to talk about all that which should be talked about, and it is difficult to recall all that which has to be recalled. Despite this, we have to remind of what has to be reminded of, and say part—a principal part—of what should be said.

We start by saying that on this day, our valiant armed forces will complete their withdrawal from Kuwait. And on this day our fight against aggression and the ranks of infidelity, joined in an ugly coalition comprising 30 countries, which officially entered war against us under the leadership of the United States of America—our fight against them would have lasted from the first month of this year, starting with the night of 16-17 [January], until this moment in the current month, February of this year.

It was an epic duel which lasted for two months, which came to clearly confirm a lesson that God has wanted as a prelude of faith, impregnability and capability for the faithful, and a prelude of an [abyss], weakness and humiliation which God Almighty has wanted for the infidels, the criminals, the traitors, the corrupt and the deviators.

To be added to this time is the time of the military and nonmilitary duel, including the military and the economic blockade, which was imposed on Iraq and which lasted throughout 1990 until today, and until the time God Almighty wishes it to last.

Before that, the duel lasted, in other forms, for years before this period of time. It was an epic struggle between right and wrong; we have talked about this in detail on previous occasions.

It gave depth to the age of the showdown for the year 1990, and the already elapsed part of the year 1991.

Hence, we do not forget, because we will not forget this great struggling spirit, by which men of great faith stormed the fortifications and the weapons of deception and the Croesus [Kuwaiti rulers] treachery on the honorable day of the call. They did what they did within the context of legitimate deterrence and great principled action.

All that we have gone through or decided within its circumstances, obeying God's will and choosing a position of faith and chivalry, is a record of honor, the significance of which will not be missed by the people and nation and the values of Islam and humanity.

Their days will continue to be glorious and their past and future will continue to relate the story of a faithful, jealous and patient people, who believed in the will of God and in the values and stands accepted by the Almighty for the Arab nation in its leading role and for the Islamic nation in the essentials of its true faith and how they should be.

These values—which had their effect in all those situations, offered the sacrifices they had offered in the struggle, and symbolized the depth of the faithful character in Iraq—will continue to leave their effects on the souls.

They will continue to reap their harvest, not only in terms of direct targets represented in the slogans of their age—whether in the conflict between the oppressed poor and the unjust and opportunist rich, or between faith and blasphemy, or between injustice, deception and treachery on the one hand and fairness, justice, honesty and loyalty on the other—but also the indirect targets as well.

This will shake the opposite ranks and cause them to collapse after everything has become clear. This will also add faith to the faithful now that the minds and eyes have been opened and the hearts are longing for what the principles, values and stances should long for and belong to.

The stage that preceded the great day of the call on 2 August 1990, had its own standards, including dealing with what is familiar and inherited during the bad times, whether on the level of relations between the ruler and the ruled, or between the leader and the people he leads.

The relations between the foreigners among the ranks of infidelity and oppression and among the region's states and the world had their own standards, effects and privileges that were created by the Arab homeland's circumstances, and which were facilitated by propaganda, which no one could expose more than it has now been exposed.

The conflict was exacerbated by the vacuum that was created by the weakness of one of the two poles that used to represent the two opposite lines in the world. However, after the second of August 1990, new concepts and standards were created.

This was preceded by a new outlook in all walks of life, in relations among peoples, relations among states, and the relations between the ruler and the ruled, and by standards of faith and positions; patriotism, pan-Arabism, and humanitarianism; holy war, faith, Islam, fear and non-fear; restlessness and tranquillity; manhood and its opposite; struggle, holy war and sacrifice, and readiness to do good things and their opposite.

When new measures spring forth and the familiar, failed, traitorous, subservient and corrupt [people], and tyrants are rejected, then the opportunity for the cultivation of the pure soil will increase in its scope, and the seeds of this plant will take root deep in the good land of the revelation and the messages, and the land of prophets.

God says: "Like a goodly tree, whose root is firmly fixed, and its branches reach to the heavens. It brings forth its fruit at all times, by the leave of its Lord." [Koranic verses]

Then everything will become possible on the road of goodness and happiness that is not defiled by the feet of the invaders nor by their evil will or the corruption of the corrupt among those who have been corrupted, and who spread corruption in the land of the Arabs.

Moreover, the forces of plotting and treachery will be defeated for good. Good people and those who are distinguished by their faith and by their faithful, honorable stands of holy war will become the real leaders of the gathering of the faithful everywhere on earth, and the gathering of corruption, falsehood, hypocrisy and infidelity will be defeated and meet the vilest fate.

The earth will be inherited, at God's order, by His righteous slaves. "For the earth is God's, to give as a heritage to such of his servants as he pleaseth; and the end is best for the righteous." [Koranic verses]

When this happens, the near objectives will not only be within reach, available and possible, but also the doors will be open without any hindrance which might prevent the achievement of all the greater, remoter and more comprehensive objectives, to the Arabs, Muslims and humanity at large.

Then, also it will be clear that the harvest does not precede the seeding, and that the threshing floor and the yield are the outcome of successful seeding and a successful harvest.

The harvest in the mother of battles has succeeded. After we have harvested what we have harvested, the greater harvest and its yield will be in the time to come, and it will be much greater than what we have at present, in spite of what we have at present in terms of the victory, dignity and glory that was based on the sacrifices of a deep faith which is generous without any hesitation or fear.

It is by virtue of this faith that God has bestowed dignity upon the Iraqi mujahedeen, and upon all the depth of this course of holy war at the level of the Arab homeland and at the level of all those men whom God has chosen to be given the honor of allegiance, guidance and honorable position, until He declares that the conflict has stopped, or amends its directions and course and the positions in a manner which would please the faithful and increase their dignity.

O valiant Iraqi men, O glorious Iraqi women. Kuwait is part of your country and was carved from it in the past.

Circumstances today have willed that it remain the state in which it will remain after the withdrawal of our struggling forces from it. It hurts you that this should happen.

We rejoiced on the day of the call when it was decided that Kuwait should be one of the main gates for deterring the plot and for defending all Iraq from the plotters. We say that we will remember Kuwait on the great day of the call, on the days that followed it, and in documents and events, some of which date back 70 years.

The Iraqis will remember and will not forget that on 8 August 1990, Kuwait became part of Iraq legally, constitutionally and actually. They remember and will not forget that it remained throughout this period from 8 August 1990, and until last night, when withdrawal began, and today we will complete withdrawal of our forces, God willing.

Today certain circumstances made the Iraqi Army withdraw as a result of the ramifications which we mentioned, including the combined aggression by 30 countries. Their repugnant siege has been led in evil and aggression by the machine and the criminal entity of America and its major allies.

These malicious ranks took the depth and effectiveness of their aggressiveness not only from their aggressive premeditated intentions against Iraq, the Arab nation and Islam, but also from the position of those who were deceived by the claim of international legitimacy.

Everyone will remember that the gates of Constantinople were not opened before the Muslims in the first struggling attempt, and that the international community [placed] dear Palestine's freedom and independence in oblivion.

Whatever the suspect parties try, by virtue of the sacrifices and struggle of the Palestinians and Iraqis, Palestine has returned anew to knock at the doors closed on evil.

Palestine returned to knock on those doors to force the tyrants and the traitors to a solution that would place it at the forefront of the issues that have to be resolved; a solution that would bring dignity to its people and provide better chances for better progress.

The issue of poverty and richness, fairness and unfairness, faith and infidelity, treachery and honesty and sincerity, have become titles corresponding to rare events and well-known people and trends that give priority to what is positive over what is negative, to what is sincere over what is treacherous and filthy, and to what is pure and honorable over what is corrupt, base and lowly. The confidence of the nationalists and the faithful mujahedeen and the Muslims has grown bigger than before, and great hope more and more.

Slogans have come out of their stores to strongly occupy the facades of the pan-Arab and human holy war and struggle. Therefore, victory is [great] now and in the future, God willing.

Shout for victory, O brothers; shout for your victory and the victory of all honorable people, O Iraqis. You have fought 30 countries, and all the evil and the largest machine of war and destruction in the world that surrounds them. If only one of these countries threatens anyone, this threat will have a swift and direct effect on the dignity, freedom, life, or freedom of this country, people and nation.

The soldiers of faith have triumphed over the soldiers of wrong, O stalwart men. Your God is the one who granted your victory. You triumphed when you rejected, in the name of faith, the will of evil which the evildoers wanted to impose on you to kill the fire of faith in your hearts.

You have chosen the path which you have chosen, including the acceptance of the Soviet initiative, but those evildoers persisted in their path and methods, thinking that they can impose their will on their Iraq, as they imagined and hoped.

This hope of theirs may remain in their heads, even after we withdraw from Kuwait. Therefore, we must be cautious, and preparedness to fight must remain at the highest level.

O you valiant men; you have fought the armies of 30 states and the capabilities of an even greater number of states which supplied them with the means of aggression and support. Faith, belief, hope and determination continue to fill your chests, souls and hearts.

They have even become deeper, stronger, brighter and more deeply rooted. God is great; God is great; may the lowly be defeated.

Victory is sweet with the help of God.

BUSH RESPONSE TO HUSSEIN RADIO SPEECH

On February 26, 1991, after Saddam Hussein's radio speech announcing an Iraqi withdrawal from Kuwait, President Bush angrily declared in a short statement at the White House that the war would continue because Hussein's announcement failed to meet the coalition's conditions for a cease-fire.

Saddam's most recent speech is an outrage. He is not withdrawing. His defeated forces are retreating. He is trying to claim victory in the midst of a rout. And he is not voluntarily giving up Kuwait.

He is trying to save the remnants of power and control in the Middle East by every means possible. And here, too, Saddam Hussein will fail.

Saddam is not interested in peace, but only to regroup and fight another day. And he does not renounce Iraq's claim to Kuwait. To the contrary, he makes clear that Iraq continues to claim Kuwait. Nor is there any evidence of remorse for Iraq's aggression or any indication that Saddam is prepared to accept the responsibility for the awful consequences of that aggression.

He still does not accept UN Security Council resolutions or the coalition terms of February 22, including the release of our POWs, all POWs, third-country detainees, and an end to the pathological destruction of Kuwait.

The coalition will therefore continue to prosecute the war with undiminished intensity. As we announced last night, we will not attack unarmed soldiers in retreat. We have no choice but to consider retreating combat units as a threat and respond accordingly. Anything else would risk additional United States and coalition casualties.

The best way to avoid further casualties on both sides is for the Iraqi soldiers to lay down their arms as nearly 30,000 Iraqis already have. It is time for all Iraqi forces in the theater of operation—those occupying Kuwait, those supporting the occupation of Kuwait—to lay down their arms. And that will stop the bloodshed.

From the beginning of the air operation nearly six weeks ago, I have said that our efforts are on course and on schedule. This morning, I am very pleased to say that coalition efforts are ahead of schedule. The liberation of Kuwait is close at hand.

And let me just add that I share the pride of all of the American people in the magnificent, heroic performance of our armed forces. May God bless them and keep them.

BUSH ANNOUNCES CEASE-FIRE

On February 27, 1991, President George Bush delivered a televised speech from the White House in which he announced the liberation of Kuwait and a cease-fire in the Gulf war.

Kuwait is liberated. Iraq's army is defeated. Our military objectives are met. Kuwait is once more in the hands of Kuwaitis, in control of their own destiny. We share in their joy, a joy tempered only by our compassion for their ordeal.

Tonight, the Kuwaiti flag once again flies above the capital of a free and sovereign nation, and the American flag flies above our embassy.

Seven months ago, America and the world drew a line in the sand. We declared that the aggression against Kuwait would not stand, and tonight America and the world have kept their word.

This is not a time of euphoria, certainly not a time to gloat. But it is a time of pride: pride in our troops, pride in the friends who stood with us in the crisis, pride in our nation and the people whose strength and resolve made victory quick, decisive, and just. And soon, we will open wide our arms to welcome back home to America our magnificent fighting forces.

No one country can claim this victory as its own. It was not only a victory for Kuwait, but a victory for all the coalition partners.

This is a victory for the United Nations, for all mankind, for the rule of law, and for what is right.

After consulting with Secretary of Defense [Dick] Cheney, the chairman of the Joint Chiefs of Staff [Gen. Colin L.] Powell [Jr.], and our coalition partners, I am pleased to announce that at midnight tonight, Eastern Standard Time, exactly one hundred hours since ground operations commenced, and six weeks since the start of Operation Desert Storm, all United States and coalition forces will suspend offensive combat operations.

It is up to Iraq whether this suspension on the part of the coalition becomes a permanent cease-fire. Coalition political and military terms for a formal cease-fire include the following requirements:

Iraq must release immediately all coalition prisoners of war, third-country nationals, and the remains of all who have fallen.

Iraq must release all Kuwaiti detainees. Iraq also must inform Kuwaiti authorities of the location and nature of all land and sea mines.

Iraq must comply fully with all relevant United Nations Security Council resolutions. This includes a rescinding of Iraq's August decision to annex Kuwait and acceptance in principle of Iraq's responsibility to pay compensation for the loss, damage, and injury its aggression has caused.

The coalition calls upon the Iraqi government to designate military commanders to meet within forty-eight hours with their coalition counterparts, at a place in the theater of operations to be specified, to arrange for military aspects of the cease-fire.

Further, I have asked Secretary of State [James A.] Baker [III] to request that the United Nations Security Council meet to formulate the necessary arrangements for this war to be ended.

This suspension of offensive combat operations is contingent upon Iraq's not firing upon any coalition forces, and not launching Scud missiles against any other country. If Iraq violates these terms, coalition forces will be free to resume military operations.

At every opportunity, I have said to the people of Iraq that our quarrel was not with them, but instead with their leadership, and above all with Saddam Hussein. This remains the case. You, the people of Iraq, are not our enemy. We do not seek your destruction. We have treated your POWs with kindness. Coalition forces fought this war only as a last resort, and looked forward to the day when Iraq is led by people prepared to live in peace with their neighbors.

We must now begin to look beyond victory and war. We must meet the challenge of securing the peace. In the future, as before, we will consult with our coalition partners. We've already done a good deal of thinking and planning for the postwar period.

And Secretary Baker has already begun to consult with our coalition partners on the region's challenges. There can be and will be no solely American answer to all these challenges, but we can assist and support the countries of the region and be a catalyst for peace.

In this spirit, Secretary Baker will go to the region next week to begin a new round of consultations.

This war is now behind us. Ahead of us is the difficult task of securing a potentially historic peace. Tonight, though, let us be proud of what we have accomplished. Let us give thanks to those who risked their lives.

Let us never forget those who gave their lives.

May God bless our valiant military forces and their families, and let us all remember them in our prayers. Good night, and may God bless the United States of America.

Bibliography

Books

Abir, Mordechai. *Saudi Arabia in the Oil Era: Regime and Elites, Conflict and Collaboration.* Boulder, Colo.: Westview Press, 1988.

Abrahamian, Evrand. *Iran Between Two Revolutions.* Princeton, N.J.: Princeton University Press, 1982.

Afkhami, Gholam R. *The Iranian Revolution: Thanatos on a National Scale.* Washington, D.C.: Middle East Institute, 1985.

Ajami, Fouad. *Arab Predicament: Arab Political Thought and Practice since 1967.* New York: Cambridge University Press, 1981.

____. *The Vanished Imam: Musa al Sadr and the Shia of Lebanon.* Ithaca, N.Y.: Cornell University Press, 1986.

Amos, John W. *Arab-Israeli Military Political Relations: Arab Perceptions and the Politics of Escalation.* Elmsford, N.Y.: Pergamon Press, 1979.

____. *Palestinian Resistance: Organization of a Nationalist Movement.* Elmsford, N.Y.: Pergamon Press, 1981.

Anderson, Irvine H. *Aramco, the United States, and Saudi Arabia: A Study of the Dynamics of Foreign Policy, 1933-1950.* Princeton, N.J.: Princeton University Press, 1981.

Ansari, Hameid. *Egypt, the Stalled Society.* Albany: State University of New York Press, 1986.

Antonius, George. *The Arab Awakening.* New York: Capricorn Books, 1965.

Avineri, Shlomo. *The Making of Modern Zionism: The Intellectual Origins of the Jewish State.* New York: Basic Books, 1981.

Ayoob, Mohammed. *Middle East in World Politics.* New York: St. Martin's Press, 1981.

Bar-Siman-Tov, Yaacov. *The Israeli-Egyptian War of Attrition, 1969-1970.* New York: Columbia University Press, 1980.

____. *Israel, the Superpowers, and the War in the Middle East.* New York: Praeger, 1987.

Benvenisti, Meron. *The West Bank Handbook: A Political Lexicon.* Boulder, Colo.: Westview Press, 1986.

Bhatia, Shyam. *Nuclear Rivals in the Middle East.* New York: Routledge, 1988.

Bidwell, Robin. *The Two Yemens.* Boulder, Colo.: Westview Press, 1983.

Bill, James A. *The Eagle and the Lion: The Tragedy of American-Iranian Relations.* New Haven: Yale University Press, 1988.

Braun, Aurel, ed. *The Middle East in Global Strategy.* Boulder, Colo.: Westview Press, 1987.

Bruton, Henry J. *The Promise of Peace: Economic Cooperation between Egypt and Israel; a Staff Paper.* Washington, D.C.: Brookings Institution, 1981.

Brzezinski, Zbigniew. *Power and Principle.* New York: Farrar Strauss Giroux, 1983.

Bulloch, John. *The Persian Gulf Unveiled.* New York: Congdon and Weed, 1985.

Carter, Jimmy. *The Blood of Abraham: Insights into the Middle East.* Boston: Houghton Mifflin, 1985.

Cattan, Henry. *The Palestine Question.* New York: Croom Helm, 1988.

Cole, Juan R. I., and Nikki R. Keddie. *Shi'ism and Social Protest.* New Haven: Yale University Press, 1986.

Congressional Quarterly. *The Iran-Contra Puzzle.* Washington, D.C.: Congressional Quarterly, 1987.

Cottam, Richard W. *Iran and the United States: A Cold War Case Study.* Pittsburgh: University of Pittsburgh Press, 1988.

____. *Nationalism in Iran.* Pittsburgh: University of Pittsburgh Press, 1979.

Cottrell, Alvin J., ed. *The Persian Gulf States: A General Survey.* Baltimore: Johns Hopkins University Press, 1980.

Cottrell, Alvin J., and Michael L. Moodie. *The United States and the Persian Gulf, Past Mistakes and Present Needs.* New York: Strategy Information Center, 1984.

Dann, Uriel. *The Great Powers in the Middle East, 1919-1939.* New York: Holmes and Meier, 1988.

Darius, Robert G., John W. Amos II, and Ralph H. Magnus. *Gulf Security into the 1980s.* Stanford, Calif.: Hoover Institution Press, 1984.

Dawisha, Adeed I. *Syria and the Lebanese Crisis.* New York: St. Martin's Press, 1980.

Dayan, Moshe. *Breakthrough: A Personal Account of the Egypt-Israel Peace Negotiations.* New York: Knopf, 1981.

Deeb, Marius. *The Lebanese Civil War.* New York: Praeger, 1980.

Devlin, John F. *Modern Syria in an Ancient Land.* Boulder, Colo.: Westview Press, 1983.

Elazar, Daniel J. *The Camp David Framework for Peace: A Shift toward Shared Rule.* Washington, D.C.: American Enterprise Institute for Public Policy Research, 1979.

Esposito, John L., ed. *Islam and Development.* Syracuse, N.Y.: Syracuse University Press, 1980.

Fahmy, Ismail. *Negotiating for Peace in the Middle East.* Baltimore: Johns Hopkins University Press, 1983.

Fisher, Michael M. J. *Iran: From Religious Dispute to Revolution.* Cambridge: Harvard University Press, 1980.

Fisher, W. B. *The Middle East.* New York: Methuen, 1978.

Frankel, William. *Israel Observed.* New York: Thames Hudson, 1981.

Freedman, Robert O. *Soviet Policy toward the Middle East since 1970.* 3d ed. New York: Praeger, 1982.

Ghanem, Shukri M. *OPEC: The Rise and Fall of an Exclusive Club.* New York: Kegan Paul International, 1986.

Golan, Galia. *The Soviet Union and the Palestinian Liberation Organization.* New York: Praeger, 1980.

Gold, Dore. *America, the Gulf, and Israel: CENTCOM and Emerging U.S. Regional Security Policies in the Middle East.* Boulder, Colo: Westview Press, 1989.

Haley, P. Edward, and Lewis W. Snider, eds. *Lebanon in Crisis, Participants and Issues.* Syracuse, N.Y.: Syracuse University Press, 1979.

Hameed, Mazher A. *Arabia Imperiled: The Security Imperatives of the Arab Gulf States.* Washington, D.C.: Middle East Assessments Group, 1986.

Harris, William W. *Taking Root: Israeli Settlement in the West Bank, the Golan, and Gaza-Sinai, 1967-1980.* New York: John Wiley and Sons, 1980.

Heikal, Mohammed. *Autumn of Fury: The Assassination of Sadat.* New York: Random House, 1983.

Heller, Mark A. *A Palestinian State: The Implications for Israel.* Cambridge: Harvard University Press, 1983.

Helms, Christine Moss. *Iraq: Eastern Flank of the Arab World.* Washington, D.C.: Brookings Institution, 1984.

Hitti, Philip K. *Islam and the West.* Melbourne, Fla.: Krieger, 1979.

Hinnebusch, Raymond A. *Peasant and Bureaucracy in Ba'thist Syria.* Boulder, Colo: Westview Press, 1989.

Hof, Frederic C. *Galilee Divided: The Israel-Lebanon Frontier, 1916-1984.* Boulder, Colo.: Westview Press, 1985.

Hourani, Albert. *The Emergence of the Modern Middle East.* Berkeley: University of California Press, 1981.

Hudson, Michael. *Arab Politics: The Search for Legitimacy.* New Haven: Yale University Press, 1977.

———. *The Precarious Republic: Political Modernization in Lebanon.* Boulder, Colo.: Westview Press, 1984.

Hurewitz, J. C. *Middle East Politics: The Military Dimension.* Boulder, Colo.: Westview Press, 1984.

———. *Struggle for Palestine.* New York: W. W. Norton, 1950.

Issac, Rael J. *Party and Politics in Israel: Three Visions of a Jewish State.* New York: Longman, 1980.

Jabber, Paul, et al. *Great Power Interests in the Persian Gulf.* New York: Council on Foreign Relations, 1989.

Johns, Richard, and David Holden. *House of Saud.* New York: Holt, Rinehart, and Winston, 1981.

Katouzian, Homa. *The Political Economy of Modern Iran: Despotism and Pseudo-Modernism, 1926-1979.* New York: Columbia University Press, 1981.

Kauppi, Mark V., and R. Craig Nation. *The Soviet Union and the Middle East in the 1980s: Opportunities, Constraints, and Dilemmas.* Lexington, Mass.: Lexington Books, 1983.

Keddie, Nikki. *Roots of Revolution: An Interpretive History of Modern Iran.* New Haven: Yale University Press, 1981.

Kenen, I. L. *Israel's Defense Lines: Her Friends and Foes in Washington.* Brooklyn, N.Y.: Prometheus Books, 1981.

Kerr, Malcolm. *The Arab Cold War.* New York: Oxford University Press, 1971.

Khadduri, Majid. *The Gulf War: The Origins and Implications of the Iraq-Iran Conflict.* New York: Oxford University Press, 1988.

———. *Political Trends in the Arab World.* Westport, Conn.: Greenwood Press, 1983.

Khalaf, Samir. *Lebanon's Predicament.* New York: Columbia University Press, 1987.

Khalidi, Walid. *Conflict and Violence in Lebanon.* Cambridge: Harvard University Press, 1979.

Khouri, Fred J. *The Arab-Israeli Dilemma.* 3d. ed. Syracuse, N.Y.: Syracuse University Press, 1985.

Kramer, Martin. *Political Islam.* Beverly Hills, Calif.: Sage Publications, 1980.

———. *Shi'ism, Resistance, and Revolution.* Boulder, Colo.: Westview Press, 1987.

Kupchan, Charles A. *The Persian Gulf and the West: The Dilemmas of Security.* Boston: Allen Unwin, 1987.

Lacey, Robert. *The Kingdom.* New York: Avon, 1983.

Laqueur, Walter, and Barry Rubin. *The Israel-Arab Reader: A Documentary History of the Middle East.* New York: Penguin, 1984.

Ledeen, Michael, and William Lewis. *Debacle: The American Failure in Iran.* New York: Random House, 1981.

Lewis, Bernard. *The Jews of Islam.* Princeton: Princeton University Press, 1984.

———. *The Political Language of Islam.* Chicago: University of Chicago Press, 1988.

Lewis, Norman N. *Nomads and Settlers in Syria and Jordan, 1800-1980.* New York: Cambridge University Press, 1987.

Licklider, Roy. *Political Power and the Arab Oil Weapon: The Experience of Five Industrial Nations.* Berkeley: University of California Press, 1988.

Lippmann, Thomas W. *Egypt after Nasser: Sadat, Peace, and the Mirage of Prosperity.* New York: Paragon House, 1988.

Long, David E., and Bernard Reich, eds. *The Government and Politics of the Middle East and North Africa.* 2d. ed. Boulder, Colo.: Westview Press, 1986.

Lukacs, Yehuda, and Abdulla M. Battah, eds. *The Arab-Israeli Conflict: Two Decades of Change.* Boulder, Colo.: Westview Press, 1988.

Lustick, Ian. *Arabs in the Jewish State: Israel's Control of a National Minority.* Austin: University of Texas Press, 1980.

Lytle, Mark H. *The Origins of the Iranian-American Alliance, 1941-1953.* New York: Holmes and Meier, 1987.

Martin, David C., and John Walcott. *Best Laid Plans: The Inside Story of America's War against Terrorism.* New York: Harper and Row, 1988.

McDermott, Anthony. *Egypt from Nasser to Mubarak: A Flawed Revolution.* London: Croom Helm, 1988.

Miller, Aaron David. *Search for Security: Saudi Arabian Oil and American Foreign Policy.* Chapel Hill: University of North Carolina Press, 1980.

Morris, Benny. *The Birth of the Palestinian Refugee Prob-*

lem 1947-1949. New York: Cambridge University Press, 1988.

Mroz, John E. *Beyond Security: Private Perceptions Among Arabs and Israelis*. Elmsford, N.Y.: Pergamon Press, 1981.

Munson, Henry. *Islam and Revolution in the Middle East*. New Haven: Yale University Press, 1988.

Muslih, Muhammad. *The Origins of Palestinian Nationalism*. New York: Cambridge University Press, 1988.

Nakhleh, Emile A. *The Persian Gulf and American Policy*. New York: Praeger, 1982.

Nakhleh, Khalil, and Elia Zureik, eds. *The Sociology of the Palestinians*. New York: St. Martin's Press, 1980.

Neumann, Robert G., et al. *Revitalizing U.S. Leadership in the Middle East*. Washington, D.C.: Center for Strategic and International Studies, 1988.

Norton, Augustus Richard. *Amal and the Shia: Struggle for the Soul of Lebanon*. Austin: University of Texas Press, 1987.

Peck, Malcolm C. *The United Arab Emirates: A Venture in Unity*. Boulder, Colo.: Westview Press, 1986.

Peretz, Don. *Government and Politics of Israel*. 2d ed. Boulder Colo.: Westview Press, 1984.

____. *Intifada: The Palestinian Uprising*. Boulder, Colo.: Westview Press, 1989.

____. *The Middle East Today*. 5th ed. New York: Praeger, 1988.

Peterson, J. E. *Yemen: The Search for a Modern State*. Baltimore: Johns Hopkins University Press, 1982.

Piscatori, James, ed. *Islam in the Political Process*. Cambridge: Cambridge University Press, 1983.

Piscatori, James, and George S. Harris, eds. *Law, Personalities, and Politics of the Middle East: Essays in Honor of Majid Khadduri*. Boulder, Colo.: Westview Press and Washington, D.C.: The Middle East Institute, 1987.

Quandt, William. *Decade of Decisions*. Berkeley: University of California Press, 1977.

____, ed. *The Middle East: Ten Years after Camp David*. Washington, D.C.: Brookings Institution, 1988.

Rabinovich, Itamar. *The War for Lebanon, 1970-1983*. Ithaca, N.Y.: Cornell University Press, 1983.

Rafael, Gideon. *Destination Peace: Three Decades of Israeli Foreign Policy*. New York: Stein and Day, 1981.

Ramazani, R. K. *The United States and Iran: The Patterns of Influence*. New York: Praeger, 1982.

Randall, Jonathan C. *Going All the Way: Christian Warlords, Israeli Adventurers, and the War in Lebanon*. New York: Viking Press, 1983.

Reich, Bernard. *The Powers in the Middle East: The Ultimate Strategic Arena*. New York: Praeger, 1986.

Richards, Alan, and John Waterbury. *A Political Economy of the Middle East*. Boulder, Colo.: Westview Press, 1989.

Ro'i, Yaacov, ed. *The USSR and the Muslim World: Issues in Domestic and Foreign Policy*. London: Allen Unwin, 1984.

Rubin, Jeffrey Z. *Dynamics of Third Party Intervention: Kissinger in the Middle East*. New York: Praeger, 1983.

Sachar, Howard M. *History of Israel*. New York: Knopf, 1976.

Safran, Nadav. *From War to War*. New York: Pegasus, 1969.

Salibi, Kemal S. *Crossroads to Civil War, Lebanon 1858-1976*. New York: Caravan Books, 1976.

Seale, Patrick. *The Struggle for Syria: A Study of Postwar Arab Politics, 1945-1958*. 2d. ed. New Haven: Yale University Press, 1987.

Sella, Amnon. *Soviet Political and Military Conduct in the Middle East*. New York: St. Martin's Press, 1981.

Shaked, Haim, and Itamar Rabinovich, eds. *The Middle East and the United States*. New Brunswick, N.J.: Transaction Books, 1980.

Sharabi, Hisham, ed. *The Next Arab Decade: Alternative Futures*. Boulder, Colo.: Westview Press, 1988.

Shawcross, William. *The Shah's Last Ride: Fate of an Ally*. New York: Simon and Schuster, 1988.

Shipler, David K. *Arab and Jew: Wounded Spirits in the Promised Land*. New York: Times Books, 1986.

Shlaim, Avi. *Collusion Across the Jordan: King Abdullah, the Zionist Movement, and the Partition of Palestine*. New York: Columbia University Press, 1988.

Sick, Gary. *All Fall Down: America's Tragic Encounter with Iran*. New York: Random House, 1985.

Sluglett, Marion-Farouk, and Peter Sluglett. *Iraq since 1958: From Revolution to Dictatorship*. New York: Methuen, 1988.

Smooha, Sammy. *Arabs and Jews in Israel Vol. 1: Conflicting and Shared Attitudes in a Divided Society*. Boulder, Colo.: Westview Press, 1989.

Spiegel, Steven L. *The Other Arab-Israeli Conflict: Making America's Middle East Policy from Truman to Reagan*. Chicago: University of Chicago Press, 1985.

St. John, Ronald Bruce. *Qaddafi's World Design: Libyan Foreign Policy, 1969-1987*. London: Saqi Books, 1987.

Stone, Julius. *Israel and Palestine: Assault on the Law of Nations*. Baltimore: Johns Hopkins University Press, 1981.

Stookey, Robert W. *South Yemen: A Marxist Republic in Arabia*. Boulder, Colo.: Westview Press, 1982.

Stowasser, Barbara Freyer. *The Islamic Impulse*. Washington: D.C.: Center for Contemporary Arab Studies, 1987.

Tahir-Kheli, Shirin, and Shaheen Ayubi. *The Iran-Iraq War*. New York: Praeger, 1983.

Tillman, Seth P. *The United States in the Middle East*. Bloomington: Indiana University Press, 1982.

Tivnan, Edward. *The Lobby: Jewish Political Power and American Foreign Policy*. New York: Simon and Schuster, 1987.

Toubia, Nahid. *Women of the Arab World*. London: Zed Books, 1989.

Touval, Saadia. *The Peace Brokers*. Princeton, N.J.: Princeton University Press, 1982.

Traverton, Gregory, ed. *Crisis Management and the Super Powers in the Middle East*. Montclair, N.J.: Allanheld, 1981.

Vance, Cyrus. *Hard Choices*. New York: Simon and Schuster, 1983.

Waterbury, John. *The Egypt of Nasser and Sadat*. Princeton, N.J.: Princeton University Press, 1983.

Watt, W. Montgomery. *Islamic Fundamentalism and the Modern World*. New York: Routledge, Chapman, and Hall, 1989.

Weinbaum, Marvin G. *Egypt and the Politics of U.S. Economic Aid*. Boulder, Colo.: Westview Press, 1986.

Wells, Samuel F., and Mark Bruzonsky. *Security in the Middle East: Regional Change and Great Power Strategies*. Boulder, Colo.: Westview Press, 1987.

Wenner, Manfred W. *Modern Yemen, 1918-1966*. Baltimore: Johns Hopkins University Press, 1967.

Worsfold, W. Basil. *Palestine of the Mandate.* Philadelphia: Porcupine Press, 1980.

Wright, Robin. *Sacred Rage: The Wrath of Militant Islam.* New York: Simon and Schuster, 1984.

Yaniv, Avner. *Dilemmas of Security: Politics, Strategy, and the Israeli Experience in Lebanon.* New York: Oxford University Press, 1987.

Yodfat, Aryeh. *The Soviet Union and the Arabian Peninsula: Soviet Policy towards the Persian Gulf and Arabia.* New York: St. Martin's Press, 1983.

———. *The Soviet Union and the Iranian Revolution.* New York: St. Martin's Press, 1983.

Zaalouk, Malak. *Power, Class, and Foreign Capital in Egypt: The Rise of the New Bourgeoisie.* London: Zed Books, 1989.

Zeine, Zeine N. *Arab-Turkish Relations and the Emergence of Arab Nationalism.* Westport, Conn.: Greenwood Press, 1981.

———. *The Struggle for Arab Independence.* 2d. ed. New York: Caravan Books, 1977.

Articles

Abukhalil, As'ad. "Internal Contradictions in the PFLP: Decision Making and Policy Orientation." *Middle East Journal* (Summer 1987): 361-378.

Al-Dajani, Ahmed Sidgi. "The PLO." *Journal of Palestine Studies* (Spring 1980): 81-98.

Alexander, Nathan. "The Foreign Policy of Libya: Inflexibility Amid Change." *Orbis* (Winter 1981): 819-846.

Ali, Sheikh R. "Holier than Thou: The Iran-Iraq War." *Middle East Review* (Fall 1984): 50-57.

Aliboni, Roberto. "The Strategic and Regional Balance in the Middle East and the Red Sea Region." *Atlantic Community Quarterly* (Spring 1981): 37-49.

Allen, Calvin H. "Oman: A Separate Place." *Wilson Quarterly* (New Year's Edition 1987): 48-79.

Al-Qutub, Ishaq Y. "Refugee Camp Cities in the Middle East: A Challenge for Urban Development Policies." *International Sociology* (March 1989): 91-108.

Al-Rumaihi, Mohammed. "Kuwaiti-American Relations: A Case of Mismanagement." *American-Arab Affairs* (Summer 1984): 77-80.

Anderson, Ewan W. "The Vulnerability of Arab Water Resources." *Arab Affairs* (Summer/Fall 1988): 73-81.

Anderson, Lisa. "Libya's Qaddafi: Still in Command?" *Current History,* February 1987, 65-68.

Ansari, Hameid. "Egypt: Repression and Liberalization." *Current History,* February 1987, 77-80.

"Bahrain: A MEED Special Report." *Middle East Economic Digest,* October 17-23, 1987, 20-45.

Barnaby, Frank. "The Nuclear Arsenal in the Middle East." *Technology Review* (May/June 1987): 27-34.

Bar-on, Mordechai. "Trend in the Political Psychology of Israeli Jews." *Journal of Palestine Studies* (August 1987): 21-36.

Bassiouni, M. Chelif. "An Analysis of Egyptian Peace Policy toward Israel: From Resolution 242 (1967) to the 1979 Peace Treaty." *New Outlook* (January 1981): 27-33.

Beinin, Joel. "The Communist Movement and Nationalist Political Discourse in Nasirist Egypt." *Middle East Journal* (Autumn 1987): 568-584.

Belfiglio, Valentin J. "Middle East Terrorism." *International Problems* (Summer 1987): 21-28.

Bill, James A. "Resurgent Islam in the Persian Gulf." *Foreign Affairs* (Fall 1984): 108-127.

Bishara, Ghassan. "Israel's Power in the U.S. Senate." *Journal of Palestine Studies* (Autumn 1980): 58-79.

Blitzer, Wolf. "Israel and Reagan: Looking Ahead." *SAIS Review* (Winter 1981): 121-128.

Brand, Laurie. "Palestinians in Syria: The Politics of Integration." *Middle East Journal* (Autumn 1988): 621-680.

"The Brookings Report: Toward Arab-Israeli Peace." *Journal of Palestine Studies* (Autumn 1988): 172-178.

Brown, L. Carl. "The Middle East: Patterns of Change, 1947-1987." *Middle East Journal* (Winter 1987): 26-39.

Campbell, John C. "Middle East: The Burdens of Empire." *Foreign Affairs* (Spring 1979): 613-632.

———. "Soviet Strategy in the Middle East." *American-Arab Affairs* (Spring 1984): 74-82.

Carter, Jimmy. "The Middle East Consultation: A Look to the Future." *Middle East Journal* (Spring 1988): 187-192.

———. "Middle East Peace: New Opportunities." *Washington Quarterly* (Summer 1987): 5-14.

Chernousov, Mikhail. "Iran Retrospect." *New Times,* January 1980, 27-30.

Chomsky, Noam. "The United States and the Middle East." *Journal of Palestine Studies* (Spring 1987): 25-42.

Christison, Kathleen M. "Myths about Palestinians." *Foreign Policy* (Spring 1987): 109-127.

Chubin, Shahram. "The Soviet Union and Iraq." *Foreign Affairs* (Spring 1983): 921-949.

———. "U.S. Security Interests in the Persian Gulf in the 1980s." *Daedalus* (Fall 1980): 31-65.

Cooley, John K. "The Libyan Menace." *Foreign Policy* (Spring 1981): 74-83.

Cooper, Mary H. "Persian Gulf Oil." *Editorial Research Reports,* October 30, 1987, 566-575.

Cordesman, Anthony. "The Gulf Crisis and Strategic Interests: A Military Analysis." *American-Arab Affairs* (Summer 1984): 8-15.

Cottam, Richard W. "Inside Revolutionary Iran." *Middle East Journal* (Spring 1989): 168-185.

Cottam, Richard W., et al. "The United States and Iran's Revolution." *Foreign Policy* (Spring 1979): 3-34.

Dann, Uriel. "The Kurdish National Movement in Iraq." *Jerusalem Quarterly* (Fall 1978): 131-144.

Dawisha, Adeed I. "Iraq: The West's Opportunity." *Foreign Policy* (Winter 1980/1981): 134-153.

Dawisha, Karen. "The USSR in the Middle East: Superpower in Eclipse." *Foreign Affairs* (Winter 1982/1983): 438-451.

Day, Arthur. "Hussein's Constraints, Jordan's Dilemma." *SAIS Review* (Fall 1987): 81-94.

Deeb, Mary-Jane. "Shia Movements in Lebanon: Their Formation, Ideology, Social Basis, and Links with Iran and Syria." *Third World Quarterly* (April 1988): 683-698.

"Defending the Gulf: A Survey." *Economist,* June 6, 1981, 1-38.

Eban, Abba. "Camp David: The Unfinished Business." *Foreign Affairs* (Winter 1978/1979): 343-354.

Eilts, Hermann Frederick. "Improve the Framework." *Foreign Policy* (Winter 1980/1981): 3-20.

Elon, Amos. "Letter from Israel." *New Yorker,* February 13, 1989, 74-80.

Feith, Douglas J. "The Oil Weapon Demystified." *Policy Review* (Winter 1981): 19-39.

Felton, John. "U.S., PLO Move to Jump-start Peace Process." *Congressional Quarterly Weekly Report,* December 17, 1988, 3512-3514.

Fishelson, Gideon. "The Economics of Peace." *New Outlook* (September/October 1986): 16-18.

Freedman, Robert O. "The Soviet Union, Syria, and the Crisis in Lebanon: A Preliminary Analysis." *Middle East Annual* (1983): 103-157.

"From Arabia Felix to Arabia Deserta." *Middle East* (September 1983): 60-63.

Gilboa, Eytan. "The Palestinian Uprising: Has It Turned American Public Opinion Around?" *Orbis* (Winter 1989): 21-37.

Gimlin, Hoyt. "Egypt's Strategic Mideast Role." *Editorial Research Reports,* February 24, 1989, 106-115.

Golan, Galia. "The Soviet Union and the Israeli Action in Lebanon." *International Affairs* (Winter 1982/1983): 7-16.

Goodman, Melvin A., and Carolyn McGiffert Ekedahl. "Gorbachev's 'New Directions' in the Middle East." *Middle East Journal* (Autumn 1988): 571-586.

Haddad, Yvonne. "The Anguish of Christians in the Middle East and American Foreign Policy." *American-Arab Affairs* (Fall 1988): 56-74.

Halliday, Fred. "Gorbachev and the 'Arab Syndrome': Soviet Policy in the Middle East." *World Policy Journal* (Summer 1987): 415-442.

Hamad, Jamil. "Learning from History: The Lessons of Arab-Israeli Errors." *International Relations* (November 1987): 176-186.

Hirsch, Seev. "Trade Regimes and the Middle East Peace Process." *World Economy,* March 1987, 61-74.

Hochstein, Joseph M. "Israel's Forty-Year Quandary." *Editorial Research Reports,* April 15, 1988, 186-199.

Hudson, Michael. "Public Opinion, Foreign Policy, and the Crisis of Legitimacy in Arab Politics." *Journal of Arab Affairs* (Fall 1986): 131-160.

———. "United States Policy in the Middle East: Opportunities and Dangers." *Current History,* February 1986, 49-52.

Hunter, Robert E. "Seeking Middle East Peace." *Foreign Policy* (Winter 1988/1989): 3-21.

Hunter, Shireen T. "After the Ayatollah." *Foreign Policy* (Spring 1987): 77-97.

———. "Iran and the Spread of Revolutionary Islam." *Third World Quarterly* (April 1988): 730-749.

Ibrahim, Saad Eddin. "Whither the Arab Future?" *Arab Affairs* (Winter 1986/1987): 124-130.

Indyk, Martin. "Reagan and the Middle East: Learning the Art of the Possible." *SAIS Review* (Fall 1987): 111-138.

Ismael, Jacqueline S. "Social Policy and Social Change: The Case of Iraq." *World Today,* May 1981, 235-248.

Jackson, Henry F. "Sadat's Perils." *Foreign Policy* (Spring 1981): 58-73.

James, Alan. "The United Nations on Golan: Peacekeeping Paradox?" *International Relations,* May 1987, 64-84.

Kassim, Anis F. "The Palestine Liberation Organization's Claim to Status: A Juridical Analysis Under International Law." *Denver Journal of International Law and Policy* (Winter 1980): 1-33.

Kemp, Geoffrey. "Middle East Opportunities." *Foreign Affairs* (America and the World Edition, 1989): 139-158.

Khalidi, Walid. "Regiopolitics: Toward a U.S. Policy on the Palestinian Problem." *Foreign Affairs* (Summer 1981): 1050-1063.

Khalidi, Rashid. "The Uprising and the Palestinian Question." *World Policy Journal* (Summer 1988): 497-517.

Kimura, Shuzo. "Japan's Middle East Policy: Impact of the Oil Crisis." *American-Arab Affairs* (Summer 1987): 62-78.

Knauerhase, Ramon. "Saudi Arabia Faces the Future." *Current History,* February 1986, 75-78.

Kollek, Teddy. "Jerusalem: Present and Future." *Foreign Affairs* (Summer 1981): 1041-1049.

Kunihelm, Bruce R. "What the Saudis Really Want: A Primer for the Reagan Administration." *Orbis* (Spring 1981): 107-121.

"Kuwait: A MEED Special Report." *Middle East Economic Digest,* July 11-17, 1987, 16-38.

Kuutab, Jonathan. "The Children's Revolt." *Journal of Palestine Studies* (Summer 1988): 26-35.

Laqueur, Walter. "Why the Shah Fell." *Commentary,* March 1979, 47-55.

Lebovic, James H., and Ashfaq Ishaq. "Military Burden, Security Needs, and Economic Growth in the Middle East." *Journal of Conflict Resolution* (March 1987): 106-138.

Lederman, Jim. "Dateline West Bank: Interpreting the Intifada." *Foreign Policy* (Fall 1988): 230-246.

Levy, Walter J. "Oil: An Agenda for the 1980s." *Foreign Affairs* (Summer 1981): 1079-1101.

Long, David. "U.S.-Saudi Relations: A Foundation of Mutual Needs." *American-Arab Affairs* (Spring 1983): 12-22.

Lustick, Ian S. "Israel's Dangerous Fundamentalists." *Foreign Policy* (Fall 1987): 118-139.

Marcus, Jonathan. "The Politics of Israel's Security." *International Affairs* (London), September 1989, 233-46.

Mattar, Philip. "The Mufti of Jerusalem and the Politics of Palestine." *Middle East Journal* (Spring 1988): 227-240.

Moench, Richard U., ed. "The Impact of Fluctuating Oil Prices on State Autonomy in the Middle East." *Arab Studies Quarterly* (Spring 1988): 155-238.

Moubarak, Walid E. "The Kuwait Fund in the Context of Arab and Third World Politics." *Middle East Journal* (Autumn 1987): 538-552.

Mylroie, Lori. "The Baghdad Alternative." *Orbis* (Summer 1988): 339-354.

Neumann, Robert G., and Shireen T. Hunter. "Crisis in the Gulf: Reasons for Concern but Not Panic." *American-Arab Affairs* (Summer 1984): 16-21.

Oden, Toby. "Japan and the Middle East: A MEED Special Report." *Middle East Economic Digest* (December 1987): 3-40.

Oren, Michael B. "Escalation to Suez: The Egyptian-Israeli Border War, 1949-1956." *Journal of Contemporary History,* April 1989, 347-374.

Page, Stephen. "Moscow and the Arabian Peninsula." *American-Arab Affairs* (Spring 1984): 83-91.

Parsons, Anthony. "Iran and Western Europe." *Middle East Journal* (Spring 1989): 218-229.

Parsons, Anthony. "The Middle East and World Peace." *International Relations,* November 1986, 176-186.

Peres, Shimon. "A Strategy for Peace in the Middle East." *Foreign Affairs* (Spring 1980): 887-901.

Peretz, Don. "Intifadeh: The Palestinian Uprising." *Foreign Affairs* (Summer 1988): 965-980.

Peterson, J. E. "American Policy in the Gulf and the Sultanate of Oman." *American-Arab Affairs* (Summer

1983): 117-130.

———. "Defending Arabia: Evolution of Responsibility." *Orbis* (Fall 1984): 465-488.

———. "The Political Status of Women in the Arab Gulf States." *Middle East Journal* (Winter 1989): 34-50.

Precht, Henry. "Ayatollah Realpolitik." *Foreign Policy* (Spring 1988): 109-128.

Prichett, Diane Tueller. "The Syrian Strategy on Terrorism." *Conflict Quarterly* (Summer 1988): 27-48.

Quandt, William. "Camp David and Peacemaking in the Middle East." *Political Science Quarterly* (Spring 1986): 357-377.

———. "The Gulf War: Policy Options and Regional Implications." *American-Arab Affairs* (Summer 1984): 1-7.

———. "Riyadh Between the Superpowers." *Foreign Policy* (Fall 1981): 37-56.

Ramati, Yohanan. "A PLO State and Israel's Security." *Midstream*, April 1989, 3-6.

Renfrew, Nita M. "Who Started the War?" *Foreign Policy* (Spring 1987): 98-108.

Roberts, Herbert R. "The Reagan Administration and the Middle East: Peace, Palestinians, and Israelis." *Scandinavian Journal of Development Alternatives* (March 1987): 44-57.

Rouleau, Eric. "Khomeini's Iran." *Foreign Affairs* (Fall 1980): 1-20.

Roumani, Maurice M. "The Sephardi Factor in Israeli Politics." *Middle East Journal* (Summer 1988): 423-435.

Rubinstein, Alvin Z. "The Soviet Union's Imperial Policy in the Middle East." *Middle East Review* (Fall 1982): 19-24.

Said, Edward W. "Inside Islam." *Harper's*, January 1981, 25-32.

———. "Irangate: A Many-sided Crisis." *Journal of Palestine Studies* (Summer 1987): 27-49.

Salpeter, E. "Agonizing Reappraisal in Israel." *New Leader*, January 9, 1989, 5-6.

Satloff, Robert. "Jordan and Reverberations of the Uprising." *Current History*, February 1989, 85-88.

Saunders, Harold. "Iran: A View from the State Department." *World Affairs* (Spring 1987): 219-224.

Sciolino, Elaine. "Iran's Durable Revolution." *Foreign Affairs* (Spring 1983): 893-920.

Segal, David. "The Iran-Iraq War: A Military Analysis." *Foreign Affairs* (Summer 1988): 946-963.

Shlaim, Avi, and Avner Yaniv. "Domestic Politics and Foreign Policy in Israel." *International Affairs* (Spring 1980): 242-262.

Shultz, George P.. "Working for Peace and Freedom." *Department of State Bulletin*, July 1987, 7-10.

Sick, Gary. "Trial by Error: Reflections on the Iran-Iraq War." *Middle East Journal* (Spring 1989): 230-246.

Sivan, Eduard. "The Islamic Republic of Egypt." *Orbis* (Winter 1987): 43-53.

Sterner, Michael. "The Iran-Iraq War." *Foreign Affairs* (Fall 1984): 128-143.

Sullivan, William H. "Dateline Iran: The Road Not Taken." *Foreign Policy* (Fall 1980): 175-186.

———. "Iran: A View from Iran." *World Affairs* (Spring 1987): 215-218.

Teter, D. Park. "Iran between East and West." *Editorial Research Reports*, January 26, 1979, 67-84.

Troxler, Nancy C. "The Gulf Cooperation Council: The Emergence of an Institution." *Millennium* (Spring 1987): 1-19.

Tuma, E. H. "Institutionalized Obstacles to Development: The Case of Egypt." *World Development*, October 1988, 1185-1198.

Viorst, Milton. "The Impact of the American Media on U.S. Middle East Policy." *American-Arab Affairs* (Summer 1987): 122-126.

———. "Jordan: A Moderate's Role." *Atlantic*, March 1981, 4-5.

Weiler, Joseph. "The Trojan Horse? European Political Cooperation, the Alliance, and the Arab-Israeli Conflict." *Harvard International Review* (November/December 1986): 20-25.

Weinbaum, Marvin. 'The Internationalization of Domestic Conflict in the Middle East." *Middle East Review* (Fall 1987): 31-42.

Welt, Leo G. " New Directions in Middle East Trade: Offsets and Countertrade." *American-Arab Affairs* (Winter 1986/1987): 88-93.

Wizarat, Talat. "The Role of the Gulf Cooperation Council in Regional Security." *Strategic Studies* (Winter 1987): 69-78.

Wright, Robin. "The Islamic Resurgence: A New Phase?" *Current History*, February 1988, 53-56.

Zartman, I. William, and A. G. Kluge. "The Sources and Goals of Qaddafi's Foreign Policy." *American-Arab Affairs* (Fall 1983): 59-69.

Index

Page numbers in **boldface** refer to biographical sketches.

Abbasid Islamic Empire, 128
Abd al-Rahim Ahmed, 29
Abd al-Rahman, 128
Abd-ul-Ilah (regent of Iraq), **239**
Abduh, Muhammad, 135, 247
Abdul Hamid, 186
Abdullah ibn Hussein (emir of Transjordan), 9, 178-179, **239**, 248, 251
Abdullah al-Salem al-Sabah, **239**
Abu al-Abbas, 128
Abu Bakr, 126, 127
Abu Dhabi
  Buraimi oasis dispute, 91, 213
  natural gas reserves, 213
  oil
    development from, 89
    reserves, 102, 213
  in UAE federation, 90, 212-213
Abu Gharbiyah, Bahjat, 29
Abu Hanifa, 132
Abu Jihad (Khalil Wazir), 246, 293
Abu Musa (Sa'id Musa al-Muragha), 28
Abu Musa (Gulf island), 90, 213, 262
Abu Nidal (Mazen Sabry al-Banna), 63, 198, 287, 288, 363
Abu'l Abbas, Muhammad, 29, 63, 287, 289, 290
Achille Lauro hijacking, 29, 36, 63, 287
ADC (American Arab Anti-Defamation Committee), 55
ADF (Arab Deterrent Force), 191
al-Afghani, Jamal al-Din, 135
Afghanistan, 39-40, 67, 274
Ahmad ibn Said, 209
Ahmadiyyah Movement, 134
AIPAC (American-Israel Public Affairs Committee), 54-55, 66, 73
Airborne Warning and Control System (AWACS) planes, 58, 72, 76, 78, 81, 218, 278-279
Ajman, 90, 213
ALA (Arab Liberation Army), 12
Alawi Moslems, 224
Alexander the Great, 124
ALF (Arab Liberation Front), 29

Algeria
  Arab League membership, 21, 141
  arms sales to
    by Soviets, 68
    suppliers (box), 85
  and the Gulf crisis, 323
  Maghreb Union, 4
  natural gas reserves, 104, 105
  oil
    crude, prices of (1973-1988), 108
    nationalization acts, 110
    production (1979-1987), 121
    reserves (1974-1988), 117
  Rejectionist Front, 27
  U.S. aid to, 77
Ali ibn Abi Talib, 127
Ali, Salim Rubayyi', 236, 270
Aliyah, 14-15
Allenby, Edmund, 247
Allon, Yigal, 267
Aly, Abdel Monem Said, 142
Amal organization, 33, 34, 189, 190, 193, 228
American Arab Anti-Defamation Committee (ADC), 55
American-Israeli Public Affairs Committee (AIPAC), 54-55, 66, 73
American Jewish community
  Biltmore Conference (1942), 11, 248
  lobbying efforts, 54-55, 73
American University of Beirut, 186
American Zionist Council, 54
Amman summit conference (1987), 5, 37, 141, 180, 292, 307-308 (text)
Amnesty International, 154, 172
al-Amri, Hasan, 234
Anderson, Terry A., 297
Anglo-American Committee of Inquiry, 249
Anglo-Persian Oil Company, 109, 151, 247, 251
Angola, 120
ANM (Arab National Movement), 18-19, 29
Aoun, Michel, 4, 183, 188, 194, 228, **239**, 294, 359
Arab-Americans, lobbying efforts, 55
Arab Civil Aviation Organization, 56
Arab Cooperation Council, 4, 164
Arab Deterrent Force (ADF), 191
Arab Federation, 255
Arab Fund for Economic and Social Development, 164

Arab-Israeli conflicts. *See also* Arab-Israeli peace efforts; Egyptian-Israeli peace treaty; Israeli-occupied lands; Palestine.
  Arab unification attempts (box), 20-21
  arms rivalry and, 70-72
  Balfour Declaration and, 8, 15, 40, 43, 168, 225, 247
  European colonialism and, 9-12, 247-248
  hostilities
    border clashes, 16-17
    Gaza raid (1956), 16, 169, 254
    Israeli invasions of Lebanon, 33-34, 59-60, 145, 169, 190, 192, 270, 280, 281
    1973 Arab-Israeli war, 24-27, 47, 169-170, 263-264.
    Six-Day War, 18-19, 22-23, 45-46, 143, 169, 179, 258-259
    Suez Canal crisis (1956), 17-18, 43-44, 143, 253-254
    War of Attrition (1969), 23, 46
    War of 1948, 13, 16, 43, 250
  Hussein of Jordan's role, 177
  inter-Arab rivalries, 18
  intifada, 1-2, 37-38, 65, 141, 172, 292
  Lebanon as microcosm, 195
  origins of, 7-8
  Palestinian guerrilla movement, 23
  postwar refugee problems, 16
  Zionist movement and, 10-12
Arab-Israeli peace efforts. *See also* Egyptian-Israeli peace treaty.
  autonomy talks, 32-33, 53, 174-175, 279
  Bourguiba peace proposal, 257-258
  Camp David agreements, 31-33, 50-52, 73-74, 271, 302-304 (text)
  Eisenhower peace plan, 255
  Fahd plan, 58, 221, 278, 306 (text)
  Fez summit proposal, 35, 62, 281, 306 (text)
  Geneva Conference, 48, 49
  Habib shuttle diplomacy, 33-34, 58, 59, 60, 192, 277
  Hussein-Arafat initiative, 35-36, 64-65, 180, 268, 281-282
  Israeli peace plan, 259
  Johnson peace plan, 259
  Kissinger shuttle diplomacy, 26-27, 47-48, 144, 264, 266
  Peres initiative, 36-37, 65

Reagan initiative, 35, 60, 62, 281, 306 (text)
Rogers plan, 23, 46, 262
Shamir's election plan, 66, 174, 296
Shultz initiative, 37-38, 65, 141, 293
Sinai II agreement, 26-27, 48
Arab League
  ADF in Lebanon, 191
  Amman summit (1987), 5, 37, 141, 180, 292, 307-308 (text)
  background (box), 20-21
  condemnation of Israeli-Egyptian peace treaty, 53, 56
  Egypt's relations with, 5, 32, 56, 141
  established, 249
  Fez summit, 35, 62, 281, 306 (text)
  and the Gulf crisis, 323, 356, 357
  and the intifada, 38
  Palestine partition opposition, 12, 250
  PLO, endorsement of, 26, 181, 265, 301-302 (text)
  PLO membership, 21, 30, 141, 267
Arab Liberation Army (ALA), 12
Arab Liberation Front (ALF), 29
Arab National Movement (ANM), 18-19, 29
Arab nationalism
  Egypt's influence, 139
  in Iraq, 94
  Lebanese leadership, 186
  rise of (box), 20-21
  Soviet influence and, 44-45
Arab Organization for Industrialization, 56
Arab politics, 323-328
Arab Revolt of 1936-1939, 10
Arabia, 125
Arabian American Oil Company (ARAMCO), 109, 220, 248, 276
The Arabs: A Comprehensive History (Mansfield), 11
Arabs, definition and origin (box), 11
Arafat, Yasir. *See also* Palestine Liberation Organization.
  biographical sketch, **239**
  Egyptian support, 141
  Fatah organization, 19, 23, 27, 66
  and the Gulf crisis, 326-327, 338
  Hussein of Jordan relationship, 35-36, 64-65, 180, 268, 281-282
  and the intifada, 2, 37-38, 65
  Moscow visit, 56
  recognition of Israel, 3, 38, 65, 295, 311 (text)
  Syria, expulsion from, 282
  terrorism renunciation, 3, 38, 295, 311 (text)
  UN addresses, 30, 65, 265, 295
ARAMCO (Arabian American Oil Company), 109, 220, 248, 276
Arens, Moshe, 68, 171, **239**
Argentina, 320
Argov, Shlomo, 280
Arif, Abdul Rahman, 162, **239**, 258
Arif, Abdul Salem, 162, **239**, 257, 258
Arms Control and Disarmament Agency, U.S., 69
Arms sales. *See also* United States foreign aid, military.
  AWACS controversy, 58, 72, 76, 78, 81, 218, 278-279
  ballistic missiles, 84-86
  chemical weapons, 6, 83-85, 96, 295
  congressional role in (box), 81
  escalation of, 5-6, 70-72

by European countries
  Egypt, 71-72
  Gulf states, 80
  Iraq, 71-72
  Israel, 16
  Jordan, 71-72
  Saudi Arabia, 71-72, 78-79
to Middle East and North Africa (box), 85
nuclear technology, 6, 290
by Soviet Union
  Algeria, 68
  Egypt, 16, 24, 41, 43, 68, 70, 75
  Iran, 258
  Iraq, 68, 82-83, 162
  Libya, 68
  PLO, 47
  Syria, 24, 25, 41, 68, 82
Tripartite Declaration and, 16, 43, 70, 251
by United States
  client list (box), 73
  congressional role (box), 81
  Gulf States, 81-82
  Iran, 64, 72
  Jordan, 79-80, 182
  Saudi Arabia, 58, 72, 76, 78-79, 278-279
Army of South Lebanon (ASL), 34
Arnett, Peter, 339
Ashkenazi Jews, 167, 171
ASL (Army of South Lebanon), 34
Aspin, Les (D-Wis), 361, 363
al-Assad, Hafez
  accession to power, 226, 261
  biographical sketch, **240**
  domestic stability under, 223, 228
  feud with Iraq, 37
  and the Gulf crisis, 319, 323, 361
  and Lebanon intervention, 191
  Moscow visit, 56, 68, 291
  in 1973 Arab-Israeli war, 24-26
  Soviet influence over, 47
  "strategic parity" policy, 173
Aswan High Dam, 17, 43, 140, 143, 253
al-Atasi, Louai, **240**
al-Atasi, Nureddin, **240**, 258, 261
Atassi, Hashim, 252
Ataturk (Mustafa Kemal), 128, 248
Atherton, Alfred Leroy, Jr., 144, 148
al-Attas, Haider Abu Bakr, 236, **240**, 288
Attlee, Clement R., 40
Australia, 320
Autoemancipation (Pinsker), 168
AWACS (Airborne Warning and Control System) planes, 58, 72, 76, 78, 81, 218, 278-279
Ayubi, Nazih N. M., 142
Aziz, Abdul, 213
Aziz, Tariq, 94, 100
  diplomacy before Gulf war, 330-331, 361, 362, 363
  Geneva statement, 383 (text)
  letter to Arab League, 317, 355
  letter to United Nations, 344, 367
  Soviet plan, 344, 366, 387 (text)

Ba'athism
  in Iraq, 162-163
  Lebanese wing, 189
Badr, Zaki, 147
Baghdad Pact, 17, 43, 44, 151, 162, 253, 256. *See also* CENTO.

Bahrain
  Arab League membership, 21, 141
  arms purchases, 72, 82, 85, 206
  British influence over, 88-90, 206
  economic diversification, 206-207
  and Gulf Cooperation Council, 80, 98, 105, 206, 279
  and the Gulf crisis, 319, 323, 368
  history of, 88-90, 206
  Iranian coup attempt, 91, 206
  Iran's claim to, 90, 207
  key facts, 205
  oil, development from, 89
  pearl industry in, 88, 89, 205
  Shi'ite's in, 90, 206
Baker, James A., III, 66, 296, 298, 330-331, 334, 349, 356, 357, 361, 362, 363, 365, 368, 382-383 (text)
Bakhtiar, Shahpur, 153, **240**, 272
al-Bakr, Ahmed Hassan, 162, **240**, 259, 273, 325
Balfour, Arthur James, 8, 40
Balfour Declaration, 8, 15, 40, 43, 168, 225, 247
Ballistic missiles, 84-86
Bangladesh, 319, 320
Bani-Sadr, Abolhassan, 153, **240**, 275, 278
al-Banna, Mazen Sabry (Abu Nidal), 63, 198, 287, 288, 363
Banu Hashim, 125
Bar-Lev Line, 23, 169
al-Barzani, Mustafa, **240**, 266
Bazargan, Mehdi, 153, **240**, 272
Begin, Menachem
  biographical sketch, **240**
  Camp David talks, 31-33, 50-52, 73-74, 271
  Irgun leadership, 12
  Lebanese Front, support of, 191
  as prime minister, 170, 268
  resignation, 171, 283
  Rogers Plan rejection, 23
Beheshti, Ayatollah Mohammed, 154, 278
Belgium, 320, 358
Ben-Gurion, David, 10, 13, 14, 169, **240**, 250
Ben-Zvi, Isaac, 14, **240**, 252
Bendjedid, Chadli, 38
Benvenisti, Meron, 172
Bernadotte, Folke, 250
Berri, Nabih, 193, 194, **240-241**, 286
Bessmertnykh, Aleksandr, 339, 365
Biden, Joseph R., Jr. (D-Del.), 58
Biltmore Conference (1942), 11, 248
al-Bitar, Salah, **241**, 257
Black Muslims, 134
Black September, 27, 262, 263
Bonaparte, Napoleon, 142
Boumediene, Houari, 56
Bourguiba, Habib, 257
Boycott of Israel Office (Arab League), 21
Brady, Nicholas, 357
Brandt, Willy, 330, 362
Brezhnev, Leonid, 46, 136, 263, 281
Britain. *See* Great Britain.
British National Oil Corporation, 117
Buckley, William, 63, 297
Bulgaria, 320
Bunche, Ralph J., 16, 250-251
Buraimi oasis dispute, 90-91, 213
Burma Road, 13
Bush, George. *See also* Persian Gulf crisis; United States.
  and the Gulf crisis

announces cease-fire, 344, 367, 390 (text)
announces war, 339, 385-386 (text)
on invasion of Kuwait, 318-319, 372-375 (text)
on Iraqi withdrawal, 344, 389-390 (text)
on troop deployments, 318-320, 328-329, 370-371 (text), 379-380 (text)
summit with Gorbachev, 357, 372 (text)
on terrorism, 66-67
relations with Egypt, 142, 148
Byzantine Empire, 124

Cable News Network (CNN), 334, 339
Cairo Agreement (1969), 27
Cairo Conference (1921), 9, 248
Cairo Conference (1977), 270
Camp David agreements, 31-33, 50-52, 73-74, 271, 302-304 (text)
Canada
aid to Iranian hostages, 275
crude oil prices, 108
and the Gulf crisis, 319, 320, 356, 358, 365
natural gas reserves, 105
oil consumption, 104
CAO (Communist Action Organization), 189
Carlucci, Frank C., 82
Carter, Jimmy
arms commitments to Israel, 73-74
arms sales attempts, 72, 75, 76, 81
energy and conservation programs, 106, 273
and Iranian hostage crisis, 154, 274-277
peace efforts
Camp David talks, 31, 49-50, 144, 271
Mideast trip, 52, 272
Carter Doctrine, 87, 275
CENTO (Central Treaty Organization), 44, 162, 256. *See also* Baghdad Pact.
Chad, 3-4, 203, 276, 290, 291, 294
al-Chalabi, Fahdil, 118
Chamoun, Camille, 197, **241**, 252
Chehab, Fuad, 187-189, **241**, 255
Chemical weapons, 6, 83-85, 96, 161, 293, 295, 346
Cheney, Dick, 319, 328, 339, 356, 358, 361, 366
Chiang Kai-shek, 144
Children of Gebalawi (Mahfouz), 145
China
Egypt's recognition of, 17
and the Gulf crisis, 321, 322, 330, 356, 361
missile sales to Saudi Arabia, 86
oil reserves, 105
OPEC talks, 120
Chou En-lai, 143
Christian, George, 45
Churba, Joseph, 90
Churchill, Winston, 9, 144
Cicippio, Joseph J., 290, 297, 298
Clark, Ramsey, 362
Clark, William P., 58
Common Market (European Economic Community), 113, 157
Communist Action Organization (CAO), 189
Conference of Presidents of Major Jewish Organizations, 54-55
Congress, U.S. *See also* United States policy.

Arab and Israel lobbying (box), 54-55
arms sales
to Israel, 72-73
role in (box), 81
to Saudi Arabia, 76, 78-79
Eisenhower Doctrine, 44, 187-188, 254
Connally, John, 362
Constantinople Delimitation Protocol (1913), 92
Coptic Christian Church, 146-147
Cox, Percy, 317
Craxi, Bettino, 63
Crowe, William, Jr., 329, 361
Cuba, 322, 356, 359, 361
Cyprus, arms purchases by, 85
Cyrus the Great, 151
Czechoslovakia, 70, 75, 320

Daher, Michel, 228
D'Arcy, William Knox, 109, 151, 247
Da'wa movement, 91, 94, 164
Dayan, Moshe, 19, 22, 30, 49, 52, **241**, 264, 268, 274
Dayr Yassin massacre (1948), 13
de Lesseps, Ferdinand, 142
Democratic Front for the Liberation of Palestine (DFLP), 29
Denmark, 320
Der Judenstaat (Herzl), 14
DFLP (Democratic Front for the Liberation of Palestine), 29
Dine, Thomas A., 54
Djibouti, 21, 141, 323
Dodge, David, 297
Douglas, Leigh, 289
Draper, Morris, 277
Druze Moslems, 184, 188, 224, 227
Dubai
oil, development from, 89
in UAE federation, 90, 213
Dugan, Michael J., 358
Dulles, John Foster, 17, 70, 143, 255

Eagleburger, Lawrence, 364
Eban, Abba, **241**, 259
Ebeid, Mona Makram, 145
Economic Unity Council (Arab League), 21
Ecuador
crude oil production (1979-1987), 121
oil revenues (1974-1988), 117
Edde, Raymond, 267
Eden, Anthony, 70
Egypt
agriculture, 140
Arab League
membership in, 21, 32
readmission, 141, 298
suspension from, 56, 273
Arab nationalism
growth of, 20-21
leadership role, 139
Arafat's visit, 35
arms sales to
by Britain, 71-72
by France, 71
by Soviet Union, 16, 24, 41, 43, 68, 70, 75
suppliers (box), 85
by United States, 73, 75-76

ballistic missiles in, 86
chemical weapons in, 84
"Cold Peace" with Israel, 145
economic problems, 147-148
foreign relations
Britain, 251-254
China, recognition of, 17
Israel normalization, 53, 275
Jordan, disputes with, 18, 254
Soviet Union, 46-47, 75, 145, 262
Syria, union with, 18
Yemeni civil war, 143
Gaza raid (1955), effect of, 16
Gaza Strip, annexation of, 9, 13, 43, 254
and the Gulf crisis
aftermath of, 349, 368
Arab League diplomacy, 317, 323, 355
coalition participation, 315, 319, 320, 341, 344, 345, 356, 364
demonstrations, 323
economic implications, 315, 328, 349, 357, 358
inter-Arab rivalries, 18
Islamic resurgence and, 146-147
key facts (box), 140
land reform, 142
map, 141
in 1948 war with Israel, 13, 16, 43
1952 revolution, 142
1973 Arab-Israel war, 24-27, 47, 144, 167-170, 263-264
OPEC talks, 120
and Palestinian peace movement, 141-142
peace efforts
Cairo Conference (1977), 270
Sadat's Israeli initiative, 31, 49, 144, 269-270
political parties, 145-146
population problems, 140
Six-Day War with Israel, 18-19, 22-23, 45-46, 143, 169, 179, 258-259
Suez Canal crisis (1956), 17-18, 43-44, 143, 253-254
terrorism, response to, 63
UAR membership, 18, 21, 143, 226, 232, 255, 256
U.S. aid to, 77, 147-148
War of Attrition (1969), 23, 46
Egyptian-Israeli peace treaty
Arab reaction to, 32, 53, 56, 273
Camp David agreements and, 31-33, 51-52, 73-74, 271
highlights of
Israeli security, 51-52, 73-74
Palestinian self-rule negotiations, 51
Sinai withdrawal, 52
U.S. oil guarantee to Israel, 53
signing of, 52, 144, 273
Soviet reaction to, 56
text of, 304-306
Eilts, Hermann F., 50
Eisenhower, Dwight D., 16, 43-44, 110, 143, 162, 254, 255, 338
Eisenhower Doctrine, 44, 187-188, 254
El Al Airlines, 63
Elijah Muhammad, 134
Elon, Amos, 14
England. *See* Great Britain.
Eshkol, Levi, **241**, 260
Ethiopia, arms purchases by, 85

Europe (western). *See also individual countries.*
  and Arab oil embargo (1973), 112, 113
  arms sales to Middle East, 70-72, 78-79, 80
  colonialism in Middle East, 9-12
  Iran, relations with, 156-157
  Nazi persecution, 10, 11, 15
  oil consumption, 104
  U.S. Libyan raid, response to, 63
European Economic Community (Common Market), 113, 157
Evron, Ephraim, 278

Fadlallah, Muhammad Hussein, **241**
Fahd ibn Abdul Aziz (king of Saudi Arabia), 36, 116, 120, 215, 218, 221-222, **241**, 280, 318, 319, 356, 357, 360, 371-372 (text)
Fahd peace plan, 58, 221, 278, 306 (text)
Fahmy, Ismail, 269
Faisal I (Faisal ibn Hussein) (king of Iraq), 9, 162, **241**, 247, 248
Faisal II (king of Iraq), 44, 162, 178, 179, **241**, 252, 324
Faisal ibn Abdul Aziz al-Saud (king of Saudi Arabia), 217, **241**, 255, 256, 257, 266
Faisal ibn Musaed, 266
Fard, W. D., 134
Farouk I (king of Egypt), 142, 145, **241**, 252
Fatah ("conquest") organization, 19, 23, 27, 29, 66
Fatah Uprising, 28
Federation of Arab Republics, 262
Fez summit peace proposal, 35, 62, 281, 306 (text)
Fisher, W. B., 11
Fitzwater, Marlin, 339, 366, 387 (text)
Five Pillars of Islam, 130
FLM (Free Lebanon Militia), 33, 189, 192
Ford, Gerald R., 48, 81, 173, 266
France
  arms sales
    to Israel, 16, 17
    policy of, 70-72
    to Saudi Arabia, 71
  colonialism in Middle East, 9-12
  and the Gulf crisis, 319, 321, 331, 355, 356, 358, 363, 365
  Lebanese peacekeeping force, 192-193
  Lebanon creation, 184, 186-187
  Suez Canal crisis (1956), 17-18, 43-44, 143
  Syria, rule over, 9, 225
  Tripartite Declaration, 16, 43, 70, 251
Franjieh, Suleiman, 31, 190, 228, **241**, 266
Free Lebanon Militia (FLM), 33, 189, 192
From War to War (Safran), 21
Fuad I (king of Egypt), **241**
Fuad II (king of Egypt), 252
Fujairah, 90, 213
Fulbright, J. William (D-Ark.), 41

Gabon, 117, 121
Galilee, 13
Galili, Israel, 171
Gaza Strip. *See also* Israeli-occupied lands.
  Camp David agreement on, 50-51
  Egyptian control of, 9, 13, 43, 254
  intifada, 1-2, 37-38, 65, 141, 172, 292
  Israeli raid (1956), 16, 169, 254

Jordan's claim relinquished, 38
  refugee camps in, 16
GCC (Gulf Cooperation Council), 80, 98, 99 (map), 105, 155, 205, 221
Gemayel, Amin, 34, 61, 62, 183, 188, 193, 228, **242,** 281
Gemayel, Bashir, 34, 60, 188, 192, **242,** 281
Gemayel, Pierre, 187, 188, **242**
Geneva Conference, 48, 49
Germany, 315, 320-321, 348, 358, 363, 365
Ghali, Butros, 247
al-Ghashni, Ahmed Hussein, 234, 270
Ghawshah, Samir, 29
Ghotbzadeh, Sadegh, 153
Glaspie, April, 318, 336, 355, 375-377 (text)
Glass, Charles, 292, 297
Glubb, John, 179
Golan Heights
  after Six-Day War, 22, 45
  Israeli annexation, 59, 279
  in 1973 Arab-Israeli war, 24-25, 169
Goodman, Alan Harry, 280
Goodman, Robert, Jr., 283
Gorbachev, Mikhail, 40, 68, 156, 157, 291, 344, 351-352, 357, 359, 360, 365, 366, 372 (text)
Great Britain
  arms sales, 70, 71-72, 78-79
  Balfour Declaration, 8, 15, 40, 43, 168, 225, 247
  colonialism in Middle East, 9-12, 162, 247-248, 317
  Egyptian relations, 251-254
  and the Gulf crisis, 319, 320, 339, 344, 345, 346, 355, 356, 357, 358, 360, 362, 363
  hostages in Iraq, 322, 330, 357
  Lebanese peacekeeping force, 192-193
  Libyan bombing, support of, 63
  oil
    crude, prices of (1973-1988), 108
    Iranian nationalization of company, 251
    Mideast reserves, 42, 105, 109
    North Sea production, 101, 117
    "red line" agreement, 109
  Palestine reassessment, 10, 249-250
  Palestine, retreat from, 11, 168-169, 250
  Persian Gulf, role in, 88-90, 206, 317
  Suez Canal crisis (1956), 17-18, 43-44, 143, 253-254
  Tripartite Declaration, 16, 43, 70, 251
Greater Land of Israel Movement, 30
Greece, 42, 320
Green Book (Qaddafi), 201
"Greenhouse" effect, 122
Gromyko, Andrei A., 249
Gulbenkian, Calouste, 109
Gulf Cooperation Council (GCC), 80, 98, 99 (map), 105, 155, 205, 221, 279
Gush Emunim organization, 30, 267

Habash, George, 18-19, 27, 28, 30, **242,** 268
Habib, Philip C., 33-34, 58, 59, 60, 192, 277, 280
Habra, Hissene, 294
Haddad, Saad, 33, 62, 189, 191, 192
Hadith-Sunnah, 129
al-Hafez, Amin, 226, 257
Haganah, 10, 11, 12-13
Haig, Alexander M., Jr., 58, 59, 60, 277
Hamadai, Muhammad Ali, 194, 291

Hamadi, Saadun, 278
al-Hamdi, Ibrahim, 234
Hammani, Said, 270
Hammarskjold, Dag, 255
Hammer, Armand, 110
Hanafis sect, 125
Hanbali school of thought, 132
Hance, Kent, 120
Hanifi school of thought, 132
Harriman, W. Averell, 251
Hassan ibn Talal (crown prince of Jordan), **242**
Hassan II (king of Morocco), 21, 37, 202
Hatfield, Mark (R-Ore.), 58
Hawatmeh, Nayef, 29
Heath, Edward, 330, 362
Hegira, 126
Helou, Charles, 188, 189-190, **242**
Henderson-Pollard, Anne, 287
Herut party, 30
Herzl, Theodor, 14, 168
Herzog, Chaim, **242,** 295
Hess, Moshe, 168
Higgins, William R., 67, 293, 297, 298
Hijackings. *See* Terrorism.
Hindawi, Nezar, 289
Hisadrut, 10
Hizballah organization, 34, 67, 189, 193
Holliman, John, 339
Holocaust, 10, 11
Holy War Army, 12
Hope-Simpson Report (1930), 10
Horner, Charles A., 364
al-Hoss, Selim, 183, 228, 294
Hostages. *See* Terrorism.
Hoveida, Amir Abbas, **242**
Howe, Geoffrey, 287
Howell, W. Nathaniel III, 362
Hubayka, Elie, 194
Hurd, Douglas, 357
Hussein Ala, 251
Hussein ibn Ali (Sherif Hussein), 9, 178, 216, 225, **242,** 247
Hussein, Saddam. *See also* Iraq; Persian Gulf crisis.
  accession to power, 162, 273
  Arab nations, relations with, 164-165
  biographical sketch, **242, 324-325** (box)
  decision to fight coalition, 336-339
  feud with Assad, 37
  Glaspie meeting, 318, 355, 375-377 (text)
  Gulf war, 339-346, 363-367, 381-382 (text), 388-389 (text)
  invasion of Kuwait, 315-323, 355
  pan-Arabist image, 323-325, 338
  power, challenges to and consolidation of, 5, 159, 164, 347, 367-368
  and Shi'ite appeasement, 94
  war with Iran, objectives, 163
Hussein ibn Talal (king of Jordan)
  Amman summit conference (1987) and, 5, 37, 141, 180, 292, 307-308 (text)
  Arafat relationship, 35-36, 64-65, 180, 268, 281-282
  assassination attempt, 261
  and the Bedouins, 178
  biographical sketch, **242**
  British support of, 18
  and Camp David agreements, 32, 52, 180
  and the Gulf crisis, 327-328, 338, 341, 356, 365
  Moscow visit, 68
  Peres meeting, 180

PLO, relations with, 23, 30, 179-180
Reagan arms proposals and, 79-80
and Reagan peace initiative, 35, 62
and Six-Day War, 22, 179
West Bank announcement, 2, 38, 65, 177, 181, 309 (text)
al-Husseini, Hajj Amin, 12

Ibadhi Moslems, 209
Ibn Saud (king of Saudi Arabia), 20, 43, 216, **242**, 247, 248
Ibrahim, Saad Eddin, 146
Idris I (king of Libya), 197, 198, 200, **242**, 260
Immigration and Naturalization Service v. Chadha, 81
India, Moslem population in, 124
Indonesia
    Moslem population, 124
    oil
        crude, prices of (1973-1988), 108
        dependence on, 116
        production (1979-1987), 121
        reserves (1974-1988), 117
Integration and Development in Israel (Matras), 15
International Energy Agency, 106, 113
Intifada, 1-2, 37-38, 65, 141, 172, 292
Iran. *See also* Iran-Iraq war.
    arms sales to
        by Soviets, 258
        suppliers (box), 85
        by United States, 64, 72
    Baghdad Pact, 17, 43, 151, 162, 253
    chemical weapons use, 6, 84
    covert initiative by United States, 64, 72, 155, 289, 290
    domestic problems, 156, 348
    ethnic traditions, 150
    foreign policy
        Abu Musa and the Tunbs, claim to, 90, 213, 262
        and Arab neighbors, 92, 323
        Bahrain, claim to, 90
        Iraq, rivalry with, 92-94
        Islamic revolution precept, 91
        Saudi feud, 119, 348
        Soviet Union, 42, 67, 89, 156, 295, 298
        United States, 151, 154, 274-277
        Western Europe, 156-157, 348
    and the Gulf crisis
        aftermath of, 347-348
        Iraqi rebels, aid to, 348, 368
        Iraqi warplanes, sheltering of, 342, 348, 365
        neutrality, 347-348, 365
        peace agreement with Iraq, 347, 356, 357
    history of, 151-152
    IRP (Islamic Republican party), role of, 153-154
    key facts (box), 150
    map, 151
    Mujaheddin, repression of, 154
    natural gas reserves, 105
    oil
        crude, prices of (1973-1988), 108
        oil company nationalization, 151, 251
        production (1979-1987), 121
        reserves, 102, 105, 149
        revenues (1974-1988), 117

revolution of 1979
    coalition of forces, 152
    export attempts, 91
    government under Khomeini, 154, 348
    overthrow of shah, 152-153, 272
    power consolidation, 153-154
    Revolutionary Guards, 153
    Shatt al-Arab waterway, control of, 92-93, 94, 159, 163
    Shi'ite majority, 150-151
    Soviet expansionism (1946), 42, 89, 151
    subversive activities of, 91-92
    U.S. aid to, 77
    U.S. embassy hostage crisis, 154, 274-277
    "White Revolution," 151-152
Iran-contra scandal, 63-64, 72, 155, 289, 290
Iran-Iraq war
    cease-fire, 3, 64, 94, 96-97, 155, 294
    chemical weapons use, 6, 83-84, 96
    economic implications, 97, 155
    internationalization attempts, 96
    Iranian offensives, 96, 163
    Iranian response, 95-96, 154-155
    Iraqi attacks, 94-95, 154-155
    Iraqi debts, 316
    Iraqi objectives, 163
    maps of Persian Gulf area, Shatt al-Arab, 97
    missile use in, 86, 119
    oil prices and, 97, 116, 118-121
    peace agreement (1990), 347, 356
    regional implications, 97-98, 163, 164
    Soviet policy, 98-100, 163
    tanker attacks, 96, 104, 155
    U.S. policy, 64, 98, 155
Iraq. *See also* Iran-Iraq war; Persian Gulf crisis; Saddam Hussein.
    agricultural potential, 160
    Arab Federation, 255
    Arab League membership, 21, 141
    Arab nationalism and, 20-21, 162-163, 323-326
    arms sales to
        by Britain, 71-72
        by France, 71
        by Soviet Union, 68, 82-83, 162
        suppliers (box), 337
        by United States, 73
    Ba'athism in, 162-163
    Baghdad Pact, 17, 43, 151, 162, 253
    ballistic missiles in, 84, 86, 340-341
    chemical weapons use, 6, 83-84, 161, 293, 294, 346
    Communist party in, 161
    demography, 160
    Egypt, disputes with, 18, 162
    foreign relations, 164
    Gulf war
        air war, 339-343, 363-366
        aftermath, 347, 367-368
        decision to fight, 336-339
        diplomacy before, 330-331, 338-339, 363
        ground war, 343-346, 366-367
    history of, 162
    invasion of Kuwait
        American and Saudi response, 318-319
        anti-Iraq coalition, 319-321
        Arab reaction, 323-325, 326-328, 356
        attack, 317-318, 355
        attrocities, 318, 365, 366
        claims to Kuwait, 317
        depopulation of Kuwait, 318, 358

economic motivations, 316-317
        hostages, 322-323, 330, 356, 357, 362
        linkage to Palestinian issue, 325-326
        oil policies, 317
        UN sanctions, 321-322, 335-336
    Iran, rivalry with, 92-94, 347-348, 357-358
    key facts (box), 160
    Kurds' autonomy movement, 6, 9, 161, 293, 294, 347
    Lebanon, involvement in, 194, 359-360
    map, 161
    in 1948 war with Israel, 13, 16
    1958 coup, 44, 162, 255
    nuclear plant attack, 57-59, 67, 277-278
    oil
        crude, prices of (1973-1988), 108
        nationalization, 111, 262
        pipeline construction program, 97, 104, 160, 164
        production (1979-1987), 121
        reserves, 102, 105, 159-160
        revenues (1974-1988), 117
    pan-Arab movement in, 162-163, 323-325
    Rejectionist Front, 27
    religious and ethnic divisions, 160-161
    Shatt al-Arab waterway, control of, 92-93, 159, 163, 347
    Shi'ites in, 91, 94, 160-161, 347
    Soviet influence, 46, 163, 351-352
    U.S. aid to, 77
Irgun Zvai Leumi (militia), 11, 12, 13
IRP (Islamic Republican party), 153
al-Iryani, Abd al-Rahman, 234
Isa bin Sulman al-Khalifa (emir of Bahrain), 206, **242**
Islam. *See also* Shi'ite Moslems.
    Abbasid Islamic Empire, 128
    after Muhammad, 126-128
    and Arabization (box), 11
    articles of faith, 130, 132
    calendar, 124
    canon law, 132
    common heritage, 123
    confession of faith, 128-129
    doctrine's sources
        consensus, 129-130
        Hadith-Sunnah, 129
        inference by analogy, 131
        Koran, 129
    facts about (box), 124
    Five Pillars of, 130
    fundamentalist movements, 135
    ideological diversity, 123
    in Iran
        fundamentalism, 91-92, 135
        ideal state idea, 91
        power of, 133, 150-151
    Jerusalem, importance to, 8, 124
    Mecca
        history of, 125
        militants' seizure of Grand Mosque in, 274
        pilgramage to (box), 131
        riots in, 91-92, 119, 218, 292
    modernization, impact of, 133-135
    Muhammad's role, 125-126
    Ottoman Empire, 8, 14, 20, 88, 92, 128
    as political force, 135-136
    predestination belief, 132
    resurgence movement, 132-133, 146
    in Saudi Arabia
        canon law penalties, 132
        political influence, 135

women's role, 136
schisms and sects of (box), 127
in the Soviet Union (box), 136
Umayyad Empire, 127-128
in the United States (box), 134
western hostility to, 123-124, 133
Islamic Amal, 189
Islamic Conference Organization. *See* Organization of the Islamic Conference.
Islamic Development Fund, 164
Islamic Front for the Liberation of Bahrain, 91
Islamic Republican Party (IRP), 153
Islamic Revolutionary Movement, 61, 91
Isma'il, Abd al-Fattah, 236, **242-243**, 270, 275
Israel. *See also* Arab-Israeli conflicts; Arab-Israeli peace efforts; Egyptian-Israeli peace treaty; Israeli-occupied lands; Palestine; Persian Gulf crisis.
Arab population, 168, 171
arms sales to
by France, 16, 17
suppliers (box), 85
by United States, 24, 25, 41-42, 57, 70-71, 72-75
by West Germany, 70
Ashkenazim, 167, 171
economy, 167, 174
foreign relations, 173-174
Egypt, normalization with, 53, 275
Jordan, 173
Soviet Union, 39, 68, 250
Syria, 173
United States. *See U.S. relations, this heading.*
and Gulf crisis,
aftermath of, 350-351
Jerusalem killings, 326, 359, 360
Palestinian issue, 325-327, 350-351
retaliation question, 341-342
Scud attacks, 340-342, 364
U.S. relations, 341-342, 350-351, 362
history, 168-169
Jewish heritage (box), 14-15
key facts (box), 168
kibbutzim, founding of, 14-15
map, 41, 169
military power
arms industry in, 73
and arms procurement, 70-72
ballistic missiles, 85-86
chemical weapons, 84
Gaza raid (1956), 16, 169, 254
and the intifada, 1-2, 37-38, 65, 292
invasions of Lebanon, 33-34, 59-60, 145, 169, 192, 270, 280, 281
Iraqi nuclear plant attack, 57-58, 67, 277
Lavi plane, 74
in 1948 war, 13, 16
nuclear arsenal report, 6, 290
National Unity Government, 171, 172-173
parliamentary government
1977 elections, 170
1981 elections, 170-171
1984 elections, 171-172
1988 elections, 172-173
premiership rotation, 171, 290
proportional representation, 170
PLO recognition of, 38, 65

Pollard spy case, 287, 289
postwar immigration, 167-168
proclaimed, 13, 43, 250
role of religion, 169
Sadat's visit to, 31, 49, 144, 269
Sephardim, 168, 171
settlements in occupied land. *See* Israeli-occupied lands.
Shin Beth affair, 289
UN admission, 250
U.S. relations
arms grants and sales, 72-75, 77
importance of, 173, 350-351
lobbying efforts (box), 54-55
oil commitment, 53
support for, 39, 41-42, 43
water, importance of, 167
Israel Defense Force, 10, 13
Israeli-occupied lands. *See also* Gaza Strip; West Bank.
Arab rights in, 269
autonomy proposal, 32-33, 53, 174-175, 279
in Camp David agreements, 51
Golan Heights annexation, 59, 279
human rights violations in, 172
intifada, 1-2, 37-38, 65, 141, 172, 292
Shamir election plan, 66, 174, 296
unauthorized settlements, 30
The Israelis: Founders and Sons (Elon), 14
Italy
and the Gulf crisis, 319, 320, 358
Lebanese peacekeeping force, 192-193
Libya, colonization of, 200
terrorist release, 63

Ja'afari school of thought, 132
Jabotinsky, Vladamir, 170
Jabotinsky, Ze'ev, 11
Jabril, Ahmed, 29
Jackson, Jesse L., 283
Jacobsen, David P., 290, 297
Jadid, Salah, 226
Jaja, Samir, 188, 194
Jalloud, Abdel Sallem, 201, 202
Japan
and Arab oil embargo (1973), 112, 113
energy source diversification, 106
and the Gulf crisis, 315, 320-321, 322, 356, 357, 358, 365
oil consumption, 104
trade with Gulf states, 89
Jarring, Gunnar V., 23, 24, 46
Jenco, Lawrence M., 290, 297
Jennings, Peter, 361
Jerusalem
British evacuation, 13
division of, 43, 250
Islam, importance to, 8, 124
Israeli capture, 22, 258-259
Sadat's visit to, 31, 49, 144, 269
Jewish Agency, 10, 11
Jewish diaspora, 7
Jewish heritage (box), 14-15
Jewish National Fund, 10
Jewish Settlement Police, 11
The Jewish State (Herzl), 168
Johnson, Lyndon B., 45, 70, 73, 257, 259
Joint Political Military Group, 74
Jones, David, 361

Jordan
Arab Federation, 255
Arab League membership, 21, 141
Arab Legion and, 12, 178
arms sales to
by Britain, 71-72
by France, 71
suppliers (box), 85
by United States, 73, 79-80, 182
civil war, 179-180, 261
demography, 178
economy, 182
Egypt, disputes with, 18, 254
and the Gulf crisis
airspace, defense of, 341-342
Arab politics, 323, 356
economic implications, 328, 357, 358
Iraq, support for, 323, 327-328, 365
refugees, 328, 358
UN sanctions, 321, 356
geography, 177-178
history of, 9, 43, 178-181
and the intifada, 180-181
key facts (box), 178
map, 179
in 1948 war with Israel, 13, 16
Palestinian refugees in, 16, 178
PLO activities in, 27-28, 179-181
political restraints, 181-182
riots (1989), 5, 182, 296
Saudi aid, 182
Six-Day War and, 179
U.S. aid, 77, 182
West Bank claims, 32, 38, 43, 65, 141, 177, 181, 309-310
Jumblatt, Kamal, 187, 188, 190, **243**, 268
Jumblatt, Walid, 188, 193, 194, **243**

Ka'bah shrine, 125, 126, 131
Kaifu, Toshiki, 365
Kamel, Muhammed Ibrahim, 49, **243**
Karami, Rashid, 188, 194, **243**, 255, 266, 291
Kassim, Abdul Karim, 162, **243**, 255, 256-257, 324
Kataeb (Phalange) party, 188
Kemal, Mustafa (Ataturk), 128, 248
Kemp, Jack F. (R-N.Y.), 58
Kennedy, Edward M. (D-Mass), 361
Kenya, arms purchases by, 85
Keren Hayesod, 10
Khalaf, Salah, **243**
Khalid bin Abdul Aziz (king of Saudi Arabia), 218, **243**, 280
Khalid ibn al-Walid, 126
Khalifa bin Hamad al-Thani, 211, **243**
al-Khalifa tribe, 88, 206
Khalil, Mustafa, 52, 53, 273
Khamenei, Ayatollah Ali, 5, 92, 150, 155, 156, **243**, 298, 358
Khayrallah, Sajida, 325
Khomeini, Ahmad, 157
Khomeini, Ayatollah Ruhollah
biographical sketch, **243**
death of, 5, 92, 155, 298, 315
exile period, 152
government structure under, 154
hatred of Iraqi regime, 161
and Iran-Iraq war, 95-96, 154-155, 294
return to Iran, 114, 153, 272

Rushdie death sentence, 133, 145, 157, 296
Shevardnadze meeting, 68
al-Khoury, Bishara, 186-187, **243**, 252
Khrushchev, Nikita, 136
Kibbutzim, 14-15
Kilburn, Peter, 289, 297
King-Crane Commission, 40, 247
Kirkpatrick, Jeane, 278
Kissinger, Henry, 25, 26-27, 47-48, 113, 144, 264, 266, 361
Kitchener, Herbert, 247
Klinghoffer, Leon, 36, 287
al-Kodsi, Nazem, 256
Kohl, Helmut, 320
Koran, 129
Kurdish people, 6, 93, 161, 294
Kuwait
    airliner hijackings, 285, 293
    Arab League membership, 21, 141, 256
    arms purchases, 73, 80-81, 85
    British influence over, 88-90, 208
    financial aid to United States, 321
    government and economy, 208
    and Gulf Cooperation Council, 80, 98, 105, 279
    history of, 88-90, 207-208
    invasion and occupation of, 317-323, 344, 355, 356
    Iranian terrorism in, 91, 92, 208
    Iraq oil dispute, 317, 355
    Iraq war aid, 119, 208
    key facts, 207
    liberation of, 344, 345, 366, 367
    modernization conflicts, 135-136
    oil
        companies, control of, 111
        crude, prices of (1973-1988), 108
        development from, 89, 109
        industry investments, 120
        production (1979-1987), 121
        reserves, 102, 105
        revenues (1974-1988), 117
        tanker reflagging, 64, 80, 96, 155, 208, 291, 292
    Palestinians in, 349
    postwar conditions, 348-349, 368
    resistance fighters, 344, 348-349, 355
    U.S. aid to, 77
Kuwatly, Shukri, 225, **243**

Lahad, Antoine, 34, 189, 193
Lavi fighter plane, 74
Lawrence, T. E., 20, 247
al-Lawzi, Ahmed, 262
League of Arab States. See Arab League.
League of Nations, 8, 40. See also United Nations.
Leahy, Patrick J. (D-Vt.), 61
Lebanese Communist party, 189
Lebanese Front, 188
Lebanese National Movement (LNM), 188, 190
Lebanese National Resistance Front (LNRF), 188
Lebanon
    Arab League membership, 21, 141
    Arab nationalism in, 20-21, 186
    armies and militias (box), 188
    armistice with Israel (1949), 16
    arms purchases, 73, 85

Chehabism, 187-189
civil war
    Aoun's defeat, 359-360
    causes of, 190
    PLO and, 30-31
    Syrian intervention, 4, 191-192, 193-194, 227-228
    Syrian-Maronite conflict, 194, 227
    tripartite agreement, 194
    U.S. involvement, 192-193
confessional representation system, 186
economic deterioration, 184
family political power, 187
French colonial rule, 9, 186-187
geographic vulnerability, 183-184
and the Gulf crisis, 323
hostages in, 63-64, 72, 193, 297
Israeli air strikes (1981), 57, 277, 278
Israeli invasions of, 33-34, 59-60, 145, 169, 190, 192, 270, 280, 281
key facts (box), 184
map, 185
National Covenant of 1943, 185, 187
in 1948 war with Israel, 13, 16
Ottoman period, 185
Palestinian refugees in, 16, 185
pan-Arab sentiment, 187
parties and factions (box), 188-189
PLO
    activities in, 27-28, 190
    evacuation, 34, 60, 192, 281, 283
    refugees, 189
religious diversity, 184-185
Socialist Front alliance, 187
Syrian influence, 61, 62
U.S. relations
    aid to, 77
    Beirut embassy evacuation, 299
    Marines, deployment of, 60, 61 (box)
    multinational peacekeeping force, 192-193
LEHI (Stern Gang), 11, 12, 13, 248
Levin, Jeremy, 285, 297
Levy, David, 171, 362
Libya. See also al-Qaddafi, Muammar.
    Arab League membership, 21, 141
    arms sales to
        by Soviet Union, 68, 83, 201, 202
        suppliers (box), 85
        by United States, 73
    ballistic missiles in, 86
    Chad merger agreement, 276
    Chad, war with, 3-4, 203, 290, 291, 294
    chemical weapons production, 6, 84, 295
    economic problems, 202
    foreign relations
        Arab world, 202-203
        radicalism of, 197
        Soviet Union, 67, 197, 202, 203
        United States, 63, 77, 202-203, 208
        Western Europe, 203
    foreign workers in, 199
    geography, 198
    and the Gulf crisis, 323
    history of, 199-201
    independence of, 200-201, 252
    Italian colonial rule, 200
    key facts (box), 198
    map, 199
    mineral resources, 198
    1969 revolution, 110, 197, 201

oil
    crude, prices of (1973-1988), 108
    marketability of, 198-199, 200-201
    nationalization acts, 110, 199
    production (1979-1987), 121
    reserves, 105
    revenues (1974-1988), 117
political repression, 202
Rejectionist Front, 27
terrorism and, 63, 197, 288
U.S. air raid (1986), 197, 289
LNM (Lebanese National Movement), 188, 190
LNRF (Lebanese National Resistance Front), 188
Lobbying
    American Jewish community, 54-55, 73
    Arab-American lobby, 55
    Israel lobby, 54-55
Lovers of Zion, 14
Lugar, Richard G. (R-Ind.), 58, 80, 361
Lukman, Rilwanu, 118, 120

MacArthur, Douglas, 358
MacDonald, Ramsay, 10, 248
Maghreb Union, 4
al-Maghreby, Mahmoud Soliman, 260
Mahdism movement, 135
Mahfouz, Naguib, 145
Malaysia, 120
Maliki school of thought, 132
Mansfield, Peter, 11
Mansour, Hassan Ali, **243**, 257
Massacres. See also Terrorism.
    Dayr Yassin (1948), 13
    Sabra-Shatila refugee camp (1982), 193, 281
Matras, Judah, 15
Mauritania
    Arab League membership, 21, 141
    and the Gulf crisis, 323, 325
    Maghreb Union, 4
McCain, John (R-Ariz.), 336
McCarthy, John, 299
McCloskey, Robert J., 45
McFarlane, Robert C., 58, 282, 289, 290
McHenry, Donald, 275
McMahon, Henry, 9, 247
Mecca. See also Islam.
    history of, 125
    seizure of Grand Mosque in, 274
    pilgrimage to (box), 131
    riots in, 91-92, 119, 218, 292
Medina al-Manura, 126
Meese, Edwin, III, 290, 293
Meguid, Esmat Abdel, 291
Meir, Golda, 46, **243-244**, 260, 261, 264
Meloy, Francis, 267
Mexico
    natural gas reserves, 105
    oil
        crude, prices of (1973-1988), 108
        reserves, 101, 105
    OPEC talks, 120
The Middle East: A Physical, Social, and Regional Geography (Fisher), 11
Middle East Business Survey, 55
Middle East Treaty Organization, 253
Missiles, ballistic, 84-86
Mitchell, George J. (D-Maine), 335
Mitterand, Francois, 358

Modai, Yitzhak, 364
Mohieddin, Khalid, 146
Mondale, Walter F., 50
Montazeri, Ayatollah Hussein Ali, 155, **244,** 287, 290, 296
Morocco
  Arab League membership, 21, 141
  arms purchases, 85
  and the Gulf crisis, 319, 320, 323
  Maghreb Union, 4
Moslem Brotherhood, 92, 144, 146, 201, 228
Moslem Students Association, 134
Mossadeq, Muhammad, 151, 153, **244,** 252
Mousavi, Mir Hossein, **244**
Moynihan, Daniel Patrick (D-N.Y.), 266
Mu'awiyah ibn Abi Sufyan, 126, 127
Mubarak al-Sabah, 88
Mubarak, Hosni, 35, 36, 68, 140-142, 145, **244,** 279, 317, 319, 323, 341, 349, 355, 357
al-Mudarasi, Hadi, 90, 206
Muhammad (Prophet), 125-126
Muhammad Ali, 142
Muhammad, Ali Nasser, 234, 235, 236, **244,** 275, 288
Muhammad Ali Shah, 151, 247
Muhammad al-Muntazar, 127
Muhsin, Zuhayr, 266
Mujaheddin
  in Iran, 153-154
  in Iraq, 164
Murabitun, 189
al-Muragha, Sa'id Musa (Abu Musa), 28
Murphy, Anne-Marie, 289
Murphy, Robert, 188
Musawi, Hussein, 189
Muskie, Edmund S., 275
Mussolini, Benito, 200
Mustafa Kemal (Ataturk), 128, 248
Mutasser, Mahmud, 257

NAAA (National Association of Arab Americans), 55
Nabavi, Behzad, 276-277
Naff, Alixa, 55
Naguib, Muhammad, **244,** 252, 253
Nakesone, Yasuhiro, 330
Nasir, Musa, 256
Nasser, Gamal Abdel. *See also* Egypt.
  accession to power, 252
  biographical sketch, **244**
  Communists, attitude toward, 45
  death of, 46, 143, 261
  "Egyptianization" policy, 254
  foreign policy of, 142-143
  Saddam Hussein, influence on, 324, 338
  and 1952 revolution, 142
  presidential election, 253
  Qaddafi, influence on, 197-198, 201
  role in Arab world, 18, 21, 142-143, 324
  Soviet arms deal, 16, 70, 143
  Suez Canal crisis and, 17, 43-44, 143, 253-254
  and War of Attrition, 23
National Association of Arab Americans (NAAA), 55
National Front for the Liberation of Palestine (NFLP), 19
Nationalism
  Arab. *See* Arab nationalism.
  Jewish heritage and (box), 14-15
Natural gas, 104, 105, 211, 212, 213, 219

Navon, Yitzhak, **244**
Nazer, Hisham M., 118
Nazi persecution, 10, 11, 15
Neeman, Yuval, 287
Nehru, Jawaharlal, 143
Netherlands, 320
The New Arab Social Order (Ibrahim), 146
New Zealand, 320
NFLP (National Front for the Liberation of Palestine), 19
Nicaraguan contra rebels, U.S. aid to, 64, 72
Niger, 320
Nigeria
  arms purchases, 85
  oil
    disputes, 116
    production, 108, 121, 332
    reserves, 105
    revenues (1974-1988), 117
Nimeiry, Gaafer, 56
Nixon, Richard, 26, 46, 61, 73, 106, 144, 265
Nobel Peace Prize, 51, 271
Noriega, Manuel, 346
North, Oliver, 289
North Yemen
  Arab League membership, 21, 141
  arms purchases, 73, 85, 234
  border disputes, 232
  economy, 232-233
  Egyptian aid, 18, 234
  foreign aid to, 77, 233
  government, 234-235
  key facts (box), 232
  map, 233
  oil production, 233
  qat problem, 233
  Zaydi-Shafi'i split, 233-234
Norway, 320
Nuclear energy, 106
Nuclear Nonproliferation Treaty, 79
Nuclear weapons, 6, 290
Nunn, Sam (D-Ga.), 361
Nusseibeh, Sari, 365

OAPEC (Organization of Arab Petroleum Exporting Countries), 25, 56, 110, 112, 141
Obeid, Abdul Karim, 67, 298
Occidental Petroleum Company, 110
Oil. *See also* Organization of Petroleum Exporting Countries; Persian Gulf crisis.
  Arab ban on sale to Egypt, 56
  Arab embargo (1973), 25, 26, 87, 105, 112-114, 217, 263-264
  Iran-Iraq war and, 97, 118-121
  Iraq-Kuwait dispute, 317
  Iraqi pipeline construction, 97, 104, 160, 164
  from Persian Gulf
    British control, 42
    discovery and development, 89-90
    importance of, 87
    Kuwaiti tanker reflagging, 64, 80, 96, 155, 208, 291, 292
    production advantages, 102-104
    supply and disposition (1986), 103
    transportation problems, 104-105
    vast reserves, 101, 102-105
  pipelines (map), 95
  prices
    crash (1986), 4, 116-118
    of crude (1973-1988) (table), 108

    increases (1978-1980), 105-106
    oil company control of, 109-110
    and Saudi production increase (1986), 92, 116-118, 220
    and U.S. dollar, 107-108
    volatility, 118
  production leaders (chart), 113
  U.S.
    consumption and imports (chart), 107
    guarantee to Israel, 53
    imports from OPEC nations (table), 111
    policy on, 106
  world demand, 101-102, 104 (box), 115
  world reserves (chart), 105
Oman
  Arab League membership, 21, 141
  arms purchases, 73, 85
  British influence in, 90, 209
  Buraimi oasis dispute, 91, 213
  foreign relations
    Soviet Union, 68, 210
    U.S. aid, 77, 209
  and Gulf Cooperation Council, 80, 98, 105, 279
  and the Gulf crisis, 319, 323, 368
  history of, 88, 209-210
  key facts, 209
  OPEC talks, 120
  political independence movement, 210
  support of Sadat, 56, 209
OPEC. *See* Organization of Petroleum Exporting Countries.
Organization of Arab Petroleum Exporting Countries (OAPEC), 25, 56, 110, 112, 141
Organization of Petroleum Exporting Countries (OPEC). *See also* Oil.
  Committee of Three, 118
  crude oil production (1979-1987) (table), 121
  divisions within, 115-116
  early agreements, 110-111
  and embargo of 1973, 112-114
  forecasts, 121-122
  formation, 110, 256
  and Gulf crisis, 315, 317, 333, 355
  Iran-Iraq war and, 119
  and NOPEC nations, 120
  oil revenues (1974-1988) (table), 117
  petrodollar investments, 108-109
  price setting (1973), 112
  production ceilings, 115-116
  Saudi role in, 114, 115-117, 220
  Saudi-Iranian feud, 119
  U.S. imports from (table), 111
Organization of the Islamic Conference (Islamic Conference Organization), 56, 123, 135, 141
The Other Arab-Israeli Conflict (Spiegle), 59
Ottoman Empire, 8, 14, 20, 88, 92, 128, 185-186, 225, 247-248, 317, 323
Oueddei, Goukouni, 276
Ozal, Turgut, 364

Padfield, Philip, 289
Pahlavi, Muhammed Reza (shah of Iran, 1941-1979), 114, 151, 152-153, 161, **244,** 248, 272, 274, 276
Pahlavi, Reza Shah (shah of Iran, 1925-1941), 151, **244,** 248

Pakistan, 319, 320
Palestine
  Anglo-American Committee of Inquiry, 249
  British retreat from, 11-12, 168-169, 250
  early Jewish settlements, 8
  Jewish diaspora, 7
  Jewish immigration to, 14-15, 40, 168-169
  partition of, 12, 43, 169, 249-250
  PNC independence announcement (1988) (text), 310
Palestine Liberation Front (PLF), 29, 36, 63
Palestine Liberation Organization (PLO). See also Arafat, Yasir.
  and Achille Lauro hijacking, 29, 36, 63, 287
  Arab League endorsement of, 26, 265, 301-302 (text)
  Arab League membership, 21, 30, 141, 267
  cease-fire with Israel (1981), 33-34, 59
  Egyptian support, 141
  establishment of, 18-19
  factions (box), 28-29
  Fez summit and, 35, 62, 281
  and the Gulf crisis, 323, 326-327, 350-351
  governing bodies (box), 28
  internal fissures, 30, 282
  and the intifada, 2-3
  in Jordan, 27-28, 178, 179
  and Lebanese civil war, 30-31
  Lebanon, evacuation from, 34, 60, 192, 281, 283
  political symbolism of, 28-30
  recognition of Israel, 38, 65, 142, 295
  Rejectionist Front, 27
  Shamir's election plan and, 66, 174
  Soviet arms sales to, 47
  Soviet support, 48
  Syrian feud, 35-36, 227-228, 282
  talks with United States, 3, 38, 65-66, 142, 284, 295
  UN admission, 30
Palestine National Council (PNC), 28, 38, 65, 142, 259, 268, 295, 310
Palestinian people. See also Israeli-occupied lands; Palestine Liberation Organization.
  defined (box), 9
  and the Gulf crisis, 323, 325-327, 350-351
  and the intifada, 1-2, 37-38, 65, 141, 172, 292, 315, 326, 350-351, 359, 360
  in Jordan, 16, 178
  in Kuwait, 349, 368
  in Lebanon, 16, 185
  Lebanon massacre, 193
  political organizing efforts, 18-19
  War of 1948, effect on, 13, 43
Panama, invasion of, 346
Pan-Arab movement, 162-163
Pan-Islamism movement, 135
Party of the Islamic Call. See Da'wa movement.
Pasha, Maher, 252
Passfield White Paper, 10, 248
Paul VI (pope), 266
Pearl industry, 88, 89, 205, 207
Peel Commission, 10
Pelletreau, Robert H., Jr., 66, 295
Percy, Charles H. (R-Ill.), 58
Peres, Shimon, 21, 35, 65, 170, 171-173, 180, 244, 268, 290
Peres initiative, 36-37, 65

Perez Alfonzo, Juan Pablo, 109, 110
Pérez de Cuéllar, Javier, 285, 292, 294, 331, 338, 356, 357, 363, 365
Perle, Richard, 361
Persian Gulf. See also individual countries.
  Buraimi oasis dispute, 90-91
  defense concerns, 105
  and the Gulf Cooperation Council, 80, 98, 105, 205
  history of, 87-90
  oil
    discovery and development, 89-90
    importance of, 87, 205
    price increases (1978-1980), 105-106
    production advantages, 102-104
    reserves in, 101, 102-105
    tanker escorts, 64
    transporatation problems, 104-105
  population of, 87
  region (map), 89, 205
  strategic importance, 87
  territorial disputes, 90-91
  Trucial System in, 88
Persian Gulf Crisis. See also Iraq; United Nations.
  aftermath of, 346-353
    Egypt, 349
    Kuwait, 348-349
    Iran, 347-348
    Iraq, 347
    Saudi Arabia, 349
    Soviet Union, 351-352
    Syria, 349-350
  air war, 339-343, 363-366
  attrocities, 318
  cease-fire, 344, 367, 390 (text)
  ground war, 343-346, 366-367
    battle plan, 343, 345 (map)
  hostages, 322-323, 330, 381-382 (text)
  invasion of Kuwait, 317-318, 355-356
  Iraqi war decision, 337-339
  Iraqi withdrawal from Kuwait, 344, 388-389 (text)
  Israel's role in, 341-342
  Jordan's role in, 327-328
  multinational coalition
    contributions to (box), 320
    members, 319-321
  oil prices, effect on, 332-333
  Palestinian role in, 326-327
  peace initiative, 343-344
  prelude to, 316-317
  sanctions against Iraq, 321, 380-381 (text)
  Scud attacks, 340-341, 364
  Soviet peace plan, response to, 387-388 (text)
  United Nations resolutions on
    Resolution 660, 369 (text)
    Resolution 661, 369 (text)
    Resolution 665, 372 (text)
    Resolution 672, 379 (text)
    Resolution 673, 379 (text)
    Resolution 678, 380 (text)
  U.S. role in
    Bush administration strategy, 328-329
    conditions for ending war, 344, 386-387 (text)
    constitutional debate, 329-330, 384 (text)
    diplomacy, 330-331, 382-383 (text)
    troop deployments, 318-319, 328, 370-371 (text), 379-380 (text)
    war decision, 331-336, 385-386 (text)

PFLP (Popular Front for the Liberation of Palestine), 19, 27, 28, 30, 179, 261, 268
PFLP-GC (Popular Front for the Liberation of Palestine-General Command), 29, 229
Phalange (Kataeb) party, 188
Physicians for Human Rights, 172
Pinsker, Leo, 168
PLF (Palestine Liberation Front), 29, 36, 63
PLO. See Palestine Liberation Organization.
PNC (Palestine National Council), 28, 38, 65, 142, 259, 268, 295, 310
Podgornyi, Nikolai V., 261
Poland, 320
Polhill, Robert, 291, 297
Pollard, Jonathan Jay, 287, 289
Polyakov, Vladimir, 278
Popular Front for the Liberation of Palestine (PFLP), 19, 27, 28, 30, 179, 261, 268
Popular Front for the Liberation of Palestine-General Command (PFLP-GC), 29, 229
Popular Palestinian Struggle Front (PPSF), 29
Portugal, 320
Powell, Colin, 342, 343, 364, 366
Primakov, Yevgenii, 351, 359, 360, 366
Progressive Socialist party (PSP), 188-189

Qaboos bin Said, 56, 209, **244-245**
al-Qaddafi, Muammar, 24
  Arab unity efforts, 197, 201
  ascent to power, 201, 260
  assassination attempts, 285
  biographical sketch, **245**
  foreign policy aspects, 63, 197-198
  Islamic fundamentalism, 133, 197
  Nasser's influence on, 197-198, 201
  political philosophy, 197, 201-202
  Soviet arms buildup and, 83
al-Qadi, Isam, 29
Qat production, in North Yemen, 233
Qatar
  Arab League membership, 21, 141
  arms purchases, 73, 82, 85
  British influence in, 211
  government and economy, 211-212
  and Gulf Cooperation Council, 80, 98, 211, 279
  and the Gulf crisis, 319, 323, 365, 368
  key facts, 210-211
  natural gas reserves, 105, 211, 212
  oil
    companies, control of, 111-112
    production (1979-1987), 121
    revenues (1974-1988), 117
  Shi'ites in, 91
Quandt, William, 315
Queen, Richard I., 276

Rabin, Leah, 268
Rabin, Yitzhak, 48, 170-171, 172-173, **245,** 264-265, 267-268
Rafsanjani, Ali Akbar Hashemi, 5, 92, 155, 157, **245,** 296, 298, 348, 365, 368
Rajavi, Massoud, 153
Ramadan, 130, 329
Ramadan, Taha Yasin, 100, 291

Ras al-Khaimah, 90, 213, 262
Rasmara, Ali, 251
Reagan, Ronald
    arms sales policy, 72, 81
    energy policy, 106, 115
    Iran-contra affair, 64, 72, 290
    Israeli relations, 57-59, 74
    Jordan, relations with, 79-80
    Kuwaiti tanker reflagging, 64, 80
    peace initiative (1982), 35, 60, 62, 281, 306
        (text)
    Saudi arms sales, 76, 78-79, 81, 278-279
    terrorism, response to, 62-63, 286
Reed, Frank H., 290, 297
Reiger, Frank, 297
Rejectionist Front, 27
Revisionist Zionism, 30
Rhodesia, 321
al-Rifai, Zaid Samir, 5, 182, **245**, 296
Roberts, USS, 64
Rockefeller, John, 109
Rogers, William P., 23, 46
Rogers Plan, 23, 46, 262
Rohan, Michael, 260
Roman Empire, 124
Rome and Jerusalem (Hess), 168
Roosevelt, Franklin D., 43, 144, 217
Ross, Dennis, 99
Rumaila oilfield, 317, 355, 360
Rushdie, Salman, 133, 145, 157, 296
Rusk, Dean, 45, 73
Russia. *See* Soviet Union.
Ryabov, Y. A., 100

al-Sabah, Jaber al-Ahmed (emir of Kuwait),
    208, **245**, 286, 317, 348-349, 355, 359,
    368, 377 (text)
al-Sabah, Mubarak, 208
al-Sabah, Saad al-Abdullah, 360, 368
al-Sabah, Sabah al-Salem, 258
Sabry, Aly, 257
al-Sadat, Anwar. *See also* Egypt.
    accession to presidency, 24, 46, 144, 261
    assassination of, 78, 144-145, 279
    biographical sketch, **245**
    Camp David talks, 31-33, 50-52, 144, 271
    goals and vision, 144
    Israel peace treaty signing, 21, 144, 273
    in 1973 Arab-Israeli war, 24-27, 47, 144
    Soviet expulsion order, 47, 75, 262
    Soviet relations with, 46-47, 75
    visit to Israel, 31, 49, 144, 269
Sadat, Jihan, 147
Sadr, Musa, 192
al-Sadr, Sayyid Muhammed Bakr, 94, 161,
    164
Safran, Nadav, 21, 47
Said bin Taimur, 209, 244
Said, Sayyid, 88
Saiqa, 29
Saladin, 324
Salafiyah movement, 135
Salam, Saeb, **245**
Salih, Ali Abdullah, 234-235, **245**, 270
al-Sallal, Abdullah, 234, 256
Samuel, Marcus, 109
Sanjabi, Karim, 271
al-Sanusi, Muhammad bin Ali, 200
al-Sanusi, Muhammad Idris, 200
Saratoga, USS, 362
Sarkis, Elias, 190, 191, **245**, 267

Sartawi, Issam, 280, 282
The Satanic Verses (Rushdie), 133, 145,
    157, 296
Saud ibn Faisal, **245**
Saud IV (king of Saudi Arabia), 217, **245**,
    256
Saudi Arabia
    Arab League membership, 21, 141
    Arab nationalism in, 20-21
    arms sales to
        AWACS controversy, 58, 72, 76, 78, 81,
            218, 278-279
        by Britain, 71-72, 78-79
        by China, 86
        by France, 71
        suppliers (box), 85
        by United States, 73, 76, 78-79, 363
    ballistic missiles in, 86
    Buraimi oasis dispute, 90-91, 213
    economy, 219
    Fahd peace plan, 58, 221, 278, 306 (text)
    foreign labor in, 216
    foreign relations
        Egypt, disputes with, 18, 217
        Iran, feud with, 119, 221
        Iraq war aid, 98, 119, 221
        Jordan, aid to, 182
        North Yemen, border disputes with,
            232
        peacemaker role, 221-222
        with United States, 77, 217, 218, 222
    geography, 215
    government and politics, 217-219
    and Gulf Cooperation Council, 80, 98,
        105, 221, 279
    and the Gulf Crisis
        aftermath of, 333, 349, 368
        Arab politics, 323, 327, 358, 360
        coalition participation, 320, 339, 341,
            345, 360
        financial aid to United States, 321
        invasion of Kuwait, response to, 318-
            319
        oil policies, 332-333
        Soviet Union, relations with, 352, 356
    history of, 216-217
    Islam, influence on, 133, 135, 218
    Islamic penalties, 132
    key facts (box), 216
    map, 217
    Mecca riots, 91-92, 119, 218
    military, 319
    natural gas reserves, 105, 219
    in 1948 war with Israel, 13, 16
    Nuclear Nonproliferation Treaty, signing
        of, 79
    oil
        companies, control of, 111-112, 220, 276
        crude, prices of (1973-1988), 108
        embargo of 1973, role in, 217
        industry investments, 120, 219
        OPEC influence, 114, 115-117, 220
        petrodollar investments, 109
        production (1979-1987), 121
        production increase (1986), 92, 116-
            118, 220
        reserves, 102, 105, 219
        revenues (1974-1988), 117
    women's role in, 136
Schlesinger, James, 361
Schwarzkopf, H. Norman, 339, 344, 346,
    364, 365, 367
Scowcroft, Brent, 359

Scranton, William, 260
SDI (Strategic Defense Initiative), 86, 174
al-Sebai, Youssef, 270
Seib, Gerald F., 291
Senegal, 320
Sephardic Jews, 168, 171
al-Sha'bi, Qahtan, 232, 236
Shafi'i school of thought, 132
Shah of Iran. *See* Pahlavi, Muhammed
    Reza.
Shalom, Avraham, 289
Shamir, Yitzhak
    biographical sketch, **245**
    election plan for occupied lands, 66, 174,
        296
    and the Gulf crisis, 350, 362, 368
    Peres initiative, opposition to, 37, 65
    PLO negotiations, opposition to, 3
    premiership rotation, 171-173, 290
Sharjah, 89, 90, 213
Sharon, Ariel, 25, 59, 171, **245-246**, 279,
    290
Shatt al-Arab waterway, 92-93, 94, 97
    (map), 159, 163
Shaw, Bernard, 339
Shaw Report (1930), 10
Shaykh Muhammad ibn 'Abd al-Wahhab,
    135
Sheehan, Edward R. F., 48
Shenuda (Coptic pope), 147
Sherif Hussein (Hussein ibn Ali), 9, 178,
    216, 225, **242**, 247,
Shevardnadze, Eduard, 63, 68, 145, 229,
    296, 318, 356, 358, 362
Shi'ite Moslems. *See also* Islam.
    in Bahrain, 90, 206
    founding of, 127
    in Gulf Arab countries, 91-92
    in Iran, 150-151
    in Iraq, 91, 94, 160-161, 347
    Ja'afari school of thought, 132
    kidnappings by, 63-64
    in Lebanon, 34, 63, 189
    Obeid kidnapping, 67, 298
    TWA hijacking by, 34, 62
al-Shishakli, Adib, 226, 252
Shultz, George P., 3, 37-38, 60, 65, 70, 80,
    141, 173, 293
Sicherman, Harvey, 148
Silo, Fawzi, 252
Sinai II agreement, 26-27, 48
Sinai Peninsula
    Camp David agreements on, 51
    Israeli withdrawal from, 52
    Jewish settlements in, 51
    1973 Arab-Israeli war in, 25
Singh, Mithileshwar, 291, 295
Six-Day War of 1967, 18-19, 22-23, 45-46,
    169, 179, 258-259
SLA (South Lebanon Army), 189
al-Solh, Rashid, **246**, 266
al-Solh, Riyad, 186-187
Somalia
    Arab League membership, 21, 141
    arms purchases, 85
    and the Gulf crisis, 323
South Africa, 321
South Lebanon Army (SLA), 189
South Yemen
    Arab League membership, 21, 141
    arms purchases, 85
    ballistic missiles in, 86
    civil war, 236, 288

economy, 235-236
foreign aid to, 235
geography, 235
government, 236
independence of, 259
map, 233
oil production, 235-236
Rejectionist Front, 27
Soviet influence, 236, 274
U.S. aid to, 77
Yemeni Socialist party, 29, 236
Soviet Union
  Arab nationalists and, 44-45
  Arab-Israeli conflicts and
    Geneva Conference, 48, 49
    in 1948 war, 41
    reaction to peace treaty, 56
    Six-Day War, 45
    Suez Canal crisis (1956), 43-44
    UN Resolution 242, 22-23
    and War of Attrition, 23, 46
  arms sales
    to Algeria, 68
    to Egypt, 16, 24, 41, 43, 68, 70, 75
    to Iran, 258
    to Iraq, 68, 82, 162, 337
    to Libya, 68, 83
    to PLO, 47
    to Syria, 24, 25, 41, 68, 82, 229
  expansionism
    Afghanistan, 39-40, 67, 274
    Greece, 42
    Iran, 42, 89
    Turkey, 40, 42
  foreign relations
    Egypt, 46-47, 145, 262
    Iran, 67, 156, 295, 298
    Iraq, 47
    Israel, 68
    Libya, 67, 197, 202, 203
    South Yemen, 236, 274
    Syria, 47, 229
    Turkey, 40
  and the Gulf crisis
    aftermath of, 352
    citizens in Iraq, 361
    coalition, support for, 319, 320, 351-352, 356, 357, 358-359
    diplomacy, 351-352, 359, 360, 366, 372 (text), 386 (text)
    informed of offensive, 339
    peace initiative, 343-344, 366
    UN Security Council, role in, 321, 353
  Islam in (box), 136
  Israel, recognition of, 39, 43
  Mideast policy
    Arab alliances, 39, 67-68
    in Iran-Iraq war, 98-100
    military aid, 82-83
    military bases (map), 71
    and Shevardnadze tour, 68, 229, 296
    under Gorbachev, 68
  natural gas reserves, 105
  oil consumption, 104
  oil reserves, 105
Spain, 320
Spiegle, Stephen, 59
SSNP (Syrian Socialist Nationalist party), 189
Stack, Lee, 248
Stalin, Joseph, 42, 136
Standard Oil Trust, 109
Stark, USS, 165, 291

Steen, Alann, 291, 297
Stern Gang, 11, 12, 13, 248
Sternhal, Ze'ev, 172
Stethem, Robert D., 286
Stoessel, Walter J., 58
Strait of Hormuz, 87, 89 (map), 104
Strategic Defense Initiative (SDI), 86, 174
Strategic petroleum reserve, 106, 332-333, 359
Sudan
  Arab League membership, 21, 141
  and the Gulf crisis, 323
  self-government, 252
  support of Sadat, 56
  U.S. aid to, 77
Suez Canal
  British-Egyptian Suez Pact (1959), 255
  Crisis of 1956, 17-18, 43-44, 143, 253-254
  Egyptian blockade, 251
  in 1973 Arab-Israeli war, 25
  reopening, 266
Sufism, 127
Suleiman the Magnificent, 128
Sunni Moslems, 127
  schools of thought, 132
Sutherland, Thomas, 297
Sweden, 320
Sykes-Picot agreement, 9, 225, 247
Syria. *See also* al-Assad, Hafez.
  Arab League membership, 21, 141
  Arab nationalism, 20-21, 226
  arable land in, 224
  armistice with Israel (1949), 16
  arms sales to
    by Soviet Union, 24, 25, 41, 68, 82
    suppliers (box), 85
    by United States, 73
  ballistic missiles in, 86
  chemical weapons production, 84
  demography, 224
  economic problems, 228
  French colonial rule, 9, 225
  geography, 223-224
  and the Gulf crisis,
    aftermath of, 349-350, 368
    Arab politics, 323, 356
    coalition participation, 315, 319, 320, 341, 344, 345, 356
    demonstrations, 323
    economic implications, 349-350, 357, 358
  history of, 224-226
  key facts (box), 224
  Lebanon
    forces in, 33, 59-60, 191-192, 193-194, 227-228
    influence in, 61, 62, 227
  map, 225
  Moslem Brotherhood in, 92, 228
  in 1948 war with Israel, 13, 16
  in 1973 Arab-Israeli war, 160-170
  oil company nationalization, 257
  Ottoman rule influence, 225
  PLO feud, 35-36, 227-228, 229
  political instability, 225-226
  refugee camps in, 16
  Six-Day War with Israel, 22, 169
  Soviet influence, 47, 229
  UAR membership, 18, 21, 143, 226, 232, 242, 256
  U.S. aid to, 77
Syrian Socialist Nationalist party (SSNP), 189

al-Tal, Wasfi, 180, **246**, 262
Talal (king of Jordan), 179, **246**, 251, 252
Talfah, Kairallah, 324
Tapline (Trans-Arabian Pipeline), 110
Tarassov, Gennadi, 68
Tarifi, Jamil, 298
Tariki, Abdullah, 110
Tehran Protocol (1911), 92
Tekoah, Yosef, 265
Terrorism. *See also* Massacres.
  Achille Lauro hijacking, 29, 36, 63, 287
  against British, 11
  Berlin discotheque bombing, 63, 289
  Bush's response to, 67
  El Al Airlines attack, 63, 288
  Entebbe hijacking, 267
  Heathrow bomb, 289
  Iranian involvement, 91-92
  Japan Air Lines hijacking, 263
  kidnappings in Lebanon, 193, 297
  in Kuwait, 91, 92, 208
  Kuwaiti airliner hijackings, 285, 293
  Lebanon, U.S. Marines attacks in, 61 (box), 62, 193, 283
  Libyan support, 63, 197, 288
  Lockerbie Pan Am bombing, 229, 295
  Lod Airport attack, 262
  Maalot school tragedy, 265
  Olympic hostage crisis, 262
  PFLP hijackings, 27, 46, 261
  PLO rejection of, 38, 65, 295, 311 (text)
  Reagan's response to, 62-63
  TWA bombing, 63, 288-289
  TWA hijacking (1969), 260
  TWA hijacking (1985), 34, 62, 193-194, 286
  U.S. hostages in Iran, 154, 274-277, 297 (table)
Texas Railroad Commission, 120
Thatcher, Margaret, 117, 289, 318, 355, 356
Tito, Josip Broz, 142
Tonkin Gulf Resolution, 336
Tracy, Edward A., 290, 297
Trans-Arabian Pipeline (Tapline), 110
Transjordan. *See also* Jordan
  after 1948 war, 43, 178, 250
  Arab nationalism, growth of, 20-21
  origin of, 9, 178, 248
Treaties
  Baghdad Pact, 17, 43, 44, 151, 162, 253
  Nuclear Nonproliferation Treaty, 79
  on Shatt al-Arab waterway, 92
  Treaty of Erzerum (1847), 92
  Treaty of Sanaa, 232
  Treaty of Sevres, 162
  Treaty of Uqayr, 207, 208
  Tripartite Declaration, 16, 43, 70, 251
  Trucial Oman Levies, 90
Trucial States. *See* United Arab Emirates.
Trucial System, 88
Truman, Harry S, 40, 42, 249, 250, 358
Truman Doctrine, 42-43
Tunbs (Gulf islands), 90, 213, 262
Tunisia
  Arab League membership, 21, 141
  arms purchases, 85
  and the Gulf crisis, 323
  Maghreb Union, 4
  peace proposal, 257-258
  U.S. aid to, 77
Turkey
  Baghdad Pact, 17, 43, 151, 162, 253

and the Gulf crisis, 318, 319, 320, 321, 328, 357, 358, 363, 364, 365
Kurdish refugees in, 294
role of Islam in, 133
Soviet expansionism (1945), 42
Soviet Union, importance to, 40
U.S. aid to, 77
Turner, Jesse J., 291, 297

U Thant, 259
UAE. *See* United Arab Emirates.
UAR (United Arab Republic), 18, 21, 44, 143, 226, 232, 255, 256
Ulbricht, Walter, 257
Umar ibn al-Khattab, 126, 127
Umayyad Islamic Empire, 127, 224
Umm al-Qaiwain, 90, 213
UNDOF (United Nations Disengagement Observer Forces), 26
UNEF (United Nations Emergency Force), 18, 254, 258
UNIFIL (United Nations Interim Forces in Lebanon), 33, 192
United Arab Emirates (UAE)
Arab League membership, 21, 141
arms purchases, 73, 85
Buraimi oasis dispute, 90-91, 213
economic cooperation, 214
foreign relations
Arab regional stability, 214
Soviet Union, 68, 214
formation of, 90, 213, 262
government of, 213
and Gulf Cooperation Council, 80, 98, 105, 279
and the Gulf crisis, 317, 319, 323, 355, 368
history of, 213
key facts, 212
oil
companies, control of, 111-112
crude, prices of (1973-1988), 108
production (1979-1987), 121
reserves, 105
revenues (1974-1988), 117
United Arab Republic (UAR), 18, 21, 44, 143, 226, 232, 255, 256
United Nations
Arafat's speeches to, 30, 65, 265, 295
Bahraini plebiscite, 90
chemical weapons conference, 84
Conciliation Commission for Palestine, 16
Disengagement Observer Forces (UNDOF), 26
Emergency Force (UNEF), 18, 254, 258
and the Gulf crisis, 321, 322, 326, 330, 352-353, 369 (text), 372 (text), 377-379 (text)
Interim Force in Lebanon (UNIFIL), 33, 192
Iran-Iraq war cease-fire, 94, 96-97, 294, 307 (text)
Palestine partition, 12, 43, 249-250
Relief and Works Agency (UNRWA), 16, 43
Resolution 242, 22-23, 24, 38, 45, 50, 259, 270, 301 (text), 326, 350, 368
Resolution 338, 25-26, 263, 301 (text), 326, 350, 368
Resolution 479, 95
Resolution 598, 97, 292, 307 (text)

Iranian acceptance (text), 308
Resolution 660, 321, 369 (text)
Resolution 661, 321, 356, 369 (text)
Resolution 665, 321, 372 (text)
Resolution 672, 359, 379 (text)
Resolution 673, 326, 379 (text)
Resolution 678, 330, 361, 380 (text)
Special Committee on Palestine (UNSCOP), 12, 249-250
Truce Supervision Organization (UNTSO) force, 273
Zionism resolution, 266
United States. *See also* Persian Gulf crisis.
and the Gulf crisis
aftermath of, 349, 352-353, 367-368
battle plan, 343
Bush administration strategy, 328-329
conditions for ending war, 344, 386-387 (text)
congressional approval of war, 336, 384 (text)
constitutional debate, 329-330
diplomacy, 330-331, 361, 363, 382-383 (text)
Israeli relations, 326, 341-342, 350, 359-360, 364
response to Iraqi invasion, 318-319, 355-356
troop deployments, 318-320, 328, 361, 370-371 (text), 379-380 (text)
UN sanctions, 321
war decision, 331-336, 385-386 (text)
Islam in (box), 134
natural gas reserves, 105
oil
Arab embargo, 112, 217, 263-264
consumption by, 104, 107
imports from OPEC nations (table), 111
state delegations to OPEC, 120
United States foreign aid. *See also* Arms sales, by United States.
economic
to Egypt, 75-76, 147-148
Jordan, 80, 182
Middle East (1946-1988), 77
military
AWACS to Saudi Arabia, 58, 72, 278-279
to Egypt, 75-76, 148
to Israel, 25, 73
Middle East (1946-1988), 77
United States policy
arms sales
congressional role in (box), 81
fundamental assumptions of, 72
list (1950-1987), 73
Baghdad Pact, 17, 43, 44, 151
Carter Doctrine, 87, 275
Eisenhower Doctrine, 44
energy, 106
conservation debate, 122
oil import ceiling, 114-115
foreign relations
Iran-contra affair and, 63-64, 72, 155
Iranian hostage crisis, 154, 274-277
Italy, 63
Jordan, 182
Libya, sanctions against, 202-203, 288
Saudi Arabia, 222
Iran-Iraq war, 64, 98, 155
Israel, relations with
arms sales, 70-71, 72-75

arms sales suspension, 57, 58, 74
commitment to, 39, 41-42, 72-75
importance of, 173
Lebanon invasions, 33-34, 58, 59-60
Lebanon, relations with
Beirut embassy evacuation, 299
Gemayel's government, 62
multinational peacekeeping force, 192-193
lobbying efforts, Arab and Israel (box), 54-55
military presence in Mideast
AWACS sales to Saudi Arabia, 58, 72, 278-279
bases, map of, 71
Libya air raid, 197, 289
Persian Gulf area, 105
U.S. Marines in Lebanon, 60, 61 (box)
objectives of, 39
Palestine partition, 40, 249-250
peace efforts
Camp David agreements, 31-33, 50-52, 73-74, 144, 271
Habib shuttle diplomacy, 33-34, 58, 59, 60, 192, 277
Hussein-Arafat initiative, response to, 36, 64-65
Kissinger shuttle diplomacy, 26-27, 47-48, 144, 264, 266
mediator role, 48, 56-57, 66
PLO talks, 3, 38, 65-66, 284
Reagan initiative, 35, 60, 62, 281, 306 (text)
Rogers Plan, 23, 46, 293
Shultz initiative (1988), 37-38, 65, 141, 293
in Suez crisis (1956), 43-44, 143
terrorism, response to, 62-63, 67
Tripartite Declaration, 16, 43, 70, 251
Truman Doctrine, 42-43
UNRWA (UN Relief and Works Agency), 16, 43
UNSCOP (United Nations Special Committee on Palestine), 12, 249-250
UNTSO (United Nations Truce Supervision Organization) force, 273
Utab tribe, 88
Uthman ibn 'Affan, 126-127

Vance, Cyrus R., 49, 53, 270, 271, 275
Vanunu, Mordechai, 290
Velayati, Ali Akbar, 156, **246**, 358
Venezuela, 105, 108, 109, 117, 121, 332, 357
Vietnam War, 319, 329, 334, 335, 336-337, 339, 361
Vincennes, USS, 64, 295

al-Wahhab, Muhammad ibn Abd, 216
Wahhabi Moslems, 135, 216
Waite, Terry, 291
Waldheim, Kurt, 362
Wall Street Journal, 118
Wallace Muhammad, 134
Waller, Calvin A. H., 362
War of Attrition (1969), 23, 46
War of Ramadan, 47*n*. *See also* Arab-Israeli conflicts, 1973 Arab-Israeli war.
War Powers Resolution, 60, 61, 329
Waring, Robert, 267

Wazir, Khalil (Abu Jihad), **246,** 293
Webster, William, 83, 84, 335, 362, 380-381
  (text)
Weinberger, Caspar W., 58, 59, 74
Weir, Benjamin F., 286, 297
Weizman, Ezer, **246,** 273, 275
Weizmann, Chaim, 168, **246,** 247, 248, 250,
  252
West Bank. *See also* Israeli-occupied lands.
  autonomy talks, 32-33, 53
  Camp David agreement on, 50-51
  intifada, 1-2, 37-38, 65, 141, 172, 292
  Israeli occupation, 22
  Jordan annexation, 9, 13, 30, 43
  Jordan's claim relinquished, 2, 38, 65,
    177, 181, 309-310 (text)
  refugee camps in, 16
West Germany
  arms sales, 70
  chemical weapons technology sales, 6, 83-
    84, 295
WHO (World Health Organization), 66
Wilson, Woodrow, 40

Women, in Islamic society, 136, 203
World Health Organization (WHO), 66
World War I, 15, 88, 142, 247
World War II, 10-11, 89, 140
World Zionist Organization, 10, 11

Yahya, Imam, 231-232
Yamani, Ahmed Zaki, 112, 116, 118, 217,
  220, **246,** 276, 290
Yasdi, Ibrahim, 153
Yemen
  Arab nationalism, 20-21, 232
  civil war, 143, 256-257
  and the Gulf crisis, 315, 322, 323, 360
  history of, 231-232
  unification attempts, 231
Yemen Arab Republic. *See* North Yemen
Yemen, People's Democratic Republic. *See*
  South Yemen.
Yergin, Daniel, 117
Yishuv, 8, 10-11, 41, 168

Yom Kippur War, 24, 47*n. See also* Arab-
  Israeli conflicts, 1973 Arab-Israeli war.
Young, Andrew, 274
Young Turks, 20

Zaghlul, Saad, 247
Zahedi, Gazollah, 252
Zamir, Yitzhak, 289
Zarara oil field, 91
Zaydism, 231
Zayed ibn Sultan al-Nahayan, 90, 213, 214,
  246, 262
al-Zayim, Husni, 225
Zghorta Liberation Army/Marada, 188
Zionism
  conflicts within, 8-9
  and Jewish heritage, 14
  revisionist, 30
  roots of, 7-8, 168
  self-reliance, increase of, 10-11
  UN resolution on, 266
Zoroastrianism, 125